By the early 1970s a revolution had taken place in the perception and practice of art: it had become redefined as a vehicle for ideas. Conceptual art challenged traditional notions of art's objecthood through its new uses

processes and existing cultural forms, especially from the

up artistic fields in unprecedented ways. The term concept

in the mid 1960s to describe the diverse practices of an internationally influential group of artists who held in common the conviction that art should raise fundamental questions concerning its own definition and the contexts in which it intervenes. As a critique of traditional media and aesthetics, conceptual art continues to exert its influence across the spectrum of contemporary art and provides an indispensible key to its understanding.

The advent of conceptual art marked a major shift in the history not only of art but of ideas. As a philosopher and critical writer on art and aesthetics, Peter Osborne describes and contextualizes in his Survey the distinct ways in which artists contested the aesthetic definition of the artwork by highlighting the role of ideas in the production of meaning from visual forms. The Works section illustrates the most influential artworks associated with conceptual art, as well as those of its most significant precursors and of recent artists who draw upon its legacy. Critical writing by conceptual artists is integral to their practice. In the Documents section essential writings by artists and critics who shaped the movement are juxtaposed with those of thinkers and philosophers whose influence was crucial to its development.

CW01666063

THEMES AND
MOVEMENTS

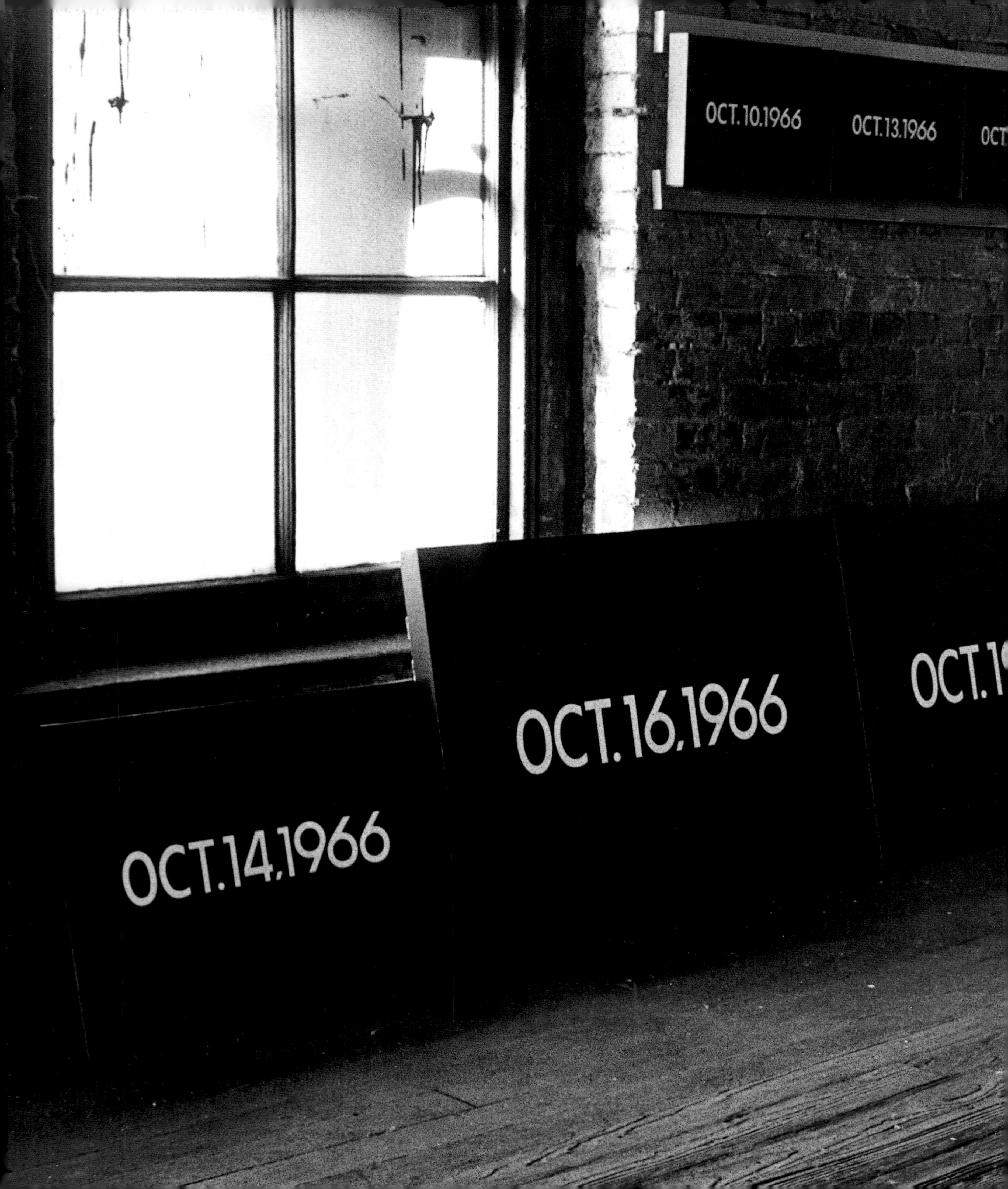
OCT.10,1966
OCT.13,1966
OCT.16,1966
OCT.14,1966

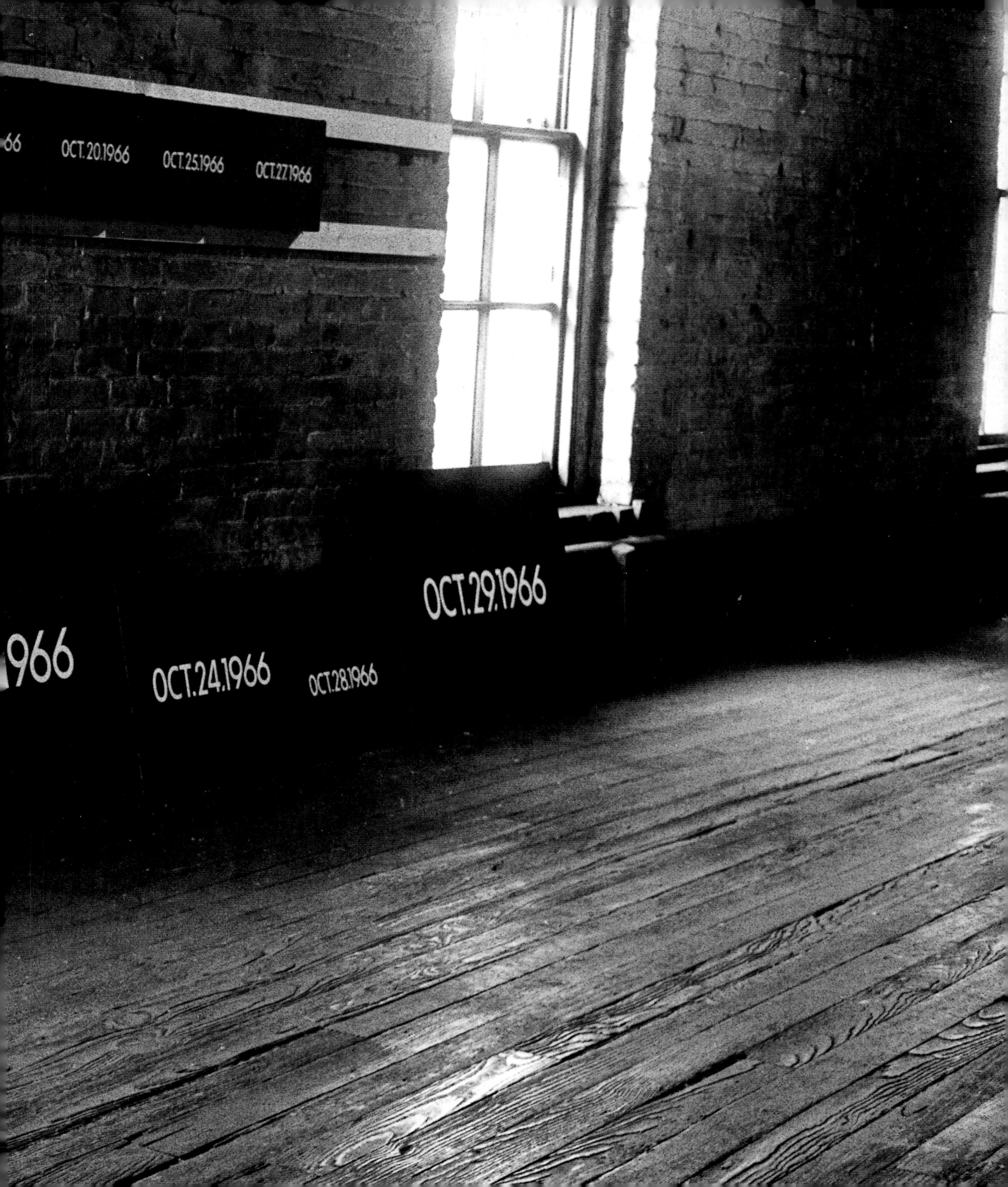
OCT.20.1966
OCT.25.1966
OCT.27.1966
OCT.29.1966
OCT.24.1966
OCT.28.1966

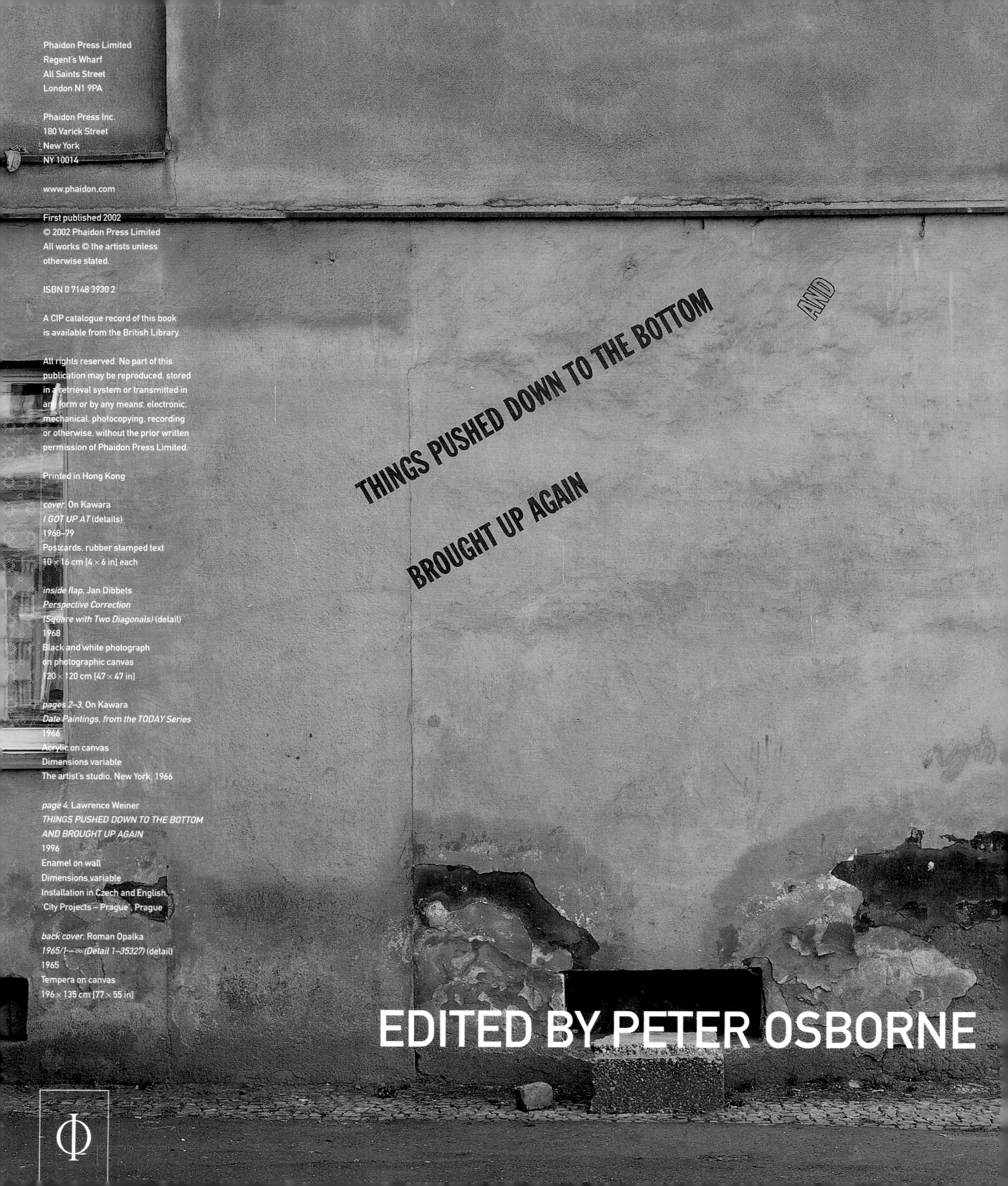

Phaidon Press Limited
Regent's Wharf
All Saints Street
London N1 9PA

Phaidon Press Inc.
180 Varick Street
New York
NY 10014

www.phaidon.com

First published 2002
© 2002 Phaidon Press Limited
All works © the artists unless
otherwise stated.

ISBN 0 7148 3930 2

A CIP catalogue record of this book
is available from the British Library.

All rights reserved. No part of this
publication may be reproduced, stored
in a retrieval system or transmitted in
any form or by any means, electronic,
mechanical, photocopying, recording
or otherwise, without the prior written
permission of Phaidon Press Limited.

Printed in Hong Kong

cover, On Kawara
I GOT UP AT (details)
1968–79
Postcards, rubber stamped text
10 × 16 cm [4 × 6 in] each

inside flap, Jan Dibbets
Perspective Correction
(Square with Two Diagonals) (detail)
1968
Black and white photograph
on photographic canvas
120 × 120 cm [47 × 47 in]

pages 2–3, On Kawara
Date Paintings, from the TODAY Series
1966
Acrylic on canvas
Dimensions variable
The artist's studio, New York, 1966

page 4, Lawrence Weiner
THINGS PUSHED DOWN TO THE BOTTOM
AND BROUGHT UP AGAIN
1996
Enamel on wall
Dimensions variable
Installation in Czech and English,
'City Projects – Prague', Prague

back cover, Roman Opalka
1965/1–∞ (Detail 1–35327) (detail)
1965
Tempera on canvas
196 × 135 cm [77 × 55 in]

EDITED BY PETER OSBORNE

CONCEPTUAL ART

WORKS page 52

PRE-HISTORY: 1950–1960 page 53

INSTRUCTION, PERFORMANCE, DOCUMENTATION page 66

PROCESS, SYSTEM, SERIES page 90

WORD AND SIGN page 112

APPROPRIATION, INTERVENTION, EVERYDAY page 130

POLITICS AND IDEOLOGY page 148

INSTITUTIONAL CRITIQUE page 164

AFTERWARDS page 176

PRE-FACE

BY PETER OSBORNE

This book is a re-examination of a major turning-point in contemporary art. Conceptual art was the point at which the conception of the artwork as an object of visual or, more broadly, spatial experience and pleasure was most directly and radically challenged.

Forgoing a narrowly linguistic definition of conceptual art in favour of a more historically and critically inclusive approach, the book offers a typology of six main kinds of conceptual art – six different ways in which artists contested the aesthetic definition of the artwork by highlighting the role of ideas in the production of meaning from visual forms. This is the basis of a new critical history of conceptual art – a history not only of works but of ideas. More than any other form of contemporary art, conceptual art was a locus for the artistic interpretation of philosophical ideas. Critical writings by conceptual artists are as much a part of this history as their works. This volume includes writings by conceptual artists along with those by philosophers and theorists who influenced them, and critics and historians who have reflected upon the movement.

Section One, 'Pre-history, 1950–1960', presents the main precursors of conceptual art in the USA, Europe and Japan. Section Two, 'Instruction, Performance, Documentation', locates the emergence of the first properly 'conceptual' artworks in the transposition of the score from music and dance into the institutional context of the gallery and in the exhibition of the documentation of performance events. Section Three, 'Process, System, Series', is concerned with a kind of conceptual art, linked to Minimalism, that explores the properties of ideal systems of logical, mathematical and spatio-temporal relations. Section Four, 'Word and Sign', considers that type of work most often associated with the 'conceptual' label: art centred on language, in the form of painted, printed or written texts. The works in the next three sections share a rejection of established conceptions of the autonomy of the artwork, but each of these three types of conceptual art challenges it in a different way. Section Five, 'Appropriation, Intervention, Everyday', deals with an art that intervenes in, and refunctions, other cultural forms in such a way as to serve as a model for alternative cultural practices and forms of imagining. Section Six, 'Politics and Ideology', focuses on art that reflects on and conveys explicitly political conceptual contents. Section Seven, 'Institutional Critique', is devoted to works that thematize the relations of power that make up the institutional conditions for the production and reception of art in general. Section Eight, 'Afterwards', samples a range of the 'post-conceptual' installation art that dominates the international art world today.

SUR-
BY PETER OSBORNE
VEY

The event that made conceivable the realization that it was possible to 'speak another language' and still make sense in art was Marcel Duchamp's first unassisted readymade. With the unassisted readymade, art changed its focus from the form of the language to what was being said. Which means that it changed the nature of art from a question of morphology to a question of function. This change – one from 'appearance' to 'conception' – was the beginning of 'modern' art and the beginning of 'conceptual' art.

All art
(after Duchamp)
is conceptual
(in nature)
because art only exists conceptually.

Joseph KOSUTH, 'Art after Philosophy', 1969

Definitions make bad philosophy, but for a time at least they made good art. Any attempt at a definition of conceptual art immediately runs up against the problem that definition is one of the main things at stake in conceptual art itself. Conceptual art, one might say, is art *about* the cultural act of definition – paradigmatically, but by no means exclusively, the definition of 'art'. Whatever else it may be, conceptual art is first and foremost an art of *questions* and it has left in its wake a whole series of questions about itself.

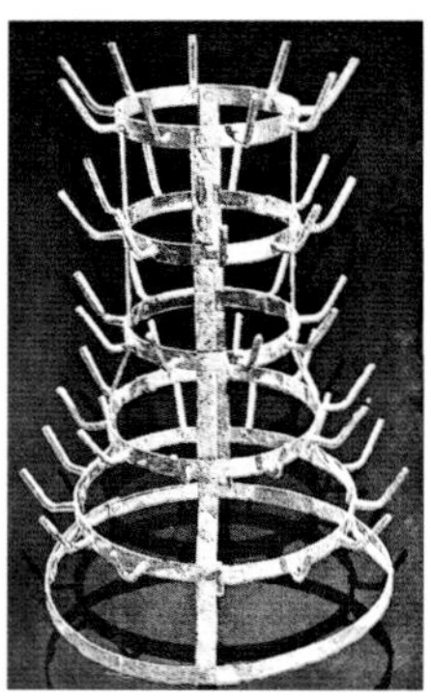

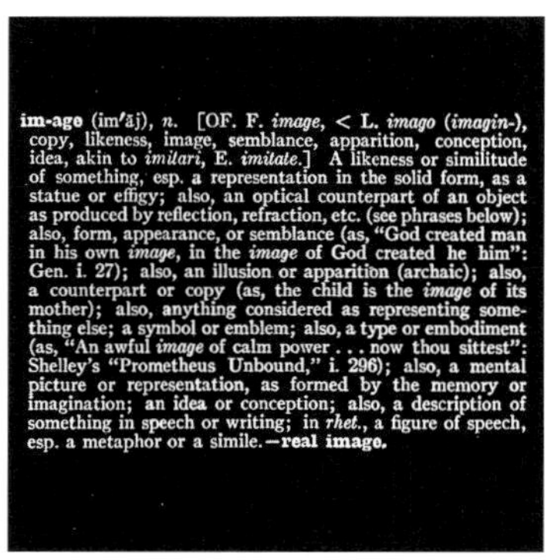

Marcel DUCHAMP, Sèche-bouteilles [Bottle Rack], 1914 [lost]. Retouched photograph by Duchamp of second version, 1936 [lost] from Boîte-en-valise [Box-in-a-valise], 1941
Joseph KOSUTH, Titled [Art as Idea as Idea] [image], 1965–67

What justification is there for naming a distinct kind of art as 'conceptual'? What type of classification is being employed?

Is conceptual art a medium-based art, for example, comparable to painting and sculpture: an art made of concepts and therefore of *language* – as the artist Henry Flynt proposed in his essay 'Concept Art' (1961)?[1] Or does the idea of conceptual art belong to a different field of enquiry? Is it best conceived in more narrowly historical terms, as the art of a particular movement: the 'dematerialization' of the art object, 1966–1972, in the Americas, Europe, England, Australia and Asia, for instance – as documented by Lucy Lippard in 1973?[2] But what about more recent work and art from other places – Soviet Russia, Eastern Europe and China – included, for example, in the 1999 exhibition 'Global Conceptualism'?[3] Or should this work be considered neo-conceptual? If so what is its specific difference? Alternatively, is conceptual art better understood more generally, such that one might talk of conceptual painting, conceptual sculpture, conceptual photography and conceptual architecture? Indeed, is not all contemporary art in some relevant sense 'conceptual'? Is there, then, such a thing as a completely non-conceptual art? What could it be? Something purely aesthetic perhaps, what Duchamp called the 'purely retinal'?[4] If so, what could the 'aesthetic' and 'conceptual' have in common to make both 'art'?

If not, what is the relationship between conceptual art and the conceptual dimension of other kinds of art?

These are just some of the questions raised by the avant-garde art of the 1960s and early 1970s that continue to resonate today. Conceptual art is a category of the 1960s and the Sixties is disputed territory for more than art-historical reasons.[5] Most recent writing about conceptual art is associated with one or other of three genres of political writing about the legacy of the Sixties: the right-wing jeremiad about collapsing standards and a 'culture of complaint'; the left-wing story of heroic failure, or theoretical triumph in practical defeat; and the progressivist narrative of a postmodern liberalism ('beyond left and right') for which the 1960s has become the harbinger of a new, post-political age.

Conservative critics have singled out conceptual art's anti-aesthetic intellectualism as the source of a reductive and relativistic, instrumental use of art, which threatens the very basis of the polity in collective cultural life.[6] On the Left, this same intellectualism is praised for its distance from an aesthetic purism that would promote the development of our perceptual faculties while leaving all other aspects of social experience untouched (although conceptual art's related attempt to side-step the appropriative mechanisms of the market and the museum is nonetheless acknowledged to have failed).[7] Finally, for postmodern liberals, the legacy of conceptual art is the inauguration of a genuinely democratic art space, in which all previous conventions of medium-specificity have been abandoned, along with the distinction between autonomous ('high') and commodity ('low') art, in a semiotic free-for-all.[8] Here, conceptual art is neither triumphant as 'politically correct' multiculturalism (as it is for the Right), nor defeated as culture but victorious as theory (as it is for the Left), but simply surpassed, disappearing into its post-conceptual product without remainder. Conceptual art remains a disputed idea. Whether viewed as an aberration, a heroic failure, a stepping-stone to the present, or an unfinished project, its neuroses continue to speak to us in a number of registers (artistic, theoretical, political), in a number of different ways.[9]

One reason for this is that the avant-garde of the 1960s rediscovered and refashioned some of the basic devices invented by the European avant-garde between the two World Wars (Dada, Surrealism, Futurism, Constructivism, Productivism), under new social and artistic conditions. In the process, it transformed their meanings, not just with respect to its own practices, but with regard to those of the earlier period as well.[10] Conceptual art forms a crucial link in a particular cultural-political history – what the artist and critic

Jeff Wall has called 'the dream of a modernism with social content' – that continues to this day.[11] There is also the question of the role of conceptual strategies in the more commercial post- (and neo-) conceptual art of today. Since the beginning of the 1990s, the international art world has been dominated by a formally diverse array of 'post-conceptual' objects and practices that combine the freedom of means characteristic of the art of the late 1960s and early 1970s with the market orientation and antipathy to theory that distinguished the reaction against that art during the 1980s. The aspiration to intellectual rigour for which conceptual art is justly famous, in its investigation of what Rosalind Krauss has dubbed the 'post-medium condition',[12] promises to provide a critical standpoint from which the art of the present might be judged. Conversely, the new uses to which conceptual strategies have been put in recent art throw the canonical works of the 1960s and 1970s into sharper relief.

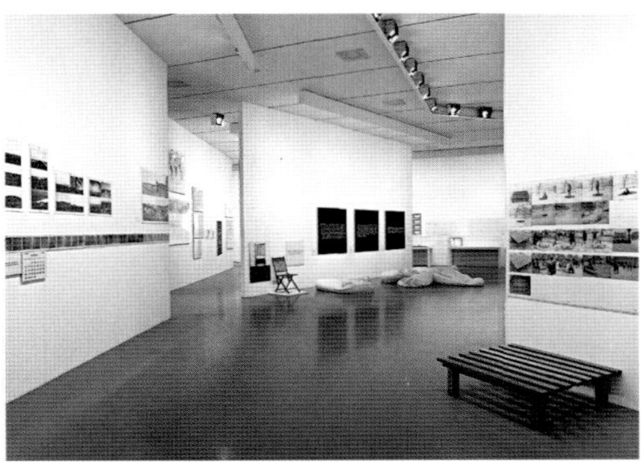

Installation view, 'Information', The Museum of Modern Art, New York, 1970

Historically, the practices to which the term 'conceptual art' is now used to refer were pretty much an 'extended free-for-all'[13] and it was some years before this designation became generally accepted. Ursula Meyer published her anthology of the movement, *Conceptual Art*, in 1972, but Gregory Battcock's critical anthology of 1973 was entitled *Idea Art* and the meandering subtitle of Lucy Lippard's *Six Years: the dematerialization of the art object ...*, also from 1973, refers to '*so-called* conceptual or information or idea art', registering the contested and open nature of the terms.[14] A similar diversity is to be found in the titles of the key exhibitions of the period. None of the four most important relevant shows of 1969 in the USA and Europe used the term 'conceptual art'. What is often regarded as the first conceptual art exhibition, curated by New York dealer Seth Siegelaub in vacant office space in the McLendon Building at 44 East 52nd Street, is generally referred to by its dates alone, 'January 5–31, 1969' – although it also bore the negative legend '0 Objects, 0 Painters, 0 Sculptures'. The seminal European show, organized by Harald Szeemann at the Kunsthalle in Bern that spring, 'When Attitudes Become Form', was subtitled 'Works–Concepts–Processes–Situations–Information', suggesting a fluid network of related forms – although its second subtitle, 'Live in Your Head', indicates its preference for the mentalistic. Lucy Lippard's Seattle Art Museum exhibition in the autumn was named after the number of inhabitants of the city, '557,087'. The smaller show at the Städtischen Museum, Leverkusen, Germany, in October, was called 'Konzeption–Conception' – although one of its exhibits refers to it as 'Conceptual Art – No Objects', indicating a more explicit, but in the end misleading, working title.

The first two exhibitions to embrace the term 'conceptual art' took place in the spring and summer of 1970 in New York and Turin respectively: 'Conceptual Art, Conceptual Aspects' – a show of mostly language-based work on paper – at the New York Cultural Center and 'Conceptual Art, Arte Povera, Land Art' organized by Germano Celant, the originator of the term 'Arte Povera'. The large international group show at the Museum of Modern Art, New York, in July 1970 was simply, and more broadly, entitled 'Information'; and the exhibition that followed at New York's Jewish Museum was still more explicit in its technological interpretation of such work: 'Software: Information Technology – Its New Meaning for Art'. Elsewhere that year, the more focused exhibition at Camden Arts Centre, London, curated by Charles Harrison, assistant editor of *Studio International*, who became the General Editor of the conceptual art journal *Art–Language* in summer 1972, was called 'Idea Structures', highlighting its relationship to the 'primary structures' of minimalist sculpture.[15]

Such terminological variety points to a tension that runs through much of the work itself between critical-formal concerns with artistic definition and identity and broader interests in cultural, social and political experimentation.[16] For a label like 'conceptual art' is far more than just an empirical designation. Rather, it functions as a summary or condensation of the most historically significant aspects of practices which can be thought of under a variety of descriptions. Thus, each critical term imposes its own retrospective unity on the history of art by proposing a standpoint from which to think what is most distinctive about the art of its time.[17] In this respect, the now established dominance of the term 'conceptual art' is less the retrospective victory of one particular artistic faction over its rivals (as some complain) than the consequence of a deeper need for historical intelligibility. The idea of conceptual art raises the retrospective search for universal determinations of 'art' to the highest theoretical power, by directly challenging the definition of the artwork as an object of visual or, more broadly, spatial experience and pleasure. As such, it represents a turning point in the recent history of art with important implications for the relationship of art to other forms of cultural experience.

Lineages of Negation

As both a critical-curatorial category and a form of practical artistic self-understanding, 'conceptual art' was the product of 'a chaotic network of ideas',[18] grounded in often seemingly opposed responses to a common situation: the crisis of formalist modernism. It crystallized into a recognizable artistic movement during the high Sixties (1967–70), only to break up in disarray by 1975, in a rapidly changing economic and political environment. It is conventional to privilege Minimalism in the immediate pre-history of this process, in part because of the inspirational role of Sol LeWitt's 1967 *Artforum* essay, 'Paragraphs on Conceptual Art'.[19] However, it is useful to take both a longer and a broader view, so that Minimalism itself may appear in proper perspective, as one of at least four genealogical lines, or lineages of negation, out of which conceptual art emerged as a distinctive and internally complex field of art practice.

The range of work which can retrospectively – but nonetheless legitimately – be classified as 'conceptual' predates the movement that bears its name by several years and includes, crucially, work by Yoko Ono and others who would become associated with Fluxus. It also extends beyond what is usually considered the movement's demise in the mid 1970s, in part as a result of the subsequent globalization of the Western art world (to include the Soviet Union and China within its frame of reference, for example), in part through the continuation of individual careers. However, one should be wary of replacing too narrowly historical and critically sectarian a definition of conceptual art, such as Kosuth's '*purely* conceptual art' (see 'Word and Sign', below), by the more general notion of 'conceptualism' – understood to denote a broad change in 'attitude' towards the art object as 'materially constituted and visually privileged'.[20] For such an inclusive attitudinal definition marks out a terrain that almost all contemporary art inhabits: 'conceptual*ism*' is more or less coextensive with 'contemporary art'.[21] Yet for all its conceptuality, most contemporary art has a far less critical, and less troubled, relationship to the object of visual perception than a properly – that is, polemically – conceptual art. I shall thus adopt a relatively historically inclusive, but nonetheless critically focused approach that picks out works in which the conceptual element is predominant, in any of four main ways, corresponding to the four genealogical lines of negation that feed into conceptual art and constitute it as a historical form.

Conceptual art was the product of successive and overlapping revolts against four defining features of the artwork as previously understood within the art institutions of the West, and as epitomized in particular in Clement Greenberg's discussion of modernist painting:[22] *material objectivity*, *medium specificity*, *visuality* and *autonomy*. Each rebellion contested a dimension of the aesthetic definition of the artwork by drawing attention to the role of ideas in the production of meaning from visual experience. But each did so in a significantly different way. Each form of negation thus had as its positive outcome a different set of resources or strategic options for a distinctive type of conceptual art, as follows:

1 *The negation of material objectivity* as the site of the identity of the artwork by the temporality of 'intermedia' acts and events. This led to a type of conceptual art linked to the history of performance in music and dance.

2 *The negation of medium* by a generic conception of 'objecthood', made up of ideal systems of relations. This led to a form of conceptual art closely related to the history of Minimalism.

3 *The negation of the intrinsic significance of visual form* by a semiotic or, more narrowly, linguistically-based conceptual content. This produced a type of conceptual art connected to academic philosophy and the history of the readymade.

4 *The negation of established modes of autonomy of the artwork* by various forms of cultural activism and social critique. This generated a range of forms of conceptual art associated with the legacy of the historical avant-gardes of the 1920s in the politics of the 1960s, and with Constructivism and Productivism in particular.[23]

This final kind of work may be divided into three sub-categories:

i) works that use as their primary means intervention into, and the refunctioning of, existing cultural forms of publicity ('media') in order to transfigure, and thereby help to transform, the structures of everyday life;

ii) works that are explicitly focused on political-ideological conflicts and promote awareness of particular alternative or subaltern ideological positions;

iii) works that direct their attention to the relations of power at play within art institutions themselves.

This typological schema generates six kinds of conceptual art, corresponding to the six central chapters in the Works and Documents sections of this book. The first three ('Instruction, Performance, Documentation'; 'Process, System, Series'; and 'Word and Sign') are characterized, primarily, by formal-critical concerns of artistic definition; the second three ('Appropriation, Intervention, Everyday'; 'Politics and Ideology'; and 'Institutional Critique') represent different varieties of cultural-political intervention. The work of any particular artist is likely to be spread across several categories. Indeed, individual works may fall into more than one category, according to which aspect one takes to be most significant in any particular interpretative context. Most works are multi-dimensional in this sense. The schema is both critical and historical: it summarizes the main artistic rationales or forms of intelligibility of the works, presenting them within a critical, as well as a broadly chronological, narrative. However, the temporality of interpretation (the temporality of the schema) is more complicated than the order of the narrative suggests.

Thus, the *chronological* priority of a Fluxus-type of performance-based 'intermedia' conceptual art may be contrasted with the *critical* priority of the subsequent minimalist conceptual art, associated principally with LeWitt. For it is the latter that makes the retrospective interpretation of the former as a type of 'conceptual art' possible. Both kinds of art rejected the restrictions of the received conceptions of artistic media (painting, sculpture, music, dance), however modernistically attenuated. However, Fluxus did so through an experimental practice of *multiple* yet disjunctive mediations between different forms of art (in the notion of *inter*media, the 'between' is opposed to the simple combinations of 'multi-media'),[24] while minimalist conceptual art did so on the basis of the *unity* of a new conception of art (art as idea). It is only from the unitary critical standpoint of the latter ('conceptual art') that the distinctive conceptual character and content of the former (Fluxus-type intermedia art) becomes, retrospectively, legible and so enters into a common field with alternative variants of conceptual art.

Conversely, the incorporation of certain Fluxus-type works into the canon of conceptual art has the effect of expanding and enriching the critical purchase of the term in a way that helps overcome the restrictions and contradictions of more exclusive, and critically canonical, linguistically-based definitions. In this respect, both the denial of the 'conceptuality' of his work by prominent Fluxus artist George Brecht and the early coinage of the term 'concept art' by his contemporary, Henry Flynt, are equally misleading. For Flynt did not propose concept art as representative of the condition of art in general – as Kosuth did, for example. Rather, the opposite. He proposed it, on the analogy of medium-based arts, as part of a strategy of *depletion* of the concept of art.[25] However, this does not mean that both should not be included in a broader historical categorization, as competing conceptions of conceptual work. Such is my proposal here.

Instruction, Performance, Documentation

Works by artists associated with Fluxus have generally been excluded from the canon of conceptual art. Indeed, it is only recently that Fluxus has become recognized as central to the art of the 1960s. There are a number of reasons for this, including: its basis in musical modernism, rather than the visual arts; a critical tendency to treat performance as a separate art category; difficulties of documentation inherent to performance-related works; its elements of anti-art activism and independent systems of distribution; and its internationalism.[26] There has been inadequate recognition of the contribution of performance-based work to the logic of conceptual art in general. However, it is not as performances as such that Fluxus-type art activities should be considered a part of conceptual art, but rather in the articulated unity of the 'intermedia' relations between their scores/instructions, performances and documentation.

The idea of performance groups together a wide range of activities in a way that is anathema to medium-based modernist critics. Including everything from dance, theatre and music to impromptu, often absurd or scatological interventions into conventional settings, and public stagings of private or banal everyday acts, its history as a means of disrupting established artistic categories and exploring the possibilities of new forms dates back at least as far as the Futurist evenings organized by Marinetti in the years before the First World War. However, it was only in the 1950s that performance began to be recognized as a category in its own right, beyond mere provocation, in much the same way that a generic idea of 'the object' was to attain its own ambiguous artistic positivity a decade later.[27] Its importance for conceptual art derives from this generic character, and in particular from the opportunities it afforded for experimental transformations in the relations between its elements, beyond the confines of established forms, such as the musical concert and dramatic play.

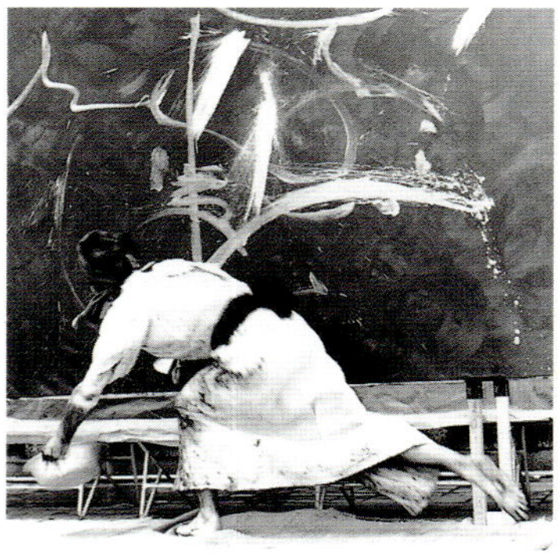

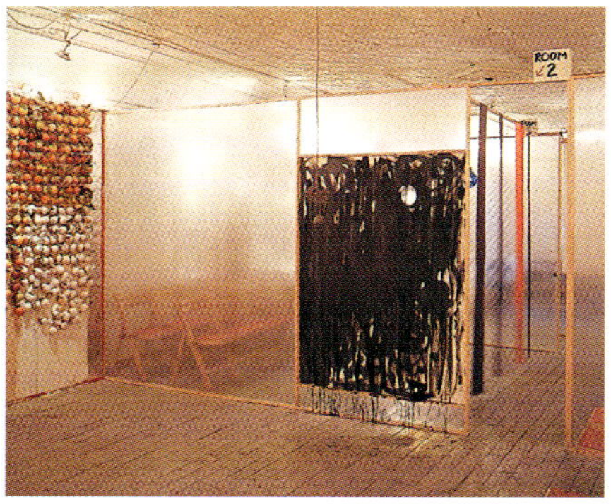

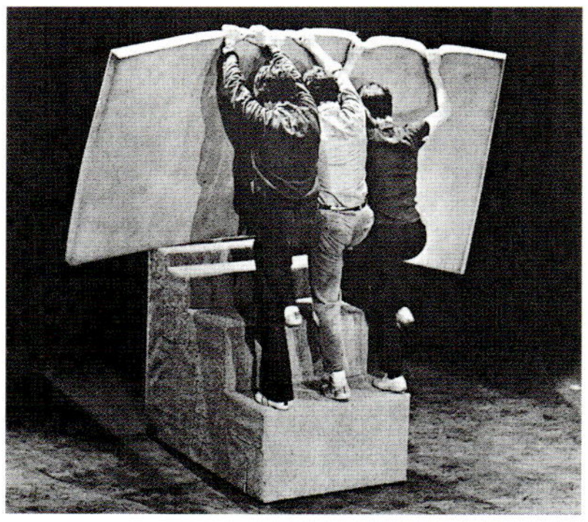

Georges MATHIEU, Painting performance on the roof of a department store, Osaka, September 1957
Allan KAPROW, 18 Happenings in 6 Parts [detail], Reuben Gallery, New York, 1959
Yvonne RAINER, Stairs, from The Mind Is a Muscle, 1966. l. to r., David Gordon, Steve Paxton, Yvonne Rainer

It is tempting to see the contribution of performance to conceptual art as lying in the conception of the work as an act or event, constituted through and disappearing into time, and thus sustaining itself over time, and into history *only at the level of its idea*. However, this is to neglect the importance of prospective and retrospective constructions of a more enduring, but nonetheless partial, actuality for the work through its 'scoring' and documentation, respectively. On the one hand, performance might be considered a paradoxical 'dematerialization' or dissolution of objecthood into time, through movement, in the very act of embodiment of the work. On the other hand, performance is always accompanied by supplementary means of representation which prefigure, retain (generally photographically) or reconstitute it, 're-materializing' it through various material modes of registration of its ideal form. (This must be so, if only in memory and oral recollection, if the act is to attain any social reality.) Philosophically puzzling as the status of such means of representation may be, they are the very stuff of the dramatic, literary and modern musical arts.[28] However, a change occurs when generic performance pieces – neither music nor theatre nor dance, as such, nor an established combination of forms (such as opera) – are located in the context of painting and sculpture. A change in the status of their linguistic (or more broadly, their notational) and their photographic registers ensues, which transforms them into a type of conceptual art.[29]

Tendencies towards a generic concept of performance as the model for a new (non-object-based) concept of art can be found across a range of arts in the mid 1950s: from John Cage's musical experiments with silence and noise (often in collaboration with Merce Cunningham's dancers) at Black Mountain College, North Carolina; through the transformations of Pollock-type action painting into performances, most notably by Georges Mathieu and the Gutai group in Japan, Yves Klein in France, and Robert Rauschenberg in the USA (but also, in a different way, more focused on process, by the young Robert Morris in California); to the developments in movement and dance associated with Ann Halprin's Dancer's Workshop Company in San Francisco of the late 1950s, and through it, the Judson Dance Theatre in New York in the early 1960s.[30] More broadly, the Situationist International offered a collective vision of performance as social intervention, in its continuation of the surrealist dream of overcoming the distinctions between art, politics and everyday life through critically 'constructed situations' which modified the urban environment in subversive ways. Similarly abolishing the division between performance and observation, but in the more restricted cultural setting of the New York art world, Allan Kaprow's Happenings became a catalyst for a series of often absurdist but increasingly political mixed-media events.[31] However, there is a specificity to certain of the performance-related practices developed by artists associated with Fluxus that distinguishes them from their predecessors. It can be traced in the evolution of the 'score-event' out of the event-score.[32]

The score is the decisive contribution of musical modernism to conceptual art. Cage's attention to the performative elements of sound-making required radical innovations in both the content and visual form of scores, as all aspects of his dramatically expanded conception of musical performance became scored.[33] At the same time, in Cage, the score both remained focused on sound and retained something of its privileged, independent status within musical culture as the site for establishing the identity of the work. Cage's scoring of performances thus pointed in opposite directions at once: away from the traditional priority of the score, as a self-sufficiently 'musical' entity, over other (not previously scored) aspects of performance; and back towards an expanded conception of the score. Artists such as George Brecht generalized from Cage's example, by focusing on the event-structure, idea and implications of simple acts of all sorts. In short, they scored 'events' as such. In doing so,

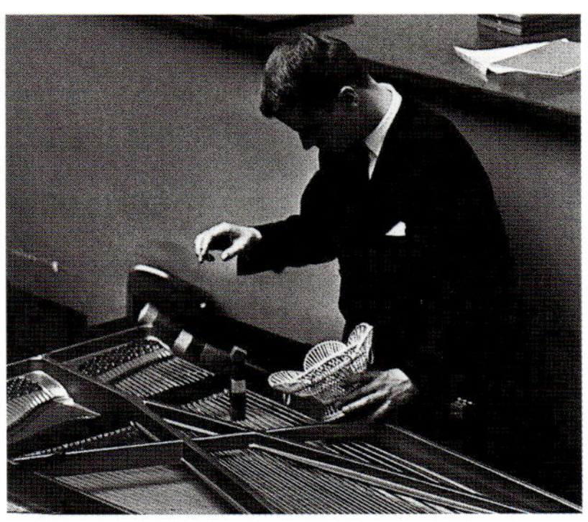

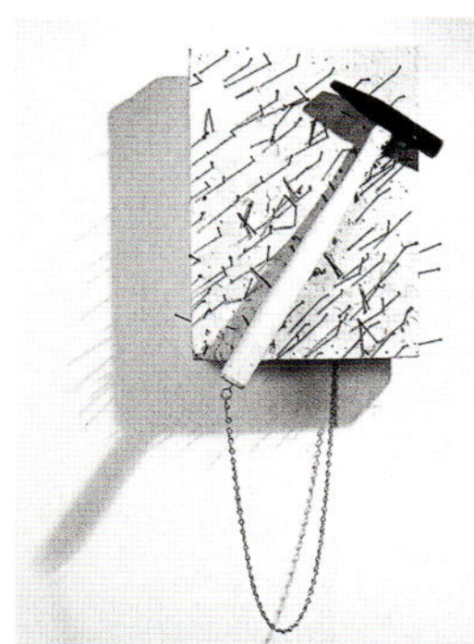

George BRECHT, Incidental Music, 1961. Performance at Fluxus Internationale Festspiele Neuester Musik, Wiesbaden, 1962
Yoko ONO, Painting to Hammer a Nail, 1961. First exhibited at AG Gallery, New York, July 1961
Yoko ONO, Painting to Hammer a Nail, 1961. Instruction for painting [detail], first exhibited at Sogetsu Art Center, Tokyo, 1962

they relocated into the context of the score certain central features of the improvisational dance of the period: a simplicity of elements; a formal structure allied to contingency, chance and random systems of relations; and an emphasis on the quotidian.[34] Thus generalized, and transposed into the medium of language, the score became an instruction. When exhibited independently, in the context of the visual arts, the instruction became a type of conceptual art we might call the 'score-event'.

If the instruction piece is the first form or genre of conceptual art, Yoko Ono's *Instructions for Paintings* (produced for exhibition at the Sogetsu Art Center, Tokyo, in May 1962) and Robert Morris' *Card File* (completed on 31 December 1962 and first exhibited at the Green Gallery, New York, in 1963) may be considered the first works of conceptual art. The variety of instances or 'versions' of Ono's *Instructions* may serve to illustrate the complexity and productive instability of the genre.

Ono's *Instructions for Paintings* began life in the closely related but qualitatively distinct form of the *Instruction Paintings* shown at the AG Gallery in New York in July 1961 as part of the exhibition *Paintings and Drawings by Yoko Ono*. These thirteen works – or rather thirteen versions of eleven works (two, *Painting to See in the Dark* and *Waterdrop Painting*, appeared in two versions) – were each composed of two main elements: (i) ink and wax on canvas, some with additional materials, (ii) an oral recital of instructions associated with each painting, and an explanation of the work to visitors, personally, by the artist or (in her absence) the gallerist. The title of each work was displayed on the wall, floor or table alongside the canvas, in the conventional manner. In addition, three of the canvases had instructions exhibited in written form alongside them, on cards. All thirteen canvases are now lost, along with two of the three instruction cards. (The sole surviving element of the exhibition is the instruction card for *Painting in Three Stanzas*.) However, all thirteen paintings and the three instruction cards are documented in photographs by George Maciunas of their installation in the gallery.[35]

At this stage, Ono appears to have conceived the works as performance-based expansions of paintings, in which the instructions at once draw attention to the event-structure of paintings, prolong it or keep it open by specifying what is required for the piece to be completed, and thereby invite the viewer to participate in the work, either directly (*Painting to be Stepped On*) or imaginatively (*Painting to See in the Dark*). At the same time, the instructions summarize the painting-events in a way that makes them repeatable, like a musical score, prioritizing the ideal content of the instruction over any particular performance. Hence, the lack of concern to preserve the results – the canvases – beyond their photographic documentation. The canvases themselves are no more privileged within the economy of the work than the photographs. Both are material traces of the work in process. Various elements of the paintings were inherently perishable: the 'live plant' in *Painting in Three Stanzas*, for example, and the wetness of *Waterdrop Painting*. The (subsequently exhibited and published) instruction for *Smoke Painting* states that it 'ends when the whole canvas or painting is gone'.[36] Nonetheless, at this point, Ono did not consider the instructions themselves exhibitable as works; rather, they seem to have had much the same status as the scores of La Monte Young's series of *Compositions*: publishable in the manner of scores, but not exhibitable in a gallery context. Independent exhibition of the instructions themselves was the next, crucial stage.

The *Instructions for Paintings* were exhibited in the lobby of the Sogetsu Art Center, Tokyo, from 24 May 1962 as the fourth part of a four-part programme, *Works of Yoko Ono*, otherwise comprising *Music*, *Events* and *Poems*. This time instructions alone were exhibited, in Ono's translation into Japanese, in calligraphic script on paper by her then-husband, the composer Ichiyanagi Toshi. The programme lists ten such works by individual names – eight from the AG Gallery show, with the word 'painting' replaced by the more generic 'piece' – and twenty-eight generically entitled *An Imaginary Piece*. Twenty-two of the thirty-eight text sheets have survived. Ono had apparently wanted the instructions typed, but was unable to get access to a typewriter with Japanese characters. Wishing to avoid the personalism of her own hand, she had them copied by Ichiyanagi (a practised copier of musical scores) in a way intended to counter their reception in terms of the decorative tradition of calligraphic display, which, one might venture, was probably nonetheless the historical condition of possibility of their exhibition.[37] Thus were generated what may be considered the first wholly language-based works of visual art. They were subsequently published in printed form, in English, along with over a hundred other instruction pieces in Ono's self-published book, *Grapefruit*, in July 1964. (About one third of the total also appeared in Japanese translation.) At this point the generic title *An Imaginary Piece* became *Painting to be Constructed in Your Head* – a translation which is now regularly applied, retrospectively, to the Sogetsu exhibition works.[38]

Ono thus passed from performance via painting to conceptual art within a single year, through works which demand to be understood simultaneously as paintings, sets of instructions and encapsulations of an infinity of potential acts. These works raise a number of issues at the heart of conceptual art: (i) the *ideal* character of the work relative to the diversity of its material manifestations or means; (ii) its *linguistic* definition; (iii) the *infinity* of its possible realizations; (iv) its dependence on the *participation* of its audience for its realization. The unity of the work is rendered ideal by its dispersal across an irreducible plurality of instantiations across different media, including documentary forms; while it is the performance character of the instructed event as 'action' that imparts to this ideality a linguistic form.[39] However, it should be noted that any strict *identity* between the work's idea and its linguistic form is already destabilized in Ono's instruction pieces by the variety of linguistic expressions associated with each work, produced by the necessity for translation between English and Japanese.[40] It is the gap between the (multiple) linguistic forms and conceptually ideal content of the work, on the one hand, and any particular concrete realization or performative enactment (material or imaginary), on the other, that sustains an infinity of possible realizations; while it is the work's dependence on others for such realizations that marks its interactive or participatory nature. The precise character of this dependence is registered in the grammatical mood of the work's linguistic element: in Ono's case, the imperative.

It is interesting, in this regard, to compare Ono's instructions with Robert Morris' various performance-based objects of the early 1960s, such as *Performer Switch* (1960) and *Box with the Sound of its Own Making* (1961), up to and including the columns, portals and L-beams that made up his 1964 Green Gallery show, some of which originated as props in performance pieces;[41] and with Richard Serra's *Verb List* from 1967–68, and the associated group of works, *Casting*, *Splashing*, etc. All three share a linguistic definition of their contents in terms of a specification of acts, or a narrative context in relation to which an object is to be situated. Where they differ is in the grammar of their linguistic elements, and hence their temporality. There are important differences here between the future-oriented imperative form of instruction works, the perpetual participal present of Serra's *Verb List* and the documentary completion of certain of the performed objects. It is notable, for example, the extent to which Morris' and Serra's objects depend upon their titles to establish relations to the acts of their production within the frozen objecthood of their results. (This is particularly true of *Casting* and *Splashing*, which set up an unresolved tension between the permanent activity of their linguistic present and the completed character of their material form.) Unlike the studied anonymity of so much abstract painting and sculpture – with their strings of 'untitled's and numbered works – here, titles are very much part of the works, and in this sense not really (merely) 'titles' at all.[42]

Instruction pieces are temporally and spatially more expansive than documentary types of conceptual work, such as Bruce Nauman's early photographs and videos, On Kawara's diary series, *I Read* and *I Went*, Richard Long's walks or Douglas Huebler's appropriations of strictly delimited sets of spatio-temporal relations. Freed from musical or dramatic conventions of performance, and open to interpretation in performance by anyone, instruction pieces are unbounded, in principle, by any particular context. This both draws attention to the indeterminacy or *infinity* inherent in their linguistic expression and confers a participatory dimension to the work, requiring its audience to 'complete' it, albeit only in this instance and often only imaginatively. Such open-ended imaginative completion both clinches the conceptual character of the work and challenges the modernist conception of the artwork as an autonomous or self-sufficient entity.[43]

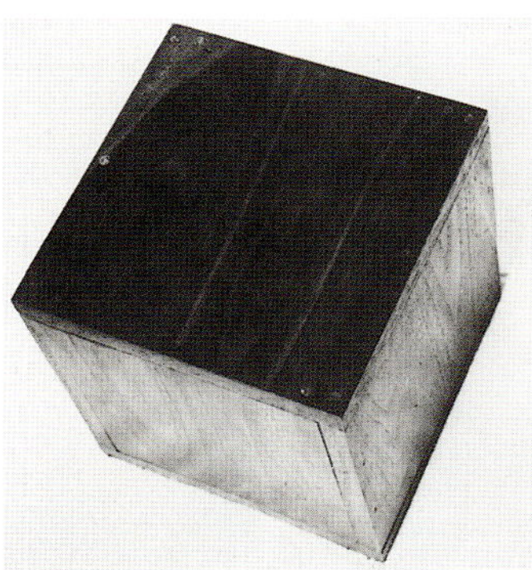
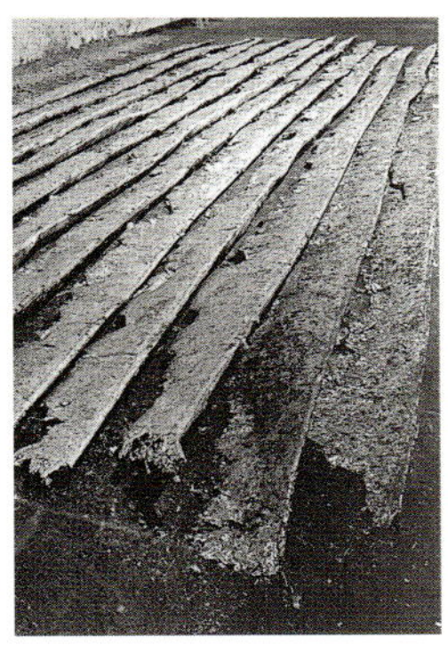
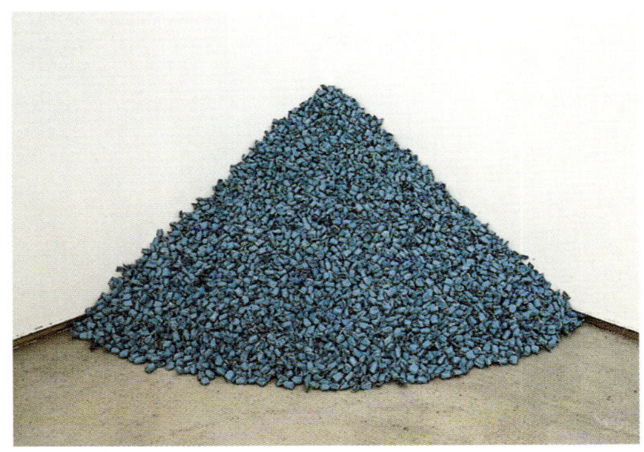

Robert MORRIS, Box with the Sound of Its Own Making, 1961
Richard SERRA, Casting, 1969
Felix GONZALEZ-TORRES, Untitled [Portrait of Marcel Brient], 1992

The solicitation of the audience in the participation of the work was part of an attempt to displace both the contemplative forms of spectatorship associated with modernist aestheticism and the presumption of art institutions that an artwork should belong to a set of recognizable types of material object, amenable to the relations of private property. It led to a strong interest in alternative forms of distribution and a number of new 'communicational' genres, such as mail art. George Brecht's notebook entry for 8 August 1959, for example, suggests that scores be 'available on printed cards or sheets of paper, to be sent to anyone'.[44] A similar practice was popularized during the 1990s, in a gallery context, by Felix Gonzalez-Torres, with his takeaway stacks of poster works and piles of sweets.[45] Even the British group of 'analytical' conceptual artists, Art & Language, hoped that their work would produce 'not a form of responsive emotion but a form of responsive activity', a critical conversation or inquiry. Such work was to achieve its intended form of distribution, 'not through being beheld or otherwise institutionalized, but through being criticized, elaborated, extended, or otherwise worked on'.[46]

The reproducibility of such art, inherent in its linguistic definition, is echoed in the importance to it of photographic documentation as its foremost representational means.[47] At the same time, the abiding requirement of some legible material trace, to which the centrality of photography attests, marks the only *partially* 'conceptual' character of the work.

Process, System, Series

It is conventional to think of conceptual art as Western art's linguistic turn. Yet the conceptual work that emerged out of the minimalist negation of medium by a generic conception of 'objecthood' was less concerned with language than with ideal systems of logical, mathematical and spatio-temporal relations. If there is a basic unit of intelligibility within minimalist or systems-based conceptual art, it is neither the act/event nor the word, but the *number*; if there is a syntactic structure common to such art, it is not the sentence, but the *formula*; and if there is a discipline in which it is grounded, it is neither composition nor linguistics, but *geometry*. Philosophically, this work is closer to a pre-aesthetic, rationalist metaphysics of the beautiful as an order of perfection, than to the post-aesthetic premises of a conceptual art grounded in either a philosophy of the act/event or a philosophy of language. Its closest artistic predecessor is serialism in modern music.

In so far as Minimalism may be associated with a recognition of the importance of language to art, it occurs not in the use of linguistic elements within artworks themselves, but in its heightened awareness of the role of *critical discourse* in the production and experience of art. If, as Charles Harrison has claimed, minimalist theory was 'the most coherent and the most powerful avant-garde discourse of the mid-1960s', this was not merely because of its 'cultural adjacency to the discourse of Abstractionism',[48] but because of its rigorous examination (and explosion) of the limits to legitimate artistic activity laid down by one particular, dominant critical paradigm: Clement Greenberg's understanding of modernist painting. A distinctive type of conceptual work exploring the properties of ideal systems of logical, mathematical and spatio-temporal relations emerged from the elaboration of conceptions of reduction and objecthood forged at the limits of formalist modernism by Frank Stella, Donald Judd, Morris and LeWitt, in the early to mid 1960s. At the same time, a related body of work was produced (notably, by Andy Warhol and Ed Ruscha) that was broadly similar in its formal structures of modular units, serial systems and repetitive ordering, but grounded technologically and socially (rather than mathematically) in relation to machino-facture, photography, film and the commodity form. Subsequently, in the late 1960s and early 1970s, these two kinds of work increasingly converged in a conceptual art that reflected upon the relations between these formal-mathematical and social dimensions.

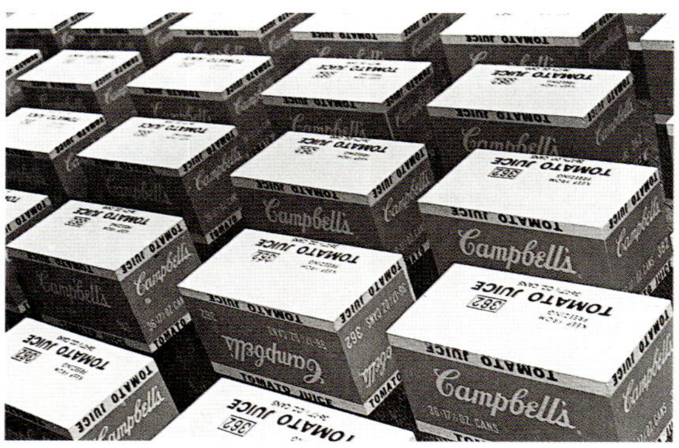

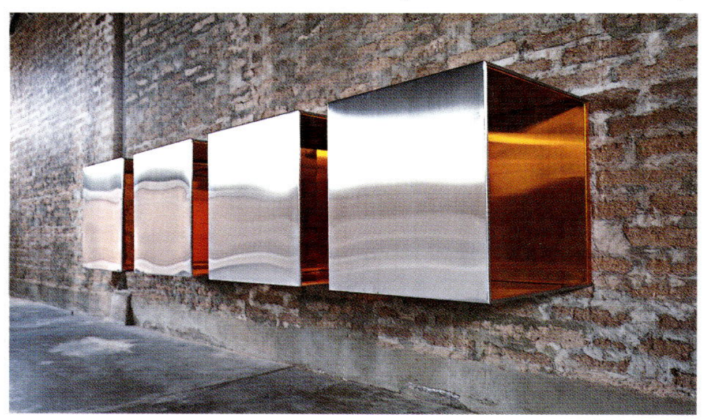

Andy WARHOL, Campbell's Box [Tomato Juice], 1964. Detail of installation, Stable Gallery, New York, 1964
Donald JUDD, Untitled, 1966

According to Judd, what he termed the 'specific object' of minimalist art 'resembles sculpture more than it does painting, but ... is nearer to painting'.[49] It was nearer to painting (modernist painting) in its abstract structural logic: not just its emphasis on surface, but in the subordination of its parts to the whole. Following Stella in the use of symmetry to abolish internal, compositional relations, minimalist objects were simple geometric 'unitary' forms. However, Robert Morris argued, the new work did not just take relationships out of the object, its three-dimensionality introduced them into the actual ('literal') space it inhabited. As a result, the object became 'but one' of the terms of a new relational aesthetic. (The other two were its site – at this point, still usually a gallery or museum space – and the embodied viewer.)[50] One of the consequences of this expansion in the spatial range and character of aesthetic significance was that it ceased to be possible to separate 'decisions which are relevant to the object as a thing in itself, from those decisions external to its physical presence', such as placement.[51] Furthermore, in so far as these decisions were no longer compositional, but rather selective and constructive (constructing the object from a pregiven stock of materials and ideal geometrical forms), they preceded the fabrication of the object. As a result, Morris argued: 'the arbitrary and incremental are abolished in favour of compulsory development. The weight of the art act is thereby shifted from judgements about termination to decisions for initiation. The *a priori* idea hovers over and informs the work.'[52]

Minimalism reconstituted objects as art via art ideas. What Morris called 'the cultural infrastructure of forming' to which these objects belonged was no longer that of the history of either painting or sculpture, but the technologies of industrial production. The referential connections established by its logic of production are 'to manufactured objects and not to previous art' – except the readymade, of course (of which more below).[53] This connection was reinforced by both the materials used in minimalist work and the frequent recourse to self-regulating series and systems of rules governing the production of the work (especially in LeWitt), in order to achieve a non-hierarchical wholeness: structural closure through mechanical self-completion. Such unity and seriality takes an immediately industrialized form in photography and film. In the work of Ruscha and Warhol, in particular, seriality appears as part of the everyday experience of images of commodities, in a world in which time itself is divided up into an infinite series of (saleable) units of equal measure. Hotels, gasoline stations, trucks on the freeway – or, in Ono's *Film No. 4* (1966), bottoms – all line up to be counted. The day is itself one such temporal unit, marked out in the ongoing series of *Infinity* or *Detail Paintings* begun in 1965 by the Polish artist Roman Opalka (each painting is a 'detail' of the infinite series) and in On Kawara's *Date Paintings*, produced from 1966 onwards. Bounded only by the prospective deaths of their producers, these series meditate on time, repetition, individuality and mortality. However, it is in the work of Sol LeWitt and Mel Bochner that the conceptual character of these procedures was most directly exposed.

Any broad similarities between Morris' and LeWitt's works of the mid 1960s conceal a fundamental difference in the directions in which they were headed. For while Morris was attracted to an expanded sculptural version of Greenbergian formalism, for which the idea of 'truth to materials', in a physical sense, remained central, LeWitt was moving towards an increasingly instrumental separation of means and ends. Thus, precisely what Morris identified as 'problematic' about schemes of 'repetitive and progressive ordering of multiple unit work' – namely, 'the fact that any order for multiple units is an imposed one that has no inherent relation to the physicality of the existing units' – was for LeWitt the distinctive point of the work. As Morris put it: 'Permuted, progressive, symmetrical organizations have a dualistic character in relation to the matter they distribute ... They ... separate ... from what is physical by *making relationships themselves another order of facts*.'[54] The ideal, *a priori* element of this kind of work was thus by no means restricted to its process of production: it changed the essential character of the work itself from that of an object of aesthetic perception to another kind of art. It is this difference that LeWitt famously summed up as establishing a 'conceptual' art, in his 'Paragraphs on Conceptual Art' of summer 1967.

LeWitt was not the first to characterize works of art as 'conceptual'. The term had been used in a loose, descriptive manner for a number of years. Lucy Lippard had written of 'conceptual extremism' as a characteristic of the art of the day in a review of Carl Andre in September 1965; and Barbara Rose had described the work of Kenneth Noland and Ellsworth Kelly (Greenberg's paradigms of 'post-painterly abstraction') as 'conceptual paintings'.[55] However, it was with LeWitt's 'Paragraphs' that the term was first used systematically to identify a distinct kind of art. It quickly took a hold in the US art world as a unifying framework for the understanding of an emergent body of work. For the essay had implications far beyond anything LeWitt himself was producing as art. At the same time, while expanding the horizon projected by his art, it still remained in certain key respects constrained by it.

LeWitt was a reluctant critic. His statement for the catalogue of *Art in Process II: The Visual Development of a Structure* (1966) begins: 'I find it difficult to write a statement that will be a correct summation of my philosophy. The work itself seems to subvert such statements, while the total of one's work creates its own philosophy ... The new work combines [with] the reality of the old and destroys the idea in which it was conceived. It cannot be understood except in the context of the other work, the original idea being lost in a mess of drawings, figurings, and other ideas.'[56] Just a year later, in 'Paragraphs', however, this notion of the *oeuvre* destroying the idea behind new work had receded in favour of that of a new kind of art in which 'the idea or concept' is indeed 'the most important aspect': 'What the work of art looks like isn't too important. It has to look like something if it has physical form. No matter what form it may finally have it must begin with an idea.' Furthermore, LeWitt claimed, crucially: 'The idea itself, even if not made visual, is as much a work of art as any finished product.' This suggests that the idea is not just 'the most important aspect', but can *itself* be a work of art. Is the physical reality of the work, then, merely optional? LeWitt does not go quite so far: 'It is the process of conception *and realization* with which the artist is concerned.' Realization remains central, not only as a clue to conception, but as what the artist is thinking about. As a result, it is the 'intervening steps' – that 'mess of drawings, figurings, and other ideas' – expanded now into 'scribbles, sketches, drawing, failed work, models, studies, thoughts, conversations', that come to the fore, as being 'sometimes more interesting than the final product'.[57]

It was an exhibition by Mel Bochner of drawings, diagrams and notations by various other artists that marked the inauguration of process-based conceptual art in the New York art world. *Working Drawings and Other Visible Things on Paper Not Necessarily Meant to Be Viewed as Art* opened at the School of Visual Arts Gallery in December 1966, more than six months prior to the publication of LeWitt's *Artforum* essay. It took the form of four books of photocopies mounted on white pedestals, containing project drawings by minimalist sculptors, alongside architectural plans, blueprints and other types of scientific diagram from commercial publications. It combined a process-based sense of art as idea with the new, cheap reproductive method of photocopying, thereby inaugurating the distinctively conceptual form of the 'xeroxbook'. The critic and theorist Benjamin Buchloh has called it 'the first truly conceptual exhibition (both in terms of materials being exhibited and in terms of presentational style)'.[58] The presentational style of Ono's Tokyo *Instructions* – wall-mounted calligraphy – and the residual sculptural qualities of Morris' *Card File* are still transitional, in this regard. This exhibition did not have 'the look' of anything previously exhibited as visual art; although it did set the tone for what would quickly become a distinctively 'conceptual' look: more like an office or a publisher's lobby than a gallery. Indeed, Bochner had already presented a magazine article as a conceptual form in his collaboration with Robert Smithson, about the American Museum of Natural History, 'The Domain of the Great Bear', published in *Art Voices* in the Fall issue of 1966.

Despite his emphasis on the intellectual aspect of artistic production, LeWitt himself was hostile to philosophy and other theoretical disciplines. ('The mathematics used by most artists', he insisted, 'is simple arithmetic or simple number systems.') For LeWitt, conceptual art is 'not theoretical or illustrative of theories'; it is not even 'necessarily logical'. Rather 'the logic of a piece or a series of pieces is a device that is used at times only to be ruined.' On the contrary, 'ideas are discovered by intuition'.[59] Indeed, he would shortly insist upon the 'mystical' rather than the 'rationalistic' character of such art, describing it is as constituted by 'illogical judgements'.[60] One reason for this is that LeWitt's art practice is structured around an exploration of the continuities and disjunctions between conceptual and perceptual logics that throws the rationality of its own mathematical formalism into doubt. The simplest serial formula becomes disorienting and can appear pointless once realized systematically in three-dimensional form. There is an absurdism in systematicity here that adds a Beckettian humour to the work. Yet this is the only 'reason' to be found within such formal systems, and LeWitt pursued it relentlessly.[61]

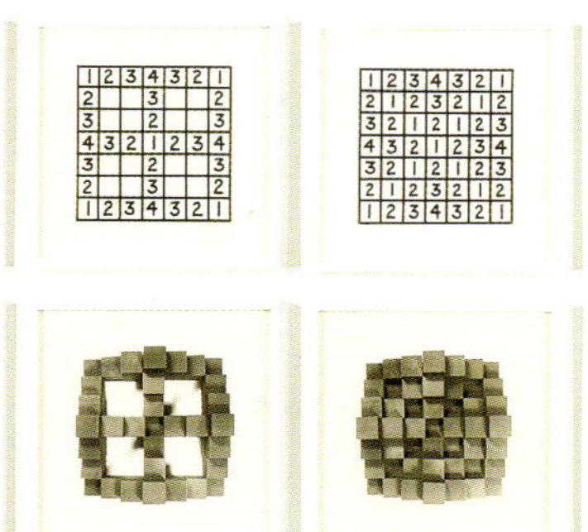

Mel BOCHNER, 36 Photographs and 12 Diagrams, 1966 [detail]

This ironic, yet obsessional, dual (conceptual and perceptual) relation to a formal processual rationality is characteristic of a large body of work from the late 1960s and early 1970s, in an increasingly socially and politically inflected mode: from Adrian Piper (LeWitt's conceptual heir) and Eva Hesse in the USA, through Art & Language in Britain, to Daniel Buren and Niele Toroni in France, Hans Haacke and Hanne Darboven in Germany, and Gostomski and Kozlowski in Poland. Setting out from the difference between an ideational order of facts and the perceptual experiences of order associated with its realization, this approach led to a more general preoccupation with the relations between different systems of representation. In *36 Photographs and 12 Diagrams* (1966), for example, Bochner sets out two parallel systems of representation of the permutational development of some temporary sculptures: mathematical schema and photographic image. A strategy that would become well-known later in the work of artists such as Joseph Kosuth, Martha Rosler and Victor Burgin, this multiplication of systems of representation of the same idea draws attention to the arbitrary nature of the sign and thereby downplays the intrinsic significance of any particular visual form.[62]

Closer to LeWitt's concern with realization, Adrian Piper's early work focused on the relations between the 'here and now' (or 'indexical present') of the artist, the work and the viewer, on the one hand, and the objectivity of formal-mathematical systems of spatio-temporal representation, on the other. As such, it provides an important link between the process-based intellectual concerns of LeWitt's conceptual art and the performance-based work of Vito Acconci, in whose magazine *0 to 9* Piper's work first appeared. The relations of recognition inherent in performance would subsequently themselves become the subject of the various performances of Piper's own racial and gender identity that make up the bulk of her subsequent work.

Process-based conceptual Minimalism staged a 'perceptual withdrawal'[63] from the artwork as traditionally conceived, by reducing the intelligibility of perceptual experience to that of an invisible conceptual logic. It pushed Judd's modernist reduction one stage further: from reduction to 'objecthood' to reduction to idea. Nonetheless, this art remained largely tied to the perceptual space of realization. It made few attempts to express its ideas directly, through words alone. This was to be the focus of the self-proclaimedly more 'purely' conceptual, analytical or theoretical, language-based conceptual art that followed.

Word and Sign

Language is at stake, and in play, in conceptual art in a variety of ways. We saw one in the context of performance, in the evolution of instruction works out of the musical score. There, language functioned to designate potential acts, which might subsequently be undertaken or may take place only imaginatively, 'in the head'. Similarly, but in a more extended way, in LeWitt's conception, the whole, often linguistic paraphernalia of preparatory work and thinking was considered as good a representation of an art idea – that 'other order of facts' – as its fabricated product, if not better. The use of language as a medium for art was most direct, and most contentious, however, when it was conceived as the privileged means for the *negation of visuality* as the distinguishing quality of modern art. 'Reading' opposes itself to 'looking', here, as a different kind of visual attention, much closer to thinking and imagining than the supposedly purely perceptual discipline prized by modernist aestheticism as the distinctive value of art. At the same time, language was increasingly used as a theoretical model for the ontological status of all artworks as special kinds of 'statement' or 'proposition'.

The making of art in the form of written or printed texts might seem like a simple change of activity: from 'art' (and artefactuality) to 'literature', but this fails to grasp the peculiar function of texts in the institutional context of visual art. Texts acquire new, and inherently unstable, artistic and cultural functions by being placed in the spaces of art, and claimed as themselves artworks. How they function there is as much a product of the rules and critical orthodoxies governing such spaces, as it is of the character of the texts themselves. It is these contextual factors (including relations to other cultural forms of language-use, such as critical and theoretical writing) that distinguish the use of language in the conceptual art of the 1960s and 1970s from prior artistic occurrences, most notably in the work of Marcel Duchamp.

Duchamp haunts conceptual art with the spectre of redundancy: the idea that he might have done it all before, that his whole oeuvre might have 'already achieved the reduction of art in general to its necessary and sufficient conditions', and that conceptual art thus merely 'projected into the future what already belonged to the past'.[64] For if, as Kosuth put it, '*All* art (after Duchamp) is conceptual (in nature) because art only exists conceptually',[65] then what can be so different, or so important, about a particular body of art claiming the mantle of 'the conceptual' for itself? The answer lies in the impact of the critical self-consciousness of art's conceptual character upon particular art practices, in the attempt to render this conceptual character explicitly and consistently within the structure of artworks themselves. To understand why the burden of such an attempt came to fall so heavily (at times exclusively) upon language, it is necessary to turn, first, to the history of the readymade prior to conceptual art, and second, to the philosophical theories of meaning prevalent in the 1960s.

For Duchamp, language added 'colour' to objects, both by complicating optical experience with non-painterly forms and, via its semantic content, by 'operating' on them – changing our cognitive relations to their visual form, in complex ways. However, in order for this to work (for the visual elements to appear as terms in a linguistic operation), it was necessary to neutralize the aesthetic affect of the object. Hence the importance of the readymade, as the means for the production of a 'visual indifference' to the object: 'the total absence of good or bad taste ... in fact a complete anaesthesia'.[66] Only thus, it seemed, could art escape the aestheticism of the 'purely retinal'. Furthermore, it is important to remember that for Duchamp, initially at least, the readymade was *not* a 'work of art'.

The first readymades, from 1914 (preceding the use of the word 'readymade', which came when Duchamp arrived in the USA, the following year), were merely 'distractions', much like the 'experiments' out of which the *Large Glass* emerged: part of the renunciation of aesthetics, the attempt to 'escape taste' and, at the same time, through Duchamp's inscriptions on them, to make semiotic play with the relationship between objecthood, language and vision.[67] When the readymade was inserted into the context of art with the famous urinal, *Fountain* (1917) – its ironic claim to art status registered linguistically, in its title – it was, paradoxically, only via the reception of the documentation of its *failure* to be considered as art (by the organizers of the Independents' Show in New York, who rejected it) that it eventually became so. Its status as a non-art *object* was in this sense confirmed, simultaneously with the recognition of the *act* of its submission as an intervention into the field of art. This recognition retrospectively provided the object with art status (in paradoxical *addition* to its non-art status), by virtue of its standing in for, or material documentation of, the act of its submission or nomination as art. In this respect, *Fountain* was 'anti-art' in the full dialectical sense of the term, closer to Dada than is now generally acknowledged, although markedly less political in the tenor of its rejection of the conventions of the art institution.[68] However, with the reception of *Fountain* into the museum, and the recognition of anti-art as a legitimate genre within an expanded conception of art, the urinal itself (or rather, more trickily, its copy) inevitably acquired the aura of art 'objecthood'. With the negation of *Fountain*'s anti-institutional impulse – or at least, its consignment to history – came the return of its aesthetic dimension.

Duchamp was well aware of the danger of 'repeating indiscriminately this form of expression'. He thus decided to limit his production of readymades to a small number (something of a paradoxical act, given their basis in mass production), lest they be 'contaminated' by what he called the 'habit-forming drug' of spectatorship: taste.[69] But he could not stop their aestheticization. For 'indifference to taste' is relative, in each instance, to a historically constituted (and thus transitory) set of aesthetic norms, and as such is intrinsically susceptible to inversion. To put it another way: Duchamp's 'aesthetic indifference' is still a principle of aesthetics. Duchamp *liked* 'aesthetically indifferent' objects. It is not the same thing as indifference to aesthetics *tout court*. Duchamp's aesthetically indifferent objects stand in for, or allegorize, indifference to aesthetics, in a way which is eroded by time. Whatever appears aesthetically indifferent, in any particular time and place, is always in danger of becoming the basis for a new form of aesthetic differentiation. And this is precisely what happened to Duchamp's readymades, in the context of Minimalism, after they had made it into the museums.[70]

In its aspiration to aesthetic indifference, Duchamp's readymade was thus an ambiguous, unstable, transitional form. Like Cage's early scores, it pointed in opposite directions: in this case, (1) towards Pop art, commodity aesthetics and minimalist sculpture, and (2) towards an art that would be genuinely indifferent to aesthetics, and hence 'purely conceptual' in kind. It is in this latter sense that the readymade may be considered the 'beginning' of conceptual art; as well as also being the source of its antagonist, Pop art. Language-based conceptual art may be understood as an attempt both to restore and to radicalize the original anti-aesthetic impulse of the readymade, through the 'visual indifference' and ideal conceptual content of language as a 'readymade' signifying material. Thus, rather than using language as just one element of a work (albeit the 'operative' one), a significant body of language-based conceptual art of the 1960s and early 1970s aspired to make art out of wholly linguistic means. In the process, it transformed the essentially negative gesture of Duchamp's 'visual indifference' into a new, linguistically defined artistic positivity: 'conceptual art'.[71]

This practical artistic movement was reinforced and legitimated by a new theoretical orthodoxy that maintained that meaning is to be understood on the model of language – indeed, that all meaning is in some sense fundamentally 'linguistic'. This idea was the product of the analytical 'revolution' in Anglo-American philosophy, in the first half of the twentieth century, known as the 'linguistic turn'.[72] It was reinforced during the 1960s by the elaboration in France of a general theory of signs, 'semiology', which took Ferdinand de Saussure's general linguistics as its theoretical model.[73] Its reception in the art world was fostered by the growing recognition (implicit in Minimalism) that even the 'pure opticality' so valued in abstract painting by medium-specific modernists was, in fact, the product of a sophisticated critical discourse about experience, rather than an immediate quality of experience itself.

It is hard to exaggerate the impact of these ideas on the community of conceptually oriented artists in New York and London during the latter part of the 1960s. As Lucy Lippard and John Chandler put it at the time: 'The studio is again becoming a study.'[74] This was as much an effect of deep-rooted economic and cultural changes within advanced capitalist societies (especially, in educational provision) as of more narrowly intra-artistic developments. The generation of US artists who came to prominence during the 1960s were the first to have attended universities. At the same time, there was a massive expansion in art education and the related network of institutions (galleries, museums, journals, dealers) that make up the international art world.[75] This expansion took place in the context of a new kind of affluent 'counter-cultural' social and political radicalism. Avant-garde reaction against the anti-intellectualism of the art world was, at the same time, reaction against its elitism and social conservatism. It took the form of a virulent antipathy towards the notion of the 'aesthetic' received from late nineteenth-century aestheticism into modernist criticism. 'Aesthetics' became a sign of everything conservative, outdated and intellectually redundant. Precisely what was to replace it, however, and how the 'conceptual' character of the new language-based art was to be interpreted, was a topic of fierce and occasionally acrimonious dispute. For there was a multitude of competing philosophical positions on the precise nature of linguistic meaning from which to choose, and an immense variety of different ways to use language, practically, to make art. It was from the experimental interaction between critical positions and art practices here (with artists increasingly producing their own criticism, critics becoming artists, and theoretical criticism itself becoming a medium for art) that the creative ambiguity of the language-based art of the period derived. As one participant has retrospectively described it: 'Conceptual Art was never quite sure where "the work" was.'[76]

The diversity of projects and positions can be sampled by a comparison of the four artists represented in what is often regarded as the paradigmatically 'conceptual' US exhibition, curated by Seth Siegelaub at 44 East 52nd Street, New York, *January 5–31, 1969*: Robert Barry, Douglas Huebler, Joseph Kosuth and Lawrence Weiner. The show was motivated by

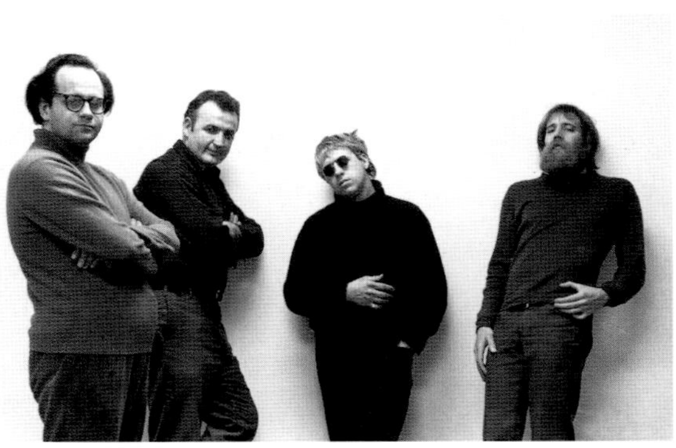

l. to r., Robert BARRY, Douglas HUEBLER, Joseph KOSUTH, Lawrence WEINER, 'Art without Space' symposium, New York, 1969

Siegelaub's conception of a reversal of the distinction between 'primary' and 'secondary' information, which allowed for the exhibition catalogue to take precedence over the exhibits. In Siegelaub's words: '... when art does not any longer depend upon its physical presence, when it has become an abstraction, it is not distorted and altered by its representation in books and catalogues. It becomes primary information, while the reproduction of conventional art in books or catalogues is necessarily secondary information. For example, a photograph of a painting is different from a painting, but a photograph of a photograph is just a photograph, or the setting of a line of type is just a line of type. When information is primary, the catalogue can become the exhibition and a catalogue auxilary to it, whereas in the January, 1969 show the catalogue was primary and the physical exhibition was auxiliary to it ... it's turning the whole thing around.'[77] Nonetheless, the differences between the four artists are instructive. For in staging different aspects of language-based art practice, each was reacting against the 'visuality' of the conventional art object in a different way. Barry was concerned with (in)visibility; Huebler with space and time, location and duration (the fundamentals of Kant's conception of 'aesthetic'); Kosuth with definition; and Weiner with the specification of relations between materials.

Lucy Lippard and John Chandler famously proposed the notion of 'dematerialization' as a way of summing up what was historically novel about an art that was dependent upon linguistic means.[78] Yet as Barry's, Huebler's, Kosuth's and Weiner's works of this period all show, the rejection of visuality as the defining quality of the significance of a work does not necessarily involve a retreat from 'matter', so much as an expansion of the means through which it may be understood to become artistically significant. For example, as Terry Atkinson argued: 'It certainly does not follow that because an object is invisible, or is less visible than it was, or is less visible than another object, that any process of dematerialization has taken place.'[79] Much of Barry's work was invisible, yet emphatically material; Huebler's work referred to past events, but via a combination of indexical traces (photographs) and printed matter (written language); and Weiner considered even those of his works that were realized in language alone – at this time, taking the form of short printed 'statements' – to represent an expansion of the notion of 'sculptural materials'. Kosuth alone considered space, and thus by implication, materiality, to be 'irrelevant' to his work.[80] In line with this view, in his critical writings Kosuth was insistent that he alone was a Conceptual artist in the proper (capitalized) sense of the term – free of all morphological, stylistic or object-based concerns.[81]
Yet ironically, retrospectively, the works that fall most clearly into Kosuth's derogatory category of 'stylistic' conceptualism are probably his own. The divide he proposed between 'pure' conceptual art and 'morphological' conceptual art quickly became a gulf into which the strong programme of a theoretical or analytical conceptual art would vanish for ever.

Barry's most distinctive works proceed in direct opposition to the 'dematerialization' thesis. They used invisible materials (principally soundwaves and inert gases) to draw attention to the manner in which 'matter' has been redefined by modern physics in such a way as to disconnect it from the traditional assumption of visibility – an assumption that forms the basis of the formalist/modernist ideology of visuality as a 'reduction to materials'. If art investigates the aesthetic properties of 'matter', this work seems to argue, then it should be as much about its (invisible) physico-chemical constituents as any immediately perceivable properties of their more complex combinations into 'objects'. However, since they are invisible, 'theoretical entities' (in the parlance of the philosophy of science), the presence of such properties must be indicated via language. *88 MC Carrier Wave (WBAI – FM)*, 1968, was made of radio waves at 88 megacycles and 5.4 kilowatts, for example; while *1600 KC Carrier Wave (AM)*, 1968, was produced at 1600 kilocycles, 60 milliwatts and 110 volts AC/DC. However, despite their imperceptibility, these are in no way merely or purely 'linguistic' works, but materially actual installations in Barry's studio, documented in Seigelaub's catalogue in the traditional manner, with photographs, (descriptive) title and list of materials. They enact a natural-scientific deconstruction of Greenberg's supposedly 'physicalist' ideology of medium-specific modern art, by drawing attention to the conceptual dimension of all reference to materiality.

Huebler's early 'location' and 'duration' pieces have a similar structure of linguistic and photographic reference. However, this is necessitated not by any 'invisibility' intrinsic to their matter, but by their reference to past events. They draw attention to the strict spatio-temporal limits of visibility as 'presence' and yet exceed these limits in their referential function. Huebler used random spatial and temporal rules for the production of his photographic documentation – photographing the same space at exactly one minute intervals, for example, or a series of spaces a fixed distance apart – in order to avoid 'aesthetic' compositions of scenes. In the presentation of the pieces, photography and language appear as equivalent but alternative 'readymade' forms of primary information. The conceptual process of 'mapping' inherent in Huebler's procedure led him to an interest in maps themselves (a common concern among conceptual artists),[82] which became a further representative source in his system of referencing, leading to what he called 'Site Sculptural Projects', based on cartographic relations. The multiplicity of ('non-aesthetic') representational forms – written descriptions, photographs, maps – was intended to produce a fluctuation of meaning, irreducible to any single form, and hence to draw attention to the ideality of meaning itself.

In 1971, Huebler formalized the principle behind his procedure into a discrete but uncompletable work, *Variable Piece No. 70 (In Process)*, also known as *Everyone Alive*, in which he pledged to '... photographically document, to the extent of his capacity ... the existence of everyone alive in order to produce the most authentic and inclusive representation of the human species that may be assembled in that manner'. When, in the 1980s, Huebler's work took a turn towards fictional narratives and mass-popular forms (especially, the comic strip), and even returned to the use of painting, in his *Crocodile Tears* project, this was subsumed into *Variable Piece No. 70* as, for example, *Variable Piece No. 70 (In Process) Global, 1981, Crocodile Tears: Inserts 'Woody Wright'*. (Woody Wright is a fictional character in the narrative).[83] The whole of Huebler's (now considerably formally expanded) output thus remained a single work, in the manner of Opalka's *Details* or *Infinity Paintings*, or On Kawara's various related series; but here, with the whole world, actual *and* fictional, as its immediate subject matter, rather than just the artist's own life. In this way, an interest in the fluctuation of meaning around the specification of spatio-temporal variables turned into a meditation on the fictional (and hence conceptual) character of narrative itself. As *Variable Piece No. 70 (In Process)* continued to develop, photographs of particular individuals began to appear labelled as parodic examples of different 'types' of person: 'At least one person who is always the life of the party'; 'At least one person for whom reality is richer than the artist's fantasies', and so on.[84] But the images were randomly paired with the descriptions, drawing attention to the way in which meaning is produced through the imposition onto singular individuals of conceptual forms.

Unlike Fluxus artists for whom the word 'piece' principally evoked a reference to music, Huebler's use of the term to describe his works foregrounds their necessarily partial, 'piecemeal' character as part of an ongoing life-project. In a similar quotidian manner, Weiner used the term 'statement' not in a formal linguistic sense, equivalent to the more technical 'proposition', but on the model of bank statements: factual documents giving an account of the way things stand in a direct, prosaic manner.[85] Rather than referring to present but invisible states of affairs, or to past events, Weiner's 'statements' are distinguished by a studied neutrality, produced by their linguistic form, the passive voice: *an amount of bleach poured onto a rug and allowed to bleach* (1968), for example. This produces a certain conclusiveness in the reference to materials, while leaving their spatio-temporal specification wholly indeterminate. The statements are thus timeless and placeless. They are open to future realizations, but, crucially, without any instruction or imperative that they be realized. Indeed, Weiner associated such instructions with authoritarianism.[86] Hence his famous 'statement of intent', published for the first time in the catalogue of *January 5–31, 1969*:

> *The artist may construct the piece.*
> *The piece may be fabricated.*
> *The piece need not be built.*
> *Each being equal and consistent with the intent of the artist, the decision as to condition rests with the receiver upon the occasion of receivership.*[87]

There are a number of things of interest about this statement. At first sight, it looks much like the tenth of LeWitt's 'Sentences on Conceptual Art', published in May of 1969 in the first issue of *Art–Language*, in which Weiner's 1968 *Statements* were themselves reproduced: a straightforward declaration of the independence of 'art as idea' from its, nonetheless possible, physical manifestation. In LeWitt's words: 'Ideas alone can be works of art; they are in a chain of development that may eventually find some form. All ideas need not be made physical.'[88] But on closer inspection there are significant differences. For when LeWitt writes of 'ideas alone' he is thinking psychologically, about events occurring in the artist's 'mind'.[89] True, he distinguished concepts from ideas ('The concept and idea are different. The former implies a general direction while the latter are the components. Ideas implement concepts'), but he nonetheless saw the work as 'a conductor from the artist's mind to the viewer's' that 'may never reach the viewer', or indeed, 'may never leave the artist's mind'. The 'pieces' that Weiner states, on the other hand, are *linguistically determinate*. There is no question of their having an existence as 'idea' until they are formulated as statements; and no question of them being 'pieces' until these formulations are actualized in some system of communication, in this case writing. Weiner considered language a '*sculptural* material' that 'gains its sculptural qualities by being read',[90] producing the perception of form in the imagination of the reader. His work is thus very much about materials, in a two-fold sense: (i) the materials to which reference is made in the statements, out of which the work may, or may not, be fabricated/constructed (bleach and a rug, one standard dye marker and the sea, etc.); and (ii) the linguistic materials through which the reference is made. Furthermore, these linguistic materials are themselves 'materials' in an ambiguous, two-fold sense: (a) in their ideal/conceptual linguistic content, and (b) in the literal materiality of any particular realization of them as writing or speech – ink on paper in small lower-case letters in Royal Typewriter face, for example, in the 1968 publication *STATEMENTS*.

Weiner draws upon all three of these senses of 'materials' in his work: linguistic content, materiality of graphic form and the constituents of the objects to which reference is made. Indeed, he constructs a reflective play between them, at the level of meaning, out of the *in*determinacy inherent in the idea of materials as such. This linguistically based semantic play, internal to each piece, makes Weiner's work central to conceptual art. At the same time, its inherent indeterminacy (reminiscent of Kant's notion of aesthetic judgement) explains why Weiner felt that the word 'conceptual' didn't really 'fit' his work. For set beside the propositional positivism of Kosuth's dogmatic critical definition of 'purely' conceptual art (see below), his materials were decidedly 'erratic'.[91] Furthermore, although 'the piece need not be built', it should not be considered indifferent to the concrete possibilities of its construction/fabrication. Rather, it is constituted through such possibilities, not merely abstractly (as in LeWitt), but via the specific contingencies of its conditions of reception: those 'decisions as to condition' that 'rest with the receiver upon the occasion of receivership'. That each of Weiner's three conditions (construction by the artist, fabrication by others, linguistic specification alone) is 'equal and consistent with the intent of the artist' *distributes* the work, ontologically, across several different states, some of which may never be realized. This is one reason why, at its best, 'Conceptual Art was never quite sure where "the work" was':[92] because it was never just in one place, or even one *kind* of place – not even, contra LeWitt, in the artist's or anyone else's 'mind' or 'head'.

Making this apparent, in opposition to the monistic materialism of Greenberg's late modernist criticism, was the most critically productive use of written language in the art of the 1960s. As Robert Smithson put it, in 1967: 'The power of a word lies in the very inadequacy of the context [in which] it is placed, in the unresolved or partially resolved tensions of disparates. A word fixed or a statement isolated without any decorative or 'cubist' visual format, becomes a perception of similarities in dissimilars – in short a paradox.'[93] However, this does not mean that the visual dimension of linguistic inscription is irrelevant, even when it is the function of such inscription to *negate* the intrinsic significance of visual form. On the contrary, it is precisely its 'unmarked' or neutral *visual* quality that performs the negation. In Weiner's early work, and that of many others of the period, this was achieved via design decisions associated with 'publishing', rather than with 'art'. Such concerns inscribe conceptual art into a history of relations between experimental typography and modern art that dates back to Futurism and Dada. In Weiner's case, the heritage of Constructivism, specifically, El Lissitsky, was one influence.[94] There was thus always, from the outset, within language-based conceptual art, the danger of a repetition of the contradiction or 'negation of the negation' inherent in the 'visual indifference' of the readymade: the danger that conceptual art would acquire, and be valued for, a 'look'.

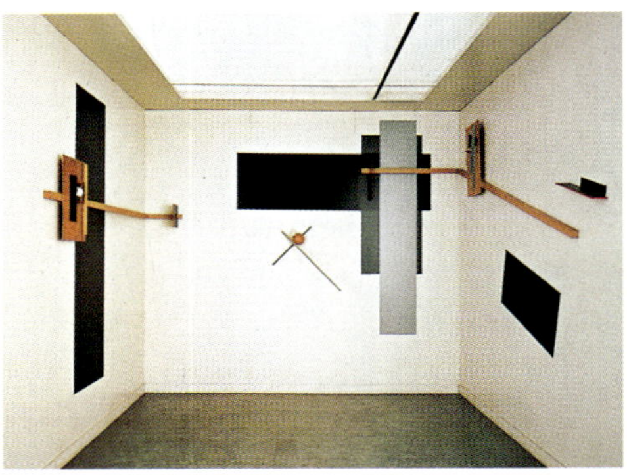

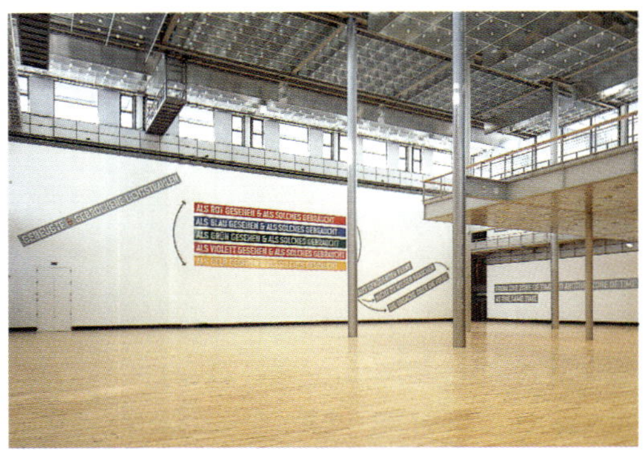

El LISSITZKY, Proun Room, Grand Berlin Art Exhibition, 1923. Reconstruction, Stedelijk Van Abbemuseum, Eindhoven, 1965

Lawrence WEINER, BENT & BROKEN SHAFTS OF LIGHT, installation view, Kunstmuseum Wolfsburg, Germany, 2000

Weiner's treatment of language as a sculptural material acknowledged this, at least implicitly, from the beginning, and his work was consequently much less threatened by it, at least in principle, than art which presumed it had left 'the visual' behind altogether. In fact, Weiner's work rapidly became more self-consciously graphically stylized during the 1970s and 1980s, as it migrated from the page to the wall, and from the gallery to more public locations, in line with his desire for a wider audience and changes in the cultural form of art institutions themselves. Kosuth, on the other hand, was insistent, for philosophical reasons, that 'the object is conceptually irrelevant to art'.[95] He was thus more vulnerable to the word as, in Smithson's fine phrase, 'an agent of disaster' for an artist.[96]

Smithson attributed both the 'fear' of language among artists and the 'delight' it causes them to the fact that 'nobody knows what it is'.[97] Kosuth set out to master this fear through philosophy and he chose a philosophy of a peculiarly reassuring kind: logical positivism, the 'analytical' philosophy of language produced in Vienna between the two World Wars and popularized in the English-speaking world by the British philosopher A.J.Ayer.[98] Kosuth was less concerned with the properties of language as an artistic material, than with a particular use of language, the 'analytical proposition', as a theoretical model for the work of art itself. In tracing conceptual art back to Duchamp's readymade, it was not the cultural dynamics of its 'visual indifference' that he was interested in (he *presupposed* this), but its 'meta-artistic' function of questioning the nature of art by *stipulating* that some particular thing is 'art' that otherwise falls outside the established extension of the term. 'Being an artist now means to question the nature of art', Kosuth argued,[99] in line with the Duchampian avant-garde of the late 1950s and 1960s (which was something quite different from questioning the limits of a medium). Unlike Fluxus, however, for whom this questioning functioned as an opening onto an infinity of possible activities, each of which raised new questions (since it is in the nature of art that the question as to its nature cannot be answered), Kosuth proposed that each work of art was a distinct self-legitimating answer or analytical art 'proposition'.

The idea that works of art function as 'propositions' has a rich history: in the late 1950s, Yves Klein called his monochromes 'Monochrome Propositions', for example; while in Brazil in the early 1960s Lygia Clark used the term to describe the participatory sculptural forms which emerged to replace her earlier Concretist constructivist work.[100] The notion is implicit in any rhetorical conception of art as a mode of assertion or the carrier of an argument. What is specific to Kosuth is his importation into art-critical discourse of the logical positivist notion of an 'analytical' proposition: a proposition with an ideal, *tautological* content that is true by virtue of relations of meaning alone, and hence provides 'no information what-so-ever about any matter of fact'. Works of art, Kosuth claimed, *are* analytical propositions. As such, each work of art is 'a *definition* of art'.[101]

Furthermore, Kosuth made this critical conception the explicit basis of his art practice: the idea that art is an idea (in the form of an analytical proposition) became his particular art idea. Hence the collective subtitle of his most famous series of works: *Art as Idea as Idea*. The idea that each work of art is a definition of art was initially conveyed in a sub-series ironically entitled *Titled (Art as Idea as Idea)*, through the symbolism of enlarged photostats of dictionary definitions of key words, such as 'painting', 'object' and 'meaning', which provided the final element in the title distinguishing each individual work: *Titled (Art as Idea as Idea) (meaning)*, for example. Kosuth's 'pure' or analytical conceptual art thus took up the baton of the meta-artistic side of Duchamp's practice, transforming its anti-art negativity into a new conceptual positivism. More specificially, Kosuth transformed the merely *abstract* negation of the aesthetic conception of art performed by the anti-art element of Duchamp's readymade into a *determinate* artistic negation, by producing 'conceptual art' as the third term in a dialectical triad: aesthetic object–readymade–conceptual art. As a result, his 'conceptual art' remained internal to the modernist conception of the autonomy of the artwork.

In fact, Kosuth received Duchamp's readymade into the context of a quite specific version of the idea of artistic autonomy as self-referentiality: Ad Reinhardt's understanding of monochrome painting as 'art as art'.[102] Duchamp's ready-mades were interpreted by Kosuth, in the wake of LeWitt's 'Paragraphs', as a radicalization and inversion of the logic of Reinhardt's position: from the idea of 'art as art' to 'art as idea (as idea)'. Ayer added the final layer: the reinterpretation of self-referentiality as analyticity. Duchamp + LeWitt + Reinhardt + Ayer = Kosuth. This was a convoluted and heady brew. Yet the works themselves were far from incompre-hensible: their enlarged reproductions of lexicographical and philosophical texts were clearly coded references to intellectual reflection upon the way meaning was being produced by the work, while their typographical designs had an immediate reference and appeal familiar from the advertising industry. Kosuth's *conception* of art was so radically anti-aesthetic that he made little attempt to *produce* 'visual indifference'. Quite the reverse, in fact. There was no need, because the object was 'conceptually irrelevant'. As Jeff Wall has argued: ' [Kosuth's work] presents the vestiges of the instrumentalized 'value-free' academic disciplines character-istic of the new American-type universities ... in the fashionable forms of 1960s advertising ... In this sense [his] conceptualism is the *doppelgänger* of Warhol-type Popism in its helpless ironic mimicry, not of knowledge, but of the mechanisms of the falsification of knowledge, whose despotic and seductive forms of display are copied to make art objects.'[103]

Directly contrary to his self-understanding, Kosuth carried out an *aestheticization* of logical positivism. This was quite alien to the conceptual art of someone like LeWitt, with his aversion to the 'slick art' that results when an artist 'learns his craft too well'.[104] It turned out not to be enough to conceive the object as a mere 'by-product of the need to record the idea'; or to argue that: 'to consider the objects produced within the [theoretical] framework ... as 'looking-at' objects rather than 'reading-about' objects is to look for first-order-visual information where there is *no intention* to produce such information'.[105] For this is precisely what the art institution does to 'objects', regardless of the artist's intention. Here, for all its apparent sophistication, Kosuth's philosophical conception lagged behind Weiner's laconic notion of language as sculptural material.

But what if one were to disrupt the context, or create a new one, in order to break down the distinction between artist and critic, artwork and critical writing? Then, surely, the problem of visuality would be transformed. The conceptual artist would not have to make works separately from criticism, in order to embody theoretical positions developed elsewhere (in the manner of Kosuth), but could present the process and proceeds of theoretical analysis as themselves a new sort of 'art'; at least, for as long as the classification of practices into art and non-art practices retains its significance as a measure of cultural value. This was the experimental project of the British group Art & Language, founded in 1968, in their journal *Art–Language*. Art & Language sought to explore 'the possibilities of a theoretical analysis as a method for (possibly) making art'[106] in a number of overlapping contexts: (i) conversation and writing within the group, (ii) teaching on the Art Theory course at Coventry School of Art in England, (iii) the journal and (iv) the conventional but contested gallery/museum spaces of the art world. This complication of 'context' is important. For whereas Kosuth's conceptual art aimed to disrupt the relationships between works of art, exhibition catalogues and critical writing, it operated within the self-enclosed space of the New York gallery world. The project of Art & Language was more closely tied to art educa-tion and involved the idea of an alternative art community, as part of a wider socialist politics.[107] This placed the issue of language-use in far stronger relief. It also meant that their writing was often more a (partial) record of ongoing conversations than the exclusive focus for their formulation of ideas.

Conversation, and the idea of a conversational community, were (and remain) central to Art & Language's art practice, which, during this period, largely took the form of 'more or less elaborate models and projections of the complexity of a conversational world':[108] most famously *Index 01* (1972), a massive cross-referential index system mapping relations of compatibility, incompatibility and lack of relational value between 350 separate texts, exhibited at *Documenta 5* in eight filing cabinets, with enlarged typescripts specifying the relations between texts displayed on the walls. This was in many ways a systematic philosophico-linguistic reprise of Morris' *Card File* by way of Bochner's *Working Drawings and Other Visible Things on Paper Not Necessarily Meant to be Viewed as Art*. The conversational world recreated there began as analysis of 'the language-use of the art society'[109] and its philosophical complexity was prodigious. For whereas Kosuth anchored his work in the fixed position of Ayer's logical positivism, Art & Language had embarked on an extended intellectual voyage. Setting out from the social conception of language in Wittgenstein's later work (the 'language-games' of the *Philosophical Investigations*), its horizon soon expanded to include most of the Anglo-American philosophy of language of the time. As such, Art & Language attempted to internalize philosophy as a disciplinary practice into their art practice, or rather, to make art out of philosophical conversations.[110] These conversations began as conversations about art, but they rapidly developed a logic of their own. For example, what began as an interest in what might count as an art object soon turned into an interest in what might count as an object, *per se*; while what started out as a collective attempt to resolve certain theoretical issues became more of a means for sustaining the collectivity of the group or, in their own Beckettian idiom, for simply 'going on': maintaining a marginalized syndicalist art community as a way of holding certain questions open in the face of the commodification of conceptual art itself.[111]

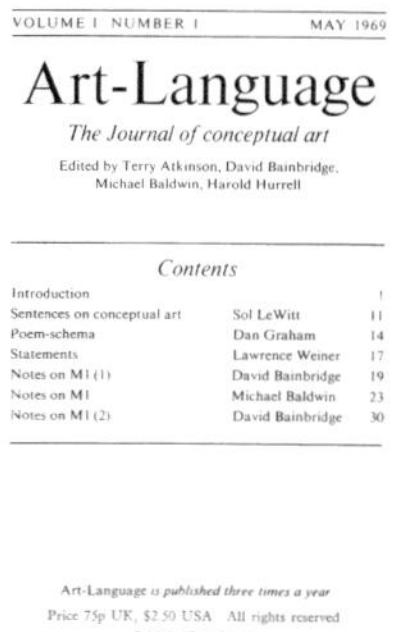
VOLUME I NUMBER I MAY 1969

Art-Language

The Journal of conceptual art

Edited by Terry Atkinson, David Bainbridge, Michael Baldwin, Harold Hurrell

Contents

Introduction		1
Sentences on conceptual art	Sol LeWitt	11
Poem-schema	Dan Graham	14
Statements	Lawrence Weiner	17
Notes on M1 (1)	David Bainbridge	19
Notes on M1	Michael Baldwin	23
Notes on M1 (2)	David Bainbridge	30

Art-Language *is published three times a year*
Price 75p UK, $2.50 USA All rights reserved
Printed in Great Britain

ART & LANGUAGE, Art-Language, Vol. 1, No. 1, May 1969

Unlike Kosuth, Art & Language recognized that they needed to *produce* 'visual indifference': that it mattered not what the work was like, but what it was unlike (an object of aesthetic appreciation). However, in retrospect, they came to accept the inevitably 'quasi-decorative' status of *Index 01*, the most complete representation of their conversational world. 'The formal blandishments of the pictorialism of the text' (and its installation) could not be avoided, if the text was to carry the burden of *immanently* negating the 'visuality' of the artwork. After a brief highly politicized phase in the mid 1970s, Art & Language reinvented their artistic practice via this very dilemma. They subsequently sought to internalize into their productions, not philosophy, but reflection on the history of conceptual art itself. The issue would no longer be how to make art with words, but how to reinvest the work of art (with or without words) with the reflexive, 'essay-like' character of writing, with which it had previously been endowed by the interpretative schema of modernist criticism.[112] In the meantime, other artists had side-stepped the threat of aestheticization lurking within the linguistic manifestations of the 'purely conceptual' by rejecting the notion of artistic autonomy upon which it depended, in order to produce art at the interface with other cultural forms.

The three kinds of conceptual art discussed so far each sought to negate, or do away with, a different aspect of the artwork as previously conceived: *material objectivity*, *medium specificity*, *visuality*. However, all three continued to operate within the bounds of the idea of art as an autonomous cultural realm. The final three types of conceptual art all question this presumption. Indeed, each functions conceptually by virtue of the way in which it negates, or does away with, a particular boundary that sets art apart from other cultural practices. Each one focuses on art's relations to a discrete social sphere: (i) everyday forms of publicity or 'media', (ii) politics, (iii) the social relations of power internal to the art institution itself. However, in each instance, the expansion of art's cultural functions results in a kind of anti- or post-autonomous art which is nonetheless ultimately, paradoxically, still autonomous, because its additional functions are freely chosen by the artist, often in a merely projective, suggested or imagined manner. Such art responds to 'no external function or practical command'. In this respect, post-autonomous conceptual art is a 'liminal type' of autonomous art.[113]

Appropriation, Intervention, Everyday

Since the mid 1980s, the term 'appropriation' has been used to refer to the reproduction by one artist of another artist's work. Originally, however, and more fundamentally, it denotes the transposition of an object from an *extra*-artistic context into an artistic one, and its consequent re-functioning, in such a way as both to mark and to challenge the idea of art as a set of special kinds of object. Duchamp's readymades were the first works of appropriation (reducing collage to a single element), but the practice soon became a common one within Surrealism, with the imagistic use of found objects of every sort. Surrealism mined the cultural-historical unconscious of the readymade, bringing to the surface the everyday traces of repressed desires. By the early 1960s, this dissenting, subaltern strand of modern art had begun to find its way into Western art museums as a legitimate kind of 'art'. In the process, however, its critical force was diminished, as the age of the objects in question distanced them from the everyday world of the present, re-establishing the divide between the artwork and the everyday object that the readymade had (initially so shockingly) collapsed. At the same time, in the aftermath of Minimalism, the position of the opposite or contrary to the artwork shifted from the industrially manufactured object to the products of the new technologies of mass communication: radio, film, television, newspapers and colour magazines. In this context, it was no longer physical objects that were to be appropriated but visual formats or whole cultural forms. Correspondingly, the mode of appropriation could no longer be simple recontextualization and titling, but required a more complex engagement and negotiation with the other cultural forms. At its best, appropriation became a mode of artistic intervention into the cultural uses of media: a model for alternative cultural practices. It is in functioning as a model that the conceptual character of such work lies.[114]

What are now widely regarded as two of the most important works of art of the 1960s appeared as articles in art magazines: Dan Graham's *Homes for America* (1966) and Robert Smithson's *The Monuments of Passaic* (1967), in *Arts Magazine* and *Artforum*, respectively. Graham explains the trajectory of his magazine works in terms of a complication of the strategy of Duchamp's readymade. His inspiration was Dan Flavin's installations of fluorescent lights. These are usually understood in the context of Minimalism in terms of their formal qualities as 'specific objects'. For Graham, however, what was most interesting about Flavin's work was its use of a material that was 'both part of the gallery apparatus and part of the larger, existing (non-art) system of electric lighting in general use'. Flavin refunctioned as art a non-art part of the art gallery system. In Flavin's work, electric lighting thus signifies in a dual, ambiguous way, referring to two contexts at once: neither simply the gallery apparatus nor simply the outside world. As Graham saw, the same is true of photography as a reproductive medium and, more particularly, the magazine. Graham became interested in these 'general cultural frameworks' upon which gallery art is dependent, as both 'a reaction against the gallery experience' and 'a response to contradictions' within it. In particular, he noted the Duchampian tendency to raise everyday objects to the status of art, instead of 'reducing gallery objects to the common level of the everyday object'. Returning to the original non-art status of the readymade, in a new historical context, he began to focus on everyday, non-art instances of the kind of formal and serial qualities associated with conceptual Minimalism, in which these qualities function as carriers of distinctive socio-political contents.[115]

Initially, Graham had hoped to use his formal yet nonetheless 'artless' documentary photographs of suburban tract housing in a popular magazine like *Esquire*, as a kind of artistic imitation of a photo-essay, lurking invisibly within a non-art context – like a Flavin in a shop selling fluorescent lighting, perhaps. This would have been a further dialectical twist of Duchamp's idea of the 'reciprocal' readymade: not 'use a Rembrandt as an ironing board' (Duchamp's example),[116] but 'use a "readymade" ironing board as an ironing board', or something like that. However, this never came about; although Graham did produce equivalent works in the context of advertising, such as *Detumescence* (1966–69), an advertisement he placed in various magazines for a qualified medical writer to describe sexual detumescence in the human male. Instead, Graham used the occasion of an invitation to write for *Arts Magazine* to reconfigure his photographs as illustrations to a short critical essay on the permutational use of prefabricated modular units in suburban housing. However, the magazine relaid the piece using a different image (ironically, by Walker Evans, whose photographic style Graham had himself appropriated into the context of Minimalism).

The piece thus came to exist in two separate forms – or rather, it was distributed *across* two separate forms: the published pages of the magazine and Graham's original paste-up. It was subsequently exhibited in a third form as a lithographic print, *Homes for America* (1966–70, two panels in mixed media, each 102 x 77 cm), which contained additional photographs. In fact, there is now a fourth version, published in a collection of Graham's writings, which includes further additional photographs by him, and within which the original layout is itself reproduced as an illustration.[117] In this version, the entire text thus appears twice, once in miniature. It is this distributive form, split between a singular 'original' layout and (amended) mass reproductions, that makes *Homes for America* such an important work, as a model of the threshold condition between art and non-art that it had set out to explore. By a quirk of fate, *Homes* manages to stage its inaugural intention to remain outside the grasp of art, within art, and thus to be a peculiar kind of non-art art, via the documentation of the history of its reception.[118] In this respect, it is the *Fountain* of the 1960s.

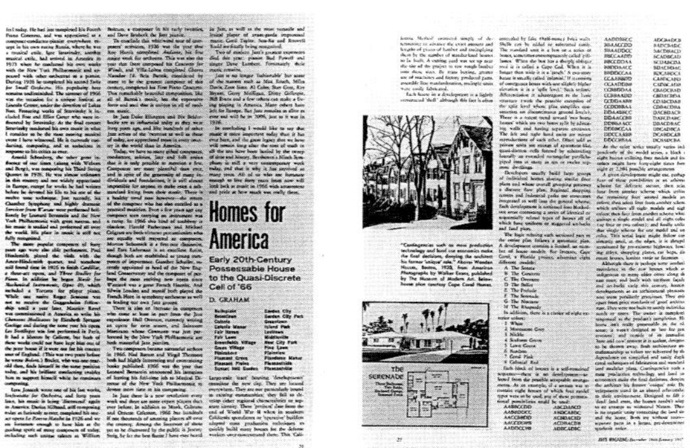
Homes for America
Early 20th-Century Possessable House to the Quasi-Discrete Cell of '66
D. GRAHAM

Smithson's *The Monuments of Passaic* has a visual form broadly similar to Graham's *Homes*, but a rather different status as a work. Smithson was already well-known as an artist-writer who innovated with the essay form. Apart from criticism on Donald Judd and essays in *Artforum* on monumentality and entropy, which drew heavily on the architectural imagination of science fiction, he had already published in other art magazines two pieces that experimented with unusual mixtures of narrative and visual genres. Distributed across these essays is a sculptural approach to architectural and mathematical space and a strong interest in popular representations of scientific knowledge. ('The Domain of the Great Bear', for example, written with Mel Bochner, was about the American Museum of Natural History.)[119] *The Monuments of Passaic* brings these interests together in the form of a travelogue in which the everyday industrial architecture in the town of Passaic, New Jersey, is parodically invested with a new monumentality, by a compulsively photographic, Instamatic eye. Like the suburbs of Graham's *Homes*, Passaic appears as a place without a past, 'just what passes for a future', new constructions of roads, homes, industrial plants: 'ruins in reverse'. It gains what meaning it has from its strange timelessness, its 'clumsy eternity', echoing clichés of infinity with its 'chain of adjectives disguised as stores', its blandness and lack of particular interest. 'If the future is "out of date" and "old-fashioned",' Smithson writes, 'then I have been in the future.'[120]

Like Graham's *Homes*, but in a more subjectively invested (complexly temporalized rather than strictly structural) manner, Smithson's *Monuments* exhibits an extraordinary capacity to refigure everyday experience, endowing it with artistic meaning, via the strategic deployment or refunctioning of photojournalistic form. This power to refigure, traditionally associated with the classical genres of autonomous art and literature, depends here on an extra-aesthetic, 'popular' cultural context, which nonetheless allows for, or opens onto, an 'artistic' reading, through the reception of the work into the critical context of avant-garde auto-critique. The art magazine functions here as a kind of relay between commercial and artistic cultures. It is the privileged instance in a wide array of photojournalistic art practices: some explicitly diaristic (On Kawara, Opalka); others focused on particular means of communication, such as the mail (On Kawara, Eleanor Antin, Susan Hiller) or advertising (Graham, Kosuth); or means of exchange, such as money (Akasegawa Genpei, Tibor Hajas); or travel, such as passports (Komar and Melamid); or, more simply, on mundanely repetitive tasks (Morris, Buren, Braco Dimitrijevic, Mierle Laderman Ukeles, Ilya Kabakov).[121]

The impact of such appropriations as cultural interventions depends upon the social significance of the site in question, the contingencies of the moment and the deeper historical resonances of their play with forms. Thus, the series of works precipitated by Akasegawa's *Model 1000-Yen Notes: Printed Work* (1963), based on his arrest for forgery and subsequent trial and conviction, attest to both the highly charged symbolic significance of printed money and a number of distinctive features of the situation of the avant-garde in Japanese society.[122] In contrast, Dan Graham's advertising works received no replies, created no reaction and exist solely through their representations in art history, as emblems of the invisibility of an art reduced wholly to 'the

Dan <u>GRAHAM</u>, Homes for America, 1966. As published with Walker Evans photographs in Arts Magazine, 1966 common level of the everyday object'. In between, a wide range of 'outreach' work was produced by artists working with community groups of various sorts, such as the Artists' Placement Group in Britain, and Stephen Willats' Social Resource Projects.[123]

Gordon Matta-Clark's literal physical interventions into buildings, such as *Splitting* (1974), were well-known in the New York art community at the time. But their deeper historical resonances are only now beginning to be felt, in the wake of transformations in thinking about architectural and urban space that took place during the 1980s and 1990s, many of which were prefigured in the work of conceptual artists such as Smithson, Graham, Christo and Matta-Clark himself. (Graham's *Alteration to a Suburban House* [1978] is of particular importance here.)[124] A similar historical status may be attributed to Ukeles' *Hartford Wash* (1973).[125] Here, it is the abiding significance of gender in the social division of labour, its inscription into the everyday rhythms of institutional life and its consequent social effacement that endow the piece with its enduring significance. By the early 1970s, the conceptual art communities in Europe and the USA had become increasingly preoccupied with radical Left politics as the discursive and practical framework within which to situate their interventions. Their work began to converge with what had always been the dominant concern of conceptually oriented art in Latin America: the critique of ideology.

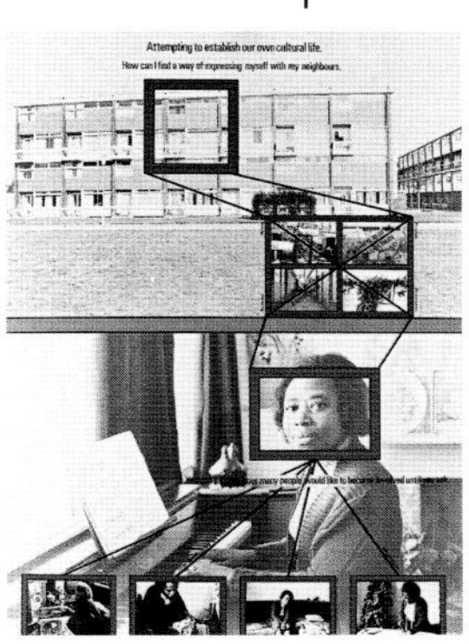

Stephen WILLATS, Learning to Live within a Confined Space, 1978 [1 of 4 panels]

Politics and Ideology

'Ideological content' is the key term of Latin American conceptual art. In distinction from the more formal ideational concerns of most US and European conceptual art (the act/event, mathematical series, linguistic propositions or the structures of cultural forms), this was an art for which 'ideology itself became the fundamental "material identity" of the conceptual proposition'.[126] It began as a communicational, media-based art, but rapidly outstripped these parameters to include direct, and often violent, political actions. Such art did not understand itself in terms of the label 'conceptual art'. (This was imported after 1969, in the wake of Kosuth's international success and used by derivative local variants of North American conceptual art). Nonetheless, both its discursive forms and explicitly cognitive content made it directly conceptual in nature. Conceptual art in Latin America may be understood as a reaction against the European and US artistic models fostered by post-Second World War modernization projects in the region (mainly, various types of Lyrical Abstraction and Abstract Expressionism) in the context of those projects' perceived failures. It was the displacement of art practices from officially sponsored art institutions into the socio-political domain that this involved which made the substitution of the art object with conceptual forms necessary.[127] Conversely, it has been argued that the political practices of certain guerrilla groups themselves performed a directly artistic cultural function.[128]

In Brazil and Argentina, where military coups toppled constitutional regimes in 1964 and 1966 respectively, it is impossible to distinguish an art of cultural appropriation and intervention from an explicitly political art, aimed at ideological subversion, collective participation and cultural recoding. Avant-garde activity centred on artistic and political interventions into systems of mass communications, of a far more direct and public kind than the discreet modifications of magazine formats within the art world by Graham and Smithson. This approach was first theorized in the Argentine manifesto 'A Media Art' (1966). Arguing that the 'ultimate characteristic' of the media is the 'de-realization of objects', and that 'works of art are, in reality, pretexts to start up the apparatus of the media' (since it is only through media images that the majority of people consume art), its authors saw the possibility of a new 'art of the media' where '"what is said" is not fundamentally important but instead thematizes the media as media'. The form of this new art was to be the publication, via press releases and reviews, of written and photographic reports of events that had never taken place.[129]

The theoretical basis of the project was a transposition of Barthes's understanding of advertising as the making of modern myths, and Marshall McLuhan's analysis of 'the medium as the message', into the political conditions of Latin America. The model for the new art was Roberto Jacoby's (May 1966) proposal for a show to consist entirely of information, taking the form of a standard exhibition catalogue, presented as if there were an accompanying exhibition, which wouldn't actually exist.[130] This is an interesting inversion of the logic of Siegelaub's subsequent 'January 5–31, 1969' show in New York. For whereas

Siegelaub's show was conceived in line with Kosuth's dictum that 'the object is conceptually irrelevant to art', Jacoby's proposal aimed to draw attention to the *illusory* power of media (such as the catalogue) to make the object *actually* irrelevant. For Jacoby it was the social reality of the power of informational media that was the issue, rather than the propositional (and therefore supposedly ideal) character of such art. The conceptual content of media art was thus posited as the social power of systems of communication to misrepresent the world: ideology.

In the aftermath of the coup in Argentina, public representations were subjected to immediate political scrutiny and, frequently, repression, leading to a rapid political radicalization of the avant-garde art community. In 1968, a number of artists from Rosario, Sante Fe and Buenos Aires joined together to form the Grupo de Artistas de Vanguardia (Group of Avant-Garde Artists) which affiliated itself to the Argentinian General Federation of Labour (CGT). Their aim was to counter a government campaign of disinformation regarding degenerating conditions in the province of Tucumán, following the closure of the majority of its sugar refineries. In developing a collective artistic practice, they went beyond Jacoby's idea of a media art to posit the necessity of creating 'an artistic object capable, on its own, of producing modifications as effective as a political act'; that is, to install a new 'said'. Such creations were seen as 'collective and violent' acts 'destroying the bourgeois myth of the new forms of art.'[131] At the same time, they maintained and developed media art's conception of 'informational circuits' as the site of intervention, extending it towards the creation of what (in the German context) Kluge and Negt would call an alternative 'proletarian public sphere'.[132]

In the production of a work called *Tucumán Burns* (1968) they set out to create 'an informational circuit to demonstrate the distortion that the activities in Tucumán suffer from a mass media that holds official power along with the bourgeois class'. Gathering facts about both the situation in Tucumán and its media coverage, with the help of the labour movement, the group staged a series of events including: a press conference, the distribution of posters and fliers in union halls, cultural centres and among students, and a large multi-media exhibition at the CGT offices in Rosario and Buenos Aires. However, the exhibition was closed by the police shortly after its opening in Buenos Aires, thereby falling victim to the very censorship it aimed to expose, and bringing to a close a brief but intense period of political conceptual art radicalism.[133]

In Brazil, the need for artists to take positions on social and political problems appeared equally pressing. The state of Brazilian avant-garde art in 1967 was summed up by Hélio Oiticica under the heading of a 'new objectivity' as follows: '(1) general constructive will; 2) a move towards the object, as painting is negated and superseded; 3) the participation of the spectator (bodily, tactile, visual, semantic, etc.); 4) an engagement and a position on political, social and ethical problems; 5) a tendency towards collective propositions and consequently the abolition, in the art of today, of 'isms' ... ; 6) a revival of, and new formulations in, the concept of anti-art.' Oiticica ends his manifesto with the rallying cry 'BY ADVERSITY WE LIVE!'[134] The terminology of a new 'objectivity' is distracting in the context of conceptual art, with its echoes of *Neue Sachlichkeit*, the Weimar movement in literature and painting; although its resonance with the broader historical spirit of the 1920s avant-gardes is apposite. More important is the emphasis Oiticica comes to place on new concepts of anti-art and their relations to 'collective propositions' and participation: 'The old problem of 'making a new art', or of knocking down cultures, is no longer formulated in this way – the correct formulation would be to ask: what propositions, promotions and measures must one draw upon to create a wide-ranging condition of popular participation in these new open propositions, in the creative sphere to which these artists elected themselves.'[135] Here, 'intervention' becomes the production of participation.

This was essentially a politicization of Brazilian Neo-Concretism, the movement that had emerged in 1959 as a vitalist reaction against the 'dangerous hypertrophy of rationalism' in Max Bill's systematic-concrete version of Bauhaus Constructivism. Neo-concretism is associated with organic models of art, but these were analogies for the phenomenological affect of the artwork as an 'almost-body', rather than a naturalism of form. In fact, it sought explicitly to 'reconvoke the problem of expression in incorporating the new conceptual dimensions created by Constructivist non-figurative art'.[136] It is best-known in the North through the works of Lygia Clark, who collaborated with Oiticica on a number of works, and later lived for many years in exile in Paris. Clark conceived her works as 'propositions' or 'proposals' in which the object was wholly subordinate to 'the instant of the act', which she considered 'the only living reality'. Furthermore, the work was not to count in and for itself, but instead as 'a simple springboard for the freedom of the spectator-author'. Propositions were to be realized: 'It is not a question here of participation for participation's sake, nor of aggression for its own sake, but rather for the participant to invest his or her gesture with meaning and for this act to be nourished by thought, in the process of bringing the participant's freedom of action to light.'[137] In the context of military dictatorship, the idea of art as what Mario Pedrosa called 'the advent of freedom' was open to immediate political interpretation. From 1968 onwards, as censorship of the arts intensified, Clark, Oiticica and Lygia Pape staged increasingly collective participatory events, in an experimental search for a new definition of 'the public'. Pape's *O Divisor* (*The Divisor*, 1968) was a huge white sheet (98 × 98 feet) cut with holes for people to put their heads through. Oiticica

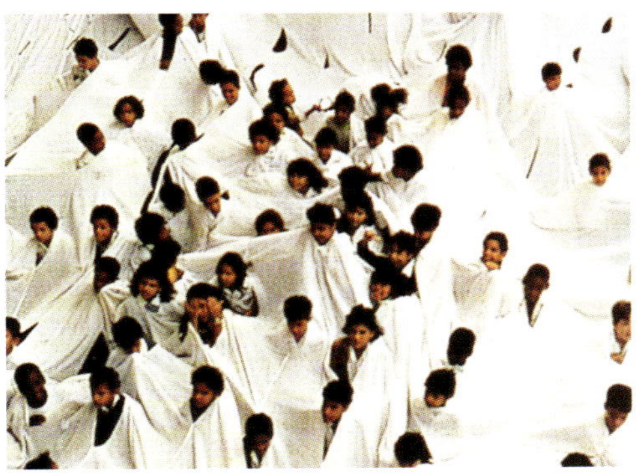

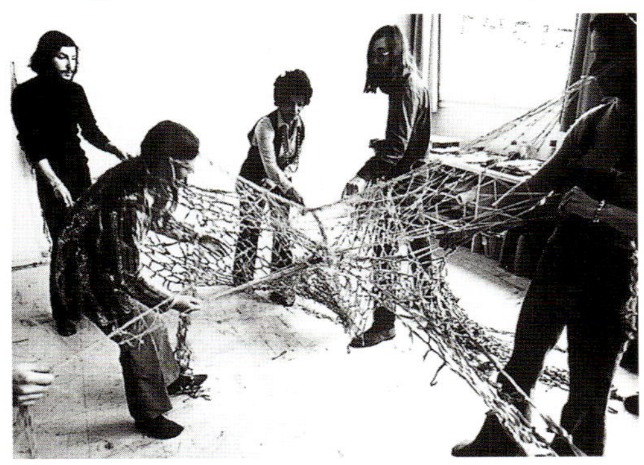

Lygia PAPE, O Divisor [The Divisor], Rio de Janeiro, 1968
Lygia CLARK, Rede de elástico [Elastic net], from Collective Body, Rio de Janeiro, 1973

constructed works which took the form of beds, tents, cabins and nests – environments to be inhabited and transformed by the public. (*Ninhos* [*Nests*] was installed in 'Information' at the Museum of Modern Art, New York, in 1970.) Clark embarked on a series, *Humanity, Living Structure of a Cellular and Biological Architecture* (1969), also known as *Collective Body*, in which people were linked together by a web of elastic bands. This art was act-based and participatory in the manner of Fluxus, and poetic and associational in the manner of Arte Povera, but it shunned the readymade for remaining tied to the domain of the alienated object. It had a fragile materiality, for economic as well as symbolic reasons, and its political content was metaphysical and allegorical, rather than sociologically specific, in part as a result of living under censorship. (These are also attributes of conceptual art in Eastern Europe.)[138] However, another Brazilian artist, Cildo Meireles, combined the readymade with the ideas of media art to reinvent intervention as a process of 'insertion' into what he called 'ideological circuits'.

During 1969, Meireles worked in the Experimental Unit of the Museum of Modern Art in Rio de Janeiro on a project 'centralizing experiences concerning the codification and decodification of languages'.[139] His *Insertions into Ideological Circuits: Coca-Cola Project* (1970) and *Insertions into Ideological Circuits: Banknote Project (Who Killed Herzog?)* (1973) recodified objects by removing them from their distributive chains, inscribing subversive messages on them and returning them to circulation in everyday life. In the *Coca-Cola Project*, for example, Meireles silkscreened critical comments about Brazilian politics onto the side of empty bottles; they were more or less invisible until the bottles were refilled in the factory, at which point the messages became legible. This was a deployment of the critical communicational logic of media art beyond the media itself – which required another kind of critique to Jacoby's, under the conditions of military censorship. It assigned a directly political role to the linguistic dimension of the readymade. The medium was a consumer object of everyday life that was at the same time a symbol of US imperialism.

Meanwhile, under very different circumstances, conceptual artists in North America and Europe were also becoming politically radicalized, by the movement against the war in Vietnam.[140] This did not just involve a change in conceptual 'content', but a shift in the relationship between content and visual form. Photo-texts, evoking the montage of the 1920s, became the staple of political conceptual art. Martha Rosler's *Bringing the War Home* (1969–72) combined the violent images of media coverage of the war (the first televised war in history) with advertising images of interior designs in suburban US homes, of the kind previously appropriated into Pop art in Britain by Richard Hamilton. This use of mass media images as a documentary vehicle of political *truth* was a tactic exploited most directly in the Art Workers' Coalition poster *Q: And Babies? A: And Babies* (1970), in which a colour photograph of the bodies of dead Vietnamese women and children strewn across a road was overprinted with the question and answer in tabloid type.

The great ideological divide of the day can be tabulated in terms of six main political issues, as follows:

–	+
war	peace activism
colonialism/imperialism	national liberation
nationalism	internationalism
class/privilege	social equality
racism	civil rights
sexism	women's and gay liberation

In the late 1960s and early 1970s, these were overlapping, interacting concerns that defined a Left political culture of great vibrancy and innovation. As the 1970s progressed, however, the political focus began to shift from the top towards the bottom of the list. Correspondingly, within conceptual art, the move away from an analytical interest in 'art language' took the direction, first, of a (generally Marxist) ideological analysis of advertising and other socially dominant sign systems, and then a (generally psychoanalytical) feminism. These shifts are epitomized in the work of the British artist-critic Victor Burgin.

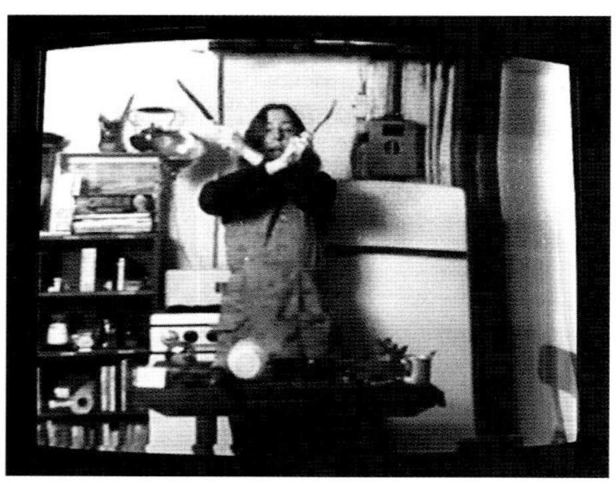

Martha ROSLER, Semiotics of the Kitchen, 1975

Burgin pioneered the theoretically based photo-text in Britain. Setting out from an analytical interest in perception and signification, stimulated by Minimalism (in works such as *Photo Path*, 1967–69, and *Performance/Narrative*, 1971), he rejected what he came to see as 'the esoteric pseudo-science' of Art & Language's preoccupation with philosophy, in favour of questions about art's function and use. Insisting that art is only ever 'partially' autonomous, he argued that: 'The optimum function of art ... is to modify institutionalized patterns of orientation towards the world and thus to serve as an agency of socialization. (No art activity therefore is to be understood apart from the codes and practices of the society which contains it; art in use is bracketed ineluctably within ideology.) ... we must accept the responsibility of producing an art which has more than just *Art* as its content.'[141] This represented a decisive shift within the self-understanding of Anglophone conceptual art away from the analytical philosophy of language towards a Marxist semiotics, in the tradition of Roland Barthes' reading of Saussure. More specifically, it represented a return to the political coordinates of Soviet Constructivism, from which Lawrence Weiner had drawn only formal inspiration, in order to produce a new 'socialist formalism'. This 'consolidation of conceptualist practices along socialist lines', deemed 'implicit from their inception', meant, in particular, a systematic engagement with advertising as the socially dominant form of mass media imagery.[142] Burgin's photo-texts from 1973 to 1976 are polemical appropriations of media culture which are at once directly political in their (also often theoretical) textual content and popular in their use of images. Focusing on private property and class consciousness, works such as *Possession* (1976) appeared in the streets as posters (500 copies in the centre of Newcastle-upon-Tyne), as well as in art magazines and galleries, where they were aggregated into series, such as the powerful *UK 76* (eleven panels, 40 × 60 ins, 1976).[143] Some of the same images would subsequently be reused in different contexts.[144]

The turn to street photography as an updated version of a Baudelairean 'painting of modern life' with which Burgin started to experiment in the late 1970s (especially after he began to travel) marks the point at which his interest in the political economy of everyday life became inflected decisively in the direction of gender and sexuality, and its theoretical focus shifted accordingly from Marx to Freud (or more precisely, to the French psychoanalyst Jacques Lacan). This was representative of a general change in the theoretical culture of politicized conceptual artists. It led to a more dramatic use of photojournalism, as analytical commentary and sexual-political critique, than the understated, more literary modes of Graham and Smithson. (See, for example, Martha Rosler's 1975 video work, *Semiotics of the Kitchen*.) In Britain, it was complemented by the more austerely conceptual documentary and theoretical ritual of Mary Kelly's *Post-Partum Document* (1973–79): a visual record and analysis of the mother/child relationship during the first six years of the artist's son's life. Conceived as an installation in six consecutive sections of documentation in mixed media, comprising 135 small units, the work had a complex exhibition history, and was later published as a book.[145]

Post-Partum Document is exemplary in its combination of an autobiographical focus on an archetypically 'private' domain of women's experience (child rearing) with 'objective' techniques of data-recording (quantification of food intake, for example) and a psychoanalytical account of the stages of child development. In its subjective, diaristic dimension, it evoked the consciousness-raising of early Women's Liberation, while its objective side mimicked the empirical procedures of the biological and social sciences. Each section was completed by a short theoretical text ('Experimentum Mentis'), unifying the narrative, via a summary of its respective developmental phase in terms of Lacan's theory of sexual difference. (Lacanian diagrams were also deployed in the documentation, baffling most of even the most knowing viewers.) The model for the documentary format was a collective work in which Kelly had collaborated with Kay Hunt and Margaret Harrison, *Women and Work: A Document on the Division of Labour in Industry* (1975), the result of a two-year study of the division of labour in a metal box factory in Bermondsey, initiated by Hunt. It consisted of photographic records of the work process, statistical tables, photocopied documents and accounts on relevant Parliamentary Acts. *Post-Partum Document* extends the conception of labour in *Women and Work* to the domestic sphere and approaches it through the psychoanalytical problematic of desire: 'It is not only the infant whose future personality is formed at this crucial moment, but also the mother whose "feminine psychology" is sealed by the sexual division of labour in childcare.'[146] It thereby implicitly raised the question of the status of the art object as an object of desire (beyond 'disinterest'), since the child's fetishistic attachments to particular objects are mirrored in the fetishistic character of their presentation as 'art', as they are also in the artist's attachment to Lacanian theory.

Kelly's *Post-Partum Document* is the canonical work of feminist conceptual art in Britain. It may be read as a gender critique of the erasure of desire from the purportedly purely logical relations of 'compatibility and incompatibility' in Art & Language's *Index*. In Britain in the 1970s, feminist art was part of a lively and contentious socialist art scene. In the USA, on the other hand, where 'women's art' movement was stronger, it was largely disconnected from organized Left politics and the more general theoretical debates such politics involved at that time. Feminist conceptual art in the USA thus tended to be less theoretical than its British counterpart and less ambivalent in its affirmation of women's history.[147]

The US work of equivalent emblematic significance to Kelly's *Post-Partum Document* is Judy Chicago's *The Dinner Party* (1974–79): a triangular table with 39 place settings, celebrating both historical and mythological women, through the traditionally 'female' handicrafts of ceramics and sewing and a 'central core' vaginal iconography. Nine hundred and ninety nine 'women of achievement' are honoured on the tiles of the central 'heritage floor'. Chicago executed the work in collaboration with teams of women connected to Womanhouse, a co-operative women's art space in Los Angeles. It was also published as a book, diaristically recording the progress of the project, providing biographical and mythological information about the women represented, and reproducing colour images of the sculpted ceramic plates.[148] The conceptual character of the piece resides in the primacy of its allegorical and ideological content, in its counterposition to the effacement of gender in the industrial techniques of fabrication in Minimalism. Nonetheless, one would be hard pressed to find two more contrasting versions of feminist art practice: the unequivocal affirmation of female anatomy, mythology and 'traditional' skills represented by *The Dinner Party* and the abstruse theoretical abstractions of Kelly's portrayal of the contradictory and conflictual psychic investments of motherhood. Yet each relies on a metaphysics of sexual difference (one biological, the other psycho-symbolic – focused on the moment of the infant's entry into language) and each is fundamentally about identity.

Adrian Piper was the only African-American among the first-generation conceptual artists in New York and one of very few women. Early on, because of her name, curators who had yet to meet her frequently assumed she was a white man. She was also the only conceptual artist to take up philosophy professionally, in the academy – an even more alienating environment for a young black woman in the early 1970s than the New York art world. Continuing her art practice while studying philosophy, she moved her art away from formal philosophical concerns with space, time and indexicality towards issues of social identity: in particular, the fears, anxieties and other fantasies occasioned by visual markers of racial and sexual difference. In *The Mythic Being* (1972–75), a multiple series of manually modified photographs, performances, advertisements and posters, Piper dons an Afro wig and takes on a masculine persona to perform provocative acts, such as *Cruising White Women* (1975) and *Getting Back* (1975), an assault on a young white man in a park. At other times, the mythic being is captured in a portrait (*I Embody Everything You Most Fear and Hate*, 1975), addresses the viewer directly via bubble captions (*I/You (Her)*,

1974) or can be seen sitting at home typing out a key sentence about the self from the transcendental deduction in Kant's *Critique of Pure Reason* (*A180 (Kant) Nos. 1–6*, 1975). Piper's is a confrontational political art designed to induce reactions in the viewer, but it was also self-reflective about the status of the performance artist as a 'self-conscious object'.[149]

Institutional Critique

The institutional aspect of the artwork was a recurrent concern within conceptual art from its Duchampian beginnings (*Fountain*), via the various certificates designating zones, persons or objects as 'art' issued by Klein, Manzoni and Morris in the late 1950s and early 1960s, through to the explicitly institutional and museological works of Daniel Buren, Marcel Broodthaers and Hans Haacke in the late 1960s and 1970s. Benjamin Buchloh has characterized the trajectory of conceptual art during the 1960s as a move from 'an aesthetic of administration and legal organization and institutional validation' to 'the critique of institutions'.[150] However, as we shall see, the institutionally affirmative and critical dimensions of this kind of conceptual art are more intricately interwoven than such a portrayal implies. The critical interpretation of Duchamp was once again the vantage point from which artists set out.

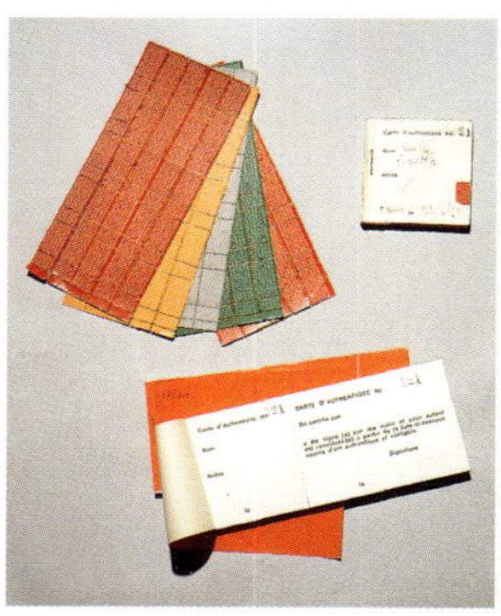

Piero MANZONI, *Ricevutta: Declaration of Authenticity*, 1961

We saw above (in 'Word and Sign') how the founding anti-institutional impulse of *Fountain* was negated by the very process of its recognition as anti-art: the recognition of *Fountain* as a testing of the limits of the institutional definition of art was at the same time a recognition of its artistic legitimacy within the conventions of the avant-garde, and hence of its candidacy for subsequent incorporation into the museum.[151] It is less frequently acknowledged that, unlike Dada, this blunting of the readymade's anti-institutional force was something that Duchamp actively sought. Duchamp was intimately engaged in the institutional fabrication of his persona as an avant-garde artist and of his *oeuvre* as a museum artefact: promulgating the myth of his withdrawal from art after 1923 into chess; acting as a middleman for purchases of his work from others for his main collectors; rebuying some of his own work in order to produce small-scale reproductions; helping install the collection in Philadelphia; designing the first book about himself in order to put his work into wider circulation; holding back the 'publication' of his final work until his death; and even acting as the executor of the estates of his two main patrons.[152] In this respect, he represents not only the hitherto most radical *negation* of established conceptions of both the art object and the artist, but also the subsequent *installation* of these negations into the heart of a reformed art establishment.

When it is claimed that the conceptual practices of the 1960s confronted 'the full range of the implications of Duchamp's legacy for the first time',[153] it is in this dual and contradictory sense that his legacy must be construed. For conceptual art contained at least two very different understandings of Duchamp's success in nominating a urinal as a work of art. At one extreme was an individualistic and voluntaristic nominalism of artistic intention; at the other, a recognition of the ideologico-political function of art institutions as the ultimately determining parameter of their powers. In between, a range of work drew attention to particular institutional conditions of artistic production and reception in a variety of more or less critical or affirmative ways.

The first position was epitomized by Kosuth, with his inflated conception of the stipulative power of the individual artist and his corresponding idea of art as 'a presentation of the artist's intention'. Kosuth's account is an institutional one to the extent to which an individual work becomes 'a kind of proposition within art's language' only when it is presented within 'the context of art'.[154] However, the context of art – so rich in Duchamp – is reduced by Kosuth to no more than a social space set aside for the realization of the artist's intention. Kosuth's implicit answer to the complex institutional question of how someone acquires the power of nomination is modelled on the *persona* of Duchamp: an artist is anyone who 'questions the nature of art'. This was the main way in which Duchamp's readymade was received in the USA in the late 1950s and early 1960s.

But there was a crucial difference between Kosuth's situation and that of Duchamp. Kosuth, along with others of his generation, lacked a pre-established artistic persona, such as Duchamp had derived from his period of infamy as a painter. Hence the importance of the critical writings of the first generation of conceptual artists to the status of their work as 'art': as guarantors and guardians of their right to nomination. Barthes' death of the author/artist was rapidly followed by 'the birth of the artist as self-curator'.[155] This led to an inflation in the cultural authority of the artist's critical discourse. Conceptual art required new modes of institutional validation. It was the heightened awareness of institutional factors as conditions of art which this produced that led to the second, more critical understanding of Duchamp's nominations as moves within an institutional game. This gave rise to a new kind of conceptual art that took the laying bare of the institutional conditions of 'art' as its main theme: institutional critique.

The art falling under the heading of 'institutional critique' takes as the object of its interventions the totality of institutional conditions that contribute to the understanding of something as 'art'. In the art of Daniel Buren, for example, an obstinately visual object (a constantly repeated form of stripe painting) was used in a consistently strategic manner both to draw attention to and to transgress the institutional conditions or 'frame' of art-making. From 1967 onwards Buren's work took the form of: 'Vertically striped sheets of paper, the bands of which are 8.7 cms wide, alternate white and coloured ... stuck over internal and external surfaces: walls, fences, display windows, etc; and/or cloth/canvas support, vertical stripes, white and coloured bands each 8.7 cms, the two ends covered with dull white paint.'[156] The paint at the ends functioned to distinguish these 'paintings' from readymades. For Buren took Duchamp's readymades to have obscured the very institutional conditions *Fountain* had initially brought to light, through which readymades themselves were able to function as art.[157] Buren's art lay in the placing of these paintings both inside and outside art institutions in such a way as (i) to reveal the constitutive power of their locational frame or boundary to produce meaning, and (ii) to comment on particular institutional circumstances.

In using as his means such a patently 'visual' object (recognizable in any particular instance as a painterly image in the tradition of Mondrian, Newman and Stella), in an art institutional context, Buren was self-consciously working within the existing limits of 'art'. In reducing the composition of the object to zero (by repeating a standard formula), making decisions as to size and location his only artistic variables, and also locating his work outside institutional spaces, Buren sought to achieve a 'complete rupture with art': 'a work capable of upsetting all that has until now been expected of art'.[158] This oscillation between a language of limits and a language of rupture, characteristic of Buren's writings, demonstrates a dialectical subtlety in his manner of playing the game of institutional critique that was often missing in other artists. His stated ambition was 'not of fitting in more or less adequately with the [existing institutional] game, nor even of contradicting it, but of abolishing its rules by playing with them, and playing another game, on another or the same ground, as a dissident'.[159] However, the philosophical depth of this strategy (linked to his exploration of the problematic of repetition) courted the danger of going unrecognized. His work was often misunderstood in terms of other, less subtle but more established conceptual paradigms.[160]

Self-consciousness of 'art as curation' achieved a more immediate artistic expression in Marcel Broodthaers' gradually evolving project *Musée d'Art Moderne, Département des Aigles (Museum of Modern Art, Eagles Department*, 1968–72). As with a number of conceptual artists who began as poets (such as Vito Acconci), Broodthaers' work retained a strong narrative and fictional element. Having, by one account, become an artist partially as a surrogate for the financially unattainable role of collector, Broodthaers set out to sublimate what he called his 'bad faith' as an 'art lover' by 'inventing something insincere'.[161] What better than his own series of collections for a museum? The multiplicity of mediums characteristic of Broodthaers' work stems from its mimesis of the organizational structure of the museum. It began with a series of curatorial classifications – a *Nineteenth-Century Section* (1968), a *Documentary Section* (1969), a *Cinema Section* (1971–72) and so on. Finally, however, when the last sections were installed at Documenta 5 (1972, at which point the *Museum of Modern Art* was conflictingly renamed *Museum of Old Master Art: 20th-Century Gallery*), sections for *Publicity* and *Literature* were added, in which the effigy of the eagle, images and photographic documentation of the museum displays were shown. This simultaneously extended the scope of the work beyond the art content of the museum and produced an equivalence between its 'art' and 'non-art' activities. This reinforced the equivalence that had already been established within the 'art' sections by the 'figure' labels attached to objects (Fig.1, Fig.2, etc. – including the projection screen in the *Cinema Section*, thereby reclassifying elements of film images as objects) and by the numbering of exhibits in the *Figures Section (The Eagle from the Oligocene to the Present)* (1972). Beneath each number in this section was printed the Magritte-like legend, 'This is not a work of art'.

Broodthaers' *Museum of Modern Art* recapitulates the institutional logic of the generic concept of art as a 'post-medium' condition, brought about by the homogenizing effect of the conditions of display of historically received medium-specific forms of art.[162] However, it is not itself a multi-media or intermedia work, but a *trans*media work of art fiction. As such, however, it approaches the condition of spectacle. In Buren's words, it was 'an object and an alibi for the museum it pretended to challenge'.[163] The problem of the appropriation of institutional critique by the institution itself, as a new legitimating device, plagues institutional critique in all but its most radical forms. On the other hand, work which is resistant to such appropriation risks the Pyrrhic victory of not being shown, at least in major art institutions, unless it can inadvertently pull off *Fountain*'s original trick of being publicly rejected. The first half of 1971 saw three, rather different, such occasions in major Western art museums: the removal of Buren's work from the Guggenheim International Exhibition the day before the opening (February); the cancellation of Haacke's one-person show at the Guggenheim, New York, a few weeks before its planned April opening (March); and the closure after only five days of Robert Morris' Tate Gallery retrospective (May).

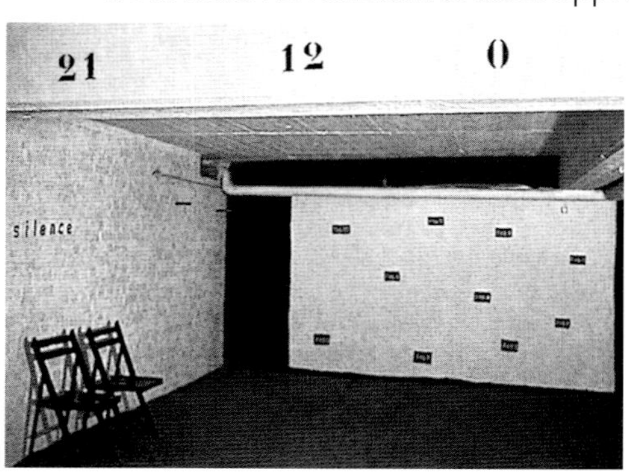

Marcel BROODTHAERS, Musée d'Art Moderne, Département des Aigles: Section Cinéma [Museum of Modern Art, Eagles Department: Cinema Section], Kunsthalle Dusseldorf, 1972

Morris' design for his retrospective at the Tate Gallery involved three interactive spaces, each of which was dedicated to different types of physical relations between the spectators, the objects, and the broader structures. In Morris' words: 'The progression is from the manipulation of objects, to constructions which adjust to the body's presence, to situations where the body itself is manipulated. I want to provide a situation where people can become more aware of themselves and their own experience rather than more aware of some version of my experience.'[164] This was a participatory transposition of the logic of Morris' earlier performance pieces, from the theatre to the gallery, with visitors taking the place of the dancers, in the utopian spirit of the participatory works from Brazil mentioned earlier, but in a far more sympathetic institutional and political setting. Neither Morris nor the curator appear to have anticipated the extent of the anarchic engagement with the installations that followed (including some 'minor accidents'), precipitating the closure. The opportunity to break the established rules of spectator behaviour produced a psychic release of carnivalesque excess, giving momentary social substance to a Cagean aesthetic of indeterminacy and chance.[165] Six days after the closure, the show reopened as a conventional, non-interactive, sculptural display.

Morris' retrospective briefly expanded, and then reinstated, the boundary of acceptable public behaviour in museums. Buren's piece challenged the architectural frame of the museum as a container of objects, by disrupting the architectural dominance of Frank Lloyd Wright's Guggenheim building over its exhibits. It thereby also raised a series of questions about 'site specific' work. The offending piece was one part of a two-part display of Buren's signature stripes, inside and outside the gallery space. Outside, a canvas 1.5m high by 10m wide was stretched across 88th Street between the museum and the building opposite; inside a canvas 20 metres high and 10 metres wide was suspended in the building's central shaft, from just below the skylight to a few metres above head height at ground level. It was the latter which caused problems. For by engaging on an architectural scale with the dynamics of the building itself, and its renowned subjugation of exhibits in its central spiral space to an aspect of the architecture, it threw a harsh light on the accommodation of the other artists' work to their allotted niches. More specifically, it was claimed, it significantly impeded the viewing of these works from a distance, across the spiral. Flavin's work, in particular, was affected because of the way it used light to highlight parts of the building, utilizing its architecture in a positive, affirmative manner.[166]

Buren's piece sought to draw attention to the conditions of spectatorship at the Guggenheim as well as the institutional conservatism of so-called 'site specific' minimalist sculpture in its complicity with those conditions, and its consequent reproduction of a conventional conception of art as the object of perceptual experience. Sixteen of the other artists in the show signed a petition protesting against the removal of Buren's piece and Carl Andre withdrew his work from the show in solidarity with Buren. Flavin, Judd, de Maria, Heizer and Kosuth refused to sign. The dispute drew a clear line between the perceptual phenomenology of minimalist contextualism and the conceptual logic of a political contextual art. However, there was little public comment on the removal at the time and awareness of its emblematic significance has been left to a belated political art history. By contrast, the cancellation of Haacke's show intensified the offending works' effects, giving rise to sustained critical debate in the art press at the time and subsequent work by Haacke about the Guggenheim itself.

Haacke's early work was a European variant of systems-based conceptual art. Starting with physical and biological systems (*Condensation Cube*, 1963–65, and *Live Airborne System*, 1965/68), Haacke had by the end of the 1960s extended his approach to what he called 'real-time social systems'. His Guggenheim show, 'Hans Haacke: Systems', was to include all three types of work, but it was the issues raised by his presentation of the system of private property in housing in New York City that proved intractable to the Guggenheim director and trustees. Haacke had already deployed sociological surveys as part of a participatory institutional critique at the Howard Wise Gallery in 1969 and in his contribution to 'Information' (*MOMA-Poll*, 1970). At the Guggenheim, he proposed to show two works based on an investigation of Manhattan real estate holdings: one about the real-estate partnership of Sol Goldman and Alex DiLorenzo; the other, *Shapolsky et al.*, about the network of corporations owned by the Shapolsky family. The latter comprised 142 photographs of individual buildings, along with typewritten sheets, charts, diagrams and maps detailing real-estate transactions. Haacke extended the tradition of the political art of the 1920s into the institutional context of the 1970s using the techniques of the conceptual art of the 1960s.

The Guggenheim objected to the reference to actual individuals, claiming both the danger of legal liability and the inappropriateness of such reference in a work of art. It was this latter that occasioned most debate.[167] Thomas M. Messer, the director of the Guggenheim, used the expression 'a form of photojournalism' to justify his exclusion of the work. Yet, as we have seen, photojournalism is a strategic tool of a whole range of conceptual art.[168] Haacke later rendered explicit the connection between the politics of his offending pieces and their exclusion by the Guggenheim (the system of private property) in a serial work, *Solomon R. Guggenheim Board of Trustees* (1974) detailing the economic and political interests of the companies run by the Guggenheim's trustees. The two offending *Manhattan Real Estate Holdings* works were eventually shown in New York at the New Museum of Contemporary Art in 1986–87, in an exhibition called 'Unfinished Business'.

In each of these cases (Morris, Buren, Haacke), the avant-garde character of the work was established in a classical manner by its being cast outside the boundaries of 'art' by authoritative institutional decree. Other types of institutional critique, such as work by Michael Asher, were largely content to restrict themselves to an internal exploration of the ideological content of the gallery's and the museum's institutional histories and architectural forms. This latter type of work subsequently became a staple of mainstream art institutions. Its extreme contextualism restricts the social content of its critique to what is immanent to these institutions themselves. It is in this sense that Jeff Wall accused it of 'defeatism': 'a displacement or repression of [the] deeper ... issue ... of the reinvention of social content in modernist art'.[169] For Wall, conceptual art's critique of 'art' ultimately failed, or remained incomplete, because of the inadequacy of its artistic formulation of the problem of social content. In opposition to the impasse of institutional critique, Wall offered *the city* as the 'single grand subject' of a renewed conceptual art and *architecture* as 'the decisive or determining art form' – understood as 'the discourse of siting the effects of power generated by publicity, information and bureaucracy in the city'.[170]

However, in the meantime, art institutions were busy transforming themselves into broader cultural agencies, in order to sponsor a variety of types of site-based work outside literal gallery or museum spaces. As a result, whatever its physical site, critical work became increasingly institutionalized in its mode of address. Art that had derived its rationale from its extra-institutional status (as an emblem of the possibility of an alternative artistic culture of everyday life) became a symbol of the cultural power of art institutions themselves. In the process, new conceptual work – whether inside or outside the architectural space of gallery and museum – increasingly took the post-conceptual form of installation.

Afterwards: Installation and Neo-Conceptualism

By the beginning of the 1980s, whatever unity conceptual art had possessed as a polemical rejection of 'the visual', had been replaced by a more general post-conceptual interest in the strategic uses of both traditional artistic and mass-media visual forms. In Europe, artists such as Sophie Calle, James Coleman and Willie Doherty explored the legacy of the photo-text. In the USA, Sherrie Levine, Louise Lawler and Allan McCollum appropriated existing works in various ways; while Jenny Holzer, Barbara Kruger, Felix Gonzalez-Torres and Krzysztof Wodiczko found public spaces for interventions manipulating mass-media imagery. This return to a (non-strategic) use of the visual was accompanied by an increased emphasis on installation, as the act of realizing a work in a specific context, inside or outside the gallery. The idea of installation as a discrete form of art – 'installation art' – was a product of the 1980s. By the mid 1990s, it had become the dominant artform in a rapidly globalizing art world, comparable in its impact on the condition of art in general (and hence on the ontological status of 'art') to the conceptual art of the late 1960s.[171] It was the outcome of an increased preoccupation with the problem of realization. For if, as conceptual art had insisted, the artwork cannot be considered identical to any particular physical entity, but it nonetheless (*contra* a 'purely' conceptual art) depends for its effectiveness upon the character of such manifestations, then the relationship between idea and entity – realization – becomes crucial.

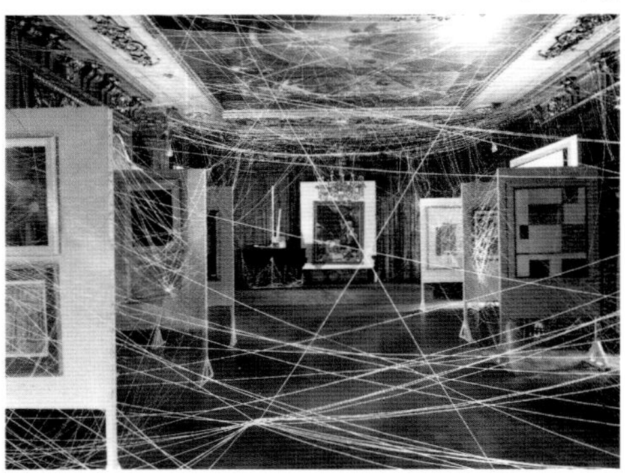

Marcel DUCHAMP, One Mile of String, installation view, 'First Papers of Surrealism', 551 Madison Avenue, New York, 1942

Until the 1980s, the term 'installation' was used in the art world in its everyday sense of fixing into position some pre-existing thing. Works, in the sense of objects, were 'installed' in spaces of exhibition. Once the work became identified with an idea, however, or a linguistically specifiable content, and its realization became (potentially) multiple, each realization came to be identified with a particular time and place. Installation was no longer simply the fixing into position of some previously fabricated thing. Rather, in a new and deeper sense, it became the *in situ* production of the work itself as a physical entity. As Buren recognized as early as 1971, '*installation* [came] to replace *exhibition*'.[172] What the institution recognizes as the work (the physical entity) became the *product* of the installation of the idea. Herein lies the distinctively post-conceptual character of installation art, the most enduring legacy of conceptual art.[173]

In order to avoid the impression of an object, positioned in a pre-existing space, installations need to exhaust the space they inhabit. Hence their affinity to the 'environments' of the 1960s, which require spectators to enter inside them. Installations work at the level of gallery space or enclose or articulate their own space. Retrospectively, the first works of installation art in this specific sense are probably Duchamp's *1,200 Bags of Coal*, installed on the ceiling of the 'International Exhibition of Surrealism' in New York in 1938; followed by his *One Mile of String*, which traversed the 'First Papers of Surrealism' exhibition in New York in 1942. As Brian O'Doherty put it, *1,200 Bags of Coal* was 'the first time an artist subsumed an entire gallery in a single gesture'.[174] Hence, once again, the inescapability of Duchamp, the fear that he might have done it all before, that the future might already belong to the past[175] – even the future of post-conceptual art. In consuming or, better, producing their own space, installations are not merely 'theatrical', in Michael Fried's famous sense of occupying literal space,[176] but at their best act as relays between the social sites of their materials (in the widest sense) and their own sites as art. In so doing, they perform a conceptual function, often in tension with the more immediate affects of their objecthood.[177] This general conceptual function, at work in a wide variety of current art practices, may be distinguished from the more self-conscious relation to 'the conceptual' characteristic of the neo-conceptualisms of the 1980s and 1990s.

Neo-conceptualism involves a knowing repetition of the conceptual strategies of the 1960s under the very different political and artistic conditions of the last two decades. It takes a variety of forms, depending on the institutional and geo-political sites of its production. Thus, for example, the dissident ('post') state-socialist conceptual work originating in Russia and China is distinct from both the slick US art world neo-conceptualisms of Jeff Koons and Haim Steinbach, on the one hand, and the UK art school neo-conceptualism of artists such as Liam Gillick, Simon Patterson and Gavin Turk, on the other. Each adopts conceptual strategies for the negation of a merely aesthetic contemplation of the artwork, but each uses them in different ways, to different ends, in different contexts, to widely differing effect. Each has a different relationship to the history of conceptual art. However, they are none the less bound together as 'neo-conceptual' work by the context of their reception – the increasingly global international art world. Both the 'Moscow conceptualism' of Victor Pivovarov, Ilya Kabakov, and Vitaly Komar and Aleksandr Melamid, and the more recent Chinese conceptual art of Wenda Gu and Zhang Huan, draw upon indigenous artistic and cultural traditions (Socialist Realism, Constructivism and political satire; calligraphy and Confucianism). But it is their affinities with the conceptual art of the 1960s which have made possible their reception into the international art world, to which they then relate through their (predominantly nationally coded) differences.[178] And this reception has itself conditioned subsequent work, not only via the westward migration of artists but more broadly through the internalization of its mores.

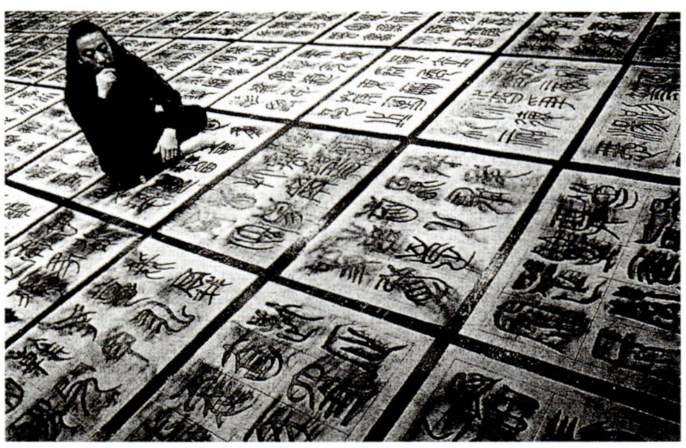

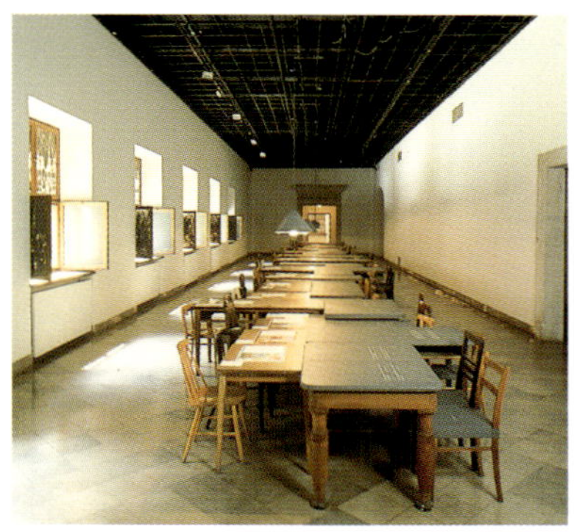

Wenda GU, pseudo characters [cobiezi], 1985
Ilya KABAKOV, Joseph KOSUTH, Corridor of Two Banalities (detail), 1994

Emblematic of this sudden (post-1989) historical confluence is Kabakov's and Kosuth's joint work *Corridor of Two Banalities*, installed in the Ujazdowski Castle in Warsaw in 1994. This is a neo-conceptual work of genuine historical depth, in which Kosuth's trademark quotations also function as citations of the style of his own paradigmatically 'conceptual' work; while the symmetrical structure of the installations produces a formal equivalence between Kosuth's and Kabakov's starkly contrasting texts that transposes Kabakov's part of the work, directly and ironically, into the context of conceptual art. This is at once a socialist critique of the disengaged stance of linguistically based Western conceptual art and a transfiguration into art, via just such a conceptual stance, of a slice of Soviet collective life.

Both the historical depth and dialectical reflexivity of *Corridor of Two Banalities* set it apart from the more academic, art-historically knowing New York neo-conceptual art of the 1980s and the London neo-conceptualism of the 1990s. The 1980s saw a proliferation of market-oriented fusions of Pop, Minimalism, abstract painting and conceptual art, exemplified at its extremes by Jeff Koons' 'neo-geo' objects and neo-expressionist painting. British neo-conceptual art is in many ways a provincial extension of this trend, with a populist inflection. It is characterized by a fundamental dualism of object and idea, whereby the work operates at two quite distinct levels at the same time, without mediation between them. On the one hand, it makes a populist aesthetic appeal at the level of the post-minimalist object (Damien Hirst's 'What the *fuck* is wrong with visual candy?');[179] on the other, it assumes an art-historical context within which the object can function semiotically as a mere bearer of conceptual relations. This stance of ironic stylization is part of a general 'postmodern' historicism in which past artistic forms and styles are treated indifferently as readymade materials for contemporary production. Much of this kind of neo-conceptual work is best treated under the rubric of 'postmodernism', in contrast to both the deeper conceptual function of post-conceptual installation art and a genuinely historically reflexive neo-conceptual art. Recent work by conceptual artists who came to prominence in the 1960s, such as Graham, Weiner and Art & Language engages both of these latter critical categories in complex ways; as does that of other conceptually oriented artists such as Rodney Graham and Miyajima Tatsuo.

As a critique of medium and autonomy, the impact of conceptual art thus continues to be felt across the whole field of current art practices. As a polemical rejection of visuality and objecthood *per se*, its moment has passed; but its critical challenge remains.

1 '*Concept art* is first of all an art of which the material is *concepts*, as e.g. the material of music is sound. Since *concepts* are closely bound up with language, concept art is a kind of art of which the material is language.' Henry Flynt, 'Concept Art', in La Monte Young (ed.), *An Anthology of Chance Operations, Indeterminacy, Improvisation, Concept Art, Anti-Art, Meaningless Work, Natural Disasters, Stories, Diagrams, Music, Dance, Constructions, Compositions, Mathematics, Plans of Action*, New York, 1963. The essay was written in 1961. George Maciunas' *Expanded Arts Diagram* (1968) credits Flynt with formulating the idea as early as 1954.

2 See *Six Years: The dematerialization of the art object from 1966 to 1972: a cross-reference book of information on some aesthetic boundaries: consisting of a bibliography into which are inserted a fragmented text, art works, documents, interviews, and symposia, arranged chronologically and focused on so-called conceptual or information or idea art with mentions of such vaguely designated areas as minimal, anti-form, systems, earth, or process art, occurring now in the Americas, Europe, England, Australia, and Asia (with occasional political overtones), edited and annotated by Lucy Lippard*, Praeger Publishers, New York, 1973. See also, Lucy R. Lippard, 'Escape Attempts', in Ann Goldstein and Anne Rorimer (eds), *Reconsidering the Object of Art: 1965–1975*, The Museum of Contemporary Art, Los Angeles; MIT Press, Cambridge, Massachusetts, 1995, 17–39.

3 See *Global Conceptualism: Points of Origin, 1950s–1980s*, Queens Museum of Art, New York, 1999.

4 Pierre Cabanne, *Dialogues with Marcel Duchamp*, Da Capo, New York, n.d., 77.

5 See Thomas Crow, *The Rise of the Sixties: American and European Art in the Era of Dissent 1955–1969*, Harry N. Abrams, New York, 1996.

6 See, for example, Robert Hughes, *Culture of Complaint: The Fraying of America*, Harvill, London, 1994.

7 See Jeff Wall, 'A Draft for "Dan Graham's Kammerspeil" (1981)', in his *Dan Graham's Kammerspeil*, Art Metropole, Toronto, 1991, where it is Benjamin Buchloh who is taken to personify this position.

8 See, for example, the various works criticized by Hal Foster in his *Recodings: Art, Spectacle, Cultural Politics*, Bay Press, Seattle, 1985.

9 John Roberts, 'Photography, Iconophobia and the Ruins of Conceptual Art', in *The Impossible Document: Photography and Conceptual Art in Britain, 1966–1976*, Camerawork, London, 1997, 7–45; Michael Newman, 'Conceptual Art from the 1960s to the 1990s: An Unfinished Project?', *Kunst & Museum Journaal*, Vol.VII, Nos. 1–3 (1996), 95–104; reprinted in this volume, 288–89.

10 See Hal Foster, *The Return of the Real: The Avant-Garde at the End of the Century*, MIT Press, Cambridge, Massachusetts, 1996, ch.1.

11 Jeff Wall, *Dan Graham's Kammerspeil*, *op. cit.*, 100. For others, the dream is over. See, for example, T.J. Clark, *Farewell to an Idea: Episodes from a History of Modernism*, Yale University Press, New Haven, 1999.

12 Rosalind Krauss, *'A Voyage on the North Sea': Art in the Age of the Post-Medium Condition*, Thames and Hudson, London, 1999.

13 Roberta Smith, 'Conceptual Art', in Nikos Stangos (ed.), *Concepts of Modern Art*, Thames and Hudson, London, 1981, 256.

14 Ursula Meyer, *Conceptual Art*, Dutton, New York, 1972; Gregory Battcock, *Idea Art: A Critical Anthology*, Dutton, New York, 1973; Lippard, *Six Years* (see note 2, above), emphasis added.

15 'Primary Structures: Young American and British Sculptors' (Jewish Museum, New York, 1966) was a landmark exhibition in the development of Minimalism as a recognizable movement.

16 This tension remains visible in the competing curatorial strategies of recent retrospectives. Both *L'art conceptual, une perspective* (ARC Musée d'art moderne de la Ville de Paris, 1989) and *Global Conceptualism* (1999) were preoccupied with issues of classification, while *Reconsidering the Object of Art, 1965–1975* and *Out of Actions: Between Performance and the Object, 1949–1979* (Museum of Contemporary Art, Los Angeles, 1995 and 1998, respectively) side-stepped them in favour of a more empiricist historiography. This registers a difference between the art-critical cultures of Europe and the US East coast, on the one hand, and the West coast, on the other.

17 As Adorno put it in *Aesthetic Theory*: 'The universal determinations of art are what art developed into. The [current] historical situation of art, which has lost any sense of art's very *raison d'être*, turns to the past in the hope of finding the concept of art, which retrospectively acquires a sort of unity. This unity is not abstract but is, rather, the unfolding of art according to its own concept. At every point, therefore, the theory of art presupposes concrete analyses, not as proofs and examples but as its own condition.' Theodor W. Adorno, *Aesthetic Theory* (1970), trans. R. Hullet-Kentor, Minnesota University Press, Minneapolis, 1997, 263.

18 Lippard, *Six Years*, *op. cit.*, p.5.

19 Sol LeWitt, 'Paragraphs on Conceptual Art', *Artforum*, 5:10 (Summer 1967), 79–83; reprinted in Charles Harrison and Paul Wood (eds), *Art in Theory, 1900–1990: An Anthology of Changing Ideas*, Blackwell, Oxford, 1992, 834–87; reprinted in this volume, 213–14.

20 Jon Bird and Michael Newman, 'Introduction', in Jon Bird and Michael Newman (eds), *Rewriting Conceptual Art*, Reaktion Books, London 1999, 5–6. See also the definitions offered in the 'Foreword' to *Global Conceptualism*, viii: *conceptual art* – 'a term used to denote an essentially formalist practice developed in the wake of Minimalism'; *conceptualism* – 'a broader attitudinal expression that summarized a wide variety of practices which, in radically reducing the role of the art object, reimagined the possibilities of art vis-à-vis the social, political and economic realities within which it was being made', respectively. The use of the notion of 'attitude' here appears to derive from the eclecticism of the 1969 exhibition 'When Attitudes Become Form'.

21 Bird and Newman, 'Introduction', 3.

22 Clement Greenberg, 'Modernist Painting' (1960), in his *The Collected Essays and Criticism, Volume 4: Modernism with a Vengeance, 1957–1969*, edited by John O'Brian, University of Chicago Press, Chicago, 1993, 85–93.

23 See John E. Bolt (ed.), *Russian Art and the Avant-Garde: Theory and Criticism*, Thames and Hudson, London, 1988, Parts III-IV.

24 Dick Higgins, 'Intermedia', *The Something Else Newsletter*, February 1966; reprinted in Higgins, *A Dialectic of Centuries: Towards a Theory of the New Arts*, Printed Editions, New York, 1976, 12–17.

25 Flynt, 'Concept Art', *op. cit.*, and *Fragments and Reconstructions from a Destroyed Oeuvre, 1959–1963*, Backworks, New York, 1982, 8; Joseph Kosuth, 'Art after Philosophy' in his *Art after Philosophy and After: Collected Writings, 1966–1990*, MIT Press, Cambridge, Massachusetts, 1991, 19. Kosuth's essay was first published serially in *Studio International* in 1969. Ina Blom's 'Postscript on Concept Art' to her 'Boredom and Oblivion', in Ken Friedman (ed.), *The Fluxus Reader*, Academy Editions, Chichester, 1998, 86–88, provides an excellent short reading of Flynt's essay. Flynt's antipathy towards conceptual art as a historical movement extends to his refusal to grant permission for the reprinting of his seminal essay, 'Concept Art', in this volume.

26 The characterization of Fluxus remains a matter of dispute. It is tempting to classify it as an art movement (albeit with strong anti-art tendencies) on the models of Dada and Surrealism. This was how it was perceived by George Maciunas, who was not so much its founder as its 'branding' figure and its main organizational force. However, both the group of artists associated with it and the kinds of work they produced pre-existed it and continued independently, as well as under the Fluxus banner. In this respect, Fluxus is perhaps best conceived as a *forum or platform* for certain kinds of art activity and a *mechanism of publicity and distribution* for such works; hence, as structured around a relationship between performance and print. See Owen Smith, 'Developing a Fluxable Forum' and Dick Higgins, 'Fluxus: Theory and Reception' in *The Fluxus Reader*, *op. cit.*, 3–21 and 217–36.

27 See RoseLee Goldberg, *Performance Art: From Futurism to the Present*, Thames and Hudson, London, 1988.

28 See Nelson Goodman, *Languages of Art: An Approach to a Theory of Symbols*, Hackett, Indianapolis, 2nd ed. 1976; extract reprinted in this volume, 202–6.

29 Cf. de Duve's claim that it was through the readymade's claim on the name 'painting' that Duchamp inaugurated a generic, nominalistic conception of 'art' – a claim that was prepared within the history of painting itself by the metaphysical implications of the metaphor of the 'language' of colour. Thierry de Duve, *Pictorial Nominalism: On Marcel Duchamp's Passage from Painting to the Readymade* (1984), trans. Dana Polan, University of Minnesota Press, Minneapolis, 1991, chs. 6 and 7.

30 Mary Emma Harris, *The Arts at Black Mountain College*, MIT Press, Cambridge, Massachusetts, 1987; Alexandra Munroe, 'To Challenge the Mid-Summer Sun: The Gutai Group', in Alexandra Munroe (ed.), *Japanese Art After 1945: Scream Against the Sky*, Harry N. Abrams, New York, 1994, 83–123; *Gutai*, Galerie Nationale du Jeu de Paume, Paris, 1999; Maurice Berger, *Labyrinths: Robert Morris, Minimalism and the 1960s*, Harper and Row, New York, 1989, 24–6, 81–106.

31 In *18 Happenings in 6 Parts*, performed at the Reuben Gallery, New York in 1959, for example, spectators were issued instructions as to how to act in response, Pavlov-fashion, to the ringing of a bell.

32 Kaprow appeared on the same bill with Fluxus artist-to-be George Brecht several times during 1960, in performances variously described as 'New Music' (Living Theatre, NY, March), 'Happenings? Events! Situations?' (Pratt Institute, Brooklyn, May), 'Sound Theatre–Happenings' (Reuben Gallery, June). However, the distinction between the 'happening' and the Fluxus-type 'event' can be seen in the contrast between Kaprow's *18 Happenings in 6 Parts* and Brecht's exhibition of objects with related instructions in the same gallery later that year, called *Towards Events*. Happenings offered a type of brief collective temporal fulfilment, while the temporality of events was self-consciously interruptive and ontologically destabilizing. In fact, Brecht considered objects as themselves, *inherently*, events – a view he justified theoretically on the basis of the sub-atomic structure of matter. Events were to reveal the event-structures of objects. See *George Brecht: Notebooks I–IV*, Verlag der Buchhandlung Walter König, Cologne, 1991, 1997 – Brecht's notes from Cage's composition classes at the New School for Social Research in New York, in the late 1950s. Kaprow attended Cage's class in 1957.

33 There is a convergence of concrete music and concrete poetry here in their mutual concentration, not only on the totality of 'concrete' features of the event of sound performance, but on the corresponding properties of the score/poem as a visual artefact. This later aspect was the subject of the exhibition 'Between Poetry and Painting' at the Institute of Contemporary Arts, London, in 1965. The Japanese word *Gutai* translates as 'concrete' in this sense.

34 See Yvonne Rainer, 'A Quasi Survey of some "Minimalist" Tendencies in the Quantitatively Minimal Dance Activity Midst the Plethora, or an Analysis of *Trio A*', in Battcock (ed.), *Minimal Art*, *op. cit.*, 267.

35 See Jon Hendricks (ed.), *Paintings and Drawings by Yoko Ono: July 17–30 1961, Preview July 16, Sunday*, Galeria 56, Budapest, 1993. According to Bruce Altschuler, an unsigned typescript in the Silverman collection mentions that fifteen instruction paintings were shown, but there is no documentation of the extra two, should the typescript be correct. See Bruce Altshuler, 'Instructions for a World of Stickiness: The Early Conceptual Work of Yoko Ono', in Alexandra Munroe with Jon Hendricks, *Yes Yoko Ono*, Japan Society; Harry N. Abrams, New York, 2000, 71, n. 7.

36 Ono had performed at least three of the paintings before, at events in her Chambers Street loft, consuming the completed canvas of a fourth, *Kitchen Piece* (1960), in a version of the destructive *Smoke Painting*. The other two were *Painting to be Stepped On* and *Shadow Painting*. See Altshuler in *ibid.*, 71, n. 30; Joan Rothfuss, 'Somewhere for the Dust to Cling: Yoko Ono's Paintings and Early Objects', in *ibid.*, 94.

37 *Ibid.*, 99, n. 12; 95.

38 Later that month, in an exhibition in Kyoto, Ono introduced a further

terminological innovation to describe the articulated unity of instruction and object, 'instructure', defined as: 'Something that emerged from instructions and yet is not quite emerged – not quite structured – never quite structured ... like an unfinished church with a sky ceiling.' (Yoko Ono, 'On Instructure' (1964), in *ibid.*, 284.) This unfinished – indeed, unfinishable – quality was highlighted by the title of Ono's show at the Indica Gallery, London, in November 1966, 'Unfinished Paintings and Objects'; although there was a marked return to visuality there in the production of an optical unity for the works – however neutral – by painting most of them white. Such minimal optical unity – the black-on-white of text-on-paper, the grey-on-grey of theory – would soon become familiar visual signs of the negation of the visual as a marked quality in art, in subsequent conceptual work.

39 'Action' is to be distinguished here from mere, physiologically defined, 'behaviour'. See Arthur C. Danto, *Analytical Philosophy of Action*, Cambridge University Press, Cambridge, 1973. Danto's formulation of the philosophical idea of 'basic actions' was contemporaneous with (but seemingly independent of) the revolution in the vocabulary of movement in modern dance.

40 This is a philosophical problem of language that later, more 'analytical' conceptual artists would almost wholly neglect; as, indeed, critics often neglect the complex political significance of the fact that various language-based works by Japanese artists, such as On Kawara, are in English.

41 At the time, Morris was closely associated with La Monte Young and other artists who would become part of Fluxus, as well as Yvonne Rainer and the Judson Dance Group, and he performed at Ono's Chamber Street loft – a venue that Duchamp attended when Ono's *Painting to be Stepped On* was on show. (Duchamp appears not to have noticed it.) Morris was originally to have been a contributor to La Monte Young's *An Anthology*, but he withdrew his piece (a manifesto on 'Blank Form', reprinted in this volume, 195) in reaction against Maciunas' leadership of Fluxus. See Berger, *Labyrinths*, *op. cit.*, ch.1, 'Duchamp and I'.

42 It was reflection on the constitutive role of titles in painting that led to Duchamp's startling inversion of the metaphor of the 'language of colour', in his decision to use *words* to 'add colour' to his work, and thereafter to reconceive painting as an interplay between language, thought and vision, in the readymades and *Large Glass*. Later, Duchamp would remark with regard to *L'avoir l'apprenti dans le soleil* that it is '[a]s far as possible from a descriptive title, in fact a suppression of the very concept of the "title"'. See de Duve, *Pictorial Nominalism*, *op. cit.*, 141; 207, n. 70. The dual, performative and linguistic (and hence 'conceptual') character of Morris' early objects derives directly from his reception of Duchamp. Duchamp used instructions in his *Green Box*, first published in English in 1960, and read by Morris that year. Morris' *Litanies* (1961) is a handwritten performance/copy of the text of 'Litanies of the Chariot' from Duchamp's *Green Box*. There are numerous other such homages to Duchamp in Morris' work of this period.

43 There is a tension between the anti-art activism of this conception (anyone can become an artist) and the quietism of the Zen experience of infinity with which it is often combined (and to which Cage's music, for example, aspired), which involves a dissolution or emptying of subjectivity: the achievement of a state of 'zero'. In so far as there is a unitary conception of the work here it lies on the side of the subject – not within the work itself, but in its affects – and it is associated with emptiness. However, the temporal logic of the avant-garde is inherently opposed to the quietism of Zen spirituality.

44 Quoted by Altshuler, 'Instructions for a World of Stickiness', *op. cit.*, 71, n. 12.

45 See the various examples in *Felix Gonzalez-Torres*, Solomon R. Guggenheim Museum, 1996.

46 Charles Harrison, 'Conceptual Art and the Suppression of the Beholder', in his *Essays on Art & Language*, Blackwell, Oxford, 1991, 51.

47 For an account of the centrality of photography to conceptual art, see Jeff Wall, '"Marks of Indifference": Aspects of Photography in, or as, Conceptual Art', in Goldstein and Rorimer (eds), *Reconsidering the Object of Art*, *op. cit.*, 247–67; and Roberts, *The Impossible Document*, *op. cit.*

48 Harrison, 'Conceptual Art and the Suppression of the Beholder', *op. cit.*, 45.

49 Donald Judd, 'Specific Objects', *Arts Yearbook*, 8, New York, 1965; reprinted in Charles Harrison and Paul Wood (eds), *Art in Theory, 1900–1990*, *op. cit.*, 811.

50 Robert Morris, 'Notes on Sculpture, Part 2' (1966) in his *Continuous Project Altered Daily: The Writings of Robert Morris*, MIT Press, Cambridge, Massachusetts, 1993, 15–17.

51 *Ibid.*, 20.

52 Morris, 'Some Splashes in the Ebb Tide' (1973), in *Continuous Project*, *op. cit.*, 129.

53 Morris, 'Notes on Sculpture, Part 3: Notes and Non Sequiturs' (1967), in *Continuous Project*, *op. cit.*, 27. It is this connection to manufactured objects that links Minimalism to Pop art. Minimalism and Pop may be understood as formal aesthetic reflections of a particular historical stage of commodity production and consumption, respectively.

54 Morris, 'Anti-Form' (1968), in *Continuous Project*, *op. cit.*, 41–3, emphasis added.

55 Lucy R. Lippard, 'New York Letter: Carl Andre', *Art International*, 20 September 1965, 58–59; Barbara Rose, 'ABC Art', 278. Note should also be taken of Flynt's 1961 'Concept Art' (see note 1, above) and Edward Kienholz's series (1963–67) of *Concept Tableaux*, such as *Art Show*, 1963.

56 Sol LeWitt, *Artist's Statement* in *Art in Process II*, Finch College, New York, 1966.

57 LeWitt, 'Paragraphs on Conceptual Art', *op. cit.*, 834–36, emphases added.

58 Benjamin H.D. Buchloh, 'Conceptual Art 1962–1969: From the Aesthetics of Administration to the Critique of Institutions', *October*, 55 (Winter 1990), 105–43; 109. Extracts reprinted in this volume, 224; 273

59 LeWitt, 'Paragraphs on Conceptual Art', *op. cit.*, 834–35.

60 LeWitt, 'Sentences on Conceptual Art', in *Art–Language*, 1:1 (1969); reprinted in *Art in Theory*, *op. cit.*, 837–9; reprinted in this volume, 222.

61 Cf. Rosalind Krauss, 'LeWitt in Progress' (1977), in her *The Originality of the Avant-Garde and Other Modernist Myths*, MIT Press, Cambridge, Massachusetts, 1986, 244–58.

62 See Ferdinand de Saussure, *Course in General Linguistics*. Extract reprinted in this volume, 225–26.

63 Buchloh, 'Conceptual Art', *op. cit.*, 116.

64 Thierry de Duve, *Kant After Duchamp*, MIT Press, Cambridge, Massachusetts, 1996, 377; 415.

65 Kosuth, 'Art after Philosophy', *op. cit.*, 18, emphasis added.

66 Marcel Duchamp, 'Apropos of "Readymades"' (1961), in *The Writings of Marcel Duchamp*, ed. Michel Sanouillet and Elmer Peterson, Da Capo, n.d., New York (reprint of the Oxford University Press edition, 1973) 141. Cf. Cabanne (ed.), *Dialogues*, *op. cit.*, 48. This role is also played in Duchamp's work by technical drawing and other geometrical techniques, although these also have other functions.

67 Cabanne (ed.), *Dialogues*, *op. cit.*, 47, 42, 48. The first readymade, *Sèche-bouteilles* (*Bottle Rack*, 1914), carried a sentence inscribed on its base.

68 See *ibid.*, 55–56. Duchamp admits the Dada 'spirit' of the piece (in the context of his relations to Picabia), but denies any direct influence. A dialectical understanding of the term 'anti-art' acknowledges that anti-art must occupy the field of art in order to oppose it, and that anti-art is thus a peculiar, paradoxical or liminal kind of art, in the same way that in the novel an anti-hero is a certain type of hero.

69 Duchamp, 'Apropos of "Readymades"', 142. Cf. Cabanne (ed.), *Dialogues*, *op. cit.*, 48.

70 This is the historical significance of Pop, as the dialectical counterpart and contemporary antagonist to conceptual art. Pop art brought to the surface and highlighted, explored and exploited the repressed aesthetic dimension of the readymade, making explicit the transition implicit in the history of its reception, from aesthetic indifference to an aesthetics of indifference: the aesthetics of the (socially indifferent) commodity's distributional form.This move was prepared by the initial reception of Duchamp in the USA, during the 1950s, in Rauschenberg's assemblages and Jasper Johns' flag, target and number paintings, which appropriated the readymade back into the context of painting as the readymade image.

71 Duchamp remarked: 'there doesn't have to be a lot of the conceptual for me to like something. What I don't like is the completely nonconceptual ... '. Cabanne, *Dialogues*, *op. cit.*, 78. In contrast, a lot of language-based conceptual art sought the completely conceptual.

72 See Richard Rorty (ed.), *The Linguistic Turn*, Chicago University Press, Chicago, 1967.

73 See Roland Barthes, 'Myth Today', in *Mythologies* (1957), trans. Annette Lavers, Jonathan Cape, London, 1972, 109–58; and *Elements of Semiology* (1964), trans. Annette Lavers and Colin Smith,Hill and Wang, New York, 1973 (this translation first appeared from Jonathan Cape in 1967). Barthes' famous essay 'The Death of the Author' was first published in the US avant-garde journal *Aspen*, in its special double issue 5+6, Fall/Winter 1967, a box containing works in several different media, including audio tape and film. This issue of *Aspen* has been described by Alexander Alberro as the first exhibition of conceptual art. Victor Burgin recalls that stumbling across the translation of *Elements of Semiology* in 1967 'changed my life'. 'Interview with Victor Burgin', in Roberts (ed.), *The Impossible Document*, *op. cit.*, 97.

74 Lucy R. Lippard and John Chandler, 'The Dematerialization of Art', *Art International*, 12: 2 (February 1968); extract reprinted in this volume, 218–20.

75 For a sociological account of this expansion, in its heartland, New York, see Diana Crane, *The Transformation of the Avant-Garde: The New York Art World, 1940–1985*, Chicago University Press, Chicago, 1987.

76 Mel Ramsden, 'Artist's Language 1', *Art–Language*, New Series, No. 3, September 1999, 37.

77 Seth Siegelaub, in Lippard, *Six Years*, *op. cit.*, 125.

78 Ironically, this was in direct opposition to the materialist semiotics characteristic of the avant-garde literary studies of the day, associated most famously with Julia Kristeva and the French journal *Tel Quel*.

79 Terry Atkinson, 'Concerning the Article "The Dematerialization of Art"' (1968); extract reprinted in this volume, 220–22.

80 See 'Art without Space: A Symposium Moderated by Seth Seigelaub with Lawrence Weiner, Robert Barry, Douglas Huebler and Joseph Kosuth', 1969; reprinted in this volume, 229–30.

81 Kosuth, 'Art after Philosophy', *op. cit.*, 25–31.

82 See Peter Wollen, 'Mappings: Situationists and/or Conceptualists', in Bird and Newman (eds), *Rewriting Conceptual Art*, *op. cit.*, 27–46.

83 Cf. Mike Kelley, 'Shall We Kill Daddy?', in Marianne Van Leeuw and Anne Pontégnie, *Origin and Destination: Alighiero E. Boetti, Douglas Huebler*, Societé des Expositions du Palais des Beaux Arts de Bruxelles, 1997, 155–72.

84 The titles of images 11 and 24 of *98/Variable Piece No. 70: 1971*, April 1994.

85 Phyllis Rosenzweig, 'Interview with Lawrence Weiner', in *Lawrence Weiner: Works in the Passage of Time*, Hirshhorn Museum and Sculpture Garden, Smithsonian Institution, Washington, D.C., 1990, – quoted in Birgit Pelzer, 'Dissociated Objects: The Statements/Sculptures of Lawrence Weiner, *October*, 90 (Fall 1999), 78.

86 Alexander Alberro and Alice Zimmerman, 'not how it should were it to be built but how it could were it to be built', in Alberro, *et al.*, *Lawrence Weiner*, Phaidon Press, London, 1998, 49.

87 *January 5–13 1969: 0 Objects 0 Paintings 0 Sculptures*, n.p.

88 LeWitt, 'Sentences on Conceptual Art', *op. cit.*, Weiner's 'Statements' were reprinted in a reduced format, identical to that of LeWitt's 'Sentences'. In their original published form, each statement had appeared half-way down a separate right-hand page. However, *Art–Language*'s desire to produce an equivalence between the two texts

was frustrated by LeWitt's concluding sentence: 'These sentences comment on art, but are not art.' Weiner's 'Statements', on the other hand, most definitely were.

89 *Ibid*.

90 'Benjamin H.D. Buchloh in conversation with Lawrence Weiner', in Alberro, *et al*., *Lawrence Weiner*, *op. cit*., 12; 28.

91 'Art without Space', *op. cit*., 99

92 See note 79, above.

93 Robert Smithson, 'Language to be Looked at and/or Things to be Read' (1967, Dwan Gallery Press Release), 61; extract reprinted in this volume, 228–29.

94 'Benjamin H.D. Buchloh in Conversation with Lawrence Weiner', in Alberro, et al., *Lawrence Weiner*, *op. cit*., 20. Weiner's source appears to have been Camilla Gray's *The Great Experiment: Russian Art 1863–1922* (1962). More broadly, see Johanna Drucker, *The Visible Word: Experimental Typography and Modern Art, 1909–1923*, Chicago University Press, Chicago, 1994, ch. 3; extract reprinted in this volume, 238–39.

95 Kosuth, 'Art after Philosophy', *op. cit*., 26

96 Robert Smithson, 'Draft for "Language to be Looked at and/or Things to be Read', Smithson Archives, roll 3834, frame 0166, quoted in Timothy Martin, *Robert Smithson: Writings, Sculptures, Earthworks*, Ph.D thesis, University of London, 1999, 144.

97 *Ibid*.

98 A.J. Ayer, *Language, Truth and Logic* (1936; 1946), Penguin, Harmondsworth, 1971.

99 Arthur R. Rose, 'Four Interviews', *Arts Magazine*, 43: 4 (February 1969), 23; Kosuth repeats this passage in 'Art after Philosophy', *op. cit*., 18

100 See Lygia Clark's writings from 1964–65 reprinted as 'Nostalgia of the Body', *October*, 69 (Summer 1994), 99–102; reprinted in this volume, 242.

101 Kosuth, 'Art after Philosophy', *op. cit*., 20. For an account of some of the philosophical investments of analytical conceptual art, see Peter Osborne, 'Conceptual Art and/as Philosophy', in Bird and Newman, *Rewriting Conceptual Art*, *op. cit*., 47–65.

102 Ad Reinhardt, 'Art as Art' (1962), in Barbara Rose (ed.), *Art as Art: The Selected Writings of Ad Reinhardt*, University of California Press, Berkeley and Los Angeles, 1975, 53–56.

103 Jeff Wall, *Dan Graham's Kammerspeil*, *op. cit*., 100; 102.

104 LeWitt, 'Sentences on Conceptual Art', *op. cit*., 839. LeWitt was probably thinking of Judd's 'specific objects', but the remark applies equally to Kosuth, whose aesthetic draws equally from Minimalism and Pop. Kosuth's 'craft' should be understood here as the facility with which he illustrates the idea of art as idea, as much as his graphic design itself.

105 Atkinson, 'Concerning the Article "The Dematerialization of Art"', *op. cit*., 54–55, emphasis added.

106 'Introduction', *Art–Language*, 1: 1, *op. cit*., 10.

107 Two of the three original members of the group (Mike Baldwin and David Bainbridge) were sacked from Coventry School of Art in 1971 for advocating language as the main medium of their students' art practice. It was only at this point that the art market was considered as an alternative source of finance for the group. For a retrospective account of those years by the third faculty member, see Terry Atkinson, 'If We Are Historical and Logical Monsters Then So Much the Better ... v2', *Art–Language*, New Series, No. 3 (September 1999), 62–75. As Atkinson puts it: 'It tends to be overlooked that Art & Language began as a teaching operation as much as anything else.', 71.

108 Michael Corris and Neil Powell, 'An Attempt at a Textual Analogue of a Possible Art & Language Exhibition', in *ibid*., 6.

109 'Introduction', *Art–Language*, 1:1, *op. cit*., 10.

110 See Osborne, 'Philosophy and/as Conceptual Art', *op. cit*., 62–65.

111 Cf. Atkinson, 'If We Are Historical and Logical Monsters', *op. cit*., 68; 70; Corris and Powell, 'An Attempt at a Textual Analogue', *op. cit*., 5. There is much in common between the sense of embattled isolation and the contorted, opaque prose of *Art–Language*, on the one hand, and Beckett's late work, on the other.

112 Charles Harrison, 'Artist's Writing', in *Art–Language*, New Series, No. 3, 30; Atkinson, 'If We Are Historical and Logical Monsters', in *ibid*., 75; Harrison, 'Artist's Writing', in *ibid*., 27; 33. See also Terry Atkinson, *The Index, The World War One Moves and the Ruins of Conceptualism*, Cornerhouse, Manchester/Irish Museum of Modern Art, Dublin, 1992. The 'return to modernism' involved here is most apparent in the writings of Charles Harrison, the group's academic representative and chief apologist.

113 Jeff Wall, 'Marks of Indifference', *op. cit*., 257; and Jeff Wall, 'Introduction: Partially Reflective Mirror Writings' in *Dan Graham, Two-Way Mirror Power*, *op. cit*., xvii.

114 In this respect, appropriation is related to the situationist concept of *détournement* ('the re-use of pre-existing artistic elements in a new ensemble'), raised to the level of cultural form. On the situationist analysis, ours is an era in which 'the greatest seriousness advances masked in the ambiguous interplay between art and its negation ...', '*Détournement* as Negation and Prelude', in Ken Knabb (ed.), *Situationist International Anthology*, Bureau of Public Secrets, Berkeley, California, 1989, 55–56. See, for example, Stephen Willats, 'Prescriptions for Task-Oriented Methodologies in Constructing Operational Models of Art Practice' (1973), in his *Changing Everything*, South London Gallery, London, 1998, 72–96.

115 Dan Graham, 'My Works for Magazine Pages: "A History of Conceptual Art"' (1985), in *Two-Way Mirror Power*, *op. cit*., 10–13.

116 *The Writings of Marcel Duchamp*, *op. cit*., 142.

117 Dan Graham, *Rock My Religion: Writings and Art Projects, 1965–1990*, ed. Brian Wallis, MIT Press, Cambridge, Massachusetts, 1993, 14–23.

118 Cf. Jeff Wall, 'Marks of Indifference', *op. cit*., 257; David Campany, 'Conceptual Art History or, A Home for *Homes for America*', in Bird and Newman (eds), *Rewriting Conceptual Art*, *op. cit*., 121–39; 137.

119 Robert Smithson, 'Donald Judd' (1965); 'Entropy and the New Monuments' (1966); 'Towards the Development of an Air Terminal Site' (1967); 'The Domain of the Great Bear' (with Mel Bochner, 1966); 'Quasi-Infinities and the Waning of Space' (1966) – in *Robert Smithson: The Collected Writings*, *op. cit*., 4–6; 10–23; 52–60; 26–33; 34–37, respectively. The last of these, from *Arts Magazine*, produces a visual equivalent between its notes and images by interspersing them, in similar dimensions, in a circle around a central block of text. Bochner's magazine work has been neglected in the revival of critical interest in the genre generated by the republication of Graham's and Smithson's pieces in recent years. See Mel Bochner, 'The Beach Boys – 100%', *Arts Magazine*, March 1967; 'Alphaville, Godard's Apocalypse', *Arts Magazine*, Vol. 42, No. 7, May 1968. Its reception has perhaps been adversely affected by his scepticism about the term 'conceptual art', in contrast to Graham's retrospective embrace of it. 'For a variety of reasons I do not like the term 'conceptual art'. Connotations of an easy dichotomy with perception are obvious and inappropriate. The unfortunate implication is of a somewhat magical/mystical leap from one mode of existence to another. The problem is the confusion of idealism and intention. By creating an original fiction, 'conceptualism' posits its special non-empirical existence as a positive (transcendental) value.' – 'Excerpts from Speculation (1967–1970)', *Artforum*, June, 1970. This is a position Bochner shares with Smithson and several other artists who are more prominently described as 'conceptual', such as Lawrence Weiner.

120 'A Tour of the Monuments of Passaic, New Jersey', in *Robert Smithson: The Collected Writings*, *op. cit*., 73–74. Interestingly, although it restores Smithson's original title, this edition makes no reference to its original layout in *Artforum*; despite the fact that several other pieces in the volume are reproduced as originally set in their magazine forms. The emphasis is, rather, on the recovery of Smithson 'the writer'. This is unfortunate, since it detracts from the cultural specificity (and extra-artistic determinants) of Smithson's intervention.

121 The emphasis on photojournalism as the unifying category here derives from Jeff Wall's writings: *Dan Graham's Kammerspeil*, *op. cit*.; 'Marks of Indifference', *op. cit*; and 'Monochrome and Photojournalism in On Kawara's Paintings', in Lynne Cooke and Karen Kelly (eds), *Robert Lehman Lectures on Contemporary Art*, Dia Center for the Arts, New York, 1996, 135–56.

122 Akasegawa produced 'forgeries' of an infamous forged 1000-Yen note, identifiable by its serial number, displayed them in a gallery and used them as invitations to the show – but he printed them on one side only. He was arrested after someone was apprehended trying to use one as money. His trial included a four-hour Happening, staged to explain to the judge what a Happening was. It led to a number of works based on the state's impounding of objects in Akasegawa's possession, as well as a later large scale (90 × 180 cm) reproduction of the note called *Morphology of Revenge* (1968). See Nam June Paik, 'To Catch Up or Not to Catch Up with the West: Hijikata and Hi Red Center', in Munroe, *Scream Against the Sky*, *op. cit*., 80–81 (Akasegawa was one of the three members of Hi Red Center); Reiko Tomii, 'Concerning the Institution of Art: Conceptualism in Japan', in *Global Conceptualism*, *op. cit*., 15–29.

123 See Artist Placement Group Statement (London, 1990) reprinted in this volume, 249; Stephen Willats, *West London Social Resource Project*, London, 1973; Oliver Cieslik, 'Mutual Geography: Stephan Willats' Project Works', in Stephen Willats, *Living Together*, Tramway Glasgow, 1994, 61–75. See also Stephen Willats, *Conceptual Living*, Victoria Miro Gallery, London, 1991.

124 See Pamela M. Lee, *Object to be Destroyed: The Work of Gordon Matta-Clark*, MIT Press, Cambridge, Massachusetts, 2000; Dan Graham, 'Gordon Matta Clark' (1983), in his *Rock My Religion*, *op. cit*., 194–205; Wall, *Dan Graham's Kammerspeil*, *op. cit*. Wall reads Graham's *Alterations to a Suburban Home* as a historical critique of the 'defeatism' of conceptual art. See also Robert Smithson, 'Ultramoderne' (1967), in his *Collected Writings*, *op. cit*., 62–65.

125 See Helen Molesworth, 'Cleaning Up in the 1970s: The Work of Judy Chicago, Mary Kelly and Mierle Laderman Ukeles', in Bird and Newman (eds), *Rewriting Conceptual Art*, 107–22.

126 Mari Carmen Ramírez, 'Tactics for Thriving on Adversity: Conceptualism in Latin America, 1960–1980', in *Global Conceptualism*, *op. cit*., 55.

127 *Ibid*., 54; 60.

128 Luis Camnitzer, 'Contemporary Colonial Art' (1969), in Alberro and Stimson (eds), *Conceptual Art*, *op. cit*., 229–30. Camnitzer was thinking of the Tupamaros in Uruguay, in particular.

129 Eduardo Costa, Raúl Escari, Roberto Jacoby, 'A Media Art (Manifesto)' (1966); extract reprinted in this volume, 255.

130 Alberro, 'A Media Art: Conceptualism in Latin America in the 1960s', in Bird and Newman (eds), *Rewriting Conceptual Art*, *op. cit*., 141.

131 Mari Teresa Gramuglio and Nicolás Rosa, 'Tucumán Burns' (1968), in Alberro and Stimson (eds), *Conceptual Art*, *op. cit*., 76–77; translation amended.

132 Alexander Kluge and Oskar Negt, *Public Sphere and Experience: Towards an Analysis of the Bourgeois and Proletarian Public Sphere* (1972), trans. Peter Labanyi, *et al*., Minnesota University Press, Minneapolis, 1993.

133 Gramuglio and Rosa 'Tucumán Burns', *op. cit*., 78–79; Alberro, 'A Media Art', *op. cit*., 144–46.

134 Hélio Oiticica, 'General Scheme of the New Objectivity' (1967), in Alberro and Stimson (eds), *Conceptual Art*, *op. cit*., 40; 42; reprinted in this volume, translation amended, 255–56.

135 *Ibid*., 42.

136 Amilcar de Castro, Ferreira Gullar, Franz Weissmann, Lygia Clark, Lygia Pape, Reynaldo Jardim, Theon Spanudis, 'Neo-Concretist Manifesto' (1959), reprinted in *October*, 69 (Summer 1994), 91–95. On its original publication in *Jornal do Brasil*, 22 March 1959, the manifesto was attributed to Gullar alone.

137 Lygia Clark, 'Concerning the Instant' (1965), 'Concerning the Magic of the Object' (1965), in *October*, 69, *op. cit*., 99–101.

138 Camnitzer pointed out that 'In 1968, in the Whitney Sculpture Annual, the average investment in materials alone, per sculpture ... [was] more than the annual income of the majority of the inhabitants in

underdeveloped countries'. 'Contemporary Colonial Art', Alberro and Stimson (eds), *Conceptual Art*, *op. cit.*, 228. In this respect, '"arte povera" was more influential for some artists because of the evocations of the title than for the actual work'. Camnitzer, in Blake Stimson, 'Dada–Situationism/ *Tumamaros* – Conceptualism: An Interview with Luis Camnitzer', in Alberro and Stimson (eds), *Conceptual Art*, *op. cit.*, 498. This was also the period of the invention of a 'Third Cinema' in Latin America, which made an aesthetic virtue out of its poverty of means.

139 Ramírez, 'Tactics for Thriving on Adversity', *Global Conceptualism*, *op. cit.*, 65.

140 There was also a direct, politicizing influence of Latin American artists on the conceptual art community in New York. Not only did Oiticica and Meireles exhibit in New York, but Lucy Lippard (a key figure in the movement and one of the prime movers in the Art Workers' Coalition, set up in New York in 1969) visited Rosario and met with the Tucumán Arde group. Blake Stimson, 'Dada–Situationism/ Tumamaros–Conceptualism', in Alberro and Stimson (eds), *Conceptual Art*, *op. cit.*, 496–97.

141 Victor Burgin, 'In Reply', *Art–Language*, 2: 2 (Summer 1972), 32–34; reprinted in this volume, 238. Burgin was responding to dismissive remarks in Terry Atkinson and Michael Baldwin, 'Unnatural Rules and Excuses', *Art–Language*, 2:1 (February 1972), 19; 21; 23 – themselves a reaction to Burgin's 'Rules of Thumb', *Studio International*, 161: 933 (May 1971), 237–39, in which he had construed Art & Language as recasting the position of *l'art pour l'art*. Burgin was one of five artists whose work Charles Harrison had added to the exhibition 'When Attitudes Become Form', when it moved from the Kunsthalle Bern to the Institute of Contemporary Arts, London, in autumn 1969. Burgin attributes Harrison with 'single-handedly' giving a platform to conceptual art in Britain in the early 1970s. 'Interview with Victor Burgin', in Roberts (ed.), *The Impossible Document*, *op. cit.*, 87. After 1973, having linked up with Art & Language, Harrison would play a more partisan role. See note 113, above.

142 Victor Burgin, 'Socialist Formalism', *Studio International*, 191: 980 (March–April, 1976), 148–54; reprinted in this volume, 256–58.

143 See Victor Burgin, *Between*, Basil Blackwell, Oxford/Institute of Contemporary Arts, London, 1986, 8–39.

144 See, for example, Victor Burgin, *Some Cities*, Reaktion Books, London, 1996, in which images are selected from a range of works over a twenty-year period and recontextualized into a continuous travelogue, transforming Burgin's *oeuvre* into the autobiography of his search for photographic representations of a certain type of socio-psychic space . The theoretical coordinates of this space are sketched in his *In/Different Spaces: Place and Memory in Visual Culture*, University of California Press, Berkeley and Los Angeles, 1996.

145 Mary Kelly, *Post-Partum Document*, Routledge and Kegan Paul, London, 1983.

146 *Ibid.*, 1.

147 Lucy Lippard, 'Issue and Tabu', in *Issue: Social Strategies by Women Artists*, Institute of Contemporary Arts, London, 1980, 3. Rosler is the exception in this regard. Lippard curated the first all women conceptual art exhibition, 'C. 7,500' (named after the population of Valencia, California, its first location) in 1973, 'by way of exasperated reply ... to those who say "there are no women making conceptual art"'. But it did not include Rosler. It travelled to the Earham Street Gallery, London, in April 1974. (See Rozsika Parker and Griselda Pollock, 'Fifteen Years of Feminist Action: From Practical Strategies to Strategic Practices', in Rozsika Parker and Griselda Pollock (eds), *Framing Feminism: Art and the Women's Movement 1970–1985*, Pandora, London, 1987, 76, n. 5; and '1974 Dossier: "*Ca.*7,500" (1–3)', in *ibid.*, 194–99.)

Exhibitions of work by women artists are not necessarily exhibitions of feminist art; although they may nonetheless, at certain times, be feminist exhibitions. The notion of 'feminist conceptual art' is still more fraught. As Griselda Pollock has argued, feminist art practices cannot be adequately comprehended as modifications of existing artistic trends, since their strategic rationale is political, in a manner designed 'to shift our attention from the conventional ways we consume works of art as objects and stress the conditions of production of art as a matter of texts, events, representations whose effects and meanings depend upon their conditions of reception.' (Griselda Pollock, 'Feminism and Modernism', in *ibid.*, 80). The matter is yet more complicated, in fact, since this definition of feminist art practice is itself theoretically indebted to conceptual art.

148 Judy Chicago, *The Dinner Party: A Symbol of our Heritage*, Anchor/ Doubleday, New York, 1979.

149 See Adrian Piper, 'Preparatory Notes for The Mythic Being' (1973–74), in Piper, *Out of Order, Out of Sight, Vol.1*, *op. cit.*, 91–139. The as-yet-unpublished philosophical project on which Piper has been working for the last twenty years is 'Rationality and the Structure of the Self'.

150 Buchloh, 'Conceptual Art 1962–1969: From the Aesthetic of Administration to the Critique of Institutions', *op. cit.*, 119.

151 It is important to remember that it was an avant-garde institution, the Independents' Show, that rejected *Fountain*, not a mainstream one. Duchamp was testing the limits of 'art' by testing the limits of the avant-garde's own conception of such tests. For an account of the avant-garde as a generational logic of 'reference, deference, and difference', see Griselda Pollock, *Avant-Garde Gambits, 1888–1893: Gender and the Colour of Art History*, Thames and Hudson, London, 1992.

152 See Martha Buskirk, 'Thoroughly Modern Marcel' *October*, 70, 113–25.

153 Buchloh, 'Conceptual Art 1962–1969', 107.

154 Kosuth, 'Art after Philosophy', *op. cit.*, 19–20. 'This is a Portrait of Iris Clert if I say so' reads the famous telegram sent by Robert Rauschenberg to his dealer, Iris Clert, in 1961, as his contribution to an exhibition of portraits – simultaneously enacting and parodying this position. 'If someone calls it art, it's art', Judd declared in 1965, more straightforwardly. In 'Art after Philosophy', Kosuth quotes this phrase of Judd's twice (17; 20).

155 Harrison, *Essays on Art & Language*, *op. cit.*, 93–94.

156 Daniel Buren, 'Beware' (1969/70), in Alberro and Stimson (eds), *Conceptual Art*, *op. cit.*, 146.

157 Daniel Buren, 'Critical Limits' (1970), in his *Five Texts*, John Weber Gallery, New York, and Jack Wendler Gallery, London, 1973. Cf. Buchloh, 'Conceptual Art 1962–1969', *op. cit.*, 138.

158 Buren, 'Beware', *op. cit.*, 155; Daniel Buren, *Reboundings*, trans. Philippe Hunt, Daled and Gevaert, Brussels, 1977, 68.

159 Buren, *Reboundings*, *op. cit.*, 73.

160 See Douglas Crimp, 'Daniel Buren's New York Work', in R.H. Fuchs, *et al.*, *Discordance/Cohérence*, Stedelijk Van Abbemuseum, Eindhoven, 1976, 75–78.

161 Marcel Broodthaers, quoted by Douglas Crimp, 'This is Not a Museum of Art', in his *On the Museum's Ruins*, MIT Press, Cambridge, Massachusetts, 1993, 200–34; 200–1.

162 Cf. Rosalind Krauss, *'A Voyage on the North Sea': Art in the Age of the Post-Medium Condition*, *op. cit.* Krauss doesn't use the term 'transmedia', but rather claims 'fiction' itself as Broodthaers' 'post-medium' medium. Yet this lacks precisely the differential specificity she claims his work reveals as a condition of a new concept of medium.

163 Buren, *Reboundings*, *op. cit.*, 63. This essay was Buren's response to Documenta 5, in which he had himself participated, spreading his painting through discrete sections of the show in order to produce an 'Exhibition of an Exhibition'. Buren's own mode of (critical) institutional self-validation was to produce critiques of shows in which he had participated. 'Beware' (*'Mise en garde'*) was written for the catalogue of the 'Konzeption' show in Leverkusen, but subsequently rewritten to incorporate criticisms of other work in the show. The version to which reference is made above is *'Mise en garde No. 3'*.

164 Robert Morris, Letter to Michael Compton, 5 March 1971, quoted in Jon Bird, 'Minding the Body: Robert Morris's 1971 Tate Gallery Retrospective', in Bird and Newman (eds), *Rewriting Conceptual Art*, *op. cit.*, 97.

165 *Ibid.*, 101–6. Like Robert Smithson (in his views on entropy), Morris was influenced by Ehrenzweig's concept of de-differentiation in *The Hidden Order of Art* (1967).

166 Flavin, who was the main instigator of the dispute, was later awarded the top prize from the exhibition. See Alexander Alberro, 'The Turn of the Screw: Daniel Buren, Dan Flavin, and the Sixth Guggenheim International Exhibition', *October*, 80, Spring 1997, 57–84.

167 For an overview of this debate, see Rosalyn Deutsche, 'Property Values: Hans Haacke, Real Estate, and the Museum', in her *Evictions: Art and Spatial Politics*, MIT Press, Cambridge, Massachusetts, 1996, 159–92.

168 Thomas M. Messer, 'Guest Editorial', *Arts Magazine*, 45:8 (Summer 1971) 5; quoted by Deutsche, *Evictions*, *op. cit.*, 179.

169 Wall, *Dan Graham's Kammerspeil*, *op. cit.*, 82, n. 4. For a defence of Asher's work as a paradigm of the critical negations of a post-conceptual functionalism – which Wall contests – see Benjamin Buchloh, 'Context-Function-Use Value: Michael Asher's Re-Materialization of the Artwork', in *Michael Asher: Exhibitions in Europe 1972–1977*, Stedelijk Van Abbemuseum, Eindhoven, 1980.

170 Wall, *Dan Graham's Kammerspeil*, *op. cit.*, 21; 28; 33; 11.

171 For some, rather unsatisfactory, histories (because they fail to recognize the depth of the category), see Nicholas de Oliveira, Nicola Oxley and Michael Petry, *Installation Art*, Thames and Hudson, London, 1994; Julie H. Reiss, *From Margin to Center: The Spaces of Installation Art*, MIT Press, Cambridge and London, 1999; Erika Suderburg, 'On Installation and Site Specificity', in Erika Suderburg (ed.), *Space, Site, Intervention: Situating Installation Art*, Minnesota University Press, Minneapolis, 2000, 1–22.

172 Daniel Buren, 'The Function of the Studio' (1971), *October*, 10 (Fall 1979), 56.

173 Installation is usually considered a post-minimalist form, because of the centrality to it of issues of site specificity and gallery space. However, this is to neglect the ideation inherent in the multiple realizations of particular works (especially clear in the case of an artist like Weiner). It is symptomatic that for Judd, for example, the problem of installation was essentially a quest for permanence. See Donald Judd, 'On Installation' (1982) – originally titled 'The Importance of Permanence' – reprinted in James Meyer, *Minimalism*, Phaidon, London, 2000, 266–68. Rather, installation is the point of convergence of the legacies of Minimalism and conceptual art. Hence its ubiquity.

174 Brian O'Doherty, *Inside the White Cube: The Ideology of Gallery Space* (1976), University of California Press, Berkeley and Los Angeles, 1999, 69.

175 See note 64, above.

176 Michael Fried, 'Art and Objecthood' (1967), reprinted in his *Art and Objecthood: Essays and Reviews*, University of Chicago Press, Chicago, 1998, 148–72.

177 See James Meyer, 'The Functional Site: or, The Transformation of Site Specificity', in Suderburg (ed.), *Space, Site, Intervention*, *op. cit.*, 23–27.

178 Harald Szeemann, the curator of 'When Attitudes Become Form' in 1969, also curated the 1999 Venice Biennale, where the Chinese work achieved its greatest international prominence to date.

179 Damien Hirst, *I Want to Spend the Rest of My Life Everywhere, with Everyone, One to One, Always, Forever, Now*, Booth-Clibborn Editions, London, 1997, 198–99.

WORK-S

VITO ACCONCI
BAS JAN ADER
AKASEGAWA GENPEI
ELEANOR ANTIN
ARAKAWA
ARMAN
ART & LANGUAGE
ART WORKERS COALITION
MICHAEL ASHER
TERRY ATKINSON
JOHN BALDESSARI
MICHAEL BALDWIN
ROBERT BARRY
BERND & HILLA BECHER
JOSEPH BEUYS
MEL BOCHNER
ALIGHIERO BOETTI
OSCAR BONY
GEORGE BRECHT
MARCEL BROODTHAERS
STANLEY BROUWN
DANIEL BUREN
VICTOR BURGIN
IAN BURN
JOHN CAGE
SOPHIE CALLE
JUDY CHICAGO
CHRISTO &
JEANNE-CLAUDE
LYGIA CLARK
JAMES COLEMAN
HANNE DARBOVEN
GUY DEBORD
JAN DIBBETS
BRACO DIMITRIJEVIC
WILLIE DOHERTY
MARCEL DUCHAMP
HAMISH FULTON
ROBERT GOBER
FELIX GONZALEZ-TORRES
ZBIGNIEW GOSTOMSKI
DAN GRAHAM
GRUPO DE ARTISTAS DE
VANGUARDIA
HANS HAACKE
TIBOR HAJAS
MARGARET HARRISON
EVA HESSE
HI RED CENTER
SUSAN HILLER
JOHN HILLIARD
JENNY HOLZER
DOUGLAS HUEBLER
KAY HUNT
ALFREDO JAAR
JASPER JOHNS
ILYA KABAKOV
TADEUSZ KANTOR
ALLAN KAPROW
ON KAWARA
MARY KELLY
EDWARD KIENHOLZ
YVES KLEIN
KOMAR & MELAMID
JOSEPH KOSUTH
CHRISTINE KOZLOV
JAROSLAW KOZLOWSKI
BARBARA KRUGER
SHIGEKO KUBOTA
JOHN LATHAM
LOUISE LAWLER
SHERRIE LEVINE
SOL LEWITT
RICHARD LONG
ALLAN MCCOLLUM
GEORGE MACIUNAS
PIERO MANZONI
GORDON MATTA-CLARK
MATSUZAWA YUTAKA
CILDO MEIRELES
ANA MENDIETA
MIYAJIMA TATSUO
ROBERT MORRIS
MURAKAMI SABURO
BRUCE NAUMAN
N.E. THING CO.
(IAIN & INGRID BAXTER)
HÉLIO OITICICA
YOKO ONO
ROMAN OPALKA
NAM JUNE PAIK
ADRIAN PIPER
VICTOR PIVOVAROV
MEL RAMSDEN
ROBERT RAUSCHENBERG
MARTHA ROSLER
EDWARD RUSCHA
CAROLEE SCHNEEMANN
RICHARD SERRA
SHIMAMOTO SHOZO
MIEKO (CHIEKO) SHIOMI
SHIRAGA FUJIKO
SHIRAGA KAZUO
ROBERT SMITHSON
MICHAEL SNOW
NIELE TORONI
MIERLE LADERMAN
UKELES
JEFF WALL
ANDY WARHOL
LAWRENCE WEINER
HANNAH WILKE
FRED WILSON
KRZYSZTOF WODICZKO
LA MONTE YOUNG
ZHANG HUAN

PRE-HISTORY: 1950–1960

The immediate precursors of conceptual art are to be found in the revival of avant-gardism in the period following the Second World War, in a complex series of cultural exchanges between Europe, the USA and Japan. Two figures stand out as sources of the new ideas: the French artist and inventor of the 'readymade' Marcel Duchamp (who had moved to America during the First World War) and the American composer and Zen Buddhist John Cage. However, it was at the limits of painting that avant-garde activities largely continued to be concentrated. In the USA, Robert Rauschenberg and Jasper Johns transformed painting with everyday objects and chance events, questioning its privileged status as a special kind of object. In Japan, the performance-based work of the Gutai group extended the trajectory of *informel* and action painting into ritualized acts of disruption. While in France and Italy, Yves Klein and Piero Manzoni developed parallel avant-garde practices, highlighting the ideal content of the experience of art, out of their alternative understandings of the metaphysical meaning of the monochrome. In each case, the expansion to destruction of the idea of painting stimulated an interest in the ephemeral and the immaterial that prefigured much of the more self-consciously 'conceptual' work that followed.

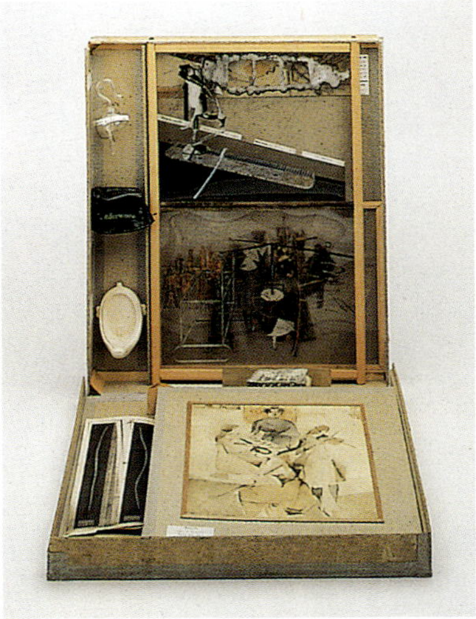

Marcel DUCHAMP
De ou par Marcel Duchamp ou Rrose Sélavy [Boîte, Series B]
Begun in Paris, 1941, completed in New York, 1942-54
Box containing miniature replicas of the artist's work
39 × 35 × 8 cm [16 × 14 × 3 in]

With the invention of readymades in 1913 – everyday found objects, significantly titled by the artist – Duchamp began a critical artistic practice of questioning the nature of art objects and their context. This laid the foundations for the conceptual art which would emerge in the 1960s. A further stage in his inquiry developed when he made a miniature collection of replicas of his works contained in a box which was portable like a suitcase. He thus displayed facsimiles of his earlier works as an 'art collection' with its own separate status. Duchamp began working on the *Boîte* in 1933 and first issued it in its deluxe version, the *Boîte-en-valise (Box in a valise)* in 1941. From then until his death in 1968 he made twenty-four further editions, such as the one illustrated here. Their titles, meaning 'from or by Marcel Duchamp or Rrose Sélavy', refer to the name he took for his female alter ego, a pun on 'eros, c'est la vie'.

John CAGE
4'33" [detail]
1952
Original version of score
in proportional notation
28 × 21.5 cm [11 × 8.5 in]
Edition Peters No. 6777a

4'33", which has become known as 'Silence', may be performed by any instrumentalist or combination of instrumentalists. Performers are instructed by the score to sit silently before the audience for the duration of the piece, four minutes and thirty-three seconds. Any sound element entering the work comes from incidental noises made by the audience or audible noise from outside the performance space. It was first performed by the pianist and composer David Tudor in Woodstock, New York, in 1952. At this time Cage and Tudor both taught in New York and at Black Mountain College, North Carolina. This score, made by Cage in 'proportional notation' after the first performance, indicates time spatially:
1 page = 7 inches = 56 seconds.

After studying Zen Buddhist and other Asian systems of thought at Columbia University in the 1940s Cage expanded the boundaries of his musical composition, giving equal status to elements which in the West had been considered as 'negatives' of that which constitutes music. Hence silence was given the same status in his work as intentionally produced sound. Similarly, random 'chance operations' were considered to be as artistically meaningful as intentionally produced events, both in scores and their performance. Initially Cage devised mathematical charts to obtain random numerical values as the basis of his scores. In the winter of 1950 he was given a copy of the *I Ching*, the ancient Chinese book of divination, which he then used as a source of chance operations.

John CAGE

45' for a Speaker [detail]

1954

Typeset extract from score, originally published in John Cage, *Silence*, 1968

'Before writing this piece I composed *34' 46.776" for Two Pianists*. These piano parts shared the same numerical rhythmic structure but were not fixed together by means of a score. They were mobile with respect to one another. In each case the structural units became different in actual time-length by use of a factor obtained by chance operations. Having been asked to speak at the Composers' Concourse in London (October 1954), I decided to prepare for that occasion a lecture using the same structure, thus permitting the playing of music during the delivery of the speech. The second pianist's part had turned out to be 31' 57.9864". When I applied the chance factor to the numerical rhythmic structure in the case of the speech, I obtained 39' 16.95". However, when the text was completed, I found I was unable to perform it within that time-length. I needed more time. I made experiments, reading long lines as rapidly as I could. The result was two seconds for each line, 45' for the entire piece ... The piano parts had included noises and whistles in addition to prepared piano tones. For the speaker, I made a list of noises and gestures. By means of chance operations, determining which noise or gesture and when it was to be made, I added these to the text ... '

– John Cage, notes for *45' for a Speaker*, in *Silence*, 1968

10"
(Hiss)
Time,
Which is the title of this piece,
(so many minutes
20" so many seconds),
is what we
and sounds
happen in. Whether early or late:
in it.
It is not a question of counting.
30" Our poetry now
is the realization
that we possess nothing.
Anything therefore (Slap table)
is a delight
(since we do not possess it)
40" and thus need (Cough)
not fear.
This composition involves a flexible use of
The number 10,000: that
is to say 100 x 100 (sq. rt.).
The actual time-lengths
50" *are changing.* This
work has no score. It should be abolished. "A statement concerning the
arts is no statement concerning the arts." It
consists of single parts. Any of them may
be played together or eliminated and at any
time. "To me teaching is an expedient, but I do
4'00" not teach external signs." Like a long book if a
long book is like a mobile. "The ignorant be-
cause of their attachment to existence seize on signified
or signifying." No beginning no ending. Harmony, so called,
is a forced abstract vertical relation which blots out the spontaneous
transmitting nature of each of the sounds forced into it. It is
10" artificial and unrealistic. Form, then, is not something
off in the distance in solitary confinement:
It is right here right now. Since it is
something we say about past actions,
it is wise
to drop it.

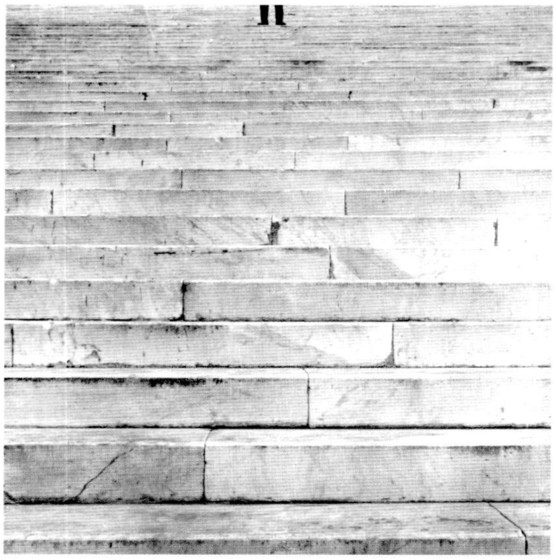
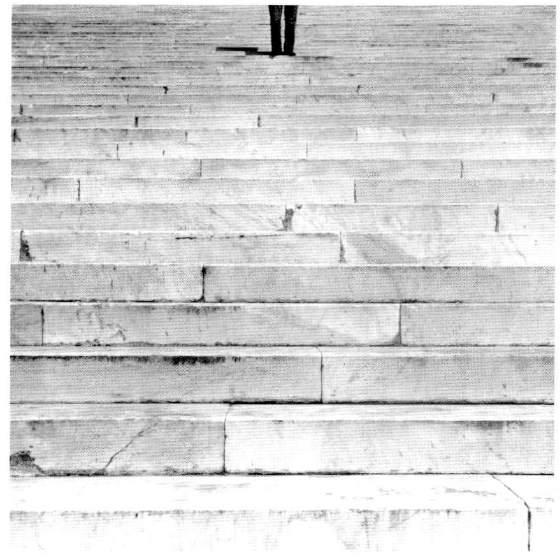
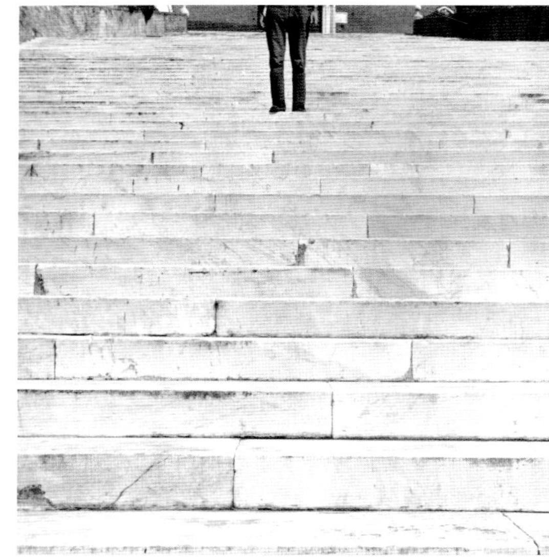

Robert RAUSCHENBERG

Cy and Roman Steps

1952

5 black and white photographs

40.5 × 40.5 cm [16 × 16 in] each

Rauschenberg began taking photographs in 1949, before he turned to painting. These early photographs are formally and conceptually related to one of his earliest works, *This is the First Half of a Print Designed to Exist in Passing Time* (1949), in which fourteen woodcuts display increasing numbers of horizontal white lines on a black ground. This progression is echoed in *Cy and Roman Steps* by the approaching legs and finally the torso of Rauschenberg's friend, the American painter Cy Twombly. Both works document temporality through an incremental sequence.

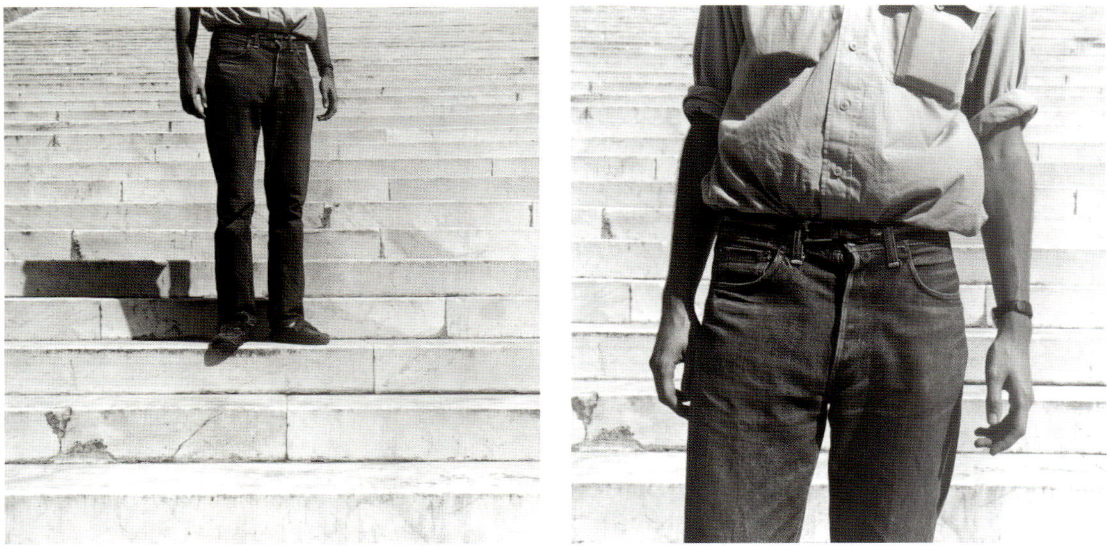

Robert RAUSCHENBERG

Erased De Kooning Drawing

1953

Traces of ink and crayon on paper with hand-lettered ink label in gilt frame

63.5 × 56 cm [25 × 22 in]

Collection, San Francisco Museum of Modern Art

In 1953 Rauschenberg approached the Abstract Expressionist painter Willem de Kooning, whose work he admired, and proposed making an artwork in reverse by erasing one of his drawings. De Kooning consented to this and supplied Rauschenberg with a heavily worked drawing so that erasing it would also require intensive work. Rauschenberg later framed the erased drawing. His ambiguous act of erasure, both a homage and a work of sabotage, has been seen as a neo-Dadaist, anti-art gesture as well as a refusal of expressionist art's existential connotations. However, the erasure also functions conceptually as a means of opening up the field of art activity, similar to the use of the 'negative' element of silence by the composer John Cage, with whom Rauschenberg worked closely during this period.

Robert RAUSCHENBERG
White Painting
1951
Oil on canvas
3 panels, 183 × 274.5 cm [72 × 108 in] overall
Collection, San Francisco Museum of Modern Art

In the early 1950s Rauschenberg produced several series of monochrome paintings. The *White Paintings* were followed by *Black Paintings* (1951–52) and *Red Paintings* (1953). Although these monochromes have textured surfaces, they do not draw attention to the individuality of the brushstrokes. Instead, they function as *tabula rasa* or environmental mirrors, recording on their surface varying light conditions and the shadows cast on them by spectators or performers. In 1951, Rauschenberg installed some of the *White Paintings* as the background for a 'concerted action' in which he performed alongside the dancer Merce Cunningham, the composer John Cage, the pianist David Tudor and the poet Charles Olsen at Black Mountain College, North Carolina. This event was a precursor of 'intermedia' Fluxus actions and Happenings.

Jasper JOHNS

Flag

1954-55

Encaustic, oil and collage on fabric mounted on plywood

107 × 154 cm [42 × 60.5 in]

Collection, The Museum of Modern Art, New York

Flag is one of a series of works of this period which make literal Johns' assertion of the painting as an object. The *Target* and *Flag* paintings drew upon 'readymade' designs, which Johns took to be so familiar to viewers that they would not be noticed in themselves. Instead, it is the thick encaustic texture of the surfaces and the three-dimensional nature of the paintings to which attention is drawn. However, on reflection, neither the surface nor the representational element of the work predominate but are equalized, emphasizing both the work's purely objective existence and the way the image of the flag functions as a sign.

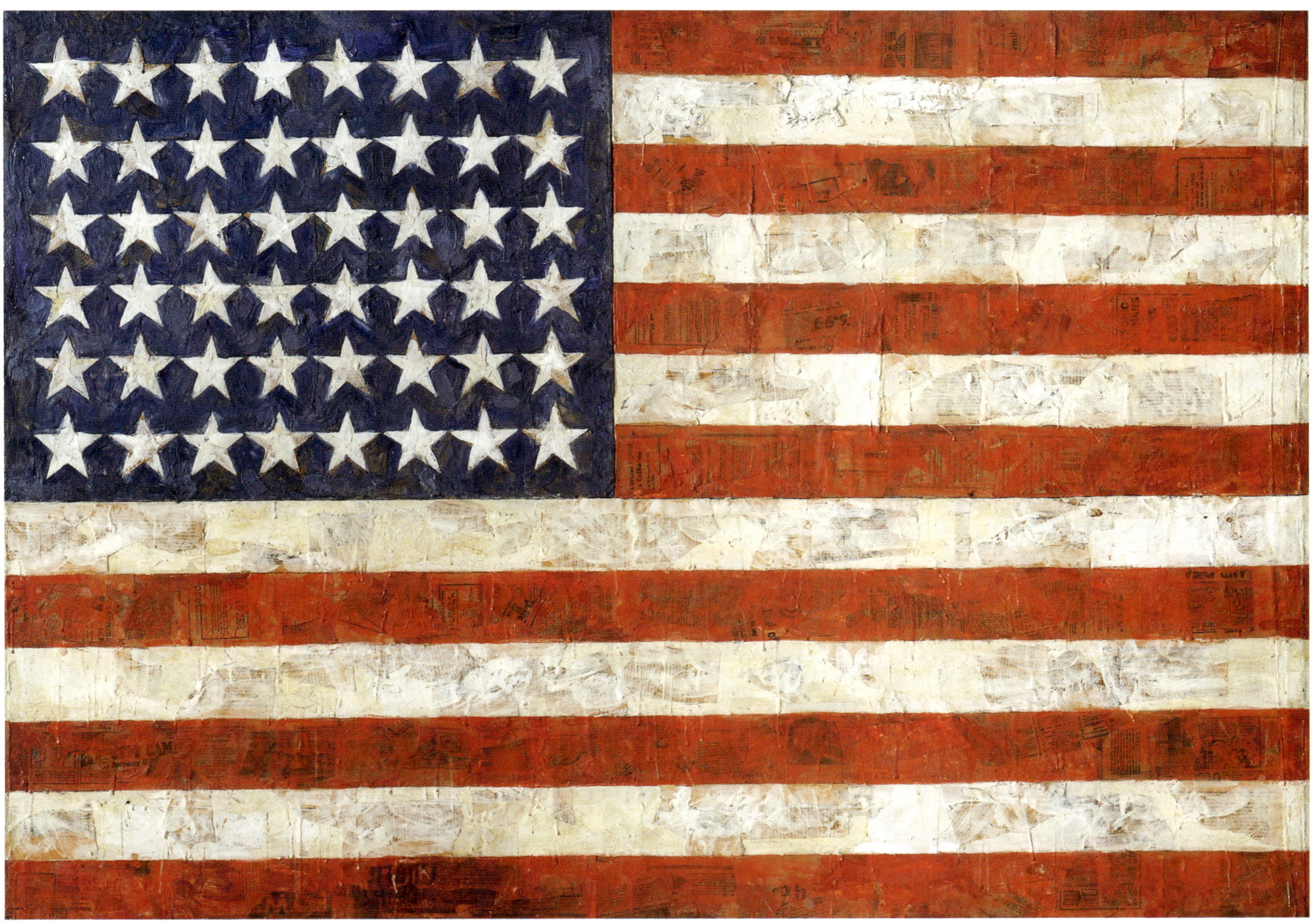

SHIRAGA Fujiko

Work

1955

Japanese paper

Central sheet, 345 × 138.5 cm [136 × 54.5 in]

Left and right sheets, 168 × 91.5 cm [66 × 36 in] each

Collection, Takamatsu City Museum of Art, Japan

Three large sheets of Japanese paper were creased and uncreased by Shiraga in a random manner and then displayed. 'Work' (in Japanese, 'Sakuhin', which means literally 'made item') was used by several members of the Gutai group as a description which was not a title and not the same as 'untitled', but which drew attention to the object as 'something made', as opposed to something that represents, imitates or alludes to any other thing or meaning beyond itself.

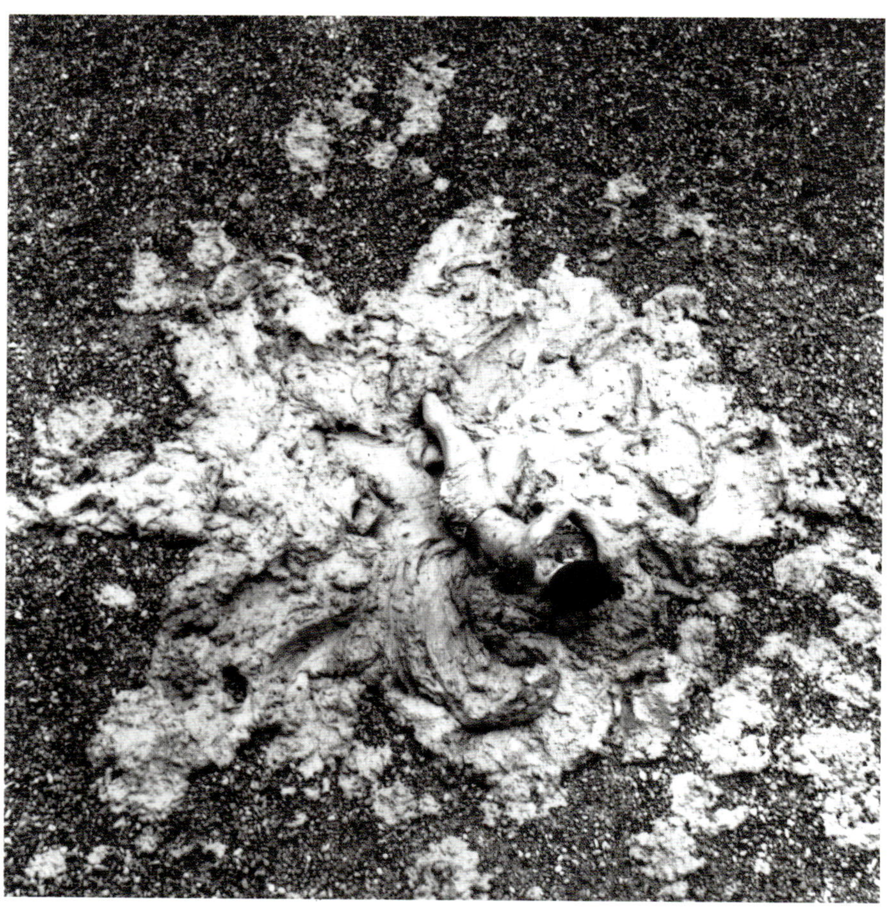

SHIRAGA Kazuo

Challenging Mud

1955

'First Gutai Art Exhibition', Ohara Kaikan Hall, Tokyo

Shiraga performed this work by writhing in a pool of thick mud, 'fighting' it like a wrestler to produce a 'painting' which used the mud as a medium bearing the imprint of his physical struggle with matter. Despite the influence of this and other actions by members of the group on the Happenings of Allan Kaprow and others in the USA, the Gutai artists' focus in the mid 1950s was on avant-garde means of reinvigorating the idea of painting, not on its transformation into other artforms. Retrospectively, however, Shiraga's action can be viewed as transforming 'painting' into a process-oriented and time-based activity, which remained only in the form of photographic documentation, as the record of an event, instantiating an idea.

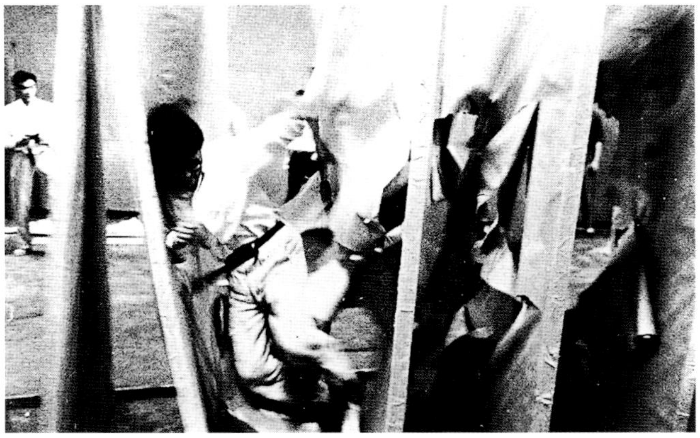

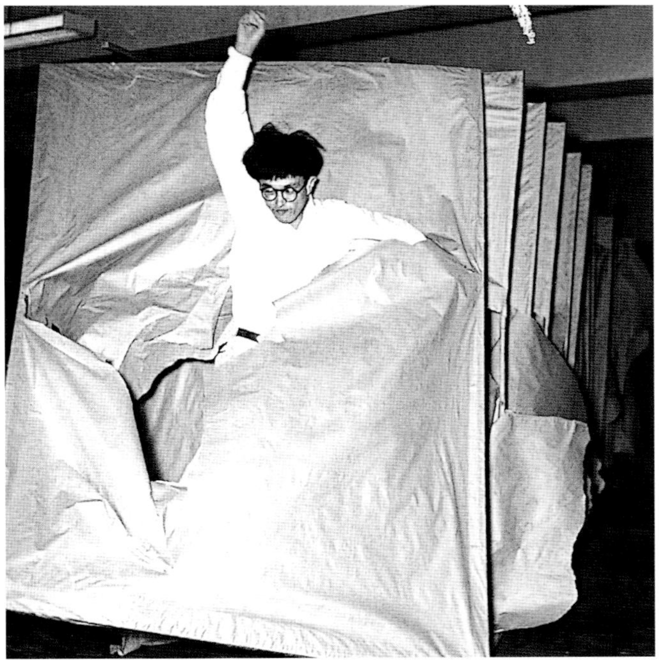

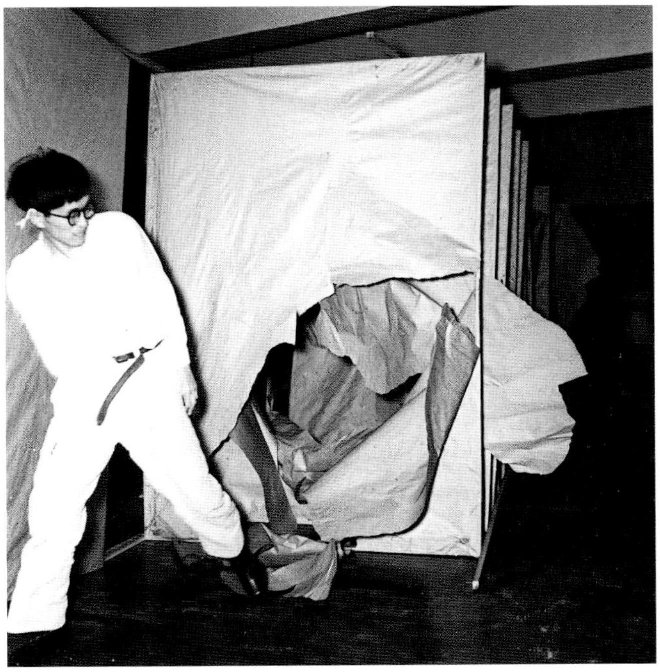

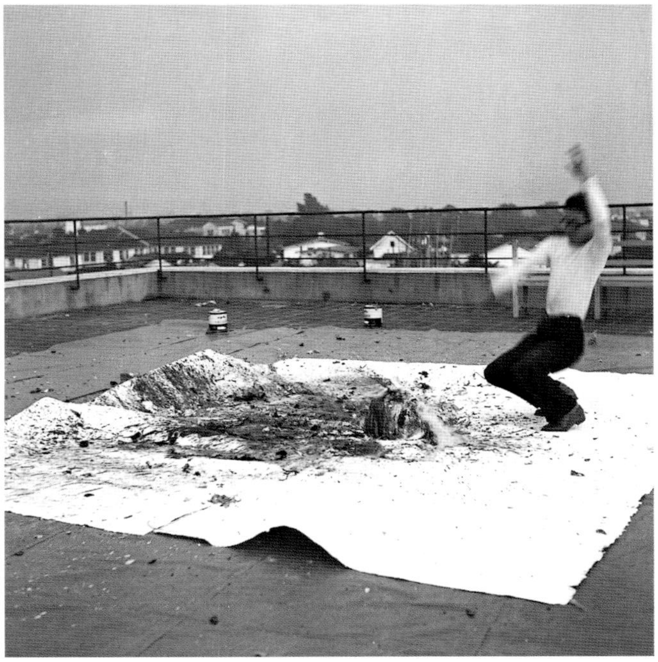

above

SHIMAMOTO Shozo

Making a Painting by Throwing Bottles of Paint

1956

'Second Gutai Art Exhibition', Ohara Kaikan Hall, Tokyo

In this action Shimamoto threw jars of paint at unstretched canvases laid on the ground, producing glass-encrusted surfaces on which the mingled red, orange and black paint reinforced a sense of the gesture's destructiveness. An extreme negation of the painting as a pictorial object was set in counterbalance with the energy of the creative act. In an earlier action of the same year Shimamoto had used cylinders placed inside a cannon to explode paint on to the surface of vertically placed canvases. Few of these works have survived owing to the violence of the process, which literally destroyed them as they were being created.

left

MURAKAMI Saburo

At One Moment Opening Six Holes

1955/56

Tokyo

This work was performed by the artist at the First Gutai Art Exhibition in Tokyo in 1955 and again the following year when it was documented photographically and retitled *Breaking through Many Paper Screens*. Murakami set up a row of wooden framed paper screens each measuring 183 × 366 cm [6 × 12 ft]. He then hurled himself through them. In succession his body burst through this series of flat surfaces, associated with painting and drawing, dramatically rupturing their status as potential picture planes. Murakami drew upon Japanese martial arts traditions, describing this action as a manifestation of concentrated consciousness: 'We must not keep on aimlessly adjusting and manipulating the canvas. Instead, our sense must be internally concentrated to a point from which it bursts on to the canvas and assumes a tangible form.'

– Murakami Saburo, *Gutai*, 1955

Yves KLEIN
Monochrome Blue IKB 48
1956
Oil on wood
150 × 125 cm [59 × 49 in]
Collection, Moderna Museet, Stockholm

In 1956 Klein exhibited twenty monochrome surfaces painted on unframed canvases at the Galerie Colette Allendy, Paris, under the title 'Yves: Propositions Monochromes'. Made with pure pigments applied to the canvas using a binder, each was a different shade of red, blue, yellow/gold, or their combination to produce orange, green or purple. The pigment continued around the sides of each canvas, creating an all-over effect which reduced the visual presence of the canvas and its underlying wooden stretcher. Klein regarded both the idea of the monochrome and the associations of the particular colours he used as manifestations of the immaterial. He attempted to remove all 'external impurities' such as line and form, from painting, leaving only the particles of coloured pigment as an indication of freedom from materiality. Klein had begun formulating his first theories about the monochrome in 1946 as the result of studying both Asian and European (Rosicrucian) mystical writings. From 1952–53 he studied Judo in Japan. During 1956 he developed a 'trinity' of standardized pigment colours: a red named Monopink (MP), a gold named Monogold (MG) and the intense ultramarine he named International Klein Blue (IKB).

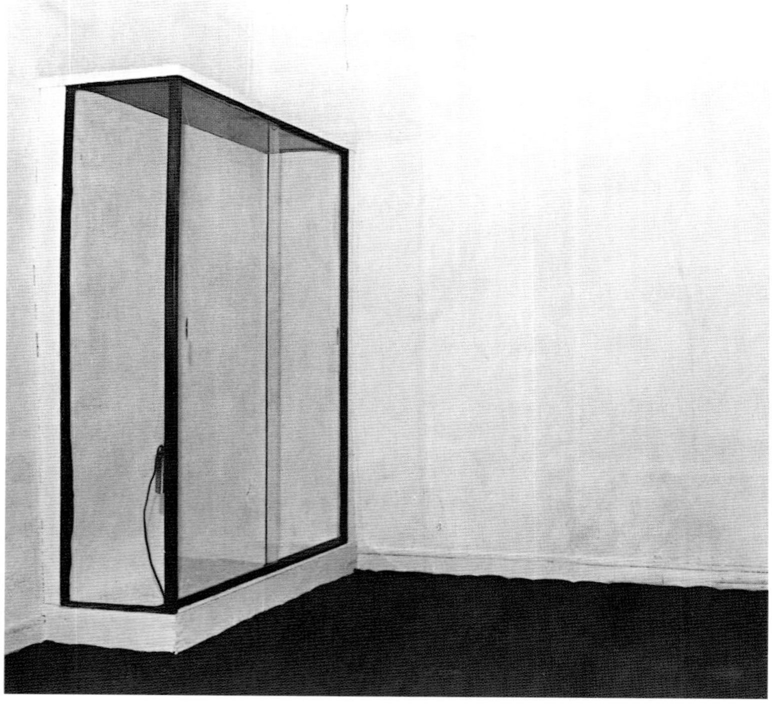

Yves KLEIN
Le vide [The Void]
1958
Galerie Iris Clert, Paris

In April 1958 Klein devised an exhibition at Galerie Iris Clert, Paris, which he titled 'La spécialisation de la sensibilité à l'état matière première en sensibilité picturale stabilisée' ('The Specialization of Sensibility in the State of Raw Material into Stabilized Pictorial Sensibility'). The element of colour in Klein's 'immaterial' monochrome canvases was now displaced onto the frontage of the gallery which was painted deep blue. Inside the gallery there were no monochrome paintings or objects. Klein had removed all the furniture except for one vitrine which contained nothing. The vitrine's frame and all the walls had been painted white. Klein titled this work *Le vide* (*The Void*) which became the name by which the exhibition was remembered. The complete emptiness of the spaces of display replaced the material presence of exhibited objects. For Klein this absence opened up the possibility of sensibility itself becoming the only content of the work.

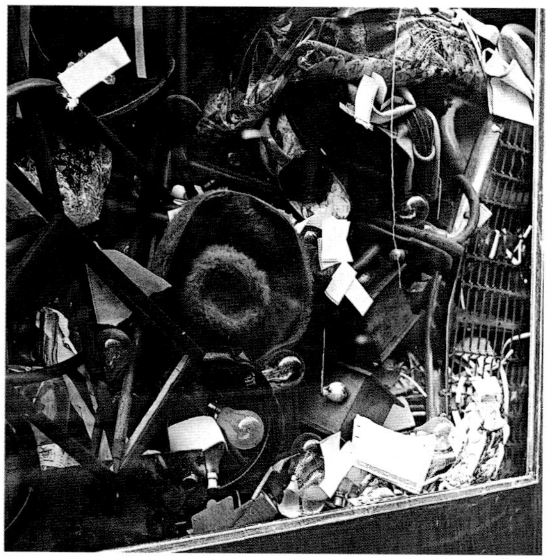

ARMAN
Le Plein [Full]
1960
Accumulation of found objects, Galerie Iris Clert, Paris

Le Plein, conceived as a subversive response to Yves Klein's *Le Vide*, exemplifies the perspective of Nouveau Réalisme. Arman's exhibition opened four days before the official manifesto of the group, by the critic Pierre Restany, was released on 27 October 1960. This characterized the movement as embracing 'the tearing up of posters … the allure of the object, of the household rubbish or the scraps of the dining room … the passionate adventure of the real perceived in itself and not through the prism of conceptual or imaginative transcription'. Arman filled the Iris Clert gallery with junk he found in the street, presenting the exact opposite of Klein's dematerialization. However, ironically given the stated aims of the Nouveau Réalistes, this was a conceptual act that placed the artist in the Duchampian guise of a collector, a position which Arman explored in his subsequent works comprising accumulations of similar objects.

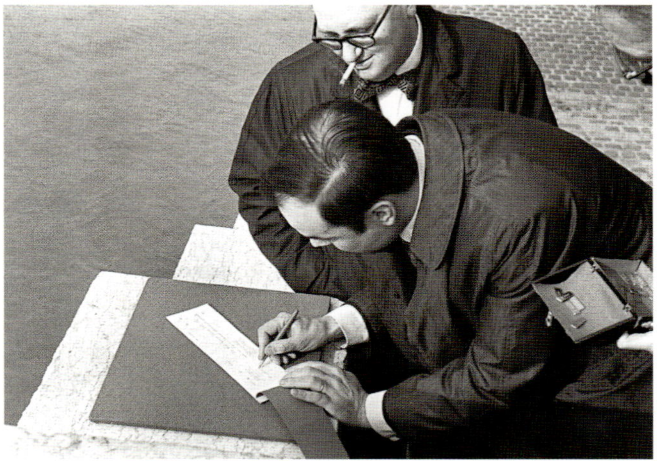

Yves <u>KLEIN</u>

Volumes de sensibilité picturale immatérielle [Zones of Immaterial Pictorial Sensibility]

1959

Transaction, Paris, 1962

In 1959 Klein took his investigation of the 'immaterial' one stage further than in his previous works. He began to issue certificates, printed by the Iris Clert gallery in Paris, to record the exchange of 'zones of immaterial pictorial sensibility' in return for gold. The transactions took place along the banks of the river Seine. Klein exchanged numbered 'zones' for specified quantities of gold. He then cast the gold away into the river. In some cases the certificate was also burned. This transaction took place on 10 February 1962. A Monsieur Blancfort gave the artist 160 grams of pure gold in 16 ingots in exchange for a certificate for 'zone' No. 1, Series 4.

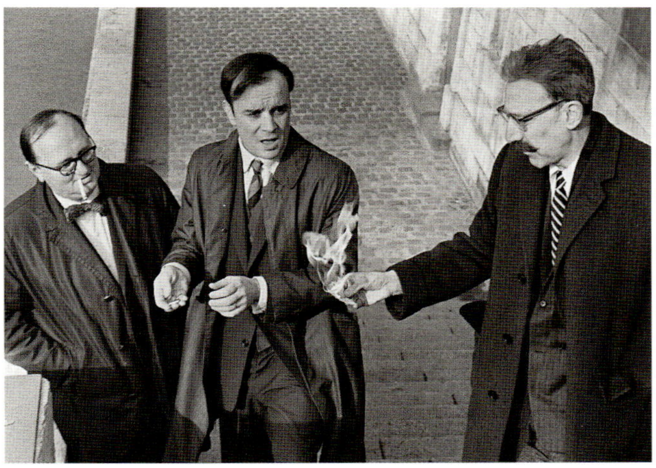

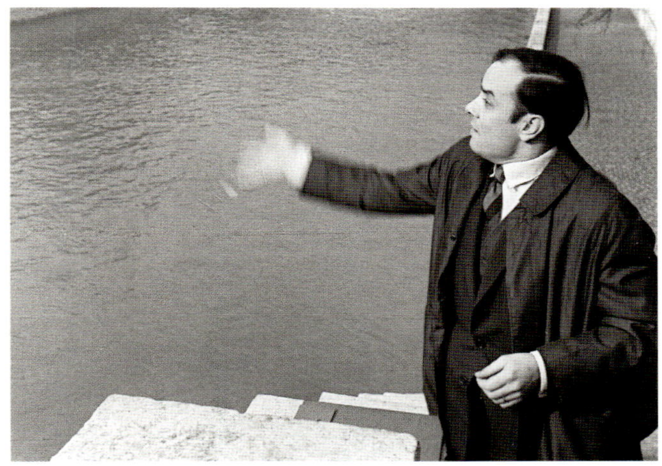

Guy <u>DEBORD</u>

Naked City

Illustration de l'hypothése des plaques tournantes en psychogeographique [Illustration of the hypothesis of turning signs in psychogeography]

1957

Collage on paper

33 × 47.5 cm [13 × 19 in]

Made in the year the Situationist International was founded by Debord, the artist Asger Jorn and others, this work, collaged from a Paris map, exemplifies two of the Situationists' fundamental precepts. It combines the *dérive*, or 'drift' down city streets, 'a technique of transient passage through varied ambiences' in an urban environment, with a *detournement*, 'the rearrangement of what was already there', in order to create, or at least prefigure, a new city. The Situationists were committed to an art that would not only criticize traditional forms but change the structure of urban society by focusing on 'the free construction of daily life'. Debord defined the 'psychogeography' in the title as 'the study of the specific effects of the geographical environment, consciously organized or not, on the emotions and behaviour of individuals'.

– quotations from Guy Debord, 'Definitions', 1958

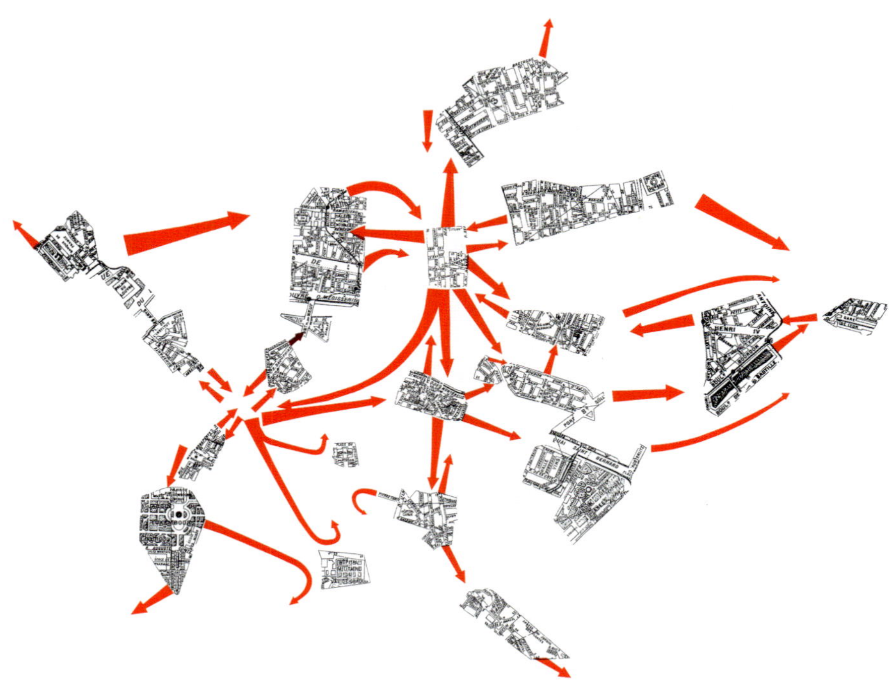

below

Piero MANZONI

Linea m. 19.11 [Line 19.11 Metres Long]

1959

Ink on paper in cardboard cylinder

h. approx. 20.5 cm [8 in]

l. extended, 19.11 m. [62.5 ft]

Manzoni began to make lines of varying length in 1959. Each of these works is a single, unbroken line drawn in ink on a strip of paper which was then rolled up and placed in a sealed, cylindrical container bearing a description of the contents and the artist's name. 'Time is a different thing from what is measured by the hands of a clock. The *Linea* does not measure metres or kilometres, but is zero, not zero as the end, but as the beginning of an infinite series.'
– Piero Manzoni, Artist's statement, 1960

Manzoni insisted that the lines should not be unfurled but should remain closed in their containers, because otherwise they would 'disappear'. He stressed that it was the idea and not the object that he was offering for sale: 'The nature of the *Linea* is eternal and infinite, the concept is everything. I put the *Linea* in a container so that people can buy the idea of the *Linea*. I sell an idea, an idea closed in a container.'
– Piero Manzoni, Artist's statement, 1961

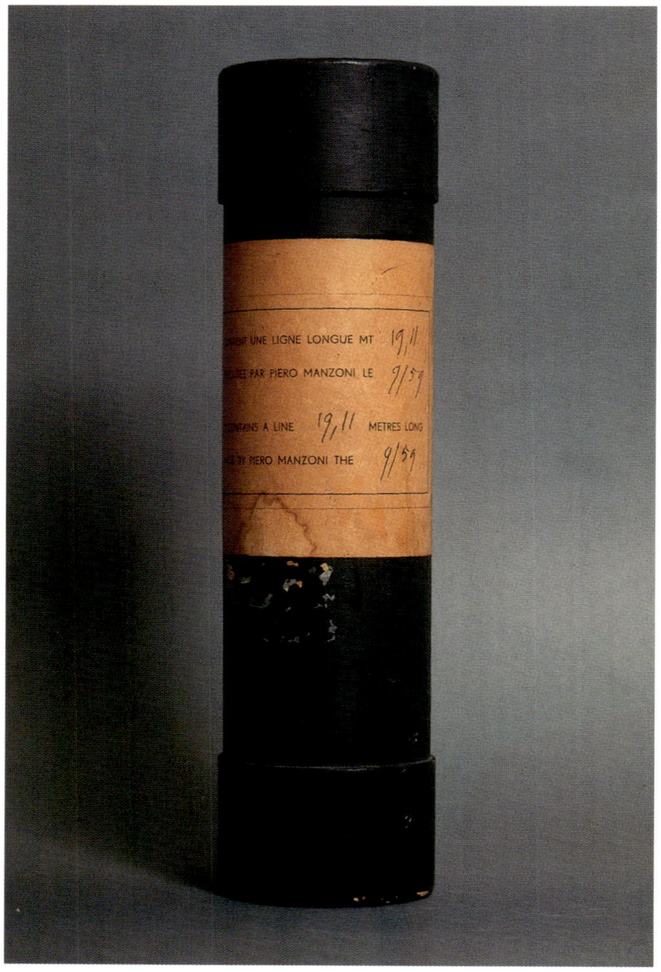

Composition 1960 #2

Build a fire in front of the audience. Preferably, use wood although other combustibles may be used as necessary for starting the fire or controlling the kind of smoke. The fire may be of any size, but it should not be the kind which is associated with another object, such as a candle or a cigarette lighter. The lights may be turned out.

After the fire is burning, the builder(s) may sit by and watch it for the duration of the composition; however, he (they) should not sit between the fire and the audience in order that its members will be able to see and enjoy the fire.

The composition may be of any duration.

In the event that the performance is broadcast, the microphone may be brought up close to the fire.

5·5·60

La Monte YOUNG

Composition 1960 No. 2

1960

Score, from An Anthology, 1963

Young's first works of 1956–58 were 12-note compositions in the tradition of Schoenberg. In 1959 he studied with Stockhausen in Darmstadt, Germany, and during the same period encountered the work of John Cage. (Cage's lecture 'Indeterminacy' was published in 1959 in Stockhausen's journal *Die Riehe*.) In 1960 he studied electronic music at the New School for Social Research in New York, where he met Cage, George Maciunas and others. He began to experiment with scores for events, expanding the concept of what constitutes musical performance. Audible sound was present in some scores but not in others, such as *Composition 1960 No. 5*, in which the instruction was to release butterflies into the performance area. The sound of their wings might be inaudible to the human ear, yet conceptually it would still be acknowledged as a sound that existed. The scores were published by Young alongside scores by other artists associated with the Fluxus group, in the book *An Anthology* (1963).

opposite

Nam June PAIK

Performance of La Monte Young's Composition 1960 No. 10 to Bob Morris [Zen for Head]

1962

'Fluxus International Festival of New Music', Städtisches Museum, Wiesbaden, Germany

Collection, Städtisches Museum, Wiesbaden, Germany

Paik's performance was an interpretation of LaMonte Young's score *Composition 1960 No. 10*: 'Draw a straight line and follow it', which Young had dedicated to the artist Robert Morris. Paik dipped his head, hands and tie in a bowl of ink mixed with tomato juice and drew a line by dragging his head along a roll of paper laid on the floor. By using his head, the locus of mental processes of creation and understanding, as a 'paintbrush' to make the line, Paik drew attention, from his own Zen-influenced perspective, to the close relationship between concept and action in the score. His gesture opened up a series of questions about the relation between action and object: how art is made, presented and received; and how and by whom the boundaries of art are determined.

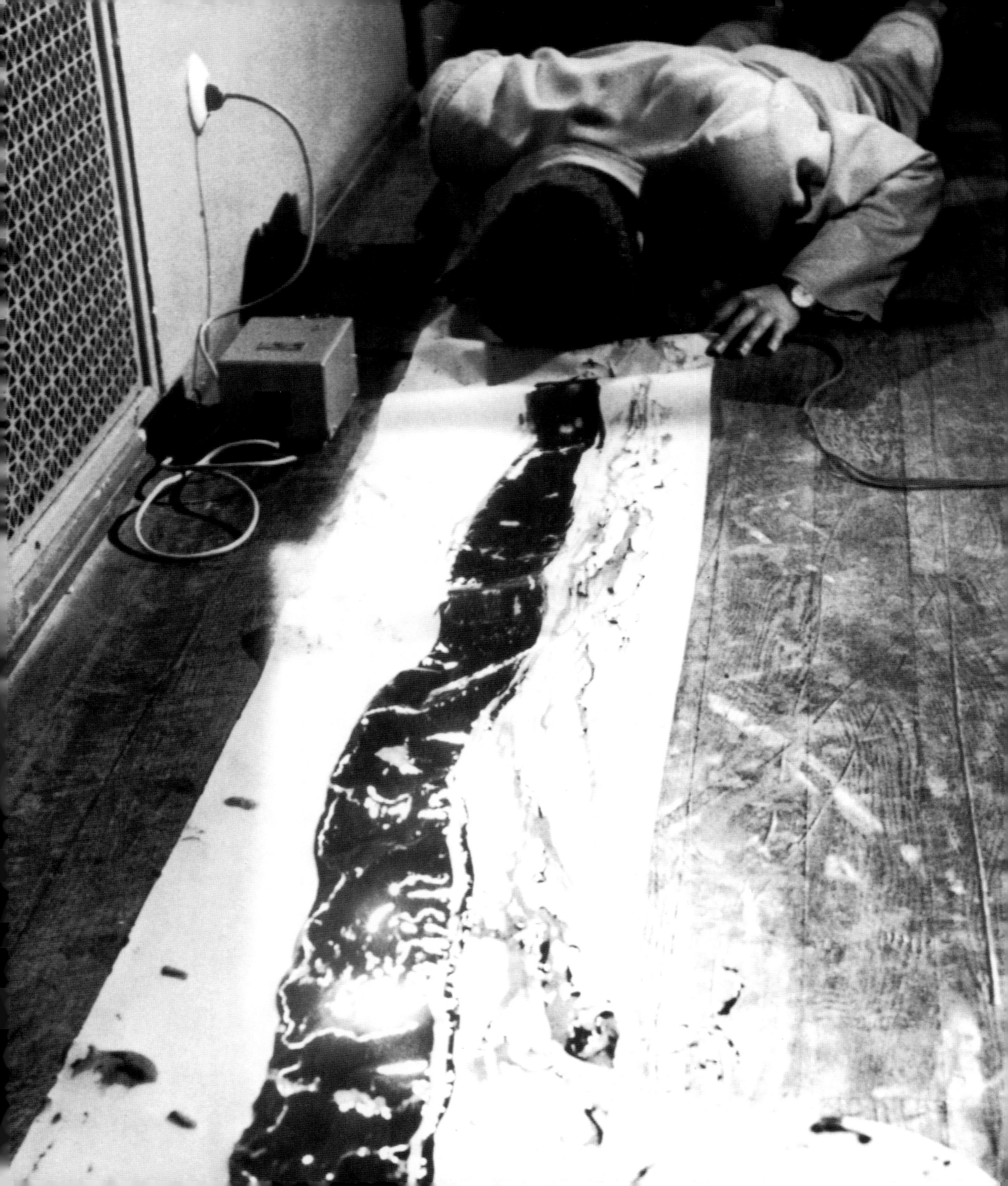

INSTRUCTION, PERFORMANCE, DOCUMENTATION

The early 1960s saw an explosion of performance-based 'intermedia' art of all kinds in which works were distributed across and between a plurality of media. The first works of conceptual art – in which a work's meaning was rendered independent of the visual properties of its material presentation, in any particular instance – emerged out of changes in the relationships between scores, their realization and the documentation of performed events. In this respect, conceptual art was a product of the transposition of ideal conceptions of the artwork, prevalent in music and dance, into the institutional context of the visual arts. Yoko Ono exhibited 'instructions' for paintings. Robert Morris constructed a card file describing events that occurred during its making, classified under subject headings and cross-referenced. George Brecht displayed objects as events. Hi Red Center videoed and conserved 'relics' of private preparations for surviving a nuclear blast. John Latham chewed a copy of Clement Greenberg's book *Art and Culture* and preserved the result. Bruce Nauman took templates of the left half of his body at ten-inch intervals. On Kawara compiled folders recording systematically what he read, where he went and who he met. Tadeusz Kantor sent a letter the size of a wall. Richard Long and Hamish Fulton exhibited documentation of walks.

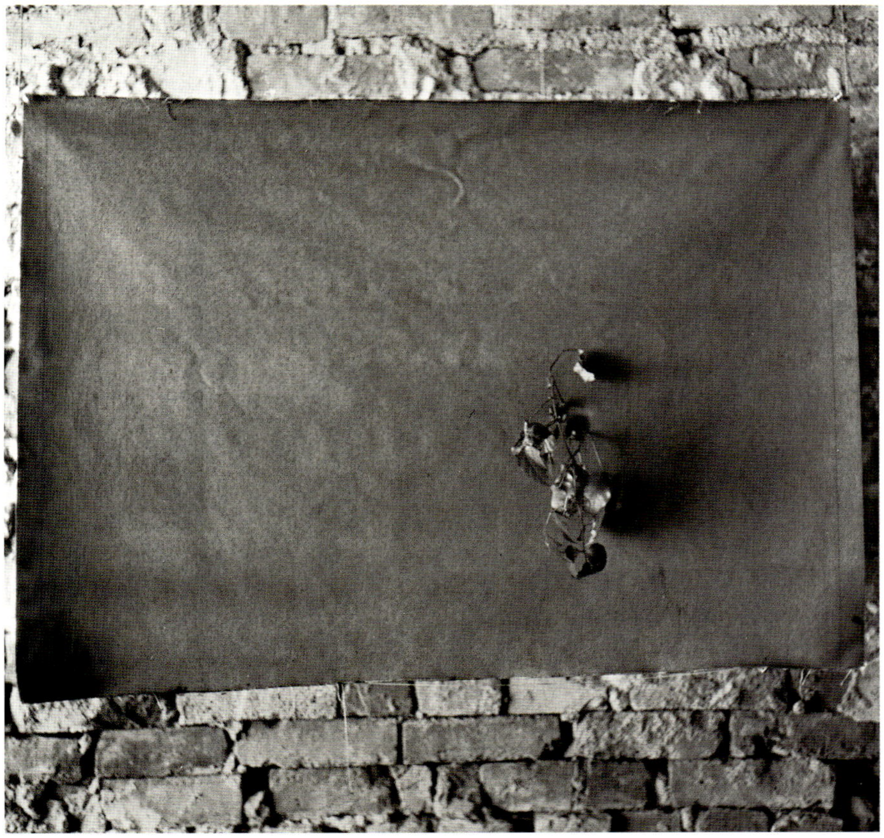

Yoko ONO

Painting in Three Stanzas [from Instruction Paintings]

1961

Ink on canvas with live plant; instruction card, ink on paper

Canvas, 76 × 107 cm [30 × 42 in]

Card, 9 × 27 cm [3.5 × 11 in]

Installation, AG Gallery, New York

Ono's first formal presentation of *Instruction Paintings* took place in 1961 at the AG Gallery in New York, at the instigation of George Maciunas; some had been shown previously during performance events at Ono's loft in Chambers Street. The instructions for the paintings were either explicit in the title or were recounted by Ono or Maciunas verbally to their visitors while escorting them round the gallery. The works required the visitors' creative participation. Some invited active engagement, for example *Painting to be Stepped On*, or *Smoke Painting*, which the viewer was invited to set alight. *Painting in Three Stanzas* is one of three works which were accompanied by instruction cards, as handwritten exhibition labels. The paintings and the instruction cards were documented photographically by George Maciunas. The instruction for this work suggests three stages – growth, decay and rebirth – which require imaginative rather than physical participation from the viewer:

'It ends when it is covered with leaves.
It ends when the leaves wither.
It ends when it turns to ashes.
And a new vine will grow. —— '

– Yoko Ono, text of instruction card, handwritten in English by Ichiyanagi Toshi.

三楽章の絵．

キャンバスに煙草で小さな穴をあけ，しめった綿を入れた袋に種を入れキャンバスの後につるし，毎日水をやる。

一楽章．キャンバスがつたにおほわれる迄．

二楽章．つたが枯れるまで．

三楽章 キャンバスが燃されて灰になる迄．

楽章の終りごとに写真をとっておく。

Yoko ONO

Painting in Three Stanzas

[from Instructions for Paintings]

1962

Ink on paper

1 of 22 works, approx. 25 × 36 cm [10 × 14 in] each

Ono first exhibited the *Instructions for Paintings* on the lobby wall of Sogetsu Kaikan Hall in conjunction with a multi-media event including performances by herself and others at Sogetsu Art Center, Tokyo, in May 1962. Ono dispensed entirely with the physically realized paintings and exhibited only the instructions, inscribed in Japanese calligraphic script by the composer Ichiyanagi Toshi. She hoped in this way to avoid any trace of the artist's hand. Like the *Instruction Paintings*, the works required the viewer to complete them. They were finally completely removed from an exhibition to a reading context in 1964 when published as typeset text in both Japanese and English, in Ono's book *Grapefruit*.

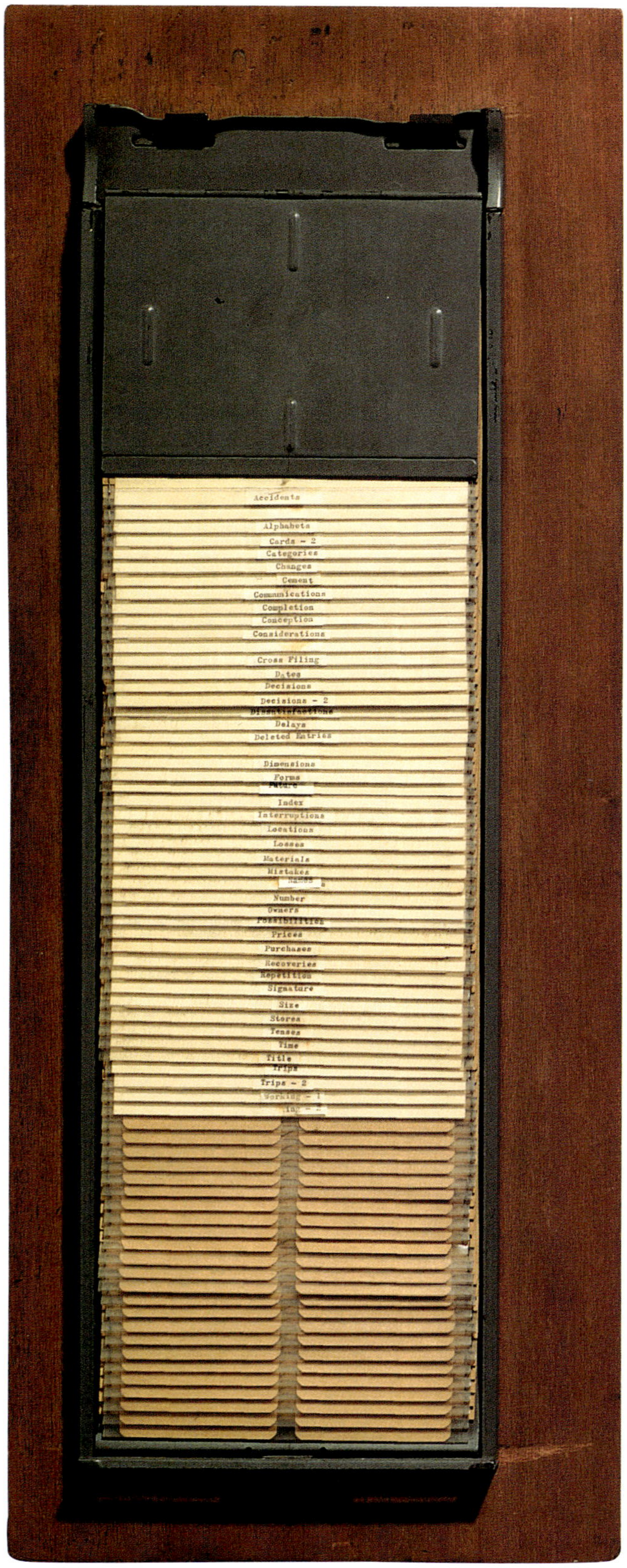

left and below

Robert MORRIS

Card File

1962

Metal and plastic wall file mounted on wood, containing 44 index cards

68.5 × 26.5 × 5 cm [27 × 10.5 × 2 in]

Collection, Musée Nationale d'Art Moderne, Centre Georges Pompidou, Paris

First exhibited in 1963 at the Green Gallery, New York, *Card File* is a vertically mounted wall file of alphabetically indexed cards which record the steps the artist followed in the conception and making of the work. The cards range across quite different categories of thought and action which are randomly systematized, as evidenced by the sequence of labels, such as 'Index; Interruptions; Locations; Losses; Materials; Mistakes; Names; Number; Owners; Possibilities; Prices; Purchases; Recoveries; Repetition' – and so on. On the cards themselves are typed an assortment of remarks that indicate the artist's thought processes and chance circumstances which contributed to the process. Thus we are informed of where Morris bought the cards, that he lost some of them, rediscovered them, conceived the work in the New York Public Library, was interrupted by the artist Ad Reinhardt, and so on. There are also cross-references, leading the reader through a circuitous route which confounds traditional notions of consciously intended artistry. A new form of 'assisted' readymade object, which incorporated a self-enclosed system denoted by written signs, the *Card File* has been considered by some to be the first 'purely' conceptual work of art, because of its predominantly linguistic nature.

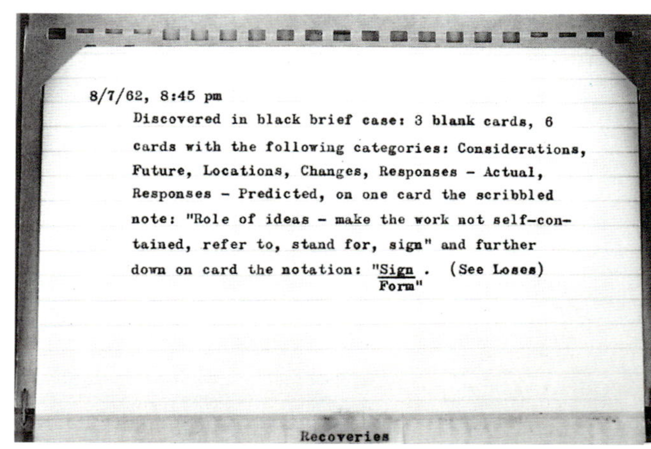

opposite

Robert MORRIS [with Carolee SCHNEEMANN]

Site

1964

Rehearsal photograph. First performed at Stage 73, New York, 1964

Morris' early work was influenced by his involvement with Yvonne Rainer's New York dance company which focused on everyday actions, emphasizing ways in which the body resisted and responded to the force of gravity. *Site* was conceived as a 'dance' which played out a set of relations between objects treated as equivalent through the use of the colour white. Morris wore white overalls and a mask. Accompanied by continuous noise from a drill hidden in a white box on the stage, he dismantled and moved a set of three large sheets of white plywood. The removal of the last board revealed the naked figure of Carolee Schneemann (painted white), lying motionless, propped against cushions on a draped board, in the guise of the subject of Manet's painting *Olympia* (1863). Thus the modernist notion of the picture plane was subverted by being staged as live and layered, collapsing the distinction between real and illusionistic space. Morris then reassembled the boards as before. A number of sculptural structures made by Morris in this period were first used as props in experimental dance performances before being exhibited in a gallery context.

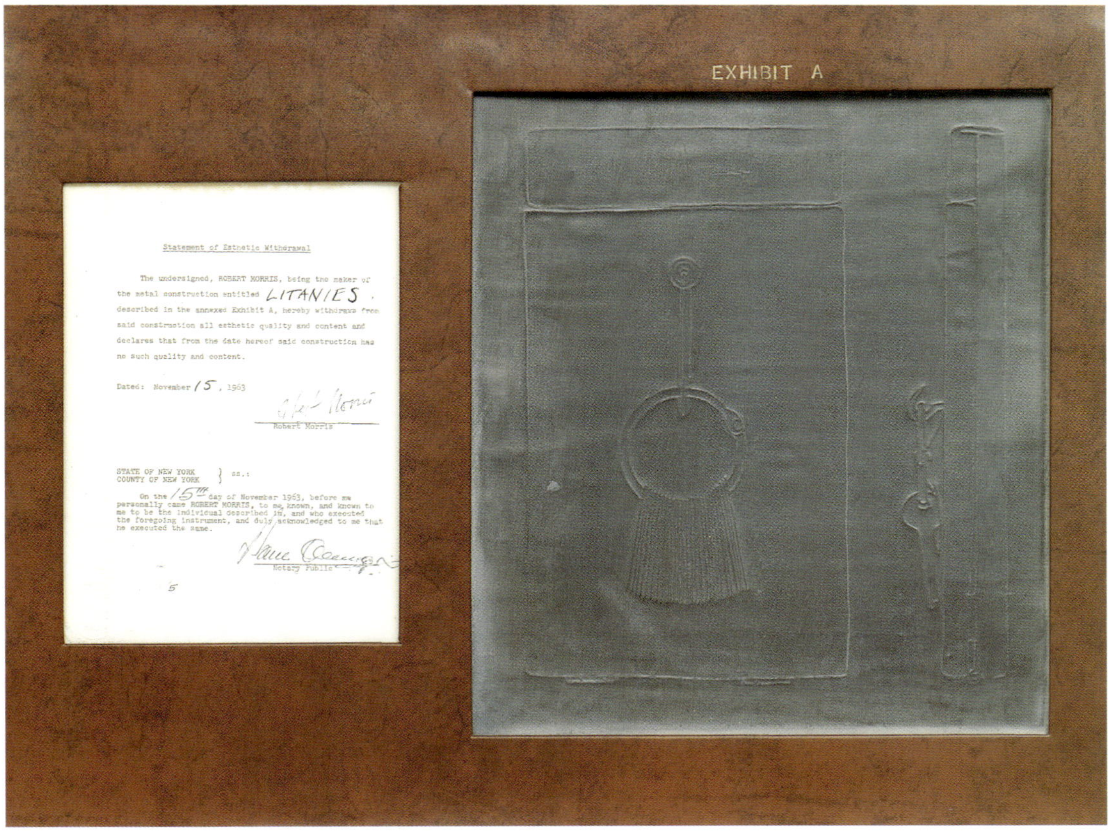

Robert MORRIS
Statement of Aesthetic Withdrawal
1963
Typed and notarized statement on paper; sheet of lead over wood, mounted in imitation leather mat
45 × 60.5 cm [18 × 24 in]
Collection, The Museum of Modern Art, New York

Morris made this work in response to a collector who had not paid for his earlier sculpture made in the same year, *Litanies*, a lead-covered box from which hang twenty-seven keys, one of which is inscribed with a litany quoted in Marcel Duchamp's *Boîte Vert (Green Box*, 1934). In withdrawing all aesthetic quality and content from *Litanies* by means of a legalistic-looking statement Morris produced a new work which challenged fundamentally the notion of artistic intent as the source of the aesthetics and meaning of a work of art.

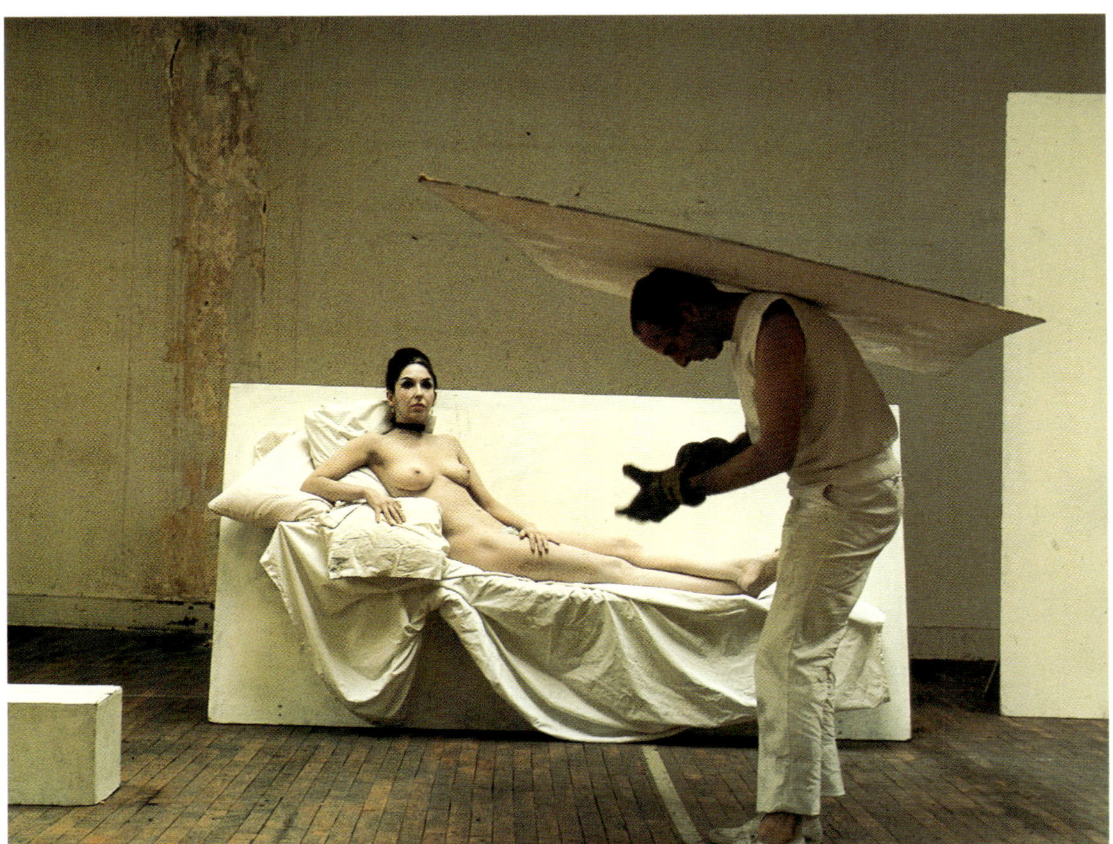

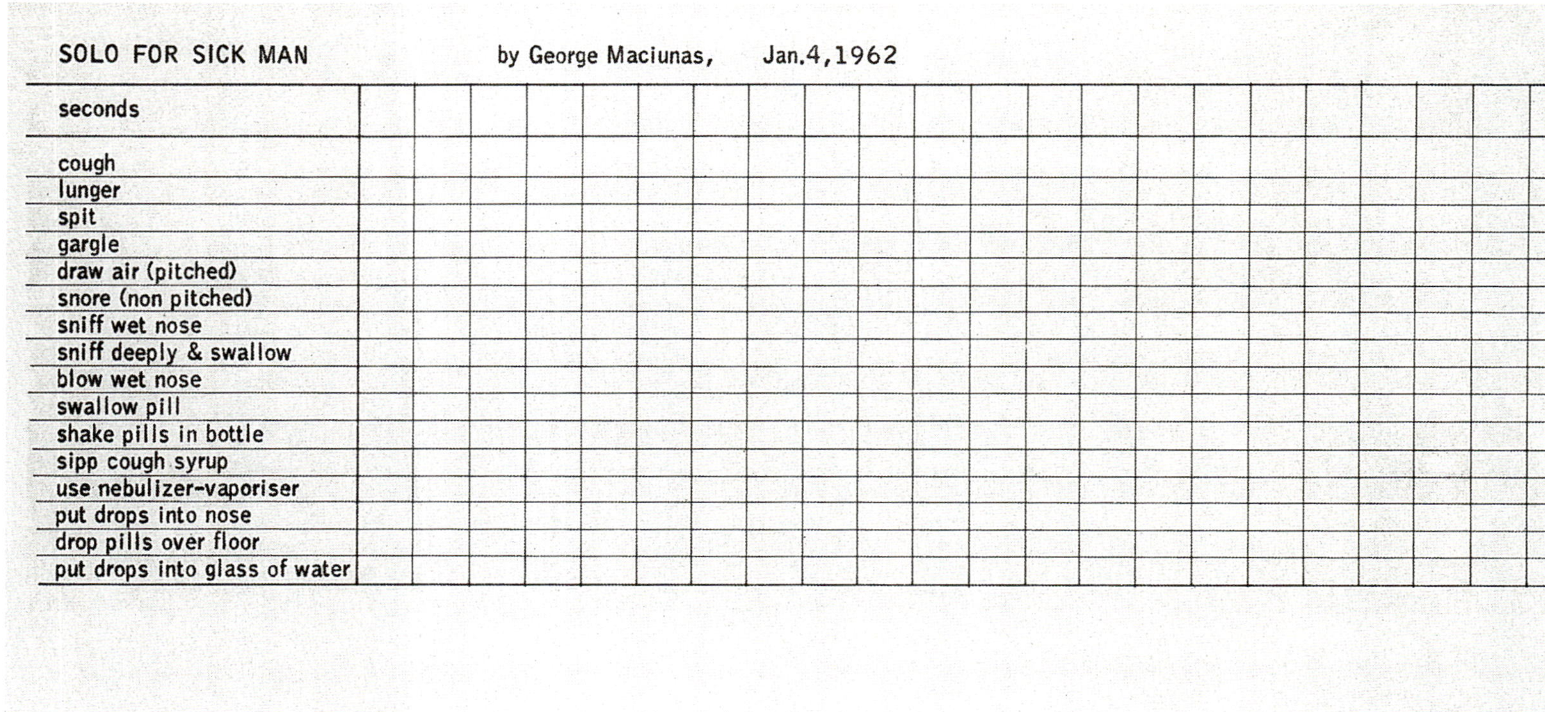
SOLO FOR SICK MAN by George Maciunas, Jan.4,1962

seconds
cough
lunger
spit
gargle
draw air (pitched)
snore (non pitched)
sniff wet nose
sniff deeply & swallow
blow wet nose
swallow pill
shake pills in bottle
sipp cough syrup
use nebulizer-vaporiser
put drops into nose
drop pills over floor
put drops into glass of water

George MACIUNAS
Solo for Sick Man
1962
Score
Ink on paper
14 × 28 cm [5.5 × 11 in]

Solo for Sick Man was created while Maciunas was travelling in Europe several months before the first series of Fluxus concerts in Germany. Informed by the emerging notion that any sound could be conceptualized as music, it is a comically self-referential 'score' intended to be performed by anyone. With a grid which suggests a blank score to be notated by the participant as required, the work also introduces mundane aspects of everyday life as its material, in this case poor health, which Maciunas had suffered since his childhood.

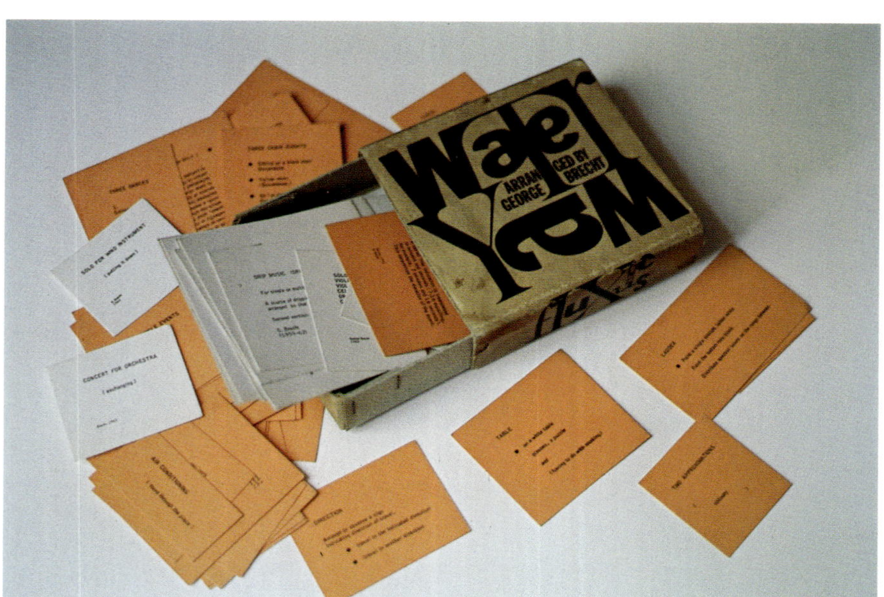

George BRECHT
Water Yam
1963
Cardboard box containing 54 scores printed black on orange card, 19 printed on white card [total 73]
15 × 16.5 × 4.5 cm [6 × 6.5 × 2 in]
First Fluxus edition, assembled by George Maciunas

Brecht had been distributing scores for events from the late 1950s before they were assembled in a boxed edition. The concept of the event was fundamental to his work, collapsing the temporality of performance into the physicality of an object so that an event score could simply be an instruction to perceive or reflect upon something. *Water Yam* exists in many editions, the first of which was assembled by George Maciunas in 1963. The 73 event scores of the first edition are non-specific, so that they may be interpreted in a number of ways by the reader. They usually comprise a title and itemized instructions. Distribution via printed ephemera, books and editioned objects formed an essential part of the Fluxus ethos of democratic participation. Boxed editions such as *Water Yam* were intended to be open-ended works which could be expanded. A later edition contains 99 scores and two additional works.

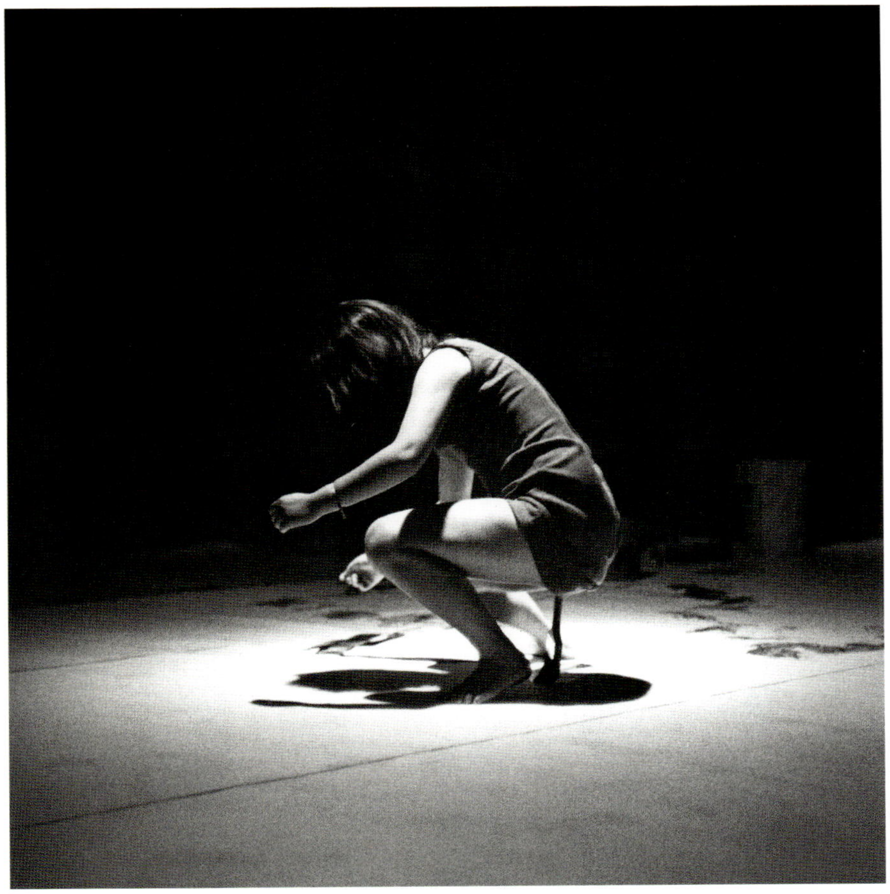

Shigeko KUBOTA

Vagina Painting

1965

'Perpetual Fluxus Festival', Cinematheque, 85 East 4th Street, New York

Kubota first encountered John Cage's scores in 1963, through her participation in Ongaku, the Tokyo-based experimental music group. In 1964 she left Japan for New York and began to work closely with members of the Fluxus group.

For this event, the artist placed a large sheet of paper on the floor and on it made gestural brushstrokes in red paint. The paintbrush was attached to the crotch of her underwear. Symbolically referring to her vagina as a source of inscription, Kubota introduced a female perspective into the characteristic Fluxus performance of 'chance operations'. The work suggested an alternative to both the aggressive technique of action painting and the continuing assumption that a woman's artistic role was as a subject directed by the male artist. Implicitly Kubota's action criticized other performances such as the use of women as 'human paintbrushes' by Yves Klein in his *Anthropometries* series of the late 1950s and early 1960s.

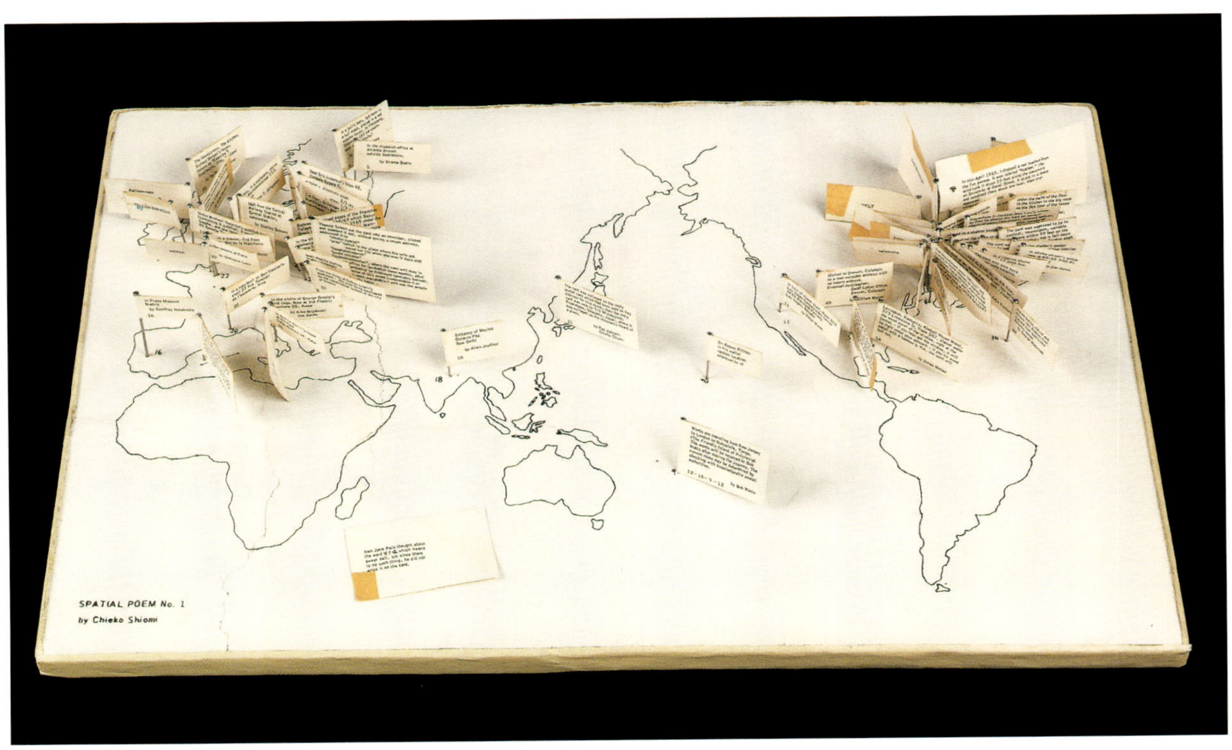

Mieko [Chieko] SHIOMI

Spatial Poem No. 1

1965

Fluxus edition; stencilled map on board, 69 printed cards with pins, cardboard box

30 × 46 × 2.5 cm [12 × 18 × 1 in]

This is the first in a series of nine separately scored 'global events' which took place over ten years. Shiomi devised a themed event and sent out letters to potential participants, usually artists, inviting them to carry it out in some way chosen by themselves, to record their action or thought and to send her the resulting documentation. She then placed the responses, printed on cards, on to a map of the world, indicating the geographical location of each participant. In 1976 the entire project was published in Osaka as the artist's book *Spatial Poem*.

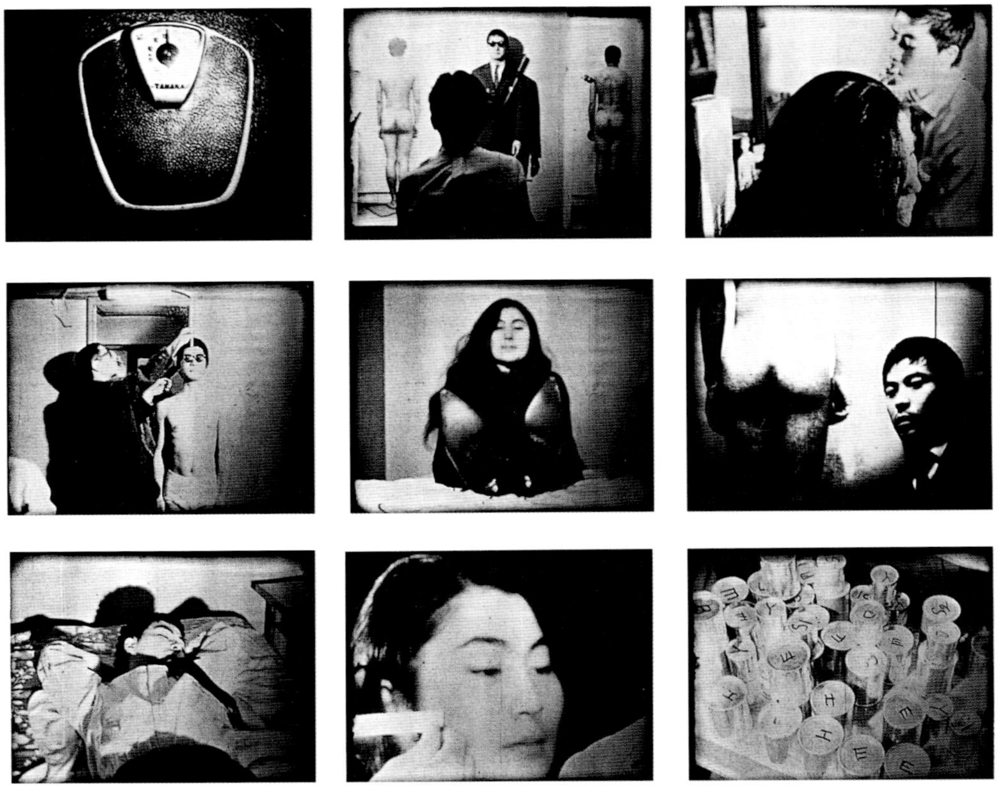

HI RED CENTER
Shelter Plan [The Imperial Hotel Physical]
1964
Video transferred from 16mm film documentation by Jonouchi Motoharu
21 min., black and white, silent
Collection, Metropolitan Art Museum, Tokyo

Hi Red Center, founded in 1962 by Takamatsu Jiro, Akasegawa Genpei and Nakanishi Natsuyuki, staged public, participatory events in Tokyo. Drawing attention to unspoken political issues in the everyday life of post-war urban Japan, they called their actions 'agitations'. For this event, in which Yoko Ono also participated, they constructed a bomb shelter at the Imperial Hotel, Tokyo, on 26–27 January 1964. Guests were invited to the 'Hi Red Center suite' where their bodies were measured for individually customized bomb shelters.

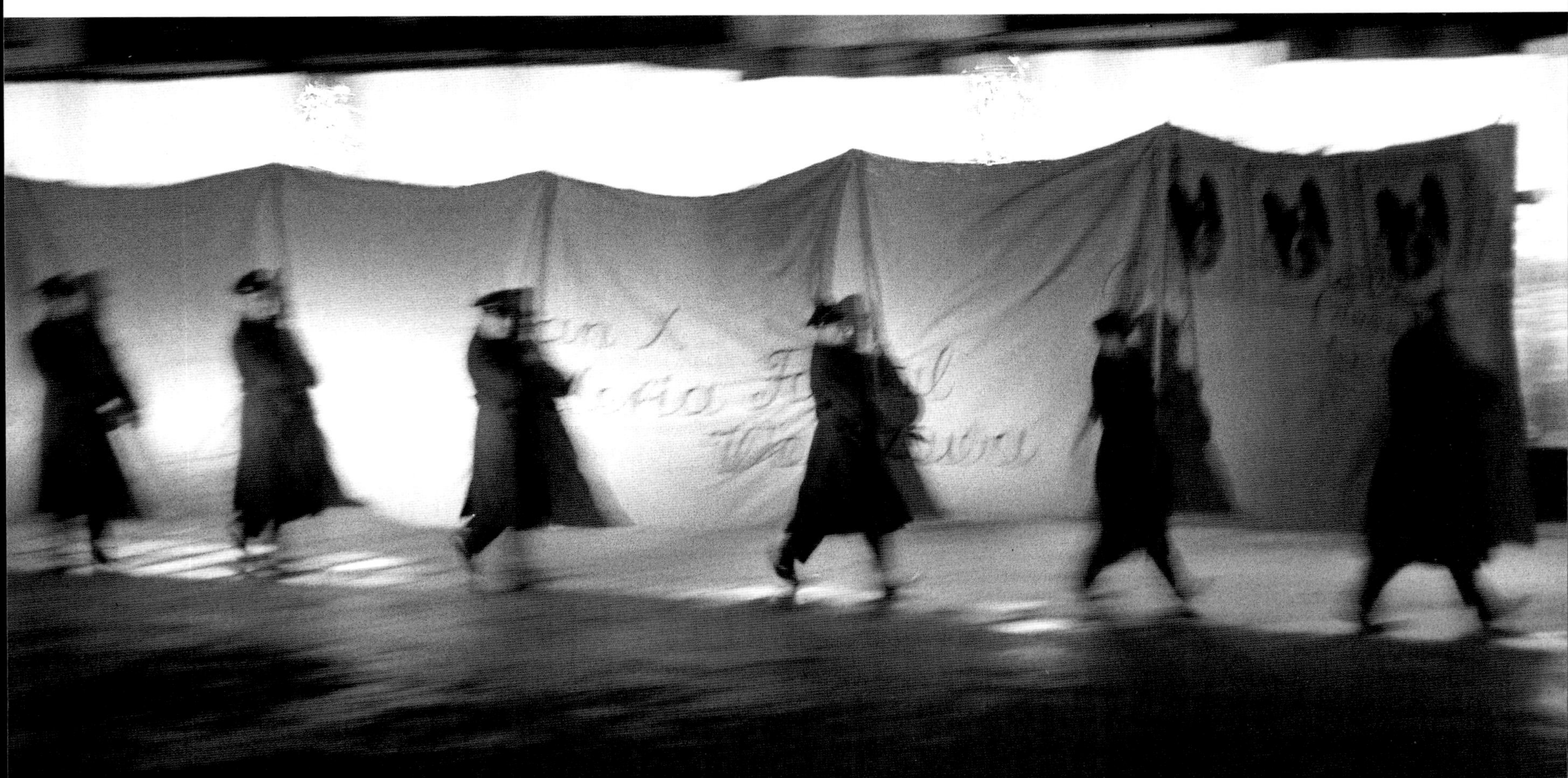

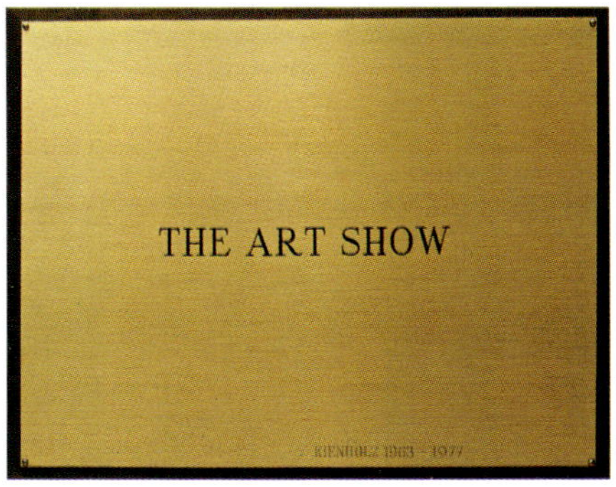

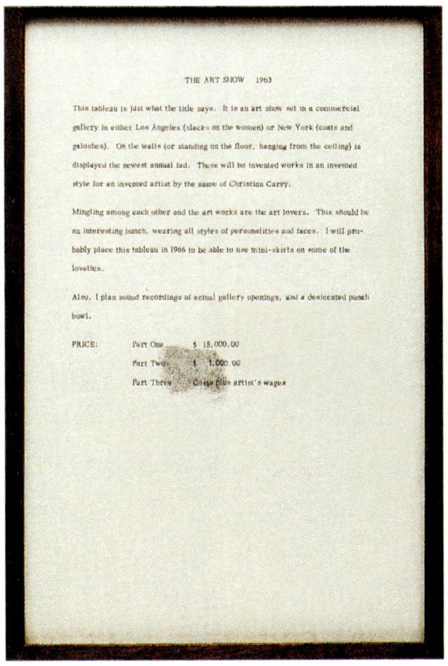

THE ART SHOW 1963

This tableau is just what the title says. It is an art show set in a commercial gallery in either Los Angeles (slacks on the women) or New York (coats and galoshes). On the walls (or standing on the floor, hanging from the ceiling) is displayed the newest annual fad. These will be invented works in an invented style for an invented artist by the name of Christian Carry.

Mingling among each other and the art works are the art lovers. This should be an interesting bunch, wearing all styles of personalities and faces. I will probably place this tableau in 1966 to be able to use mini-skirts on some of the lovelies.

Also, I plan sound recordings of actual gallery openings, and a desiccated punch bowl.

PRICE:	Part One	$ 15,000.00
	Part Two	$ 1,000.00
	Part Three	Costs plus artist's wages

Edward KIENHOLZ
The Art Show
1963
Brass title plaque with framed instructions
Plaque, 23.5 × 30 cm [9 × 12 in]
Framed instructions, 34 × 23.5 cm [14 × 9 in]

Kienholz began making lifesize assemblage sculptures in the form of tableaux in the early 1960s, using found materials to form human figures and objects in room-sized environments. As they were large and labour intensive he decided to offer the works for sale as concepts before fabricating them. The resulting *Concept Tableaux* each consist of a metal plaque inscribed with the title and a framed written description of the work to be constructed. The purchaser (who paid a price estimated to be that of the completed sculpture) had the option of commissioning a 'working drawing' for an additional sum specified on the written description. As a third option, the artist would construct the sculpture on payment of costs and 'artist's wages'. This agreement was ratified in a contract signed by the purchaser.

opposite
Tadeusz KANTOR
Letter
1967
Fabric, paper, ink
2 × 14 m [6.5 × 46 ft]
Galerie Foksal, Warsaw

Kantor arranged for the delivery by eight post office employees of a giant envelope – 14 metres long and 2 metres high – to the Galerie Foksal in Warsaw. This was one of the events of this period that marked a shift from Kantor's theatrical performances to interventions in everyday life. The concept developed from staged performances he had produced in the late 1950s and early 1960s in which giant objects appeared, sometimes operating as costumes and enveloping the actors. *Emballage*, or wrapping, became one of Kantor's signature techniques.

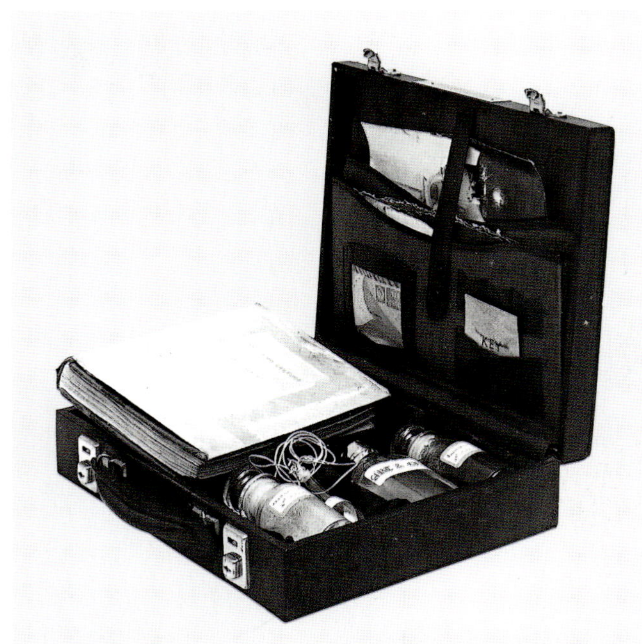

John LATHAM
Art and Culture
1966-69
Book, labelled vials filled with powders and liquids, letters, photostats and other materials in leather case
8 × 28 × 25 cm [3 × 11 × 10 in]
Collection, The Museum of Modern Art, New York

In 1966 Latham withdrew a copy of Clement Greenberg's collection of essays *Art and Culture* from the library of St Martin's School of Art, London, where he taught. This widely used text epitomized the formalist principles of late modernist painting. He organized a festive event at his home, titled *Still and Chew*, where he invited guests to tear and chew the pages of Greenberg's book and, when necessary, to spit out the product into a flask provided. Greenberg's text was thus reconstituted as indigestible matter. Latham transformed the product into a brew by adding chemicals and yeast and, when the library requested the book the following year, decanted the distilled mass into a glass jar, labelled it 'Art and Culture' and returned it. The following day he was dismissed from his teaching post. Latham's artwork titled *Art and Culture* is a leather briefcase containing the elements that went into *Still and Chew* – powders, liquids, letters, photostats – and the invitation he sent for the event. It includes a copy of Greenberg's book and Latham's letter of dismissal, among other relics of the event.

Bruce NAUMAN

Eleven Colour Photographs

[details]

1966-70

right

Coffee Thrown Away Because

It Was Too Cold

right, below

Self-portrait as a Fountain

2 of 11 colour photographs

50 × 60 cm [20 × 24 in] each

After viewing a Man Ray retrospective at Los Angeles County Museum of Art, Nauman made a series of eleven colour photographs at the end of 1966, published by Leo Castelli, New York, in 1970. Man Ray's lack of concern with consistency of meaning or style encouraged Nauman to incorporate aspects of thought and activity which had hitherto been outside the boundaries of his art. He devised a series of ironic scenes based on aspects of everyday life which he enacted in his studio, presenting them as photographs combined with mundane or punning titles. *Self-Portrait as a Fountain* referred to Duchamp's readymade and is also linked with another piece Nauman made in 1966, a window-shade around the edge of which he placed the text 'The true artist is an amazing luminous fountain', a verbal proposition to which the *Self-Portrait* adds a further level of irony through literal enaction.

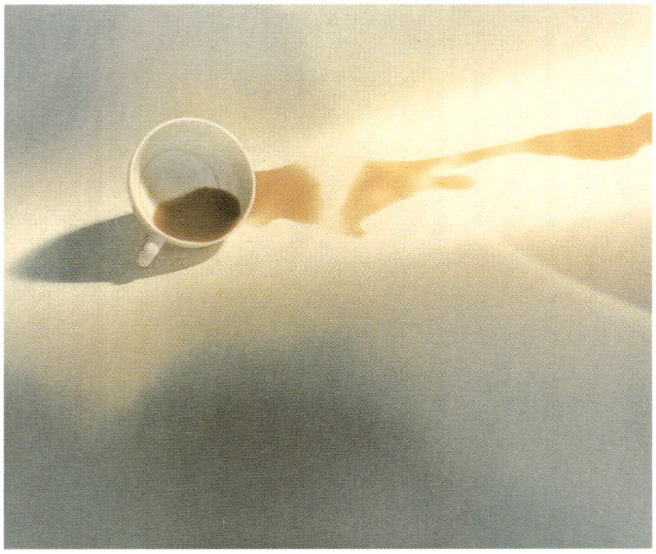

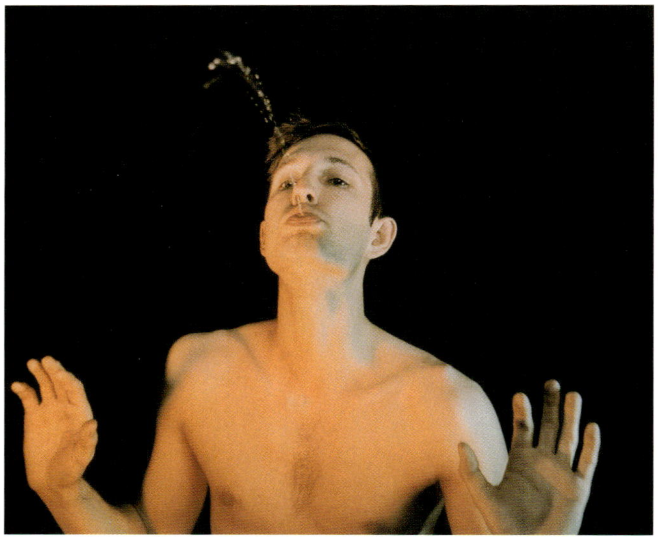

opposite

Bruce NAUMAN

Neon Templates of the Left Half of My Body Taken at Ten-Inch Intervals

1966

Neon tubing on clear glass tubing suspension frame

178 × 23 × 15 cm [70 × 9 × 6 in]

By 1966 Nauman was beginning to use his own body as a standard of measurement to expand the notion of the 'life model' into a field outside the concerns of traditional sculpture. The templates taken from the left half of his body correspond to seven body parts: head, shoulder, chest, waist, thigh, knee and calf, recalling the standard art school ideal of the human body as seven heads high. However, this 'life study' is far removed from traditional representational norms. The full verbal description of the process of making the work signals that the action and the concept are as important as any formal sculptural issues. The neon outlines, conveying no obvious reference to the subject's body, are dependent on the title for their decipherment.

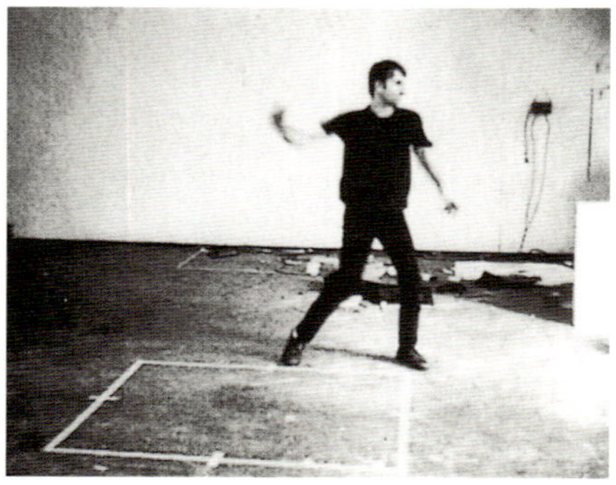

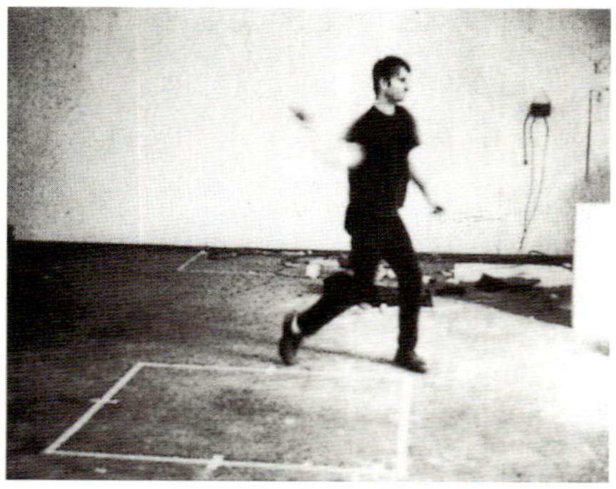

Bruce NAUMAN

Bouncing Two Balls between the Floor and Ceiling with Changing Rhythms

1967-68

16mm film

10 mins., black and white, sound

In 1966 Nauman set up a studio in an abandoned grocery store in San Francisco. Here he paced the space thinking about 'the fundamental question of what an artist does when left alone in the studio. My conclusion was that as I was an artist and I was in the studio, then whatever I was doing in the studio must be art ... At this point art became more of an activity and less of a product.'

– Bruce Nauman, quoted in Neal Benezra, *et al., Bruce Nauman*, 1994

He began by using 16mm film to document simple activities, setting up situations which relied on a tension created by the varying difficulty of the action. In this work he attempted to get a rhythm going with the two balls, bouncing them alternately off the floor and the ceiling, once or several times, and catching them in between bounces. He found he could not keep control of the game and became frustrated. The film is a ten-minute loop, the duration of a standard roll of 16mm film.

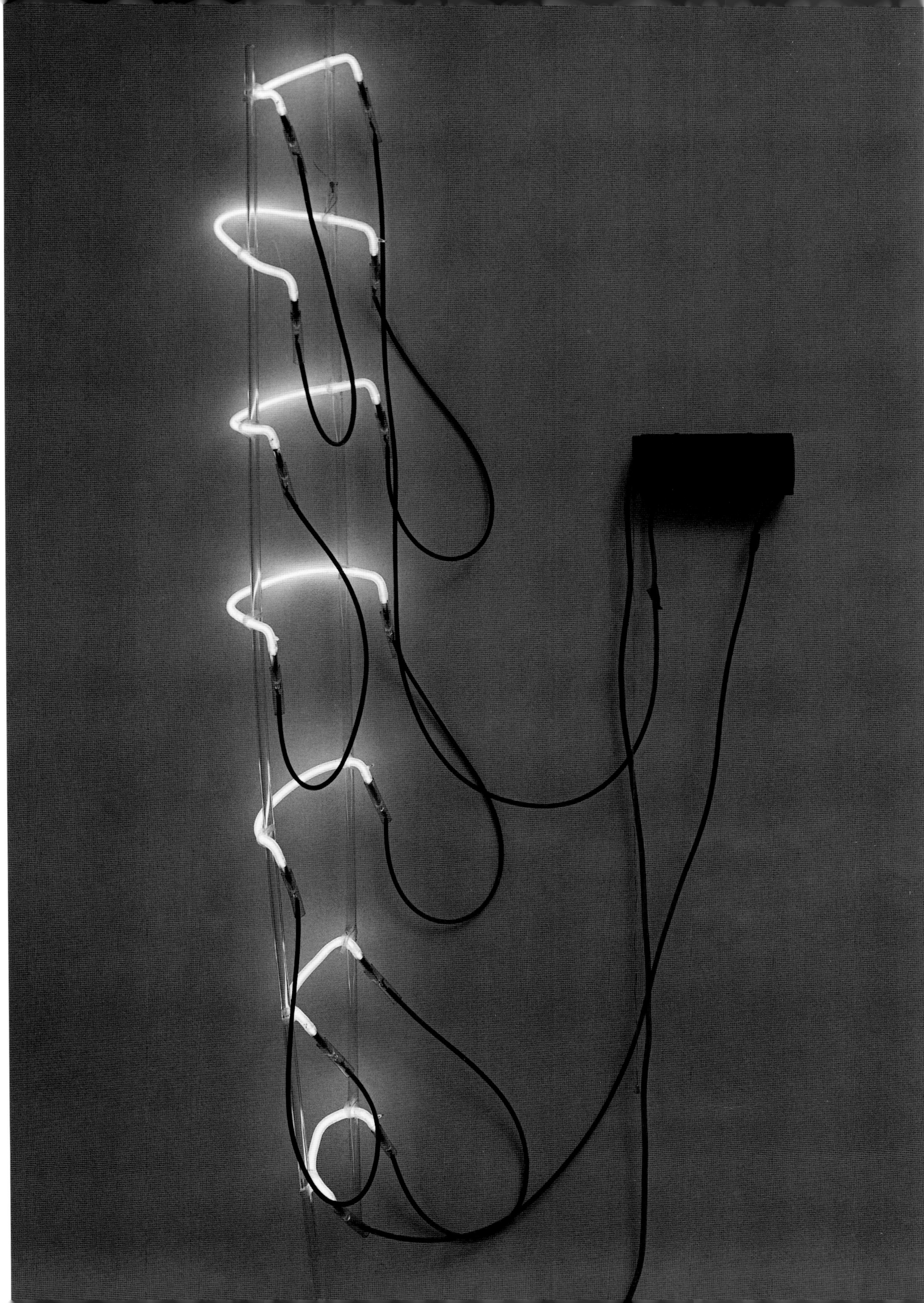

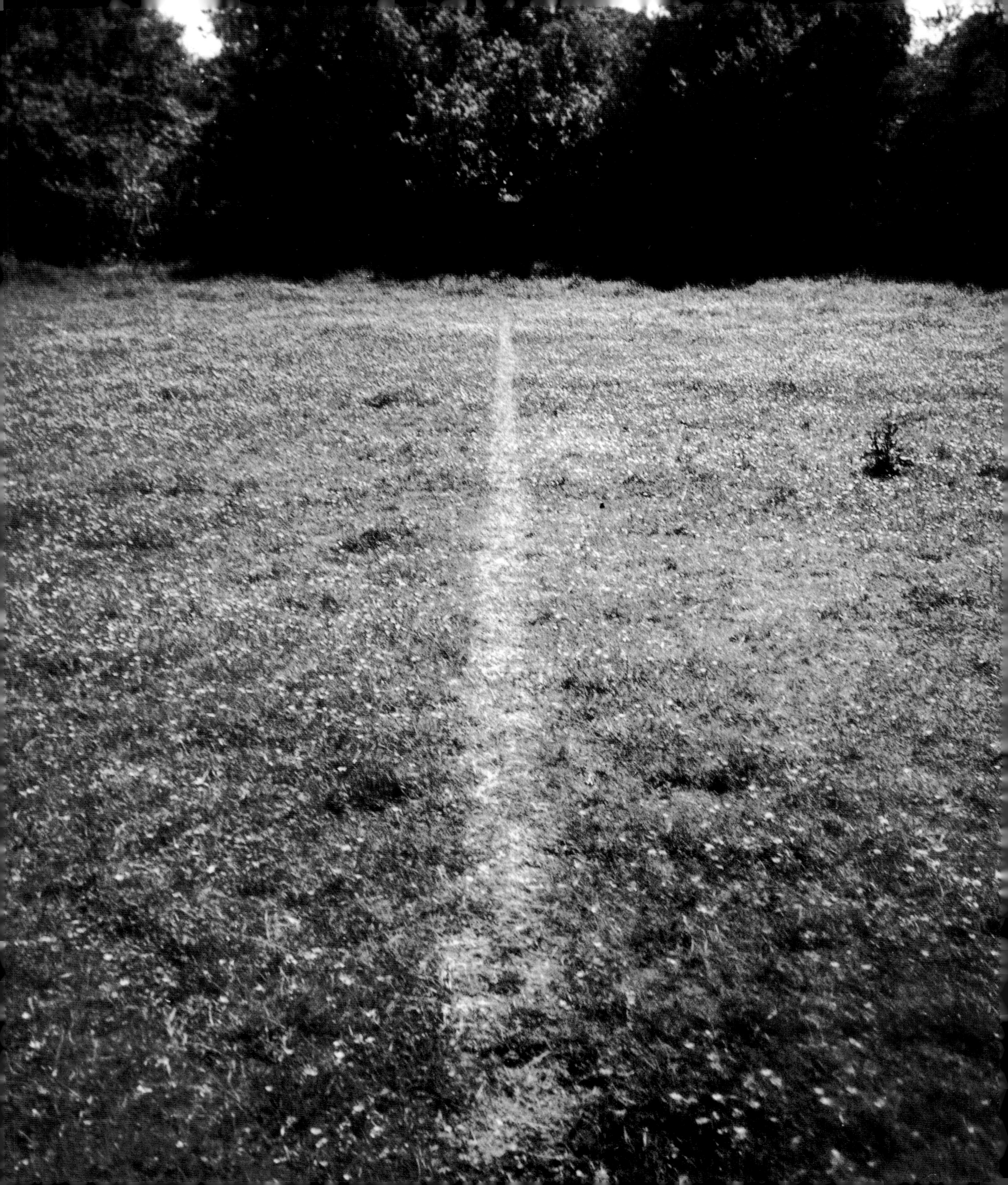

Richard LONG

A Line Made by Walking

1967

Black and white photograph, text

37.5 × 32 cm [15 × 12.5 in]

Somerset, England

Long made this work by walking repeatedly backwards and forwards so that a line was 'drawn' in the flattened grass of the field.

Since the mid 1960s Long has made works which centre on the act of walking in natural environments. Often during the course of the journey he also makes ephemeral marks or simple sculptural assemblages using the materials to hand, such as sticks or stones. The record of these private actions is mediated through the most economical of means, such as a short descriptive title or list, a map in which the route is marked, a single photograph, or the placement in an exhibition space of natural materials from a landscape visited, assembled by the artist into a basic form such as a line or a circle. Different works may be made of just one of these elements or a combination of them.

April, 1967

Times of Lifts from London to Andorra and from Andorra to London

England		
London	8.30a.m.	April 9th
Lydd Airport	10.15a.m.	April 9th
Lydd Airport	11.00a.m.	April 9th
France		
Le Touquet Airport	11.20a.m.	April 9th
Le Touquet Airport	11.30a.m.	April 9th
1 km. south of Etaples	1.25p.m.	April 9th
Montreuil	1.40p.m.	April 9th
Montreuil	2.2.p.m.	April 9th
4 kms. south of Beauvais	3.50p.m.	April 9th
4 kms. south of Beauvais	3.50p.m.	April 9th
Paris	7.15p.m.	April 9th
Paris Port D' Clichy	7.18p.m.	April 9th
Paris Port D'Orleans (metro)	7.50p.m.	April 9th
Paris Port d'Orleans (bus)	8.00p.m.	April 9th
Outskirts of Paris Route N20 toOrleans	8.30pm.	April 9th
Outskirts of Paris Route N20 to Orleans	9.25p.m.	April 9th
Petrol Station on Route N20 to Orleans	10.00p.m.	April 9th
Petrol Station on Route N20 to Orleans	10.30p.m.	April 9th
Unmarked Area on Route N20 to Orleans	11.00p.m.	April 9th
Unmarked Area on Route N20 to Orleans	11.15p.m.	April 9th
5 kms. south of Orleans	11.50p.m.	April 9th
5 kms. south of Orleans	5.40 a.m.	April 10th
Sallris	6.20a.m.	April 10th
Sallris	8.20a.m.	April 10th
Chateauroux	9.50a.m.	April 10th
Chateauroux	10.15a.m.	April 10th
89 kms. north of Limoges	10.40a.m.	April 10th
89 kms. north of Limoges	12.20p.m.	April 10th
Toulouse (centre)	8.50p.m.	April 10th
Toulouse (centre)	9.20p.m.	April 10th
Toulouse (outskirts)	9.30p.m.	April 10th
Toulouse (outskirts)	11.5p.m.	April 10th
Saverdun	11.45p.m.	April 10th
Saverdun	7.30a.m.	April 11th
Saverdun (outskirts)	7.40a.m.	April 11th
Saverdun (outskirts)	7.45a.m.	April 11th
France/Andorra frontier	10.00a.m.	April 11th
Andorra		
Pas de la Casa (bus)	11.45a.m.	April 11th
Andorra (centre)	12.50p.m.	April 11th
Andorra (centre)	4.05p.m.	April 11th
Encamp	4.10p.m.	April 11th
Encamp	4.30p.m.	April 11th
Pas de la Casa	5.20p.m.	April 11th
France/Andorra frontier	5.45p.m.	April 11th
France		
Crossroads of Bourge Madame and Ax les Thermes	6.05p.m.	April 11th
Crossroads of Bourge Madame and Ax les Thermes	6.35p.m.	April 11th
Ax les Thermes	7.00p.m.	April 11th
Ax les Thermes	7.25p.m.	April 11th
Tarascon	7.55p.m.	April 11th
Tarascon	8.10p.m.	April 11th
Unmarked area north of Tarascon	8.30p.m.	April 11th
Unmarked area north of Tarascon + 8 kms	11.30p.m.	April 11th
Toulouse	11.30a.m.	April 12th
3 kms. north of Toulouse	11.50a.m.	April 12th
Montauban	12.30p.m.	April 12th
Montauban	5.50p.m.	April 12th
Cahors	6.45p.m.	April 12th
Cahors	9,20p.m.	April 12th
Brive	12.15a.m.	April 13th
Brive	10.25a.m.	April 13th
Uzerche	11.5 a.m.	April 13th
Uzerche	12.00	April 13th
Paris	8.10p.m.	April 13th
Paris Port d'Orleans (metro)	9.00p.m.	April 13th
Paris (Clignancourt)	9.05 p.m.	April 13th
Paris (Clignancourt)	10.10p.m.	April 13th
Paris outskirts	10.30p.m.	April 13th
Paris outskirts	6.30a.m.	April 14th
Beauvais	7.10a.m.	April 14th
Beauvais	8.45a.m.	April 14th
Abbeville	9.50a.m.	April 14th
Abbeville	11.25a.m.	April 14th
Wailly Beauchamp	12.15p.m.	April 14th
Wailly Beauchamp	1.10p.m.	April 14th
Montreuil	1.20p.m.	April 14th
Montreuil	3.25p.m.	April 14th
Boulogne	4.00p.m.	April 14th
Boulogne	4.40p.m.	April 14th
Calais	5.05p.m.	April 14th
Calais	6.10p.m.	April 14th
Gravelines	7.05p.m.	April 14th
Gravelines	7.10pm.	April 14th
Dunkerque	7.30p.m.	April 14th
Dunkerque (car ferry)	2.28a.m.	April 15th
England		
Dover	6.10a.m.	April 15th
Dover	6.55a.m.	April 15th
London	9.05a.m.	April 15th

Hamish FULTON

Times of Lifts from London to Andorra and from Andorra to London

1967

Text on paper

Dimensions variable

One of Fulton's earliest projects, this work recorded in words and figures the elements of time, distance and physical location in a journey made by the artist with two fellow students at St Martin's School of Art, London, Rodney McDonald and Alistair Milne. The group hitch-hiked to Andorra and back again. It was agreed that during the journey the participants would stay together, making them aware of a collective identity, and would travel continuously. The project was completed with the recording and listing of each lift, place, date and time. The measurement of time and distance was thus formally structured in a relationship with the actuality of place.

Since 1973 Fulton's work has centred on specific walks, made alone. In the late 1990s he resumed making some works which are participatory.

He began to use photographs in addition to text while visiting Utah, South Dakota, Wyoming and Montana in 1969. These were initially of a snapshot quality and postcard sized. The photographs are without human presence, except occasionally for the traces of other travellers encountered in the landscape. It was also at this time that Fulton resolved that his work would centre on respect for, and engagement with the experience of nature. He has only rarely made any alterations to the environments he encounters, and these are always ephemeral, such as a row of small sticks tracing the sun's shadow.

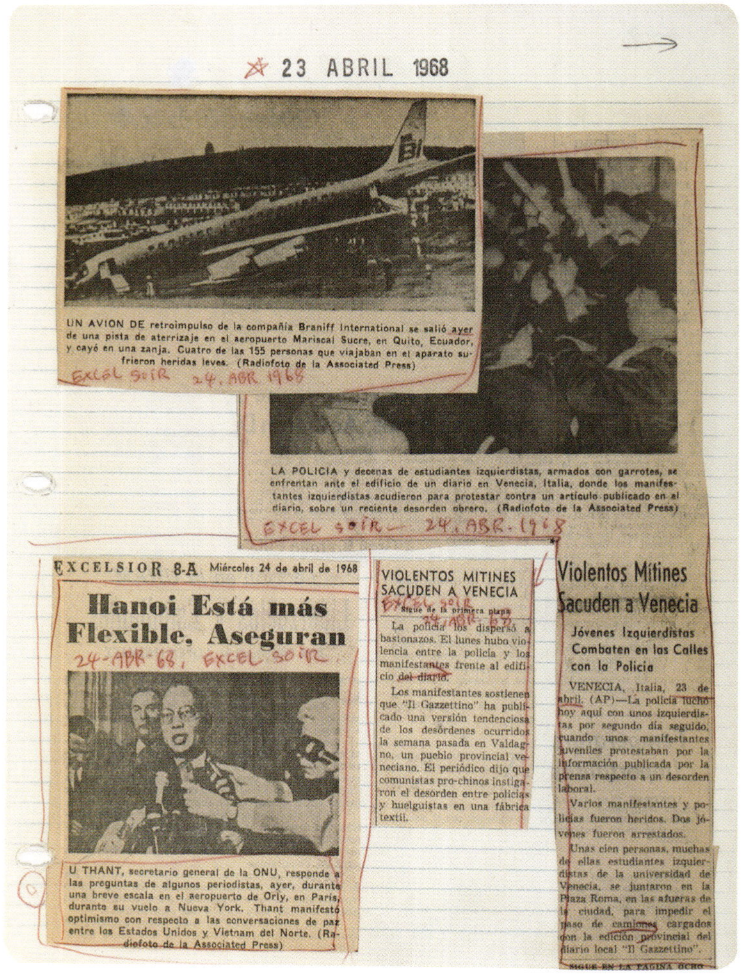

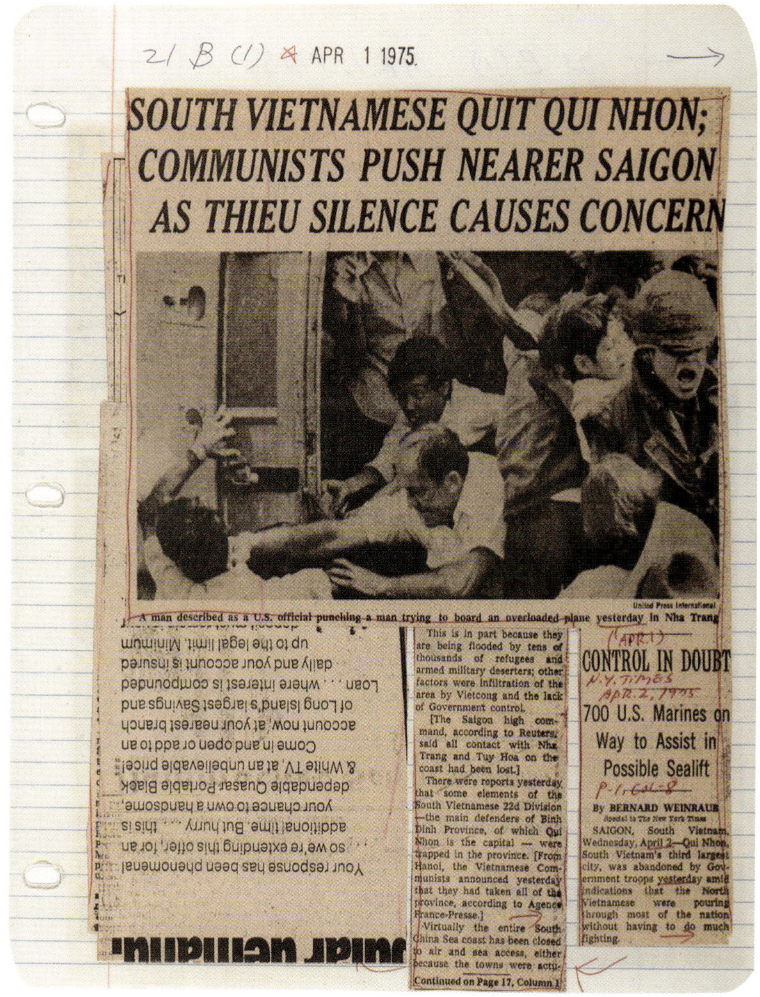

On KAWARA
I READ [details]
1966 to the present
Newspaper cuttings in clothbound loose leaf binders
29 × 27.5 × 8.5 cm [11.5 × 11 × 3.5 in] each

From 1966 onwards Kawara generally enclosed, with each *Date Painting* from the *TODAY Series* in its box (see page 93), a cutting from a newspaper which he had read on that day. *I READ* is a parallel project which he began at the same time as the *TODAY Series*, comprising newspaper cuttings only, collected according to the same criteria and assembled in chronological order in a loose leaf notebook. The work defines itself in relation to the artist's own consciousness of time and place, as the event it records is not primarily the news documented on the page but his reading of it. The cuttings suggest a historical context for Kawara's artistic activity yet their arbitrariness discourages a reading of history as meaningful in itself – news of trivial matters is as likely to be the day's cutting as news of major events. The work invites the reader to be conscious of the everyday forms which define the experience of time.

On KAWARA

I WENT [details]

1968–79

Red biro on photocopied maps in clothbound loose leaf binders

29 × 27.5 × 8.5 cm [11.5 × 11 × 3.5 in] each

In 1968 Kawara began three series of works in addition to the *TODAY Series*: *I GOT UP AT* – local postcards he sent, rubber-stamped with the address where he was staying and that of the friend who was the recipient, the date and the time when he rose; *I MET* – a list of people he met during a day, typed on to a paper sheet and date-stamped; and *I WENT* – a tracing in red biro onto a photocopied local map of his movements during one day in an area he was living in or visiting. These series were added to consistently every day, and each was ended on 17 September 1979. In the case of *I WENT* the process of recording his movement in this way gave rise to what the artist describes as a 'double-consciousness', involving concurrent horizontal and vertical points of view. It was as if he were at the same time observing his movements from above and navigating at ground level.

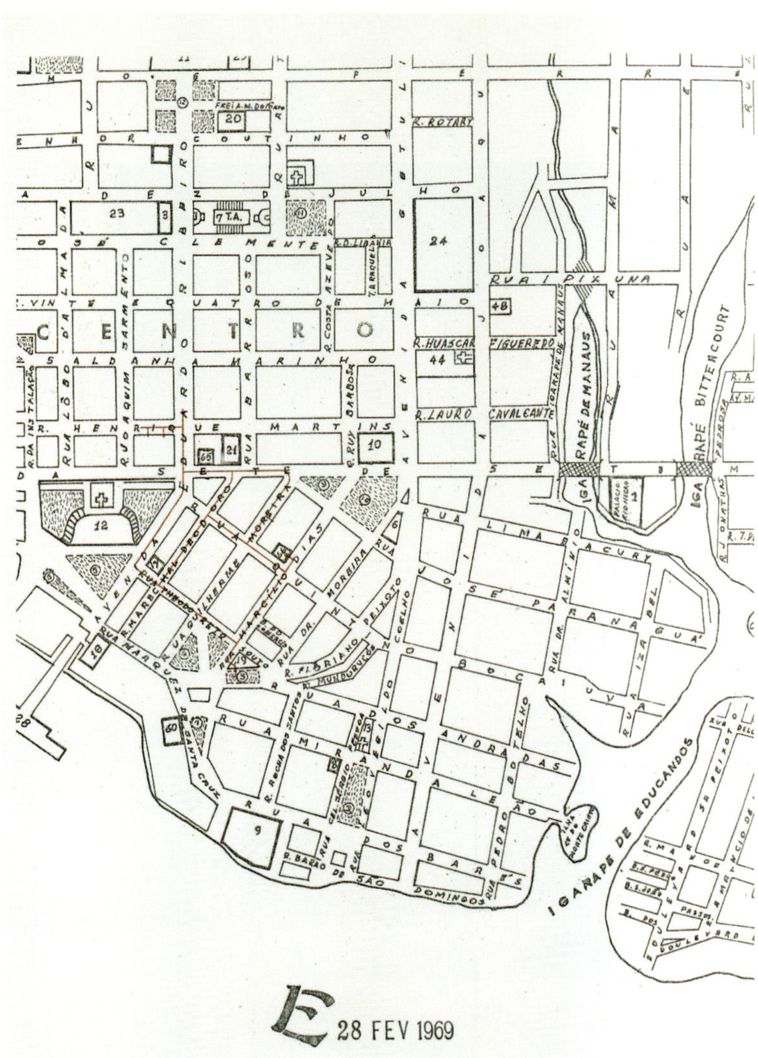

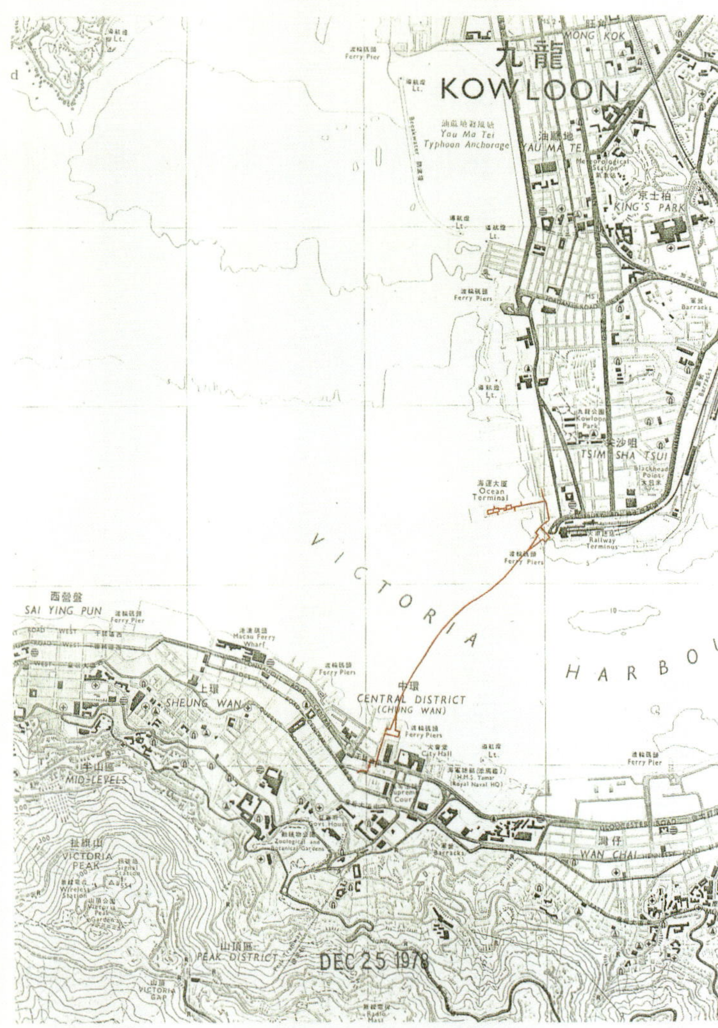

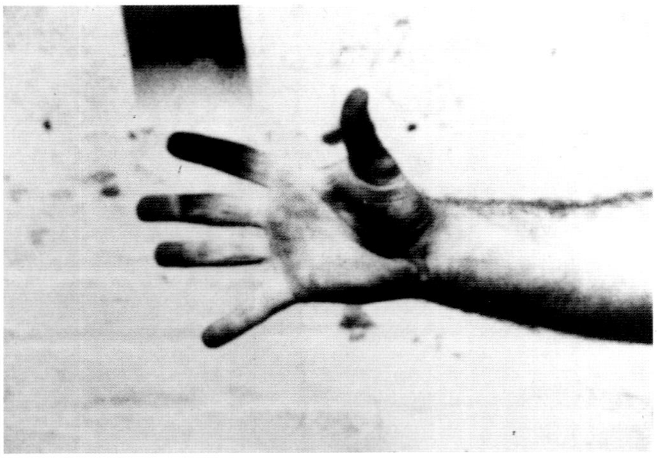

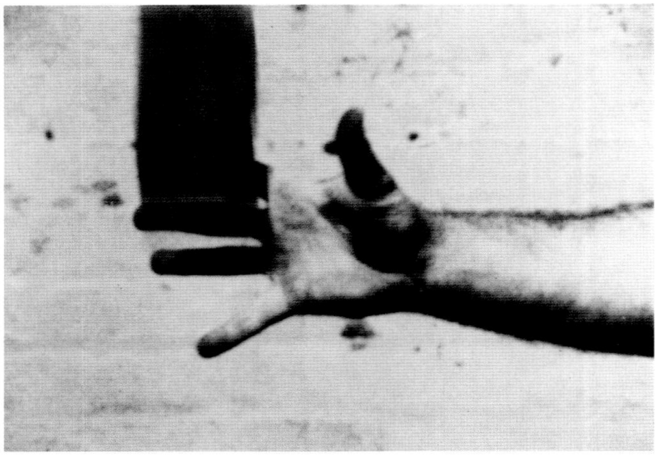

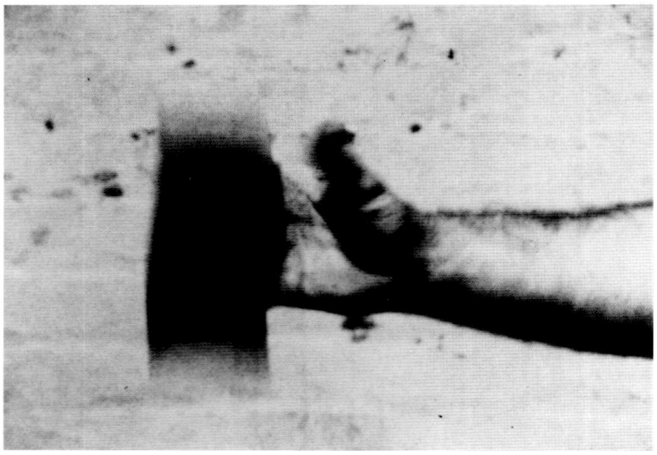

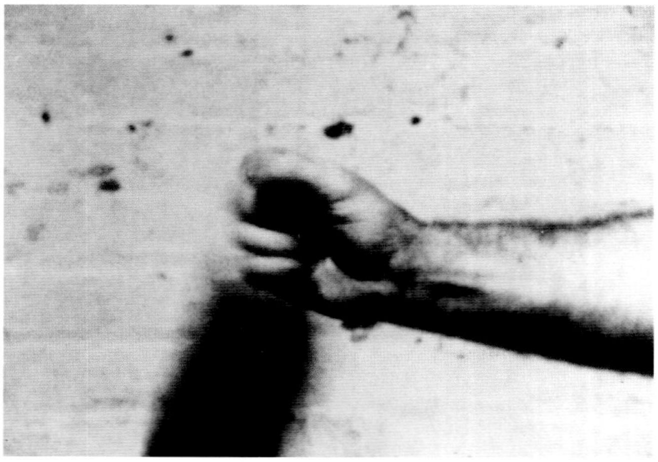

Richard SERRA

Hand Catching Lead

1968

16mm film

3.5 min., black and white, silent

Interest by a documentary filmmaker in recording Serra's working process resulted in the artist himself making his first film work, in which he aimed to explore 'some sort of filmic analogy ... just by using my hand as a device'. He had recently seen Yvonne Rainer's 5-minute experimental film *Hand Movie* (1968), in which she explored links between the material reductiveness of Minimalism and the reduced bodily gestures of her experimental choreography. In Serra's film a succession of falling pieces of lead enter the camera's frame, at the centre of which is the artist's hand, attempting to catch the pieces as they fall. His hand either fails to catch the pieces or immediately releases them, so that the activity reads as purposeless. The passage of the falling lead through the filmic frame imitates the movement of the celluloid strip of film through first the camera and then the projector, manifesting Serra's sculptural interest in 'using material for the sake of its manipulative possibilities'. The repetitive seriality of this work also echoes minimalist structures, including the serial musical composition of Philip Glass, who at that time was working alongside Serra in the same studio.

– quotations from 'The Films of Richard Serra: An Interview', *October*, 10, Fall 1979

to roll
to crease
to fold
to store
to bend
to shorten
to twist
to dapple
to crumple
to shave
to tear
to chip
to split
to cut
to sever
to drop
to remove
to simplify
to differ
to disarrange
to open
to mix
to splash
to knot
to spill
to droop
to flow

to curve
to lift
to inlay
to impress
to fire
to flood
to smear
to rotate
to swirl
to support
to hook
to suspend
to spread
to hang
to collect
of tension
of gravity
of entropy
of nature
of grouping
of layering
of felting
to grasp
to tighten
to bundle
to heap
to gather

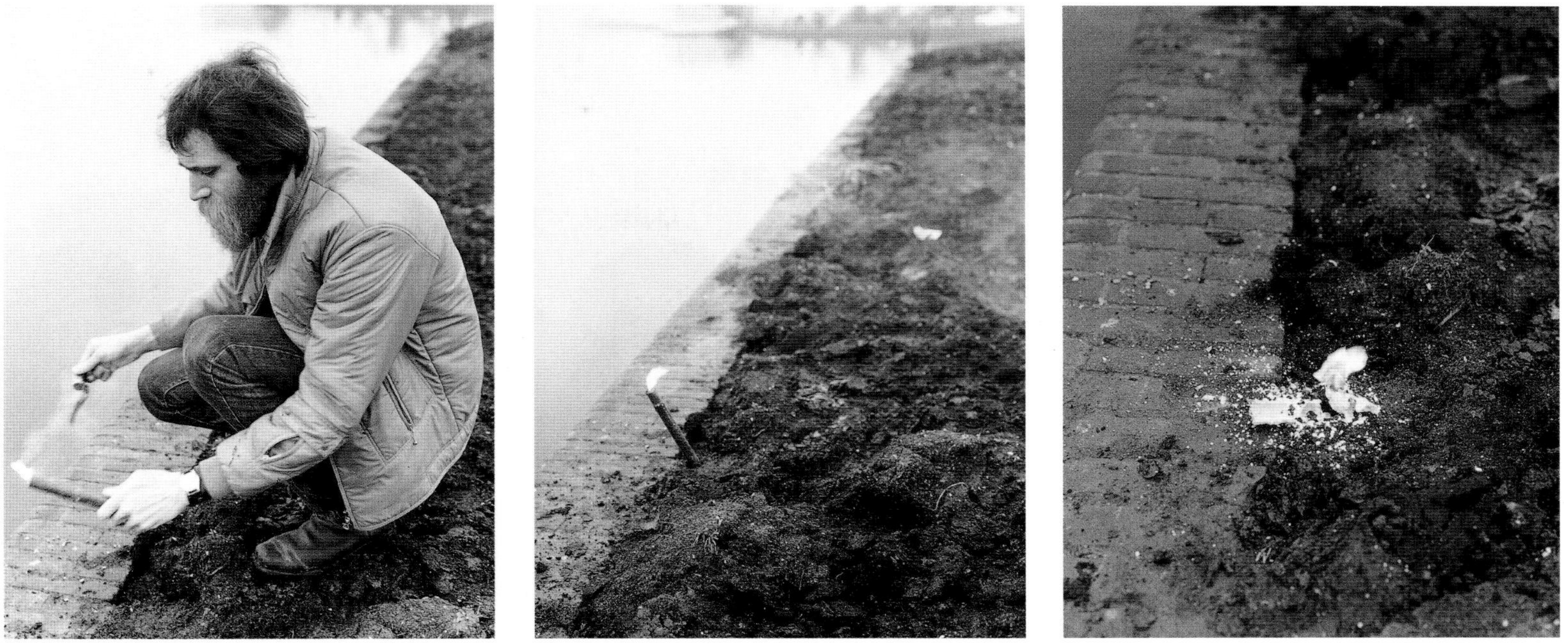

Lawrence WEINER
THE RESIDUE OF A FLARE IGNITED UPON A BOUNDARY
1968
Construction of the work by the artist
'Op losse schroeven: situaties en cryptostructuren',
Stedelijk Museum, Amsterdam, 1969

For the group show 'Op losse schroeven: situaties en cryptostructuren' ('On loose screws: situations and cryptic structures'), organized by Wim Beeren at the Stedelijk Museum, Amsterdam in 1969, Weiner physically made the work THE RESIDUE OF A FLARE IGNITED UPON A BOUNDARY beside the water at the city's edge. This was documented by the photos above but these, like other documentation elsewhere, were never exhibited. They exist solely as a record of what the piece could look like if it were made. Within the museum the work was presented in the form of the statement only, on paper. One month later, at 'When Attitudes Become Form', curated by Harald Szeemann at the Kunsthalle in Bern, Weiner made in the museum A 36" × 36" REMOVAL TO THE LATHING OR SUPPORT WALL OF PLASTER OR WALLBOARD FROM A WALL. This was accompanied by the statement, on a card placed nearby.

Between 1968 and 1970 Weiner's relationship to sculpture underwent a radical transition. In spring 1968 he had installed a sculpture comprising a grid of hemp twine stapled to 34 stakes, with a notch removed from one corner of the grid, on a playing field at Windham College, Putney, Vermont, for the show 'Carl Andre, Robert Barry, Lawrence Weiner', organized by Seth Siegelaub. The work didn't survive long, as the students wanted to use the playing area. Weiner came to realize, however, that the work remained intact as the proposition in language - the statement - from which its physical execution followed. It was only necessary for him to propose works in the form of general or specific statements (see page 124). All other conditions of the presentation and reception of the work would be provided for by a general Statement of Intent he devised in 1969, which has accompanied his work ever since:

The artist may construct the piece.
The piece may be fabricated.
The piece need not be built.
Each being equal and consistent with the intent of the artist, the decision as to condition rests with the receiver upon the occasion of receivership.

opposite
Richard SERRA
Verb List Compilation: Actions to Relate to Oneself [detail]
1967-68
Printed text on paper
Dimensions variable

First published in Grégoire Müller's *The New Avant-Garde: Issues for the Art of the Seventies* (New York, 1972), this list of verbs and several mainly abstract nouns preceded a series of photographs of Serra in action hurling molten lead. The list, like the photographs, formed a portrait of the artist at work; the focus here being on the linguistic character of the action rather than on its product. In Serra's list there are no objects, only transitive verbs and nouns which suggest grammatically the energies operating on physical materials.

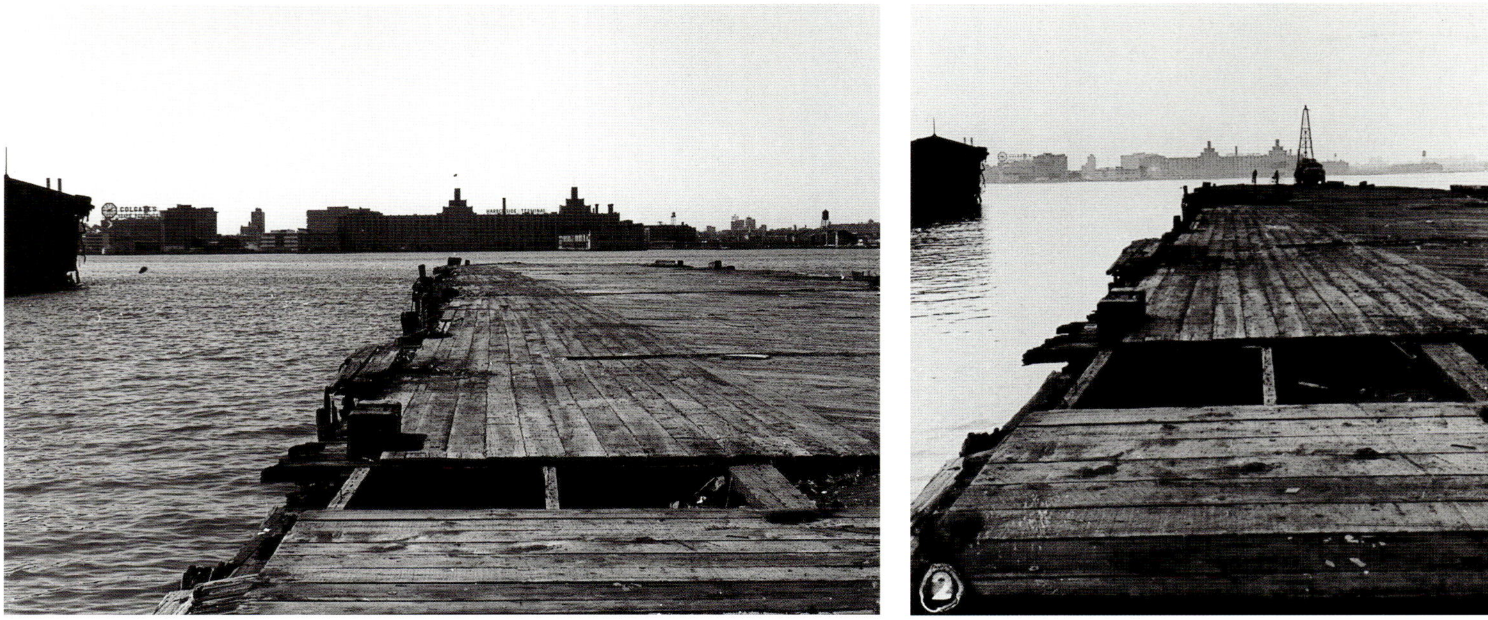

Douglas HUEBLER

Location Piece No. 7 [details]

1971

Pier 18, New York

8 documentation photographs

Dimensions variable

In February and March 1971 the critic and curator Willoughby Sharp invited a number of artists to make works at the abandoned site of Pier 18 on the Hudson river, New York, shortly before its demolition. Documentation of the work by the photographic team of Shunk-Kender was exhibited in 'Pier 18' at The Museum of Modern Art, New York, from June to August 1971.

Huebler asked Shunk-Kender to select and photograph two views of Pier 18 that they considered the most aesthetic, from a 'long range' position, and to make two second photographs representing the most aesthetic 'short range' view. They were asked to make X marks in chalk to indicate both positions from which they had taken the photographs. Several weeks later the artist obtained proof prints of the photographs from the photographers, visited the site and, locating the chalk marks, photographed the same views, duplicating almost exactly the photographers' originals. The four originals and their copies were then juxtaposed without attribution, together with Huebler's statement describing the process, to constitute the final form of this piece.

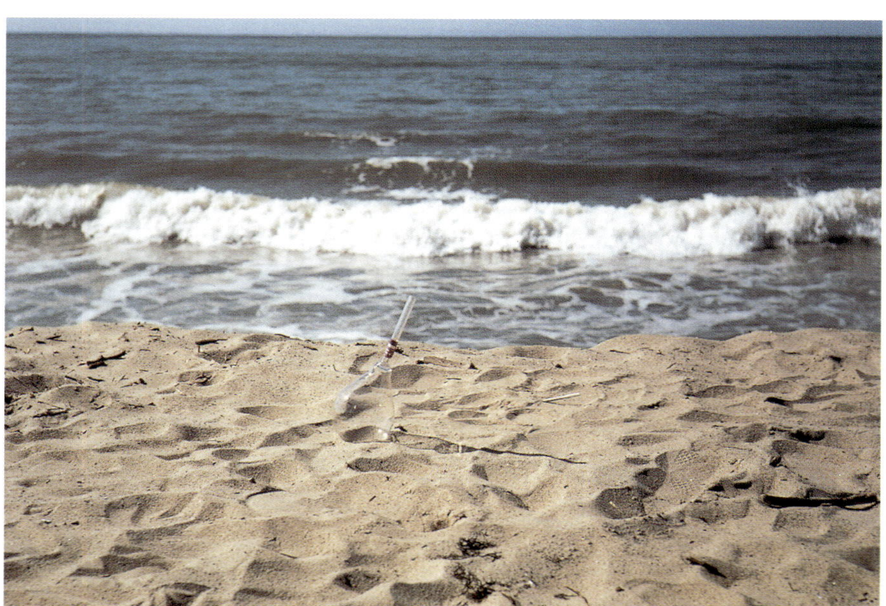

Robert BARRY

Inert Gas Series: Argon [from a measured volume to indefinite expansion]

1969

Pacific Ocean, Santa Monica

On 4 March 1969, on a beach in Santa Monica, California, one litre of Argon was returned to the atmosphere. This was one of a series of releases of different gases which Barry made in March and April of that year. 'I chose to work with inert gas because there was not the constant presence of a small object or device that produced the art. Inert gas is a material that is imperceptible – it does not combine with any other element ... It continues to expand forever in the atmosphere, constantly changing, and it does all of this without anybody being able to see it.'
– Robert Barry, Artist's statement, in Ursula Meyer, *Conceptual Art*, 1970

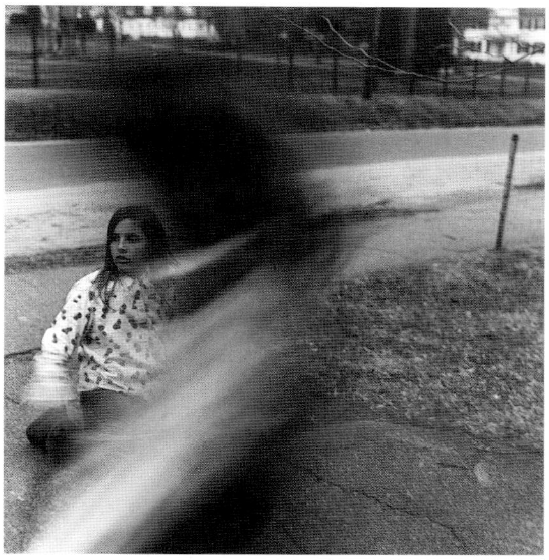

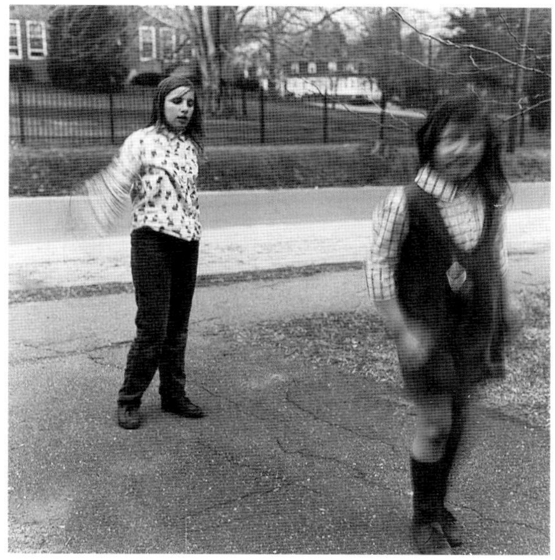

Douglas HUEBLER
Duration Piece No. 4 [details]
1968
Bradford, Massachusetts
9 documentation photographs, text
Dimensions variable

'Photographs of two children playing "jump-rope" were made in the following order: I. Three photographs were made at 10 second intervals. II. Three photographs were made at 20 second intervals. III. Three photographs were made at 30 second intervals. The nine photographs have been scrambled out of sequence and join with the statement to constitute the form of this piece.'
– Douglas Huebler, September 1968

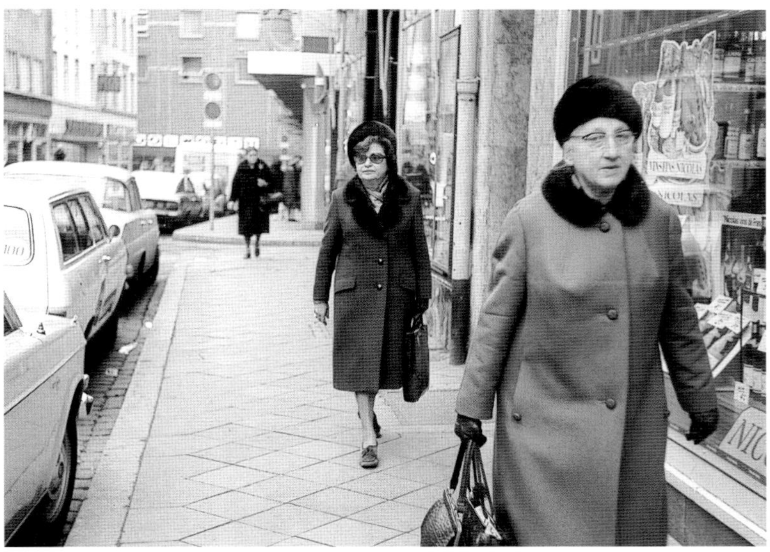

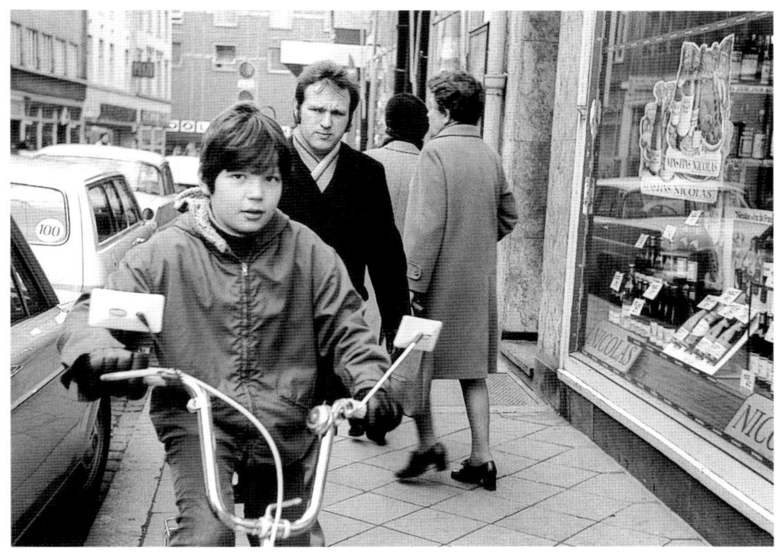

Douglas HUEBLER
Variable Piece No. 70 [In Process] Global [details]
1971–97
Documentation photographs, text
Dimensions variable

This is an early piece of documentation from a work in progress that began in 1971 and continued until the artist's death in 1997. Each documentation was accompanied by the following statement which applies to the whole series: 'Throughout the remainder of the artist's lifetime he will photographically document, to the extent of his capacity, the existence of everyone alive in order to produce the most authentic and inclusive representation of the human species that may be assembled in that manner. Editions of this work will be periodically issued in a variety of topical modes: "100,000 people", "1,000,000 people", "10,000,000 people", "people personally known by the artist", "look-alikes", "overlaps", etc.'
– Douglas Huebler, November 1971

Vito ACCONCI
Following Piece
1969
New York

'Each day I pick out, at random, a person walking in the street.

I follow a different person every day; I keep following until that person enters a private place (home, office, etc.) where I can't get in.'

Following Piece took place over 23 days in New York in October 1969 as part of 'Street Works IV', a series of events organized by New York's Architectural League. Acconci documented his activity with black and white photographs and diaristic lists itemizing the times of his sightings and the activity, such as boarding a train, of the person he was following. Among the notes he wrote for this project he recorded these observations:

'Adjunctive relationship: I add myself on to another person (I give up control/ I don't have to control myself/I become dependent on the other person/I need that other person, that other person doesn't need me) ...

(My time and space are taken up, out of myself, into a larger system.)

Fall into position in a system. I can be substituted for, I can be replaced. My positional value counts here, not my individual characteristics.'

– quotes from Vito Acconci, notes for *Following Piece*, 1969

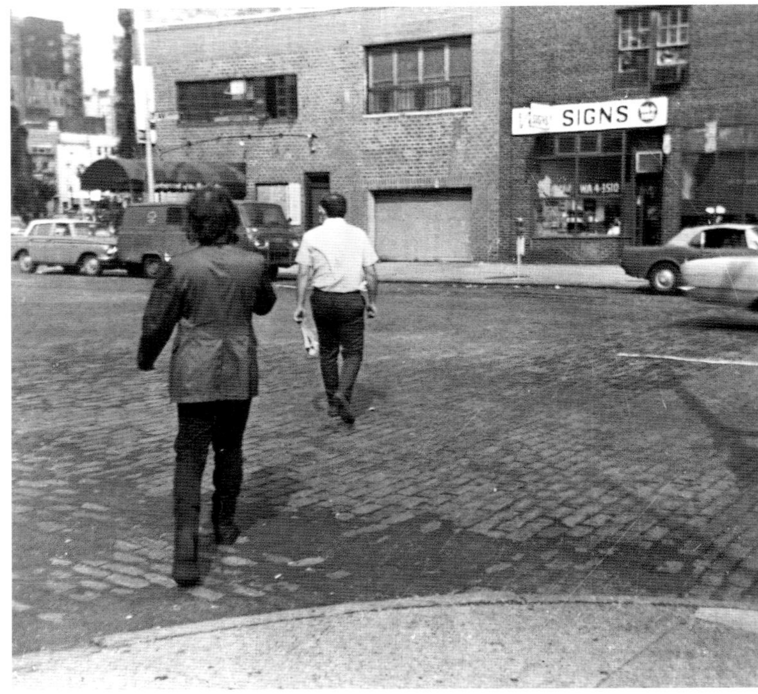

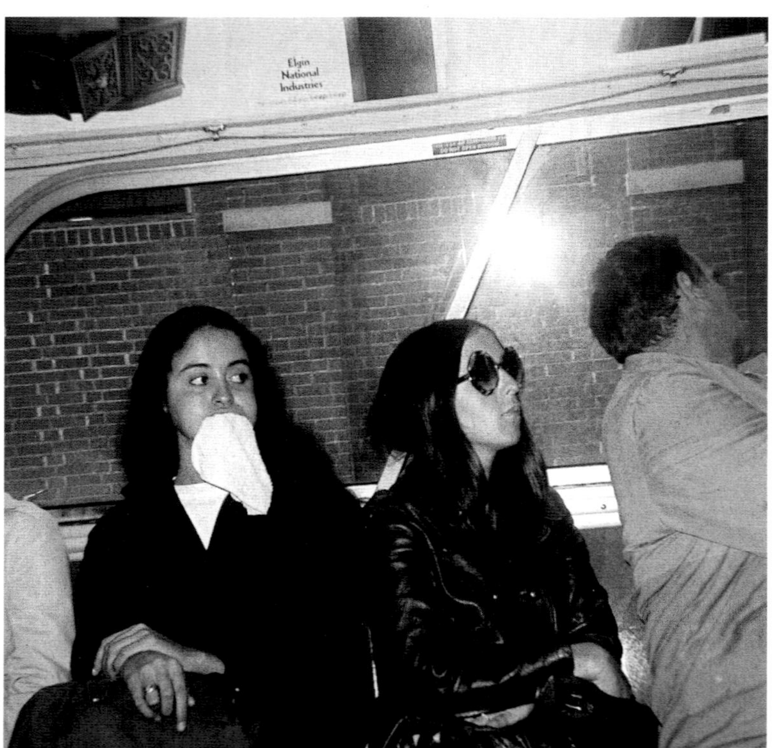

Adrian PIPER
Catalysis IV [detail]
1970–71
2 black and white documentation photographs, text
Photograph, 12.5 × 12.5 cm [5 × 5 in]

In 1970 Piper abandoned working with abstract conceptual drawing and text on paper and began to use her own social presence as a 'catalytic agent' for change. She appeared in public environments in New York, provoking passers-by to confront their attitudes towards others by various disruptive actions. In the *Catalysis* series she would travel by bus with a towel stuffed in her mouth, or shop in smart stores in a shirt painted with a 'Wet Paint' sign, among other strategies.

'Because the artist is the embodiment of a particular creative process, artworks can abandon the intermediary of the discrete form and base themselves on this type of impact. The artist himself becomes the catalytic agent inducing change in the viewer; the viewer responds to the catalytic presence of the artist as artwork. This is not to be confused with life as art or the artist's personality as art. The aesthetic formality and artifice of the work temporarily replace or veil the personal attributes of the artist ... As a discrete form himself, an artist possesses all the potential strengths of secondary discrete forms without any of their intrinsic difficulties.'

– Adrian Piper, 'Art as Catalysis', 1970

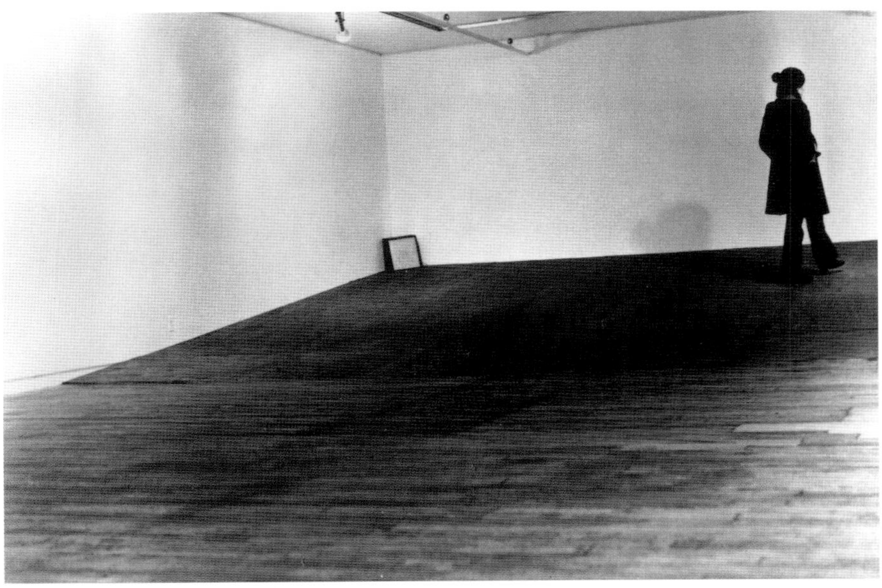

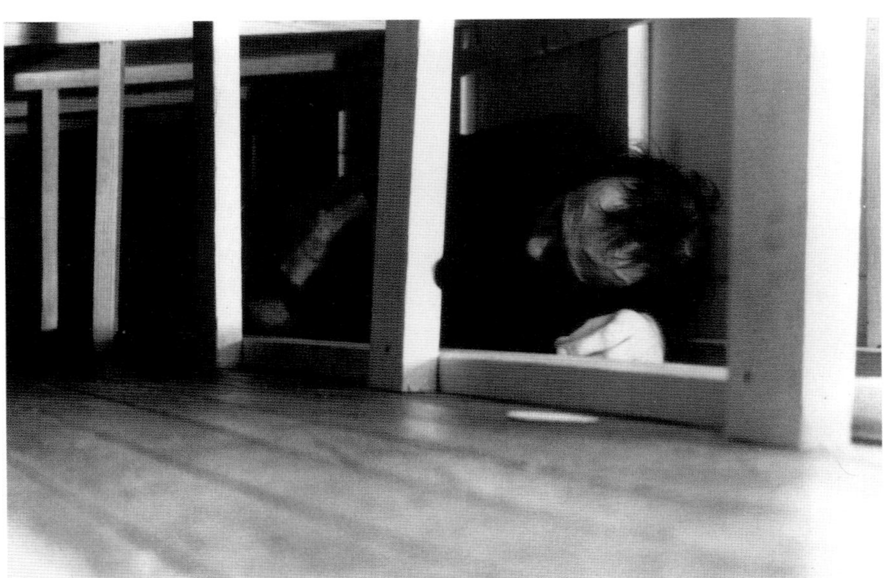

Vito ACCONCI

Seedbed

1972

Sonnabend Gallery, New York

In January 1972, in a room at the Sonnabend Gallery, New York, Acconci built a low wooden ramp merging with the existing floor. Over two weeks, each visitor who opened the door, entered and walked onto the ramp would hear Acconci's voice:

'I'm doing this with you now ... you're in front of me ... you're turning around ... I'm moving towards you ... leaning towards you ... Under the ramp: I'm moving from point to point, covering the floor ... I'm turned to myself: turned onto myself: constant contact with my body (rub my body in order to rub it away, rub something away from it, leave that and move on): masturbating: I have to continue all day – cover the floor with sperm, seed the floor ... I can form an image of you, dream about you, work on you ... I can go on as I think of you, you can reinforce my excitement, serve as my medium ... '

– Vito Acconci, notes for *Seedbed*, 'Power Field – Exchange Points – Transformations', *Avalanche*, 1972

Concealed below as he fantasized about people whom he could not see and who could not see him, Acconci mediated the action he was performing through his verbal commentary, spoken into a microphone broadcast by a speaker above. Negotiating this altered environment and hearing the artist's disembodied statements, visitors found themselves implicated in a relationship of the kind described by the psychologist Curt Lewin as a 'power field', situated in what the sociologist Erving Goffman named a 'performance area'. Goffman and Lewin were among the theoretical sources Acconci drew upon in his work from 1969 onwards.

Jeff WALL

Landscape Manual [details]

1969

Artist's book

28 × 21.5 cm [11 × 8.5 in]

Landscape Manual is a 64-page book, published in Vancouver in an edition of 400. Displaying a price of 25 cents on the front cover, it simulates a cheap technical manual. Its typewritten text is annotated and corrected roughly by hand. Illustrating the text are black and white photographs of such ordinary suburban features as cars, roads, houses and waste ground, all viewed through a car windscreen. The text provides a running commentary on the process of taking the photographs, making the 'manual' and, ultimately, framing a 'landscape'. This was an early manifestation in Wall's work of a conceptual relationship to photography and its genres.

FROM AND FOR A WORK IN PROGRESS

Toward a defeatured landscape on all levels, without any sense of loss, negation, subversion, etc.---reams of tiny photographs.

The beginning of a continuing interpenetration with as yet untaken photographs, with as yet unreceived signals from the as yet existenceless future. This date, September 27, 1969, 7:15 p.m., will mark the"outset" of this endless experiment.

The work in progress: sequences, interspersed with situations and spaces of a specific, dense nature---a sequence which is subtly altered, manipulated in a particular way, one procedure from a vault of endless possibilities. I myself sit here---or possibly ride in a car---and am somewhat more than just a "recording machine".

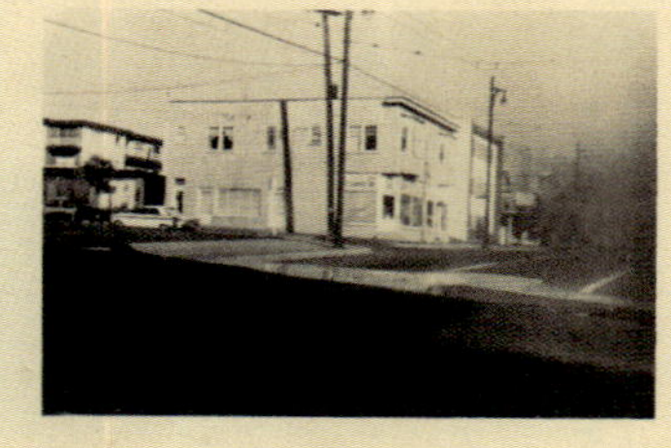

The outlines of the region of concrete reactions---reactions "lived" in complex (i.e.--timeless) time & remembered in "neural" time--complex but different. Instead of being an [redacted] expository work, the work should be a particular procedure itself, carried out as the writing (etc.) is carried out, becoming, in effect indistinguishable from the procedure itself---not subordinate to any other particular physical etc. process, but instead, as concrete as any other particular procedure. Typewriting [redacted] as "physical" [redacted] activity: interadtion with materials, etc., as interaction with stone, steel, ## clay, etc. Interaction with materials as primarily "structural"; i.e.--participation in any process is a [redacted] condition of relating which demands a complete structural "metaphysics", and we can see more & more clearly that this demand & its response should be made as <u>consciously</u> as possible. When words are used, this necessity obviously becomes most apparent---(close attention to interface of vagueness/clarity---apparent "opposition" of mistakes to "correct procedure")

Look carefully <u>onto</u> the page; pattern might see the surface as a (preliminary) [redacted], a particular articulation of many [redacted] simultaneous functions, propositions, etc.---this "surface" articulation a particular and necessary structure, and, as such, intimately related to extended regions of abstraction, each x simpler than the previous---all connected in "crystalline" organic fashion, like the interchange on the broad high-speed freeway under the wheels of a car (1968 Dodge Monaco convertible), then the gleaming approaches, the long straight secondary highways with rutted gravel shoulders, and further and further away, the complex and simultaneous network of suburban drives, crescents and avenues---the white lines carrying speakers out of hearing range. The road-landscape exists, then, as a region of <u>primary</u> involvement, carried to the page with real, primary words and actual chemical photographs.

VAST DEFEATURED REGION

The "regions" which make up the content of the ongoing system are of little importance in & for themselves. Because what we know, or what we actually work with when we work at all, is an awareness of structures---when we make abstractions from these structures to qualitatively different kinds of structures---we understand that what we are doing involves a manipulation of elements or of maybe "objects" which are not important to us except in the manner in which we manipulate them.

I am riding in a car; the sun breaks and slants in through the windows. The car is full of noise---the engine, the wind tearing in through rolled-down windows and wide-open vents under the dashboard. On my lap lies a camera in a leather case. My hands are at my sides and I am looking to my right out the window. Books and papers oover the back seat. The landscape issues out through the rear windows of the car and slips away much too quickly to be contained; nevertheless, from time to time I snap a photograph through one of the car's windows.

mo t documents"

1

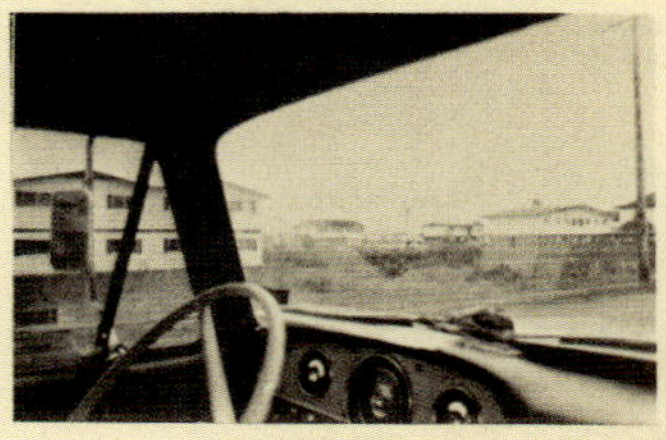

photo: final activity of art (in delirious housing development)

Note: left-hand rear-view mirror suddenly registering housing development factor.
Also: reflection of window in puddle (confluence of speeding mirror-images.

obviously only just begun. Sit as you are sitting now chart your activities, thoughts, observations, etc.---hold the charts up to the light see what corresponds with what. Obviously, this kind of charting has only just begun.

INDEXED UNREELED

Some among us might want to undercut or subvert all possibilities, all dry roads of "meaning", establishing instead only a silent sophisticated well-considered domain apparently without problems of sequence, hierarchy or iconology--by fixing once and for all the principles of actual organization. Nevertheless, the illness remains. Subversion in these terms (subversion/destruction of one specific continuum of "meaning") is always merely an attempt at reformulating the <u>center of importance</u> in particular structures. As long as one kind of organization is absolutely preferred to another, then the genuine field awareness cannot be grasped. In "functional" terms, one always chooses, makes distinctions, etc.---as I choose this varied and synthetic process over some other. The question confronting the man the table the small pile of mechanical images is why are <u>necessary</u> attachments made between things?? Why would you try to make "sense" out of the apparent "noise" of this picture [redacted] game?? Stop trying to shut off the bothersome noise---the symbols which you dont choose the symbols which "impose themselves" upon you and suddenly ---quiet. Immense fields precise as focussed film spread easily effortlessly beneath the eye the lens the hand raised in front of the face. In the moving car, sitting the way you are sitting now, the vacant sequences form beneath the tires, all the windows show blank and the sun glinting across the silvery dashboard fixtures the speedometer set at a steady 33 or 34 miles an hour. Look down into your hand: there is a small photograph you did not choose representing a landscape you do not know. Look out the windΘow, scatter the photos, return the image of the landscape back to the "source"; beneath the tires of the car the terms of your consciousness girlish fond hands proffer city chemistry the consclusions (ANALYTICAL) [redacted]---continuous possibilities for accepting a deep symbio-

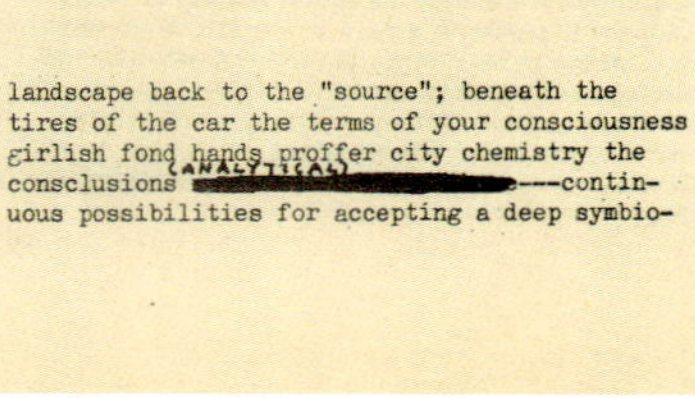

picture-game landscape

34

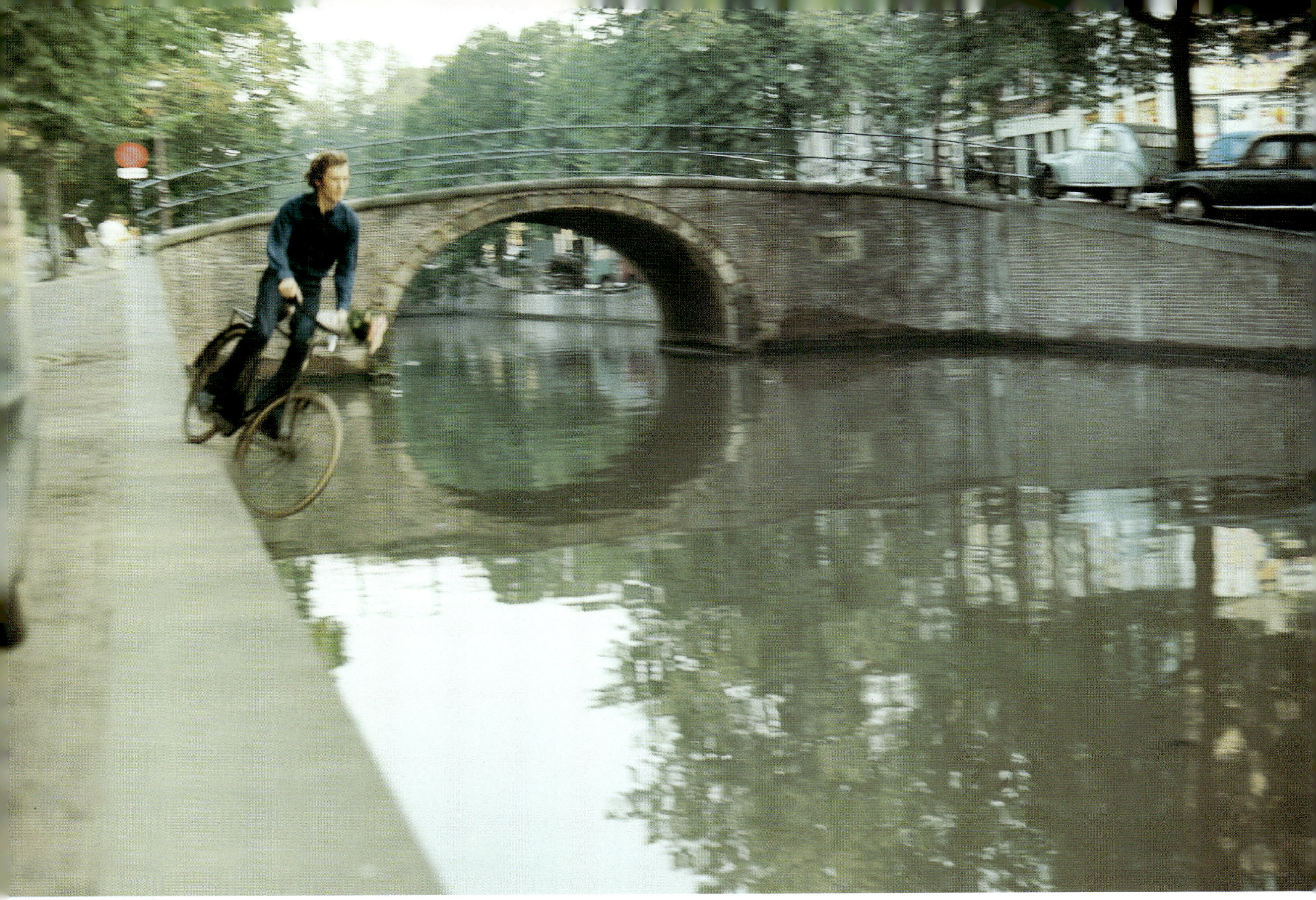

Bas Jan ADER

Fall II

1970

Production still from one of two 16mm films, *Fall I* and *Fall II*, 22 of which were published as black and white photographs in the artist's book *Fall*, Amsterdam, 1970

'When I fell off the roof of my house, or into a canal, it was because gravity made itself master over me.' – Bas Jan Ader, *Avalanche*, 1971

Fall I is a short 16mm black and white film in which Ader falls from a chair on the roof of a 1920s-style bungalow in Los Angeles and rolls down its slope to the ground. *Fall II*, another short film, depicts the artist cycling along the side of one of Amsterdam's canals until he suddenly swerves and plunges into the water. Ader used the act of falling, in these and several other works documented as photographs, to investigate the transitional relationships between the acting-out of the fall; the real-life moment in which the artist actually falls, relinquishing dramatic control; and the representation of the event through documentation.

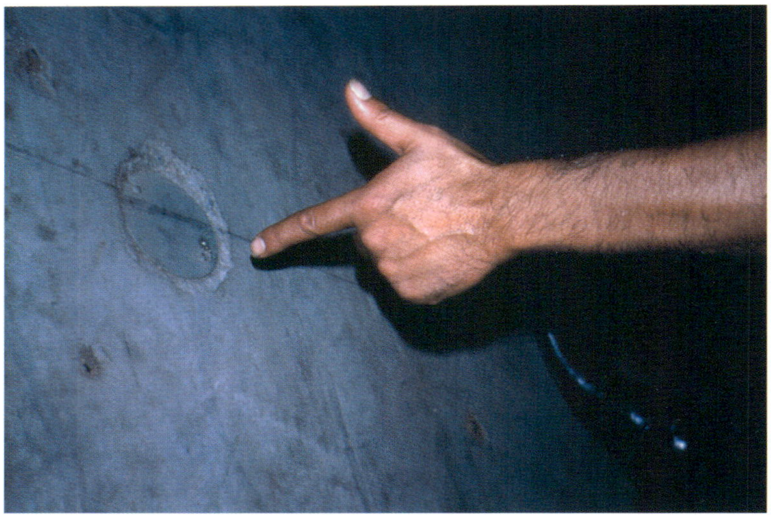

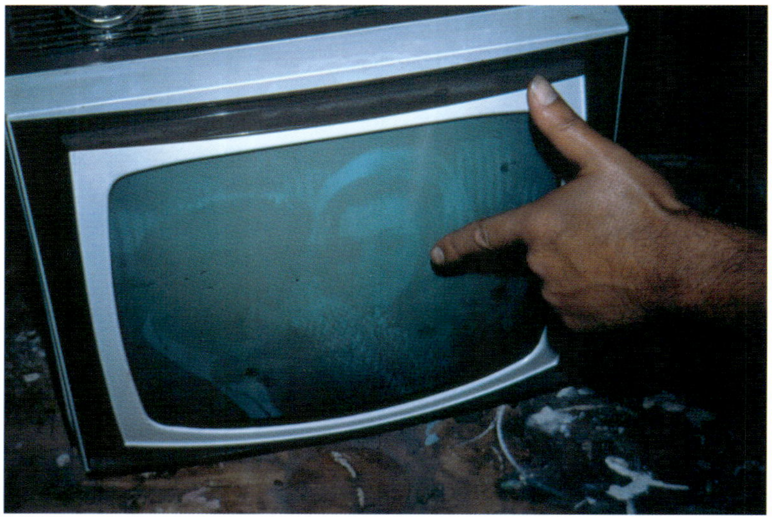

above

John BALDESSARI

A Person Was Asked to Point

1969

Colour photographs mounted on museum board

2 from the series, 73.5 × 108 cm [29 × 42.5 in] each

This work is a literal interpretation of a critical comment on conceptual art attributed to the painter Al Held, who was reported to have said 'All conceptual art is just pointing at things'. Baldessari photographed the hand of his friend the jazz musician George Nicolaidis as he pointed at various mundane objects that caught his attention. This work became the basis of Baldessari's next series, the *Commissioned Paintings*, opposite.

right

John BALDESSARI

Cremation Project, July 24, 1970 [details]

1970

Ashes, bronze urn in the shape of a book, certificate, 6 documentation photographs, text

Urn, 2.5 × 20 × 24 cm [1 × 8 × 9.5 in]

By late summer 1969 Baldessari became overwhelmed by the quantity of artworks that filled his studio. Invited to participate in the exhibition 'Konzeption/Conception' (Städtisches Museum, Leverkusen, Germany), he sent a series of notes, to be reproduced in the exhibition's catalogue, including a text titled 'The world has too much art – I have made too many objects – what to do?' One of the answers he provided was: 'Burn all my paintings, etc., done in past few years. Have them cremated in a mortuary. Pay all fees, receive all documents. Have event recorded at County Recorder's. Send out announcements? Or should it be a private affair? Keep ashes in urn.'

In December that year he had a one-day studio exhibition. What was unsold was publicly cremated. Afterwards he posted a notice in the *San Diego Union* stating: 'Notice is hereby given that all works of art done by the undersigned between May 1953 and March 1966 in his possession as of July 24, 1970, were cremated on July 24, 1970, in San Diego, California.' The completed project, comprising photographic documentation, a bronze plaque and an urn containing the ashes, was exhibited in 'Software' at the Jewish Museum, New York, in September 1970.

– quotations from the artist in Coosje Van Bruggen, *John Baldessari*, 1990

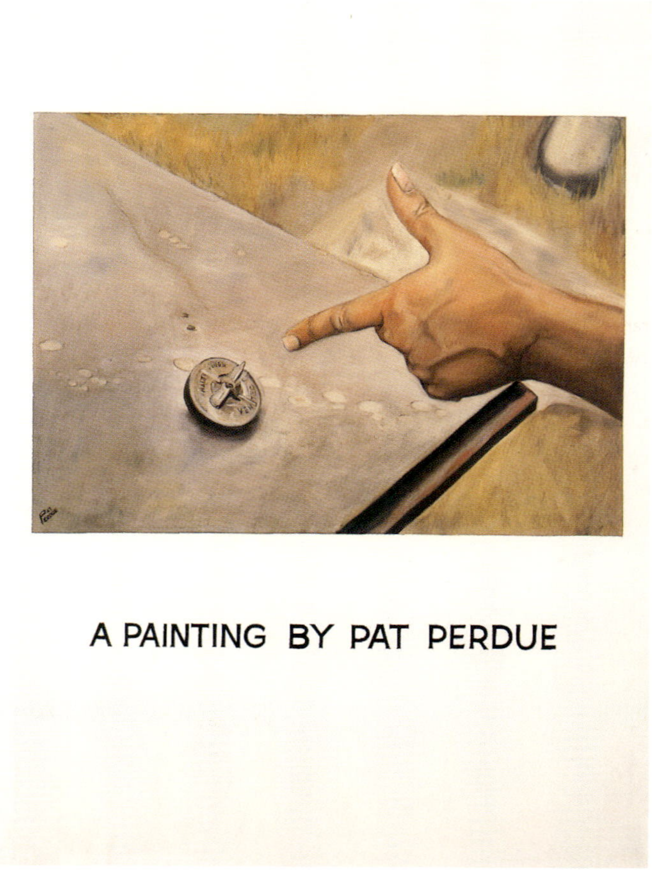

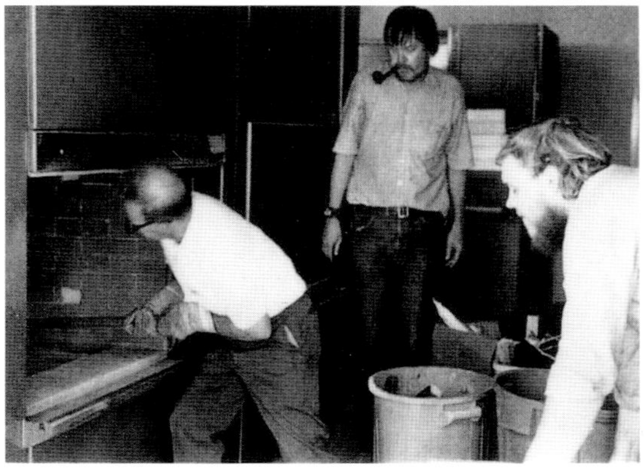

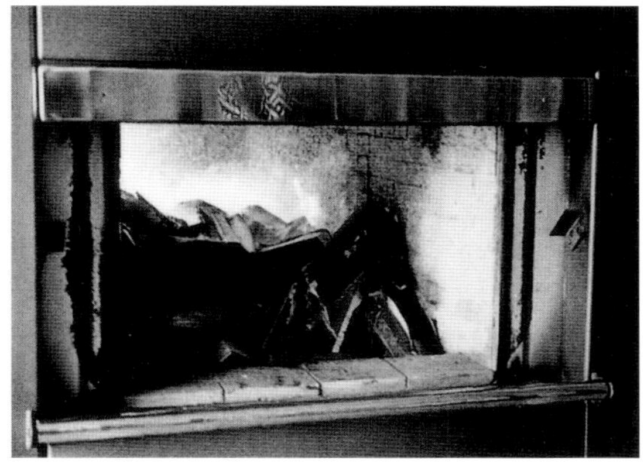

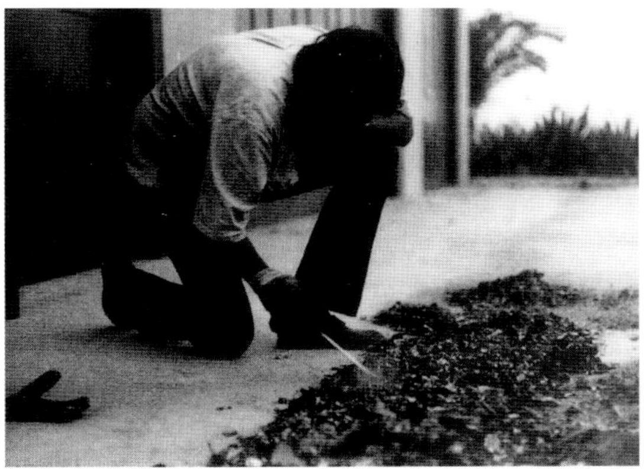

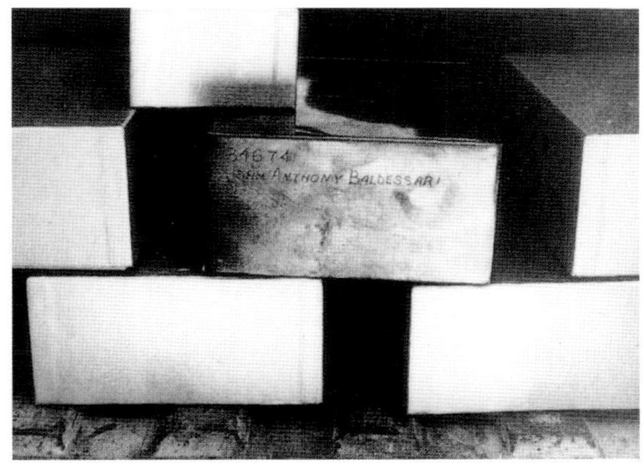

opposite

John BALDESSARI

Commissioned Paintings [detail]

1969

Acrylic or oil on canvas

150.5 × 115.5 cm [59 × 45.5 in] each

'These are paintings done on commission. I had long been fascinated by Sunday painting. The procedure: first I visited many amateur art exhibits. When I discovered a painter I asked if he or she would do a painting on commission. Then I delivered a standard canvas with an area delineated to the proportions of a 35mm transparency. The problem of providing interesting subject matter (to avoid their usual choice of schooner ships, desert cactii, moonlit oceans, etc.) was solved by a series I had just finished which involved someone walking around and pointing to things that were interesting to him. I presented each artist with approximately a dozen of these slides from which to choose. They were asked to paint a rendition as faithfully as possible, the idea being that the art would emerge. Upon completion, each painting was taken to a sign painter and the artist's name affixed thus "A Painting by ... " It was important that the paintings were exhibited as a group so that the spectator could practice connoisseurship, for example comparing how the extended forefinger in each was painted ... '

– John Baldessari, in *John Baldessari: Paintings 1966-68*, Stedelijk Van Abbemuseum, Eindhoven, 1981

PROCESS, SYSTEM, SERIES

Abstraction and reduction had been central features of modernist art in the late 1950s and early 1960s. Minimalism took these processes beyond the traditional boundaries of painting and sculpture and explored them at the level of 'objecthood' in general, often in serial form. Serial and systems-based conceptual art took this process of generalization one step further: from objecthood to idea. By the mid 1960s, ideal systems of logical, mathematical and spatio-temporal relations, and our modes of reference to them, had become the very 'stuff' of art. Art ideas can be represented in a whole host of ways. For Mel Bochner and Sol LeWitt, working drawings, notes, diagrams and lists became as good, or better, representations of art ideas as the fabrication of objects. John Baldessari, Bernd and Hilla Becher, John Hilliard, Edward Ruscha, Michael Snow and Andy Warhol exploited the seriality inherent in photography and film. On Kawara and Roman Opalka continued to paint, but in serial form. Hanne Darboven, Dan Graham and Adrian Piper worked with numbers and words. Hans Haacke explored parallels between physical, biological and social systems. Daniel Buren and Niele Toroni used sameness as a signature of difference.

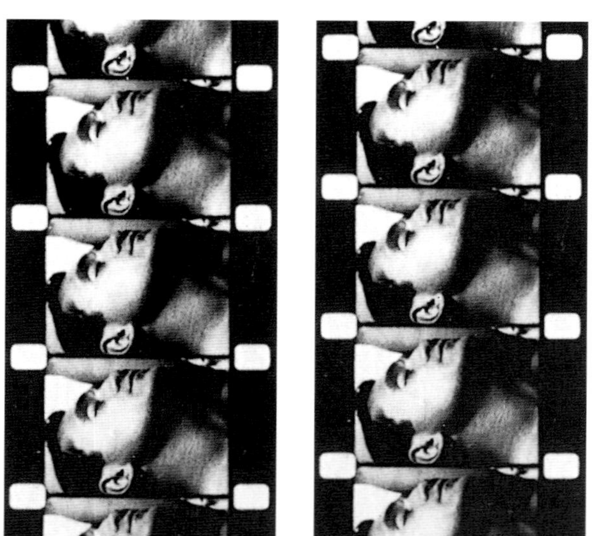

Andy WARHOL
Sleep
1963
16mm film
6 hours, 16 frames per second, black and white, silent

The third of Warhol's films, *Sleep* was shot on a hand-wound 16mm Bolex camera fitted with a motor to enable him to run 100 feet of film continuously without pausing to rewind. He filmed six 100-foot rolls of 16mm film, each, comprising uninterrupted takes of his friend the poet John Giorno asleep, taken from various angles. These are repeated, permutated and projected at a slower speed than that of the original filming (16 frames per second instead of the normal 24), finally slowing to freeze-frames. The whole film lasts six hours. By slowing the film down he created a transformation of mundane reality through a heightened awareness to detail. Equally, however, the work emphasizes the endless repetition and 'artlessness' which the media of mechanical reproduction make available.

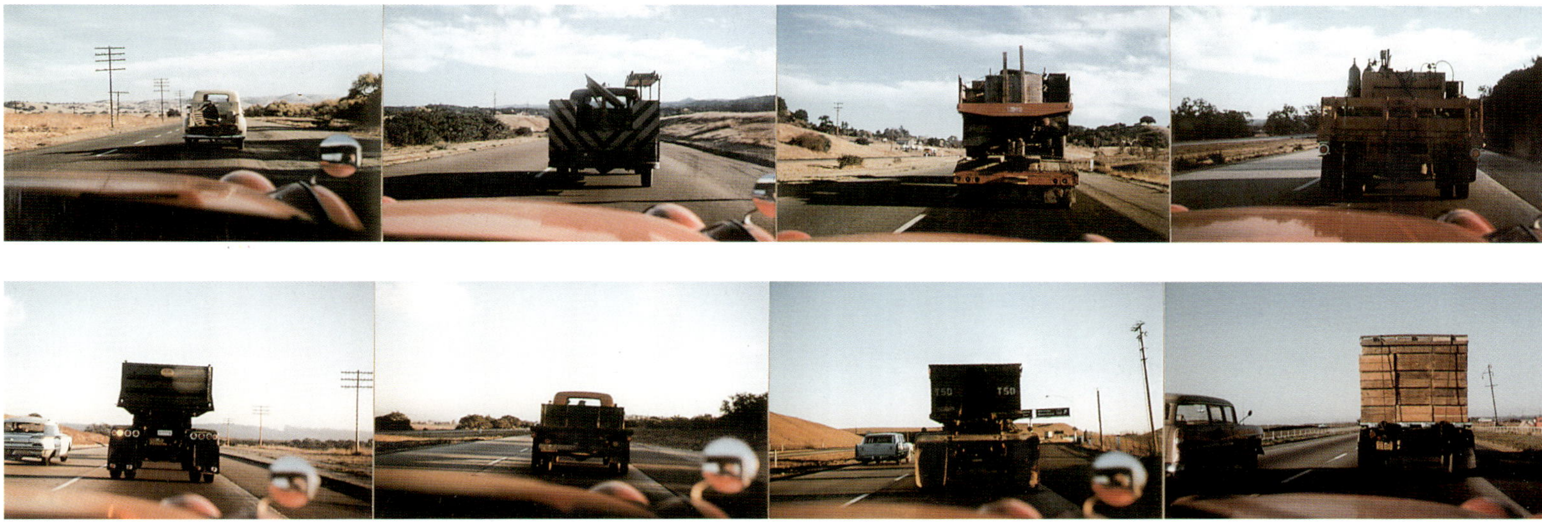

John BALDESSARI

The Back of All the Trucks Passed While Driving from Los Angeles to Santa Barbara, California, Sunday 20 January, 1963 [details]

1963

Thirty-two 35 mm slides

Colour print, dimensions variable

Baldessari made this work during a single day in 1962. In this period he drove every day to the cliff area by La Jolla to paint whatever caught his attention. The works became increasingly abstract, and he began to notice objects around him which resembled areas of these paintings. He began to photograph outdoor surfaces, such as the backs of trucks, using these snapshots as sources for new paintings, which in turn suggested new photographs. This is one of the few works which Baldessari did not destroy when he rejected painting entirely in 1970. Instead he exhibited the photographs no longer as a 'study' for a painting but as an independent work.

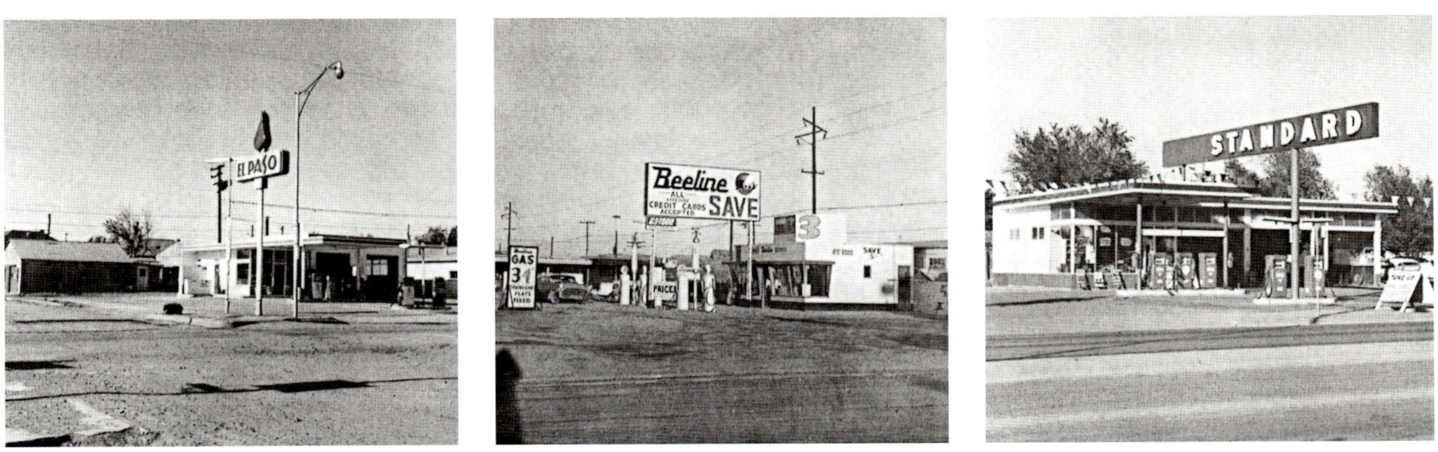

Edward RUSCHA

Twenty Six Gasoline Stations [details]

1962

Artist's Book

18 × 14 cm [7 × 5.5 in]

In a small, cheap book, his first artist's book, Ruscha printed these snapshots of gasoline stations alongside titles giving their name and location, such as *TEXACO, SUNSET STRIP, LOS ANGELES*. 'The title came before I even thought about the pictures. I like the word "gasoline" and I like the specific quality of "twenty-six" ... Above all, the photographs I use are not "arty" in any sense of the word ... they are technical data like industrial photography. To me, they are nothing more than snapshots ... My pictures are not that interesting, nor the subject matter. They are simply a collection of "facts"; my book is more like a collection of "readymades".' – Edward Ruscha, interview with John Coplans, *Artforum*, February 1965

Roman OPALKA

1965/1- ∞ [Detail 1-35327]

1965

Tempera on canvas

196 × 135 cm [77 × 53 in]

This is an ongoing series begun in 1965 in which Opalka maps infinity in relation to the individual action of counting. He began the first painting with the number one at the top left hand of the canvas, proceeding sequentially to fill the entire canvas with numbers up to 35327, when there was no more space. The second canvas followed on directly from the first, beginning with the number 35328. Every canvas is the same size: 196 by 135 cm. The numbers are white. Initially they were painted onto a black ground; in 1972 Opalka began adding white to the background paint to make it grey. In each new painting he increases the quantity of white by one per cent. Eventually this will result in a merging of figure and ground as the background becomes white. Each painting is begun with a loaded brush, replenished only when it is almost empty of paint, to produce gradations of intensity. The artist makes a tape recording of himself reciting the numbers as he is painting them; on completing each canvas he records his face in a photographic self-portrait. Thus the sequential numerical progression is accompanied by a record of the artist's physical ageing. The ultimate disappearance of the counting mechanism as the numbers fade into the background evokes the progression of individual mortality.

A detail of this painting is reproduced on the back cover of this book.

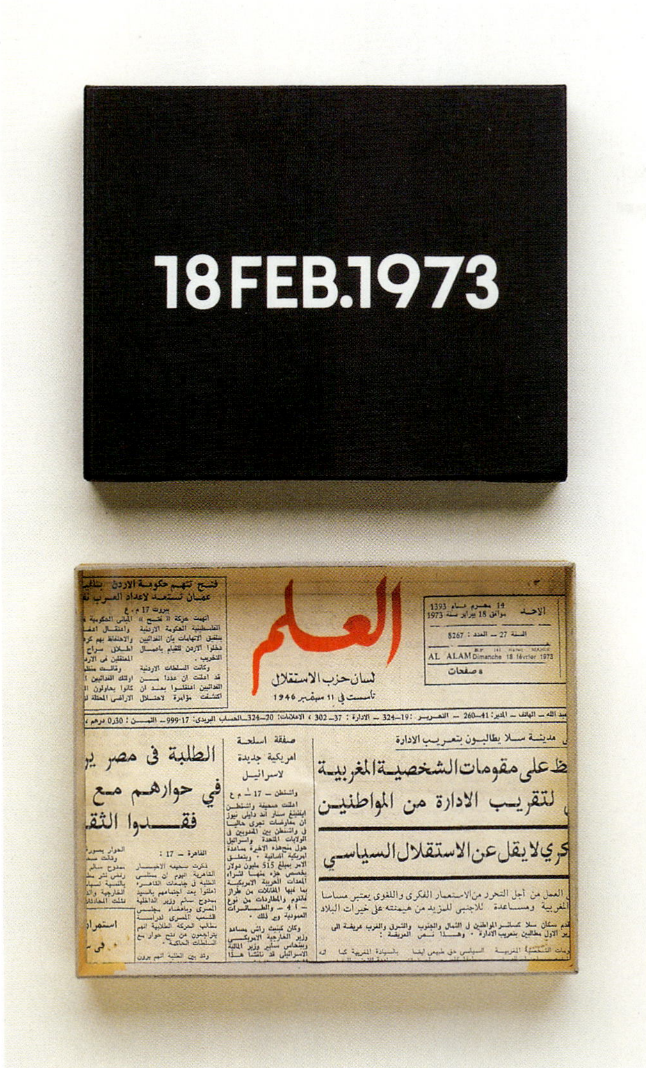

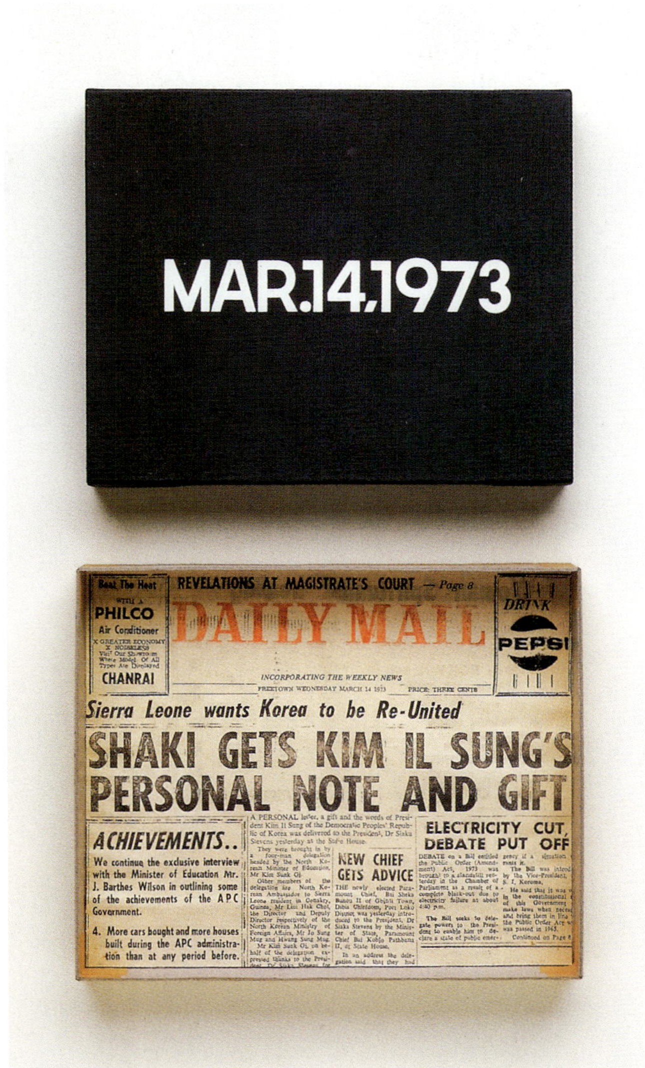

On KAWARA

above

18 FEB. 1973

above right

MAR. 14, 1973

1973

Acrylic on canvas

20 × 25.5 cm [8 × 10 in] each

From the *TODAY* series, 1966 to the present

In 1966 Kawara made his first *Date Paintings*, which collectively form an ongoing project, the *TODAY Series*. Each work is a painting, simply, of the date on which it was made. Ranging in size, the paintings are made using acrylic on pre-stretched canvas, supported on wooden frames 2 inches (5 cm) deep. The text, often using an abbreviation of the month, is painted in white, located at the centre of the rectangle, against a background painted a plain colour from a limited range varying from blue or red to black or a dark sober colour. The process is exacting and time-consuming. Four coats of paint are applied for the ground, with enough time elapsing between for drying, followed by a rubbing down in preparation for subsequent coats. The outlines of the text are drawn and then filled in with several coats of white paint with the use of tapered brushes, a ruler and set square, a scalpel and a brush for dusting. Further time is spent making minute adjustments to correct imperfections. If the painting is not finished by the end of the day, by midnight it is destroyed.

Each *Date Painting* is subtitled and registered in a journal with details of its size, colour and date, and finally stored in a cardboard box made to size. On the lid of the box is a label with the corresponding date. Inside, in the case of most of the earlier *Date Paintings*, but less frequently in later works, is a cutting of news the artist read in a local newspaper on the same day.

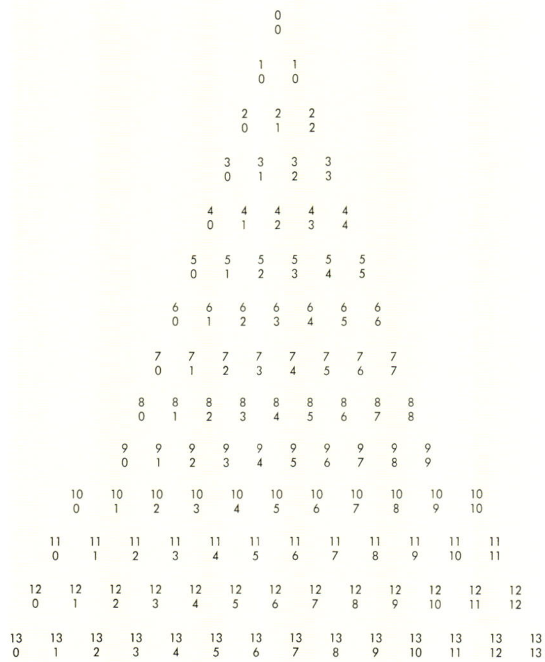
0
0

1 1
0 0

2 2 2
0 1 2

3 3 3 3
0 1 2 3

4 4 4 4 4
0 1 2 3 4

5 5 5 5 5 5
0 1 2 3 4 5

6 6 6 6 6 6 6
0 1 2 3 4 5 6

7 7 7 7 7 7 7 7
0 1 2 3 4 5 6 7

8 8 8 8 8 8 8 8 8
0 1 2 3 4 5 6 7 8

9 9 9 9 9 9 9 9 9 9
0 1 2 3 4 5 6 7 8 9

10 10 10 10 10 10 10 10 10 10 10
0 1 2 3 4 5 6 7 8 9 10

11 11 11 11 11 11 11 11 11 11 11 11
0 1 2 3 4 5 6 7 8 9 10 11

12 12 12 12 12 12 12 12 12 12 12 12 12
0 1 2 3 4 5 6 7 8 9 10 11 12

13 13 13 13 13 13 13 13 13 13 13 13 13 13
0 1 2 3 4 5 6 7 8 9 10 11 12 13

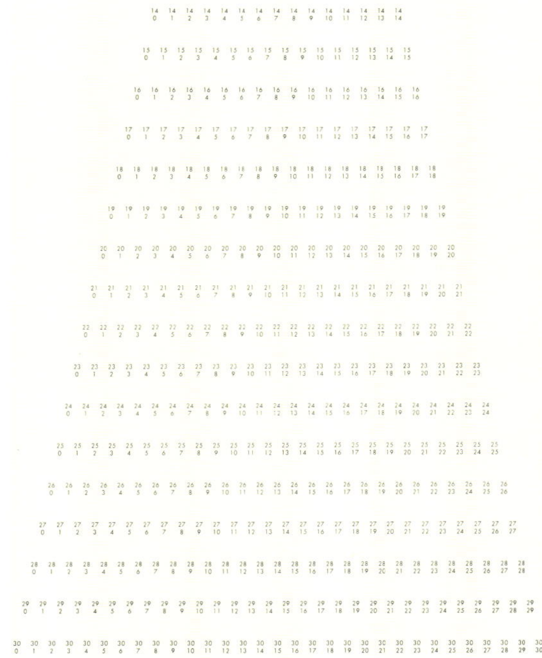
14 14 14 14 14 14 14 14 14 14 14 14 14 14 14
0 1 2 3 4 5 6 7 8 9 10 11 12 13 14

15 15 15 15 15 15 15 15 15 15 15 15 15 15 15 15
0 1 2 3 4 5 6 7 8 9 10 11 12 13 14 15

16 16 16 16 16 16 16 16 16 16 16 16 16 16 16 16 16
0 1 2 3 4 5 6 7 8 9 10 11 12 13 14 15 16

17 17 17 17 17 17 17 17 17 17 17 17 17 17 17 17 17 17
0 1 2 3 4 5 6 7 8 9 10 11 12 13 14 15 16 17

18 18 18 18 18 18 18 18 18 18 18 18 18 18 18 18 18 18 18
0 1 2 3 4 5 6 7 8 9 10 11 12 13 14 15 16 17 18

19 19 19 19 19 19 19 19 19 19 19 19 19 19 19 19 19 19 19 19
0 1 2 3 4 5 6 7 8 9 10 11 12 13 14 15 16 17 18 19

20 20 20 20 20 20 20 20 20 20 20 20 20 20 20 20 20 20 20 20 20
0 1 2 3 4 5 6 7 8 9 10 11 12 13 14 15 16 17 18 19 20

21 21 21 21 21 21 21 21 21 21 21 21 21 21 21 21 21 21 21 21 21 21
0 1 2 3 4 5 6 7 8 9 10 11 12 13 14 15 16 17 18 19 20 21

22 22 22 22 22 22 22 22 22 22 22 22 22 22 22 22 22 22 22 22 22 22 22
0 1 2 3 4 5 6 7 8 9 10 11 12 13 14 15 16 17 18 19 20 21 22

23 23 23 23 23 23 23 23 23 23 23 23 23 23 23 23 23 23 23 23 23 23 23 23
0 1 2 3 4 5 6 7 8 9 10 11 12 13 14 15 16 17 18 19 20 21 22 23

24 24 24 24 24 24 24 24 24 24 24 24 24 24 24 24 24 24 24 24 24 24 24 24 24
0 1 2 3 4 5 6 7 8 9 10 11 12 13 14 15 16 17 18 19 20 21 22 23 24

25 25 25 25 25 25 25 25 25 25 25 25 25 25 25 25 25 25 25 25 25 25 25 25 25 25
0 1 2 3 4 5 6 7 8 9 10 11 12 13 14 15 16 17 18 19 20 21 22 23 24 25

26 26 26 26 26 26 26 26 26 26 26 26 26 26 26 26 26 26 26 26 26 26 26 26 26 26 26
0 1 2 3 4 5 6 7 8 9 10 11 12 13 14 15 16 17 18 19 20 21 22 23 24 25 26

27 27 27 27 27 27 27 27 27 27 27 27 27 27 27 27 27 27 27 27 27 27 27 27 27 27 27 27
0 1 2 3 4 5 6 7 8 9 10 11 12 13 14 15 16 17 18 19 20 21 22 23 24 25 26 27

28 28 28 28 28 28 28 28 28 28 28 28 28 28 28 28 28 28 28 28 28 28 28 28 28 28 28 28 28
0 1 2 3 4 5 6 7 8 9 10 11 12 13 14 15 16 17 18 19 20 21 22 23 24 25 26 27 28

29 29 29 29 29 29 29 29 29 29 29 29 29 29 29 29 29 29 29 29 29 29 29 29 29 29 29 29 29 29
0 1 2 3 4 5 6 7 8 9 10 11 12 13 14 15 16 17 18 19 20 21 22 23 24 25 26 27 28 29

30 30 30 30 30 30 30 30 30 30 30 30 30 30 30 30 30 30 30 30 30 30 30 30 30 30 30 30 30 30 30
0 1 2 3 4 5 6 7 8 9 10 11 12 13 14 15 16 17 18 19 20 21 22 23 24 25 26 27 28 29 30

Dan GRAHAM
Scheme [details]
1965
Printed text on paper
28 × 21.5 cm [11 × 8.5 in] each
First published in Robert Smithson, 'Quasi-infinities and the Waning of Space', *Arts Magazine*, New York, 1966

Scheme was designed for use either as a single page or to be extended indefinitely in book form. The series of numbers appear in two-line groups. The top line of each group is a repetition of the same number; the second line starts at zero and follows a numerical sequence until it shows as many numbers as there are digits in the line above. From this scheme there results a progressive enlargement in the form of a triangle, the base of which is determined by the width of the sheet of paper. This is the earliest of the works Graham conceived as existing outside of conventional exhibition contexts, in the form of a proposal to be carried out by a magazine or book editor.

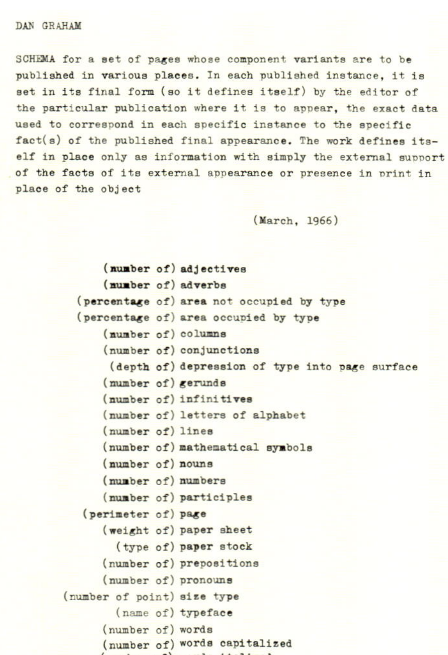
DAN GRAHAM

SCHEMA for a set of pages whose component variants are to be published in various places. In each published instance, it is set in its final form (so it defines itself) by the editor of the particular publication where it is to appear, the exact data used to correspond in each specific instance to the specific fact(s) of the published final appearance. The work defines itself in place only as information with simply the external support of the facts of its external appearance or presence in print in place of the object

(March, 1966)

(number of) adjectives
(number of) adverbs
(percentage of) area not occupied by type
(percentage of) area occupied by type
(number of) columns
(number of) conjunctions
(depth of) depression of type into page surface
(number of) gerunds
(number of) infinitives
(number of) letters of alphabet
(number of) lines
(number of) mathematical symbols
(number of) nouns
(number of) numbers
(number of) participles
(perimeter of) page
(weight of) paper sheet
(type of) paper stock
(number of) prepositions
(number of) pronouns
(number of point) size type
(name of) typeface
(number of) words
(number of) words capitalized
(number of) words italized

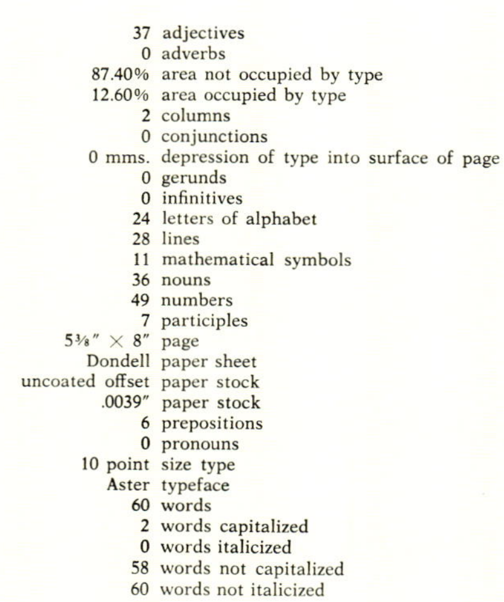
37 adjectives
0 adverbs
87.40% area not occupied by type
12.60% area occupied by type
2 columns
0 conjunctions
0 mms. depression of type into surface of page
0 gerunds
0 infinitives
24 letters of alphabet
28 lines
11 mathematical symbols
36 nouns
49 numbers
7 participles
5⅜" × 8" page
Dondell paper sheet
uncoated offset paper stock
.0039" paper stock
6 prepositions
0 pronouns
10 point size type
Aster typeface
60 words
2 words capitalized
0 words italicized
58 words not capitalized
60 words not italicized

Dan GRAHAM
Schema
1966
Printed text on paper
28 × 21.5 cm [11 × 8.5 in]
Generic form (*far left*) first published in *Aspen*, No. 5/6, New York, 1966

This work was published in various specific forms, as on the near left, in several English and German language magazines after its first appearance in *Aspen*, No. 5/6, in 1966 as a generic form which existed as an instruction or invitation, to be completed with the specific details by the editor of the publication in which it appeared. '*Schema* lines up syntax as arithmetic. An attempt to inventory what is impossible to inventory, it also plays with the limits of formulating a system as such. Graham borrows its inconclusive character from the mathematician Kurt Gödel (1906–78), whose theorum of incompleteness stated that within any system there are elements that cannot be proved.'
– Birgit Pelzer, *Dan Graham*, London, 2000

Sol LEWITT

Serial Project No. 1 [A,B,C,D]

1966

Baked enamel on aluminium

51 × 414 × 414 cm [20 × 163 × 163 in]

Collection, The Museum of Modern Art, New York

In 1966 LeWitt expanded his series of individual geometric structures into larger ensembles. In *Aspen*, No. 5/6 (1966), he described the work in detail with accompanying diagrams. 'Serial compositions are multipart pieces with regulated changes. The differences between the parts are the subjects of the composition ... Chance, taste, or unconsciously remembered forms would play no part in the outcome. The serial artist does not attempt to produce a beautiful or mysterious object but functions merely as a clerk cataloguing the results of his premise ... The premise governing this series is: to place one form within another and include all major variations in two and three dimensions. This is to be done in the most succinct manner, using the fewest measurements.' The project comprises four three-part progressions of box-like square and rectangular, open and closed forms. Each quarter, A, B, C or D, consists of three rows of three elements. They are arranged such that the progressive growth of structures is mirrored along the central axis of the grid. The work may be shown as a whole ensemble or as separated components.

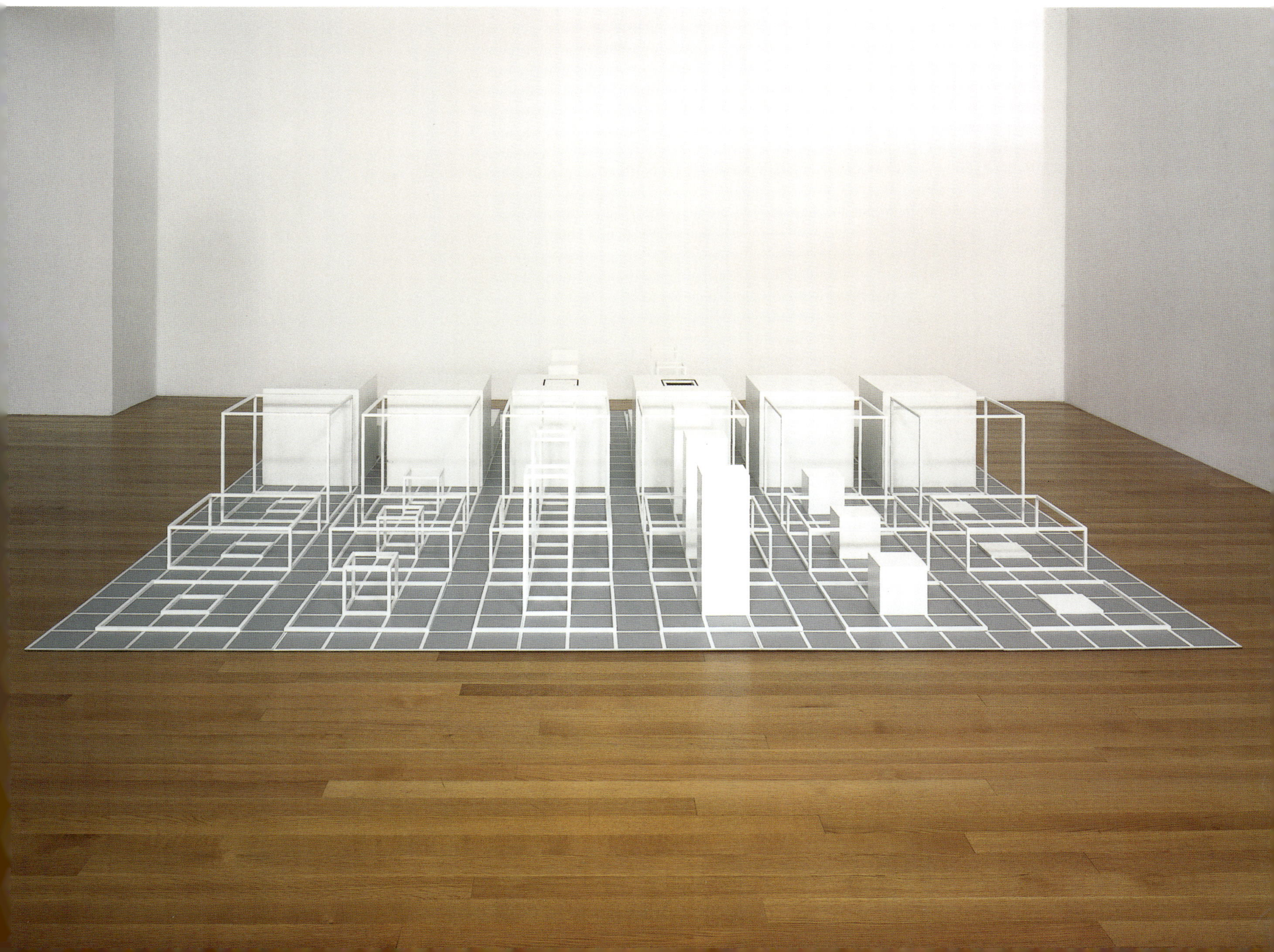

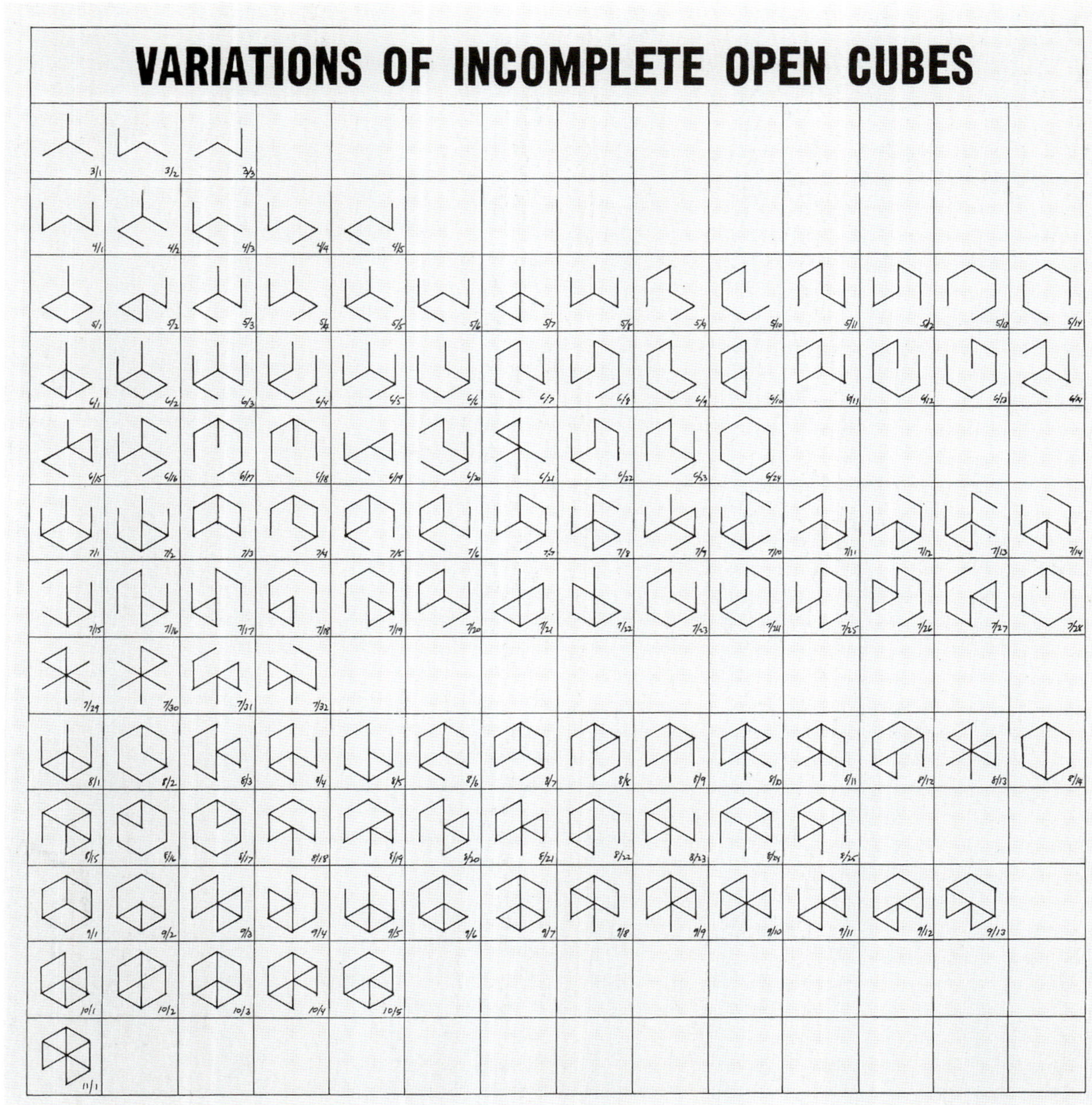

Sol LEWITT

Schematic Drawing for Incomplete Open Cubes

1974

Printed announcement for exhibition at John Weber Gallery, New York

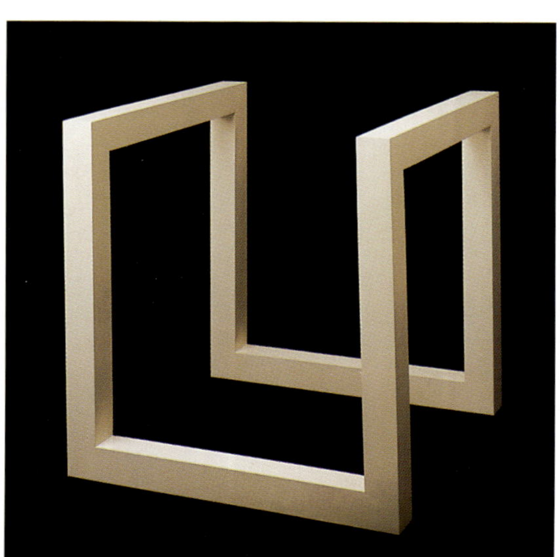

Sol LEWITT

Incomplete Open Cube 8/3

1974

Painted aluminium

106.5 × 106.5 × 106.5 cm [42 × 42 × 42 in]

Collection, Minneapolis Institute of Arts

LeWitt began making cube-based open structures in 1965, first constructed in painted wood and then, in a rejection of their handmade quality, in industrially fabricated metal. In the work described by the schematic drawing above, variations of open cubes are laid out on the floor and the related two-dimensional drawings of them are hung in frames on the walls. The drawings and the sculptures thus become interdependent parts of the total installation. The variations follow the sequence: 3 drawings of 3 sides of a cube, 5 of 4 sides, 14 of 5 sides, 24 of 6 sides, 32 of 7 sides, 25 of 8 sides, 13 of 9 sides, 5 of 10 and 1 of 11 sides, totalling 122 incomplete open cubes.

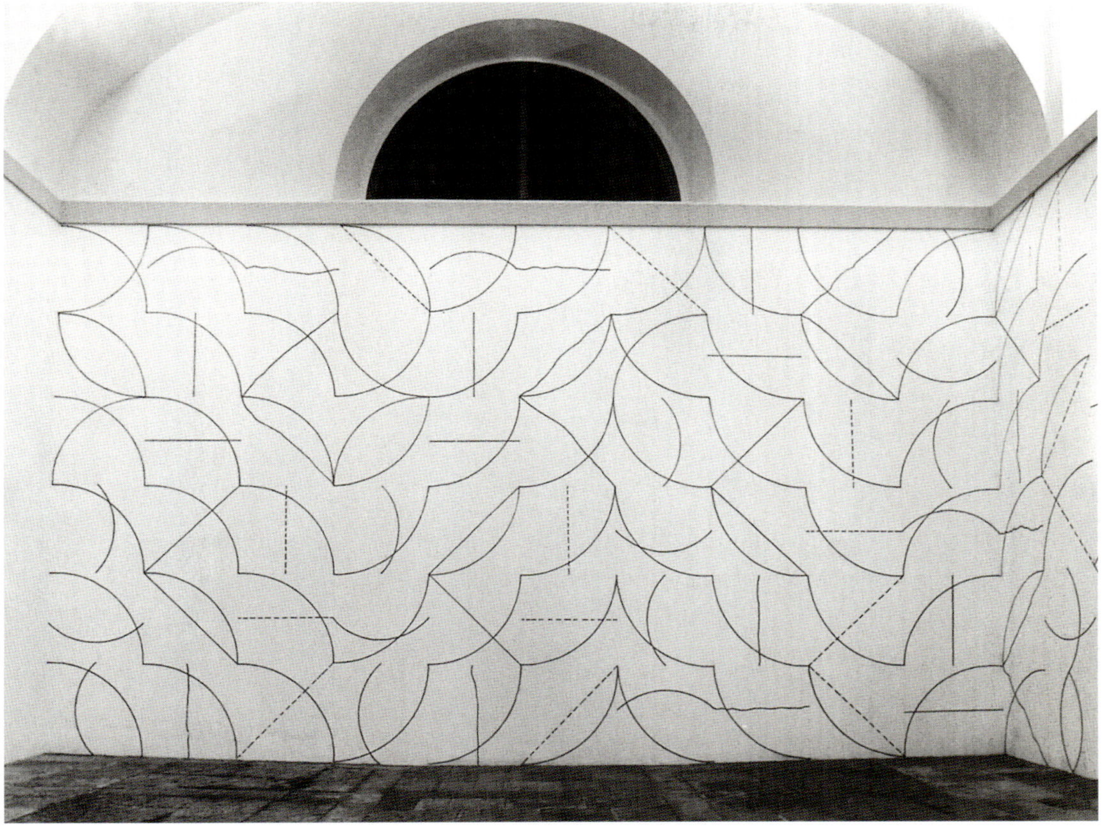

Sol LEWITT
Wall Drawing No. 146
All two-part combinations of blue arcs from corners and sides, and blue straight, not straight and broken lines
1972
Blue crayon
Dimensions variable
Installation, Panza di Biumo Collection, Varese
Collection, Solomon R. Guggenheim Museum, New York

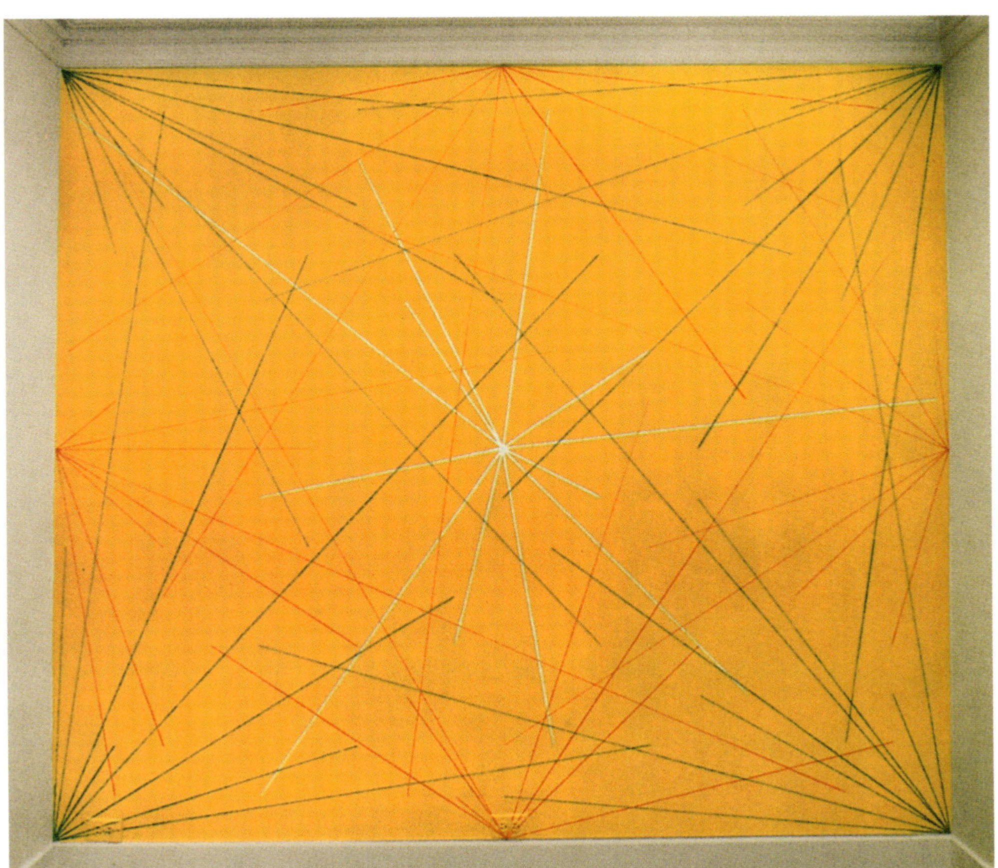

Sol LEWITT
Wall Drawing No. 280
A six-inch (15 cm) grid covering a yellow wall. Blue lines from the four corners, red lines from the midpoints of the four sides, white lines from the centre to points on the grid
1976
Red, blue and white crayon, black pencil grid, yellow wall
Dimensions variable
First installation, Hallwalls, Buffalo, New York

From 1968 LeWitt devised a system of drawing, applied directly onto walls and executed by others, following a set of instructions. 'An ink drawing on paper accompanies the wall drawing. It is rendered by the artist while the wall drawing is rendered by assistants. The ink drawing is a plan for but not a reproduction of the wall drawing; the wall drawing is not a reproduction of the ink drawing. Each is equally important.' – Sol LeWitt, 'Wall Drawings', *Sol LeWitt*, New York, 1978

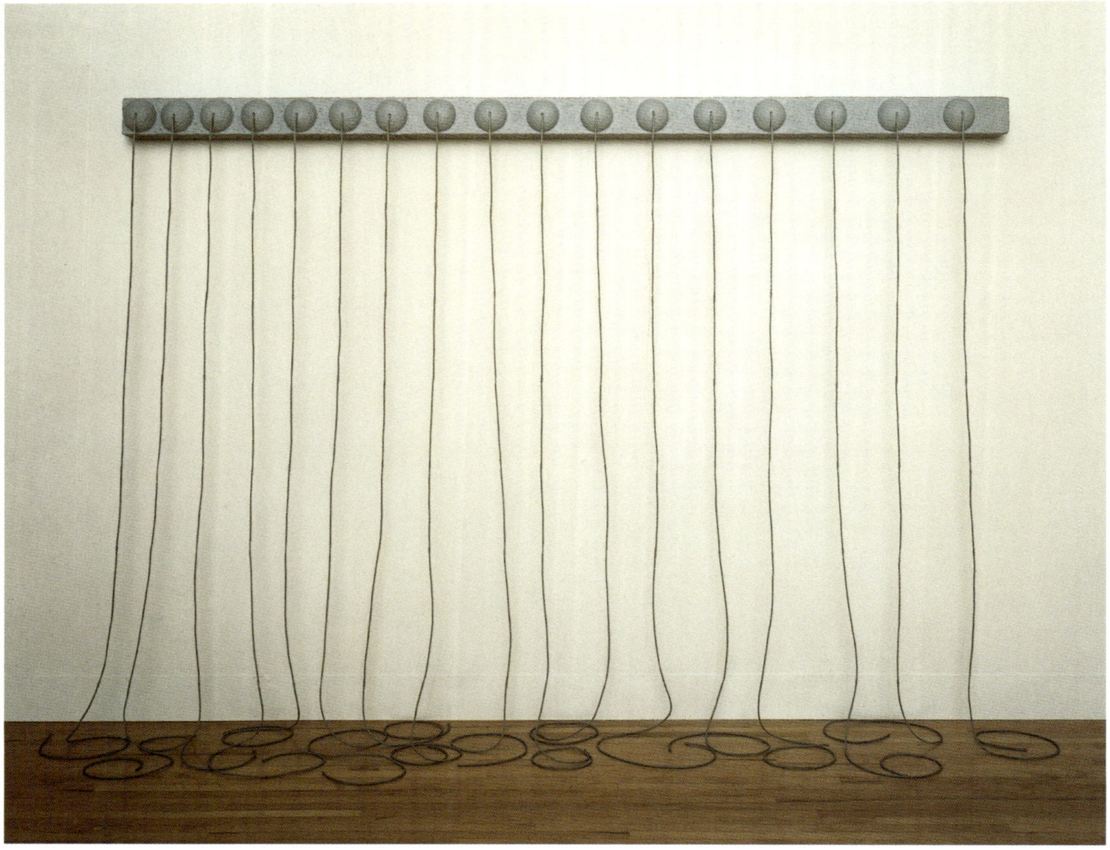

above

Eva HESSE

Addendum

1967

Papier mâché, wood, cord

Wood, 12.4 × 303 × 12.4 cm [5 × 119 × 5 in]

This work was exhibited in 'Art in Series', at Finch College, New York, in 1967. It consists of a horizontal row of unevenly spaced domes, from which long cords extend to the floor below. Although the forms allude to body parts, Hesse carefully kept these organic referents ambiguous. By combining the seriality found in the work of the Minimal artists with soft and irregular materials, she developed a highly personal sculptural idiom. 'For me the great involvement is for a purpose – to arrive at an end – not that much of a thing in itself ... I am interested in finding out through working on the piece some of the potential and not the preconceived ... As you work, the piece itself can define or redefine the next step, or the next step combined with some vague idea.'

– Eva Hesse, interview with Cindy Nemser, *Artforum*, 9: 8, May 1970

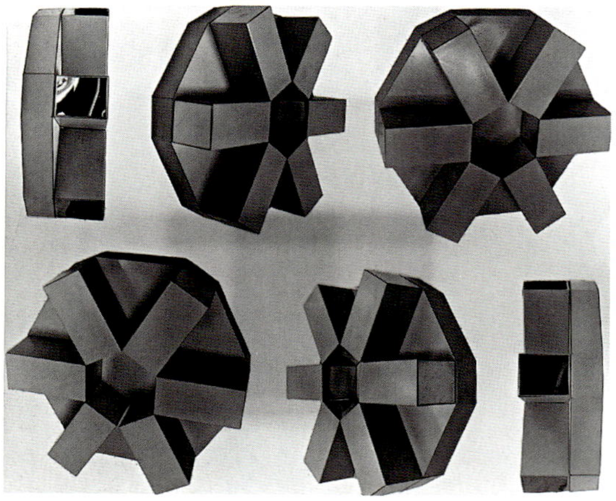

below left

Robert SMITHSON

The Cryosphere

1966

Painted steel with chrome inserts

6 units, 43 × 43 × 15 cm

[17 × 17 × 6 in] each

In a 1972 interview with Paul Cummings, Smithson linked this work's hexagonal units with ice crystals. Also hexagonal, they represent the lowest possible level of energy and can be regarded as water's entropic state. This association, combined with the sculptures' inert quality, conveys a 'degree zero' reduction of form and concept. This was reinforced by Smithson's text describing the work reproduced below, which may in itself be considered a conceptual work. It was first published in the catalogue for 'Primary Structures' at the Jewish Museum, New York, in 1966.

'THE CRYOSPHERE

BLOCK ENCODEMENT # 1

010010010010010010 × 12M = 72(1) + 144(0)

1. 010010010010010010 is the tentative sequence for the placement of the six solid hexagonal modules.

2. Each module has 12 mirror surfaces (12M).

3. 6 modules are visible.

4. 12 modules are invisible.

5. 72 mirror surfaces are visible.

6. 144 mirror surfaces are invisible.

7. $66^{2/3}$% of the entire work is invisible.

8. Invent your sight as you look. Allow your eyes to become an invention.

9. Colour by Krylon Inc.

Surf Green, No. 2002

Pigment ... 2.92%

Titanium Dioxide ... 100.00%

Tinting material less than ... 5.00%

Non-volatile (from vehicle) ... 9.08%

Cellulose Nitrate, Coconut Oil

Modified Alkyd, Phthalate Esters

Plasticizer, GL-358 Phenolic Resin

Penetrant

Volatile ... 48.00%

Ketones, Esters, Alcohols

Aromatic Hydrocarbons

Propellent ... 40.00%

Halogenated Hydrocarbons ... 100.00%

10. Phases of one module as photographed by Gretchen Lambert. Intervals of height measured in inches from the floor to camera aperture. (See phased-detail)

Clock position: 9 10 11 1 2 3

Height (inches): $61^{1/2}$ $55^{1/2}$ $39^{1/2}$ $39^{1/2}$ $55^{1/2}$ $61^{1/2}$.'

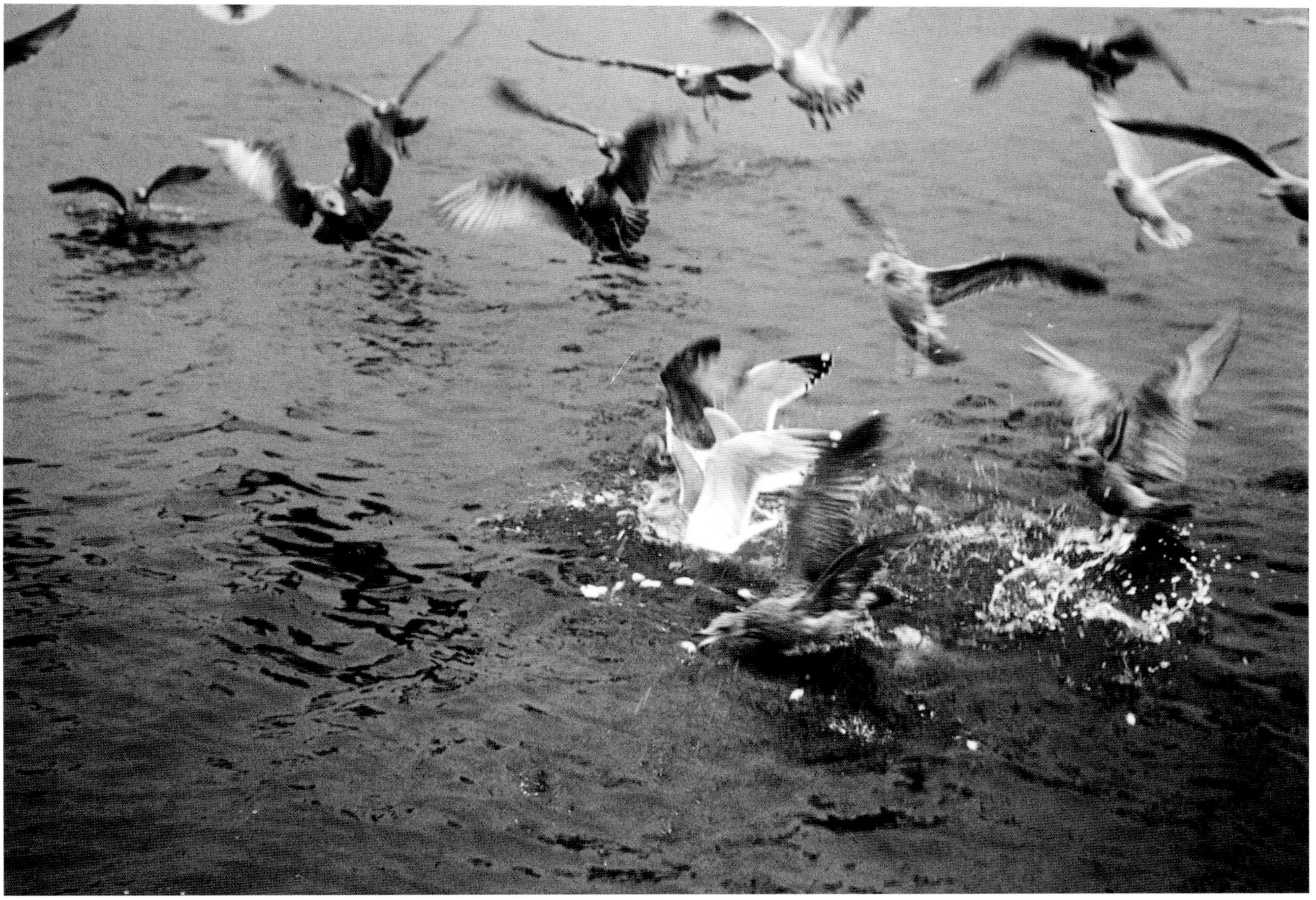

above
Hans HAACKE
Live Airborne System
1965/68
Black and white documentation photograph
Dimensions variable

right
Hans HAACKE
Condensation Cube
1963-65
Plexiglas cube, water, light
100 × 100 × 100 cm [39.5 × 39.5 × 39.5 in]

In the early 1960s Haacke became interested in the self-organizing properties of systems. As an alternative to creating finished products as the objective evidence of his artistic subjectivity, he sought a form of art that is in process, similar to the systems whereby natural elements, flora and fauna adapt to or transform their environments. *Live Airborne System* documents seagulls feeding on crumbs floating on the surface of water, its title drawing attention to this natural survival system. *Condensation Cube* is one of a series of Plexiglas cubes of various dimensions, partially filled with water and sealed. Light warms the interior, the water evaporates and condenses. 'The process of condensation does not end. The box has a constantly but slowly changing appearance which never repeats itself. The conditions are comparable to a living organism which reacts in a flexible manner to its surroundings. The image of condensation cannot be precisely predicted. It is changing freely, bound only by statistical limits.'
– Hans Haacke, Artist's statement, 1965

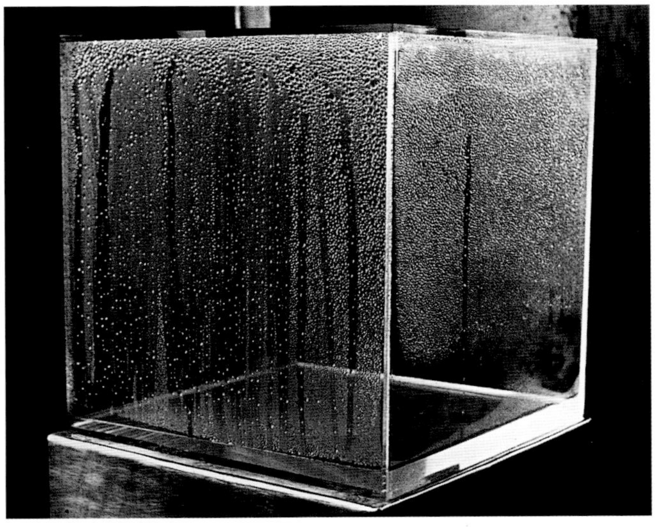

Mel BOCHNER
Working Drawings and Other Visible Things on Paper Not Necessarily Meant to be Viewed as Art
1966
4 identical looseleaf notebooks, each with 100 Xerox copies of studio notes, working drawings and diagrams collected and xeroxed by the artist, displayed on 4 sculpture stands
Installation view, The School of Visual Arts Gallery, New York

As a teacher at the School of Visual Arts in New York Bochner was invited to organize a Christmas show of drawings. He approached fellow artists including Andre, Flavin, Hesse, Judd, LeWitt, and asked them for drawings that weren't necesarily 'works of art'. Due to lack of funds, it was not possible either to frame or photograph the works, so Bochner made photocopies. He collated these in four identical A4 notebooks, displayed on standard white plinths. In addition to the drawings, each book included diverse printed ephemera from 'non-art' sources. The pages were arranged alphabetically. On the final page was an assembly diagram of the Xerox machine used. This was the first 'Xeroxbook', which emphasized the creative process over its results. It blurred the distinction between curator and artist and gave rise to a kind of work which could (at least hypothetically) be endlessly replicated.

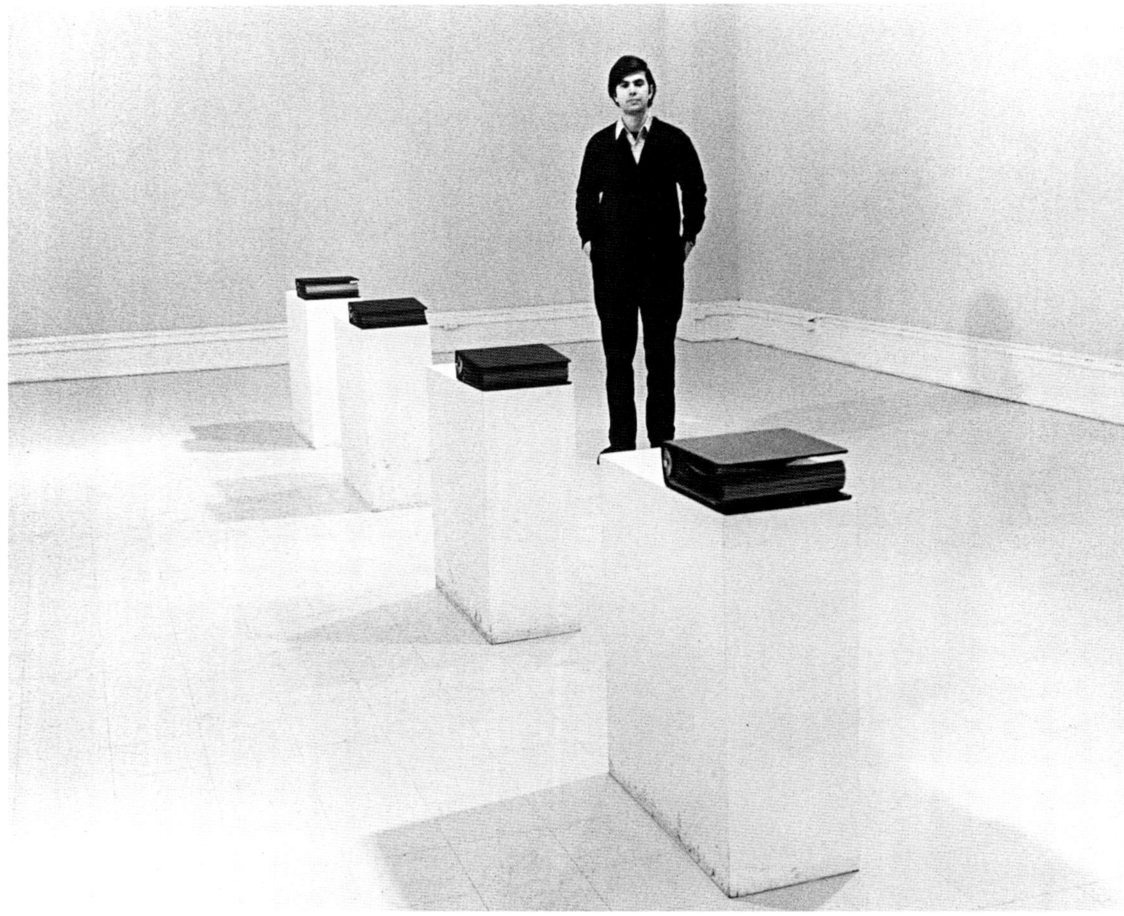

Mel BOCHNER
Measurement Room
1969
Tape and Letraset on wall
Dimensions variable
Collection, The Museum of Modern Art, New York

Bochner first created this work at Galerie Heiner Friedrich, Munich, where it was titled *Measurement: Room*. He marked each of the lengths of the architectural features of the room (wall surfaces, windows, doors) with a line of tape bisected by the notation (in feet and inches) of its exact measurement. He used Letraset to denote the figures. The lines of tape were always placed close to another line marking their referent: for example, the horizontal lines marking the width of the wall ran as a line, continuous between wall planes, a few inches from the floor; the measurements of the vertical height of the door and the distance from its moulding to the ceiling were traced beside it. No measurements were repeated. Bochner's measurements made visible the geometric existence of the room: 'When I measure a room, it objectifies the emptiness of the space. The measurements project a mental construct of the space onto the space itself.' Much of Bochner's subsequent work has been concerned with the application of the principles of logic and mathematics to the physical world, emphasizing incongruities.
– quotation from the artist, *Mel Bochner: Thought Made Visible 1966–1973*, 1995

Mel BOCHNER

Axiom of Indifference [details]

1973

Masking tape, coins, text

Dimensions variable

First shown at the Sonnabend Gallery, New York, this work comprises eight squares made by masking tape on the floor, four on each side of a wall dividing two rooms. Three coins lie on the floor in relation to each square. There are two configurations: one square directly above the other and one square diagonally touching another. Handwritten text denotes the coins' variable placement in relation to the squares: some; all; in; out. Four statements, 'some are in', 'some are out', etc., appear on the four squares directly next to the wall, the primary level. At the secondary level, on the four squares further away from the wall, Bochner has used 'not in' and 'not out' to add another level of variation which contradicts the first level by substituting it with its opposite, on the other side of the wall. All the statements containing the word 'out' are on one side of the wall; all those containing the word 'in' are on the other. On the 'out' side the coins are 'heads' up; on the 'in' side they are 'tails' up. The logic of propositions expressed in language and mathematics is thus brought into a subtle critical relationship with their physical realization.

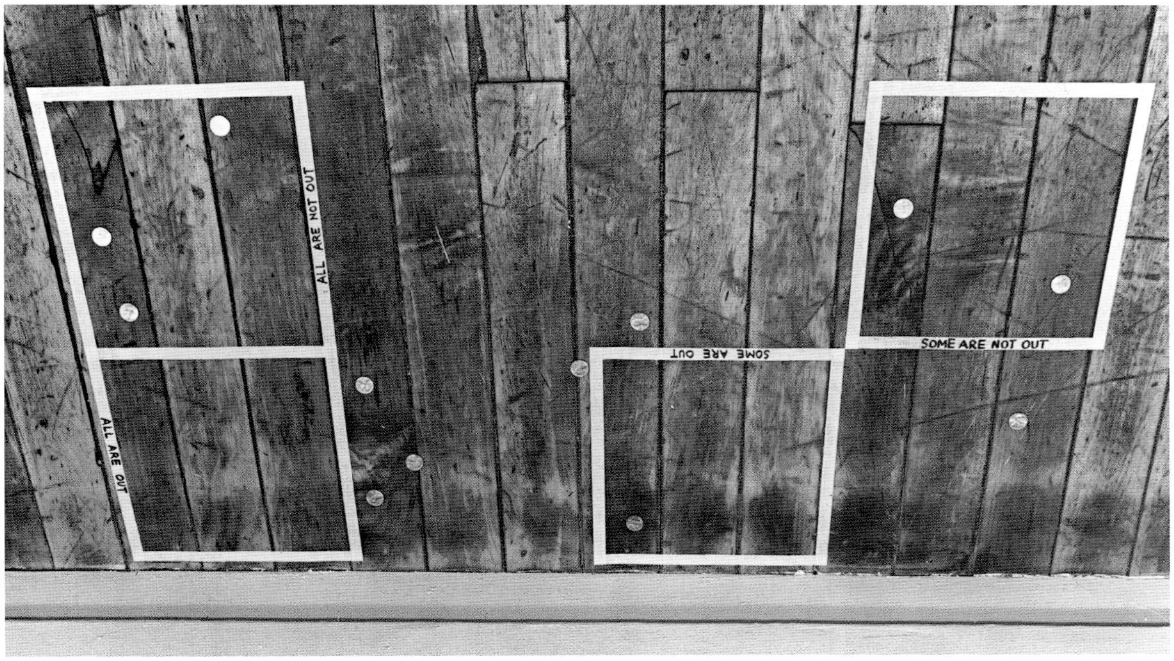

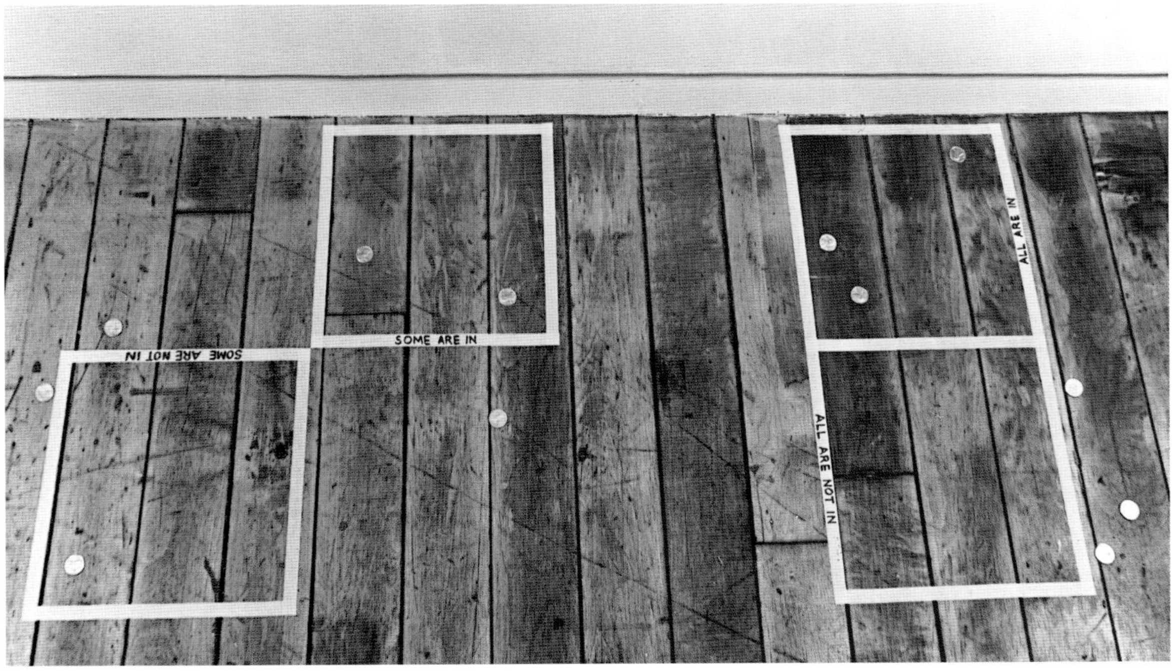

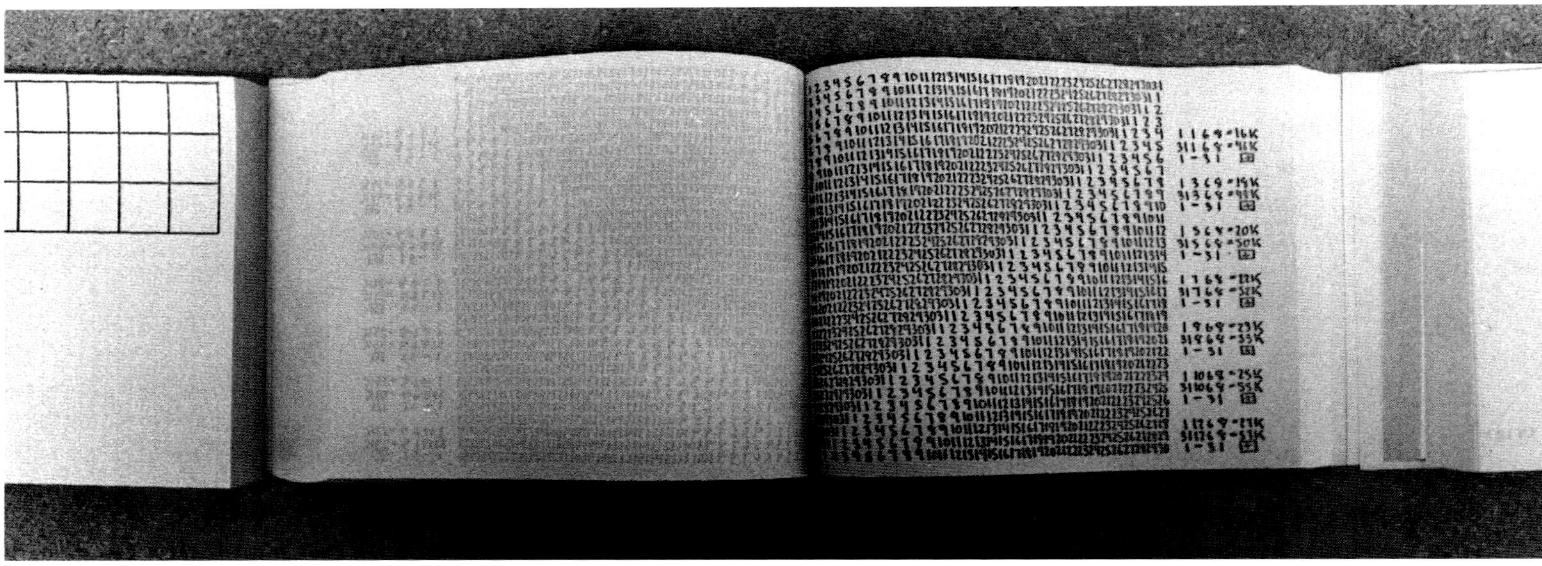

Hanne DARBOVEN
1968 [detail]
1968
6 Xerox books of drawings
20.5 × 28 cm [8 × 11 in] each

'I only use numbers because it is a way of writing without describing.'
– Hanne Darboven, *Artforum*, 12: 2, October 1973

In the late 1960s Darboven began to create numerical sequences based on the four to six digits used to delineate the date in a standard Gregorian calendar (omitting the first two digits of the year). She has made many permutations following the system she derived by adding up the digits and then extrapolating them, resulting in countless combinations. She has worked both with numbers and, from the early 1970s, handwritten text in this systematized way, exhibiting her drawings in forms varying from large wall installations to artist's books. The underlying schemes of Darboven's works are highly complex and their execution laborious and time consuming. Her concept of art fuses dedicated production time (art as 'work') with time demarcated as system and sequence. For Darboven, numbers provide a structure similar to that of a grid and permit endless continuation while remaining rooted in the reality of the everyday through their reference to calendar time.

Christine KOZLOV
271 Blank Sheets of Paper Corresponding to 271 Days of Concepts Rejected
1968
Paper
28 × 21.5 × 2.5 cm [11 × 8.5 × 1 in]

This is a one-inch high stack of sheets of standard size typing paper. Apart from the top page, which describes the work by stating its title, all the sheets are blank. By referring to rejected concepts this work alludes to the process of selection, vital to any artist's creative activities. It accords rejection/selection a status equal to representation. Employing typing paper, emblematic of text-based communication in an office environment, rather than a traditional artist's type of drawing paper, the work emphasizes processes of thinking over those of making. The annulment of representation, through negations of various kinds, was the principal theme of Kozlov's work for a decade from the mid 1960s onwards.

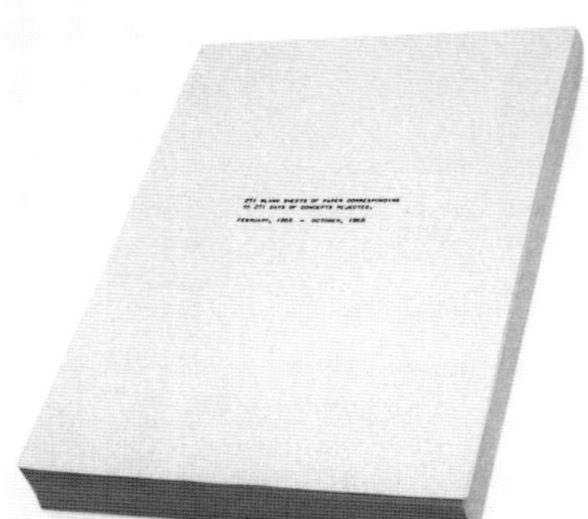

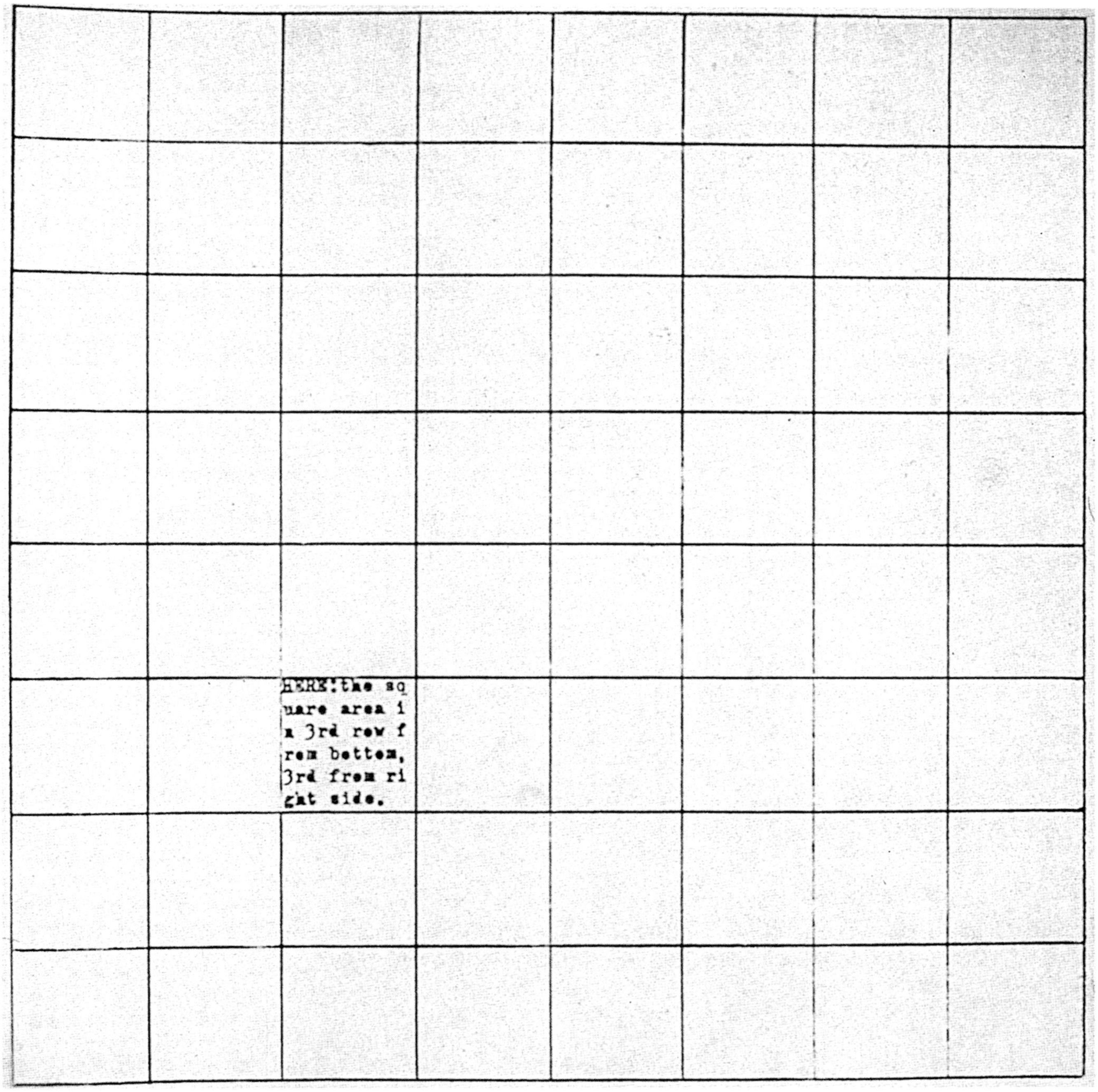

Adrian PIPER

Here and Now

1968

Artist's book folio with 60 loose leaves

20 × 20 × 1 cm [8 × 8 × 0.5 in]

Piper records that in 1968 she aligned her work closely with the principles formulated and demonstrated by Sol LeWitt in 1967. During 1968 and 1969 she made a series of works published in the format of a printed page or loose leaf, in many of which drawn grids were notated in written or numerical form with specific co-ordinates or references of various kinds. These works explored 'the construction of finite systems ... that serve to contain an idea within certain formal limits and to exhaust the possibilities of the idea set by those limits ... For me my early conceptual work succeeded in so far as it illuminated the contrast between abstract atemporality and the indexical, self-referential present.'

– Adrian Piper, 'On Conceptual Art', *Out of Order, Out of Sight, Volume I: Selected Writings in Meta-Art 1968–1992*, 1996

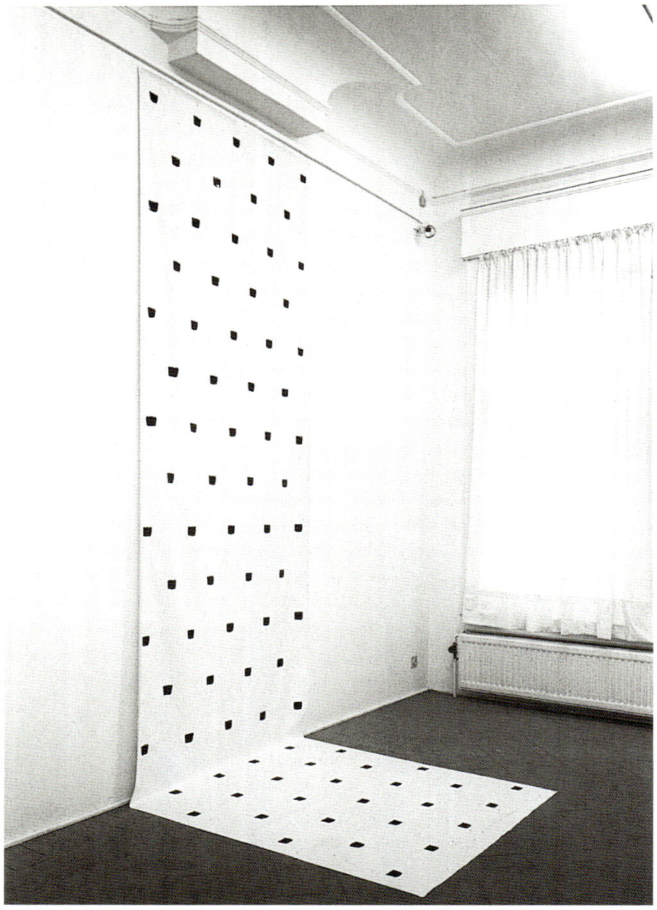

Niele TORONI

Imprints of no. 50 brush repeated at regular intervals of 30 cm

1966-67

Acrylic on canvas

Dimensions variable

Painting made for installation at Wide White Space, Antwerp, 1975

Conceived in 1966 and first publicly exhibited in 1967, Toroni's series of paintings, all of the same title, reduce the expressive faculties of painting to objective fact. They replace a focus on the materiality of painted surfaces – exemplified by abstract painting of the preceding generation – with a focus on the repetitive process itself of paint's application to a surface. Since 1967 Toroni has used the following statement to describe his working method:

On the given support a brush no. 50 is applied at regular distances 30cm
NB: support: canvas, cloth, paper, oil-cloth, wall ground . . . , generally white surfaces.
to apply: to place a thing upon another one so as to cover it and stick on it, or leave an imprint.
brush no. 50: flat paintbrush 50mm wide.

The paint is controlled by filling the brush with sufficient, but not excess, quantities of paint to avoid dripping but to ensure an adequate mark. No one imprint is more eye-catching than another, resulting in an effect similar to mechanically produced reproduction. Variation is achieved through the use of different coloured paints, different grounds as specified above, and larger or smaller areas covered.

Robert BARRY

4 Red Squares

1967

Acrylic on canvas

4 panels on white wall

152 × 152 cm [60 × 60 in] overall

From 1963 to 67 Barry made paintings which referred, increasingly as the series progressed, to spatial conditions that lie beyond the canvas itself. The untitled paintings shown at his first solo exhibition (Westerly Gallery, New York, 1964) were square monochromes in which the colour field was punctuated by regular small squares of unpainted canvas. The outer edges of the canvas were also left unpainted, and the installation of the works was described in the press release as an overall continuum. In 1966 he exhibited brightly coloured monochromes whose outer edges of unpainted canvas protruded several inches from the wall, negating the traditional dividing boundary between pictorial and architectural space. Subsequently, his small monochromes of 1967 were accompanied by specifications which related their placement to the entire wall of the space in which they are exhibited – such as one painting installed at the exact centre, or four paintings, each installed a specified distance from each corner. Barry then progressed by late 1967 to works which no longer required the presence of a canvas to delineate spatial relationships. He began to use string, and by 1968 was using invisible materials 'to produce energy, detect it, measure it and define its form'. (see page 82.)
– Robert Barry, in Arthur R. Rose, 'Four Interviews: with Barry, Huebler, Kosuth, Weiner', *Arts Magazine*, 43:4, February 1969

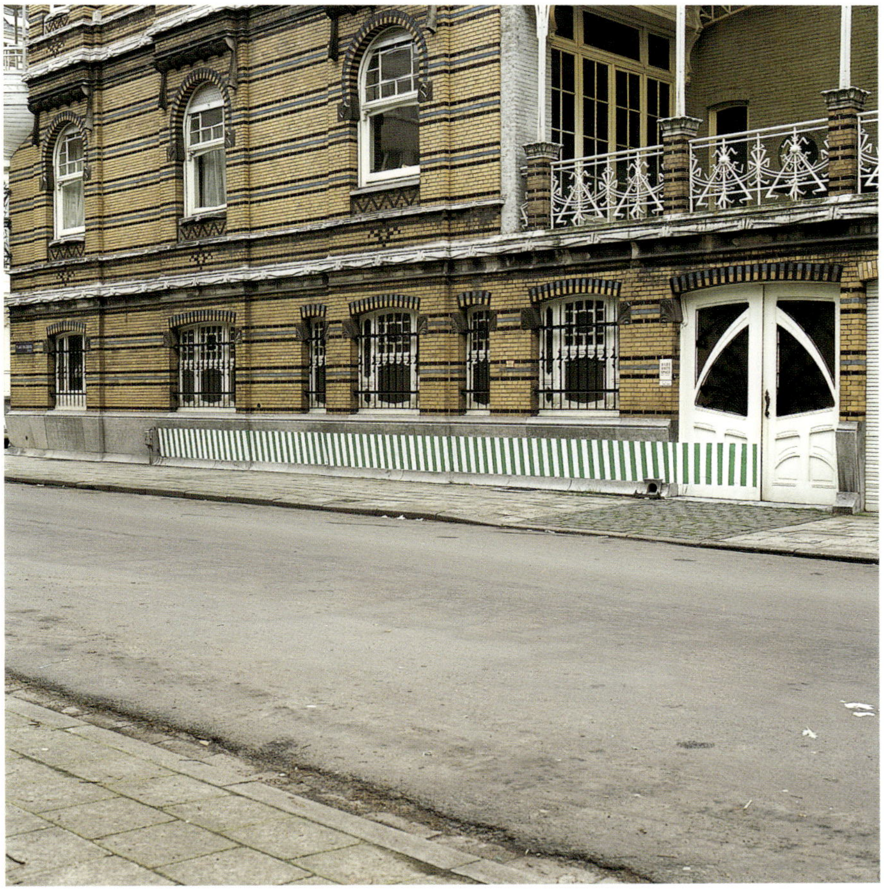

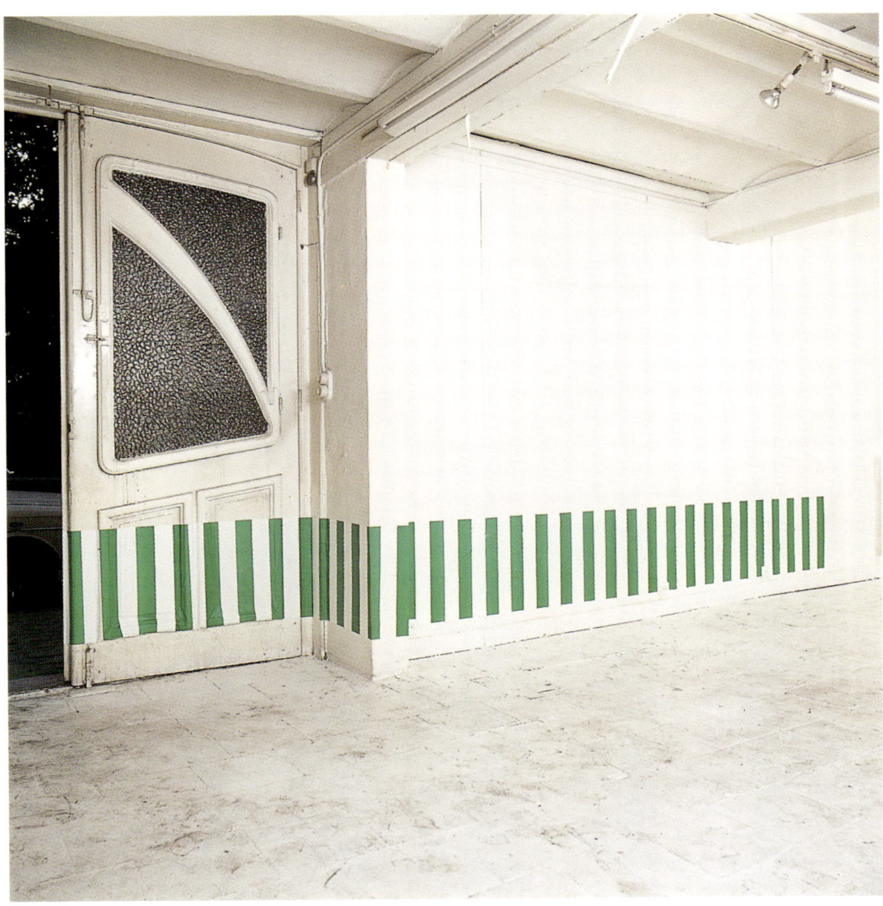

Daniel BUREN
Work in situ
1969
Paper with alternating green
and white vertical stripes each 8.7 cm wide
h. 52 cm [20.5 in]
Wide White Space, Antwerp

From 1967 onwards Buren's work took the form of: 'Vertically striped sheets of paper, the bands of which are 8.7 cms wide, alternate white and coloured … stuck over internal and external surfaces: walls, fences, display windows, etc; and/or cloth/canvas support, vertical stripes, white and coloured bands each 8.7 cms, the two ends covered with dull white paint.'
– Daniel Buren, 'Beware', 1969–70

In May 1968, as part of the 'Salon de Mai' at the Musée d'art moderne de la Ville de Paris, he adhered a rectangle of green and white striped paper, over 50 feet long and 15 feet high, to a wall in the galleries. He then hired two 'sandwich men' to wander the Paris streets with the same stripes displayed on their boards, thus linking and questioning the divide between art and non-art spaces.

The relationship between inside and outside of a given exhibition space was further explored in projects such as this work, repeated over several years at Wide White Space, Antwerp, in which the entrance door becomes the focal point for a convergence of stripes installed on the outside and inside of the building. In this case the striped paper installation was made from sections which were printed on the other side so that they also served as the invitation for the exhibition. For each installation (green, 1969; red, 1971; yellow, 1972; blue, 1973; brown, 1974) the colour was chosen by the gallery itself. 'The work starts on the outside of the gallery, at the very bottom (foundation wall) of the building, the only place where the paper can be affixed without any problems. The paper strips trace the outline of the entrance to the gallery, make their way inside and continue as far as the end of the gallery.'
– Daniel Buren, *Photos-Souvenirs, 1965–1988*, Institut d'Art Contemporain, Villeurbanne, 1988

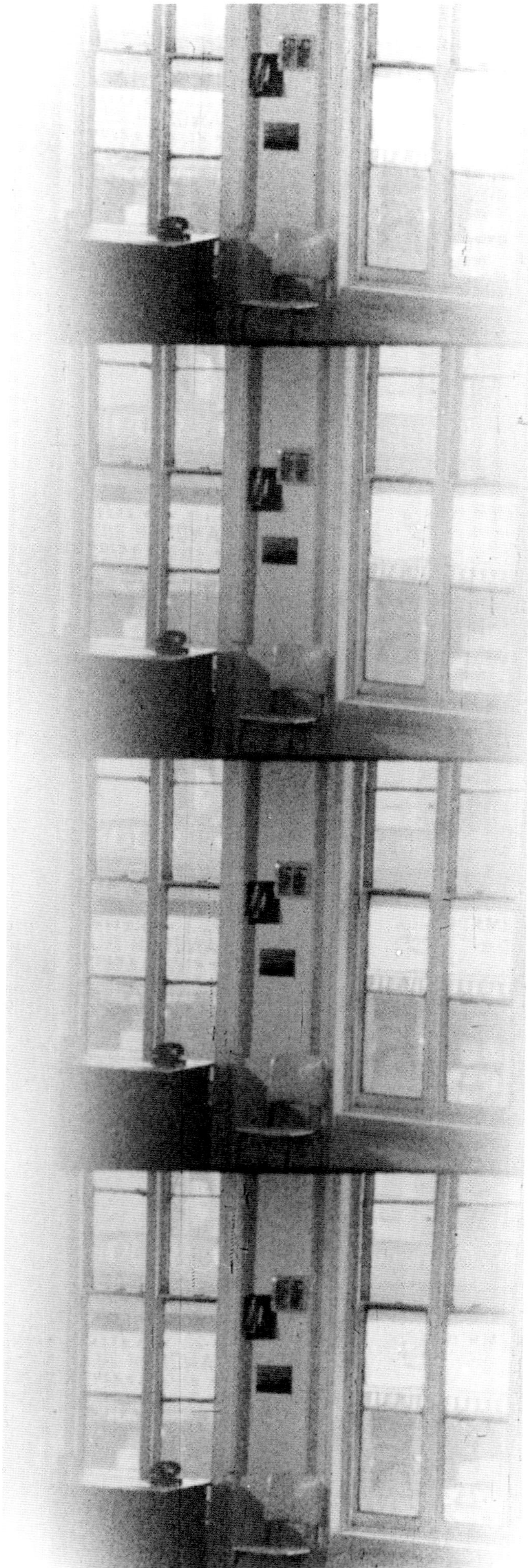

Michael SNOW
Wavelength
1966-67
16mm film
45 mins., colour, sound

The apparent structure of *Wavelength* is a 45-minute continuous forward zoom, the camera moving from a general view of a loft space finally to frame a photograph of the sea pinned to the wall of the loft. The sound track comprises a continuous sound wave rising from its lowest to its highest note (50 to 12,000 cycles per second). There are also sounds relating to the sparse action taking place in the room. Two men bring in and leave a bookcase. Two young women enter, drink coffee while listening to the radio and then leave. After indiscernible noises of broken glass or blows, a man (Snow's contemporary the filmmaker Hollis Frampton) appears and then collapses out of the frame. One of the young women comes in and speaks on the telephone, telling someone that she thinks the collapsed man is dead. The apparently continuous zoom is interrupted by the editor's splicing of the numerous rolls of 16mm film required, the insertion of various coloured filters, dramatic changes in lighting caused by the transition from day to night and back again and the transition between cameras of variable focal length accompanied by slight changes in axis and shifts in perpective. Flares at the end of the reels and double exposures have been deliberately included, resulting in a film which emphasizes its processes of making over its self-referential and inconclusive narrative content.

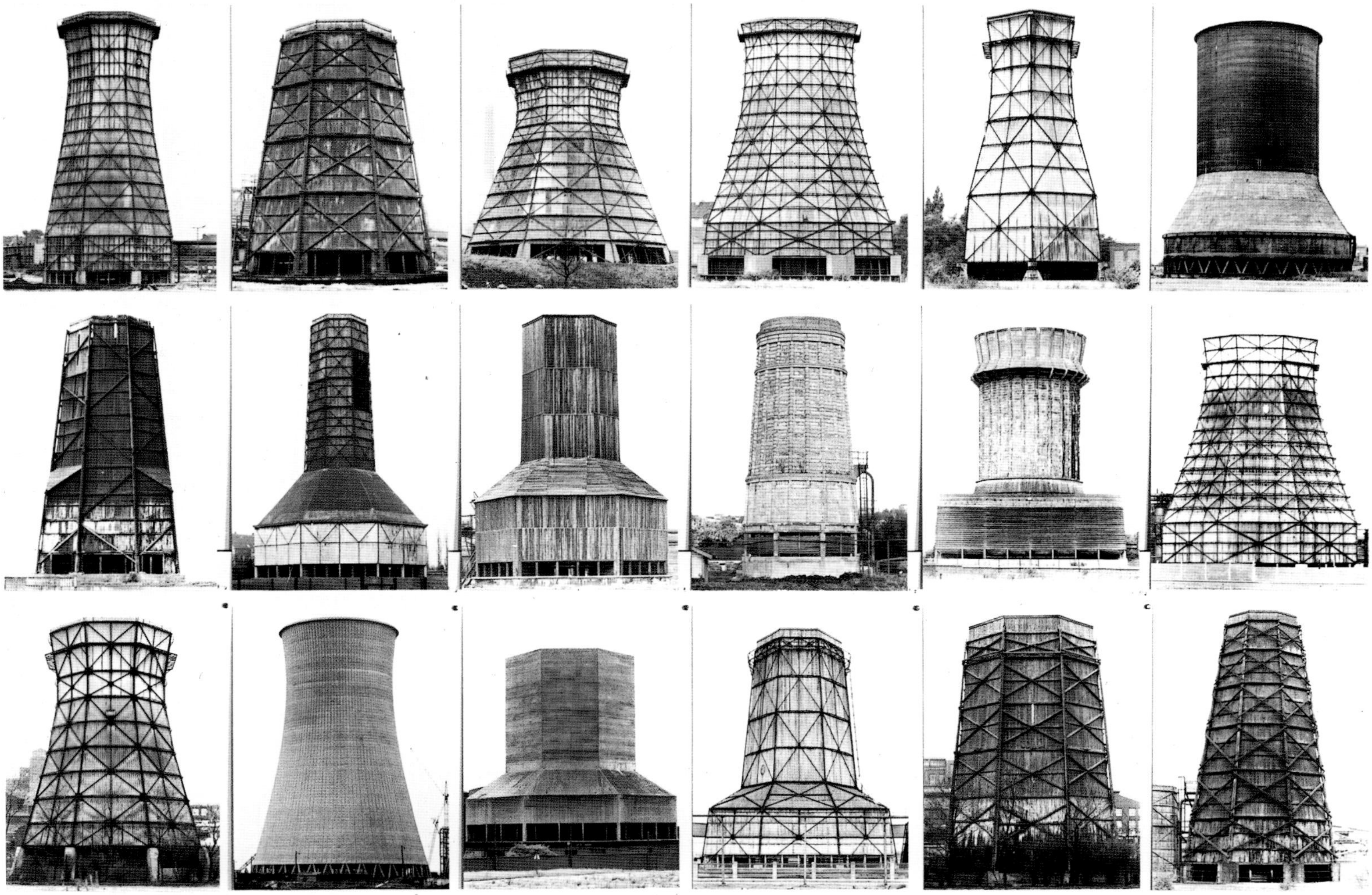

Bernd and Hilla BECHER

Anonymous Sculpture [detail]

1959-72

30 black and white photographs; text panel with reproduction

207.5 × 188.5 cm [81.5 × 74 in] overall

Collection, The Museum of Modern Art, New York

The Bechers began their collaboration in 1959. Photographs from their series, usually titled generically as 'Cooling Towers', 'Framework Houses' and so on were first exhibited internationally in the late 1960s. This group of thirty photographs of cooling towers was exhibited and also published in a book format under the title *Anonymous Sculpture*. This suggested that these buildings became 'readymades' through the act of photographing them, while also acknowledging the monumental achievement of the unrecorded workers who constructed them. The photographs were juxtaposed with a separate panel comprising a diagram and text describing the functioning of a typical cooling tower. The Bechers photograph mainly industrial or vernacular buildings, displaying them as groups of equally scaled, similar structures. To maintain as much objectivity as possible, the buildings are photographed in even light against a cloudless sky, with no human figures or other distracting elements.

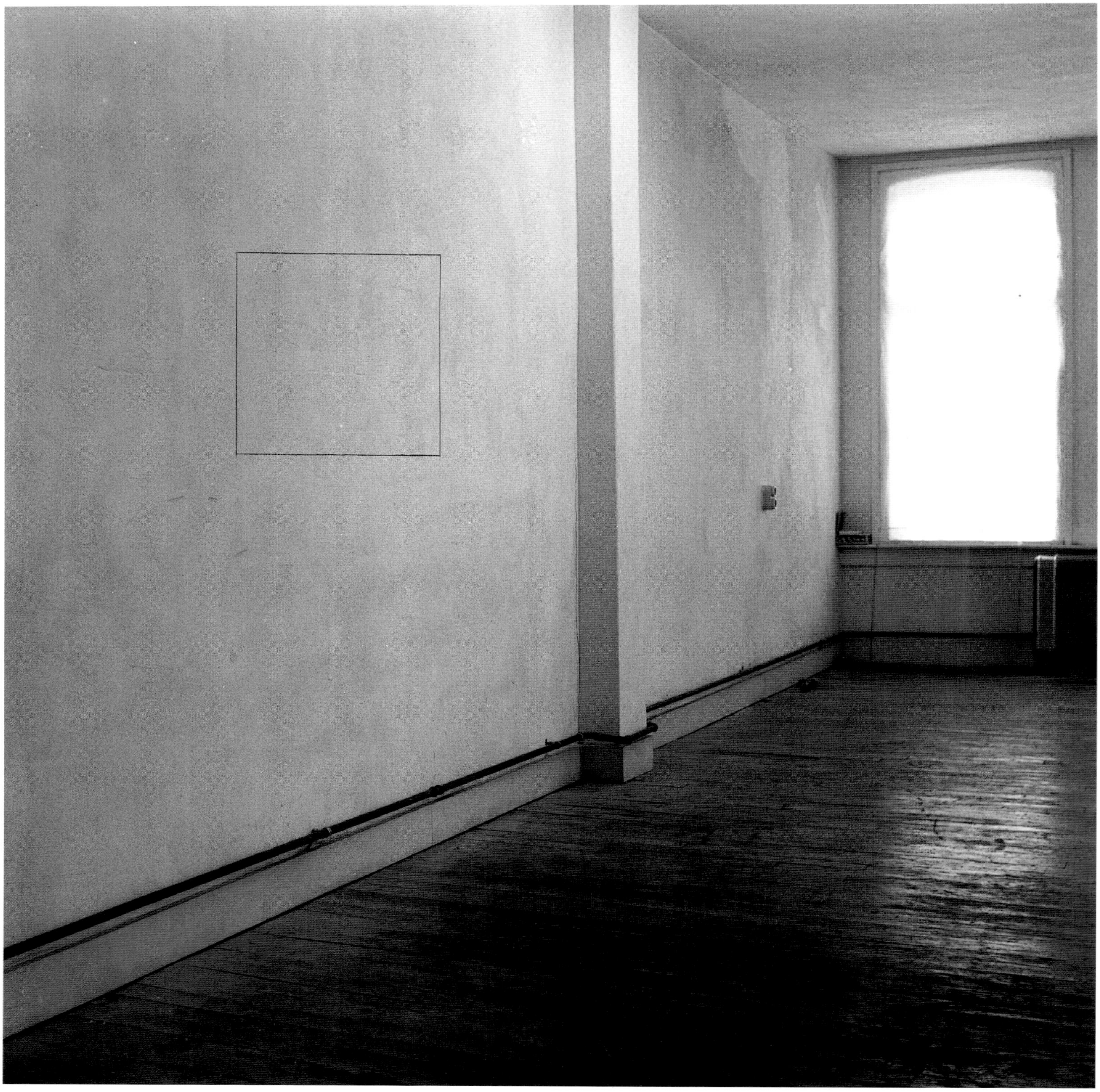

Jan DIBBETS

My Studio I, 1: Square on Wall [from Perspective Correction series]

1969

Black and white photograph on photographic canvas

110 × 110 cm [43 × 43 in]

Collection, Stedelijk Museum, Amsterdam

In this series of works produced in various sites, Dibbets used devices to negate the basis of our acceptance of perspectival illusion in pictorial representation. A geometric shape was either drawn or constructed by various means on site; however, the photographic documentation makes it appear as if this regular shape is not in the environment pictured, but superimposed upon it. It appears to be 'true' to the flatness of the picture plane. The 'correction' thus creates a further level of illusion which negates the original illusion of three-dimensionality.

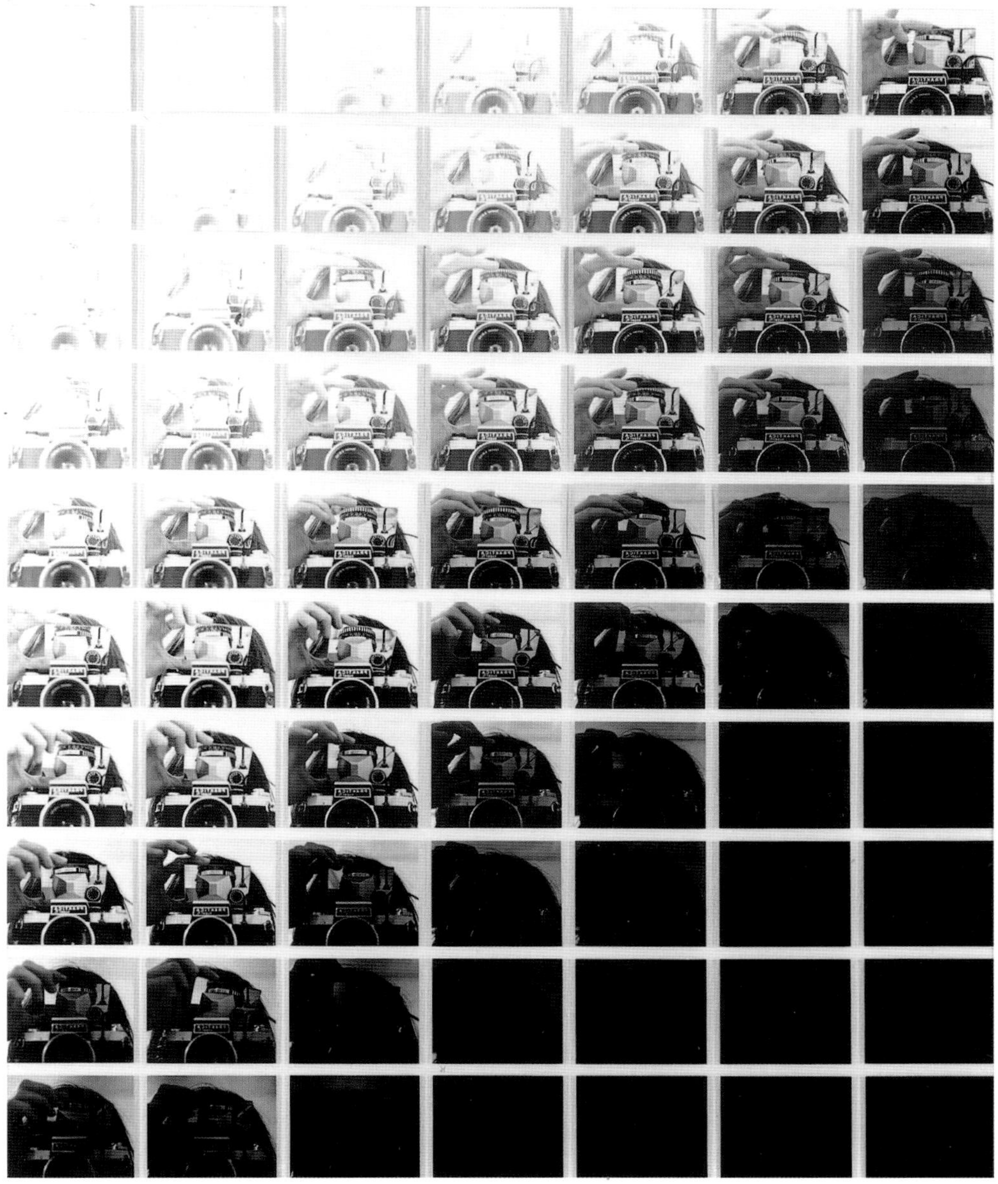

John HILLIARD

Camera Recording Its Own Condition [7 Apertures, 10 Speeds, 2 Mirrors]

1971

Black and white photographs on card mounted on Perspex

216 × 183 cm [85 × 72 in]

Collection, Tate Gallery, London

This self-reflexive work is described by its title. It comprises a series of seventy (7 × 10) versions of the same image of Hilliard taking a photograph of his camera. He uses two mirrors, the larger presenting a reversed image of its subject and the smaller reflecting, reversing and thereby making legible the camera's settings and controls. As the title indicates, the variations of settings structure the work as well as being recorded by it. The seventy photographs depict all the possible combinations of aperture size and shutter speed available in this particular camera, an East German manufactured Praktica. The exposures are 'correct' over a diagonal axis, where the camera's settings are legible reflected in the small mirror held above it. On either side of the diagonal axis, where the film is either over- or under-exposed, legibility becomes increasingly difficult and eventually impossible at the top left and bottom right corners of the grid.

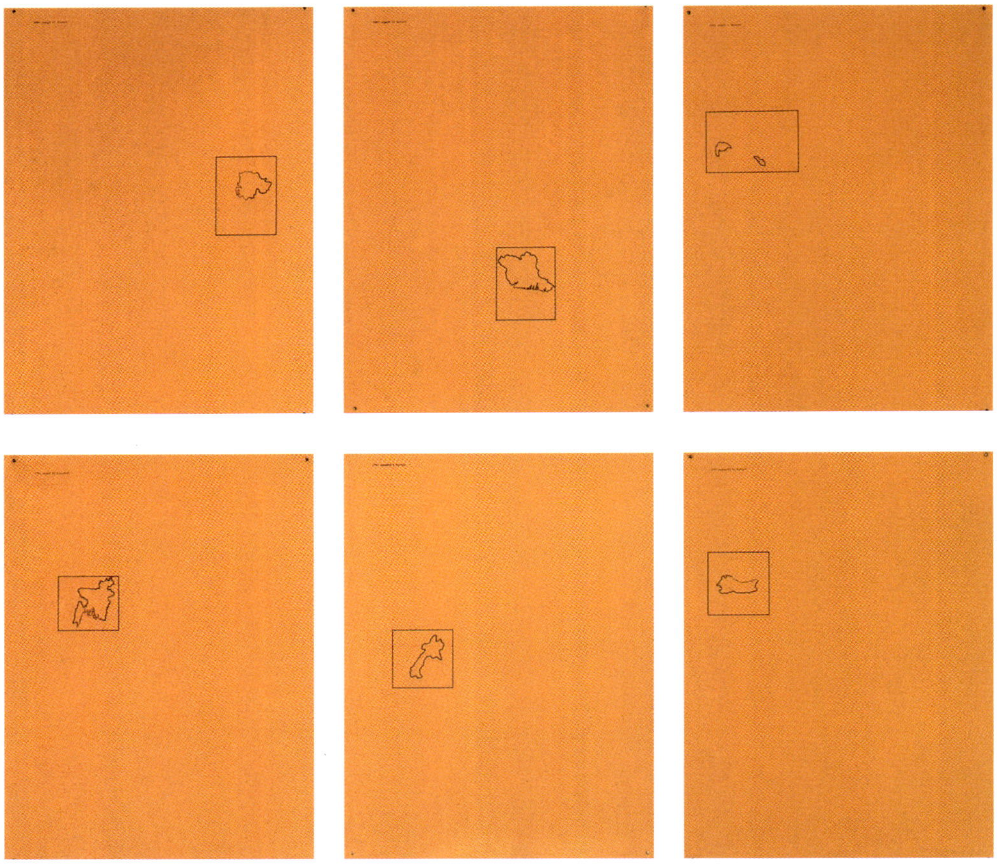

Alighiero BOETTI

Duodeci formi di giugno 1967 [Twelve forms from June 1967] [details]

1967–71

Etched copper

6 of the 12 panels, 59 × 43 cm [23 × 17 in] each

Initiated in 1967 but not completed until 1971, this is a series of twelve copper sheets, each etched with the shape of a political territory which was in a state of war on 10 June 1967. It anticipates themes Boetti explored in later works, such as political divisions of the world, mapping, tracing, classification and allowing works to develop over a number of years. For Boetti, dates of no significance in the present acquired retrospective significance: 'Do you know why dates are so important? Because if you write, say "1970" on a wall, it seems like nothing, absolutely nothing, but in thirty years' time … every day that passes makes the date more beautiful; time is doing the work, that's all that's working! Dates have this beauty: the more time passes, the more beautiful they become.'

– Alighiero Boetti, interview with Mirella Bandini, 1972

opposite

Zbigniew GOSTOMSKI

Fragment of the System [It Begins in Wroclow] [detail]

1970

Altered map and text on paper

Dimensions variable

A system of circles and diagonals was superimposed on a city map. A written schema, extracted below, describes three spatial constructions evolved from these symbols. Here composition is replaced by repetition of the symbols in a potentially infinite expansion in space and time. In the work of Gostomski and his Polish contemporaries such as Jaroslaw Koslowski, schemata and documentation interplay with spatial constructions to form a self-reflexive commentary on art's boundaries.

O / on the plan of the city, on its suburbs, and beyond its limits, covering an increasingly extensive space …

1. O – an element X in diameter, X in attitude

2. / – an element with dimensions X x X x X …

Realization of the O / must strictly follow the offered scheme, while the spots in which O / will exist must not be infringed upon. The spots where O, / or Ø, appear, are meaningless, and their form is expressionless …

The starting point for realization may be any place chosen out of those marked by an O, or /, or Ø on the plan.

When spots for O / are sorted out, any distance between elements may be accepted that would correspond fairly enough with distances stated on the plan. The distance, once it has been chosen, will be binding for the whole realization – it must not undergo a slightest modification … The initial working assumption determines the whole future action, for any and all whereabouts or situations as might emerge there for O / to exist …

The present work is conceived as steady and unending, developing uniformly in all directions, increasingly extending in space …

O /
It begins in Wroclaw.
It could be started anywhere.
It begins in a definite area,
but it need not end there.
It is potentially endless.
It is unchanging in its form,
but perpetually changing in its situation.

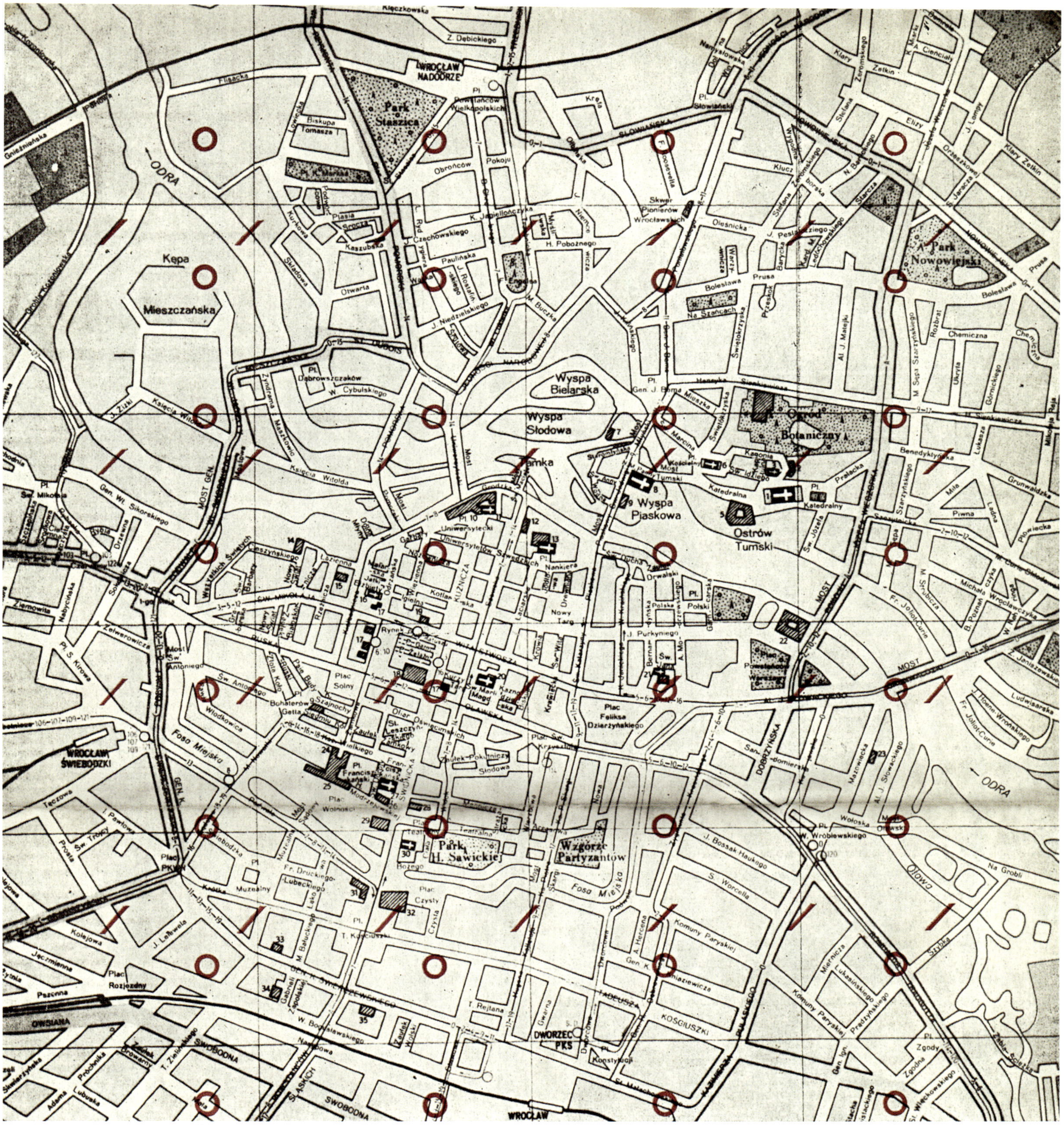

ODRA
Kępa
Mieszczańska
Park Staszica
WROCŁAW NADODRZE
Wyspa Bielarska
Wyspa Słodowa
Wyspa Piaskowa
Ostrów Tumski
Ogród Botaniczny
Park Nowowiejski
Park H. Sawickiej
Wzgórze Partyzantów
Plac Solny
Plac Feliksa Dzierżyńskiego
WROCŁAW ŚWIEBODZKI
DWORZEC PKS
WROCŁAW
Plac Rozjezdny
Plac PKWN
Plac Wolności
Plac Czysty
Fosa Miejska

WORD AND SIGN

Language can be seen as the 'signature' style of conceptual art. The late 1960s witnessed a proliferation of texts in art galleries and a breakdown of the distinction between spaces of exhibition and publication. The stencilled techniques of sign painting had acquired a growing currency in Pop art in the early 1960s. As the decade progressed, they were increasingly deployed in the service of a modernist reflexiveness about meaning in painting. This placed as much emphasis on the semantic content of the painted words as on their visual form. By 1967, for Mel Ramsden, Ian Burn and John Baldessari, a painting had become a site for linguistic statements, like a page. Conversely, the page became as legitimate a site for art as the canvas, the plinth or the gallery wall. In 1968, Seth Siegelaub curated an exhibition in the form of a photocopied book, the 'Xeroxbook', and Lawrence Weiner published his famous 'Statements' in book form. Meanwhile, Joseph Kosuth was developing the theory that all art functions analogously to a certain type of linguistic proposition – that works of art are 'propositions as to art's nature'. For others, such as Robert Smithson and the British group Art & Language, language was the site of new problems for art, as well as a model for understanding it. More generally, language became one more means in a newly unlimited conception of artistic materials.

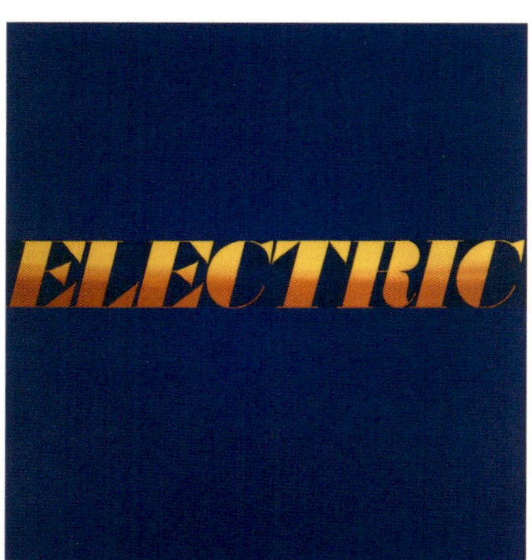

Edward RUSCHA
Electric
1963
Oil on canvas
183 × 170 cm [72 × 67 in]
Collection, Albright-Knox Art Gallery, Buffalo

In the early 1960s Ruscha made a series of paintings which explored the possibility of language standing in for the representational properties of visual imagery. Each work is centred on a single painted word, denoting the subject matter. Stylistically derived from the lettering found on hand-painted signs, in printed advertising or on product labels, the text as a painted image replaces the particulars of visual realism and individual expression with a sign that floats, unanchored to a specific context.

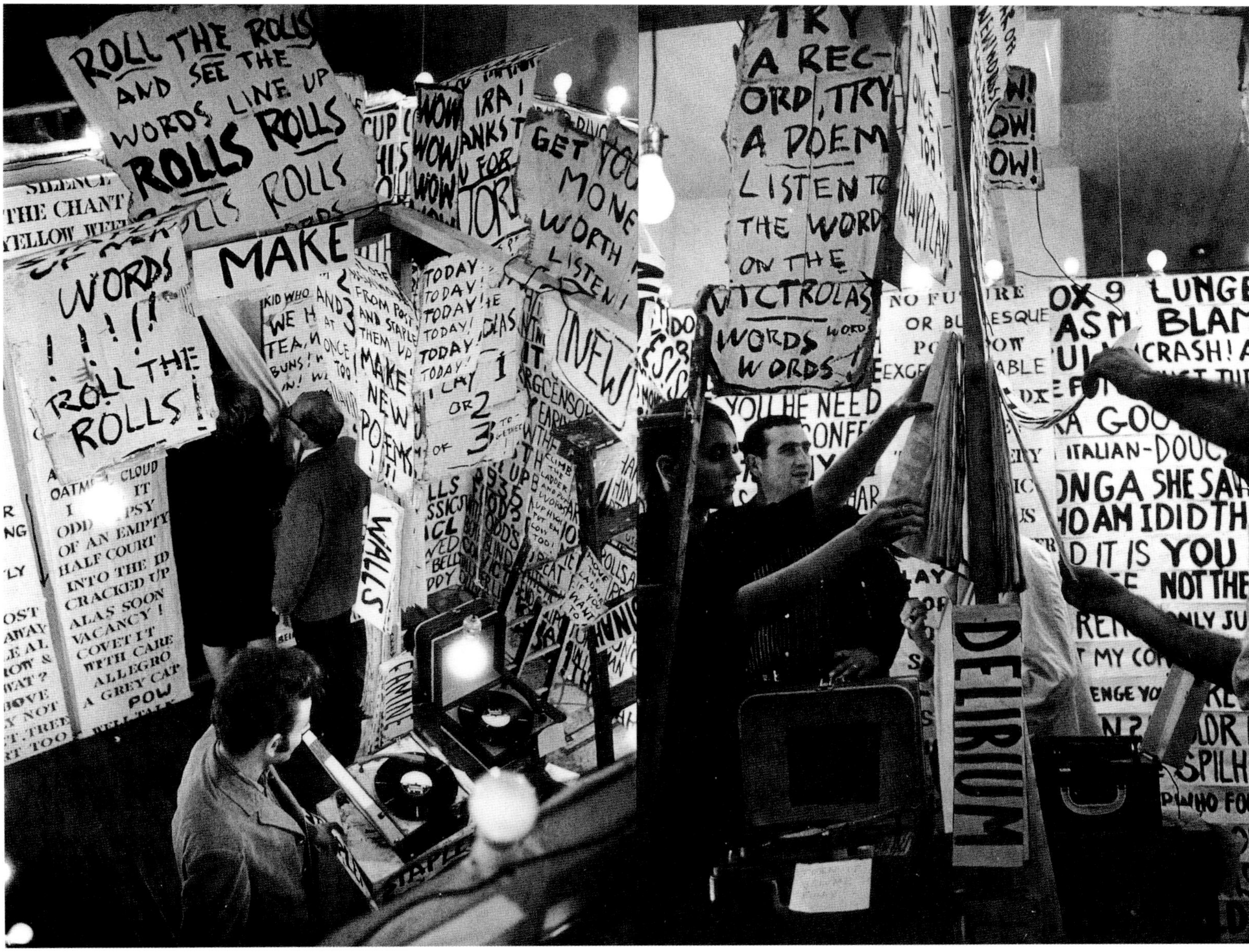

Allan KAPROW

Words [detail]

1961

Rearrangeable environment with lights and sound

Dimensions variable

Installation view, Smolin Gallery, New York, 1962

At the beginning of the 1960s Kaprow began to experiment with environments as an expansion of his assemblages which in turn had evolved from painting. The environments filled an entire gallery space, forcing the viewer to encounter the work physically and to interact with it. *Words* departed from the traditional stasis of the artwork in several ways, being a 'rearrangeable' environment which used lights and the sounds of records playing in addition to its central feature, banners covered in hand painted words, some of which visitors were encouraged to 'roll' to make their own combinations of words. By presenting words as 'images' and inviting viewers to become active writers/artists in this environment, the work questioned existing distinctions between artist and audience on both a formal and a social level.

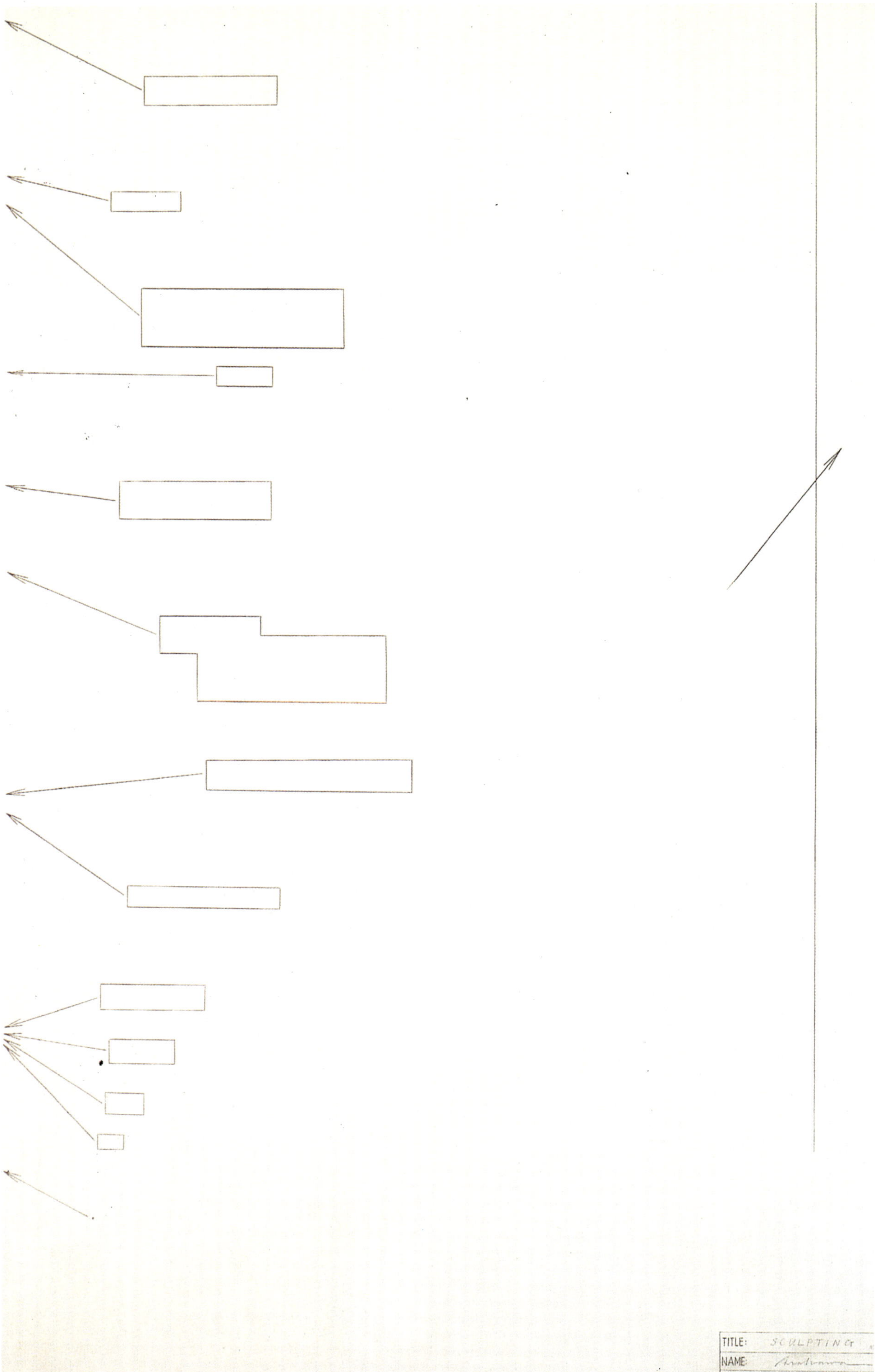

ARAKAWA

Sculpting No. 1

1961-62

Acrylic and pencil on canvas

183 × 122 cm [72 × 48 in]

'I have systematically tried to learn the true limitation of painting by staying within instead of exiting from the medium.'

– Arakawa, interview with Madeline Gins, *Flash Art*, 133, April 1987

This drawing belongs to an initial series of diagrammatic works in which Arakawa explored the potential of drawing and painting for the representation of mental process. Drawn in pencil, they consist of linear configurations and words on bare white canvas. The juxtaposition of graphic and linguisitic elements questions systems of perception. Arrows pointing to the edges of the canvas destabilize the notion of a unitary whole and suggest that the line and the rectangles in the drawing are destined to be removed. The drawing thus evokes a process of taking apart rather than construction, inverting the traditional notion of building up as implied by the word 'sculpting'. Instead of abandoning painting as Duchamp had, Arakawa aimed at constructing a new form of painting which could transcend materiality. His paintings operate as a stimulus to an invisible work completed in the mind of the viewer.

MATSUZAWA Yutaka

¥ Dead Body ¥ Remains

1964

Printed text on paper

38.5 × 26 cm [15 × 10 in]

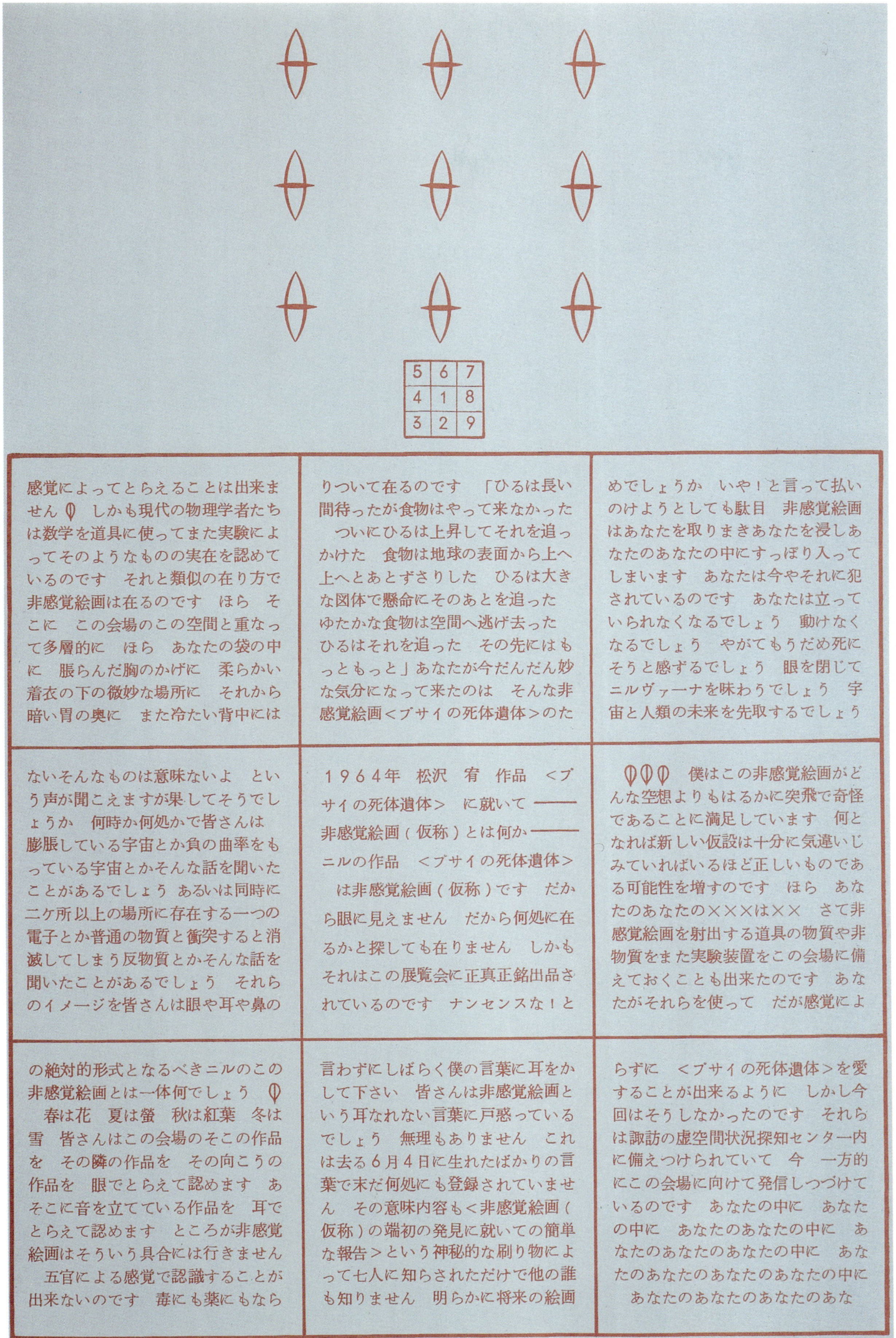

5	6	7
4	1	8
3	2	9

１９６４年　松沢　宥　作品　＜ブサイの死体遺体＞　に就いて――非感覚絵画（仮称）とは何か――ニルの作品　＜ブサイの死体遺体＞　は非感覚絵画（仮称）です　だから眼に見えません　だから何処に在るかと探しても在りません　しかもそれはこの展覧会に正真正銘出品されているのです　ナンセンスな！と

言わずにしばらく僕の言葉に耳をかして下さい　皆さんは非感覚絵画という耳なれない言葉に戸惑っているでしょう　無理もありません　これは去る６月４日に生れたばかりの言葉で未だ何処にも登録されていません　その意味内容も＜非感覚絵画（仮称）の端初の発見に就いての簡単な報告＞という神秘的な刷り物によって七人に知らされただけで他の誰も知りません　明らかに将来の絵画

の絶対的形式となるべきニルのこの非感覚絵画とは一体何でしょう
　春は花　夏は螢　秋は紅葉　冬は雪　皆さんはこの会場のそこの作品を　その隣の作品を　その向こうの作品を　眼でとらえて認めます　あそこに音を立てている作品を　耳でとらえて認めます　ところが非感覚絵画はそういう具合には行きません
　五官による感覚で認識することが出来ないのです　毒にも薬にもなら

ないそんなものは意味ないよ　という声が聞こえますが果してそうでしょうか　何時か何処かで皆さんは膨脹している宇宙とか負の曲率をもっている宇宙とかそんな話を聞いたことがあるでしょう　あるいは同時に二ケ所以上の場所に存在する一つの電子とか普通の物質と衝突すると消滅してしまう反物質とかそんな話を聞いたことがあるでしょう　それらのイメージを皆さんは眼や耳や鼻の

感覚によってとらえることは出来ません　しかも現代の物理学者たちは数学を道具に使ってまた実験によってそのようなものの実在を認めているのです　それと類似の在り方で非感覚絵画は在るのです　ほら　そこに　この会場のこの空間と重なって多層的に　ほら　あなたの袋の中に　脹らんだ胸のかげに　柔らかい着衣の下の微妙な場所に　それから暗い胃の奥に　また冷たい背中には

りついて在るのです　「ひるは長い間待ったが食物はやって来なかった
　ついにひるは上昇してそれを追っかけた　食物は地球の表面から上へ上へとあとずさりした　ひるは大きな図体で懸命にそのあとを追った　ゆたかな食物は空間へ逃げ去った　ひるはそれを追った　その先にはもっともっと」あなたが今だんだん妙な気分になって来たのは　そんな非感覚絵画＜ブサイの死体遺体＞のた

めでしょうか　いや！と言って払いのけようとしても駄目　非感覚絵画はあなたを取りまきあなたを浸しあなたのあなたの中にすっぽり入ってしまいます　あなたは今やそれに犯されているのです　あなたは立っていられなくなるでしょう　動けなくなるでしょう　やがてもうだめ死にそうと感ずるでしょう　眼を閉じてニルヴァーナを味わうでしょう　宇宙と人類の未来を先取するでしょう

　僕はこの非感覚絵画がどんな空想よりもはるかに突飛で奇怪であることに満足しています　何となれば新しい仮設は十分に気違いじみていればいるほど正しいものである可能性を増すのです　ほら　あなたのあなたの×××は××　さて非感覚絵画を射出する道具の物質や非物質をまた実験装置をこの会場に備えておくことも出来たのです　あなたがそれらを使って　だが感覚によ

らずに　＜ブサイの死体遺体＞を愛することが出来るように　しかし今回はそうしなかったのです　それらは諏訪の虚空間状況探知センター内に備えつけられていて　今　一方的にこの会場に向けて発信しつづけているのです　あなたの中に　あなたの中に　あなたのあなたの中に　あなたのあなたのあなたの中に　あなたのあなたのあなたのあなたの中に
　あなたのあなたのあなたのあな

¥ Dead Body ¥ Remains is a handbill of which 10,000 copies were printed by Matsuzawa and distributed in Japan. It states '*¥ Dead Body ¥ Remains* is a non-perceptual painting (tentative title). Therefore it is invisible' and reproduces three geometric diagrams, each divided into nine sections, simulating a Shingon mandala configuration. Shingon is a school of Japanese Buddhism embraced by Matsuzawa, which teaches the attainment of spiritual enlightenment through disciplines of body, speech and mind. By presenting printed words as art, inviting viewers to complete the work in their imagination, Matsuzawa brought the Shingon contemplative practice of visualization into Japanese avant-garde art practice. This work is considered by some to be the first manifestation of conceptual art in Japan.

Matsuzawa initially studied architecture in Japan but discarded this when he was introduced to the philosophy of religion while on a Fulbright Scholarship in the USA. In addition to his study of esoteric Buddhist teachings, other influences on his work include Symbolist and Surrealist poetry and theories of quantum physics. He established a 'Void Conditioning Monitoring Centre' in the mountains of Nagano Prefecture from which he disseminated his work by various means, such as postcards with the phrase 'The picture which is not seen and which cannot be seen'.

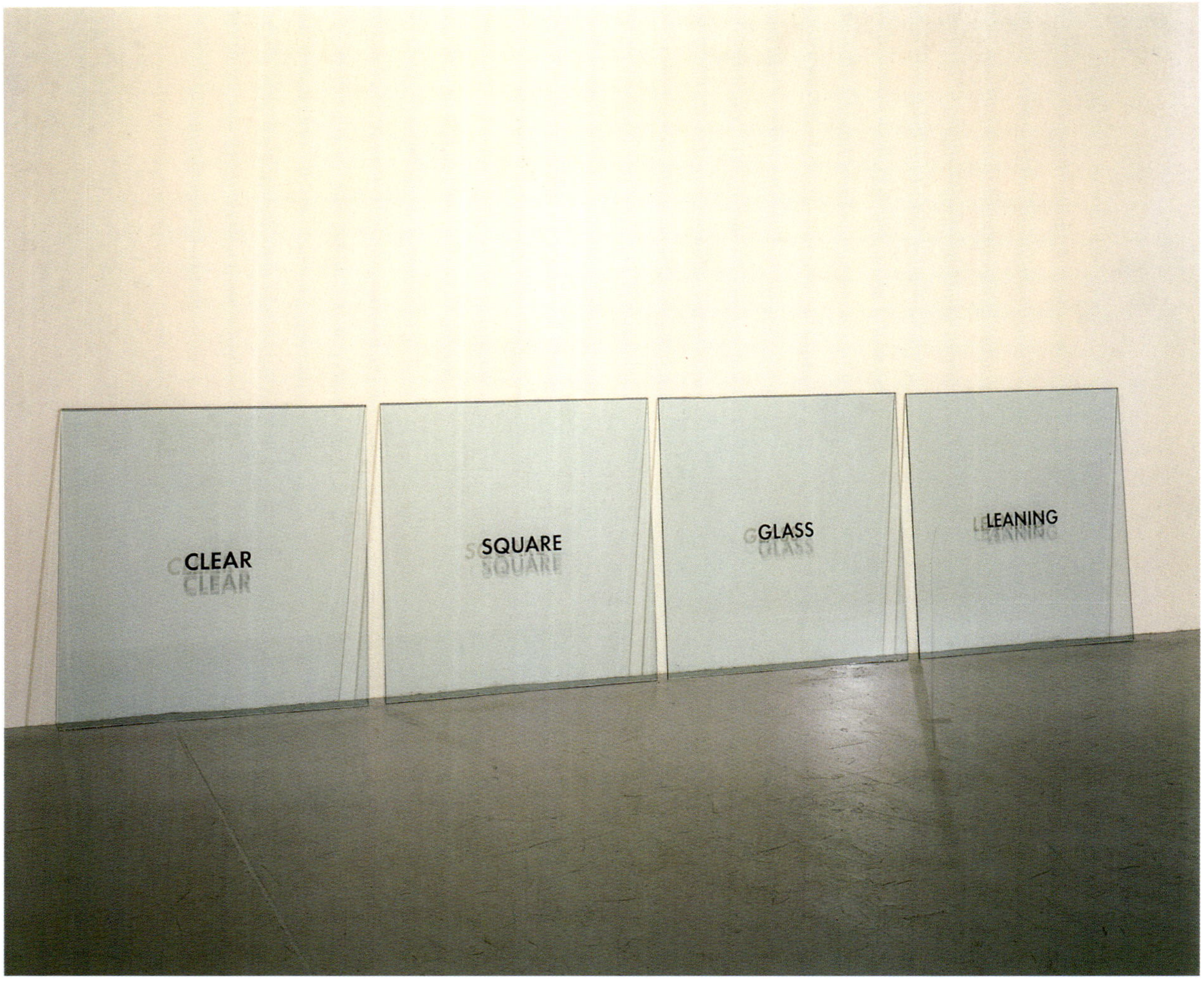

Joseph KOSUTH
Clear Square Glass Leaning
1965-67
4 glass plates, silkscreened text
91.5 × 91.5 cm [36 × 36 in] each

Kosuth had the idea of juxtaposing textual description with its physical reference in 1965. In *Clear Square Glass Leaning* each of the four words of the title is silkscreened on to one of four sheets of clear, square glass propped side by side against the wall. Reading the words and looking at the glass occur at the same time and produce the same meaning. The relationship between photography and written language as alternative forms of reference is the subject of the tripartite, retrospectively titled *Proto-Investigations* conceived in the same year, to which *One and Three Chairs* belongs. These present three versions of a utilitarian object – the physical object, a life-size photograph of it and an enlarged facsimile of its dictionary definition – placed alongside each other. The object, in this case a chair, is flanked by the two representations, emphasizing the conceptual relationships and disparities between it, its definition and its visual image.

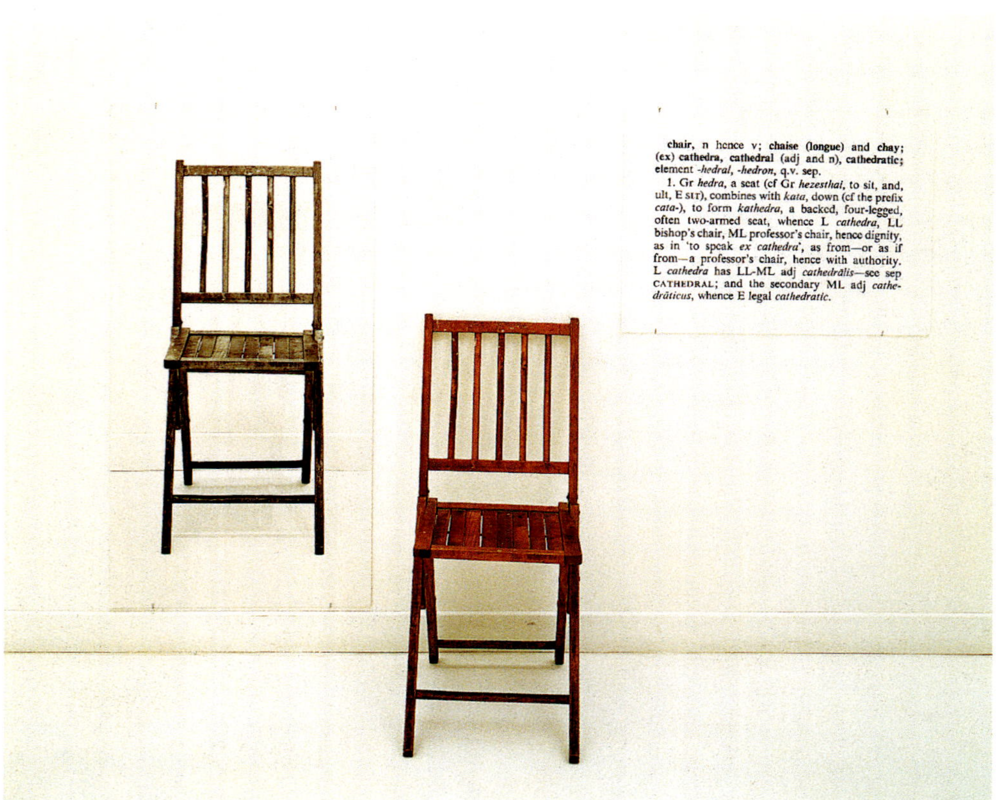

Joseph KOSUTH
One and Three Chairs
1965-67
Photograph of chair to scale, wooden folding chair, photographic enlargement of dictionary definition
Dimensions variable

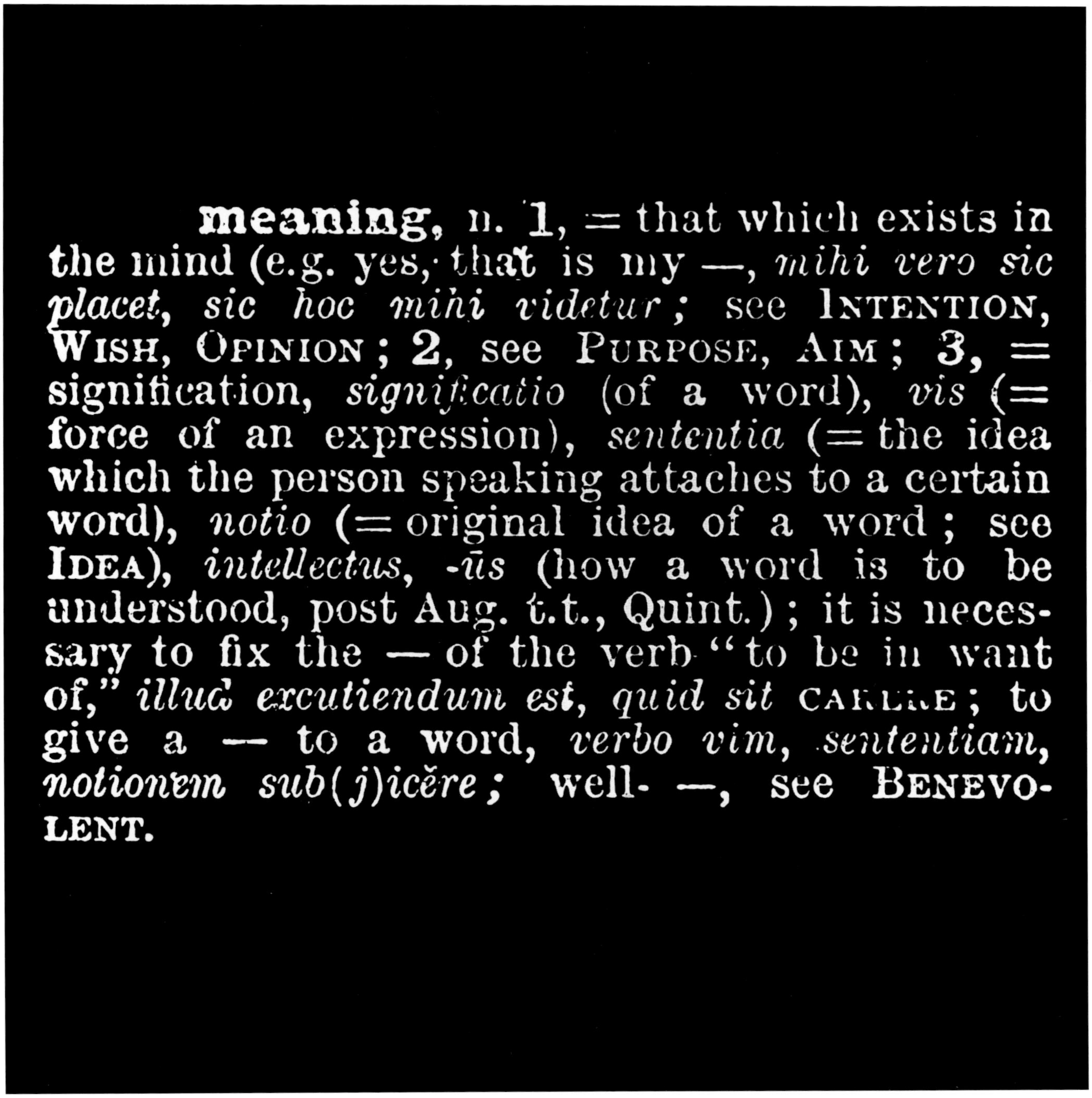

Joseph KOSUTH

Titled [Art as Idea (as Idea)] [meaning]

1967-68

Photographic enlargement of dictionary definition

Dimensions variable

Kosuth subtitled his *First Investigation* (1967-68) *Art as Idea as Idea*, with reference to a statement made by the artist Ad Reinhardt in 1962 that 'art is art-as-art and everything else is everything else'. With this series he discarded the physical object and its photographic representation and focused exclusively on language in the form of appropriated dictionary definitions of adjectival qualities and abstract nouns. Kosuth realized that the definitions alone were sufficient to supply the 'idea' of the idea which was his art practice: 'When I began to re-think my ideas of art, I had to re-think that thinking process, and it begins with the making process ... "Art as idea" was obvious; ideas or concepts as the work itself. But this is a reification – it's using the idea as an object, to function within the prevailing formalist ideology of art. The addition of the second part – "Art as Idea as Idea" – intended to suggest the real creative process, and the radical shift was in changing the idea of art itself.'
– Joseph Kosuth, *Art after Philosophy and After: Collected Writings, 1966–1990*, 1991

Joseph KOSUTH
The Eighth Investigation, Proposition 3 [A.A.I.A.I.]
1971
Installation with texts, table, chairs, clocks
Dimensions variable
Installation view, Leo Castelli Gallery, New York, 1971

Kosuth's *Eighth, Ninth* and *Tenth Investigations* evolved from the earlier *Information Room* (1970) – a room-sized installation comprising multi-disciplinary texts set on reading tables which the public were invited to peruse. *The Eighth Investigation, Proposition 3 (A.A.I.A.I.)* was first installed at the Leo Castelli Gallery, New York. Like the *Information Room* it offers reading material, bound in files, set out for the viewer's intellectual consumption. Here it is set on three sides of a square table around which clocks on the wall display different times. The texts are reproduced philosophical discussions about the expressive capacity of the written word. The clocks emphasize the passing of time – an ineliminable dimension, however it is measured or expressed.

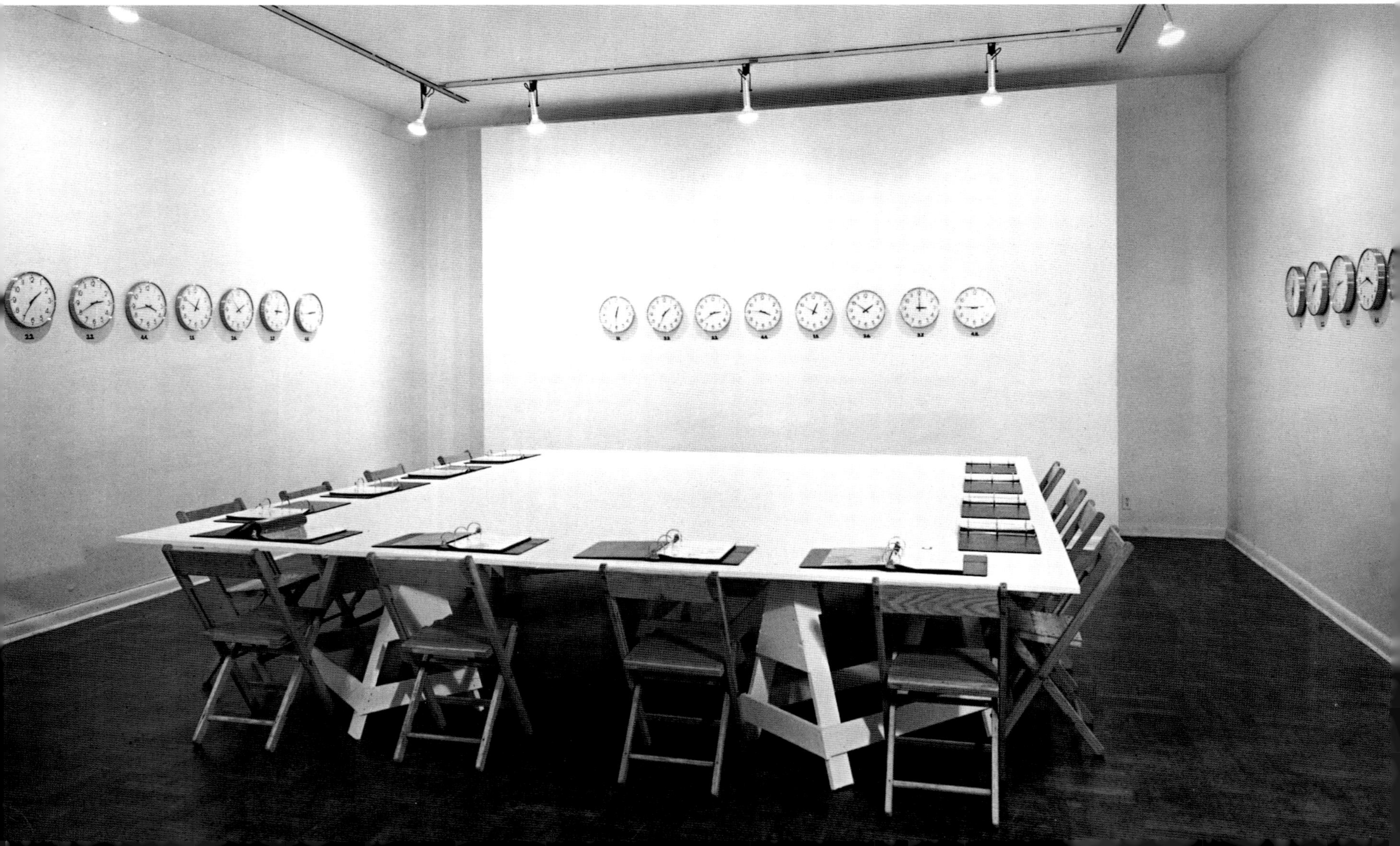

Air Show

The fog bank is a macroscopic aggregate. There is no theoretical primacy here for this macroscopic aspect. That is, its importance or unimportance is shown up by raising and answering internal questions to the framework.

There is no rhapsody here.

The macroscopic aggregate can be subjected to a micro-reductive examination. The horizontal dimensions of a 'column' of air, atmosphere, 'void' etc. can be indicated and established (for all 'external' and practical purposes) by a visible demarcation in terms of horizontal dimensions, axis, etc. This could be done in a number of ways: e.g. through the indication of some points of contiguity with other 'things', or through the computation of a particular physical magnitude - e.g. temperature or pressure differences, etc. (this is not necessarily to advocate an instrumental situation). None of this is to say that a complete, if only 'factual' or constructual, specification is to be expected.

Obviously, when one talks of a column, there is some reference to a visual situation (from whence the vocabulary may or may not find support). There is a comparison to be made here between the 'air-conditioning situation' and the fog bank, in which the obvious physical differences between the 'matter' which constitutes the indicators of this or that 'boundary' can be made out. This is not to describe the difference between boundaries per se, nor is it to exclude the possibility of regarding 'boundaries' as 'entifications' of geometrical gaps.

Mostly, anyway, the questions of 'demarcation' are external ones of a practical nature. Still, they remain securely rooted in the perusal tradition, so long as one considers them in the context of particularizing charateristics at an observational level.

A lot of emphasis was placed on the microscopic mechanical aspects of procedure and process in the air-conditioning situation; it's easy to raise and answer the same sort of question here, The objection to doing this is based in a rejection of the problems of 'visualization' (and 'identification' in that context) on theoretical grounds. The microscopic picture has a counterweight origin in the macroscopic aspect of a situation. Whilst articulation on and identification of air as a 'thing' conforms to this tradition, the molecular mechanical concept of 'particle', 'flux', (of energy) and the 'thing', 'particle' identity systems

(1) *By 'measure of identifiability' I mean there are some bodies which are more easily identifiable than is, say, a molecule of hydrogen. To identify a molecule of hydrogen considerable instrumental refinement is needed to aid normal vision.*

appear to be incompatible. What is interesting about thermodynamics is that it is restricted to the formulation of necessary conditions for an occurrence (Cf. remarks on nomological implications, connections etc. as appropriate to these considerations, below.)

There is a challenge to the million years habit of identifying 'things'. The recognizance of something as something is another question bound up with aspects of things, and not solely with 'identification' per se. The structure of kinetic theory, for example, is built on the (extralinguistic, extralogical) mechanics of so-called 'common-sense' objects. There is a rooted assumption that the laws and concepts of Newtonian mechanics, 'proved' by experience to be valid for 'day to day objects', continue to have the same meaning beyond the macroscopic-microscopic domain as they do within it. The kinetic theory represents the micro-reductive approach to the study of the properties of material aggregates. It interprets thermal phenomena in terms of properties and interactions of the constituents of material assemblies. Thermodynamics, on the other hand, is not based on any definite assumptions as to the ultimate constitution of matter. The foundations are in very few general empirical principles (appertaining to the behaviour of complex thermal systems.)

Since the Greeks, speculation concerning the identity of matter has run directly toward the atomic theory. Bridgeman held that there seems to be no logical or empirical justification for this. Rather, it seemed to him that it was a psychological fact that the search to 'identify' things demands the atomic particle concept. Persistently, even in a science like meteorology, which treats critically of thermal systems, the methodological and definitory approach is such that it draws exclusively from the kinetic theory of identity. (It is of interest to point out, here, that the meteorological phenomena which are most self-important (disruptive, etc.) are usually those with a visible aspect (macroscopic). 'Invisible fog' is self-contradictory in all common contexts of usage (i.e. 'Invisible' contradicts the formal sign 'fog' or 'cloud'. And both signs refer to the characteristics (in terms of 'visibility') of the meteorological objects to which they are assigned.)

The point here is not to make the gravamen of the discussion that people compulsively picture both assemblies which are such that they do fit the 'picturing' function and assemblies such that they do not. The suggestion is, rather, that the concept of identities like flux of heat and flux of energy might be inchoative; and that not

Terry ATKINSON, Michael BALDWIN

Air Show [detail]

1966

Text on paper

Dimensions variable

Pages 1 and 2

A collaborative project by Atkinson and Baldwin prior to the founding of Art & Language. *Air Show* first took form as an essay within *Frameworks 1966–67*, later published by Art & Language Press in 1968 in a numbered edition of 200. It is a proposal for exhibitions which transcend the gallery as the physical, traditionally defined premises for art, by the presentation of tabulated theoretical physics: 'In displaying these names and numbers we were suggesting a dimensional "vocabulary" in which an item nominated as "art" in terms of everyday expression might be "seen". Among the questions proposed by all this is: "If we inaugurated a reform of our ordinary language so as to include the language of physics, and in particular, this shorthand of relations between quantities, what would befall our sense of dematerialization *vis à vis* the nomination of a quantity of air as 'art', and what would happen consequently and correspondingly to our 'aesthetic' language?"'
– Michael Baldwin, Charles Harrison, Mel Ramsden, *Art & Language in Practice: Vol. 1: Illustrated Handbook*, 1999

Terry Atkinson Michael Baldwin

Key:

1 Group of related properties (conjoined '&')
2–5 Four part disjunction of related properties (four components)
6 'Extreme' of group of related properties (conjoined)
7,8 Disjunction of 'extremes'
9 'Intermediates' of group (conjoined)
10,11 Disjunction of 'Intermediates'
12 Relational predicate 'warmer'. Although it appears on separate sheet, it would be senseless to see it either conjoined or disjoined with adjacents – so a careful gimmick would be gratuitous. (that is: up to now, the 'space between the sheets' has meant 'or' – here it can't – so the syntax is shown).
13–18 Six part disjunction – each of two components – the top one with a higher 'subscript' than the bottom one. The last disjunction contains the relevant elements for a definition of the relational predicate (that is: when each term has a thing to describe) (or in the case of 'warmer', a relation between things, states, etc.)

HOT

WARM

COOL

COLD

1

ART & LANGUAGE
Hot-Cold [details]
1967–68
Letterpress artist's book
Dimensions variable

Hot–Cold was published as a small book by Art & Language Press in 1968. '"Hot" and "cold" behave perhaps like the words for complementary colours. We do not say that something is red-ish green. In the Minimalist and post-Minimalist world of phenomenological simplicity – of uninflected shapes, colours and quantities – the grammar of the predicates of simple sensations remained relatively unexamined. This book functions perhaps as an index of possible experiences involving the non-visual sensations of heat.'
– Michael Baldwin, Charles Harrison, Mel Ramsden, *Art & Language in Practice*, 1999

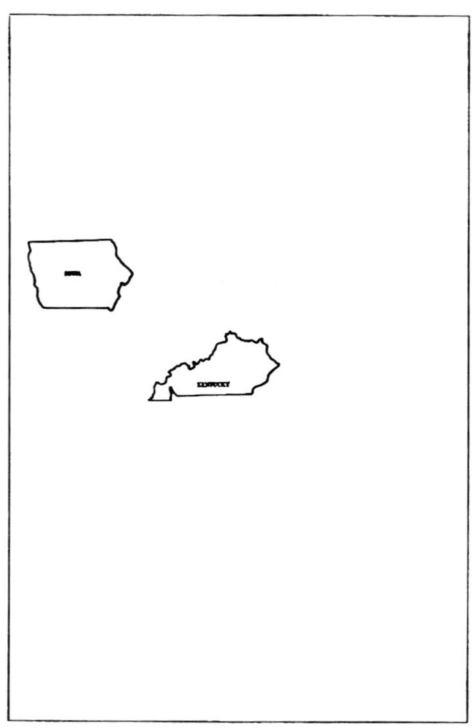

Map to not indicate: CANADA, JAMES BAY, ONTARIO, QUEBEC, ST. LAWRENCE RIVER, NEW BRUNSWICK, MANITOBA, AKIMISKI ISLAND, LAKE WINNIPEG, LAKE OF THE WOODS, LAKE NIPIGON, LAKE SUPERIOR, LAKE HURON, LAKE MICHIGAN, LAKE ONTARIO, LAKE ERIE, MAINE, NEW HAMPSHIRE, MASSACHUSETTS, VERMONT, CONNECTICUT, RHODE ISLAND, NEW YORK, NEW JERSEY, PENNSYLVANIA, DELAWARE, MARYLAND, WEST VIRGINIA, VIRGINIA, OHIO, MICHIGAN, WISCONSIN, MINNESOTA, EASTERN BORDERS OF NORTH DAKOTA, SOUTH DAKOTA, NEBRASKA, KANSAS, OKLAHOMA, TEXAS, MISSOURI, ILLINOIS, INDIANA, TENNESSEE, ARKANSAS, LOUISIANA, MISSISSIPPI, ALABAMA, GEORGIA, NORTH CAROLINA, SOUTH CAROLINA, FLORIDA, CUBA, BAHAMAS, ATLANTIC OCEAN, ANDROS ISLANDS, GULF OF MEXICO, STRAITS OF FLORIDA.

Terry ATKINSON, Michael BALDWIN
Map to not indicate ...
1967
Letterpress print on paper
Dimensions variable
Collection, Tate Gallery, London

This is one of three maps created collaboratively by Atkinson and Baldwin prior to the founding of Art & Language. 'The map is designed to indicate "not indicating". Iowa and Kentucky are indicated in one mode – delineated sub-areas labelled "Iowa" and "Kentucky" within the whole map area, the size of which, obviously, is dependent upon the scale used and the shape of which, obviously, is dependent upon which area is mapped. The second mode is a list of proper names succeeding the phrase "map to not indicate". This list of names indicates the relevant areas not indicated on the map above it.' In the map works language supersedes the traditional mode of cartography, the drawn line.
– quotations from Michael Baldwin, Charles Harrison, Mel Ramsden, *Art & Language in Practice*, 1999

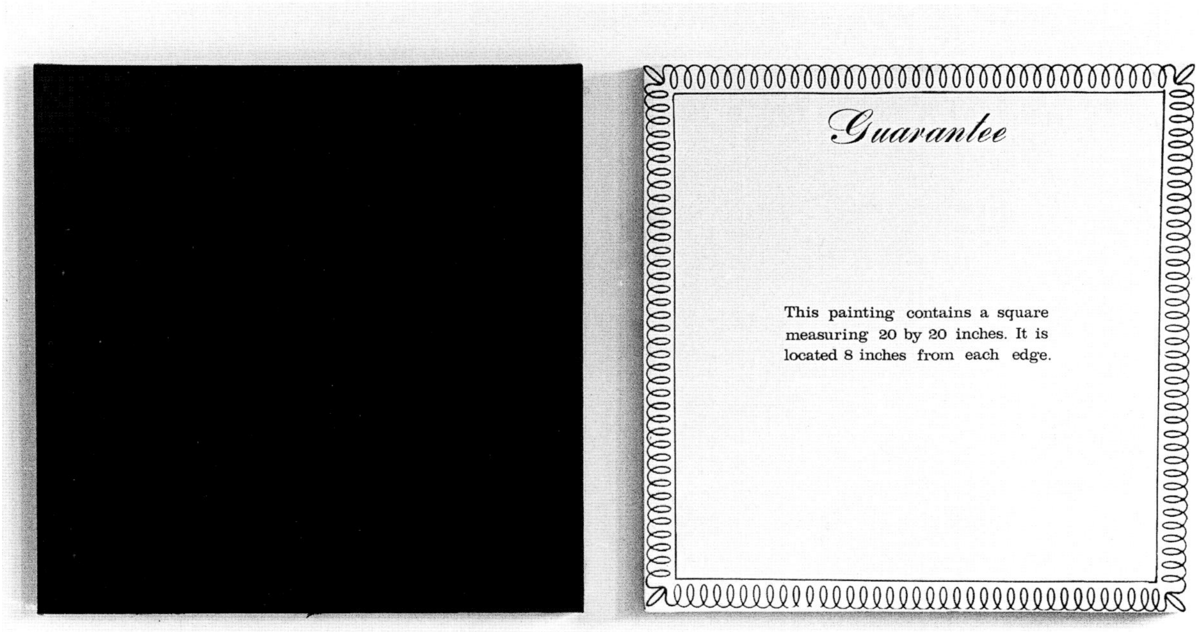

Mel RAMSDEN
Guaranteed Painting
1967-68
Acrylic on hardboard, photostat text on paper
51 × 51 cm [20 × 20 in] each

In this work the text 'guarantees' the contents of the accompanying painting. 'These works parodied the artist's "certificates" used, for example by Dan Flavin, to authenticate a particular arrangement of fluorescent tube lighting as "authentically a Dan Flavin". It also parodied the guarantees provided with consumer goods like washing machines and refrigerators.'
– Michael Baldwin, Charles Harrison, Mel Ramsden, *Art & Language in Practice*, 1999

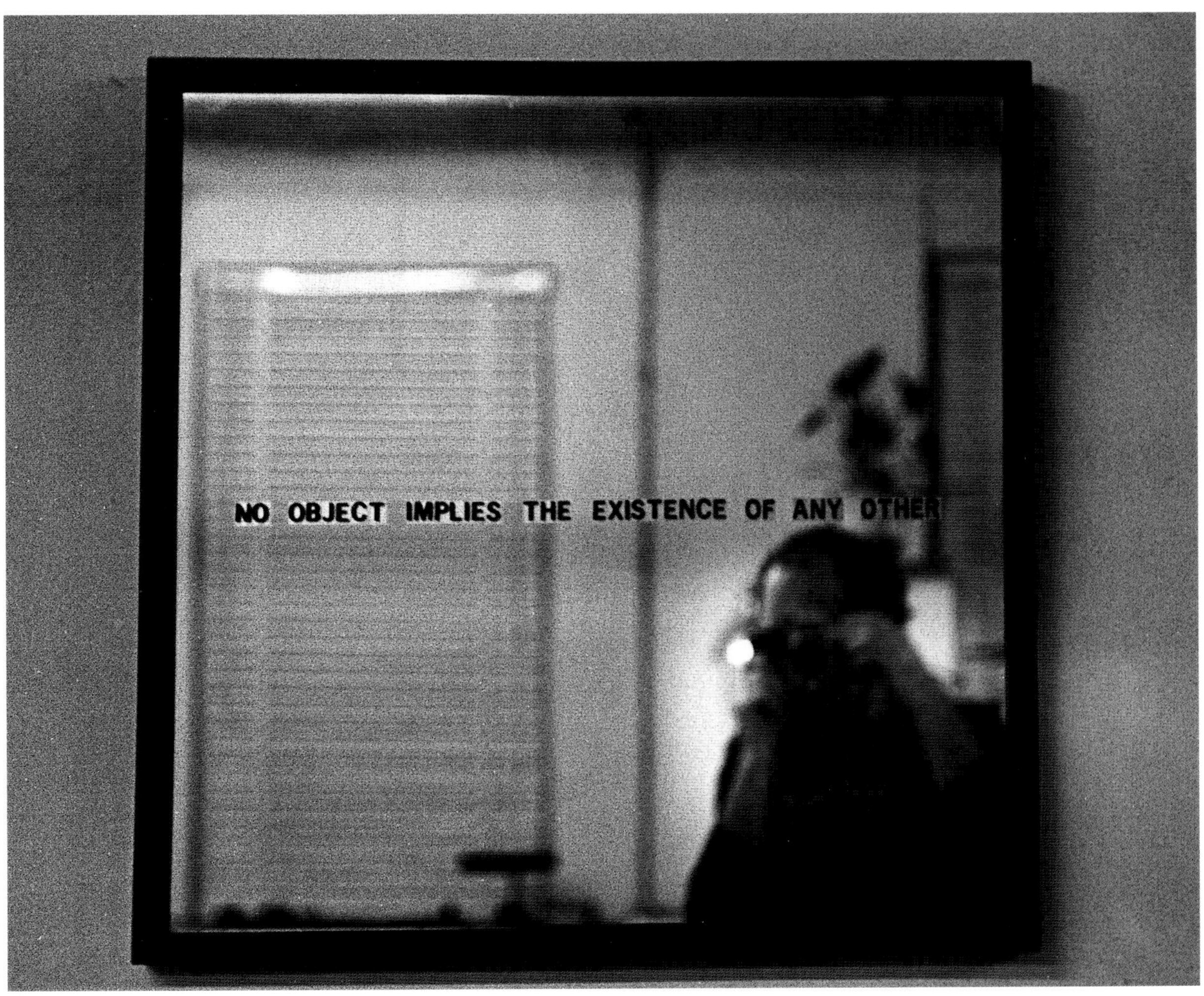

Ian BURN
No Object Implies the Existence of Any Other
1967
Framed mirror, text
Dimensions unknown

Burn and Mel Ramsden had both moved to England from Australia in 1965 after meeting at the National Gallery School, Melbourne. During the next two years Burn progressed from colour field to 'minimal' style monochrome painting in explorations of 'propositions' about what a painting might be, for example: 'six different exactly identical paintings', which became *Yellow Premiss* (1965). From 1967 to 68 he made a series of *Mirror Pieces* in which viewing was refracted by varying degrees of reflectability in the glass used. These were followed by mirror works in which text was incorporated to add a further interruption to the visual experience and to make discursive the viewer's phenomenological encounter with the work.

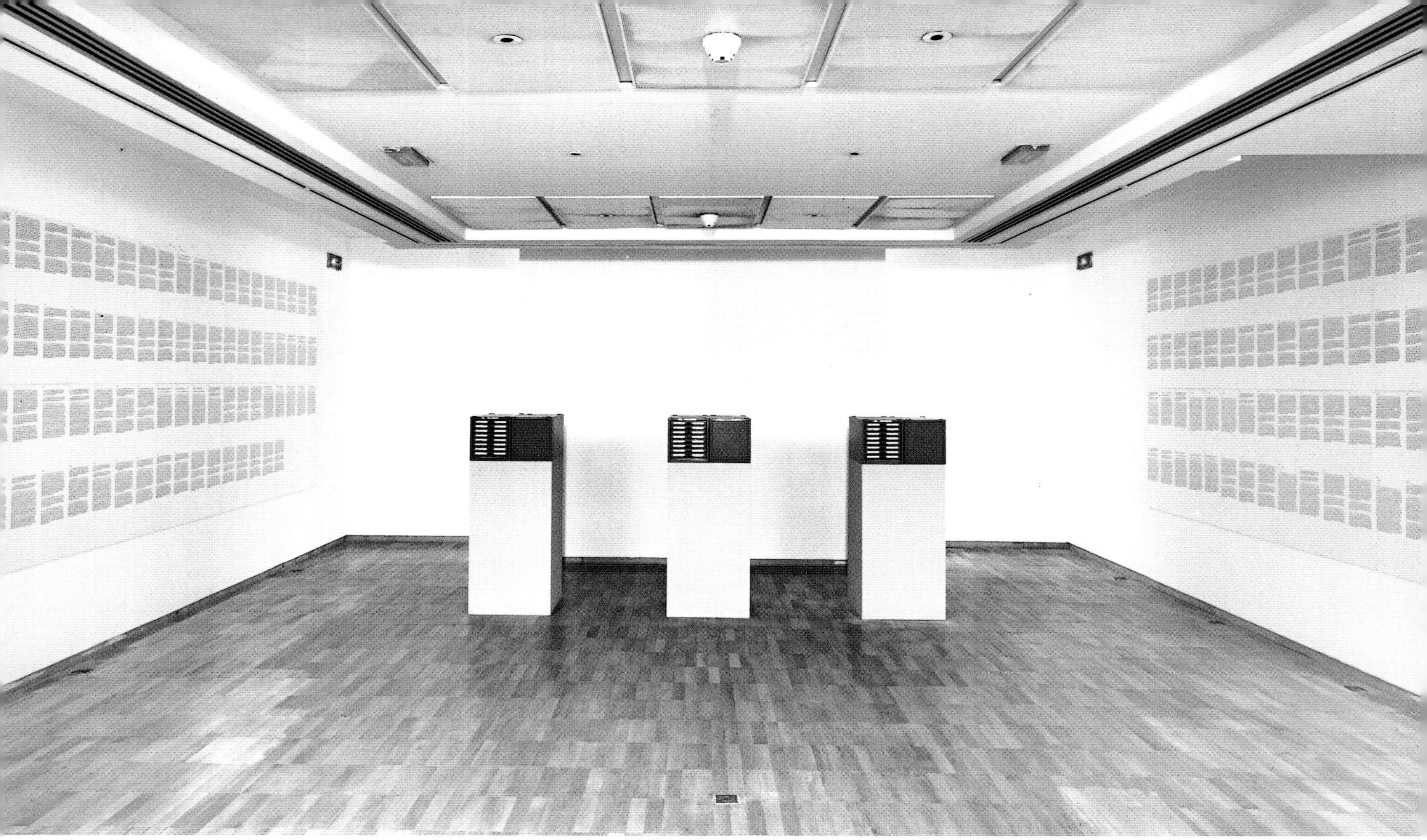

ART & LANGUAGE
Index 001
1972
Texts on paper, index cards, index file boxes
Dimensions variable
Installation view, Documenta 5, Kassel, Germany, 1972

The series of Art & Language *Indexes* began as a project for Documenta 5 in 1972. The indexes present large volumes of textual information organized into various systems which challenge the viewer's ability to make sense of it according to habitual means of classification. 'The principal motif of the series was the nature of the identities of artist and onlooker. In participating ... the "spectator" "produces" a conceptual possibility whereby the work is realized ... '
– Michael Baldwin, Charles Harrison, Mel Ramsden, *Art & Language in Practice*, 1999

opposite
Robert SMITHSON
A Heap of Language
1966
Pencil on paper
16.5 × 56 cm [6.5 × 22 in]

In this small pencil drawing a two-dimensional form reminiscent of an 'earthwork' is constructed from handwritten words, beginning at the top with 'language', underneath which are layers of words and expressions all of which relate to language, progressing from 'phraseology, speech, tongue, lingo, vernacular', through words describing written language, translation, dialect, the study of handwriting and so on, and ending with 'cipher'. The words function both as units of language and as the 'objects' from which the 'heap' is formed, inviting speculation about the relationship between form, language and the physical world.

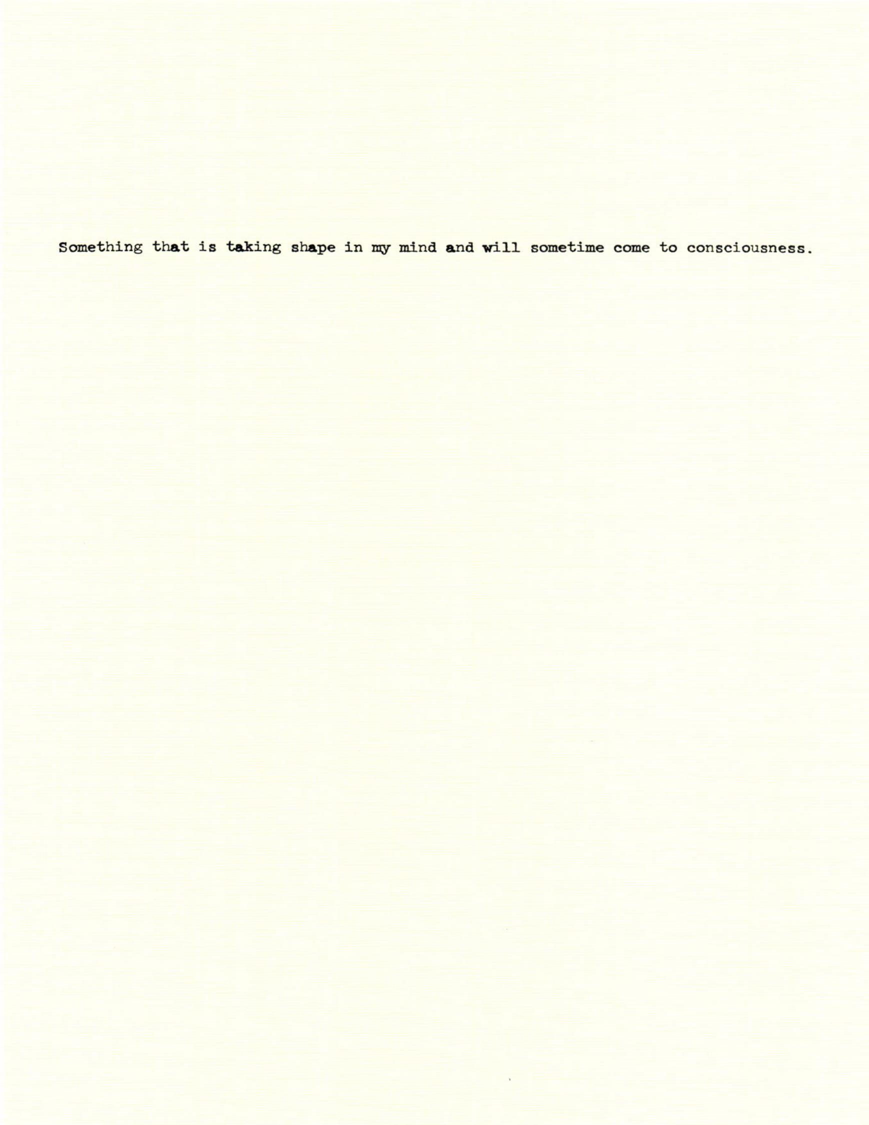

left

Robert BARRY

Something … [detail]

1969

Typed text on paper

28 × 22 cm [11 × 8.5 in] each

At the end of the 1960s, as the material of Barry's work became visually imperceptible – carrier waves of different frequencies, ultrasonic sound, microwaves, electronic energy fields, radioactive substances and inert gases – he rejected for the most part photographic documentation, using it only to prove that 'there was nothing to photograph'. Language, as in this example which is part of a series, became increasingly important. Not the material but the mental realization of its presence became the work's focus, communicated through language. Barry attempted to express his concepts as neutrally as possible, using 'as brief as possible a description in fairly technical language … [which was] as impersonal as possible'.

– Robert Barry, interview with Patricia Norvell, in Alexander Alberro and Patricia Norvell (eds), *Recording Conceptual Art*, 2001

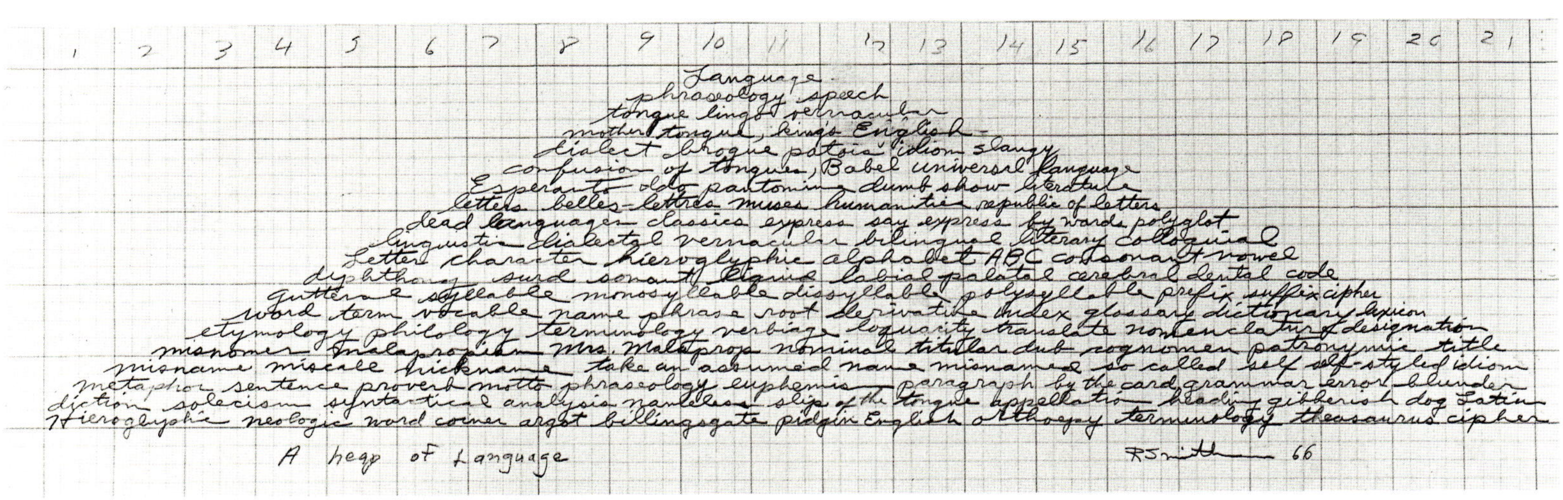

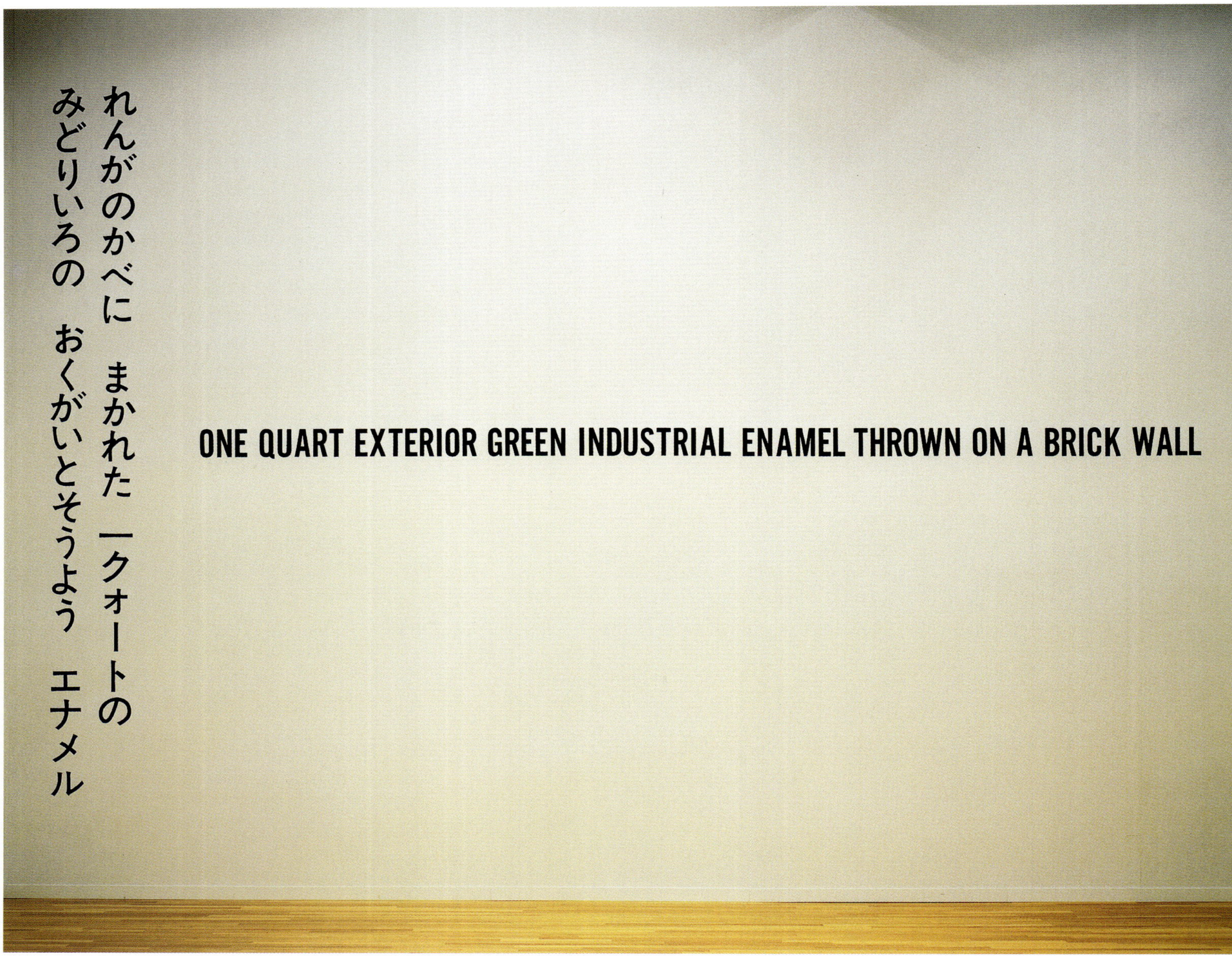

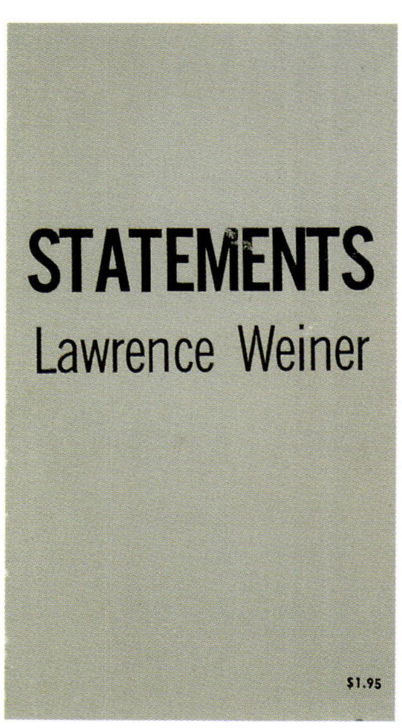

Lawrence WEINER

STATEMENTS

1968

Artist's book

18 × 10 cm [7 × 4 in]

Published by Seth Siegelaub and The Louis Kellner Foundation, New York

In 1968 Weiner realized that a construction in language could function as 'sculpture' as adequately as a fabricated object. As a proposition or 'statement', each work need not be confined to an existence in one realized form, place or time but might be constructed in different contexts. In December 1968 he published a series of statements in a book of that title, available cheaply at $1.95. One statement is printed on each page, all in lowercase, in a small typewriter font. The book is divided into general statements – such as: *an amount of paint poured directly upon the floor and allowed to dry* and specific statements, such as: *one quart exterior green industrial enamel thrown on a brick wall*. When asked to exhibit his work in galleries, Weiner decided that the statements could be placed directly on the wall, as in the example above, temporarily installed at the Museum of Contemporary Art, Tokyo, in 1995.

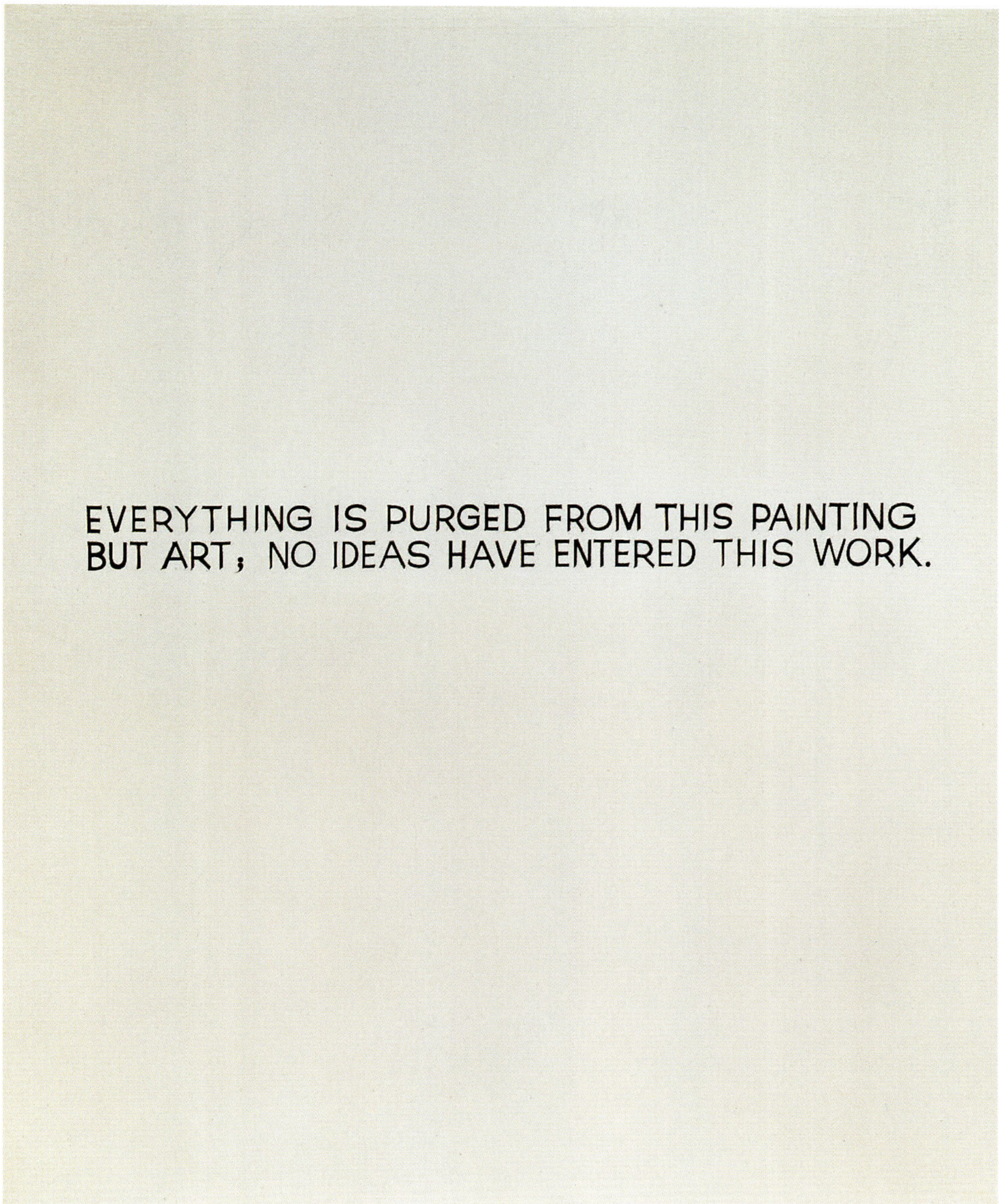

John BALDESSARI
Everything is Purged from This Painting but Art; No Ideas Have Entered This Work
1966-68
Acrylic on canvas
150 × 115 cm [59 × 45 in]

This is part of a series of painted statements, a number of which were quoted from textbooks on art theory and technique. From his experience of teaching in National City, California, a small town near the Mexican border, in the mid 1960s, Baldessari realized that 'high art' had little relevance to most citizens' everyday lives. He gave up traditional painting and began to work with photography and text.

'I was weary of doing relational painting and began wondering if straight information would serve. I sought to use language not as a visual element but as something to read. That is, a notebook entry about painting could replace the painting. And visual data that was less pleasing artistically than as documentation, as in a store catalogue or police photograph ... I was attempting to make something that didn't emanate art signals. The only art signal I wanted was the canvas ... it was important that I was the strategist. Someone else built and primed the canvases and took them to the sign painter ... and the sign painter was instructed not to attempt to make attractive, artful lettering but to letter the information in the most simple way.'
– John Baldessari in *John Baldessari: Paintings 1966–68*, 1981

Victor BURGIN

All Criteria …

1970

Printed text on paper

Two sheets, 30 x 21 cm [12 x 8.5 in] each

Collection, Tate Gallery, London

'It may no longer be assumed that art, in some mysterious way, resides in materials.'
– Victor Burgin, 'Situational Aesthetics', *Studio International*, 178:915, October 1969

Burgin's instruction-based works of the late 1960s, such as *Photopath* below, were followed by a series of language-based pieces which no longer had a relation to physical fabrication or the visual representation of material objects. These works include *This Position* (1969), *Any Moment* (1970) and *All Criteria* (1970). They could be presented as printed sheets in an exhibition space or as pages in a publication. They each comprise a series of statements, reminiscent of philosophical propositions or the rules of a cryptic game, which describe in abstract a series of spatial and temporal relationships, centred on the position of the viewer. As general statements they provide a template which the viewer can fill in with specifics.

1
ALL CRITERIA BY WHICH YOU MIGHT DECIDE THAT ANY SERIES OF BODILY ACTS, DIRECTLY KNOWN TO YOU AT ANY MOMENT PREVIOUS TO THE PRESENT MOMENT, CONSTITUTES A DISCRETE EVENT

2
ALL CRITERIA BY WHICH YOU MIGHT ASSESS THE SIMILARITY OF ANY ONE EVENT TO ANY OTHER EVENT

3
ANY SERIES OF SIMILAR EVENTS DIRECTLY KNOWN TO YOU PREVIOUSLY TO THE PRESENT MOMENT

4
ANY OBJECT WITHIN 3 WHICH YOU KNOW TO BE THE SAME INDIVIDUAL THROUGHOUT 3 AND TOWARDS WHICH ANY BODILY ACTS WERE DIRECTED

5
ALL CRITERIA BY WHICH YOU MIGHT ASCRIBE INDIVIDUALITY TO THINGS OTHER THAN OBJECTS

6
ALL INDIVIDUALS WITHIN 3 OTHER THAN OBJECTS

7
A HYPOTHETICAL EVENT IN SERIES WITH 3 OCCURRING LATER THAN THE PRESENT MOMENT

8
AN OBJECT WITHIN 7 WHICH IS THE SAME INDIVIDUAL AS 4

9
ALL HYPOTHETICAL INDIVIDUALS WITHIN 7 OTHER THAN OBJECTS

10
ALL INDIVIDUALS WHICH ARE BOTH MEMBERS OF 9 AND OF 6

11
ANY OBJECT DIRECTLY KNOWN TO YOU AT THE PRESENT MOMENT TOWARDS WHICH ANY BODILY ACT IS DIRECTED

12
ALL INDIVIDUALS DIRECTLY KNOWN TO YOU AT THE PRESENT MOMENT OTHER THAN OBJECTS

13
THE SUBSTITUTION OF 11 FOR 8 AND FOR 4

14
THE SUBSTITUTION OF 12 FOR 9 AND FOR 6

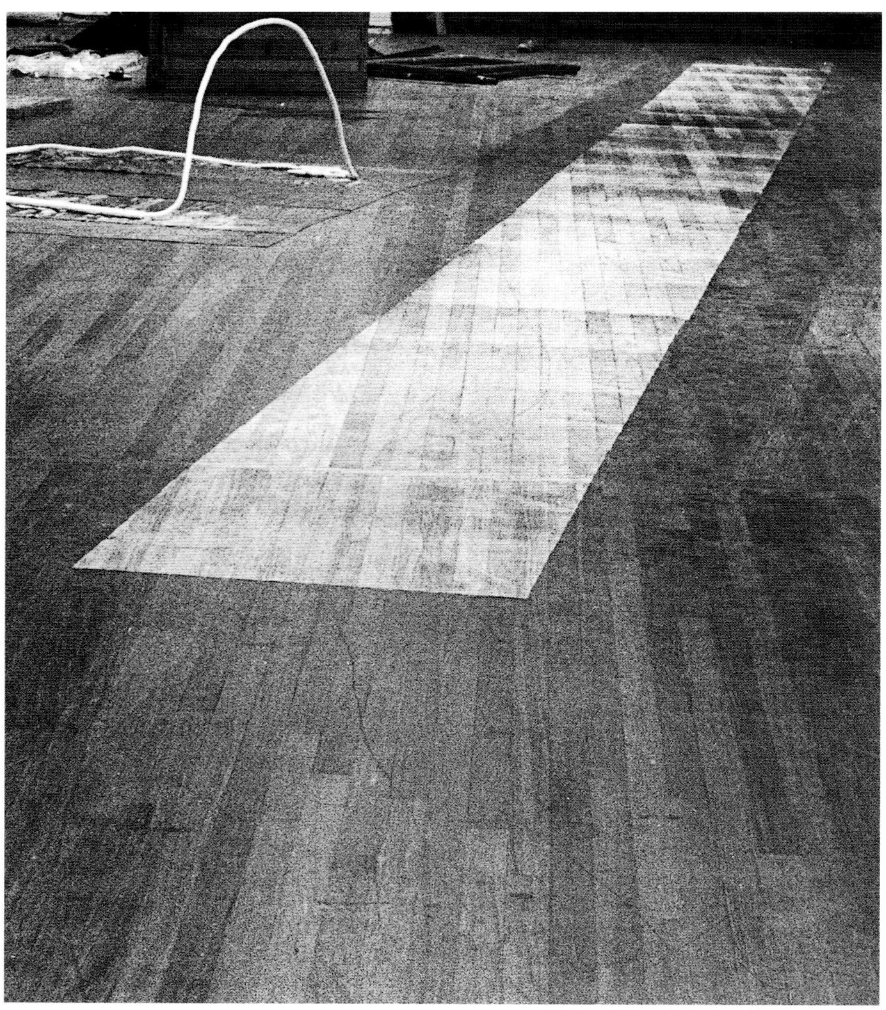

Victor BURGIN

Photopath

1967–69

Photographs affixed to floor

Dimensions variable

Installation view, 'When Attitudes Become Form', Institute of Contemporary Arts, London, 1969

'A path along the floor, proportions 1 × 21 units, photographed. Photographs printed to the actual size of objects and prints attached to the floor so that the images are perfectly congruent with their objects.'
– Victor Burgin, written instruction, 1967, for work fabricated in 1969 as *Photopath*

For the London version of the exhibition 'When Attitudes Become Form' in 1969, Burgin fabricated one of approximately fifteen works he had made as written instructions on index cards in 1967. Twenty-one photographs of twenty-one continuous sections of the gallery's floorboards were printed actual size and stapled to the boards so that the woodgrain and the image were exactly congruent.

'It was a piece of "sculpture" in as much as it was material on the floor, in an art gallery, and had no other function than to be looked at by an art audience. But it was very ephemeral at the same time – just paper – photographs that only showed what was already there. So there was a play, a paradox, on seeing and not seeing, revealing while concealing. I was reading Wittgenstein, and I was interested in a passage where he talks about thinking of something and looking at it at the same time. The photograph on the floor was supposed to be some sort of analogue of the act; also, it was an inchoate anti-capitalist gesture, because it would make no sense to move it – you couldn't collect it, it could only be where it was.'
– Victor Burgin, interview with Tony Godfrey, *Block*, 7, 1982

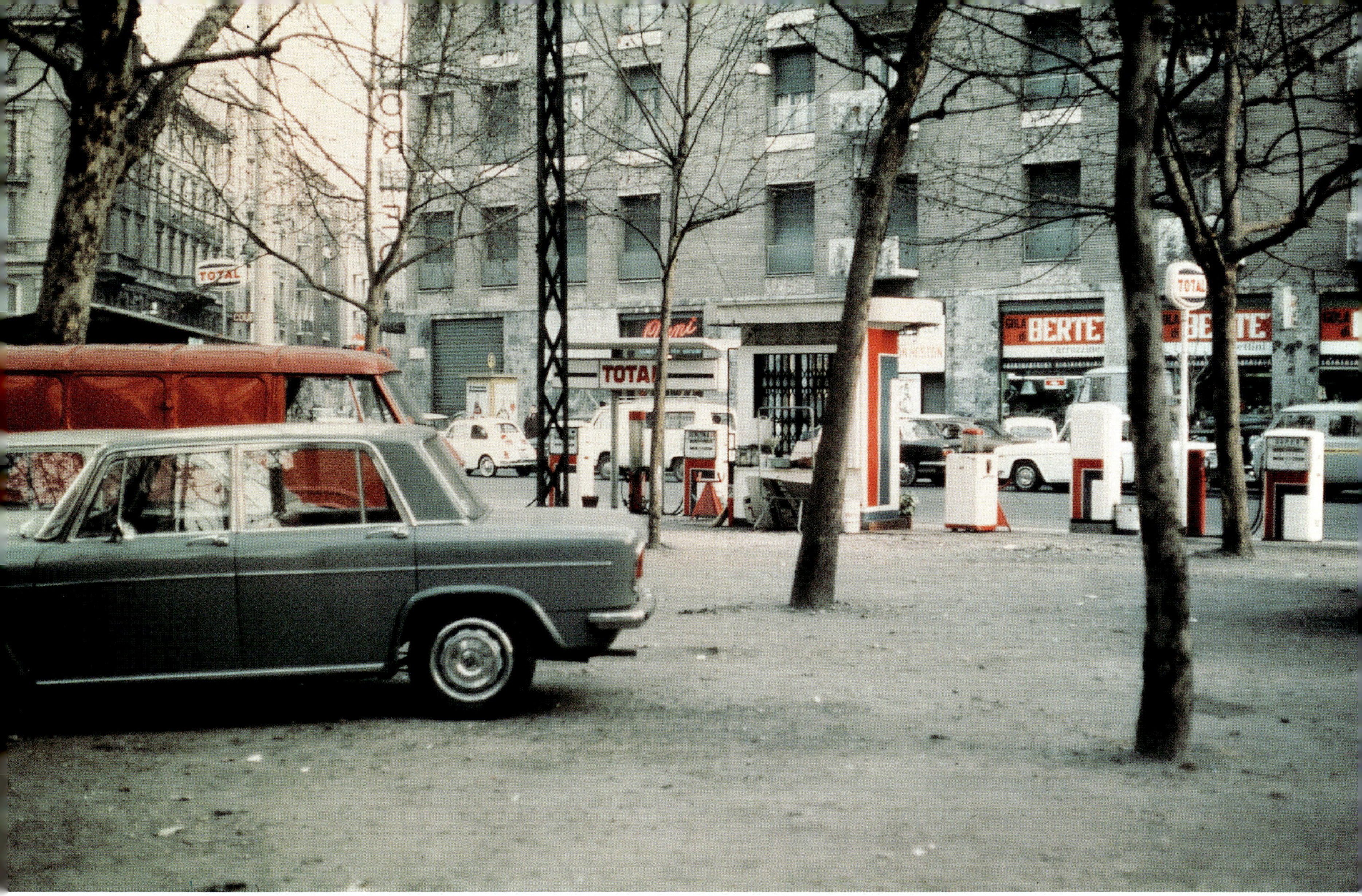

James COLEMAN

Slide Piece

1972–73

Repeated projected image with synchronized audio narration

Dimensions variable

This work comprises the full-scale projection of a single slide image in a darkened room, accompanied by an audiotape. The slide is a photograph of a deserted city square in Milan, the city Coleman had come to from his native Dublin to pursue his studies. The audiotape recording contains verbal descriptions of the square made by nearly a dozen individuals invited by the artist to contribute *in situ*. They are all delivered in the voice of a single narrator and are noticeably different. The unifying voice of the narrator operates to emphasize the differences between the various participators' approaches to selecting significant elements in the square.

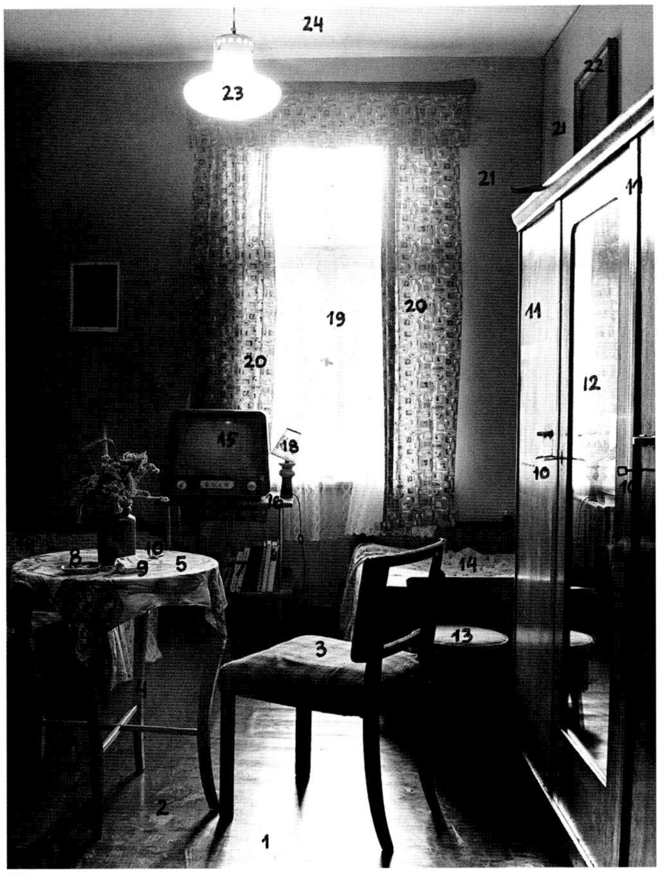

What is it?
Qu'est que c'est?
Was ist das?
Co to jest?

It is a metaphysics.
C'est une métaphysique.
Das ist eine Metaphysik.
To jest metafizyka.

Is it a metaphysics?
Est-ce une metaphysique?
Ist das eine Metaphysik?
Czy to jest metafizyka?

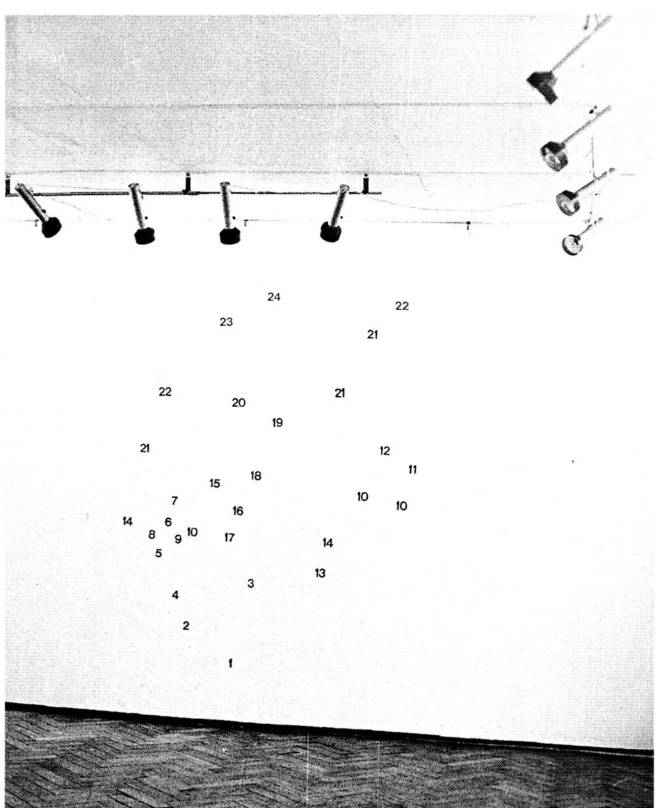

Jaroslaw KOZLOWSKI

above

Metaphysics [detail]

1972

Black and white photograph, text

left

Ics [detail]

1974

Letraset numerals on wall

Dimensions variable

These are the first and third parts of the series *Metaphysics, Physics, Ics* (1972–74). In *Metaphysics*, numbers are written on an actual photograph of a domestic room, exhibited opposite various phrases in the form of text. *Physics* is a wall projection of the same photograph. The numbers are now written on the wall, labelling the objects in the image, as before. A recorded voice recites, in English, French, German and Polish, three phrases corresponding to each number. In *Ics* the numbers originally written on the wall are replaced by Letraset numbers, with no projected image. Recorded voices describe the now invisible objects. 'I would not make a too clear-cut distinction between object and idea. It seems to me that there is instead a constant "change of places"; transformation of one into the other. Objects may be good carriers of ideas, ideas are often reified. Each such "transformation", regardless of its direction, introduces momentary chaos, confusion, which results in a most interesting demystification of either the object or the idea. There opens a kind of "crack", through which we may gain insight into what is usually hidden, inaccessible, camouflaged ...'
– Jaroslaw Kozlowski, Artist's statement, 1974

Victor PIVOVAROV

Projects for a Lonely Man [detail from series]

1971

Enamel on masonite

170 × 130 cm [67 × 51 in]

In the Soviet environment prior to Perestroika, Pivovarov's cultural influences were predominantly verbal; he hardly encountered visual art until his university studies. 'A word is the main tool of Russian culture and its power is that of a law.' Like Ilya Kabakov, with whom he worked closely in the early 1970s, he produced illustrated albums in which text and image have an equal importance. The series of *Projects for a Lonely Man* conceptualize a notion of freedom which is very different from the individualism of Western existentialism: '*Projects for a Lonely Man* show that there are four degrees of loneliness: 1) tragic, or existential loneliness, 2) melancholic, or cosmic loneliness, 3) meditative, or metaphysical loneliness, and 4) joyful, or absolute loneliness. The *Projects* offer an extreme lack of freedom on the level of actual being but they bring the man to the fourth degree which, though coalescing with the physical death of the lonely man, means reaching true freedom and unification with the infinite.'
– quotations from Victor Pivovarov, *Revolver Revue*, 1993

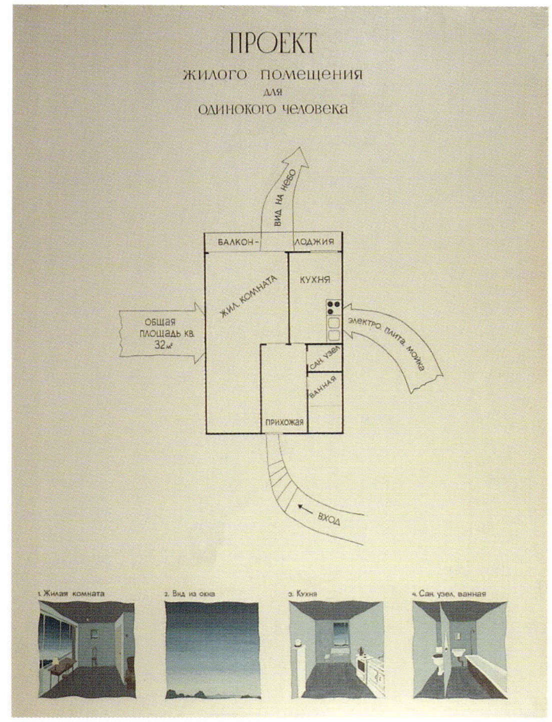

below

Ilya KABAKOV

Ekaterina Lvovna Soyka: Whose Mug Is This? [from The Communal Kitchen]

1982

Enamel on masonite panel, enamel tin mug

70 × 120 cm [27.5 × 47 in]

Kabakov had introduced a distrust of the purely visual into his paintings and illustrations of the late 1960s when he included verbal commentaries by a 'fictional beholder' within works such as the painting *Answers of the Experimental Group* (1969). The suppression of the viewing of alternative art led Kabakov to invent the viewer and introduce him or her into the artwork itself, in a series of illustrated albums of the early 1970s based on different characters. This developed into a collective presence when Kabakov began to introduce the 'speech' of communal dwellings into paintings and installations, at first presented in his studio at the end of the 1970s. These also incorporated household articles, such as the mug in this work.

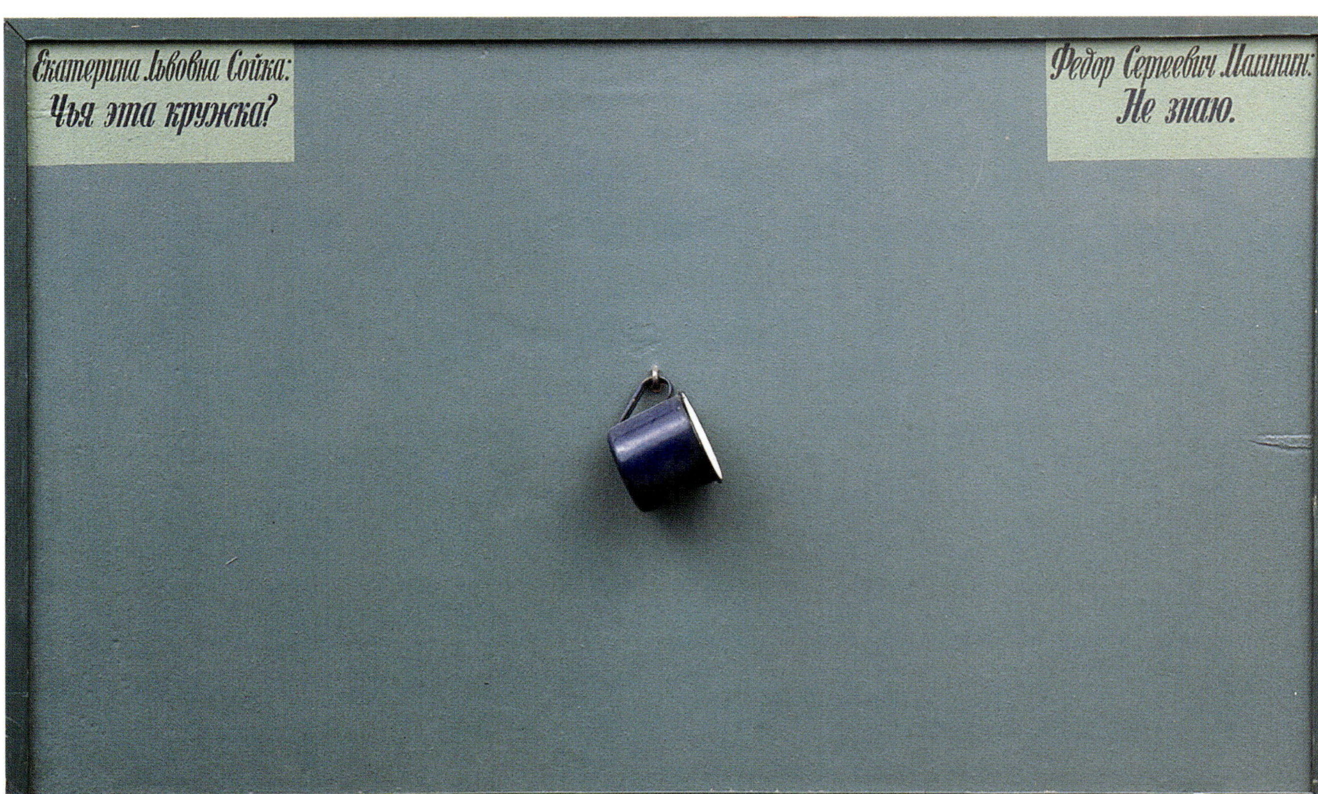

APPROPRIATION, INTERVENTION, EVERYDAY

The multiplication of material means for making art and, in particular, the proximity to publishing of certain kinds of conceptual art, opened up the possibility of new relationships between art and everyday commercial cultural forms, outside the gallery system. In this context, a series of new sub-genres of appropriation art emerged. These included Akasegawa Genpei's money art; On Kawara's mail art; Robert Smithson and Dan Graham's magazine art; Mierle Laderman Ukeles' maintenance art and Gordon Matta-Clark's modifications of buildings. Intervening in quotidian activities, these artists introduced new elements of reflexiveness and activism into everyday life. In some cases, these interventions were almost invisible; in others, they became the object of protracted and controversial legal proceedings. Either way, their documentation for art institutions, upon which their status as art depends, made documentary photography the meta-genre of a culturally activist conceptual art.

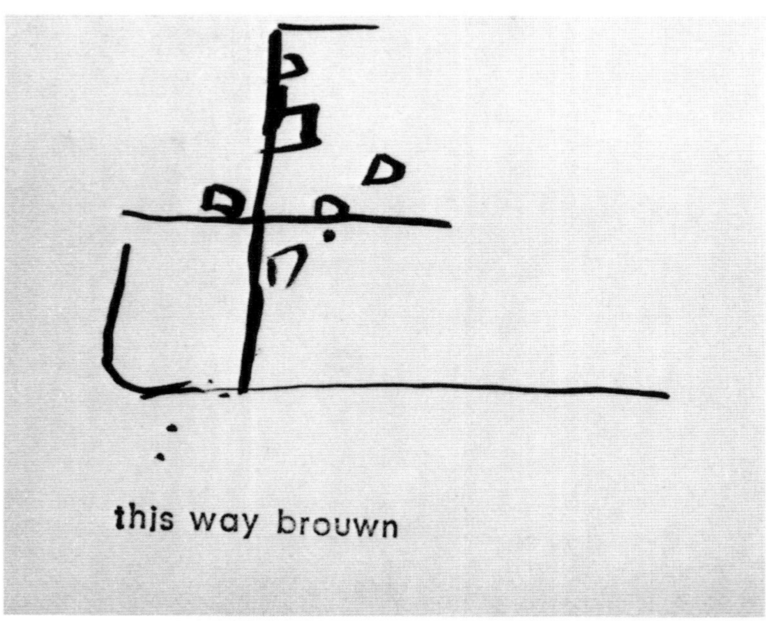

Stanley BROUWN
this way brouwn [detail]
1961
Ink and rubber stamp on paper
From the series of works, approx. 21 × 29 cm [8 × 11.5 in] each

Brouwn's work is concerned with measuring distance, particularly through walking. In 1960 he began making *pedestrian steps on paper*, laying sheets of paper in the street to collect the footprints of people walking by. The footprints resemble monoprints both in their smudged appearance and in their one-off nature. However their source is anonymous members of the public rather than the hand (or foot) of the artist. Similarly, the *this way brouwn* series depends on choices offered to the public for its creation. It comprises sheets of paper, each bearing a diagrammatic drawing and the stamped words 'this way brouwn'. Brouwn stood in the street and requested directions from people passing by. The pedestrians were asked to explain on paper how to walk from one point to another. 'A *this way brouwn* is produced in the time it takes for the pedestrian to give his explanation. No second thoughts, no polishing and touching up the result ... there are no good *this way brouwns*. There are no bad *this way brouwns*.'
– Stanley Brouwn, *this way brouwn, 25–2–61 / 26–2–61, Zeichnungen 1*, 1971

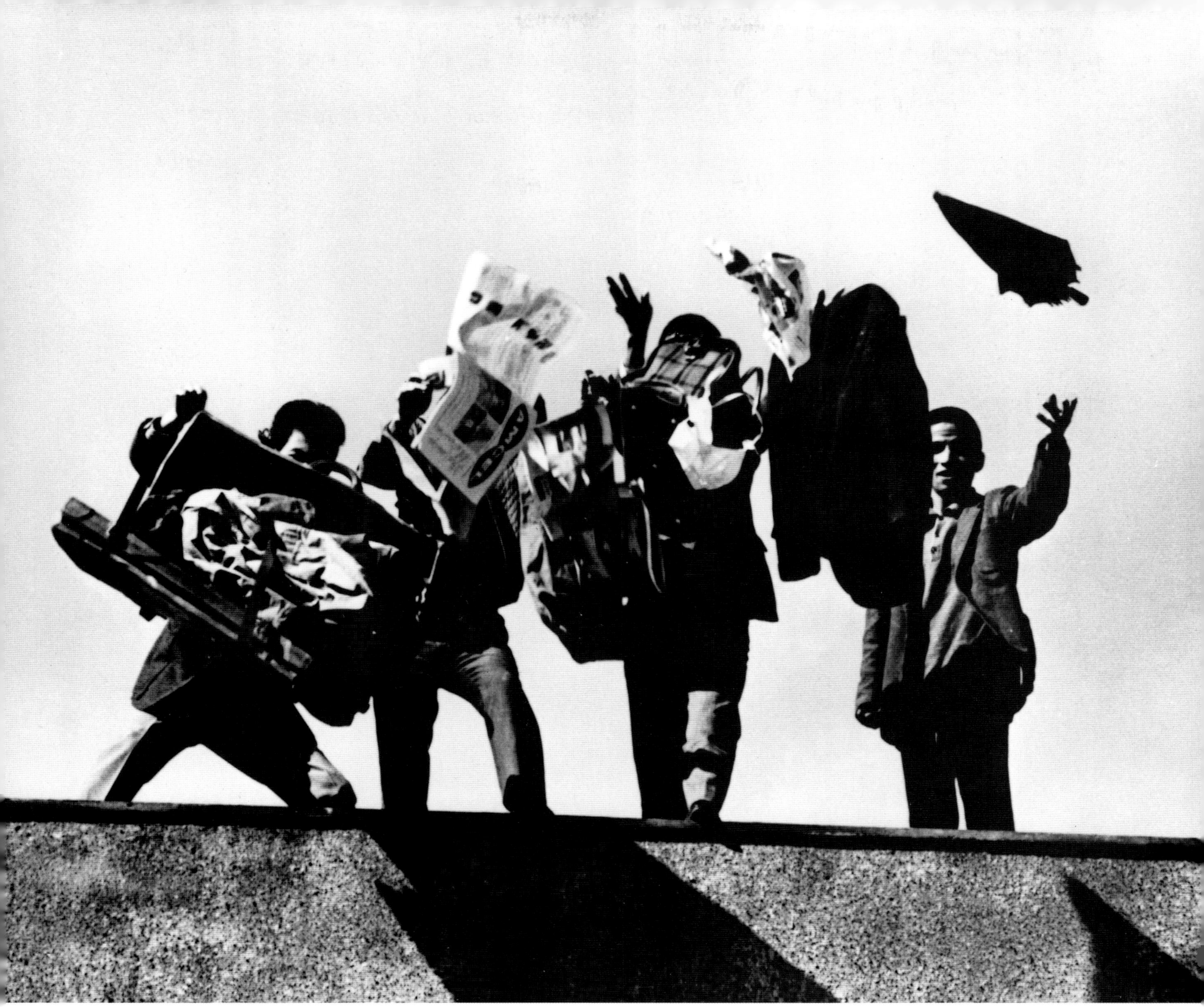

HI RED CENTER

The Ochanomizu Drop [Dropping Event]

1964

Tokyo

This event was performed in and around the Ochanomizu section of downtown Tokyo on 10 October 1964. Members of the Hi Red Center group dropped old clothes and everyday objects from the roof of Ikenobo Kaikan hall and watched them land on the street below. They then packed the dropped things in a suitcase, placed it in a public locker and sent the locker key to a name they picked at random from the phone book. Six days later, dressed in surgical masks and gowns bearing Hi Red Center '!' arm bands, the group scrubbed the pavements of the down-at-heel Ginza district, which had recently been 'spruced up' for the Tokyo Olympics. This second event was titled *Movement to Promote the Clean-up of the Metropolitan Area (Be Clean!)*. These were among a series of 'agitations' in which the group intervened in everyday city life to draw attention to its political undercurrents.

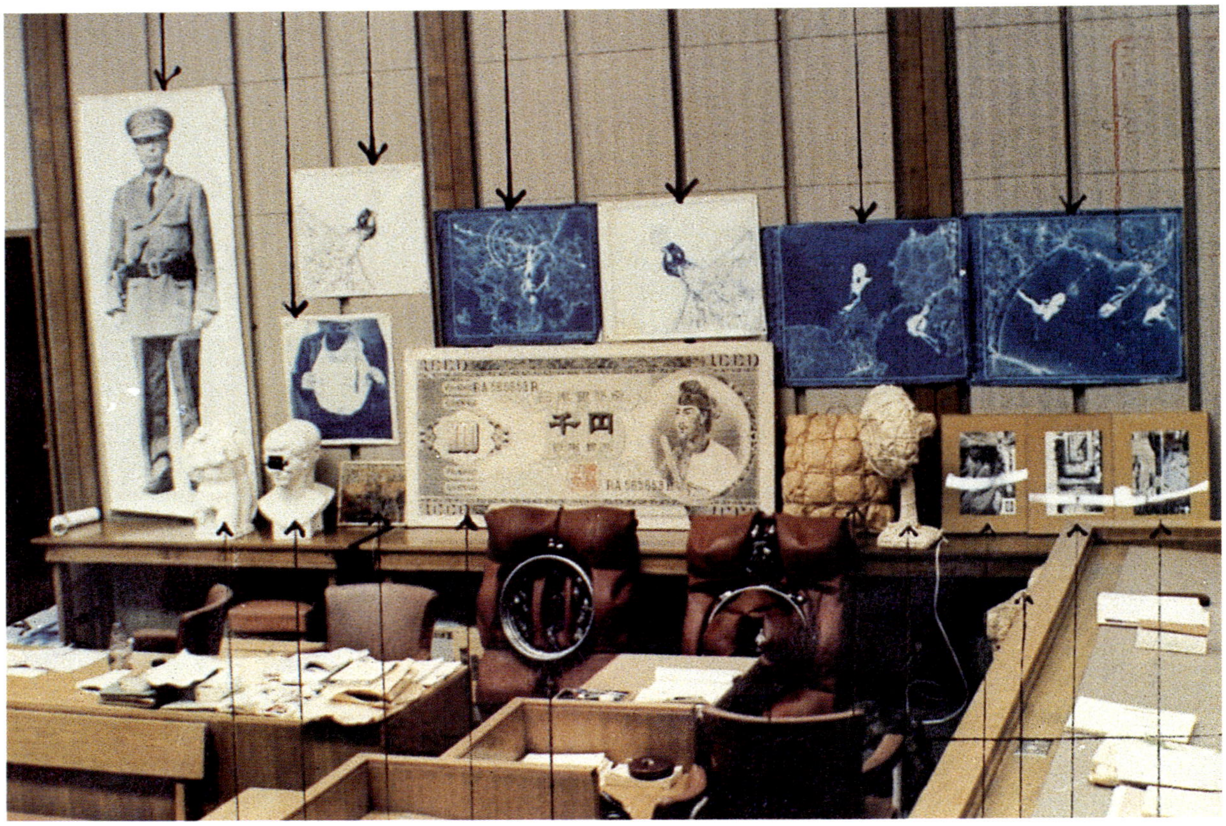

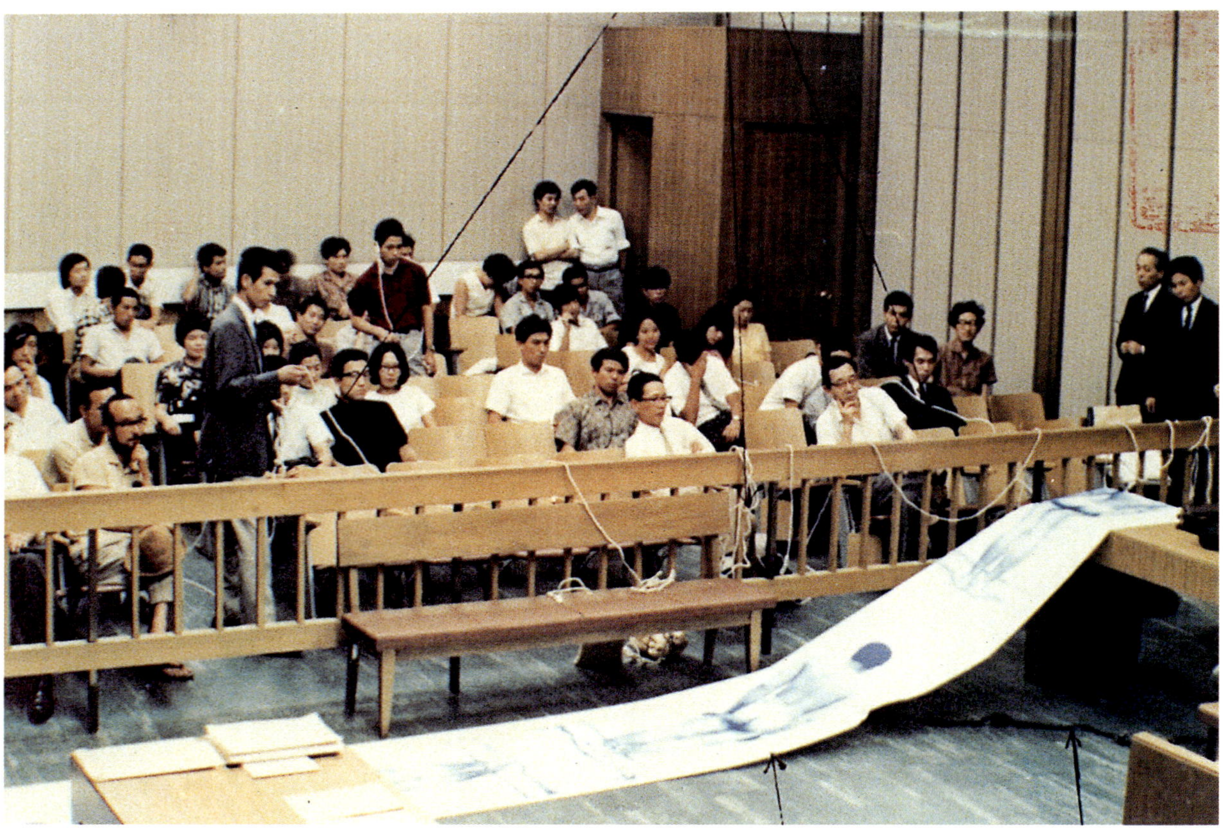

AKASEGAWA Genpei

Model 1000-Yen Note Incident

1963-73

left

Documentation of impounded objects

below left

One Thousand Yen Note Trial, Tokyo District Court, 1966

In 1963 Japanese police had been unsuccessfully tracking the counterfeiter of a 1000-Yen note. To their embarrassment the serial number became public knowledge. Akasegawa, one of the three founding members of the group Hi Red Center, made a forgery of the forgery, printing the note in full colour and size and using the same serial number. To make it obvious that it was a forgery he printed only one side, leaving the other side white. He sent out the bills as invitations to an exhibition and pasted them to the gallery wall as well as to the wall of the boarding house room where he lived. One night a stranger attempted to use his one-sided money and it came to the attention of the police. Its origin was traced to Akasegawa and his lodgings were raided. A highly publicized trial followed, where the artist was defended by respected art historians and critics. A four-hour Happening was enacted during the trial to demonstrate the nature of Akasegawa's artistic practice.

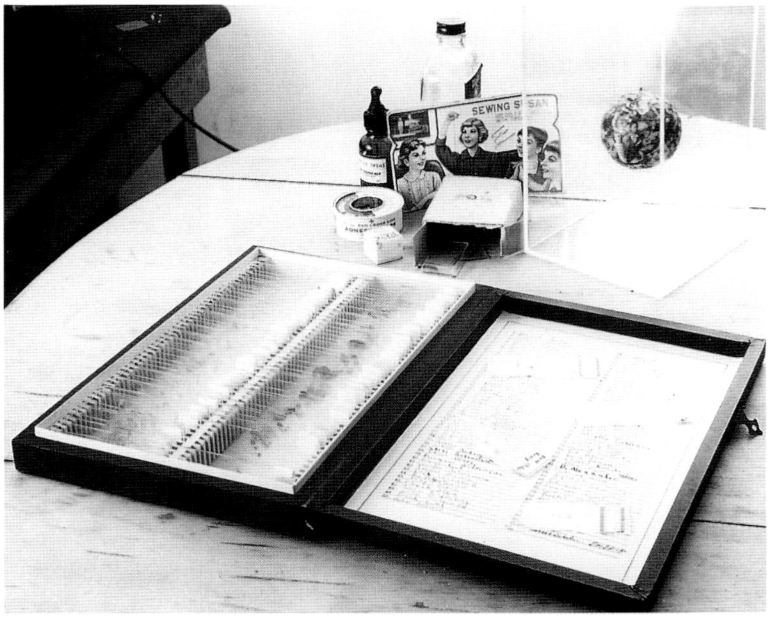

Eleanor ANTIN

Blood of the Poet Box

1965-68

Wooden box with 100 glass slides of poets' blood specimens and specimen lists

29 × 20.5 × 4 cm [11.5 × 8 × 1.5 in]

A compartmentalized box, reminiscent of Marcel Duchamp's collection of miniaturized versions of his work in a suitcase, the *Boîte-en-valise* (1941–68), this work comprises one hundred glass microscope slides bearing the blood samples of one hundred poets. The donors include the poets Allen Ginsberg, Lawrence Ferlinghetti, Gerard Malanga and the artist's husband, David Antin. The slides are labelled with the donor's name and the date the sample was collected. The work ironically subjects notions of artistic pre-eminence, treasured in the form of relics, to a pseudo-scientific objectivism. The multiple nature of the collection reduces individual poetic identity to a collective and equalized set of mundane data.

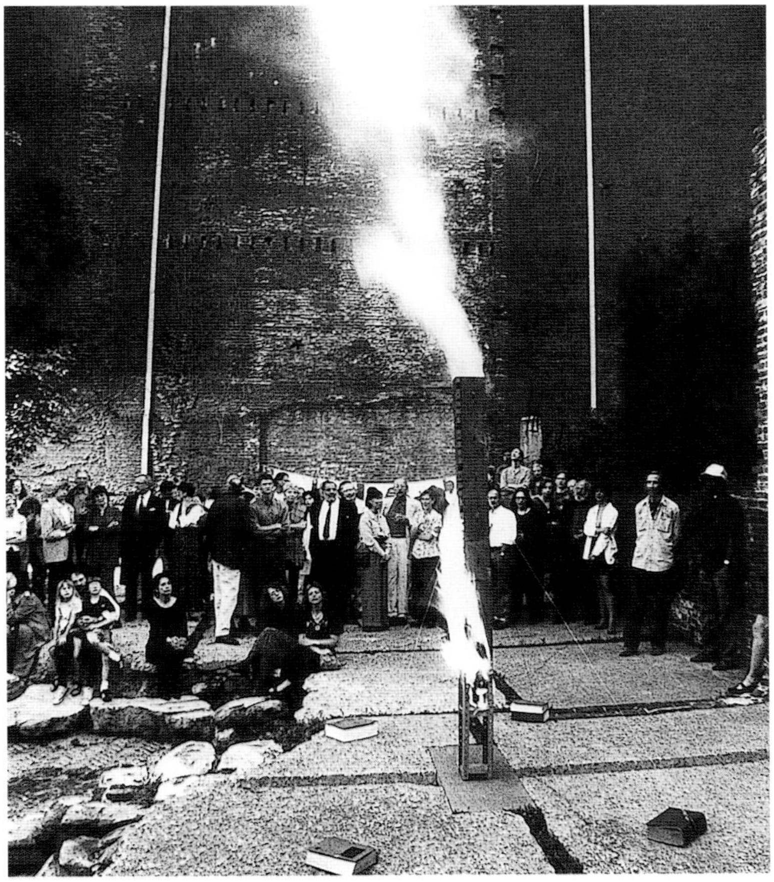

John LATHAM

Skoob Tower Ceremony

1966

Thames South Bank event related to Destruction in Art Symposium, Institute of Contemporary Arts, London

In his work of the 1960s Latham focused on the transformation of objects into events, often through reversal or destruction. He invented the term 'noit', the opposite of the suffix '-tion', through which verbs are converted to nouns, to signify a reversal of the process of crystallization of action into fixity. Books were used in a variety of ways, initially in assemblage works – a 1959 relief mural consists of books stuck to canvas, some facing towards the wall, others opening to the viewer. From 1964 to 1966, assemblages known as *Skoob Towers* ('skoob' being 'books' spelt backwards) were set alight and burned in 'ceremonies' such as the South Bank event which was part of the Destruction in Art Symposium organized by a committee which included the 'auto-destructive' artist Gustav Metzger among others. Latham referred to these events as 'reverse order sculpture'. 'The *Tower Ceremony* contradicts a general notion about sculpture which is regarded as definitive – that sculpture is concerned with permanence. The tower is made to carry a sculptural idea. The proposition is that in disappearing a sculpture in this way it will be more memorable – and therefore more permanent than if it were carved in granite or fabricated in polyester. I think there is a case for art collections to carry evidence objects – documents by record of certain episodes that will register our changing attitude to time.'
– John Latham, interview with Charles Harrison, *Studio International*, May 1968

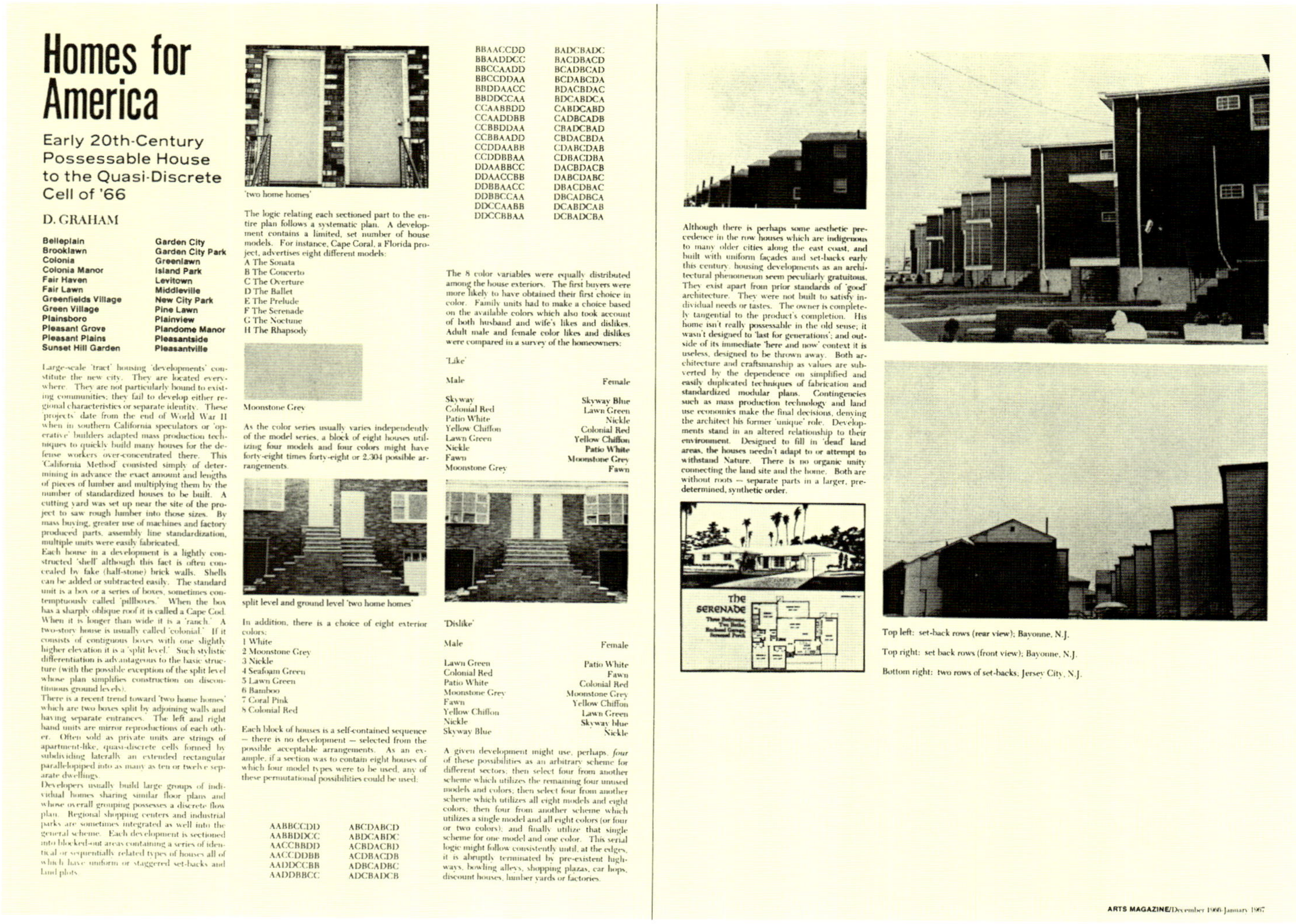

Homes for America

Early 20th-Century Possessable House to the Quasi-Discrete Cell of '66

D. GRAHAM

Belleplain	**Garden City**
Brooklawn	**Garden City Park**
Colonia	**Greenlawn**
Colonia Manor	**Island Park**
Fair Haven	**Levitown**
Fair Lawn	**Middleville**
Greenfields Village	**New City Park**
Green Village	**Pine Lawn**
Plainsboro	**Plainview**
Pleasant Grove	**Plandome Manor**
Pleasant Plains	**Pleasantside**
Sunset Hill Garden	**Pleasantville**

Large-scale 'tract' housing 'developments' constitute the new city. They are located everywhere. They are not particularly bound to existing communities; they fail to develop either regional characteristics or separate identity. These 'projects' date from the end of World War II when in southern California speculators or 'operative' builders adapted mass production techniques to quickly build many houses for the defense workers over-concentrated there. This 'California Method' consisted simply of determining in advance the exact amount and lengths of pieces of lumber and multiplying them by the number of standardized houses to be built. A cutting yard was set up near the site of the project to saw rough lumber into those sizes. By mass buying, greater use of machines and factory produced parts, assembly line standardization, multiple units were easily fabricated.

Each house in a development is a lightly constructed 'shell' although this fact is often concealed by fake (half-stone) brick walls. Shells can be added or subtracted easily. The standard unit is a box or a series of boxes, sometimes contemptuously called 'pillboxes.' When the box has a sharply oblique roof it is called a Cape Cod. When it is longer than wide it is a 'ranch.' A two-story house is usually called 'colonial.' If it consists of contiguous boxes with one slightly higher elevation it is a 'split level.' Such stylistic differentiation is advantageous to the basic structure (with the possible exception of the split level whose plan simplifies construction on discontinuous ground levels).

There is a recent trend toward 'two home homes' which are two boxes split by adjoining walls and having separate entrances. The left and right hand units are mirror reproductions of each other. Often sold as private units are strings of apartment-like, quasi-discrete cells formed by subdividing laterally an extended rectangular parallelopiped into as many as ten or twelve separate dwellings.

Developers usually build large groups of individual homes sharing similar floor plans and whose overall grouping possesses a discrete flow plan. Regional shopping centers and industrial parks are sometimes integrated as well into the general scheme. Each development is sectioned into blocked-out areas containing a series of identical or sequentially related types of houses all of which have uniform or staggered set-backs and land plots.

'two home homes'

The logic relating each sectioned part to the entire plan follows a systematic plan. A development contains a limited, set number of house models. For instance, Cape Coral, a Florida project, advertises eight different models:
A The Sonata
B The Concerto
C The Overture
D The Ballet
E The Prelude
F The Serenade
G The Noctune
H The Rhapsody

Moonstone Grey

As the color series usually varies independently of the model series, a block of eight houses utilizing four models and four colors might have forty-eight times forty-eight or 2,304 possible arrangements.

split level and ground level 'two home homes'

In addition, there is a choice of eight exterior colors:
1 White
2 Moonstone Grey
3 Nickle
4 Seafoam Green
5 Lawn Green
6 Bamboo
7 Coral Pink
8 Colonial Red

Each block of houses is a self-contained sequence – there is no development – selected from the possible acceptable arrangements. As an example, if a section was to contain eight houses of which four model types were to be used, any of these permutational possibilities could be used:

AABBCCDD	ABCDABCD
AABBDDCC	ABDCABDC
AACCBBDD	ACBDACBD
AACCDDBB	ACDBACDB
AADDCCBB	ADBCADBC
AADDBBCC	ADCBADCB
BBAACCDD	BADCBADC
BBAADDCC	BACDBACD
BBCCAADD	BCADBCAD
BBCCDDAA	BCDABCDA
BBDDAACC	BDACBDAC
BBDDCCAA	BDCABDCA
CCAABBDD	CABDCABD
CCAADDBB	CADBCADB
CCBBDDAA	CBADCBAD
CCBBAADD	CBDACBDA
CCDDAABB	CDABCDAB
CCDDBBAA	CDBACDBA
DDAABBCC	DACBDACB
DDAACCBB	DABCDABC
DDBBAACC	DBACDBAC
DDBBCCAA	DBCADBCA
DDCCAABB	DCABDCAB
DDCCBBAA	DCBADCBA

The 8 color variables were equally distributed among the house exteriors. The first buyers were more likely to have obtained their first choice in color. Family units had to make a choice based on the available colors which also took account of both husband and wife's likes and dislikes. Adult male and female color likes and dislikes were compared in a survey of the homeowners:

'Like'

Male	Female
Skyway	Skyway Blue
Colonial Red	Lawn Green
Patio White	Nickle
Yellow Chiffon	Colonial Red
Lawn Green	Yellow Chiffon
Nickle	Patio White
Fawn	Moonstone Grey
Moonstone Grey	Fawn

'Dislike'

Male	Female
Lawn Green	Patio White
Colonial Red	Fawn
Patio White	Colonial Red
Moonstone Grey	Moonstone Grey
Fawn	Yellow Chiffon
Yellow Chiffon	Lawn Green
Nickle	Skyway blue
Skyway Blue	Nickle

A given development might use, perhaps, *four* of these possibilities as an arbitrary scheme for different sectors; then select four from another scheme which utilizes the remaining four unused models and colors; then select four from another scheme which utilizes all eight models and eight colors; then four from another scheme which utilizes a single model and all eight colors (or four or two colors); and finally utilize that single scheme for one model and one color. This serial logic might follow consistently until, at the edges, it is abruptly terminated by pre-existent highways, bowling alleys, shopping plazas, car hops, discount houses, lumber yards or factories.

Although there is perhaps some aesthetic precedence in the row houses which are indigenous to many older cities along the east coast, and built with uniform façades and set-backs early this century, housing developments as an architectural phenomenon seem peculiarly gratuitous. They exist apart from prior standards of 'good' architecture. They were not built to satisfy individual needs or tastes. The owner is completely tangential to the product's completion. His home isn't really possessable in the old sense; it wasn't designed to 'last for generations'; and outside of its immediate 'here and now' context it is useless, designed to be thrown away. Both architecture and craftsmanship as values are subverted by the dependence on simplified and easily duplicated techniques of fabrication and standardized modular plans. Contingencies such as mass production technology and land use economics make the final decisions, denying the architect his former 'unique' role. Developments stand in an altered relationship to their environment. Designed to fill in 'dead' land areas, the houses needn't adapt to or attempt to withstand Nature. There is no organic unity connecting the land site and the home. Both are without roots – separate parts in a larger, predetermined, synthetic order.

Top left: set-back rows (rear view); Bayonne, N.J.

Top right: set back rows (front view); Bayonne, N.J.

Bottom right: two rows of set-backs, Jersey City, N.J.

ARTS MAGAZINE/December 1966-January 1967

Dan GRAHAM

Homes for America

1966

Printed texts and photographs as magazine layout

2 panels, 101.5 × 84.5 cm [40 × 33 in] each

Original artist's paste-up

After a brief period exhibiting artists such as Dan Flavin, Donald Judd and Sol LeWitt in the early 1960s Graham moved beyond the confines of the New York gallery system. He bought a cheap Kodak Instamatic camera and photographed the suburban houses and diners in his native New Jersey, attracted to the non-artistic, democratic quality of amateur photography. He realized that the notion of 'specific objects' which his contemporaries such as Donald Judd, who coined this term in 1965, were seeking to establish through the reductive forms of Minimalism, could equally be applied to contexts outside of the institutions of art and thus related back to people's everyday lives. 'I wanted to show that Minimalism was related to a real social situation that could be documented.'
– Dan Graham, interview with Mike Metz', *Two-way Mirror Power: Selected Writings by Dan Graham on His Art*, 1999

Homes for America described different types of mass-produced housing in suburban developments that could be ordered from a catalogue. The page layout echoed both the brochures and the serial logic of real estate development and prefabricated housing. Graham intended to publish the work in a mass-circulation magazine such as *Esquire*, which was a focus of humanistic, sociological articles, of which he was critical, about these suburbs and which often used photographs by Walker Evans and his contemporaries as illustration. Eventually *Arts Magazine* accepted Graham's work for publication in winter 1966 but altered his original layout substituting a Walker Evans photograph for Graham's images of contemporary housing. Graham subsequently re-made the work in several versions.

Mel BOCHNER, Robert SMITHSON

The Domain of the Great Bear [details]

1966

Black and white photographs, text

Pages 1 and 2 from magazine project for *Art Voices*,

New York, Fall 1966

This magazine project was published in *Art Voices*, New York, in the autumn of 1966. It took the reader on a tour of the American Museum of Natural History and Hayden Planetarium in New York, but was presented in a way that departed from the customary division between an artwork and a published article. Pointed visual and written juxtapositions were made between the institution – its sometimes absurd signs of administrative authority or the presence of commercial sponsorship – and the sublime natural and cosmic domains it attempted to represent.

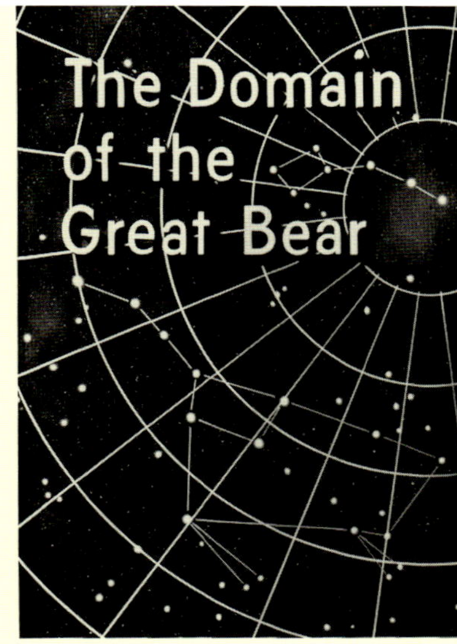

By Mel Bochner & Robert Smithson

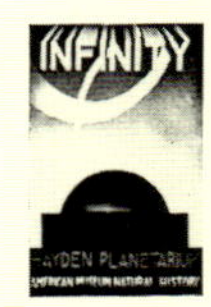

FOR SOME, INFINITY IS THE PLANETARIUM, A FROZEN WHIRLPOOL AT THE END OF THE WORLD, A VAST STRUCTURE OF CONCENTRIC CIRCLES, ROUND WHOSE BORDERS ONE MAY FIND AN INTERMINABLE COLLECTION OF IDEAS AS OBJECTS, A REPOSITORY OF MODEL UNIVERSES. HERE ALSO IS THE DOMAIN OF THE GREAT BEAR.

Nature is an infinite sphere, whose center is everywhere and whose circumference is nowhere.
—PASCAL

in the center of the infinite

Borges speaks of a labyrinth that is a straight line, invisible and unceasing. Overwhelming in its symmetries, the architecture of the planetarium is more labyrinthian. Circular, insular, windowless, it renders the mind itself invisible. An artistic conception of the inconceivable, it conforms to no outer necessity. Edges blur as one tries to distinguish an outline. The ambulatories become vast interminable spaces; traversing them becomes an interstellar journey. Once such expectations occur, there no longer exist any realities. Just vague disorders and contingencies. The planetarium becomes the same size as the universe; which it is. Perplexed, dizzied, one encounters here a cosmic nostalgia. Vertigo at contemplating man's most futile gesture—patrimony of the infinite. Above the staircase a sign:

SOLAR SYSTEM
☛
& REST ROOMS

The walls of the original sections of the building have a clotted surface and are painted sky-blue. They are a last refuge from the sleek and streamlined. There is a toneless, bleak feeling in the blank stone facing, the wide stretches of deserted corridor, the dark shrouded corners. A supernatural, immobilizing effect. But the light of recently installed exhibitions is bleaching out the dim uncertainties of 1934. New notions of the future and space, more optimistic and satisfying, are supplanting the dreary void. Formica and fluorescent, chrome and plexiglass are replacing the beaverboard, textured cement, glass and plywood. The dismal maroons and blacks are being repainted aqua, chartreuse, cerise or tangerine.

The conundrum, however, remains.

captives of the planets

At first only the image of a yellow light bulb is visible, suspended from the ceiling. A small globe of yellow incandescent light sunk in a dim background. Slowly other groupings of lights appear, advancing or retreating sluggishly as they move out from the center along wider and wider tracks. In orbit about the second order of lamps, further diminished lights revolve, sometimes indistinct, sometimes overlapping, hanging from boxes and armatures or other less simple shapes. This is the Solar System.

On the floor, in the center of the circular room, beneath the sun, is a twelve-foot reproduction of the Aztec Calendar Stone. The core of the design is a face of the Sun God. Its close-set eyes are crossed. Its expression vaguely cruel. On either side of the Sun, claws enclosed in circles are grasping human hearts.

About the stone in concentric rows are the seats. In the seats, in stupor, the audience. . . . Captives of the Planets. The atmosphere is violet, silent and inert. A recorded lecture drones in a basal monotone. Vacancy adds to the lifelessness. The axes of the system cut four aisles through the tightly wound rings of chairs. The aisles terminate in four sets of double doors at the outermost reaches. The doors, once closed, expel temporality. Enormous lengths of time are compressed into the room. Light-years pass in minutes. Life so extended becomes negligible. The cycle of the planets occurs and reoccurs. The Solar System, this mechanical collection of tracks, boxes, bulbs, gears, armatures, rods, seems tired, torpid. A chamber of ennui. And fatigue. It is endless, if only the electricity holds out.

All photos courtesy of American Museum of Natural History

"Under the great dome, the lecturer, with a complicated series of buttons, dials and switches to manipulate, and with over two thousand possible combinations at his command, is virtually in control of the universe."

Hayden Planetarium Guide Book

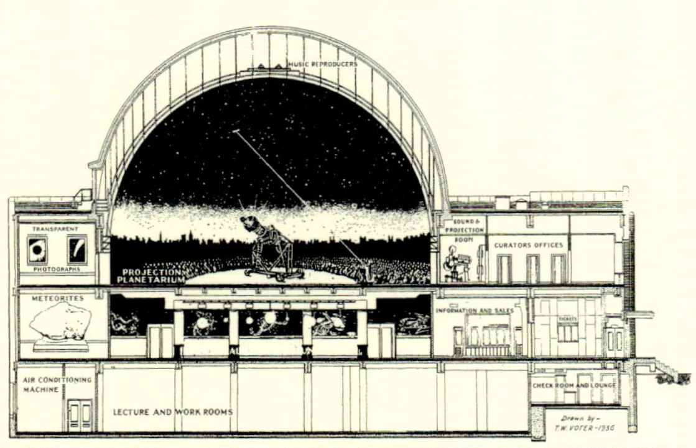

LONGITUDINAL SECTION OF THE HAYDEN PLANETARIUM

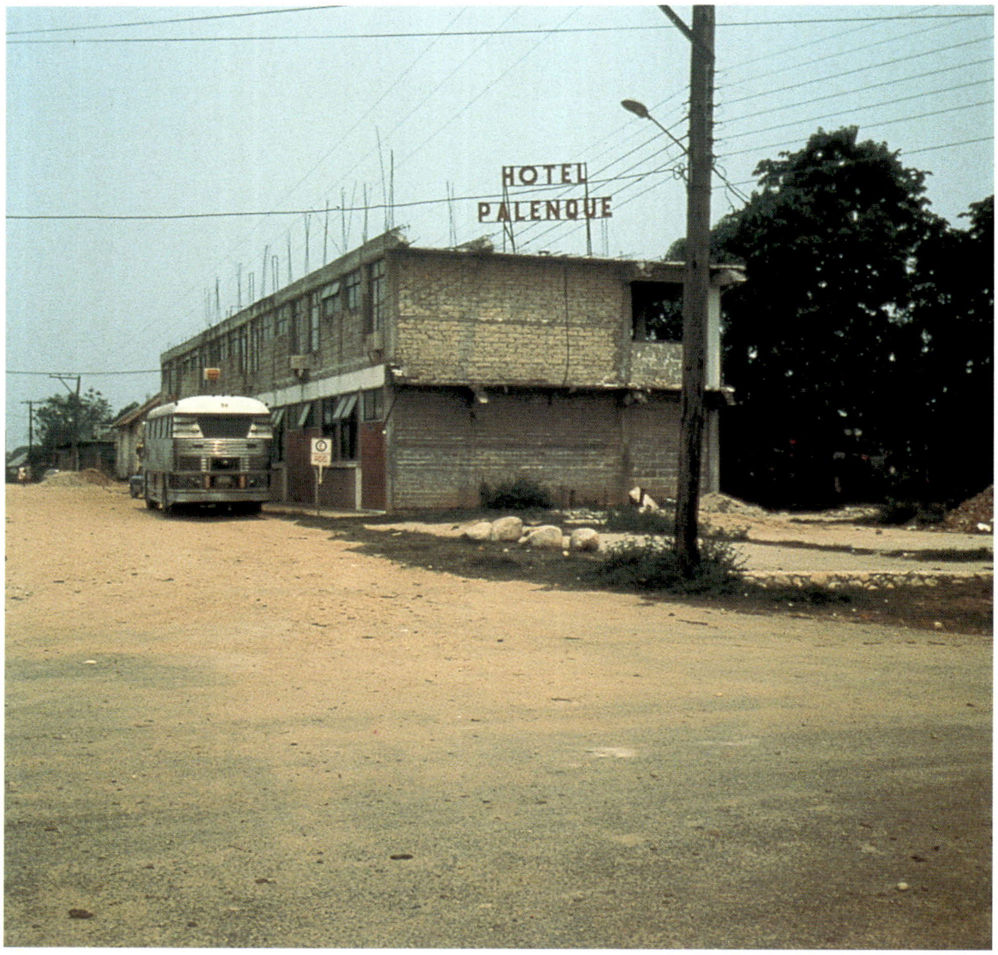

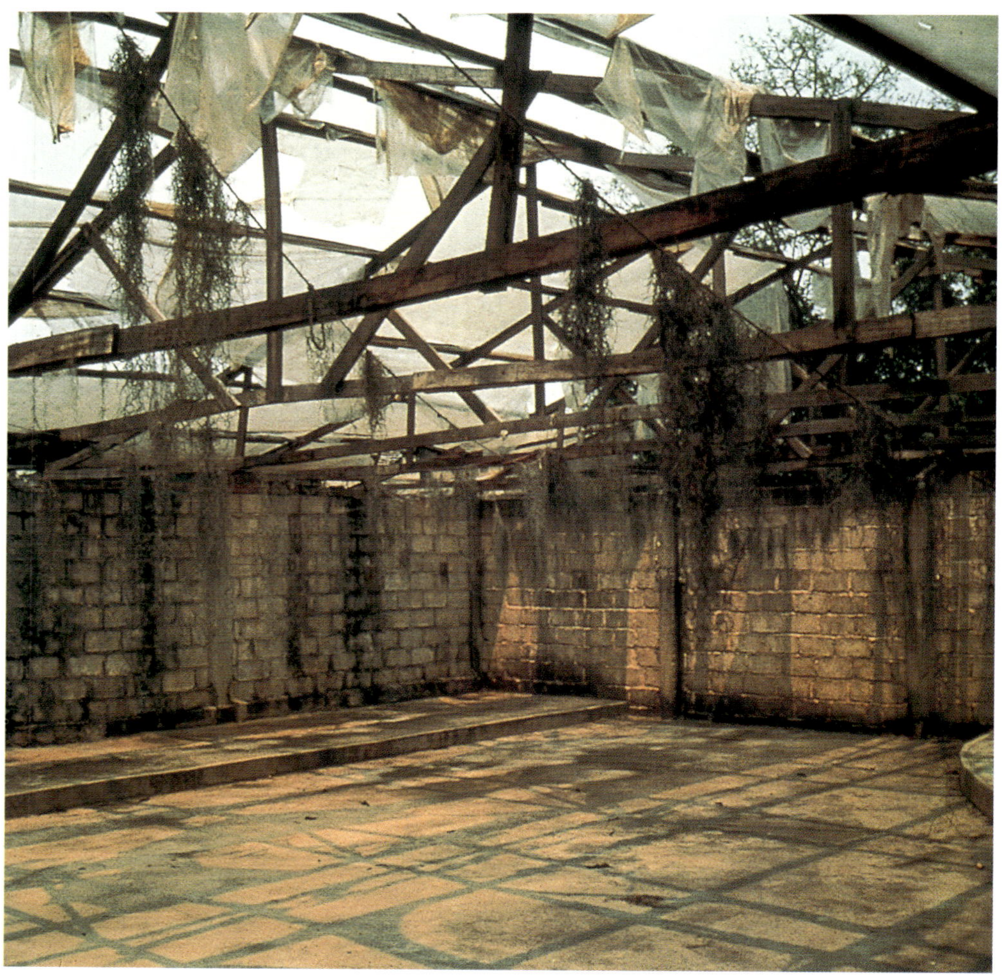

Robert SMITHSON

Hotel Palenque [details]

1969-72

Photographs taken in Yucatan, Mexico, in 1969, presented as slides in lecture delivered to architecture students at the University of Utah in 1972

Collection, Solomon R. Guggenheim Museum, New York

'Most tourists to Palenque are concerned with ruins of past civilizations; Smithson, however, was fascinated with the ruins of his own time. When he visited Palenque, he photographed the town's hotel and later used the slides in a lecture he gave to architecture students. Playing on his audience's expectations to see ruins of great buildings, Smithson presented ruins of an unimportant, run-down hotel that was being torn down in some places and newly built in others. The hotel was not razed at once, he informed the students, but instead it was destroyed slowly, with sensitivity. The lecture was conversational, its organization an extemporaneous exploration of the building, its tone ironic. At first, the students, who had expected a traditional slide lecture, were puzzled; they didn't laugh at any of Smithson's jokes. Only after Smithson had talked for twenty minutes did they laugh when they comprehended how he had undermined current architectural premises.

'In the lecture Smithson extolled an architecture that defies functionalism. He was drawn particularly to the rooflessness of parts of the hotel and the consequent tropical green interiors, to an empty swimming pool with a suspension bridge over it, and to an inoperative dance floor with its own live Spanish moss.'

– Robert Hobbs, *Robert Smithson: Sculpture*, 1981

Robert SMITHSON
Non-site [Slate from Bangor, Pa.] [detail]
1968
Wood, slate
15 × 101.5 × 81 cm [6 × 40 × 32 in]

'In June 1968 my wife, Nancy, Virginia Dwan, Dan Graham and I visited the slate quarries in Bangor-Pen Argyl, Pennsylvania. Banks of suspended slate hung over a greenish-blue pond at the bottom of a deep quarry. All boundaries and distinctions lost their meaning in this ocean of slate ... The brittleness of the site seemed to sway around one, causing a sense of displacement. I collected a canvas bag full of slate chips ... How can one contain this "oceanic" site? I have developed the *Non-site*, which in a physical way contains the disruption of the site. The container is in a sense a fragment of itself, something that could be called a three-dimensional map ... It is a three-dimensional perspective that has broken away from the whole, while containing the lack of its own containment ...'
– Robert Smithson, 'A Sedimentation of the Mind: Earth Projects', 1968

In this work from the series Smithson made throughout 1968, the frame-like metal container that holds the slate has a trapezoid form which follows the lines of one-point perspective. This highlights a disparity between illusionism and formalism on the one hand, and on the other, alternative ways of communicating our experience of natural phenomena. Integral to the exhibition of the *Non-sites* were accompanying wall-mounted statements, maps and diagrams.

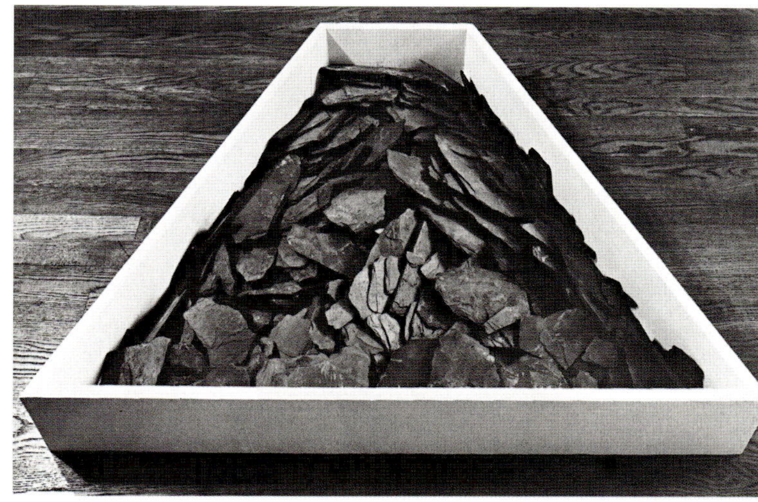

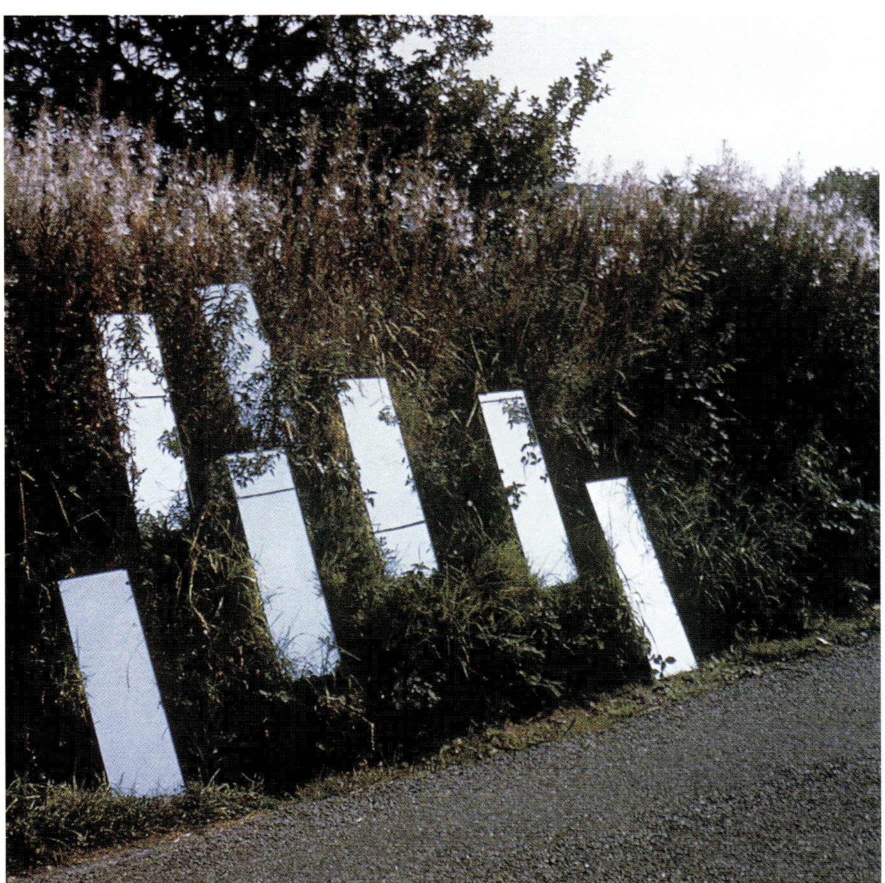

Robert SMITHSON
Mirror Displacement [Grassy Slope], England
1969
Colour photograph from 35mm slide
1 of 3 slides, dimensions variable

In 1968 Smithson began a series of works in which he placed mirrors in natural environments and documented them with slides, a number of which were then printed as photographs. Some of these 'slide works' were titled *Mirror Displacement*, referring to the way the mirrors intervened in the landscape through their reflections and refractions.

Describing the progression of his mirror works from his other *Non-site* series, Smithson wrote: 'I'm using a mirror because the mirror in a sense is both the physical mirror and the reflection: the mirror as a concept and abstraction; then the mirror as a fact within the mirror of the concept. So that's a departure from the other kind of contained, scattering idea. But still the bi-polar unity between the two places is kept. Here the site/non-site becomes encompassed by mirror as a concept – mirroring, the mirror being a dialectic.'
– Robert Smithson, interview with William C. Lipke, 1969

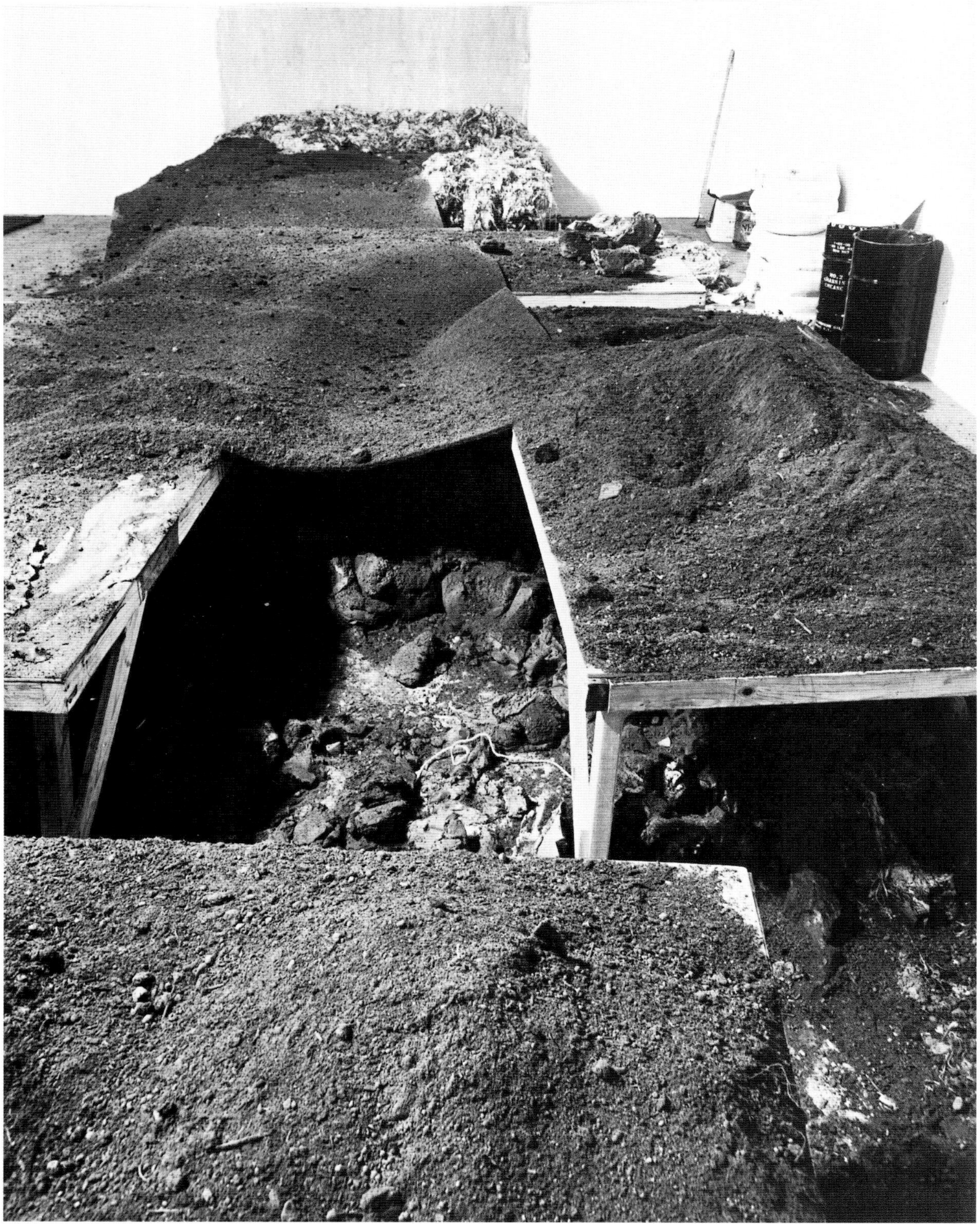

Robert MORRIS

Continuous Project Altered Daily

1969

Clay, earth, asbestos, cotton, water, wood, grease, threadwaste, electric light, photographs, etc., recorded sound

Leo Castelli Warehouse, New York

Between 1 and 22 March 1969 Morris visited the Leo Castelli Warehouse space on West 108th Street, New York, on each day of this project's duration. Here he worked intuitively and experimentally with a range of materials including clay, earth, asbestos, cotton, water, planks of wood, grease, threadwaste, electric lights, photographs, muslin and recorded sound. At the end of each day he documented the space photographically. Activities included rubbing clay on the wall, 'aimlessly throwing it around' and, on the last day, recording the clean-up, and playing the recording back as he took the last photograph – an image of the tape recorder alone in an empty space in front of the earlier photographs arranged on the back wall. The order of the exhibition space was transformed into a chaotic building site, open for public viewing every afternoon from Tuesday to Saturday. The work emphasized randomness and the properties of 'non-art' materials. It attempted to resist the formal closure of an art 'object' and of systems of production, display and viewing.
– quotations from Morris' unpublished journal entries during the work in progress, cited in *Robert Morris: The Mind/Body Problem*, 1994

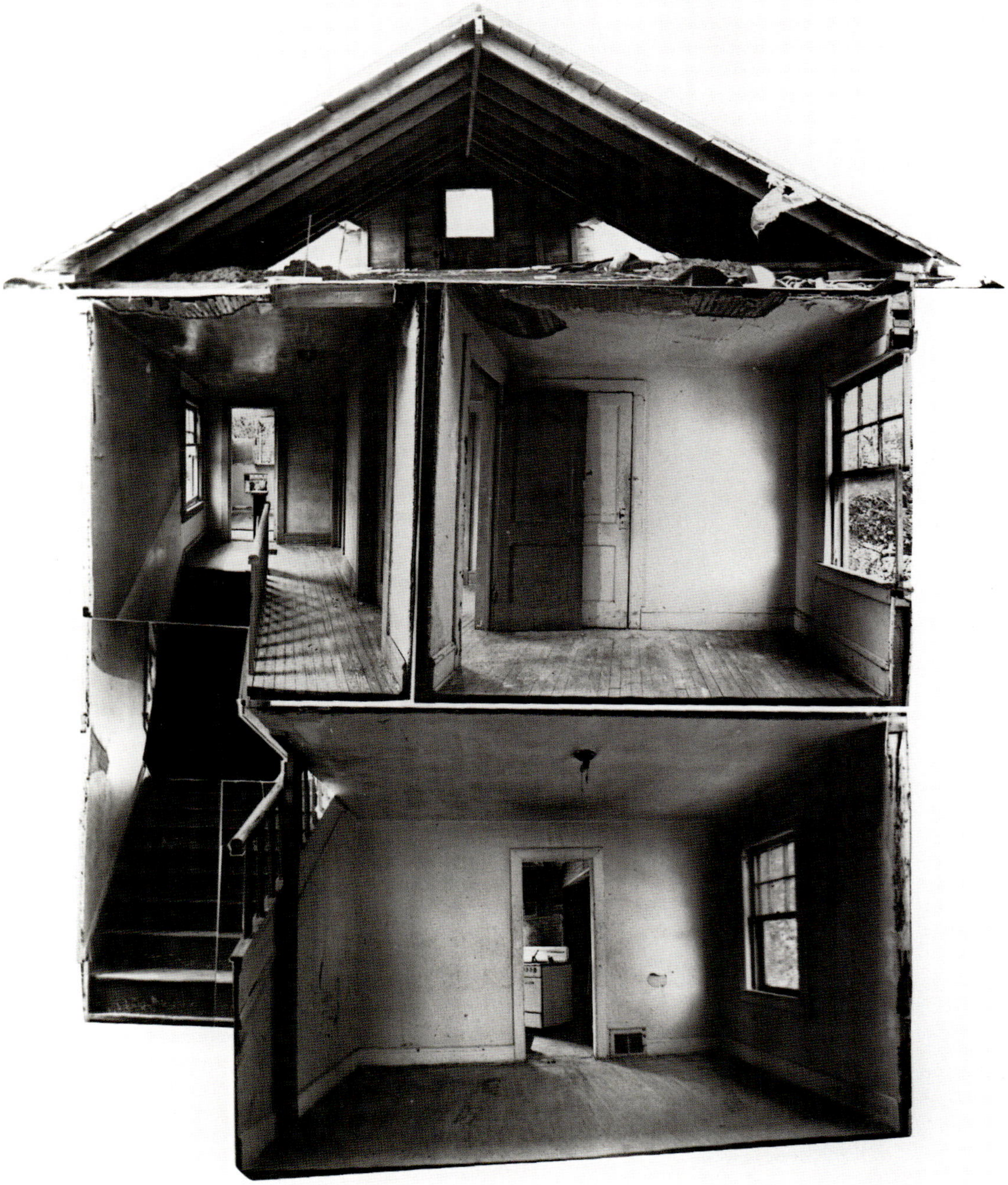

Gordon MATTA-CLARK
Splitting
1974
322 Humphrey Street, Englewood,
New Jersey
left
Photomontage of section
below
Documentation photograph
Dimensions variable

Matta-Clark described his work as a process of 'unbuilding'. When he proposed a project to cut a house in two, his New York gallery, Holly Solomon, secured 322 Humphrey Street, Englewood, New Jersey, a house scheduled for demolition. After clearing the house of debris left by its former occupants, Matta-Clark used a chainsaw to make two parallel vertical cuts through the middle of the building. With assistance he then lowered the back half of the house by the height of a cinder block, creating a wedge of space which literally split the house in two. He also removed the four corners of the roof and cleaved through the internal staircase, creating a gap which widened as the viewer ascended. Matta-Clark described the making of *Splitting* as akin to 'juggling with syntax'; this was experienced physically by visitors to the house who found that the normal vertical and horizontal axes which organize domestic architecture did not tally with their perceptual horizons.

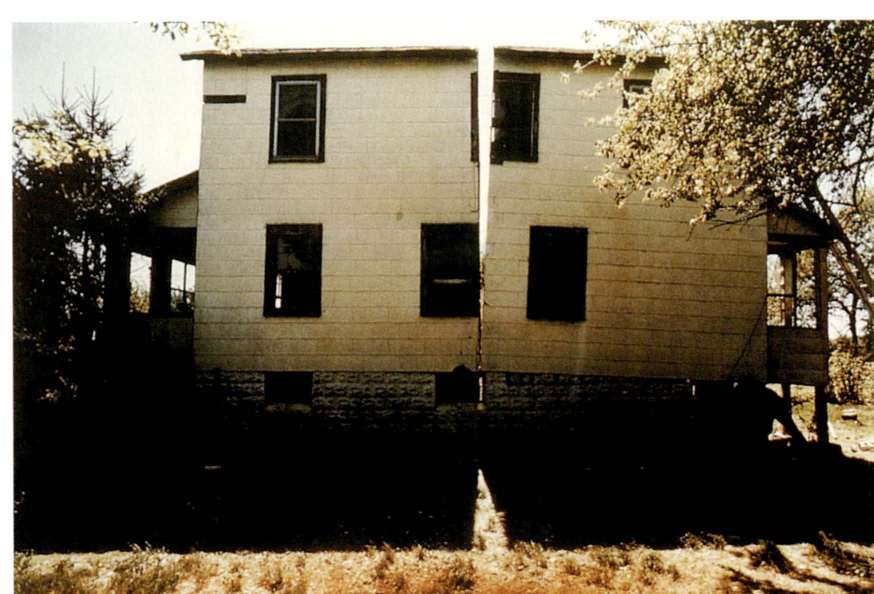

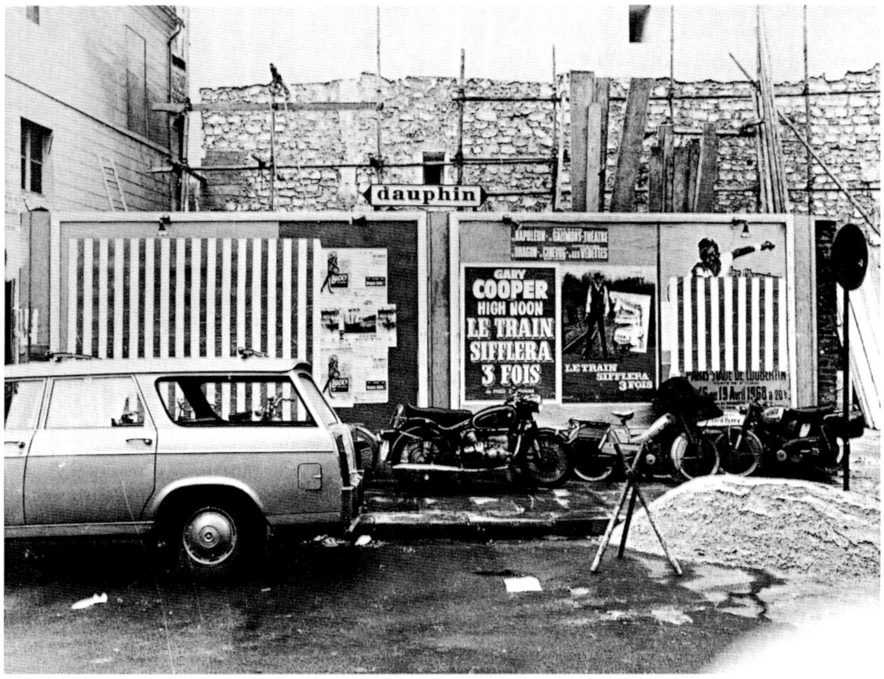

Daniel BUREN
Affichages sauvages [Wild Signboards]
1968
Paris
Photo/souvenir

In the middle of the night in March 1968 'Buren pasted single, rectangular sheets of green and white striped paper on approximately two hundred billboards and surfaces with signs throughout Paris and its environs. He placed the striped rectangles randomly over or beside existing texts, advertisements or graffiti, thus juxtaposing stripes – his sign for painting – with signs having nothing to do with art ... Unsigned by the artist and possessing only the "backing" of the signboard, the two hundred "paintings", dispersed throughout the urban landscape, commingled with the everyday reality of street images and messages.'
– Anne Rorimer, *New Art in the 60s and 70s: Redefining Reality*, 2001

This was the most ambitious of Buren's first works *in situ*. Made anonymously, without the permission or support of public, commercial or artistic organizations, his intervention effaced his authorship, drawing attention instead to the work's physical environment, and juxtaposed different art and non-art representational systems.

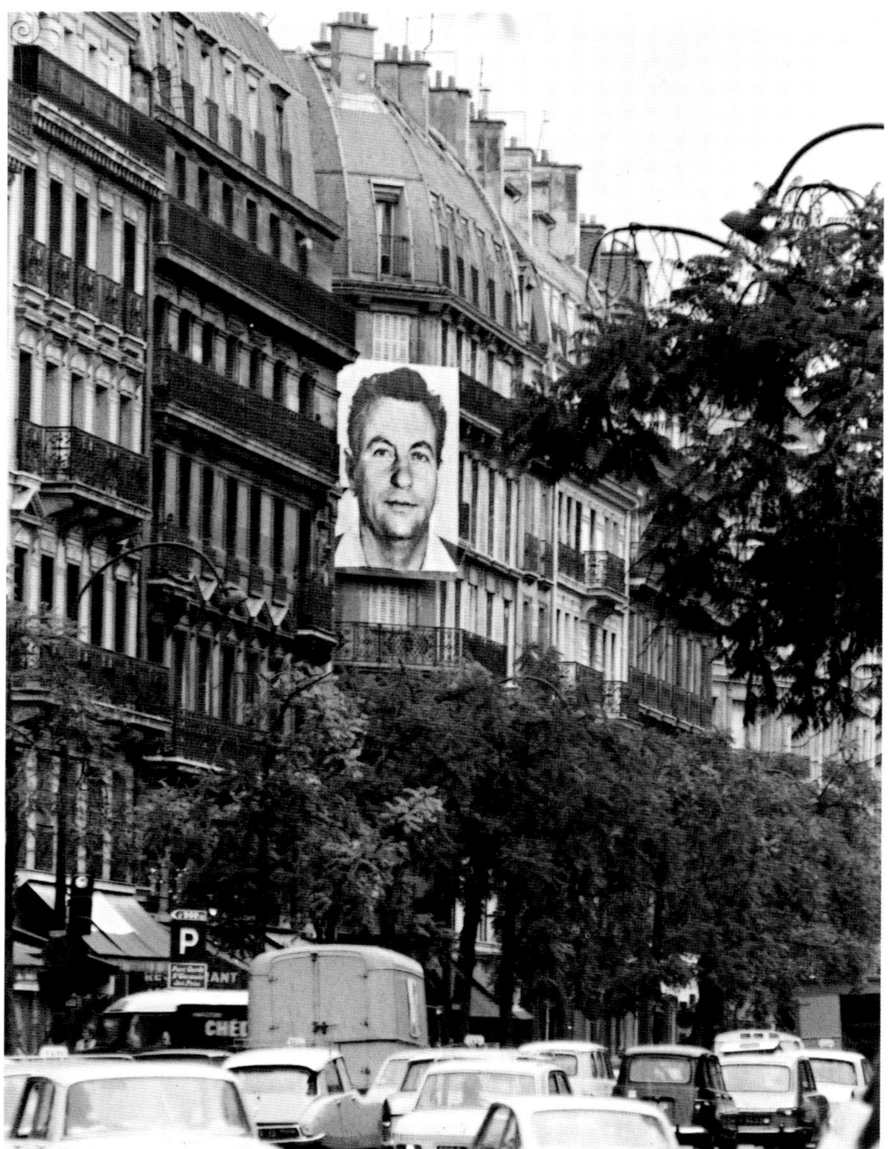

Braco DIMITRIJEVIC
Casual Passer-by I Met at 11.09 p.m., Paris, 1971
1971
Documentation photograph of portrait photograph *in situ*,
Boulevard St. Germain, Paris
Portrait, 5.5 × 4.5 m [18 × 15 ft]
Collection, Centre Georges Pompidou, Paris

At the beginning of the 1970s Dimitrijevic began to photograph people he met at random in the street. He then exhibited their portraits, often greatly enlarged, on public sites which are normally reserved for portraits of politicians, celebrities or advertising, such as banners, billboards, the backs of buses or sandwich boards. One of the first of these works was sited on the Boulevard St. German, Paris, in 1971. The work was later repeated in many cities, including Berlin, London and New York. Dimitrijevic also fabricated monuments to casual passers-by, in the form of portrait busts which were classical in appearance but inscribed with a personal message. In these works the artist posed broad questions about the ascription of fame, power and historical significance to individuals marked out from the rest of society. In 1976 he coined the term 'Post History' to explore the possibility that differing ideologies and forms of representation can co-exist.

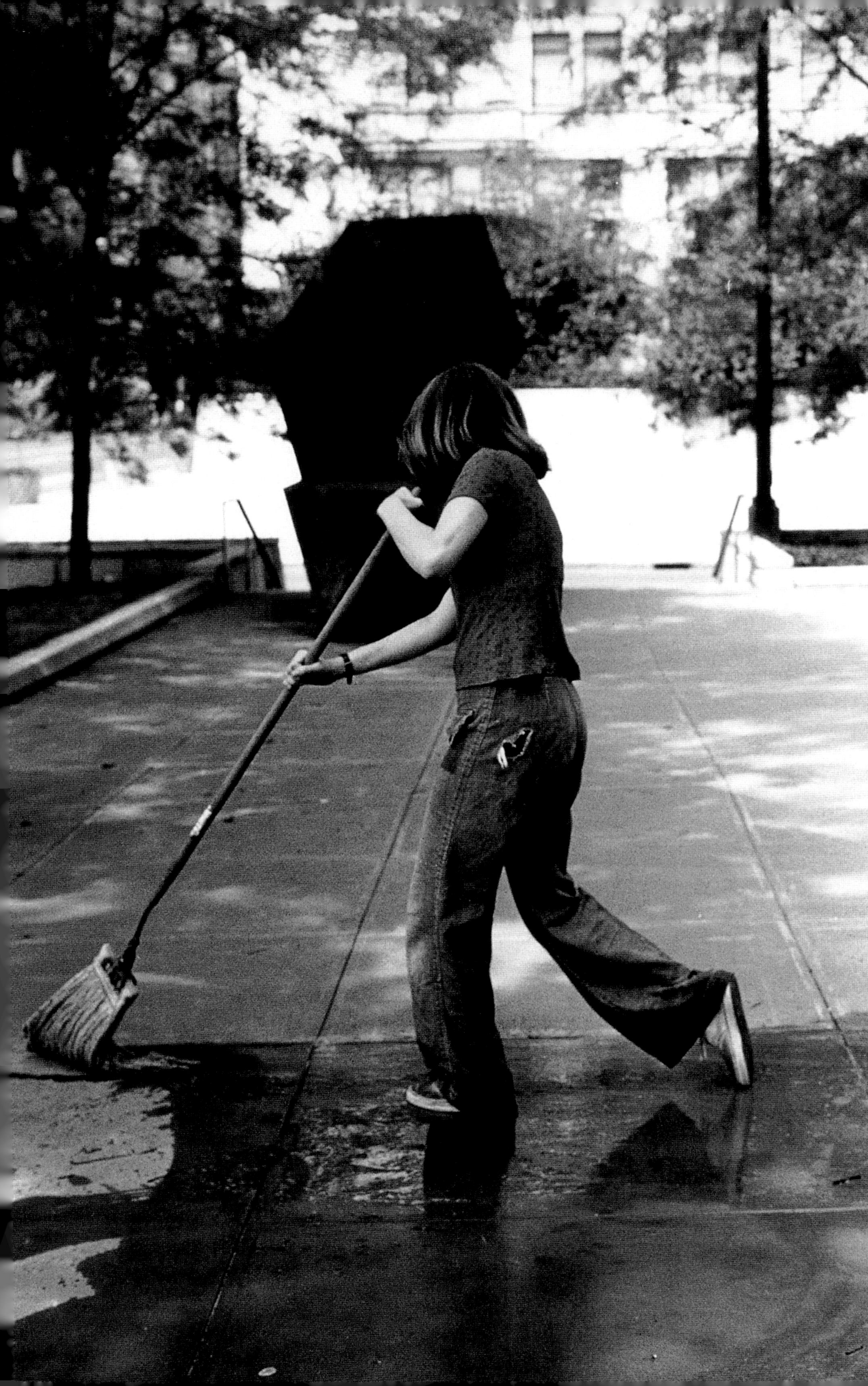

Mierle Laderman UKELES
Hartford Wash: Washing, Tracks, Maintenance: Outside
1973
Hartford, Connecticut
Documentation photograph

Ukeles first carried out everyday maintenance activities in public urban spaces, during public hours, in a series of seventeen actions, between 1973 and 1976. These actions provoked the viewer to reconsider the cultural importance of public maintenance and sanitation, and to view differently those who are assigned these tasks and their social and cultural significance. Ukeles has continued to work in this field. In 1990 she recorded these observations:

' ... We are, all of us whether we desire it or not, *in relation to* Sanitation, implicated, dependent – if we want the City, and ourselves, to last more than a few days. I am – along with every other citizen who lives, works, visits or passes through this space – a co-*producer* of Sanitation's work-product, as well as a *customer* of Sanitation's work.

In addition, because this is a thoroughly *public* system, I – we – are all *co-owners* – we have a *right to a say* in all this.

We are, each and all, bound to Sanitation, to restrictiveness ...

Waste is our immediate unwanted past. Do we "conserve" its energy through transformation, or do we drown in it? We are facing an environmental crisis, because we are running out of space to put it "away". To begin to accept as "ours" the difficult social task of dealing with "our" waste at the highest, not the most mediocre, level of intelligence and creativity ... people need to understand how they connect one to the other across our society, in all *its* scale.

We need holistic, inter-connected perceptual models of how we connect and how we add up.

As a first step we certainly need to peel away and separate ourselves from the ancient, transcultural, alienating notion and aura of the caste-stigma of waste-worker, of "garbageman", which has always translated, trickily, into "their" waste, not "ours"; they're "dirty", we're "clean".

Sanitation is the City's first *cultural* system, not its displaced-housekeeper caste-system. To do Sanitation is to husband the City as home. I think it can serve as a model for democratic imagination ... '

– Mierle Laderman Ukeles, ''Sanitation Manifesto!', *The Act*, 2:1, 1990

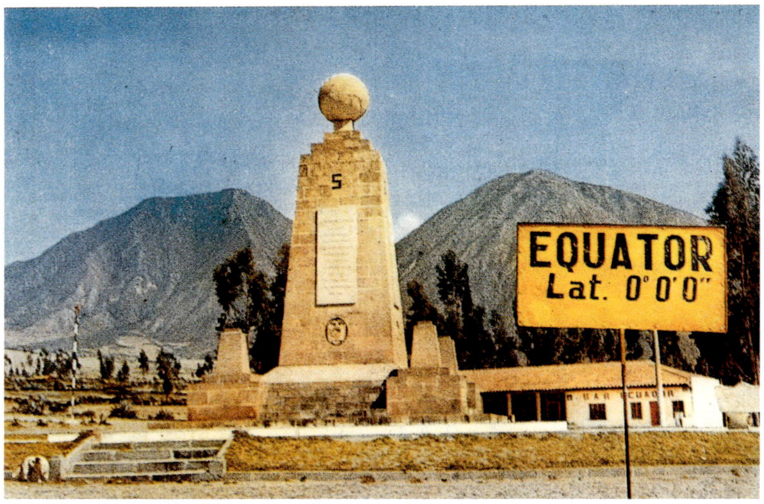

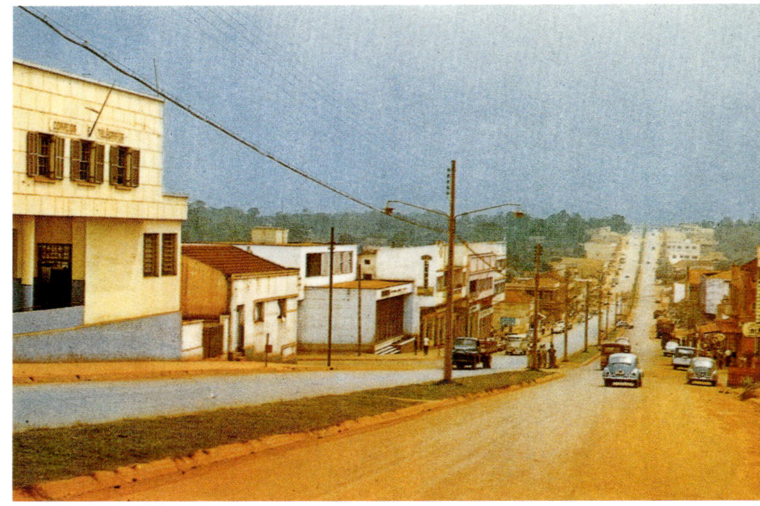

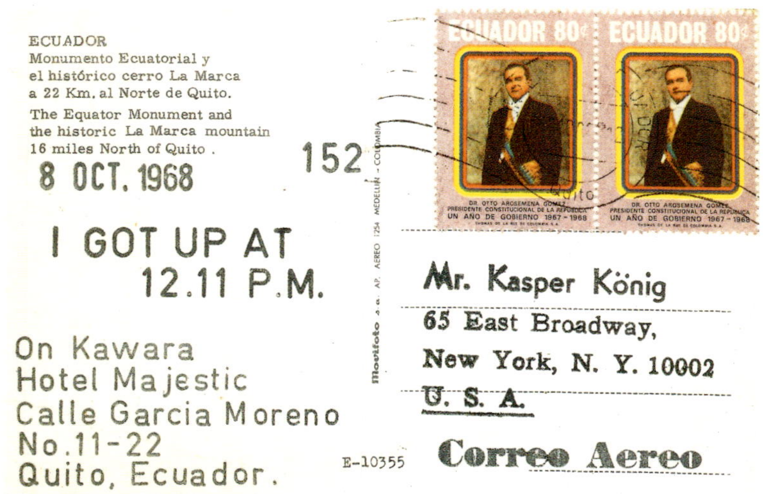

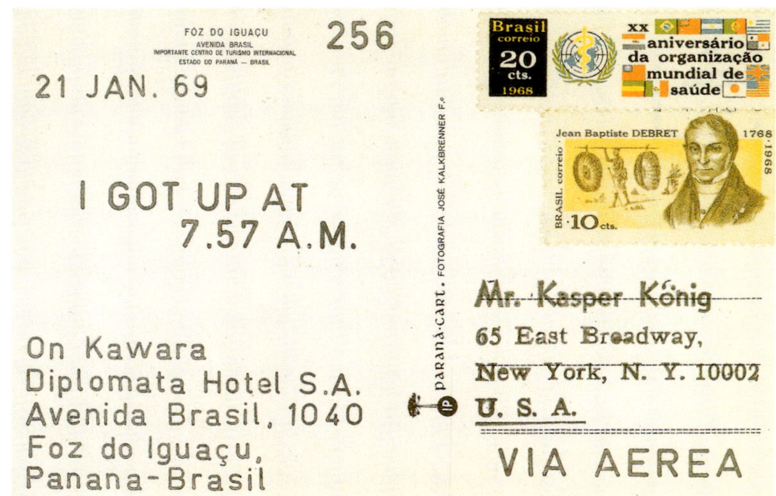

On KAWARA
I GOT UP AT [details]
1968-79
Postcards, rubber stamped text
10 × 15 cm [4 × 6 in] each

This work was begun in 1968 and continued until 1979. Every day Kawara would mail postcards which depicted the place where he was situated to two different people he knew. On the back of the card he rubber-stamped the exact time at which he had risen, prefaced by the date and the words 'I got up at', and followed by the address where he was staying or living. Three 'readymade' systems of communication were used to make this work: postcards, a rubber stamp and the postal system. The generic and multiple nature of these media and communication systems is brought into relationship with the specificity of the moment when Kawara awoke to consciousness of his surroundings each day.

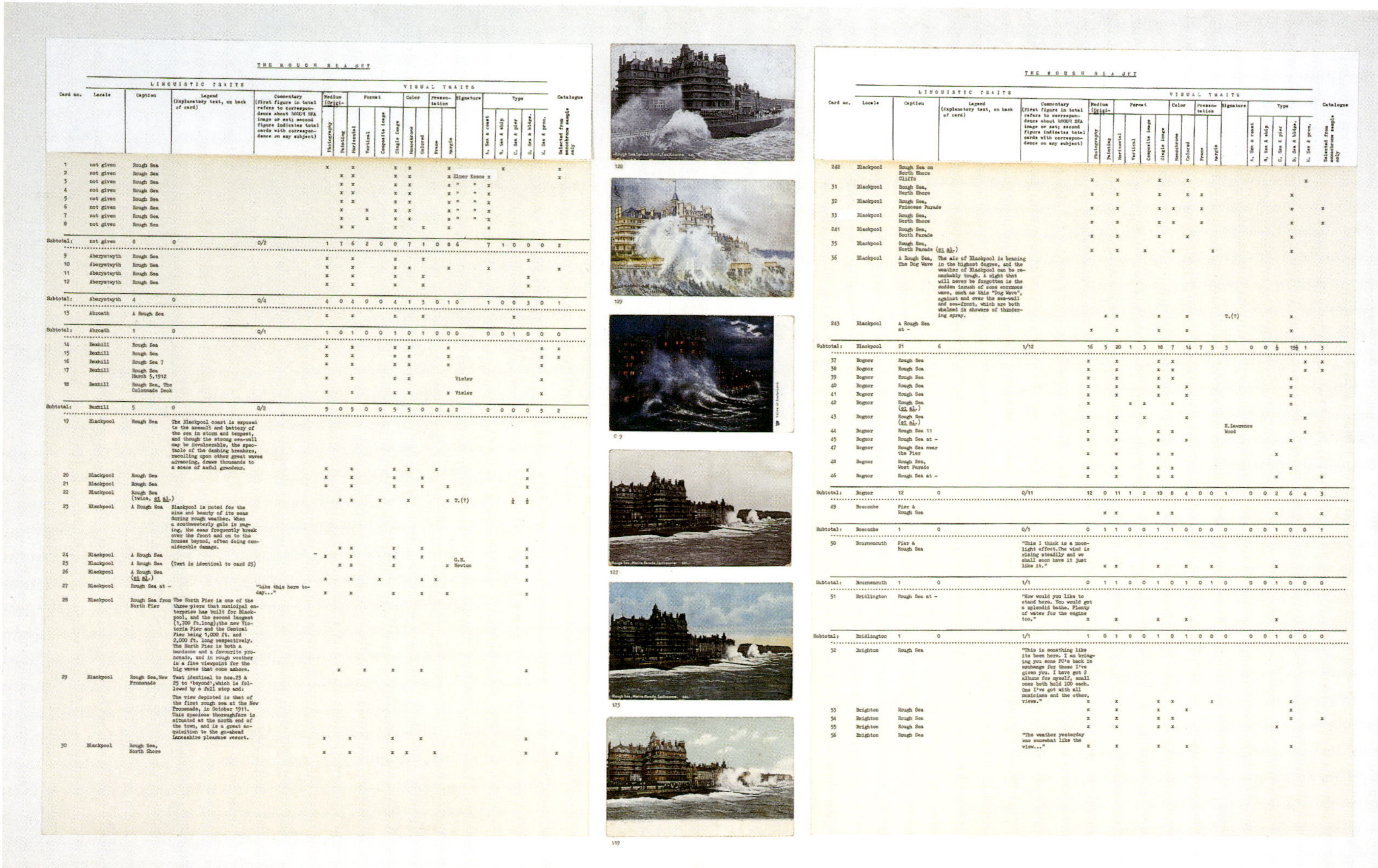

Susan HILLER

Dedicated to the Unknown Artists [details]

1972-76

305 postcards, charts, maps, 1 book, 1 dossier, mounted on 14 panels

Panels, 66 × 104 cm [28 × 36 in] each

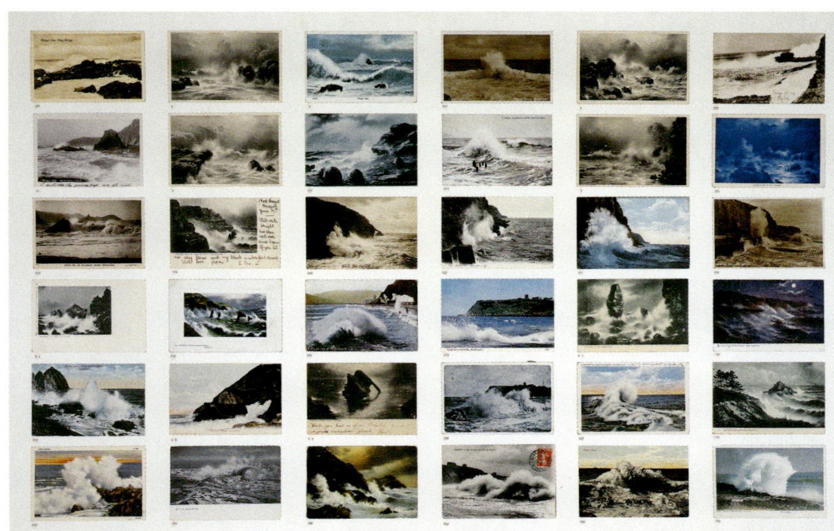

Hiller worked for several years with a particular genre of seaside postcard which she collected from numerous British coastal locations. These striking depictions of tumultuous waves were always captioned 'rough sea'. Hiller took the stance of acting as curator for the productions of the unknown artists who created this previously unrecognized body of image-text works. She established a typology of the images and analysed factors such as the complex and intriguing relationships between painting and photography in their production.

Dedicated to the Unknown Artists is an extensive museological project, combining visual presentation with textual analysis and charts that document data such as the messages on the backs of the 'rough sea' postcards when these comment on the picture or caption. By giving common, ephemeral cultural materials the same kind of serious attention a curator would give to recognized artworks, Hiller highlights the potential status of these seemingly simple artefacts as art, in terms of the imaginative creativity and complexity of meaning they manifest. The work draws our attention to fluctuations in the relationship of verbal description and image, and suggests various interpretations of the forces of nature, often expressed in a gendered form. In Hiller's tabulations, slight differences are carefully noted, drawing viewers into a close scrutiny of each image and raising the question, what makes these pictures notable, their similarities or their differences? Her questioning of 'originality' as a condition for any canonical validation can be directly related to a female exclusion from the canon. By implicitly involving viewers in an awareness of this issue, the work subtly connects them to a broader social inquiry.

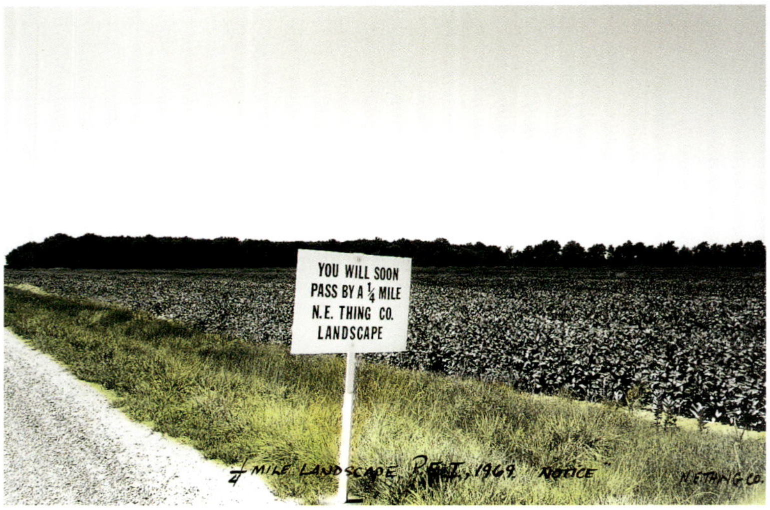

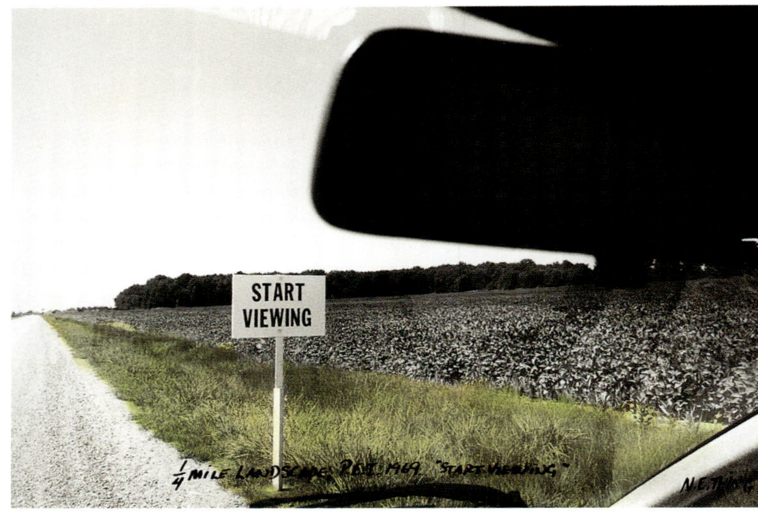

N.E. THING CO. (Iain and Ingrid BAXTER)
Quarter Mile Landscape [Prince Edward Island]
1969
4 panels, 3 hand tinted silver prints, 1 map with watercolour
and pencil on paper
53 × 81 cm [21 × 32 in] each

'It is the visual Unknown that challenges the N.E. Thing researchers. Like researchers anywhere, they seek to add to the world's store of knowledge – by exploratory research on the frontiers of basic theory, by product research for results in specific tangible forms, by production research for processes that yield precise end products. These probings of the where and how of visual things and their combinations are efforts to discover distinct properties or effects and the means of putting them into operation.'
N.E. Thing Co., company statement, 1968

Between 1966 and 1978 Iain and Ingrid Baxter produced works from their home in Vancouver under the mock-corporate name of N.E. Thing Co. (or NETCO). Rather than criticize the commercial institutions of art by adversarial means, they decided to position themselves and their audience ironically in relation to the art market by presenting themselves as a corporation. They produced works such as the above, in which the 'company' identifies as art, and therefore as valuable property, a segment of roadside grass verge (denoted on the map in the fourth panel), and installations in which they would transform an area of a museum into a mock corporate head-quarters with 'products' for sale. By this means they were able to draw viewers into ironic situations where artistic and commercial concepts intersect as abstract ideas.

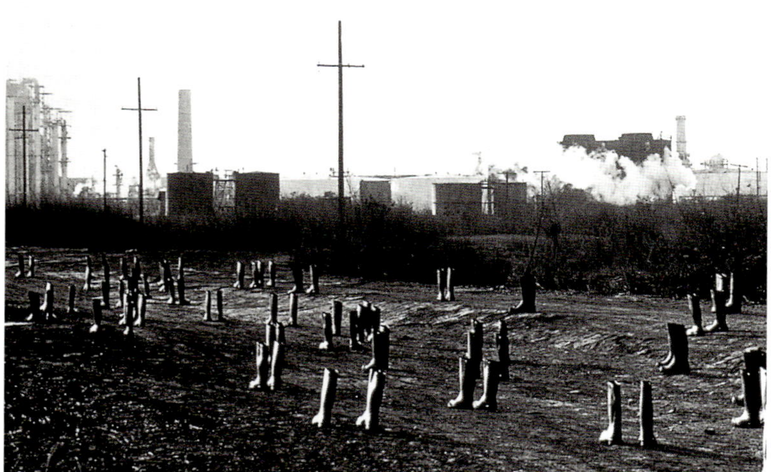

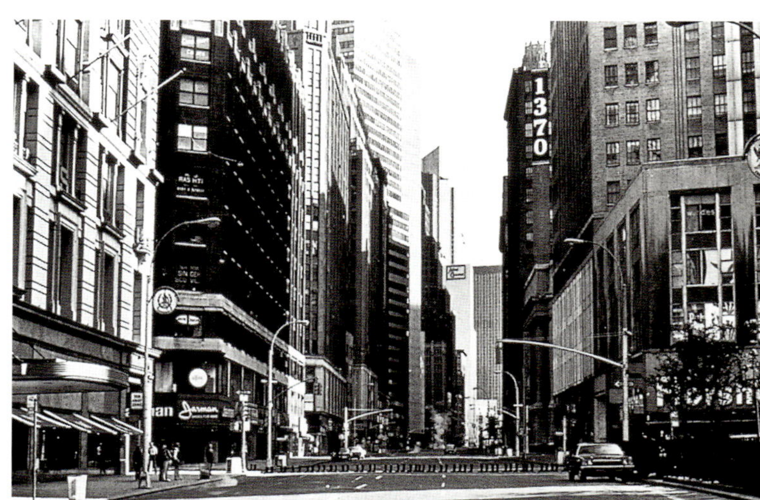

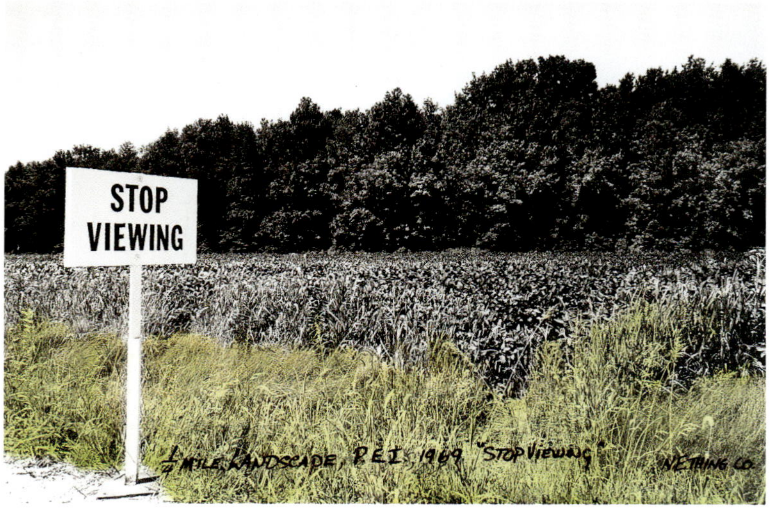

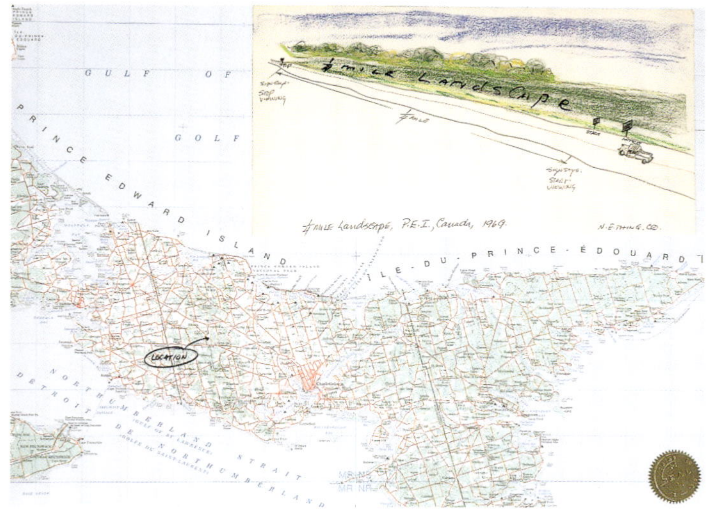

Eleanor ANTIN

100 Boots

1971–73

Black and white photographs mailed as postcards

11.5 × 18 cm [4.5 × 7 in]

For this work Antin mailed a series of fifty-one photographs made into postcards to around 1,000 adressees over two and a half years. Using fifty pairs of black rubber boots she had bought in an Army and Navy store, she created a persona (which she referred to in the singular as 'he') whose 'journey' the cards document. The photographs of the boots posed by Antin were taken by Richard Steinmetz at various locations in and between California and New York, where eventually the boots are seen marching towards the front door of the Museum of Modern Art for an actual exhibition of the cards in 1973. Each photograph is accompanied by a few words describing the location. The work parodically highlights the ways in which documentary photography is not a neutral form but is often complicit in a prefigured conceptual reconstruction of events.

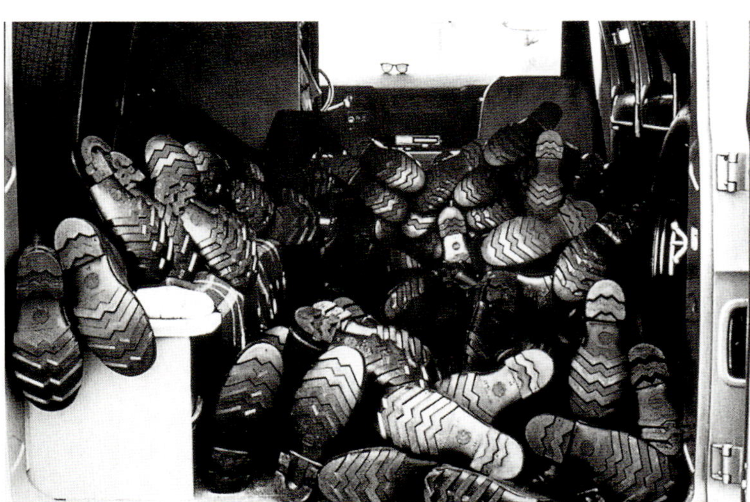

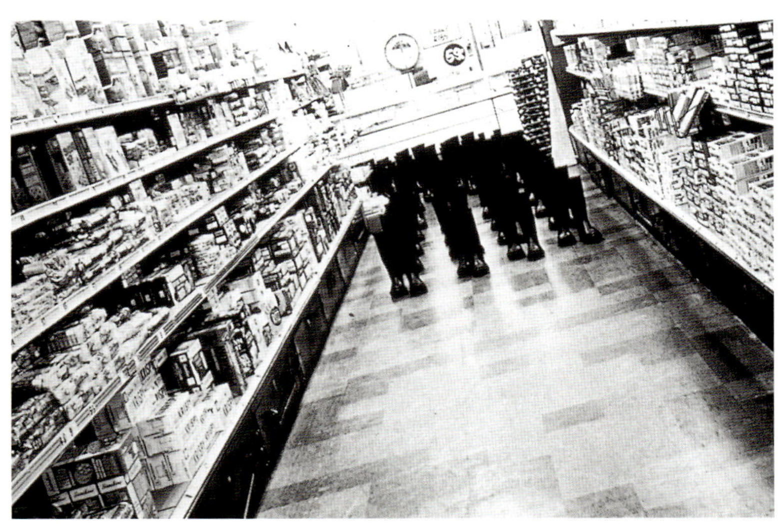

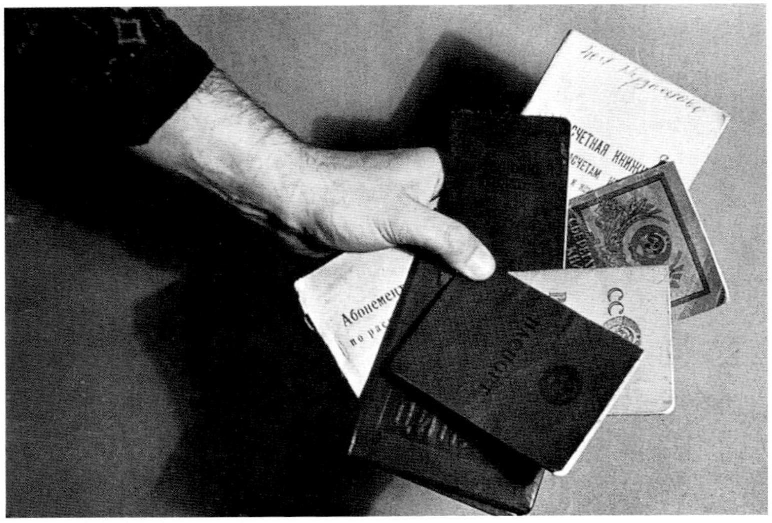

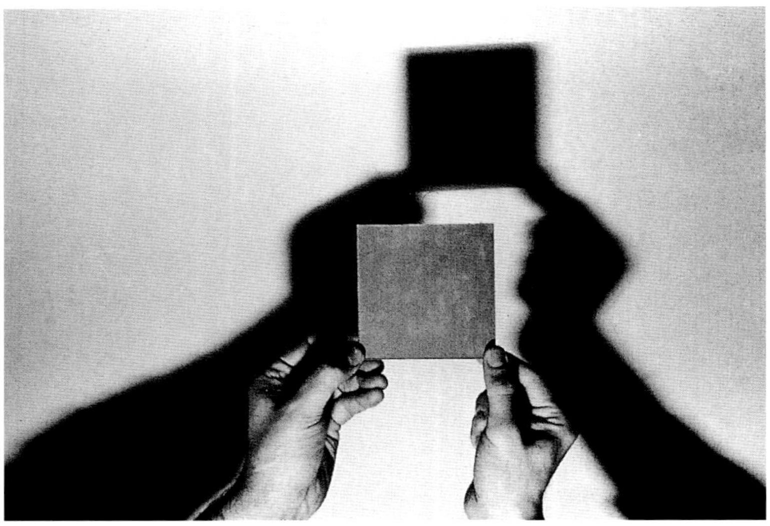

Vitaly KOMAR and Aleksandr MELAMID

Documents: Ideal Document

1975

13 Perspex panels, text, 3 photographs

Overall, 122 × 152 cm [48 × 60 in]

To make this work Komar and Melamid appropriated and reconfigured documents used by the bureaucracy of the Soviet Union. They selected twelve types of official papers, including marriage and birth certificates, a trade union book and a domestic passport. Each document was measured and its dimensions replicated with a Plexiglas panel. A thirteenth panel was created using the square root of the figure arrived at by computing the mean surface area of all twelve documents. This 'ideal square' was painted red, invoking Kasimir Malevich's *Red Square* painting of 1915. The work as a whole refers to the geometric art produced by the earlier Soviet avant-garde, ironically suggesting that geometric abstraction may both resolve and negate political oppression, by creating its ideal form and at the same time denuding it of verbal meaning.

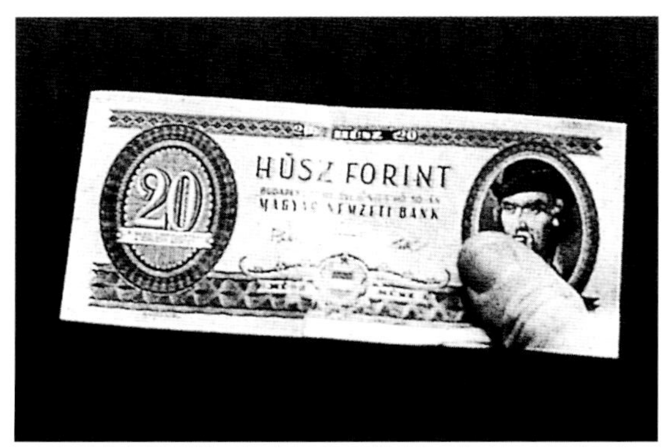

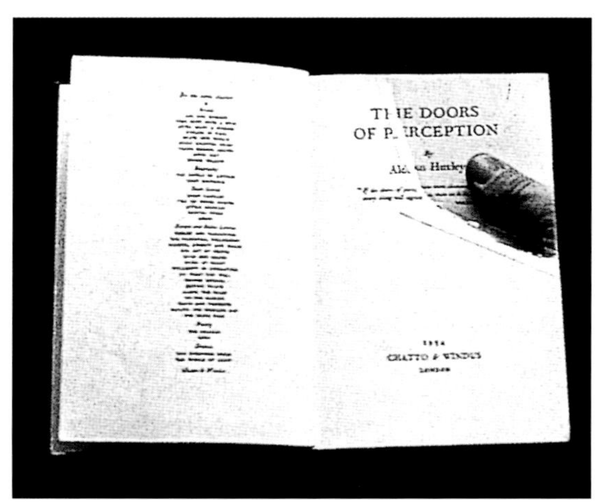

Tibor HAJAS

right

Restoration 2: Restored Money

1976

Bank note, photograph

46 × 33 × 4 cm [18 × 13 × 1.5 in]

below right

Restoration 5 [Restored Huxley]

Photograph inserted into book

Restored Money is a hybrid created from a twenty florin banknote and a lifesize photograph of the same banknote taped together. On the photograph the artist's thumb is clearly visible, half-covering the head of the historical Hungarian figure printed on the note. Hajas was a poet who became Hungary's most influential performance artist. His few conceptual works deal with the difference between the real and photographed or photocopied replications. *Restored Money*, visually dominated by the section of thumb, suggests that the human element is what might be missing (and needing restoration) in the exchange of currency. A photograph of Hajas' thumb 'restores' the living human to his other *Restorations*, such as in *5 (Restored Huxley)*, where it appears on the top right-hand corner of the title page of the book *The Doors of Perception* by Aldous Huxley.

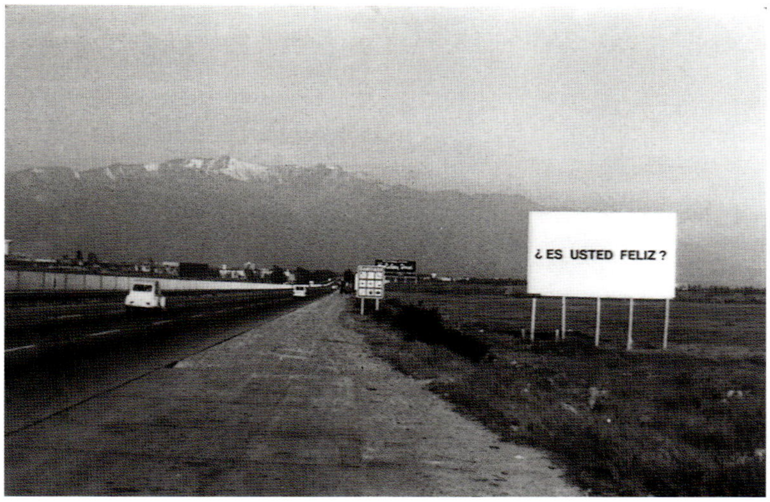

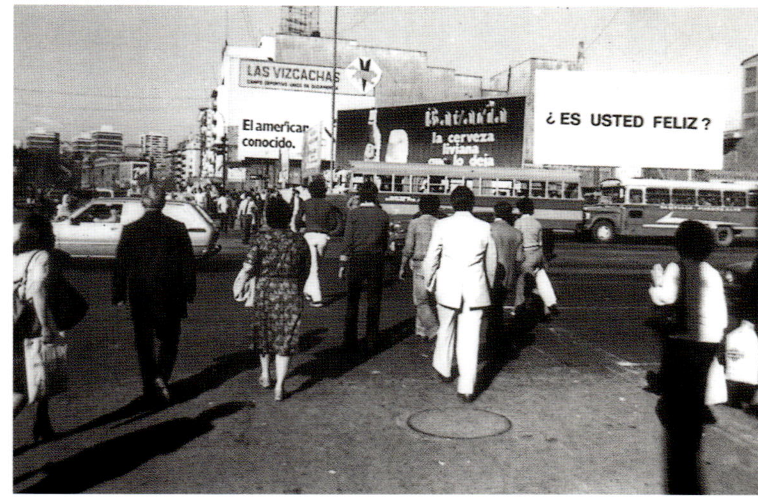

Alfredo JAAR

Studies on Happiness [details]

1979–81

Public interventions, various sites, Santiago de Chile

The works shown above, in which the message 'Are You Happy?' was placed on billboards and other sites such as public clocks, are part of the series *Studies on Happiness*, which Jaar initiated in 1979 in Santiago de Chile, during the military dictatorship. The project offered its audience a unique space for discussion and interaction, which dared to challenge the authoritarian atmosphere of the period. At that historical moment video was a new medium to the majority of Chileans. Video recording was used in the work, alongside other activities, such as the use of questionnaires and displays to record personal statements and opinions, as a means of engaging in open democratic participation. The work was conceived and presented in seven distinct phases: research and conceptualization (when Jaar collected statistics and made graphs of percentages of the public who were happy or unhappy); a survey; interviews; portraits of happy and unhappy people; situations of confrontation (public presentation of happy and unhappy people and a video installation); public interventions (such as the billboards above); and the final presentation of the project as an interactive video piece entitled *An Open Work – A Non-Stop Record*.

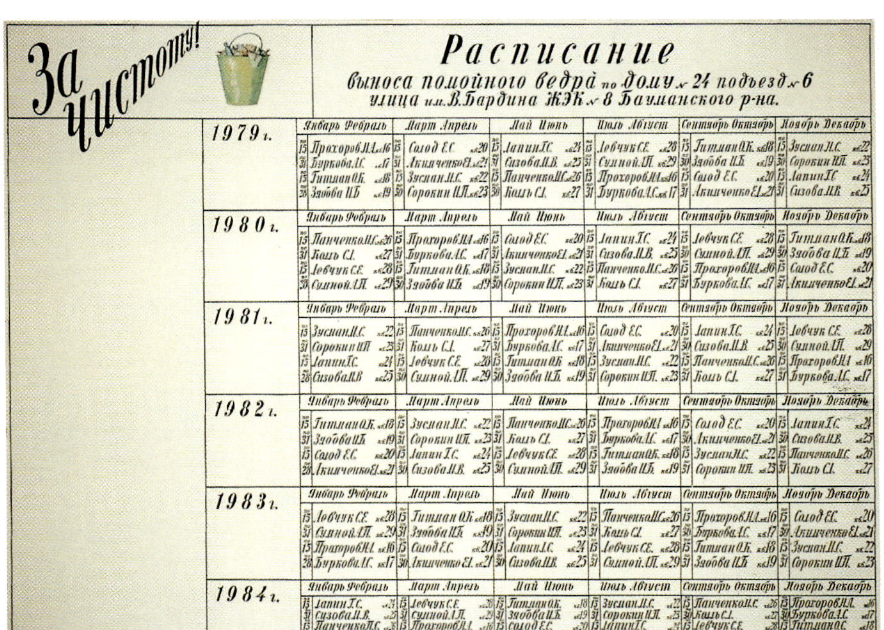

Ilya KABAKOV

Carrying Out the Slop Pail

1980

Enamel on masonite panel

150 × 210 cm [59 × 82.5 in]

Collection, Kunstmuseum, Basel

'3A

Cleanliness!

Schedule for Carrying out the Slop Pail in House No. 24, Entrance No. 6, V. Bardin Street, Zhek No. 8 of the Bauman region

1979

January–February

15 Prokhorov N.A. apt. 16

31 Burkova A.S. apt. 17 ... '

This is one of a series of paintings Kabakov made at the close of the 1970s which resemble the boards used in public offices in the Soviet Union at that time to display announcements, information, lists of names, charts and instructions. The use of text on a white background suggests Western conceptual art, yet rather than the text engaging with questions of art's definition, in an abstract form, it reflects upon the social world of communication within Soviet bureaucracy.

POLITICS AND IDEOLOGY

By the end of the 1960s art communities in capitalist societies had become increasingly politicized by authoritarian uses of state power: be it dictatorship (in Latin America), the violation of civil rights or the waging of imperialist war (the USA in Vietnam). In the context of social struggles, art took on an explicitly political role as artists became aware of its significance as an ideological form. The idea of art as an intervention – with a definite conceptual-political content – into the 'ideological circuits' of a society, through its media apparatus, was developed in Argentina and Brazil by Roberto Jacoby and Cildo Meireles, respectively. Also in Brazil, Hélio Oiticica and Lygia Clark emphasized the collective, participatory character of an art of 'propositions' that was at the same time an 'advent of freedom'. In Europe and the USA, class politics, women's liberation and anti-racism became significant artistic concerns. In works by Victor Burgin, Hans Haacke, Mary Kelly, Adrian Piper, Martha Rosler and others, new relationships between texts and images made theoretically based photo-text the dominant form of political conceptual art.

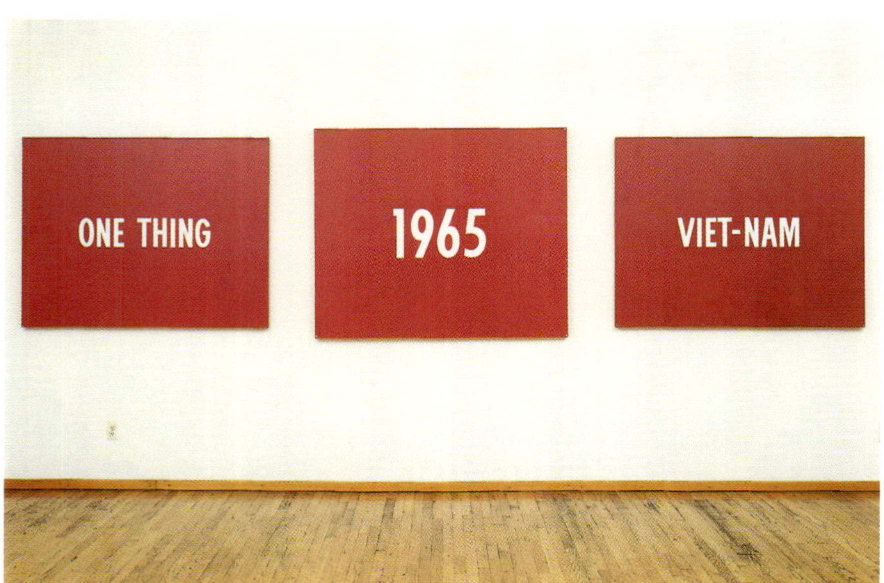

On KAWARA
Title
1965
Acrylic on canvas
Centre panel, 130 × 160 cm [51.5 × 63 in]
left and right panels, 117 × 130 cm [46 × 51.5 in] each

Unlike the *Date Paintings*, begun in 1966, this earlier work was not made in the place to which it refers. Rather, it is about the idea of Vietnam, which in 1965 underwent massive bombing by US forces. Kawara had witnessed the aftermath of Hiroshima and Nagasaki's destruction by US atomic bombs, and now lived in New York.

The left-hand canvas, 'ONE THING', is a development from *Nothing, Something, Everything* (1964) which consisted of the word 'SOMETHING' placed across a rectangle outlined in pencil. Rather than pointing to the the internal logic of the artwork, the texts in both of these works draw attention to the status of knowledge. Kawara, like the majority of people even in much of Vietnam, relied on the media for information about the war. The three elements of the work produce an arresting stillness in contrast to this flow of information and misinformation, focusing the mind on a different level of consciousness and of conscience.

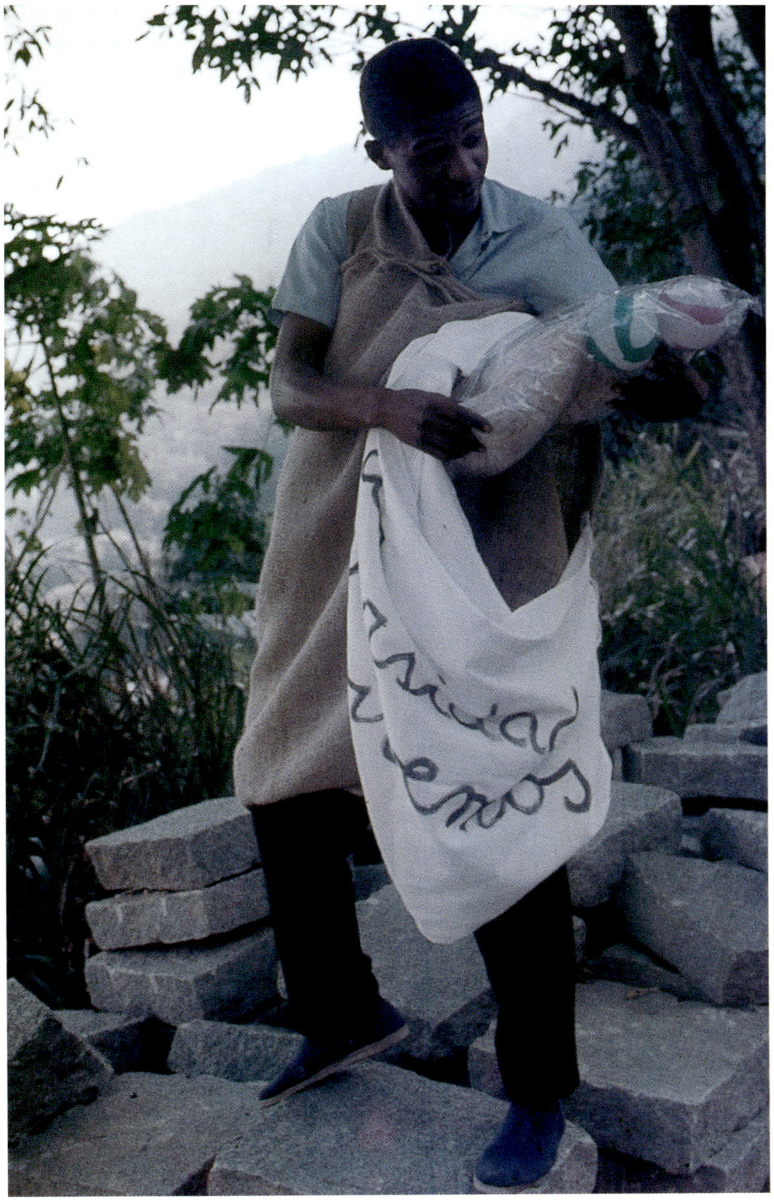

left
Hélio OITICICA
Parangolé
Nildo of Mangueira with P-16 Cape 12: De adversida vivemos
[On adversity we live]
1967
Acrylic on canvas with plastic, newspaper, burlap and pigment
Dimensions variable

Begun in 1964, the *Parangolés*, which have no exact translation in English, are transformable art works which take the form of capes, each of which has a different structure and character, usually inspired by a particular person or collaboratively made. A number of them were made for samba dancers from the Mangueira *favela*, a typical Brazilian shanty town, elements of which Oiticica imaginatively reconstructed inside art galleries in environments such as *Tropicaliá* (1967) and *Eden* (1969). When the *Parangolés* are worn or danced in, the participant veils and unveils its various layers, in which different materials symbolize aspects of the political message carried by their titles, which in some cases, as on the left, are incorporated as text onto the work itself.

right
Lygia CLARK
Máscaras abismo (Abyss masks)
1968
Eye masks, nylon mesh sacking, air-filled plastic bags, stones
Dimensions variable
Example worn by the artist

The *Abyss Masks*, which hang upon the head and partially cover the body, include a blindfold so that the subject feels a strong sense of volume, space and weight, not distanced by sight, in relation to the inward body and to objects, such as a bag filled with air, pressed gently between the hands, on a cavity of which which rests a pebble. The weight of the pebble counteracts the weightlessness of the air, and vice versa. In the context of military dictatorship and censorship of the arts the blindfold also has political connotations.

From 1966 onwards Clark, a leading member of the Brazilian Neo-Concrete movement in Rio de Janeiro, gradually moved away from constructivist sculpture and began to use everyday found objects to make 'relational objects' which invited a participatory engagement through the senses. Often the works are designed to make participants aware of their other senses and the totality of their bodies by restricting or submerging the visual sense. Clark considered her works to be 'propositions' or 'proposals' which bring to light participants' freedom of action. After 1968 they took on increasingly collective forms.

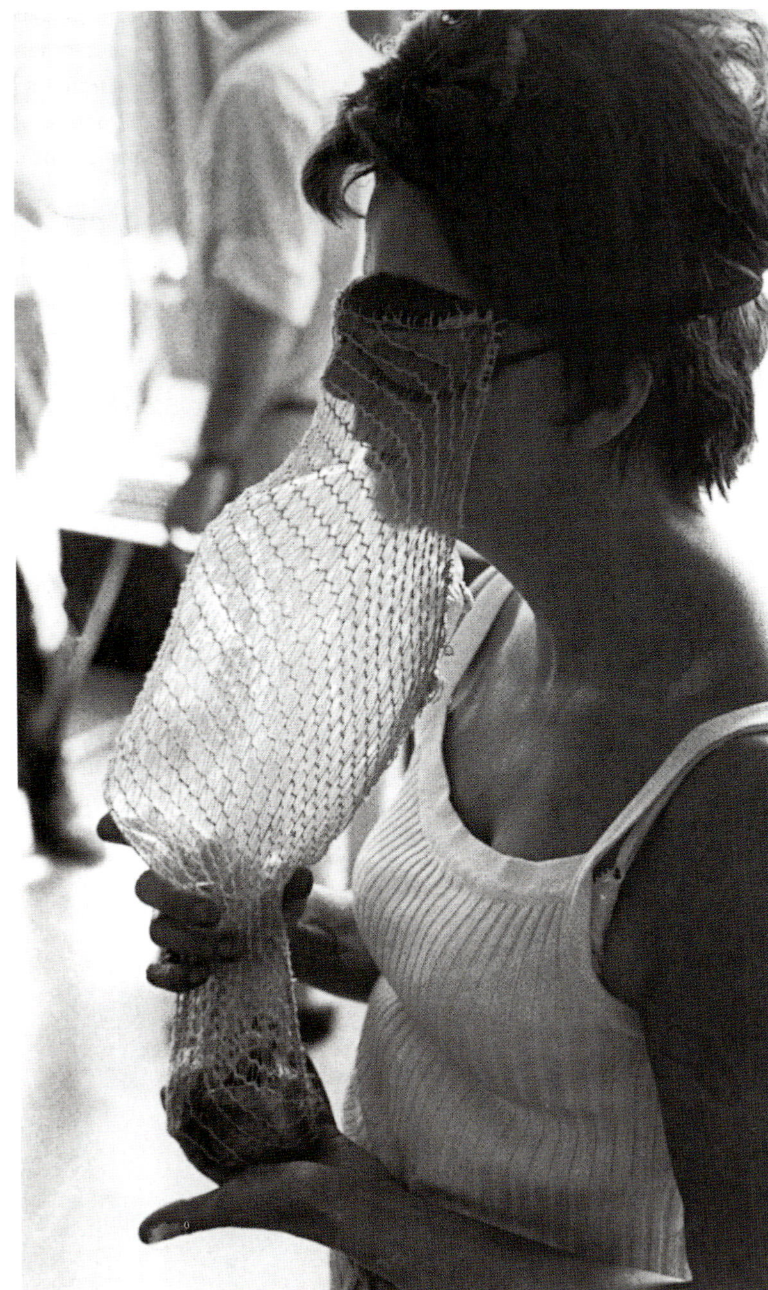

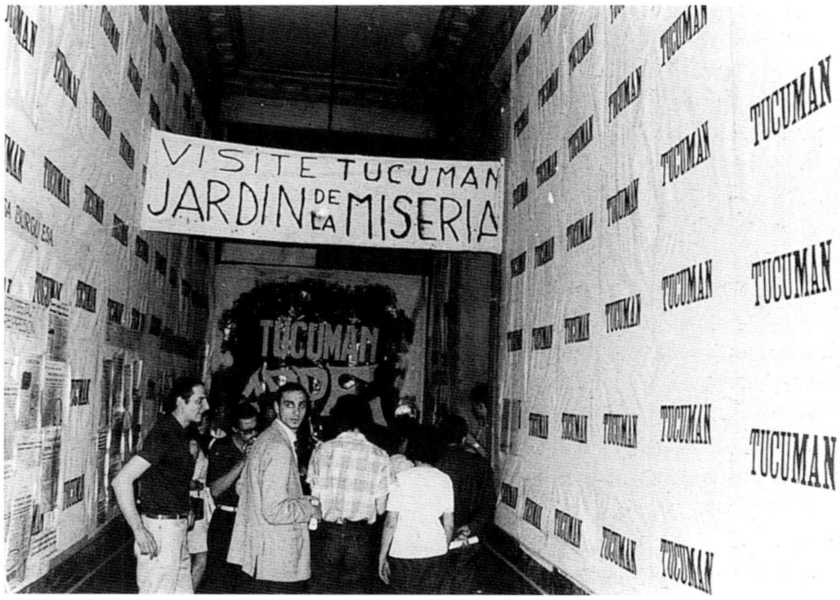

GRUPO DE ARTISTAS DE VANGARDIA/CGT

Tucumán Arde [Tucumán Burns]

1968

Detail of installation, Rosario, Argentina

Tucumán is a small province in north-western Argentina where a harsh plan of economic rationalization by the Argentinian government in the late 1960s led to the closure of most of the local sugar refineries, the province's principal source of income, leaving massive unemployment and poverty. To suppress protest, the government used the media to create a smokescreen, promoting a largely fictional new industrialization project which would 'quickly' restore employment to the area.

In response, a group of artists from Rosario, Santa Fe and Buenos Aires formed the Grupo de Artistas de Vanguardia (Group of Avant-Garde Artists). They affiliated themselves with the Argentinean General Confederation of Labour (Confederación General del Trabajo, or CGT) in order to create this work in 1968. The group researched the facts and publicized them by every means available, initially using posters and fliers and eventually installing large multi-media exhibitions in trade union halls in Rosario and Buenos Aires. The installations included posters, placards, photo-murals, newspaper montages, tape recordings and statistical graphs indicating rates of infant mortality, tuberculosis and illiteracy in the Tucumán region. Juxtaposed with this was the full range of government-sponsored misinformation. The extreme discrepancies functioned to raise political consciousness and to educate viewers about the informational circuits of the state.

Cildo MEIRELES

Inserções em circuitos ideologicos: projeto Coca-Cola

[Insertions into Ideological Circuits: Coca-Cola Project]

1970

Messages transferred onto Coca Cola bottles in circulation

Collection, New Museum of Contemporary Art, New York

Meireles made this work in Rio de Janeiro. It took two forms: in the first project, he temporarily removed recyclable Coca-Cola bottles from circulation. Onto them he transferred small messages in white text such as 'Yankees Go Home', and then placed them back in circulation. In the second, the 'Banknote Project', he similarly removed banknotes from circulation, placing rubber stamped messages on them about such things as the 'disappearance' of political opponents of the Brazilian government, before returning them into circulation. The 'readymade' here is not an industrial object transferred into the realm of art but a social system of distribution which is endowed with a new artistic and political function. The works 'concentrated on isolating and defining the concept of the circuit, by taking advantage of a pre-existing system of circulation. In this sense the texts on the Coca-Cola bottles and on the banknotes functioned as a kind of mobile grafitti.' 'The work is the operation and not the objects ... The *Insertions* dissolve the notion of authority.'
– quotations from the artist, *Cildo Meireles*, 1999

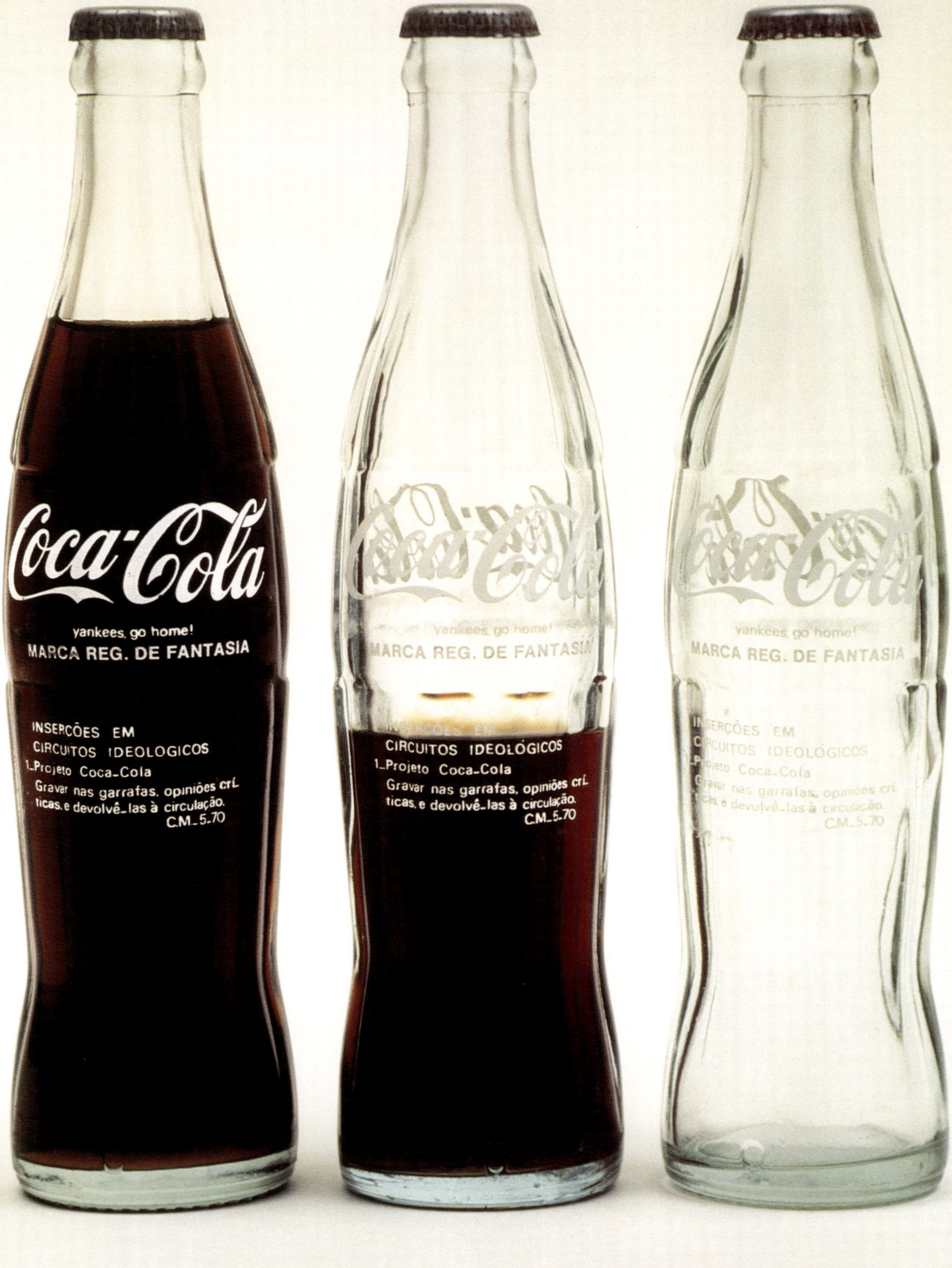
Coca-Cola
yankees, go home!
MARCA REG. DE FANTASIA
INSERÇÕES EM
CIRCUITOS IDEOLÓGICOS
1_Projeto Coca-Cola
Gravar nas garrafas, opiniões crí_
ticas, e devolvê_las à circulação.
C.M._5_70

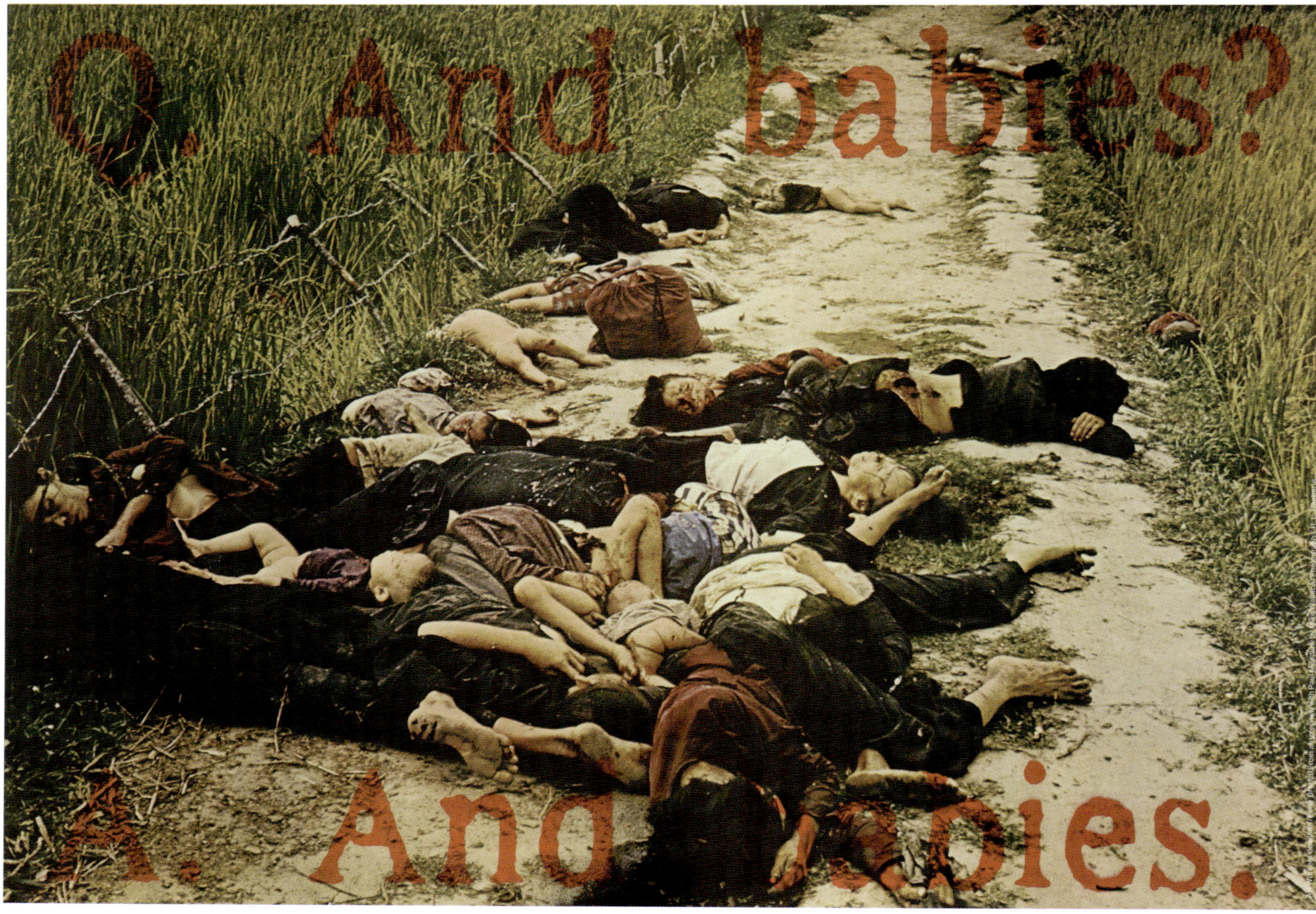

ART WORKERS COALITION [Ronald HAEBERLE and Peter BRANDT]
Q. And babies?
A. And babies
1970
Colour lithograph
63.5 × 96.5 cm [25 × 38 in]
Collection, The Museum of Modern Art, New York

The Art Workers Coalition, whose members included Carl Andre, Mel Bochner and Robert Morris, made this poster in 1970, using a war reportage photograph which had first appeared in a newspaper in Cleveland, Ohio, and shortly after on US national television in the winter of 1969. The bodies depicted were the victims of a 'neutralization' mission by American forces in March 1968 at a small village in South Vietnam. Although the soldiers were not fired on by the inhabitants, they burned the village, raped and mutilated women, sparing no one, including the elderly and infants, all of whom were killed. Over one hundred of the villagers were massacred in the ditch shown in the photograph. The poster was distributed around the world. Some members of the Coalition made a protest in New York's Museum of Modern Art, where they held it up in front of Picasso's painting *Guernica*, his protest against the inhumanity of the Spanish Civil War. Many of the museum's trustees were the same people who owned the companies that produced the machinery of war and benefited financially from it. The work raised devastating questions about the underlying political conditions of official culture.

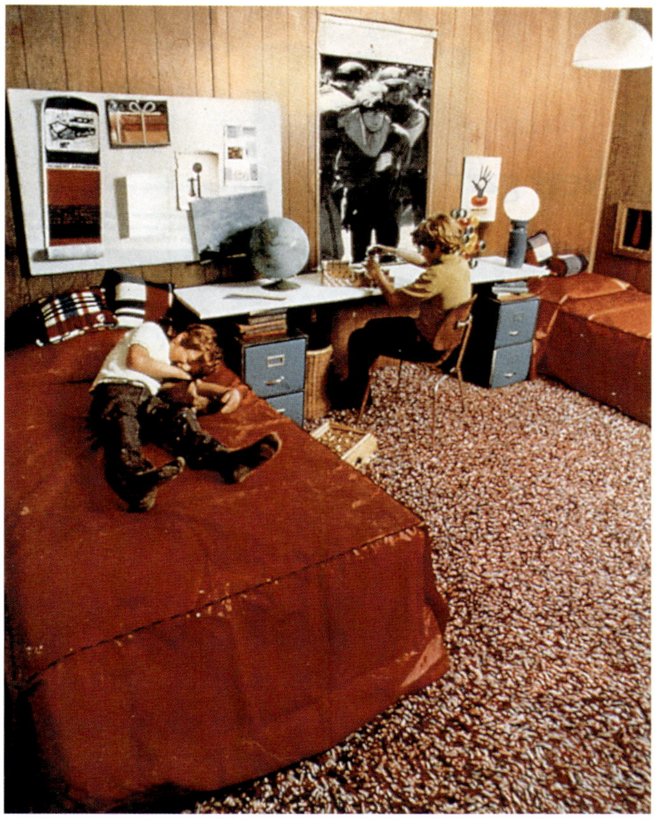

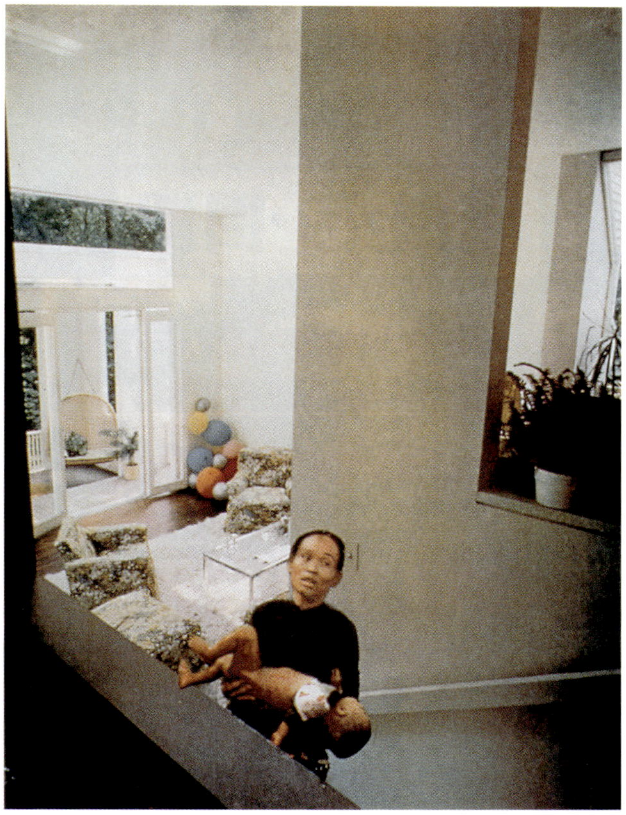

Martha <u>ROSLER</u>

Bringing the War Home [details]

1969-72

Photomontages printed as photographs

2 from the series of 20, 61 × 51 cm [24 × 20 in] each

In the late 1960s Rosler began inserting images of the Vietnam war into pictures of American home interiors. *Life* and other mainstream American magazines provided her source material. Such elements as maimed and shell-shocked Vietnamese women and children, American soldiers in combat uniform and cannons firing were placed in disturbing juxtaposition with scenes of comfortable home life. The photographs were published in the California-based alternative press during the early 1970s but were not exhibited in an art context until 1991. They grew out of Rosler's involvement with anti-war activities and her frustration with images presented on television and in print media. Rosler's work unveiled the horrors of war which had been concealed or distanced by the dominant media sources, drawing attention to and challenging the passive complicity of ordinary citizens.

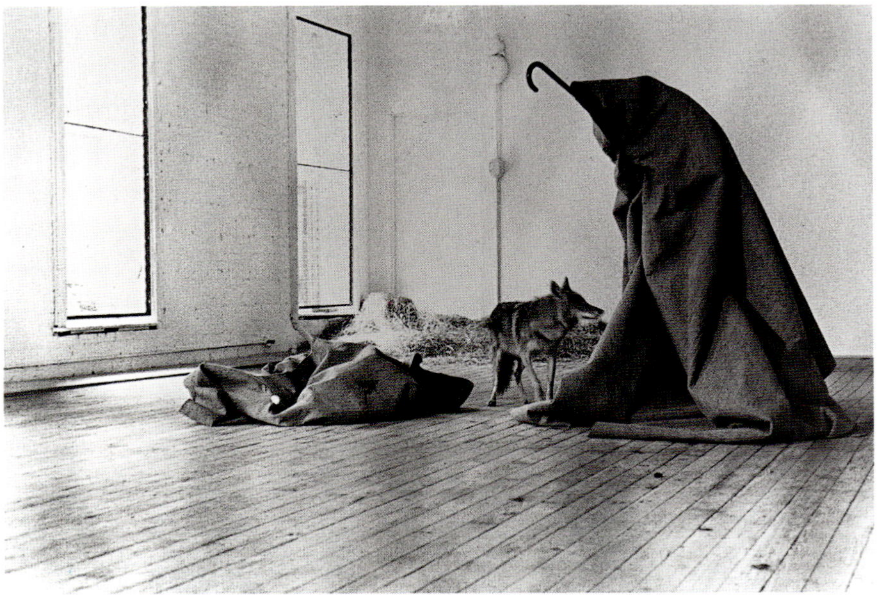

Joseph <u>BEUYS</u>

I Like America and America Likes Me

1974

René Block Gallery, New York

When invited to exhibit at René Block's new gallery in New York in 1974, in the aftermath of the US engagement in the Vietnam war, Beuys decided as a political gesture to be carried, wrapped entirely in felt, by ambulance from the plane at JFK Airport to the inside of the gallery. Thus he did not see anything outside this space nor did his feet touch American ground. Inside the gallery an area had been caged in and filled with straw, and a wild coyote brought in. Beuys lived alongside the coyote for five days. He entered covered with the felt and carrying a shepherd's staff. Long periods of mutual observation, silence and sleep were occasionally broken when Beuys interacted with the coyote by making sounds or movements or offering it objects. Beuys played the role of mediator between the native American wilderness, symbolized by the coyote, and US-based capitalism, symbolized by one of the materials also introduced into the space, a stack of copies of the *Wall Street Journal*. At the end of the five days Beuys returned in the same manner as he had arrived.

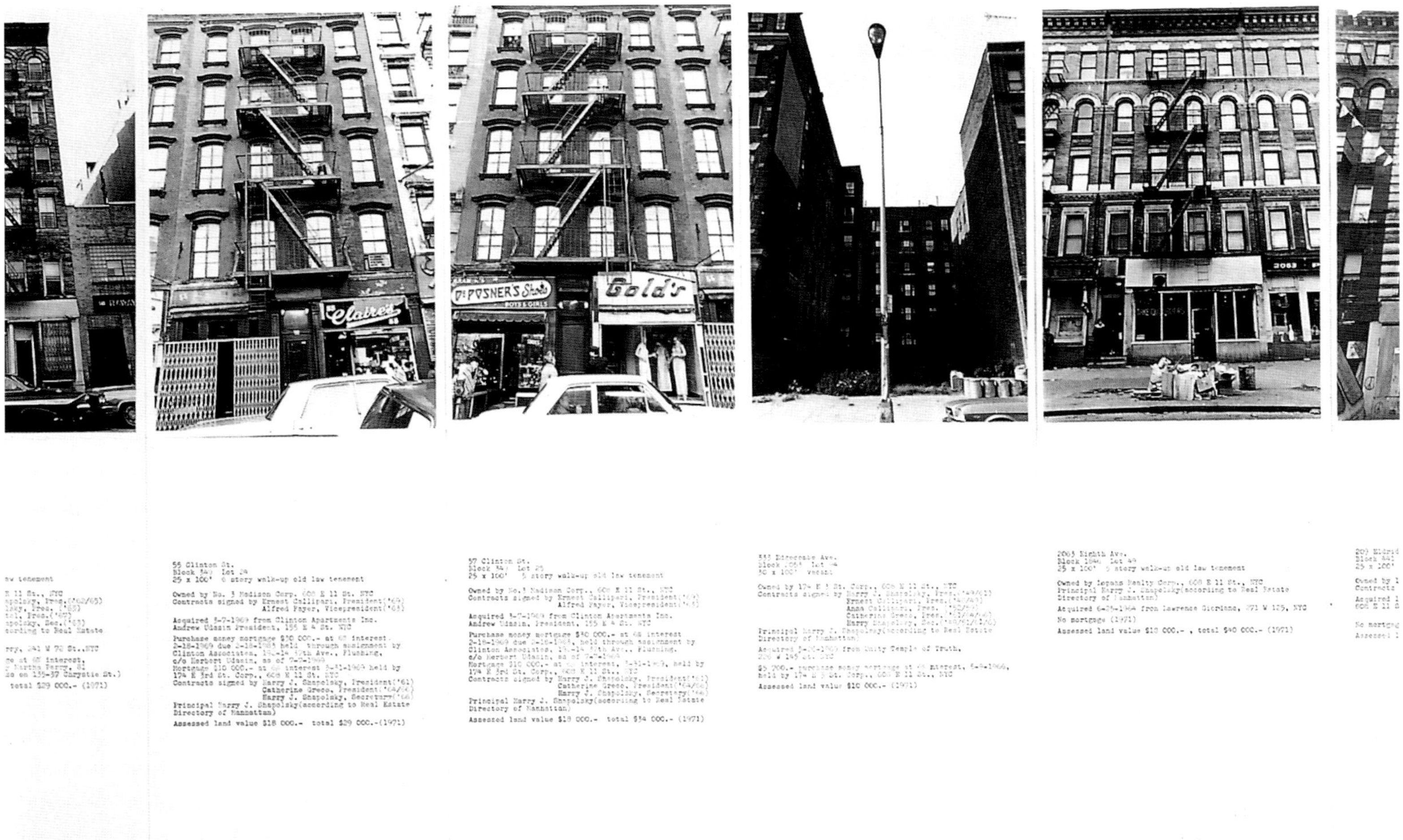

Hans HAACKE

Shapolsky et al. Manhattan Real Estate Holdings, a Real-Time Social System, as of 1 May 1971 [detail]

1971

2 maps, 142 black and white photographs with typewritten data sheets framed in 23 sets of 6 per frame and 1 set of 4 per frame, 6 charts and 1 explanatory panel

Dimensions variable

Following his earlier investigations of natural systems, Haacke turned his attention to economic systems – in this case a system of planned impoverishment of urban neighbourhoods by a group of real-estate speculators led by a notorious rent extractor, Harry Shapolsky. In 1971 the clan of Shapolsky family members owned the largest concentration of real estate under the control of a single group in New York. Haacke researched the work using public records at the New York County Clerk's Office. The work comprises two photo-enlarged maps of the Lower East Side and Harlem; 142 photos of building façades and empty lots; 142 typewritten sheets giving information about the properties; six charts documenting business transactions of the real estate group and one explanatory panel.

This work, along with two others, cost Haacke his solo exhibition at the Solomon R. Guggenheim Museum, New York, planned in 1971. The director of the museum rejected the works and, on Haacke's refusal to withdraw them, cancelled the exhibition six weeks before the scheduled opening. The exhibition's curator was also asked to leave when he defended the works. A protest demonstration was held by artists inside the museum and over one hundred pledged to boycott the Guggenheim until it changed its policy.

opposite

Martha ROSLER

The Bowery in Two Inadequate Descriptive Systems [detail]

1974–75

Black and white photographs, text

45 panels, 20.5 × 25.5 cm

[8 × 10 in] each

This is a series of black and white photographs of storefronts and other street elements in the Manhattan 'skid row' district known as the Bowery. Each is accompanied by a typewritten text comprising clusters of words and phrases, all of which are idioms, both familiar and archaic, for alcoholics, inebriation and alcoholism. As the title indicates, image and text here provide two inadequate means of describing a particular reality, in this case that of the deprived people who inhabit the area's streets, towards whom, in her refusal to depict them, Rosler avoids adopting a distanced or 'concerned' position. While the texts describe a physical and mental state, the images offer backgrounds empty of the people implicitly referred to, neither affirming nor denying them. The work thus resists the notion of photographic transparency and objectivity. Rosler has, however, pointed out that her critique 'doesn't mean that photography and, in particular, documentary, can't work in a project of social change, only that photography's role has to be re-thought'.
– Martha Rosler, conversation with the author quoted by Laura Cottingham in *Inside the Visible*, 1995

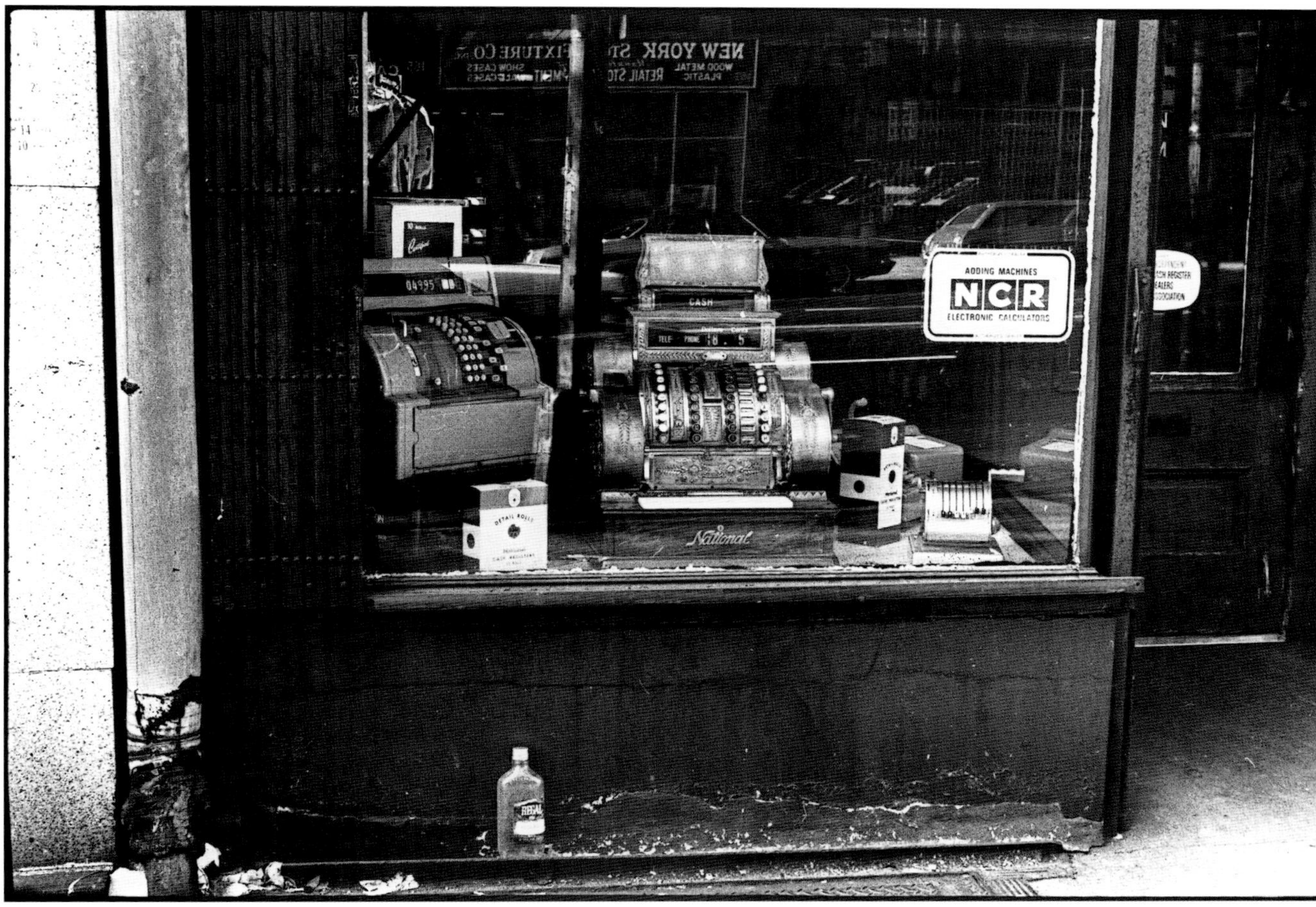

plastered stuccoed

rosined shellacked

vulcanized

inebriated

polluted

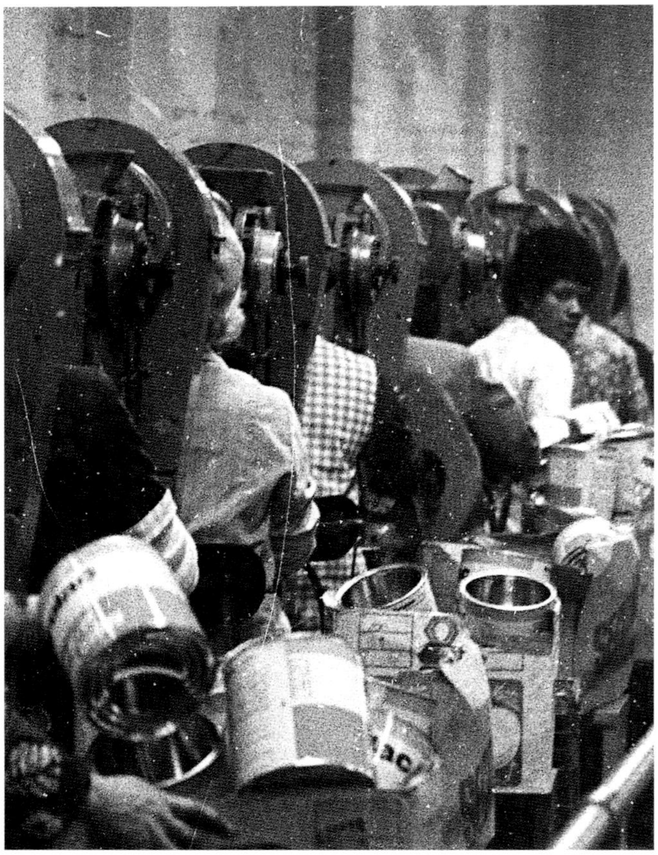

```
 6:00 AM: GET UP, GET BABY
          DRESSED, FED
 7:00 AM: TAKE BABY TO
          MINDER
 7:15 AM: GO TO WORK
 8:00 AM: START WORK
12.30 PM: DINNER BREAK
          GO SHOPPING
 1:30 PM: START WORK
 5:00 PM: FINISH WORK
 5:30 PM: GET BABY FROM
          MINDER
 6:00 PM: PREPARE BABY'S
          MEAL
 7:30 PM: PUT HIM TO BED
 8:00 PM: PREPARE MEAL FOR
          HUSBAND AND SELF
 9:00 PM: BABY'S WASHING
          CLEAN UP
12:00 PM: GO TO BED

JOANNA MARTIN, AGE 21
1 SON  AGE 1

SHRINK WRAP OPERATOR
FULL TIME   8:00 AM - 5:00 PM
```

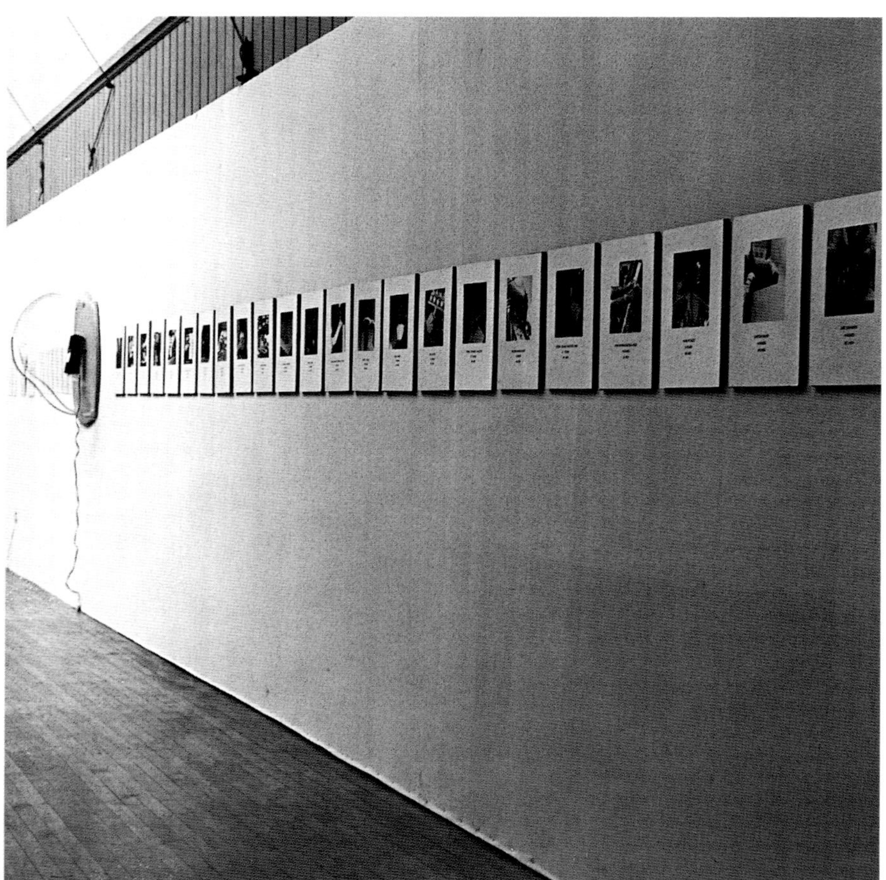

Margaret HARRISON, Kay HUNT, Mary KELLY

Women & Work: A Document on the Division of Labour in Industry

1973–75

Black and white photographs, charts, tables, photocopied documents, film loops, audiotapes

Dimensions variable

above

Details of chart and photograph from documentation

left

Installation view, South London Art Gallery

Women & Work was a documentary installation about the implementation of the Equal Pay Act in a metal box factory. After meeting the artists Margaret Harrison and Mary Kelly in other political art contexts in London and agreeing to form a collaboration, Kay Hunt initiated the project at a South London factory similar to one where her female relatives had worked in the past. The completed project was shown at the South London Art Gallery in 1975. Like the work of Harrison's partner the artist Conrad Atkinson, the project was rooted in working-class experience and used all available forms of information and display to convey the interwoven complexities and iniquities of the system. It constructed a feminist perspective by foregrounding the role of gender in working situations. The project questioned the authoritative position of the artist outside the field of investigation and incorporated subjective material from the participants. The female workers discussed not only their factory work and conditions but also their unpaid labour in the home and their feelings about their roles. Schedules of workers' daily activities, from getting up in the morning to going to bed at night, were displayed alongside excerpts from Parliamentary Acts and statistical information about employment in the factory.

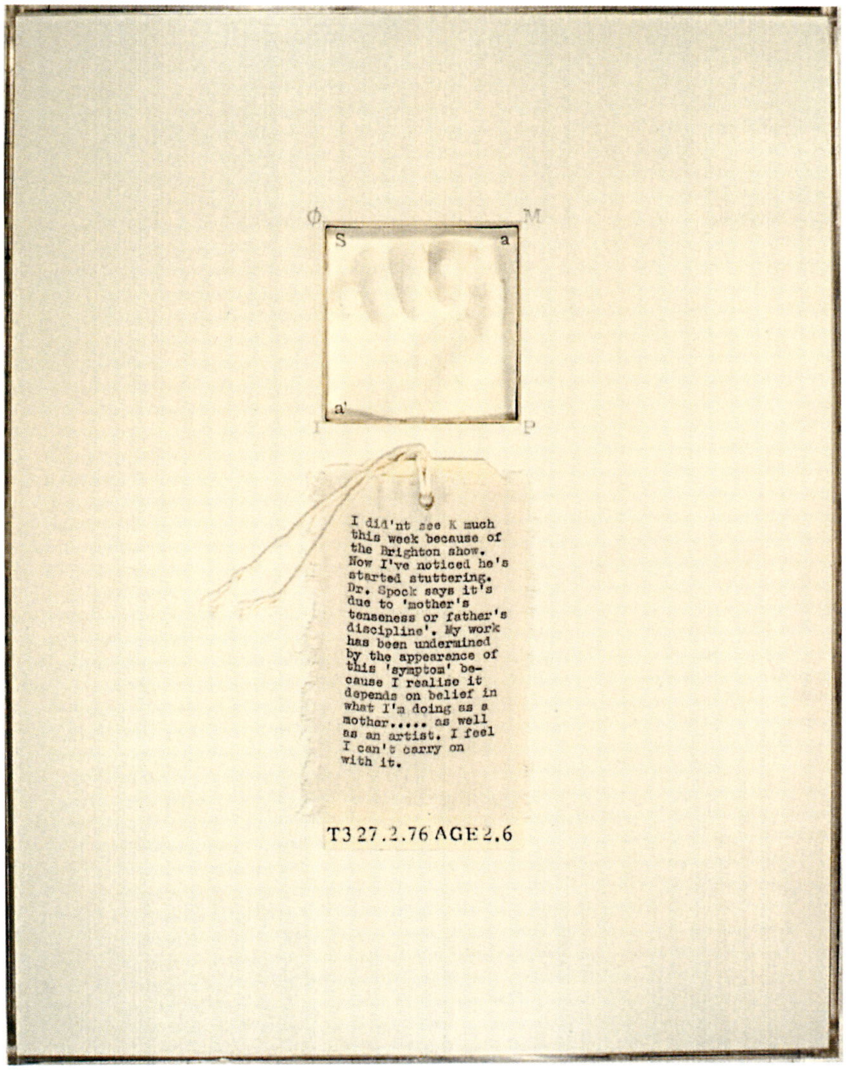

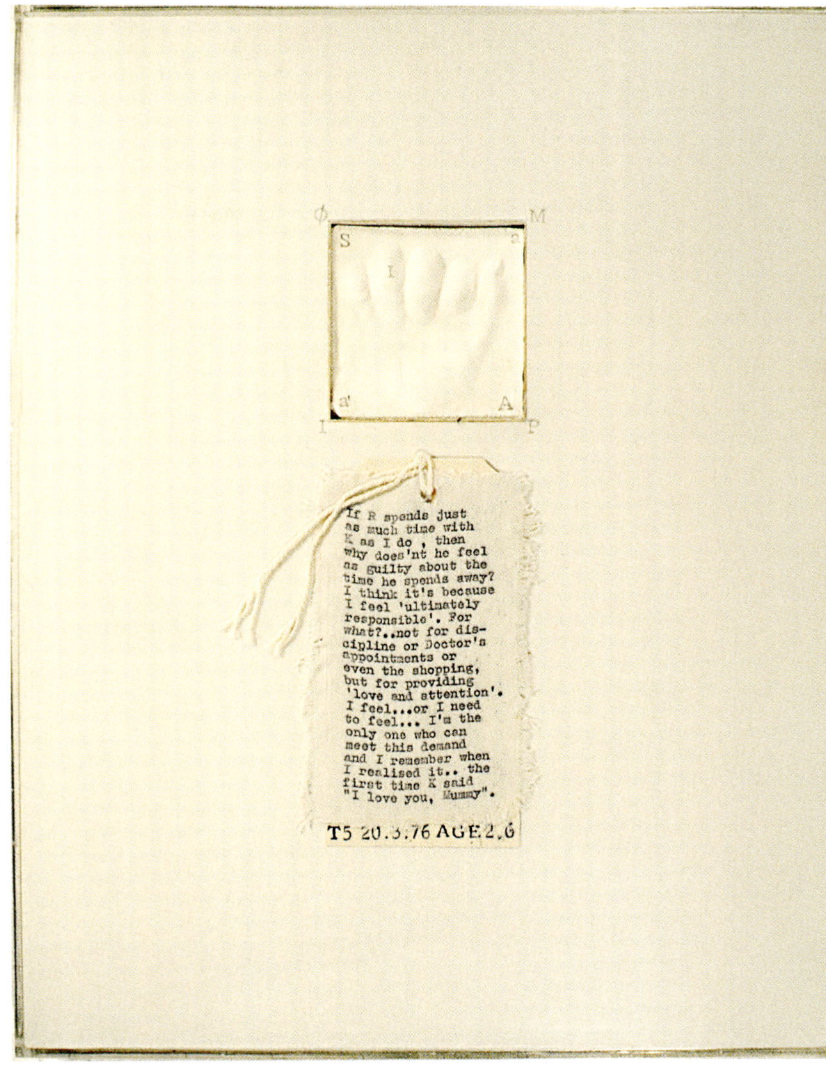

Mary <u>KELLY</u>
Post-Partum Document
1973-79
Documentation IV, Transitional Objects, Diary and Diagram [details]
Perspex units, white card, body/hand imprint in clay, plaster
of Paris, cotton fabric, string
2 of the 8 units, 35.5 × 28 cm [14 × 11 in] each
Collection, Zurich Museum

In 1973 *Post-Partum Document* 'was conceived as an ongoing process of analysis and visualization of the mother/child relationship. It was born as an installation in six consecutive sections, comprising in all 135 small units. It grew up as an exhibition, adapted to a variety of genres ... and finally reproduced itself in the form of a book.'
– Mary Kelly, 'Preface', *Post-Partum Document*, 1983

The project analysed the artist's experience of motherhood; it inserted the voice of female subjectivity into the language of conceptual art, while also explicitly contesting the naturalization of women's practice. Her investigation led Kelly to depart from psychoanalytic orthodoxy to posit a concept of maternal fetishism. The work suggests that if a baby fulfils in fantasy the plenitude denied by 'lack' of the phallus (according to Freud's account of the castration complex), the growing distance and thus 'loss' of the maturing child represents a renewed threat, in response to which the mother's memorabilia – shoes, locks of hair, etc. – both commemorate the loss and defend against it. The 'transitional objects' of the mother as well as the child are documented, not as surrogates but as emblems of desire, drawing attention to the fetishistic nature of representation itself.

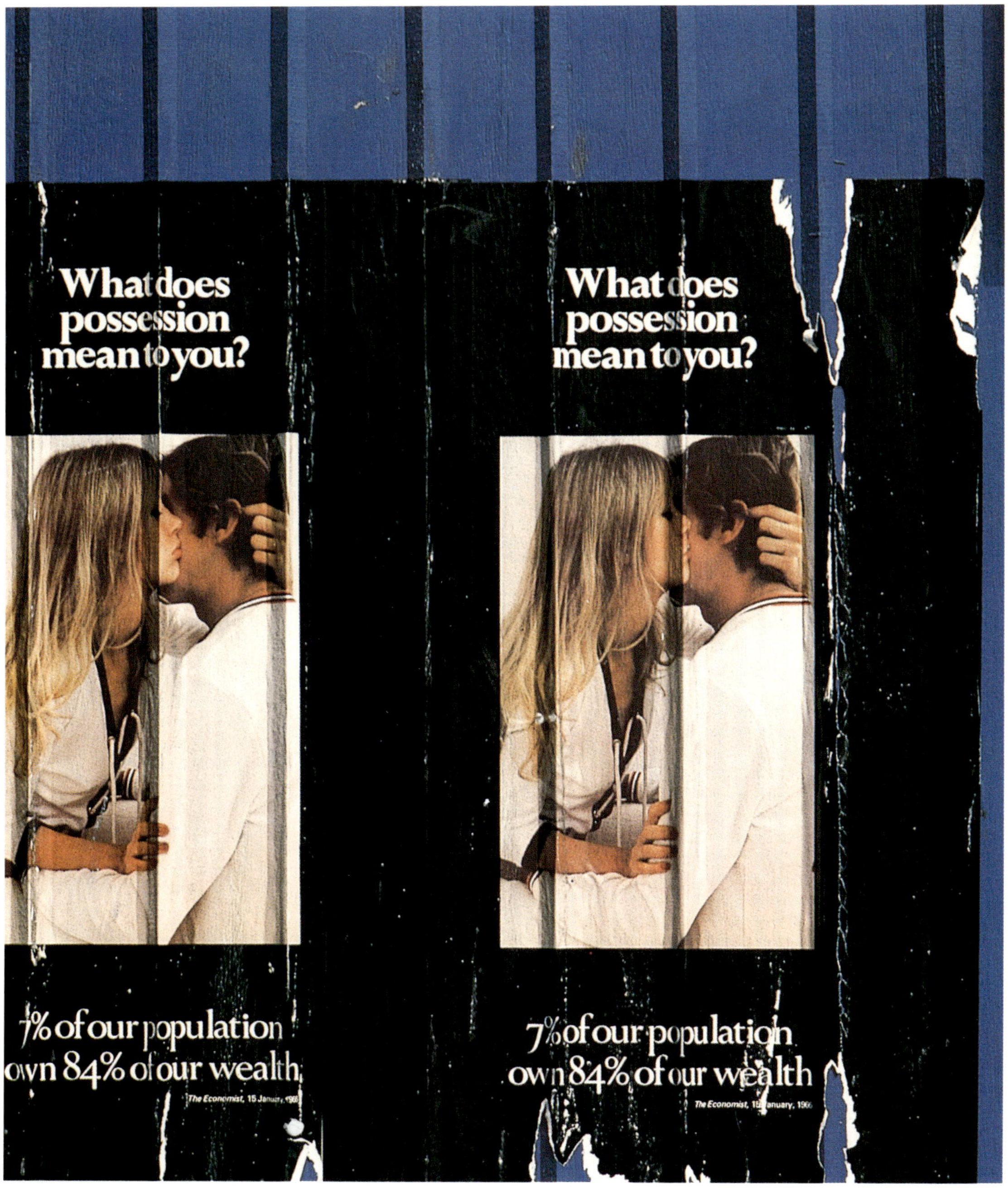

Victor BURGIN
Possession
1976
Offset poster
109 × 84 cm [43 × 33 in]
Detail of poster installation in the streets of Newcastle upon Tyne, 1976

In 1976 Burgin was invited to create a poster work for a group exhibition in Newcastle upon Tyne. He used as its basis a found image from a 'stock' picture library used by advertising companies. He juxtaposed the image with a quotation taken from *The Economist*. In a reworking of the *détournement* strategy of the Situationists, the work reconfigures existing visual and verbal messages so that they act as agents in their own subversion. By this means the work unveils the concealed relations of power interconnecting the fields of sexuality, economics and social hierarchy. The works were pasted up on existing poster sites in the streets, allowing for the widest possible viewing. They were intended to engage the viewer's attention initially as if they were real advertisements for products.

'At that time, I had the feeling that the world was saturated with images, and that there was no point in manufacturing more ... I felt that an artist's job was to take already existing images and rearrange them so that new meanings appeared ... My strategy was a kind of guerilla semiotics: capturing images and turning them against themselves.'
– Victor Burgin, interview with Régis Durand, *Art Press*, 130, November 1988

opposite
Victor BURGIN
UK 76 [details]
1976
Black and white photograph and text mounted on board
2 of 11 photographs, 102 × 152 cm [40 × 60 in] each

Burgin's use of appropriated imagery from sources such as advertising introduced, within the widely used text and image format of much conceptual art, psychoanalytic and feminist perspectives into the interpretation of signs in late capitalist culture. In this series, comprising eleven photographic panels, texts written by the artist in the style of promotional or journalistic copy are superimposed on images of everyday reality such as factory workers or council housing estates. Ironic contradictions emerge between the world depicted visually and the imaginary world of fetishization and commodification conveyed by the text. A verbal and a visual complex of signs are juxtaposed to reveal the concealed assumptions which underlie each.

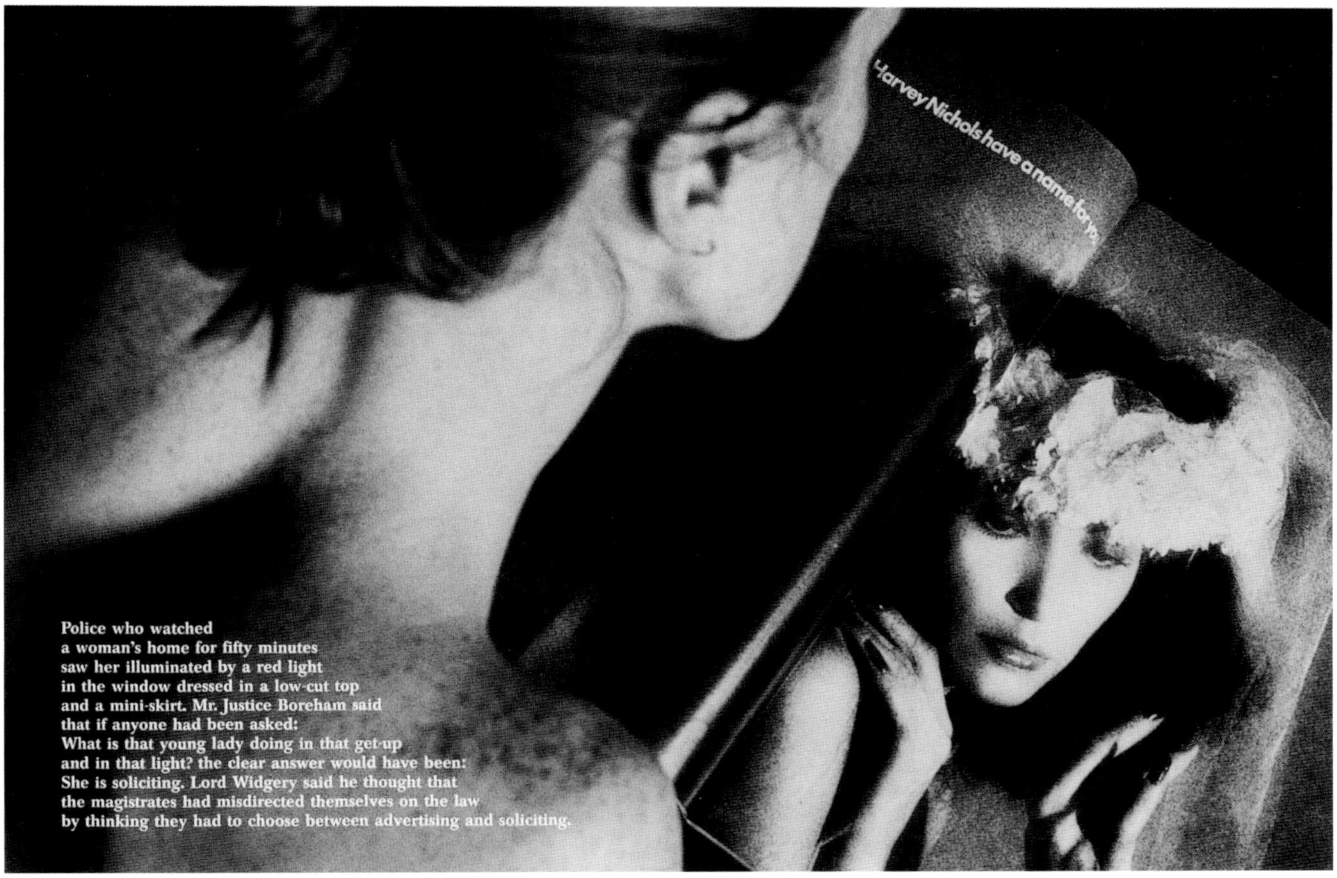
Harvey Nichols have a name for yo
Police who watched
a woman's home for fifty minutes
saw her illuminated by a red light
in the window dressed in a low-cut top
and a mini-skirt. Mr. Justice Boreham said
that if anyone had been asked:
What is that young lady doing in that get-up
and in that light? the clear answer would have been:
She is soliciting. Lord Widgery said he thought that
the magistrates had misdirected themselves on the law
by thinking they had to choose between advertising and soliciting.

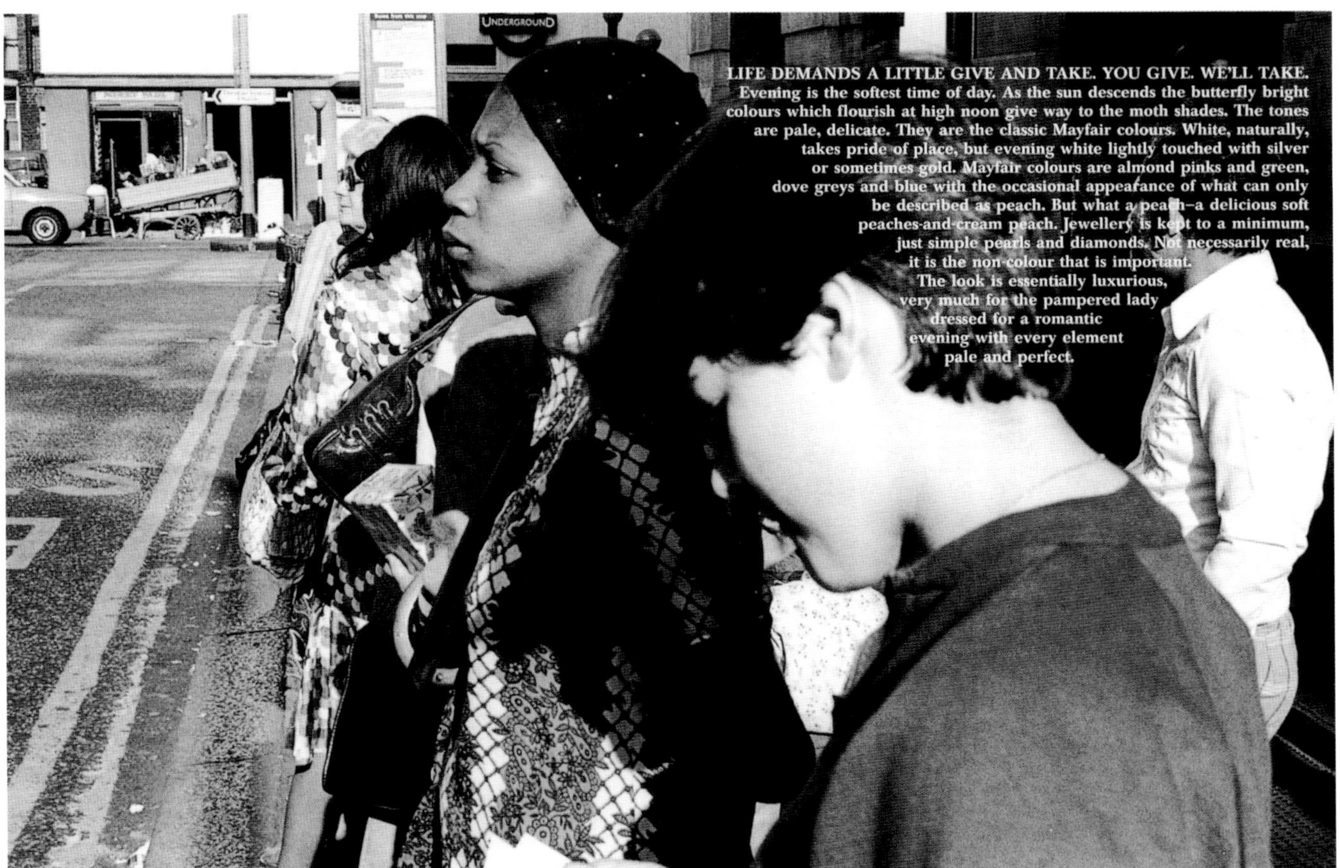
UNDERGROUND
LIFE DEMANDS A LITTLE GIVE AND TAKE. YOU GIVE. WE'LL TAKE.
Evening is the softest time of day. As the sun descends the butterfly bright
colours which flourish at high noon give way to the moth shades. The tones
are pale, delicate. They are the classic Mayfair colours. White, naturally,
takes pride of place, but evening white lightly touched with silver
or sometimes gold. Mayfair colours are almond pinks and green,
dove greys and blue with the occasional appearance of what can only
be described as peach. But what a peach–a delicious soft
peaches-and-cream peach. Jewellery is kept to a minimum,
just simple pearls and diamonds. Not necessarily real,
it is the non-colour that is important.
The look is essentially luxurious,
very much for the pampered lady
dressed for a romantic
evening with every element
pale and perfect.

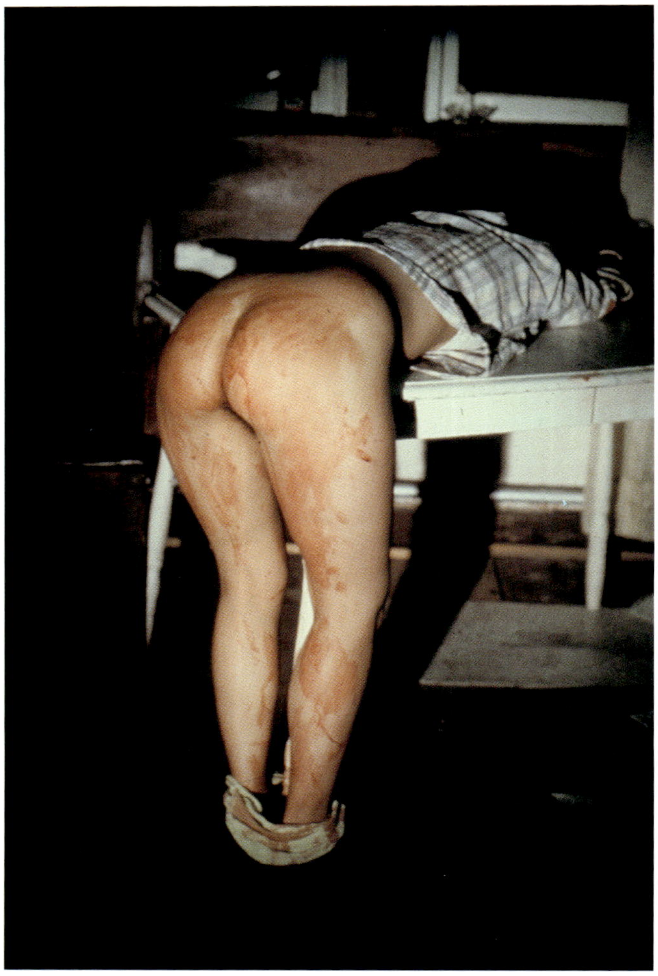

Ana MENDIETA

Rape Scene

1973

Moffit Street, Iowa City, Iowa

Mendieta distanced herself from conceptual art, referring to it as a predominantly male domain of 'clean' work in contrast to her own often visceral preoccupations. Despite this, there is an investigation in her own work of a central issue in conceptual art: the reinterpretation or transformation of Marcel Duchamp's idea of the readymade. In her most confrontational work, the *Rape Scenes*, which she performed several times in different locations in the area where a real rape had taken place, she devised a context where her own body acted as a politicized form of 'readymade'.

A fellow student at the Iowa University campus had been raped and murdered. In one version of this work Mendieta invited friends and colleagues to her apartment, leaving the door slightly ajar. When they entered they saw a brutal post-rape scene which she had created around her as a tableau, with her still body posed at the centre. The unpreparedness of the viewers and the specificity of the recent actual incident countered the possibility that she would be seen as an anonymous object in a theatrical tableau. In this way the work offered a form of resistance and redress by politically reappropriating the objectification of the female body.

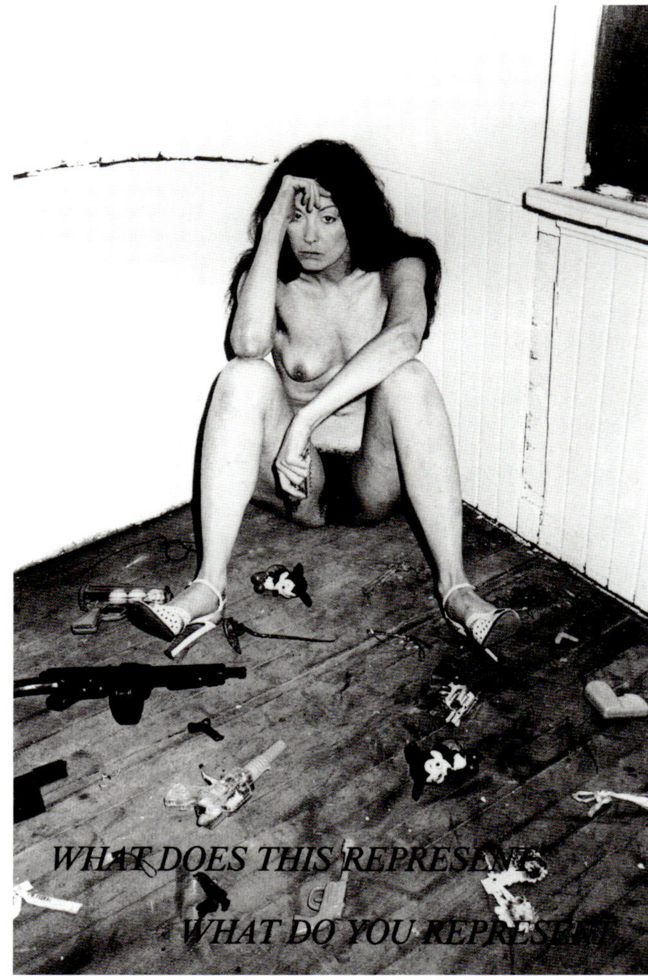

Hannah WILKE

What Does This Represent? What Do You Represent? [Reinhardt]

1978-84

Black and white photograph

152.5 × 101.5 cm [60 × 40 in]

In 1945 the painter Ad Reinhardt drew a two-part cartoon. In the first picture a man points at an abstract painting, jeering, 'What does this represent?' In the second, the painting is redrawn so that its elements now resemble an angry face staring at the man. It retorts: 'What do you represent?' In Wilke's work Reinhardt's ironic reversal is redirected towards reflection on the gendering of representations. This work is part of Wilke's *So Help Me Hannah* series of self-portrait performances, recorded on video between 1979 and 1985 and then made into works using photographic documentation and text. Each image is overprinted with quotations from male artists and philosophers.

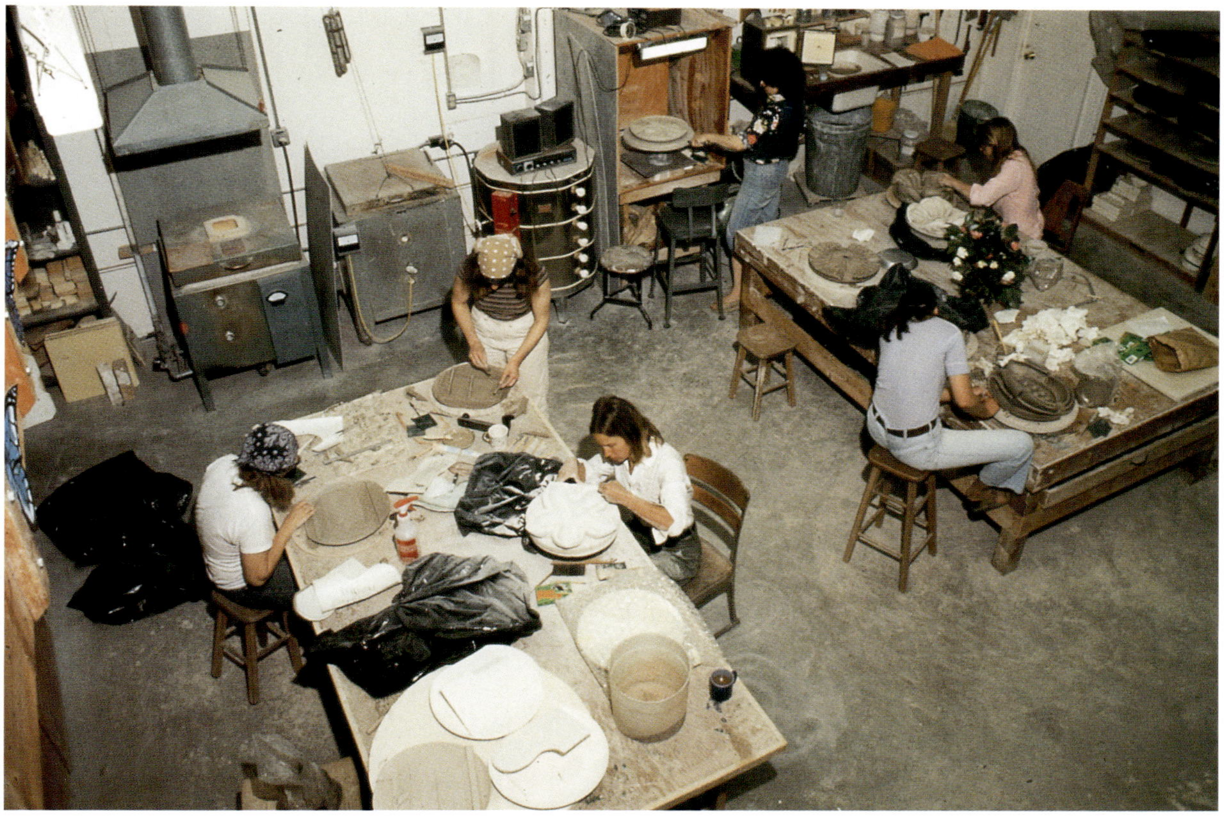

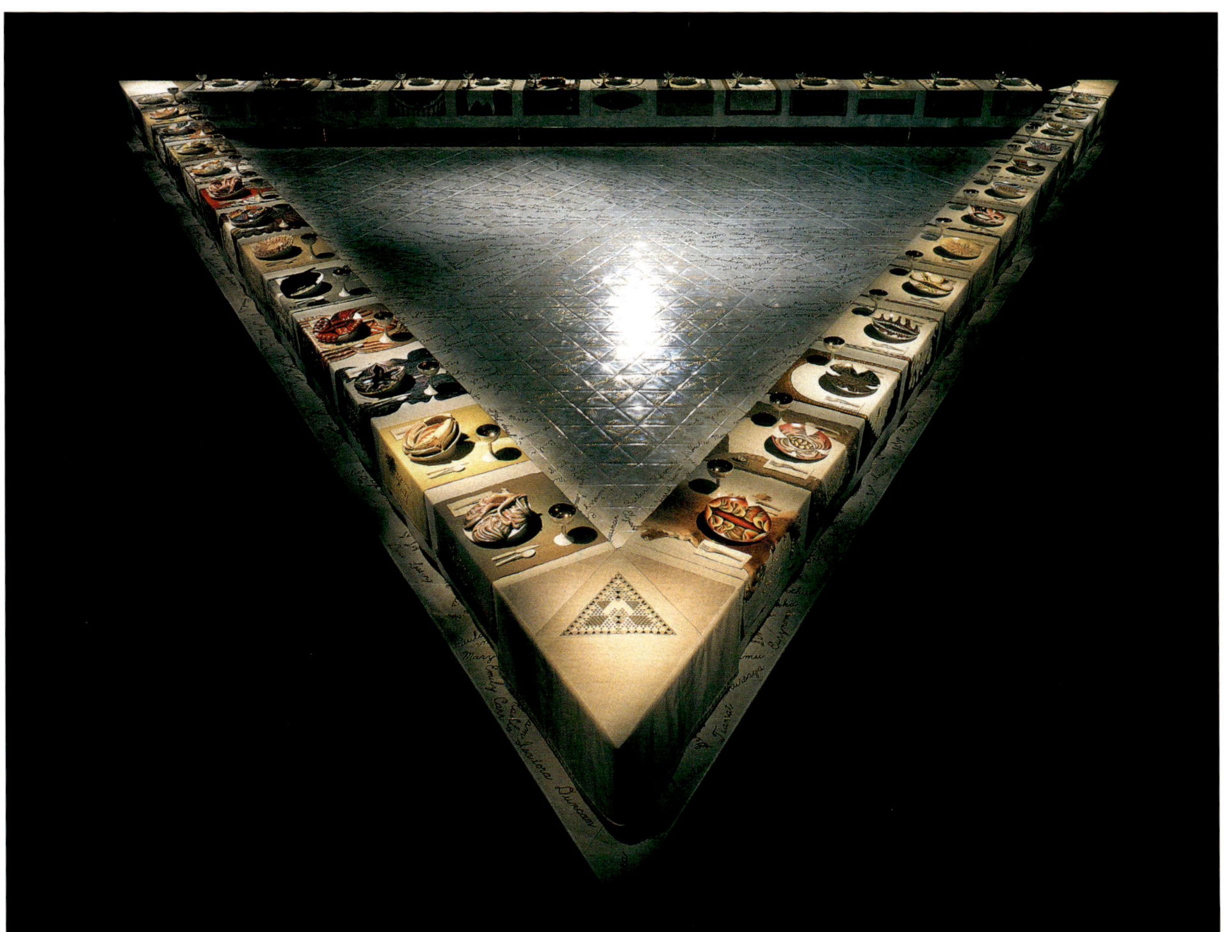

Judy CHICAGO

left

Workers in The Dinner Party Ceramic Studio

below left

The Dinner Party

1974-79

Wood, ceramic, fabric, needlework, metal, paint

1463 × 1280 × 91.5 cm

[576 × 504 × 36 in]

Over a hundred women collaborated on this monumental project. Thirty-nine place settings, each commemorating a female historical or mythological figure, are placed around an equilateral triangle formed from three tables. Each of the thirty-nine women is represented on a hand-painted plate by an abstract form based on 'central core' vulvic imagery, an embroidery and a chalice. On the base tiles are inscribed a further 999 names. The work's chronological sequence traces the social origins and decline of matriarchy, its replacement by patriarchy, the institutionalization of male oppression and women's response to it. The work toured internationally and attracted some of the largest crowds ever to view a museum exhibit.

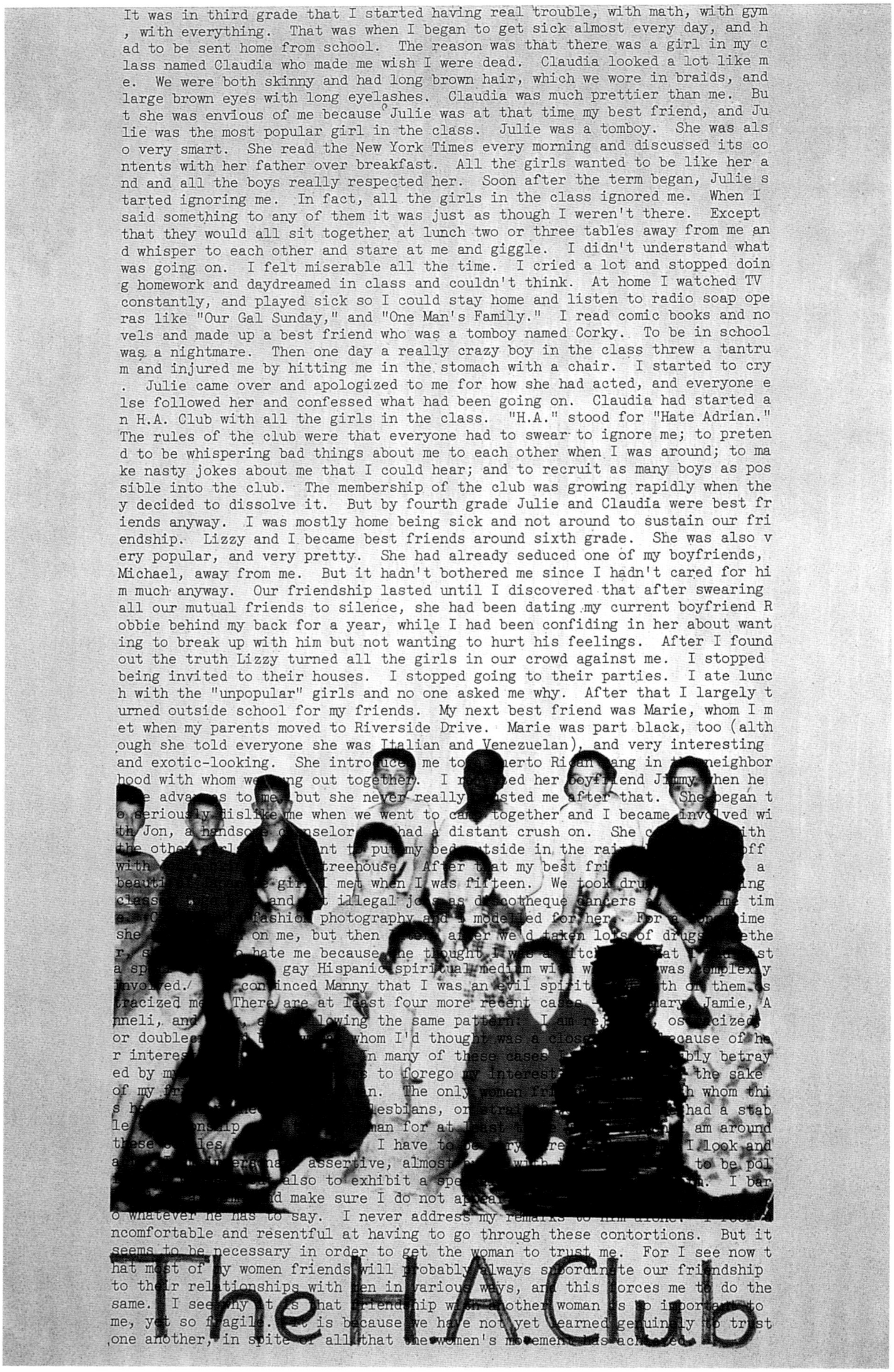

left

Adrian PIPER

Political Self-Portrait No. 1

[Sex]

1979

Black and white photostat

with image and text

75 × 48 cm [29.5 × 19 in]

opposite

Adrian PIPER

Aspects of the Liberal Dilemma

[detail]

1978

Black and white photograph from

mixed media installation

45.5 × 45.5 cm [18 × 18 in]

In her *Political Self-Portraits* (1978–80), Piper superimposed over images of her face and body detailed autobiographical texts written from the perspectives of gender, race and class which have contributed to her marginalization as an artist, using autobiographical content to serve an ideological function. Other works made during the same period, such as *Aspects of the Liberal Dilemma*, take the form of installations using materials such as found photographs isolated from their original context.

'The main issues and preoccupations of my work have become increasingly focused on political content, specifically racism, racial stereotyping and xenophobia. This is one direct consequence of having chosen to work with materials, that is, language and conceptual symbols, which can refer to content beyond themselves: it forces a choice of content and therefore a recognition of what content is most pressingly important. And the indexical present has provided the major strategy of my work, which is direct, immediate and confrontational. Racism is not an abstract, distanced issue out there that only affects all those unfortunate other people. Racism begins with you and me, here and now, and consists in our tendency to try to eradicate each other's singularity through stereotyped conceptualization.'

– Adrian Piper, 'On Conceptual Art', *Out of Order, Out of Sight, Volume I: Selected Writings in Meta-Art 1968–1992*, 1996

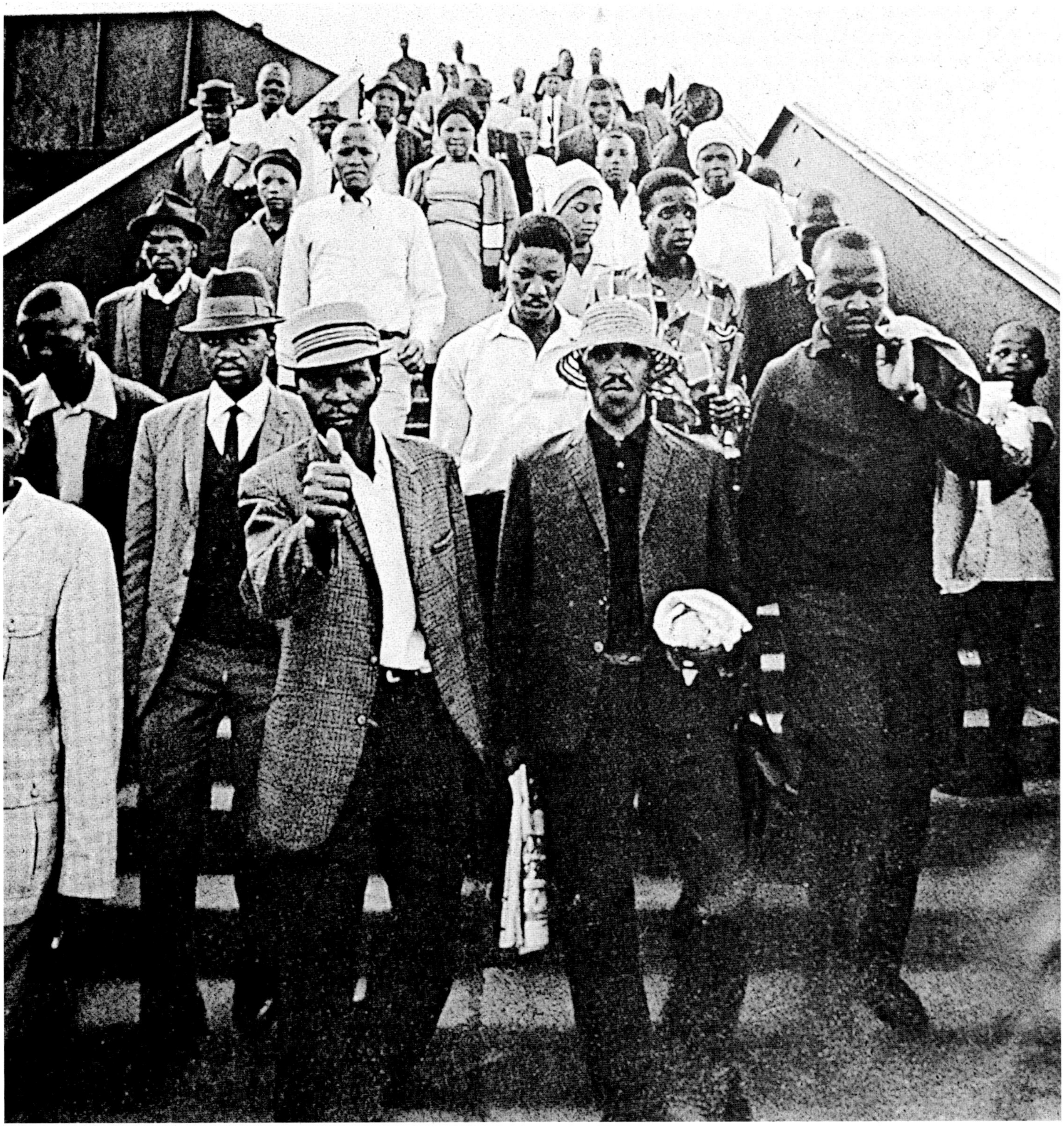

INSTITUTIONAL CRITIQUE

The institutional dimension of the artwork was at issue within conceptual art from the outset, since conceptual art violated so many of the established conventions about how art should look and what kind of thing it should be. During the 1970s, in part as a reaction to conceptual art's own institutional success, it moved to the fore. Art falling under the heading of 'institutional critique' takes as its conceptual materials the institutional conditions that contribute to the understanding of something as 'art'. It functions as critique by drawing attention to the various ways in which these conditions are sustained and function through inequalities of power. Daniel Buren's strategy was to use a single, obstinately unchanging visual form to highlight the alchemy by which galleries turn objects into 'art'. Marcel Broodthaers undertook a full-scale parodic reconstruction of a museum collection. Hans Haacke used the sociological techniques of polling and research into property ownership to lay bare the class relations within museums themselves. Michael Asher engaged in rearrangements of the architectural fabric of museums and galleries, to draw attention to their repressed histories and ideological effects.

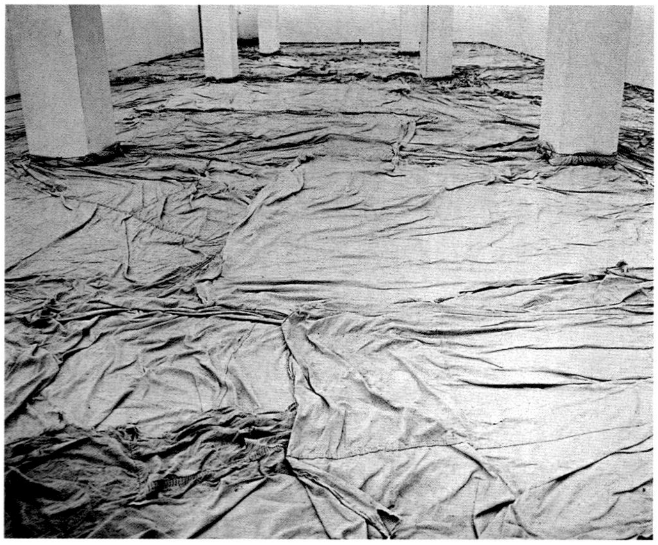

CHRISTO and JEANNE-CLAUDE
Wrapped Floor and Stairway
1969
White paint, painters' cotton dropcloths, rope
260 sq m [2,800 sq ft]
Museum of Contemporary Art, Chicago
In conjunction with the wrapping of the Museum of Contemporary Art in Chicago, described opposite, the Christos made a complimentary work for the interior. The museum's lower gallery was emptied of all contents and painted white. When the painters had finished they removed their dropcloths. The Christos then took the off-white cotton dropcloths and laid them down, secured by ropes, throughout the floor areas, covering 2,800 square feet.

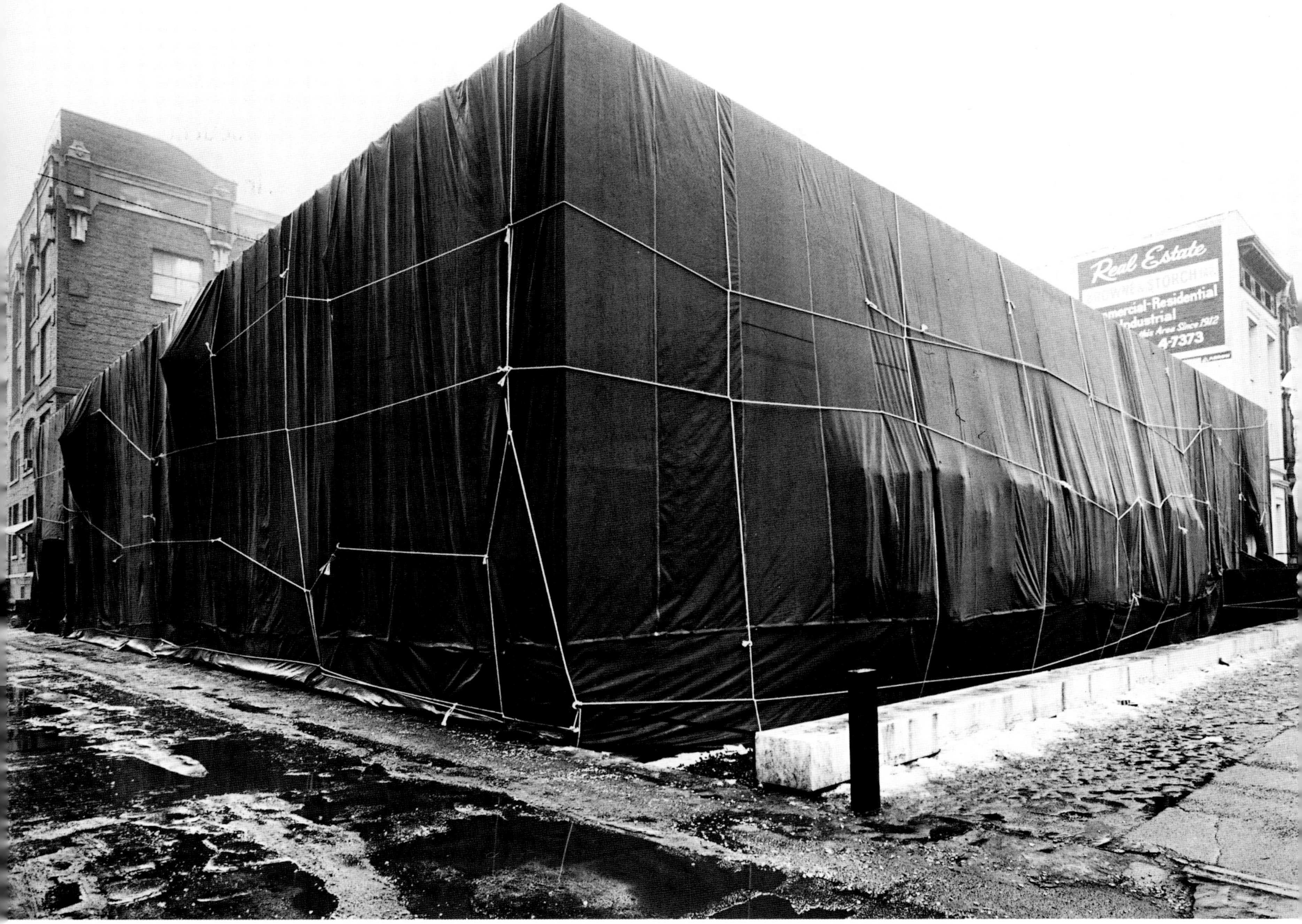

CHRISTO and JEANNE-CLAUDE

Chicago Museum of Contemporary Art, Wrapped

1969

Tarpaulins, Manila rope

900 sq m [10,000 sq ft]

Christo began to wrap objects in 1958 and together with Jeanne-Claude conceived the first project for wrapping a public building in 1961. The first such building to be wrapped was the Kunsthalle, Bern, in 1968. This was followed in January 1969 by the Museum of Contemporary Art in Chicago. Students from the School of the Art Institute of Design were engaged by the artists to wrap the structure in 10,000 square feet of tarpaulin, lending greater physical presence to this architecturally undistinguished building. The museum's Director Jan van der Marck noted in the exhibition brochure that this 'packaged monument suceeds in parodying all the associations a museum evokes: a mausoleum, a repository for precious contents, an intent to "wrap up" all of art history'. Although the Christos do not regard themselves as conceptual artists they have been highly influential within this field as critics of the institutions of power (they have always rejected funding from external sources of any kind) and for the participatory, democratic nature of their public projects.

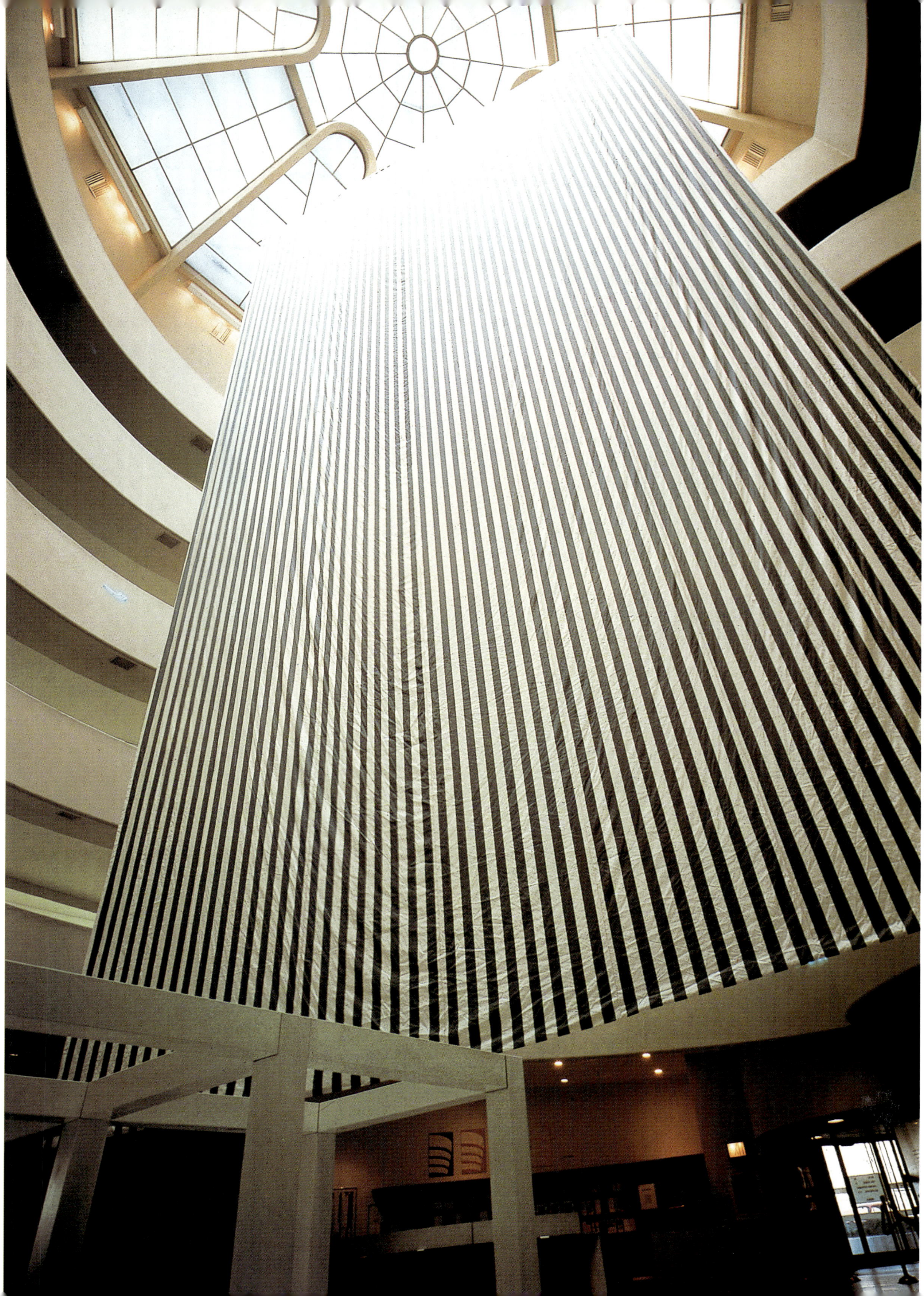

opposite

Daniel BUREN

Visible Recto Verso Painting

1971

Acrylic on canvas

20 × 10 m [65.5 × 33 ft]

VI Guggenheim International, Solomon R. Guggenheim Museum, New York

[removed from exhibition]

Buren was invited, alongside Carl Andre, Dan Flavin, Donald Judd and others, to participate in the Guggenheim International exhibition in 1971. He devised two works related to this specific location, the Solomon R. Guggenheim Museum in New York: a canvas 1.5 metres high by 10 metres wide was stretched across 88th Street between the museum and the building opposite; in the atrium of the museum a canvas 20 metres high and 10 metres wide was suspended from just below the skylight to a few metres above head height at ground level. The painting inside the museum thus competed in scale and effect with a notorious characteristic of Frank Lloyd Wright's building – that it dominated architecturally over its exhibits. The painting also obscured views of other artworks, such as Flavin's fluorescent light installation, which had been conceived to highlight aspects of the architecture. After a petition from sixteen participants, Buren's work was removed. Andre then withdrew his work in solidarity. The dispute highlighted the contrast between ideas of 'site specific' context related to perceptual phenomena and an art such as Buren's which focused on the underlying politics of institutional presentation.

below

Marcel BROODTHAERS

Un coup de dés jamais n'abolira le hasard. Image [details]

1969

Artist's book, black ink on tracing paper

First edition, Wide White Space, Antwerp/Michael Werner, Cologne

The title of this work alludes to Stéphane Mallarmé's poem of 1897 *Un Coup de dés jamais n'abolira le hasard* (*Casting the dice once will never abolish chance*). This poem was one of the most influential precursors of concrete poetry in the 1950s and 1960s, in which the appearance and the meaning of words are reconfigured by their spatial and typographic relationships on the page. In Broodthaers' version, the patterns of Mallarmé's typography remain but the words have been replaced by black bands. These emphasize both the absence of any text and an increased visual and spatial presence – poetic language has been replaced by a mute abstract pattern. The work negates in equal measure the competing forms of literary and visual communication. Suspended in between, it suggests the conceptual space of a generic notion of 'art'.

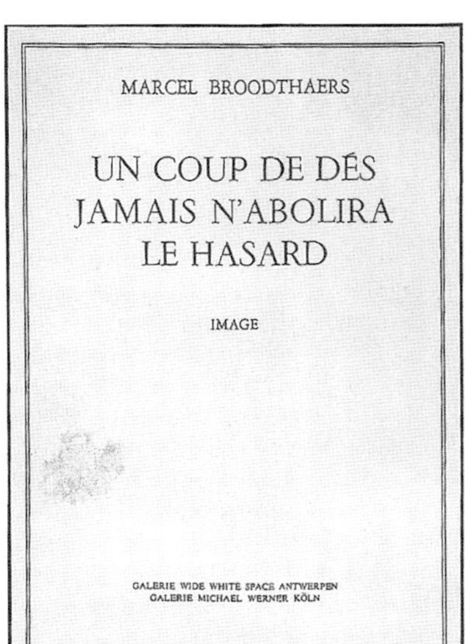

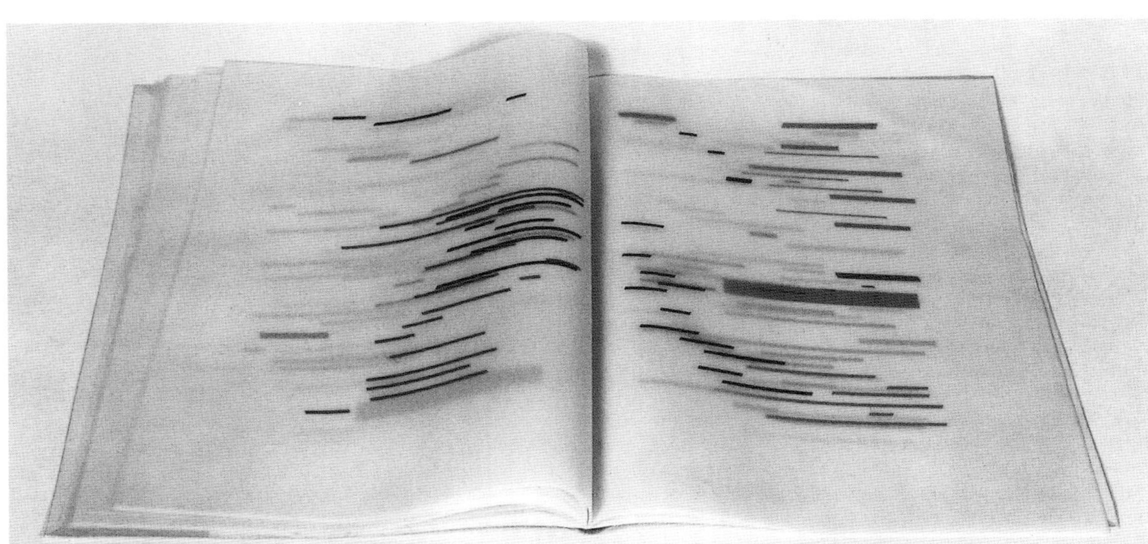

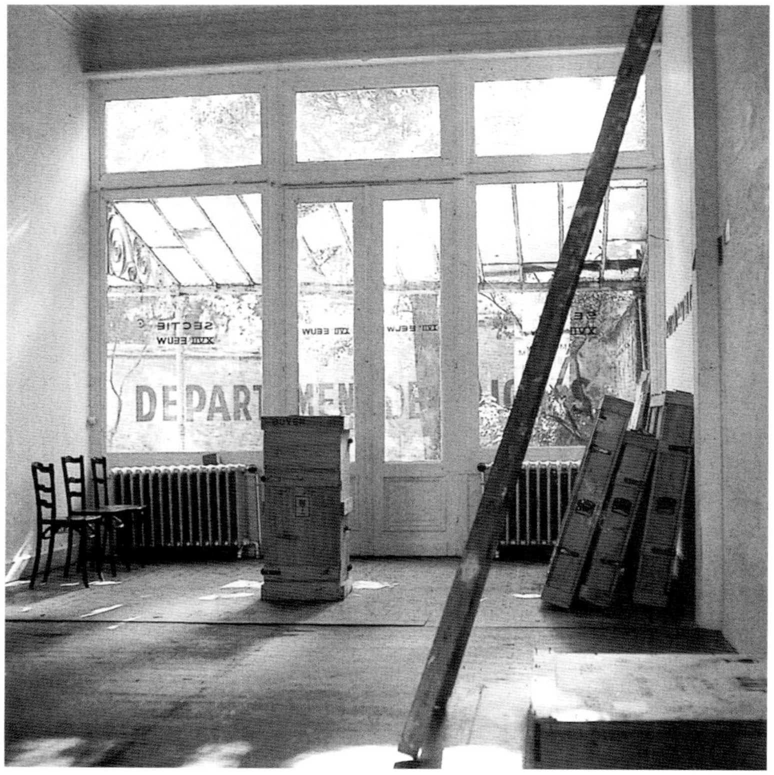

Marcel BROODTHAERS
Musée d'Art Moderne, Département des Aigles [Museum of Modern Art, Eagles Department]
1968-72
Section XVIIe Siècle [Seventeenth-Century Section, detail]
Antwerp, 1969

Broodthaers' museum was a complex, itinerant work which deliberately avoided the status of a permanent collection or a permanent location. It appeared in the following different forms (here translated from the French): 'Nineteenth-Century Section', installed in his house in Brussels (1968); 'Literary Section', also at the apartment (1968–70); 'Seventeenth-Century Section', Antwerp (1969); 'Nineteenth-Century Section (repeat)', Kunsthalle, Dusseldorf (1970); 'Cinema Section', Dusseldorf (1971); 'Financial Section', Galerie Michael Werner, Cologne (1971); 'Figures Section (The Eagle from the Oligocene to the Present)', Kunsthalle, Dusseldorf (1972); 'Publicity Section, Section of Modern Art' and 'Museum of Ancient Art, Twentieth-Century Gallery', Documenta 5, Kassel, Germany (1972).

In its first form in Broodthaers' house the museum consisted of an arrangement of empty wooden packing crates for art, marked 'fragile', 'this way up', etc. and a series of postcards reproducing nineteenth-century paintings from the Louvre and other museums, which relegated these works of art to the status of souvenirs.

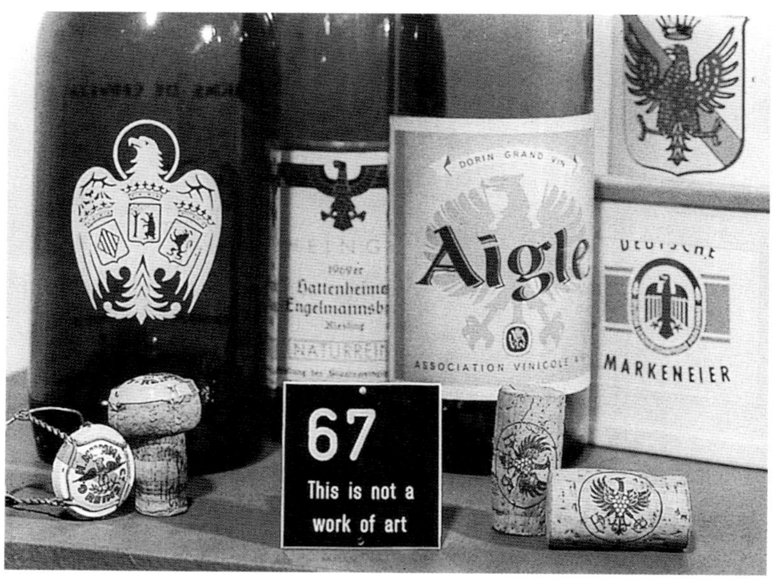

Marcel BROODTHAERS
Musée d'Art Moderne, Département des Aigles [Museum of Modern Art, Eagles Department]
1968-72
left and opposite
Section des Figures [Figures Section, details]
Kunsthalle, Dusseldorf, 1972

At the Kunsthalle, Dusseldorf, in 1972, the 'Figures Section' displayed hundreds of artefacts loaned by 43 museums as well as private collectors. The unifying theme of this exhibit was representations of the eagle in diverse forms from around the world and across history, ranging from painting and sculpture, etc., to everyday objects of use. No recognizable system of classification was apparent at first sight, but a very specific system emerged to visitors as they viewed the exhibits. Each piece was accompanied by a small black plastic label on which a catalogue number was engraved in white, beneath which was the statement 'This is not a work of art', in French, German and English alternately. This referred both to Duchamp's *Fountain* (1917), and to Magritte's famous 1929 painting (*La Trahaison des Images*) of a pipe under which is inscribed 'Ceci n'est pas une Pipe'. The statement on the labels raised the question of whether the artist, by means of language, possesses the authority to determine whether an object has the status of an artwork. Rather, was it not due to the existence of museums and the authority conferred by exhibition, that Duchamp and Magritte were able to make their assertions? By founding the museum in 1968, Broodthaers invited the viewer to recognize the concealed assumptions which empower museums to confer cultural, social, political and economic value upon their contents.

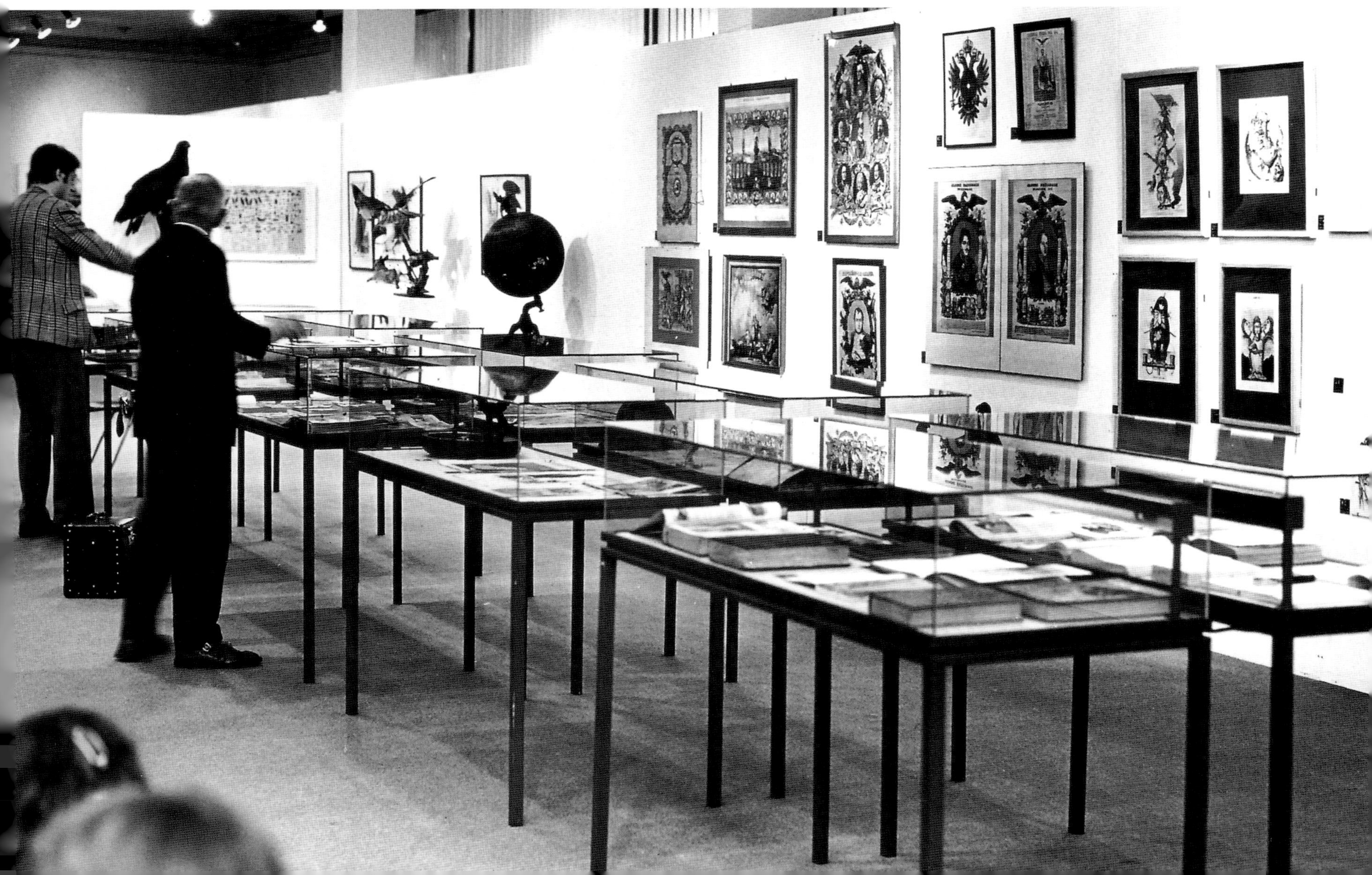

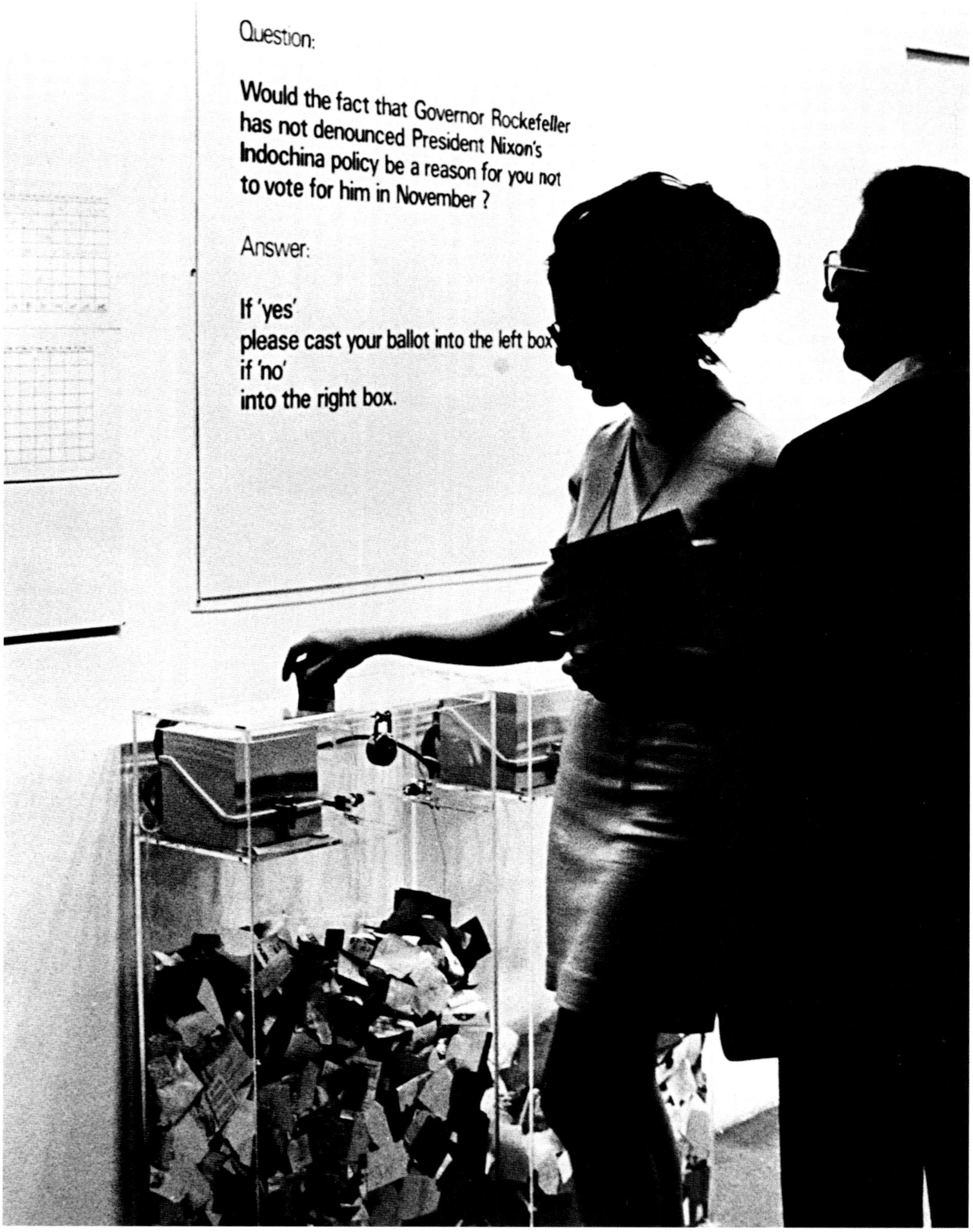

Hans HAACKE
MOMA Poll
1970
2 ballot boxes with counter
102 × 51 × 24.5 cm
[40 × 20 × 9.5 in] each
'Information', The Museum
of Modern Art, New York

Haacke made several polls for museum visitors, including a *Visitors' Profile* (a twenty-question questionnaire) for visitors to Documenta 5 in 1972. The *MOMA Poll* was installed at the Museum of Modern Art, New York, for the duration of the 'Information' exhibition in 1970. It comprised two transparent acrylic ballot boxes, one marked 'yes' and the other 'no'. Each box was equipped with a photo-electrically triggered counting device to register the paper votes.

At the museum entrance visitors were given ballot papers coloured according to the individual's status as a full-paying visitor, holder of a courtesy pass, or visitor on a Monday when admission to the museum was free. The question of the poll refers to Nelson Rockefeller, the Republican governor of the state of New York who was running for re-election in 1970. At the time he was also a member of the museum's board of trustees. He had previously served both as president and chairman. Two months before the show opened, President Nixon had ordered the bombing and invasion of Cambodia by US military forces, despite that country's declared neutrality in the Indochina conflict. After four students were shot dead by the National Guard during a student demonstration against this policy, many artists in New York called for the temporary closing of museums as a gesture of protest. At the close of the exhibition the counters of the ballot boxes registered 25,566 votes (68.7%) 'yes' and 11,563 (31.3%) 'no'.

Hans HAACKE

On Social Grease [details]

1975

Engraved plaques, magnesium mounted on aluminium

4 of 6 plaques, 76 × 76 cm [30 × 30 in] each

This is a series of six plaques, each comprising a magnesium plate mounted on aluminium and bearing a photo-engraved quotation. Those quoted are C. Douglas Dillon, director general of New York's Metropolitan Museum, 1970–78; Nelson Rockefeller, former director general and chairman of the Museum of Modern Art, New York, vice-president of the United States, 1974–77; Frank Stanton, trustee, board member and director of many museums and corporate giants; David Rockefeller, Nelson's brother, vice president of the Museum of Modern Art; Richard M. Nixon, president of the United States, 1968–74; and Robert Kingsley, a powerful corporate figure in the arts. Haacke's work ironically draws public attention to the links between powerful commercial and political interests within the arts. Both the sponsorship of art exhibitions and the collection of art by large corporations developed with a new intensity in the early 1970s. Haacke was later to use the exposure of these relationships more overtly as the topic of his work.

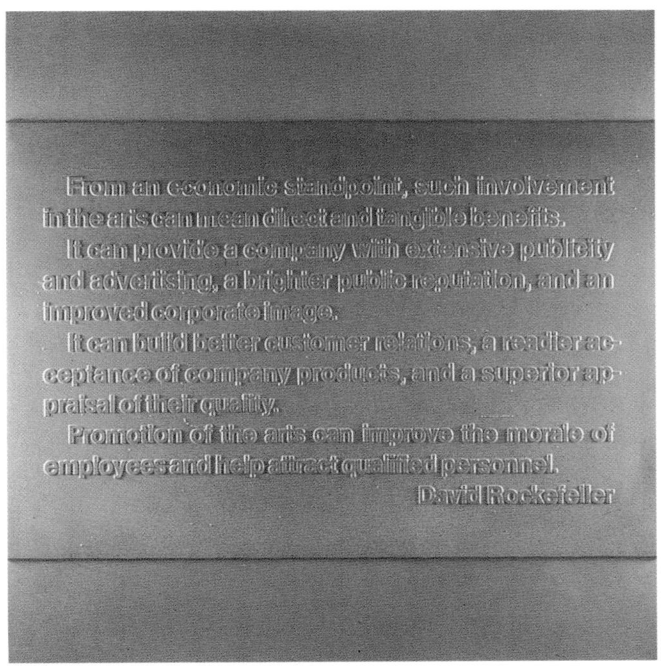

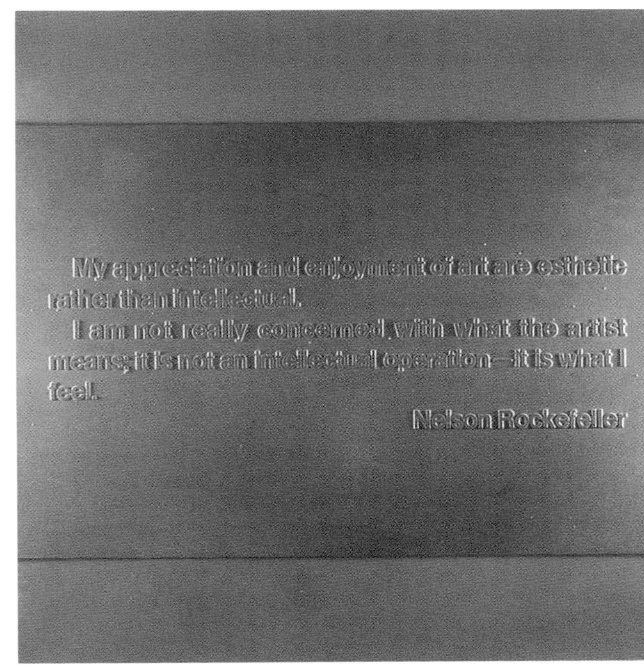

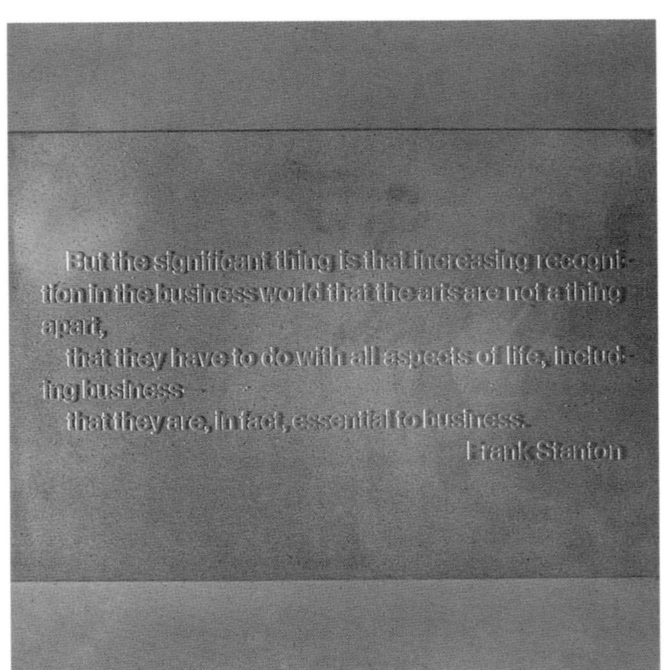

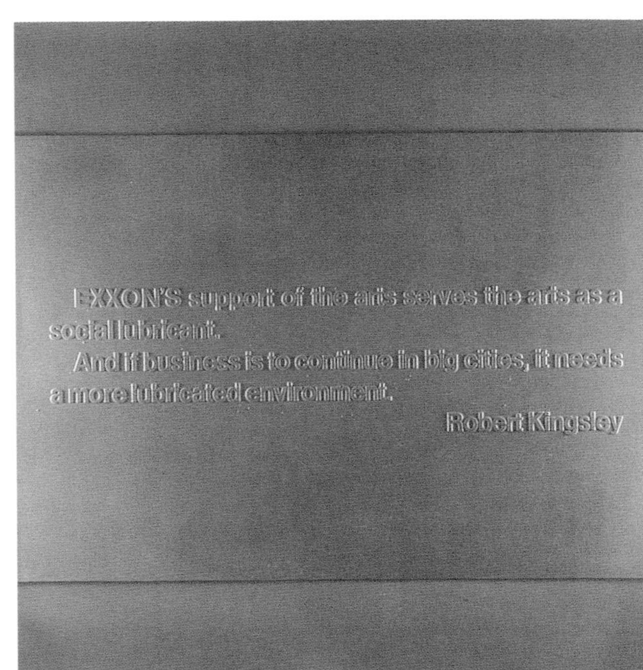

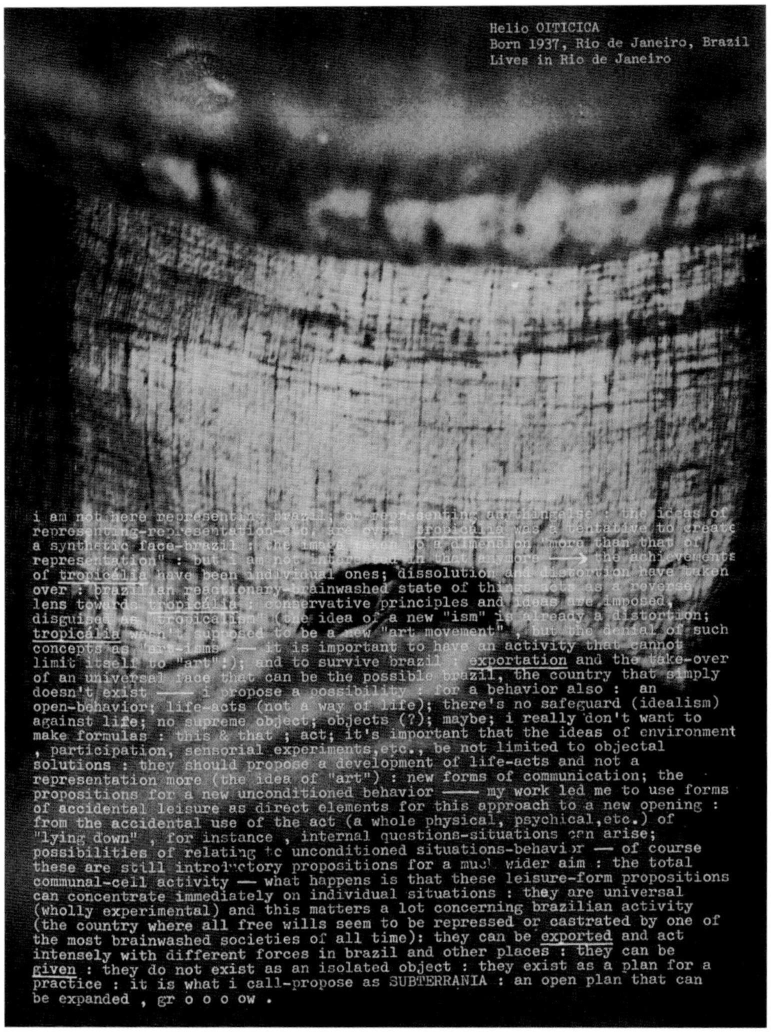

left

Hélio OITICICA

below

Jan DIBBETS

Artist's pages for *Information* catalogue, The Museum of Modern Art, New York, 1970

When the Museum of Modern Art in New York presented its first large-scale exhibition of conceptual art, 'Information', curated by Kynaston McShine in 1970, it was aware of the scrutiny directed towards it due to the emerging critique of art institutions by many of the participating artists, groups such as the Art Workers Coalition and figures such as the independent curator Seth Siegelaub. The format of the exhibition catalogue attempted to erase the usual signs of the institution and to accommodate the wishes of the artists. Typeset in a typewriter fount, illustrated with grainy black and white photographs and printed on newsprint-style paper, it had the appearance of an artist-produced project, resembling 'alternative' publications such as the *Whole Earth Catalog*. Each artist was allocated a page and offered as open a set of options as possible for the way the page could be used. The precedent for this presentation had been set by Seth Siegelaub, who devised formats such as the 'Xeroxbook' in 1968, and subsequently several catalogues, as art-as-information, independent of art support systems of any kind. Here the museum was attempting to imitate such radical gestures, yet it was unable to disentangle itself from its authoritative position. Jan Dibbets' contribution, below, let the museum's own typed form serve as a disclosure of its hierarchical list of what might be included. Oiticica used his page explicitly to refute the notion that he was 'representing' his country Brazil, at that time under a military dictatorship, or any other category such as an art movement. He refers to *Tropicália*, an environment which recreated aspects of the physical experience of a Brazilian *favela* or shanty town within an art gallery, and, by introducing them into a different context, offered both a critical distance and the utopian possibility of creating different conditions of existence in everyday life.

Jan DIBBETS
Born 1941, Weert, the Netherlands
Lives in Amsterdam, the Netherlands

How do you want to be represented in the catalogue? A page is the size of this sheet and each artist will have one page.

Photographs of the piece in the show?

Photographs of a previous piece?

Other photographs,

By a statement?

In any other way?

BY this paper.

6 April 1970
Date

Jan Dibbets
Signature

43

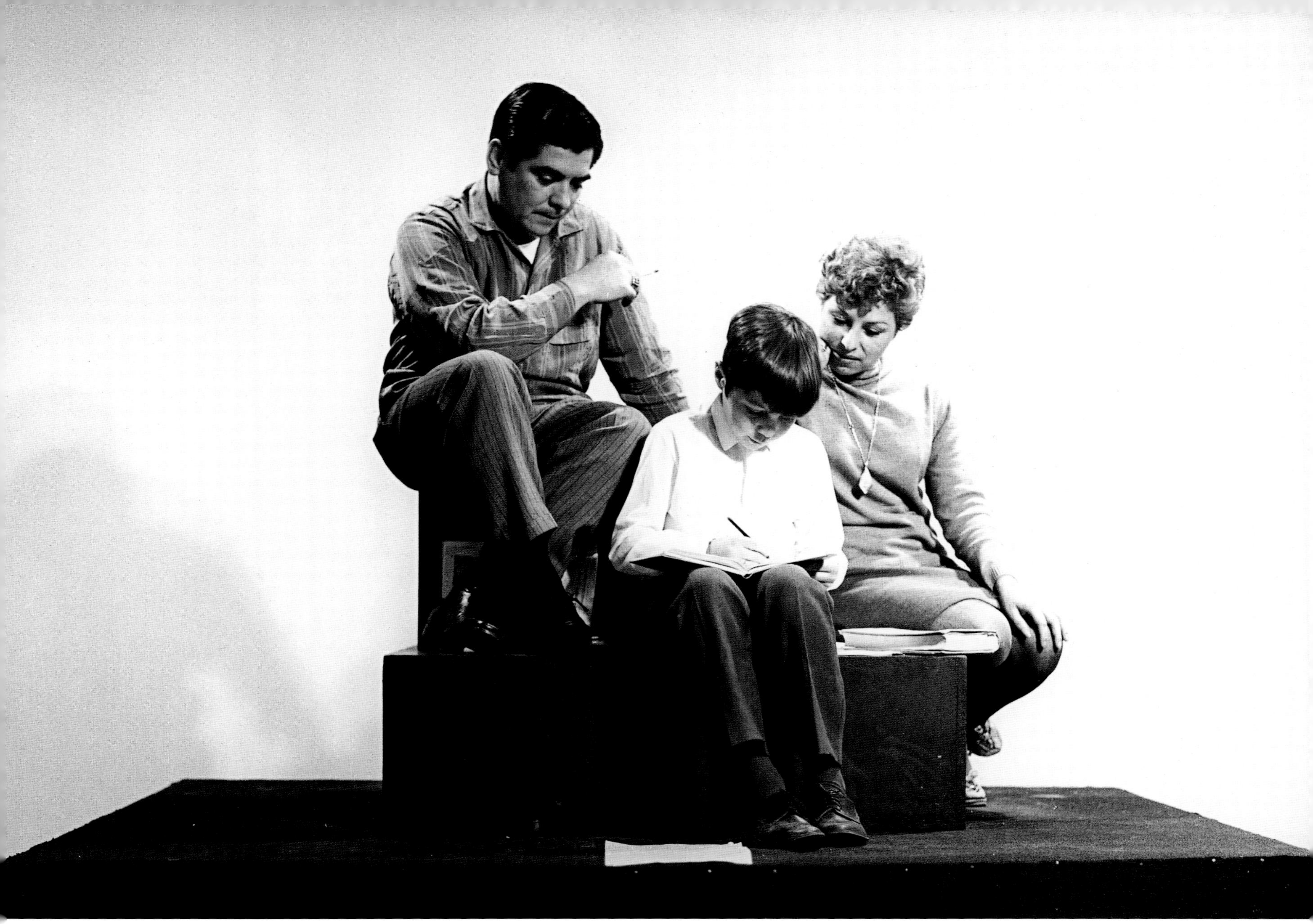

Oscar BONY
La familia obrera [Proletarian Family]
1968
Documentation photograph of event, 'Experiencias 68',
Instituto Torcuato di Tella, Buenos Aires
Dimensions variable

Bony arranged for a working family to pose on a plinth as works of art during exhibition hours, at the Instituto Torcuato di Tella, Buenos Aires, in 1968, in return for a fee which was twice their normal salary. The museum label accompanying the work shown above stated: 'Luis Ricardo Rodriguez, whose profession is metallurgic worker, is receiving twice what he earns in his regular job just for being exhibited, with his wife and son, while this show is on.' From 1962–65 the artist Alberto Greco had made street performances in Buenos Aires and elsewhere, called the *Vivo dito* series, in which he either signed his name on people or objects or drew a circle around them to label them as 'living works of art'. In Bony's work this iconoclastic gesture is incorporated into a wider project of critique of the museum as an authenticator of culture which is complicit with the economic and political authorities.

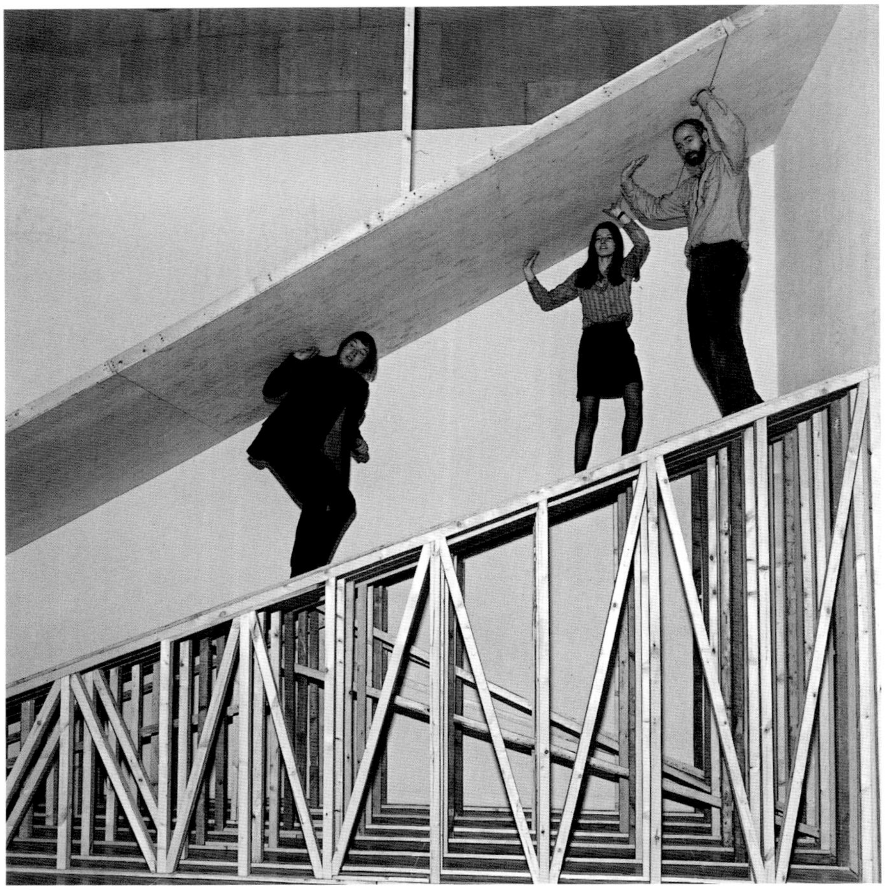

Robert MORRIS

Installation views, 'Robert Morris', Tate Gallery, London, 1971

left

Robert Morris (right) and visitors interacting with works in the initial installation

below

Second installation of the exhibition after temporary closure

For a retrospective at the Tate Gallery, London, Morris designed a series of structures, based on earlier sculptures, which invited the physical participation of the public. These structures included balancing platforms, a large granite column, brass, steel, aluminium, stone and wood weights hanging on ropes over a steel ramp, climbing slots and nets, a tunnel and a suspended tightrope wire. In the back of the exhibition catalogue, a poster describing the three different sections of structures made the claim that 'these pieces ... render physical and practical what was left to empathy and imagination in the earlier sculptures. They represent an art that goes beyond the making, selling, collecting and looking-at kind of art, and proposes a new role for the artist in relation to society.' Five days after the exhibition opened it was closed by the museum as a result of 'minor accidents' as well as the 'exuberant and excited behaviour' of some visitors whose actions had damaged a number of the structures. The exhibition was subsequently re-opened in a more traditional form. Despite the museum's high claim to be opening its doors to a new form of art, the practical reality proved more of a challenge than the institution was able to take on. By inviting audience participation/engagement of such a physical nature with the work, Morris not only broke the boundaries of the traditional art object but also the boundaries of acceptable (and non-destructive) social behaviour. – quotation from Michael Compton and David Sylvester, *Robert Morris*, 1971

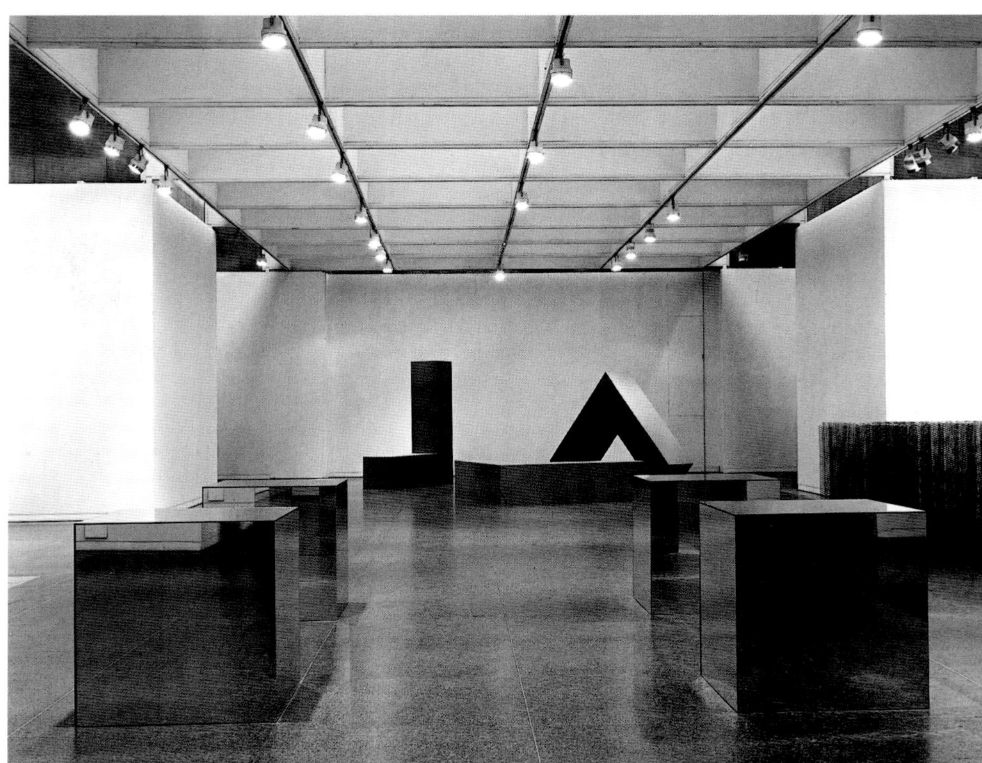

Michael ASHER
Untitled
1973
Galleria Toselli, Milan

Asher had the walls and ceiling of this private Milan gallery sandblasted so that all traces of white paint were removed and the underlying plaster exposed. Once the gallery was sand-blasted only natural light was used to light the interior. 'Traditionally, the white interior of a commercial gallery presented an artist's production within an architectural setting of false autonomy. If, through its absence, the viewer was reminded of the white paint an interesting question was then raised: How does the white "partition" of paint affect the context of art usually seen on that support surface?'
– Michael Asher, *Writings 1973–1983 on Works 1969–1979*, 1983

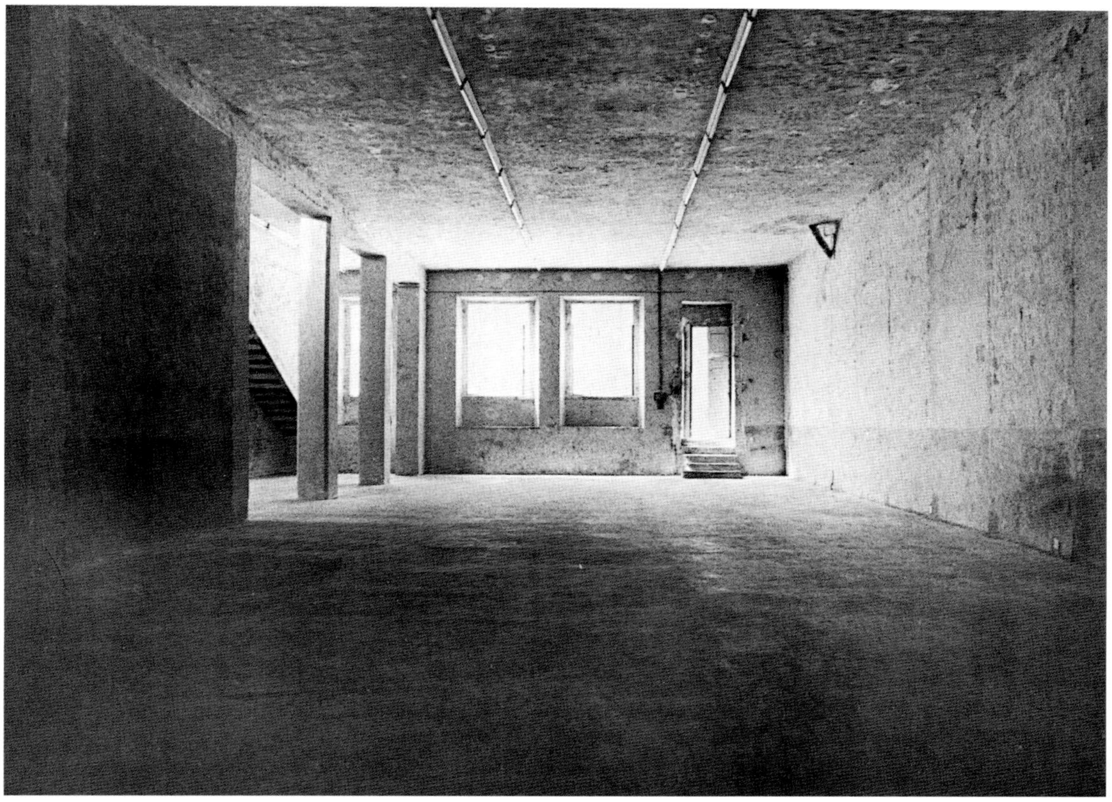

Michael ASHER
Untitled
1974
Claire Copley Gallery,
Los Angeles

Here Asher removed the partition between a gallery and its office. Viewers 'were confronted with the way in which they had been traditionally lulled into viewing works of art and, simultaneously, the gallery structure and its operational procedures. Works had been perceived from a safe cultural distance which generally prevented the viewer from questioning the issues involved. Without that questioning a work of art could remain enclosed in its abstract aesthetic context, creating a situation where the viewer could mystify its actual and historical meaning ... This work laid bare the contradictions inherent within the gallery structure and its constituent elements.'
– Michael Asher, *Writings 1973–1983 on Works 1969–1979*, 1983

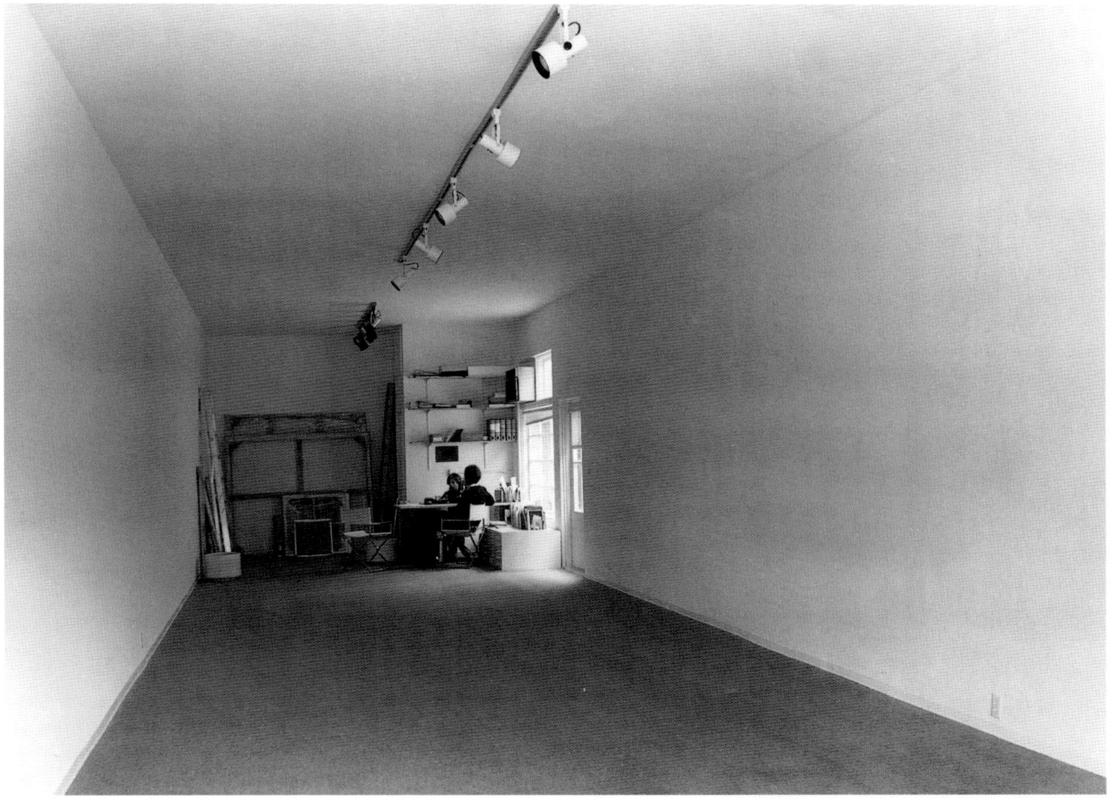

AFTERWARDS

By the beginning of the 1980s, whatever unity conceptual art had once possessed as a polemical rejection of 'the visual' had been replaced by a post-conceptual interest in the strategic uses of both traditional artistic and mass-media visual forms. This was accompanied by an increased emphasis on installation, as the act of realizing a work in a specific context, inside or outside the gallery. Jenny Holzer, Barbara Kruger, Felix Gonzalez-Torres and Krzysztof Wodiczko sought public spaces for their interventions. Sophie Calle and Willie Doherty explored the legacy of the photo-text. In China, new kinds of conceptual art were emerging in opposition to domestic artistic conditions. Zhang Huan used Confucian practices of self-discipline as conceptual technique. Internationally, new uses of installation by artists of the 1960s and 1970s generations, such as Dan Graham and Lawrence Weiner, addressed the expanded space of a globalized art world.

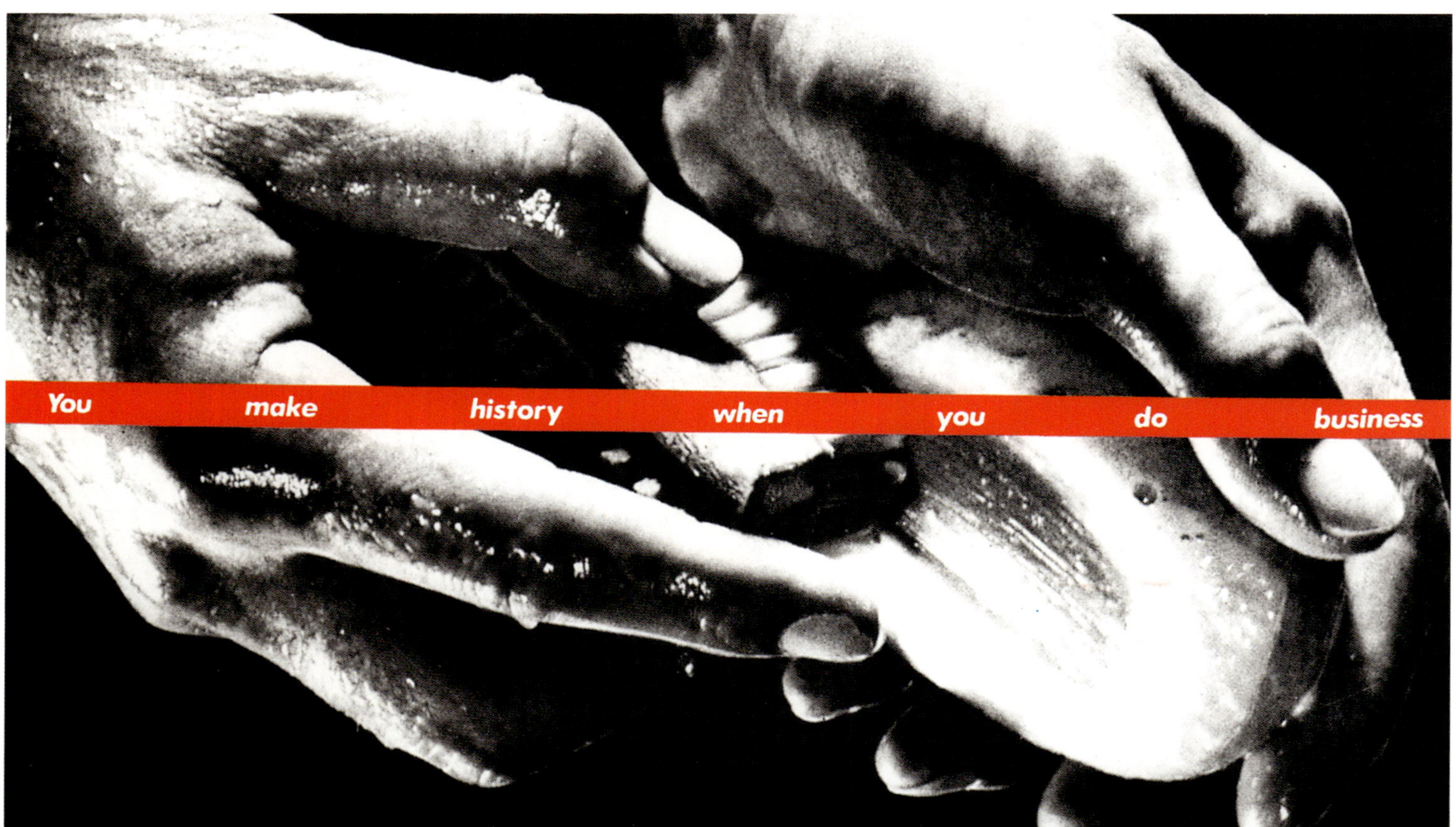

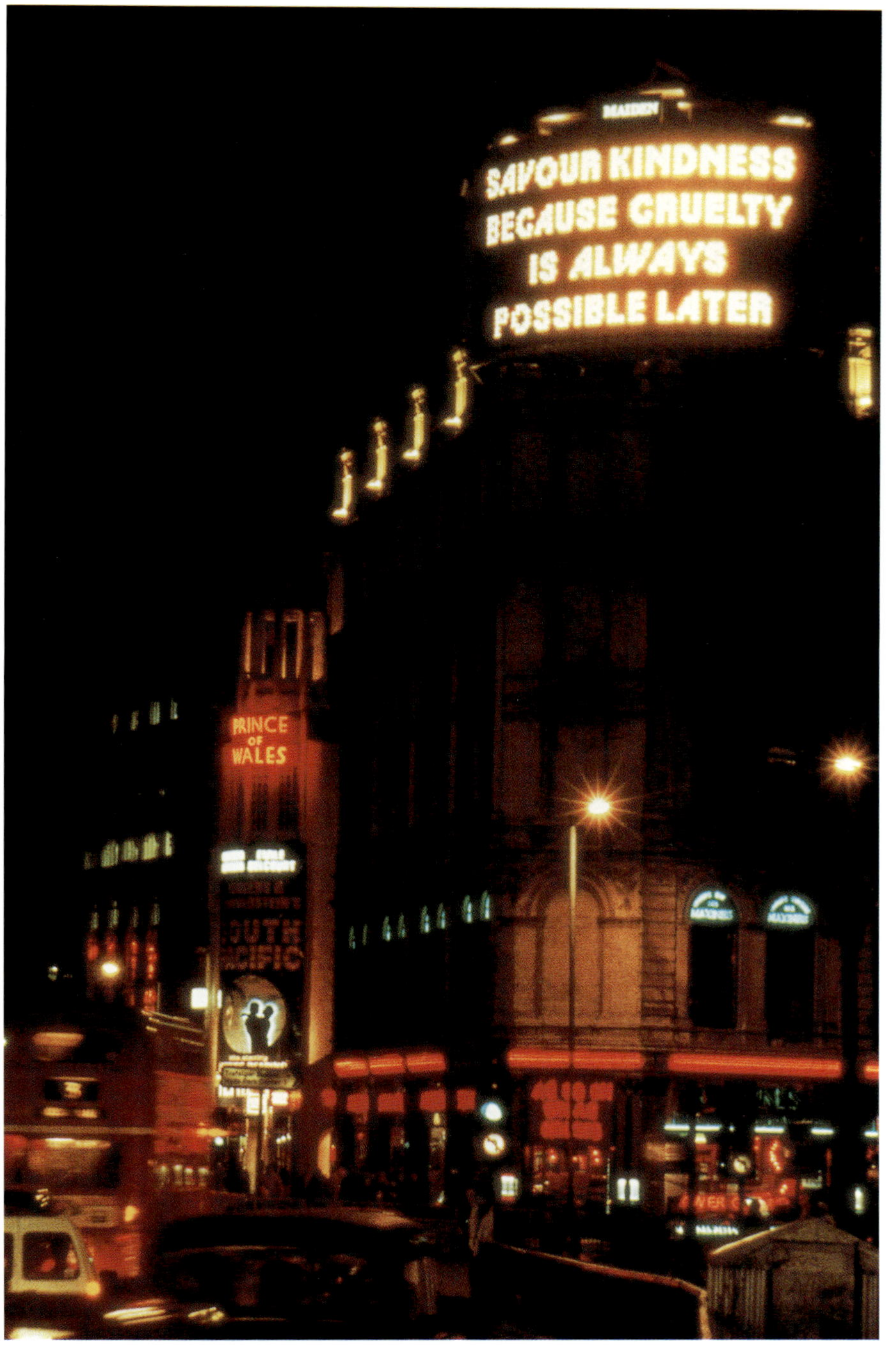

Jenny HOLZER
Survival [detail]
1983-85
Spectacolor sign
460 × 910 cm [181 × 358 in]
Piccadilly Circus, London,
1988-89

Holzer's first series of texts, *Truisms* (1977–79) were initially pasted anonymously on walls in Manhattan, in the form of cheaply printed posters in black type on white paper. Later, along with other related series, such as this detail from *Survival*, these texts were presented and distributed in a wide variety of forms ranging from the electronic signs in Times Square, New York, and elsewhere to T-shirts, billboards, cash till receipts, baseball caps and postcards.

Holzer adapted a form derived from existing language-based practices in conceptual art, for interventionist, more directly politicized use. She extensively researches social statements, such as truisms, from a wide range of literary and popular cultural sources. This material is adapted to construct texts that mimic authoritative voices in mass culture. By making the statements gender neutral and presenting them as if they are familiar and accepted, Holzer draws attention to the subliminal influences of social conditioning.

opposite
Barbara KRUGER
Untitled [You make history when you do business]
1982
Photomontage with text
122 × 244 cm [48 × 96 in]

Kruger began making image and text montages in the early 1980s. Formerly involved in commercial graphic design, she was critically aware of the increasingly pervasive media strategies whereby individuals are persuaded to conform to the social, economic and ideological agendas of dominant groups. Like Holzer, she investigates the ways in which we receive verbal and visual messages circulated by anonymous sources of power, and seeks to intercept this process, reversing its logic. When personal pronouns are used in the context of this work, rather than being invested with the coercive authority of advertising or propaganda, they reveal ways in which the position of the individual subject within the language system is indefinite. The gender of the 'I', 'you', 'we' is also non-determined, so that rather than 'masculine' or 'feminine' positions emerging there is instead an interplay between positions of activity and passivity, which reveals the patterns of power relations and suggests ways of redirecting them.

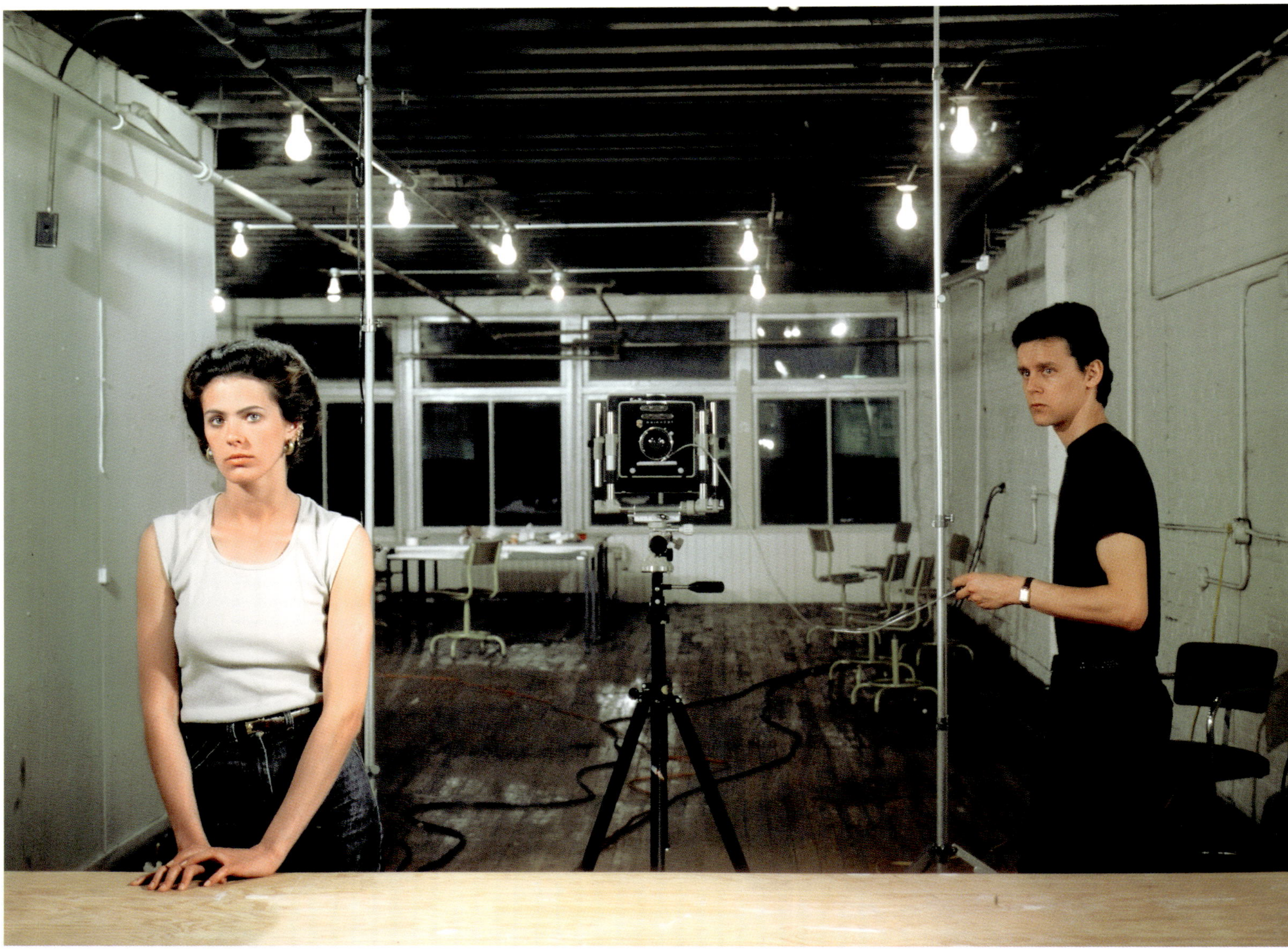

Jeff WALL
Picture for Women
1979
Transparency in light box
163 × 229 cm [64 × 90 in]
Collection, Centre Georges Pompidou, Paris

Noting the camera held by the photographer (Wall), the viewer registers that he is positioned in front of a mirror which he is photographing. It is hard to tell which way he is looking and it is only by imagining the scene diagrammatically that it can be ascertained that he is looking at the woman's reflection in the mirror and not looking at her back in the studio space. The woman is on the same side of the picture plane as the photographer. She becomes, therefore, a viewer rather than just a subject, hence the mode of address in the work's title. Her eyes are fixed just past the viewer's gaze. The optical viewpoint of the spectator is represented by the camera, which serves as the 'vanishing point' of the picture. The viewer thus understands that the camera has photographed itself in the mirror, yet the camera itself is an 'unknowing' eye – it represents us without seeing us, functioning simultaneously as an 'eye' and as a blind spot. In representing this paradox in a photograph which refers to Manet's famous painting of a serving woman standing in front of a bar mirror (*A Bar at the Folies-Bergère*, 1882), Wall draws upon early modernism's radical questioning of the picture plane in painting and applies its principles to photography. Whereas in painting the materiality of the painted surface testifies to the presence of the picture plane, in photography the picture plane is normally invisible. This work makes it visible, attempting to resolve a disparity with painting so that photography can take over the field that belonged, before modernism, to genre painting.

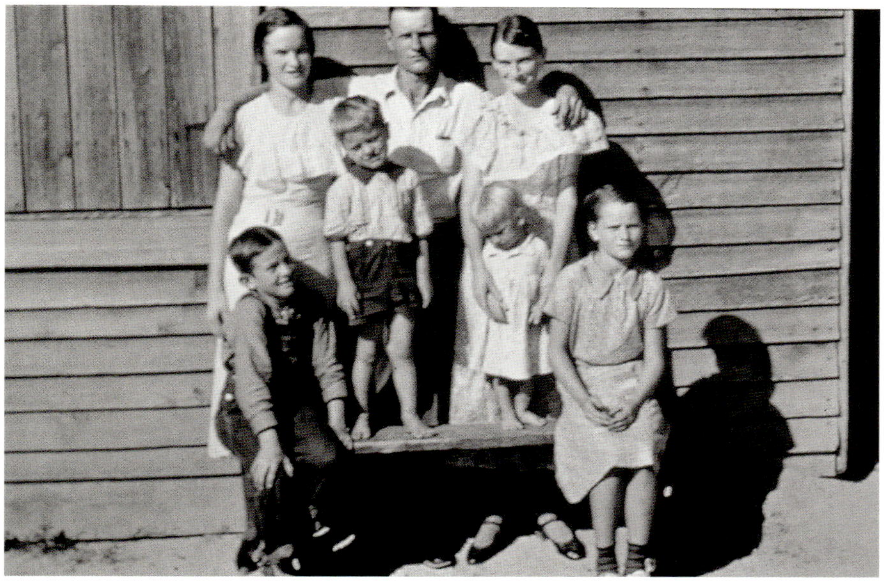

Sherrie LEVINE

Untitled [After Walker Evans No. 2]

1981

Gelatin silver print

20.5 × 25.5 cm [8 × 10 in]

Collection, Metropolitan Museum of Art, New York

Levine appropriates as 'readymades' not objects from outside an artistic context but those artefacts which are already canonized as important and valuable artworks. In many of her works the original photographs, sculptures or paintings she re-presents are by male artists who in turn 'appropriated' subject matter which they regarded as 'other' to themselves – women, poverty, the natural world, the exotic. Levine's act of re-appropriation highlights the paternal authority invested in the original image while at the same time drawing attention to the dilemmas of an artist, in the post-conceptual era, attempting to establish a renewed relationship with past forms of representation.

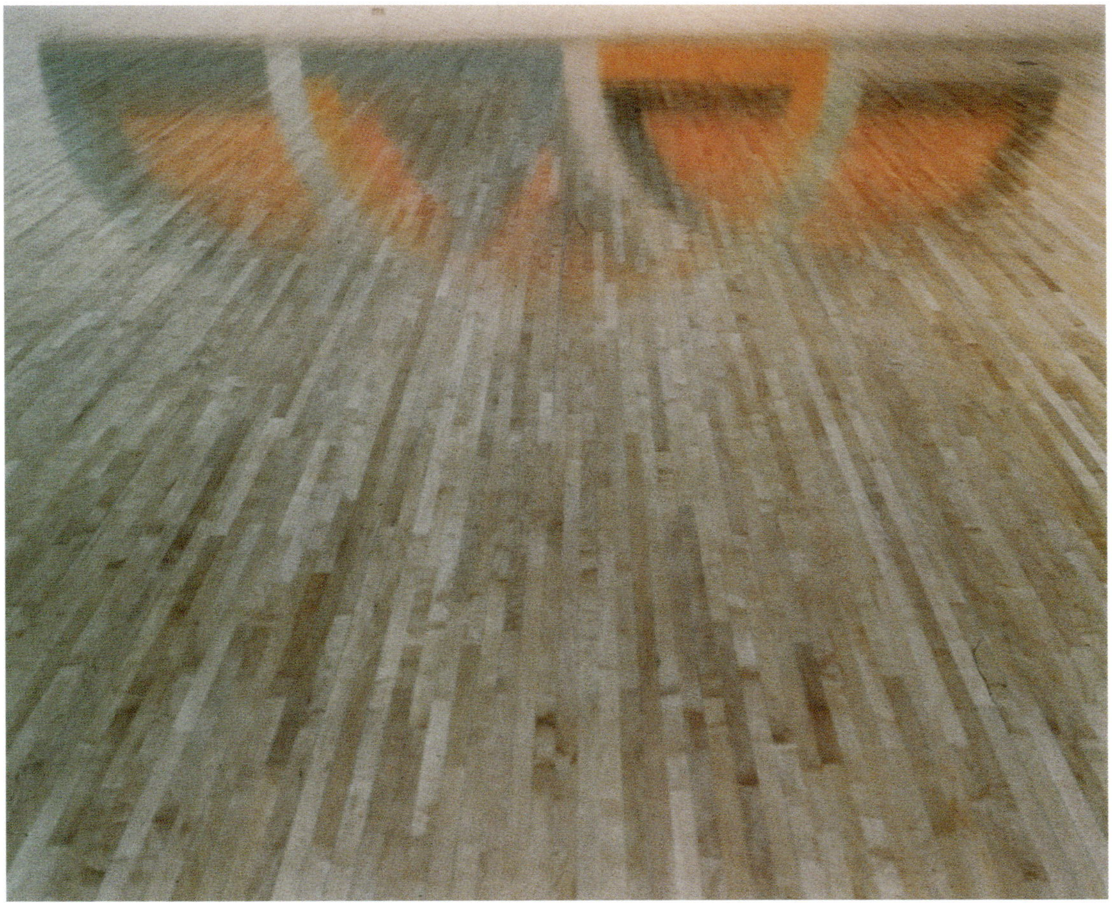

Louise LAWLER

How Many Pictures

1989

Cibachrome print

122 × 157 cm [48 × 62 in]

In the sheen of highly polished floor-boards the reflection of a large painting by Frank Stella can be discerned. Lawler's work draws upon the institutional critique of her conceptual art predecessors by focusing on what seem insignificant details – such as the particular way works of art are arranged in a gallery, an office or the home of an art collector, or the format of an exhibition invitation or a press release. Although seemingly inconsequential, all of these aspects of presentation function as competing signs alongside the artworks themselves. They position the art and to a significant extent determine its reception and meaning.

Allan MCCOLLUM
Plaster Surrogates
1982-85
Enamel on hydrostone
Dimensions variable
Installation, Lisson Gallery, London, 1985
Each of these works is a plaster mould in the shape of a painting, including the frame, but with blackness where the image should be. Produced and installed in numbers of several hundred, they suggest the absence of the aura of the artwork in the age of mechanical reproduction. At the same time, paradoxically, through their variations and as an aesthetically pleasing spectacle in their own right they are endowed with a presence which contrasts with the negation they imply. As a 'collection' they raise further questions about individuality, replication and the status of painting.

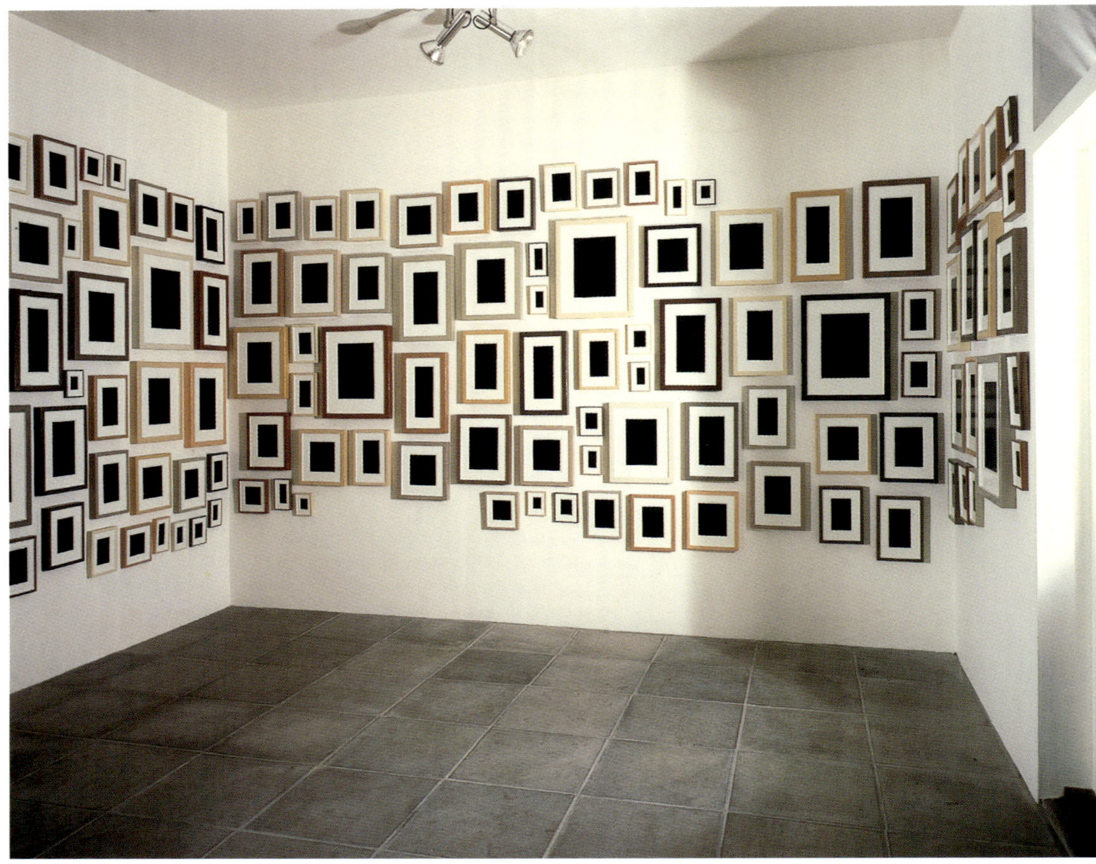

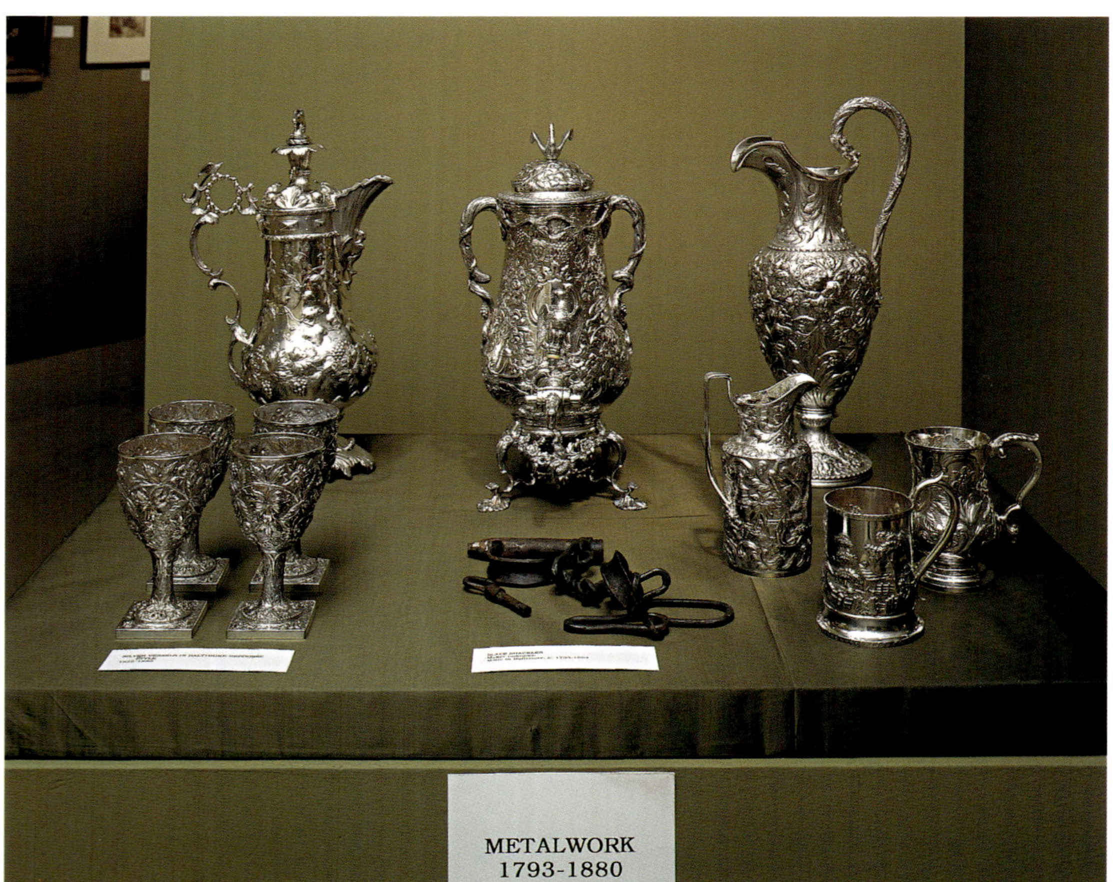

Fred WILSON
Mining the Museum
1992
Installation of rearranged objects from the collection Maryland Historical Museum, Baltimore
'I am fascinated by images and ideas that are present but go unnoticed by the average viewer. As art generally involves looking, I find art and museums fertile territory to mine.' Fine metalwork fabricated by African Americans in the nineteenth century is juxtaposed here with iron shackles. Wilson has made a number of projects where he works with the collections and archives of museums, using both exhibits and normally unseen materials to draw attention to the way 'otherness' has been represented, or repressed, in institutional presentations over the last century due to the 'disfiguring lens of colonial and racial ideas of its time'.
– quotations from Fred Wilson, Artist's statement, *The Museum as Muse*, 1999

Robert GOBER
Untitled
1992
Plaster, wood, wire lathe, steel, latex, paint, newspapers, etc.
Site-specific installation, Dia Center for the Arts, New York

This installation occupied an entire floor of the former warehouse space at the Dia Center for the Arts, New York. In the central space Gober had the walls painted with woodland scenes by scene painters, reversed in sections, like wallpaper. Four high *trompe-l'oeil* barred windows revealed a painted blue sky. Eight hand-modelled sinks were attached to the walls. The sinks were kept at a constant, partially filled level of water by the functioning taps. Refabricated boxes of rat poison were laid on the floor at various points. Large stacks of newspapers appeared throughout the installation; these were facsimiles of recent newspaper pages altered to varying degrees by the artist. Subjects included cases of anti-gay discrimination, premature death, maltreatment of children, neglect of the AIDS crisis, as well as mundane news of everyday events. All of these features were typical of Gober's installations during this period, in which fabricated and illusionistic items, a number of which, such as the sinks, referred to Duchamp's readymades, confronted viewers with the duplicity which pervades popular forms of representation in the late twentieth century.

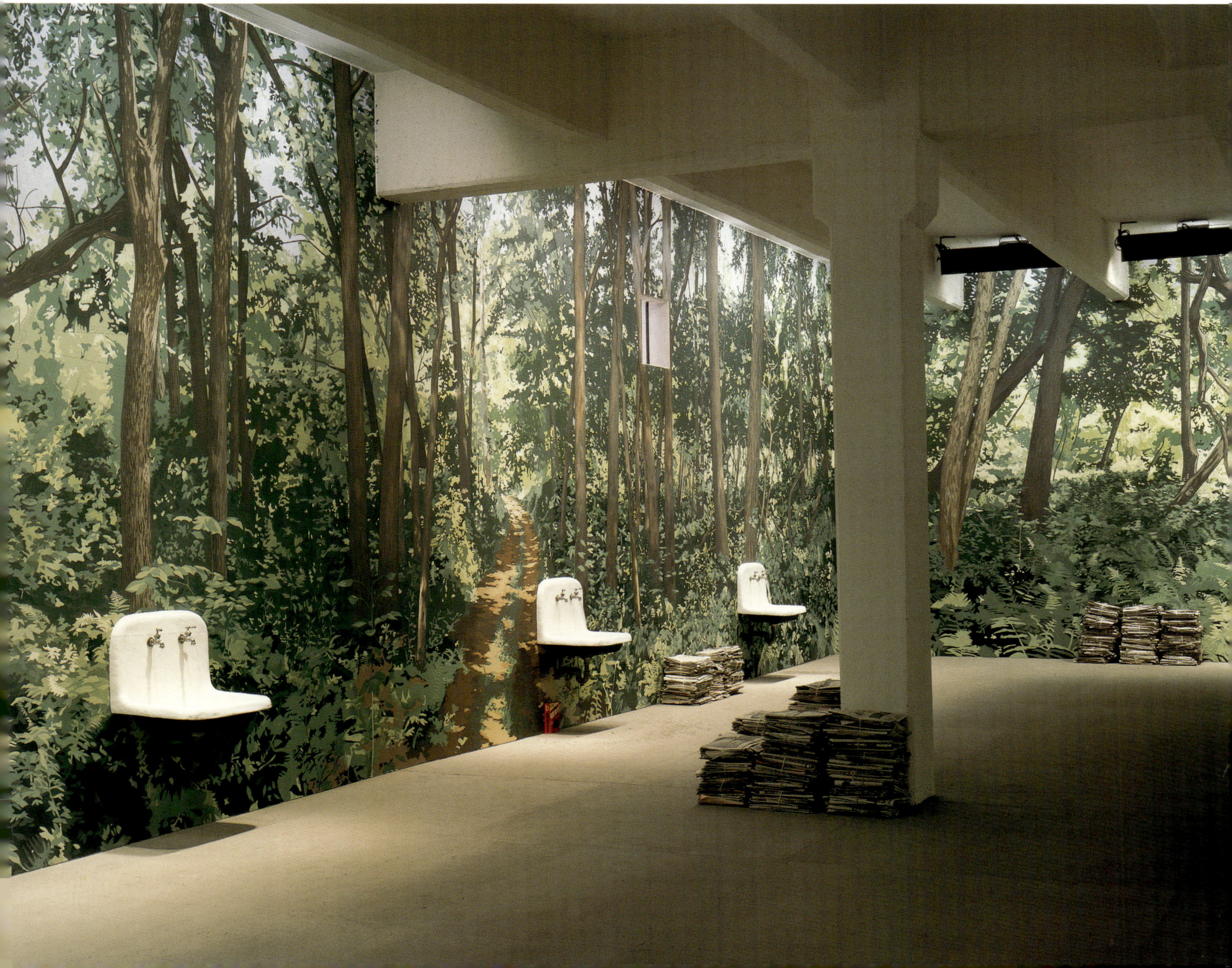

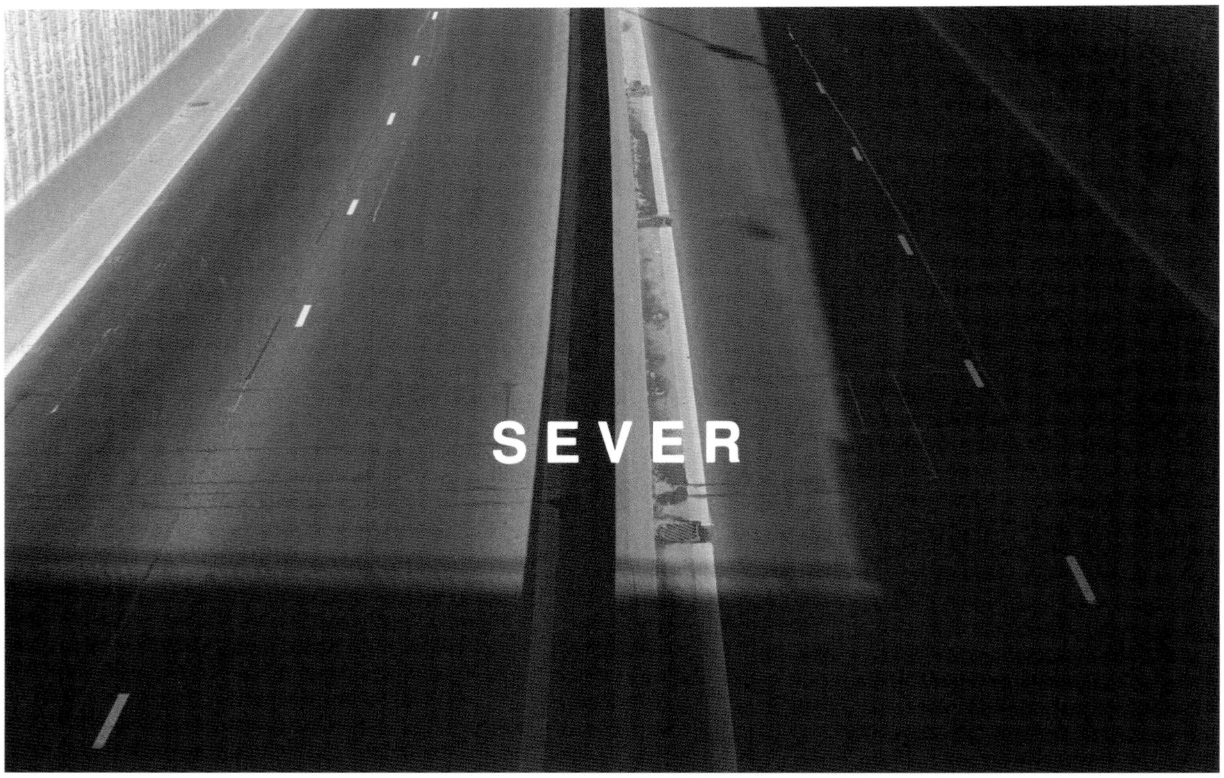

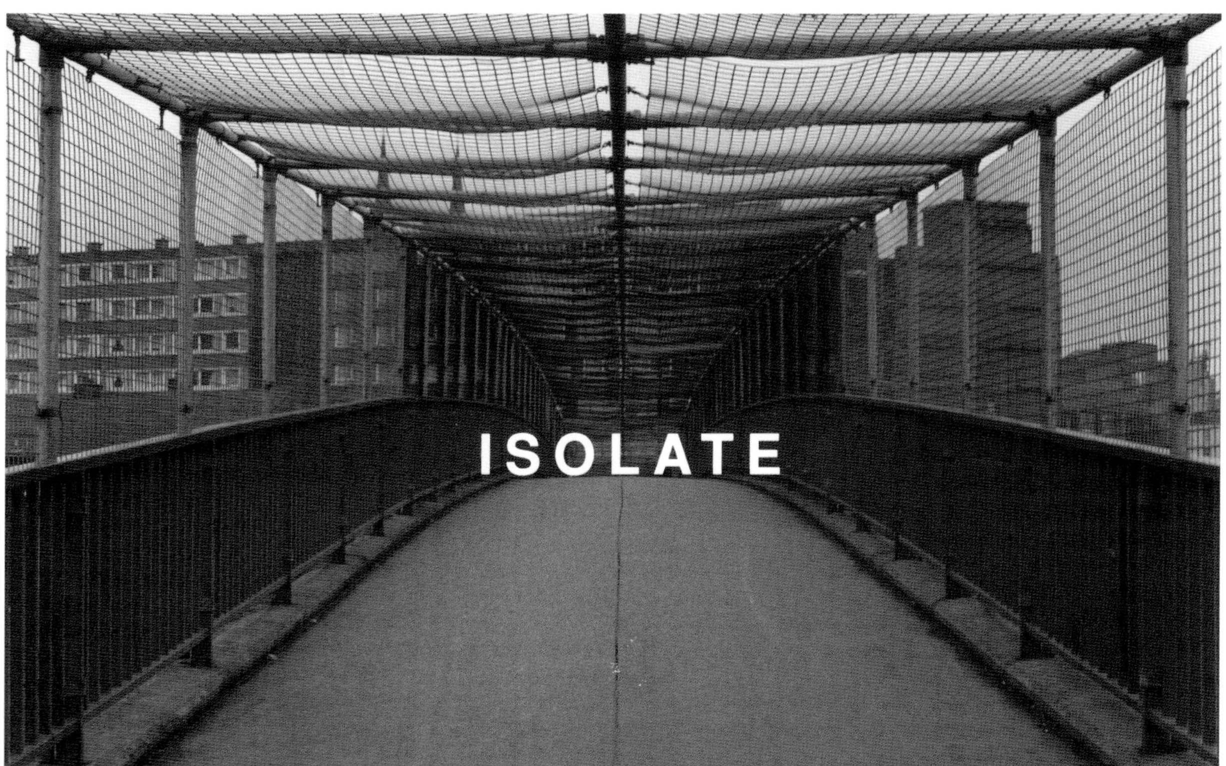

Willie DOHERTY
Strategy: Sever/Isolate
1989
2 black and white photographs mounted on aluminium
Diptych, 122 × 183 cm
[48 × 72 in] each

From 1985 to 1992 Doherty adopted a formal strategy which allowed him to engage with international currents in art while addressing the immediate political situation in his home town, Derry. He produced a series of black and white photo-text works which reference the practice of conceptual artists who combine language with photography. In Doherty's works border roads, rural landscapes, inner city areas and military barriers are punctuated by texts that implicate the image. The texts were often taken from sectarian grafitti or political speeches. By 'anchoring' a caption to an image, Doherty was also referring to the ideological function of advertising. In works such as this diptych, a reference to film noir can be seen in the oblique angles and accentuated depth of field. The works adopt – and provide an alternative, resistant language to – the strategies of the photographic, filmic and television media through which politically charged information and misinformation is circulated.

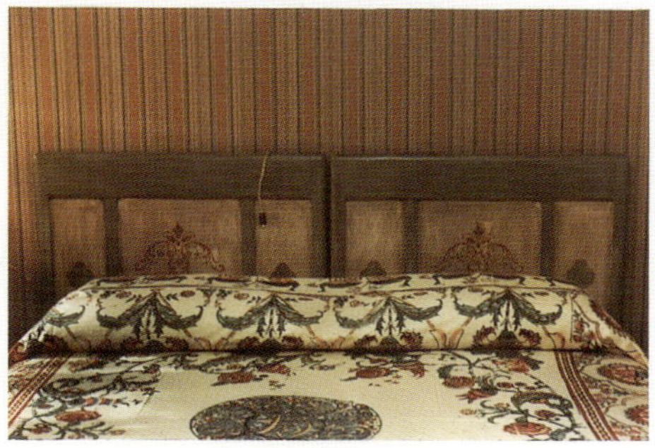

C H A M B R E 2 8

Mardi 3 mars 1981. *J'entre au 28. Les lits jumeaux sont défaits. A gauche on dort avec deux oreillers, à droite, sans. Je remarque le pyjama d'homme en soie rouge et noire, posé sur la chaise et les babouches brodées (pointure 38). Ce sont les seuls éléments d'occupation visibles avec la valise et le sac de voyage, tous deux fermés à clé. Les armoires sont vides hormis trois sous-vêtements blancs (deux culottes et un tricot de corps) dans le tiroir supérieur de la commode, quelques affaires de toilette (rasoir, blaireau, dentifrice et brosse à dents...) et des médicaments dans le bidet de la salle de bains. Il n'y a rien d'autre à voir. Je fais le ménage et quitte la chambre.*

Mercredi 4. *Les valises sont toujours fermées à clé. Les babouches et le pyjama à leurs places respectives. Aujourd'hui, l'occupant du lit de droite s'est confectionné un petit oreiller avec un coussin du sofa protégé par une serviette. A gauche, maintenant un seul oreiller. Je remarque que la table adossée au lit a été tournée en sens inverse de façon à bloquer le tiroir contre le lit. Je la remets à l'endroit. En fait, le tiroir est vide.*

Jeudi 5. *Deux paires de bottes (pointures 38 et 42) ont fait leur apparition. Les valises sont toujours fermées à clé. Les trois sous-vêtements n'ont pas bougé. Et toujours au même endroit, le pyjama et les babouches. Pour une fois les oreillers sont restés tels que je les avais disposés. Ils n'ont pas touché à la table.*

Vendredi 6. *La situation est la même (pyjama, babouches, valises, salle de bains, table, sous-vêtements, bottes). C'est mon dernier jour de service à l'hôtel C. Je laisse à ma remplaçante le soin d'observer les variations des oreillers du 28. Aujourd'hui celui de gauche, qui tombe légèrement du lit, garde l'empreinte arrondie d'une présence. J'y vois comme un signe d'adieu.*

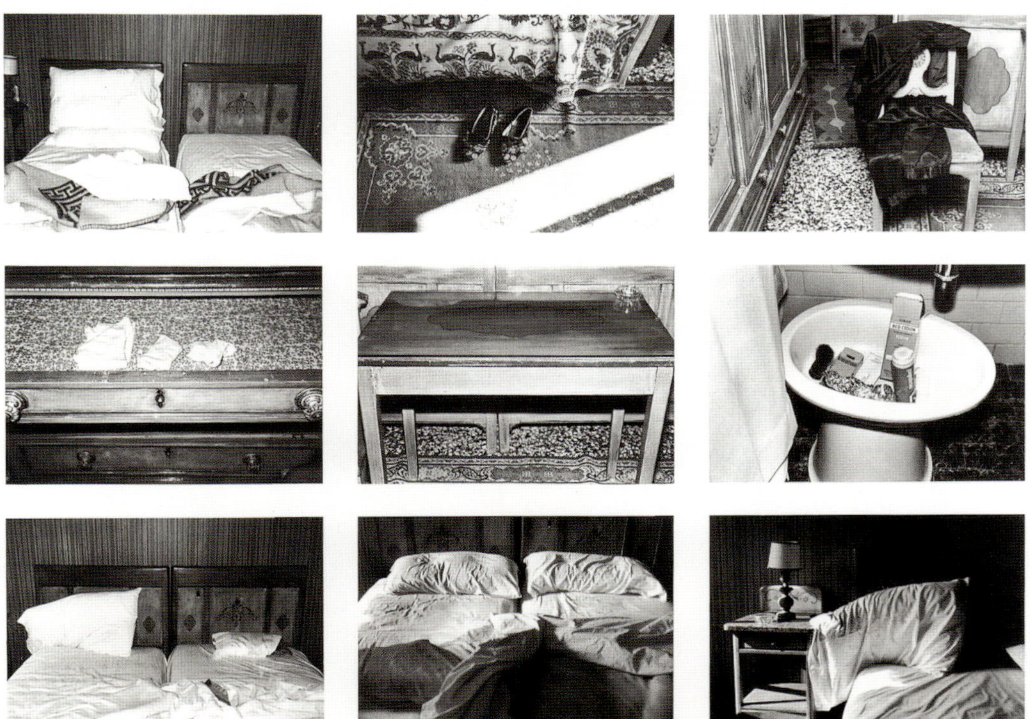

Sophie CALLE
Chambre 28, 3 Mars [from Hotel]
1981-90
Black and white and colour photographs, text
2 panels from the series,
102 × 142 cm [40 × 56 in] each

'On Monday 16 February 1981, after a year of approaches and waiting, I managed to get myself hired as a temporary chambermaid, replacing another during a period of three weeks, in a Venetian hotel: Hotel C. I was responsible for twelve rooms on the fourth floor. During my working hours I examined the personal effects of travellers, the signs of hotel clients' provisional installation, their succession one after the other in the same room. Through details, I observed lives which remained closed to me. On Friday 5 March my period of replacement came to an end.' Calle recorded the succession of anonymous travellers, and the evidence of their stay, through diary entries and photographs. She noted such details as the contents of the wastepaper bin, personal objects left lying around beside the bed and in the bathroom, clothing and even clients' diary entries. Each room is documented by two panels. One contains a colour photograph of the bed in the particular room, accompanied by Calle's diary entries relevant to that room. The other comprises a grid of black and white photographs of those idiosyncratic personal details which caught the artist's interest.
– quotations from the artist, in *Sophie Calle: à suivre*, 1991

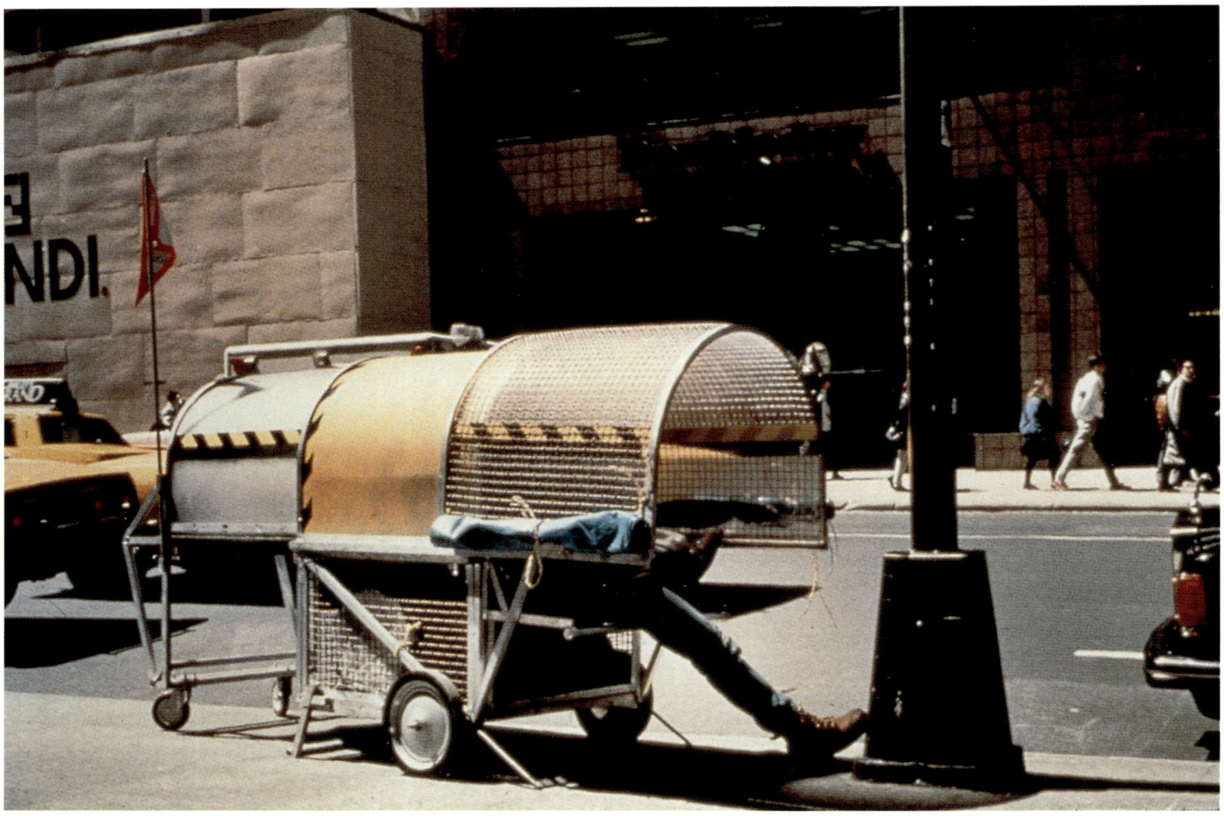

Krzysztof WODICZKO
Homeless Vehicle
1987–88
above
Documenation photograph
122 × 157 cm [48 × 62 in]
below right
Project drawing

'This vehicle is neither a temporary nor a permanent solution to the housing problem, nor is it intended for mass production. Its point of departure is a strategy for survival for urban nomads-evicts in the existing economy.'
– Krzysztof Wodiczko, David Lurie, statement for *Homeless Vehicle Project*, 1987

Since the late 1980s Wodiczko has developed a series of devices for survival, communication and empowerment designed to be used by homeless people and immigrants. Renowned for his public art interventions through the use of projection, in 1986 he collaborated with the artist Jana Sterbak on a related work, *The Homeless Projection: A Proposal for the City of New York*, in which images of the homeless were projected on to public buildings.

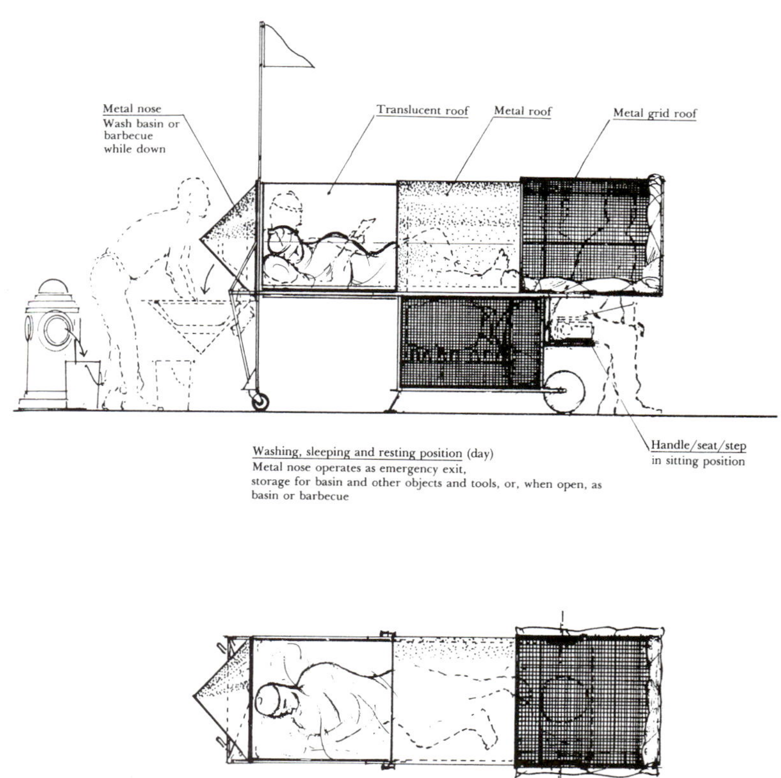

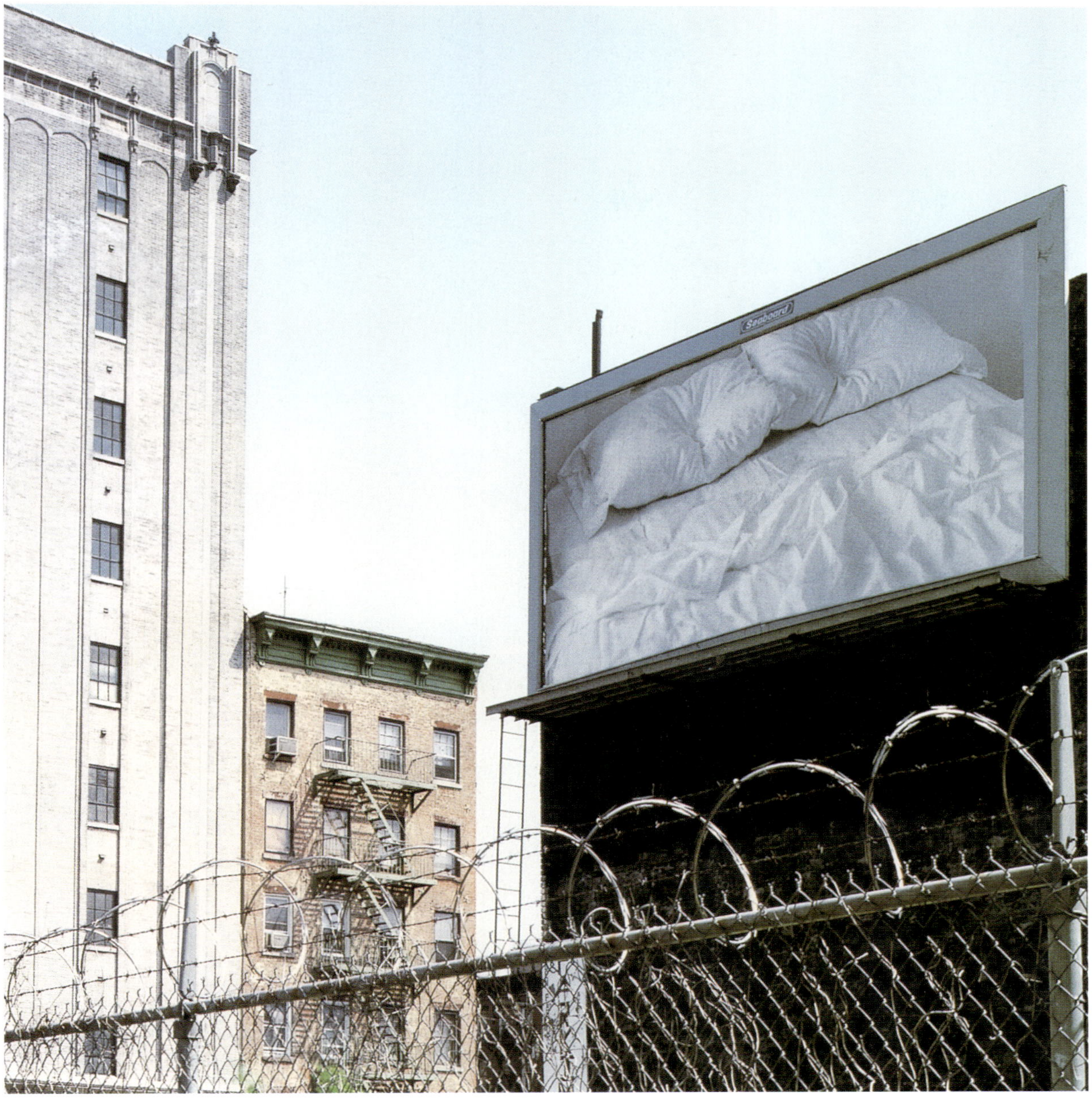

Felix GONZALEZ-TORRES
Untitled
1991
Billboard
2nd Avenue at East 2nd Street, New York; one of 24 street locations of installation organized by The Museum of Modern Art, New York

'There is no private space any more. Our intimate desires, fantasies, dreams are ruled and intercepted by the public sphere.'
– Felix Gonzalez-Torres, Artist's statement, 1991

In 1991 twenty-four billboards throughout Manhattan and the surrounding boroughs of New York displayed a black and white photograph of an empty but recently shared double bed, its pillows still bearing the fresh indentations of two people's heads. The image had a specific personal significance for the artist, as a testament of mourning for his life companion who had died that year, and also alluded to the invasion of private life by a punitive public sphere affecting people with AIDS. However the subversive power of the image lies, as he intended, in its refusal to cohere into a singularly coded representation. As in many of his other photographic works a visual sign of absence, such as a physical trace or a cast shadow, produces meaning, signifying differently for different viewers.

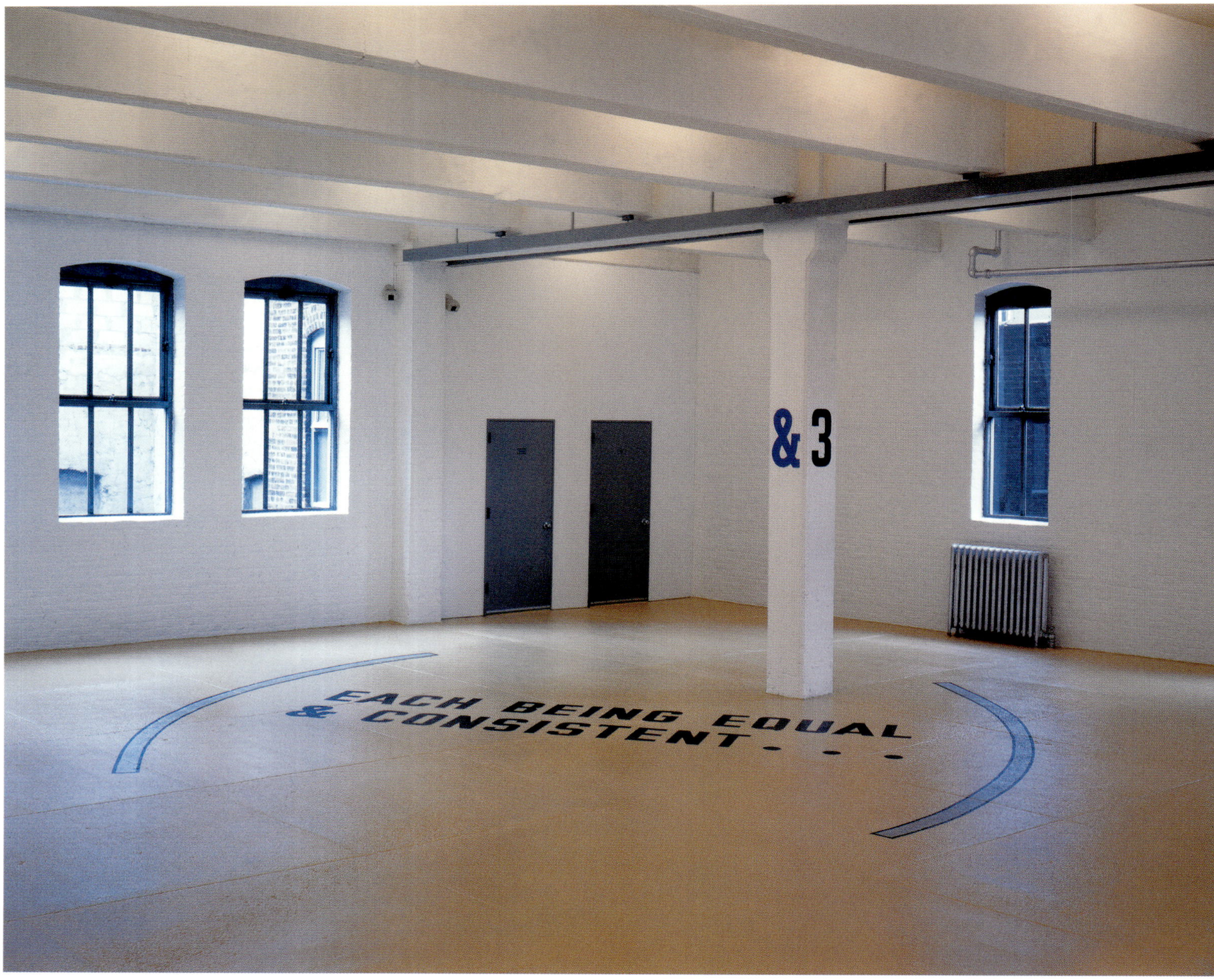

Lawrence WEINER
DISPLACEMENT [detail]
1991-92
Painted text
Dimensions variable
'DISPLACEMENT', Dia Center for the Arts, New York

This temporary installation is an example of works, both temporary and permanent, that Weiner has made in public sites. Although his statements painted on the surfaces of buildings draw attention to the presence of the physical world, they are not intended to be 'site specific' in relation to their given location. The statements always have an existence which is independent from any instance of their inscription: 'The work gains its sculptural qualities by being read, not by being written.'
– Lawrence Weiner, interview with Benjamin Buchloh, *Lawrence Weiner*, 1998

DISPLACEMENT highlights the role of translation: 'Just as translation implies transport, displacement, placement and an exhibition site, it operates on different levels at different times: the studio work, which consists of translating the material into a statement; public presentation of its translation; and finally, realization of the statement by others, a translation into their own reality that opens the field of interpretation ... [the work provides] reference points that will help them situate themselves in relation to objects: to understand, in material terms, where they are.'
– Birgit Pelzer, 'Dissociated Objects: The Statements/Sculptures of Lawrence Weiner', *October*, 90, 1999

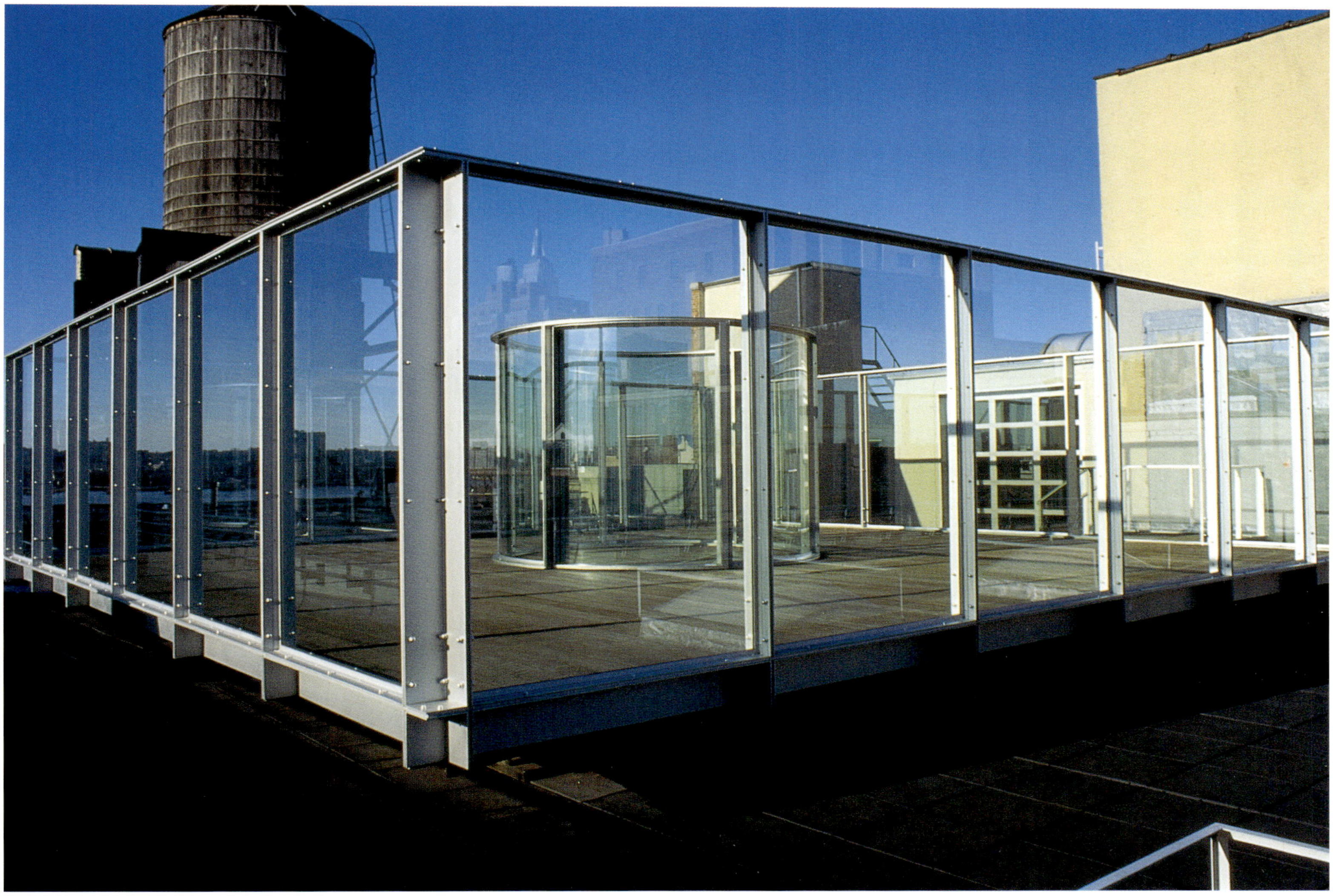

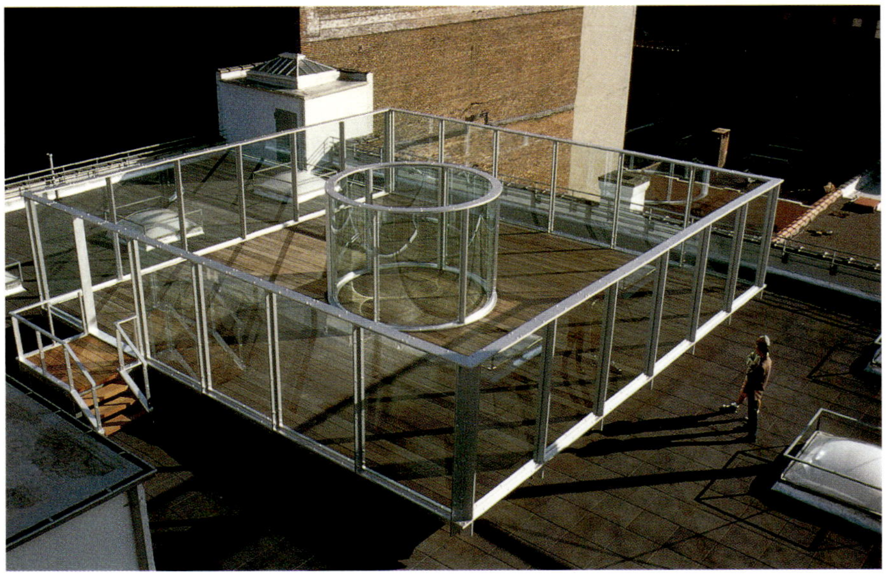

left and above

Dan GRAHAM

Two-way Mirror Cylinder inside Cube and Video Salon, Rooftop Park for Dia Center for the Arts

1981-91

Two-way mirror glass, transparent glass, steel, wood, rubber

2.4 × 11 × 11 m [8 × 36 × 36 ft]

Permanent installation, Dia Center for the Arts, New York

This project is 'an urban panopticon that transposes the atrium onto the rooftop of the institution, with a view of Manhattan and the Hudson river. For Graham the atrium characteristic of many corporate buildings represents a world within a world, a temporary refuge that brings the outside into an inside of transitions. In a peculiar shift, it brings back to the city the Utopia promised by the suburban haven, away from yet close to the city. The city park created by Graham's pavilion proclaims its social function. In the spirit of the alternative spaces of the 1970s, it offers a coffee bar and a place for viewing videos and for performance events. Forming a 360-degree horizon, it turns the city into a cinematic panorama.'

– Birgit Pelzer, *Dan Graham*, 2001

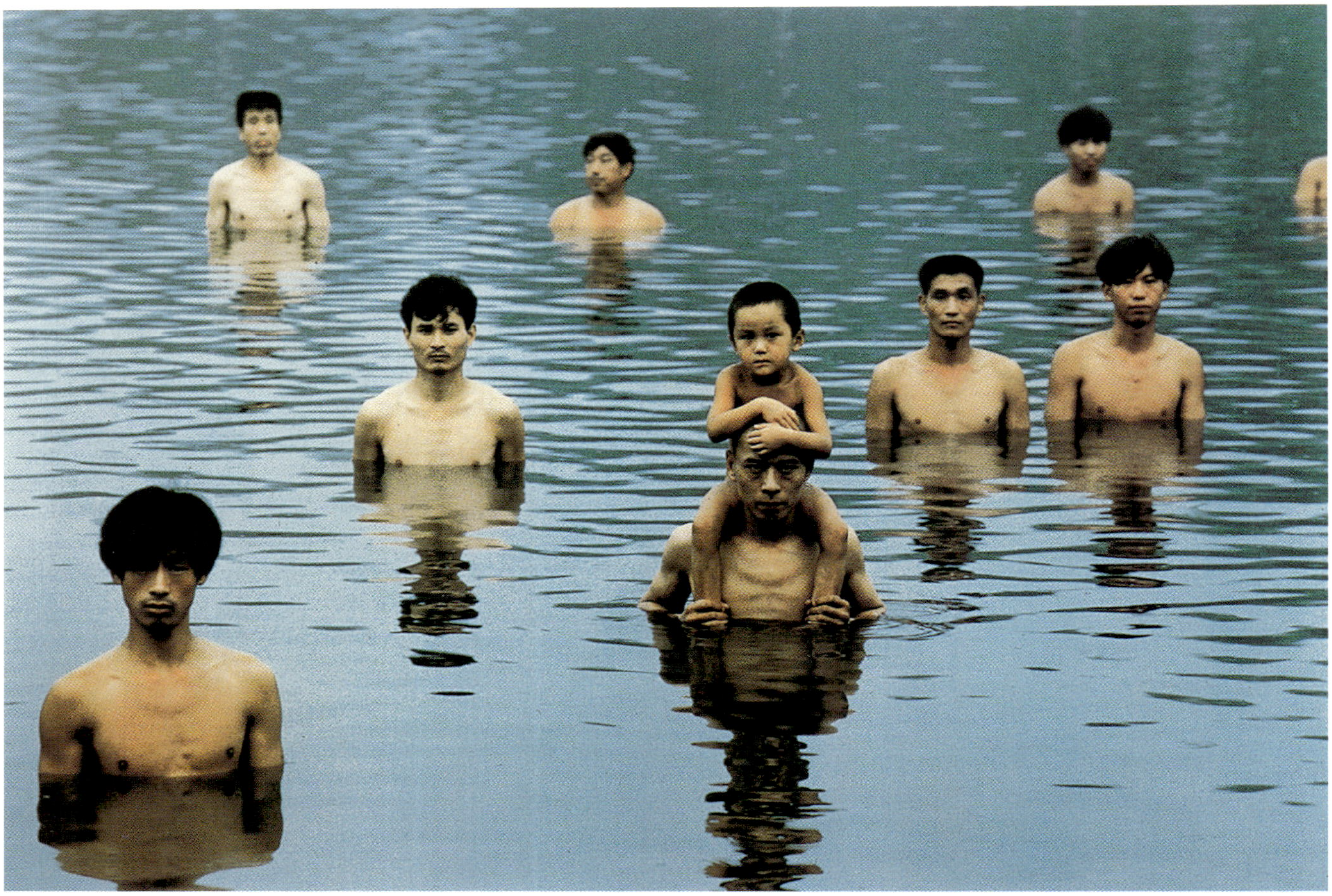

<u>ZHANG</u> Huan
To Raise the Water Level in a Fish Pond [detail]
1997
Beijing
Documentation photograph
102 × 152 cm [40 × 60 in]

In 1997 Zhang invited a large group of people to stand in a fish pond. Their collective presence raised the level of the water. The participants were all people who had lost their jobs as the result of China's recent industrial modernization programme. The curious logic of the action they carried out provoked reflection on the rigid and alienating logic of political forces beyond their control which had affected the course of their lives. This action was part of a series of related works made between 1994 and 1998 in the deprived Dong Cun (east village) district on the outskirts of Beijing, such as *To Add One Metre to an Unknown Mountain* (1995), in which participants lay on top of one another, at the top of a mountain, to achieve the required height.

opposite
<u>MIYAJIMA</u> Tatsuo
Revive Time [detail]
1999
2,450 blue light-emitting LED units
Dimensions variable
Installation view, 48th Venice Biennale, 1999

Commissioned for the Japanese Pavilion at the Venice Biennale in 1999 this work, unlike most of Miyajima's installations, has a specific reference, acting as a form of countdown for the end of the twentieth century and the beginning of the twenty-first. The light emitted from the electronic units is not red, orange or green, the colours usually used by the artist, but blue, which for him symbolizes death – with reference to the numbers of deaths caused in the twentieth century, the 'numerical' era of technologically and industrially determined societies.

Since 1988 Miyajima has produced works using numerical electronic signs which exist in many versions, all following the concept he has schematized as: 1. Keep changing, 2. Connect with everything, 3. Continue forever. This notion is related to the technology of the 'counter gadget', a small digital machine which displays two figures that count repeatedly from 1 to 99, then back to 1. In installations numerous counter gadgets are displayed together in a darkened room. Each follows a different rhythm. Together they comprise a metaphor for the paradoxical coexistence of difference with similarity which characterizes individuals within species. The work mirrors the continual change inevitable in all forms of existence, while aiming to 'continue forever' through the replaceability of machine parts. The arabic numerals displayed are intended to be understood by people across all nations and cultures.

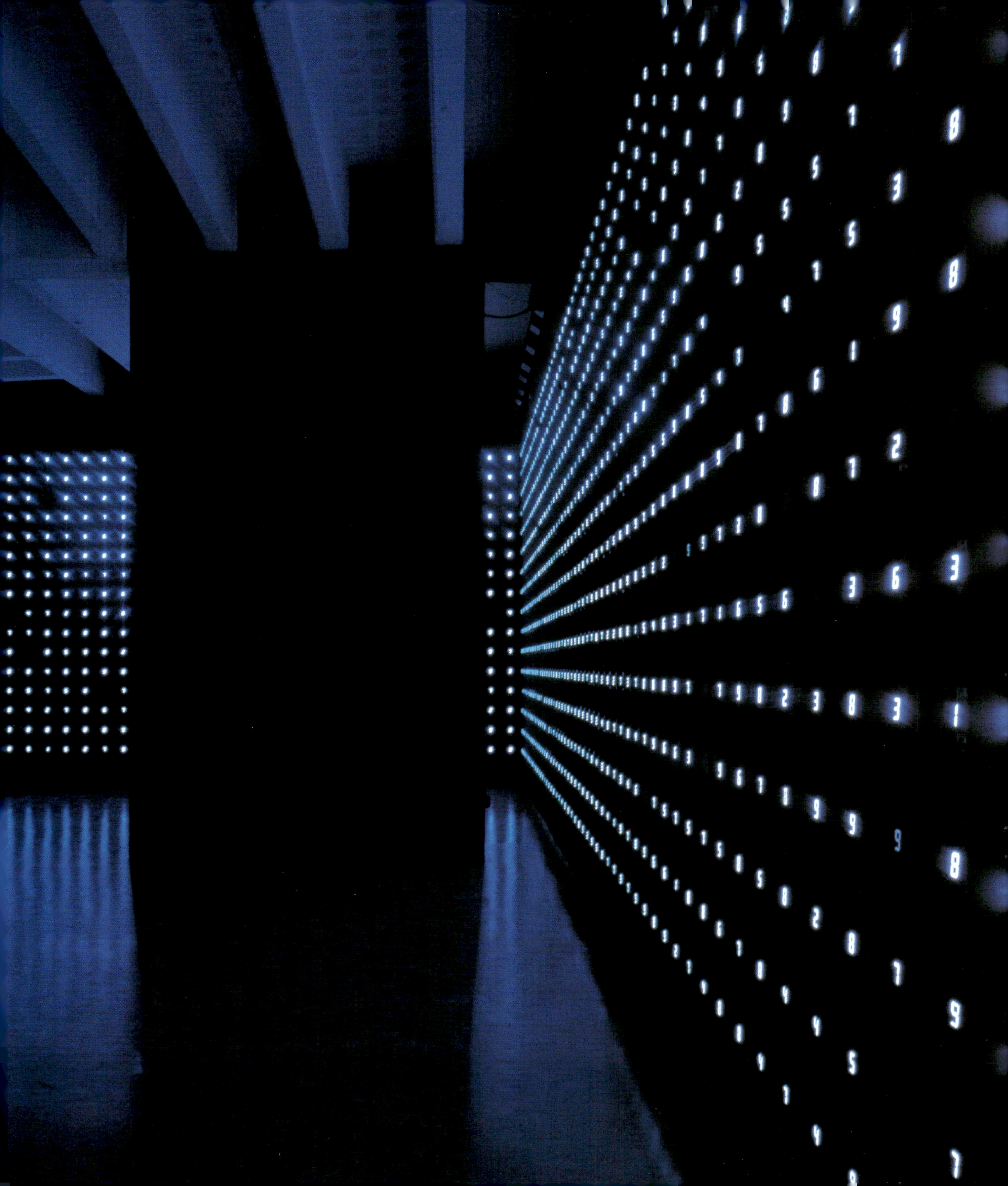

DOCU-
MENTS

VITO ACCONCI
THEODOR W. ADORNO
ALEXANDER ALBERRO
ART & LANGUAGE
ARTIST PLACEMENT GROUP
MICHAEL ASHER
TERRY ATKINSON
ROLAND BARTHES
JEAN BAUDRILLARD
SAMUEL BECKETT
MEL BOCHNER
BENJAMIN H.D. BUCHLOH
DANIEL BUREN
VICTOR BURGIN
IAN BURN
JACK BURNHAM
JOHN CAGE
LUIS CAMNITZER
JOHN CHANDLER
LYGIA CLARK
MICHEL CLAURA
EDUARDO COSTA
ROGER CUTFORTH
GUY DEBORD
MARCEL DUCHAMP
JOHANNA DRUCKER
ANTON EHRENZWEIG
RAÚL ESCARI
HAL FOSTER
IRVING GOFFMAN
NELSON GOODMAN
DAN GRAHAM
MAX HORKHEIMER
ROBERTO JACOBY
JASPER JOHNS
ALLAN KAPROW
MARY KELLY
YVES KLEIN
JOSEPH KOSUTH
JAROSLAW KOZLOWSKI
GEORGE KUBLER
THOMAS S. KUHN
JOHN LATHAM
CURT LEWIN
SOL LEWITT
LUCY R. LIPPARD
GEORGE MACIUNAS
ANDRÉ MALRAUX
HERBERT MARCUSE
KARL MARX
CILDO MEIRELES
GUSTAV METZGER
ROBERT MORRIS
MICHAEL NEWMAN
BRIAN O'DOHERTY
HÉLIO OITICICA
YOKO ONO
ROZSIKA PARKER
ADRIAN PIPER
MEL RAMSDEN
MARTHA ROSLER
FERDINAND DE SAUSSURE
SETH SIEGELAUB
ROBERT SMITHSON
MIERLE LADERMAN UKELES
JEFF WALL
LUDWIG WITTGENSTEIN

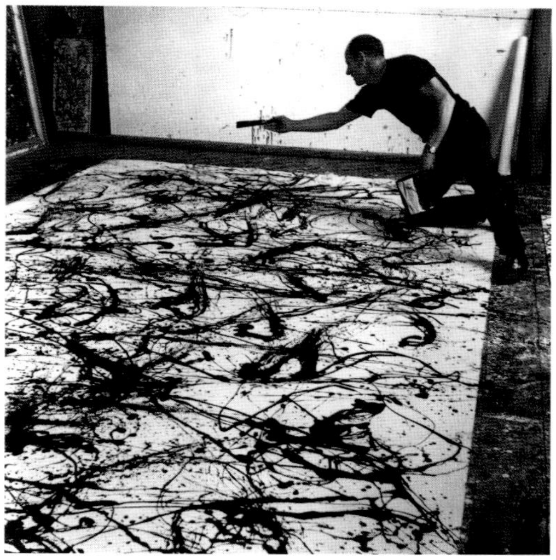

1. [see page 194]
Jackson POLLOCK
Painting in his studio
c. 1950
East Hampton

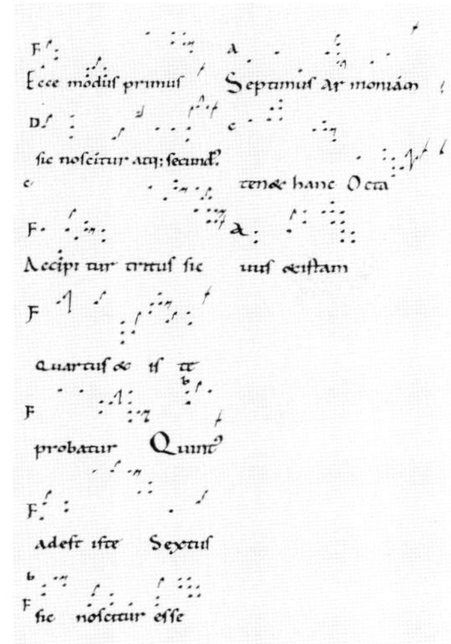

2. [see page 203]
Page of manuscript,
late eleventh century
Fol. 127 v. from Lat.
7211, Bibliothèque
Nationale, Paris

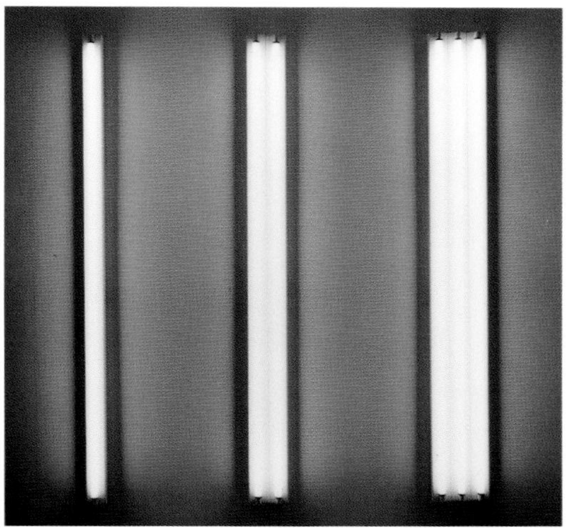

3. [see page 213]
Dan FLAVIN
the nominal three
[to William of Ockham]
1964-69
Cool white fluorescent
light
h. 244 cm
[96 in]

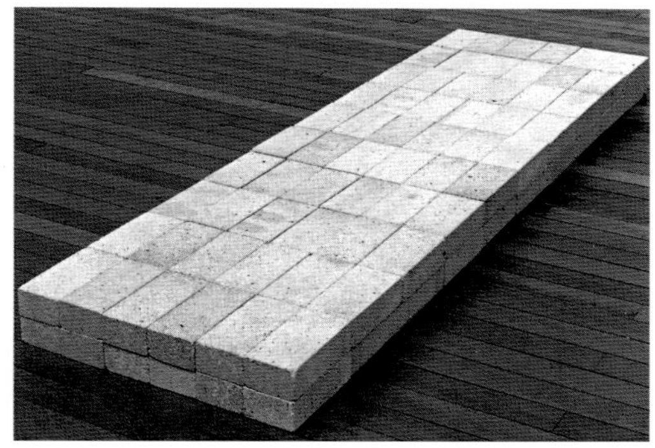

4. [see page 213]
Carl ANDRE
Equivalent VIII
1966
120 fire-bricks
13 × 69 × 229 cm
[5 × 27 × 90 in]

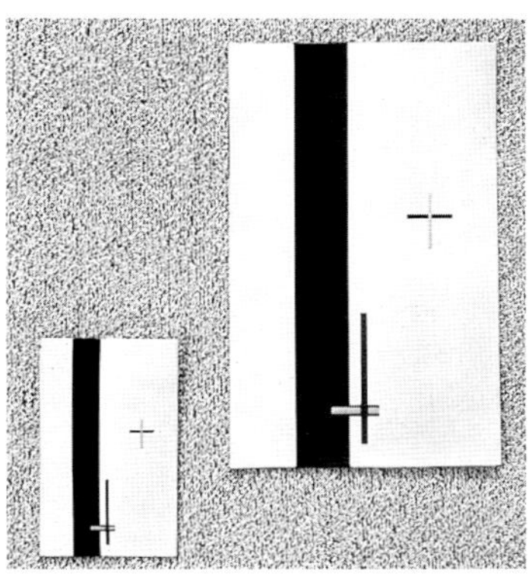

5. [see page 216]
Laszlo MOHOLY-NAGY
Compositions ordered
by telephone referring
to colour grid
['telephone pictures']
1923
Baked enamel
Dimensions variable

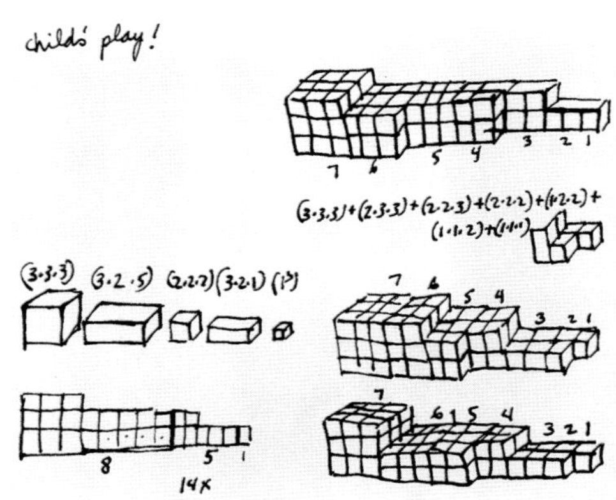

6. [see page 219]
Mel BOCHNER
Untitled ['child's
play!': Study for
Seven-Part Progression]
1966
Ink on paper
14 × 18 cm
[5.5 ×7 in]

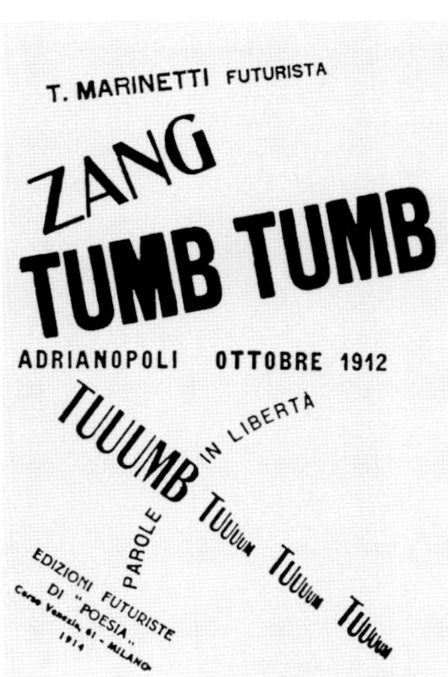

7. [see page 239]
Filippo Tommaso
MARINETTI
Zang Tumb Tuum
1914
Title page

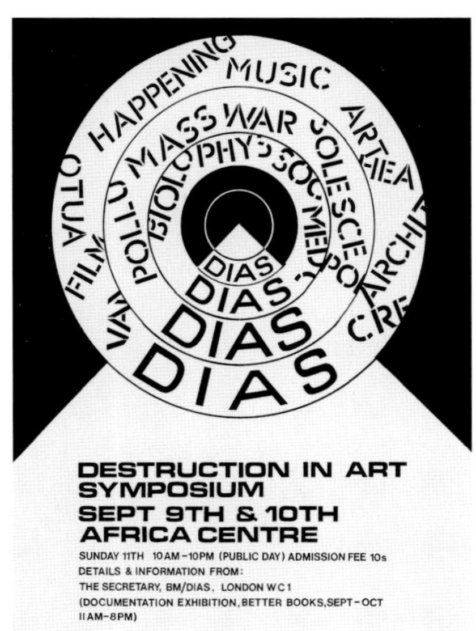

8. [see page 242]
Gustav METZGER, DIAS
Committee
Poster for Destruction
in Art Symposium
1966
Africa Centre, London

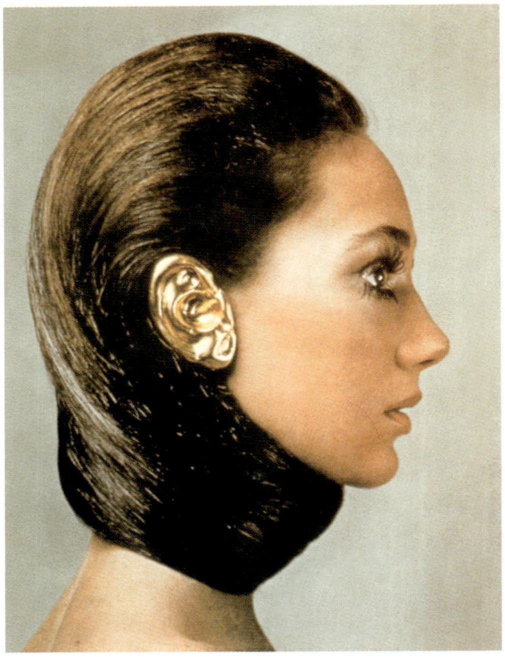

9. [see page 255]
Eduardo COSTA
Fashion Fictions
[detail]
1966-69
Colour photographs
of model wearing gold
props, published in
Vogue magazine

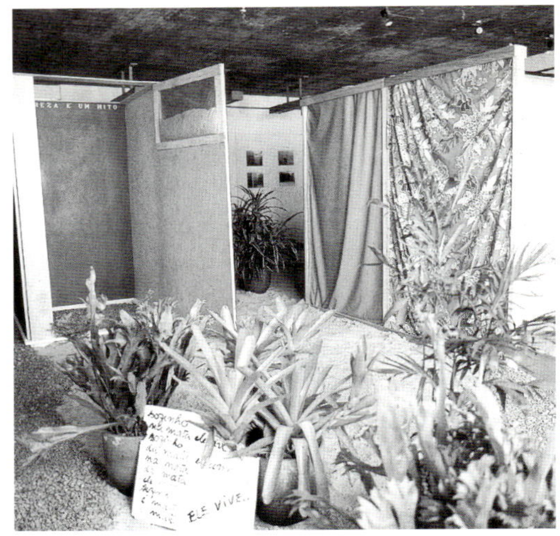

10. [see page 255]
Hélio OITICICA
Tropicália
1967
Wood, canvas, sand,
plants, text, etc
Dimensions variable
Reconstruction, State
University, Rio de
Janeiro, 1990

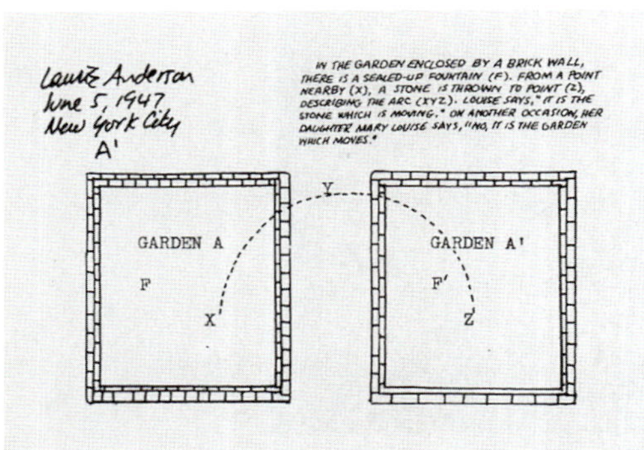

11. [see page 261]
Laurie ANDERSON
Work on card for
'C.7,500', organized
by Lucy R. Lippard
1973
30 printed index cards
10 × 15 cm
[4 × 6 in] each

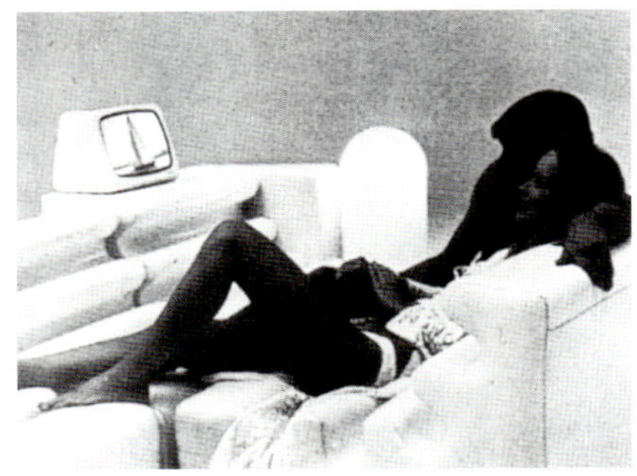

12. [see page 269]
Guy DEBORD
La Societé du Spectacle
[Society of the
Spectacle]
1973
Film of détourned images
with reading of text
from Debord's 1967 book

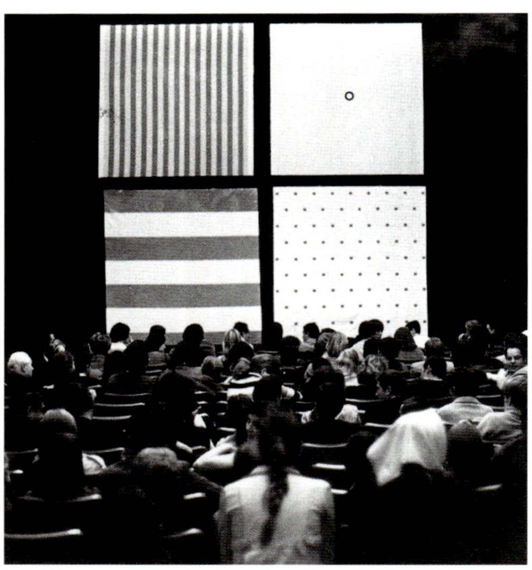

13. [see page 271]
Daniel BUREN, Olivier
MOSSET, Michel
PARMENTIER, Niele
TORONI
Manifestation, Musée
des Arts Décoratifs,
Paris, June 1967

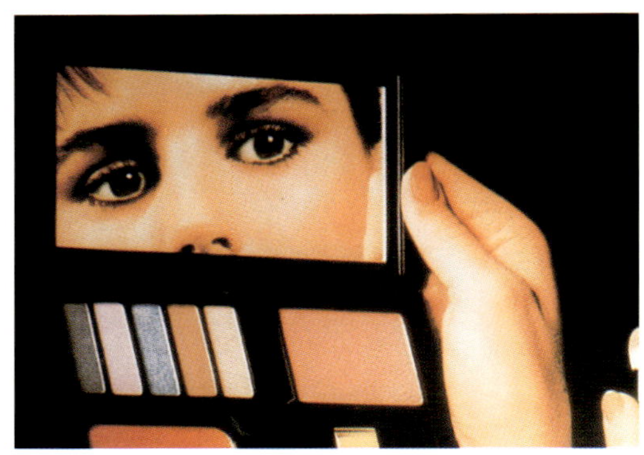

14. [see page 288]
Richard PRINCE
Untitled
1982
Ektacolor print
69 × 101.5 cm
[27 × 40 in]

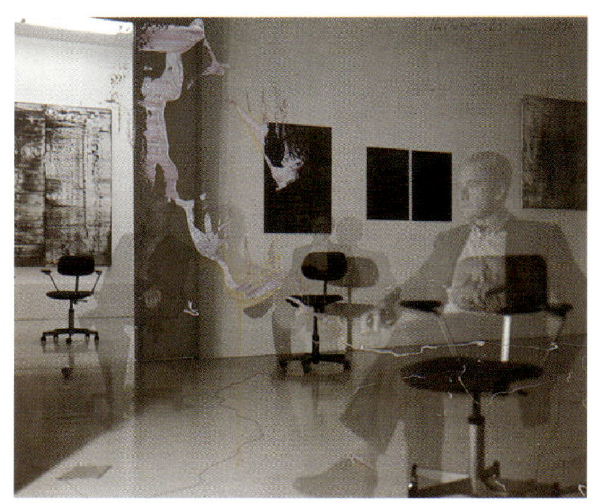

15. [see page 289]
Gerhard RICHTER
Self-Portrait Three
Times 25.1.90
1990
Oil on photograph
50 × 60 cm
[19.5 × 23.5 in]

PRE-HISTORY: 1950–1960

The history of conceptual art is in many ways the history of the belated artistic reception of Marcel Duchamp's 'readymades'. In the USA in the 1950s, Duchamp's influence spread through the teachings and writings of the composer John Cage. In Europe, it was metaphysical interpretations of monochrome painting by Yves Klein and others which first led to self-consciously 'immaterial' works. An alternative trajectory out of abstract painting passed through performance via an interest in process. After the death of Jackson Pollock in 1956, Allan Kaprow reinterpreted his legacy as that of a 'destruction' of painting. In a manner similar to aspects of the work of the Gutai group in Japan, Kaprow extended Pollock's emphasis on painting as a bodily act into staged engagements with objects of everyday life in Environments and Happenings. The marginal and often temporary nature of the sites of such events provoked an interest in context that converged with the strategic, institutional dimension of Duchamp's thought. By the early 1960s, Robert Morris had arrived at the view that art is 'primarily a situation'.

Marcel DUCHAMP
Apropos of 'Readymades' [1961]

In 1913 I had the happy idea to fasten a bicycle wheel to a kitchen stool and watch it turn.

A few months later I bought a cheap reproduction of a winter evening landscape, which I called *Pharmacy* after adding two small dots, one red and one yellow, in the horizon.

In New York in 1915 I bought at a hardware store a snow shovel on which I wrote 'in advance of the broken arm'.

It was around that time that the word 'readymade' came to mind to designate this form of manifestation.

A point which I want very much to establish is that the choice of these 'readymades' was never dictated by aesthetic delectation.

This choice was based on a reaction of visual indifference with at the same time a total absence of good or bad taste ... in fact a complete anaesthesia.

One important characteristic was the short sentence which I occasionally inscribed on the 'readymade'.

That sentence instead of describing the object like a title was meant to carry the mind of the spectator towards other regions more verbal.

Sometimes I would add a graphic detail of presentation which, in order to satisfy my craving for alliterations, would be called 'readymade aided'.

At another time wanting to expose the basic antinomy between art and readymades I imagined a 'reciprocal readymade': use a Rembrandt as an ironing board!

I realized very soon the danger of repeating indiscriminately this form of expression and decided to limit the production of 'readymades' to a small number yearly. I was aware at that time that, for the spectator even more than for the artist, art is a habit forming drug and I wanted to protect my 'readymades' against such contamination.

Another aspect of the 'readymade' is its lack of uniqueness ... the replica of a 'readymade' delivering the same message; in fact nearly every one of the 'readymades' existing today is not an original in the conventional sense.

A final remark to this egomaniac's discourse:

Since the tubes of paint used by the artist are manufactured and ready made products we must conclude that all the paintings in the world are 'readymades aided' and also works of assemblage.

Marcel Duchamp, 'Apropos of "Readymades"' (1961), *Art and Artists*, 1:4 (July 1966) 47; reprinted in *The Writings of Marcel Duchamp* (Oxford and New York: Oxford University Press, 1973) 141–42.

John CAGE
Robert Rauschenberg [1953]

To whom
No subject
No image
No taste
No object
No beauty
No message
No talent

No technique (no why)
No idea
No intention
No art
No feeling
No black
No white (no *and*)

After careful consideration, I have come to the conclusion that there is nothing in these paintings that could be changed, that they can be seen in any light and are not destroyed by the action of shadows.

Hallelujah! the blind can see again; the water's fine.

John Cage, 'Robert Rauschenberg' (1953). Statement which accompanied the exhibition of Robert Rauschenberg's *White Paintings* in 1953 at the Stable Gallery, New York; reprinted in *John Cage*, ed. Richard Kostelanetz (London and New York: Allen Lane, 1971) 111-12.

Yves KLEIN

Writings [1956–58]

[1956] At the Galerie Colette Allendy I exhibited some twenty monochrome surfaces, all in different colours: greens, reds, yellows, purples, blues, oranges ... and so found myself at the start of my career in this style ... I was trying to show colour, but I realized at the private view that the public were prisoners of a preconceived point of view and that, confronted with all these surfaces of different colours, they responded far more to the interrelationship of the different propositions, they reconstituted the elements of a decorative polychromy.

[1957] It was then that I remembered the colour blue, the blue of the sky in Nice that was at the origin of my career as a monochromist. I started work towards the end of 1956 and in 1957 I had an exhibition in Milan which consisted entirely of what I dared to call my 'Epoque bleue'.

[1957] My monochrome pictures are not my definite works, but the preparation for my works. They are the left-overs from the creative processes, the ashes. My pictures, after all, are only the title-deeds to my property which I have to produce when I am asked to prove that I am a proprietor.

[1958] I had left the visible, physical blue at the door, outside, in the street. The real blue was inside, the blue of the profundity of space, the blue of my kingdom, of our kingdom! ... the immaterialization of blue, the coloured space that cannot be seen but which we impregnate ourselves with ... A space of blue sensibility within the frame of the white walls of the gallery.

[1958] I want to take as the canvas for my next picture the entire surface of France. This picture will be called 'The Blue Revolution'. It isn't the fact of my taking power in France that interests me, but rather the possibility of creating a monochrome picture in my new manner: 'The Refinement of Sensibility'.

Yves Klein, extracts from journals, documents and talks; first published in English as 'Selected Writings' (1928-1962), trans. Barbara Wright, in *Yves Klein* (London: Tate Gallery, 1974) 30-65.

Allan KAPROW

The Legacy of Jackson Pollock [1958]

The tragic news of Pollock's death two summers ago was profoundly depressing to many of us. We felt not only a sadness over the death of a great figure, but also a deep loss, as if something of ourselves had died too. We were a piece of him: he was, perhaps, the embodiment of our ambition for absolute liberation and a secretly cherished wish to overturn old tables of crockery and flat champagne. We saw in his example the possibility of an outstanding freshness, a sort of ecstatic blindness [...]

He created some magnificent paintings. But he also destroyed painting. If we examine a few of the innovations [...] it may be possible to see why this is so.

For instance, the act of painting. In the last seventy-five years the random play of the hand upon the canvas or paper has become increasingly important. Strokes, smears, lines, dots became less and less attached to represented objects and existed more and more on their own, self-sufficiently. But from Impressionism up to, say, Maxim Gorky, the idea of an 'order' to these markings was explicit enough. Even Dada, which purported to be free of such considerations as 'composition', obeyed the Cubist aesthetic. One coloured shape balanced (or modified or stimulated) others, and these in turn were played off against (or with) the whole canvas, taking into account its size and shape – for the most part quite consciously. In short, part-to-whole or part-to-part relationships, no matter how strained, were a good fifty per cent of the making of a picture (most of the time they were a lot more, maybe ninety per cent). With Pollock, however, the so-called dance of dripping, slashing, squeezing, daubing and whatever else went into a work placed an almost absolute value upon a diaristic gesture. He was encouraged in this by the Surrealist painters and poets, but next to his their work is consistently 'artful', 'arranged' and full of finesse – aspects of outer control and training. With the huge canvas placed upon the floor, thus making it difficult for the artist to see the whole or any extended section of 'parts', Pollock could truthfully say that he was 'in' his work. Here the direct application of an automatic approach to the act makes it clear that not only is this not the old craft of painting but it is perhaps bordering on ritual itself, which happens to use paint as one of its materials.

But I used the words 'almost absolute' when I spoke of the diaristic gesture as distinct from the process of judging each move upon the canvas. Pollock, interrupting his work, would judge his 'acts' very shrewdly and carefully for long periods before going into another 'act'. He knew the difference between a good gesture and a bad one. This was his conscious artistry at work, and it makes him a part of the traditional community of painters. Yet the distance between the relatively self-contained works of the Europeans and the seemingly chaotic, sprawling works of the American indicates at best a tenuous connection to 'paintings'. (In fact, Jackson Pollock never really had a *malerisch* sensibility. The painterly aspects of his contemporaries, such as Robert Motherwell, Hans Hofmann, Willem de Kooning, Mark Rothko, and even Clyfford Still, point up at one moment a deficiency in him and at another moment a liberating feature. I choose to consider the second element the important one.)

I am convinced that to grasp at Pollock's impact properly, we must be acrobats, constantly shuttling between an identification with the hands and body that flung the paint and stood 'in' the canvas and submission to the objective markings, allowing them to entangle and assault us. This instability is indeed far from the idea of a 'complete' painting. The artist, the spectator and the outer world are much too interchangeably involved here. (And if we object to the difficulty of complete comprehension, we are asking too little of the art.)

Then Form. To follow it, it is necessary to get rid of the usual idea of 'Form', i.e., a beginning, middle and end, or any variant of this principle – such as fragmentation. We do not enter a painting of Pollock's in any one place (or hundred places). Anywhere is everywhere, and we dip in and out when and where we can. This discovery has led to remarks that his art gives the impression of going on forever – a true insight that suggests how Pollock ignored the confines of the rectangular field in favour of a continuum going in all directions simultaneously, *beyond* the literal dimensions of any work. (Though evidence points to a slackening of the attack as Pollock came to the edges of many of his canvases, in the best ones he compensated for this by tacking much of the painted surface around the back of his stretchers.) The four sides of the painting are thus an abrupt leaving off of the activity, which our imaginations continue outward indefinitely, as though refusing to accept the artificiality of an 'ending'. In an older work, the edge was a far more precise caesura: here ended the world of the artist; beyond began the world of the spectator and 'reality'.

We accept this innovation as valid because the artist understood with perfect naturalness 'how to do it'. Employing an iterative principle of a few highly charged elements constantly undergoing variation (improvising, as in much Asian music), Pollock gives us an all-over unity and at the same time a means to respond continuously to a freshness of personal choice. But this form allows us equal pleasure in participating in a delirium, a deadening of the reasoning faculties, a loss of 'self' in the Western sense of the term. This strange combination of extreme individuality and selflessness makes the work remarkably potent but also indicates a probably larger frame of psychological reference. And for this reason any allusions to Pollock's being the maker of giant textures are completely incorrect. They miss the point, and misunderstanding is bound to follow.

But given the proper approach, a medium-sized exhibition space with the walls totally covered by Pollocks offers the most complete and meaningful sense of his art possible.

Then Scale. Pollock's choice of enormous canvases served many purposes, chief of which for our discussion is that his mural-scale paintings ceased to become paintings and became environments. Before a painting, our size as spectators, in relation to the size of the picture, profoundly influences how much we are willing to give up consciousness of our temporal existence while experiencing it. Pollock's choice of great sizes resulted in our being confronted, assaulted, sucked in. Yet we must not confuse the effect of these with that of the hundreds of large paintings done in the Renaissance, which glorified an idealized everyday world familiar to the observer, often continuing the actual room into the painting by means of *trompe l'oeil*. Pollock offers us no such familiarity, and our everyday world of convention and habit is replaced by the one created by the artist. Reversing the above procedure, the painting is continued out into the room. And this leads me to my final point: Space. The space of these creations is not clearly palpable as such. We can become entangled in the web to some extent and by moving in and out of the skein of lines and splashings can experience a kind of spatial extension. But even so, this space is an allusion far more vague than even the few inches of space-reading a Cubist work affords. It may be that our need to identify with the process, the making of the whole affair, prevents a concentration on the specifics of before and behind so important in a more traditional art. But what I believe is clearly discernible is that the entire painting comes out at us (we are participants rather than observers), right into the room. It is possible to see in this connection how Pollock is the terminal result of a gradual trend that moved from the deep space of the fifteenth and sixteenth centuries to the building out from the canvas of the Cubist collages. In the present case the 'picture' has moved so far out that the canvas is no longer a reference point. Hence, although up on the wall, these marks surround us as they did the painter at work, so strict is the correspondence achieved between his impulse and the resultant art.

What we have, then, is art that tends to lose itself out of bounds, tends to fill our world with itself, art that in meaning, looks, impulse seems to break fairly sharply with the traditions of painters back to at least the Greeks. Pollock's near destruction of this tradition may well be a return to the point where art was more actively involved in ritual, magic and life than we have known it in our recent past. If so, it is an exceedingly important step and in its superior way offers a solution to the complaints of those who would have us put a bit of life into art. But what do we do now?

There are two alternatives. One is to continue in this vein. Probably many good 'near-paintings' can be done varying this aesthetic of Pollock's without departing from it or going further. The other is to give up the making of paintings entirely – I mean the single flat rectangle or oval as we know it. It has been seen how Pollock came pretty close to doing so himself. In the process, he came upon some newer values that are exceedingly difficult to discuss yet bear upon our present alternative. To say that he discovered things like marks, gestures, paint, colours, hardness, softness, flowing, stopping, space, the world, life, death might sound naïve. Every artist worth his salt has 'discovered' these things. But Pollock's discovery seems to have a peculiarly fascinating simplicity and directness about it. He was, for me, amazingly childlike, capable of becoming involved in the stuff of his art as a group of concrete facts seen for the first time. There is, as I said earlier, a certain blindness, a mute belief in everything he does, even up to the end. I urge that this not be seen as a simple issue. Few individuals can be lucky enough to possess the intensity of this kind of knowing, and I hope that in the near future a careful study of this (perhaps) Zen quality of Pollock's personality will be undertaken. At any rate, for now we may consider that, except for rare instances, Western art tends to need many more indirections in achieving itself, placing more or less equal emphasis upon 'things' and the relations between them. The crudeness of Jackson Pollock is not, therefore, uncouth; it is manifestly frank and uncultivated, unsullied by training, trade secrets, finesse – a directness that the European artists he liked hoped for and partially succeeded in but that he never had to strive after because he had it by nature. This by itself would be enough to teach us something.

It does. Pollock, as I see him, left us at the point where we must become preoccupied with and even dazzled by the space and objects of our everyday life, either our bodies, clothes, rooms, or, if need be, the vastness of Forty-second Street. Not satisfied with the suggestion through paint of our other senses, we shall utilize the specific substances of sight, sound, movements, people, odours, touch. Objects of every sort are materials for the new art: paint, chairs, food, electric and neon lights, smoke, water, old socks, a dog, movies, a thousand other things that will be discovered by the present generation of artists. Not only will these bold creators show us, as if for the first time, the world we have always had about us but ignored, but they will disclose entirely unheard-of happenings and events, found in garbage cans, police files, hotel lobbies; seen in store windows and on the streets; and sensed in dreams and horrible accidents. An odour of crushed strawberries, a letter from a friend, or a billboard selling Drano; three taps on the front door, a scratch, a sigh, or a voice lecturing endlessly, a blinding staccato flash, a bowler hat – all will become materials for this new concrete art.

Young artists of today need no longer say, 'I am a painter' or 'a poet' or 'a dancer'. They are simply 'artists'. All of life will be open to them. They will discover out of ordinary things the meaning of ordinariness. They will not try to make them extraordinary but will only state their real meaning. But out of nothing they will devise the extraordinary and then maybe nothingness as well. People will be delighted or horrified, critics will be confused or amused, but these, I am certain, will be the alchemies of the 1960s.

Allan Kaprow, 'The Legacy of Jackson Pollock', *ARTnews*, 57:6 (1958) 24-26, 55-57; reprinted in Allan Kaprow, *Essays on the Blurring of Art and Life*, ed. Jeff Kelley (Berkeley and Los Angeles: University of California Press, 1993) 1-9.

Robert MORRIS

Blank Form [1960–61]

From the subjective point of view there is no such thing as nothing – Blank Form shows this, as well as might any other situation of deprivation.

So long as the form (in the broadest possible sense: situation) is not reduced beyond perception, so long as it perpetuates and upholds itself as being an object in the subject's field of perception, the subject reacts to it in many particular ways when I call it art. He reacts in other ways when I do not call it art. Art is primarily a situation in which one assumes an attitude of reacting to some of one's awareness as art.

Blank Form is still in the great tradition of artistic weakness – taste. That is to say I prefer it – especially the content (as opposed to 'antiform' for the attempt to contradict one's taste). Blank Form is like life, essentially empty, allowing plenty of room for disquisitions on its nature and mocking each in its turn.

Blank Form slowly waves a large grey flag and laughs about how close it got to the second law of thermodynamics.

Some examples of Blank Form sculpture:

1 A column with perfectly smooth, rectangular surfaces, 61 × 61 × 244 cm [2 × 2 × 8 ft], painted grey.
2 A wall, perfectly smooth and painted grey, measuring 61 × 61 × 244 cm [2 × 2 × 8 ft].
3 A cabinet with simple construction, painted grey and measuring 30.5 × 61 × 183 cm [1 × 2 × 6 ft] – that is, a cabinet just large enough to enter.

Robert Morris, texts written for *An Anthology*, ed. La Monte Young (New York: Jackson Mac Low and La Monte Young, 1963), deleted by the author prior to publication. Reprinted as 'Blank Form' (1960-61) in John Hanhardt and Barbara Haskell, *Blam! The Explosion of Pop, Minimalism and Performance 1958-64* (New York: Whitney Museum of American Art/W.W. Norton, 1984) 101.

John CAGE

26 Statements re. Duchamp [1963]

History

The danger remains that he'll get out of the valise we put him in. So long as he remains locked up –

The rest of them were artists. Duchamp collects dust.

The check. The string he dropped. The *Mona Lisa*. The musical notes taken out of a hat. The glass. The toy shotgun painting. The things he found. Therefore, everything seen – every object, that is, plus the process of looking at it – is a Duchamp.

Duchamp Mallarmé?

There are two versions of the ox-herding pictures. One concludes with the image of nothingness, the other with the image of a fat man, smiling, returning to the village bearing gifts. Nowadays we have only the second version. They call it neo-Dada. When I talked with M.D. two years ago he said he had been fifty years ahead of his time.

Duchamp showed the usefulness of addition (moustache). Rauschenberg showed the function of subtraction (De Kooning). Well, we look forward to multiplication and division. It is safe to assume that someone will learn trigonometry. Johns

Ichiyanagi Wolff

We have no further use for the functional, the beautiful, or for whether or not something is true. We have only time for conversation. The Lord help us to say something in reply that doesn't simply echo what our ears took in. Of course we can go off as we do in our corners and talk to ourselves.

There he is, rocking away in that chair, smoking his pipe, waiting for me to stop weeping. I still can't hear what he said then. Years later I saw him on MacDougall Street in the Village. He made a gesture I took to mean OK.

'Tools that are no good require more skill.'

A duchamp

Seems Pollock tried to do it – paint on glass. It was in a movie. There was an admission of failure. That wasn't the way to proceed. It's not a question of doing again what Duchamp already did. We must nowadays nevertheless at least be able to look through what's beyond – as though we were in it looking out. What's more boring than Marcel Duchamp? I ask you. (I've books about his work but never bother to read them.) Busy as bees with nothing to do.

He requires that we know that being an artist isn't child's play: equivalent in difficulty – surely – to playing chess. Furthermore a work of our art is not ours alone but belongs also to the opponent who's there to the end.

Anarchy?

He simply found that object, gave it his name. What then did he do? He found that object, gave it his name. Identification. What then shall we do? Shall we call it by his name or by its name? It's not a question of names.

The air.

We hesitate to ask the question because we do not want to hear the answer. Going about in silence.

One way to write music: study Duchamp.

Say it's not Duchamp. Turn it over and it is.

Now that there's nothing to do, he does whatever anyone requires him to do: a magazine cover, an exhibition, a movie sequence, etc., *ad infinitum*. What did she tell me about him? That he gave himself except for two days a week (always the same days, Thursdays, Sundays)? That he's emotional? That he formed three important art collections? The phonograph.

Theatre

John Cage, '26 Statements re. Duchamp' (1963), *A Year From Monday* (Middletown: Wesleyan University Press, 1967) 70-72.

Jasper JOHNS
Marcel Duchamp (1887–1968) [1968]

The self attempts balance, descends. Perfume – the air was to stink of artists' egos. Himself, quickly torn to pieces. His tongue in his cheek.

Marcel Duchamp, one of this century's pioneer artists, moved his work through the retinal boundaries which had been established with Impressionism into a field where language, thought and vision act upon one another. There it changed form through a complex interplay of new mental and physical materials, heralding many of the technical, mental and visual details to be found in more recent art.

He said that he was ahead of his time. One guesses at a certain loneliness there. Wittgenstein said that '"Time has only one direction" must be a piece of nonsense'. In the 1920s Duchamp gave up, quit painting. He allowed, perhaps encouraged, the attendant mythology. One thought of his decision, his willing this stopping. Yet on one occasion, he said it was not like that. He spoke of breaking a leg. 'You don't mean to do it', he said.

The Large Glass. A greenhouse for his intuition. Erotic machinery, the Bride, held in a see-through cage – 'a Hilarious picture'. Its cross-references of sight and thought, the changing focus of the eyes and mind, give fresh sense to the time and space we occupy, negate any concern with art as transportation. No end is in view in this fragment of a new perspective. 'In the end you lose interest, so I didn't feel the necessity to finish it.'

He declared that he wanted to kill art ('for myself') but his persistent attempts to destroy frames of reference altered our thinking, established new units of thought, 'a new thought for that object'.

The art community feels Duchamp's presence and his absence. He has changed the condition of being here.

Jasper Johns, 'Marcel Duchamp (1887-1968)', *Artforum* 7:3 (November 1968) 6; reprinted in *Jasper Johns, Writings, Sketchbook Notes, Interviews*, ed. Kirk Varnedoe (New York: The Museum of Modern Art, 1996) 22.

Robert MORRIS
Notes on Sculpture. Part 4: Beyond Objects [1969]

Jasper Johns established a new possibility for art ordering. The *Flags* and *Targets* imply much that could not be realized in two dimensions. The works undeniably achieved a lot in their own terms. More even than in Pollock's case, the work was looked at rather than into, and painting had not done this before. Johns took painting further towards a state of non-depiction than anyone else. The *Flags* were not so much depictions as copies, decorative and fraudulent, rigid, stuffed, ridiculous counterfeits. That is, these works were not depictions according to past terms that had, without exception, operated within the figure-ground duality of representation. Johns took the background out of painting and isolated the thing. The background became the wall. What was previously neutral became actual, while what was previously an image became a thing.

The *Flags* and *Targets* were the first paintings to use a strict *a priori* ordering. One of the outcomes of this way of working was to throw a heretofore unimagined weight on the edge. This weight was not one of relational significance to the interior image (Stella later developed this relationship) so much as the assertion of a final, absolute limit that was a part of the experience of the entire work. Painting had previously been a more or less diaphanous surface that ended at the edge. Johns' works were definite shapes that were flat. The whole process was not one of stripping art down but of reconstituting art as an object.

Johns established new rules to the game. These were general rules and, with the exception of Stella's work, were not to be applied further to painting. The coexistence of the image with the physical extension of the object and the *a priori* mode of working are descriptive of three-dimensional objects – what they are and how they get made. Obviously, the acceptance of the art object as a constructed thing and its removal from a depicting ground to a field of real space were more suitable for full development in three dimensions.

The symmetrical internal divisions of Johns, Stella and much subsequent 1960s painting were not as new or as radical as was the holistic structural feature of making the total image congruent with the physical limits of the work. Conversely, the fully three-dimensional work of the 1960s that perpetuated symmetrical internal divisions maintained painterly, decorative concerns, as these features are applied redivisions of a more total whole. That is to say, it is a method of setting things beside each other rather than a method of construction which, by its nature, is literally a holistic tying together of material. It was the structure underlying a constructed object as art that Johns illuminated. The complete manifestation of this structure could never be realized so long as the work remained on the wall. In the most literal way, flags and targets are only half objects: both are flat, targets have only one side. Johns probably never intended the realization of the constructed object. Even the *Beer Cans* are depictions.

Part of the possibility for the success of the project of reconstituting objects as art had to do with the state of sculpture. It was terminally diseased with figurative allusion. The object mode in three dimensions was a new start. Whereas painting has only been able to mutate, carrying constantly the germ of depiction, sculpture stopped dead and objects began [...]

Robert Morris, 'Notes on Sculpture. Part 4: Beyond Objects' (April 1969); reprinted in *Continuous Project Altered Daily: The Writings of Robert Morris* (Cambridge, Massachusetts: MIT Press; New York/ Solomon R. Guggenheim Museum, 1993) 51-53.

INSTRUCTION, PERFORMANCE, DOCUMENTATION

The first works of conceptual art emerged in the context of avant-garde performance culture. Initially, they were understood as a form of 'neo-Dada', which adopted the anti-art practices of Dadaism in the service of a radical expansion of the notion of art. For some, such as Yoko Ono, this involved thinking of art as part of the 'mind-world' and of everyone as a potential artist. Others, such as Robert Morris and John Latham, maintained less mentalistic, more embodied conceptions of art as 'event'. Adrian Piper stressed the role of art as a 'catalysis' for social interaction. Some artists, such as Vito Acconci, came to conceptual art from a background in concrete poetry, where the staccato rhythms of Samuel Beckett's late prose style were keenly felt.

George MACIUNAS
Neo-Dada in Music, Theatre, Poetry, Art [1962]

Neo-Dada, its equivalent, or what appears to be neo-Dada manifests itself in very wide fields of creativity. It ranges from 'time' arts to 'space' arts; or more specifically from literary arts (time-art), through graphic-literature (time-space-art) to graphics (space-arts) through graphic-music (space-time-arts) to graphless or scoreless music (time-art), through theatrical music (space-time-art) to environments (space-arts). There exist no borderlines between one and the other extreme. Many works belong to several categories and also many artists create separate works in each category. Almost each category and each artist however, is bound with the concept of Concretism ranging in intensity from pseudo concretism, surface concretism, structural concretism, method concretism (indeterminacy systems), to the extreme of concretism which is beyond the limits of art, and therefore sometimes referred to as anti-art, or art-nihilism. The new activities of the artists therefore could be charted by reference to two co-ordinates: the horizontal co-ordinate defining transition from 'time' arts to 'space' arts and back to 'time' and 'space', etc., and the vertical co-ordinate defining transition from extremely artificial art, illusionistic art, then abstract art (not within the subject of this essay), to mild concretism, which becomes more and more concrete, or rather non-artificial until it becomes non-art, anti-art, nature, reality.

Concretists in contrast to illusionists prefer unity of form and content, rather than their separation. They prefer the world of concrete reality rather than the artificial abstraction of illusionism. Thus in plastic arts for instance, a concretist perceives and expresses a rotten tomato without changing its reality or form. In the end, the form and expression remain [the] same as the content and perception – the reality of rotten tomato, rather than an illusionistic image or symbol of it. In music a concretist perceives and expresses the material sound with all its inherent polychromy and pitchlessness and 'incidentalness', rather than the immaterial abstracted and artificial sound of pure pitch or rather controlled tones denuded of its pitch-obliterating overtones. A material or concrete sound is considered one that has close affinity to the sound-producing material – thus a sound whose overtone pattern and the resultant polychromy clearly indicates the nature of material or concrete reality producing it. Thus a note sounded on a piano keyboard or a bel-canto voice is largely immaterial, abstract and artificial since the sound does not clearly indicate its true source or material reality – common action of string, wood, metal, felt, voice, lips, tongue, mouth, etc. A sound, for instance, produced by striking the same piano itself with a hammer or kicking its underside is more material and concrete since it indicates in a much clearer manner the hardness of hammer, hollowness of piano sound box and resonance of string. A human speech or eating sounds are likewise more concrete for the same reason of source recognizability. These concrete sounds are commonly, although inaccurately, referred to as noises. They may be pitchless to a large extent, but their pitchlessness makes them polychromic, since the intensity of acoustic colour depends directly on pitch obliterating inharmonic overtones.

Further departure from the artificial world of abstraction is affected by the concept of indeterminacy and improvisation. Since artificiality implies human pre-determination, contrivance, a truer concretist rejects pre-determination of final form in order to perceive the reality of nature, the course of which, like that of man himself, is largely indeterminate and unpredictable. Thus an indeterminate composition approaches greater concretism by allowing nature [to] complete its form in its own course. This requires the composition to provide a kind of framework, an 'automatic machine' within which or by which, nature (either in the form of an independent performer or indeterminate-chance compositional methods) can complete the artform, effectively and independently of the artist-composer. Thus the primary contribution of a truly concrete artist consists in creating a *concept* or a *method* by which form can be created independently of him, rather than the form or structure. Like a mathematical solution such a composition contains a beauty in the method alone.

The furthest step towards concretism is of course a kind of art-nihilism. This concept opposes and rejects art

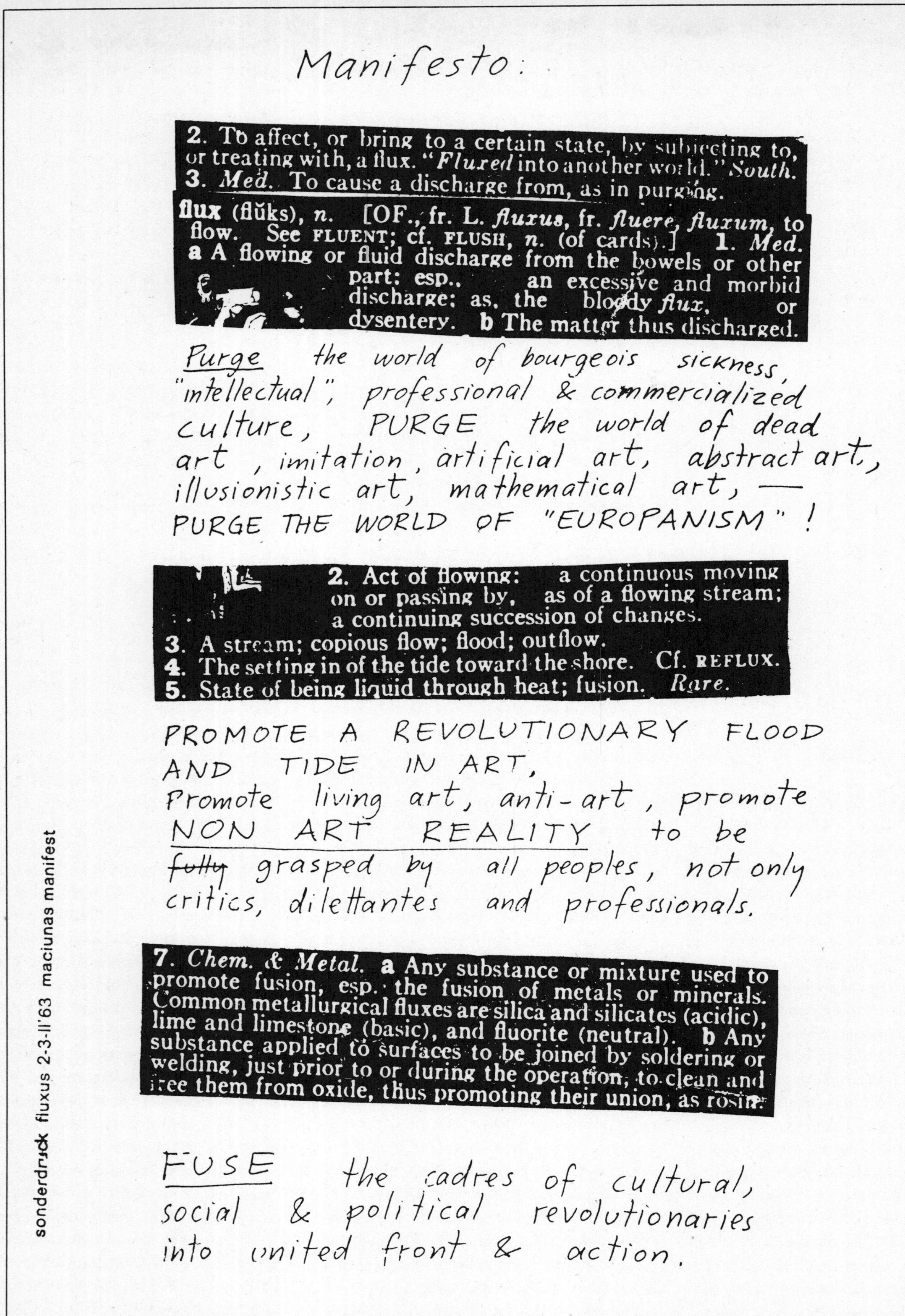

Manifesto:

2. To affect, or bring to a certain state, by subjecting to, or treating with, a flux. "*Fluxed* into another world." *South.*
3. *Med.* To cause a discharge from, as in purging.

flux (flŭks), *n.* [OF., fr. L. *fluxus*, fr. *fluere*, *fluxum*, to flow. See FLUENT; cf. FLUSH, *n.* (of cards).] **1.** *Med.* **a** A flowing or fluid discharge from the bowels or other part; esp., an excessive and morbid discharge: as, the bloody *flux*, or dysentery. **b** The matter thus discharged.

Purge the world of bourgeois sickness, "intellectual", professional & commercialized culture, PURGE the world of dead art, imitation, artificial art, abstract art, illusionistic art, mathematical art, — PURGE THE WORLD OF "EUROPANISM"!

2. Act of flowing: a continuous moving on or passing by, as of a flowing stream; a continuing succession of changes.
3. A stream; copious flow; flood; outflow.
4. The setting in of the tide toward the shore. Cf. REFLUX.
5. State of being liquid through heat; fusion. *Rare.*

PROMOTE A REVOLUTIONARY FLOOD AND TIDE IN ART,
Promote living art, anti-art, promote NON ART REALITY to be ~~fully~~ grasped by all peoples, not only critics, dilettantes and professionals.

7. *Chem. & Metal.* **a** Any substance or mixture used to promote fusion, esp. the fusion of metals or minerals. Common metallurgical fluxes are silica and silicates (acidic), lime and limestone (basic), and fluorite (neutral). **b** Any substance applied to surfaces to be joined by soldering or welding, just prior to or during the operation, to clean and free them from oxide, thus promoting their union, as rosin.

FUSE the cadres of cultural, social & political revolutionaries into united front & action.

sonderdruck fluxus 2-3-II'63 maciunas manifest

George MACIUNAS, *Manifesto*, 1963

itself, since the very meaning of it implies artificiality whether in creation of form or method. To approach closer affinity with concrete reality and its closer understanding, the Art-nihilist or anti-artists (they usually deny those definitions) either create 'anti-art' or exercise nothingness. The 'anti-art' forms are directed primarily against art as a profession, against the artificial separation of a performer from audience, or creator and spectator, or life and art; it is against the artificial forms or patterns or methods of art itself; it is against this purposefulness, formfulness and meaningfulness of art; Anti-art is life, is nature, is true reality – it is one and all. Rainfall is anti-art, a babble of a crowd is anti-art, a sneeze is anti-art, a flight of a butterfly, or movements of microbes are anti-art. They are as beautiful and as worth to be aware of as art itself. If man could experience the world, the concrete world surrounding him (from mathematical ideas to physical matter) in the same way he experiences art, there would be no need for art, artists and similar 'nonproductive' elements.

George Maciunas, 'Neo-Dada in Music, Theatre, Poetry, Art' version of a draft first read by Arthur C. Caspari, in German, at the Fluxus concert 'Après John Cage', Wuppertal, West Germany, 1962; reprinted in Clive Philpot, Jon Hendricks (eds.), *Fluxus: Selections from the Gilbert and Lila Siverman Fluxus Collection* (New York: The Museum of Modern Art, 1989) 25-27.

Samuel BECKETT
Imagination Dead Imagine [1965]

No trace anywhere of life, you say, pah, no difficulty there, imagination not dead yet, yes, dead, good, imagination dead imagine. Islands, waters, azure, verdure, one glimpse and vanished, endlessly, omit. Till all white in the whiteness the rotunda. No way in, go in, measure. Diameter three feet, three feet from ground to summit of the vault. Two diameters at right angles AB CD divide the white ground into two semicircles ACB BDA. Lying on the ground two white bodies, each in its semicircle. White too the vault and the round wall eighteen inches high from which it springs. Go back out, a plain rotunda, all white in the whiteness, go back in, rap, solid throughout, a ring as in the imagination the ring of bone. The light that makes all so white no visible source, all shines with the same white shine, ground, wall, vault, bodies, no shadow. Strong heat, surfaces hot but not burning to the touch, bodies sweating. Got back out, move back, the little fabric vanishes, ascend, it vanishes, all white in the whiteness, descend, go back in. Emptiness, silence, heat, whiteness, wait, the light goes down, all grows dark together, ground, wall, vault, bodies, say twenty seconds, all the greys, the light goes out, all vanishes. At the same time the temperature goes down, to reach its minimum, say freezing-point, at the same instant that the black is reached, which may seem strange. Wait, more or less long, light and heat come back, all grows white and hot together, ground, wall, vault, bodies, say twenty seconds, all the greys, till the initial level is reached whence the fall began. More or less long, for there may intervene, experience shows, between end of fall and beginning of rise, pauses of varying length, from the fraction of the second to what would have seemed, in other times, other places, an eternity. Same remark for the other pause, between end of rise and beginning of fall. The extremes, as long as they last, are perfectly stable, which in the case of the temperature may seem strange, in the beginning. It is possible too, experience shows, for rise and fall to stop short at any point and mark a pause, more or less long, before resuming, or reversing, the rise now fall, the fall rise, these in their turn to be completed, or to stop short and mark a pause, more or less long, before resuming, or again reversing, and so on, till finally one or the other extreme is reached. Such variations of rise and fall, combining in countless rhythms, commonly attend the passage from white and heat to black and cold, and vice versa. The extremes alone are stable as is stressed by the vibration to be observed when a pause occurs at some intermediate stage, no matter what its level and duration. Then all vibrates, ground, wall, vault, bodies, ashen or leaden or between the two, as may be. But on the whole, experience shows, such uncertain passage is not common. And most often, when the light begins to fail, and along with it the heat, the movement continues unbroken until, in the space of some twenty seconds, pitch black is reached and at the same instant say freezing-point. Same remark for the reverse movement, towards heat and whiteness. Next most frequent is the fall or rise with pauses of varying length in these feverish greys, without at any moment reversal of the movement. But whatever its uncertainties the return sooner or later to a contemporary calm seems assured, for the moment, in the black dark or the great whiteness, with attendant temperature, world still proof against enduring tumult. Rediscovered miraculously after what absence in perfect voids it is no longer quite the same, from this point of view, but there is no other. Externally all is as before and the sighting of the little fabric quite as much a matter of chance, its whiteness merging in the surrounding whiteness. But go in and now briefer lulls and never twice the same storm. Light and heat remain linked as though supplied by the same source of which still no trace. Still on the ground, bent in three, the head against the wall at B, the arse against the wall at A, the knees against the wall between B and C, the feet against the wall between C and A, that is to say inscribed in the semicircle ACB, merging in the white ground were it not for the long hair of strangely imperfect whiteness, the white body of a woman finally. Similarly inscribed in the other semicircle, against the wall his head at A, his arse at B, his knees between A and D, his feet between D and B, the partner. On their right sides therefore both and back to back head to arse. Hold a mirror to their lips, it mists. With their left hands they hold their left legs a little below the knee, with their right hands their left arms a little above the elbow. In this agitated light, its great white calm now so rare and brief, inspection is not easy. Sweat and mirror notwithstanding they might well pass for inanimate but for the left eyes which at incalculable intervals suddenly open wide and gaze in unblinking exposure long beyond what is humanly possible. Piercing pale blue the effect is striking, in the beginning. Never the two gazes together except once, when the beginning of one overlapped the end of the other, for about ten seconds. Neither fat nor thin, big nor small, the bodies seem whole and in fairly good condition, to judge by the surfaces exposed to view. The faces too, assuming the two sides of a piece, seem to want nothing essential. Between their absolute stillness and the convulsive light the contrast is striking, in the beginning, for one who still remembers having been struck by the contrary. It is clear however, from a thousand little signs too long to imagine, that they are not sleeping. Only murmur ah, no more, in this silence, and at the same instant for the eye of prey the infinitesimal shudder instantaneously suppressed. Leave them there, sweating and icy, there is better elsewhere. No, life ends and no, there is nothing elsewhere, and no question now of ever finding again that white speck lost in whiteness, to see if they still life still in the stress of that storm, or of a worse storm, or in the black dark for good, or the great whiteness unchanging, and if not what they are doing.

Samuel Beckett, 'Imagination Dead Imagine' (1965, original text in French, translated into English by the author, 1966), *No's Knife: Collected Shorter Prose 1945-1966* (London: Calder and Boyars, 1967) 161-64.

Robert MORRIS
Notes on Dance [1965]

My involvement in theatre has been with the body in motion. However changed or reduced the motion might have been or however elaborate the means used might have been, the focus was this movement. In retrospect this seems a constant value which was preserved. From the beginning I wanted to avoid the pulled-up, turned-out, antigravitational qualities that not only give a body definition and role as 'dancer' but qualify and delimit the movement available to it. The challenge was to find alternative movement.

I was not the first to attempt such alternatives. Simone Whitman, together with others, had already explored the possibilities inherent in a situation of 'rules' or gamelike structures which required the performer to respond to cues which might, for example, indicate changes in height or spatial position. A fair degree of complexity of these rules and cues effectively blocked the dancer's performing 'set' and reduced him to frantically attempting to respond to cues – reduced him from performance to action. In 1961 Simone Whitman held a concert in a loft in New York. This concert involved the use of such devices as a 45 degree inclined plane about eight feet square with several ropes coming from the top of it. Performers were allowed to climb up the plane, pass between each other and rest when tired – all by means of the ropes. Here the rules were simple and did not constitute a game situation but rather indicated a task while the device, the inclined plane, structured the actions. (This single example does not do justice to the implications this seemingly simple concert held.) Here focused clearly for the first time were two distinct means by which new actions could be implemented: rules or tasks and devices (she termed them 'constructions') or objects.

While possibilities for generating movement by task situations or devices had become clearly established, it was essentially an indirect method in both cases. Movement had not been approached directly but had resulted, willy-nilly, from going about getting this or that task accomplished – moving over a dominating eccentric surface, etc.

By the uses of objects which could be manipulated I found a situation which did not dominate my actions or subvert my performance. In fact the decision to employ objects came out of considerations of specific problems involving space and time. For me, the focus of a set of specific problems involving time, space, alternate forms of a unit, etc., provided the necessary structure. While dance technique and chance methods were both irrelevant to me I would never have denied the value, necessity even, of perpetuating structural systems. But for my purposes the need for such systems was for syntactical rather than methodological bases. My efforts were bound up with the didactic and demonstrative and were not concerned with the establishment of a set of tools by which works could be generated.

The objects I used held no inherent interest for me but were means for dealing with specific problems. For example, the establishment of an inverse ratio between movement, space, and duration was implemented by the use of a T-like form which I could adjust and move away from, adjust again and move away from, and so on until the sequence of movements according to the ratio had been completed. Or again, the establishment of a focus shifting between the egocentric and the exocentric could be accomplished by swinging overhead in a fully lighted room a small light at the end of a cord. The lights in the room fade as the cord is slowly let out until finally in total darkness only the moving point of light is visible as it revolves in the large space above the heads of the audience. Both of the above instances occurred in *Arizona* (1963), the first dance I made.

An element of the work as persistent as the use of objects is the coexistence of the static and the mobile – e.g., a sequence of ten Muybridge slides of a nude man lifting a stone followed by a similar movement by a nude male performer executed in the same space and illuminated by the beam of the slide projector (*Waterman Switch*, 1965); or the rotation of the upper torso through 90 degrees over a five minute period – the movement itself being imperceptible – accompanied by a taped description of strenuous movements (*Arizona*); or a taped verbal description of actions which occur at a remove in time (*Waterman Switch*); or the illumination of a runner with stroboscopic-type light which, because of the briefness of the illumination, gives a static image (*Check*, 1964). In one form or another the static coexisting with the mobile occurs in every work.

Time, in so far as considerations of length are concerned, has seemed irrelevant. Since the movement situations were primarily those of either demonstration or exposition, time was not an element of usage but a necessary condition; less a focus than a context. Only at those points where there was no movement did time function as an isolated, observable focus – i.e., durations of stillness were not used as punctuations for the movement but in the attempt to make duration itself palpable.

Space, like time, was reduced to context, necessity; at most a way of anchoring the work, riveting it to a maximum frontality [...]

Robert Morris, 'Notes on Dance' *Tulane Drama Review*, 10:2 (Winter 1965) 179-83; reprinted in *Happenings and Other Acts*, ed. Mariellen R. Sandford, (London and New York: Routledge, 1995) 168-71.

Yoko ONO

To the Wesleyan People [1966]

When a violinist plays, which is incidental: the arm movement or the bow sound?

Try arm movement only.

If my music seems to require physical silence, that is because it requires concentration to yourself – and this requires inner silence which may lead to outer silence as well.

I think of my music more as a practice (*gyo*) than a music.

The only sound that exists to me is the sound of the mind. My works are only to induce music of the mind in people.

It is not possible to control a mind-time with a stop watch or a metronome. In the mind-world, things spread out and go beyond time.

There is a wind that never dies.

My paintings, which are all instruction paintings (and meant for others to do), came after collage and assemblage (1915) and happening (1905) came into the art world. Considering the nature of my painting, any of the above three words or a new word can be used instead of the word, painting. But I like the old word painting because it immediately connects with 'wall painting' painting, and it is nice and funny.

Among my instruction paintings, my interest is mainly in 'painting to construct in your head'. In your head, for instance, it is possible for a straight line to exist – not as a segment of a curve but as a straight line. Also, a line can be straight, curved and something else at the same time. A dot can exist as a 1, 2, 3, 4, 5, 6 dimensional object all at the same time or at various times in different combinations as you wish to perceive. The movement of the molecule can be continuum and discontinuum at the time. It can be with colour and/or without. There is no visual object that does not exist in comparison to or simultaneously with other objects, but these characteristics can be eliminated if you wish. A sunset can go on for days. You can eat up all the clouds in the sky. You can assemble a painting with a person in the North Pole over a phone, like playing chess. This painting method derives from as far back as the time of the Second World War when we had no food to eat, and my brother and I exchanged menus in the air.

There maybe a dream that two dream together, but there is no chair that two see together.

I think it is possible to see a chair as it is. But when you burn the chair, you suddenly realize that the chair in your mind did not burn or disappear.

The world of construction seems to be the most tangible, and therefore final. This made me nervous. I started to wonder if it were really so.

Isn't a construction a beginning of a thing like a seed? Isn't it a segment of a larger totality, like an elephant's tail? Isn't it something just about to emerge – not quite structured – never quite structured ... like an unfinished church with a sky ceiling? Therefore, the following works:

A Venus made of plastic, except that her head is to be imagined.

A paper ball and a marble book, except that the final version is the fusion of these two objects which come into existence only in your head.

A marble sphere (actually existing) which, in your head, gradually becomes a sharp cone by the time it is extended to the far end of the room.

A garden covered with thick marble instead of snow – but like snow, which is to be appreciated only when you uncover the marble coating.

One thousand needles: Imagine treading them with a straight thread.

I would like to see the sky machine on every corner of the street instead of the coke machine. We need more skies than coke.

Dance was once the way people communicated with God and godliness in people. Since when did dance become a pasted-face exhibitionism of dancers on the spotlighted stage? Can you not communicate if it is totally dark?

If people make it a habit to draw a somersault on every other street as they commute to their office, take off their pants before they fight, shake hands with strangers whenever they feel like, give flowers or part of their clothing on streets, subways, elevator, toilet, etc, and if politicians go through a tea house door (lowered, so people must bend very low to get through) before they discuss anything and spend a day watching the fountain water dance at the nearest park, the world business may slow down a little but we may have peace. To me this is dance.

All my works in the other fields have an 'Event bent' so to speak. People ask me why I call some works Event and others not. They also ask me why I do not call my Events, Happenings.

Event, to me, is not an assimilation of all the other arts as Happening seems to be, but an extrication from the various sensory perceptions. It is not 'a get togetherness' as most happenings are, but a dealing with oneself. Also, it has no script as happenings do, though it has something that starts it moving – the closest word for it may be a 'wish' or 'hope'.

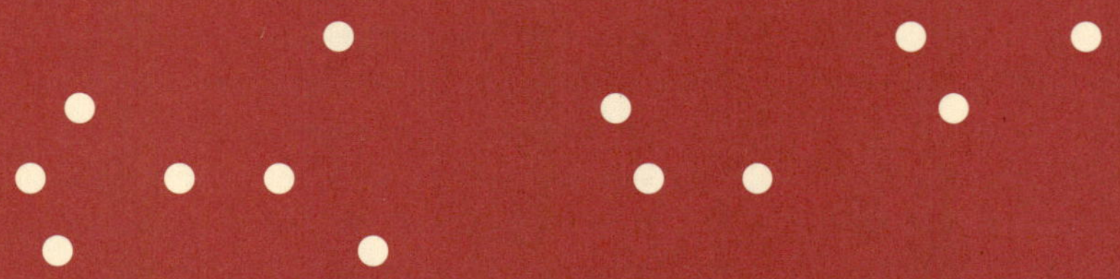

A dot can exist as a 1, 2, 3, 4, 5, 6 dimensional object all at the same time or at various times in different combinations as you wish to perceive

Yoko ONO, 'To the Wesleyan People (who attended the meeting) - a footnote to my lecture of January 13th, 1966', *The Stone*, 1966

At a small dinner party last week, we suddenly discovered that our poet friend whom we admire very much was colour blind. Barbara Moore said, 'That explains about his work. Usually people's eyes are blocked by colour and they can't see the thing.'

After unblocking one's mind, by dispensing with visual, auditory and kinetic perceptions, what will come out of us? Would there be anything? I wonder. And my Events are mostly spent in wonderment [...]

People talk about happening. They say that art is headed towards that direction, that happening is assimilating the arts. I don't believe in collectivism of art nor in having only one direction in anything. I think it is nice to return to having many different arts, including happening, just as having many flowers. In fact, we could have more arts 'smell', 'weight', 'taste', 'cry', 'anger' (competition of anger, that sort of thing), etc. People might say, that we never experience things separately, they are always in fusion, and that is why 'the happening', which is a fusion of all sensory perceptions. Yes, I agree, but if that is so, it is all the more reason and challenge to create a sensory experience isolated from other sensory experiences, which is something rare in daily life. Art is not merely a duplication of life. To assimilate art in life, is different from art duplicating life.

But returning to having various divisions of art, does not mean, for instance, that one must use only sounds as means to create music. One may give instructions to watch the fire for 10 days in order to create a vision in ones mind.

The mind is omnipresent, events in life never happen alone and the history is forever increasing its volume. The natural state of life and mind is complexity. At this point, what art can offer (if it can at all – to me it seems) is an absence of complexity, a vacuum through which you are led to a state of complete relaxation of mind. After that you may return to the complexity of life again, it may not be the same, or it may be, or you may never return, but that is your problem [...]

Yoko Ono, 'To the Wesleyan People (who attended the meeting) – a footnote to my lecture of January 13th, 1966', first published as an insert in *The Stone* (New York: Judson Gallery, 1966).

John LATHAM

Eventstructure [1967]

Structure now is Eventstructure. The separation of time from space, things from goings on – gives a very thin and unstable worldpicture that necessitated an explosion of non-existent 'entities' by which the world is explained or described ... semantic schizophrenia.

An artist works now with the whole historical context tied into the single move. What used to be called a medium is now a series – painting is such a series, so is theatre or writing, one uses the tradition to measure from. There is only one medium, that every artist uses within his chosen series, and it is, simply, DIFFERENCE.

The key to Eventstructure turned when I realized that a work is simultaneously five categories of dissociated events, each in some degree a meaning carrier. Sensuality doesn't tell this, but a whole new principle of control in form becomes intelligible, offering a critique to behaviour that puts current language in startling lights. The borderline between steady-state 'things' and change-of-state 'events' is arbitrary. It rests on a particular time measure characteristic of brains and it is necessary to see the relations between the frequency of small events and the durations of longer ones. A 'thing' is experienced as such because it is a compulsive image. Change-of-state 'things' as in live nature are also compulsive images but on different time-co-ordinates. Long-term cycles are another range of compulsive images. What we experience as life is the collision of relatively stable (compulsive) images, the 'Energy' of which is a function of the stability or compulsiveness latent in the structure. What I hear of atomic physics has no quarrel with this nor the hesitations in theoretical psychology, but whereas these departments speak different languages, Eventstructure provides a framework for a non-specialist to get a good grip of any subject and relate it to any other. It gives the artist a basis for regarding any situation as carrying potential opportunities for action.

So far as Skoob is concerned – paintings, spray gunnery, roller-painting and plumbing books, and film – these have been comparable to painting (as we think of it), to books, to writing as we think of it, and so on; they are in some degree all of them and the difference between them has carried the meaning. Music too, particularly with film. And there is another category of event, in the referring and referred to. This is usually called 'literary', a term of abuse but probably applied to notions that don't construct too well anyway.

The reversed book idiom began in 1954 with a spray-gun mark. From the standpoint of mathematics this offered an absolute non-reducible primitive event, the incidence of a vanishing-small black on an extensive white over a minimal instant; followed by a proliferation of similar characteristics all comparable in simple terms, giving a primary explosion. The incidence of a book in this situation was dramatic on all series (too good taste) and took several years to digest. A good half dozen of them were obscure because the series was not clear; there's not much of a tradition in visual maths but there was something important about the surface white becoming volume under information (black) saturation, the frequency of the individual marks and the inference of non-existence as part of frequency. There was something kinetic about the static form that didn't tell until it became clear that the time-signature of motion is different in category from the time-signature of frequency. The static was felt to be more kinetic than movement in a work but in a way that didn't appear to the 'kinetic' movement. The actual moving peopled events like the play and the bookplumbing are comparable as much to lab experiment activity as to other art.

An artist in the social event has a function of priority regulator and experimenter, operating on levels between his group and the life of the planet. They are in collision most of the time. We have just been passing through a phase in which priorities were thought to work out independently of individual preference, and profit-motive has been the most respectable for individual behaviour.

Eventstructure as currently understood has taken the intervening thirteen years to develop and while seeming to be totally viable it is not mature and is not to be assimilated in a day either.

The final episode in the series 'Bookplumbing' at Better Books was called 'Windfoamdream', during which a boy was papered up in a hammock and hoisted to the ceiling – being connected to the world below by way of a long plastic pipe, a very accurate sound carrier.

What went on below was a mounting 'storm' situation with quantities of paper chopped and circulated by fans, black rain and lightning represented by an abstract film. Crowd noises from a tape-recorder with volume control. The foam was a chemical mixture poured into book constructions. When the storm was over the boy was blown free of his hammock by inflatables.

The wordless play – now 'Juliet and Romeo' – starts with a SKOOB film made from a piece that hangs in the Tate Gallery. Two figures move into the stage in front of the screen heavily dressed in paper books and other paraphernalia. They are left almost blind and immobile at the end of the film except for some simple characteristic movements. They collide, and having come to each others' notice they conduct a slow process of identification through insult, anger, excitement and so on until they are free of paper. The play ends with a decapitation. The new production introduces inflatables by Jeffrey Shaw.

John Latham, 'Eventstructure', *Studio International* (September 1967) 82.

Nelson GOODMAN

Score, Sketch and Script

[1968]

You see no experiment can be repeated exactly. There will always be something different ... What it comes to when you say you repeat an experiment is that you repeat all the features of an experiment which a theory determines are relevant. In other words you repeat the experiment as an example of the theory.
Sir George Thomson[1]

1 SCORE

A score is character in a notational system. Even in musical notation not every character is a score, but I count as a score every character that may have compliants. This excludes purely syncategorematic characters, for example, without requiring of a score either that it be a complete composition or that it be actually nonvacant. I have broadened the application of 'score' to embrace characters of the sort described in any notational system,[2] not merely in musical notation. Similarly, I often call the compliants of such characters performances where these compliants are not by ordinary usage performed or even events at all; and I often call the compliance-classes works, even when these classes are such – e.g., fortuitous aggregates of natural objects – as not to be works in any usual sense. All this I think may help to keep before us both the cardinal example of music and the more general principles illustrated.

A score, we found, defines a work but is a peculiar and privileged definition, without competitors. A class is uniquely determined by a score, as by an ordinary definition; but a score, unlike an ordinary definition, is also uniquely determined by each member of that class. Given the notational system and a performance of a score, the score is recoverable. Identity of work and of score is retained in any series of steps, each of them either from compliant performance to score-inscription, or from score-inscription to compliant performance, or from score-inscription to true copy. This is ensured by the fact, and only by the fact, that the language in which a score is written must be notational – must satisfy the five stated requirements. No inherent partitioning of the subject-matter is presumed; and performances of a work may vary widely and in many respects.

Redundancy, as noted earlier, is a common and minor violation of notationality. The net effect is that in a chain of the sort described, the score-inscriptions may not all be true copies of one another; yet all will be semantically equivalent – all performances will be of the same work. Work-preservation but not score-preservation is ensured; and in so far as work-preservation is paramount, and score-preservation incidental, redundancy is tolerable.

None of our usually natural languages is a notational system. Such *discursive languages* meet the two syntactic requirements but are exempt from the three semantic requirements. Accordingly, a definition or set of coextensive definitions is seldom uniquely determined by a member of the class defined. And as we have seen, ambiguity is not always to blame; a wheelbarrow belongs to many different compliance-classes of object-English – complies, that is, with many extensionally diverse descriptions, such as 'wooden object', 'wheeled vehicle', etc. In such a language there is no such thing as *the* definition, or set of equivalent definitions, that the given object satisfies. But in a notational system, or even a system, or even a system that misses notationality only through redundancy, all scores for a given performance are coexistive – have all the same performances as compliants.

2 MUSIC

So far, I have been discussing matters of general theory without examining closely any of the presumably notational systems actually used in the arts. Standard musical notation offers a familiar and at the same time a remarkable case. It is at once complex, serviceable and – like Arabic numerical notation – common to the users of many different verbal languages. No alternative has gained any currency; and apparently no other culture, such as the Chinese or Indian, has developed any comparably effective musical notation over the centuries. The variety and vitality of recent rebellions against it testify to the authority it has acquired.[3]

Ordinary musical notation has sometimes been thought to owe its origin to the introduction of keyboard instruments, with their separate keys and spaced tones; but the question just when either a true notation or a true keyboard instrument emerged is so elusive that the hypothesis hardly admits of any conclusive historical investigation. And the hypothesis is antecedently implausible; musical notation no more needed to wait upon invention of the clavichord than alphabetical notation needed to wait upon the invention of the typewriter. Development of a notational scheme or system does not depend upon an intrinsic segregation of marks or objects into disjoint and differentiated sets, but is often achieved in the face of virtual continuity in both realms.

In some early mediaeval musical manuscripts, marks were placed higher or lower over syllables or words of a song to indicate pitch. Only later did horizontal lines come to be added. At first these lines may have functioned as mere guides for judging absolute position, like the graduation-marks on a thermometer taken as an analogue instrument. When the lines and the spaces between them become characters of the system, with placement of a syllable or note-sign serving only to pick out one of these characters, elements of a genuine notation emerge. However, I am primarily concerned here not with origins or development but with how fully the language of musical scores qualifies as a truly notational system.

That the syntactic requirements are in general met is quite clear. A note-mark may, indeed, be so placed that we are in doubt about whether it belongs to one note-character or another, but in no case does it belong to both. Ostensible note-marks do not count as inscriptions in the system unless and until they are determined to belong to one character rather than to any other. Most characters of a musical score, whether numerals or letters or neither, are syntactically disjoint and differentiated. The symbol scheme is thus substantially notational, and the language of scores truly a language. But is this language a notational system? Does it satisfy the semantic requirements?

If we consider piano scores alone, the language is highly redundant since, for example, the same sound-events comply simply with the characters for *c*-sharp, *d*-flat, *e*-triple-flat, *b*-double-sharp, and so on;[4] but redundancy, as we have seen, is not altogether fatal. A more crucial question arises when we consider scores for other instruments as well. In a violin score the characters for *c*-sharp and *d*-flat have no compliants in common.[5] Now if two characters thus have some compliants jointly (in piano scores) and others severally, the two compliance-classes properly intersect, flagrantly violating the requirement of semantic disjointness. What this account misses, though, is that since every performance is on one instrument or another, each of the two characters can be considered a vacant atomic character that combines with different specifications of instrument to form different prime characters. The compliance-classes of the two resultant prime characters occurring in piano scores are identical; the compliance-classes of the two resultant prime characters occurring in violin scores are disjoint. Neither pair nor the pair of atomic vacant characters nor the set of all six characters violates the rule of semantic disjointness by more than the redundancy mentioned.

If we suppose the series of whole note, half-note, quarter-note, eighth-note, etc., to be continued without end, the semantic requirement of finite differentiation will be violated. For then by tying note-signs together we can construct characters for notes differing in duration by less than any given fraction of a beat. Hence no sounding of a note could be determined to comply with at most one character. Now of course in any given score or corpus of scores, the number of note-signs, and of flags on any of them, is finite. But there must furthermore be a tacit or express limit on the number of flags permitted by the system at all; otherwise recovery of score from performance will not be even theoretically possible, identity of work from performance to performance will not be ensured, and the primary purpose of a notational system will not be served. Theoretically, any limit would do. Tradition seems to set it for the present at five flags – the 1/128 note.

The main corpus of peculiarly musical characters of the system thus appears on the whole to meet the semantic as well as the syntactic requirements for a notation. The same cannot be said for all the numerical and alphabetical characters that also occur in scores.

First, some compositions are written with a 'figured bass' or 'continuo', allowing performers certain options. Now so long as such scores determine comparatively broad but still mutually disjoint classes of performances,[6] they cause no trouble; what counts is not specificity but separateness. But a system that permits alternative use of figured-bass and specific notation, without rigidly prescribing the choice in every case, materially violates the conditions upon notational systems; for the compliance-classes of some of its characters are properly included in the compliance- classes of other, more general characters. Two score-inscriptions, one in figured-bass and the other in specific notation, even though they have some common compliant performance, will not thereby be semantically equivalent; and two performances complying with the former may severally comply with two specific scores that have no compliant in common. The comprehensive language of musical scores, in so far as it offers free choice between figured-bass and specific notation, is thus not truly notational. Rather, it comprises two notational subsystems; and the one in use must be designated and adhered to if identification of work from performance to performance is to be ensured.

Much the same can be said concerning the free cadenza. The performer, again, is given wide scope; and scores providing for free cadenzas have compliance-classes that properly include those of other scores with their solo passages all specified note by note. Unless there is a way of determining in every case whether a solo passage is to be fully specified or indicated as a free cadenza, we must again recognize that the language of musical scores is not purely notational but divides into notational subsystems.

Trouble of a different sort arises from the verbal notation used for the tempo of a movement. That the words come from ordinary object-language does not of itself matter, 'Notational' does not imply 'nonverbal'; and not every selection of characters, along with their compliance-classes, from a discursive language violates the conditions for notationality. What matters is whether the borrowed vocabulary meets the semantic requirements. Now just what is the vocabulary of tempo? It contains not only the more common terms like 'allegro', 'andante', and 'adagio', but indefinitely many others like the following, taken from a few programmes of chamber music:[7] *preso, allegro vivace, allegro assai, allegro spiritoso, allegro molto, allegro non troppo, allegro moderato, poco allegretto, allegretto quasi-minuetto, Minuetto, minuetto con un poco di moto, rondo alla Polacaa, andantino mosso, andantino grazioso, fantasia, affetuoso e sostenuto, moderato e amabile.* Apparently almost any words may be used to indicate pace and mood. Even if unambiguity were miraculously preserved, semantic disjointness would not be. And since a tempo may be prescribed as fast, or as slow, or as between fast and slow, or as between fast and between-fast-and-slow, and so on without limit, semantic differentiation goes by the board, too.

Thus the verbal language of tempos is not notational. The tempo words cannot be integral parts of a score in so far as the score serves the function of identifying a work from performance to performance. No departure from the indicated tempo disqualifies a performance as an instance – however wretched – of the work defined by the score. For these tempo specifications cannot be accounted integral parts of the defining score, but are rather auxiliary directions whose observance or nonobservance affects the quality of a performance but not the identity of the work. On the other hand, metronomic specifications of tempo do, under obvious restrictions and under a system universally requiring them, qualify as notational and may be taken as belonging to the score as such.

I have been able to discuss here, rather sketchily, only a few salient samples of relevant questions concerning the standard language of musical scores. The results suggest, however, that it comes as near to meeting the theoretical requirements for notationality as might reasonably be expected of any traditional system in constant actual use, and that the excisions and revisions needed to correct any infractions are rather plain and local. After all, one hardly expects chemical purity outside the laboratory.

Since complete compliance with the score is the only requirement for a genuine instance of a work, the most miserable performance without actual mistakes does count as such an instance, while the most brilliant performance with a single wrong note does not. Could we not bring our theoretical vocabulary into better agreement with common practice and common sense by allowing some limited degree of deviation in performances admitted as instances of a work? The practising musician or composer usually bristles at the idea that a performance with one wrong note is not a performance of the given work at all; and ordinary usage surely sanctions overlooking a few wrong notes. But this is one of those cases where ordinary usage gets us quickly into trouble. The innocent-seeming principle that performances differing by just one note are instances of the same work risks the consequence – in view of the transitivity of identity – that all performances whatsoever are of the same work. If we allow the least deviation all assurance of work-preservation and score-preservation is lost; for by a series of one-note errors of omission, addition and modification, we can go all the way from Beethoven's *Fifth Symphony* to *Three Blind Mice*. Thus while a score may leave unspecified many features of a performance, and allow for considerable variation in others within prescribed limits, full compliance with the specifications given is categorically required. This is not to say that the exigencies that dictate our technical discourse need govern our everyday speech. I am no more recommending that in ordinary discourse we refuse to say that a pianist who misses a note has performed a Chopin *Polonaise* than that we refuse to call a whale a fish, the earth spherical, or a grayish-pink human white.

The overwhelming monopoly log held by standard musical notation has inevitably inspired rebellion and alternative proposals. Composers complain variously that scores in this notation prescribe too few features or too many or the wrong ones, or prescribe the right ones too precisely or not precisely enough. Revolution here as elsewhere may aim at more or at less or at different control of the means of production.

One simple system devised by John Cage is roughly as follows: dots, for single sounds, are placed within a rectangle; across the rectangle, at varying angles and perhaps intersecting, run five straight lines for (severally) frequency, duration timbre, amplitude and succession. The significant factors determining the sounds indicated by a dot are the perpendicular distances from the dot to these lines.[8] This system is not notational; for without some stipulation of minimal significant units of angle and distance, syntactic differentiation is wanting. So long as no limit is set upon the smallness of the difference in position that makes a difference in character, no measurement can ever determine that any mark belongs to one character rather than to any number of others. Similarly, under this system, no measurement can ever determine that a performance complies with one mark rather than others. Furthermore, depending upon just how the symbols are interpreted, syntactic and semantic disjointness may be lacking. The point is not that a work is less rigidly prescribed than by a standard score; for the character-classes and the compliance-classes of a notational system may be of any size so long as they are disjoint and differentiated. Under the proposed system there are no disjoint and differentiated characters or compliance-classes, no notation, no language, no scores.

The objection may be raised that the lack of syntactic differentiation here hardly matters if we have the original drawing and photographic means of reproducing it within any desired or consequential degree of accuracy. But however small the inaccuracy of reproduction, a chain of successive reproductions of reproductions can result in departing to any degree from the original. True enough, we can detect significant deviation by direct comparison with the original (if it is available); yet for two significantly different originals there may be a third (or a copy) that does not differ significantly from either. To arrive at a notation here calls not only for a limit upon significant deviation but also for a means of ensuring disjointness of characters.

Now I am by no means pronouncing upon whether adoption of a system like that described might nevertheless be a good idea. I am neither qualified nor called upon to make such a judgement. I am simply pointing out that much more is involved than a mere shift from one notational system to another. Nor am I quibbling about the proper use of such words as 'notation', 'score' and 'work'. That matters little more than the proper use of a fork. What does matter is that the system in question furnishes no means of identifying a work from performance to performance or even of a character from mark to mark. Nothing can be determined to be a true copy of Cage's autograph diagram or to be a performance of it. There are only copies *after* and performances *after* that unique object as there are only drawings and paintings after a sketch [...]

3 SKETCH

Because a painter's sketch, like a composer's score, may be used as a working guide, the crucial difference in their status might go unnoticed. The sketch, unlike the score, is not in a language or notation at all, but in a system without either syntactic or semantic differentiation. And while the Cage system described takes certain relationships of dot to line as the only pertinent ones, none among the pictorial properties of a sketch can be dismissed as irrelevant. But in neither case can anything be determined to belong to or to comply with at most one character. Thus, whereas a true score picks out a class of performances that are the equal and only instances of a musical work, a sketch does not determine a class of objects that are the equal and only instances of a work of painting. Unlike the score, the sketch does not define a work, in the strong sense of 'define' explained earlier, but rather *is* one.

Now this is not to deny that a notational system might be established such that sketches belong to its characters. Obviously sketches and also paintings can be sorted into disjoint and differentiated classes in any of various ways; and any of a multitude of correlations can be set up. But quite as obviously, to have two realms that can be so sorted and correlated is not yet to have a system. Only when custom or express stipulation actually effects or selects a classification of each realm and a correlation of the two do we have a system. Such a selection has already been made in the case of standard musical notation, but not in the case of sketches. No pictorial respects are distinguished as those in which a sketch must match another to be its equivalent, or a painting match a sketch to be an instance of what the sketch defines. And no magnitude of difference in any respect is set as the threshold of significance. Differences of all kinds and degrees, measurable or not, are on equal footing. Hence no classes of sketches are picked out as the characters, and no classes of pictures as the compliance-classes, of a notational system.

In short, the sketch – as a sketch – differs from the score not in functioning as a character in a language of a different kind but in not functioning as a character in a *language* at all.[9] The notational language of musical scores has no parallel in a language (notational or not) of sketches.

4 PAINTING

That we have ready at hand no notational system for painting does not settle the question whether such a system is possible. Taken at its face value, the question can be answered with an unhesitating but trivial *yes*. For examples of such notational languages are easily constructed. A library-like decimal system assigning a numeral to each painting according to time and place of production would meet all five requirements. Far afield is the objection that no one can tell by inspection, without further information, whether a given painting complies with a given numeral; for likewise no one can tell by inspection, *without further information*, whether a given performance complies with a musical score. One has to be able to interpret the score as one has to be able to interpret the numeral; and to know how to interpret a character is to know what complies with it.

The compliance-classes for the language just described will indeed be unit-classes, so that identification of a work from instance to instance will always be from sole instance to same sole instance, but there are no requirements upon the size of the compliance-classes of a notational system. And the uniqueness of instance in painting is irrelevant here since exactly the same question about the possibility of a notational system arises for etching, and is to be answered in the same way. If impressions are assigned numerals according to the plate printed from, the compliance-class of a numeral will usually have many members. Indeed, nothing precludes taking each plate itself as the unique inscription of character having its impressions as its compliants. Hence for painting and etching alike, notational languages are readily devised.

Yet, clearly, this straight-faced answer to the literal question asked misses the main point. For the question of real interest here is whether by means of a notational system the work of painting or etching can be freed of dependence upon a particular author or upon a place or date or means of production. Is it theoretically possible to write a score so defining a work of painting or etching that objects produced by others, before or since the usually designated original or originals, and by other means (than, e.g., the 'original' plate) may comply with the score and qualify as equal instances of the work? In short, could the institution of a notational system transform painting or etching from an autographic into an allographic art?

Some reasons that have been given for a negative answer are plainly beside the point. That a visual work is more complex and subtle than a musical performance would – even if true – not matter. For a score need not – indeed cannot – specify all aspects of the compliants nor even every degree of difference in any aspect; a score, as in figured-bass or free-cadenza notation, may be summary in the extreme. Nor does the difficulty of making perfect reproductions of a painting have anything to do with confinement of the work to the unique original.[10] The performances of the most specific score are by no means exact duplicates of one another, but vary widely and in many ways. A moderately good copy and the original painting resemble each other more closely than to performances of a Bach suite by Piatigorsky and Casals.

Yet there are constraints. Although a notational system may pick out any set of disjoint and finitely differentiated classes in any realm as compliance-classes, not every compliance-class of every such system counts as a work. Standard musical notation might be reinterpreted so that its compliance-classes cut wildly across the standard ones or even contain no musical performances at all. Or a notational system might classify pictures according to size or shape. But in none of these cases does a compliance-class any more constitute a work than the animals in a zoo form a species, or the performances of a musical composition make up a society. Whether the compliance-classes for a system are works (or societies) depends partly upon their relationship to the classes accounted works (or societies) in antecedent practice.

Special care must be taken here. While it would be quite wrong to suppose that a class becomes a work by being assigned a character in a notational system, it would also be quite wrong to suppose that no class is a work unless it has been antecedently considered so. On the one hand, the antecedent classification stands as licence and touchstone for a notational system; only in reference to this classification can there be a charge of material error or a claim of material correctness. On the other hand, the antecedent classification is normally partial and provisional. It submits only sample classes, each only by samples. Adoption of a notational language thus effects a double protection: from the samples of the several classes to the complete classes, and from the sample classes to the complete classification of the field of reference. This involves a choice among alternatives; and some actual departures from the antecedent classification may be made for the sake of better systematization. In sum, the problem of developing a notational system for an art like music amounted to the problem of arriving at a real definition of the notion of a musical work.

Where a pertinent antecedent classification is lacking or is flouted, a notational language effects only an arbitrary, nominal definition of 'work', as if it were a word newly coined. With no prototype, or no recognition of one, there are no material grounds for choosing one systematization rather than any other. But in the case of painting, a work is antecedently identified with (the unit-class of) an individual picture; and in the case of etching, with the class of impressions printed from an individual plate. Now the question is whether by application of a notational system works of painting or etching could legitimately be identified with quite different classes. This would call not just for such minor adjustments as occur in any systematization but for a drastic overhaul that would lump together in each compliance-class many antecedently different works. A notational system effecting such a reclassification may of course be applied at will; but scores in it will not constitute real definitions of works of painting. To repudiate the antecedent classification is to disenable the only authority competent to issue the needed licence.

Thus the answer to the significant question about a notational system for painting is *no*. We can devise a notational system that will provide, for works of painting and etching, real definitions that depend upon history of production. We can devise a notational system that will provide purely arbitrary nominal definitions that do not depend upon history of production. But we cannot devise a notational system that will provide, for such works, definitions that are both real (consonant with antecedent practice) and independent of history of production.

In sum, an established art becomes allographic only when the classification of objects or events into works is legitimately projected from an antecedent classification and is fully defined, independently of history of production, in terms of a notational system. Both authority and means are required; a suitable antecedent classification provides the one, a suitable notational system the other. Without the means, the authority is unexercised; without the authority, the means are footless.

5 SCRIPT

A script, unlike a sketch, is a character in a notational scheme and in a language but, unlike a score, is not a notational system. The syntactic but not all the semantic requirements are met. 'Script' here is thus not confined to cursive inscriptions or to the work of playwrights and film writers. In general, the characters of natural and of most technical languages are scripts; for even if ambiguity is avoided, the compliance-classes of such a language are seldom either disjoint or differentiated from one another.

While most scripts are verbal, notationality obviously does not turn upon the look of marks. We do not arrive at a notational system if we substitute a numeral for each word of English.[11] And we do not sacrifice notationality – although we surely jettison practicality – if we translate standard musical notation into a sub-language of English in such a way that the vocabulary of admitted words meets our five requirements.

One might suppose that scripts but not scores can assert or denote. But we have already seen that means of effecting assertion (or question or command) can be added to or subtracted from a system without affecting notationality; and the idea that scores do not denote seems no better founded. Offhand, indeed, the relation between a term and what it denotes appears quite different from that between a score and its performances or between a letter and its utterances; but no very clear principle seems to underlie this distinction. The criteria that distinguish notational systems from other languages are in terms of interrelationships among compliance-classes, and provide no good grounds for refusing to say that a character in a language of either sort denotes what complies with it.[12]

Even less can be said for the notion that while we need only know how to recognize a performance of a musical score or an utterance of a phonetic score, we have to understand a script. In both cases, we have to know how to determine what complies with the character. Where a language has few prime characters and fairly simple principles of compliance, so that confident and almost automatic use is acquired rather easily, we tend to regard the language as an instrument we operate. Where the prime characters are many and the principles of compliance are complex, so that interpretation of a character often calls for some deliberation, we tend to speak of having to understand the language. But this difference in complexity, besides being a matter of degree, does not at all coincide with the distinction between notational systems and other languages. For a notational system may have a denumerable infinity of prime characters and an intricate compliance-relation, while a discursive language may have only two characters – say the words 'red' and 'square', with red things and square things as their compliants.

A script, then, differs from a score not in being verbal or declarative or denotational or in requiring special understanding, but simply in being a character in a language that is either ambiguous or lacks semantic disjointness or differentiation. But this prosaic distinction is more consequential than might appear, both in ways already observed and in its bearing upon some currently touchy philosophical questions [...]

1 In 'Some Thoughts on Scientific Method', Lecture of 2 May 1963, printed in *Boston Studies in the Philosophy of Science*, Vol. II (New York: Humanities Press, 1965) 85.

2 Not, be it observed, 'in any notational *scheme*'. The usage here adopted counts only characters of notational *systems* as scores.

3 I do not say to its merits, aesthetic or otherwise [...]

4 I oversimplify here by ignoring features other than pitch, but the central point is unaffected [...]

5 This may be disputed. I am told that a tone of, say, 333 vibrations per second is accepted for either character. But we may regard such a tone as either actually compliant with both characters or (like the missing of one note) as merely within tolerable limits of deviation in practice. For purposes of illustrating a general point, I choose the latter interpretation here. A more relational notation is still compatible with notationality.

6 The question whether these compliance-classes are in fact disjoint can be answered only by careful examination of the notation in use and some delicate decisions concerning its interpretation.

7 Chosen casually from programmes of works played at the Marlboro Music Festival, Marlboro, Vermont, during six weeks in the summer of 1961.

8 See *Concert for Piano and Orchestra, Solo for Piano* (New York: Henmar Press, Inc., 1960) 53, fig. BB [reproduced in this volume, 191].

9 Of course, nothing prevents a given mark from functioning as an inscription in a notation (or in several different notations) and also as a sketch in a nonlinguistic system (or in several such systems).

10 Widespread acceptance of this easy and inept explanation has inhibited efforts towards real understanding of the matter. Philosophers of art are not immune from the error; see, for example, Joseph Margolis, 'The Identity of a Work of Art', *Mind*, 68 (1959) 50.

11 Lexicographical order might be taken as the basis for assigning numerals to words. But if we want to assign a numeral to every string of letters, and we place no limit on the length of a string, lexicographical ordering becomes astoundingly complex. However, numerals may be assigned to all such strings on the basis of the different and very simple ordering that begins with lexicographical ordering of all one-letter strings, proceeds to lexicographical ordering of all two-letter strings, and so on.

12 This is not to say that everything a symbol refers to complies with it; exemplification, though a mode of reference, does not constitute compliance.

Nelson Goodman, 'Score, Sketch and Script', *Languages of Art: An Approach to a Theory of Symbols* (Indianapolis: Bobbs-Merrill, 1968; second edition, Indianapolis: Hackett Publishing Company, Inc., 1976) 177-201.

Vito ACCONCI
Some Notes on Activity and Performance [1970]

1 ACCESSIBILITY (AVAILABILITY) OF PERSON

If the artist is a performer, in action, his presence alone produces signs and marks. The information he provides necessarily concerns the source of information, himself, and cannot be solely about some absent object; the information pertains to the general relationship of the individual to what is transpiring.

If the artist cannot be continuously on exhibit, he can present a situation on which, because of everyday living, he is required to act, wherever he may be at the time. (There might be exhibited, for example, an object that the artist must sometime or other need, and therefore go to pick up or send for; the object exhibited is there in preparation for his use.)

Generating expression – and hence making the information available – need not be an official end of the action but only a side-effect. The intention of the performer can be to make unwitting moves, observable behaviour unoriented to the assessment an observer might be making of it.

2 ADAPTIVE LINES OF ACTION

A performance can consist of performing (adhering to the terms of) a particular element (a rule, a space, a previous performance, another person.) The performer can balance between tactics – selecting an immediate action from his available repertoire – and strategy – choosing where he wishes to be at a future time.

The performance can be set up as a learning process. When the performer makes a move, the consequences of his behaviour can control his next move. The use of feedback can steady and bring into unison one stage of the performance, after which can come change as new material is imported and adapted to.

The performer can work as a producer; the performance pattern can be linear – a series of additions of material and energy. Or he can work as a consumer; the pattern can be radial – lines of material and energy converging on him for his use.

3 DRIFT

If there is a lag in feedback, the direction of the performance can be changed. A line of action can be weakened by emergent forces in the surrounding field; the consequences of an action can become increasingly unpredictable.

The performance can begin with an alarm reaction to a stimulus, when the performer is groping because he has not yet specifically developed a system to cope with the task at hand. The performance can take up time as the performer goes through a stage of resistance and adaptation, developing a specific channel of defence. The performance can continue to a stage of exhaustion, when the specific channel of adaptation is broken down – the reaction spreading over different areas – and momentum is retained for a while after the shut-off of power.

The exhaustion is reversible if the performer can rest, as part of the performance – if he can 'mark time', as things come in and out of focus – or if he can pass without serious resistance to another pattern.

4 DEPRIVATION, STIGMA, AND INVASION OF PRIVACY

In the stage of exhaustion, the performer is potentially vulnerable. A performance can provide an occasion for wearing out his channels of resistance and rules of order; it can shift into explicit focus what is ordinarily unattended to; it can produce a deprivation that calls for supernormal reactions in an attempt at stabilization.

How the performer acts, in a certain situation, can be revealed to be at variance with the category and attributes that are socially demanded of him. He can be reduced from a 'whole' person to a 'tainted' and discredited one.

The subject of a performance can be the control (or lack of control) of personal information. The performance can be a means of developing a handicap, or a stigma, that would make control more difficult.

5 STRATEGY AND INTERACTION

If the performer comes into contact with another party (another performer, or an observer), the situation can be one that the performer assesses while the other party is trying to penetrate that assessment; the other party can realize that the performer's assessment includes, as one of its features, the fact that the other party will try to penetrate it.

When assessment is the basis of an activity, the performer can become a parasite on the other party, or he can absorb him. (A performance can use, for example, techniques of spying, following, imitating; an exhibit can propose that some personal possessions of the artist, such as his clothes, can be borrowed and used for the duration of the exhibition.)

A performance can be a series of conditional avowals, where the performer will pursue a given course of action if the other party engages (or does not engage) in another course of action. What can be at stake in a performance is not a location (and its occupation) but the capacity to move more or less at will.

Vito Acconci, 'Some Notes on Activity and Performance', *Interfunktionen* (Cologne, 1970) 138-42.

Adrian PIPER
Art as Catalysis [1970]

'Since some such originative sources are present in soulless things, and others in things possessed of soul, and in soul, and in the rational part of the soul, clearly some potencies will be non-rational and some will be accompanied by a rational formula. This is why all arts, i.e. all productive forms of knowledge, are potencies; they are originative sources of change in another thing, or in the artist himself considered as other. And each of those which are accompanied by a rational formula is alike capable of contrary effects, but one non-rational power produces one effect; e.g., the hot is capable only of heating, but the medical art can produce both disease and health.'
– Aristotle, *Metaphysics*, 1046b

One reason for making and exhibiting a work is to induce a reaction or change in the viewer. The stronger the work, the stronger its impact and the more total (physiological, psychological, intellectual, etc.) the reaction of the viewer. The strength of such a work is a function of the viewer's response to it. The work is a catalytic agent, in that it promotes a change in another entity (the viewer) without undergoing any permanent change itself. The value of the work may then be measured in terms of the strength of the change, rather than whether the change accords positively or negatively with some aesthetic standard. In this sense, the work as such is nonexistent except when it functions as a medium of change between the artist and the viewer.

Separating the work from the artist (giving it discrete formal/external existence) gives it independent status as an artwork but decreases its potential strength as a catalytic agent. There is a time and space lapse between the creative process of the artist in conceiving and executing the work and the experience of the viewer in perceiving it. The viewer experiences only that part of the work retained in the immediate exhibit situation. The process leading up to the final work (which intrinsically involves the artist's presence) can be mentally inferred, and this inference can constitute an important part of the perception of the work. The work is a product, each of which may influence the interpretation of the work differently; but the artist is the embodiment of that particular process. This aspect of the work is eliminated by the artist when he eliminates his own presence from the discrete form of the final product as it is exhibited: In eliminating himself from the work, he is alienating process from product. A complete experience of the work as a total process is replaced by an incomplete experience of its end product alone, plus the viewer's projection of an inferred history or biography of the product.

The characteristics of any discrete form that occupies its own time and/or space apart from the artist limit the viewer's reaction to the work. Verbal documentation and verbally transmitted information have impact almost exclusively on an intellectual, contemplative level. The impact of static sculptural form is on an almost exclusively physical or sensory level: when a strong work manipulates a set of physical conditions in an exciting way, it is a way that produces a unique affective response in the viewer.

Media documentation (photos, movies, tapes, video, etc.) requires a psychological displacement in time and space by the viewer – a mental recreation of the documented conditions. The success of this effort precedes and influences appreciation of the work itself. Another possibility is that the media are utilized by the viewer as is verbal information, and apprehended on a similarly intellectual level. A third possibility is that the media convey the work on the same level as movies or news broadcasts: The psychic impact is there but on a removed level rather than an immediate and personal one. The impact of the work is then in proportion to one's success in suspending disbelief for the duration of the work.

Events and happening-type situations often share many of the same limitations of other discrete forms, when they are separated from the artists and their own creative processes. When an artificial series of actions are performed, the viewer perceives a similarly incomplete end product. When an artificial environment is created, the viewer relinquishes his role as essentially passive 'substance' on which the catalytic agent works in order to become part of the catalytic agent. In either case the potential impact of the work is diminished: In the former case, the final work is incomplete; in the latter, the role of the viewer is incomplete (being temporarily superseded by the role of 'participating artist').

The strongest impact that can be received by a person in the passive capacity of viewer is the impact of human confrontation (within oneself or between people). It is the most aggressive and the most threatening, possibly because the least predictable and the least controllable in its consequences.

Because the artist is the embodiment of a particular creative process, artworks can abandon the intermediary of the discrete form and base themselves on this type of impact. The artist himself becomes the catalytic agent inducing change in the viewer; the viewer responds to the catalytic presence of the artist as artwork. This is not to be confused with life as art or the artist's personality as art. The aesthetic formality and artifice of the work temporarily replace or veil the personal attributes of the artist.

The potential impact may then increase because (1) it is based on direct and immediate confrontation; and (2) it is aesthetically a more complete viewing experience. The time and space occupied by the total artwork process is exactly the same as that occupied by the viewer. The viewing experience cannot be fragmented by projections in time or hypothetical constructs about the nature of the work. As a discrete form himself, an artist possesses all the potential strengths of secondary discrete forms without any of their intrinsic difficulties.

Adrian Piper, 'Art as Catalysis' (August, 1970), reprinted as a section of 'Talking to Myself: The Ongoing Biography of an Art Object', *Out of Order, Out of Sight, Volume I: Selected Writings in Meta-Art, 1968-1992* (Cambridge, Massachusetts: MIT Press, 1996) 32-34.

PROCESS, SYSTEM, SERIES

A significant strand of conceptual art developed out of the mathematical side of minimalist sculptors' interest in process. As Sol LeWitt and Mel Bochner increasingly focused on the intellectual aspects of their art, their writings became as central to their role as artists as the physical fabrication of their works. The publication of LeWitt's 'Paragraphs on Conceptual Art' in *Artforum* in the summer of 1967 introduced the idea of conceptual art to the international art community. Bochner and Jack Burnham explored the more specific ideas of 'serial art' and 'systems aesthetics', respectively. Adrian Piper developed LeWitt's ideas in an explicitly philosophical direction. Artists began to draw upon an ever-wider range of theoretical resources. Two books of particular influence were Curt Lewin's *Principles of Topological Psychology* (1936), which was reissued in 1966, and George Kubler's *The Shape of Time* (1962). Lucy Lippard and John Chandler summed up the cumulative effect of these developments in the swiftly disputed idea of a 'dematerialization' of art. A similar artistic interest in logico-mathematical processes was characteristic of the development of conceptual art in Poland, represented here by the writing of Jaroslaw Kozlowski. More recently, critics such as Benjamin Buchloh have drawn attention to the conceptual dimension of serial form in the early American Pop art of Andy Warhol and Edward Ruscha.

Curt LEWIN
Principles of Topological Psychology [1936]

THE MATHEMATICAL CONCEPT OF SPACE

In order to settle the question of whether the facts that exist psychologically, i.e. those which have psychological effects, show spatial relationships, one has to go back to the mathematical concept of space. The person who is not a mathematician as a rule thinks of space as *physical* space. He pictures mathematical space as a geometrical structure extending in every direction without limits, a structure which can be visualized to a certain degree and within which one can determine direction and distance exactly by measurement.

Mathematics, in the course of its long history, has developed a concept of space which is in no way limited to physical space or to space which can be visualized. It has progressed from the investigation of three-dimensional to that of *n*-dimensional space, from Euclidian space to curved space, from metrical to non-metrical space.

The nature of the things whose system constitutes a mathematical space is entirely irrelevant for modern mathematics. It does not matter whether one thinks of them as physical objects, temperatures, numbers, colours, events, or anything else. Only certain relationships and the possibility of certain operations are relevant. It is these which finally define space.

As far as mathematics is concerned there is therefore no fundamental objection to applying the mathematical concept of space to psychological facts. The crucial point is whether the relationships that characterize space in mathematics can be applied adequately to psychological facts, and whether one can co-ordinate psychological processes univocally to mathematical operations.

(In order to avoid misunderstanding in terminology it should be noted that one does not think of mathematical space as necessarily unlimited in all directions. One also designates as space a series of numbers, a sphere, or a finite line of any curvature.)

Topological Space. – The mathematical concept of space can be developed from different fundamental relationships. From the point of view of psychology it is especially interesting that one can use the part-whole relationship as the basic one. This basic theorem states that for any two objects, *U* and *V*, of a system for which certain conditions hold, the following relationship shall or shall not be valid: *U* is a part of *V* (that is equivalent to '*V* includes *U*'). By means of certain monotonous series of inclusion one can characterize the concept of a 'point'[1] and further the concept of 'surrounding'.

Space thus defined is called topological space. By this term is meant that we are dealing with mathematical relationships which can be characterized without measurement. No distances are defined in topological space. A drop of water and the earth are, from a topological point of view, fully equivalent. A cube and a sphere also are not distinguishable. Nevertheless these nonmetrical spaces exhibit important characteristics which are fundamental also for metrical space. There is a highly developed branch of mathematics which has grown around the concept of connectedness. It deals with separated and connected spaces, with the different kinds of connectedness, with the relationship of part sets in different regions, with boundaries, with cuts, etc. Problems of dimension can also be treated on the basis of topological concepts without recourse to metrical properties.

It is now generally recognized that the whole-part relationship, and the relationships of the parts to each other, play a fundamental role in psychology. This is true for all branches of psychology. The concept of connectedness, for instance the distinction between separate and connected regions, the distinction between different groupings of regions, is as we have shown above of prime importance for characterizing both the person and the psychological environment. Changes of connection, especially the uniting and separating of regions, are just as important for the psychology of perception as for the psychology of intention, satisfaction or friendship. The basic idea of a person in an environment is in its conceptual content a statement of a certain topological relationship between two regions.

Certain binary relationships, i.e. relationships between two points of topological space, play an essential role in topology. In this place we must call attention to the topological concept of 'path' that connects two points. How parts of a space are connected can be determined to a large extent by the possibility of such paths and the fact that the path does or does not intersect certain boundaries. We will see that the concept of path plays a fundamental role in the constitution of psychological spaces. One can co-ordinate certain psychological facts which have the function of a psychological connection between two psychological 'points' to a 'path' which mathematically connects two points. For instance, any kind of locomotion of the person in the quasi-physical, the quasi-social or the quasi-conceptual field can be designated as a connecting process which corresponds to a topological path.

In addition to the locomotions of the person or other parts of the psychological space we must call attention to that type of real connection which one can call 'dynamic communication'. The fact that certain regions in the psychological environment and within the person influence other regions, both of the environment and of the person, may be taken as a criterion for connectedness in the topological sense [...]

Metrical Space. – One can ask whether it is possible to go beyond topological determinations and apply metrical concepts to psychological regions. Metrical space is characterized by the fact that one can coordinate to any two points, *x*, *y*, of the space a distance $\overline{xy} \leqq 0$ for which certain axioms hold, especially the triangle axiom. One distinguishes Euclidian and non-Euclidian space according to the particular kind of metrics employed. Common to both is the fact that there are differences in magnitude and that one can use measurement and numbers in characterizing spatial relationships.

Certainly at the present time there are no metrical determinations available concerning psychological life space. It is clear that a double distance in physical space generally does not correspond to a double distance in psychological space. There is no doubt that very different quasi-physical distances often correspond to equal physical distances. A special investigation is necessary to determine whether the triangle axiom whose applicability is the premise for all measurement of distance holds also for quasi-physical fields. It might seem to be impossible to measure in the exact meaning of the word quasi-social or quasi-conceptual distances. The same difficulties appear with the problem of magnitude of layers or regions of the person, or the distance between them.

Not only the concept of distance but also that of direction goes beyond purely topological determinations. Mathematically there is a close relationship between measurement of angles and measurement of distances. As a matter of fact the determination of directions in the psychological life space is as difficult as that of distance.

On the other hand, the history of psychology seems to show that it is impossible to represent psychological causal interconnections without making use of the concept of direction. It is presupposed in the concept of 'direction of a movement' as well as in the concepts of 'tendency' or 'force'. The concept of 'difference of direction' or of 'opposing direction' can hardly be avoided, for instance in the theory of conflict.

Neither can we ignore the fact that in certain cases one can speak definitely about direction, or at least changes in direction. This is true not only for the quasi-physical, but also for the quasi-social or quasi-conceptual fields. The same is true of the determination of distance. Despite all obvious objections to any exact measurement in the psychological life space it seems to be possible sometimes to make definite statements about distance or at least changes of distance. Such a change of distance takes place, for instance, when one approaches his goal in the quasi-social space. One can even compare regions within the life space with each other as to their magnitude, for instance, regions of free movement [...]

Curt Lewin, *Principles of Topological Psychology*, trans. Fritz Heider, Grace M. Heider (New York: McGraw-Hill, 1936; reprinted 1966) 52-56.

George KUBLER
The Shape of Time [1962]

FORMAL SEQUENCES

Every important work of art can be regarded both as a historical event and as a hard-won solution to some problem. It is irrelevant now whether the event was original or conventional, accidental or willed, awkward or skilful. The important clue is that any solution points to the existence of some problem to which there have been other solutions, and that other solutions to this same problem will most likely be invented to follow the one now in view. as the solutions accumulate, the problem alters. The chain of solutions nevertheless discloses the problem.

Linked Solutions. The problem disclosed by any sequence of artifacts may be regarded as its mental form, and the linked solutions as its class of being. The entity composed by the problem and its solutions constitutes a form-class. Historically only those solutions related to one another by the bonds of tradition and influence are linked as a sequence.

Linked solutions occupy time in a great variety of ways, discussed in the remainder of this book. They disclose a finite yet uncharted domain of mental forms. Most of these are still open to further elaboration by new solutions. Some are closed, completed series belonging to the past.

In mathematical usage a series is the indicated sum of a set of terms, but a sequence is any ordered set of quantities like the positive integers.[1] A series therefore implies a close grouping, and a sequence suggests an open-ended, expanding class. The mathematical distinction is worth keeping in this discussion.

In general, formal sequences exceed the ability of any individual to exhaust their possibilities. An occasional person, born by chance into favouring time, may contribute beyond the usual measure of a single life-span, but he cannot alone simulate in his life the corporate activity of a whole artistic tradition.

The mathematical analogy for our study is topology, the geometry of relationships without magnitudes or dimensions, having only surfaces and directions. The biological analogy is speciation, where form is manifested by a large number of individuals undergoing genetic changes.

Where are the boundaries of a formal sequence? Because history is unfinished business, the boundaries of its divisions continually move, and will continue to move for as long as men make history. T.S. Eliot was perhaps the first to note this relationship when he observed that every major work of art forces upon us a reassessment of all previous works.[2] Thus the advent of Rodin alters the transmitted identity of Michaelangelo by enlarging our understanding of sculpture and permitting us a new objective vision of his work.[3]

For our purposes here, the boundaries of a sequence are marked out by the linked solutions describing early and late stages of effort upon a problem. With a sequence having many stages, there was a time when it had fewer. More new ones may be added in the future. The sequence can continue only when the problem is given greater scope by new needs. As the problem expands, both the sequence and its early portions lengthen.

Open and closed sequences. When problems cease to command active attention as deserving of new solutions, the sequence of solutions is stable during the period of inaction. But any past problem is capable of reactivation under new conditions. Aboriginal Australian bark-painting is an open sequence in the twentieth century, because its possibilities are still being expanded by living artists, but Greek vase-painting is an arrested sequence because the modern painter needed to renew his art at 'primitive' sources rather than among the images of the Hellenic world. The transparent animals and humans of Australian painting, and the rhythmic figures of African tribal sculpture, correspond more closely to contemporary theories of reality than to the opaque and unequivocal body forms of Greek art.

The method imposed by such considerations is analytical and divisive rather than synthetic. It discards any idea of regular cyclical happening on the pattern of 'necessary' stylistic series by the biological metaphor of archaic, classic and baroque stages. Sequence classing stresses the internal coherence of events, all while it shows the sporadic, unpredictable and irregular nature of their occurrence. The field of history contains many circuits which never close. The presence of the conditions for an event does not guarantee the occurrence of that event in a domain where man can contemplate an action without committing it.

Simple biographical narration in the history of art tends to display the entire historical situation in terms of an individual's development. Such biography is a necessary stage of reconstruction, but a formal sequence designates chains of linked events by an analysis which requires us to do the opposite: to perceive the individual in terms of his situation.

Sequence classing allows us to bridge the gap between biography and the history of style with a conception less protean than biological or dialectic theories of the dynamics of style, and more powerfully descriptive than biography. Its dangers and its limitations will be readily apparent. In the long run, the conception of a sequence may serve as a scaffolding which it may be convenient to discard later on, after it has given access to previously invisible portions of the historical edifice.

It is disturbing to those who value the individuality of a thing to have that individuality diminished by classifications and generalizations. We are caught between difficulties: single things are extremely complicated entities, so complicated that we can pretend to understand them only by generalizing about them. One way out is frankly to accept the complexity of single things. Once their difficulty is conceded, it is possible to find aspects that can be used in comparisons. No such trait now known is unitary or fundamental: every trait of a thing is both a cluster of subordinate traits as well as a subordinate part of another cluster [...]

The closest definition of a formal sequence that we now can venture is to affirm it as a historical network of gradually altered repetitions of the same trait. The sequence might therefore be described as having an armature. In cross section let us say that is shows a network, a mesh or a cluster of subordinate traits; and in long section that it has a fibre-like structure of temporal stages, all recognizably similar, yet altering in their mesh from beginning to end.

Two questions immediately arise: in the first place, are formal sequences not indefinitely numerous? No, because each corresponds to a conscious problem requiring the serious attention of many persons for its successful resolution. There are no linked solutions without there having been a corresponding problem. There is no problem where there is no awareness. The contours of human activity as a whole are therefore congruent with those of the totality of formal sequences. Each class of forms consists of a real difficulty and of real solutions. In the course of time, most of these solutions may have been destroyed, but that difficulty is only an apparent one, for our determinations of sequence can if necessary be founded upon only one surviving solution or example. Such determinations are of course provisional and incomplete. Yet every object attests to the existence of a requirement for which it is the solution, even when that object is only a late copy in a long series of coarsened products far removed from the clarity and sharpness of an original.

In the second place, are we going to consider all man-made objects or only a selection of them? Where is the minimal boundary? We are concerned mainly with works of art rather than with tools, and we are interested more in long durations than in brief ones, which tell us less about our subject. Tools and instruments commonly have extremely long durations. Upon occasion these extend so far that it is difficult to note great changes, as, for example, in the minor inflections that record the passage of civilizations in the cooking pots of a deep refuse midden. A working rule is that the simpler tools record very large durations, and that the more complicated tools record brief episodes of special needs and inventions.

Fashions. The minimal boundary perhaps lies near the limits of fashion. Fashions in dress are among our briefest durations. A fashion obeys demands to which the longer evolutions are impervious. A fashion is the projection of a single image of outward being, resistant to change during its brief life, ephemeral, expendable, receptive only to copying but not to fundamental variation. Fashions touch the limit of credibility by violating the precedent and by grazing the edge of the ridiculous. They belong not to a connected chain of solutions, but they constitute, each fashion in turn, classes of only one member each. A fashion is a duration without substantial change: an apparition, a flicker, forgotten with the round of the seasons. It is like a class, but it differs from a sequence by having no appreciable dimension in time [...]

SERIAL POSITION, AGE AND CHANGE

In mathematical usage, series and sequence differ as closed and open classes of events. In the foregoing pages we assumed that most classes are open-ended sequences. Here, however, we will assume that most classes can be treated as closed series. The difference between the two points of view depends upon the viewer's position, whether he wishes to be inside or outside the events in question. From the inside, most classes look like open sequences; from outside they seem to be closed series. In order to reconcile both positions, let us say that the conception of the formal sequence outlined in the preceding section allows us to assemble the ideas of things, with their first realizations and with the consequent mass of replicas, as events into connected finite series.

The rule of series. Every succession may be stated in the following propositions: 1) in the course of an irreversible finite series the use of any position reduces the number of remaining positions; 2) each position in a series affords only a limited number of possibilities of action; 3) the choice of an action commits the corresponding position; 4) taking a position both defines and reduces the range of possibilities in the succeeding position.

Stated differently: every new form limits the succeeding innovations in the same series. Every such form is itself one of a finite number of possibilities open in any temporal situation. Hence every innovation reduces the duration of its class. The boundaries of a class are fixed by the presence of a problem requiring linked solutions: classes may be small or large: we are here concerned only with their internal relationships and not with their dimensions or magnitudes.

One more proposition allows us to qualify the mode of duration. Each series, originating in its own class of forms, has its own minimal duration for each position, depending upon the effort required. Small problems require small effort; large ones demand more effort and so consume more time. Any effort to shortcut the circuit leads to failure. The rule of series requires each position to be occupied for its corresponding period before the next position can be taken. In purely technological domains this is self-evident: the steam engine was invented before the locomotive, but the *mise au point* of a locomotive required many more parts, each consuming its portion in the economy of the time sequence, than a steam engine alone. In works of art the rule of minimal durations is even more rigorous, marked by collective attitudes of acceptance or rejection [...] These cannot be short-circuited by fortuitous discoveries as in the technological fields. For example, the discovery of a luminous paint was no help to the painter engaged in an attempt to record on canvas the play of light in nature: he was bound to achieve his unconventional aim with conventional materials.

Our procedure is rather to recognize the recurrence of a need in differing stages of its gratification, and the persistence of a problem throughout various efforts to solve it. Every need evokes a problem. The juncture of each need with successive solutions leads to the conception of sequence. It is a conception much narrower yet more labile than that of any biological metaphor, for it considers only human needs and their satisfaction, in a one-to-one correspondence between needs and things, without the intermediary of any other irrelevant entity like 'life-cycle'. The main difficulty arises in the specification of 'needs', but we have carefully sidestepped that question by restricting the discussion to relationships rather than to magnitudes.

Systematic age. We need here to study the nature of durations. To speak of sequences or series, that is, of specified needs and their successive stages of satisfaction, is to mark a variety of durations. No duration, however, can be discussed save in respect to its beginning, middle and end, or to its early and its late moments. In one duration, we are agreed that 'late' cannot precede 'early'. Hence we may speak of the *systematic age* of each item in a formal series according to its position in the duration.

Easily recognized visual properties mark the systematic age of any item, once we have identified its series. It is not the purpose of this book to dwell upon the techniques and kinds of chronological discrimination, yet certain fundamental observations are indispensable. Early solutions (promorphic) are technically simple, energetically inexpensive, expressively clear. Late solutions (neomorphic) are costly, difficult, intricate, recondite and animated. Early solutions are integral in relation to the problem they resolve. Late ones are partial in being addressed more to the details of function or expression than to the totality of the same problem. Our terms, promorphs and neomorphs, have the permission of the best dictionaries, and they avoid the promiscuous contamination of terms such as 'primitive' and 'decadent', and 'archaic' or 'baroque'. But these determinations depend upon defining the pertinent form-class, for otherwise the visual properties of late solutions in one class may deceptively resemble those of early solutions in another class. Late and early are perforce relative to a defined starting point. They will inevitably remain as parameters until some absolute measure of visual position in time is devised [...]

1 *Mathematics Dictionary*, ed. Glenn James and R.C. James (Princeton, 1959) 349-50.

2 T.S. Eliot, 'Tradition and the Individual Talent', *Selected Essays, 1917-32* (New York, 1932) 5.

3 André Malraux has appropriated the 'Eliot effect' in several passages of *The Voices of Silence* (New York, 1954) 67, 317, 367, where major artists are represented as altering their respective traditions retroactively by their own novel contributions.

George Kubler, *The Shape of Time: Remarks on the History of Things* (New Haven: Yale University Press, 1962) 33-9, 53-56.

Sol LEWITT
Serial Project No. 1 (ABCD) [1966]

Serial compositions are multi-part pieces with regulated changes. The differences between the parts are the subject of the composition. If some parts remain constant it is to punctuate the changes. The entire work would contain sub-divisions that could be autonomous but that comprise the whole. The autonomous parts are units, rows, sets or any logical division that would be read as a complete thought. The series would be read by the viewer in a linear or narrative manner even though in its final form many of these sets would be operating simultaneously, making comprehension difficult. The aim of the artist would not be to instruct the viewer but to give him information. Whether the viewer understands this information is incidental to the artist; one cannot foresee the understanding of all one's viewers. One would follow one's predetermined premise to its conclusion, avoiding subjectivity. Chance, taste or unconsciously remembered forms would play no part in the outcome. The serial artist does not attempt to produce a beautiful or mysterious object but functions merely as a clerk cataloguing the results of the premise.

The premise governing this series is to place one form within another and include all major variations in two and three dimensions. This is to be done in the most succinct manner, using the fewest measurements. It would be a finite series using the square and cube as its syntax. A more complex form would be too interesting in itself and obstruct the meaning of the whole. There is no need to invent new forms. The square and cube are efficient and symmetrical. In order to free a square within a larger square, the larger square is divided into nine equal parts. The centre square would be equally distant from the outer square and exactly centred. A single measurement is used as the basis for the series.

The set contains nine pieces. They are all of the variations within the scope of the first premise. The first variation is a square within a square. The other variations follow: a cube within a square; a square within a cube; an outer form raised to the height of the inner cube; the inner cube raised to the height of the outer, larger cube; a cube within a cube, and all cross matchings of these forms. The first set contains nine pieces. These pieces are laid out on a grid. The grid equalizes the spacing and makes all of the pieces and spaces between of equal importance. The individual pieces are arranged in three rows of three forms each. In each row there are three different parts and three parts that are the same. The inner forms of one row of three are read in sequence, as are the outer forms.

The sets of nine are placed in four groups. Each group comprises variations on open or closed forms.

In cases in which the same plane is occupied by both the inside and outside forms, the inside plane takes precedence. This is done so that there is more information given the viewer. If it were otherwise more forms would be invisible, impeding the viewer's understanding of the whole set. When the larger form is closed and the top of the smaller form is not on the same plane as the larger – but lower – the smaller form is placed inside. If the viewer cannot see the interior form, one may believe it is there or not but one knows which form one believes is there or not there. The evidence given him or her by the other pieces in the set, and by reference to the other sets will inform the viewer as to what should be there. The sets are grouped in the most symmetrical way possible. Each set mirrors the others, with the higher pieces concentrated in the centre.

Sol LeWitt, 'Serial Project No. 1 (ABCD)', *Aspen Magazine*, 5-6 (1966); reprinted in *Sol LeWitt* (New York: The Museum of Modern Art, 1978) 170-71.

Mel BOCHNER
Serial Art, Systems, Solipsism [1967]

'Go to the things themselves.'
– Edmund Husserl

'No object implies the existence of any other.'
– John Hume

'There is nothing more to things than what can be discovered by listing the totality of the descriptions which they satisfy.'
– A.J. Ayer

If it can be safely assumed that all things are equal, separate and unrelated, we are obliged to concede that they (things) can be named and described but never defined or explained. If, furthermore, we bracket-out all questions that, due to the nature of language, are undiscussible (such as why did this or that come to exist, or what does it mean) it will then be possible to say that the entire being of an object, in this case an art object, is in its appearance. Things being whatever it is they happen to be, all we can know about them is derived directly from how they appear.

What is thought about art is usually only thought about because it has been thought about that way before. Whatever art is, it is, and criticism, which is language, is something different. Language comes to terms with art by creating parallel structures or transposing, both of which are less than adequate. (That doesn't mean, however, I think that it is true that nothing can be said except about language itself.)

Criticism has traditionally consisted of one of three approaches: 'impressionable' criticism, which has concerned itself with the effects of the work of art on the observer – individual responses; 'historical' criticism, which has dealt with an *a posteriori* evolution of forms and techniques – what is between works; and 'metaphorical' criticism, which has contrived numerous analogies – most recently to scientism. What has been generally neglected is a concern with the object of art in terms of its own material individuality – the thing itself.

Two criteria are important if such an attempt is to be made. First, the considerations should be concrete (deal with the facts of the thing itself). Second, they should be simplificatory (provide an intellectually economic structure for the group of facts obtained). The latter is necessary because description alone can never adequately locate things. In fact, it very often confers upon them an enigmatic position. Nonetheless it offers more interesting possibilities than the impressionistic, historic, or

WHEN AN ARTIST USES A CONCEPTUAL FORM OF ART, IT MEANS THAT ALL OF THE PLANNING AND DECISIONS ARE MADE BEFOREHAND AND THE EXECUTION IS A PERFUNCTORY AFFAIR. THE IDEA BECOMES A MACHINE THAT MAKES THE ART. THIS KIND OF ART IS NOT THEORETICAL OR ILLUSTRATIVE OF THEORIES; IT IS INTUITIVE, IT IS INVOLVED WITH ALL TYPES OF MENTAL PROCESSES AND IT IS PURPOSELESS. IT IS USUALLY FREE FROM THE DEPENDENCE ON THE SKILL OF THE ARTIST AS A CRAFTSMAN. IT IS THE OBJECTIVE OF THE ARTIST WHO IS CONCERNED WITH CONCEPTUAL ART TO MAKE HIS WORK MENTALLY INTERESTING TO THE SPECTATOR, AND THEREFORE USUALLY HE WOULD WANT IT TO BECOME EMOTIONALLY DRY. THERE IS NO REASON TO SUPPOSE, HOWEVER, THAT THE CONCEPTUAL ARTIST IS OUT TO BORE THE VIEWER. IT IS ONLY THE EXPECTATION OF AN EMOTIONAL KICK, TO WHICH ONE CONDITIONED TO EXPRESSIONIST ART IS ACCUSTOMED, THAT WOULD

DETER THE VIEWER FROM PERCEIVING THIS ART.

Sol LEWITT, 'Paragraphs on Conceptual Art', *Artforum*, Summer 1967 metaphoric approach.

Everything that exists is three-dimensional and 'takes up' space (space considered as the medium in which the observer lives and moves). Art objects are qualitatively different from natural life yet are coextensive with it. This 'intrusion factor' is the basis of the *unnaturalness* of all art.

The above is relevant to an examination of certain art being done today. This work cannot be discussed on either stylistic or metaphoric grounds. What it can be said to have in common, though, is a heightened artificiality because of the clearly visible and simply ordered structure it uses. For some artists order itself is the work of art. Others manipulate order on different levels creating both conceptual and perceptual logic. These different kinds of order and the way in which resultant works of art exist in their environments are what I would like to examine.

Carl Andre works within a strict, self-imposed modular system. He uses convenient, commercially available objects like bricks, Styrofoam planks, ceramic magnets, cement blocks, wooden beams. Their common denominators are density, rigidity, opacity, uniformity of composition, and roughly geometric shape. A number of *a priori* decisions govern his various pieces. One and only one kind of object is used in each. Individual pieces are specifically conceived for the conditions of the place in which they are to occur. The arrangement of the designated units is made on an orthogonal grid by use of simple arithmetic means. (The word 'arrangement' is preferable to 'composition'. 'Composition' usually means the adjustment of the parts, i.e. their size, shape, colour, or placement, to arrive at the finished work, whose exact nature is not known beforehand. 'Arrangement' implies the fixed nature of the parts and a preconceived notion of the whole.) The principal means of cohesion in Andre's pieces is weight (gravity), the results of another *a priori*: no use of adhesives or complicated joints. This necessitates their appearance on the floor in horizontal configurations, like rows or slabs. Although earlier pieces made of Styrofoam planks are large and space consuming (a principal quality of Styrofoam being its 'bloatedness'), recently Andre's work has tended to be more unassuming. Height is a negligible dimension in these recent pieces, probably partly because of the instability of unadhered stacks. At any rate this causes the pieces to exist below the observer's eye-level. They are made to be 'looked down upon', impinging very slightly on common space. It is, however, just this persistent slightness that is essentially unavoidable and their bald matter-of-factness that makes them in a multiple sense *present*.

Artists like Andre are further differentiated (as all artists are) by their individual methodology, which in relation to the methodology of the past can only be termed systematic. Systematic thinking has generally been considered the antithesis of artistic thinking. Systems are characterized by regularity, thoroughness, and repetition in execution. They are methodical. It is their consistency and the continuity of application that characterizes them. Individual parts of a system are not in themselves important but are relevant only in the way they are used in the enclosed logic of the whole.

One of the first artists to make use of a basically progressional procedure was Dan Flavin. A salient example of this is his 1964 *Nominal Three – To Wm. of Ockham*. ('Posit no more entities than are necessary'. – William of Ockham.) The simple series involved can be graphically visualized as (1 + [1 + 1] + [1 + 1 + 1]).

Flavin, however, is difficult to come to terms with in even a quasi-objective discussion. For, although his placement of fluorescent lamps parallel and adjacent to one another in varying numbers of sizes is 'flat-footed' and obvious, the results are anything but. It is just these 'brilliant' results that confound and compound the difficulties [...]

For the solipsist reality is not enough. He denies the existence of anything outside the self-enclosed confines of his own mind. (Sartre refers to solipsism as 'the reef', for it 'amounts to saying that outside me nothing exists'. Schopenhauer speaks of the solipsist as 'a madman shut up in an impregnable blockhouse'.) Viewed within the boundaries of thought, the random dimensions of reality lose their qualities of extension. They become flat and static. Serial art in its highly abstract and ordered manipulation of thought is likewise self-contained and nonreferential. Such diverse artists as Edward Muybridge, Jasper Johns, Larry Poons, Sol LeWitt, Don Judd, Jo Baer, Robert Smithson, Hanne Darbroven, Dorothea Rockburne, Ed Ruscha, Eva Hess, Paul Mogensen, Dan Graham, Alfred Jensen, William Kolakoski, and myself have used serial methodology. Seriality is premised on the idea that the succession of terms (divisions) within a single work is based on a numerical or otherwise predetermined derivation (progression, permutation, rotation, reversal) from one or more of the preceding terms in that piece. Furthermore the idea is carried out to its logical conclusion, which, without adjustments based on taste or chance, is the work. No stylistic or material qualities unite the artists using this approach because what form the work takes is unimportant (some of these artists have ceased to make 'things'). The only artistic parallel to this procedure would be in music. J.S. Bach's *Art of the Fugue* or works by Schoenberg, Stochhausen, and Boulez exhibit similar ideas about how works of art can be made based on the application of rigorous governing logics rather than on personal decision making.

Sol LeWitt's serial work takes a particularly flat, nonemphatic position. His complex, multipart structures are the consequence of a rigid system of logic that excludes individual personality factors as much as possible. As a system it services to enforce the boundaries of his work as 'things-in-the-world' separate from both maker and observer.

LeWitt's recent West Coast exhibition (one-quarter of the proposal he exhibited at the Dwan Gallery, New York City, 'Scale Models' exhibition) is an interesting example of seriality. First, a governing set of decisions are made. The first cause is an open frame square placed on the floor in the center of a larger square, ration 1:9, which in extension becomes a cube within a cube, ration 1:27. The next limitation that is made are the three height variables:

1) LOW – the height of the cross-section of the bar of which the entire ensemble is constructed.

2) MEDIUM – the height of one cube (arbitrary).

3) HIGH – three times the height of 2).

Then the variable combinations of open frame and/or closed volume are considered in the four binomial possibilities: open inside – open outside; open inside – closed outside; closed inside – open outside; close inside – closed outside. No mathematics are involved in operations like these. Happily there seems to be little or not connection between art and mathematics. When numbers are used it is generally as convenient regulating device, a logic external to both the time and place of application.

When one encounters a LeWitt, although an order is immediately intuited, how to apprehend or penetrate it is nowhere revealed. Instead one is overwhelmed with a mass of data – lines, joints, angles. By controlling so rigidly the conception of the work and never adjusting it to any predetermined ideas of how a work of art should look, LeWitt arrives at a unique perceptual breakdown of conceptual order into visual chaos. The pieces situate in centers usurping most of the common space, yet their total volume (the volume of the bar itself) is negligible. Their immediate presence in reality as separate and unrelated things is asserted by the demand that we go around them. What is most remarkable is that they are seen moment to moment spatially (due to a mental tabulation of the entirety of other views), yet do not cease at every moment to be flat.

Some may say, and justifiably, that there is a 'poetry' or 'power' or some other quality to this work that an approach like the above misses. But aspects like those exist for individuals and are difficult to communicate using conventional meanings for words. Others may claim that given this they are still bored. If this is the case, their boredom may be the product of being forced to view things not as sacred but as they probably are – autonomous and indifferent.

Mel Bochner, 'Serial Art, Systems, Solipsism', *Arts Magazine* (Summer 1967); reprinted in Gregory Battcock (ed.), *Minimal Art: A Critical Anthology*, (Berkeley and Los Angeles: University of California Press, 1968) 92-102.

Sol LEWITT
Paragraphs on Conceptual Art [1967]

The editor has written me that he is in favour of avoiding 'the notion that the artist is a kind of ape that has to be explained by the civilized critic'. This should be good news to both artists and apes. With this assurance I hope to justify his confidence. To continue a baseball metaphor (one artist wanted to hit the ball out of the park, another to stay loose at the plate and hit the ball where it was pitched), I am grateful for the opportunity to strike out for myself.

I will refer to the kind of art in which I am involved as conceptual art. In conceptual art the idea of concept is the most important aspect of the work.[1] When an artist uses a conceptual form of art, it means that all of the planning and decisions are made beforehand and the execution is a perfunctory affair. The idea becomes a machine that makes the art. This kind of art is not theoretical or illustrative of theories; it is intuitive, it is involved with all types of mental processes and it is purposeless. It is usually free from the dependence on the skill of the artist as a craftsman. It is the objective of the artist who is concerned with conceptual art to make his work mentally interesting to the spectator, and therefore usually he would want it to become emotionally dry. There is no reason to suppose, however, that the conceptual artist is out to bore the viewer. It is only the expectation of an emotional kick, to which one conditioned to expressionist art is accustomed, that would deter the viewer from perceiving this art.

Conceptual art is not necessarily logical. The logic may be used to camouflage the real intent of the artist, to lull the viewer into the belief that he understands the work, or to infer a paradoxical situation (such as logic vs. illogic).[2] The ideas need not be complex. Most ideas that are successful are ludicrously simple. Successful ideas generally have the appearance of simplicity because they seem inevitable. In terms of idea the artist is free to even surprise himself. Ideas are discovered by intuition.

What the work of art looks like isn't too important. It has to look like something if it has physical form. No matter what form it may finally have it must begin with an idea. It is the process of conception and realization with which the artist is concerned. Once given physical reality by the artist the work is open to the perception of all, including the artist. (I use the word 'perception' to mean the apprehension of the sense data, the objective understanding of the idea and simultaneously a subjective interpretation of both.) The work of art can only be perceived after it is completed.

Art that is meant for the sensation of the eye primarily would be called perceptual rather than conceptual. This would include most optical, kinetic, light and colour art.

Since the functions of conception and perception are contradictory (one pre-, the other post-fact) the artist would mitigate his idea by applying subjective judgement to it. If the artist wishes to explore his idea thoroughly, then arbitrary or chance decisions would be kept to a minimum, while caprice, taste and other whimsies would be eliminated from the making of the art. The work does not necessarily have to be rejected if it does not look well. Sometimes what is initially thought to be awkward will eventually be visually pleasing.

To work with a plan that is pre-set is one way of avoiding subjectivity. It also obviates the necessity of designing each work in turn The plan would design the work. Some plans would require millions of variations, and some a limited number, but both are finite. Other plans imply infinity. In each case, however, the artist would select the basic form and rules that would govern the solution of the problem. After that the fewer decisions made in the course of completing the work, the better, This eliminates the arbitrary, the capricious and the subjective as much as possible. That is the reason for using this method.

When an artist uses a multiple modular method he usually chooses a simple and readily available form. The form itself is of very limited importance; it becomes the grammar for the total work. In fact it is best that the basic unity be deliberately uninteresting so that it may more easily become an intrinsic part of the entire work. Using complex basic forms only disrupts the unity of the whole. Using a simple form repeatedly narrows the field of the work and concentrates the intensity to the arrangement of the form. This arrangement becomes the end while the form becomes the means.

Conceptual art doesn't really have much to do with mathematics, philosophy or any other mental discipline. The mathematics used by most artists is simple arithmetic or simple number systems. The philosophy of the work is implicit in the work and is not an illustration of any system of philosophy.

It doesn't really matter if the viewer understands the concepts of the artist by seeing the art. Once out of his hand the artist has no control over the way a viewer will perceive the work. Different people will understand the same thing in a different way.

Recently there has been much written about minimal art, but I have not discovered anyone who admits to doing this kind of thing. There are other art forms around called primary structures, reductive, rejective, cool and mini-art. No artist I know will own up to any of these either. Therefore I conclude that it is part of a secret language that art critics use when communicating with each other through the medium of art magazines. Mini-art is best because it reminds one of the mini-skirts and long-legged girls. It must refer to very small works of art. This is a very good idea. Perhaps 'mini-art' shows could be sent around the country in matchboxes. Or maybe the mini-artist is a very small person, say under five feet tall. If so, much good work will be found in the primary schools (primary school primary structures).

If the artist carries through his idea and makes it into visible form, then all the steps in the process are of importance. The idea itself, even if not made visual, is as much a work of art as any finished product. All intervening steps – scribbles, sketches, drawings, failed work, models, studies, thought, conversations – are of interest. Those that show the thought process of the artist are sometimes more interesting than the final product.

Determining what size a piece should be is difficult. If an idea requires three dimensions then it would seem any size would so. The question would be what size is best. If the thing were made gigantic then the size alone would be impressive and the idea may be lost entirely. Again, if it is too small, it may become inconsequential. The height of the viewer may have some bearing on the work and also the size of the space into which it will be placed. The artist may wish to place objects higher than the eye level of the viewer, or lower. I think the piece must be large enough to give the viewer whatever information he needs to understand the work and placed in such a way that will facilitate this understanding. (Unless the idea is of impediment and requires difficulty of vision or access.)

Space can be thought of as the cubic area occupied by a three-dimensional volume. Any volume would occupy space. It is air and cannot be seen. It is the interval between things that can be measured. The intervals and measurements can be important to a work of art. If certain distances are important they will be made obvious in the piece. If space is relatively unimportant it can be regularized and made equal (things placed equal distances apart), to mitigate any interest in interval. Regular space might also become a metric time element, a kind of regular beat or pulse. When the interval is kept regular whatever is irregular gains more importance.

Architecture and three-dimensional art are of completely opposite natures. The former is concerned with making an area with a specific function. Architecture, whether it is a work of art or not, must be utilitarian or else fail completely. Art is not utilitarian. When three-dimensional art starts to take on some of the characteristics of architecture such as forming utilitarian areas it weakens its function as art. When the viewer is dwarfed by the large size of a piece this domination emphasizes the physical and emotive power of the form at the expense of losing the idea of the piece.

New materials are one of the great afflictions of contemporary art. Some artists confuse new materials with new ideas, There is nothing worse than seeing art that wallows in gaudy baubles. By and large most artists who are attracted to these materials are the ones that lack the stringency of mind that would enable them to use the materials well. It tales a good artist to use new materials and make them into a work of art. The danger is, I think, in making the physicality of the material so important that it becomes the idea of the work (another kind of expressionism).

Three-dimensional art of any kind is a physical fact. This physicality is its most obvious and expressive content. Conceptual art is made to engage the mind of the viewer rather than his eye or emotions. The physicality of a three-dimensional object then becomes a contradiction to its non-emotive intent. Colour, surface, texture and shape only emphasize the physical aspects of the work. Anything that calls attention to and interests the viewer in this physicality is a deterrent to our understanding of the idea and is used as an expressive device. The conceptual artist would want to ameliorate this emphasis on materiality as much as possible or to use it in a paradoxical way. (To convert it into an idea.) This kind of art, then, should be stated with the most economy of means. Any idea that is better stated in two dimensions should not be in three dimensions. Ideas may also be stated with numbers, photographs, or words or any way the artist chooses, the form being unimportant.

These paragraphs are not intended as categorical imperatives but the ideas stated are as close as possible to my thinking at this time. These ideas are the results of my work as an artist and are subject to change as my experience changes.[3] I have tried to state them with as much clarity as possible. If the statements I made are unclear it may mean the thinking is unclear. Even while writing these ideas there seemed to be obvious inconsistencies (which I have tried to correct, but others will probably slip by). I do not advocate a conceptual form of art for all artists. I have found that it has worked well for me while other ways have not. It is one way of making art; other ways suit other artists. Nor do I think all conceptual art merits the viewer's attention. Conceptual art is only good when the idea is good.

1 In other forms of art the concept may be changed in the process of execution.

2 Some ideas are logical in conception and illogical perceptually.

3 I dislike the term 'work of art' because I am not in favour of work and the term sounds pretentious. But I don't know what other term to use.

Sol LeWitt, 'Paragraphs on Conceptual Art', *Artforum*, 5:10 (Summer 1967) 79-84; reprinted in Alexander Alberro; Blake Stimson (eds.) *Conceptual Art: a Critical Anthology* (Cambridge, Massachusetts: MIT Press, 1999) 12-16.

Jack BURNHAM
Systems Aesthetics [1968]

A polarity is presently developing between the finite, unique work of high art, i.e., painting or sculpture, and conceptions which can loosely be termed 'unobjects', these being either environments or artifacts which resist prevailing critical analysis. This includes works by some primary sculptors (though some may reject the charge of creating environments), some gallery kinetic and luminous art, some outdoor works, happenings, and mixed media presentations. Looming below the surface of this dichotomy is a sense of radical evolution which seems to run counter to the waning revolution of abstract and non-objective art. The evolution embraces a series of absolutely logical and incremental changes, wholly devoid of the fevered iconoclasm which accompanied the heroic period from 1907 to 1925. As yet the evolving aesthetic has no critical vocabulary so necessary for its defence, nor for that matter a name or explicit cause.

In a way this situation might be likened to the 'morphological development' of a prime scientific concept – as described by Thomas Kuhn in *The Structure of Scientific Revolutions* (1962). Kuhn sees science at any given period dominated by a single 'major paradigm'; that is, a scientific conception of the natural order so pervasive and intellectually powerful that it dominates all ensuing scientific discovery. Inconsistent facts arising through experimentation are invariably labelled as bogus or trivial – until the emergence of a new and more encompassing general theory. Transition between major paradigms may best express the state of present art. Reasons for it lie in the nature of current technological shifts.

The economist J.K. Galbraith has rightly insisted that until recently the needs of the modern industrial state were never served by complete expression of the aesthetic impulse. Power and expansion were its primary aims.

Special attention should be paid to Galbraith's observation. As an arbiter of impending socio-technical changes his position is pivotal. For the Left he represents America's most articulate apologist for Monopoly Capitalism; for the Right he is the socialist *éminence grise* of the Democratic Party. In *The New Industrial State* (1967) he challenges both Marxist orthodoxies and American mythologies premised upon *laissez-faire* Capitalism. For them he substitutes an incipient technocracy shaped by the evolving technostructure. Such a drift away from ideology has been anticipated for at least fifty years. Already in California think-tanks and in the central planning committees of each soviet, futurologists are concentrating on the role of the technocracy, i.e., its decision-making autonomy, how it handles the central storage of information, and the techniques used for smoothly implementing social change. In the automated state power resides less in the control of the traditional symbols of wealth than in information.

In the emergent 'superscientific culture' long-range decision making and its implementation become more difficult and more necessary. Judgment demands precise socio-technical models. Earlier the industrial state evolved by filling consumer needs on a piecemeal basis. The kind of product design that once produced 'better living' precipitates vast crises in human ecology in the 1960s. A striking parallel exists between the 'new' car of the automobile stylist and the syndrome of formalist invention in art, where 'discoveries' are made through visual manipulation. Increasingly 'products' – either in art or life – become irrelevant and a different set of needs arise: these revolve around such concerns as maintaining the biological livability of the Earth, producing more accurate models of social interaction, understanding the growing symbiosis in man-machine relationships, establishing priorities for the usage and conservation of natural resources, and defining alternate patterns of education, productivity and leisure. In the past our technologically-conceived artifacts structured living patterns. We are now in transition from an *object-oriented* to a *systems-oriented culture*. Here change emanates, not from *things*, but from *the way things are done*.

The priorities of the present age revolve around the problems of organization. A systems viewpoint is focused on the creation of stable, on-going relationships between organic and non-organic systems, be these neighbourhoods, industrial complexes, farms, transportation systems, information centres, recreation centres, or any of the other matrixes of human activity. All living situations must be treated in the context of a systems hierarchy of values. Intuitively many artists have already grasped these relatively recent distinctions, and if their 'environments' are on the unsophisticated side, this will change with time and experience.

The major tool for professionally defining these concerns is systems analysis. This is best known through its usage by the Pentagon and has more to do with the expense and complexity of modern warfare than with any innate relation between the two. Systems analysts are not cold-blooded logicians; the best have an ever-expanding grasp of human needs and limitations. One of the pioneers of systems applications, E.S. Quade, has stated that 'Systems analysis, particularly the type required for military decisions, is still largely a form of art. Art can be taught in part, but not by the means of fixed rules ... '[1] Thus 'The Further Dimensions'[2] elaborated upon by Galbraith in his book are aesthetic criteria. Where for some these become the means for tidying up a derelict technology, for Galbraith aesthetic decision-making becomes an integral part of any future technocracy. As yet few governments fully appreciate that the alternative is biological self-destruction.

Situated between aggressive electronic media and two hundred years of industrial vandalism, the long held idea that a tiny output of art objects could somehow 'beautify' or even significantly modify the environment was naïve. A parallel illusion existed in that artistic influence prevails by a psychic osmosis given off by such objects. Accordingly lip service to public beauty remains the province of well-guarded museums. Though the early stages of industrialism it remained possible for decorative media, including painting and sculpture, to embody the aesthetic impulse; but as technology progresses this impulse must identify itself with the means of research and production. Obviously nothing could be less true for the present situation. In a society thus estranged only the didactic function of art continues to have meaning. The artist operates as a quasipolitical *provocateur*, though in no concrete sense is he an ideologist or a moralist. 'L'art pour l'art' and a century's resistance to the vulgarities of moral uplift have insured that.

The specific function of modern didactic art has been to show that art does not reside in material entities, but in relations between people and between people and the components of their environment. This accounts for the radicality of Duchamp and his enduring influence. It throws light on Picasso's lesser position as a seminal force. As with all succeeding formalist art, Cubism followed the tradition of circumscribing art value wholly within finite objects.

In an advanced technological culture the most important artist best succeeds by liquidating his position as artist vis-à-vis society. Artistic nihilism established itself through this condition. At the outset the artist refused to participate in idealism through craft. 'Craft-fetishism,'[3] as termed by the critic Christopher Caudwell, remains the basis of modern formalism. Instead the significant artist strives to reduce the technical and psychical distance between his artistic output and the productive means of society. Duchamp, Warhol and Robert Morris are similarly directed in this respect. Gradually this strategy transforms artistic and technological decision-making into a single activity – at least it presents that alternative in inescapable terms. Scientists and technicians are not converted into 'artists', rather the artist becomes a symptom of the schism between art and technics. Progressively the need to make ultrasensitive judgments as to the uses of technology and scientific information becomes 'art' in the most literal sense.

As yet the implication that art contains survival value is nearly as suspect as attaching any moral significance to it. Though with the demise of literary content, the theory that art is a form of psychic preparedness has gained articulate supporters.

'Art, as an adaptive mechanism, is reinforcement of the ability to be aware of the disparity between behavioural pattern and the demands consequent upon the interaction with the environment. Art is rehearsal for those real situations in which it is vital for our survival to endure cognitive tension, to refuse the comforts of validation by affective congruence when such validation is inappropriate because too vital interests are at stake...'[4]

The post-formalist sensibility naturally responds to stimuli both within and outside the proposed art format. To this extent some of it does begin to resemble 'theatre', as imputed by Michael Fried. More likely though, the label of 'theatricality' is a red herring disguising the real nature of the shift in priorities. In respect to Mr. Fried's argument,[5] the theatre was never a purist medium, but a conglomerate of arts. In itself this never prevented the theatre from achieving 'high art'. For clearer reading, rather than maintaining Mr. Fried's adjectives, 'theatrical' or 'literalist' art, or the phrase used until now in this essay, 'post-formalist aesthetic', the term *systems aesthetic* seems to encompass the present situation more fully.

The systems approach goes beyond a concern with staged environments and happenings; it deals in a revolutionary fashion with the larger problem of boundary concepts. In systems perspective there are no contrived confines such as the theatre proscenium or picture frame. Conceptual focus rather than material limits define the system. Thus any situation, either in or outside the context of art, may be designed and judged as a system. In as much as a system may contain people, ideas, messages, atmospheric conditions, power sources, etc., a system is, to quote the systems biologist, Ludwig von Bertalanffy, a 'complex of components in interaction',[6] comprised of material, energy and information in various degrees of organization. In evaluating systems the artist is a perspectivist considering goals, boundaries, structure, input, output and related activity inside and outside the system. Where the object almost always has a fixed shape and boundaries, the consistency of a system may be altered in time and space, its behaviour determined both by external conditions and its mechanisms of control.

5. Moholy-Nagy

In his book, *The New Vision*, Moholy-Nagy described fabricating a set of enamel on metal paintings. These were executed by telephoning precise instructions to a manufacturer. An elaboration of this was projected recently by the director of the Museum of Contemporary Art in Chicago, Jan van der Marck, in a tentative exhibition, 'Art by Telephone'. In this instance the recorded conversation between artist and manufacturer was to *become part of the displayed work of art*. For systems, information, in whatever form conveyed, becomes a viable aesthetic consideration.

Fifteen years ago Victor Vasarely suggested mass art as a legitimate function of industrial society. For angry critics there existed the fear of undermining art's fetish aura, of shattering the mystique of craft and private creation. If some forays have been made into serially produced art, these remain on the periphery of the industrial system. Yet the entire phenomenon of reproducing an art object *ad infinitum* is absurd; rather than making quality available to a large number of people, it signals the end of concrete objects embodying visual metaphor. Such demythification is the Kantian Imperative applied aesthetically. On the other hand, a systems aesthetic *is* literal in that all phases of the life cycle of a system are relevant. There is no end product which is primarily visual, nor does such an aesthetic rely on a 'visual' syntax. It resists functioning as an applied aesthetic, but is revealed in the principles underlying the progressive reorganization of the natural environment.

Various postures implicit in formalist art were consistently attacked in the later writings of Ad Reinhardt. His black paintings were hardly rhetorical devices (nor were his writings) masking Zen obscurities; rather they were the means of discarding formalist mannerism and all the latent illusionism connected with post-realistic art. His own contribution he described as:

'The one work for the fine artist, the one painting, is the painting of the one-sized canvas ... The single theme, one formal device, one colour-monochrome, one linear division in each direction, one symmetry, one texture, one free-hand brushing, one rhythm, one working everything into dissolution and one indivisibility, each painting into one overall uniformity and non-irregularity.'[7]

Even before the emergence of the anti-formalist 'specific object' there appeared an oblique type of criticism, resisting emotive and literary associations. Pioneered between 1962 and 1965 in the writings of Donald Judd, it resembles what a computer programmer would call an entity's 'list structure', or all the enumerated properties needed to rebuild an object *physically*. Earlier the phenomenologist Maurice Merleau-Ponty asserted the impossibility of *conceptually* reconstructing an object from such a procedure. Modified to include a number of perceptual insights not included in a 'list structure', such a technique has been used to real advantage by the anti-novelist, Alain Robbe-Grillet. A web of sensorial descriptions is spun around the central images of a plot. The point is not to internalize scrutiny in the Freudian sense, but to infer the essence of a situation through detailed examination of surface effects. Similar attitudes were adopted by Judd for the purpose of critical examination. More than simply an art object's list structure, Judd included phenomenal qualities which would never have shown up in a fabricator's plans, but which proved necessary for the 'seeing' of the object. This cleared the air of much criticism centred on meaning and private intention.

It would be misleading to interpret Judd's concept of 'specific objects' as the embodiment of a systems aesthetic. Rather object art has become a stage towards further rationalization of the aesthetic process in general – both by reducing the iconic content of art objects and by Judd's candidness about their conceptual origins. However, even in 1965 he gave indications of looking beyond these finite limits.

'A few of the more general aspects may persist, such as the work's being like an object or even being specific, but other characteristics are bound to develop. Since its range is wide, three-dimensional work will probably divide into a number of forms. At any rate, it will be larger than painting and much larger than sculpture, which, compared to painting, is fairly particular ... Because the nature of three dimension isn't set, given beforehand, something credible can be made, almost anything.'[8]

In the 1966 '68th American Show' at the Chicago Art Institute, the sculptor Robert Morris was represented by two large, L-shaped forms which were shown the previous year in New York. Morris sent plans of the pieces to the carpenters at the Chicago museum where they were assembled for less than the cost of shipping the originals from New York. In the context of a systems aesthetic possession of a privately fabricated work is no longer important. Accurate information takes priority over history and geographical location.

Morris was the first essayist to describe precisely the relation between sculpture style and the progressively more sophisticated use of industry by artists. He has lately focused upon material-forming techniques and the arrangement of these results so that they no longer form specific objects but remain uncomposed. In such handling of materials the idea of *process* takes precedence over end results: 'Disengagement with preconceived enduring forms and orders of things is a positive assertion.'[9] Such loose assemblies of materials encompass concerns that resemble the cycles of industrial processing. Here the traditional priority of end results over technique breaks down; in a systems context both may share equal importance, remaining essential parts of the aesthetic.

Already Morris has proposed systems which move beyond the confines of the minimal object. One work proposed to the City of New York last fall was later included in Willoughby Sharp's 'Air Art' show in a Y.M.H.A. gallery in Philadelphia. In its first state Morris' piece involved capturing steam from the pipes in the city streets, projecting this from nozzles on a platform. In Philadelphia such a system took its energy from the steam bath room. Since 1966 Morris' interests have included designs for low relief earth sculptures consisting of abutments, hedges and sodden mounds, visible from the air and not unlike Indian burial mounds. 'Transporting' one of these would be a matter of cutting and filling earth and resodding. Morris is presently at work on one such project and unlike past sculptural concerns, it involves precise information from surveyors, landscape gardeners, civil engineering contractors and geologists. In the older context, such as Isamu Noguchi's sunken garden at Yale University's Rare Book Library, sculpture defined the environment, with Morris' approach the environment defines what is sculptural.

More radical for the gallery are the constructions of Carl Andre. His assemblies of modular, unattached forms stand out from the works of artists who have comprised unit assembly with the totality of fixed objects. The mundane origins of Andre's units are not 'hidden' within the art work as in the technique of collage. Andre's floor reliefs are architectural modifications – though they are not subliminal since they visually disengage from their surroundings. One of Andre's subtler shows took place in New York last year. The viewer was encouraged to walk stocking-footed across three areas, each 12 by 12 feet and composed of 144 one-foot-square metal plates. One was not only invited to see each of these 'rugs' as a grid arrangement in various metals, but each metal grid's thermal conductivity was registered through the soles of the feet. Sight analysis diminishes in importance for some of the best new work; the other senses and especially kinaesthesis makes 'viewing' a more integrated experience.

The scope of a systems aesthetic presumes that problems cannot be solved by a single technical solution, but must be attacked on a multileveled, interdisciplinary basis. Consequently some of the more aware sculptors no longer think like sculptors, but they assume a span of problems more natural to architects, urban planners, civil engineers, electronic technicians and cultural anthropologists. This is not as pretentious as some critics have insisted. It is a legitimate extension of McLuhan's remark about Pop art when he said that it was an announcement that the entire environment was ready to become a work of art.

As a direct descendant of the 'found object', Robert Smithson's identifying mammoth engineering projects as works of art ('Site-Selections')[10] makes eminent sense. Refocusing the aesthetic away from the preciousness of the work of art is in the present age no less than a survival mechanism. If Smithson's 'Site-Selections' are didactic exercises, they show a desperate need for environmental sensibility on a larger than room scale. Sigfried Giedion pointed to specific engineering feats as *objets d'art* thirty years ago. Smithson has transcended this by putting engineering works into their natural settings and treating the whole as a time-bound web of man-nature interactions [...]

The components of systems – whether these are artistic or functional – have no higher meaning or value. Systems components derive their value solely through their assigned context. Therefore it would be impossible to regard a fragment of an art system as a work of art in itself – as say, one might treasure a fragment of one of the Parthenon friezes. This became evident in December 1967 when Dan Flavin designed six walls with the same alternate pattern of 'rose' and 'gold' 8-foot fluorescent lamps. This 'Broad Bright Gaudy Vulgar System', as Flavin called it, was installed in the new Museum of Contemporary Art in Chicago. The catalogue accompanying the exhibition scrupulously resolves some of the important aesthetic implications for modular systems.

'The components of a particular exhibition upon its termination are replaced in another situation. Perhaps put into non-art as part of a different whole in a different future. Individual units possess no intrinsic significance beyond their concrete utility. It is difficult either to project into them extraneous qualities, a spurious insight, or for them to be appropriated for fulfilment or personal inner needs. The lights are transformed. There are no symbolic transcendental redeeming or monitary added values present.'[11] [...]

Formalist art embodies the idea of deterministic relations between a composition's visible elements. But since the early 1960s Hans Haacke has depended upon the invisible components of systems. In a systems context, invisibility, or invisible parts, share equal importance with things seen. Thus air, water, steam and ice have become major elements in his work. On both coasts this has precipitated interest in 'invisible art' among a number of young artists. Some of the best of Haacke's efforts are shown outside the gallery. These include his *Rain Tree*, a tree dripping patterns of water; *Sky Line*, a nylon line kept aloft by hundreds of helium filled white balloons; a weather balloon balanced over a jet of air; and a large-scale nylon tent with air pockets designed to remain in balance one foot off the ground.

Haacke's systems have a limited life as an art experience, though some are quite durable. He insists that the need for empathy does not make his work function as with older art. Systems exist as on-going independent entities away from the viewer. In the systems hierarchy of control, *interaction* and *autonomy* become desirable values. In this respect Haacke's *Photo-Electric Viewer Programmed Co-ordinate System* is probably one of the most elegant responsive environments made to date *by an artist* (certainly more sophisticated ones have been conceived for scientific and technical purposes). Boundary situations are central to his thinking.

'A "sculpture" that physically reacts to its environment is no longer to be regarded as an object. The range of outside factors affecting it, as well as its own radius of action, reach beyond the space it materially occupies. It thus merges with the environment in a relationship that is better understood as a "system" of interdependent processes. These processes evolve without the viewer's empathy. He becomes a witness. A system is not imagined, it is real.'[12]

Tangential to this systems approach is Allan Kaprow's very unique concept of the Happening. In the past ten years Kaprow has moved the Happening from a rather self-conscious and stagy event to a strict and elegant procedure. The Happening now has a sense of internal logic which was lacking before. It seems to arise naturally from those same considerations which have crystalized the systems approach to environmental situations. As described by their chief inventor, the Happenings establish an indivisibility between themselves and everyday affairs; they consciously avoid materials and procedures identified with art; they allow for geographical expansiveness and mobility; they include experience and duration as part of their aesthetic format; and they emphasize practical activities as the most meaningful mode of procedure.[13] As structured events the Happenings are usually reversible. Alterations in the environment may be 'erased' after the Happening, or as a part of the Happening's conclusion. While they may involve large areas of space, the format of the Happening is kept relatively simple, with the emphasis on establishing a participatory aesthetic.

The emergence of a 'post-formalist aesthetic' may seem to some to embody a kind of absolute philosophy, something which, through the nature of its concerns cannot be transcended. Yet it is more likely that a 'systems aesthetic' will become the dominant approach to a maze of socio-technical conditions rooted only in the present. New circumstances will with time generate other major paradigms for the arts.

For some readers these pages will echo feelings of the past. It may be remembered that in the fall of 1920 an ideological schism ruptured two factions of the Moscow Constructivists. The radical Marxists, led by Vladimir Tatlin, proclaimed their rejection of art's false idealisms. Establishing themselves as 'Productivists', one of their slogans became: 'Down with guarding the traditions of art. Long live the constructivist technician.'[14] As a group dedicated to historical materialism and the scientific ethos, most of its members were quickly subsumed by the technological needs of Soviet Russia. As artists they ceased to exist. While the Productivist programme might have had some basis as a utilitarian aesthetic, it was crushed amid the Stalinist anti-intellectualism that followed.

The reasons are almost self-apparent. Industrially underdeveloped, food and heavy industry remained the prime needs of the Soviet Union for the next forty years. Conditions and structural interdependencies which naturally develop in an advanced industrial state were then only latent. In retrospect it is doubtful if any group of artists had either the knowledge or political strength to meaningfully affect Soviet industrial policies. What emerged was another vein of formalist innovation based on scientific idealism; this manifested itself in the West under the leadership of the Constructivist emigres, Gabo and Pevsner.

But for our time the emerging major paradigm in art is neither an *ism* nor a collection of styles. Rather than a novel way of rearranging surfaces and spaces, it is fundamentally concerned with the implementation of the art impulse in an advanced technological society. As a culture producer, man has traditionally claimed the title, *Homo Faber: man the maker* (of tools and images). With continued advances in the industrial revolution, he assumes a new and more critical function. As *Homo Arbiter Formae* his prime role becomes that of *man the maker of aesthetic decisions*. These decisions – whether they are made concertedly or not – control the quality of all future life on the Earth. Moreover these are value judgments dictating the direction of technological endeavour. Quite plainly such a vision extends beyond political realities of the present. This cannot remain the case for long.

1 Quade, E. S. (November 1964), 'Methods and Procedures' in *Analysis for Military Decisions* (Santa Monica: The Rand Corp.), p. 153.

2 Galbraith, John Kenneth (1967), *The New Industrial State* (Boston: Houghton Mifflin Co.), pp. 343-353.

3 Caudwell, Christopher (pseud.) (1937), *Illusion and Reality: A Study of the Sources of Poetry* (London: MacMillan and Co.), p. 111.

4 Peckham, Morse (1965), *Man's Rage for Chaos: Biology, Behaviour & the Arts* (New York: Schocken Books, 1967),

p. 314.

5 Fried, Michael (Summer, 1967), 'Art and Objecthood', *Artforum*, p. 15.

6 Bertalanffy, Ludwig von (1967), *Robots, Men and Minds* (New York: George Braziller Inc.), p. 69.

7 Anonymous (September 1, 1967), 'Ad Reinhardt, Painter, Is Dead, Reduced Color to Bare Minimum' in *The New York Times*, p. 33.

8 Judd, Donald (1965), 'Specific Objects' in *Contemporary Sculpture* (New York: The Arts Digest, Inc.), p. 78.

9 Morris, Robert (April 1968), 'Anti Form', *Artforum*, p. 35.

10 Smithson, Robert (Summer 1967), 'Towards the Development of an Air Terminal Site', *Artforum*, pp. 36-40.

11 Flavin, Dan (with introduction by) (December 1967) *Dan Flavin: Pink and Gold*, exhibition catalogue (Chicago: The Museum of Contemporary Art).

12 Haacke, Hans (with statement by) (January 1968), *Hans Haacke*, exhibition catalogue (New York: Howard Wise Gallery).

13 Kaprow, Allen (March 1966), 'The Happenings are Dead - Long Live Happenings', *Artforum*, pp. 36-39.

14 Gabo, Naum (1957), *Gabo: Constructions, Sculptures, Paintings, Drawings, Engravings* (Cambridge: Harvard University Press), p. 153.

Jack Burnham, 'Systems Aesthetics', *Artforum*, 7:1, September 1968.

Lucy R. LIPPARD, John CHANDLER

The Dematerialization of Art

[1968]

During the 1960s, the anti-intellectual, emotional/intuitive processes of art-making characteristic of the last two decades have begun to give way to an ultra-conceptual art that emphasizes the thinking process almost exclusively. As more and more work is designed in the studio but executed elsewhere by professional craftsmen, as the object becomes merely the end product, a number of artists are losing interest in the physical evolution of the work of art. The studio is again becoming a study. Such a trend appears to be provoking a profound dematerialization of art, especially of art as object, and if it continues to prevail, it may result in the object's becoming wholly obsolete.

The visual arts at the moment seem to hover at a crossroad that may well turn out to be two roads to one place, though they appear to have come from two sources: art as idea and art as action. In the first case, matter is denied, as sensation has been converted into concept; in the second case, matter has been transformed into energy and time-motion. If the completely conceptual work of art in which the object is simply an epilogue to the fully evolved concept seems to exclude the *objet d'art*, so does the primitivizing strain of sensuous identification and envelopment in a work so expanded that it is inseparable from its non-art surroundings. Thus the extremely cool and rejective projects of Judd, LeWitt and others have a good deal in common with the less evolved but perhaps eventually more fertile synaesthetic ambitions of Robert Whitman, Robert Rauschenberg and Michael Kirby, or the dance of Yvonne Rainer and Alex Hay, among others. This fact is most clearly illustrated by the work of Robert Morris, who has dealt with idea as idea, idea as object, and idea as performance. In fact, the performance media are becoming a no-man's- or every-man's land in which visual artists whose styles may be completely at variance can meet and even agree. As the time element becomes a focal point for so many experiments in the visual arts, aspects of dance, film and music become likely adjuncts to painting and sculpture, which in turn are likely to be absorbed in unexpected ways by the performing arts.

Another possibility that permits a combination of art as idea and art as action is the use of a serial scheme, though the recent 'Art in Series' exhibition at the Finch College Museum of Art, organized by Mel Bochner, while a good show, indicated that only the most basic of tenets of serialism have so far been adapted to the plastic arts. Static by tradition, painting and sculpture have until lately lagged behind music, poetry and film in the use of serial methods.

Motion is the source of pattern-making, and it might seem that film rather than painting or sculpture would be the visual art most suited to the portrayal of motion and time. But paintings like those of Larry Poons and sculpture such as Sol LeWitt's offer successful means of presenting time-motion without anything actually moving (as, in another way, do Oldenburg's soft sculptures). They are like time exposures in photography, revealing time-space patterns that are invisible to someone seeing them in sequence alone. They are like chords in music, where the pattern is discovered in the vertical and simultaneous arrangements of the elements rather than horizontally and sequentially, as in melody. Thus these time exposures are double exposures or multiple exposures. LeWitt's serial projects are made up of parts which, though each part can be seen separately, as sculpture, and in sequence, can also be seen simultaneously as one thing. (One of LeWitt's influences, and also one of Duchamp's, was Muybridge.) However, the parts do sometimes call attention to themselves with the unfortunate results that the whole lacks the unity of a chord; it is in the mind, or in the working drawing that sketches all the possibilities, rather than in the eye, that the whole attains its completely realized simplicity and unity. A series is an appropriate vehicle for an ultra-conceptual art, since thinking is ratiocination, or discovering the fixed relations, ratios and proportions between things, in time as well as in space.

A highly conceptual art, like an extremely rejective art or an apparently random art, upsets detractors because there is 'not enough to look at', or rather not enough of what they are accustomed to looking *for*. Monotonal or extremely simple-looking painting and totally 'dumb' objects exist in time as well as in space because of two aspects of the viewing experience. First, they demand more participation by the viewer, despite their apparent hostility (which is not hostility so much as aloofness and self-containment). More time must be spent in immediate experience of a detail-less work, for the viewer is used to focusing on details and absorbing an impression of the piece with the help of these details. Secondly, the time spent looking at an 'empty' work, or one with a minimum of action, seems infinitely longer than action-and-detail-filled time. This time element is, of course, psychological, but it allows the artist an alternative to or extension of the serial method. Painter-sculptor Michael Snow's film *Wavelength*, for instance, is tortuously extended within its forty-five minute span. By the time the camera, zeroing in very slowly from the back of a large loft, reaches a series of windows and finally a photograph of water surface, or waves, between two of them, and by the time that photograph gradually fills the screen, the viewer is aware of an almost unbearable anticipation that seems the result of an equally unbearable length of time stretched out at less than normal rate of looking; the intensity is reinforced by the sound, which during most of the film is monotonal, moving up in pitch and up in volume until at the end it is a shrill hum, both exciting and painful [...]

Dematerialized art is post-aesthetic only in its increasingly nonvisual emphases. The aesthetic of principle is still an aesthetic, as implied by frequent statements by mathematicians and scientists about the beauty of an equation, formula, or solution: 'Why should an aesthetic criterion be so successful so often? Is it just that it satisfies physicists? I think there is only one answer – nature is inherently beautiful' (physicist Murray Gell-Mann); 'In this case, there was a moment when I knew how nature worked. It had elegance and beauty. The goddam thing was gleaming' (Nobel prizewinner Richard Feynman).[1] The more one reads these statements, the more apparent it becomes that the scientist's attempt to discover, perhaps even to impose order and structure on the universe, rests on assumptions that are essentially aesthetic. Order itself, and its implied simplicity and unity, are aesthetic criteria.

The disintegration [of art] Schillinger predicted is obviously implicit in the breakup since 1958 or so of traditional media, and in the introduction of electronics, light, sound, and, more important, performance attitudes into painting and sculpture – the so far unrealized intermedia revolution whose prophet is John Cage. It is also implied by the current international obsession with entropy. According to Wylie Sypher, for example: 'The future is that in which time becomes effective, and the mark of time is the increasing disorder towards which our system tends ... During the course of time, entropy increases. Time can be measured by the loss of structure in our system, its tendency to sink back into that original chaos from which it may have emerged ... One meaning of time is a drift towards inertia'.[2]

Today many artists are interested in an order that incorporates implications of disorder and chance, in a negation of actively ordering parts in favour of the presentation of a whole [...]

There is a decided element of humour in most of this work which is by no means to say that it is not serious; the best comedy is always serious art; one would completely misunderstand Aristophanes, Swift, Chaplin or Beckett if one assumed that they were not serious artists, just as one would misunderstand Democritus if one did not keep in mind that he was known as the 'laughing philosopher', or the cynic Menippus if one forgot that he was known as 'the secret dog who bites as he laughs' (*ridendo dicere verum*). The sort of humour these artists are concerned with is really wit, an Anglo-Saxon word that originally meant 'mind' or the powers of reasoning and thinking. One of its meanings is 'the mental faculties in their normal condition of sanity', as in 'to keep one's wits about him', and the word gradually came to designate 'the ability to make clever, ironic or satirical remarks usually by perceiving the incongruous and expressing it in a surprising or epigrammatic manner'.

Taking this literary parallel into consideration, it is not surprising that the main twentieth-century sources for a dematerialized art are found in Dada and Surrealism [...]

The danger, or fallacy, of an *ultra*-conceptual art is that is will be 'appreciated' for the wrong reasons, that it will, like Duchamp's *Bottle Rack* or *Large Glass*, come to be mainly an ingratiating object of aesthetic pleasure instead of the stringently metaphysical vehicle for an idea intended. The idea has to be awfully good to compete with the object, and few of the contemporary ideas ... are finally that good. Nevertheless, the 'thinness', both literal and allusive, of such themes as water, steam, dust, flatness, legibility, temporality, continues the process of ridding art of its object quality. Some of these artists hold that the idea is self-generating and self-conclusive, that building the sculpture or painting the painting is simply the traditional, expected step finally unnecessary to the aesthetic, but very little of their work is really conceptual to the point of excluding the concrete altogether. On the other hand, ideas like Oldenburg's trench or LeWitt's buried cube[3] are both tangible and intangible, simple and complex. They open up art to the intellect without delivering it into any other cultural or transcultural area. Visual art is still visual even when it is invisible or visionary. The shift of emphasis from art as product to art as idea has freed the artist from present limitations – both economic and technical. It may be that works of art that cannot be realized now because of lack of means will at some future date be made concrete. The artist as thinker can project a visionary and utopian art that is no less art than concrete works. Architecture provides many precedents for this kind of unmaterialized art; Wright's mile-high skyscraper is no less art for not having a concrete expression. Moreover, since dealers cannot sell art-as-idea, economic materialism is denied along with physical materialism.

Nonvisual must not be confused with nonvisible; the conceptual focus may be entirely hidden or unimportant to the success or failure of the work. The concept can determine the means of production without affecting the product itself; conceptual art need not communicate its concepts. The audience at a Cage concert or a Rainer dance performance will never know what the conceptual framework of the work is. At the other extreme is LeWitt's contention: 'Logic may be used to camouflage the real intent of the artist, to lull the viewer into the belief that he understands the work, or to infer a paradoxical situation (such as logic versus illogic). The ideas need not be complex. Most ideas that are successful are ludicrously simple. Successful ideas generally have the appearance of simplicity because they seem inevitable'.[4]

Thus the difficulty of abstract conceptual art lies not in the idea but in finding the means of expressing that idea so that it is immediately apparent to the spectator. In math or science, the simpler the explanation or formula, the more satisfying it seems to be, and to reduce the great complexity of the universe to a single simple equation or metaphor is the goal. Even the simple progression of 1, 2, 3, in Dan Flavin's 1964 fluorescent piece *the nominal three (to William of Okham)* or the 1, 2, 3, 4 of David Lee's dark hanging plexiglass panels at Finch, are enough to satisfy the initial demands of a rational art. Even the most apparently elaborate schemes, such as Larry Poon's multiple inversions, though they require more deliberation to detect, once found are only slightly more complicated than the simple ones. Perhaps this, or the 'camouflage' mentioned by LeWitt, is the reason for the popularity of hermetic motifs today. Hermeticism of one kind or another, manifested as enclosure or monotonality and near invisibility, as an incommunicative blank façade or as excessive duration, helps maintain the desired aloofness in a work confronted by the ordinary or suspiciously avid spectator, while at the same time it satisfies the artist's desire for difficulty and endears itself to the spectator willing to commit himself on a deeper meaning.

Much recent conceptual art is illustration in a sense, in the form of drawings or models for nearly impossible projects that will probably never be realized, or in many cases, need no further development. According to Joseph Kosuth: 'All I make are models. The actual works of art are ideas. Rather than "ideals", the models are a visual approximation of a particular art object I have in mind'.[5] Mel Bochner's contribution to the Finch serial show – *Sixteen Isomorphs* – is a model after the fact – a model for a piece already executed, and dismantled. Its sixteen modules are serial photographs of a project set up in small black blocks specifically to be photographed.

The interest in rough working drawings, which has become something of a fetish among Primary Structurists, is indicative of a sneaking nostalgia for a certain executionary *éclat* denied them in the work itself. On the other hand, Bochner's working drawing show at the School of Visual Arts last year [1967], consisting of five identical loose-leaf notebooks filled with Xerox copies of the 'exhibits' (including lists, notes, specifications for bills from fabricators, contributions by poets and architects) brought up another point: the concept of drawing as pseudo-painting was banished and drawing was brought back to its original function as a sketch or medium for working out ideas – visual or intuitive. Nevertheless, the emphasis on diagrams and projects, on models and working drawings rather than the finished pieces, is usually accompanied by the existence of the finished pieces, and these are finally successful only if the idea – original or not – has been successfully translated into visual terms. All of the artists mentioned here were presumably attracted to visual art in order to express something concretely. They began by making work strongly visual in character – conventional painting and sculpture – and they may return to it at any time. Duchamp's example of almost total abstention is not likely to attract many, although certain highly intelligent but formally unoriginal artists will continue to make 'art' that is largely an illustration of ideas rather than either visual or ultra-conceptual; their œuvre becomes a veritable Smithsonian of collected fact and invention – technological artifacts. Of course the use of the object of art as a vehicle for ideas is nothing new. In the course of art history it was only in the late nineteenth century that an alternative was offered by the proposal that art is strictly 'retinal' or sensuous in effect – a proposition that has come down to us as the formal or modernist mainstream.[6] Throughout history, art has been not merely descriptive but has been a vehicle for ideas – religious, political, mystical; the object has been taken on faith. What something looks like and what it is about may be complementary but not necessarily (rarely) identical.

Sol LeWitt sees ultra-conceptual art as a 'blind man's art' or 'nonvisual art' whose logic is conceptual and whose visual appearance is incidental, regulated entirely by the concept rather than by the appearance. 'The idea becomes a machine that makes the art', he has said. His most recent projects, like a good deal of other serially based art, are planned entirely conceptually but contain a few visual aspects that make no 'sense' to the viewer, such as a shape that must be completely contained in another one and taken on faith rather than seen, or an odd proportion that just doesn't seem to work visually. A 'nonvisual structure' is nonvisual because it does not inspire the usual response to art; it does not make compositional sense, just as the nonrelational primary painting or structure disregards compositional balance. In this way it may incorporate the irrational as well as the rational, disorder as well as order.

Some of the most rationally conceived art is visually nonsense. The extent to which rationality is taken can be so obsessive and so personal that rationality is finally subverted and the most conceptual art can take on an aura of the utmost irrationality. Hanne Darboven makes sheets of serial drawings on graph paper – endless permutations based on complex numerical combinations; the more she makes, the more offshoots become possible, and even hundreds of drawings based on a précis of a précis of a précis of one combination only imply the ultimate infinity. Her decisions on which to follow and which to leave are aesthetic. Darboven's is a kind of blind man's art too; the works themselves have analogies with Braille; they pass directly from the intellectual to the sensuous, almost entirely bypassing the visual. The illegible but fundamentally orderly tangle of lines connecting point to point is *felt* by the mathematical layman more than it is understood rationally or visually. Often there is not even a perceptible pattern. Carl Andre's bricks and metal plaques appear simple but stem from an extremely complex motivation; he offers clastic art as an alternative to plastic art: 'Whereas plastic art is a repeated record or process, clastic art provides the particles for an ongoing process'.[7] Like Darboven and Andre, and like Eva Hesse in her infinitely repeated identical shapes or rows of curiously exotic but understated forms, many ultra-conceptual artists seem to saturate their outwardly sane and didactic premises with a poetic and condensatory intensity that almost amounts to insanity. How normal is normal art, after all? [...]

Idea art has been seen as art about criticism rather than art-as-art or even art about art. On the contrary, the dematerialization of the object might eventually lead to the disintegration of criticism as it is known today. The pedantic or didactic or dogmatic basis insisted on by many of these artists is incorporated in the art. It bypasses criticism as such. Judgement of ideas is less interesting than following the ideas through. In the process, one might discover that something is either a good idea, that is, fertile and open enough to suggest infinite possibilities; or a mediocre idea, that is, exhaustible; or a bad idea, that is, already exhausted or with so little substance that it can be taken no further. (The same can be applied to style in the formal sense, and style except as an individual trademark tends to disappear in the path of novelty.) If the object becomes obsolete, objective distance becomes obsolete. Sometime in the near future it may be necessary for the writer to be an artist as well as for the artist to be a writer. There will still be scholars and historians of art, but the contemporary critic may have to choose between a creative originality and explanatory historicism.

Ultra-conceptual art will be thought of by some as 'formalist' because of the spareness and austerity it shares with the best of painting and sculpture at the moment. Actually, it is as antiformal as the most amorphous or journalistic expressionism. It represents a suspension of realism, even formal realism, colour realism, and all the other 'new realisms'. However, the idea that art can be experienced in order to extract an idea or underlying intellectual scheme as well as to perceive its formal essence *continues from* the opposing formalist premise that painting and sculpture should be looked at as objects *per se* rather than as references to other images and representation. As visual art, a highly conceptual work still stands or falls by what it looks like, but the primary, rejective trends in their emphasis on singleness and autonomy have limited the amount of information given, and therefore the amount of formal analysis possible. They have set critic and viewer thinking about what they see rather than simply weighing the formal or emotive impact. Intellectual and aesthetic pleasure can merge in this experience when the work is both visually strong and theoretically complex.

Some thirty years ago, Ortega wrote about the 'new art'; 'The task it sets itself is enormous; it wants to create from nought. Later, I expect, it will be content with less and achieve more'.[8] Fully aware of the difficulty of the new art, he would probably not have been surprised to find that a generation or more later the artist has achieved more with less, has continued to make something of 'nought' fifty years after Malevich's *White on White* seemed to have defined nought for once and for all. We still do not know how much less 'nothing' can be. Has an ultimate zero point been arrived at with black paintings, white paintings, light beams, transparent film, silent concerts, invisible sculpture, or any of the other projects mentioned above? It hardly seems likely.

1 Quoted in Lee Edson, 'Two Men in Search of the Quark', *New York Times Magazine*, 8 October 1967.

2 Wylie Sypher, *Loss of Self in Modern Literature and Art* (New York: Vintage, 1962) 73-74. The word has also been applied to differing areas of recent art by Robert Smithson and Piero Gilardi; it appears as the title of a short story by Thomas Pynchon and as a theme of Beckett's, etc.

3 Reference is here made to the examples of 'ultra-conceptual or dematerialized art' cited earlier in Lippard and Chandler's essay, quoted below [ed.]: '*Claes Oldenburg*: numerous monument projects, including *Placid City Monument*, a trench dug and filled again by union gravediggers behind the Metropolitan Museum (accepted by the New York City sculpture exhibition, Fall 1967) [...] *Sol LeWitt*: 'nonvisual' serial projects incorporating conceptual logic and visual illogic; exhibition at the Konrad Fischer Gallery, Dusseldorf, January 1968, of a series of hidden cubes indicated by lines drawn from their bases; project for a buried cube to be interred at a Texas airport.'

4 Sol LeWitt, 'Paragraphs on Conceptual Art', *Artforum* (Summer, 1967) 80.

5 *Non-Anthropomorphic Art by Four Young Artists: Four Statements* (Lannis Gallery, February 1967)

6 Marcel Duchamp, interviewed by J.J. Sweeney, 'Eleven Europeans in America', *Museum of Modern Art Bulletin*, 13:4-5 (New York: The Museum of Modern Art, 1926).

7 Quoted in Dan Graham, 'Carl Andre', *Arts Magazine* (January 1968).

8 José Ortega y Gasset, *The Dehumanization of Art* (New York: Doubleday, Anchor, 1956) 50.

Lucy R. Lippard, John Chandler, 'The Dematerialization of Art', *Art International*, 12:2 (February 1968); reprinted in Lucy R. Lippard, *Changing: Essays in Art Criticism* (New York: Dutton, 1971) 255-76.

Terry ATKINSON
Concerning the Article 'The Dematerialization of Art'
[1968]

[...] I have some enquiries I wish to advance relating to the usage of the word 'dematerialization' with precise regard as to its correctness in describing and relating the process of disestablishing a precept which had been assumed to be a necessary condition of the visual art menage (i.e. that there be a 'looking at' object). There seems to be in your article a strongly emphasized palaeontological framework of reference according to the data you offer from Schillinger's evolutionary categorical chronology of art-making procedures, hence I deduce you are using 'dematerialization' to describe a process which has connections with processes which have been slowly forming its own structure. Nevertheless, after careful consideration, I can only perceive that your usage of 'dematerialization' is a metaphorical one (I know that I am pointing out what is probably the most obvious of facts); there is not, I realize, anything of necessity wrong with metaphorical usage. But I think in the case of the process I understand your article to be concerned with, such a usage has a number of shortcomings in as far as the process of dematerialization is not in any strict sense the process (I emphasize as I understand it) you are describing [...]

The Oxford English Dictionary defines 'dematerialization' as 'to deprive of material qualities'. It would seem appropriate here to define matter as follows: a specialized form of energy which has the attributes of mass and extension in time, and with which we become acquainted through our bodily senses. It is more than plain then that when a material entity becomes dematerialized it does not simply become non-visible (as opposed to invisible), it becomes an entity which cannot be perceived by any of our senses. As far as material qualities go it is simply a non-entity. Thus it seems to me that if you are talking about art-objects dematerializing,[1] then you would be obliged to talk about objects of which there was now no material trace; if, on the other hand, you are talking or implying, by virtue of the metaphorical licence, that some artists today are using immaterial entities to demonstrate ideas, then you would be talking of ideas that had never had any material concretization. It certainly does not follow that because an object is invisible, or is less visible[2] than it was, or is less visible than another object,[3] that any process of dematerialization has taken place. If I might be permitted to make more specific reference to your article I would like to continue in the postliminary manner.

All the examples of art-works (ideas) you refer to in your article are, with few exceptions, art-objects. They may not be an art-object as we know it in its traditional matter-state, but they are nevertheless matter in one of its forms, either solid-state, gas-state, liquid-state. And it is on this question of matter-state[4] that my caution with regard to the metaphorical usage of dematerialization is centred upon. Whether for example, one calls Carl Andre's 'substance of forms' empty space or not does not point to any evidence of dematerialization because the term 'empty space' can never, in reference to terrestrial situations, be anything more than a convention describing how space is filled rather than offering a description of a portion of space which is, in physical terms, empty. Andre's empty space is in no sense a void ... Consequently, when you point, among many others, to an object made by Atkinson, 'Map to not indicate etc', that it has 'almost entirely eliminated the visual-physical element', I am a little apprehensive of such a description. The map is just as much a solid-state object (i.e., paper with ink lines upon it) as is any Rubens (stretcher-canvas with paint upon it) and as such comes up for the count of being just as physically-visually perusable as the Rubens [...]

I wish at this point to reiterate briefly some of the aspects of your article which have interested me and which I have touched upon in the foregoing. Matter is a specialized form of energy; radiant energy is the only form in which energy can exist in the absence of matter. Thus when dematerialization takes place, it means, in terms of physical phenomena, the conversion (I use this word guardedly) of a state of matter into that of radiant energy; this follows that energy can never be created or destroyed. But further, if one were to speak of an art-form that used radiant energy, then one would be committed to the contradiction of speaking of a formless form, and one can imagine the verbal acrobatics that might take place when the romantic metaphor was put to work on questions concerning formless-forms (non-material) and material forms. The philosophy of what is called aesthetics relying finally, as it does, on what it has called the content of the art work is, at the most, only fitted with the philosophical tools to deal with problems of an art that absolutely counts upon the production of matter-state entities. The shortcomings of such philosophical tools are plain enough to see inside this limit of material objects; once this limit is broken these shortcomings hardly seem worth considering as the sophistry of the whole framework is dismissed as being not acceptable to an art procedure that records its information in words, and the consequent material qualities of the entity produced (i.e., typewritten sheet, etc) do not necessarily have anything to do with the idea. That is, the idea is 'read about' rather than 'looked at'. That some art should be directly material and that other art should produce a material entity only as a necessary by-product of the need to record the idea is not at all to say that the latter is connected by any process of dematerialization to the former.

Here in England, I have been and still am a participant in what could loosely be called a think-tank[5] (at the risk of being accused of using metaphorical technological jargon reminiscent of McLuhan) which had been working with 'objectless' quiddities (I use this phrase for the patent want of a better one) developed inside what I can, at the moment, only call a framework of mention.[6] Such a framework uses only theoretical entities and as such does not come up for the count as either material or immaterial art. The ideas are recorded in typewritten word form as the nature of the ideas can only be satisfactorily developed in such a form (or in audio form on magnetic tape). One reads the written information just as one reads any written information [...]

At the moment I can only refer to the technique that Michael Baldwin and myself have used in attempting to formulate the theoretical entities constructed in the 'Air-Conditioning Show', the 'Air Show' and the 'Time Show' as a technique where the contents is separated off from the notion of making an art-object. Maybe something like a technique of content-isolation (I am wary of such a description; but I must admit, at the cost of being a little anecdotal, that the term appeals to me by virtue of the fact that Clement Greenberg has pontificated to the effect that it is no use talking about the content of an art-work, which if I guess correctly means he can't talk about these particular works at all.) It is, to put it more approximately than precisely, the artist working with what, in the visual-art context, is traditionally recognized as the medium of the art-critic and art-historian. Perhaps I can explicate the methodology of such a technique a little more. If it is pointed out in the theoretical frameworks (used by Michael Baldwin and myself) that the situations are no more than synallagmatically related to the internal introduction (i.e. inside the framework of what I call mention) of new descriptive terms, etc., which provide a consistent and appropriate non-eliminative context for nomological implication (i.e. if there are any rules governing such a framework they are, in consequence of the nature of the structure of the framework, open-ended and thus difficult to identify as rules), then questions about objects made will, obviously, be seen to entail answers, the natures of which will in the end only be cognizable with objects produced as a by-product of the need to record the content of the idea, hence to consider the objects produced within the framework (i.e. typewritten sheets) as 'looking-at' objects rather than 'reading-about' objects is to look for first-order-visual information where there is no intention to produce such information.[7]

In view of the immediately preceding paragraph I wish to develop a few ideas and thoughts with regard to another interesting postulation you have made in the 'Dematerialization' article. I quote: 'that dematerialized art is post-aesthetic only in its increasing non-visual emphases ... ' Nobody concerned with problems (pertaining to your article) that I know of here in England is likely to want to make a major issue of argument over whether or not 'the aesthetic of principle is still an aesthetic';[8] however, I have a few reflective notes which may be of some small relevance here. Equations, formulae, theoretical entities, etc., are normally recorded in written-sign-word form and obviously any aesthetic criteria applied to them are usually related to how effectively the written format expresses the information relevant to the state, situation, etc., it is seeking to describe/explain. If I may be allowed to pursue an analogy here, consider the following. A man has in his possession a map which he knows contains the information instructing him how to get from A to B, but because he has not had an adequate course in map-reading he cannot read the map. If he then says the map has great beauty, then he cannot be judging this map to have beauty according to the information presented by the map as a map, but is talking of the map in some other way. Now when a scientist talks of the beauty of an equation, his beauty is judged according to the nature of his course in equation-reading[9] which provides him with the basis for making judgements concerning how good an equation is. If he is simply looking at the object 'equation' then his judgement of the beauty of the equation is according some other kind of beauty to it. If, for instance, the scientist is reading-looking at the equation, then if he is reading it wrongly then he is not applying criteria according to another kind of beauty; rather, questions of true or false come in here. Judgements pertaining to another kind of beauty bring in questions relating to relevant or irrelevant before questions of truth or falsehood are examined. I quote further from your article: ' ... the more one reads these statements, the more apparent it becomes that the scientist's attempt to discover, perhaps even to impose order and structure on the universe, rests on assumptions that are essentially aesthetic. Order itself, and its implied simplicity and unity, are essential aesthetic criteria'. Now the search for a completely coherent theory of anti-matter (i.e. quark theory) is a fascinating one, and I certainly would not dispute Richard Feynman's claim that he has experienced revelata and therefore is aware of certain things or phenomena that most of us are not. But, and I think it is a considerable but, statements such as 'nature is inherently beautiful' (Gell-Mann), and 'It had elegance and beauty. The goddam thing was gleaming', whilst maybe showing evidence of the two physicists' 'aesthetic' sophistication do not in themselves have anything to do with the effectiveness of an equation, formula, theory, etc.

The principles of aesthetics are an accepted area of philosophical investigation,[10] but the aesthetic of principle is quite another. I wonder if there is (to use a metaphor) a danger of putting the cart before the horse. Obviously, I am open to any discussion you wish to raise. By using a phrase such as 'the aesthetic of principle'[11] do you somehow intend to imply the principle of the aesthetic of beauty? Are you hinting at some kind of meta-aesthetic? It seems that here we are not only up against the diffficulty of constructing a framework allowing a general definition of goodness and its consequent directive to examine the varieties of goodness,[12] but also, here, you seem to be implying that our seeking after a thorough analysis of our compulsion to seek after what we think is goodness is not the sole area that comes under the heading of aesthetics, but that aesthetics is extended to the construction of the aesthetic of principle theory (a kind of theory of principles?) in addition to its more conventional applications. Such a notion implies that the framework that is set up to examine what the nature of aesthetics is has the nature (framework) of what it is trying to examine as the foundations of its own framework. There is, obviously, something not quite right here. A principal is defined, in one sense at least, as a theoretical basis. An aesthetic of theoretical basis? Imagine books written entitled *The Aesthetics of the Principles of Literary Criticism* or *The Aesthetics of the Principles of Thermodynamics*. What is often judged as good about a principle is that it is the foundation of a certain theory(ies) or construct. Would then two books, to be purely speculative, trace the origins of, say, the principles of literary criticism and those of thermodynamics to the same principle of principles? I am open to your suggestions on such a point, but I think that such a usage of aesthetic as the aesthetic of principle calls for a stringent examination of whether there is any valid hierarchy in the concepts of principle, aesthetics and criteria. I will be in New York over Easter. I would welcome an exchange of views with you.

Yours in good faith. Terry Atkinson

PS. Although neither David Bainbridge, Michael Baldwin nor Harold Hurrell have seen this letter. I sign with some considerable confidence for them.

1 Dematerialization especially relates to the form of a radiant energy as this is the only form in which energy can exist in the absence of matter. Such a factor is discussed in a little more detail later in this paper.

2 When I use the term 'less visible' I admit to a somewhat everyday usage of the description of the quality of being visible. There are more fundamental questions implied here than I have gone into. For example, when we

say a car is less visible in a fog than it is on a clear day, it does not mean that we see any the worse on a foggy day (i.e. our seeing mechanism is not functioning any the worse). On a foggy day we see the unclear image of the car just as clearly as we see the distinct image of the car on a clear day.

3 (Relating to note 2.) That is we see that the object that is less visible is as clearly less visible as the object that is more visible is as clearly more visible.

4 There is a modest theory-object pertaining to the use of a solid-state to liquid-state to gas-state conversion process which I sketched together in May, 1967. I may yet publish it along with the other small theories, theory-objects I worked upon between February and May of 1967. I would not include in this category the 'Air-Conditioning Show' that I worked upon with Michael Baldwin during this period nor many of the still not formulated ideas I worked upon (and still am working upon) with both Bainbridge and Michael Baldwin, as I think these ideas are of a much more comprehensive nature.

5 I am using the term 'think-tank' here to refer to the loose confederation that has existed between Harold Hurrell, David Bainbridge, Michael Baldwin and myself. On the 'Air-Conditioning Show', 'Air Show' and 'Time Show' and also on 'Frameworks' Michael Baldwin and myself worked particularly closely together, and the present project concerning the hardware MI in the main engineered by David Bainbridge has entailed much explication and theorizing by all four of us.

6 The concept of 'framework of mention' was as far as I know first used by Michael Baldwin in the context of the 'Air Show' that he and myself worked upon during September and October 1967. Since, we have formulated some considerable explication and extrapolation of the device in 'Frameworks'.

7 Consequently, there is a section in 'Frameworks' in second order visual-information form explaining that in the 'Air-Conditioning', 'Air' and 'Time' shows there is no intention to present first order visual information forms.

8 It should be noted here that I am assuming when you use the 'aesthetic of principle' you are stating an aesthetic that is judged by you to be post-visual-aesthetic. The question of the aesthetic of principle is dealt with in a little more detail later in the paper.

9 Perhaps it is as well here to confirm that I am aware that to interpret art-objects (first order visual information) it is obviously a considerable help to have had an adequate course in object reading, thus it should be clear that I am not maintaining, when I call art objects first order visual information, that I am maintaining that a comprehensivce reading of an art-object can be done naTvely, but rather one is reading about the object one is looking at through this act of 'looking at'. Whereas if, say, one is reading-looking at the letter R, usually one is not examining the form of the R (except that it be recognizable as R) but rather seeing how it fits in aggregate with other letters to form, for example, the word red.

10 e.g. *Principia Ethica*, G.E. Moore (etc., etc., etc.)

11 Refer note 9.

12 Georg Henrik von Wright, *The Varieties of Goodness* (London: Routledge and Kegan Paul, 1963).

Terry Atkinson,'Concerning the article "The Dematerialization of Art"' (letter to Lucy Lippard and John Chandler, 2 November 1968); extract reprinted in Alexander Alberro; Blake Stimson (eds.) *Conceptual Art: A Critical Anthology* (Cambridge, Massachusetts: MIT Press, 1999) 52-58.

Sol LEWITT

Sentences on Conceptual Art [1969]

1 Conceptual Artists are mystics rather than rationalists. They leap to conclusions that logic cannot reach.
2 Rational judgements repeat rational judgements.
3 Illogical judgements lead to new experience.
4 Formal Art is essentially rational.
5 Irrational thoughts should be followed absolutely and logically.
6 If the artist changes his mind midway through the execution of the piece he compromises the result and repeats past results.
7 The artist's will is secondary to the process he initiates from idea to complete. His wilfulness may only be ego.
8 When words such as painting and sculpture are used, they connote a whole tradition and imply a consequent acceptance of this tradition, thus placing limitations on the artist who would be reluctant to make art that goes beyond the limitations.
9 The concept and idea are different. The former implies a general direction while the latter are components. Ideas implement the concept.
10 Ideas alone can be works of art; they are in a chain of development that may eventually find some form. All ideas need not be made physical.
11 Ideas do not necessarily proceed in logical order. They may set one off in unexpected directions but an idea must necessarily be completed in the mind before the next one is formed.
12 For each work of art that becomes physical there are many variations that do not.
13 A work of art may be understood as a conductor from the artists' mind to the viewers. But it may never reach the viewer, or it may never leave the artists' minds.
14 The words of one artist to another may induce an ideas chain, if they share the same concept.
15 Since no form is intrinsically superior to another, the artist may use a form, from an expression of words, (written or spoken) to physical reality, equally.
16 If words are used, and they proceed from ideas about art, then they are art and not literature; numbers are not mathematics.
17 All ideas are art if they are concerned with art and fall within the conventions of art.
18 One usually understands the art of the past by applying the conventions of the present thus misunderstanding the art of the past.
19 The conventions of art are altered by works of art.
20 Successful art changes our understanding of the conventions by altering our perceptions.
21 Perception of ideas leads to new ideas.
22 The artist cannot imagine his art, and cannot perceive it until it is complete.
23 One artist may mis-perceive (understand it differently than the artist) a work of art but still be set off in his own chain of thought by that misconstrual.
24 Perception is subjective.
25 The artist may not necessarily understand his own art. His perception is neither better nor worse than that of others.
26 An artist may perceive the art of others better than his own.
27 The concept of a work of art may involve the matter of the piece or the process in which it is made.
28 Once the idea of the piece is established in the artist's mind and the final form is decided, the process is carried out blindly. There are many side-effects that the artist cannot imagine. These may be used as ideas for new works.
29 The process is mechanical and should not be tampered with. It should run its course.
30 There are many elements involved in a work of art. The most important are the most obvious.
31 If an artist uses the same form in a group of works, and changes the material, one would assume the artist's concept involved the material.
32 Banal ideas cannot be rescued by beautiful execution.
33 It is difficult to bungle a good idea.
34 When an artist learns his craft too well he makes slick art.
35 These sentences comment on art, but are not art.

Sol LeWitt, 'Sentences on Conceptual Art' *Art-Language: The Journal of Conceptual Art*, 1:1 (May 1969) 11-13.

Adrian PIPER

Idea, Form, Context [1969]

IDEA

1 Good ideas are necessary and sufficient for good art.
2 A good idea is too broad in scope to be stated directly; it can be implied only in a given set of conditions. A well-constructed set of conditions allows great breadth of implication in a direction defined by the idea.
3 There are two basic kinds of art idea: ideas that use life conditions (such as physical forces, concrete material, or sensory phenomena), and ideas that use ideas or theories about life conditions (such as physics, Gestalt psychology, philosophy, geometry, math). Both kinds of idea are inherent in a work, but the predominance of one leads the viewer to infer the other.
4 The first kind of art idea reorganizes specific life conditions to form a unique, artificial entity that takes its place in life as a new condition among existing conditions. Responding to this kind of idea usually involves adapting the new life condition into an existing perspective, relating it to past experience, learning to feel comfortable with it.

One is required to reason inductively from the new life conditions among existing perspectives; it adds to the sum total of ideas about life, rather than to life itself. Responding to this kind of idea usually involves adapting an existing life condition to a new perspective; redefining past experience in light of it; learning to feel uncomfortable with it. One is required to reason inductively from the existing life condition to a new or unfamiliar idea about that condition. By doing this, the implications of the (or any) familiar life conditions are broadened in one's consciousness.

5 The first kind of idea has the effect of broadening one's perspective. The first adds to reality; the second adds to mind. Reality adds to mind inductively; mind adds to reality deductively.

FORM

1 Form is separate from, but necessary for, the realization of an idea.

2 The function of form is to communicate as much of an idea as possible, to eliminate those aspects of a given set of conditions that are irrelevant to the idea, and to retain only those aspects that clarify the idea. Ideally, an idea should have no form at all. With no perceptual energy filtered out in the process of communication, apprehension of the set of conditions and its implications would then have total impact on the understanding.

3 The less a form is intrinsically interesting, the more suitable it is as a communicative medium. Concrete visual and spatial forms are intrinsically interesting. They embody their own perceptual character and communicate their own perceptual significance; they indiscriminately convey the chaos inherent in any situation, thus obscuring or nullifying the possibility of apprehending the idea. (Chaos as an idea can be conveyed with complete clarity in a non-concrete form.)

4 Forms that traditionally convey information about things external to themselves, such as spoken or written language, records, tapes, slides, films, television, photographs, maps or diagrams, are interesting only in so far as what they refer to is interesting. They eliminate irrelevant aspects of a set of conditions by simply not referring to them. They need have little intrinsic interest if they are used in a traditional, non-experimental way. They are thus more suitable for conveying an idea.

CONTEXT

1 Context is separate from, but necessary for, presenting a realized idea.

2 An artificial context is unimportant in an idea that deals directly with life conditions.[1] A work of this nature is itself a unique life condition. It remains an adjunct to reality; art of, but separate from, any set of familiar life conditions (those of the home, gallery or outdoor environment).

3 An artificial context is important for presenting the kind of art idea that deals with ideas about life conditions.[2] The context must present an existing life condition in a way that emphasizes and broadens its implications beyond the routine pattern in which it normally occurs.

4 The form of this kind of idea should be adapted to the artificial context used. This further minimizes the significance of the form and allows maximum control in conveying the idea.

5 In an event context, both time and space factors are controlled. Forms that control both time and space factors include films, television, sometimes slides, and sometimes spoken language. These forms are thus most easily adaptable to the event context.

6 In a spatial context (such as a gallery or outdoor environment), the space factor is controlled. Forms that may control the space factor alone include diagrams, maps, photographs and slides. Gallery contexts also, however, control the time factor in a more subtle way. The adaptability of these forms to the gallery context may therefore be questioned.

7 In an aural information context (telephone, radio, loudspeaker), the time factor alone is controlled. Forms that control the time factor alone include tapes, records, and sometimes spoken language. These forms are thus most easily adaptable to an aural information context.

8 Books, folders, and other similarly unsituated sets of information control neither the time nor the space factor. Forms that control neither the time nor the space factor include written language, maps, diagrams and photographs. These forms are thus most easily adaptable to an unsituated information context.

9 Any context is an existing life condition that normally occurs in a routine pattern. The information presented in an artificial context may therefore convey something about that context itself as an existing life condition. When this is the case, the artificial context becomes a member in the set of conditions that supports the idea. The idea may then be completely based on ideas about life conditions and may not manipulate reality in any way.

IDEA, FORM, CONTEXT

1 The major premises of the preceding three articles can be restated in the following ways:

a) Idea: [The existence of an] idea is necessary and sufficient for [the existence of] art; idea is equivalent to art.[3]

b) Form: [The existence of] form is necessary but not sufficient for [realizing an] idea; [realizing an] idea is sufficient but not necessary for [the existence of] form. [The existence of] idea is not equivalent to [the existence of] form.[4]

c) Context: [The existence of] context is necessary but not sufficient for form [through which an idea has been realized]; form [through with an idea has been realized] is sufficient but not necessary for [the existence of] context. [The existence of] form is not equivalent to [the existence of] context.[5]

2 From these premises, this conclusion follows: [The existence of] context is necessary but not sufficient for [conveying an] art idea; [conveying an] art idea is sufficient but not necessary for [the existence of] context.[6] [Conveying an] art idea is not equivalent to [the existence of] context. From this argument taken as a whole, both form and context are shown to be secondary considerations; necessary but not sufficient for art. The primary consideration in art is idea.

3 However, the relative importance of form and context in an idea are factors by which the general nature of certain ideas may be determined.

4 When form is important and context unimportant, the idea is generally formal[7] in nature.

5 When both form and context are important, the idea is generally environmental[8] in nature.

6 When both form and context are unimportant,[9] the idea is generally conceptual after the aesthetic developed in the work of Sol LeWitt.[10]

7 When form is unimportant and context is important, the idea is generally ideal[11] in nature.

8 When the considerations of form and context are of secondary importance to an art idea, the relative importance of form and context are elements by which the nature of the art may be analyzed.

1 See 'Idea', number 4.

2 See 'Idea', number 5.

3 See 'Idea', number 1.

4 See 'Form', number 1.

5 See 'Context', number 1.

6 Some conditions in which [conveying an] art idea is sufficient but not necessary for [the existence of] context are discussed in 'Context', number 9.

7 The term *formal* is used as a convenient method of summarizing the ideas discussed in 'Form', number 3, and 'Context', number 2.

8 The term *environmental* is used as a convenient method of summarizing the ideas discussed in 'Form', number 3, and 'Context', number 3.

9 As discussed in 'Form', number 2 and 'Context', number 2.

10 See Sol LeWitt, 'Paragraphs on Conceptual Art', *Artforum* 5, no. 10 (Summer 1967) 79-83 [see above, 213-14].

11 The term *ideal* is used as a convenient method of summarizing the ideas discussed in 'Idea', number 5, 'Form', numbers 2 and 4, and 'Context', numbers 3-9.

Adrian Piper, 'Idea, Form, Context' (1969), *Out of Order, Out of Sight, Volume II: Selected Writings in Art Criticism, 1967-1992*, (Cambridge, Massachusetts: MIT Press, 1996) 5-12.

Jaroslaw KOZLOWSKI Continuum (a Gloss to Andrzej Kostolowski's Thesis 'On the End of Art') [*c.* 1973]

'Whatever is, may not become faded by means of any division, even the most extreme.
To a great one, there is always some even greater thing.'
– Anaxagoras of Clazomene

1 A hypothesis: Art as a *continuum*.

2 In Brouwer's approach: *'a set is a rule on whose grounds, following a selection of any digit group within the sequence of 1, 2, 3, 4, 5, ..., one achieves a certain*

determined mark or not, or, the process gets obstructed and its outcome finally annihilated, whereas for each n>1, following each non-obstructed sequence of n - 1 acts of selection, at least one digit group may be quoted which, selected as an nth digital group, will not result in an obstruction of the process. Each sequence of marks (usually, not presentable in a ready-made form) thus established out of infinite sequence of selection acts, will be called an element of the set.'

3 In accordance with intuition, Brouwer thus describes infinite countable sets as a *limitless sequence* of acts of selection. In a *continuum*, there are no finished elements; instead, it is a centre of 'free happening (emergence) of things'. Finite sets, in turn, are characterized by a creation process being obstructed. Whenever a sequence suddenly ends, it gets 'obstructed'; or, whenever an already constructed element gets annihilated, a finite set is established.

4 For Brouwer, the principle of complete induction, connected with the sequence of natural numbers, that is, with the most obvious form of revelation of a *continuum*, is an empty form, emerging as a result of the passage from the past into the future, against a simultaneous disregard of any particular features. *'Mathematics emerges when, out of an object featuring an ambiguity resulting from the passage of time, we can extract any characteristics owned by this object. The empty form thus created, of common contents of all those dualities, reappears in an infinite manner as a pre-intuition of mathematics, creating new mathematical objects.'*

5 Infinity = the possibility of a limitless, reason-based construction.

6 Having replaced, by analogy, in item 4, above, the term 'mathematics' by the notion of 'art', and applied into item 5, above, the hypothesis quoted in item 1, we arrive at the following concept:

1° Art is created whenever, out of an object to which the feature of duality pertains, ensuing from the fact of the passage of time, we have abstracted any and all characteristics thereof. The empty form thus created, of common contents of all those dualities, reappears in an infinite manner as a pre-intuition of art, creating new facts of art.

2° Art = the possibility of a limitless reason-based construction.

Jaroslaw Kozlowski, 'Continuum' (*c.* 1973), translated by Tristan Korecki, in Pawel Polit and Piotr Wozniakiewicz (eds.) *Conceptual Reflection in Polish Art. Experiences of Discourse: 1965-1975* (Warsaw: Ujazdowski Castle Centre for Contemporary Art, 2000) 249-50.

Benjamin H.D. BUCHLOH
Edward Ruscha's Books
[1990]

[...] Among the key strategies of future Conceptual art that were initiated by Ruscha in 1963 were the following: to choose the vernacular (e.g., architecture) as referent; to deploy photography systematically as the representational medium; and to develop a new form of distribution (e.g., the commercially produced book as opposed to the traditionally crafted *livre d'artiste*.)

Typically, reference to architecture in any form whatever would have been unthinkable in the context of American-type formalism and Abstract Expressionism (or within the European post-war aesthetic for that matter) until the early 1960s. The devotion to a private aesthetic of contemplative experience, with its concomitant absence of any systematic reflection of the social functions of artistic production and their potential and actual publics, had, in fact, precluded any exploration of the interdependence of architectural and artistic production, be it even in the most superficial and trivial of architectural décor. It was not until the emergence of Pop art in the early 1960s, in particular in the work of Bernd and Hilla Becher, Claes Oldenburg and Edward Ruscha, that the references to monumental sculpture (even in its negation as the *Anti-Monument*) and to vernacular architecture reintroduced (even if only by implication) a reflection on public architectural and domestic space, thereby foregrounding the absence of a developed artistic reflection on the problematic of the contemporary publics.

In January 1963 (the year of Duchamp's first American retrospective, held at the Pasadena Art Museum), Ruscha, a relatively unknown Los Angeles artist, decided to publish a book entitled *Twenty Six Gasoline Stations*. The book, modest in format and production, was as removed from the tradition of the artist's book as its iconography was opposed to every aspect of the official American art of the 1950s and early 60s: the legacy of Abstract Expressionism and Colour Field painting. The book was, however, not so alien to the artistic thought of the emerging generation, if one remembers that the year before an unknown artist from New York by the name of Andy Warhol had exhibited a serial arrangement of thirty-two stencilled paintings depicting Campbell's Soup cans arranged like objects on shelves in the Ferus Gallery. While both Warhol and Ruscha accepted a notion of public experience that was inescapably contained in the conditions of consumption, both artists altered the mode of production as well as the form of distribution of their work such that a different public was potentially addressed.

Ruscha's vernacular iconography evolved to the same extent as Warhol's had from the Duchamp and Cage legacy of an aesthetic of 'indifference', and from the commitment to an anti-hierarchical organization of a universally valid facticity, operating as total affirmation. Indeed, random sampling and aleatory choice from an infinity of possible objects (Ruscha's *Twenty Six Gasoline Stations*, Warhol's *Thirteen Most Wanted Men*) would soon become essential strategies of the aesthetic of Conceptual art: one thinks of Alighiero Boetti's *The Thousand Longest Rivers*, of Robert Barry's *One Billion Dots*, of On Kawara's *One Million Years*, or, most significantly in this context, of Douglas Huebler's lifelong project, entitled *Variable Piece No. 70*. This work claims to document photographically *'the existence of everyone alive in order to produce the most authentic and inclusive representation of the human species that may be assembled in that manner. Editions of this work will be periodically issued in a variety of topical modes: "100,000 people", "1,000,000 people", "10,000,000 people", ... etc.'* Or again, there are the works by Stanley Brouwn or Hanne Darboven where in each case an arbitrary, abstract principle of pure quantification replaces traditional principles of pictorial or sculptural organization and/or compositional relational order.

In the same manner that Ruscha's books shifted the formal organization of the representation, the mode of presentation itself became transformed: instead of lifting photographic (or print-derived) imagery from mass-cultural sources and transforming these images into painting (as Warhol and the Pop artists had practiced it), Ruscha would now deploy photography directly, in an appropriate printing medium. And it was a particularly laconic type of photography at that, one that explicitly situated itself as much outside of all conventions of art photography as outside of those of the venerable tradition of documentary photography, least of all that of 'concerned' photography. This devotion to a deadpan, anonymous, amateurish approach to photographic form corresponds exactly to Ruscha's iconographic choice of the architectural banal. Thus at all three levels – iconography, representational form, mode of distribution – the given forms of artistic object no longer seemed acceptable in their traditionally specialized and privileged positions [...]

Benjamin H.D. Buchloh, 'Conceptual Art 1962-1969: From the Aesthetics of Administration to the Critique of Institutions', *October*, 55 (Winter 1990) 119-22.

WORD AND SIGN

Conceptual artists drew on a wide array of theoretical resources. The main influences upon the linguistic self-consciousness of the day were Saussure's semiology and Wittgenstein's logical positivism. Central to artists' understandings of their 'revolutionary', paradigm-shifting position in the history of art was Thomas Kuhn's distinction between 'revolutionary' and 'normal' science. LeWitt had popularized the phrase 'conceptual art', but it was Joseph Kosuth in his three-part article in *Studio International* in 1969–70, 'Art after Philosophy', who first attempted to give the notion a strict philosophical form. However, there was little agreement among artists on philosophical issues. The British group Art & Language made philosophical enquiry into 'the language-use of the art society' the focus of their activities. For some artists, such as Victor Burgin, this was a new form of art-for-art's sake. From the historical perspective of subsequent criticism, use of the printed word was less novel than it appeared at the time. It connects conceptual art, despite itself, to a tradition of experimental typography.

Ferdinand de SAUSSURE Course in General Linguistics [1915]

[...] Language, once its boundaries have been marked off within the speech data, can be classified among human phenomena, whereas speech cannot.

We have just seen that language is a social institution; but several features set it apart from other political, legal, etc. institutions. We must call in a new type of facts in order to illuminate the special nature of language.

Language is a system of signs that express ideas, and is therefore comparable to a system of writing, the alphabet of deaf-mutes, symbolic rites, polite formulas, military signals, etc. But it is the most important of all these systems.

A science that studies the life of signs within society is conceivable; it would be an art of social psychology and consequently of general psychology; I shall call it *semiology* (from Greek *semeîon* 'sign'). Semiology would show what constitutes signs, what laws govern them. Since the science does not yet exist, no one can say what it would be; but it has a right to existence, a place staked out in advance. Linguistics is only a part of the general science of semiology; the laws discovered by semiology will be applicable to linguistics, and the latter will circumscribe a well-defined area within the mass of anthropological facts [...]

In short, the characteristic that distinguishes semiological systems from all other institutions shows up clearly only in language where it manifests itself in the things which are studied least, and the necessity or specific value of a semiological science is therefore not clearly recognized. But to me the language problem is mainly semiological, and all developments derive their significance from that important fact. If we are to discover the true nature of language we must learn what it has in common with all other semiological systems; linguistic forces that seem very important at first glance (e.g., the role of the vocal apparatus) will receive only secondary consideration if they serve only to set language apart from the other systems. This procedure will do more than to clarify the linguistic problem. By studying rites, customs, etc. as signs, I believe that we shall throw new light on the facts and point up the need for including them in a science of semiology and explaining them by its laws [...]

NATURE OF THE LINGUISTIC SIGN

1 *Sign, Signified, Signifier*

Some people regard language, when reduced to its elements, as a naming-process only – a list of words, each corresponding to the thing that it names. For example: [fig. in original of a tree opposite its Latin name 'arbor'.]

This conception is open to criticism at several points. It assumes that ready-made ideas exist before words; it does not tell us whether a name is vocal or psychological in nature (*arbor*, for instance, can be considered from either viewpoint); finally, it lets us assume that the linking of a name and a thing is a very simple operation – an assumption that is anything but true. But this rather naïve approach can bring us near the truth by showing us that the linguistic unit is a double entity, one formed by the associating of two terms.

We have seen in considering the speaking-circuit that both terms involved in the linguistic sign are psychological and are united in the brain by an associate bond. This point must be emphasized.

The linguistic sign unites, not a thing and a name, but a concept and a sound-image. The latter is not the material sound, a purely physical thing, but the psychological imprint of the sound, the impression it makes on our senses. The sound-image is sensory, and if I happen to call it 'material', it is only in that sense, and by way of opposing it to the other term of the association, the concept, which is generally more abstract.

The psychological character of our sound-images becomes apparent when we observe our own speech. Without moving our lips or tongue, we can talk to ourselves or recite mentally a selection of verse. Because we regard the words of our language as sound-images, we must avoid speaking of the 'phonemes' that make up the words. This term, which suggests vocal activity, is applicable to the spoken word only, to the realization of the inner image in discourse. We can avoid that misunderstanding by speaking of the *sounds* and *syllables* of a word provided we remember that the names refer to the sound-image.

The linguistic sign is then a two-sided psychological entity that can be represented by the drawing:

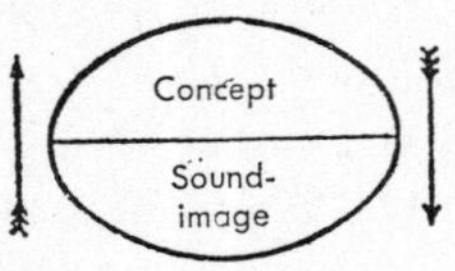

The two elements are intimately united, and each recalls the other. Whether we try to find the meaning of the Latin word *arbor* or the word that Latin uses to designate the concept 'tree', it is clear that only the associations sanctioned by that language appear to us to conform to reality, and we disregard whatever others might be imagined.

Our definition of the linguistic sign poses an important question of terminology. I call the combination of a concept and a sound-image a *sign*, but in current usage the term generally designates only a sound-image, a word, for example, (*arbor*, etc.). One tends to forget that *arbor* is called a sign only because it carries the concept 'tree', with the result that the idea of the sensory part implies the idea of the whole.

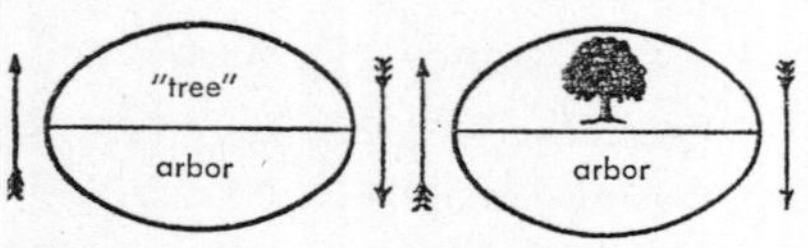

Ambiguity would disappear if the three notions involved here were designated by three names, each suggesting and opposing the others. I propose to retain the word *sign* [*signe*] to designate the whole and to replace *concept* and *sound-image* respectively by *signified* [*signifié*] and *signifier* [*signifiant*]; the last two terms have the advantage of indicating the opposition that separates them from each other and from the whole of which they are parts. As regards sign, if I am satisfied with it, this is simply because I do not know of any word to replace it, the ordinary language suggesting no other.

The linguistic sign, as defined, has two primordial characteristics. In enunciating them I am also positioning the basic principles of any study of this type.

2. *Principle I: The Arbitrary Nature of the Sign*

The bond between the signifier and the signified is arbitrary. Since I mean by sign the whole that results from the associating of the signifier with the signified, I can simply say: *the linguistic sign is arbitrary*.

The idea of 'sister' is not linked by any inner relationship to the succession of sounds *s-ö-r* which serves as its signifier in French; that it could be represented equally by just any other sequence is proved by differences among languages and by the very existence of different languages: the signified 'ox' has as its signifier *b-ö-f* on one side of the border and *o-k-s* (*Ochs*) on the other.

No one disputes the principle of the arbitrary nature of the sign, but it is often easier to discover the truth than to assign to it its proper place. Principle I dominates all the linguistics of language; its consequences are numberless. It is true that not all of them are equally obvious at first glance; only after many detours does one discover them, and with them the primordial importance of the principle.

One remark in passing: when semiology becomes organized as a science, the question will arise whether or not it properly includes modes of expression based on completely natural signs, such as pantomime. Supposing that the new science welcomes them, its main concern will still be the whole group of systems grounded on the arbitrariness of the sign. In fact, every means of expression used in society is based, in principle, on collective behaviour or – what amounts to the same thing – on convention. Polite formulas, for instance, though often imbued with a certain natural expressiveness (as in the case of a Chinese who greets his emperor by bowing down to the ground nine times), are nonetheless fixed by rule; it is this rule and not the intrinsic value of the gestures that obliges one to use them. Signs that are wholly arbitrary realize better than the others the ideal of the semiological process; that is why language, the most complex and universal of all systems of expression, is also the most characteristic; in this sense linguistics can become the master-pattern for all branches of semiology although language is only one particular semiological system.

The word *symbol* has been used to designate the linguistic sign, or more specifically, what is here called the signifier. Principle I in particular weighs against the use of this term. One characteristic of the symbol is that it is never wholly arbitrary; it is not empty, for there is the rudiment of a natural bond between the signifier and the signified. The symbol of justice, a pair of scales, could not be replaced by just any other symbol, such as a chariot.

The word *arbitrary* also calls for comment. The term should not imply that the choice of the signifier is left entirely to the speaker (we shall see below that the individual does not have the power to change a sign in any way once it has become established in the linguistic community); I mean that it is unmotivated, i.e. arbitrary in that it actually has no natural connections with the signified [...]

3. *Principle II: The Linear Nature of the Signifier*

The signifier, being auditory, is unfolded solely in time from which it gets the following characteristics: (a) it represents a span, and (b) the span is measurable in a single dimension; it is a line.

While Principle II is obvious, apparently linguists have always neglected to state it, doubtless because they found it too simple; nevertheless, it is fundamental, and its consequences are incalculable. Its importance equals that of Principle I; the whole mechanism of language depends upon it. In contrast to visual signifiers (nautical signals, etc.) which can offer simultaneous groupings in several dimensions, auditory signifiers have at their command only the dimension of time. Their elements are presented in succession; they form a chain. This feature becomes readily apparent when they are represented in writing and the spatial line of graphic marks is substituted for succession in time [...]

Ferdinand de Saussure, *Cours de linguistique générale* (Paris, 1915); trans. Wade Baskin, *Course in General Linguistics* (London: Peter Owen, 1959) 15-17, 65-70.

Ludwig WITTGENSTEIN Tractatus Logico-Philosophicus [1921]

1' The world is all that is the case.

1.1 The world is the totality of facts, not of things.

1.11 The world is determined by the facts, and by their being *all* the facts.

1.12 For the totality of facts determines what is the case, and also whatever is not the case.

1.13 The facts in logical space are the world.

1.2 The world divides into facts.

1.21 Each item can be the case or not the case while everything else remains the same.

2 What is the case – a fact – is the existence of states of affairs.

2.01 A state of affairs (a state of things) is a combination of objects (things).

2.011 It is essential to things that they should be possible constituents of states of affairs.

2.012 In logic nothing is accidental: if a thing *can* occur in a state of affairs, the possibility of the state of affairs must be written into the thing itself.

2.0121 It would seem to be a sort of accident, if it turned out that a situation would fit a thing that could already exist entirely on its own.

If things can occur in states of affairs, this possibility must be in them from the beginning. (Nothing in the province of logic can be merely possible. Logic deals with every possibility and all possibilities are its facts.)

Just as we are quite unable to imagine spatial objects outside space or temporal objects outside time, so too there is *no* object that we can imagine excluded from the possibility of combining with others.

If I can imagine objects combined in states of affairs, I cannot imagine them excluded from the *possibility* of such combinations.

2.0122 Things are independent in so far as they can occur in all *possible* situations, but this form of independence is a form of connection with states of affairs, a form of dependence. (It is impossible for words to appear in two different roles: by themselves, and in propositions.)

2.0123 If I know an object I also know all its possible occurrences in states of affairs.

(Every one of these possibilities must be part of the nature of the object.)

A new possibility cannot be discovered later.

2.01231 If I am to know an object, though I need not know its external properties, I must know all its internal properties.

2.0124 If all objects are given, then at the same time all *possible* states of affairs are also given.

2.013 Each thing is, as it were, in a space of possible states of affairs. This space I can imagine empty, but I cannot imagine the thing without the space.

2.0131 A spatial object must be situated in infinite space. (A spatial point is an argument-place.)

A speck in the visual field, though it need not be red, must have some colour: it is, so to speak, surrounded by colour-space. Notes must have *some* pitch, objects of the sense of touch *some* degree of hardness, and so on.

2.014 Objects contain the possibility of all situations.

2.0141 The possibility of its occurring in states of affairs is the form of an object.

2.02 Objects are simple.

2.0201 Every statement about complexes can be resolved into a statement about their constituents and into the propositions that describe the complexes completely.

2.021 Objects make up the substance of the world. That is why they cannot be composite.

2.0211 If the world has no substance, then whether a proposition had sense would depend on whether another proposition was true.

2.0212 In that case we could not sketch any picture of the world (true or false).

2.022 It is obvious that an imagined world, however different it may be from the real one, must have *something* – a form – in common with it.

2.023 Objects are just what constitute this unalterable form.

2.0231 The substance of the world *can* only determine a form, and not any material properties. For it is only by means of propositions that material properties are represented – only by the configuration of objects that they are produced.

2.0232 In a manner of speaking, objects are colourless.

2.0233 If two objects have the same logical form, the only distinction between them, apart from their external properties, is that they are different.

2.02331 Either a thing has properties that nothing else has, in which case we can immediately use a description to distinguish it from the others and refer to it; or, on the other, there are several things that have the whole set of their properties in common, in which case it is quite impossible to indicate one of them.

For if there is nothing to distinguish a thing, I cannot distinguish it, since otherwise it would be distinguished after all.

2.024 Substance is what subsists independently of what is the case.

2.025 It is form and content.

2.0251 Space, time, and colour (being coloured) are forms of objects.

2.026 There must be objects, if the world is to have an unalterable form.

2.027 Objects, the unalterable, and the subsistent are one and the same.

2.0271 Objects are what is unalterable and subsistent; their configuration is what is changing and unstable.

2.0272 The configuration of objects produces states of affairs.

2.03 In a state of affairs objects fit into one another like the links of a chain.

2.031 In a state of affairs objects stand in a determinate relation to one another.

2.032 The determinate way in which objects are connected in a state of affairs is the structure of the state of affairs.

2.033 Form is the possibility of structure.

2.034 The structure of a fact consists of the structures of states of affairs.

2.04 The totality of existing states of affairs is the world.

2.05 The totality of existing states of affairs also determines which states of affairs do not exist.

2.06 The existence and non-existence of states of affairs is reality.

(We also call the existence of states of affairs a positive fact, and their non-existence a negative fact.)

2.061 States of affairs are independent of one another.

2.062 From the existence or non-existence of one state of affairs it is impossible to infer the existence or non-existence of another.

2.063 The sum-total of reality is the world.

2.1 We picture facts to ourselves.

2.11 A picture presents a situation in logical space, the existence and non-existence of states of affairs.

2.12 A picture is a model of reality.

2.13 In a picture objects have the elements of the picture corresponding to them.

2.131 In a picture the elements of the picture are the representatives of objects.

2.14 What constitutes a picture is that its elements are related to one another in a determinate way.

2.141 A picture is a fact.

2.15 The fact that the elements of a picture are related to one another in a determinate way represents that things are related to one another in the same way.

Let us call this connection of its elements the structure of the picture, and let us call the possibility of this structure the pictorial form of the picture.

2.151 Pictorial form is the possibility that things are related to one another in the same way as the elements of the picture.

2.1511 *That* is how a picture is attached to reality; it reaches right out to it.

2.1512 It is laid against reality like a measure.

2.15121 Only the end-points of the graduating lines actually *touch* the object that is to be measured.

2.1513 So a picture, conceived in this way, also includes the pictorial relationship, which makes it into a picture.

2.1514 The pictorial relationship consists of the correlations of the picture's elements with things.

2.1515 These correlations are, as it were, the feelers of the picture's elements, with which the picture touches reality.

2.16 If a fact is to be a picture, it must have something in common with what it depicts.

2.161 There must be something identical in a picture and what it depicts, to enable the one to be a picture of the other at all.

2.17 What a picture must have in common with reality, in order to be able to depict it – correctly or incorrectly – in the way it does, is its pictorial form.

2.171 A picture can depict any reality whose form it has.

A spatial picture can depict anything spatial, a coloured one anything coloured, etc.

2.172 A picture cannot, however, depict its pictorial form: it displays it.

2.173 A picture represents its subject from a position outside it. (Its standpoint is its representational form.) That is why a picture represents its subject correctly or incorrectly.

2.174 A picture cannot, however, place itself outside its representational form.

2.18 What any picture, of whatever form, must have in common with reality, in order to be able to depict it – correctly or incorrectly – in any way at all, is logical form, i.e. the form of reality.

2.181 A picture whose pictorial form is logical form is called a logical picture.

2.182 Every picture is *at the same time* a logical one. (On the other hand, not every picture is, for example, a spatial one.)

2.19 Logical pictures can depict the world.

2.2 A picture has logico-pictorial form in common with what it depicts.

2.201 A picture depicts reality by representing a possibility of existence and nonexistence of states of affairs.

2.202 A picture represents a possible situation in logical space.

2.203 A picture contains the possibility of the situation that it represents.

2.21 A picture agrees with reality or fails to agree; it is correct or incorrect, true or false.

2.22 What a picture represents it represents independently of its truth or falsity, by means of its pictorial form.

2.221 What a picture represents is its sense.

2.222 The agreement or disagreement of its sense with reality constitutes its truth or falsity.

2.223 In order to tell whether a picture is true or false we must compare it with reality.

2.224 It is impossible to tell from the picture alone whether it is true or false.

2.225 There are no pictures that are true *a priori*.

3 A logical picture of facts is a thought [...]

1 The decimal numbers assigned to the individual propositions indicate the logical importance of the propositions, the stress laid on them in my exposition. The propositions n.1, n.2, n.3, etc. are comments on proposition no. n; the propositions n.m1, n.m2, etc. are comments on proposition no. n.m; and so on.

Ludwig Wittgenstein, *Tractatus Logico-Philosophicus* (1921); trans. D.F. Pears and B.F. McGuiness (London: Routledge, 1961) 5-10.

Thomas S. KUHN
The Nature and Necessity of Scientific Revolutions [1962]

What are scientific revolutions and what is their function in scientific development? [...] scientific revolutions are here taken to be those non-cumulative developmental episodes in which an older paradigm is replaced in whole or in part by an incompatible new one. There is more to be said, however, and an essential part of it can be introduced by asking one further question. Why should a change of paradigm be called a revolution? In the face of the vast and essential differences between political and scientific development, what parallelism can justify the metaphor that finds revolutions in both?

One aspect of the parallelism must already be apparent. Political revolutions are inaugurated by a growing sense, often restricted to a segment of the political community, that existing institutions have ceased adequately to meet the problems posed by an environment that they have in part created. In much the same way, scientific revolutions are inaugurated by a growing sense, again often restricted to a narrow subdivision of the scientific community, that an existing paradigm has ceased to function adequately in the exploration of an aspect of nature to which that paradigm itself had previously led the way. In both political and scientific development the sense of malfunction that can lead to crisis is prerequisite to revolution. Furthermore, though it admittedly strains the metaphor, that parallelism holds not only for the major paradigm changes, like those attributable to Copernicus and Lavoisier, but also for the far smaller ones associated with the assimilation of a new sort of phenomenon, like oxygen or X-rays. Scientific revolutions [...] need seem revolutionary only to those whose paradigms are affected by them. To outsiders they may, like the Balkan revolutions of the early twentieth century, seem normal parts of the developmental process. Astronomers, for example, could accept X-rays as a mere addition to knowledge, their paradigms were unaffected by the existence of the new radiation. But for men like Kelvin, Crookes and Roentgen, whose research dealt with radiation theory or with cathode ray tubes, the emergence of X-rays necessarily violated one paradigm as it created another. That is why these rays could be discovered only through something's first going wrong with normal research.

This genetic aspect of the parallel between political and scientific development should no longer be open to doubt. The parallel has, however, a second and more profound aspect upon which the significance of the first depends. Political revolutions aim to change political institutions in ways that those institutions themselves prohibit. Their success therefore necessitates the partial relinquishment of one set of institutions in favour of another, and in the interim, society is not fully governed by institutions at all. Initially it is crisis alone that attenuates the role of political institutions as we have already seen it attenuate the role of paradigms. In increasing numbers individuals become increasingly estranged from political life and behave more and more eccentrically within it. Then, as the crisis deepens, many of these individuals commit themselves to some concrete proposal for the reconstruction of society in a new institutional framework. At that point the society is divided into competing camps or parties, one seeking to defend the old institutional constellation, the others seeking to institute some new one. And, once that polarization has occurred, *political recourse fails*. Because they differ about the institutional matrix within which political change is to be achieved and evaluated, because they acknowledge no supra-institutional framework for the adjudication of revolutionary difference, the parties to a revolutionary conflict must finally resort to the techniques of mass persuasion, often including force. Though revolutions have had a vital role in the evolution of political Institutions, that role depends upon their being partially extra-political or extra-institutional events [...]

The historical study of paradigm change reveals very similar characteristics in the evolution of the sciences. Like the choice between competing political institutions, that between competing paradigms proves to be a choice between incompatible modes of community life. Because it has that character, the choice is not and cannot be determined merely by the evaluative procedures characteristic of normal science, for these depend in part upon a particular paradigm, and that paradigm is at issue. When paradigms enter, as they must, into a debate about paradigm choice, their role is necessarily circular. Each group uses its own paradigm to argue in that paradigm's defence.

The resulting circularity does not, of course, make the arguments wrong or even ineffectual. The man who premises a paradigm when arguing in its defence cart nonetheless provide a clear exhibit of what scientific practice will be like for those who adopt the new view of nature. That exhibit can be immensely persuasive, often compellingly so. Yet, whatever its force, the status of the circular argument is only that of persuasion. It cannot be made logically or even probabilistically compelling for those who refuse to step into the circle. The premises and values shared by the two parties to a debate over paradigms are not sufficiently extensive for that. As in political revolutions, so in paradigm choice – there is no standard higher than the assent of the relevant community. To discover how scientific revolutions are effected, we shall therefore have to examine not only the impact of nature and of logic, but also the techniques of persuasive argumentation effective within the quite special groups that constitute the community of scientists [...]

Thomas S. Kuhn, *The Structure of Scientific Revolutions*, (Chicago: University of Chicago Press, 1962) 92-97.

Robert SMITHSON
Language to be Looked at and/or Things to be Read [1967]

Language operates between literal and metaphorical signification. The power of a word lies in the very inadequacy of the context [in which] it is placed, in the unresolved or partially resolved tension of disparates. A word fixed or a statement isolated without any decorative or 'cubist' visual format, becomes a perception of similarity in dissimilars – in short a paradox. Congruity could be disrupted by a metaphorical complexity within a literal system. Literal usage becomes incantory when all metaphors are suppressed. Here language is built, not written. Yet discursive literalness is apt to be a container for a radical metaphor. Literal statements often conceal violent analogies. The mind resists the false identity of such circumambient suggestions, only to accept an equally false logical surface. Banal words function as a feeble phenomena that fall into their own mental bogs of meaning. An emotion is suggested and demolished in one glance by certain words. Other words constantly shift or invert themselves without ending, these could be called 'suspended words'. Simple statements are often based on language fears, and sometimes result in dogma or non-sense. Words for mental processes are all derived from physical *things*. References are often reversed so that the 'object' takes the place of the 'word'. A is A is never A is A, but rather X is A. The misunderstood notion of a metaphor has it that A is X – that is wrong. The scale of a letter in a word changes one's visual meaning of the word. Language thus becomes monumental because of the mutations of advertising. A word outside of the mind is a set of 'dead letters'. The mania for literalness relates to the breakdown in the rational belief in reality. Books entomb words in a synthetic *rigor mortis*; perhaps that is why 'print' is thought to have entered obsolescence. The mind of this death, however, is unrelentingly awake.

Eton Corrasable

[My sense of language is that it is matter and not ideas

– i.e., 'printed matter'. R.S. 2 June 1972]

Robert Smithson, 'Language to be Looked at and/or Things to be Read', Dwan Gallery press release, 1967; reprinted in *Robert Smithson: The Collected Writings*, ed. Jack Flam, (Berkeley and Los Angeles: University of California Press, 1996) 61.

Robert BARRY, Douglas HUEBLER, Joseph KOSUTH, Seth SIEGELAUB, Lawrence WEINER Art without Space [1969]

Seth Siegelaub What we will hopefully be concerning ourselves with is the nature of the art whose primary existence in the world does not relate to space, not to its exhibition in space, not to its imposing things on the walls [...]

Lawrence Weiner **I disagree wholeheartedly that there could ever be an art without space *per se*. It's just another catch all. Anything that exists has a certain space around it; even an idea exists within a certain space.**

Douglas Huebler **I would agree altogether. Whatever you do involves space. I think the essential thing is that we are not concerned (*I* am not concerned; I should speak for myself) with the specific space wherein the so-called art image exists. There doesn't have to be a museum, gallery or anything for what I do, because the environment does not affect what I do and it is not affected by what I have done.**

Robert Barry **I honestly think there isn't an artist here whose work in some way doesn't have to do with some kind of spatial experiences. For instance, if an art is involved in objects – say there is a tangible three-dimensional object – then it is implied that there is space around it, or that it is *in* space. In fact, space is really defined by the objects that are in it. The object determines the nature of the space that it is in, and you can't really think about absolute space or space without objects. If we are not in close proximity to the object, that doesn't mean that we can't project ourselves. Say Lawrence does something in the Arctic Circle; there is obviously a space between me and the Arctic Circle and that space is very important. Maybe we are just dealing with a space that is different from the space that one experiences when confronting a traditional object.**

Joseph Kosuth **The point is, of course, that we are talking about space in the context of art. In other words, an artist using space as conceptually relevant to whatever his artistic proposition is. I would separate myself from what has been said already because space really has absolutely nothing to do with my work (unless I do a work that is *about* space and then, of course, there are subsequent questions about that). When you are talking about something as rarefied as art is, you begin to realize that words like space have very functional meanings, and when we bring up space in the context of art, considering twentieth-century sculpture and other kinds of interest in space (and the word space, of course, in the 1950s was very much part of the terminology of art), I think the subject is loaded. It has to do with physical objects and the place for them. I don't find those the issues. It's just not relevant to the work I'm doing.**

Barry **I use the word space in two specific senses; one, as an interest or subject matter of the work and, two, which is how I meant it, the space as a condition for the awareness of the work, in other words, a space in which you become aware of the work. For instance, Doug Huebler says he is involved with space. He has tried to document it, distances, time space, things of this nature, but by space I refer to the lack of space.**

Weiner **I don't understand how you can think that something that is a fact of life is not germane. To use Joseph's term – 'rarefied atmosphere of art', etc. – you may be able not to concern yourself with the spatial problem in making art. You may not consider space an art material, but the fact that you are occupying a certain amount of space in a pure physical sense means that you are dealing with space whether you want to or not. Like you can say, I am not terribly interested in oxygen, but you are breathing it.**

Kosuth **But we are talking in the context of art. You conjecture that everything is relevant to art. I don't agree with that. It is very clear that in the nature of art, beginning with the twentieth century, there was a shift in the visual experience from morphological to conceptual. Once you start realizing the implications of that, then you begin to realize that art doesn't have any subject matter; it has only what the artist uses in it.**

Siegelaub Gentlemen, do you have any feelings about how your work relates to the community at large, to the other art that is being made?

Barry **Part of the nature of art is that it is out there in the community, part of what it is in other people's minds, so that it has to be out there ... My own art actually exists in the minds of other people as part of its very nature. Once I present my art, I don't have much control over what other people think of it, but certainly that's part of reality.**

Kosuth **I think that obviously the way art lives is through influencing other artists, but not by the physical residue that exists in museums. Some places exhibit the palettes with the paintings, with an equal amount of pride, because they are both just residues of an artist's activities ... One could make a case for artists just existing conceptually.**

Huebler **I tend to agree and disagree with what Bob said about not being able to affect what happens to the work once it goes out. Some very bad interpretations are made, and you can't help that, but at the same time when the work gets out there again and again, if it is in any way unfamiliar or has any kind of strength, or resonance, it begins to condition that community, which is kind of what I think Joseph is saying. It is an additive process ... The thing that does tie us together in some way is that we are making art that doesn't have an object as the residue. What we call art is not visual, so it can exist in a number of contexts, for some of us at least.**

Barry **Yes. We all make objects that don't have any space around them except the personal experience of space, which is more subjective than our experience of colour, which registers directly on our eyes. We have to learn about depth and space, make judgments about it. Music is a very spatial experience. I think we can experience space in a less physical way and that's the kind of space I'm talking about.**

Weiner **You bring up a very strange problem here. You bring in the subjective. Space for me would be almost an energy, since it doesn't matter to me whether my works are built or not built, or whether I build them or somebody else builds them. It is all exactly the same work, once it is presented or communicated. I believe the work itself produces a certain amount of energy, which in turn displaces a certain amount of space ... The only thing is, they don't have any way yet of determining this objective space, walking over it and chalking it out and saying this is the space that Weiner's idea in 1968 took up.**

Barry **I think space would be more frightening if it were found to be very objective. Maybe there is too much objective art around. People try to get away from their art, depersonalize it, dehumanize it, have someone else make it, or they try to take away any kind of humanistic elements. In my own work I don't. I try to put myself into it, or I try to realize the fact that art is something that is made by human beings, and when I present it, I present it to other human beings, and that is really what it is about.**

Weiner **As I see it, it's an imposition to impose my personal life on the art that attempts to present something to people that is not just about me. It is all about materials, and it is about the world they live in, perhaps, but it is not about themselves, their own personal, everyday lives, which is what I try to take out of my art.**

Siegelaub I would like to ask each of you what exactly you consider your work to be about, the subject matter of your art.

Weiner **I really believe the subject matter of my art is – art.**

Siegelaub What separates your art from Douglas Huebler's?

Weiner **The fact that I made it and he didn't.**

Huebler **I think everything is available as subject matter and I really mean everything. I concern myself with time, space, and things that are going on in the world, and everything. Not in the sense of trying to restate or interpret or express anything, but to take something out of the world just long enough and use just enough of that to throw something out, bring something back, that I can call an image. The way what is brought back is *presented* is just the package. The act of perceiving is what concerns me rather than what is perceived, because it is more interesting to find out what it is we do when we do perceive.**

Barry **I have always considered the viewer. Art is about man himself ... It is about myself, the world around me. It is also about things that I don't know, about using the unknown.**

Kosuth **I don't think art is about man any more than it is about the fact that it is made by man. There are other issues. My own art, my own attempt is to deal with**

abstraction in a way that is real for me and not a metaphoric kind of abstraction or one that grew morphologically out of traditional art, but an abstraction in what abstraction really means.

Siegelaub Much of the work you men are involved in concerns itself with the use of language, which is a radical condition of the art. I'd like to know how you think about it and particularly in reference to how it differs from poetry or literature.

Weiner This is a major problem with me because sharing my work could be done by publishing a book, just the statements *per se* of the work. It would be just as good as if the work were built. As for poetry, poetry is inherently involved in the medium of language as well as the content. I may utilize the medium in an attempt to get across *only* the content, in the most concise package I'm capable of at that moment. Inherent beauty or exciting ramifications of the language don't terribly interest me, but I don't see how you can differentiate poetry from art without the proper information. First you might see it as a poem, but with the correct information, you would accept it as it is intended. Perhaps the art I make and the art the rest of the gentlemen sitting here make differs from previous art in that it relies upon information, whereas previously the art was just presented. Nobody even knew terribly much about the art, how to cope with it.

Huebler The language as information is absolutely necessary. Getting back to the space thing. The person who sits and looks at a TV set in any room and watches the man in the spacecraft, or stepping on the moon, makes a literal spatial jump that goes beyond any perceptual frame he could possibly have. Then there is the information that tells him that that picture is not contained in that frame; that picture is like 240,000 miles away, or however far the moon is, and it absolutely demands language. I don't think any of us jumping over into language are interested in pure information, or pure poetry, but it would be a kind of McLuhan world where we do transcend the space that we can ordinarily perceive.

Barry In my work the language itself isn't the art. It doesn't even describe or detail the art much. I use language as a sign to indicate that there is art, the direction in which the art is, and to prepare someone for the art ... to communicate your ideas through language.

Kosuth Yes, when you deal with language you deal with it conceptually and when you deal with things conceptually, you deal with them in a most general way. My recourse is a way of making it clear that I'm using language to go beyond language. One begins to realize that if one uses language, as a medium it becomes invisible, so that you don't focus on any specifics, which implies a sort of stance, a kind of philosophy. Composition and taste are specific but language is very neuter because it is used in so many ways.

Huebler If I might pose this: the idea of words as a convention and by extension the popular use of them as a more general condition, doesn't that parallel the use of the picture frame for 60,000 years in which the rectangular painting became a convention? Isn't it subject to the same changes and pressures? What are you laughing about, Weiner?

Weiner Well, the ease with which you throw that out on the table belies what you are saying, because the picture-frame convention was a very real thing. The painting stopped at that edge. When you are dealing with language, there is no edge that the picture drops over or drops off. You are dealing with something completely infinite. Language, because it is the most non-objective thing we have ever developed in this world, never stops.

Kosuth Your analogy works better for poetry, in the sense that poetry has as much to do with words as *material*. I think that's why most of the concrete poets are now starting to do theatre and getting out of concrete poetry [Acconci, Perreault, Hannah Weiner, etc.]. They realize the sort of decadence that follows from that sort of materialism. They are trying to say things about the world that are illogical in terms of language.

Siegelaub One becomes very much aware of the speed with which this art travels, of the way it is rapidly transferred from continent to continent or city to city, by virtue of its portability, more quickly than other art.

Barry I haven't found that people understand it any faster [...]

Weiner I don't have that trouble because I'm working within the realm of complete generalities. There can be no misreadings. If somebody chooses, when they receive a piece, to build it themselves, they can't do it wrong. They can do it in a way that might displease me personally but not aesthetically. They can't do it wrong.

Kosuth Conceptually.

Weiner Not conceptually. They just can't do it wrong. You like the word conceptual. For you, it's fine. It fits you. I don't really see it fitting me. I don't think there is a preconceived concept because the material is so erratic.

Kosuth If you make a statement, say your work is so much paint poured; if you follow that concept, you can't do anything wrong because you are following that concept, right?

Weiner Well, the concept is not necessarily a conceptual situation.

Kosuth I mean the conceptual has to do with the fact that you can deal with what I'm saying, and that those words have meanings; those words are the conception. I wasn't making any rarefied art-context use of the word conceptual. I was just using the word's standard meaning. You use language, so conceptual is applicable, whether you like it or not, baby.

Robert Barry, Douglas Huebler, Joseph Kosuth, Lawrence Weiner, 'Art Without Space' symposium moderated by Seth Siegelaub, broadcast on WBAI-FM, New York, 2 November 1969; excerpts from transcripts published in Lucy R. Lippard, *Six Years: The Dematerialization of the Art Object from 1966 to 1972* (London: Studio Vista, 1973; reprinted: Berkeley and Los Angeles: University of California Press, 1997) 127-33.

ART & LANGUAGE

Introduction, *Art-Language*

[1969]

[...] Suppose the following hypothesis is advanced: that this editorial, in itself an attempt to evince some outlines as to what 'conceptual art' is, is held out as a 'conceptual art' work. At first glance this seems to be a parallel case to many past situations within the determined limits of visual art, for example the first Cubist painting might be said to have attempted to evince some outlines as to what visual art is, whilst, obviously, being held out as a work of visual art. But the difference here is one of what shall be called 'the form of the work'. Initially what conceptual art seems to be doing is questioning the condition that seems to rigidly govern the form of visual art – that visual art remains visual.

During the past two years, a number of artists have developed projects and theses, the earliest of which were initially housed pretty solidly within the establishment constructs of visual art. Many of these projects etc. have evolved in such a manner that their relationship to visual art conventions has become increasingly tenuous. The later projects particularly are represented through objects, the visual form of which is governed by the form of the conventional signs of written language (in this case English). The content of the artist's idea is expressed through the semantic qualities of the written language. As such, many people would judge that this tendency is better described by the category-name 'art-theory' or 'art criticism'; there can be little doubt that works of 'conceptual art' can be seen to include both the periphery of art criticism and of art theory, and this tendency may well be amplified. With regard to this particular point, criteria bearing upon the chronology of art theory may have to be more severely and stringently accounted for, particularly in terms of evolutionary analogies. For example the question is not simply: 'Are works of art theory part of the kit of the conceptual artist, and as such can such a work, when advanced by a conceptual artist come up of the count as a work of conceptual art?' But also: 'Are past works of art-theory now to be counted as works of conceptual art?' What has to be considered here is the intention of the conceptual artist. It is very doubtful whether an art theoretician could have advanced one of his works as a work of 'conceptual art' (say) in 1964, as the first rudiments of at least an embryonic awareness of the notion of 'conceptual art' were not evident until 1966. The intention of the 'conceptual artist' has been separated off from that of the art theoretician because of their previously different relationships and standpoint towards art, that is, the nature of their involvement in it.

If the question is formed the other way round, that is, not as 'Does art-theory come up for the count as a possible sector of 'conceptual art'?' but as, 'Does 'conceptual art' come up for the count as a possible sector of art-theory?' then a rather vaguely defined category is being advanced as a possible member of a more established one. Perhaps some qualification can be made for such an assertion. The development of some work by certain artists both in Britain and the USA does not, if their intentions are to be taken into account, simply mean a matter of a transfer of function from that of artist to count various theoretical constructs as artworks. This has contingently meant, either (1) If they are to be 'left alone' as separate, then re-defining carefully the definitions of both art and art theory, in order to assign more clearly what kind of entity belongs to which category. If this is take up it usually means that the definition of art is expanded, and art theoreticians then discuss the consequences and possibilities of the new definitions, the traditional format of the art theoretician discussing what the artist has implied, entailed etc., by his 'creative act'. Or (2) To allow the peripheral area between the two categories some latitude of interpretation and consequently account the category 'art theory' a category which the category 'art' might expand to include. The category 'maker of visual art' has been traditionally regarded as solely the domain of the visual-art object producer (i.e. the visual-art artist). There has been a hierarchy of languages headed by the 'direct read-out from the object' language which has served as the creative core, and then various support languages acting as explicative and elucidatory tools to the central creative core. The initial language has been what is called 'visual', the support languages have taken on what shall be called here 'conventional written sign' language-form. What is surprising is that although the central core has been seen to be an ever evolving language no account up to the present seems to have taken up the possibility of this central core evolving to include and assimilate one or other or all of the support languages. It is through the nature of the evolution of the works of 'conceptual art' that the implicated artists have been obliged to take account of this possibility. Hence these artists do not see appropriateness of the label 'art theoretician' necessarily eliminating the appropriateness of the label 'artist'. Inside the framework of 'conceptual art' the making of art and the making of a certain kind of art theory are often the same procedure.

With a context such as this the initial question can be posed with a view to a more specific enquiry. The question: 'Can this editorial, in itself an attempt to evince some outlines as to what 'conceptual art' is, come up for the count as a work of conceptual art? Firstly, the established notions of what the presentation of art and the procedures of art-making entail have to be surveyed. The question 'Can this editorial come up for the count as a work of art within a developed framework of the visual art convention?' can only be answered providing some thorough account is given of what is meant be 'developed' here. At the present we do not, as a norm, expect to find works of visual art in magazines, we expect critical, historical, etc. comment upon them, photographic reproductions etc. The structures of the identity of art-objects have consecutively been placed under stress by each new movement in art, and the succession of new movements has become more rapid this century. In view of this phenomenon perhaps the above question can be altered to: 'Can this editorial come up for the count as a member of the extended class 'visual art work'?' Here 'extended' replaces 'developed' and can, perhaps, be made to point out the problem as follows:

Suppose an artist exhibits an essay in an art exhibition (as a print might be exhibited). The pages are simply laid out flat in reading order behind glass within a frame. The spectator is intended to read the essay 'straight', as a notice might be read, but because the essay is mounted in an art ambience it is implied that the object (paper with print upon it) carries conventional visual art content. The spectator being puzzled at nor really being able to grasp any direct visual art read-out meaning starts to read it (as a notice might be read). It goes as follows:

'On why this is an essay'

The appearance of this essay is unimportant in any strong sense of visual-art appearance criteria. The prime requirement in regard of this essay's appearance is that is reasonably legible. Any decisions apart from this have been taken with a view to what it should not look like as a point of emphasis over what it should look like. These secondary decisions are aimed at eliminating as many appearance similarities to established art-objects as possible.

Thus if the essay is to be evaluated in terms of the content expressed in the writing (WHICH IT IS), then in an obvious established sense many people would say that if it has a connection with art at all, that it fits better into the category 'art-criticism' or 'art theory'. Such a statement at least admits the observation that when an artist uses '(a piece of) writing' in this context then he is not using such an object in the way that art audiences are accustomed to it being used. But further it admits of a rather more bigoted view, that is, this essay belongs more to art criticism or art theory because it is formed of writing and in this sense it looks more like art criticism or art theory than it looks like art; that is, that this object (a piece of writing) does not have sufficient appearance criteria to be identified as a member of the class 'art object' – it does not look like art. This observation has a strong assumption behind it that the making of a traditional art object (i.e. one to be judged within the visual evaluative framework) is a necessary condition for the making of art. Suppose there are some areas (say) pertaining to art at present which are of such a nature that they need not, maybe cannot, any longer meet the requirements which have previously been required as a necessary mode of an object coming up for the count as a member of the class 'art work'. This necessary mode is formulated as follows, (say) the recognition of art in the object is through some aspect(s) of the visual qualities of the object as they are directly perceived.

The question of 'recognition' is a crucial one here. There has been a constantly developing series of methods throughout the evolution of the art whereby the artist has attempted to construct various devices to ensure that his intention to count the object as an art object is recognised. This has not always been 'given' within the object itself [...]

The concept of using 'declaration' as a technique for making art was used by Terry Atkinson and Michael Baldwin for purposes of the 'Air-conditioning Show' and 'Air Show' which were formulated in 1967. For example the basic tenet of the 'Air Show' was a series of assertions concerning a theoretical usage of a column of air comprising a base of one square mile and of unspecified distance in the vertical dimension. No particular square mile of the earth's surface was specified. The concept did not entail any such particularized location. A quote from some of the preliminary notes from the 'Air Show' will perhaps serve to elucidate the concept further:

'A persistent objection that there has so far been no indication that the 'Air Shows' etc. are any more than fictional entities (in so far as it doesn't seem to matter if that is what they are), whereas paintings, sculptures, etc. are real things – concrete entities, offering actual concrete experiences, can be answered only by the evincing of possible instrumental 'tests' etc. (observations): when an assertion is made to the effect that a sculpture, say, is made of 'real' gold etc. there is an implication that it is not made of an imitation, or that it is not defective in some way. Something like that can be said of the 'Air Show' – but not about the situation (i.e. the described state of affairs) – it is said of the concept: the question as to whether or not one can say that something is 'real' here, is not one that comes up naturally, the circumstances in which such a question might arise might be those in which one is looking for concept defects (being fictional).

The objector is just asserting that these 'things' don't occur in a series of persual (perceptual) situations' [...]

The existential object upon which the 'content' [...] is formulated (i.e. paper with print on it) is not the art object; the art object is not an object which can be directly perceived, the 'object' component is merely specified. Once having established writing as a method of specifying points in an enquiry of this kind, there seems no reason to assume that enquiries pertaining to the art area should necessarily have to use theoretical objects simply because art in the past has required the presence of a concrete object before art can be thought of as 'taking place'; having gained the use of such a wide ranging instrument as 'straight' writing, then objects, concrete and theoretical, are only two types of entity which can count, a whole range of other types of entities become candidates for art usage. Some of the British artists involved in this area have constructed a number of hypotheses using entities which might be regarded as alien to art. Most of these enquiries do not exhibit the framework of the established art-to-object relationship and (if you like) they are not categorically asserted as members of the class 'art object', nor for that matter is there a categorical assertion that they are art ('work'); but such a lack of absolute assertion does not prohibit them from being tentatively asserted as having some important interpellations for the art area.

Terry Atkinson, David Bainbridge, Michael Baldwin, Harold Hurrell, 'Introduction', *Art-Language: The Journal of Conceptual Art*, 1:1 (May 1969) 1-6.

Joseph KOSUTH
Art after Philosophy [1969]

[...] The function of art, as a question, was first raised by Marcel Duchamp. In fact it is Marcel Duchamp whom we can credit with giving art its own identity. (One can certainly see a tendency towards this self-identification of art beginning with Manet and Cézanne through to Cubism,[1] but their works are timid and ambiguous by comparison with Duchamp's.) 'Modern' art and the work before seemed connected by virtue of their morphology. Another way of putting it would be that art's 'language' remained the same, but it was saying new things. The event that made conceivable the realization that it was possible to 'speak another language' and still make sense in art was Marcel Duchamp's first unassisted readymade. With the unassisted readymade, art changed its focus from the form of the language to what was being said. Which means that it changed the nature of art from a question of morphology to a question of function. This change – one from 'appearance' to 'conception' – was the beginning of 'modern' art and the beginning of 'conceptual' art. All art (after Duchamp) is conceptual (in nature) because art only exists conceptually.

The 'value' of particular artists after Duchamp can be weighed according to how much they questioned the nature of art; which is another way of saying 'what they *added* to the conception of art' or what wasn't there before they started. Artists question the nature of art by presenting new propositions as to art's nature. And to do this one cannot concern oneself with the handed-down 'language' of traditional art, since this activity is based on the assumption that there is only one way of framing art propositions. But the very stuff of art is indeed greatly related to 'creating' new propositions.

The case is often made – particularly in reference to Duchamp – that objects of art (such as the readymades, of course, but all art is implied in this) are judged as *objets d'art* in later years and the artists' *intentions* become irrelevant. Such an argument is the case of a preconceived notion of art ordering together not necessarily related facts. The point is this: aesthetics, as we have pointed out, are conceptually irrelevant to art. Thus, any physical thing can become an *objet d'art*, that is to say, can be considered tasteful, aesthetically pleasing, etc. But this has no bearing on the object's application to an art context; that is, its *functioning* in an art context. (E.g. if a collector takes a painting, attaches legs, and uses it as a dining table it's an act unrelated to art or the artist because, as art, that wasn't the artist's *intention*.)

And what holds true for Duchamp's work applies as well to most of the art after him. In other words, the value of Cubism is its idea in the realm of art, not the physical or visual qualities seen in a specific painting, or the particularization of certain colours or shapes. For these colours and shapes are the art's 'language', not its meaning conceptually as art. To look upon a Cubist 'masterwork' *now* as art is nonsensical, conceptually speaking, as far as art is concerned. (That visual information which was unique in Cubism's language has now been generally absorbed and has a lot to do with the way in which one deals with painting 'linguistically'. [E.g. what a Cubist painting meant experimentally and conceptually to, say, Gertrude Stein, is beyond our speculation because the same painting then 'meant' something different than it does now.]) The 'value' now of an original Cubist painting is not unlike, in most respects, an original manuscript by Lord Byron, or *The Spirit of St. Louis* as it is seen in the Smithsonian Institution. (Indeed, museums fill the very same function as the Smithsonian Institution – why else would the *Jeu de Paume* wing of the Louvre exhibit Cézanne's and Van Gogh's palettes as proudly as they do their paintings?) Actual works of art are little more than historical curiosities. As far as *art* is concerned Van Gogh's paintings aren't worth any more than his palette is. They are both 'collector's items'.[2]

Art 'lives' through influencing other art, not by existing as the physical residue of an artist's ideas. The reason why different artists from the past are 'brought alive' again is because some aspect of their work becomes 'usable' by living artists. That there is no 'truth' as to what art is seems quite unrealized.

What is the function of art, or the nature of art? If we continue our analogy of the forms art takes as being art's *language* one can realize then that a work of art is a kind of *proposition* presented within the context of art as a comment on art. We can then go further and analyze the types of 'propositions'.

A.J. Ayer's evaluation of Kant's distinction between analytic and synthetic is useful to us here: 'A proposition is analytic when its validity depends solely on the definitions of the symbols it contains, and synthetic when its validity is determined by the facts of experience.'[3] The analogy I will attempt to make is one between the art condition and the condition of the analytic proposition. In that they don't appear to be believable as anything else, nor about anything (other than art), the forms of art most clearly finally referable only to art have been forms closest to analytical propositions.

Works of art are analytic propositions. That is, if viewed within their context – as art – they provide no information whatsoever about any matter of fact. A work of art is a tautology in that it is a presentation of the artist's intention, that is, he is saying that a particular work of art is art, which means, is a *definition* of art. Thus, that it is art is true *a priori* (which is what Judd means when he states that 'if someone calls it art, it's art').

Indeed, it is nearly impossible to discuss art in general terms without talking in tautologies – for to attempt to 'grasp' art by any other 'handle' is to merely focus on another aspect or quality of the proposition which is usually irrelevant to the art work's 'art condition'. One begins to realize that art's 'art condition' is a conceptual state. That the language forms which the artist frames his propositions in are often 'private' codes or languages is an inevitable outcome of art's freedom from morphological constrictions; and it follows from this that one has to be familiar with contemporary art to appreciate it and understand it. Likewise one understands why the 'man on the street' is intolerant to artistic art and always demands art in a traditional 'language'. (And one understands why formalist art 'sells like hot cakes'.) Only in painting and sculpture did the artists all speak the same language. What is called 'Novelty Art' by the formalists is often the attempt to find new languages, although a new language doesn't necessarily mean the framing of new propositions: e.g. most kinetic and electronic art.

Another way of stating in relation to art what Ayer asserted about the analytic method in the context of language would be the following: The validity of artistic propositions is not dependent on any empirical, much less any aesthetic, presupposition about the nature of things. For the artist, as an analyst, is not directly concerned with the physical properties of things. He is concerned only with the way (1) in which art is capable of conceptual growth and (2) how his propositions are capable of logically following that growth.[4] In other words, the propositions of art are not factual, but linguistic in *character* – that is, they do not describe the behaviour of physical, or even mental objects; they express definitions of art, or the formal consequences of definitions of art. Accordingly, we can say that art operates on a logic. For we shall see that the characteristic mark of a purely logical inquiry is that it is concerned with the formal consequences of our definitions (of art) and not with questions of empirical fact.[5]

To repeat, what art has in common with logic and mathematics is that it is a tautology; i.e., the 'art idea' (or 'work') and art are the same and can be appreciated as art without going outside the context of art for verification.

On the other hand, let us consider why art cannot be (or has difficulty when it attempts to be) a synthetic proposition. Or, that is to say, when the truth or falsity of its assertion is verifiable on empirical grounds. Ayer states:

'... *The criterion by which we determine the validity of an* a priori *or analytical proposition is not sufficient to determine the validity of an empirical or synthetic proposition. For it is characteristic of empirical propositions that their validity is not purely formal. To say that a geometrical proposition, or a system of geometrical propositions, is false, is to say that it is self-contradictory. But an empirical proposition, or a system of empirical propositions, may be free from contradiction, and still be false. It is said to be false, not because it is formally defective, but because it fails to satisfy some material criterion.*'[6]

The unreality of 'realistic' art is due to its framing as an art proposition in synthetic terms: one is always tempted to 'verify' the proposition empirically. Realism's synthetic state does not bring one to a circular swing back into a dialogue with the larger framework of questions about the nature of *art* (as does the work of Malevich, Mondrian, Pollock, Reinhardt, early Rauschenberg, Johns, Lichtenstein, Warhol, Andre, Judd, Flavin, LeWitt, Morris, and others), but rather, one is flung out of art's 'orbit' into the 'infinite space' of the human condition.

Pure Expressionism, continuing with Ayer's terms, could be considered as such: 'A sentence which consisted of demonstrative symbols would not express a genuine proposition. It would be a mere ejaculation, in no way characterizing that to which it was supposed to refer.'

Expressionist works are usually such 'ejaculations' presented in the morphological language of traditional art. If Pollock is important it is because he painted on loose canvas horizontally to the floor. What *isn't* important is that he later put those drippings over stretchers and hung them parallel to the wall. (In other words, what is important in art is what one *brings* to it, not one's adoption of what was previously existing.) What is even less important to art is Pollock's notions of 'self-expression' because those *kinds* of subjective meanings are useless to anyone other than those involved with him personally. And their 'specific' quality puts them outside of art's context.

'I do not make art', Richard Serra says, 'I am engaged in an activity; if someone wants to call it art, that's his business, but it's not up to me to decide that. That's all figured out later.' Serra, then, is very much aware of the implications of his work. If Serra is indeed just 'figuring out what lead does' (gravitationally, molecularly, etc.) why should *anyone* think of it as art? If he doesn't take the responsibility of it being art, who can, or should? His work certainly appears to be empirically verifiable: lead can do and be used for many physical activities. In itself this does anything but lead us into a dialogue about the nature of art. In a sense then he is a primitive. He has no idea about art. How is it then that we know about 'his activity'? Because he has told us it is art by his actions *after* 'his activity' has taken place. That is, by the fact he is with several galleries, puts the physical residue of his activity in museums (and sells them to art collectors – but as we have pointed out, collectors are irrelevant to the 'condition of art' of a work). That he denies his work is art but plays the artist is more than just a paradox. Serra secretly feels that 'arthood' is arrived at empirically. Thus, as Ayer has stated: 'There are no absolutely certain empirical propositions. It is only tautologies that are certain. Empirical questions are one and all hypotheses, which may be confirmed or discredited in actual sense-experience. And the propositions in which we record the observations that verify these hypotheses are themselves hypotheses which are subject to the test of further sense-experience. Thus there is no final proposition.'[7]

What one finds all throughout the writings of Ad Reinhardt is this very similar thesis of 'art-as-art', and that 'art is always dead, and a "living" art is a deception'.[8] Reinhardt had a very clear idea about the nature of art, and his importance is far from being recognized.

Forms of art that can be considered synthetic propositions are verifiable by the world, that is to say, to understand these propositions one must leave the tautological-like framework of art and consider 'outside' information. But to consider it as art it is necessary to ignore this same outside information, because outside information (experiential qualities, to note) has its own intrinsic worth. And to comprehend this worth one does not need a state of 'art condition'.

From this it is easy to realize that art's viability is not connected to the presentation of visual (or other) kinds of experience. That this may have been one of art's extraneous functions in the preceding centuries is not unlikely. After all, man in even the nineteenth century lived in a fairly standardized visual environment. That is, it was ordinarily predictable as to what he would be coming into contact with day after day. His visual environment in the part of the world in which he lived was fairly consistent. In our time we have an experientially drastically richer environment. One can fly all over the earth in a matter of hours and days, not months. We have the cinema, and colour television, as well as the man-made spectacle of the lights of Las Vegas or the skyscrapers of New York City. The whole world is there to be seen, and the whole world can watch man walk on the moon from their living rooms. Certainly art or objects of painting and sculpture cannot be expected to compete experientially with this?

The notion of 'use' is relevant to art and its 'language'. Recently the box or cube form has been used a great deal within the context of art. (Take for instance its use by Judd, Morris, LeWitt, Bladen, Smith, Bell and McCracken – not to mention the quantity of boxes and cubes that came after.) The difference between all the various uses of the box or cube form is directly related to the differences in the intentions of the artists. Further, as is particularly seen in Judd's work, the use of the box or cube form illustrates very well our earlier claim that an object is only art when placed in the context of art.

A few examples will point this out. One could say that if one of Judd's box forms was seen filled with debris, seen placed in an industrial setting, or even merely seen sitting on a street corner, it would not be identified with art. It follows then that understanding and consideration of it as an art work is necessary *a priori* to viewing it in order to 'see' it as a work of art. Advance information about the concept of art and about an artist's concepts is necessary to the appreciation and understanding of contemporary art. Any and all of the physical attributes (qualities) of contemporary works if considered separately and/or specifically are irrelevant to the art concept. The art concept (as Judd said, though he didn't mean it this way) must be considered in its whole. To consider a concept's parts is invariably to consider aspects that are irrelevant to its art condition – or like reading *parts* of a definition.

It comes as no surprise that the art with the least fixed morphology is the example from which we decipher the nature of the general term 'art'. For where there is a context existing separately of its morphology and consisting of its function one is more likely to find results less conforming and predictable. It is in modern art's possession of a 'language' with the shortest history that the plausibility of the abandonment of that 'language' becomes most possible. It is understandable then that the art that came out of Western painting and sculpture is the most energetic, questioning (of its nature), and the least assuming of all the general 'art' concerns. In the final analysis, however, all of the arts have but (in Wittgenstein's terms) a 'family' resemblance.

Yet the various qualities relatable to an 'art condition' possessed by poetry, the novel, the cinema, the theatre, and various forms of music, etc., is that aspect of them most reliable to the function of art as asserted here.

Is not the decline of poetry relatable to the implied metaphysics from poetry's use of 'common' language as an art language?[9] In New York the last decadent stages of poetry can be seen in the move by 'Concrete' poets recently towards the use of actual objects and theatre.[10] Can it be that they feel the unreality of their art form?

'We see now that the axioms of a geometry are simply definitions, and that the theorems of a geometry are simply the logical consequences of these definitions. A geometry is not in itself about physical space; in itself it cannot be said to be 'about' anything. But we can use a geometry to reason about physical space. That is to say, once we have given the axioms a physical interpretation, we can proceed to apply the theorems to the objects which satisfy the axioms. Whether a geometry can be applied to the actual physical world or not, is an empirical question which falls outside the scope of geometry itself. There is no sense, therefore, in asking which of the various geometries known to us are false and which are true. In so far as they are all free from contradiction, they are all true. The proposition which states that a certain application of a geometry is possible is not itself a proposition of that geometry. All that the geometry itself tells us is that if anything can be brought under the definitions, it will also satisfy the theorems. It is therefore a purely logical system, and its propositions are purely analytic propositions.'
— A. J. Ayer[11]

Here then I propose rests the viability of art. In an age when traditional philosophy is unreal because of its assumptions, art's ability to exist will depend not only on its *not* performing a service – as entertainment, visual (or other) experience, or decoration – which is something easily replaced by kitsch culture and technology, but rather, it will remain viable by *not* assuming a philosophical stance; for in art's unique character is the capacity to remain aloof from philosophical judgements. It is in this context that art shares similarities with logic, mathematics and, as well, science. But whereas the other endeavours are useful, art is not. Art indeed exists for its own sake.

In this period of man, after philosophy and religion, art may possibly be one endeavour that fulfills what another age might have called 'man's spiritual needs'. Or, another way of putting it might be that art deals analogously with the state of things 'beyond physics' where philosophy had to make assertions. An art's strength is that even the preceding sentence is an assertion, and cannot be verified by art. Art's only claim is for art. Art is the definition of art [...]

The 'purest' definition of conceptual art would be that it is inquiry into the foundations of the concept 'art', as it has come to mean. Like most terms with fairly specific meanings generally applied, 'conceptual art' is often considered as a *tendency*. In one sense it is a tendency of course because the 'definition' of 'Conceptual Art' is very close to the meanings of art itself.

But the reasoning behind the notion of such a tendency, I am afraid, is still connected to the fallacy of morphological characteristics as a connective between what are really disparate activities. In this case it is an attempt to detect stylehood. In assuming a primary cause-effect relationship to 'final outcomes', such criticism bypasses a particular artist's intents (concepts) to deal exclusively with his 'final outcome'. Indeed most criticism has dealt with only one very superficial aspect of this 'final outcome', and that is the apparent 'immateriality' or 'anti-object' similarity amongst most 'conceptual' works of art. But this can only be important if one assumes that objects are necessary to art – or to phrase it better, that they have a definitive relation to art. And in this case such criticism would be focusing on a negative aspect of the art [...]

This is not to say that a particular 'art investigation' may or may not employ objects, material substances, etc. within the confines of its investigation. Certainly the investigations carried out by Bainbridge and Hurrell are excellent examples of such a use.[12] Although I have proposed that all art is finally conceptual, some recent work is clearly conceptual in intent whereas other examples of recent art are only related to conceptual art in a superficial manner. And although this work is in most cases an advance over Formalist or 'Anti-Formalist' (Morris, Serra, Sonnier, Hesse, and others) tendencies, it should not be considered 'Conceptual Art' in the *purer* sense of the term.

Three artists often associated with me (through Seth Siegelaub's projects) – Douglas Huebler, Robert Barry, and Lawrence Weiner – are not concerned with, I do not think, 'Conceptual Art' as it was previously stated. Douglas Huebler, who was in the 'Primary Structures' show at the Jewish Museum (New York), uses a non-morphologically art-like form of presentation (photographs, maps, mailings) to answer iconic, structural sculpture issues directly related to his formica sculpture (which he was making as late as 1968). This is pointed out by the artist in the opening sentence of the catalogue of his 'one-man show' (which was organized by Seth Siegelaub and existed only as a catalogue of documentation): 'The existence of each sculpture is documented by its documentation'. It is not my intention to point out a *negative* aspect of the work, but only to show that Huebler – who is in his mid-forties and much older than most of the artists discussed here – has not as much in common with the aims in the *purer* versions of 'Conceptual Art' as it would superficially seem.

The other men – Robert Barry and Lawrence Weiner – have watched their work take on a 'Conceptual Art' association almost by accident. Barry, whose painting was seen in the 'Systemic Painting' show at the Guggenheim Museum, has in common with Weiner the fact that the 'path' to conceptual art came via decisions related to choices of art materials and processes. Barry's post-Newman/Reinhardt paintings 'reduced' (in physical material, not 'meaning') along a path from two-inch square paintings, to single lines of wire between architectural points, to radio-wave beams, to inert gases, and finally to 'brain energy'. His work then seems to exist conceptually only because the material is invisible. But his art does have a physical state, which is different than work which only exists conceptually.

Lawrence Weiner, who gave up painting in the spring of 1968, changed his notion of 'place' (in an Andrean sense) from the context of the canvas (which could only be specific) to a context which was 'general', yet all the while continuing his concern with specific materials and processes. It became obvious to him that if one is not concerned with 'appearance' (which he wasn't, and in this regard he preceded most of the 'Anti-Form' artists) there was not only no need for the fabrication (such as in his studio) of his work, but – more important – such fabrication would again invariably give his work's 'place' a specific context. Thus, by the summer of 1968, he decided to have his work exist only as a proposal in his notebook – that is, until a 'reason' (museum, gallery, or collector) or as he called them, a 'receiver' necessitated his work to be made. It was in the late Fall of that same year that Weiner went one step further in deciding that it didn't matter whether it was made or not. In that sense his private notebooks became public.[13]

Purely conceptual art is first seen concurrently in the work of Terry Atkinson and Michael Baldwin in Coventry, England; and with my own work done in New York City, all generally around 1966.[14] On Kawara, a Japanese artist who has been continuously travelling around the world since 1959, has been doing a highly conceptualized kind of art since 1964 [...]

1 As Terry Atkinson pointed out in his introduction to *Art-Language* 1:1, the Cubists never questioned *if* art had morphological characteristics, but *which* ones in *painting* were acceptable.

2 When someone 'buys' a Flavin he isn't buying a light show, for if he was he could just go to a hardware store and get the goods for considerably less. He isn't 'buying' anything. He is subsidizing Flavin's activity as an artist.

3 A.J. Ayer, *Language, Truth and Logic* (New York: Dover, 1946) 78.

4 Ibid., 57.

5 Ibid., 57.

6 Ibid., 90.

7 Ibid., 94.

8 *Ad Reinhardt: Paintings*, 12.

9 It is poetry's use of common language to attempt to *say the unsayable* which is problematic, not any inherent problem in the use of language within the context of art.

10 Ironically, many of them call themselves 'Conceptual Poets'. Much of this work is very similar to Walter de Maria's work and this is not coincidental; de Maria's work functions as a kind of 'object' poetry, and his intentions are very poetic: he really wants his work to change men's lives.

11 Ayer, 82.

12 *Art-Language* 1:1.

13 I did not (and still do not) understand this last decision. Since I first met Weiner, he defended his position (quite alien to mine) of being a 'Materialist'. I always found this last direction (e.g. *Statements*) sensical in *my* terms, but I never understood how it was in his.

14 I began dating my work with the *Art as Idea as Idea* series.

Joseph Kosuth, 'Art after Philosophy', *Studio International*, 178:915-17 (October, November, December 1969) 134-37, 160-61, 212-13; reprinted in Alexander Alberro; Blake Stimson (eds.) *Conceptual Art: A Critical Anthology* (Cambridge, Massachusetts: MIT Press, 1999) 164-77.

Ian BURN
Dialogue [1970]

1 Artists are exploring language to create access to ways of seeing.
2 Perception is no longer a direct and unified act, through language it has become fragmented and dispersed.
3 Language has become an integral part and tool of activity.

1 Language and the product are separate and independent.
2 Language influences and alters the perceiving and recognizing of material and products.
3 Language reduces the role of perception and brings into use new material, areas for ideas and processes beyond previous perceiving.

1 Language has more relevance in terms of idea.
2 The product ceases to have a focal centre: perceiving becomes scanning rather than focusing, taking in a field of no particular emphasis rather than directing interest.
3 The viewing is an experience outside of the idea and its structure, visual interest has become arbitrary.

1 Language suggests, through the idea and the viewer, a kind of dialogue or 'conversation'.
2 This creates an actual area of the work.
3 Participating in the dialogue gives the viewer a new significance; rather than listening, he becomes involved in reproducing and inventing part of that dialogue.

Ian Burn, 'Dialogue', *Art-Language*, 1:2 (February 1970) 22.

Terry ATKINSON
From an Art & Language Point of View [1970]

One can assume that whether or not in the long run the artists associated directly with Art and Language Press are called conceptual artists is of no matter, one hopes anyway that in the future there will be new, younger artists bringing fresh ideas to the identity of the Press thus affecting its identity no matter what it is or what it is called. What this essay is concerned with is the Art and Language view of the conceptual field in general and as a means of detailing out this view some critiques of some conceptual artists in particular. Knowing the way that Joseph Kosuth's articles in the recent October and November *Studio International* have been received by many sectors of the Conceptual Art fraternity, one would hardly expect this essay to be received any more favourably by the same sectors of the fraternity. The essay is, nevertheless, an honest attempt to articulate a viewpoint of which over the past eighteen months or so, the Art and Language artists have become increasingly convinced. It is an attempt to point out some of the inconsistencies which the Art and Language artists feel to be involved in much recent work. It is hoped that the pointing out of these inconsistencies will help clarify the work of the Art and Language artists if only by virtue of showing a considerable gap in both method and technique between them and some other conceptual artists [...]

CONCEPTUAL ART AND SOME CONCEPTUAL ARTISTS
An early attempt in classifying, and in classifying attempting to make some sense of, the actions from 'Minimal' across 'Conceptual' art is the Chandler-Lippard document 'The Dematerialization of Art' (*Art International*, February, 1968). Since this document was published much of the work it refers to and attempts to place, still remains, to my mind, in a cloudy and unclarified ambience. Such an ambience is merely an aggregated result of what I think is a profuse amount of mumbo-jumbo and witch-doctor talk by many of the artists and writers surveyed by the document and perhaps even more so in the case of many artists and writers who have gathered beneath the Conceptual flag since. The article itself can be seen, in the main, to be uncontroversial in its descriptive aspects, and some of its prophetic notions seem to be fairly sound. It is not a serious aim of this paper to challenge the article, but there are points in the Chandler-Lippard writing that offer a sufficiently appropriate grip on an initial avenue into an extrapolation of an Art and Language point of view to warrant their use. Firstly one can say that a title using such a notion as dematerialization must at many points be referring to our concept, or concepts, of matter; and this regardless of how metaphorical usage is being deployed. This concern with concepts of matter is an extremely commensurate sector for thematic understanding of an Art and Language point of view. An examination of such concepts is the most relevant means of cementing this paper into a reasonably coherent pattern.

Cited in the 'Dematerialization' document, one can point out the following examples of work as relevant to the complex and expanding notion of the material domain and also the complex and expanded usage (i.e. both methodological and technical procedures) problems that the 'messing about' with such materials should have held out if many of the artists had possessed more acutely developed 'radar' for scanning assertions in the material domain. Such assertions rested fairly and squarely upon the most entrenched and traditionally familiar operated (within the art sector) taxonomy of the material domain, in these cases particularly the art object domain.

1 Robert Morris: projects for jets of steam as sculpture (Gas-state matter)
2 Carl Andre: the negative of the first brick show in which empty space was the substance of the forms. (Here the substance would be air-gas-state matter).
3 Hans Haacke: condensation (possibly solid-state to liquid-state to gas-state matter) and frost (solid-state matter) sculptures. An interesting point about the condensation notion would be ascertaining whether Haacke is using 'condensation' as a straight noun in which case one assumes one can point to these condensation sculptures much as one points to condensation on a car windscreen, or as a process-word where somehow Haacke is holding out the process of condensing as a sculpture, in which case the notion is probably a nonsensical but more provocative one and possibly a more 'interesting' one. We will return to such notions apart from Haacke's work later.
4 Carl Andre's conical pile of sand – which cited 'the use of gravity'.
5 Sol LeWitt's non-visual sculptures using (what is called) conceptual logic and visual illogic. Projects employing the device of hiding objects.
6 Dan Flavin's light aggregates which are asserted as possessing both material and immaterial identities. I have never been at all sure exactly how this notion is supposed to work, I can only attempt to construe it as something like the following. Either, (1) that the solid-state components (e.g. the tube) is the material-identity entity and the gas (gas-state) contained within the tube is the immaterial-identity entity. or, (2) that the material-identity is constituted by both the solid-state and gas-state components and that the immaterial identity somehow refers to or describes the image as separate from the gas, or maybe refers to some aspect of what might be called an idea, or concept, and in which case in the more precise broad sense the Flavin light aggregates cannot be singled out as being more or especially significant with regard to questions of the material identity of the objects of art, from almost any other art object, (See, for example, Richard Wollheim's book *Art and its Objects*), Thus in view of this latter qualification no.(1) seems, to me at least, to be the only viably significant notion in terms of the broad framework of the 'dematerialization' writing,

However noting that many of the works characterized above do seem to offer some problematic directives with regard to the identity of art objects and in doing so have, apparently in the main in an unconscious way on the part of the artists who made them, crossed over into the most traditional philosophic domains which have embraced the examination of such problems, not specifically, obviously, with regard to the art object domain, but the more general object domain, it seems that some kind of surveillance of even the simplest formulation of the philosophic lines of enquiry would be useful on two counts. Firstly, and perhaps more positively, that such an awareness is a good ground for assessing where some of the major points of development within conceptual art are to be rooted out and secondly that such an awareness might well have prevented much of the mumbo-jumbo and witch-doctor talk which, as I have already stated, I believe many of the conceptual artists to have committed. These two factors are separated somewhat arbitrarily and in terms of the practice of conceptual art what I believe is the lack of such an awareness has meant the perpetrating of some trivial devices, and it goes (as taken from granted) that I regard such devices as extremely overrated and inflated, and the claims for the devices to be bordered on the ludicrous.

First things first; it seems that Andre, Flavin, LeWitt, Morris and Judd despite the great diversity of their work are representative in terms of their sensibility of the wing comprised of the movements from 'Minimal' across Conceptual art, it seems also that they are no longer in a controversial position with regard to their status as major artists (for the moment at any rate). There are some points which can be usefully raised about the nature of their achievements reached by 1967. These points are advanced here with a view to showing that much of the work of the younger artists of the conceptual wing has merely been, at the most, an underlining of the achievements of the older artists, and further has added nothing significantly new to the domain of art further than that series of assertions achieved by the older artists two or three years ago. Following them has mostly entailed a repetitious raising of the same questions: once given the possibility of using gas-state matter, liquid-state matter, solid-state matter entities, actual or theoretical, the mere listing of as many gas-state, liquid-state or solid-state entities as possible is little more than merely a list. Hence there is Wiener and Huebler and Long and Dibbets, Baxter and Serra and Flanagan and Saret, Nauman and Oppenheim and Hutchinson and Heizer, *et al.*, *et al.*, all working in the wonderful new expanded range of material and method and technique, with rope and sand and earth and lead and twigs, and the countless other myriads of materials, assertions about uses of energy (Richard Hamilton's assertion of Duchamp seems to offer a precedent here[1]), about 'things made of energy' (Robert Barry), about uses of gravity, assertions claiming to be working with time, techniques using tides, using the United States Mail Service, claims from a multitude of artists to be working with and using all manner of things, indeed so many claims that I wonder that if this worldly *planum* of ours is such a fertile realm then we artists should perhaps hold a harvest festival of thanksgiving both for the fertility of the material realm and for the indomitable green fingeredness of our creative selves.

But some of these claims have a strange ring, do they not? to the ones of us with perhaps a less baroque view of the concept of artistic license. The claims often have been made as if one works with energy or time or gravity much as Michaelangelo worked with marble or Manet worked with paint. Firstly there must be some examination of how these artists can be seen to be using gravity or energy, etc. that is, more how they use it than what they are using. Thus in the case of Andre's 'conical pile of sand' piece, maybe the phenomena of gravity is used in a similar way to the way Manet can be said to have used (relied upon) the adhesive qualities of paint in helping him form an image, or perhaps, better still, Pollock can be said to have used the phenomena of gravity in dropping and dripping his paint upon the canvas on the floor, and hence in forming his image. But the difference between the Andre process and the Pollock one is maybe a salient one here, in Pollock's case there is no claim to single out the 'use of gravity' component. This as far as the Chandler-Lippard writing is concerned is extremely pertinent; whereas in the case of Pollock one is asked solely to evaluate the image, the 'use of gravity' component is ignored, is not at all relevant, in the Chandler-Lippard writing the conical pile of sand, the corresponding entity to the canvas+paint entity in the Pollock process, is designated to a subservient role, the emphasis seems to be heavily upon the use of gravity, but there is a certain strangeness here because there seems to be an underlying structural implication in the document that the use of gravity can somehow be viewed as an object and consequently as evidence of dematerialization; at the most the use of gravity can be seen as an event, and events and objects are very different things.[2] The Andre notion is a more complex one still in as far as it embraces also notions of disintegration. Perhaps the point to remember about the Andre piece is that the notion of the use of gravity is singled out, and one assumes, maybe wrongly, that because it is singled out one should attach some significance to it. This is not at all to say that Andre makes any strange claim for this device, indeed from what I know of him he sees himself in the regular line of sculpture makers, that is, Brancusi and co. But the use of gravity relevant to the dematerialization of art is provocative to say the least.[3] Maybe something like the following, that the use of gravity is a former of the image in the same way that paint is a former of the image, but sand is the exact corresponding material to paint in the Andre piece and the floor is the exact corresponding material to the canvas, and this leaves gravity out on its own, or does it? All art works can be said to have had a use of gravity employed in their formation, in the Andre piece the action is simply singled out, but what Andre has produced is a perfectly conventional solid-state object, a pile of sand, the significant notion does not lie in any de-materializing, the deployment of the phenomena of gravity simply entails the dropping of solid-state matter (i.e. grains of sand) and the deployment of the process of disintegration simply entails (possibly) the change from solid-state matter to liquid and/or gas-state matter. The difficult thing here is knowing how Chandler-Lippard are operating the dematerialization notion.

Maybe there is a hang-up in the plastic arts with objects and object-making but much of the most coveted attacking of the object-making stance has been itself made from an extremely unclarified position and with an unreasonable appetite for novelty.[4] Most of the works of conceptual art are works very much bounded by our concepts of matter. Weiner's lists for example all pertain in a strong sense to matter states; any claim that he does not use objects but only ideas is simply a tediously novel aphorism, the truth of which simply rests on what is meant by 'use' in this context, and if it is simply indicative of the fact that Wiener does not make objects, that in itself is a trivial claim for significance. The notion Seth Siegelaub demonstrated in contrasting 'tedious' objects with ideas (*Art in America*, Summer, 1969) is demonstrably shaky if Siegelaub is claiming more significance for the latter category as some sort of 'god-given' necessity, that is as if there is something especially significant in simply being in the position of making such a contrast. And all this quite apart from the extremely trite quality of contrasting entities such as objects and ideas, as if the idea-users were doing more significant work than the object-makers simply because they were idea-users; on the contrary!

As far as I can see it seems quite justifiable to expect the idea-user domain to support as much rubbish as does the object-maker domain, if not more, judging by the way things are at the moment The claims for dematerialization; of not using those tedious old things, objects; of oral communication (Wilson); of using gravity or energy, etc., etc., are not simply to be valued because they exercise a little novelty and thus appear a little fresh.

If there is significance in the new work it must be in more than embellishing the achievements of Andre and Morris and LeWitt. What the group of older artists (Andre, Morris, LeWitt, Judd) had done by 1966, was to lay out from the object position fairly complex and expanded formal situations. Andre, for example, in the negative of the first brick show in which 'empty space was the substance of the forms' simply held out a substance-concept for operation of the empty space notion, which was a fairly straightforward assertion as air (empty space) is gas-state matter. In the domain of physics such notions are commonplace, but in the more metaphor dominated domain of art this appeal to physical taxonomy was treated as a species of *revelatum*, and many of the younger artists since have indulged in this rubbing of the lamp of the genie [...]

1 'Marcel Duchamp', Richard Hamilton, *Art International*, 7:10.

2 Maybe there is an assertion that there is a process going on in which the emphasis is laid very much on the event of making rather than upon the visual characteristics of the object which is made.

3 2, above, advances one notion as to its relevancy.

4 A fairly marked example of this appetite can be seen in Seth Siegelaub's remarks noted in the article 'Impossible Art - What it is', David L. Shirley, *Art in America*, May-June, 1969.

Terry Atkinson, 'From an Art & Language Point of View', *Art-Language*, 1:2 (February 1970) 25-42.

Ian BURN, Roger CUTFORTH, Mel RAMSDEN

Proceedings, the Society for Theoretical Art and Analyses [1970]

Claims that it is possible to frame effective propositions about 'art' through the manipulation of material constituents are problematic. The quasi-empirical connotations of such cases imply that the introduction of 'art' must be as a second context, i.e., 'something' to which a second status is ascribed. Objects, metonymically as 'art', represent a manipulation of material constituents depicted by a proposition without essentially inquiring into the special syntax of that proposition. An overtly syntactical approach to a state of affairs normally considered well within the bounds of material constituents might well be repudiated on the grounds of a seeming indifference to the significance of these constituents; some argument might, however, be advanced that certain of the constituents do not count (subsistently or otherwise), excepting that their function within the state of affairs is merely syntactical.

If an analogy is drawn to the customary rejection of 'the ontological argument', then such statements as 'art is' or 'art exists' can be held as misleading. While they may be grammatically or syntactically misleading, they may (or may not) necessarily be so in the terms of any possible 'facts' they are employed to record. That is, they may be 'formally improper to the facts of the logical form they are employed to record and proper to facts of quite another logical form'. So, grammatical appearances to the contrary, within such remarks the term 'art' is not introduced as a subject, nor does it function as a subject about which something is being predicated or asserted. It follows that the verb 'is' or 'exists' is not signifying any character predicated and that the term 'art' is introduced predicatively. (This predicative status is not contradicted by the argument that, in use of the term, the implication is 'condition of art' or 'covering concept of art'.) Therefore the term 'art' is introduced into the statement as an assertion which is employed to signify the character or status by which the subject is being characterized. So, while the tendency has been to direct at the term 'art' all attributes of a true subject, it is still functioning as a covert predicate.

In an expression such as 'object of art', the terms 'object' and 'art' are introduced in different ways; 'object' is introduced as a particular and functions in the statement substantively and as a subject, whereas 'of art' is assertive and predicates the subject. It can be posited that, aside from any material constituents, 'object of art' is primarily a proportional format in which a substantive term is introduced and predicated by 'as art'.

There is a distinction within the proposition between a substantive and an assertive introduction of terms; 'objects' and 'art' are terms which are mutually exclusive and are linked only as a proposition. Although both of the terms can join as a proposition they can in no way be regarded as being the proposition. The 'object' in no way contains the assertion 'of art' as an ingredient and this holds for every and any subject as 'art'. In statements like ' ... of art', the exemplary term is the assertive introduction of 'of art' rather than something which, because of the prepositional format, is somehow locatable 'in' the subject. This provides the basis for the erroneous belief that exemplary substantives must exist, that all other substantives exhibiting similar features are indeed 'art' and are classified as such. (Such instances simply disregard the assertion.) However the designating feature is not that e.g. the *Bottle Rack* [Marcel Duchamp's readymade] and painted form each possess an intrinsic element known to be 'art', but that they both belong to a class of subjects asserted 'as art'.

Grammatical distinctions such as prepositional difference: e.g. '... as...', '... in ... ', '... for ... ' are only *prima facie* evidence-of distinction in application. This can be qualified, though imprecisely, by stating that distinction cannot be evident from any knowledge of applications but can be considered to be merely grammatical. Of course this may appear particularly contradictory if, as it is posited, the context of applications originates from an essentially linguistic format. However, as has been stated previously, the component terms and the prepositional format itself are somewhat distinct. If 'as' or 'in' do not count it is in application although they may be formally-proper grammatically they are insignificant in terms of applications. In these terms then, any link-up will serve since ostensibly first context subjects cannot become intrinsic constituents of 'of art'. Within the prepositional format the terms remain exclusive, the component term 'art' designating distinct subjects.

From the prepositional linking of 'art' and 'object', a proposition of synthetic status is recognized. This suggests that 'object' does not and cannot belong to or be a property of 'of art', which is so regardless of the subject predicated. In this format there are no restrictions on elaboration, *ad infinitum*. As long as the proposition is 'about' or 'ascribing to' it will remain synthetic. The supposition here is that 'object', 'art' and 'proposition' are distinct and are only syntactically grouped because of contextual rules forming 'applications'. It is through this that 'object' and 'art' come to be regarded as propositional as well as component terms.

The stratification of almost all 'art' terminologies in order that they deal exclusively with propositional formats (of which 'art' is considered to be a component term), results in excessive confusions between 'art' and particular properties and substantives. Grammatical distinctions are valid, not in so far as they mirror 'real and true applications', but rather because the initial proposition is intrinsically linguistic. Clarification of this kind is not intended to develop any alternate temporal or spatial properties as 'art', but rather is to establish explicit grammatical groundwork for a state of affairs that has predominantly depended on certain semantic applications. (If most of the art-community had not been afflicted with an advanced logo-phobia this would be readily apparent.)

If any 'subject' can replace 'object', then within the propositional format one can postulate that this subject is merely syntactical. Then the exclusive function of the subject may only be that it occupies a syntactical role as component of the proposition.

However, the question as to whether 'art' and 'object' are open to operability apart from syntactical component terms really depends on whether the propositional format itself is dispensable. It is evident that one term is a mere matter of filling a grammatical 'hole' while the other serves as a conglomeration of vague genealogical justifications; there is not much one can do to escape the quasi nominative role that 'art' performs while holding such a status.

The contention is being held that, despite the appearance of certain substantive objects as constituents of the propositional format no empirical import should be accorded them; i.e. in the proposition '... as art' constituents rely on syntax rather than on application for their signification. They therefore appear as syntactic component terms apart from 'facts' but within a context of rules. The subject term is employed in a syntactical format with mystic penumbras, the component terms retain a fixed operation within the context of rules. The subject term is employed in a syntactical role of '... as art', while the predicate term is paradigmatic and nominative. (Both as fixed terms of the propositional format). It is particularly within this synthetic format that 'art' is able to designate 'subjects' and it then accumulates an aura of a whole genealogy of applications. (This does not help if the aim is to maintain procedures outside of any application.) The predicate term acts as the paradigmatic feature (the only one) for a number of undeniably dissimilar subjects and, as components, the terms are fixed into this mode, i.e. the designating and the merely grammatical.

Ian Burn, Roger Cutforth, 'Proceedings, Society for Theoretical Art and Analyses', *Art-Language*, 1:3 (June 1970) 1-3.

Ian BURN, Mel RAMSDEN

Notes on Analysis [1970]

[...]

1 Rather than add to the chain of almighty art icons some purported 'analytic' art is intent only on advancing bases for analysis. Other merely indicates some areas of investigation.

2 The outcome of much of the 'conceptual' work of the past two years has been to carefully clear the air of objects. One no longer feels obligated to materialize constructs and, perhaps of more consequence, one no longer feels the pressure to replace such constructs with specific 'ideas', 'proposals', etc.

The formulation of a set of art-constructs does not require justification through, nor is it contingent on, material productivity. It is now justifiable as a form of activity.

Amongst the earlier contentions of the conceptual *cum* analytic work was that no object contains any 'magical' artness which may be said to individuate it as an art-object. Given that there are no such determinable characteristics within an art object and that, furthermore, the puzzle is how such and such an art-object is picked out as an art-object, then the area of attention must, arguably, shift away from the object itself. Individuation might then be held to come about by falling back upon various contextual and behavioural prescriptions. There is an obvious need to study such prescriptions since they provide the bases for individuation and must be known prior to individuating activity.

The contention here is that the area of attention is shifting from single iconic elements (art-objects, art-works) to comprise a whole continuum of these elements in a sign-process (*semiosis*).

3 Now in order to set up within an interpreter the disposition to react in a special way, a sign must have some known fixtures. Thus one might contend that only objects with known art-object fixtures could be picked out as signs of 'the presence of art'. But since we have already denied the existence of such internal fixtures, then it is tenable to suggest that no art-object can itself qualify as a sign of 'art'. In which case art-objects must be signified by falling back upon the norms and prescriptions of a known language and, since they are designated from this language, one picks the objects out through this language (and not by suddenly being struck dumb by whatever usage that language may have been put to).

So, analytic art may not be concerned with the proliferation of designated signifieds, but with the abstract structure of this designation: the semiosis.

Now the artist's traditional line of business has been with usage (practice) rather than with sorting out the terms of the semiosis itself. He has accordingly been more preoccupied with the material ramifications of single iconic elements than with the sub-structure or continuum determining the status of these elements. Increasing abstraction means decreasing iconicity. Analytic art seeks to formulate connections between the 'grammatical' parts of this semiotic mosaic – in other words, the analytic construct explains its line of business and does not merely act from that line of business.

Now we can call upon some cautious, if logically contentious, remarks about this sign-process.

4 Initial investigation ought to manifest (i) what would be the situation of the conventional iconic art-object in the sign process, and (ii) what could be the situation (if any) of an analytic art-construct itself within this process?

i) If C (sign) sets up in D (interpreter) the reaction to E (signification), then it can be argued that C is the context or prescriptions that D must know to enable the bringing about of E: thus C displays the characteristics for D individuating E. Now if this latter event E were to stand for an art-object then it is as a significant designated by C. One might almost regard C as the language norms or 'dictionary' learnt by D and then E is an instance of this language 'spoken'.

Given this, that conventional significants (E) are designated, then such a designation obeying all the contextual and syntactical dimensions of C, need only be observable; i.e., E might conceivably be anything, on the face of this planet.

Such formidable spatio-temporal possibilities might be seen as the semantic proliferation of the designative sign-process. However, the abstract structure of such a process might be more rewardingly studied through its syntactic and pragmatic dimensions.

ii) Under the circumstances outlined in (i), it would be dumb to insist on nominating an analytic art-construct (i.e., this paper) as an 'artwork'. The contention is that the analytic construct occurs elsewhere in the semiosis.

So instead of seeking to parallel the conventional signification, an analytic construct may conceivably reproduce in itself the state of a sign: i.e., be 'language' but not 'usage', be prescription but not practice. Rather than be designated by a set of prescriptions, this construct would itself seek to state those prescriptions. Thus its meaning might be 'read out' instead of 'read in'.

Consider then: C as a sign which sets up in D the

disposition to react in a special way E. An analytic construct C need not designate any material element but rather the hope from D of a certain behaviour E. It therefore need not be thought that something is 'missing' when material elements are not included in the sign-process – rather, it is that the sign C is no longer semantically designative but has moved into the pragmatic mode: it is now prescriptive in that it signifies conduct E – not designative in nominating object E.

Finally, one can't lose material conditions by simplistic 'dematerialization'. Objects disappear because of fundamental procedural changes in the semiotic or conceptual sign-structure of the continuum itself. The apprehension of analytic art could lie in gaining an awareness of such abstract strategies [...]

Ian Burn, Mel Ramsden, *Notes on Analysis*, (New York, 1970); reprinted in *Six Years: The dematerialization of the art object from 1966 to 1972*, ed. Lucy R. Lippard, (Berkeley and Los Angeles: University of California Press, 1973) 136-37.

Victor BURGIN

In Reply [1972]

[...] A consistently ignored aspect of what might be termed 'the problem of legitimation' in art is the question of art's *use*. The elevation of theory-building to putative self-sufficiency cannot fill this absence as such moves are continuous with the same programme of abstraction – the attempt to replace a semantic function with a formal one – which led to it.

Abstraction has become a *value*, serving to legitimate 'evolutions' in 'art'. The historicism implicit in the former term is consequent upon the reification of the latter.

Any ongoing human activity in a society is liable to become institutionalized. Any social institution is in turn liable to become attributed with an ontological status independent of human activity and signification. The habitualized convenience of the singular term 'art' has encouraged the notion that art is a singular *thing*, an assumption endorsed by the presence of such undeniably concrete entities as museums. The meaning of the institution objectified by these and other presences – *ipso facto* 'the meaning of art' – is periodically reconstructed according to a variety of legitimating formulas. Historicist legitimations – those incorporating such notions as 'perpetual revolution' – lend the illusion of purposive movement to what might equally well be described as a contingent succession of collapses – bringing conservation and continuity out of impermanence and waste and providing a basis for what Edgar Wind called '... a proud art which is no one's servant, posing all its problems from within'.

I argued in 'Rules of Thumb' (*Studio International*, May, 1971) against recent recastings of the *l'art pour l'art* position. It is unlikely that an activity carried out with a declared disregard for the empirical world, yet which possesses no language of its own, will attain comparable standing with mathematics or logic. It is more likely that such an activity will acquire. the status of astrology: an esoteric pseudo-science and logic *manqué*.

If the term 'analytic' is not being used in a technical sense to indicate a *l'art pour l'art* position then it has not been made at all clear just what it is that is being analysed by artists of declared 'analytic' intent. To claim to analyse 'art' would be an essentialist nonsense. While we may analyse 'the concept of art', which empirically means this or that use of the term 'art' and whatever synonyms we might ascribe to it, the empirical study of word-uses belongs increasingly to linguistics. The recent discovery by philosophers that ethics is no longer *infra dig*[1] may be seen as acknowledging that 'values' are all that remains to *them* of the old territories of philosophical semantics. Word-usage *per se* may hardly be claimed as the special concern of art.

The exorcizing of ghosts in the art machine is a continuously necessary activity, but what is valuable as a means may be over-valued as an end: the total isolation of conceptual issues from substantive ones is as airy a piece of transcendentalism as ever any continental metaphysician dreamed up. However, although, on a number of art fronts, an abstract heaven is *de facto* being conjured, we are not *a priori* committed to occupying it.

What counts as art varies through history and between societies, as does art's function. A de-reified notion of art places it (with some qualification as we shall see later) as socio-culturally contingent, implying we should seek formation rules for art within the complex of synchronous social practices contemporary with the given work. However, apart from accounts of patronage, such studies are rare. There is no (comparably consolidated) synchronic counterpart of the diachronically oriented role of art historian. This disparity of attention has contributed to the ubiquitousness of the idea of art as a hermetic and autonomously evolving *thing*, and consequently to the divorce of the problem of legitimation from the question of *use*.

For any given economic and technological condition of a society the physical needs essential to the survival of the human organism may be equally well met within the context of a wide range of alternative customs, beliefs, values, laws, moral systems, etc. However, within the given society, what structures prevail in actuality tend to be seen as belonging to 'the nature of things'. Because of these reifications, shifts in the conventional view of what the nature of things *is* necessarily engender changes in institutionalized values and practices.

Linguistics has demonstrated that the conventional notions of 'reality' held within a society are not simply transmitted by the language of that society but are to an extent *produced* by that language. In recognition of this fact the artificial and technical languages of science were evolved to reduce the element of convention in observation statements. Thus, for Carnap, 'The basic language of the constructional system is the symbolic language of logistics ... the other languages serve only more comprehensible auxiliary languages'.

Natural languages, together with those other systems of signification for which there is no known linguistics but yet which are commonly employed in a society, at any given time 'embody' the institutional order of that society. That is to say, in Saussure's distinction, while *langue* is defined as a unified whole the forms of *parole* are differentiated to the degree to which ideological variance is tolerated – the articulation of each 'form' determining the manner of division of the world onto which it is mapped. If art has not evolved languages of its own comparable with those evolved within science it is because the special concern of art is not with the physical world *sui generis* but with the social mediation of the physical world through the agency of *signs*, its predominant orientation in regard to these is not analytical and descriptive (scientific linguistics) but synthetic and normative.

Commonly held systems of signification are the subject of an art activity aimed at assembling new codes from fragments of the old, but art typically (e.g. as when it takes as much account of connotation as of denotation) accesses that area of 'parallelism of constituents' whose explanation, for Carnap, 'lies outside the range of science'.

My contention is that art is only partially autonomous and that works of art may be only partially accounted for in terms of art 'traditions' (the totality of previous art practices). Factors external to art traditions, especially social factors, are also to be considered. These, however, are to be seen not in terms of simple determination but in terms of a dialectic. The optimum function of art within this dialectic is to modify institutionalized patterns of orientation towards the world and thus to serve as an agency of socialization. (No art activity therefore is to be understood apart from the codes and practices of the society which contains it; art in *use* is bracketed ineluctably within ideology.)

The weakness of the 'analytical' position, so far as it is clear to me, is that those who subscribe to it may find there is no appreciable disparity of function (albeit some disparity of competence) between themselves and those practitioners whose territories they have annexed (a case of the colonists going native). I believe we must accept the responsibility of producing an art which has more than just *Art* as its content, and which carries the possibility of becoming more than just the rejectamenta of our economic surplus, if the already over-historicized and in-growing discourse of the art community is to avoid total fossilization.

1 abbr. *infra dignitatem*: beneath one's dignity.[ed.]

Victor Burgin, 'In Reply', *Art-Language*, 2:2 (Summer, 1972) 32-34.

Johanna DRUCKER

Experimental Typography as a Modern Art Practice [1994]

THE TYPOGRAPHIC CONTEXT FOR EXPERIMENTAL WORK

The early twentieth-century avant-garde found no medium more suitable for both production and promotion of their formal innovations and activist agenda than the printed page. And though print lacked the cachet of up-to-the-minute modernity associated with radio broadcast technology, it remained the mass medium par excellence of the decades of the teens and twenties. Print media were affordable, available, and effective means of communication and public visibility. From the first appearance of the Futurist Manifesto of F.T. Marinetti in the pages of *Figaro*, on 10 February 1909, through the profusion of independently published magazines, handbills, invitations, posters, and other printed ephemera – everywhere one looks across the broad spectrum of artistic activities from London, Berlin, Zurich, Milan, Moscow, Paris and St Petersburg – publications proliferate. The printed form existed not merely as an incidental record of the life and spirit of the times of avant-garde activity, but as one of the primary means of its realization.

Not surprisingly, many typical features of early avant-garde practices are manifest in these printed works: a strongly self-referential investigation of the formal properties of the medium; a blurring of the line between the forms and sites of so-called high art and the forms and situations of mass media; a muddying of distinctions between image and language and a subversive attack on their fundamental properties as representation and an even more systematic attack on the conventions of literary and visual symbolic form.

The typographic experiments of the early avant-garde were created in a context in which the visuality of written forms of language had received significantly increased attention in several fields such as linguistics, poetics and the visual arts. But it is also important to note the situation of typographic experimentation within the context of commercial and artistic publishing. The typographic distinction of the avant-garde only gains its specificity from its relation to this context, and the features which function to distinguish the experimental work from commercial or fine print productions are best understood by contrast – as a function of difference, rather than inherence [...]

At its broadest, the typographic field from which experimental artistic 'inventions' are derived stretches across the spectrum of typographic printed matter from journalists to advertisements through literary publishing and fine book work. Such work provides the norms against which the experimental typography takes on its cultural significance as transgressive, and it is therefore an essential underpinning to an evaluation of the effort of the effect of the avant-garde work.

The technology of letterpress typography was flourishing at the end of the nineteenth century. Highspeed presses had been invented, along with linotype and monotype machines for rapid setting and casting of large amounts of metal type. The advertising realm had burgeoned in response to the demands of the mass market strategies of industrial production. The result was an increased interest in graphics as an interface between producer and consumer to maximize the potential of a medium which had undergone, by contrast, comparatively little change in the three centuries since its invention. The graphic traditions established in the first decades of the existence of letterpress printing had undergone only slight modification.

Within the limited graphic vocabulary of early printing there were two distinct aspects to these traditions, each exemplifying a distinct mode of typographic enunciation. By this term I intend to designate those elements of typographic practice by which the speaker, recipient, and context of the text may be identified – and any other aspects of what is commonly recognized within linguistic analysis as the enunciative apparatus. The distinctive feature of this typographic enunciation is a distinction between *marked* and *unmarked* texts, with the additional possibility of distinguishing between public and private, personal language through their typographic treatment. In general, the split between marked and unmarked texts corresponds to the split between commercial and literary uses of typography, reflecting the distinction in linguistic modes of enunciation by which these domains are frequently distinguished from each other. These distinctions became increasingly operative in the nineteenth century with the increased possibility of entrenching the different domains through graphic means.

The basic distinction between marked and unmarked typography occurred simultaneously with the invention of printing. Gutenberg printed two distinctly different kinds of documents, which embodied the characteristic features of what evolved into the two distinct traditions. On the one hand he printed bibles, with their perfectly uniform grey pages, their uninterrupted blocks of text, without headings or subheadings or any distraction beyond the occasional initial letter. These bibles are the archetype of the unmarked text, the text in which the words on the page 'appear to speak themselves' without the visible intervention of author or printer. Such a text appears to possess an authority which transcends the mere material presence of words on a page, ink impressions on parchment. By contrast, the Indulgences which he printed displayed the embryonic features of a marked typography. Different sizes of type were used to hierarchize information, to create an order in the text so that different parts of it appear to 'speak' differently, to address a reader whose presence was inscribed at the outset by an author in complicity with the graphic tools of a printer who recognized and utilized the capacity of typographic representation to manipulate the semantic value of the text through visual means.

That the tradition of the unmarked text was established with the printing of bibles is not incidental to the ways in which its mode of transcendent seeming authority comes to operate within the literary field which models itself upon that original presentation. Literary works, while they adopted certain modifications such as running heads and elaborate title pages, essentially adopted the unmarked mode of Gutenberg's biblical setting as their norm. The literary text is the single grey block of undisturbed text, seeming, in the graphic sense, to have appeared whole and complete. The literary text wants no visual interference or manipulation to disturb the linguistic enunciation of the verbal matter. All interference, resistance, must be minimized in order to allow the reader a smooth reading of the unfolding linear sequence. The aspirations of typographers serving the literary muse are to make the text as uniform, as neutral, as accessible and seamless as possible, and it remains the dominant model for works of literature, authoritative scholarly prose, and any other printed form in which seriousness of purpose collapses with the authority of the writer, effacing both behind the implicit truth value of the words themselves.

The marked text had its most vibrant spurt of development in the domain of advertising, where manipulation, practically for its own sake, motivated the development of a wide range of typefaces, styles, and conventions governing their use. Almost all the visual feats and virtuoso-seeming pyrotechnics of the late nineteenth-century advertisers' practice had been a technical possibility since the invention of moveable type [...] What had been slow in developing was a sensibility to the medium which would investigate its potential to disturb the linear order by which the cast metal forms of type had embodied the normative linear text. An influence which had prevailed with increasing popularity in the nineteenth century was the graphic sensibility of lithography, which had none of the built-in restraints of cast metal to predispose the orientation of words and letterforms, but the promptings of a commercialized market eager for novelty and effect in the advertising of products can be assigned the greatest responsibility for generating innovation [...]

The ultimate importance of the Arts and Crafts movement as an influence on early twentieth-century experimental typography was not stylistic influence, but its self-conscious attention to the visual form in which literary texts were represented and the demonstration that, even in their 'unmarked' form, type gave text a distinctly visual form and character [...]

The Dada and Futurist artists were aware of the place the particular visual properties of type, layout and graphic design had in the social realm of public language and saw that they had become sufficiently codified and organized so that they could be manipulated. They were also aware that the distinct separation of the two typographic domains, the public/commercial and the literary, made the appropriation of these publicity techniques to literary works an activity which was subversive to the visual codes on which the authority of the literary text had been established. But this notion of authority depends on an understanding of the way in which literature, as a signifying practice, obtains its definition in relation to certain fundamental critical terms. The literary mode of typographic representation, borrowing from the convention of the unmarked text, posited the existence of an absent author whose authority was reworked through the seemingly transparent, speaking-itself, character of the words on the page. The subversive disruption of this authority and its impact on the structure of subjectivity, ideology and power in the text were effected through typographic manipulation [...]

Johanna Drucker, *The Visible Word* (Chicago: University of Chicago Press, 1994) 91-103.

APPROPRIATION, INTERVENTION, EVERYDAY

The decades following the end of the Second World War were marked by an intensification of interest in ideas and objects of everyday life – economically, politically and artistically. Sociologists such as Erving Goffman studied the 'presentation of self' in everyday interaction; while the French group the Situationist International set out to intervene into daily life, displacing and reorganizing its elements (*détournement*) in a new kind of avant-garde practice. There was renewed interest in the destructive aspect of the historical avant-garde and in the body as the basis of aesthetic perception. Anton Ehrenzweig's development of the concept of 'dedifferentiation' out of a reading of Freud's notion of the unconscious as a 'primary process', in *The Hidden Order of Art* (1967), was especially influential. All of these sources fed into a culturally activist, functionalist type of conceptual art, undertaken in new contexts: from the pages of commercial magazines (Dan Graham) to the workplace (the Artist Placement Group and Mierle Laderman Ukeles) to architectural modelling (Graham, again) and buildings scheduled for demolition (Gordon Matta-Clark). In the process, as Jeff Wall subsequently argued, photography became the privileged means of conceptual representation.

Guy DEBORD
Definitions [1958]

constructed situation: A moment of life concretely and deliberately constructed by the collective organization of a unitary ambiance and a game of events.

situationist: Having to do with the theory or practical activity of constructing situations. One who engages in the construction of situations. A member of the Situationist International.

situationism: A meaningless term improperly derived from the above. There is no such thing as situationism, which would mean a doctrine of interpretation of existing facts. The notion of situationism is obviously devised by antisituationists.

psychogeography: The study of the specific effects of the geographical environment, consciously organized or not, on the emotions and behaviour of individuals.

psychogeographical: Relating to psychogeography. That which manifests the geographical environment's direct emotional effects.

psychogeographer: One who explores and reports on psychogeographical phenomena.

dérive: A mode of experimental behaviour linked to the conditions of urban society: a technique of transient passage through varied ambiances. Also used to designate a specific period of continuous dériving.

unitary urbanism: The theory of the combined use of arts and techniques for the integral construction of a milieu in dynamic relation with experiments in behaviour.

détournement: Short for: *détournement* of pre-existing aesthetic elements. The integration of present or past artistic production into a superior construction of a milieu. In this sense there can be no situationist painting or music, but only a situationist use of these means. In a more primitive sense, *détournement* within the old cultural spheres is a method of propaganda, a method which testifies to the wearing out and loss of importance of those spheres.

culture: The reflection and prefiguration of the possibilities of organization of everyday life in a given historical moment; a complex of aesthetics, feelings and mores through which a collectivity reacts on the life that is objectively determined by its economy. (We are defining this term only in the perspective of the creation of values, not in that of the teaching of them.)

decomposition: The process in which the traditional

cultural forms have destroyed themselves as a result of the emergence of superior means of dominating nature which enable and require superior cultural constructions. We can distinguish between an active phase of the decomposition and effective demolition of the old superstructures – which came to an end around 1930 – and a phase of repetition which has prevailed since then. The delay in the transition from decomposition to new constructions is linked to the delay in the revolutionary liquidation of capitalism.

Guy Debord, 'Definitions' (1958), *Internationale Situationniste*, 3 (December, 1959); reprinted in *Situationist International Anthology*, ed. Ken Knabb (Berkeley, California: Bureau of Public Secrets, 1981) 45-46.

Guy DEBORD
Détournement as Negation and Prelude [1959]

Détournement, the re-use of pre-existing artistic elements in a new ensemble, has been a constantly present tendency of the contemporary avant-garde both before and since the establishment of the SI [Situationist International]. The two fundamental laws of *détournement* are the loss of importance of each *détourned* autonomous element – which may go so far as to lose its original sense completely – and at the same time the organization of another meaningful ensemble that confers on each element its new scope and effect.

Détournement has a peculiar power which obviously stems from the double meaning, from the enrichment of most of the terms by the coexistence within them of their old senses and their new, immediate senses. *Détournement* is practical because it is so easy to use and because of its inexhaustible potential for reuse. Concerning the negligible effort required for *détournement*, we have already said, 'The cheapness of its products is the heavy artillery that breaks through all the Chinese walls of understanding' (*Methods of Détournement*, May 1956). But these points would not by themselves justify recourse to this method, which the same text describes as 'clashing head-on against all social and legal conventions'. *Détournement* has a historical significance. What is it?

'*Détournement* is a game made possible by the capacity of *devaluation*', writes Asger Jorn in his study *Détourned Painting* (May 1959), and he goes on to say that all the elements of the cultural past must be 'reinvested' or disappear. *Détournement* is thus first of all a negation of the value of the previous organization of expression. It arises and grows increasingly stronger in the historical period of the decomposition of artistic expression. But at the same time, the attempts to re-use the '*détournable* bloc' as material for other ensembles express the search for a vaster construction, a new genre of creation at a higher level.

The SI is a very special kind of movement, of a nature different from preceding artistic avant-gardes. Within culture the SI can be likened to a research laboratory, for example, or to a party in which we are situationists but nothing that we do is situationist. This is not a disavowal for anyone. We are partisans of a certain future of culture, of life. Situationist activity is a definite craft which we are not yet practising.

Thus the signature of the situationist movement, the sign of its presence and contestation in contemporary cultural reality (since we cannot represent any common style whatsoever), is first of all the use of *détournement*. We may mention, on the level of *détourned* expression, Jorn's altered paintings; Debord and Jorn's book *Mémoires*, 'composed entirely of prefabricated elements', in which the writing on each page runs in all directions and the reciprocal relations of the phrases are invariably uncompleted; Constant's projects for *détourned* sculptures; and Debord's *détourned* documentary film, *On the Passage of a Few Persons Through a Rather Brief Period of Time*. On the level of what *Methods of Détournement* calls '*ultradétournement*, that is, the tendencies for *détournement* to operate in everyday social life' (e.g. passwords or the wearing of disguises, belonging to the sphere of play), we might mention, at different levels, Gallizio's industrial painting; Wyckaert's 'orchestral' project for assembly-line painting with a division of labour based on colour; and numerous *détournements* of buildings that were at the origin of unitary urbanism. But we should also mention in this context the SI's very forms of 'organization' and propaganda.

At this point in the world's development all forms of expression are losing all grip on reality and being reduced to self-parody. As the readers of this journal can frequently verify, present-day writing always has an element of parody. 'It is necessary', states *Methods of Détournement*, 'to conceive of a parodic-serious stage where the accumulation of *détourned* elements, far from aiming at arousing indignation or laughter by alluding to some original work, will express our indifference towards a meaningless and forgotten original, and concern itself with rendering a certain sublimity.'

The parodic-serious expresses the contradictions of an era in which we find ourselves confronted with both the urgent necessity and the near impossibility of bringing together and carrying out a totally innovative collective action. An era in which the greatest seriousness advances masked in the ambiguous interplay between art and its negation; in which the essential voyages of discovery have been undertaken by such astonishingly incapable people.

Guy Debord, 'Détournement as Negation and Prelude', *Internationale Situationniste*, 3 (December, 1959); reprinted in *Situationist International Anthology*, ed. Ken Knabb (Berkeley, California: Bureau of Public Secrets, 1981) 55-56.

Erving GOFFMAN
The Presentation of Self in Everyday Life [1959]

In recent years there have been elaborate attempts to bring into one framework the concepts and findings derived from three different areas of inquiry: the individual personality, social interaction and society. I would like to suggest here a simple addition to these inter-disciplinary attempts.

When an individual appears before others, he knowingly and unwittingly projects a definition of the situation, of which a conception of himself is an important part. When an event occurs which is expressively incompatible with this fostered impression, significant consequences are simultaneously felt in three levels of social reality, each of which involves a different point of reference and a different order of fact.

First, the social interaction, treated here as a dialogue between two teams, may come to an embarrassed and confused halt; the situation may cease to be defined, previous positions may become no longer tenable, and participants may find themselves without a charted course of action. The participants typically sense a false note in the situation and come to feel awkward, flustered, and, literally, out of countenance. In other words, the minute social system created and sustained by orderly social interaction becomes disorganized. These are the consequences that the disruption has from the point of view of social interaction.

Secondly, in addition to these disorganizing consequences for action at the moment, performance disruptions may have consequences of a more far-reaching kind. Audiences tend to accept the self projected by the individual performer during any current performance as a responsible representative of his colleague-grouping, of his team, and of his social establishment. Audiences also accept the individual's particular performance as evidence of his capacity to perform the routine and even as evidence of his capacity to perform any routine. In a sense these larger social units – teams, establishments, etc. – become committed every time the individual performs his routine; with each performance the legitimacy of these units will tend to be tested anew and their permanent reputation put at stake. This kind of commitment is especially strong during some performances. Thus, when a surgeon and his nurse both turn from the operating table and the anaesthetized patient accidentally rolls off the table to his death, not only is the operation disrupted in an embarrassing way, but the reputation of the doctor, as a doctor and as a man, and also the reputation of the hospital may be weakened. These are the consequences that disruptions may have from the point of view of social structure.

Finally, we often find that the individual may deeply involve his ego in his identification with a particular part, establishment and group, and in his self-conception as someone who does not disrupt social interaction or let down the social units which depend upon that interaction. When a disruption occurs, then, we may find that the self-conceptions around which his personality has been built may become discredited. These are consequences that disruptions may have from the point of view of individual personality.

Performance disruptions, then, have consequences at three levels of abstraction: personality, interaction and social structure. While the likelihood of disruption will vary widely from interaction to interaction, and while the social importance of likely disruptions will vary from interaction to interaction, still it seems that there is no interaction in which the participants do not take an appreciable chance of being slightly embarrassed or a slight chance of being deeply humiliated. Life may not be much of a gamble, but interaction is. Further, in so far as individuals make efforts to avoid disruptions or to correct for ones not avoided, these efforts, too, will have simultaneous consequences at the three levels. Here, then, we have one simple way of articulating three levels of abstraction and three perspectives from which social life has been studied.

Erving Goffman, *The Presentation of Self in Everyday Life* (Garden City, New York: Doubleday & Company, Inc., 1959) 242–43.

Lygia CLARK
Nostalgia of the Body [1966–68]

WE REFUSE ...
What's happening around me? A whole group of people clearly sees that modern art doesn't communicate, is increasingly becoming an elitist issue. So they turn to popular art, hoping to fill the gulf that separates them from the majority. Result: they cut the ties that attach them to the development of universal art and fall back onto a form of expression that is local in character.

I see another group that clearly feels the enormous crisis of modern expression. Those who compose it try to deny art – but this negation, they find no other way to express it except, precisely, works of art.

For myself, I belong to a third group that tries to elicit the public's participation. This totally changes the meaning of art as one has understood it up to now. That's why:

We refuse representational space and the work as passive contemplation.

We refuse all myth external to humanity.

We refuse the work of art as such, and we place the emphasis on the act of realizing the proposition.

We refuse duration as a means of expression. We propose the very time of the act as a field of experience. In a world in which the subject has become a stranger to its labour, we use experience to incite awareness of the alienation in which one lives.

We refuse all transference to the object – even to an object that seems to be there only to underline the absurdity of all expression.

We refuse the artist who pretends by means of the object to give a total communication of his or her message, without the spectator's participation.

We refuse the Freudian idea of the subject conditioned by its past and we emphasize the idea of freedom.

We propose precariousness as a new idea of existence against all static crystallization within duration.

WE ARE PROPOSERS
We are proposers: we are the mill. It's up to you to blow into it the meaning of our existence.

We are proposers: our proposal is that of dialogue. Alone, we don't exist, we are at your mercy.

We are proposers: we have buried the 'work of art' as such and we call out to you so that thought will live by means of your action.

We are proposers: we are proposing neither the past nor the future to you, but the 'now'.

ARE WE DOMESTICATED?
If I were younger, I would be in politics. I feel a bit too at ease, too integrated.

Before artists were marginalized. Now, we, the proposers, are too well placed in the world. We are able to live – just by proposing. There is a place for us in society.

There is another type of person who prepares what will happen, other precursors. They, they continue to be marginalized by society. When there is a struggle with the police and I see, in Brazil, a seventeen-year-old killed (I put his photo on my wall, in my studio), I realize that he dug a place with his body for the generations that will succeed him. These young people have the same existential attitude as we, they unleash processes whose end they can't see, they open a path whose exit is unknown. But society resists them, and kills them. It's thus that they work all the more. What they try to force is perhaps more essential. They are incendiaries. It's they who shake up the world. We, sometimes I wonder if we are not a bit domesticated. That annoys me ...

Lygia Clark, 'Nosotros recusamos ... ' ('We Refuse ...', 1966), 'Nosotros somos los proponentes' (We Are the Proposers', 1968), '¿Estamos domesticados?' ('Are We Domesticated?', 1968), first published in Lygia Clark, *Livro-obra* (*Book-work*), Rio de Janeiro, 1983; reprinted posthumously in the present form under the title 'Nostalgia of the Body', *October* (Summer 1994) 105–7.

Gustav METZGER
DIAS [Destruction in Art Symposium] Preliminary Report [1967]

'The cataclysmic increase in world destructive potential since 1945 is inextricably linked with the most disturbing tendencies in modern art, and the proliferation of programmes of research into aggression and destruction in society. The organizers of DIAS [Destruction in Art Symposium], seeing the close relationship between art forms using actual destruction of material and social reality, have arranged a three day Symposium. The aim of DIAS is to create an opportunity for artists, writers, psychologists, sociologists, and other scientists to meet and exchange ideas. DIAS aims to assemble the maximum amount of information on the new art forms and related topics, and to make this information freely available.'

The above is the opening statement of a Press Release of May 1966. DIAS had been launched during the previous month. One of the decisive factors had been the decision of the new London periodical, *Art and Artists*, to issue a special number on auto-destructive art and related art forms in August 1966. This number was most helpful in establishing contact with some artists and in creating interest for the Symposium.

A number of Press Conferences were held to publicize our plans. At the first, June 15th, John Latham burned a *Skoob Tower* on the South Bank. Shortly after this we arranged a week's visit to London by two leading figures of the Dutch PROVO movement – Bernhard de Vries (a recently elected member of Amsterdam Municipal Council) and Irene van der Weetering. This visit, arranged immediately following the June rioting in Amsterdam, was part of the work of DIAS; clarifying the relationships of destruction in society and in art.

The response to DIAS, summarily described in this report, proves conclusively that the use of destructive techniques in art is a *world wide activity*. This was the first attempt to present a full review of this direction in art, and the majority of participants saw the need for maintaining contacts in the future.

More than twenty artists came to Britain specifically to take part in DIAS – while twenty-eight artists, composers and writers from abroad sent documentation on their involvement with destruction in art. This surely represents the most concentrated influx of advanced artists to London since Surrealist and Constructivist activity in the thirties. With one or two exceptions, none of the artists who came to Britain had presented their work here previously. Some of the biggest impact was made by two groups founded in recent years – the Institute of Direct Art, Vienna, most of whose members were present, and Group ZAJ of Madrid.

Artists from the following countries contributed to DIAS: Britain, USA, France, Argentina, Austria, Spain, Japan, Bolivia, Germany, Holland, Belgium, Italy, Mexico, Czechoslovakia, Iceland, N. Ireland.

Apart from the Symposium, thirty separate events were arranged, spread over a period of one month. Some sessions of the Symposium attracted over 100 people, while attendance at events varied from 20 to 100.

One of the objectives of DIAS is to encourage the diffusion of information on destructive art forms. *This aim was achieved*. The entire National Press reported the activities of DIAS and of individual artists. Artists appeared on television, and the BBC broadcast reports on DIAS on its Home, European and Overseas services. A discussion on Destruction in Art was transmitted on the Third Programme. DIAS was also featured on foreign press, television and radio.

DIAS was completely independent, and no attempt was made to receive sponsorship or financial aid from any organization. It was run on a voluntary basis and the artists paid their own expenses [...]

As a consequence of the Nitsch *Action* on September 16th at St Bride Institute, two members of the Hon. Committee, John Sharkey and Gustav Metzger, have been charged by the Director of Public Prosecutions with '... unlawfully causing to be shown and presenting an indecent exhibition contrary to Common Law'.

Gustav Metzger, *DIAS Preliminary Report* (London: DIAS, February 1967); reprinted in Hans Sohm, *Happenings & Fluxus: Materialen* (Cologne: Kölnisher Kunstverein, 1970). The Honorary Committee of DIAS (1 September 1966) was: Mario Amaya, Roy Ascott, Enrico Baj, Bob Cobbing, Ivor Davies, Jim Haynes, Dom Sylvester Houedard, Gustav Metzger, [Barry] Miles, Frank Popper, John Sharkey, Wolf Vostell.

Anton EHRENZWEIG
The Child's Vision of the World [1967]

The classical concept of the primary process (which forms unconscious phantasy) denies it any structure. Unconscious phantasy does not distinguish between opposites, fails to articulate space and time as we know it, and allows all firm boundaries to melt in a free chaotic mingling of forms. Art, on the other hand, appears the embodiment of rigorous organization. So it has been assumed that art's structure is exclusively shaped by conscious and preconscious functions, the so-called secondary process. But this will not do. In her Freud Centenary Lecture, *Psychoanalysis and Art,* Marion Milner said that a revision of the concept of the primary process was in the air; the problems raised by the nature of art pressed towards this revision.

For once the 'applied' psycho-analysis of art may backfire and modify original clinical theory. Such a development would not be new in the history of science. The science of the human body also began as medicine, but soon branched out into allied non-clinical disciplines that owed little to research into pathological phenomena and could in turn modify existing medical theory. Psycho-analysis as the science of the human mind may now have reached this stage, where non-clinical branches of research may claim to be independent enquiries that need not take over clinical theory without criticism. Psycho-analytic ego psychology – the study of creative work belongs to this field of research – has largely been nursed by Freud's analysis of the dream, which was certainly non-clinical. After a period of long stagnation ego psychology has once again attracted attention. It may be that the analysis of art can continue where the analysis of the dream has left off.

Before Freud the dream was considered the chance product of a half-paralysed mind. It was his achievement to have demonstrated its hidden meaning by referring it to a latent dream phantasy running on underneath the disconnected dream. While vindicating the dream's nonsensical content, Freud did not vindicate its seemingly chaotic structure. As I have said, he attributed it to a primary process lacking in the proper differentiation of opposites, of space and time, and indeed in any other firm structure. The formal analysis of art can make good this omission. The unconscious components of art demonstrate a deceptive chaos; for instance, the scribbles of artistic handwriting or background textures exhibit the same lack of precise structure. It has been my point in all my writings that their superficial appearance should not deceive us. They may be merely less differentiated, that is to say, they try to do too many things at once and cannot afford to distinguish (differentiate) between opposites and to articulate precise space and time. I will show that the complexity of a creative search, which has to explore many avenues, needs an advance on a broader front which keeps contradicting options open. In the solution of complex tasks the undifferentiation of unconscious vision turns into an instrument of rigorous precision and leads to results that are fully acceptable to conscious rationality. Of course, in mental illness undifferentiated material rises from the unconscious merely to disrupt the more narrowly focused modes of conscious discursive thinking; and the chaos and destruction which we are wont to associate with undifferentiated primary process phantasy overwhelm the patient's reason. In contrast to illness, creative work succeeds in coordinating the results of unconscious undifferentiation and conscious differentiation and so reveals the hidden order in the unconscious. Clinical work knows little about how creative sublimation works, because it is mainly concerned with interpreting and translating the contents of unconscious phantasy. Once the unconscious conflicts are resolved, it is left to the automatic action of the ego to sublimate the revealed unconscious drives into useful creative work. This procedure leaves the creative working of the ego obscure. The study of art's unconscious substructure and of the scanning processes in science offers the needed opportunity for observing the creative techniques of the ego and the way in which it makes use of the dispersed structure of unconscious perception. The chaos of the unconscious is as deceptive as the chaos of outer reality. In either case we need the less differentiated techniques of unconscious vision to become aware of their hidden order. The scientist has to face the fragmentation of physical facts with courage. He has to scan a multitude of possible links that could make sense out of apparent chaos. I would maintain that he needs the more dispersed (undifferentiated) structure of low-level vision in order to project the missing order into reality. At the same time – and this is the immense psychological gain – he will make a constructive use of his unconscious faculties and achieve the integration of his own ego. In creativity, outer and inner reality will always be organized together by the same indivisible process. The artist, too, has to face chaos in his work before unconscious scanning brings about the integration of his work as well as of his own personality. My point will be that unconscious scanning makes use of undifferentiated modes of vision that to normal awareness would seem chaotic. Hence comes the impression that the primary process merely produces chaotic phantasy material that has to be ordered and shaped by the ego's secondary processes. On the contrary, the primary process is a precision instrument for creative scanning that is far superior to discursive reason and logic.

The concept of undifferentiation as distinct from chaos is not easy to grasp. For the sake of a clearer exposition let me describe its character as it evolves during infancy. The undifferentiated structure of primary-process phantasy corresponds to the primitive still undifferentiated structure of the child's vision of the world. Piaget has given currency to the term 'syncretistic' vision as the distinctive quality of children's vision and of child art. Syncretism also involves the concept of undifferentiation. Around the eighth year of life a drastic change sets in in children's art, at least in Western civilization. While the infant experiments boldly with form and colour in representing all sorts of objects, the older child begins to analyse these shapes by matching them against the art of the adult which he finds in magazines, books and pictures. He usually finds his own work deficient. His work becomes duller in colour, more anxious in draughtsmanship. Much of the earlier vigour is lost. Art education seems helpless to stop this rot. What has happened is that the child's vision has ceased to be total and syncretistic and has become analytic instead. The child's more primitive syncretistic vision does not, as the adult's does, differentiate abstract details. The child does not break down the shape of some concrete object into smaller abstract elements and then match the elements of his drawings one by one. His vision is still global and takes in the entire whole which remains undifferentiated as to its component details. This gives the younger child artist the freedom to distort colour and shapes in the most imaginative and, to us, unrealistic manner. But to him – owing to his global, unanalytic view – his work is realistic. A scribble can represent a great number of objects that would look very different to the analytic spectator. However 'abstract' the infant's drawing may appear to the adult, to him himself it is a correct rendering of a concrete, individual object. His syncretistic vision allows him to disregard matching detail to detail.

I have said that the global syncretistic view is undifferentiated as to its elements. Their distortion and even complete change need not affect the identity of the object. The syncretistic neglect of detail in grasping a total object should not be dismissed as crude and primitive, or due to lack of self-critical faculties. We have to remember that the early work is better in its aesthetic achievement than the timid art of the older child. More important, syncretistic vision is never entirely destroyed and can be shown to be a potent tool in the hands of the adult artist.

E.H. Gombrich, in his already classic book *Art and Illusion*, has shown that realism in art does not simply copy the artist's subjective perceptions. Realism is only possible because conventional schemata for representing reality exist which have developed over the centuries. These the inventive artist can refine further and then match his new shapes against external reality. The initial 'making' (an intuitive act) of the schema has to be justified by 'matching' the tentative result against reality. What Gombrich implies, but never says explicitly, is that matching can be twofold; it can either be analytic or syncretistic. The matching of global shapes on the syncretistic level is freer and – wrongly – appears arbitrary to the analytic viewer. Gombrich matches usually, but not always, on the analytic level. Yet syncretism can be as precise, if not more so, than the analytic matching of detail. Picasso's incredibly convincing portraits defeat all analytic matching by jumbling up and distorting all the details of a face. But we can judge the likeness of the portrait only if we have become attuned to this kind of representation. We then no longer judge the verisimilitude of the portrait by analysing single features, but intuitively grasp the portrait as an indivisible whole. Picasso's one-time secretary, the Spanish writer Sabartés, illustrated his book on the master with a series of portraits of him painted by Picasso, which range from youthful academic realism to the most arbitrary distortions. In a late portrait Picasso reversed the position of the sitter's spectacles so that they sit upside down on the ridge of the nose. Yet the whole holds together and makes this most arbitrary of portraits the most convincing and 'realistic' of all. Only superficially does this lack of proper differentiation and spatial coherence seem chaotic. The resemblance achieved by a syncretistic portrait relies on a subtle balance which is not amenable to conscious analysis. Yet we can judge the likeness with precision. Some hidden order must guide us. The same reliability and precision is found in the young child's syncretistic grasp of reality. He may neglect abstract detail, yet his powers of recognition may be superior to the duller vision of the adult. Often some quite inconspicuous cue that escapes the more sophisticated adult may allow him to identify an object. A friend told me that his three-year-old boy could identify the make of some car which was almost totally hidden by relying on a single obscure feature in the car's bonnet. I will show that undifferentiated vision is altogether more acute in scanning complex structures. It treats all of them with equal impartiality, insignificant as they may look to normal vision. Normally our attention is drawn only to conspicuous features. These alone are then clearly differentiated. The others sink back to form an insignificant ground. Syncretistic vision is impartial because it does not differentiate figure and ground in this manner. Hence it also neglects what to analytic vision would seem important. But this neglect does not make it chaotic and still less unstructured.

In *Art and Illusion* Gombrich deals with the peculiarities of the caricature. Obviously the realism of the caricature is not based on matching analytically. The single distortions are certainly unrealistic and sometimes could not be recognized in isolation as parts of a human face. But they add up effortlessly to a global view which can bear a more striking resemblance to the sitter than a more conventional portrait. We have no rational standard whatsoever for matching the likeness analytically. The spectator has to call up in himself the young child's syncretistic vision which did not differentiate the identity of a shape by matching its details one by one, but went straight for the whole. Syncretistic vision can override photographic correctitude in detail by focusing only on the total view. Syncretistic vision appears much more flexible than analytic vision. To this extent we could reverse the usual evaluation and consider analytic vision cruder and less sensitive than (syncretistically) undifferentiated modes of vision obtaining on primitive (infantile) levels of awareness [...]

If this view of syncretistic vision is correct we can no longer say that the child, in creating his phantastic equivalents of reality, lacks self-criticism. When the analytic faculty of the child awakens around the age of eight and he learns to compare abstract details, he certainly tends to disparage his older syncretistic ways as crude and ignorant. But is this not a failure of our teaching? Is the awakening of self-criticism so self-destructive because we have failed to educate it earlier? We always tend to underestimate the child's intelligence. Even monkeys may be capable of appreciating their aesthetic efforts. In our view we have to help the infant in appreciating his work on the proper syncretistic level. There are degrees of success and failure even in the invention of the freest and most phantastic equivalent. We have seen how we can judge Picasso's phantasmagorias or the wild colour distortions of the Fauves as right or wrong, though we have not any rational standard for judging them. If the child has been properly supported in his aesthetic standards on the syncretistic level, the later awakening of his analytic self-criticism will no longer be quite so harmful. It would be useless, and even wrong, to discourage the eight-year-old child from applying his new analytic faculties to his work. We have only to prevent him from destroying his earlier syncretistic powers which remain so important even for the adult artist. This might only be achieved by surrounding the child with an adult environment of works by highly spontaneous artists such as Picasso, Klee, Miró, Matisse etc. This environment can sustain his old syncretistic vision side by side with his new analytic awareness. Encouraging the old blind 'free self-expression' against the new faculties simply will not do. If his syncretistic vision had been aesthetically trained it might well survive the onslaught of the new analytic vision and infuse vigour into his tired pattern making.

I will have a great deal more to say about the scattering of focus inherent in syncretistic vision. But let us first consider the pattern of ordinary analytic perception. From the undifferentiated mosaic of the visual field we are compelled to select a 'figure' on which attention concentrates while the rest of visual data recedes and fuses into a vague background of indistinct texture. Gestalt psychology has investigated the principles that govern the selection and formation of one particular figure in preference to others. From a number of possible constellations into which the visual stimuli can be grouped, we will tend to select the most compact, simple and coherent pattern which is said to possess properties of 'good' gestalt. The goodness of the gestalt is judged by our habitual aesthetic tastes. This makes gestalt psychology dependent on aesthetics, not too firm a ground on which to build a reliable theory. A good gestalt approximates to simple geometric patterns such as are hardly ever found in nature. But this matters little. The gestalt principle not only governs the selection of the best pattern from within the visual field, but it will also actively improve it. Little gaps and imperfections in an otherwise perfect gestalt are filled in or smoothed away. This is why analytic gestalt vision tends to be generalized and ignores syncretistic individuality.

Freud found that dreams looked particularly real not when the dream's imagery was precise and clear but when the dream was supported by a rich unconscious phantasy content. The same holds good of our waking perception. The schizophrenic, who is cut off from this anchorage, sees the world flat and unreal. Because syncretistic vision is anchored in the undifferentiated unconscious it is also more plastic and real (though less clearly defined) than the analytic vision of abstract pattern. Day-dreaming of the lazy sort need not be plastic and real in this way. The portraitist who projects landscapes into a face is wide awake. It is the privilege of the artist to combine the ambiguity of dreaming with the tensions of being fully awake. In the moment of inspiration reality will appear to him super-real and intensely plastic.

If we want to observe fine differences in abstract form we must project phantastic meaning into it. It is well known that we can judge the relative position of three dots in a circle with astonishing accuracy if we interpret them as two eyes and a mouth set in a rotund face. The slightest shifting in their position will affect their physiognomic expression. A smiling face becomes sad or threatening and vice versa. A copyist will do better if he copies this total facial expression instead of attending to detailed geometric relationships. This again goes to prove the superior scanning power of a total syncretistic vision and its better recognition of individual features, though it seems oblivious of abstract detail. In this lies the paradox of order in chaos.

The analytic vision of the eight-year-old child represents the fully developed abstract gestalt principle. The child begins to focus his attention on abstract geometric details of his drawings and compare them one by one with elements of the objects around him. No longer can he scatter his attention to the total appearance without regard to detail. The current gestalt theory ignores syncretism. It proclaims that these comparatively late gestalt tendencies are innate from birth [...]

Recent research, partly based on experiments with young animals and babies, suggests that the young animal does not see abstract shapes but scans the total object for cues that are immediately connected with real objects. To some young birds the same wooden shape suggests, say, a goose with a long neck if it is moved in one direction, and a dangerous hawk if moved backwards with the long neck now turned into a long tail. Colour alone may serve as a cue for identifying friend, enemy, parents and the like objects. A young baby will smile at a terrifying crude mask if only it has certain minimum cues suggesting the mother's face, but will show signs of fear if the cues are missing. This recognition of objects from cues rather than from the analysis of abstract detail is the beginning of syncretistic vision. Analytic vision would only obstruct the recognition of objects. Every movement of an object can profoundly affect the abstract shape of its details. The human nose looks triangular in profile and a shapeless squiggle in a frontal view. The two views have nothing in common. Yet we easily recognize a face which we have first seen in profile when it is presented later in a frontal view. If the gestalt theory had been correct and our first awareness of reality were analytic rather than syncretistic, the difficulty of identifying objects would become enormous. If we are able to discount the constant change and loss in abstract detail with such ease this must be due to the mysterious syncretistic grasp of the total shape which can be hypersensitive to individual features while ignoring meaningless abstract pattern. It is, therefore, wrong to speak of the child's primitive vision that is incapable of abstract form analysis; rather is it a superior faculty best suited to instant recognition of individual objects [...]

I am, of course, not decrying the awakening of the analytic abstract faculties during latency. Far from it; the new awareness of abstract form becomes one of the most potent tools in the hands of the artist and the scientist. Scientific abstraction is a product of unconscious dedifferentiation. It is based on a mixture of images which to conscious introspection appear incompatible and so blot each other out [...] (I will speak of *un*differentiation when referring to the static structure of unconscious image making, of *de*differentiation when describing the dynamic process by which the ego scatters and represses surface imagery.) The growth of new images in art and of new concepts in science is nourished by the conflict between two opposing structural principles. The analysis of abstract gestalt elements is pitted against the syncretistic grasp of the total object, focusing on detail against complex scanning, fragmentation against wholeness, differentiation against dedifferentiation. These polarities are aspects of the same conflict between the secondary and primary process. The new technical meaning which I have given to the terms 'undifferentiation' and 'dedifferentiation' may necessitate not only a modification of the present conception of the primary process, but also of the term 'unconscious'; images are withdrawn from consciousness not merely because of the superego's censorship of certain offensive *contents*; they may become inaccessible through their undifferentiated *structure* alone. The paradox of syncretistic vision can be explained in this way. Syncretistic vision may appear empty of precise detail though it is in fact merely undifferentiated. Through its lack of differentiation it can accommodate a wide range of imcompatible forms, for instance all the possible distortions of a face by a good caricature. Nevertheless, syncretistic vision is highly sensitive to the smallest of cues and proves more efficient in identifying individual objects. It impresses us as empty, vague and generalized only because the narrowly focused surface consciousness cannot grasp its wider more comprehensive structure. Its precise concrete content has become inaccessible and 'unconscious'.

Anton Ehrenzweig, 'The Child's Vision of the World', *The Hidden Order of Art: A Study in the Psychology of Artistic Imagination* (London: Weidenfeld and Nicholson, 1967) 3-20.

Mierle Laderman UKELES
Maintenance Art Manifesto: Proposal for an Exhibition, 'CARE' [1969]

I IDEAS

A The Death Instinct and the Life Instinct:

The Death Instinct: separation; individuality; Avant-Garde par excellence; to follow one's own path to death – do your own thing; dynamic change.

The Life Instinct: unification; the eternal return; the perpetuation and MAINTENANCE of the species; survival systems and operations; equilibrium.

B Two basic systems: Development and Maintenance. The sourball of every revolution: after the revolution, who's going to pick up the garbage on Monday morning?

Development: pure individual creation; the new; change; progress; advance; excitement; flight or fleeing.

Maintenance: keep the dust off the pure individual creation; preserve the new; sustain the change; protect progress; defend and prolong the advance; renew the excitement; repeat the flight: show your work – show it again keep the contemporaryartmuseum groovy keep the home fires burning

Development systems are partial feedback systems with major room for change.

Maintenance systems are direct feedback systems with little room for alteration.

C Maintenance is a drag; it takes all the fucking time (lit.) The mind boggles and chafes at the boredom. The culture confers lousy status on maintenance jobs minimum wages, housewives = no pay.

clean your desk, wash the dishes, clean the floor, wash your clothes, wash your toes, changes the baby's diaper, finish the report, correct the typos, mend the fence, keep the customer happy, throw out the stinking garbage, watch out don't put things in your nose, what shall I wear, I have no sex, pay the bills, don't litter, save string, wash your hair, change the sheets, go to the store, I'm out of perfume, say it again — 'he doesn't understand', seal it again – it leaks, go to work, this art is dusty, clear the table, call him again, flush the toilet, stay young.

D Art:

Everything I say is Art is Art. Everything I do is Art is Art. 'We have no Art, we try to do everything well.' (Balinese saying).

Avant-garde art, which claims utter development, is infected by strains of maintenance ideas, maintenance activities, and maintenance materials.

Conceptual & Process art, especially, claim pure development and change, yet employ almost purely maintenance processes.

E The exhibition of Maintenance Art, 'CARE' would zero in on pure maintenance, exhibit it as contemporary art, and yield, by utter opposition, clarity of issues.

II THE MAINTENANCE ART EXHIBITION: 'CARE'

Three parts: Personal, General, and Earth Maintenance.

A Part One: Personal

I am an artist. I am a woman. I am a wife. I am a mother. (Random order).

I do a hell of a lot of washing, cleaning, cooking, renewing, supporting, preserving, etc. Also (up to now separately) I 'do' Art.

Now, I will simply do these maintenance everyday things, and flush them up to consciousness, exhibit them as Art. I will live in the museum as I customarily do at home with my husband and my baby, for the duration of the exhibition (Right? or if you don't want me around at night I would come in every day), and do all these things as public Art activities: I will sweep and wax the floors, dust everything, wash the walls (i.e. 'floor paintings, dust works, soapsculpture, wall-paintings'), cook, invite people to eat, make agglomerations and dispositions of a functional refuse.

The exhibition area might look 'empty' of art, but it will be maintained in full public view.

MY WORKING WILL BE THE WORK.

B Part Two: General

Everyone does a hell of a lot of noodling maintenance work. The general part of the exhibition would consist of interviews of two kinds.

1 *– Previous individual interviews, typed and exhibited.*

Interviewees come from, say, 50 different classes and kinds of occupations that run a gamut from maintenance 'man', maid, sanitation 'man', mail 'man', union 'man', construction worker, librarian, grocerystore 'man', nurse, doctor, teacher, museum director, baseball player, sales 'man', child, criminal, bank president, mayor, moviestar, artist, etc., about:

– what you think maintenance is; – how you feel about spending whatever parts of your life you spend on maintenance activities; – what is the relationship between maintenance and freedom; – what is the relationship between maintenance and life's dreams.

2 *– Interview Room for spectators at the Exhibition: A room of desks and chairs where professional (?) interviewers will interview the spectators at the exhibition along same questions as typed interviews. The responses should be personal.*

These interviews are taped and replayed throughout the exhibition area.

C Part Three: Earth Maintenance

Everyday, containers of the following kinds of refuse will be delivered to the Museum:

– the contents of one sanitation truck;
– a container of polluted air;
– a container of polluted Hudson River;
– a container of ravaged land.

Once at the exhibition, each container will be serviced:

purified, de-polluted, rehabilitated, recycled, and conserved
by various technical (and/or pseudo technical) procedures either by myself or scientists.
These servicing procedures are repeated throughout the duration of the exhibition.

Mierle Laderman Ukeles, 'Maintenance Art Manifesto: Proposal for an Exhibiiton, CARE' (1969); reprinted in Alexander Alberro; Blake Stimson (eds.) *Conceptual Art: A Critical Anthology* (Cambridge, Massachusetts: MIT Press, 1999) 122-25.

Dan GRAHAM
Gordon Matta-Clark [1983–84]

In the 1970s, artists attempted to leave the politically coercive bonds of the art gallery. They deserted the city to make neoprimitive earth works, relocations, or simply maps of their walks in the landscape. But in the display (documentation) of this work to the public, ironically, the art gallery returned as a support. As Robert Smithson said in 1970, 'Landscape [is] co-extensive with the gallery. I don't think we're dealing with matter in terms of a back to nature movement. For me the world is a museum.'[1] Smithson wanted to deny any reading of his work in terms of the then currently fashionable ecology movement or any political reading; rather it was to be read as formalist art or as an ambiguously romantic stance.

Not only couldn't the Earth artists escape the need for the gallery to document their work, but they were in danger of taking part of nature and exhibiting it as a found object. This was a great dilemma for Gordon Matta-Clark, a young artist and friend of Smithson's. He described his first work, saying 'I made a series of visits to the ghetto area of the Lower East Side and the Bronx ... moving into spaces with a hand saw and cutting away rectangular sections of the floor or walls to create a view from one space into another. The sections were carefully removed from their original positions [and taken] to an art gallery.'[2]

Matta-Clark came to the position that work must function directly in the actual urban environment. 'Nature' was an escape, political and cultural contradictions were not to be denied. By making his removals public (similar to the chance spectacle of a demolition for casual pedestrians), the work could function as a kind of urban agitprop, like the actions of the Paris Situationists during May '68 – public intrusions or 'cuts' in the seamless urban fabric. The Situationist idea was to have their gestures interrupt the induced habits of the urban masses; this might then unrepress certain concealed realities. Similarly, Matta-Clark saw his 'cuts' as probes, opening up socially hidden information beneath the surface to: '*create repercussions in terms of what else is imposed upon by a cut ... It was kind of the thin edge of what was being seen that interested me as much, if not more than, the views that were being created ... The layering, the strata, the different things that are being severed [provided] the simplest way to create complexity ... without having to make or build anything.*'[3] [...]

'By undoing a building', Matta-Clark said, '[I] open a state of enclosure which had been preconditioned not only by physical necessity but by the industry that [proliferates] suburban and urban boxes as a context for insuring a passive isolated consumer.'[4] These deconstructions can, paradoxically, still be a form of architecture; for the effect of stripping or cutting into buildings functions to enhance or preserve the site. Matta-Clark noted that in his work *Splitting*, 'What the cutting's done is to make the space more articulated, but the identity of the building as a place, as an object, is strongly preserved, enhanced.'[5]

To strip, to eviscerate, to deconstruct a building – these are statements against professional architectural practice. To destroy and not to construct (or reconstruct) a building amounts to an inversion of functionalist doctrine. While Mies, for instance, constructed in terms of materials such as glass and steel to reveal both the material structure and the previously unrevealed interior, Matta-Clark looked for already existing 'gaps, void places that were not developed'. These only exist as negation in modern architecture. In fact, the sheer glass-and-steel openwork, like the modern bureaucratic thinking it reflects, is often a measure taken by modern architecture to cover over these contradictions (particularly contradictions in the definition of public versus private property). A Matta-Clark work reveals contradictions as they have been developed in time as stratified, archaeological layers of otherwise normal building situations. Matta-Clark's exposures, unlike Minimal, Pop, or Conceptual art allow a historical time to enter: 'There is a kind of complexity which comes from taking an otherwise completely normal, conventional, albeit anonymous situation and redefining it, retranslating it into overlapping and multiple readings of conditions past and present.'[6] [...]

Matta-Clark fragments or splinters architecture, turning it into a kind of reverse cubism or 'anti-monument', but one whose task is to reconstitute memory – not conventional memory as in the traditional monument, but that subversive memory that has been hidden by social and architectural facades and their false sense of 'wholeness'. '*[There is] a type of space we all, all of us, have stored in memory: spaces that are detailed and precise, fragments generally, at all levels of reminiscence. And of course, once you get into reminiscence, an infinite number of associations emerge. Memory seems to create a unique kind of space setting up an about-to-disintegrate level.*'[7]

Unlike the conventional monument designed to smoothly link past to present to implied future, Matta-Clark's 'monument' is profoundly pessimistic. It will be quickly demolished; as a work it is something of a useless gesture. It defies permanent symbolic form. It accepts its fate – to be remembered only as a photo/text representation as 'conceptual art' *and* to disappear into the anonymous rubble. It is close to instant ruins – a photo of what was once a spark of hope and is now erased by more dominant forms. These are negative 'monuments' or remembrances of works desired to 'open up' history and historical memory, which could lead to a critical view of present oppression.

In effect, Matta-Clark's work, although negative as to architectural practice, still hopefully opts, from the view of historical materialism, for a communication value. This is the ideal of Conceptual art: 'The determining factor is the degree to which my intervention can transform the structure into an act of communication.'[8] Matta-Clark identified his deconstructions in terms of linguistic acts: 'It's like juggling with syntax, or disintegrating some kind of established sequence of parts ... The piece is a way of imposing a presence, an idea, it's a way to disorientation by using a clear and given system.'[9]

1 Robert Smithson, quoted from 'Discussions with Heizer, Oppenheim, Smithson', *Avalanche*, 1 (Fall 1970), 62.
2 Gordon Matta-Clark, quoted in 'Interview with Gordon Matta-Clark, Antwerp, September 1977', in *Gordon Matta-Clark* (Antwerp: International Cultureel Centrum, 1977), 8.
3 Liza Bear, 'Gordon Matta-Clark: Splitting (The Humphrey Street Building)', *Avalanche*, 10 (December 1974), 34.
4 'By undoing a building there are many aspects of the social conditions against which I am gesturing: first, to open a state of enclosure which had been preconditioned not only by physical necessity but by the industry that [proliferates] suburban and urban boxes as a context for insuring a passive, isolated consumer – a virtually captive audience ... The question is a reaction to an ever less viable state or privacy, private property, and isolation.' Gordon Matta-Clark, quoted in Donald Wall, 'Gordon Matta-Clark's Building Dissections', *Arts Magazine* 50:9 (May 1976), 76.
5 Bear, 'Splitting', *op. cit.*, 37.
6 Wall, 'Building Dissections', *op. cit.*, 77.
7 Ibid., 78-9.
8 Ibid., 77.
9 Bear, 'Splitting', p. 36.

Dan Graham, 'Gordon Matta-Clark', first published in an incomplete French version in *Art Press*, XX (Paris: Summer 1983); reprinted in English in *Dan Graham, Rock My Religion, 1965-1990*, ed. Brian Wallis (Cambridge, Massachusetts: MIT Press, 1993) 194-205.

Dan GRAHAM
My Works for Magazine Pages: 'A History of Conceptual Art' [1985]

I became involved with the art system accidentally when friends of mine suggested that we open a gallery. In 1964, Richard Bellamy's Green Gallery was the most important avant-garde gallery and was just beginning to show people such as Judd, Morris and Flavin. Our gallery, John Daniels, gave Sol LeWitt a one-man show, as well as doing several group shows which included all the 'proto-Minimalist' artists whether they already showed at Green Gallery or not. We also had plans to have a one-man exhibition of Robert Smithson – then a young 'Pop' artist. However, the gallery was forced to close due to bankruptcy at the end of the first season.

If we could have continued for another two years, with the aid of more capital, perhaps we might have succeeded. Nevertheless, the experience of managing a gallery was particularly valuable for me in that it afforded the many conversations I had with Dan Flavin, Donald Judd, Jo Baer, Will Insley, Robert Smithson and others who, if they were not able to give works for thematic exhibitions, supported the gallery by recommending other artists and by dropping by to chat. In addition to a knowledge of current and historical art theory, some of these artists had an even greater interest, which I shared, in intellectual currents of that moment such as serial music, the French 'New Novel' (Robbe-Grillet, Butor, Pinget, etc.), and new scientific theories. It was possible to connect the philosophical implications of these ideas with the art that these 'proto-Minimal' artists and more established artists such as Warhol, Johns, Stella, Lichtenstein and Oldenburg or dancers such as Yvonne Rainer or Simone Forti were producing.

The Fall after the gallery failed I began experimenting myself with art works which could be read as a reaction against the gallery experience, but also as a response to contradictions I discerned in gallery artists. While American 'Pop' art of the early 1960s referred to the surrounding media world of cultural information as framework, 'Minimal' art of the middle through late 1960s seemed to be referring to the gallery's interior cube as the ultimate contextual frame of reference or support for the work. This reference was only compositional; in place of a compositional reading interior to the work, the gallery would compose the art's formal structure in relation to the gallery's interior architectural structure. That the work was equated with the architectural container tended to literalize it; both the architectural container and the work contained within were meant to be seen as non-illusionistic, neutral and objectively factual – that is, as simply material. The gallery functioned literally as part of the art. One artist's work of this period (although not always his later work) examined how specific, functional architectural elements of the gallery interior prescribed meaning and determined specific readings for the art defined within its architectural frame: Dan Flavin's fluorescent light installations.

Lighting – light fixtures – within the architectural setting of the gallery/museum is normally disregarded, or considered merely functional or minor interior decoration. As gallery space is meant to appear neutral, the lighting, which creates this neutrality as much as the white walls, and at the same time is used to highlight and centre attention on the artwork on the wall or floor, is kept inconspicuous. While the background in general makes the artworks visible, the lighting literally makes the works visible.

The lighting system, within which the specific light fixtures of a gallery arrangement function, is both part of the gallery apparatus and part of the larger, existing (non-art) system of electric lighting in general use:

'*I believe that the changing standard lighting system should support my idea within it.*'

– Dan Flavin, 'Some Remarks', *Artforum*, 1966.

Flavin's installations make use of this double functioning (inside and outside the gallery/art context) as well as the double connotation of lighting as minor decoration (interior decoration) and anonymously functional creator of the gallery's neutrality.

'*I believe that art is shedding its vaunted mystery for a common sense of keenly realized decoration. Symbolizing is dwindling – becoming slight. We are pressing downward towards no art – a mutual sense of psychologically indifferent decoration – a neutral pleasure of seeing known to everyone.*'

– Dan Flavin, 'Some Other Remarks', *Artforum*, 1966.

His arrangements of light fixtures in a gallery space depend for significance, contextually, upon the function of the gallery, and the socially determined architectural use of electric lighting. Use of electric light is related to a specific time in history. Flavin has observed that when the existing system of electric lighting has ceased to exist, his art will no longer function. Being a series of standardized, replaceable units, which, in Flavin's words, 'can be bought in any hardware store', his arrangements of fluorescent tubes within the interior or adjacent exterior architectural frame of the gallery exhibition space function only in situation installation, and upon completion of the exhibition cease to function artistically.

Perhaps I misread the implications of these works by suggesting a conscious intention to examine the relation of the value of art to the question of the gallery in which it was exhibited. I also felt that the 'solution' Marcel Duchamp had found to this problem of art's 'value' was unsatisfactory.

In his 'readymades', Duchamp brought objects which were not considered art when placed outside the gallery, into the gallery to prove dialectically that it is in fact the gallery which gives the object its value and meaning. Instead of reducing gallery objects to the common level of the everyday object, this ironic gesture simply extended the reach of the gallery's exhibition territory. In bringing the 'non-art' object into the gallery, Duchamp wished to place in apparent contradiction the conventional function of the gallery to designate certain objects as 'art' and to exclude others.

Essentially Duchamp attempted to question the aristocratic function of art and the art gallery as an institution. Because this question was only presented on a logical abstract level, his critique was itself immediately integrated back into the institutional system of gallery or museum art, becoming a kind of 'idea' art. A further problem with Duchamp's analysis is the resolution of the contradiction between gallery art and art in relation to its social value based on a historical concept; the condition of art is seen as neither social nor subject to external social change. By contrast, Flavin's fluorescent light pieces are not merely *a priori* philosophical idealizations, but have concrete relations to specific details of the architectural arrangement of the gallery, details which produce meaning.

In addition, Duchamp saw the problem of value and meaning in art as a simple binary opposition, inside the gallery or outside in the world. He failed to link this opposition of art and so-called 'non-art' to more ambiguous phenomena such as the reproduction of the art object by the media, which was meditated upon by the critic Walter Benjamin in the 1930s and was even earlier an important aspect of Constructivist art.

Through the actual experience of running a gallery, I learned that if a work of art wasn't written about and reproduced in a magazine it would have difficulty attaining the status of 'art'. It seemed that in order to be defined as having value – that is, as 'art' – a work had only to be exhibited in a gallery and then to be written about and reproduced as a photograph in an art magazine. Then this record of the no longer extant installation, along with more accretions of information after the fact, became the basis for its fame, and to a large extent, its economic value.

From one perspective, the art object can be analyzed as inseparably connected to the institution of the gallery or museum; but from another perspective it can be seen as having a certain independence, as it belongs also to the general cultural framework which the magazine is a part of. Magazines specialize in a way which replicates other social and economic divisions. Any magazine, no matter how generalized, caters to a certain market or a specific audience in a particular field. All art magazines are directed to people who are involved in the art world professionally in one way or another. Furthermore, the art magazine itself is supported by advertisements which, with one or two exceptions, come from art galleries that are presenting exhibitions. It follows that in some way the advertisers have to be taken care of in that their shows have to be reviewed and made a matter of record in the magazine. Thus these shows and works are guaranteed some kind of value and can be sold on the market as 'art'. The fact that sales do take place yields enough money for the gallery to purchase more advertisements in art magazines and to sustain the art system in general.

Art magazines ultimately depend upon art galleries for their economic support, just as the work shown in galleries depends on photographic reproduction for its value in the media. Magazines determine a place or are a frame of reference both outside and inside. Magazines specialize in a 'field' – for instance, the specialized 'world' of art and artists termed the 'art' world. *Sports Illustrated* caters to those who are interested in sports, the *American Legion* magazine caters to members of the American Legions. Art magazines cater to artists, dealers, collectors, connoisseurs, and writers who have a professional interest in art. And the art magazine itself is supported by advertisements.

Dan Graham, 'My Works for Magazine Pages: "A History of Conceptual Art"', *Dan Graham*, ed. Gary Dufour (Perth: Art Gallery of Western Australia, 1985) 8-13; reprinted in *Two-Way Mirror Power, Selected Writings by Dan Graham on his Art*, ed. Alexander Alberro, (Cambridge, Massachusetts: MIT Press, 1999) 10-13.

Jeff WALL
Dan Graham's *Kammerspiel*
[1988]

[...] In 1966 Graham redesigned Pop in the grim, grey style of 'factography' in order to present an image of the miserable consequence of architectural thought in the post-war era – the barracks-like tract house. Upon this structure his thought dwells consistently over the years. A sense of the social misery congealed across the abstract surfaces of the Pop-Minimal coalescence is retrieved as Graham marks off the affirmativeness of both types of art. Minimalism is seen through *Homes for America* (1966–67) as a repressed social semiotics which is barred from accepting itself as such by its roots in Idealist abstraction.

Homes for America is indeed a form of Pop art, in that it mimics a certain kind of magazine article the way Lichtenstein copied comic strips. However, it establishes its particular form of mimesis as both Pop and antithetical to Pop (in part by *not* being traditional artwork). More importantly, this piece of 'photojournalism' becomes the vehicle by which means the social surfaces of American culture, brightened and celebrated by Pop, are reinvested with the grey, funereal and somewhat distressing atmosphere of the Johnsian mid 1950s, the Cold War era in which corporate emblems still retained vestiges of their then-recent function as war-propaganda. The text of *Homes for America* discusses the development of tract-housing after World War II. The insistent comparison of the new suburb to a barracks or prison is articulated in language combining journalistic concreteness with a sense of the deliriously labyrinthine. Graham's text is as Borgesian as those of Robert Smithson, whose *A Tour of the Monuments of Passaic, New Jersey* (1967) is its closest parallel (and who played a part in having *Homes* commissioned as a 'think-piece' for *Arts Magazine*). Graham's intention with this work is to reveal the structural and historical isomorphism of Minimal and Pop art. The consequences for both trends of the repression are not directly linked with any particular attitude towards the political problems of urbanism since the 1920s, but the issue is evoked obliquely in the unveiling of the consequences of those problems both for architecture itself and for Pop and Minimalism, which appropriate material from the common or popular signifiers put in place by urbanism.

Thus, through a series of assumptions of roles or functions, *Homes for America* arrives at its position as unique within conceptual art. Like much conceptualism, it attempts to breach the dominance of the established art forms and to articulate a critique of them. However, unlike the more academic types of conceptual art (as practised by Art-Language, they could arrive only at a paradoxical state of establishing themselves as works of art *negatively*, by enunciating conditions for art which they had no interest in actually fulfilling) Graham's photojournalistic format demands that his work have a separable, distinguishable subject-matter. Instead of making artistic gestures which were little more than rehearsals of first principles, as Kosuth or Art-Language were to do, Graham brings into being his analysis of the institutional status of art through the dynamism of a journalistic subject which is implicitly the inner truth of purer forms of art. This is, of course, the antithesis of the formalist abolition of subject-matter. In a single gesture Graham establishes the primacy of social subject-matter as *the* historically essential problem to be posed by conceptualism, and at the same time he identifies the single grand subject which will remain central to the development of the movement's historical self-consciousness: the city. *Homes for America* is the work in which Graham recognizes that the conceptual critique indeed has an inherent subject, which he begins to investigate – the historical development of city as site of cultural conflict. This investigation begins on the ground of conceptualism by posing anew the antithesis faced by the more revolutionary artists of the 1920s and 30s: one between the isolated and exalted 'pure' work of art (the highest product of the distraught bourgeois self-consciousness) and the social machine as a whole that reproduces this distraught consciousness in the process of its own reproduction as city.

Homes for America is, however, of its own time and does not pose this historical contradiction in terms of the explicit dynamism of Lissitzky or Tatlin. Although Graham manages to identify the historical consequences of the collapse of the hopes of the utopian artists and planners of the 1920s, he cannot rekindle them. He can go no further than specifying those conditions resulting in the era when this hope appears to have been permanently eclipsed. Graham's reminiscence of the oppressive greyness of the 50s sets off a further reminiscence of the history of earlier planning schemes whose liberating rhetoric has shrunken into the gratuitous structures of the suburban grid, the garden of subjection for a lost proletariat. For Graham, as for many other young artists, in 1966, the key revelation of the city was in the shock of the absolute loss of hope. This loss was as much a stimulant for critical memory as was indignation: the city of Antonioni provoked the memory of de Chirico and Breton, as the city of Godard did that of Heartfield or Meyerhold. Although his response to this shock shares neither Smithson's black indignation nor his black humour, Graham appreciates both, and commits himself to the decipherment of this image of mechanistic domination. When Smithson leads the incensed Romantics into the desert, Graham remains in the city and suburbs.

Homes for America is the finest of the group magazine pieces of the late 1960s, all articulating the theme of the defeat of those ideals of rational, critical language by bureaucratic-commercial forms of communication and enforcement. The magazine pieces are structured as small, ironically insignificant defeats for liberationist ideas, as 'defeatist interventions' in the mechanisms of ideological dominations. They are aimed at interrupting the flow of standardized, falsified representation and language, and inducing a 'mini-crisis' for the reader or viewer by means of the inversions they create. This strategy, carried out most insidiously and brilliantly in *Detumescence* (1966/69), parallels the creation of distancing effects in everyday environments by early conceptualists such as Weiner (particularly in his series of 'removals'). Reflected in the provocations and interventions characteristic of 1960s Situationism in which an unexpected and confrontational gesture interrupts the established rhythm of relationships in a specific context, and induces a form of contestation, paradox or crisis, this approach thereby exposes the forms of authority and domination in the situation, which are normally imperceptible or veiled. The most notable artistic image of this is the unexpected 'void' or 'rupture' in the seamlessly designed social surface, and conceptualism's origins are filled with such blanks, erasures, tears and cuts. These gestures interrupt the induced habits of the urban masses, and the interruption theoretically permits social repression (which is the veiled content of habit) to emerge in a kind of hallucination provoked by the work. This liberating hallucination is the objective of the work, and its claim to value. Such Situationist intervention is also related to Pop, but inversely, as is conceptualism; it aggravates Pop irony by means of *humeur noir*, and attempts to elicit a recognition of the terroristic aspects of the normalized environment of images, things, spaces and mechanisms.

Graham's magazine pieces fuse a Situationist-inspired strategy of the 'cut', of *détournement*, with that of the mimesis of bureaucratic forms of 'factography'. The interventions designed by him remain primarily concrete, functioning through the dynamics of specific subjects. Conceptualism, in relapsing into 'radical formalism', tended to empty the 'cut' or intervention of its specific character, thereby absolutizing it as an extreme form of emblematic abstraction. Such interventions are reduced to decorativism, as is the case with many later works by Buren, for example.

Graham uses an actual text – an article, an advertisement, a chart – which constitutes its intervention through a structured difference with the norms of the genre in question. Thus, in these works, a specific social genre, existing functionally, is altered in a prescribed direction aimed at bringing out and making perceptible the underlying historical oppression.

Thus, *Homes for America*'s theme, the subjection of the romantic ideal of the harmonious garden suburb to the systems of 'land development', is presented in the pseudo-Readymade form of a 'think-piece' or popular photo-essay. This format is retained, mimetically, as the means by which the subject-matter is altered and made perceptible in a negative sense. Graham's approach accepts the existing formalism of culture – its rigidified generic structure – as a first principle, and applies pseudo-Readymade, pseudo-Pop, and authentically Situationist strategies to it. The result is formalism intensified to the qualitative crisis point. The work makes its intervention in the context of a formalized emptiness of existing genres, but does not create an antithetical emptiness, a purely abstract or emblematic intervention. In fusing the journalistic attitude which accepts the primacy of subject-matter together with the Situationist-conceptualist strategy of interventionism and *détournement*, the work establishes a discourse in which its subject matter, a critique of Minimalism and Pop via a discussion of the architectural disaster upon which they both depend, can be enlarged to the point of a historical critique of reigning American cultural development [...]

Jeff Wall, *Dan Graham's Kammerspiel* (1988) (Toronto: Art Metropole, 1991) 26-32.

John LATHAM, Barbara STEVENI Art as Social Strategy in Institutions and Organization with the Artist Placement Group (APG) London [1990]

APG arose in the mid 1960s, as a development from central themes within the art trajectory. The hundred-year old movement towards simplification summarized in Mies van der Rohe's phrase LESS IS MORE, indicated clearly that the concept of the art object was now to be subsumed by that of the *event*. It also became clear that language and art met at a point where principles of structure, within any event complex, would have to be *shown*.
Additionally, that verbal information by itself (in its syntactic relations to 'ime' and in-formation) held too many mis-interpretations of nature for social and spiritual progress to be continued.

Therefore, when APG first came into being, it was through those artists who had already invented a new form of expression, each one with a different medium, but orientated towards 'event' as distinct from object. There is no common 'style' to be seen (except in as much as the effect of the common denominator – context – might produce one), but a common understanding of the nature of art, of discovery, and of the circumstances that most facilitate discovery. It is these same circumstances derived from artistic experience and practice, that APG has taken care to manifest in its method of association of artist with organizational structures.

APG's principles have appeared disturbing for the existing art frameworks both in the market and within colleges of art. However, from the point of view of the larger economic unit, human society as a whole, this move by artists towards the social context, was right by art and right by the interpretation of history. A move in effect, from expressionist art to an art of implementation.

The principles proposed by APG for an effective form of association of artists with organizational structures therefore emphasize the following guidelines:

1 That *context* is half the work. (cf. between 6, Kunsthalle Dusseldorf 1971 and Art and Economics, APG Hayward Gallery Exhibition London December 1971).

2 That the function of *medium* in art is determined not so much by the factual object, as by the process and the levels of attention to which the work aims. (By level of attention is meant the consideration of human long-term identity.)

3 That the proper contribution of art to society is art. (APG is not concerned therefore to seek 'employment' for artists, but is run in the belief that society is starved of an important ingredient when creative people are kept outside the working parts of governments, organizations and institutions.)

4 That the status of artists within organizations must necessarily be in line with other professional persons, engaged within the organization.

5 That the status of the artist within organizations is independent, bound by invitation rather than by instructions from authority within the organizations, department, company, to those of the long-term objectives of the whole of society.

6 That, for optimum results, the position of the artist within an organization (in the initial stages at least) should facilitate a form of cross-referencing between departments.

Negotiations are contingent upon both participants having this understanding, and a mutual confidence. So APG requires intelligence and strength in art and a reciprocal response from within administrations.

(APG had previously been instrumental in placing artists within various organizations, typically industrial ones in the private and public sectors; these included in the period from 1968 to 1971 British Steel, British Airways, British Rail, Esso Petroleum, ICI, National Bus Company, Ocean Fleets and Hille International. An exhibition of the group's work was exhibited at the Hayward Gallery, London, in December 1971 under the title Art and Economics.)

METHOD OF OPERATION

The general method of procedure for APG artist association was first set out in a Memorandum drawn up jointly between artists and the British Civil Service Department in Whitehall, London in 1972. This memorandum was then addressed to other departments of the British government and subsequently artists were seconded to a number of government organizations, notably the Department of Environment where the artist was attached to the Inner Area Study in Birmingham; the Department of Health and Social Security, attached to the Personal Services and Mental Health Group of the Architects Division concerned with the future planning of mental institutions, in particular Broadmoor and Rampton Hospitals; the Peterlee Development Corporation, and the Scottish Office where the artist was attached to the Planning Department and asked to look at the aspects of the Urban Renewal of the City of Glasgow, Derelict Land and the Cartographic Department.

This procedure has recently been examined for its applicability to conditions and procedures in Germany and other European countries. An exchange of details through letters from the Department of Foreign Affairs in London with that in Bonn has ensured the common ground between German and British action in this direction. (Further details as to procedure, work of artists when on placement with these government bodies, can be obtained from the catalogue *KUNST ALS SOZIALE STRATEGIE: Ausstellung von vier Projekten* published by the Bonn Kunstverein for the occasion of the Artist Placement Group presentation 8.12.77–15.1.78 in Bonn. Additional APG presentations addressed to civic, commercial and ministerial authorities have been at Documenta 6 in Kassel, June 1977; at the Royal College of Art, London, 1977; in the Salle Dufy in the Musée d'Art Moderne, Paris, in the context of the exhibition 'Un Certain Art Anglais' in January 1979; and in Vienna in the Palais Liechtenstein, the Museum of Modern Art, under the title 'Kunst als Soziale Strategie in Institutionen und Organisation'.)

Under the general stance of The Incidental Person approach to government, APG, representing an international artist voice and engaged in an activity that has no sectional interest to serve, invites negotiations with those organizations carrying public responsibility to form associations with artists who are able and willing to work in the wider fields afforded by the administrative contexts of any country.

John Latham, Barbara Steveni, 'Art as Social Strategy in Institutions and Organization with the Artist Placement Group', London, May 1990.

Jeff WALL 'Marks of Indifference': Aspects of Photography in, or as, Conceptual Art [1995]

[...] Many of conceptual art's essential achievements are either created in the form of photographs or are otherwise mediated by them.

Reportage is introverted and parodied, manneristically, in aspects of photoconceptualism. The notion that an artistically significant photograph can any longer be made in a direct imitation of photojournalism is rejected as having been historically completed by the earlier avant-garde and by the lyrical subjectivism of 1950s art photography. The gesture of reportage is withdrawn from the social field and attached to a putative theatrical event. The social field tends to be abandoned to professional photojournalism proper, as if the aesthetic problems associated with depicting it were no longer of any consequence, and photojournalism had entered not so much a postmodernist phase as a 'post-aesthetic' one in which it was excluded from aesthetic evolution for a time. This, by the way, suited the sensibilities of those political activists who attempted a new version of proletarian photography in the period.

This introversion, or subjectivization, of reportage was manifested in two important directions. First, it brought photography into a new relationship with the problematics of the staged, or posed, picture, through new concepts of performance. Second, the inscription of photography into a nexus of experimental practices led to a direct but distantiated and parodic relationship with the art-concept of photojournalism. Although the work of many artists could be discussed in this context, for the sake of brevity I will discuss the photographic work of Richard Long and Bruce Nauman as representative of the first issue, that of Dan Graham, Douglas Huebler and Robert Smithson of the second.

Long's and Nauman's photographs document already conceived artistic gestures, actions or 'studio events' – things that stand self-consciously as conceptual, aesthetic models for states of affairs in the world, which, as such, need no longer appear directly in the picture. Long's *England 1968* (1968) documents an action or gesture, made by the artist alone, out in the countryside, away from the normal environs of art or performance. Generically, his pictures are landscapes, and their mood is rather different from the typologies and intentions of reportage. Conventional artistic landscape photography might feature a foreground motif, such as a curious heap of stones or a gnarled tree, and counterpoint it to the rest of the scene, showing it to be singular, differentiated from its surroundings, and yet existing by means of those surroundings. In such ways, a landscape picture can be thought to report on a state of affairs, and therefore be consistent with an art-concept of reportage. Long's walked line in the grass substitutes itself for the foreground motif. It is a gesture akin to Barnett Newman's notion of the establishment of a 'Here' in the void of a primaeval terrain. It is simultaneously agriculture, religion, urbanism and theatre, an intervention in a lonely, picturesque spot which becomes a setting completed artistically by the gesture and the photograph for which the gesture was enacted. Long does not photograph events in the process of their occurrence but stages an event for the benefit of a preconceived photographic rendering. The picture is presented as the subsidiary form of an act, as 'photo-documentation'. It has become that, however, by means of anew kind of photographic *mise-en-scène*. That is, it exists and is legitimated as continuous with the project of reportage by moving in precisely the opposite direction, towards a completely designed pictorial method, an introverted masquerade that plays games with the inherited aesthetic proclivities of art-photography-as-reportage.

Many of the same elements, moved indoors, characterize Nauman's studio photographs, such as *Failing to Levitate in the Studio* (1966) or *Self-Portrait as a Fountain* (1966–70). The photographer's studio, and the generic complex of 'studio photography', was the Pictorialist antithesis against which the aesthetics of reportage were elaborated. Nauman changes the terms. Working within the experimental framework of what was beginning at the time to be called 'performance art', he carries out photographic acts of reportage whose subject-matter is the self-conscious, self-centered 'play' taking place in the studios of artists who have moved 'beyond' the modern fine arts into the new hybridities. Studio photography is no longer isolated from reportage: it is reduced analytically to coverage of whatever is happening in the studio, that place once so rigorously controlled by precedent and formula, but which was in the process of being reinvented once more as theatre, factory, reading room, meeting place, gallery, museum, and many other things.

Nauman's photographs, films and videos of this period are done in two modes or styles. The first, that of *Failing to Levitate* is 'direct', rough, and shot in black and white. The other is based on studio lighting effects – multiple sources, coloured gels, emphatic contrasts – and is of course done in colour. The two styles, reduced to a set of basic formulae and effects, are signifiers for the new co-existence of species of photography which had seemed ontologically separated and even opposed in the art history of photography up to that time. It is as if the reportage works go back to Muybridge and the sources of all traditional concepts of photographic documentary, and the colour pictures to the early 'gags' and jokes, to Man Ray and Moholy-Nagy, to the birthplace of effects used for their own sake. The two reigning myths of photography – the one that claims that photographs are 'true' and the one that claims they are not – are shown to be grounded in the same praxis, available in the same place, the studio, at that place's moment of historical transformation.

These practices, or strategies, are extremely common by about 1969, so common as to be *de rigueur* across the horizon of performance art, Earth art, Arte Povera, and Conceptualism, and it can be said that these new methodologies of photographic practice are the strongest factor linking together the experimental forms of the period, which can seem so disparate and irreconcilable. This integration or fusion of reportage and performance, its manneristic introversion, can be seen as an implicitly parodic critique of the concepts of art-photography. Smithson and Graham, in part because they were active as writers, were able to provide a more explicit parody of photojournalism than Nauman or Long.

Photojournalism as a social institution can be defined most simply as a collaboration between a writer and a photographer. 'Conceptual art's intellectualism was engendered by young, aspiring artists for whom critical writing was an important practice of self-definition. The example of Donald Judd's criticism for *Arts Magazine* was decisive here, and essays like 'Specific Objects' (1964) had the impact, almost, of literary works of art. The interplay between a veteran littérateur, Clement Greenberg; a young academic art critic, Michael Fried; and Judd, a talented stylist, is one of the richest episodes in the history of American criticism, and had much to do with igniting the idea of a written critique standing as a work of art. Smithson's 'The Crystal Land', published in *Harper's Bazaar* in 1966, is a homage to Judd as a creator of both visual and literary forms. Smithson's innovation, however, is to avoid the genre of art criticism, writing a mock-travelogue instead. He plays the part of the inquisitive, *belle-lettriste* journalist, accompanying and interpreting his subject. He narrativizes his account of Judd's art, moves from critical commentary to storytelling and re-invents the relationships between visual art and literature. Smithson's most important published works, such as *The Monuments of Passaic*, and *Incidents of Mirror-Travel in the Yucatan* are 'auto-accompaniments'. Smithson the journalist-photographer accompanies Smithson the artist-experimenter and is able to produce a sophisticated apologia for his sculptural work in the guise of popular entertainment. His essays do not make the Conceptualist claim to be works of visual art but appear to remain content with being works of literature. The photographs included in them purport to illustrate the narrative or commentary. The narratives in turn describe the event of making the photographs. 'One never knew what side of the mirror one was on', he mused in *The Monuments of Passaic*, as if reflecting on the parody of photojournalism he was in the process of enacting. Smithson's parody was a way of dissolving, or softening, the objectivistic and positivistic tone of Minimalism, of subjectivizing it by associating its reductive formal language with intricate, drifting, even delirious moods or states of mind.

The Minimalist sculptural forms to which Smithson's texts constantly allude appeared to erase the associative chain of experience, the interior monologue of creativity, insisting on the pure immediacy of the product itself, the work as such, as 'specific object'. Smithson's exposure of what he saw as Minimalism's emotional interior depends on the return of ideas of time and process, of narrative and enactment, of experience, memory and allusion, to the artistic forefront, against the rhetoric of both Greenberg and Judd. His photojournalism is at once self-portraiture – that is, performance – and reportage about what was hidden and even repressed in the art he most admired. It located the impulse towards self-sufficient and nonobjective forms of art in concrete, personal responses to real-life, social experiences, thereby contributing to the new critiques of formalism which were so central to Conceptual art's project.

Dan Graham's involvement with the classical traditions of reportage is unique among the artists usually identified with Conceptual art, and his architectural photographs continue some aspects of Walker Evans' project. In this, Graham locates his practice at the boundary of photojournalism, participating in it, while at the same time placing it at the service of other aspects of his oeuvre. His architectural photographs provide a social grounding for the structural models of intersubjective experience he elaborated in text, video, performance and sculptural environmental pieces. His works do not simply make reference to the larger social world in the manner of photojournalism; rather, they refer to Graham's own other projects, which, true to Conceptual form, are models of the social, not depictions of it.

Graham's *Homes for America* (1966) has taken on canonical status in this regard. Here the photo-essay format so familiar to the history of photography has been meticulously replicated as a model of the institution of photojournalism. Like Walker Evans at *Fortune*, Graham writes the text and supplies the pictures to go along with it. *Homes for America* was actually planned as an essay on suburban architecture for an art magazine, and could certainly stand unproblematically on its own as such. By chance, it was never actually published as Graham had intended it. Thereby, it migrated to the form of a lithographic print of an apocryphal two-page spread.[1] The print, and the original photos included in it, do not constitute an act or practice of reportage so much as a model of it. This model is a parody, a meticulous and detached imitation whose aim is to interrogate the legitimacy (and the processes of legitimation) of its original, and thereby (and only thereby) to legitimate itself as art.

The photographs included in the work are among Graham's most well-known and have established important precedents for his subsequent photographic work. In initiating his project in photography in terms of a parodic model of the photo-essay, Graham positions all his picture-making as art in a very precise, yet very conditional, sense. Each photograph may be – or, must be considered as possibly being – no more than an illustration to an essay, and therefore not an autonomous work of art. Thus, they appear to satisfy, as do Smithson's photographs, the demand for an imitation of the non-autonomous. *Homes for America*, in being both really just an essay on the suburbs and, as well, an artist's print, constituted itself explicitly as a canonical instance of the new kind of anti-autonomous yet autonomous work of art. The photographs in it oscillate at the threshold of the autonomous work, crossing and recrossing it, refusing to depart from the artistic dilemma of reportage and thereby establishing an aesthetic model of just that threshold condition.

Huebler's work is also engaged with creating and examining the effect photographs have when they masquerade as part of some extraneous project, in which they appear to be means and not ends. Unlike Smithson or Graham, though, Huebler makes no literary claims for the textual part of his works, the 'programmes' in which his photographs are utilized. His works approach Conceptual art *per se* in that they eschew literary status and make claims only as visual art objects. Nevertheless, his renunciation of the literary is a language-act, an act enunciated as a maneuvre of writing. Huebler's 'pieces' involve the appropriation, utilization and mimesis of various 'systems of documentation', of which photography is only one. It is positioned within the works by a group of generically related protocols, defined in writing, and it is strictly within these parameters that the images have meaning and artistic status. Where Graham and Smithson make their works through mimesis and parody of the forms of photojournalism, its published product, Huebler parodies the assignment, the 'project' or enterprise that sets the whole process into motion to begin with. The seemingly pointless and even trivial procedures that constitute works like *Duration Piece No. 5, Amsterdam, Holland* (1970) or *Duration Piece No. 7, Rome* (1973) function as models for that verbal or written construction which, in the working world, causes photographs to be made. The more the assignment is emptied of what could normatively considered to be compelling social subject matter, the more visible it is simply as an instance of a structure, an order, and the more clearly it can be experienced as a model of relationships between writing and photography. By emptying subject matter from his practice of photography, Huebler recapitulates important aspects of the development of modernist painting. Mondrian, for example, moved away from depictions of the landscape, to experimental patterns with only a residual depictive value, to abstract works which analyze and model relationships but do not depict or represent them. The idea of an art which provides a direct experience of situations or relationships, not a secondary, representational one, is one of abstract art's most powerful creations. The viewer does not experience the 're-representation' of absent things, but the presence of a thing, the work of art itself, with all of its indwelling dynamism, tension and complexity. The experience is more like an encounter with an entity than with a mere picture. The entity does not bear a depiction of another entity, more important than it; rather, it appears and is experienced in the way objects and entities are experienced in the emotionally-charged contexts of social life.

Huebler's mimesis of the model-constructive aspects of modernist abstract art contradicts, of course, the natural depictive qualities of photography. This contradiction is the necessary centre of these works. By making photography's inescapable depictive character continue even where it has been decreed that there is nothing of significance to depict, Huebler aims to make visible something essential about the medium's nature. The artistic, creative part of this work is obviously not the photography, the picture-making. This displays all the limited qualities identified with photoconceptualism's de-skilled, amateurist sense of itself. What is creative in these works are the written assignments, or programmes. Every element that could make the pictures 'interesting' or 'good' in terms derived from art photography is systematically and rigorously excluded. At the same time, Huebler eliminates all conventional 'literary' characteristics from his written statements. The work is comprised of these two simultaneous negations, which produce a 'reportage' without event, and a writing without narrative, commentary, or opinion. This double negation imitates the criteria for radical abstract painting and sculpture, and pushes thinking about photography towards an awareness of the dialectics of its inherent depictive qualities. Huebler's works allow us to contemplate the condition of 'depictivity' itself and imply that it is this contradiction between the unavoidable process of depicting appearances and the equally unavoidable process of making objects, that permits photography to become a model of an art whose subject matter is the idea of art [...]

1 A variant, made as a collage, is in the Daled Collection, Brussels.

Jeff Wall, 'Marks of Indifference': Aspects of Photography in, or as, Conceptual Art', in Ann Goldstein; Anne Rorimer (eds.) *Reconsidering the Object of Art: 1965-1975* (Los Angeles: the Museum of Contemporary Art; Cambridge, Massachusetts: MIT Press, 1995) 247-58.

POLITICS AND IDEOLOGY

The politicization of conceptual art during the 1970s drew its theoretical inspiration from diverse sources. Foremost amongst these was Marx's analysis of the fetishism of commodities. This focus on commodification was supplemented by Roland Barthes' semiological analyses of advertising as the making of modern myths. In his essay 'Socialist Formalism', Victor Burgin traced back the left-wing interest in the visual forms of mass media to the Soviet avant-garde of the 1920s. He proposed a revival of the constructivist tradition in which politically explicit goals were pursued by formally experimental mass visual means. In the USA, the Art Workers Coalition organized artists as workers; and Seth Siegelaub drew up a model contract for the sale of artworks and the transfer of rights. Many of the feminist conceptual artists of the period concerned themselves with theoretical issues of representation, often, as in the case of Mary Kelly, from a psychoanalytic point of view. The Frankfurt School philosopher Herbert Marcuse summed up the aesthetic dimension of the political tumult of the times in the idea of a 'new sensibility'.

Karl MARX
The Fetishism of Commodities and the Secret Thereof [1867]

A commodity appears, at first sight, a very trivial thing, and easily understood. Its analysis shows that it is, in reality, a very queer thing, abounding in metaphysical subtleties and theological niceties. So far as it is a value in use, there is nothing mysterious about it, whether we consider it from the point of view that by its properties it is capable of satisfying human wants, or from the point that those properties are the product of human labour. It is as clear as noon-day, that man, by his industry, changes the forms of the materials furnished by Nature, in such a way as to make them useful to him. The form of wood, for instance, is altered by making a table out of it. Yet, for all that, the table continues to be that common, everyday thing, wood. But so soon as it steps forth as a commodity, it is changed into something transcendent. It not only stands with its feet on the ground but, in relation to all other commodities, it stands on its head, and evolves out of its wooden brain grotesque ideas, far more wonderful than 'table-turning' ever was.

The mystical character of commodities does not originate, therefore, in their use-value. Just as little does it proceed from the nature of the determining factors of value. For in the first place, however varied the useful kinds of labour or productive activities may be, it is a physiological fact that they are functions of the human organism, and that each such function, whatever may be its nature or form, is essentially the expenditure of human brain, nerves, muscles, etc. Secondly, with regard to that which forms the groundwork for the quantitative determination of value, namely the duration of that expenditure, or the quantity of labour, it is quite clear that there is a palpable difference between its quantity and quality. In all states of society, the labour-time that it costs to produce the means of subsistence must necessarily be an object of interest to mankind, though not of equal interest in different stages of development. And lastly, from the moment that men in any way work for one another, their labour assumes a social form.

Whence, then, arises the enigmatical character of the product of labour, so soon as it assumes the form of commodities? Clearly from this form itself. The equality of all sorts of human labour is expressed objectively by their products all being equally values; the measure of the expenditure of labour-power by the duration of that expenditure, takes the form of the quantity of value of the products of labour; and finally, the mutual relations of the producers, within which the social character of their labour affirms itself, take the form of a social relation between the products.

A commodity is therefore a mysterious thing, simply because in it the social character of men's labour appears to them as an objective character stamped upon the product of that labour; because the relation of the producers to the sum total of their own labour is presented to them as a social relation, existing not between themselves, but between the products of their labour. This is the reason why the products of labour become commodities, social things whose qualities are at the same time perceptible and imperceptible by the senses. In the same way the light from an object is perceived by us not as the subjective excitation of our optic nerve, but as the objective form of something outside the eye itself. But in the act of seeing there is, at all events, an actual passage of light from one thing to another, from the external object to the eye. There is a physical relation between physical things. But it is different with commodities. There, the existence of the things *qua* commodities, and the value-relation between the products of labour which stamps them as commodities, have absolutely no connection with their physical properties and with the material relations arising therefrom. There it is a definite social relation between men that assumes, in their eyes, the fantastic form of a relation between things. In order, therefore, to find an analogy, we must have recourse to the mist-enveloped regions of the religious world. In that world the productions of the human brain appear as independent beings endowed with life, and entering into relation both with one another and the human race. So it is in the world of commodities with the products of men's hands. This I call the Fetishism which attaches itself to the products of labour, so soon as they are produced as commodities, and which is therefore inseparable from the production of commodities.

This Fetishism of commodities has its origin, as the foregoing analysis has already shown, in the peculiar social character of the labour that produces them.

As a general rule, articles of utility become commodities only because they are products of the labour of private individuals or groups of individuals who carry on their work independently of each other. The sum total of the labour of all these private individuals forms the aggregate labour of society. Since the producers do not come into social contact with each other until they exchange their products, the specific social character of each producer's labour does not show itself except in the act of exchange. In other words, the labour of the individual asserts itself as a part of the labour of society, only by means of the relations which the act of exchange establishes directly between the products, and indirectly, through them, between the producers. To the latter, therefore, the relations connecting the labour of one individual with that of the rest appear, not as direct social relations between individuals at work, but as what they really are, material relations between persons and social relations between things. It is only by being exchanged that the products of labour acquire, as values, one uniform social status, distinct from their varied forms of existence as objects of utility. This division of a product into a useful thing and a value becomes practically important only when exchange has acquired such an extension that useful articles are produced for the purpose of being exchanged, and their character as values has therefore to be taken into account, beforehand, during production. From this moment the labour of the individual producer acquires socially a two-fold character. On the one hand, it must, as a definite useful kind of labour, satisfy a definite social want, and thus hold its place as part and parcel of the collective labour of all, as a branch of a social division of labour that has sprung up spontaneously. On the other hand, it can satisfy the manifold wants of the individual producer himself, only in so far as the mutual exchangeability of all kinds of useful private labour is an established social fact, and therefore the private useful labour of each producer ranks on an equality with that of all others. The equalization of the most different kinds of labour can be the result only of an abstraction from their inequalities, or of reducing them to their common denominator, viz., expenditure of human labour-power or human labour in the abstract. The twofold social character of the labour of the individual appears to him, when reflected in his brain, only under those forms which are impressed upon that labour in everyday practice by the exchange of products. In this way, the character that his own labour possesses of being socially useful takes the form of the condition, that the product must be not only useful, but useful for others, and the social character that his particular labour has of being the equal of all other particular kinds of labour, takes the form that all the physically different articles that are the products of labour have one common quality, viz., that of having value.

Hence, when we bring the products of our labour into relation with each other as values, it is not because we see in these articles the material receptacles of homogeneous human labour. Quite the contrary: whenever, by an exchange, we equate as values our different products, by that very act, we also equate, as human labour, the different kinds of labour expended upon them. We are not aware of this, nevertheless we do it.[1] Value, therefore, does not stalk about with a label describing what it is. It is value, rather, that converts every product into a social hieroglyphic. Later on, we try to decipher the hieroglyphic, to get behind the secret of our own social products; for to stamp an object of utility as a value, is just as much a social product as language. The recent scientific discovery, that the products of labour, so far as they are values, are but material expressions of the human labour spent in their production, marks, indeed, an epoch in the history of the development of the human race, but by no means, dissipates the mist through which the social character of labour appears to us to be an objective character of the products themselves. The fact that in the particular form of production with which we are dealing, viz., the production of commodities, the specific social character of private labour carried on independently, consists in the equality of every kind of that labour, by virtue of its being human labour, which character, therefore, assumes in the product the form of value – this fact appears to the producers, notwithstanding the discovery above referred to, to be just as real and final as the fact that, after the discovery by science of the component gases of air, the atmosphere itself remained unaltered.

Karl Marx, 'The Fetishism of Commodities and the Secret Thereof', *Capital: A Critique of Political Economy, Volume 1*, ed. Frederick Engels (Hamburg: 1867; London: 1887), trans. Samuel Moore, Edward Aveling, (London: Lawrence & Wishart, 1954) 76-79.

Roland BARTHES

Myth Today [1957]

What is a myth, today? I shall give at the outset a first, very simple answer, which is perfectly consistent with etymology: ***myth is a type of speech.***[1]

MYTH IS A TYPE OF SPEECH

Of course, it is not *any* type: language needs special conditions in order to become myth: we shall see them in a minute. But what must be firmly established at the start is that myth is a system of communication, that it is a message. This allows one to perceive that myth cannot possibly be an object, a concept, or an idea; it is a mode of signification, a form. Later, we shall have to assign to this form historical limits, conditions of use, and reintroduce society into it: we must nevertheless first describe it as a form.

It can be seen that to purport to discriminate among mythical objects according to their substance would be entirely illusory: since myth is a type of speech, everything can be a myth provided it is conveyed by a discourse. Myth is not defined by the object of its message, but by the way in which it utters this message: there are formal limits to myth, there are no 'substantial' ones. Everything, then, can be a myth? Yes, I believe this, for the universe is infinitely fertile in suggestions. Every object in the world can pass from a closed, silent existence to an oral state, open to appropriation by society, for there is no law, whether natural or not, which forbids talking about things. A tree is a tree. Yes, of course. But a tree as expressed by Minou Drouet is no longer quite a tree, it is a tree decorated, adapted to a certain type of consumption, laden with literary self-indulgence, revolt, images, in short with a type of social *usage* which is added to pure matter.

Naturally, everything is not expressed at the same time: some objects become the prey of mythical speech for a while, then they disappear, others take their place and attain the status of myth. Are there objects which are *inevitably* a source of suggestiveness, as Baudelaire suggested about Woman? Certainly not: one can conceive of very ancient myths but there are no eternal ones; for it is human history which converts reality into speech, and it alone rules the life and the death of mythical language. Ancient or not, mythology can only have a historical foundation, for myth is a type of speech chosen by history: it cannot possibly evolve from the 'nature' of things.

Speech of this kind is a message. It can consist of modes of writing or of representations; not only written discourse, but also photography, cinema, reporting, sport, shows, publicity, all these can serve as a support to mythical speech. Myth can be defined neither by its object nor by its material, for any material can arbitrarily be endowed with meaning: the arrow which is brought in order to signify a challenge is also a kind of speech. True, as far as perception is concerned, writing and pictures, for instance, do not call upon the same type of consciousness; and even with pictures, one can use many kinds of reading: a diagram lends itself to signification more than a drawing, a copy more than an original, and a caricature more than a portrait. But this is the point: we are no longer dealing here with a theoretical mode of representation: we are dealing with *this* particular image, which is given for *this* particular signification. Mythical speech is made of a material which has *already* been worked on so as to make it suitable for communication: it is because all the materials of myth (whether pictorial or written) presuppose a signifying consciousness, that one can reason about them while discounting their substance. This substance is not unimportant: pictures, to be sure, are more imperative than writing, they impose meaning at one stroke, without analyzing or diluting it. But this is no longer a constitutive difference. Pictures become a kind of writing as soon as they are meaningful: like writing, they call for a *lexis*.

We shall therefore take *language*, *discourse*, *speech*, etc., to mean any significant unit or synthesis, whether verbal or visual: a photograph will be a kind of speech for us in the same way as a newspaper article; even objects will become speech, if they mean something. This generic way of conceiving language is in fact justified by the very history of writing: long before the invention of our alphabet, objects like the Inca *quipu*, or drawings, as in pictographs, have been accepted as speech. This does not mean that one must treat mythical speech like language; myth in fact belongs to the province of a general science, coextensive with linguistics, which is *semiology*.

MYTH AS A SEMIOLOGICAL SYSTEM

For mythology, since it is the study of a type of speech, is but one fragment of this vast science of signs which Saussure postulated some forty years ago under the name of *semiology*. Semiology has not yet come into being. But since Saussure himself, and sometimes independently of him, a whole section of contemporary research has constantly been referred to the problem of meaning: psychoanalysis, structuralism, eidetic psychology, some new types of literary criticism of which Bachelard has given the first examples, are no longer concerned with facts except inasmuch as they are endowed with significance. Now to postulate a signification is to have recourse to semiology. I do not mean that semiology could account for all these aspects of research equally well: they have different contents. But they have a common status: they are all sciences dealing with values. They are not content with meeting the facts: they define and explore them as tokens for something else.

Semiology is a science of forms, since it studies significations apart from their content [...] Semiology, once its limits are settled, is not a metaphysical trap: it is a science among others, necessary but not sufficient. The important thing is to see that the unity of an explanation cannot be based on the amputation of one or other of its approaches, but, as Engels said, on the dialectical coordination of the particular sciences it makes use of. This is the case with mythology: it is a part both of semiology inasmuch as it is a formal science, and of ideology inasmuch as it is a historical science: it studies ideas-in-form.[2]

Let me therefore restate that any semiology postulates a relation between two terms, a signifier and a signified. This relation concerns objects which belong to different categories, and this is why it is not one of equality but one of equivalence. We must here be on our guard, for despite common parlance which simply says that the signifier expresses the signified, we are dealing, in any semiological system, not with two, but with three different terms. For what we grasp is not at all one term after the other but the correlation which unites them: there are, therefore, the signifier, the signified, and the sign, which is the associative total of the first two terms. Take a bunch of roses: I use it to signify my passion. Do we have here, then, only a signifier and a signified, the roses and my passion? Not even that: to put it accurately, there are here only 'passionified' roses. But on the plane of analysis, we do have three terms; for these roses weighted with passion perfectly and correctly allow themselves to be decomposed into roses and passion: the former and the latter existed before uniting and forming this third object, which is the sign. It is as true to say that on the plane of experience I cannot dissociate the roses from the message they carry, as to say that on the plane of analysis I cannot confuse the roses as signifier and the roses as sign: the signifier is empty, the sign is full, it is a meaning. Or take a black pebble: I can make it signify in several ways, it is a mere signifier; but if I weigh it with a definite signified (a death sentence, for instance, in an anonymous vote), it will become a sign. Naturally, there are between the signifier, the signified, and the sign, functional implications (such as that of the part to the whole) which are so close that to analyze them may seem futile; but we shall see in a moment that this distinction has a capital importance for the study of myth as semiological schema.

Naturally these three terms are purely formal, and different contents can be given to them. Here are a few examples: for Saussure, who worked on a particular but methodologically exemplary semiological system – the language of *langue* – the signified is the concept, the signifier is the acoustic image (which is mental), and the relation between concept and image is the sign (the word, for instance), which is a concrete entity.[3] For Freud, as is well known, the human psyche is a stratification of tokens or representatives. One term (I refrain from giving it any precedence) is constituted by the manifest meaning of behaviour, another, by its latent or real meaning (it is, for instance, the substream of the dream); as for the third term, it is here also a correlation of the first two: it is the dream itself in its totality, the parapraxis (a mistake in speech or behaviour) or the neurosis, conceived as compromises, as economies effected thanks to the joining of a form (the first term) and an intentional function (the second term). We can see here how necessary it is to distinguish the sign from the signifier: it is the functional union of these two terms. In Sartrean criticism, finally (I shall keep to these three well-known examples), the signified is constituted by the original crisis in the subject (the separation from his mother for Baudelaire, the naming of the theft for Genet); Literature as discourse forms the signifier; and the relation between crisis and discourse defines the work, which is a signification. Of course, this tri-dimensional pattern, which I have just described: the signifier, the signified, and the sign. But myth is a peculiar system, in that it is constructed from a semiological chain which existed before it: it *is a second-order semiological system*. That which is a sign (namely the associative total of a concept and an image) in the first system, becomes a mere signifier in the second. We must here recall that the materials of mythical speech (the language itself, photography, painting, posters, rituals, objects, etc.), however different at the start, are reduced to a pure signifying function as soon as they are caught by myth. Myth sees in them only the same raw material; their unity is that they all come down to the status of a mere language. Whether it deals with alphabetical or pictorial writing, myth wants to see in them only a sum of signs, a global sign, the final term of a first semiological chain. And it is precisely this final term which will become the first term of the greater system which is builds and of which it is only a part. Everything happens as if myth shifted the formal system of the first significations sideways. As this lateral shift is essential for the analysis of myth, I shall represent it in the following way, it being understood that the spatialization of the pattern is here only a metaphor:

It can be seen that in myth there are two semiological systems, one of which is staggered in relation to the other: a linguistic system, the language (or the modes of representation which are assimilated to it), which I shall call the *language-object*, because it is the language which myth gets hold of in order to build its own system; and myth itself, which I shall call *metalanguage*, because it is a second language, *in which* one speaks out about the first. When he reflects on a metalanguage, the semiologist no longer needs to ask himself questions about the composition of the language-object, he no longer has to take into account the details of the linguistic schema; he will only need to know its total term, or global sign, and only inasmuch as this term lends itself to myth. This is why the semiologist is entitled to treat in the same way writing and pictures: what he retains from them is the fact that they are both *signs*, that they both reach the threshold of myth endowed with the same signifying function, that they constitute, one just as much as the other, a language-object.

It is now time to give one or two examples of mythical speech. I shall borrow the first from an observation by Valéry.[4] I am a pupil in the second form in a French *lycée*. I open my Latin grammar, and I read a sentence, borrowed from Aesop or Phaedrus: *quia ego nominor leo*. I stop and think. There is something ambiguous about this statement: on the one hand, the words in it do have a simple meaning: *because my name is lion*. And on the other hand, the sentence is evidently there in order to signify something else to me. Inasmuch as it is addressed to me, a pupil in the second form, it tells me clearly: I am a grammatical example meant to illustrate the rule about the agreement of the predicate. I am even forced to realize that the sentence in no way *signifies* its meaning to me, that it tries very little to tell me something about the lion and what sort of name he has; its true and fundamental signification is to impose itself on me as the presence of a certain agreement of the predicate. I conclude that I am faced with a particular, greater, semiological system, since it is co-extensive with the language: there is, indeed, a signifier, but this signifier is itself formed by a sum of signs, it is in itself a first semiological system (*my name is lion*). Thereafter, the formal pattern is correctly unfolded: there is a signified (*I am a grammatical example*) and there is a global signification, which is none other than the correlation of the greater signifier and the signified; for neither the naming of the lion nor the grammatical example is given separately.

And here is now another example: I am at the barber's, and a copy of *Paris-Match* is offered to me. On the cover, a young negro in a French uniform is saluting, with his eyes uplifted, probably fixed on a fold of the tricolour. All this is the *meaning* of the picture. But, whether naively or not, I see very well what it signifies to me: that France is a great Empire, that all her sons, without any colour discrimination, faithfully serve under her flag, and that there is no better answer to the tractors of an alleged colonialism than the zeal shown by this Negro in serving his so-called oppressors. I am therefore again faced with a greater semiological system: there is a signifier, itself already formed with a previous system (*a black soldier is giving the French salute*); there is a signified (it is here a purposeful mixture of Frenchness and militariness); finally, there is a presence of the signified through the signifier.

Before tackling the analysis of each term of the mythical system, one must agree on terminology. We now know that the signifier can be looked at, in myth, from two points of view: as the final term of the linguistic system, or as the first term of the mythical system. We therefore need two names. On the plane of language, that is, as the final term of the first system, I shall the signifier: *meaning* (*my name is lion, a Negro is giving the French salute*); on the plane of myth, I shall call it: *form*. In the case of the signified, no ambiguity is possible: we shall retain the name *concept*. The third term is the correlation of the first two: in the linguistic system, it is the *sign*; but it is not possible to use this word again without ambiguity, since in myth (and this is the chief peculiarity of the latter), the signifier is already formed by the *signs* of the language. I shall call the third term of myth the *signification*. This word is here all the better justified since myth has in fact a double function: it points out and it notifies, it makes us understand something and it imposes it on us.

1 Innumerable other meanings of the word 'myth' can be cited against this. But I have tried to define things, not words.

2 The development of publicity, of a national press, of radio, of illustrated news, not to speak of the survival of a myriad rites of communication which rule social appearances, makes the development of a semiological science more urgent than ever. In a single day, how many really non-signifying fields do we cross? Very few, sometimes none. Here I am, before the sea; it is true that it bears no message. But on the beach, what material for semiology! Flags, slogans, signals, signboards, clothes, suntan even, which are so many messages to me.

3 The notion of word is one of the most controversial in linguistics. I keep it here for the sake of simplicity.

4 *Tel Quel*, II

Roland Barthes, 'Myth Today', *Mythologies* (Paris: Editions du Seuil, 1957); trans. Annette Lavers (New York: Hill and Wang, 1972) 109-17.

Eduardo COSTA, Raúl ESCARI, Roberto JACOBY

A Media Art (Manifesto) [1966]

In a mass society, the public is not in direct contact with cultural activities but is informed of them through the media. For example, the mass audience does not see an exhibition; it doesn't experience a happening or a soccer match first hand but, instead, sees its diffusion since it can only reach a diminished public. 'To distribute two thousand copies in a big modern city is like shooting a bullet into the air and waiting for the pigeons to fall', said Nam June Paik. Ultimately, information consumers are not interested in whether or not an exhibition occurs; it is only the image the media constructs of the artistic event that matters.

Contemporary art (principally Pop art) sometimes makes use of mass media elements and techniques, divorcing them from their natural context (on, for example, the work of Lichtenstein or in D'Arcangelo's road series), Unlike Pop art, we aim to make works of art utilizing the qualities fundamental to this medium. In this way, we undertake to give to the press the written and photographic report of a happening that has not occurred. This false report would include the names of the participants, an indication of the time and location in which it took place and a description of the spectacle that is supposed to have happened, with pictures taken of the supposed participants in other circumstances. In this way of transmitting the information, in this way of 'realizing' the non-existent event, in the differences that would arise from the separate versions that each transmission would make from the same event, the sense of the art work would appear. The work would begin to exist in the same moment that the consciousness of the spectator constitutes it as having been accomplished.

Therefore there is a triple creation:

> *the formation of the false report*
> *the transmission of the report through the existing channels of information*'
> *the reception by the spectator who constructs – based on the information received and depending on the manner that information signifies for him – the substance of a non-existent reality which he would imagine as truthful.*

This way we take on the ultimate characteristic of the media: the de-realization of objects. In this way the moment of transmission of the work of art is more privileged than its production. The creation consists of liberating its production from its transmission.

Currently, the work of art is a combination of results from a process that starts with the realization of a work (traditional) and continues until such work is converted into material transmitted by the media. Now we propose a work of art in which the moment of production disappears. In this way it will be made clear that works of art are, in reality, pretexts to start up the apparatus of the media.

From the spectator's point of view it is possible. For this kind of work of art, to have two readings: on one side, the reading of the spectator who trusts the media and believes in what he sees; on the other side, the reading of the informed spectator who is conscious of the non-existence of the art work that is being transmitted.

In this way the possibility of a new genre is open: the art of the media where 'what is said' is not fundamentally important but instead thematizes the media as media.

This report addresses not only the second type of reader but also 'notifies' some other readers and thereby also performs the first part of the work that we described.

1 The message would vary, depending on the material characteristics of the transmitting channel. 'The medium is the message' (McLuhan).

Eduardo Costa, Raul Escari, Roberto Jacoby, 'A Media Art (Manifesto)' (Buenos Aires: July 1966); first published in Oscar Masotta (ed.), *Happenings* (Buenos Aires: Jorge Alvarez, 1967) 119-22; reprinted, trans. Trilce Navarrette, in Alexander Alberro; Blake Stimson (eds.), *Conceptual Art: A Critical Anthology* (Cambridge, Massachusetts: MIT Press, 1999) 2-4.

Hélio OITICICA

General Scheme of the New Objectivity [1967]

A typical state of current Brazilian avant-garde art could be formulated as 'New Objectivity'. Its principal characteristics are: 1) general constructive will; 2) a move towards the object, as easel painting is negated and superceded; 3) the participation of the spectator (bodily, tactile, visual, semantic, etc.); 4) an engagement and a position on political, social and ethical problems; 5) a tendency towards collective propositions and consequently the abolition, in the art of today, of 'isms', so characteristic of the first half of the century (a tendency which can be encompassed by Mário Pedrosa's concept of 'Post-Modern Art'); 6) a revival of, and new formulations in, the concept of anti-art.

'New Objectivity' therefore, as a typical state of current Brazilian art, likewise distinguishes itself on the international plane from the two main currents of today: Pop and Op, and also from those connected to them: *Nouveau Réalisme* and Primary Structures (Hard Edge).

'New Objectivity' being a state, and not a dogmatic, aestheticist movement (as Cubism was, for instance, or any of the other 'isms' constituted as a 'unity of thought', but unified nevertheless by a general verification of these multiple tendencies grouped into general tendencies). One may find, if one wishes, a simile in Dada, keeping in mind the distances and differences. [...]

The problem of spectator participation is more complex, since this participation, which from the beginning was opposed to pure transcendental contemplation, manifests itself in many ways. There are, however, two well-defined modes of participation: one is that which involves 'manipulation' or 'sensorial-corporal participation'; the other, that which involves a 'semantic' participation. These two modes of participation seek, as it were, a fundamental, total, significant, nonfractioned participation, involving the two processes; that is, they are not reducible to the purely mechanical participation, but concentrate on new meanings, differing from pure transcendental contemplation. From the 'playful' propositions to those of the 'act', from the 'pure word' semantic propositions to those of the 'word in the object', in 'narrative' works and works of political or social protest, what is being sought is an objective mode of participation. This would be the internal search, inside the object, desired by the proposition of active spectator participation in the process: the individual to whom the work is addressed is invited to complete the meanings proposed by it – it is thus an open work. [...] It is useless to outline here a history of the phases and appearances of spectator participation, but it can be found in all the new manifestations of our avant-garde, from the individual works to the collective (e.g. 'happenings'). Experiences of both an individualized and a collective nature tend towards increasingly more open propositions in the sense of this participation, including those which tend to give the individual the opportunity to 'create' his work. Likewise, the preoccupation with serial production of works (which would be the playful sense elevated to the highest degree) is an important take-off point for this problem.

There is currently in Brazil the need to take positions in regard to political, social and ethical problems, a need which increases daily and requires urgent formulation, since it is the crucial issue in the creative field: the so-called plastic arts, literature, etc [...]

There are two ways to propose a collective art: the first would be to throw individual productions into contact with the public in the streets (naturally, productions created for this, not conventional productions adapted); the other is to propose creative activities to this public, in the actual creation of the work. In Brazil, the tendency towards a collective art is what really concerns our avant-garde artists [...]

In Brazil, the roles take on the following pattern: how to, in an underdeveloped country, explain and justify the appearance of an avant-garde, not as a symptom of alienation, but as a decisive factor in its collective progress? How to situate the artist's activity there? The problem could be tackled by another question: who does the artist make his work for? It can be seen, thus, that this artist feels a greater need, not only simply to 'create', but to 'communicate' something which for him is fundamental, but this communication would have to be large-scale, not for an elite reduced to 'experts', but even 'against' this elite, with the proposition of unfinished, 'open' works. This is the fundamental key to the new concept of anti-art: not only to hammer away at the art of the past, or against the old concepts (as before, still an attitude based upon transcendentalism), but to create new experimental conditions where the artist takes on the role of 'proposer', or 'entrepreneur', or even 'educator'. The old problem of 'making a new art', or of knocking down cultures, is no longer formulated in this way – the correct formulation would be to ask: what propositions, promotions and measures must one draw upon to create a wide-ranging condition of popular participation in these new open propositions, in the creative sphere to which these artists elected themselves. Upon this depends their very survival, and that of the people in this sense [...]

In conclusion, I want to evoke a sentence which, I believe, could very well represent the spirit of 'New Objectivity', a fundamental sentence which, in a way, represents a synthesis of all these points and the current situation (condition) of the Brazilian avant-garde; it could serve as a motto, the rallying cry of 'New Objectivity' – here it is: OUT OF ADVERSITY WE LIVE![1]

1 This has been translated slightly differently by authors quoted elsewhere. Oiticica's original statement in Portuguese is: Da adversidade vivemos! [ed.]

Hélio Oiticica, 'Esquema geral da nova objetividade (General Scheme of the New Objectivity)' (1967), *Nova Objetividade Brasileira* (Rio de Janeiro: Museu de Arte Moderna, 1967); extract reprinted in English in Alexander Alberro; Blake Stimson (eds.), *Conceptual Art: A Critical Anthology* (Cambridge, Massachusetts: MIT Press, 1999) 40-42.

Victor BURGIN
Socialist Formalism [1976]

While contemporary Western art practice is currently polarized between Modernism and 'conceptualism' *both* are being viewed in terms of a Modernist *politique* – in terms of a Modernist aesthetics and a Modernist version of history. The inability of most critics to deal with conceptualism on anything but an *ad hoc* basis stems from this fundamental category error, as does the failure of most conceptualists to found their practice in anything other than *laissez-faire* subjectivism. The consolidation of conceptualist practices along the socialist lines which have been implicit from their inception demands a reading of formalist aesthetics, of history, and of current priorities, different from that now predominating in the Western art community.

Conceptualism administered a rebuff to the Modernist demand for aesthetic confections and for formal novelty for its own sake. It disregarded the arbitrary and fetishistic restrictions which 'Art' placed on technology – the anachronistic daubing of woven fabrics with coloured mud, the chipping apart of rocks and the sticking together of pipes – all in the name of timeless aesthetic values. However, once beyond the official enclosures of 'legitimate' art practice many found that they had exchanged their prison for a desert. They learned that there is nothing to be made of a conceptual*ism*, defined in opposition to Modernism, other than an 'official opposition'; and that there is nothing to be made of Modernist art history other than a history of Modernism.

My remarks here, very far from being comprehensive, are intended to point off the highroad of Western bourgeois aesthetics to areas where conceptualism may be better grounded for the completion of its metamorphosis from an essentially Modernist avant-garde to a socialist art practice. They will concern Russian art in the decade following the October revolution, normally presented as a story of the arbitrary suppression of modern art by philistine communism; and (representing a general concern with 'mass media') advertising, normally not presented at all in an art context.

The Western assessment of the 'importance' of Malevich amongst modern Russian artists is readily understood: his work, his concern for 'the spiritual in art', is easily accommodated within the Western tradition of Romantic formalism. This movement of accommodation disengages all Russian art of the revolutionary period from its real historical context in order to insert it in the familiar, spuriously historical sequence 'from Cubism to Modernism' which in fact is an anti-history, an ideology. It also ignores the *difference* between Western and Russian formalism.

Modernism is typically defined in opposition to Realism. In classic Realism there is assumed an unmediated presentation of the referent through the sign (unmediated that is save for 'noise' in the physical channel of communication – problems of mediation in Realism tending to become confused with questions of technique exercised in the interests of conformity to some prevailing model of reality). Realism is primarily 'about' content and major debates within Realism concern subject-matter alone (witness the recurring 'crisis of content' in nineteenth-century painting.)

With the hindsight granted us by Saussure we can today see that classic Realism rests upon a mistaken concept of signification: the sign is assumed to be 'transparent', allowing unproblematical access to the referent. Cubism we can see as constituting a radical critique of this concept, a practice compatible with a recognition of the disjunction of signifier and signified within the sign. Post-cubist Modernism, however, did not develop as a scientific aesthetics based upon a critique of the sign, but rather as a normative aesthetics based upon a notion of territoriality.

The brand of formalism propounded by Greenberg and Fried is in direct line of descent from the attempt by Bell and Fry to 'free' art from concerns not 'peculiarly its own'. In the earlier of these two periods of formalist criticism, particularly with Bell, recourse is made to a Kantian ontology (a *noumenal* world 'behind' mere appearances) in order to justify abstraction. American Modernism ostensibly sees the art object as justified solely as an end in itself, but it remains determined by the earlier English version in that in the same movement in which it sheds idealism it loses the last vestige of any concern with content. (The ghost of idealism haunts Modernism to this day – it was minimal sculpture which came closest to a materialist abstractionism.)

In Russia the move towards the immanent modes of analysis of formalism was first accomplished by the Symbolist philologists Potebnya and Veselovsky. Their emphasis on the distinction between poetic and prosaic language isolated language itself as the primary object of literary studies.[1] The Formalist critics of *OPOYAZ* (Society for the Study of Poetic Language) and the Moscow Linguistic Circle retained this distinction, Jakobson, in a well-known dictum, declaring the proper object of literary studies to be not literature but 'literariness' (*literaturnost*).

The Russian Formalists, however, rejected the Symbolist notion of a 'higher reality'. They also rejected the Symbolist notion of form in which form, the perceivable, was conceived in opposition to content, the intelligible. They extended the notion of form to cover all aspects of a work. Todorov writes: '... the Symbolists tended to divide the literary product into form (i.e. sound), which was vital and content (i.e. ideas), which was external to art. The Formalist approach was completely opposed to this aesthetic appreciation of 'pure form'. They no longer saw form as opposed to some other internal element of a work of art (normally its content) and began to conceive it as the totality of the work's various components. Thus every element inside a work of art is, according to the exact measure of its appropriateness to it, a formal part of the whole ... This makes it essential to realize that the 'form' of a work is not its only formal element: its content may equally be formal.'[2] Russian Formalism was therefore substantially advanced beyond its Western contemporary, the formalism of Fry and Bell, in which considerations of content were arbitrarily banished in a quasi-legal ruling.

There is another important distinction to be made between Eastern and Western formalism in this period; Fredric Jameson makes it in terms of the literary context: '... the Formalists found themselves to be contemporaries of Mayakovsky and Khlebnikov, revolutionaries both in art and in politics, whereas the most influential literary contemporaries of the American New Critics were called T.S. Eliot and Ezra Pound. This is to say that the familiar split between avant-garde art and left-wing politics was not a universal but merely a local, Anglo-American phenomenon.[3] – Although the extent of overt intervention in party politics by the early Russian avant-garde is not to be overestimated, there can be no doubt that their aesthetic programmes were politically motivated and that their practices may only properly be grasped in terms of such motivations.

The first aim of the Petrograd Artists' Union, formed in May 1917 amidst the confusion following the abdication of the Czar, was its own total autonomy. State intervention in the arts was to cease. When, following the October Revolution, the newly appointed Soviet Commissar for Education, A.V. Lunacharsky, proposed a fifty per cent representation of soldiers and peasants within the Artists' Union he was rebutted and a policy of non-co-operation adopted.

The Artists' Union however was an unstable coalition of left Futurists, centre 'moderns', and right academics. After the formation, early in 1918, of *IZO*, the visual arts department of *Narkompros* (People's Commissariat of Education), Mayakovsky and Brik led the left out of the Artists' Union into cooperation with the Bolsheviks, gaining virtual control of *IZO* and instigating the eventual collapse of the Union, many of whose remaining members dispersed to the 'White' areas of Civil War Russia and from there to the West.

When the official journal of *IZO*, *Art of the Commune*, appeared in December 1918 it was effectively a Futurist journal. Its editor was Osip Brik; others involved included Shklovsky, Mayakovsky, and Malevich. Through this magazine the Futurists laid claim to having foreshadowed, in their anti-bourgeois aesthetic revolution, the political and economic revolution of 1917. Holding commanding posts in the State administration for the arts, Futurists directed museums, the new art schools, and the purchase and distribution of new works of art. Brik presented the notion of 'art into production': 'Go to the factories, this is the only task for artists ... Artists must become producers.' [...]

In 1923 the magazine *Lef* (Left Front of the Arts) was launched. Mayakovsky wrote: '... One of the slogans, one of the great achievements of *Lef* – the de-aestheticization of the productional arts, Constructivism. A poetic supplement: agit-art and economic agitation: the advertisement'.[4]

'Left Front of the Arts' was a heterogeneous grouping of artists and theorists of Futurist, Formalist or Constructivist persuasions. The Left Front therefore embraced a variety of practices from Futurist 'trans-sense' (*Zaum*) poetry to 'Productivism'. *Lef* carried frequent attacks on laboratory art When in 1922 *Vesche*, a Berlin-based Constructivist magazine, had printed a photograph of a snow-clearing locomotive alongside designs by Malevich and linked them with the caption 'supremacist object', Arvatov had commented: '*Vesche* cannot and will not understand that Malevich's little square is not an object and still less a functional object like a locomotive.' He condemned *Vesche* for its 'opportunism' and predicted: '... It is certain that the revolutionary process, even in the West, will be joined to the definitive renunciation of the "painting" in offering the painter real possibilities of production.'[5] This line of attack on Constructivist painting as 'revisionist': and 'opportunist', as a bourgeois art form, was consistently followed by Arvatov and others in *Lef*. Brik, on the editorial board and responsible for much of the development of productivist theory, continued to provide a link between left art and the Formalists – issue 5, published shortly after Lenin's death in 1924, consisted mainly of Formalist articles on the language of Lenin. Among the original Futurist poets who contributed to *Lef* were Kruchenykh, Khlebnikov and Mayakovsky (who drafted the manifestos for the first issue). All the covers of *Lef*, which include some of the earliest examples of photomontage, were designed by Rodchenko.

By the early twenties *Lef* production artists were designing everything from stamps to the new workers' clubs where all fittings were in the Constructivist style. Rodchenko worked closely with Mayakovsky on a variety of projects including books, posters, and advertising for the new *GUM* department store [...]

Publication of *Lef* was terminated by its parent body *GIZ* (State Publishing House) in 1925, when it brought out only one issue. Mayakovsky revived the journal in 1927 as *Novy Lef*, which was to be 'left of *Lef*'. In 1928 he resigned the editorship to Tretyakov. In the second issue of *Novy Lef* Tretyakov had written: '*Lef* was the form which the activities of revolutionary Futurism took in the conditions of the New Economic Policy – an association of workers in left art ... The whole of academy art ranged itself against *Lef*. Academy art was economically powerful for it had once again found its old, well-tried consumer. It demanded a licence to trade and this was obligingly granted in the shape of the formula about "assuming the cultural heritage"'.[6]

The position of *Novy Lef* on the 'cultural heritage' question was unequivocal: 'To the easel painting, which supposedly functions as "a mirror of reality", *Lef* opposes the photograph – a more accurate, rapid and objective means of fixing fact. '

To the easel painting – claimed to be a permanent source of agit – *Lef* opposes the placard, which is topical, designed and adapted for the street, the newspaper and the demonstration, and which hits the emotions with the sureness of artillery fire.

In literature, to *belles-lettres* and the related claim to 'reflection' *Lef* opposes reportage – 'factography' – which breaks with literary art traditions and moves entirely into the field of publicism to serve the newspaper and the journal.'[7]

At the end of 1928, after 24 issues, *Novy Lef* ceased publication. Left art had moved far into the public domain in its transition from Futurism to Factography,[8] but in terms of public acceptability it could not compete with traditional art forms. Artistic conservatism had been reprieved with NEP when left artists lost political influence. VAPP (All Union Association of Proletarian Writers), formed in 1920 mainly of ex-*Proletkult* members, had tempered Bogdanov's hard-line proletarianism with a more accommodating attitude to the 'fellow-travellers' (non-proletarian literary traditionalists sympathetic to communism – previously championed by Voronsky). VAPP received official support from 1925. In 1928 it reorganized as RAPP, accepting the membership of Mayakovsky in 1930 (the year of his suicide).

In 1932 the central committee of the CPSU dissolved all existing writers' and artists' associations in order to establish a single union of Soviet Writers and analogous bodies for the other arts. It was only at this point that the notion of Socialist Realism as such appears, a first definition being included in the charter of the writer's union: 'Socialist Realism, which is the fundamental method of Soviet literature and letters, requires the artist to present reality in its revolutionary course of development, in a true and historically concrete manner.'[9]

The period from 1917 to 1932 does not present the simple story of suppression preferred in the West. Decisions on aesthetic questions were entirely avoided by the party until 1925. The notion that a fully formed state aesthetic' policy was desirable did not emerge until the thirties. By 1920, however, 'laboratory art' Constructivism had already been condemned by the constructivist artists themselves as an anachronistic perpetuation of bourgeois vested interests. These productivists went on to develop, in industry and in mass media, practices compatible with their revolutionary socialist politics. In some respects they were 'overtaken on the left' by *Proletkult*, but both factions eventually foundered against the growing influence of conservatism after NEP – that moment depicted in some accounts as an improvement in post-revolutionary cultural conditions, but which the artists and critics of *Lef* recognized as a betrayal of the revolution.

We may integrate the concerns of Russian Formalism and Factography within a modern Western art problematic: the first requirement of a socialist art practice is that it should engage those codes and contents which are *in the public domain*. These present themselves, and thus ideology, as natural and whole; a socialist art practice aims to deconstruct these codes, to unpick the apparently seamless ideological surface they present.

The propaganda message is ineffective to the extent that it endorses the very codes which frame the ideology it would oppose; it is these which appropriate it as 'mere propaganda'. Anthony Wilden puts it: '... the response to the indifference of the system cannot simply be a strident dogmatism ... the first line of defence against the violence of the rhetoric of the establishment is to learn something about rhetoric. And that means to learn something about communication. But a line of defence is not enough; the victims must take the offensive. What is required – at this admittedly minimal level – is a *guerrilla rhetoric*. And for a guerrilla rhetoric, you must know what your enemy knows, why and how he knows It, and how to contest him on any ground.'[10]

Wilden is speaking here of the rhetoric of the academic establishment in which: 'The necessary isolation of a system from its context in order that it may be studied ... is generally used, implicitly to justify the isolation of the researcher from *his* context: from his past, from his social and academic position, from his future expectations, from his economic status in a hierarchical system of privilege, from his conscious or unconscious positive or neutral commitment to a set of ideological and political views – all of which one may expect to discover in various transformations in his work.'[11] Wilden's remarks, however, may be extended to all the forms of discourse which collectively constitute the symbolic representation of our official culture; not those which are encountered in the mass media.

Fortini quotes a certain communist spokesman: 'Continue as writers. We do not want to make a corporal of a man whose voice can move an army and then comments that '... the writer whose "voice can move an army" is in fact the bureaucrat of letters, the specialist in propaganda integrated in mystification.'[12] It is such specialists these who today compose commercial publicity.

Without doubt advertising constitutes one of the most massive ideological interventions in our cultural life. Why then does it receive such a disproportionately small amount of 'serious' attention compared say with cinema? One answer to this question is cultural: British intellectuals tend to have an 'English Lit' background and the analysis of (what they take to be) animated books suits them very well. Another reason is phenomenological: whereas the cinema readily constitutes itself as an object, advertising is received as an environment and as such tends to pass unremarked (like ideology itself). Nevertheless it is advertising which is closest to that mass-consumed art form, the product of an anonymous collective, which cinema becomes in imagination of 'left' film commentators when they take time off from writing about films by famous men. It is as much an autonomous category of communication as is the cinema, and should be studied as such.

1 References to literature are unavoidable when discussing the visual arts in Russia at the beginning of the present century. In addition to the early lead taken by Formalist literary criticism the political framework of art tended to be discussed primarily in terms of literature; party decisions on the arts were made first in respect of literature with other arts following suit. To make such literary references, however, is not to misrepresent the theoretical context of the visual arts, as contacts between the various arts were extensive both before the October revolution and into the late 1920s.

2 Tzvetan Todorov, 'Some approaches to Russian Formalism', *20th Century Studies* (December 1972) 10.

3 Fredric Jameson, *The Prison House of Language* (Princeton: Princeton University Press, 1972) 45.

4 Vladimir Mayakovsky, 'I Myself', quoted in Richard Sherwood, 'Documents from *Lef*', *Screen*, 12:4 (1971) 29.

5 Boris Arvatov, quoted in Giorgio Kraiski, 'Let Contre Nep', *VH101*, 7/8 (Paris, 1972).

6 Sergei Tretyakov, 'We Raise the Alarm', *Novy Let*, 2 (1927); reprinted in *Screen*, 12:4 (1971) 68.

7 'We are Searching', 'Editorial', *Novy Let*, 11, 12 (1927); reprinted in *Screen*, *op. cit.*, 67.

8 See Ben Brewster, 'Documents from *Novy Lef*'; Ibid., 59-66; also 'From Shklovsky to Brecht: A Reply', Screen, 15:2 (1974) 82-102.

9 Quoted in Lee Baxandall (ed.) *Radical Perspectives in the Arts*, 241.

10 Anthony Wilden, *System and Structure* (London: Tavistock, 1972) xxvi.

11 *Ibid.*, xxii.

12 Franco Fortini, 'The Writers' Mandate and the End of Anti-Fascism', *Screen*, 15:1 (1974) 42-43.

Victor Burgin, 'Socialist Formalism', *Studio International*, 191:980 (March-April 1976) 148-52.

Herbert MARCUSE
The New Sensibility [1969]

The new sensibility has become a political factor. This event, which may well indicate a turning point in the evolution of contemporary societies, demands that critical theory incorporate the new dimension into its concepts, project its implications for the possible construction of a free society. Such a society presupposes throughout the achievements of the existing societies, especially their scientific and technical achievements. Released from their service in the cause of exploitation, they could be mobilized for the global elimination of poverty and toil. True, this redirection of the intellectual and material production already presupposes the revolution in the capitalist world; the theoretical projection seems to be fatally premature – were it not for the fact that the awareness of the transcendent possibilities of freedom must become a driving power in the consciousness and the imagination which prepare the soil for this revolution. The latter will be essentially different, and effective, precisely to the degree to which it is carried forward by this power.

The new sensibility, which expresses the ascent of the life instincts over aggressiveness and guilt, would foster, on a social scale, the vital need for the abolition of injustice and misery and would shape the further evolution of the 'standard of living'. The life instincts would find rational expression (sublimation) in planning the distribution of the socially necessary labour time within and among the various branches of production, thus setting priorities of goals and choices: not only what to produce but also the 'form' of the product. The liberated consciousness would promote the development of a science and technology free to discover and realize the possibilities of things and men in the protection and gratification of life, playing with the potentialities of form and matter for the attainment of this goal. Technique would then tend to become art, and art would tend to form reality: the opposition between imagination and reason, higher and lower faculties, poetic and scientific thought, would be invalidated. Emergence of a new Reality Principle: under which a new sensibility and a desublimated scientific intelligence would combine in the creation of an *aesthetic ethos*.

The term 'aesthetic', in its dual connotation of 'pertaining to the senses' and 'pertaining to art', may serve to designate the quality of the productive-creative process in an environment of freedom. Technique, assuming the features of art, would translate subjective sensibility into objective form, into reality. This would be the sensibility of men and women who do not have to be ashamed of themselves anymore because they have overcome their sense of guilt: they have learned not to identify themselves with the false fathers who have built and tolerated and forgotten the Auschwitzs and Vietnams of history, the torture chambers of all the secular and ecclesiastical inquisitions and interrogations, the ghettos and the monumental temples of the corporations, and who have worshipped the higher culture of this reality. If and when men and women act and think free from this identification, they will have broken the chain which linked the fathers and the sons from generation to generation. They will not have redeemed the crimes against humanity, but they will have become free to stop them and to prevent their recommencement. Chance of reaching the point of no return to the past: if and when the causes are eliminated which have made the history of mankind the history of domination and servitude. These causes are economic-political, but since they have shaped the very instincts and needs of men, so economic and political changes will bring this historical continuum to a stop unless they are carried through by men who are physiologically and psychologically able to experience things, and each other, outside the context of violence and exploitation.

The new sensibility has become, by this very token, praxis: it emerges in the struggle against violence and exploitation where this struggle is waged for essentially new ways and forms of life: negation of the entire Establishment, its morality, culture; affirmation of the right to build a society in which the abolition of poverty and toil terminates in a universe where the sensuous, the playful, the calm and the beautiful become forms of existence and thereby the *Form* of the society itself.

The aesthetic as the possible Form of a free society appears at that stage of development where the intellectual and material resources for the conquest of scarcity are available, where previously progressive repression turns into regressive suppression, where the higher culture in which the aesthetic values (and the aesthetic truth) had been monopolized and segregated from the reality collapses and dissolves in desubliminated, 'lower', and destructive forms, where the hatred of the young bursts into laughter and song, mixing the barricade and the dance floor, love play and heroism. And the young also attack the *esprit de sérieux* in the socialist camp: miniskirts against the apparatchiks, rock 'n' roll against Soviet Realism. The insistence that a socialist society can and ought to be light, pretty, playful, that these qualities are essential elements of freedom, the faith in the rationality of the imagination, the demand for a new morality and culture – does this great anti-authoritarian rebellion indicate a new dimension and direction of radical change, and a new vision of socialism in its qualitative difference from the established societies? Is there anything in the aesthetic dimension which has an essential affinity with freedom not only in its sublimated cultural (artistic) but also in its desublimated political, existential form, so that the aesthetic can become a *gesellschaftliche Produktivkraft*: factor in the technique of production, horizon under which the material and intellectual needs develop?

Throughout the centuries, the analysis of the aesthetic dimension focused on the idea of the beautiful. Does this idea express the aesthetic *ethos* which provides the common denominator of the aesthetic and the political?

As desired object, the beautiful pertains to the domain of the primary instincts, Eros and Thanatos. The mythos links the adversaries: pleasure and terror. Beauty has the power to check aggression: it forbids and immobilizes the aggressor. The beautiful Medusa petrifies him who confronts her. 'Poseidon, the god with azure locks, slept with her in a soft meadow on a bed with springtime flowers'.[1] She is slain by Perseus, and from her truncated body springs the winged horse Pegasus, symbol of poetic imagination. Kinship of the beautiful, the divine, the poetic, but also kinship of the beautiful and unsublimated joy. Subsequently, the classical aesthetic, while insisting on the harmonious union of sensuousness, imagination, and reason in the beautiful, equally insisted on the objective (ontological) character of the beautiful, as the Form in which man and nature come into their own: fulfilment. Kant asks whether there is not a hidden connection between Beauty and Perfection (*Vollkommenheit*),[2] and Nietzsche notes: 'the Beautiful as the mirror (*Spiegelung*) of the Logical, i.e., the laws of logic are the object of the laws of the Beautiful'.[3] For the artist, the beautiful has the 'biological value' of that which is 'useful, beneficial, enhancing life' (*Lebensteigernd*)'.[4]

By virtue of these qualities, the aesthetic dimension can serve as a sort of gauge for a free society. A universe of human relationships no longer mediated by the market, no longer based on competitive exploitation or terror, demands a sensitivity freed from the repressive satisfactions of the unfree societies; a sensitivity receptive to forms and modes of reality which thus far have been projected only by the aesthetic imagination. For the aesthetic needs have their own social content: they are the claims of the human organism, mind and body, for a dimension of fulfilment which can be created only in the struggle against the institutions which, by their very functioning, deny and violate these claims. The radical social content of the aesthetic needs becomes evident as the demand for their most elementary satisfaction is translated into group action on an enlarged scale. From the harmless drive for better zoning regulations and a modicum of protection from noise and dirt to the pressure for closing of whole city areas to automobiles, prohibition of transistor radios in all public places, decommercialization of nature, total urban reconstruction, control of the birth rate – such action would become increasingly subversive of the institutions of capitalism and of their morality. The quantity of such reforms would turn into the quality of radical change to the degree to which they would critically weaken the economic, political and cultural pressure and power groups which have a vested interest in preserving the environment and ecology of profitable merchandising [...]

1 Hesiod, *Theogony*, trans. Norman O Brown (Indianapolis: Bobbs-Merrill, 1953) 61.

2 Kant, *Handschriftlicher Nachlass (Akademieausgabe)*, 622.

3 Nietzsche, *Werke*, Vol. IX (Stuttgart: Alfred Kröner, 1921) 185.

4 *Ibid.*, Vol. XVI (1911) 230.

Herbert Marcuse, *An Essay on Liberation* (Boston: Beacon Press, 1969) 23-28.

Lucy R. LIPPARD
The Art Workers' Coalition: Not a History [1970]

On April 10, 1969, some 300 New York artists and observers thereof filled the amphitheatre of the School of Visual Arts for an 'Open Public Hearing on the subject: What Should Be the Program of The Art Workers Regarding Museum Reform, and to Establish the Program of an Open Art Workers' Coalition'. The last time such a large and various group had got together for non-aesthetic reasons concerned the Artists Tenants Association's threatened loft strike in 1961, which did not take place. The hearing was preceded by a list of 13 demands to the Museum of Modern Art and demonstrations supporting them which emphasized artists' rights: legal, legislative and loosely political; they were the product of the newly-named Art Workers' Coalition (temporarily and simultaneously the Artists' Coalition). The AWC was conceived on January 3, 1969, when the kinetic artist, Takis (Vassilakis), removed a work of art, made by him but owned by the Museum of Modern Art, from the museum's 'Machine' show, on the grounds that an artist had the right to control the exhibition and treatment of his work whether or not he had sold it. Not a revolutionary proposition, except in the art world.

Despite the specific subjects announced for the Open Hearing, taped and after published verbatim by the AWC, the real content of the night was the airing of general complaints about The System, keynoted by Richard Artschwager's use of his two minutes to set off firecrackers instead of talk. The picture of frustrated violence that emerged from this motley cross-section of the art community (70 artists, architects, film-makers and critics, a number of them black, spoke) surprised the establishment at which it was aimed. As well it might, since art world complaints are made loudly, but in the relative privacy of studios and bars, rarely in public. Those who voiced them were immediately accused of opportunism by some of those who remained closet protestants. A number of speakers considered the Museum of Modern Art an unworthy object of artists' attention, but a grudging consensus agreed it was the best place to start if only because it is the seat (in all senses) of power; not enough people, time and energy were available then to tackle all the museums at once and MOMA qualified by its rank in the world, its Rockefeller-studded Board of Trustees with all the attendant political and economic sins attached to such a group, its propagation of the star system and consequent dependence on galleries and collectors, its maintenance of a safe, blue-chip collection, and particularly, its lack of contact with the art community and recent art, its disdain for the advice and desires of the artists that filled its void. The demands made in February 1969 were boiled down from 13 to 11 in June, and revised slightly as the nine-plus below to apply to all museums in March 1970:

A With regard to art museums in general the Art Workers' Coalition makes the following demands:

1 The Board of Trustees of all museums should be made up of one-third museum staff, one-third patrons and one-third artists, if it is to continue to act as the policy-making body of the museum. All means should be explored in the interest of a more open-minded and democratic museum. Art works are a cultural heritage that belong to the people. No minority has the right to control them; therefore, a board of trustees chosen on a financial basis must be eliminated.

2 Admission to all museums should be free at all times and they should be open evenings to accommodate working people.

3 All museums should decentralize to the extent that their activities and services enter Black, Puerto Rican and all other communities. They should support events with which these communities can identify and control. They should convert existing structures all over the city into relatively cheap, flexible branch-museums or cultural centres that could not carry the stigma of catering only to

the wealthier sections of society.

4 A section of all museums under the direction of Black and Puerto Rican artists should be devoted to showing the accomplishments of Black and Puerto Rican artists, particularly in those cities where these (or other) minorities are well represented.

5 Museums should encourage female artists to overcome centuries of damage done to the image of the female as an artist by establishing equal representation of the sexes in exhibitions, museum purchases and on selection committees.

6 At least one museum in each city should maintain an up-to-date registry of all artists in their area, that is available to the public.

7 Museum staffs should take positions publicly and use their political influence in matters concerning the welfare of artists, such as rent control for artists' housing, legislation for artists' rights and whatever else may apply specifically to artists in their area. In particular, museums, as central institutions, should be aroused by the crisis threatening man's survival and should make their own demands to the government that ecological problems be put on a par with war and space efforts.

8 Exhibition programmes should give special attention to works by artists not represented by a commercial gallery. Museums should also sponsor the production and exhibition of such works outside their own premises.

9 Artists should retain a disposition over the destiny of their work, whether or not it is owned by them, to ensure that it cannot be altered, destroyed or exhibited without their consent.

B Until such time as a minimum income is guaranteed for all people, the economic position of artists should be improved in the following ways:

1 Rental fees should be paid to artists or their heirs for all work exhibited where admissions are charged, whether or not the work is owned by the artist.

2 A percentage of the profit realized on the re-sale of an artist's work should revert to the artist or his heirs.

3 A trust fund should be set up from a tax levied on the sales of the work of dead artists. This fund would provide stipends, health insurance, help for artists' dependents and other social benefits.

The extent to which each 'member' agrees with each 'demand' fluctuates to the point where structural fluidity of the organization itself is unavoidable. The AWC has as many identities as it has participants at any one time (there are no members or officers and its main manner of fund-raising is a 'Frisco Circle' at meetings, and the number of participants varies as radically as does their radicality, according to the degree of excitement, rage, guilt, generated by any given issues). It has functioned best as an umbrella, as a conscience and complaint bureau incorporating, not without almost blowing inside out, groups and goals that are not only different, but often conflicting. Advocates of a tighter structure, of a real dues-paying union situation, have reason but not reality on their side. Nobody, inside or outside the coalition, has illusions about its efficiency; the difference is that everyone outside thinks it could be done better another way and from the inside that looks impossible [...]

The most controversial aspect of the AWC among artists and establishment has been its so-called 'politicization of art' term, a term usually used to cover the Black and women's programmes as well a demands that museums speak out against racism, war and repression [...]

The AWC did not begin as a political group, but its models were clearly the Black and student movements of the 1960s, and by the time of the Open Hearing it was obvious that non-art issues would assume if not priority, a major rhetorical importance. Though the Black Panthers, the Chicago Seven and other radical causes have been supported; though we have protested by telegram and testimony ecological catastrophes, budget cutbacks to museums, expressways etc., and once gave half the treasury (some £300 from sales of the books) to a Biafran woman who delivered a particularly stirring plea at a meeting, the AWC, like its predecessor and sometime colleague, the Artists and Writers Protest, has concentrated its political energies on Peace, as did the May 1970 Art Strike. On the first Moratorium Day (October 15, 1969) the AWC managed to get the Modern, the Whitney and the Jewish museums and most of the galleries to close, and (with the crucial help of the participating artists) the Metropolitan to postpone the opening of its big American painting and sculpture show till a more auspicious date, though the museum itself stayed open and, with the Guggenheim, was picketed.

The bitterest quarrel the AWC has had with the museum ... was over joint sponsorship of the Song-My massacre protest poster – a ghastly coloured photograph of the event by a *Life* photographer captioned 'Q: AND BABIES? A: AND BABIES', which was vetoed by the president of the Board of Trustees after an initial, though unexpected, executive staff acceptance of the proposal. We picketed and protested in front of *Guernica*, published 50,000 posters on our own and distributed them, free, via an informal network of artists and movement people; it has turned up all over the world. Our release read, in part: 'Practically, the outcome is as planned: an artist-sponsored poster protesting the Song-My massacre will receive vast distribution. But the Museum's unprecedented decision to make known, as an institution, its commitment to humanity, has been denied it. Such lack of resolution casts doubts on the strength of the Museum's commitment to art itself, and can only be seen as bitter confirmation of this institution's decadence and/or impotence'. Via this and other experiences we discovered that semi-private institutions are unable to buck their trustees, particularly when the issue is one that presents the trustees with a direct conflict of interest. (As Gregory Battcock said at the Open Hearing: 'The trustees of the museums direct NBC and CBS, the *New York Times* and the Associated Press, and that greatest cultural travesty of modern times – The Lincoln Center. They own AT&T, Ford, General Motors, the great multi-billion dollar foundations, Columbia University, Alcoa, Minnesota Mining, United Fruit and AMK, besides sitting on the boards of each others' museums. The implications of these facts are enormous. Do you realize that it is those art-loving, culturally committed trustees of the Metropolitan and Modern museums who are waging the war in Vietnam?')

Lucy R. Lippard, 'The Art Workers' Coalition: Not a History', *Studio International*, 17:6 (November 1970), 171-73.

Cildo MEIRELES
Insertions into Ideological Circuits [1970]

[...] When, in a philosophical definition of his work, Marcel Duchamp stated that, among other things, his aim was to free 'art from the dominion of the hand', he certainly did not imagine the point we would come to in 1970. Something that at first sight could easily be located and effectively combated tends nowadays to be located in an area that is hard to access and to apprehend: the brain.

It is clear that Duchamp's phrase is an example, now, of a lesson that has not been learnt correctly. Duchamp fought not so much against the domination of hands as against manual craftsmanship and, in short, against the gradual emotional, rational and psychological lethargy that this mechanicalness, this habituation would inevitably produce in the individual. The fact that one's hands are not soiled with art means nothing except that one's hands are clean.

Rather than against manifestations of a phenomenon, the fight is against the logic of that phenomenon. What one can see nowadays is a certain relief and a certain delight at not using one's hands. As if things were finally OK. As if at this specific moment, people did not need to start fighting against a much bigger opponent: the habits and handiwork of the brain.

Style, whether of the hands or of the brain (reason), is an anomaly. And with anomalies, it is more intelligent to abort them than to help them to live.

ART-CULTURE

If Duchamp's interference was in terms of Art (the logic of the phenomenon), it is fair to say that it applied to aesthetics, and if thereby it heralded the freeing of habit from the dominion of the hands, it is right to say that any interference in this sphere nowadays (Duchamp's collocation has the great merit of forcing ones perception of Art to shift from being a perception of artistic objects to becoming more a phenomenon of thought), given that what is being done now tends to be closer to culture than to Art, would necessarily be a political interference. Because IF AESTHETICS IS THE BASIS OF ART, IT IS POLITICS THAT IS THE BASIS OF CULTURE.

Cildo Meireles, 'Inserçoes em circuitos ideológicos' ('Insertions into Ideological Circuits'), *Malasartes*, 1 (September-November 1975) 15; reprinted in Alexander Alberro; Blake Stimson (eds.), *Conceptual Art: A Critical Anthology* (Cambridge, Massachusetts: MIT Press, 1999) 232-33.

Rozsika PARKER
Art Has No Sex. But Artists Do [1974]

Laurie Anderson: 'I've always resented the "Hey Baby" assaults because they usually come after I've passed by. They aren't attempts at communication. But ways of turning me into a thing to be coolly assessed. I decided to take my revenge by taking (stealing) their picture. One day in the middle of June I took the photographs of nine men who made unsolicited comments to me. To my disappointment, most of them seemed pleased and flattered that I had wanted to take their pictures.' Laurie Anderson exhibited the photographs and records of the men's reactions.

Eleanor Antin: 'I live in California and from 24 November to 15 December 1971 – a period of seventeen days – I planned to visit New York City with my husband and small child. We planned to stay with my mother in her Manhattan apartment ...' Eleanor Antin recorded her conversations with her mother and the compromises she made to keep the peace between them. Her exhibit consisted of descriptions and graphs of the emotional contents of their talks, ranging from 'boredom' through 'agitation' to 'provocation'.

Mierle Laderman Ukeles: 'Maintenance Art' 'Development and Maintenance the sourball of every resolution: after the revolution, who's going to pick up the garbage on Monday morning? She requested that for one hour per day during the entire run of the exhibition, all maintenance work done by the regular maintenance people was, with their consent and awareness, considered art.

11. Laurie Anderson

Laurie Anderson, Eleanor Antin and Mierle Laderman Ukeles are three of the women included in the exhibition of twenty-six American conceptual artists which was shown in London during April. Lucy Lippard, the New York writer who organized the show, gives the following definition of conceptual art: 'In conceptual art, the idea is paramount – permanence, formal or decorative values are secondary or of no concern.' The ideas, like the three described above, were exhibited in different ways; with photographs, text, tapes, drawings, forms for visitors to fill in, etc. The only factor they had in common was that each artist's work had to fit into a foolscap envelope to enable the show to tour Europe and the USA in a packing case and be seen by as wide an audience as possible.

THE GORY DETAILS

Last summer, readers may remember, we mentioned that Roselee Goldberg was planning to exhibit the show at the Royal College of Art. In retrospect the announcement was premature. We should have predicted the mental and physical problems involved in mounting an all women's show in England. Sure enough, before the show arrived, the Royal College refused to supply the small space and meagre sum of money required for it. The Arts Council was asked for funds but they too rejected the idea. Finally, Garage gallery joined the struggle and approached the Arts Council who then miraculously found the money. But not enough. The show arrived, and survived purely on voluntary labour. So ironically, the Arts Council, whose shows of conceptual art have excluded women, profited from our eagerness to see women's work.

Of course the danger is that the Arts Council will feel that they've now had their women's show, when the group of women who are trying to organize a large show of English artists' work are still finding it absolutely impossible to procure the space or the money for the project. Exhibitions like those organized by the Women's Workshop of the Artists' Union – with the artists present to explain their decision to exhibit together – are badly needed.

AN EXASPERATED REPLY

But the show went on and provided, amongst other things, a focus for very good, productive discussions on women and art. The first question raised by people who appear not to have noticed the percentage of all male shows in London was, 'why have an all women show?' Lucy Lippard, in her introduction to the catalogue, gave her reason:

'This fourth show includes only women artists, by way of exasperated reply on my own part to those who say "there are no women making conceptual art". For the record, there are a great many more than could be exhibited here. Inevitably there will be complaints about the sexual limitation of this show, to which I can only say that all curatorial limitations or whims ("German Art Since 1945", "Colour Painting", "The Cat in Art", "American Artists Under 35" etc.) are equally ridiculous and, for the curator, equally necessary.'

A cat may well respond more to 'The Cat in Art' than 'American Artists Under 35', and certainly as a woman spectator I found plenty to respond to in 'C.7,500' as the show was called (referring to the population of Valencia, California, where the exhibition originated). Lucy Lippard again suggests the reason why:

'All art no matter how "rational" comes from inside *the artist and the social and biological experience of any woman is very different from that of any man in this society. Art of course has no sex. But artists do.'*

And so do spectators. However, there was a wide spectrum of vision and experience represented within the show – by no means all the women were feminists – and concerns varied from examination of role playing, to the nature of art, perception, communication, identity and change. The idea of change was an important component of the show. Caroline Tisdall, speaking recently on alienation and the artist, said that she wanted art to be an expression of a will to change society; 'we lack a notion of art as an evolutionary activity', she said. The artists who confronted various facets of women's experience in 'C7,500' were presenting art as an 'evolutionary activity', but not in a preaching, didactic manner – more in a spirit of inquiry, both humourous and inventive.

ANALYSING THE SAINT

Laurie Anderson discovered during lectures on the history of art that she had a talent for falling asleep in public. Together with a woman photographer friend she explored the taboo on public sleeping. Her friend photographed her sleeping and they recorded both her dreams and people's reactions to the sight. One of the few places where they were not hassled was in a women's lavatory.

Agnes Denes asked artists to fill in questionnaires and she sent the answers to two different psychologists. The exhibit 'Psychograph' consisted of the questionnaires and the written analyses by the two shrinks. 'Psychograph' she writes, 'deals with approximate truth; its subject matter is artists and the aura they must, or feel they must create in order to exist and do their art. It also reveals the outside world's perception of artists, in this case the psychologists. It reveals them as well'. It did. It showed walls of defensiveness interfering with understanding and communication.

In 'Fantasy, a group work', Ryan Canby wrote, 'instead of brushes they use costumes, their environment and other people. Painting is a medium understood by and large by those trained in art schools; this new work by women artists can speak to all those who fantasize about themselves in new roles in order to stretch their identity'. The group of women that she is talking about lived out and dissected their fantasies using make-up, clothes etc. – manipulating the materials which women have previously only used in self defence. But it was Adrian Piper who presented the most thoroughly reasoned defence of using herself as material in 'Talking to Myself: The Ongoing Autobiography of an Art Object'. One reason, she says, for making and exhibiting a work is to induce a change in the viewer, and human confrontation has the greatest impact. Her argument covered 58 typed pages and I can't begin to summarize it. The art work actions that she has done include 'coating my palms with rubber cement and then browsing at a newstand' and similar 'catalytic' events. By becoming the art work herself she combined process and product and escaped the alienation of the art world.

Judith Stein in 'Anyone to tease a saint seriously' compiled descriptions of St. Bernardette ranging from the Press release for the film 'The Song of Bernadette' to an analysis of the saint's handwriting by Gini Glass Graphologist. It was a brilliant demonstration of subjectivity and how description alters according to the position, the relative knowledge and aims of the author.

'IT STINKS OF THE GHETTO'?

But perhaps even more revealing of the biased nature of description was the press coverage of 'C.7,500'. Of course I'm biased and my description of the show is selective and distorted by preconceptions but I'm seen to be writing in an overtly feminist magazine while art critics are not seen as writing in male dominated publications. They are simply seen as The Critics.

London's last large exhibition of conceptual art was all male, christened 'Art Now' and reverentially received.

When women conceptual artists exhibit together it's greeted with outrage, 'it stinks of the ghetto' with 'a whiff of the second rate'. Critics are entitled to their likes and dislikes and they are expected to pass value judgements, but one critic recently described their role as that of mediator between artist and audience. And as mediators they made a poor job of conveying to their readers the variety and diversity of this show – with the exception of Susan Smyth of *Arts Review* whose review revealed both the time and understanding she had put into it.

They fastened on the few artists who were dealing with traditional women's activities and dismissed the entire show as preoccupation with trivialities. But when men make art of activities not usually seen outside the factory, it's Art, not 'the monitoring of a humdrum, self preoccupied existence'.

'Self-preoccupied', 'narcissistic', 'self indulgent' were words constantly used in reference to the show, yet communication was a central theme – communication based on the recognition of shared experience, and an implied need for change. But then once artist and audience communicate the critic's role as mediator becomes obsolete.

Although critics attacked the artists for being self-preoccupied it didn't occur to them to ask why women artists should feel the need to question their identity as both artists and women, or whether there is a discrepancy between the stereotype of the artist and the female stereotype. Instead they viewed it in the light of established definitions – it wasn't conceptual art, it was second rate. 'Nobody is going to be convinced that an injustice is being done if the works displayed to counter it are second rate', wrote Caroline Tisdall in the *Guardian*. But if, as she claims, the works are second rate then it's *because of* the injustice being done to women. During the evening discussions in the gallery we heard repeated proof of the overwhelming discouragement and discrimination facing women in art schools and later in job opportunities. Men present pointed out that they too had a tough time as artists but there was little doubt as to who had the greatest incentive to look for alternative structures and new definitions of art and artist.

Rozsika Parker, 'Art Has No Sex. But Artists Do.', *Spare Rib*, 25 (1974) 34–5; reprinted in Rozsika Parker; Griselda Pollock (eds.), *Framing Feminism: Art and the Women's Movement 1970–85* (London and New York: Pandora, 1987) 194–96.

Mary KELLY
Notes on Reading the *Post-Partum Document* [1976]

THE DISCOURSE OF THE WOMEN'S MOVEMENT

The *Post-Partum Document* located, within the theoretical and political practice of the women's movement, a practice which foregrounds the issues of subjectivity and ideological oppression. More specifically, the *Document* is identified with the tendency that bases the notion of ideological oppression on a psychoanalytic theory of subjectivity, that is, the unconscious.[1] Freud's discovery of the unconscious had crucial implications for theorizing the process by which human subjects become constituted in ideology. If there is no ideology except in practice and by a subject, then ideological oppression is not merely false consciousness. The ideological refers not only to systems of representation but also to a non-unitary complex of social practices which have political consequences. Moreover, these consequences are not given as the direct effect of the means of signification employed in a practice. They depend on a political analysis of what is signified.[2]

For the purposes of such an analysis, the *Post-Partum Document* is the product of a practice of signification, and as such, it does not reflect but reworks the feminist ideology in which it was founded. This is primarily the ideology of consciousness-raising groups that still form a major part of the women's movement. The *Document* reiterates, at one level, the unique contribution that consciousness-raising made to political practice in general by emphasizing the subjective moment of women's oppression.[3] But, at another level, it argues against the supposed self-sufficiency of lived experience and for a theoretical elaboration of the social relations in which femininity is formed. In this sense, the *Post-Partum Document* functions as part of an ongoing debate over the relevance of psychoanalysis to the theory and practice of both Marxism and feminism. Furthermore, the debate includes a critique of the patriarchal bias underlying some of the theoretical assumptions on which the *Document* is based.[4]

THE DISCOURSE OF THE MOTHER-CHILD RELATIONSHIP

The *Post-Partum Document* describes the subjective moment of the mother-child relationship. An analysis of this relationship is crucial to an understanding of the way in which ideology functions in/by the material practices of childbirth and child care. Feeding or dressing a child depends as much on the interchange of a system of signs as teaching him/her to speak or write. In a sense, even the unconscious discourse of these moments is 'structured like a language'.[5] This underlines the fact that intersubjective relationships are fundamentally social. More precisely, every social practice offers a specific expression of a general social law and this law is the symbolic dimension which is given in language.[6]
In patriarchy, the phallus becomes the privileged signifier of this symbolic dimension.[7] Although the subject is constituted in a relation of 'lack' at the moment of his/her entry into language, it is possible to speak specifically of the woman's 'negative place' in the general process of significations or social practices that reproduce patriarchal relations within a given social formation. In childbirth, the mother's negative place is misrecognized insofar as the child is the phallus for her.[8] This imaginary relation is lived through, at the level of ideology and in the social practice of child care, as proof of the natural capacity for maternity and the inevitability of the sexual division of labour.[9]

The documentations of specific moments such as weaning from the breast, learning to speak, and entering a nursery demonstrates the reciprocity of the process of socialization, that is, the intersubjective discourse through which not only the child but also the mother is constituted as subject.

THE DISCOURSE OF WOMEN'S PRACTICE IN ART

The *Post-Partum Document* forms part of the 'problematic' of women's practice in art. The problematic includes a symptomatic reading of the visual inscriptions of women artists. Such a reading, based as much on absences as presences, suggest the way in which the realm of 'the feminine' is bounded by negative signification in the order of language and culture. Because of this coincidence of language and patriarchy, the feminine is, metaphorically, set on the side of the heterogeneous, the unnamable, the unsaid. But the radical potential of women's art practice lies precisely in this coincidence, since, in so far as the feminine is said, it is profoundly subversive.[10]

However, the *Post-Partum Document* is not an excavation of female culture, or a valorization of the female body or of feminine experience as such; it is an attempt to articulate the feminine as discourse, and therefore places the emphasis on the intersubjective relationships which constitute the female subject.[11] Currently in women's art practice, there is a proliferation of forms of signification where the artist's own person, in particular her body, is given as a signifier, that is, as object. In the *Document*, as a means of distantiation, the figure of the mother is not visibly present. Although it is a self-documentation of the mother-child relationship, here between myself and my son, the *Post-Partum Document* does not describe the unified transcendental subject of autobiography, but rather, the decentered, socially constituted subject of a mutual discourse. Moreover, this subject is fundamentally divided. There is a conscious/unconscious split which has operations characteristic of both sides: the signifying processes of drives on the one hand, and the social constraints such as family structures or modes of production on the other.[12] The means of signification used in the *Document* are scriptovisual in order to articulate the gap left by this split, that is, to show how the unconscious processes irrupt into a signifying practice and cut across the systematic order of language and, also, to show the difficulty of the symbolic order for women.

In the *Post-Partum Document*, the art objects are used as fetish objects, explicitly to displace the potential fetishization of the child and implicitly to expose the typically fetishistic function of representation.[13] The stained liners, folded vests, child's markings, and word imprints have a minimum sign value in relation to the commodity status of representations in art, but they have a maximum affective value in relation to the libidinal economy of the unconscious. They are 'representations', in the psychoanalytic sense, of the cathected memory traces.[14] These traces, in combination with the diaries, speech events and feeding charts, construct the discourse of the mother's lived experience. At the same time, they are set up in an antagonistic relationship with the diagrams, algorithms and footnotes which construct the

discourse of feminist analysis. In the context of an installation, this analysis is not meant to theorize the *Post-Partum* moment definitively, but rather to describe a process of secondary revision. In a sense, this text is also included in that process not as a topology of intention but as a rewriting of the discourse of the *Document* which is at once a repression and a reactivation of its consequences.

1 The *Post-Partum Document* is most closely associated with the debate that surfaced after the publication in 1974 of Juliet Mitchell's book *Psychoanalysis and Feminism*, and in particular with a Lacanian reading of Freud, which was in strong evidence as a theoretical tendency at the Patriarchy Conference in London in May 1976. A seminar entitled *Psychoanalysis and Feminism* was organized during the showing of the *Post-Partum Document* at the ICA New Gallery in October 1976. The relevance of psychoanalysis to ideology, feminine psychology and art practice was discussed by a panel on which I was a participant along with Parveen Adams, lecturer in psychology, Brunei University; Susan Lipshitz, psychologist, the Tavistock Institute; filmmaker Laura Mulvey; and writer Rosalind Delmar.

2 Paul Q. Hirst, 'Althusser's Theory of Ideology', *Economy and Society*, 5 (November 1976), 396; see also section on 'Representation', 407-11.

3 Rosalind Coward, 'Sexuality and Psychoanalysis', unpublished paper, 1977.

4 For a useful outline of the debate see the Editorial Collective's article on 'Psychology, Ideology and the Human Subject' in *Ideology and Consciousness*, 1 (May 1977) 5-56. The critique concerns Lacan's acceptance of the 'universality of language', cf. Luce Irigary, *Speculum de l'Autre Femme* (Paris: Editions de Minuit, 1974). See also 'Women's Exile: An Interview with Luce Irigary', trans. Couze Penn, *Ideology and Consciousness*, 1 (May 1977) 62-76

5 See Jacques Lacan, 'The Insistence of the Letter in the Unconscious', in *Structuralism* (New York: Anchor Books, 1970) 287-323.

6 Julia Kristeva, 'The System and the Speaking Subject', *Times Literary Supplement* (12 October 1973).

7 For an elaboration of the consequences in terms of sexual difference, see Jacques Lacan, 'La Signification du phallus', *Ecrits* (Paris: Editions du Seuil, 1966) 685-695.

8 Misrecognition here refers specifically to Lacan's sense of the term as in 'the function of misrecognition which characterizes the ego in all its structures', and not ideological 'misrecognitions'. See Jacques Lacan, 'The Mirror Phase as Formative of the Function of the I' *New Left Review*, 5:47-52 (1968) 71-77.

9 The sexual division of labour is not a symmetrically structured system of women inside the home, men outside it, but rather an intricate, most often asymmetrical, delegation of tasks which aims to provide a structural imperative to heterosexuality. Mary Kelly, *Post-Partum Document*, 'Footnotes and Bibliography', (ICA New Gallery, 1976) 1.

10 See Julia Kristeva, 'Signifying Practice and Mode of Production' in *La Traversée de Signée* (Paris: Editions du Seuil, 1975), trans. and intro. Geoffery Nowel-Smith, *Edinburgh Magazine*, 1 (1976).

11 In 'Art and Sexual Politics' I defined the forms/means of signification employed in women's art practice in terms of the underlying structures of 'feminine narcissism', based metaphorically on Freud's description of narcissistic object choice in 'On Narcissism: An Introduction' (1914), *Collected Papers*, *4*, 47. See also 'Women's Practice in Art', Susan Hiller and Mary Kelly in conversation, *Audio Arts*, 3:3 (1977), and 'Women and Art', *Studio International*, 3 (1977).

12 Julia Kristeva, 'The System and the Speaking Subject', *Times Literary Supplement* (12 October 1973), cf. the splitting of the subject, Marcelin Pleynet, 'de Pictura', trans. Stephen Bann, *20th Century Studies* (December 1977).

13 See Stephen Heath on fetishism and 'representation' in classic cinema and popular photography, 'Lessons from Brecht', *Screen*, 15 (Summer 1974); see also Laura Mulvey, 'Visual Pleasure and Narrative Cinema', *Screen*, 16 (Autumn 1975).

14 J. Laplanche and J.B. Pontalis, *The Language of the Self* (London: Hogarth Press, 1973) 200. For Freud, the idea/presentation/representation is to be understood as what comes from the object and is registered in mnemic systems, and not as the act of presenting an object of consciousness; ibid., 247, memory trace/mnemic trace is used by Freud to denote the way in which events are inscribed upon the memory, they are deposited in different systems and reactivated only once they have been cathected; ibid., 62, cathexis is an economic concept pertaining to the fact that a certain amount of psychical energy is attached to an idea or group of ideas, a part of the body, or an object.

Mary Kelly, 'Notes on Reading the Post-Partum Document', *Control Magazine*, 10 (1977) 10-12; reprinted in Alexander Alberro; Blake Stimson (eds.), *Conceptual Art: A Critical Anthology* (Cambridge, Massachusetts: MIT Press, 1999) 370-74.

Martha ROSLER

To Argue for a Video Representation. To Argue for a Video against the Mythology of Everyday Life [1977]

Where do ideas come from? All the myths of everyday life stitched together form a seamless envelope of ideology, the false account of everything thinkable. Ideology is a readymade always ready to stand in for a closer understanding of the world and its workings. The myths of ideology cushion us, it is true, from the paranoia that is engendered by mistrust of culture givens. But they are not nurturant. The interests served by ideology are not human interests properly defined; rather, ideology serves society in shoring up its particular form of social organization. In class society, ideology serves the interests of the class that dominates. Through the channels of mass communication, which it controls, our dominant class holds its own ideology up to our whole society as the real and proper set of attitudes and beliefs. The impetus is then strong for everyone to identify her/himself as a member of the 'middle class', a mystified category standing in for the image of the dominant class. We have all come to aspire to the condition of the *petit bourgeoisie*: to be, paradigmatically, 'one's own boss'. Thus the legitimate desire for control over one's own life is flattened out, transmuted into a desire to own one's own business – or, failing that, to construct a 'private' life in opposition to the world out there.

The eradication of craft skills and of *economically productive* family activity has lessened people's chances to gain a sense of accomplishment and worth and has increased our vulnerability to the blandishments of advertising, the most potent educational institution in our culture. As the opportunities for personal power on a human level diminish for all but a relatively small part of the population, self-confidence, trust and pleasure conceived in straightforward terms are poisoned, and we are increasingly beguiled by an accordion-like succession of mediations between ourselves and the natural and social world, mediations in the form of commodities. We are each promised personal power and fulfilment through consumption; we are as nothing unless clothed in a culture that is conceived of as a congeries of packages, each of which presents us with a bill. In pursuit of meaning and satisfaction we are led to grant the aura of life to things and to drain it from people: *we personify objects and objectify persons.* We experience alienation from ourselves as well as from others. We best comprehend ourselves as social entities in looking at photos of ourselves, assuming the voyeur's role with respect to our own images; we best know ourselves from within in looking through the viewfinder at other people and things.

The culture of corporate capitalism has metamorphosed architecture: each of us is the row to be hoed, the field to be sowed. The upward-aspiring bourgeoisie and upper ranks of the working class are led to develop superfluous skills, such as gourmet cooking or small-boat navigation, whose real significance is extravagant, well-rationalized consumerism and the cultivation of the self but which, in seeking legitimation, mimic skills once necessary to life; skills which, moreover, were tied to a form of social organization that we think of as less alienated and more familiar than our own. In pursuit of meaning, also, we are led to see meaning where there is only emptiness and sham, strength where there is only violence or money, knowledge where there is only illusion, honesty where there is only a convincing manner, status where there is only a price tag, satisfaction where there is only a cattle prod, limitless freedom where there is only a feed lot. Our entire outlook is conditioned by the love and the terror of consumption.

Commodity fetishism, the giving over of self to the thing, is not a universal trope of the psyche; it is not even a quirk of character. It is both the inescapable companion

and the serviceable pipe dream of capitalist social organization; it is Our Way of Life. It is built into the structure of society, originating in the production process and the social relations it engenders, in which one's very ability to make or to do something is transformed into a commodity of sorts in itself, saleable to the boss in exchange for 'wages'.

How does one address these banally profound issues of everyday life? It seems to me appropriate to use the medium of television, which in its most familiar form is one of the primary conduits of ideology – through both its ostensive subject matter and its overtly commercial messages. I am trying to enlist 'video', a different form of television, in the attempt to make explicit the connections between *ideas* and *institutions*, connections whose existence is never alluded to by corporate TV. Nevertheless, video is not a strategy, it is merely a mode of access.

Video itself is not 'innocent'. It too is a form of cultural commodity that often stands for a celebration of the self and its powers of invention. Yet video is useful in that it provides me with the opportunity to construct 'decoys', entities that engage in a natural dialectic with TV itself. A woman in a bare-bones kitchen, in black and white, demonstrating some hand tools and replacing their domesticated 'meaning' with a lexicon of rage and frustration is an antipodean Julia Child.[1] A woman in a red and blue Chinese coat, demonstrating a wok in a dining room and trying to speak with the absurd voice of the corporation, is a failed Mrs Pat Boone. An anachronistically young couple, sitting cramped and earnest in their well-appointed living room, attempting to present a coherent narrative and explanation of their daughter's self-starvation, are any respectably middle-class couple visited by misfortune and subjected to a 'human interest' news-show interview. A woman and child in a studio-constructed no-space, being handed can after package after can of food as Christmas charity, are a faded echo of *Queen for a Day*. An operatic presentation of a woman put through an ordeal of measurement tenuously alludes to a monumentally stretched-out version of *Truth or Consequences*.

One of the basic forms of mass culture, including television, is the narrative, especially the first-person narrative. (Melodramas, situation comedies, soap operas and so on seem to me to embody a form of first-person narrative in their protagonists.) Narrative is a homey, manageable form of address, but its very virtue, the air of subjectivity and lived experience, is also its fault. The rootedness in the *I*, which is (predictably) the most seductive encoding of *convincingness*, suggests an absolute inability to transcend the consciousness of a single individual. And consciousness is the realm of ideology, so that the logic of the first-person narrative, in particular, suggests that there is no appeal from ideology, no *metacritique*. Given the pervasive relativism of our society (according to which only the personal is knowable and all opinions are equally valid) the first-person narrative implies the irretrievability of objective truth. (The validity which we grant to 'public' figures of all kinds, which tends to include the scientific and medical establishment, is the opposite term of this pair of oppositions.) At most, one version or another of the dominant ideology is implicitly reinforced, on the basis of what happens to the protagonists or the other figures with whom they interact.

Yet this inability to speak truth is the failure not so much of narrative *per se* as of the *naturalism* that is taken to be narrative's central feature. Break the bonds of that naturalism and the problem vanishes. One can provide a critical dimension and invoke matters of truth precisely through reference to the ideological confusions that naturalism falsifies by ommission. A character speaking in contradictions or failing to manage the socially right sequence of behaviours can eloquently index the irresolvable social contradictions – starvation in the midst of plenty, the subtly aggressive impersonality of institutional charity, the racism, sexism and national chauvinism of some of the basic tenets of 'scientific' intelligence testing that are the source of ideological confusions.

In choosing representational strategies I aim for the distancing (*ostranenie*, the *Verfremdungseffekt*), the distantiation occasioned by a refusal of realism, by foiled expectations, by palpably flouted conventions. Tactically I tend to use a wretched pacing and a bent space; the immovable shot or, conversely, the unexpected edit, pointing to the mediating agencies of photography and speech; long shots rather than close ups, to deny psychological intent; contradictory utterances; and, in acting, flattened affect, histrionics or stageiness. Although video is simply one medium among several that are effective in confronting real issues of culture, video based on TV has this special virtue; it has little difficulty in lending itself to the kind of 'crude thinking', as Brecht used this phrase, that seems necessary to penetrate the waking daydreams that hold us in thrall. The clarification of vision is a first step towards reasonably and humanely changing the world.

1 The celebrity US chef and cookery TV presenter [ed.].

Martha Rosler, 'To Argue for a Video of Representation. To Argue for a Video against the Mythology of Everyday Life', originally written for a pamphlet accompanying the exhibition 'New American Filmmakers: Martha Rosler' (New York: Whitney Museum of American Art, 1977); reprinted in Alexander Alberro; Blake Stimson (eds.), *Conceptual Art: A Critical Anthology* (Cambridge, Massachusetts: MIT Press, 1999) 366-69.

Alexander ALBERRO
A Media Art: Conceptualism in Latin America in the 1960s [1999]

A number of art movements emerged in the late 1960s in the southern cone of Latin America, especially in Argentina and Brazil, that paralleled and at times preceded many of the better-known claims of Conceptual art in Europe and North America. From the beginning, however, there was a significant divergence between Latin American Conceptualists and their more post-structural counterparts in North America and Europe. Whereas the latter posited that language performed the fundamental role in the construction of the artwork (and, more generally, the subject, as in the notion that 'the subject is spoken through language'), Latin American Conceptualism, by contrast, predicated that extra-linguistic, all-encompassing mythical structures of ideology played that role.[1] Underpinning this view was a social and political movement that sought to counter the dominant hegemonic practices by appealing to anti-colonial and anti-imperialist feelings. It advocated a unique Latin American cultural perspective that would break with the bourgeois humanism that characterized post-war European and North American Modernism. This radical discourse coincided with an increasingly optimistic view of the social future. Inspired by an economic boom, a growing middle class and past development of consumer markets, that optimism – though naïve in retrospect – generated an unprecedented urban expansion, creating some of the largest megalopolises in the world.[2]

It is in this context that an art practice emerged in Latin America that not only discarded the old model of a concrete artistic work as the object of interaction between the artist and the public, but also dissolved the privileged function of the mediatory object and replaced it by the disembodied forces of mass-media communications. In other words, a basic shift took place as the central position of a material work of art was displaced by an abstract system of information, circulation and distribution produced by different media. This was, of course, a rather paradoxical outcome for an artistic avant-garde that, in the very process of revealing and exposing the limiting institutional parameters of art, suddenly found itself turning to the institutional media as the source and manifestation of art [...]

Yet in Argentina the idea of actual appropriation and manipulation of ready-made media forms and structures did not survive long, even in abstract form. The increasingly repressive social and political reality that followed the June 1966 military coup soon made such minor subversion of the prevailing system seem woefully inadequate. In response, there was an increase in the number of politically aggressive art interventions that, while still inspired by Conceptualism, bordered on direct action.[3] One of the most explosive of these, announced as *En el mundo hay salida para todos* (*In the World There is an Escape for Everyone*), consisted of an action performed by a group of artists from the industrial city of Rosario who, in collaboration with artists from Buenos Aires similarly close to Conceptual theories, locked for an hour the doors of the official 1966 Biennale of Córdoba exhibition. To the continued alarm of exhibition officials, when they finally managed to open the doors to the galleries, the artists accompanied by a group of students occupied the space and used the ensuing media attention to protest against the repressive political regime and its cultural apparatuses, such as the Biennale of Córdoba.[4] [...]

The swift shift in focus from Conceptualism that questioned the ideological bases of bourgeois art to an artistic movement that questioned all of the institutions of bourgeois culture is perhaps best exemplified by the *Tucumán Arde* (*Tucumán Burns*) project of 1968. In Tucumán, a small province in north-western Argentina, Onganía's harsh plan of economic rationalization had led to the closure of the majority of local sugar refineries. As these formed the province's principal means of income, their demise resulted in a depopulation of the area, leaving it poverty-stricken and without a strong labour force to protest against the disastrous conditions. The government, with the co-operation of the press, promoted then an 'Operativo Tucumán' in an attempt to conceal the dire situation of extreme poverty rampant in the province. A massive publicity campaign was launched that announced a largely mythical industrialization project financed by new capital industries throughout Tucumán. It was 'soon' to lead to prosperity, but in the meantime the pressing reality of the social catastrophe in Tucumán was downplayed and any remedy deferred.

In response, a group of artists from Rosario, Santa Fe and Buenos Aires formed the Grupo de Artistas de Vanguardia (Group of Avant-Garde Artists) and affiliated themselves with the Argentinean General Confederation of Labour (Confederación General del Trabajo, or CGT) in order to create a work that would 'come out of a consciousness of the current reality of the artist as an individual within the political and social context which surrounds him'.[5] This programme culminated in the 1968 action, *Tucumán Arde* (*Tucumán Burns*) that sought to expose the catastrophic policy in Tucumán by disseminating counter-information designed to subvert the mythical nature of official media information. Not only the existing situation but, more significantly, the factors that led up to it were mercilessly publicized following an intense period of research systematically carried out by the Group. Posters and fliers of Tucumán were distributed throughout Rosario and Santa Fe. Next the Group decided to escalate its action by mounting large multi-media exhibitions within meeting locales of the CGT in Rosario and Buenos Aires. The installation of the work in union halls, which drew a significantly different and larger public than was usual for more conventional art exhibitions, facilitated the political praxis of the work. The same circumstances also led to the adoption of a larger design format for the work.

Viewers of the installation were treated to an all-encompassing interior environment made of posters, placards, photo-murals, newspaper montages, tape recordings and an array of statistical graphs indicating rates of infant mortality, tuberculosis and illiteracy in the region of Tucumán. Juxtaposed to this information was the full range of government-sponsored misinformation. The dramatic discrepancy between official and factual information was theorized by the group as having the potential not only to educate but also to heighten the political consciousness of the spectators. The group also expected that the media attention occasioned by the shows would create an important vehicle for the spreading of information. The progress from handbills to exhibition displays to media stratagems underscores the growing awareness of these artists as they assessed the increased role of the media in production, transmission and, ultimately, control of information about art and politics alike.[6] [...]

A similar interest in the semiotic potential of systems of distribution pervaded Brazilian artists' moves towards Conceptual art in the 1960s. The theoretical basis for one such move was articulated in the manifesto 'General Scheme of the New Objectivity', printed in the catalogue of the 1967 exhibition 'Nova Objetividade Brasileira' ('Brazilian New Objectivity'), at the Museu de Arte Moderna, Rio de Janeiro. Written by Hélio Oiticica, the manifesto charts the principal characteristics of the new art, including 'the participation of the spectator (bodily, tactile, visual, semantic, etc.)', 'an engagement and a position on political, social and ethical problems', a 'tendency towards collective propositions' and 'a revival of, and new formulations in, the concept of anti-art'.[7] The impact that the theses of this manifesto were to have on a new generation of artists in Brazil and elsewhere on the continent may have been underestimated because of the extremely volatile and dangerous circumstances surrounding artistic production under military dictatorship. In Brazil, the army coup that toppled the constitutional regime in 1964 was followed by a reinforcement of the oppressive regime in 1968. The government, supported by Brazilian censors, immediately imposed an effective and dramatic crackdown on the arts. Within a year, the director of the Museu de Arte Moderna in Rio de Janeiro, Mauricio Roberto, was forced by the political police to take down a large exhibition of new art a few hours before the opening ceremony; a widespread international boycott of the Sao Paulo Bienal followed and persisted for over a decade but without tangible effects. In fact, many young artists, even those who did not produce work that addressed politics in any way, were taken to court or otherwise persecuted by the authorities.[8] [...]

Two dominant strategies underlie modes of Latin American Conceptualism in the 1960s, neither of which relies on dominant artistic traditions or national or regional heritage. One appropriates and manipulates ready-made media forms and structures, or, in Barthes' terms, 'myths', and highlights their ideological commitment behind their fake neutrality. The other builds upon the appropriations of the first, compounding the myths and recharging them with a radical and often political content that aims to transform the viewers' habitual perception of both artworks and artefacts of everyday life as well. It is this subversion of the mythical operation of the mass media and parallel ideological circuits – a subversion that in some cases resorts to what could properly be termed 'guerrilla' tactics – that in the context of the 1960s forms the particular character of Latin American Conceptual art. And it is this same strategy that ultimately makes Latin American Conceptualism uniquely relevant to the subsequent history of Conceptual and post-Conceptual art practices everywhere, and, in more general terms, to the history of the avant-garde in the twentieth century.

1 The refusal of artists working in Latin America to rely entirely on linguistic structures to theorize the construction of the subject, and their taking into consideration broader mythical structures, surely have to do with the fact that the dominant language (Spanish or Portuguese) was itself culturally and socially problematical, being symptomatic of the ruling class.

2 See Manuel Castells, 'La Urbanización Dependente en América Latina' (1971), in his *Imperialismo yurbanizacion en América Latina* (Barcelona, 1973) 7-26. Written in the early 1970s, Castells' essay asserts that 'Latin America has a rate of urbanization almost equivalent to that of Europe, and a rate of metropolitanization greater than that of Europe' (7). See also T. Lynn Smith, 'Why the Cities? Observations on Urbanization in Latin America', in *Latin American Problems*, ed. P.L. Astuto and R.A. Leal (New York, 1964.

3 According to Andrea Giunta, 'Arte y (re)presión: cultura crítica y prácticas conceptuales en Argentina', *Arte, historia y identidad en América: visiones comparativas*, Vol. III, ed. Gustavo Curiel, *et al.* (Mexico: DF, 1994) 881, there were two opposite strands of avant-garde art in 1960s Argentina. One, represented by Jacoby, Costa and Escari's 'Media Art', took up 'the optimistic and festive character of Pop art', while the other, represented by such artists as Leon Ferrari, was much more 'critical of the fundamental premises of Western art'. For an informative overview of the relationship between art and politics in 1960s Argentina, see John King, Art and Cultural Development: Argentina 1956-1976', in *Art from Argentina, 1920-1994*, ed. David Elliot (Oxford: Museum of Modern Art, 1994) 66-73. The account of social, economic and political developments in 1960s Latin America presented in this paper is indebted to Tulio Halperin Donghi's highly informative study *The Contemporary History of Latin America*, trans. John Charles Chasteen (Durham and London, 1993), esp. 292-337.

4 See G. Fantoni, 'Tensiones hacia la politica: del homenaje al Vietnam a la Anti-Bienal', Rev. Sisi (Buenos Aires), II:2 (1990) 34; as cited in Lisa Roberts, Pablo Suárez: A Portrait of Resistance', in *Art from Argentina* (op. cit.), 107-8. Córdoba is a city in Argentina.

5 See María Teresa Gramuglio and Nicolás Rosa, *Tucumán Arde* (Rosario, 1968), n.p. See also Sueldo, et al., Tucumán Arde [...]

6 This development was accompanied by the decision to draft a manifesto articulating the aims and methods of the Group. Collectively written and first published as a mimeograph by the CGT, the *Tucumán Arde* manifesto postulates that the first step to a genuine 'revolutionary art' is the 'awareness of the actual reality of the artist as an individual inside the political and social context that surrounds him'.

7 Hélio Oiticica, 'General Scheme of the New Objectivity' (1967) [see above, 255-56].

8 As recounted by Cildo Meireles in Nuria Enguita, 'Places for Digressions (an interview with Cildo Meireles)' (1994), in Bartolomeu Mari and Nuria Enguita, *Cildo Meireles* (Valencia: IVAM, Centre del Carme, 1995) 161.

Alexander Alberro, 'A Media Art: Conceptualism in Latin America in the 1960s', *Rewriting Conceptual Art*, eds. Michael Newman, Jon Bird, (London: Reaktion Books, 1999) 140-51.

INSTITUTIONAL CRITIQUE

The conceptual art of institutional critique involves the application of a Marxist analysis of capitalism to the social relations of the art world. This approach was pioneered during the 1930s in Germany by Walter Benjamin and Theodor Adorno. It was summed up in two post-war texts: the chapter on the 'culture industry' in Adorno and Horkheimer's *Dialectic of Enlightenment* (1947) and André Malraux's *Museum without Walls* (1953). Both were widely influential during the 1970s. This perspective was updated, radicalized and generalized in Guy Debord's situationist text *Society of the Spectacle* (1967). Artists such as Daniel Buren, Marcel Broodthaers and Michael Asher applied these ideas, in detail, to the art-institutional conditions of their day, in their writings as well as their art. Brian O'Doherty synthesized them with minimalist debates about the constitutive role of gallery space in the experience of art, in his essays on the ideology of the 'white cube'.

Theodor W. ADORNO, Max HORKHEIMER The Culture Industry: Enlightenment as Mass Deception [1944]

[...] Culture is a paradoxical commodity. So completely is it subject to the law of exchange that it is no longer exchanged; it is so blindly consumed in use that it can no longer be used. Therefore it amalgamates with advertising. The more meaningless the latter seems to be under a monopoly, the more omnipotent it becomes. The motives are markedly economic. One could certainly live without the culture industry, therefore it necessarily creates too much satiation and apathy. In itself, it has few resources itself to correct this. Advertising is its elixir of life. But as its product never fails to reduce to a mere promise the enjoyment which it promises as a commodity, it eventually coincides with publicity, which it needs because it cannot be enjoyed. In a competitive society, advertising performed the social service of informing the buyer about the market; it made choice easier and helped the unknown but more efficient supplier to dispose of his goods. Far from costing time, it saved it. Today when the free market is coming to an end, those who control the system are entrenching themselves in it. It strengthens the firm bond between the consumers and the big combines. Only those who can pay the exorbitant rates charged by advertising agencies, chief of which are the radio networks themselves; that is, only those who are already in a position to do so, or are co-opted by the decision of the banks and industrial capital, can enter the pseudo-market as sellers. The costs of advertising, which finally flow back into the pockets of the combines, make it unnecessary to defeat unwelcome outsiders by laborious competition. They guarantee that power will remain in the same hands – not unlike those economic decisions by which the establishment and running of undertakings is controlled in a totalitarian state. Advertising today is a negative principle, a blocking device: everything that does not bear its stamp is economically suspect. Universal publicity is in no way necessary for people to get to know the kinds of goods – whose supply is restricted anyway. It helps sales only indirectly. For a particular firm, to phase out a current advertising practice constitutes a loss of prestige, and a breach of the discipline imposed by the influential clique on its members. In wartime, goods which are unobtainable are still advertised, merely to keep industrial power in view. Subsidizing ideological media is more important than the repetition of the name. Because the system obliges every product to use advertising, it has permeated the idiom – the 'style' – of the culture industry. Its victory is so complete that it is no longer evident in the key positions: the huge buildings of the top men, floodlit stone advertisements, are free of advertising; at most they exhibit on the rooftops, in monumental brilliance and without any self-glorification, the firm's initials. But, in contrast, the nineteenth-century houses, whose architecture still shamefully indicates that they can be used as a consumption commodity and are intended to be lived in, are covered with posters and inscriptions from the ground right up to and beyond the roof: until they become no more than backgrounds for bills and sign-boards. Advertising becomes art and nothing else, just as Goebbels – with foresight – combines them: *l'art pour l'art*, advertising for its own sake, a pure representation of social power. In the most influential American magazines, *Life* and *Fortune*, a quick glance can now scarcely distinguish advertising from editorial picture and text. The latter features an enthusiastic and gratuitous account of the great man (with illustrations of his life and grooming habits) which will bring him new fans, while the advertisement pages use so many factual photographs and details that they represent the ideal of information which the editorial part has only begun to try to achieve. The assembly-line character of the culture industry, the synthetic, planned method of turning out its products (factory-like not only in the studio but, more or less, in the compilation of cheap biographies, pseudo-documentary novels and hit songs) is very suited to advertising: the important individual points, by becoming detachable, interchangeable and even technically alienated from any connected meaning, lend themselves to ends external to the work. The effect, the trick, the isolated repeatable device, have always been used to exhibit goods for advertising purposes, and today every monster close-up of a star is an advertisement for her name, and every hit song a plug for its tune. Advertising and the culture industry merge technically as well as economically. In both cases the same thing can be seen in innumerable places, and the mechanical repetition of the same culture product has come to be the same as that of the propaganda slogan. In both cases the insistent demand for effectiveness makes technology into psycho-technology, into a procedure for manipulating men. In both bases the standards are the striking yet familiar, the easy yet catchy, the skilful yet simple; the object is to overpower the customer, who is conceived as absent-minded or resistant.

By the language he speaks, he makes his own contribution to culture as publicity. The more completely language is lost in the announcement, the more words are debased as substantial vehicles of meaning and become signs devoid of quality; the more purely and transparently words communicate what is intended, the more impenetrable they become. The demythologization of language, taken as an element of the whole process of enlightenment, is a relapse into magic. Word and essential content were distinct yet inseparable from one another. Concepts like melancholy and history, even life, were recognized in the word, which separated them out and preserved them. Its form simultaneously constituted and reflected them. The absolute separation, which makes the moving accidental and its relation to the object arbitrary, puts an end to the superstitious fusion of word and thing. Anything in a determined literal sequence which goes beyond the correlation to the event is rejected as unclear and as verbal metaphysics. But the result is that the word, which can now be only a sign without any meaning, becomes so fixed to the thing that it is just a petrified formula. This affects language and object alike. Instead of making the object experiential, the purified word treats it as an abstract instance, and everything else (now excluded by the demand for ruthless clarity from expression – itself now banished) fades away in reality. A left-hand at football, a black-shirt, a member of the Hitler Youth, and so on, are no more than names. If before its rationalization the word had given rise to lies as well as to longing, now, after its rationalization, it is a straitjacket for longing more even than for lies. The blindness and dumbness of the data to which positivism reduces the world pass over into language itself, which restricts itself to recording those data. Terms themselves become impenetrable; they obtain a striking force, a power of adhesion and repulsion which makes them like their extreme opposite, incantations. They come to be a kind of trick, because the name of the *prima donna* is cooked up in the studio on a statistical basis, or because a welfare state is anathematized by using taboo terms such as 'bureaucrats' or 'intellectuals', or because base practice uses the name of the country as a charm. In general, the name – to which magic most easily attaches – is undergoing a chemical change: a metamorphosis into capricious, manipulable designations, whose effect is admittedly now calculable, but which for that very reason is just as despotic as that of the archaic name. First names, those archaic remnants, have been brought up to date either by stylization as advertising trade-marks (film stars' surnames have become first names), or by collective standardization. In comparison, the bourgeois family name which, instead of being a trademark, once individualized its bearer by relating him to his own past history, seems antiquated. It arouses a strange embarrassment in Americans. In order to hide the awkward distance between individuals, they call one another 'Bob' and 'Harry', as interchangeable team members. This practice reduces relations between human beings to the good fellowship of the sporting community and is a defence against the true kind of relationship. Signification, which is the only function of a word admitted by semantics, reaches perfection in the sign. Whether folksongs were rightly or wrongly called upper-class culture in decay, their elements have only acquired their popular form through a long process of repeated transmission. The spread of popular songs, on the other hand, takes place at lightning speed. The American expression 'fad', used for fashions which appear like epidemics – that is, inflamed by highly-concentrated economic forces – designated this phenomenon long before totalitarian advertising bosses enforced the general lines of culture. When the German Fascists decide one day to launch a word – say, 'intolerable' – over the loudspeakers the next day the whole nation is saying 'intolerable'. By the same pattern, the nations against whom the weight of the German 'blitzkrieg' was thrown took the word into their own jargon. The general repetition of names for measures to be taken by the authorities makes them, so to speak, familiar, just as the brand name on everybody's lips increased sales in the era of the free market. The blind and rapidly spreading repetition of words with special designations links advertising with the totalitarian watchword. The layer of experience which created the words for their speakers has been removed; in this swift appropriation language acquires the coldness which until now it had only on billboards and in the advertisement columns of newspapers. Innumerable people use words and expressions which they have either ceased to understand or employ only because they trigger off conditioned reflexes; in this sense, words are trademarks which are finally all the more firmly linked to the things they denote, the less their linguistic sense is grasped. The minister for mass education talks incomprehendingly of 'dynamic forces', and the hit songs unceasingly celebrate 'reverie' and 'rhapsody', yet base their popularity precisely on the magic of the unintelligible as creating the thrill of a more exalted life. Other stereotypes, such as memory, are still partly comprehended, but escape from the experience which might allow them content. They appear like enclaves in the spoken language. On the radio of Flesch and Hitler they may be recognized from the affected pronunciation of the announcer when he says to the nation, 'Good night, everybody!' or 'This is the Hitler Youth', and even intones 'the Führer' in a way imitated by millions. In such clichés the last bond between sedimentary experience and language is severed which still had a reconciling effect in dialect in the nineteenth century. But in the prose of the journalist whose adaptable attitude led to his appointment as an all-German editor, the German words become petrified, alien terms. Every word shows how far it has been debased by the Fascist pseudo-folk community. By now, of course, this kind of language is already universal, totalitarian. All the violence done to words is so vile that one can hardly bear to hear them any longer. The announcer does not need to speak pompously; he would indeed be impossible if his inflection were different from that of his particular audience. But, as against that, the language and gestures of the audience and spectators are coloured more strongly than ever before by the culture industry, even in fine nuances which cannot yet be explained experimentally. Today the culture industry has taken over the civilizing inheritance of the entrepreneurial and frontier democracy – whose appreciation of intellectual deviations was never very finely attuned. All are free to dance and enjoy themselves, just as they have been free, since the historical neutralization of religion, to join any of the innumerable sects. But freedom to choose an ideology – since ideology always reflects economic coercion – everywhere proves to be freedom to choose what is always the same. The way in which a girl accepts and keeps the obligatory date, the inflection on the telephone or in the most intimate situation, the choice of words in conversation, and the whole inner life as classified by the now somewhat devalued depth psychology, bear witness to man's attempt to make himself a proficient apparatus, similar (even in emotions) to the model served up by the culture industry. The most intimate reactions of human beings have been so thoroughly reified that the idea of anything specific to themselves now persists only as an utterly abstract notion: personality scarcely signifies anything more than shining white teeth and freedom from body odour and emotions. The triumph of advertising in the culture industry is that consumers feel compelled to buy and use its products even though they see through them.

Theodor W. Adorno and Max Horkheimer, *Die Dialektik der Aufklärung* (Amsterdam, 1947); trans. J. Cumming (1972), *Dialectic of Enlightenment* (London and New York: Verso, 1997) 161-67.

André MALRAUX
Museum without Walls [1951]

A Romanesque crucifix was not regarded by its contemporaries as a work of sculpture; nor Cimabue's *Madonna* as a picture. Even Pheidias' *Pallas Athene* was not, primarily, a statue.

So vital is the part played by the art museum in our approach to works of art today that we find it difficult to realize that no museums exist, none has ever existed, in lands where the civilization of modern Europe is, or was, unknown; and that, even amongst us, they have existed for barely two hundred years. They bulked so large in the nineteenth century and are so much part of our lives today that we forget they have imposed on the spectator a wholly new attitude towards the work of art. For they have tended to estrange the works they bring together from their original functions and to transform even portraits into 'pictures'. Though Caesar's bust and the equestrian *Charles V* remain for us Caesar and the Emperor Charles, *Count-Duke Olivares* has become pure Velazquez. What do we care who the *Man with the Helmet* or the *Man with the Glove* may have been in real life? For us their names are Rembrandt and Titian. The men who sat for these portraits have lapsed into nonentity. Until the nineteenth century a work of art was essentially a representation of something real or imaginary, which conditioned its existence *qua* work of art. Only in the artist's eyes was painting specifically painting, and often, even for him, it also meant a 'poetic' rendering of his subject. The effect of the museum was to suppress the model in almost every portrait (even that of a dream-figure) and to divest works of art of their functions. It did away with the significance of Palladium, of Saint and Saviour; ruled out associations of sanctity, qualities of adornment and possession, of likeness or imagination. Each exhibit is a representation of something, differing from the thing itself, this specific difference being its *raison d'être*.

In the past a Gothic statue was a component part of the Cathedral; similarly a classical picture was tied up with the setting of its period, and not expected to consort with works of different mood and outlook. Rather, it was kept apart from them, so as to be the more appreciated by the spectator. True, there were picture collections and *cabinets d'antiques* in the seventeenth century, but they did not modify that attitude towards art of which Versailles is the symbol. Whereas the modern art gallery not only isolates the work of art from its context but makes it foregather with rival or even hostile works. It is a confrontation of metamorphoses.

The reason why the art museum made its appearance in Asia so belatedly (and, even then, only under European influence and patronage) is that for an Asiatic, and especially the man of the Far East, artistic contemplation and the picture gallery are incompatible. In China the full enjoyment of works of art necessarily involved ownership, except where religious art was concerned; above all it demanded their isolation. A painting was not exhibited, but unfurled before an art-lover in a fitting state of grace; its function was to deepen and enhance his communion with the universe. The practice of pitting works of art against each other, an intellectual activity, is at the opposite pole from the mood of relaxation which alone makes contemplation possible. To the Asiatic's thinking an art collection (except for educational purposes) is as preposterous as would be a concert in which one listened to a programme of ill-assorted pieces following in unbroken succession.

For over a century our approach to art has been growing more and more intellectualized. The art museum invites criticism of each of the expressions of the world it brings together; and a query as to what they have in common. To the 'delight of the eye' there has been added – owing to the sequence of conflicting styles and seemingly antagonistic schools – an awareness of art's impassioned quest, its age-old struggle to remould the scheme of things. Indeed an art gallery is one of the places which show man at his noblest. But our knowledge covers a wider field than our museums. The visitor to the Louvre knows that he will not find the great English artists significantly represented there; nor Goya, nor Michelangelo (as painter), nor Piero della Francesca, nor Grünewald – and that he will see but little of Verneer. Inevitably in a place where the work of art has no longer any function other than that of being a work of art, and at a time when the artistic exploration of the world is in active progress, the assemblage of so many masterpieces – from which, nevertheless, so many are missing – conjures up in the mind's eye *all* the world's masterpieces. How indeed could this mutilated possible fail to evoke the whole gamut of the possible?

Of what is it necessarily deprived? Of all that forms an integral part of a whole (stained glass, frescoes); of all that cannot be moved; of all that is difficult to display (sets of tapestries); of all that the collection is unable to acquire. Even when the greatest zeal has gone into its making, a museum owes much to opportunities that chance has thrown in its way. All Napoleon's victories did not enable him to bring the Sistine to the Louvre, and no art patron, however wealthy, will take to the Metropolitan Museum the Royal Portal of Chartres or the Arezzo frescoes. From the eighteenth to the twentieth century what migrated was the portable; far more pictures by Rembrandt than Giotto frescoes have found their way to sales. Thus the Art Museum, born when the easel-picture was the one living form of art, came to be a pageant not of colour but of pictures; not of sculpture but of statues.

The Grand Tour rounded it off in the nineteenth century. Yet in those days a man who had seen the totality of European masterpieces was a very rare exception. Gautier saw Italy (but not Rome) only when he was thirty-nine; Edmond de Goncourt when he was thirty-three; Hugo as a child; Baudelaire and Verlaine, never. The same holds good for Spain; for Holland rather less, as Flanders was relatively well known. The eager crowds that thronged the Salons – composed largely of real connoisseurs – owed their art education to the Louvre. Baudelaire never set eyes on the masterpieces of El Greco, Michelangelo, Masaccio, Piero della Francesca or Grünewald; or of Titian, or of Hals or Goya – the Galerie d'Orléans notwithstanding.

What had he seen? What (until 1900) had been seen by all those writers whose views on art still impress us as revealing and important; whom we take to speaking of the same works as those we know, and referring to the same *data* as those available to us? They had visited two or three galleries, and seen reproductions (photographs, prints or copies) of a handful of the masterpieces of European art; most of their readers had seen even less. In the art knowledge of those days there was a pale of ambiguity, a sort of no man's land – due to the fact that the comparison of a picture in the Louvre with another in Madrid was that of a present picture with a memory. Visual memory is far from being infallible, and often weeks had intervened between the inspections of the two canvases. From the seventeenth to the nineteenth century, pictures, interpreted by engraving, had *become* engravings; they had kept their drawing but lost their colours, which were replaced by 'interpretation', their expression in black-and-white; also, while losing their dimensions, they acquired margins. The nineteenth-century photograph was merely a more faithful print, and the art-lover of the time 'knew' the pictures in the same manner as we now 'know' stained-glass windows.

Nowadays an art student can examine colour reproductions of most of the world's great paintings, can make acquaintance with a host of second-rank pictures, archaic arts, Indian, Chinese and Pre-Columbian sculpture of the best periods, Romanesque frescoes, Negro and 'folk' art, a fair quantity of Byzantine art. How many statues could be seen in reproduction in 1850? Whereas the modern art-book has been pre-eminently successful with sculpture (which lends itself better than pictures to reproduction in black-and-white). Hitherto the connoisseur duly visited the Louvre and some subsidiary galleries, and memorized what he saw, as best he could. We, however, have far more great works available to refresh our memories than those which even the greatest of museums could bring together. For a 'Museum without Walls' is coming into being, and (now that the plastic arts have invented their own printing-press) it will carry infinitely farther that revelation of the world of art, limited perforce, which the 'real' museums offer us within their walls.

Photography, which started in a humble way as a means of making known acknowledged masterpieces to those who could not buy engravings, seemed destined merely to perpetuate established values. But actually an ever greater range of works is being reproduced, in ever greater numbers, while the technical conditions of reproduction are influencing the choice of the works selected. Also, their diffusion is furthered by an ever subtler and more comprehensive outlook, whose effect is often to substitute for the obvious masterpiece the significant work, and for the mere pleasure of the eye the surer one of knowledge. An earlier generation thrived on Michelangelo; now we are given photographs of lesser masters, likewise of folk paintings and arts hitherto ignored: in fact everything that comes into line with what we call a style is now being photographed.

For while photography is bringing a profusion of masterpieces to the artists, these latter have been revising their notion of what it is that makes the masterpiece.

From the sixteenth to the nineteenth century the masterpiece was a work that existed 'in itself', an absolute. There was an accepted canon preconizing a mythical yet fairly well-defined beauty, based on what was thought to be the legacy of Greece. The work of art constantly aspired towards an ideal portrayal; thus, for Raphael, a masterpiece was a work on which the imagination could not possibly improve. There was little question of comparing such a work with others by the same artist. Nor was it given a place in time; its place was determined by its success in approximating to the ideal work it adumbrated.

True, this aesthetic was steadily losing ground between the Roman sixteenth and the European nineteenth centuries. Nevertheless, until the Romantic movement, it was assumed that the great work of art was something unique, the product of unconditioned genius. History and antecedents counted for nothing; the test was its *success*. This notion, narrow if profound, this Arcadian setting in which man, sole arbiter of history and his sensibility, repudiated (all the more effectively for his unawareness of it) the struggle of each successive age to work out its own perfection – this notion lost its cogency once men's sensibility became attuned to different types of art, whose affinities they glimpsed, though without being able to reconcile them with each other [...]

André Malraux, *Les Voix du silence* (Paris: Gallimard, 1951); trans. Stuart Gilbert (1953), *The Voices of Silence* (London: Paladin, 1974) 12-17.

Guy DEBORD

Society of the Spectacle [1967]

SEPARATION PERFECTED

1 In societies where modern conditions of production prevail, all of life presents itself as an immense accumulation of *spectacles*. Everything that was directly lived has moved away into a representation.

2 The images detached from every aspect of life fuse in a common stream in which the unity of this life can no longer be re-established. Reality considered *partially* unfolds, in its own general unity, as a pseudo-world *apart*, an object of mere contemplation. The specialization of images of the world is completed in the world of the autonomous image, where the liar has lied to himself. The spectacle in general, as the concrete inversion of life, is the autonomous movement of the non-living.

3 The spectacle presents itself simultaneously as all of society, as part of society, and as *instrument of unification*. As a part of society it is specifically the sector which concentrates all gazing and all consciousness. Due to the very fact that this sector is *separate*, it is the common ground of the deceived gaze and of false consciousness, and the unification it achieves is nothing but an official language of generalized separation.

4 The spectacle is not a collection of images, but a social relation among people, mediated by images.

5 The spectacle cannot be understood as an abuse of the world of vision, as a product of the techniques of mass dissemination of images. It is, rather, a *Weltanschauung* which has become actual, materially translated. It is a world vision which has become objectified.

6 The spectacle, grasped in its totality, is both the result and the project of the existing mode of production. It is not a supplement to the real world, an additional decoration. It is the heart of the unrealism of the real society. In all its specific forms, as information or propaganda, as advertisement or direct entertainment consumption, the spectacle is the present *model* of socially dominant life. It is the omnipresent affirmation of the choice *already made* in production and its corollary consumption. The spectacle's form and content are identically the total justification of the existing system's conditions and goals. The spectacle is also the *permanent presence* of this justification, since it occupies the main part of the time lived outside of modern production.

7 Separation is itself part of the unity of the world, of the global social praxis split up into reality and image. The social practice which the autonomous spectacle confronts is also the real totality which contains the spectacle. But the split within this totality mutilates it to the point of making the spectacle appear as its goal. The language of the spectacle consists of signs of the ruling production, which at the same time are the ultimate goal of this production.

8 One cannot abstractly contrast the spectacle to actual social activity: such a division is itself divided. The spectacle which inverts the real is in fact produced. Lived reality is materially invaded by the contemplation of the spectacle while simultaneously absorbing the spectacular order, giving it positive cohesiveness. Objective reality is present on both sides. Every notion fixed this way has no other basis than its passage into the opposite: reality rises up within the spectacle, and the spectacle is real. This reciprocal alienation is the essence and the support of the existing society.

9 In a world which *really is topsy-turvey*, the true is a moment of the false.

10 The concept of 'spectacle' unifies and explains a great diversity of apparent phenomena. The diversity and the contrasts are appearances of a socially organized appearance, the general truth of which must itself be recognized. Considered in its own terms, the spectacle is *affirmation* of appearance and affirmation of all human life, namely social life, as mere appearance. But the critique which reaches the truth of the spectacle exposes it as the visible *negation* of life, as a negation of life which *has become visible*.

11 To describe the spectacle, its formation, its functions and the forces which tend to dissolve it, one must artificially distinguish certain inseparable elements. When *analyzing* the spectacle one speaks, to some extent, the language of the spectacular itself in the sense that one moves through the methodological terrain of the very society which expresses itself in the spectacle. But the spectacle is nothing other than the *sense* of the total practice of a social-economic formation, its *use of time*. It is the historical movement in which we are caught.

12 The spectacle presents itself as something enormously positive, indisputable and inaccessible. It says nothing more than 'that which appears is good, that which is good appears'. The attitude which it demands in principle is passive acceptance which in fact it already obtained by its manner of appearing without reply, by its monopoly of appearance.

13 The basically tautological character of the spectacle flows from the simple fact that its means are simultaneously its ends. It is the sun which never sets over the empire of modern passivity. It covers the entire surface of the world and bathes endlessly in its own glory.

14 The society which rests on modern industry is not accidentally or superficially spectacular, it is fundamentally *spectaclist*. In the spectacle, which is the image of the ruling economy, the goal is nothing, development everything. The spectacle aims at nothing other than itself.

15 As the indispensable decoration of the objects produced today, as the general exposé of the rationality of the system, as the advanced economic sector which directly shapes a growing multitude of image-objects, the spectacle is the *main production* of present-day society.

16 The spectacle subjugates living men to itself to the extent that the economy has totally subjugated them. It is no more than the economy developing for itself. It is the true reflection of the production of things, and the false objectification of the producers.

17 The first phase of the domination of the economy over social life brought into the definition of all human realization the obvious degradation of *being* into *having*. The present phase of total occupation of social life by the accumulated results of the economy leads to a generalized sliding of *having* into *appearing*, from which all actual 'having' must draw its immediate prestige and its ultimate function. At the same time all individual reality has become social reality directly dependent on social power and shaped by it. It is allowed to appear only to the extent that it *is not*.

18 Where the real world changes into simple images, the simple images become real beings and effective motivations of hypnotic behaviour. The spectacle, as a tendency to *make one see* the world by means of various specialized mediations (it can no longer be grasped directly), naturally finds vision to be the privileged human sense which the sense of touch was for other epochs; the most abstract, the most mystifiable sense corresponds to the generalized abstraction of present-day society. But the spectacle is not identifiable with mere gazing, even combined with hearing. It is that which escapes the activity of men, that which escapes reconsideration and correction by their work. It is the opposite of dialogue. Wherever there is independent *representation*, the spectacle reconstitutes itself.

19 The spectacle inherits all the *weaknesses* of the Western philosophical project which undertook to comprehend activity in terms of the categories of *seeing*; furthermore, it is based on the incessant spread of the precise technical rationality which grew out of this thought. The spectacle does not realize philosophy, it philosophizes reality. The concrete life of everyone has been degraded into a *speculative* universe.

20 Philosophy, the power of separate thought and the thought of separate power, could never by itself supersede theology. The spectacle is the material reconstruction of the religious illusion. Spectacular technology has not dispelled the religious clouds where men had placed their own powers detached from themselves; it has only tied them to an earthly base. The most earthly life thus becomes opaque and unbreathable. It no longer projects into the sky but shelters within itself its absolute denial, its

fallacious paradise. The spectacle is the technical realization of the exile of human powers into a beyond; it is separation perfected within the interior of man.

21 To the extent that necessity is socially dreamed, the dream becomes necessary. The spectacle is the nightmare of imprisoned modern society which ultimately expresses nothing more than its desire to sleep. The spectacle is the guardian of sleep.

22 The fact that the practical power of modern society detached itself and built an independent empire in the spectacle can be explained only by the fact that this practical power continued to lack cohesion and remained in contradiction with itself.

23 The oldest social specialization, the specialization of power, is at the root of the spectacle. The spectacle is thus a specialized activity which speaks for all the others. It is the diplomatic representation of hierarchic society to itself, where all other expression is banned. Here the most modern is also the most archaic.

24 The spectacle is the existing order's uninterrupted discourse about itself, its laudatory monologue. It is the self-portrait of power in the epoch of its totalitarian management of the conditions of existence. The fetishistic, purely objective appearance of spectacular relations conceals the fact that they are relations among men and classes: a second nature with its fatal laws seems to dominate our environment. But the spectacle is not the necessary product of technical development seen as a *natural* development. The society of the spectacle is on the contrary the form which chooses its own technical content. If the spectacle, taken in the limited sense of 'mass media' which are its most glaring superficial manifestation, seems to invade society as mere equipment, this equipment is in no way neutral but is the very means suited to its total self-movement. If the social needs of the epoch in which such techniques are developed can only be satisfied through their mediation, if the administration of this society and all contact among men can no longer take place except through the intermediary of this power of instantaneous communication, it is because this 'communication' is essentially *unilateral*. The concentration of 'communication' is thus an accumulation, in the hands of the existing system's administration, of the means which allow it to carry on this particular administration. The generalized cleavage of the spectacle is inseparable from the modern *State*, namely from the general form of cleavage within society, the product of the division of social labour and the organ of class domination.

25 *Separation* is the alpha and omega of the spectacle. The institutionalization of the social division of labour, the formation of classes, had given rise to a first sacred contemplation, the mythical order with which every power shrouds itself from the beginning. The sacred has justified the cosmic and ontological order which corresponded to the interests of the masters; it has explained and embellished that which society *could not do*. Thus all separate power has been spectacular, but the adherence of all to an immobile image only signified the common acceptance of an imaginary prolongation of the poverty of real social activity, still largely felt as a unitary condition. The modern spectacle, on the contrary, expresses what society *can do*, but in this expression the *permitted* is absolutely opposed to the *possible*. The spectacle is the preservation of unconsciousness within the practical change of the conditions of existence. It is its own product, and it has made its own rules: it is a pseudo-sacred entity. It shows what it *is*: separate power developing in itself, in the growth of productivity by means of the incessant refinement of the division of labour into a parcellization of gestures which are then dominated by the independent movement of machines; and working for an ever-expanding market. All community and all critical sense are dissolved during this movement in which the forces that could grow by separating are not yet *reunited*.

26 With the generalized separation of the worker and his products, every unitary view of accomplished activity and all direct personal communication among producers are lost. Accompanying the progress of accumulation of separate products and the concentration of the productive process, unity and communication become the exclusive attribute of the system's management. The success of the economic system of separation is the *proletarianization* of the world.

27 Due to the success of separate production as production of the separate, the fundamental experience which in primitive societies is attached to a central task is in the process of being displaced, at the crest of the system's development, by non-work, by inactivity. But this inactivity is in no way liberated from productive activity: it depends on productive activity and is an uneasy and admiring submission to the necessities and results of production; it is itself a product of its rationality. There can be no freedom outside of activity, and in the context of the spectacle all activity is negated, just as real activity has been captured in its entirety for the global construction of this result. Thus the present 'liberation from labour', the increase of leisure, is in no way a liberation within labour, nor a liberation from the world shaped by this labour. None of the activity lost in labour can be regained in the submission to its result.

28 The economic system founded on isolation is a *circular production of isolation*. The technology is based on isolation, and the technical process isolates in turn. From the automobile to television, all the *goods selected* by the spectacular system are also its weapons for a constant reinforcement of the conditions of isolation of 'lonely crowds'. The spectacle constantly rediscovers its own assumptions more concretely.

29 The spectacle originates in the loss of the unity of the world, and the gigantic expansion of the modern spectacle expresses the totality of this loss: the abstraction of all specific labour and the general abstraction of the entirety of production are perfectly rendered in the spectacle, whose *mode of being concrete* is precisely abstraction. In the spectacle, one part of the world *represents itself* to the world and is superior to it. The spectacle is nothing more than the common language of this separation. What binds the spectators together is no more than an irreversible relation at the very centre which maintains their isolation. The spectacle reunites the separate, but reunites it *as separate*.

30 The alienation of the spectator to the profit of the contemplated object (which is the result of his own unconscious activity) is expressed in the following way: the more he contemplates the less he lives; the more he accepts recognizing himself in the dominant images of need, the less he understands his own existence and his own desires. The externality of the spectacle in relation to the active man appears in the fact that his own gestures are no longer his but those of another who represents them to him. This is why the spectator feels at home nowhere, because the spectacle is everywhere.

31 The worker does not produce himself; he produces an independent power. The *success* of this production, its abundance, returns to the producer as an *abundance of dispossession*. All the time and space of his world become *foreign* to him with the accumulation of his alienated products. The spectacle is the map of this new world, a map which exactly covers its territory. The very powers which escaped us *show themselves* to us in all their force.

32 The spectacle within society corresponds to a concrete manufacture of alienation. Economic expansion is mainly the expansion of this specific industrial production. What grows with the economy in motion for itself can only be the very alienation which was at its origin.

33 Separated from his product, man himself produces all the details of his world with ever increasing power, and thus finds himself ever more separated from his world. The more his life is now his product, the more he is separated from his life.

34 The spectacle is *Capital* to such a degree of accumulation that it becomes an image [...]

Guy Debord, 'I: Separation Perfected', *La Société du Spectacle* (Paris: Buchet-Chastel, 1967); trans. *The Society of the Spectacle* (Detroit: Black & Red, 1970; revised 1977), paragraphs 1-34.

Michel CLAURA
Paris Commentary [1969]

There are, I feel, a few basic ideas to be considered before discussing the work of Daniel Buren and his friends. First of all, these ideas are the outcome of an objective look at art from its beginnings. Each work of art is the fruition of its creator's sensitivity and is directed at the sensitivity of the beholder.

The forms taken by an artist's sensitivity, and indeed by its opposite, can be manifold, but it determines his choice of subject – flowers, a woman, war, his environment, movement, the contrast or harmony of colours, the contrast or harmony of form – and whatever his subject the artist's aim is to translate his personal feelings into a work of art. Artistic creation thus boils down to the exploitation of his personal problems, either by translating his problems into universal terms or sinking his own inhibitions in his work. 'Everybody, hence me', or 'me, hence everybody'. *To express himself the artist must both receive and transmit.*

If art is both an illusion in itself and the illusion of communication, what does it mean to the public? A doubtless unconscious complicity is established between artist and spectator. The artist offers an illusion which the public accepts. In so doing, the public, consciously or otherwise, in fact rejects reality. Which reduces art to the level of entertainment.

During the time that a spectator takes to look at, or even to think of, a work of art, he is no longer quite alone, alone with himself, alone in a hostile environment. Thus the complicity between the artist and his public reaches a state of blindness – the one blinding and the other allowing himself to be blinded.

It is, however, possible to find another criterion – which alone explains the fact that there is a history of art. The artist is constantly striving for greater perfection of expression. His aim is to progress, to reduce the distance between the significant and the expressed and to give greater universality to his own problems. Problems are not hard to acquire. They have not noticeably changed since man first made hand imprints on cave walls. The only development, the only progress that has been made, is exclusively in the means of expression. Thus, when all is said and done, our advance has been of a technical nature only. So far as art is concerned, the change has been in form without affecting the fundamentals. It is a purely technical development. *The history of art is the history of the technique of art.* Illusion's great attraction remains undiminished because techniques have continuously developed. Thus the outcome of the creative act can only be illusion, in that an artist's job is to select from his environment or from within himself an object, a light, a form, a movement, and to remove them from their context in order to transform them into a work of art. The illusion lies in the fact that a work of art is a space in which material or spiritual odds and ends taken out of context are deposited and which, we are persuaded, form an entity. This problem of illusion in art is the problem of communication. As art has always been a pseudo-realistic or symbolic representation of non-communicable feelings, what else could it be but the illusion of communication?

Communication takes place at the level of the artist's own proclaimed beliefs, and to see something more than this in a work of art is to bring one's own sensitivity into play. But by clinging to an illusion, this very sensitivity will be lost in the gulf which separates the significant from the expressed, intent from deed. The beholder will have had no more than the illusion of communication.

This cursory but fundamental analysis of art is possible today because art is more in evidence than ever. It is an obvious illusion, an illusion of communication, an aesthetic hedge against inflation, a technical entertainment: today art is more self-conscious than ever. Seen in this context, the attitudes of Buren and his friends are perhaps more comprehensible. On the one hand they present an objective analysis of art and on the other new concepts which, in my mind, are connected with art only in so far as they fundamentally question the whole role of art.

For more than a year Buren and three friends put on a series of demonstrations. On January 3, 1967, at the 'Salon de la Jeune Peinture' at the Paris Museum of Modern Art, the four of them painted in public from eleven in the morning until eight in the evening to show how simple their techniques are. They also distributed a leaflet which said:

> *Because painting is a game,*
> *Because painting is the application (consciously or otherwise) of the rules of composition,*
> *Because painting is the freezing of movement,*
> *Because painting is the representation (or interpretation or appropriation or disputation or presentation) of objects,*
> *Because painting is a springboard for the imagination,*
> *Because painting is spiritual illustration,*
> *Because painting is justification,*
> *Because painting serves an end,*
> *Because to paint is to give aesthetic value to flowers, women, eroticism, the daily environment, art, dadaism, psychoanalysis and the war in Vietnam,*
> We are not painters.

Throughout the day a tape-recording in French, English and Spanish repeated 'Buren, Mosset, Parmentier and Toroni advise you to use your intelligence'. That evening they withdrew their canvases from the 'Salon' saying they opposed Paris salons as the 'heritage of nineteenth-century salons' and 'galleries which abet public laziness (each gallery being a place of pilgrimage for a public intent on self-consolation)'.

On 2 June, 1967, at 9 p.m. in the auditorium of the Musée des Arts Décoratifs (entrance 5 Fr.), four canvases by Buren, Mosset, Parmentier and Toroni were displayed on a platform before 150 spectators. Nothing happened. The public waited a quarter of an hour, half an hour, an hour; still nothing happened. At a quarter past ten a leaflet was distributed which read:

> *Obviously you have come here to look at canvases by Buren, Mosset, Parmentier and Toroni. What you must look at is:*
> *a canvas 2.50m × 2.50m divided into twenty-nine equal vertical red and white stripes of which the two outer stripes are white (Buren);*
> *a black circle (interior radius 4.5 cm, exterior radius 7.8 cm), centered on a white canvas 2.50m × 2.50 m (Mosset);*
> *alternate gray and white horizontal stripes each 38 cm apart on a canvas 2.50 m × 2.50m (Parmentier);*
> *eighty-five regular blue imprints of a flat brush each 30 cm apart on a white surface 2.50m × 2.50m (Toroni).*

In October 1967 at the Fifth Paris Biennale, the four paintings were again displayed but this time photographs were projected onto them to the accompaniment of a recorded text:

Photographs	Text
Views of St. Tropez	*Art is the illusion of being somewhere else. It is not a painting by Buren (spotlight projected onto his canvas), by Mosset (idem), by Parmentier (idem), by Toroni (idem).*
	Art is the illusion of freedom. It is not etc.
Little Red Riding Hood	*Art is the illusion of dreaming. It is not etc.*
Shots of a bullfight	*Art is the illusion of sacredness. It is not etc.*
Shots of the Versailles fountains	*Art is the illusion of the marvelous. It is not etc.*
Striptease	*Art is the illusion of escape. It is not etc.*
Flowers	*Art is the illusion of nature. It is not etc.*
No projection	*Art is entertainment, art is false. Painting begins with Buren, Mosset, Parmentier and Toroni.*

After a three-minute interval, the whole thing began again, and continued throughout the exhibition.

In December 1967 three of them – Buren, Mosset and Toroni – put on a new exhibition at the former 'J' Gallery in Paris. I should add here that these three had been painting the same three pictures for more than a year. In order to stress the 'autonomy' of their canvases, each artist painted and presented both his picture and those of the other two. They stated:

> *The logic of our activities up to the present leads us today to say that to call a Buren a Buren, a Mosset a Mosset or a Toroni a Toroni is nothing but an abuse of language.*
> *Buren presents a Buren, a Mosset and a Toroni. But all three canvases were painted by Buren. Mosset presents a Mosset, a Buren and a Toroni. But all three canvases were painted by Mosset. Toroni presents a Toroni, a Buren and a Mosset. But all three canvases were painted by Toroni. This demonstration adds nothing to the paintings by Buren, Mosset and Toroni. It is an exhibition of three Burens, three Mossets and three Toronis.*

Also in December 1967, Buren and Toroni held a joint exhibition at the Flaviana Gallery in Lugano. They carried their logic a stage further and entitled the show 'Buren or Toroni or Any One Else'. 'Anyone else' was invited to paint either of the pictures usually done by Buren or Toroni and to sign it with his own name, appropriating the picture simply by painting it. There is nothing to distinguish any of the canvases, no matter who painted them. *In this demonstration the two artists are stating as clearly as possible that the thing they are painting IS.* It is therefore of little significance whether it was painted by one of themselves by someone else or by a machine. In two successive interviews which appeared in *La Galerie des Arts* (February 1968) and *Les Lettres Françaises* (March 13, 1968) Buren once again stated his case. Clearly it is no longer an artist talking, but a theoretician. Theory and art are incompatible.

The actual canvases shown by Buren, Toroni and Mosset are completely lacking in sensitivity. Humour, discomfort, anxiety, joy, calm, serenity – every human feeling is absent. This first point alone challenges our

BECAUSE PAINTING

IS A GAME,
IS THE APPLICATION (CONSCIOUSLY OR OTHERWISE) OF THE RULES OF COMPOSITION,

IS THE FREEZING OF MOVEMENT,

IS THE REPRESENTATION (OR INTERPRETATION OR APPROPRIATION OR DISPUTATION OR PRESENTATION) OF OBJECTS,

IS A SPRINGBOARD FOR THE IMAGINATION,

IS SPIRITUAL ILLUSTRATION,

IS JUSTIFICATION,

SERVES AN END,

BECAUSE TO PAINT

IS TO GIVE AESTHETIC VALUE TO FLOWERS, WOMEN, EROTICISM, THE DAILY ENVIRONMENT, ART, DADAISM, PSYCHOANALYSIS AND THE WAR IN VIETNAM,

WE ARE NOT PAINTERS.

Daniel BUREN, Olivier MOSSET, Michel PARMENTIER, Niele TORONI, quoted in Michel Claura, 'Paris Commentary', *Studio International*, 1969 basic concept of art. To reject sensitivity means abandoning personal problems. And abandoning what I have called 'personal problems' results in a picture which is no longer a transformation – by the artist – of reality into illusion.

Perhaps these attempts should be placed on a linguistic level, the search for a language which would, for the first time, specifically belong to the plastic arts. There is no longer a question of a work of art being limited to a given space, for example, where everything or nothing can be put, but of a work conceived in itself without ever taking anything whatever (being, object, idea) out of context. The result is a thing to be looked at for its own sake. It no longer represents, expresses, etc. It is no longer an illusion.

These canvases introduce a new concept of art which means that the relations between the work and the public will be changed. The problem of communication – even of non-communication – will no longer exist. There is no didactic intent. The spectator sees a work in itself, nothing else, nothing more. Buren, Mosset, Parmentier and Toroni will not be there to entertain you because the entertainment aspect of art is the transformation of what is all too true into illusion. Or, put another way, illusion is eliminated because no outside elements are introduced.

What happens to technique in their painting? It can no longer be the means by which an object is transformed into the representation of an object, into the illusion of an object, because there is no longer an object to recreate. In fact their technique is extremely simple, and if the work remains a composition (in that everything is 'composed') it has nonetheless taken on a completely new meaning. The technique is *within* the work but no longer *is* the work.

To go back once again to the Buren-Toroni exhibition at Lugano, which was, I think, the most important they have ever presented, their canvases are 'autonomous'. Hence they were able to ask literally anyone to produce them and claim them as their own. They had in fact eliminated the artists 'expression', since whoever produces one of these is not expressing himself. If there were any self-expression, the work could only be imitated, but if in addition to Buren and Toroni, absolutely anyone can produce the *'same'* canvas, this means that the painter never expresses himself on any level, whether his name is Buren, Toroni or Any One Else. If the canvas is always identical, it is because it *is, immutably.* The artist is insignificant. Thus the system of references which constitutes the language of art is no longer acceptable. This contention supports – and is supported by – the fact that the very concept of art is fundamentally questioned and in the course of being replaced by a new proposition. Because, let us not forget, these pictures existed before we came to talk about them. Logically (according co their own lights), they have painted innumerable copies of one canvas for nearly two years. Logically, because if they limited themselves to a single copy each this would have to be considered as a unique work, as *the* masterpiece, a concept they have also rejected. We do not have to consider their future. We can limit ourselves to what they show us, to their canvases. Their existence-in-themselves could be related to formalist mathematics.

We are no longer in the domain of art. But we are faced with a questioning of the whole basis of art.

Since this article was written, Buren in particular has been able to demonstrate at what point his action was coherent. He continues to prove that it is possible to elaborate a practical theory in art, on condition that one ceases to be just an artist or, in other words, that one has a total and specific vision of the innumerable problems posed by the work and its communication. Using the same material, Buren has, since March 1968, produced the same stripes printed on paper. In April he pasted pieces of paper on advertisement hoardings in Paris, showing nothing but the stripes themselves. At Prospect '68' in Dusseldorf he pasted similar pieces of paper on a surface 26 by 32 ft. (September 1968). In October, in an article in *Galerie des Arts*, Buren, discussing specific and marginal problems of art teaching, described the mechanics of creation as a social act. In the same month he had an exhibition at the Galerie Apollinaire in Milan, and used the gallery as a kind of background support rather than as an exhibition space.

Michael Claura, 'Paris Commentary', *Studio International*, 177:907 (January 1969) 47-9; reprinted in Alexander Alberro; Blake Stimson (eds.), *Conceptual Art: A Critical Anthology* (Cambridge, Massachusetts: MIT Press, 1999) 82-87.

Daniel BUREN
Function of the Museum[1]
[1970]

Privileged place with a triple role:

1 *Aesthetic.* The Museum is the frame and effective support upon which the work is inscribed/composed. It is at once the centre in which the action takes place and the single (topographical and cultural) viewpoint for the work.

2 *Economic.* The Museum gives a sale value to what it exhibits, has privileged/selected. By preserving or extracting it from the commonplace, the Museum promotes the work socially, thereby assuring its exposure and consumption.

3 *Mystical.* The Museum/Gallery instantly promotes to 'Art' status whatever it exhibits with conviction, i.e. habit, thus diverting in advance any attempt to question the foundations of art without taking into consideration the place from which the question is put. The Museum (the Gallery) constitutes the mystical body of Art.

It is clear that the above three points are only there to give a general idea of the Museum's role. It must be understood that these roles differ in intensity depending on the Museums (Galleries) considered, for socio-political reasons (relating to art or more generally to the system).

PRESERVATION

One of the initial (technical) functions of the Museum (or Gallery) is preservation. (Here a distinction can be made between the Museum and the Gallery although the distinction seems to be becoming less clear-cut: the former generally buys, preserves, collects, in order to exhibit; the latter does the same with the view of resale.) This function of preservation perpetuates the idealistic nature of all art since it claims that art is (could be) eternal. This idea, among others, dominated the nineteenth century, when public museums were created approximately as they are still known today.

Painted things are generally attitudes, gestures, memories, copies, imitations, transpositions, dreams, symbols ... set/fixed on the canvas arbitrarily for an indefinite period of time. To emphasize this illusion of eternity or timelessness, one has to preserve the work itself (physically fragile: canvas, stretcher, pigments etc.) from wear. The Museum was designed to assume this task, and by appropriate artificial means to preserve the work, as much as possible, from the effects of time – work which would otherwise perish far more rapidly. It was/is a way – another – of obviating the temporarily/fragility of a work of art by artificially keeping it 'alive', thereby granting it an appearance of immortality which serves remarkably well the discourse which the prevalent bourgeois ideology attaches to it. This takes place, it should be added, with the author's i.e. the artist's delighted approval.

Moreover, this conservatory function of the Museum, which reached its highest point during the nineteenth century and with Romanticism, is still generally accepted today, adding yet another paralysing factor. In fact nothing is more readily preserved than a work of art. And this is why twentieth-century art is still so dependent on nineteenth-century art since it has accepted, without a break, its system, its mechanisms and its function (including Cézanne and Duchamp) without revealing one of its main alibis, and further more accepting the exhibition framework as self-evident. We can once again declare that the Museum makes its 'mark', imposes its 'frame' (physical and moral) on everything that is exhibited in it, in a deep and indelible way. It does this all the more easily since everything that the Museum shows is only considered and produced in view of being set in it.

Every work of art already bears, implicitly or not, the trace of a gesture, an image, a portrait, a period, a history, an idea ... and is subsequently preserved (as a souvenir) by the Museum.

COLLECTION

The Museum not only preserves and therefore perpetuates, but also collects. The aesthetic role of the Museum is thus enhanced since it becomes the single viewpoint (cultural and visual) from which works can be considered, an enclosure where art is born and buried, crushed by the very frame which presents and constitutes it. Indeed, collecting makes simplifications possible and guarantees historical and psychological weight which reinforce the predominance of the support (Museum/Gallery) in as much as the latter is ignored. In fact, the Museum/Gallery has a history, a volume, a physical presence, a cultural weight quite as important as the support on which one paints, draws. (By extension, this naturally applies to any sculpted material, transported object or discourse inscribed in the Museum). On another level, let us say social, collecting serves to display different works together, often very unalike, from different artists. This results in creating or opposing different 'schools'/'movements' thereby cancelling certain interesting questions lost in an exaggerated mass of answers. The collection can also be used to show a single artist's work, thus producing a 'flattening' effect to which the work aspired anyway, having been exclusively conceived – willingly or not – in view of the final collection.

In summary, the collection in a Museum operates in two different but parallel ways, depending on whether one considers a group of a one-man show.[2]

a) In the case of a confrontation of works by different artists the Museum imposes an amalgam of unrelated things among which chosen works are emphasized. These chosen works are given an impact which is only due to their context – collection. Let is be clear that the collection we are speaking of and the selection it leads to are obviously economically motivated. The Museum collects the better to isolate. But this distinction is false as the collection forces into comparison things that are often incomparable, consequently producing a discourse which is warped from the start, and to which no one pays attention [...]

b) In collecting and presenting the work of a single artist (one-man show) the Museum stresses differences within a single body of work and insists (economically) on (presumed) successful works and (presumed) failures. As a result, such shows set off the 'miraculous' aspect of 'successful' works. And the latter therefore also give a better sales value to juxtaposed weaker works. This is the 'flattening' effect we mentioned above, the aim of which is both cultural and commercial.

REFUGE

The above considerations quite naturally lead to the idea, close to the truth, that the Museum acts as a refuge. And that without this refuge, no work can 'exist'. The Museum is an asylum. The work set in it is sheltered from the weather and all sorts of dangers, and most of all protected from any kind of questioning. The Museum selects, collects and protects. All works of art are made in order to be selected, collected and protected (among other things from other works which are, for whatever reasons, excluded from the Museum). If the works takes shelter in the Museum-refuge, it is because it finds there its comfort and its frame; a frame which one considers as natural, while it is merely historical. That is to say, a frame necessary to the works set in it (necessary to their very existence). This frame does not seem to worry artists who exhibit continually without ever considering the problem of the place in which they exhibit.

Whether the place in which the work is shown imprints and marks this work, whatever it may be, or whether the work itself is directly – consciously or not – produced for the Museum, any work presented in that framework, if it does not explicitly examine the influence of the framework upon itself, falls into the illusion of self-sufficiency – or idealism. This idealism (which could be compared to Art for Art's sake) shelters and prevents any kind of break ...[3]

In fact every work of art inevitably possesses one or several extremely precise frames. The work is always limited in time as well as in space. By forgetting (purposefully) these essential facts one can pretend that there exists an immortal art, an eternal work ... And one can see how this concept and the mechanisms used to produce it – place the work of art once and for all above all classes and ideologies. The same idealism also points to the eternal and apolitical Man which the prevalent bourgeois ideology would like us to believe in and preserve.

The non-visibility or (deliberate) non-indication/revelation of the various supports of any work (the work's stretcher, the work's location, the work's frame, the work's stand, the work's price, the work's verso or back etc ...) are therefore neither fortuitous nor accidental as one would like us to think.

What we have here is a careful camouflage undertaken by the prevalent bourgeois ideology, assisted by the artists themselves. A camouflage which has until now made it possible to transform 'the reality of the world into an image of the world, and History into Nature'.

1 It must be quite clear that when we speak of 'the Museum' we are also referring to all types of 'galleries' in existence and all other places which claim to be cultural centres. A certain distinction between 'museum' and 'gallery' will be made below. However the impossibility of escaping the concept of cultural location must also be stressed.

2 We are here referring more particularly to contemporary art and its profusion of exhibitions.

3 A detailed demonstration of the various limits and frames which generally constitute a work of art – painting, sculpture, object, readymade, concept ... – has been removed for technical reasons from the original text. However this subject matter can be found in other texts already published, such as: 'Critiques Limites' (a), 'Around and about' (b), 'Beware!' (c), 'Standpoints' (d), 'Exposition d'une exposition' (e).(a) Edited by Yvon Lambert Paris October 1970 (text in French)(b) in *Studio International*, London, June 1971 (c) in *Studio International*, London, March 1970 (d) in *Studio International*, London, April 1971 (e) in catalogue, *Documenta V* (text in German and French).

Daniel Buren, 'Function of the Museum' (1970), (Oxford: Museum of Modern Art, 1973) n.p; reprinted *Artforum*, 1973.

Seth SIEGELAUB
The Artist's Reserved Rights Transfer and Sale Agreement [1971]

The accompanying 3 page Agreement form has been drafted by Bob Projansky, a New York lawyer, after my extensive discussions and correspondence with over 500 artists, dealers, lawyers, collectors, museum people, critics and other concerned people involved in the day-to-day workings of the international art world.

The Agreement has been designed to remedy some generally acknowledged inequities in the art world, particularly artists' lack of control over the use of their work and participation in its economics after they no longer own it.

The Agreement form has been written with special awareness of the current ordinary practices and economic realities of the art world, particularly its private, cash and informal nature, with careful regard for the interests and motives of all concerned.

It is expected to be the standard form for the transfer and sale of all contemporary art, and has been made as fair, simple and useful as possible. It can be used either as presented here or slightly altered to fit your specific situation.

If the following information does not answer all your questions consult your attorney.

WHAT THE AGREEMENT DOES

The Agreement is designed to give the artist:

– 15% of any increase in the value of each work each time it is transferred in the future.

– a record of who owns each work at any given time.

– the right to be notified when the work is to be exhibited, so the artist can advise upon or (see Article Seven (b)) veto the proposed exhibition of his/her work.

– the right to borrow the work for exhibition for 2 months every five (5) years (at no cost to the owner).

– the right to be consulted if repairs become necessary.

– half of any rental income paid to the owner for the use of the work at exhibitions, if there ever is any.

– all reproduction rights in the work.

The economic benefits would accrue to the artist for life, plus the life of a surviving spouse (if any) plus 21 years, so as to benefit the artist's children while they are growing up. The artist would maintain aesthetic control only for his/her lifetime.

Although the contract may seem to alter the previous relationship between artist and art owner principally by putting new obligations on the owners, the Agreement really does some very good things for the collector. In return for these obligations, which are almost costless for the collector, he gets substantial benefits; the Agreement is designed:

– to give each owner the formalized right to receive from the artist (or his/her agent) a certified history and *provenance* of the work.

– to create and clarify a non-exploitative, one-to-one relationship between the artist and the owner.

– to maintain this relationship – what lawyers call 'privity' – between the artist and each successive owner of the work.

– to establish recognition that the artist maintains a moral relationship to the work, even as the collector owns and controls it.

– to give assurance to the owner that he is using the work in harmony with the artist's intentions.

WHEN TO USE THE AGREEMENT

The Agreement form has been designed to be used by the artist at the time of the FIRST TRANSFER – either by gift, or barter for things or services, or sale

of EACH INDIVIDUAL work of art –

either a painting, a sculpture, a drawing, a graphic, a

multiple, a mural, an immovable sculpture, a non-object work, or any other fine art you can think of

from the artist to ANYONE else –

either a friend, another artist, collector, museum, gynaecologist, lawyer, corporation, landlord, relative or dealer.

IMPORTANT: it is NOT for use when you lend your work to exhibitions or when you give it to your dealer on consignment. It IS for use when the dealer sells your consigned work.

In short, the Agreement form is to be used when you part with your work for keeps.

Its terms are effective and it requires a very simple procedure to keep it in effect with each successive owner of your work of art.

It requires the artist and the first owner of the work to fill out and sign the Agreement form and also, to affix a notice of the existence of the Agreement somewhere on the work of art itself.

HOW TO USE THE AGREEMENT

1 To begin, xerox or offset a number of copies of each page of the Agreement form. You will need at least 2 copies for each work you sell or give or trade away. (Save *this* copy to make future copies and so you can refer to this information.)

2 Fill out the contract forms – one copy for you, one for the new owner, and another copy of the last page only (from which you cut out the notice to affix to the work). Make sure that you fill it out legibly.

3 Follow the simple instructions in the margin of the Agreement form. Double check to make sure you have filled in the spaces that must be filled in and struck out what must be struck out.

IMPORTANT: Fill out only those parts of the Specimen TRANSFER AGREEMENT AND RECORD which identify the work and the *original* parties to the *original* Agreement [...] Be sure you fill out the specimen NOTICE.

You will note that the contract form speaks in terms of a 'sale' ('whereas Artist is willing to sell the Work to Collector and Collector is willing to purchase ... '); this doesn't mean you can't use it when you give a friend a work or pay your dentist with a painting or trade works with another artist. We have used the words 'sell' and 'purchase' only for the sake of simplicity (likewise, we use the term 'Collector' just because it is the most all-inclusive word for this purpose). Strictly speaking, even if you are giving or trading your work you are 'selling' it for the promises in the Agreement and whatever else you get.

This Agreement form is not a bill of sale or an invoice, nor is it a substitute. If the work is sold for money, prepare a separate bill of sale for your financial records.

In Article One, you enter the price OR value of the work; you, the artist, can put any value that you and the new owner agree upon. If the work is resold for a figure higher than the one you have entered as 'value', the owner will have to pay you 15% of the difference over that figure; obviously the higher the figure you put in, the better break the new owner is getting. If you are giving a friend a work or exchanging with another artist (you need two separate Agreements for the latter situation) you might want to enter a nominal value so that you would get some money, even if he/she later sells it for less than what your dealer would sell it for.

IMPORTANT: if there are rights given the artist under the Agreement form that you as the artist do not want, you strike them out. IMPORTANT: be sure to examine ARTICLE SEVEN (b); if you don't feel you must have a veto over all details of the future exhibition of the work, be sure your strike (b) out of ARTICLE SEVEN. Few collectors will want to buy a work if their right to lend it for exhibition is so restricted by someone else. If you give a work away you can leave (b) in, but that will make it very difficult for your friend to sell it. We have put (b) in because (a) is the least an artist should accept and (b) is the most he/she can ask for. If (a) is not enough for you but you don't need (b), have an attorney draft a short rider to the Agreement setting forth those specific controls over exhibition that you feel you must have.

4 You and the Collector should each sign both copies, yours and his, so they will both be legal originals.

5 Before the work is delivered, be sure that a copy of the NOTICE is affixed to the work. DO NOT cut it out of one of the originals. Put it on a stretcher bar or under a sculpture base or wherever else it will be aesthetically invisible yet easily findable. It should get a coat of clear polyurethane – or something like it – to protect it. It won't hurt to put several copies of the NOTICE on a large work.

If your work simply has no place on it for the NOTICE or your signature – in which case you should always use an ancillary document which describes the work, which bears your signature, and which is transferred as a (legal) part of the work – glue the NOTICE on the document.

PROCEDURE FOR FUTURE TRANSFERS. For future transfers, the owner makes three copies of the TRANSFER AGREEMENT AND RECORD form from his original (without the words 'SPECIMEN'). He then fills them out, entering the value or price that he and the next owner have agreed upon. Both the old and new owners sign ALL THREE copies of the dated TRANSFER AGREEMENT AND RECORD, each keeps one copy and the third is sent with the 15% payment (if any is required) to the artist or his/her agent. The old owner gives the new owner a copy of the original Agreement, so he will know his responsibilities to the artist and have the TRANSFER AGREEMENT AND RECORD form if HE transfers the work.

THE DEALER

If you have a dealer, he is going to be very important in getting people to sign the contract when he sells your work.

The dealer should make the use of the Agreement a policy of the gallery, thereby giving the artists in the gallery collective strength against those few collectors and institutions who do not really have the artist's interests at heart.

Remember, your dealer knows all the ins and outs that go down in the business of the art world. He knows the ways to get the few reluctant art buyers to sign the Agreement – the better the dealer the more ways and the more buyers he knows and the easier it will be. He can do what he does now when he wants things for his artists – give the buyer favours, exchange privileges, preferential treatment, discounts, hot tips, time, advice and all the other things that collectors expect and appreciate.

The Agreement only formalizes what dealers do now anyway; dealers try to keep track of the work they have sold, but now they can only rely on exhibition lists, catalogues, hit-or-miss intelligence and publicity to keep them up-to-date. The Agreement creates a very simple record system, which will automatically maintain a biography of each work and a chronological record of ownership. It is private, uncluttered and no dealer should ever have to hire another secretary to administer it; if each work engenders a dozen pieces of paper over the entire life of the Agreement, it will be a lot. The requirement of giving a *provenance* to the current owner is no more than what goes on today, but under this system it will be accurate and almost effortless.

A dealer shouldn't be expected to do this for nothing; it seems reasonable to compensate the dealer with some part of the 15% he/she is collecting for the artist, perhaps one-third of it.

When, as is often the case, an artist moves from one dealer to a more prestigious one, the first dealer might continue to collect whatever payments are occasioned by the resale of the earlier work.

When a dealer BUYS work directly from the artist (for resale or otherwise), they should write the intended RETAIL value of the work in their Agreement, NOT the actual amount of money the dealer is paying the artist, which would be less.

Getting the contract signed is mostly a state of mind. If your dealer does not think the benefits of the Agreement are important for you, he will have dozens of reasons why he can't get those few reluctant buyers to sign it; on the other hand, if he seriously wants you to have these benefits he will be able to overcome all those obstacles without losing a single sale.

THE FACTS OF LIFE: YOU, THE ART WORLD AND THE AGREEMENT

The general response to the preliminary draft of this Agreement form has been extremely favourable; the vast majority of people in the art world feel it is fair, reasonable and practical. A few have expressed certain reservations about whether or not people will actually use it. These reservations can be summed up in two basic statements:

– '... the economics of buying and selling art is so fragile that if you place one more burden on the collectors of art, they will simply stop buying art ... ', and

– '... I will certainly use the Agreement – if everyone else uses it ... '

The first statement is nonsense; clearly the art will be just as desirable with as without the Agreement and there is no reason why the value of any art should be affected at all, especially if this contract is standard practice in the art world – which brings us to the second statement. If there is a problem here, this statement reflects it: it is the concern of the individual artist or dealer that the insistence on the use of the contract will jeopardize their sales in a competitive market.

If we examine this notion carefully, we see it doesn't hold up.

ALL artists sell, trade and give their work to only two kinds of people:
– those who are their friends
– those who are not their friends

Obviously, your friends will not give you a hard time; they will sign the Agreement with you. The ONLY trouble will come when you are selling to someone who is not a friend. Since surely 75% of all art that is sold is bought by people who are friends of the artist or dealer – friends who dine together, see each other socially, drink together, weekend together, etc. – whatever resistance may appear will come only in respect to some portion of the 25% of your work that is being sold to strangers. Of these people, most will wish to be on good terms with you and will be happy to enter into the Agreement with you. This leaves perhaps 5% of your sales which will encounter serious resistance over the contract. Even this real resistance should decrease towards zero as the contract comes into widespread use.

In a manner of speaking, this Agreement will help you discover who your friends are.

If a collector wants to buy but doesn't want to sign the Agreement, you should tell him that all your work is sold under the contract, that it is standard for your work.

If he buys work only from those few artists who won't insist on using the Agreement he is being very foolish; non-use of this Agreement is a very dumb criterion for building one's collection.

There are other things that you can point out to the reluctant collector:
– first of all, it's not going to cost him anything unless your work appreciates in value. If that doesn't cut any ice, and he wants to keep *all* of whatever profit he might make with your work, you can simply write in a higher value for it, thus giving him a free ride for the first part of the appreciation he anticipates.
– if and when he sells your work and he owes you some payment, he doesn't necessarily have to pay you with money; you can give him credit against the purchase of a new work or take payment in services or something other than money.
– of course, if a collector buys a work without the contract when the use of the Agreement has become the standard practice for the artist, the collector will have to rely on sheer good-will when he later wants the artist (or his/her dealer) to appraise, repair or authenticate it. Why he should expect to find any good-will there is anybody's guess.

Is the collector really going to pass up your work because you want him to sign the contract? Work that he likes and thinks is worth having? If the answer is yes, given the fact that it won't cost *him* anything to give you the respect that you as the creator of the work deserve – if that will keep him from buying, he is being very stubborn and foolish and nobody can tell you how to illuminate him.

Using the contract doesn't mean that all your relationships in the art world will hereafter be strictly business or that you will have to enforce your rights down to the last penny. Friends will still be friends; you will be able to waive your rights to payments (in whole or in part), your right to make repairs, to grant reproduction rights, to be consulted – but they will be YOUR rights and the choices will be YOURS.

The Agreement form has been prepared to be used by any and all artists – known, well-known and unknown. Simply make a lot of copies and use it whenever you give, trade or sell your work. It will be effective from the moment you use it. The more artists and dealers there are using it, the better and easier it will be for everybody. It requires no organization, no dues, no government agency, no meetings, no public registration, no nothing – just your will to use it. Just plug it in and watch it go – a perfect waffle every time!

ENFORCEMENT

First, let's put this question in perspective: most people will honour the Agreement because most people honour agreements. Those few people who will try to cheat you are likely to be the same kinds who will give you a hard time about signing the Agreement in the first place. Later owners will be more likely to try to cheat you than the first owner, with whom you or your dealer have had some face-to-face contact, but there are strong reasons why both first and future owners should fulfill the contract's terms.

What happens if owner No. 2 sells your work to owner No. 3 and doesn't send you the transfer form? (He's not sending your money, either.)

Nothing happens. (You don't know about it yet.)

Sooner or later you do find out about it because it takes a lot of effort to conceal such sales and the grapevine will get the new to you (or your dealer) anyway. To conceal the sale, owner No. 3 has to conceal the work and he's not going to hide a good and valuable work just to save a little money. And if he ever wants to sell it, repair it, appraise it or authenticate it, he MUST come to you (or your dealer). When you do find out about such a transfer – and you will – you sue owner No. 2, who will be stuck for 15% of the increase based on the price to owner No. 3 OR on the value at the time you find out about it, which may be much higher. Clearly, a seller (in this case owner No. 2) would be extremely foolish to take this chance, to risk having to pay a lot of money just to save a little money.

As to falsifying values reported to the artist, there will be as much pressure from the new owner to put in a falsely high value as from the old owner to put in a low value. There are real difficulties inherent in getting two people to lie in unison, especially if it only benefits one of them – the seller. In 95% of the cases the amount of money to be paid to the artist won't be enough to compel the collectors to lie to you.

You will note that in the event you have to sue to enforce any of your rights under the Agreement, ARTICLE NINETEEN gives you the right to recover reasonable attorney's fees in addition to whatever else you may be entitled to.

SUMMATION

We realize that this Agreement is essentially unprecedented in the art world and that it just may cause a little rumbling and trembling; on the other hand, the ills it remedies are universally acknowledged to exist and no other practical way has ever been devised to cure them.

Whether or not you, the artist, use it, is of course up to you; what we have given you is a legal tool which you can use yourself to establish ongoing rights when you transfer your work. This is a substitute for what has existed before – nothing.

We have done this for no recompense, for just the pleasure and challenge of the problem, feeling that should there ever be a question about artists' rights in reference to their art, the artist is more right than anyone else [...]

Seth Siegelaub, 'The Artist's Reserved Rights Transfer and Sale Agreement', (Introduction to the Agreement Form, 24 February 1971). The Agreement was printed and distributed as a poster by the School of Visual Arts, New York, in 1971; all the information contained in the poster was also contained in the April 1971 issues of *Art News*, *Studio International* and *Arts Canada*. It is reprinted in facsimile in *Conception. Conceptual Documents 1968 to 1972*, ed. Catherine Moseley (Norwich, England: Norwich School of Art and Design, 2001), 69-76.

Robert SMITHSON
Cultural Confinement [1972]

Cultural confinement takes place when a curator imposes his own limits on an art exhibition, rather than asking an artist to set his limits. Artists are expected to fit into fraudulent categories. Some artists imagine they've got a hold on this apparatus, which in fact has got a hold of them. As a result, they end up supporting a cultural prison that is out of their control. Artists themselves are not confined, but their output is. Museums, like asylums and jails, have wards and cells – in other words, neutral rooms called 'galleries'. A work of art when placed in a gallery loses its charge, and becomes a portable object or surface disengaged from the outside world. A vacant white room with lights is still a submission to the neutral. Works of art seen in such spaces seem to be going through a kind of aesthetic convalescence. They are looked upon as so many inanimate invalids, waiting for critics to pronounce them curable or incurable. The function of the warden-curator is to separate art from the rest of society. Next comes integration. Once the work of art is totally neutralized, ineffective, abstracted, safe and politically lobotomized, it is ready to be consumed by society. All is reduced to visual fodder and transportable merchandise. Innovations are allowed only if they support this kind of confinement.

Occult notions of 'concept' are in retreat from the physical world. Heaps of private information reduce art to hermeticism and fatuous metaphysics. Language should find itself in the physical world, and not end up locked in an idea in somebody's head. Language should be an ever developing procedure and not an isolated occurrence. Art shows that have beginnings and ends are confined by unnecessary modes of *representation* both 'abstract' and 'realistic'. A face or a grid on a canvas is still a representation. Reducing representation to writing does not bring one closer to the physical world. Writing should generate ideas into matter, and not the other way around. Art's development should be dialectical and not metaphysical.

I am speaking of a dialectics that seeks a world outside of cultural confinement. Also, I am not interested in art works that suggest 'process' within the metaphysical limits of the neutral room. There is no freedom in that kind of behavioural game playing. The artist acting like a B.F. Skinner rat doing his 'tough' little tricks is something to be avoided. Confined process is no process at all. It would be better to disclose the confinement rather than make illusions of freedom.

I am for an art that takes into account the direct effect of the elements as they exist from day to day apart from representation. The parks that surround some museums isolate art into objects of formal delectation. Objects in a park suggest static repose rather than any ongoing dialectic. Parks are finished landscapes for finished art. A park carries the values of the final, the absolute and the sacred. Dialectics have nothing to do with such things. I am talking about a dialectic of nature that interacts with the physical contradictions inherent in natural forces as they are – nature as both sunny and stormy. Parks are idealizations of nature, but nature in fact is not a condition of the ideal. Nature does not proceed in a straight line, it is rather a sprawling development. Nature is never finished. When a finished work of twentieth-century sculpture is placed in an eighteenth-century garden, it is absorbed by the ideal representation of the past, thus reinforcing political and social values that are no longer with us. Many parks and gardens are re-creations of the lost paradise or Eden, and not the dialectical sites of the present. Parks and gardens are pictorial in their origin – landscapes created with natural materials rather than paint. The scenic ideals that surround even our national parks are carriers of a nostalgia for heavenly bliss and eternal calmness.

Apart from the ideal gardens of the past, and their modern counterparts – national and large urban parks – there are the more infernal regions – slag heaps, strip mines and polluted rivers. Because of the great tendency towards idealism, both pure and abstract, society is confused as to what to do with such places. Nobody wants to go on a vacation to a garbage dump. Our land ethic, especially in that never-never land called the 'art world' has become clouded with abstractions and concepts.

Could it be that certain art exhibitions have become metaphysical junkyards? Categorical miasmas? Intellectual rubbish? Specific intervals of visual desolation? The warden-curators still depend on the wreckage of metaphysical principles and structures because they don't know any better. The wasted remains of ontology, cosmology, and epistemology still offer a ground for art. Although metaphysics is outmoded and blighted, it is presented as tough principles and solid reasons for installations of art. The museums and parks are graveyards above the ground – congealed memories of the past that act as a pretext for reality. This causes acute anxiety among artists, in so far as they challenge, compete, and fight for the spoiled ideals of lost situations.

Robert Smithson, 'Cultural Confinement', *Artforum*, (October 1972); reprinted in *Robert Smithson: The Collected Writings*, ed. Jack Flam, (Berkeley and Los Angeles: University of California Press, 1996) 154-56.

Brian O'DOHERTY
Inside the White Cube: The Ideology of the Gallery Space [1976]

NOTES ON THE GALLERY SPACE

[...] All of us are now sure that the glut of history, rumour, and evidence we call the Modernist tradition is being circumscribed by a horizon. Looking down, we see more clearly its 'laws' of progress, its armature hammered out of idealist philosophy, its military metaphors of advance and conquest. What a sight it is – or was! Deployed ideologies, transcendent rockets, romantic slums where degradation and idealism obsessively couple, all those troops running back and forth in conventional wars. The campaign reports that end up pressed between boards on coffee tables give us little idea of the actual heroics. Those paradoxical achievements huddle down there, awaiting the revisions that will add the avant-garde era to tradition, or, as we sometimes fear, end it. Indeed, tradition itself [...] looks like another piece of bric-a-brac on the coffee table – no more than a kinetic assemblage glued together with reproductions, powered by little mythic motors and sporting tiny models of museums. And in its midst, one notices an evenly lighted 'cell' that appears crucial to making the thing work: the gallery space.

The history of Modernism is intimately framed by that space; or rather the history of modern art can be correlated with changes in that space and in the way we see it. We have now reached a point where we see not the art but the *space* first. (A cliché of the age is to ejaculate over the space on entering a gallery.) An image comes to mind of a white, ideal space that, more than any single picture, may be the archetypal image of twentieth-century art; it clarifies itself through a process of historical inevitability usually attached to the art it contains.

The ideal gallery subtracts from the artwork all cues that interfere with the fact that it is 'art'. The work is isolated from everything that would detract from its own evaluation of itself. This gives the space a presence possessed by other spaces where conventions are preserved through the repetition of a closed system of values. Some of the sanctity of the church, the formality of the courtroom, the mystique of the experimental laboratory joins with chic design to produce a unique chamber of aesthetics. So powerful are the perceptual fields of force within this chamber that, once outside it, art can lapse into secular status. Conversely, things become art in a space where powerful ideas about art focus on them. Indeed, the object frequently becomes the medium through which these ideas are manifested and proffered for discussion – a popular form of late Modernist academicism ('ideas are more interesting than art'). The sacramental nature of the space becomes clear, and so does one of the great projective laws of Modernism: As Modernism gets older, context becomes content. In a peculiar reversal, the object introduced into the gallery 'frames' the gallery and its laws.

A gallery is constructed along laws as rigorous as those for building a mediaeval church. The outside world must not come in, so windows are usually sealed off. Walls are painted white. The ceiling becomes the source of light. The wooden floor is polished so that you click along clinically, or carpeted so that you pad soundlessly, resting the feet while the eyes have at the wall. The art is free, as the saying used to go, 'to take on its own life'. The discreet desk may be the only piece of furniture. In this context a standing ashtray becomes almost a sacred object, just as the firehose in a modern museum looks not like a firehose but an aesthetic conundrum. Modernism's transposition of perception from life to formal values is complete. This, of course, is one of Modernism's fatal diseases.

Unshadowed, white, clean, artificial – the space is devoted to the technology of aesthetics. Works of art are mounted, hung, scattered for study. Their ungrubby surfaces are untouched by time and its vicissitudes. Art exists in a kind of eternity of display, and though there is lots of 'period' (late modern), there is no time. This eternity gives the gallery a limbo-like status; one has to have died already to be there. Indeed the presence of that odd piece of furniture, your own body, seems superfluous, an intrusion. The space offers the thought that while eyes and minds are welcome, space-occupying bodies are not – or are tolerated only as kinesthetic mannequins for further study. This Cartesian paradox is reinforced by one of the icons of our visual culture: the installation shot, *sans* figures. Here at last the spectator, oneself, is eliminated. You are there without being there – one of the major services provided for art by its old antagonist, photography. The installation shot is a metaphor for the gallery space. In it an ideal is fulfilled as strongly as in a Salon painting in the 1830s [...]

CONTEXT AS CONTENT

[...] the art of the 1970s locates its radical notions not so much in the art as in its attitudes to the inherited 'art' structure, of which the gallery space is the prime icon. The structure is questioned not by classic resentment but by project and gesture, by modest didacticism and phasing of alternatives. These are the hidden energies of the 1970s; they present a low-lying landscape which is traversed by ideas deprived of absolutes and powered by low-grade dialectics. No peaks are forced up by irreconcilable pressures. The landscape levels off partly because the genres involved in mutual recognition and avoidance (post-Minimalism, Conceptualism, Colour Field, Realism, etc.) are non-hierarchical – one is as good as another. The democracy of means contributed by the 1960s is now extended to genres, which in turn reflect a demythified social structure (the 'professions' now carry fewer rewards and diminished prestige). The Sixties still headline most people's perception of the Seventies. Indeed one of the 'properties' of Seventies art is the failure of Sixties critics to look at it. Measuring the Seventies by the Sixties is faulty but unavoidable (an artist's new phase is always judged in relation to the one previous). Nor does the skipped decade theory help – the Fifties revival turned out to be a bummer.

Seventies art is diverse, made up of non-hierarchical genres and highly provisional – indeed unstable – solutions. Major energies no longer go into formal painting and sculpture (young artists have a fairly good nose for historical exhaustion) but into mixed categories (performance, post-Minimal, video, tuning the environment), which present more temporary situations involving an inspection of consciousness. When necessary, Seventies art crosses media in a gentle, non-polemical way – understatement being a characteristic of its low profile. It tends to deal with what is immediately present to the senses and the mind, and so presents itself as intimate and personal. Thus it often appears narcissistic, unless this is understood as a mode of locating the boundary where a person 'ends' and something else begins. It is not in search of certainties, for it tolerates ambiguity well. Its intimacies have a somewhat anonymous cast since they turn privacy inside out to make it a matter of public discourse – a Seventies form of distancing. Despite this personal focus, there is no curiosity about matters of identity. There is great curiosity about how consciousness is constructed. Location is a key word. It telescopes concerns about *where* (space) and *how* (perception). *What* is perceived, one gathers from genres as widely removed as Photo-Realism and post-Minimalism, is not as important (though a dwarf called iconography schlepps around knocking at every door). Most Seventies art seems to attempt a series of verifications on an ascending scale: physical (out there); physiological (internal); psychological; and, for want of a better word, mental. These roughly correspond with available genres. The correlatives are personal space, perceptual revisions, exploration of time conventions and silence.

These verifications locate a body, mind and place that can be *occupied*, or at least partly tenanted. If Fifties man was a Vitruvian survivor and Sixties man composed of alienated parts held together by systems, Seventies man is a workable monad – figure and place, a transposition of figure and ground into a quasi-social situation. Seventies art does not reject the consequences of Fifties and Sixties art, but some basic attitudes have changed. The Sixties audience is rejected by Seventies art. Often there is an attempt to communicate with an audience that hasn't been interfered with by art, thus dislodging the wedge that 'art' has driven between perception and cognition. (The growth of alternative spaces across the country outside the formal museum structure is part of this – a change of audience, location and context that makes it possible for New York artists to do what they can't do in New York.) Seventies art remains troubled by history, yet so much of it is temporary it rejects the historical consciousness. It questions the system through which it presents itself, yet most of it passed through that system. Its makers are socially concerned but politically ineffective. Some of the dilemmas suppressed during the avant-garde era have come home to roost, and Seventies art is working through them in its rather elusive way.

With postmodernism, the gallery space is no longer 'neutral'. The wall becomes a membrane through which aesthetic and commercial values osmotically exchange. As this molecular shudder in the white walls becomes perceptible, there is a further inversion of context. The walls assimilate; the art discharges. How much can the art do without? This calibrates the degree of the gallery's mythification. How much of the object's eliminated content can the white wall replace? Context provides a large part of late modern and postmodern's art content. This is Seventies art's main issue, as well as its strength and weakness [...]

Brian O'Doherty, *Inside the White Cube: The Ideology of the Gallery Space*, first published in serial form in three issues of *Artforum*, 1976; first published in book form by Lapis Press, Santa Monica, 1986; expanded edition (Berkeley and Los Angeles: University of California Press, 1999) 13-15, 77-79.

Michael ASHER
On Works, 1969 to 1979 [1983]

[...] A critical analysis of the gallery structure was developed by a small number of artists in the late 1960s and early 1970s, at a time when they viewed their role as artists as that of individual producers with the right to control totally not only the production but also the distribution of their work. They believed that artists of previous generations had accepted uncritically and without qualification a distribution system (the gallery/market) which had often dictated the content and context of their work. These artists found themselves in a paradoxical situation; they either had to suppress the intentions of their work when it intersected with the gallery/market or they had to forgo the conventional distribution system altogether and give up their role as individual producers; or they could exhibit outside the traditional exhibition context, with the hope that a new production and distribution system could be developed. When their work conflicted with the commodity status required by the gallery system, these artists had no choice but to develop a new cultural context for their work before they could expect to function within the gallery nexus.

Interestingly enough these works were often seen as 'nonmaterial' since they seemed to function outside of the traditional context of the marketplace. Instead of deriving their cultural meaning from the conventional exhibition support, they functioned in a variety of locations. Ultimately, in the late 1970s, it was shown that these works had at least an economic materiality of their own and did not in fact operate outside of the cultural context. Some younger generation artists considered this discrepancy of theory and practice sufficient proof that once again the interdependence between production and distribution in the work of art could be totally ignored. The work as object reinstated the dealer and the distribution system to its original status. Some artists of this younger generation, possibly seeking a way out of object production and gallery/museum distribution similar to that of artists of the late 1960s and early 1970s formed production collectives, which attempted to keep their non-object-oriented production outside of the confines of the cultural industry.

Another phenomenon of the early 1970s, deriving from artists' anticommercialism and concern with the problem of commodification, was the development of the alternative space system for exhibition, although not necessarily for distribution. The alternative space relied for its funding on outside sources rather than the market for which the work was primarily produced. Alternative spaces made more works more frequently accessible than the commercial galleries, yet they falsified the work's commodity status, assuming that visibility alone would complete the reception process and that exchange value was not one of the work's features. The alternative space system provided visibility for the work regardless of specific interest, but it did not necessarily stand behind the work, with the full support necessary for reception within the culture. Paradoxically, the only way for a work to be fully received is through its initial abstraction for exchange value. To resolve these contradictions between the artist's interests and the functions and capacities of the alternative space, these institutions finally had to assume the role of being either a commercial gallery or a museum.

I felt at the time and still feel that the gallery is one essential context for the cultural reception of my work. What came under scrutiny in the Claire Copley work was the question of whether a work of art whose discourse disclosed the system of economic reproduction could possibly, at the same time, engender that economic reproduction for itself. Just as the work served as a model of how the gallery operated, it also served as a model for its own economic reproduction [...]

Michael Asher (in collaboration with Benjamin H.D. Buchloh), *Writings, 1973-1983, on works 1969-1979* (Halifax, Nova Scotia: The Press of the Nova Scotia College of Art; Los Angeles: The Museum of Contemporary Art, 1983) 100.

Benjamin H.D. BUCHLOH
Conceptual Art 1962–69: From the Aesthetics of Administration to the Critique of Institutions [1990]

[...] It was only logical that, on the occasion of Seth Siegelaub's first major exhibition of Conceptual Art, the show entitled 'January 5–31, 1969', Lawrence Weiner would have presented a formula that then functioned as the matrix underlying all his subsequent propositions. Specifically addressing the relations within which the work of art is constituted as an open, structural, syntagmatic formula, this matrix statement defines the parameters of a work of art as those of the conditions of authorship and production, and their interdependence with those of ownership and use (and not least of all, at its own propositional level, as a *linguistic definition* contingent upon and determined by *all* of these parameters in their continuously varying and changing constellations:

With relation to the various manners of use:
1. The artist may construct the piece
2. The piece may be fabricated
3. The piece need not to be built
Each being equal and consistent with the intent of the artist the decision as to condition rests with the receiver upon the occasion of receivership

What begins to be put in play here, then, is a critique that operates at the level of aesthetic 'institution'. It is a recognition that materials and procedures, surfaces and textures, locations and placement are not only sculptural or painterly matter to be dealt with in terms of a phenomenology of visual and cognitive experience or in terms of a structural analysis of the sign (as most of the Minimalist and post-Minimalist artists had still believed), but that they are always already inscribed within the conventions of language and thereby within institutional power and ideological and economic investment. However, if, in Weiner's and Barry's work of the late 1960s, this recognition still seems merely latent, it was to become manifest very rapidly in the work of European artists of the same generation, in particular that of Marcel Broodthaers, Daniel Buren and Hans Haacke after 1966. In fact an institutional critique became the central focus of all three artists' assaults on the false neutrality of vision that provides the underlying rationale for those institutions.

In 1965, Buren – like his American peers – took off from a critical investigation of Minimalism. His early understanding of the work of Flavin, Ryman and Stella rapidly enabled him to develop positions from within a strictly painterly analysis that soon led to a reversal of painterly/sculptural concepts of visuality altogether. Buren was engaged on the one hand with a critical review of the legacy of advanced modernist (and postwar American) painting and on the other in an analysis of Duchamp's legacy, which he viewed critically as the utterly unacceptable negation of painting. This particular version of reading Duchamp and the readymade as acts of petit-bourgeois anarchist radicality – while not necessarily complete and accurate – allowed Buren to construct a successful critique of both: modernist painting and Duchamp's readymade as its radical historical Other. In his writings and his interventions from 1967 onwards, through his critique of the specular order of painting and of the institutional framework determining it, Buren singularly succeeded in displacing *both* the paradigms of painting and that of the readymade (even twenty years later this critique makes the naïve continuation of object production in the Duchampian vein of the readymade model appear utterly irrelevant).

From the perspective of the present, it seems easier to see that Buren's assault on Duchamp, especially in his crucial 1969 essay *Limites Critiques*, was primarily directed at the conventions of Duchamp *reception* operative and predominant throughout the late 1950s and early 60s, rather than at the actual implications of Duchamp's model itself. Buren's central thesis was that the fallacy of Duchamp's readymade was to obscure the very institutional and discursive framing conditions that allowed the readymade to generate its shifts in the assignment of meaning and the experience of the object in the first place. Yet, one could just as well argue, as Marcel Broodthaers would in fact suggest in his catalogue of the exhibition *The Eagle from the Oligocene to Today* in Düsseldorf in 1972, that the contextual definition and syntagmatic construction of the work of art had obviously been initiated by Duchamp's readymade model first of all.

In his systematic analysis of the constituting elements of the discourse of painting, Buren came to investigate all the parameters of artistic production and reception (an analysis that, incidentally, was similar to the one performed by Lawrence Weiner in arriving at his own 'matrix' formula. Departing from Minimalism's (especially Ryman's and Flavin's) literalist dismemberment of painting, Buren at first transformed the pictorial into yet another model of opacity and objecthood. (This was accomplished by physically weaving figure and ground together in the 'found' awning material, by making the 'grid' of vertical parallel strips his eternally repeated 'tool', and by mechanically – almost superstitiously or ritualistically, one could say with hindsight – applying a coat of white paint to the outer bands of the grid in order to distinguish the pictorial object from a readymade.) At the same time that the canvas had been removed from its traditional stretcher support to become a physical cloth-object (reminiscent of Greenberg's notorious 'tacked up canvas [which] already exists as a picture'), this strategy in Buren's arsenal found its logical counterpart in the placement of the *stretched* canvas leaning as an object against support wall and floor.

This shifting of support surfaces and procedures of production led to a wide range of forms of distribution within Buren's work: from unstretched canvas to anonymously mailed sheets of printed striped paper; from pages in books to billboards. In the same way, his displacement of the traditional sites of artistic intervention and of reading resulted in a multiplicity of locations and forms of display that continuously played on the dialectic of interior and exterior, thereby oscillating within the contradictions of sculpture and painting and foregrounding all those hidden and manifest framing devices that structure both traditions within the discourse of the museum and the studio.

Furthermore, enacting the principles of the Situationist critique of the bourgeois division of creativity according to the rules of the division of labour, Buren, Olivier Mosset, Michel Parmentier and Niele Toroni publicly performed (on various occasions between 1966 and 1968) a demolition of the traditional separation between artists and audience, with each given their respective roles. Not only did they claim that each of their artistic idioms be considered as absolutely equivalent and interchangeable, but also that anonymous audience production of these pictorial signs would be equivalent to those produced by the artists themselves.

With its stark reproductions of mug shots of the four artists taken in photomats, the poster for their fourth manifestation at the 1967 Biennale de Paris inadvertently points to another major source of contemporary challenges to the notion of artistic authorship linked with a provocation to the 'audience' to participate: the aesthetic of anonymity as practiced in Andy Warhol's 'Factory' and its mechanical (photographic) procedures of production.

The critical interventions of the four into an established but outmoded cultural apparatus (represented by such venerable and important institutions as the Salon de la Jeune Peinture or the Biennale de Paris) immediately brought out in the open at least one major paradox of all conceptual practices (a paradox, incidentally, which had made up the single most original contribution of Yves Klein's work ten years before). This was that the critical annihilation of cultural conventions itself immediately acquires the conditions of the spectacle, that the insistence on artistic anonymity and the demolition of authorship produces instant brand names and identifiable products, and that the campaign to critique conventions of visuality with textual interventions, billboard signs, anonymous handouts and pamphlets inevitably ends by following the pre-established mechanisms of advertising and marketing campaigns.

All of the works mentioned coincide, however, in their rigorous redefinition of relationships between audience, object and author. And all are concerted in the attempt to replace a traditional, hierarchical model of privileged experience based on authorial skills and acquired competence of reception by a structural relationship of absolute equivalents that would dismantle both sides of the equation: the hieratic position of the unified artistic object just as much as the privileged position of the author. In an early essay (published, incidentally, in the same 1967 issue of *Aspen Magazine* – dedicated by its editor Brian O'Doherty to Stéphane Mallarmé – in which the first English translation of Roland Barthes' 'The Death of the Author' appeared), Sol LeWitt laid out these concerns for a programmatic redistribution of author/artist functions with astonishing clarity, presenting them by means of the rather surprising metaphor of a performance of daily bureaucratic tasks:

'The aim of the artist would be to give viewers information ... He would follow his predetermined premise to its conclusion avoiding subjectivity. Chance, taste or unconsciously remembered forms would play no part in the outcome. The serial artist does not attempt to produce a beautiful or mysterious object but functions *merely as a clerk cataloguing the results of his premise.*'[12] (italics added).

Inevitably the question arises how such restrictive definitions of the artist as a cataloguing clerk can be reconciled with the subversive and radical implications of Conceptual art. And this question must simultaneously be posed within the specific historical context in which the legacy of an historical avant-garde – Constructivism and Productivism – had only recently been reclaimed. How, we might ask, can these practices be aligned with that historical production that artists like Henry Flynt, Sol LeWitt and George Maciunas had rediscovered, in the early 1960s, primarily through the publication of Camilla

Gray's *The Great Experiment: Russian Art 1863–1922.*[3] This question is of particular importance since many of the formal strategies of early Conceptual Art appear at first glance to be as close to the *practices* and *procedures* of the Constructivist/Productivist avant-garde as Minimal sculpture had appeared to be dependent upon its *materials* and *morphologies*.

The profoundly utopian (and now unimaginably naïve) nature of the claims associated with Conceptual art at the end of the 1960s were articulated by Lucy Lippard (along with Seth Siegelaub, certainly the crucial exhibition organizer and critic of that movement) in 1969:

'Art intended as pure experience doesn't exist until someone experiences it, defying ownership, reproduction, sameness. Intangible art could break down the artificial imposition of 'culture' and provide a broader audience for a tangible, object art. When automatism frees millions of hours for leisure, art should gain rather than diminish in importance, for while art is not just play, it is the counterpoint to work. The time may come when art is everyone's daily occupation, though there is no reason to think this activity will be called art.'[4]

While it seems obvious that artists cannot be held responsible for the culturally and politically naïve visions projected on their work even by their most competent, loyal and enthusiastic critics, it now seems equally obvious that it was precisely the utopianism of earlier avant-garde movements (the type that Lippard desperately attempts to resuscitate for the occasion) that was manifestly absent from Conceptual art throughout its history (despite Robert Barry's onetime invocation of Herbert Marcuse, declaring the commercial gallery as 'Some places to which we can come, and for a while "be free to think about what we are going to do"'). It seems obvious, at least from the vantage of the early 1990s, that from its inception Conceptual art was distinguished by its acute sense of discursive and institutional limitations, its self-imposed restrictions, its lack of totalizing vision, its critical devotion to the factual conditions of artistic production and reception without aspiring to overcome the mere facticity of these conditions. This became evident as works such as Hans Haacke's series of *Visitor's Profiles* (1969–70), in its bureaucratic rigour and deadpan devotion to the statistic collection of factual information, came to refuse any transcendental dimension whatsoever.

Furthermore, it now seems that it was precisely a profound disenchantment with those political master-narratives that empowered most of 1920s avant-garde art that, acting in a peculiar fusion with the most advanced and radical forms of critical artistic reflection, accounts for the peculiar contradictions operating within (proto) Conceptual art of the mid to late 1960s. It would explain why this generation of the early 1960s – in its growing emphasis on empiricism and its scepticism with regard to all utopian vision – would be attracted, for example, to the logical positivism of Wittgenstein and would confound the affirmative petit-bourgeois positivism of Alain Robbe-Grillet with the radical atopism of Samuel Beckett, claiming all of them as their sources. And it would make clear how this generation could be equally attracted by the conservative concept of Daniel Bell's 'end of ideology' and Herbert Marcuse's Freudo-Marxist philosophy of liberation.

What Conceptual art achieved at least temporarily, however, was to subject the last residues of artistic aspiration towards transcendence (by means of traditional studio skills and privileged modes of experience) to the rigorous and relentless order of the vernacular of administration. Furthermore, it managed to purge artistic production of the aspiration and consumption (the last of the totalizing experiences into which artistic production had mimetically inscribed itself with credibility in the context of Pop art and Minimalism for one last time).

Paradoxically, then, it would appear that Conceptual art truly became the most significant paradigmatic change of post-war artistic production at the very moment that it mimed the operating logic of later capitalism and its positivist instrumentality in an effort to place its auto-critical investigations at the service of liquidating even the last remnants of traditional aesthetic experience. In that process it succeeded in purging itself entirely of imaginary and bodily experience, of physical substance and the space of memory, to the same extent that it effaced all residues of representation and style, of individuality and skill. That was the moment when Buren's and Haacke's work from the late 1960s onwards turned the violence of that mimetic relationship back onto the ideological apparatus itself, using it to analyze and expose the social institutions from which the laws of positivist instrumentality and the logic of administration emanate in the first place. These institutions, which determine the conditions of cultural consumption, are the very ones in which artistic production is transformed into a tool of ideological control and cultural legitimation.

It was left to Marcel Broodthaers to construct objects in which the radical achievements of Conceptual art would be turned into immediate travesty and in which the seriousness with which Conceptual artists had adopted the rigorous mimetic subjection of aesthetic experience to the principles of what Adorno had called the 'totally administered world' were transformed into absolute farce. And it was one of the effects of Broodthaers' dialectics that the achievement of Conceptual art was revealed as being intricately tied to a profound and irreversible loss: a loss not caused by artistic practice, of course, but one to which that practice responded in the full optimism of its aspirations, failing to recognize that the purging of image and skill, of memory and vision, within visual aesthetic representation was not just another heroic step in the inevitable progress of Enlightenment to liberate the world from mythical forms of perception and hierarchical modes of specialized experience, but that it was also yet another, perhaps the last of the erosions (and perhaps the most effective and devastating one) to which the traditionally separate sphere of artistic production had been subjected in its perpetual efforts to emulate the regnant episteme within the paradigmatic frame proper to art itself.

Or worse yet, that the Enlightenment-triumph of Conceptual art – its transformation of audiences and distribution, its abolition of object status and commodity form – would most of all only be shortlived, almost immediately giving way to the return of the ghostlike reapparitions of (prematurely?) displaced painterly and sculptural paradigms of the past. So that the specular regime, which Conceptual art claimed to have upset, would soon be reinstated with renewed vigor. Which is of course what happened.

1 Michel Claura, at the time the critic actively promoting awareness of the affiliated artists Buren, Mosset, Parmentier and Toroni, has confirmed in recent conversation that the reference to Warhol, in particular to his series *The Thirteen Most Wanted Men*, which had been exhibited at the Ileana Sonnabend Gallery in 1967, was quite a conscious decision.

2 Sol LeWitt, 'Serial Project No. 1, 1966', *Aspen Magazine*, 5-6, ed. Brian O'Doherty, 1967, n.p. [reprinted above, 211]

3 The importance of this publication in 1962 was mentioned to me by several of the artists interviewed during the preparation of this essay.

4 Lucy R. Lippard, 'Introduction', in *955.000* (Vancouver: The Vancouver Art Gallery, 13 January - 8 February, 1970), n.p.

Benjamin H.D. Buchloh, 'Conceptual Art 1962-1969: From the Aesthetics of Administration to the Critique of Institutions', *October*, 55 (Winter 1990) 136-43.

AFTERWARDS

Conceptual art challenged the aesthetic definition of the artwork as the object of a purely 'visual' pleasure and means of knowledge. In the process, it both expanded to infinity the material means of artistic production and endowed them with a newly strategic, self-consciously 'semiotic' function. In the international art world of the 1980s, this became the cue for a proliferation of new kinds of object-based work acting as, in Hal Foster's phrase, 'subversive signs'. There was a vogue in the art world for the writings of the post-situationist French thinker Jean Baudrillard on the 'simulacrum' and the political economy of signs. Victor Burgin reconceived conceptual art as the forerunner of postmodernism in glimpsing the possibility of 'the absence of presence'. During the 1990s, more explicitly historicist 'neo-conceptualisms' emerged, raising the question of whether conceptual art might not remain an 'unfinished project'.

Jean BAUDRILLARD
The Orders of Simulacra
[1981]

Three orders of appearance, parallel to the mutations of the law of value, have followed one another since the Renaissance:

Counterfeit is the dominant scheme of the 'classical' period, from the Renaissance to the industrial revolution;

Production is the dominant scheme of the industrial era;

Simulation is the reigning scheme of the current phase that is controlled by the code.

The first order of simulacrum is based on the natural law of value, that of the second order on the commercial law of value, that of the third order on the structural law of value [...]

THE HYPERREALISM OF SIMULATION

[...] defines a digital space, a magnetic field for the code, with polarizations, diffractions, gravitations of the models and always, always, the flux of the smallest disjunctive unities (the question/answer cell, that is like the cybernetic atom of meaning). We should compare this kind of control with the traditional repressive space, the police-space that still corresponded to a *signifying* violence. Space of reactionary conditioning that took its inspiration from the total Pavlovian disposition of programmed, repetitive aggressions, and which you find again multiplied in scale in 'hard sell' advertising and in the political propaganda of the 1930s. Raw industrial violence, aiming to induce behaviours of terror and of animal obeisance. All of that no longer has any meaning. The totalitarian, bureaucratic concentration is a scheme which dates from the era of the mercantile law of value. The system of equivalences imposes in effect the form of a general equivalent, and therefore the centralization of a global process. Archaic rationality compared to that of simulation; there is no longer a single general equivalent, but a diffraction of models that plays a regulatory role. No longer the form of the general equivalent, but that of distinctive opposition. From injunction you pass to disjunction by the code, from the ultimatum you pass to the solicitation, from the required passivity to models constructed all at once on the basis of the 'active response' of the subject, on its implication, its 'ludic' participation, etc., towards a total environmental model made out of incessant spontaneous responses of joyous feed-back and irradiating contact. This is the 'concretization of the general atmosphere', according to Nicolas Schöffer, the great festival of Participation, made out of myriads of stimuli, miniaturized tests, infinitely divisible question/answers, all magnetized by a few great models in the luminous field of the code.

Here comes the time of the great Culture of tactile communication, under the sign of the technico-luminous cinematic space of total spatio-dynamic theatre.

This is a completely imaginary contact-world of sensorial mimetics and tactile mysticism; it is essentially an entire ecology that is grafted on this universe of operational simulation, multi-stimulation and multi-response. We naturalize this incessant test of unsuccessful adaptation in assimilating it into animal mimesis. 'The adaptation of animals to the colours and forms of their milieu is a valid phenomenon for man' (Nicolas Schöffer), and the same for Indians, with their 'innate sense of ecology'! Tropisms, mimetics, empathy: the complete ecological Evangel of open systems, with positive or negative feedback, is going to rush into this breech, with an ideology of regulation by information which is only the avatar, according to a more flexible rationality, of Pavlov's reflex. So it is that we graduate from electro-shock therapy to bodily expression as a means of conditioning mental health. Everywhere the disposition of force and forcing yield to dispositions of ambience, with operationalization of the notions of need, perception, desire, etc. Generalized ecology, mystique of the 'niche' and of the context, milieu-simulation right up to 'Centres of Aesthetic and Cultural Re-Animation' foreseen in the VIIth Plan (why not?) and Centre of Sexual Leisure, constructed in the form of a breast, that will offer a 'superior euphoria due to a pulsating ambiance ... The workers from all classes will be able to penetrate into these stimulating centres'. Spatiodynamic fascination, like this 'total theatre' established 'according to a hyperbolic circular disposition turning around a cylindrical cone': no more scene, cut-off point, or 'regard': end of the spectacle as well as of the spectacular, towards the total environmental, fused together, tactile, aesthesia and no longer aesthetics, etc. We can think of the total theatre of Artaud only with black humour, his Theatre of Cruelty, of which this spatiodynamic simulation is only an abject caricature. Here cruelty is replaced by 'minimal and maximal stimulus thresholds', by the invention of 'perceptive codes calculated on the basis of saturation thresholds'. Even the good old 'catharsis' of the classical theatre of the passions has become today homeopathy by simulation. So goes creativity.

This also means the collapse of reality into hyperrealism, in the minute duplication of the real, preferably on the basis of another reproductive medium – advertising, photo, etc. From medium to medium the real is volatilized; it becomes an allegory of death, but it is reinforced by its very destruction; it becomes the real for the real, fetish of the lost object – no longer object of representation, but ecstasy of denegation and of its own ritual extermination: the hyperreal.

Realism had already begun this tendency. The rhetoric of the real already meant that the status of the latter had been gravely menaced (the golden age is that of language's innocence, where it doesn't have to add an 'effect of reality' to what is said). Surrealism is still solidary with the realism it contests, but augments its intensity by setting it off against the imaginary. The hyperreal represents a much more advanced phase, in the sense that even this contradiction between the real and the imaginary is effaced. The unreal is no longer that of dream or of fantasy, of a beyond or a within, it is that of a *hallucinatory resemblance of the real with itself*. To exist from the crisis of representation, you have to lock the real up in pure repetition. Before emerging in Pop art and pictorial neo-realism, this tendency is at work already in the new novel. The project is already there to empty out the real, extirpate all psychology, all subjectivity, to move the real back to pure objectivity. In fact this objectivity is only that of the pure look – objectivity at last liberated from the object, that is nothing more than the blind relay station of the look which sweeps over it. Circular seduction where you can detect easily the unconscious desire of no longer being visible at all.

This is certainly the impression that the new novel leaves: this rage for eliding sense in a minute and blind reality. Syntax and semantics have disappeared – there is no longer apparition, but instead subpoena of the object, severe interrogation of its scattered fragments – neither metaphor nor metonymy: successive immanence under the policing structure of the look. This 'objective' minuteness arouses a vertigo of reality, a vertigo of death on the limits of representation-for-the-sake-of-representation. End of the old illusions of relief, perspective and depth (spatial and psychological) bound to the perception of the object: it is the entire optic, the view become operational on the surface of things, it is the look become molecular code of the object.

Several modalities of this vertigo of realistic simulation are possible.

I The deconstruction of the real into details – closed paradigmatic declension of the object – flattening, linearity and seriality of the partial objects.

II The endlessly reflected vision: all the games of duplication and reduplication of the object in detail. This multiplication is presented as a deepening, that is for a critical metalanguage, and it was doubtless true in a reflexive configuration of the sign, in a dialectic of the mirror. From now on, though, this indefinite refraction is only another type of seriality. The real is no longer reflected, instead it feeds off itself till the point of emaciation.

III The properly serial form (Andy Warhol). Here not only the syntagmatic dimension is abolished, but the paradigmatic as well. Since there no longer is any formal flection or even internal reflection, but contiguity of the same – flection and reflection zero. Like those two twin sisters in a dirty picture: the charnel reality of their bodies is erased by the resemblance. How to invest your energies in one, when her beauty is immediately duplicated by the other? The regard can go only from one to the other, all vision is locked into this coming-and-going. Subtle way of murdering the original, but also singular seduction, where all attention to the object is intercepted by its infinite diffraction into itself (inverted scenario of the Platonic myth of the reunion of the separated halves of the symbol – here the sign multiplies like protozoans). This seduction is possibly that of death, in the sense that for sexual beings, death is possibly not nothingness, but simply the mode of reproduction anterior to the sexual. This generation by model along an endless chain that in effect recalls the protozoans and is opposed to a sexual mode that we tend, inaccurately, to confuse with life itself.

IV But this pure mechanization is doubtless only a paradoxical limit: the true generating formula, that which englobes all the others, and which is somehow the stabilized form of the code, is that of binarity, of digitality. Not pure repetition, but the minimal separation, the least amount of inflection between the two terms, that is to say the 'very smallest common paradigm' that the fiction of sense could possibly support. Combination of differentiation internal to the pictorial object and to the object of consummation, this simulation retreats in contemporary art to be no more than the minute difference that still separates the hyperreal from hyperpainting. The latter pretends to extend right up to a sacrificial effacement before the real, but you know how all these prestigious elements in painting resuscitate in this minute difference: all of painting takes refuge in the border that separates the painted surface and the wall. And in the signature metaphysical sign of painting and of the whole metaphysic of representation, at the limit where it takes itself for model (the 'pure look') and turns back upon itself in the compulsive repetition of the code.

The very definition of the real becomes: *that of which it is possible to given an equivalent reproduction*. This is contemporaneous with a science that postulates that a process can be perfectly reproduced in a set of given conditions, and also with the industrial rationality that postulates a universal system of equivalency (classical representation is not equivalence, it is transcription, interpretation, commentary). At the limit of this process of reproductibility, the real is not only what can be reproduced, but *that which is always already reproduced*. The hyperreal.

And so: end of the real, and end of art, by total absorption one into the other? No: hyperrealism is the limit of art, and of the real, by respective exchange, on the level of the simulacrum, of the privileges and the prejudices which are their basis. The hyperreal transcends representation (cf. J.F. Lyotard, *L'Art Vivant*, number on hyperrealism) only because it is entirely in simulation. The tourniquet of representation tightens madly, but of an implosive madness, that, far from eccentric (marginal) inclines towards the centre to its own infinite repetition. Analogous to the distancing characteristic of the dream, that makes us say that we are only dreaming; but this is only the game of censure and of perpetuation of the dream. Hyperrealism is made an integral part of a coded reality that it perpetuates, and for which it changes nothing.

In fact, we should turn our definition of hyperrealism inside out: *It is reality itself today that is hyperrealist*. Surrealism's secret already was that the most banal reality could become surreal, but only in certain privileged moments that nevertheless are still connected with art and the imaginary. Today it is quotidian reality in its entirety – political, social, historical and economic – that from now on incorporates the simulatory dimension of hyperrealism. We live everywhere already in an 'esthetic' hallucination of reality. The old slogan 'truth is stranger than fiction', that still corresponded to the surrealist phase of this aestheticization of life, is obsolete. There is no more fiction that life could possibly confront, even victoriously – it is reality itself that disappears utterly in the game of reality – radical disenchantment, the cool and cybernetic phase following the hot stage of fantasy.

It is thus that for guilt, anguish and death there can be substituted the total joy of the signs of guilt, despair, violence and death. It is the very euphoria of simulation, that sees itself as the abolition of cause and effect, the beginning and the end, for all of which it substitutes reduplication. In this manner all closed systems protect themselves at the same time from the referential – as well as from all metalanguage that the system forestalls in playing at its own metalanguage; that is to say in duplicating itself in its own critique of itself. In simulation, the metalinguistic illusion duplicates and completes the referential illusion (pathetic hallucination of the sign and pathetic hallucination of the real).

'It's a circus', 'It's theatre', 'It's a movie', old adages, old naturalistic denunciation. These sayings are now obsolete. The problem now is that of the *satellization of the real*, the putting into orbit of an indefinable reality without common measure to the fantasies that once used to ornament it. This satellization we find further naturalized in the two-rooms-kitchen shower that they have launched into orbit – to the powers of space, you could say – with the last lunar module. The banality of the earthly habitat lifted to the rank of cosmic value, of absolute decor – hypostatized in space – this is the end of metaphysics, the era of hyperreality that begins.[1] But the spatial transcendence of the banality of the two-rooms, like its cool and mechanical figuration of hyperrealism,[2] says only one thing: that this module, such as it is, participates in a hyperspace of representation – where each is already technically in possession of the instantaneous reproduction of his own life, where the pilots of the Tupolev that crashed at Bourget could see themselves die live on their own camera. This is nothing else than the short-circuit of the response by the question in the test, instantaneous process of re-conduction whereby reality is immediately contaminated by its simulacrum.

There used to be, before, a specific class of allegorical and slightly diabolical objects: mirrors, images, works of art (concepts?) – simulacra, but transparent and manifest (you didn't confuse the counterfeit with the original), that had their characteristic style and savoir-faire. And pleasure consisted then rather in discovering the 'natural' in what was artificial and counterfeit. Today, when the real and the imaginary are confused in the same operational totality, the aesthetic fascination is everywhere. It is a subliminal perception (a sort of sixth sense) of deception, montage, scenario – of the overexposed reality in the light of the models – no longer a production space, but a reading strip, strip of coding and decoding, magnetized by the signs – aesthetic reality – no longer by the premeditation and the distance of art, but by its elevation to the second level, to the second power, by the anticipation and the immanence of the code. A kind of non-intentional parody hovers over everything, of technical simulation, of indefinable fame to which is attached an aesthetic pleasure, that very one of reading and of the rules of the game. Travelling of signs, the media, of fashion and the models, of the blind and brilliant ambiance of the simulacra.

A long time ago art prefigured this turning which is that today of daily life. Very quickly the work turns back on itself as the manipulation of the signs of art: over-signification of art, 'academism of the signifier', as Levi-Strauss would say, who interprets it really as the form-sign. It is then that art enters into its indefinite *reproduction*: all that reduplicates itself, even if it be the everyday and banal reality, falls by the token under the sign of art, and becomes aesthetic. It's the same thing for production, which you could say is entering today this aesthetic reduplication, this phase when, expelling all content and finality, it becomes somehow abstract and non-figurative. It expresses then the pure form of production, it takes upon itself, as art, the value of a finality without purpose. Art and industry can then exchange their signs. Art can become a reproducing machine (Andy Warhol), without ceasing to be art, since the machine is only a sign. And production can lose all social finality so as to be verified and exalted finally in the prestigious, hyperbolic signs that are the great industrial combines, the quarter-mile-high towers or the number mysteries of the GNP.

And so art is everywhere, since artifice is at the very heart of reality. And so art is dead, not only because its critical transcendence is gone, but because reality itself, entirely impregnated by an aesthetic which is inseparable from its own structure, has been confused with its own image. Reality no longer has the time to take on the appearance of reality. It no longer even surpasses fiction: it captures every dream even before it takes on the appearance of a dream. Schizophrenic vertigo of these serial signs, for which no counterfeit, no sublimation is possible, immanent in their repetition – who could say what the reality is that these signs simulate? They no longer even repress anything (which is why, if you will, simulation pushes us close to the sphere of psychosis). Even the primary processes are abolished in them. The cool universe of digitality has absorbed the world of metaphor and metonymy. The principle of simulation wins out over the reality principle just as over the principle of pleasure.

1 The coefficient of reality is proportional to the imaginary in reverse which gives it its specific density. This is true of geographical and spatial exploration also. When there is no more territory which is virgin and therefore available for the imaginary, when the map covers the whole territory, then something like a principle of reality disappears. The conquest of space constitutes in this sense an irreversible threshold in the direction of the loss of the earthly referential. This is precisely the haemorrhage of reality as internal coherence of a limited universe when its limits retreat infinitely. The conquest of space follows that of the planet as the same fantastic enterprise of extending the jurisdiction of the real – to carry for example the flag, the technique and the two-rooms-and-kitchen to the moon – same tentative to substantiate the concepts or to territorialize the unconscious – the latter equals making the human race unreal, or to reversing it into a hyperreality of simulation.

2 Or that of the metal-plated caravan or supermarket dear to hyperrealists, or Campbell's Soup dear to Andy Warhol, or the Mona Lisa, since she too has been satellized around the planet, as absolute model of earthly art, no longer a work of art but a planetary simulacrum where everyone comes to witness himself (really his own death) in the gaze of the future.

Jean Baudrillard, *Simulacres et Simulations* (Paris: Galilée, 1981); trans. Paul Foss, Paul Patton, Philip Beitchman, 'The Orders of Simulacra', *Simulations* (New York: Semiotext(e), 1983) 83-159.

Victor BURGIN
The Absence of Presence: Conceptualism and Postmodernisms [1984]

The 'conceptual art' of the late 1960s to early 1970s was an affront to established values, hostility to the new work being often so intense as to suggest that more than merely aesthetic values were at stake. Today the excitement has died down. Recollected in tranquility conceptual art is now being woven into the seamless tapestry of 'art history'. This assimilation, however, is being achieved only at the cost of amnesia in respect of all that was most radical in conceptual art. I want to say something of what I believe has been repressed in the almost universal tendency, in the art world of the 1980s, to 'lose' an entire decade – the 1970s – as a period in which 'nothing happened'. As what characterizes the present moment in the art world is a certain notion of 'post-modernism', now being used to support a wholesale 'return to painting', then I shall address my remarks to these issues [...]

The idea of art as object began [...] with commodity connoisseurship in the Renaissance; it further developed within eighteenth-century aesthetics, primarily with Lessing, as a notion of the specificity of the 'visual' as against the 'literary'. Greenberg's aesthetics are the terminal point of this historical trajectory. There is *another* history of art however, a history of representations (hardly a dramatic revelation, and no more avant gardist, or 'fashionable', than is the Warburg Institute). For me, and some other erstwhile conceptualists, conceptual art opened onto that *other* history, a history which opens onto history. Art practice was no longer to be defined as an artisanal activity, a process of crafting fine objects in a given medium, it was rather to be seen as a set of operations performed in a *field* of signifying practices, perhaps centred on a medium but certainly not bounded by it. The field of concern was to be [...] the semiotic practices of a society seen, in their segmentation of the world, as a major factor in the social construction of the world, and thus of the values operative within it. As a statement of intent, this had the advantage of being sufficiently vague to allow *anything* to happen. The ensuing decade has been a period of working out and working through various specific responses to the problem of going beyond conceptual art. I have mentioned the re-emergence, out of conceptualism, of attention to the political; an initial, and continuing, consequence has been the production of work in which political issues of the day are represented – often, and it seems to me increasingly, by means of painting. Another response, one which has tended to eschew such means, has been based less upon a notion of the 'representation of politics' and more on a systematic attention to the *politics of representation*. It is in terms of this attention that a theory of the subject, involving a critique of humanist presuppositions, has become crucially important.

The theory of the subject which it is necessary to oppose to the traditional 'common-sense' picture of the individual is that of psychoanalysis. Psychoanalysis is a theory of the process by which the tiny human animal, the infant, is transformed into a socially functioning (or dysfunctioning) individual. It is often believed that psychoanalysis is 'only about subjective experience' to the exclusion of considerations of society and history, but nothing could be further from the truth – psychoanalysis is a theory of the *internalization* of the social in the formation of the individual. 'The motive of human society', wrote Freud, 'is in the last resort an economic one'. Just as Marx saw that the economic imperative, the need to produce the means to support life, gives rise to certain specific forms of society, so Freud saw that these same imperatives, and consequent social forms, engender particular structures of identity. One of Freud's books has the title *Civilization and its Discontents*; it contains no utopian prescription for a contented society, its message is that there can be no civilization *without* discontents. In submitting to the socioeconomic imperative the gratification of the instinctual demands of the individual must be deferred or denied, 'repressed'; as a result of this inevitable process of repression is the formation of an *unconscious* along with the conscious individual. 'To thine own self be true', wrote Shakespeare, when humanism was new; psychoanalysis shows us the difficulty, if not impossibility, of what is being asked of us here – not because of the material and social impediments which face us, but because the self we know by introspection – consciousness – does not know its unconscious; our self-image, and the images we have of others, are always to some degree *fictional*. The word 'fiction' here may bring with it such notions as 'narrative' and 'staging', a vocabulary of *representation* which is entirely appropriate to the field of human actions. To invoke Shakespeare again, 'All the world's a stage', but there is of course a difference between being in the world and being on stage; although we may speak of 'playing a role' in society, we are really thinking of such things as the jobs we may perform, we do not mean to imply that our *self*, our 'individuality' has in any way been 'written' elsewhere. The common-sense view, the one which just seems *obvious*, is that we are each born into the world as a little 'self' which is just as much simply *there* psychologically as it is physiologically – a little seed of individuality which over time sprouts to form the adult subject we eventually become; but psychoanalysis has built up a different picture: we become what we are only through our encounter, while growing up, with the multitude of representations of what we *may* become – the various positions that society allocates to us. There is no essential self which precedes the social *construction* of the self through the agency of representations. The most important question asked of any of us is a question which, at the time it is asked, we do not understand: 'Doctor, is it a boy or a girl?' – the answer to that question will determine the general form of the demands society will make of us. A normal baby has at birth either an anatomically male or female body, but it is not born with a correspondingly 'male' or 'female' psychology. For example, we are all familiar with a certain stereotype of the woman: an essentially passive and dependent creature whose emotions rule her reason and whose exclusive aim in life is homemaking and motherhood. This version of essential 'femininity' was in the quite recent past represented as being as inescapably natural to women as their biological gender. If it is more difficult to get away with such an oppressive stereotype today it is due to the achievements of the women's movement. In the field of cultural theory, feminism has set out to describe the way in which the collusion of women in their own oppression has in the past been achieved precisely *through* representation.

Feminist theorists have argued that the predominant traditional verbal and visual representations of women do not reflect, 'represent', a biologically-given 'feminine nature' – *natural*, therefore unchangeable; on the contrary, what women have to adapt to as their 'femininity', particularly in the process of growing up, is itself the *product* of representations. Representations therefore cannot be simply tested against the real, as this real is itself *constituted*, as everyday common-sense 'reality', *in* representations. (This is what it means to say: 'there is no reality outside representation'.) A search for, or contestation of, the 'truth' of the representation therefore becomes irrelevant (for all that this violates common-sense intuition); what it is to be interrogated is its *effects*. I have taken my example of the construction of subjectivity here from the recent history of feminism. It is comparatively recently that the perception and definition of the field of 'the political' has undergone a radical expansion beyond the traditional ghetto of party politics and considerations of 'class struggle' to now include, amongst other things, considerations of sexuality; 'sexuality' understood not in the reductive terms of the caricature in which it appears in the popular media, but in the complex and subtle understandings to be derived from psychoanalysis, where considerations of sexual difference are seen as governing relations within and between the individual, language, and power. It has now become possible to ask a question which could not previously even have been thought: 'What are *the forms* of visual imagery consequent upon the forms of construction of the fiction of the subject?'

I have spoken of the peculiar status of the *art object* in traditional aesthetics: an object of awe – part holy relic, part gilt-edged security. It is significant that, independently, both Marx and Freud, in their very different but mutually complementary projects, found it necessary to invoke a concept of fetishism. In Freud the fetish is that which 'stands in for' the absent female penis, reassuring the male in his anxiety that the same loss might befall *him*. As a teacher I have found that of all of Freud's ideas this is the one which provokes the most hostility and derision – especially from men. We should remember three things: first, Freud is not talking about ideas which are consciously held – they are unconscious; secondly, unconscious castration anxiety originates in early childhood when the very small boy first takes into account the fact that not all bodies are like his own – given the primitive state of his thinking and information the idea that the female body is a body from which something has been removed is a perfectly reasonable hypothesis (and subsequent knowledge will not erase the unconscious inscription of that phantasy); thirdly, in a patriarchal society, the little boy is becoming increasingly aware of the superior privileges afforded to men (TV action films alone would be enough to instill this idea) – his penis is not only a narcissistically highly-invested source of masturbatory pleasure, it is also his ticket of access to an exclusive club. No man escapes castration anxiety; although not all men become 'clinical' fetishists as a result (that is, unable to achieve sexual pleasure without the fetish), nevertheless they are all fetishists to some degree or other. Marx pointed to the fact of 'commodity fetishism' in capitalist society, Freud identified a primary contributory cause. (The consequences for a classic Marxist theory of ideology will be obvious to those familiar with it – no change in the form of the economy could have the least effect on fetishism.)

It might be objected that although clinical fetishism in *women* may be rare almost to the point of non-existence, many women nevertheless appear to fetishize the commodity. One response to this observation would be to point out that an object may be overvalued for many reasons other than fetishism. This does not, however, dispose of the question of female fetishism. The French psychoanalyst Jacques Lacan has broadened the Freudian notion of castration anxiety to include both men and women. Lacan observes that from the moment we are expelled from the womb and suffer that first physical separation from the mother's body our lives are a succession of experiences of loss (chronologically, the next painful experience of separation we must suffer is that of weaning from the breast, or its substitute). Such early experiences instill a sense of 'lack' in all of us, man and women alike, and much of our subsequent behaviour may be seen as compensatory attempts to eradicate this sense: hence the often surprisingly excessive overvaluation of some thing, or person, or idea. Lacan sees sexual difference, the presence or absence of the penis as simply the organizing metaphor for all other experiences of lack, and it is thus that he differentiates the 'phallus' – the symbolic term – from the 'penis' – the organ. The reason for this, Lacan's, often criticized '*phallocentrisrm*' is quite simply that, like Freud, he is describing the symbolic organization of the society in which we in the West actually live – which is *patriarchal*; to *describe* something does not entail either that one approves or disapproves of it, and in fact what Freud or Lacan themselves thought about the society in which they lived should be a fact of some indifference to us compared with the more critical question of what *use* we can make of their theories.

It is precisely because society *is* patriarchal that I believe we should keep in mind Freud's original account of fetishism, premised on the *male* body, when we consider the forms of our society and its cultural products. In Freud's account, the fetish is revered as irreducibly and irreplaceably *unique*; moreover, it has a punctual quality, it is not in any way diffuse or extended in space or time, it is as if *framed*. The comparison with the art object need not be laboured. The fetish is unique amongst signs (more correctly, 'signifiers'): it exists, paradoxically. to deny the existence of the very thing to which it refers – the absence of the female penis; in this it masquerades as entirely self-sufficient, not really a *sign* at all, but an *object* purely and simply. Again, the comparison with the art object is obvious. The fetish, in short, is *pure presence*, its function being precisely to deny absence, to fill the 'lack in being' – and how many times have I been told that photographs 'lack presence', that paintings are to be valued precisely *because of their* presence!

I began by referring to the hostility with which conceptual art was initially received – it was the attack upon the *object*, upon *presence*, which caused it. For a short time it seemed as if the *object*, as we know it, had indeed been got rid of. Without losing their interest in, or indeed love of, the painting and sculpture of the past, a whole generation of artist were no longer interested in repeating the hard-won successes of their forebears. This situation did not last long. An apparatus set up precisely to process *objects* soon produced a flurry of revivals of painting [...]

It seems likely that 'conceptualism' is destined, for the moment at least, to be represented as that 'movement' which, by undermining 'modernism', paved the way for 'post-modernism'. None of the 'isms' here, however, were, or are, unitary phenomena nor do such cultural phenomena simply give way to one another like television programmes in an evening's viewing. Aesthetically, culturally, politically, conceptualism comprised both tendencies for change and conservative tendencies. The same is true of this present period of 'postmodernism'. What we can see happening in art today is a return to the symbolic underwriting of the patriarchal principle by means of the reaffirmation of the primacy of *presence*. The function of the insistence upon presence is to eradicate the threat to narcissistic self-integrity (the threat to the body of 'art', the body-politic) which comes from *taking account* of difference, *division* (rather than effectively *denying* difference by valorizing one term of an opposition in order to suppress the other): division of form from content (political subject matter can be fetishized as 'presence' just as much as can the avoidance of any subject matter whatsoever); division of the private (art as 'private experience') from the social (which after all only maps the division of family life from work in industrial capitalist societies, including those in the East); division of the word from the image (I have written at length elsewhere about what a complete nonsense *that* is); division of the masculine from the feminine in the interests of producing 'men' and 'women'; division of theory from practice; division of the inside of the institution from its outside (for example, the almost complete isolation of art-historical and critical discourse from the wider analytical discourses – including psychoanalysis and semiotics – which surround them); and so on. What was radical in conceptual art, and what, I am thankful to say, has not yet been lost sight of, was the work it required – beyond the *object* – or recognizing, intervening within, realigning, reorganizing, these networks of differences in which the very definition of 'art' and what it *represents* is constituted: the glimpse it allowed us of the possibility of the absence of 'presence', and thus the possibility of *change*.

Victor Burgin, 'The Absence of Presence: Conceptualism and Postmodernisms', *1965-1975: When Attitudes Became Form* (Cambridge: Kettles Yard Gallery, 1984); reprinted in Victor Burgin, *The End of Art Theory: Criticism and Postmodernity* (London: Macmillan, 1986) 29-48.

Hal FOSTER
Subversive Signs [1985]

A writer – by which I mean not the possessor of a function or the servant of an art, but the subject of a praxis – must have the persistence of the watcher who stands at the crossroads of all other discourses (**trivialis** ***is the etymological attribute of the prostitute who waits at the intersection of three roads).***
– Roland Barthes, 'Leçon'.

The most provocative American art of the present is situated at such a crossing – of institutions of art and political economy, of representations of sexual identity and social life. More, it assumes its purpose to be so sited, to lay in wait for these discourses so as to riddle and expose them or to seduce and lead them astray. Its primary concern is not with the traditional or modernist proprieties of art – with refinement of style or innovation of form, aesthetic sublimity or ontological reflection on art as such. And though it is aligned with the critique of the institution of art based on the presentational strategies of the Duchampian readymade, it is not involved, as its minimalist antecedents were, with an epistemological investigation of the object or a phenomenological inquiry into subjective response. In short, this work does not bracket art for formal or perceptual experiment but rather seeks out its affiliations with other practices (in the culture industry and elsewhere); it also tends to conceive of its subject differently.

The artists active in this work (Martha Rosler, Sherrie Levine, Dara Birnbaum, Barbara Kruger, Louise Lawler, Allan McCollum, Jenny Holzer, Krzysztof Wodiczko ...) use many different forms of production and modes of address (photo-text collage, constructed or projected photographs, videotapes, critical texts, appropriated, arranged or surrogate art works, etc.), and yet they are alike in this: each treats the public space, social representation or artistic language in which he or she intervenes as both a target and a weapon. This shift in practice entails a shift in position: the artist becomes a manipulator of signs more than a producer of art objects, and the viewer an active reader of messages rather than a passive contemplator of the aesthetic or consumer of the spectacular. This shift is not new – indeed, the recapitulation in this work of the 'allegorical procedures'[1] of the readymade, (dadaist) photomontage and (pop) appropriation is significant – yet it remains strategic if only because even today few are able to accept the status of art as a social sign entangled with other signs in systems productive of value, power and prestige.

The situational aesthetics of this art – its special attention to site, address and audience – is prepared by the varied institutional critique of such artists as Daniel Buren, Michael Asher, Dan Graham, Hans Haacke, Marcel Broodthaers, Lawrence Weiner, John Baldessari and Joseph Kosuth. Yet if Kruger, Holzer *et al.* inherit the conceptual critique of the given parameters of art production and reception, they do so not uncritically. For just as the conceptual artists extended the minimalist analysis of the art object, so too these later artists have opened up the conceptual critique of the art institution in order to intervene in ideological representations and languages of everyday life. It is important to trace this genealogy (which is *not* intended as a conscription of these mostly feminist artists into a paternal tradition), especially in the face of the contemporary rejection of *all* institutional critique, indeed *all* avant-garde practice, under the cynical pretence that it is now 'exhausted' or 'academic' – a pretence that abets the forced resurrection of a traditionalist art largely given over to the manipulated demands of the market and the myths of the museum.

As is well known (in part because of a countermemory afforded by later artists and critics), the investigation of Buren, Asher, Haacke and Broodthaers focuses primarily on the institutional frame, and secondarily on the economic logic, of the modern art object. In critical writings and works *in situ*, these four artists (among others) have sought to reveal the ways in which the production and reception of art are institutionally predetermined, recuperated, used. Thus since 1965 Buren, with his banners and flags of alternately coloured and white (or transparent) stripes set in specific art and non-art spaces for specific periods of time, has stressed the *spatiotemporal* predisposition of the work of art by its institutional frame. And since 1969 Asher, with his (dis)placements of different gallery/museum objects, services and spaces, has fore-grounded the *functional* delimitation of all artistic activity sited there. Before his death in 1976, Broodthaers, with his fictitious museums (in which the roles of artist and curator are reversed), allegorically doubled the ways in which the museum *acculturates* heterogeneous objects and activities as art. And finally, since 1970 Haacke, with his detailed exposés of different museums, corporate benefactors and art collectors, has probed the *material* bases of the fine-art apparatus which, repressed, allows for its pretenses of social neutrality and cultural autonomy.

It was the need to expose this false idealism of art that initially led these artists to its 'mystical body', the modern museum, for it became clear that its supposedly supplemental role of 'preservation, enclosure and refuge' (Buren) actually preconditioned art production, predisposed it to an ideology of transcendence and self-sufficiency.[2] As opposed to the argument that avant-garde practice had attempted to *destroy* the institution of art,[3] these practitioners held that modern artists had not *comprehended* it – its conditions of production, exhibition and exchange; thus Buren in 1970: 'twentieth-century art is still so dependent on nineteenth-century art since it has accepted, without a break, its system, its mechanism and its function (including Cezanne and Duchamp) without revealing one of its main alibis, and furthermore accepting the exhibition framework as self-evident.'[4] To these artists transformation of this apparatus is contingent upon an exposing of its 'alibis', to which the work of Broodthaers and Haacke in particular is committed, and upon a foregrounding of its 'framework', in which Asher and Buren are engaged.

Clearly this is an important intervention, but it is a necessarily (de)limited one. It is limited, first of all, by its very attention to the institutional frame, which determines its production no less for being exposed in doing so; by its deconstructive posture, this work diminishes its own transformative potential. Secondly, posed within the gallery/museum, it is often referenced to the given forms of art (thus Buren's banners tend to be read in relation to easel painting and Asher's (dis)placements in relation to sculpture);[5] however residual, these categories are sustained even as they are demonstrated to be logically arbitrary, ideologically laden and/or historically obsolete. On a different score, the 'scientificity' of this practice tends to present the exhibitional limits of art as socially indiscriminate and sexually indifferent (this is perhaps the most obvious point of critical revision by feminist artists); it also cannot fully account for the systems of circulation in which the art work is involved *after* exhibition – the processes by which it becomes a discriminatory sign. (Of the four only Haacke *thematizes* the intertextuality of art and power, which allows him actually to use the limits of the gallery/museum as a screen for his political attacks.) Finally and familiarly, this practice runs the risk of reduction in the gallery/museum from an act of subversion to a form of exposition, with the work less an attack on the separation of cultural and social practice than another example of it and the artist less a deconstructive delineator of the institution than its 'expert'.

Such criticisms come after the fact, however, and are less failings of this practice than insights developed from it by later artists. Such legatees of conceptual art as Louise Lawler and Allan McCollum work to literalize more than to abolish the rules of art.[6] Though this may seem its own negation of institutional critique, it is instead its adaption to a code of art that now extends beyond conditions of production and exhibition. (As the 'title' of a recent work by Lawler – a photograph of a statue of Sappho and a bust of a patriarch – asks: 'Is it the work, the location or the stereotype that is the institution?') These later artists stress the economic manipulation of the art object – its circulation and consumption as a commodity-sign – more than its physical determination by its frame. And yet no less than the conceptual artists they too seek to reveal the definitional character of the supplements of art, only they tend to foreground the institutionally insignificant (the over-looked) rather than the transparent (the unseen) functions like the arrangement of pictures in galleries, museums, offices, homes, and forms like press releases and exhibition invitations which, thought to be trivial to the matter of art, in fact do much to position it, to determine its place, reception, meaning.

For Walter Benjamin the 'artistic function' as we still know it today – the isolated maker of art objects for the market – is 'incidental' to the determination of art by its exhibition (or exchange) value.'[7] It is this function, this determination that artists like Buren and Asher, Lawler and McCollum explore. But there is another 'function' that emerges when art passes from courtly patronage to the marketplace; the collector; and Lawler and McCollum are no less interested in this beast. In her 'Arrangements of Pictures' Lawler reframes in photographs the various ways in which different collectors – museums, corporations, the old and new rich – invest art with value by 'sumptuary expenditure', guarantee this value by reference to an institutional code of proper names and affiliations (a lineage of artists and works, a pedigree of owners and experts) and display it as a marker of taste, hierarchy, prestige or simply investment.[8] For his part McCollum is obsessed by the contractually adversarial rapport between artist and collector; this convention has 'inspired' him to produce thousands of surrogate paintings – objects which consist solely of a frame, mat and, for an image, a blank, with but minor differences in size and proportion.[9] With these decoys McCollum feeds the hunger for pictures felt by a social group dedicated to the mastery of both accumulation and signification but in such a way as to famish it. For he beckons the desire to spectate and buy – the desire for spectacle, for control through consumption – only to re-present the very emptiness which the picture-fetish is supposed to fill, only to turn the ritual of mutual confirmation into a charade of (mis)recognition: '*You see yourself in so far as you see me see myself, yet I see myself only as I see that I am seen. Our reciprocal surveillance is sustained through my artwork, which thrives. Our misplaced assignations of authority and our fraudulent identifications are thus mediated into a dislocated ritual of self-congratulation, strange looks, and the exchange of money for false tokens.*'[10]

This is not to suggest that these artists neglect the exhibition framework. In a 1978 show at Artists Space in New York, Lawler installed an 1824 painting of a racehorse (borrowed from the New York Racing Association) with two stage lights, one set above the picture and aimed at the viewer, the other directed outside through a gallery window. Here Lawler did indeed make 'the element of an exhibition the subject of her production',[11] but she also posed a funny, provocative conflation of exhibited painting and displayed thoroughbred that exposed them both as tokens in the sumptuary production of value and prestige. (Are not art world and racetrack alike based *on* a closed system of training and grooming, of handicapping and betting, of investment, competition and auction? After all we do call galleries 'stables.') More recently, Lawler and McCollum collaborated on an installation that fore-grounded in a different way the status of art as display: 100 hydrocal sculpture pedestals set on bases and bathed in spectacular light, titled *For Presentation and Display: Ideal Settings* (1984). Here the abstraction of modern sculpture, its passage from sited, figurative monument to siteless, autonomous sign,[12] was decoded as its 'abstraction' by the commodity-form as if sculpture had not absorbed its base in the pursuit of aesthetic purity so much as spectacle had swallowed art in the pure display of the commodity. Exhibition value, once productive of an autonomous 'artistic function', here consumed it entirely.

This displacement of art by its own support, by its own spectacle, is both a characteristic strategy and a historical demonstration of Lawler and McCollum. The functional indifference of art objects produced in the studio/gallery/museum nexus, remarked by Buren, is shown by McCollum to be no less determined by the market. His 'empty' surrogates make explicit the reduction of content to form in the exchange of like for like as well as the general equivalence of objects in a serial mode of production. For her part Lawler makes clear the division of labour that produces the hierarchical functions and generic forms of art (i.e., who creates what for whom in what order of privilege and value). This institutional order of names, services and forms is then confused by the (relative) anonymity of her interventions, by her assumption of different guises (arranger, publicist, etc.), by her production as art of such giveaways as gallery matchbooks (supplements which again seem superfluous but are crucial to the spectacle of art). Yet just as it may be unclear whether the McCollum surrogates 'dislocate' the ritual of exchange or replicate the status of the object become sign (delivered up in all its minor difference for our consumption), so too it may be unclear whether the Lawler gambits subvert the mechanisms of art exhibition, circulation and consumption or play them to the hilt. (Do her giveaways update the Duchamp readymade, substitute use value for exchange value, or aestheticize use one more time?) Like a dye in the bloodstream, the work of these artists does delineate the circulation system of art, but it also operates within its terms. If artists like Buren and Asher may become guardians of the demystified myths of the art museum, then artists like Lawler and McCollum may indeed serve as 'ironic collaborators'[13] of its market apparatus.

Other artists, no less influenced by conceptual work, have sought to reflect critically on representations outside the art apparatus and from there to turn back to address discourses within it. For these artists ideology cannot be reduced to one language, then critiqued, or the institution of art to one space, then charted. Such signs and sites are not simply given, open to manipulation only:[14] other meanings can be constructed, other publics sought out. Specifically, the position of the subject must be taken into account, and it is at the point of production of the subject rather than of the art object that this work intervenes. Barbara Kruger takes a feminist tack: through different collisions of images and texts she seeks to dispel the secular nature of representations that subject women to the gaze of a univocal male subject, 'to welcome a female spectator in the audience of men.' Jenny Holzer's is a "situationist"' strategy: in a variety of signs she presents opinions, credos, anecdotes in a way which both manifests the domination active in everyday discourse and confounds it by sheer anarchic display. In this way the work of such artists seeks to disorient the law, to call language into crisis. This is what ideology cannot afford, for it tends to operate in language that denies its status as such: stereotypical language. Yet, by the same token, this art cannot afford to take the demonstrations of institutional critique for granted. For without specific attention to its own institution this critical practice, even now well received in the gallery/museum nexus, will be recuperated as yet another avant-gardist exercise, a mere manipulation rather than an active transformation of social signs.

A strong sense of duty imprisons you.
Abuse of power comes as no surprise.
Alienation produces eccentrics or revolutionaries
Ambivalence can ruin your life.

Both Kruger and Holzer are concerned with the power at work in social representations; Holzer's site of intervention is language. As Barthes wrote: '*Language is legislation, speech is its code ... To utter a discourse is not, as is too often repeated, to communicate; it is to subjugate. ...Language – the performance of a language system – is neither reactionary nor progressive; it is quite simply fascist.*'[15]

In her texts Holzer seeks to undo this 'fascism', to display the censorious circularity of our idiolects. Her work suggests not only how language subjects us but how we may disarm it; and here again the lactic is subversive complicity: 'it is within speech that speech must be fought, led astray – not by the message of which it is the instrument, but by the play of words of which it is the theatre.'[16] With Holzer this 'theatre' becomes a bedlam of voices which mocks the certainty of personal credos and the neutrality of public discourse (e.g., of the mass media). Her texts often function as a dictionary of received ideas to deplete our *ideologemes*, to rob them of the 'fascist' power to compel.

This bedlam-effect is strongest in her *Truisms* (1977), an alphabetical list of statements which together confound all order and logic. First presented as public-information posters on New York City walls (and since as T-shirts, electronic signs, plaques, works of art), the *Truisms* not only 'place in contradiction certain ideological structures that are usually kept apart'[17] but set them into open conflict. This contestation-by-contradiction is also contextual, for the *Truisms* expose the false homogeneity of the signs on the street among which they are often placed. An encounter with them, then, is like an encounter with the Sphinx: though one is given answers, not asked questions, initiation into our Theban society is much the same: entanglement in discourse.

This entanglement is a continual displacement – to the point where the reader begins to see, first, that (s)he is not an autonomous individual of free beliefs so much as a subject inserted into language and, second, that this insertion can be changed. The experience of truistic entrapment cedes to a feeling of anarchic release, for the *Truisms* expose the coercion that is usually hidden in language, and once exposed it appears ridiculous. Essentially, this release comes of the recognition that meaning is a rhetorical construction of will more than a Platonic apprehension of an idea – that, however directed towards truth, it is finally based on power. This is not a nihilistic insight: it allows for resistance based on truth constructed through contradiction. And this indeed is the one genuine truth that the *Truisms* express: that only through contradiction can one construct a self that is not entirely subjected. (This truth, that of dialectics, denies its own closure as a truth: this is what makes it true.)

Entanglement in discourse is most extreme in the *Inflammatory Essays* (1979–82), which also appeared first as street posters and then as signs, books, art works. Here again the voices are provocative: imperative commands and subjunctive inducements mix with the impersonal mode of truth. Yet the *Essays* are more arguments than statements, and they do not taxonoimize ideologies so much as hyperbolize political rhetoric (in these tracts poles of left and right threaten to implode).[18] Thus even more than the *Truisms*, the *Essays* are concerned with the *force* of language: they exhibit how different ideologies position and pervert us as subjects of discourse. Some voices insinuate, others demand. A few almost convince, but finally each voice is convinced, conquered by its own speech. This closure is of the kind noted by Barthes in political language where reality is prejudged, and naming and judging are one: 'A history of political modes of writing would therefore be the best of social phenomenologies.'[19] Together the *Truisms* and the *Essays* evoke such a phenomenology.

In 1981 through 1983 Holzer worked (in part with Peter Nadin) on the *Living* series. With these signs and plaques Holzer functioned more in given art spaces; at the same time she drew more on everyday talk. Indeed, the language of the *Living* series is omnivorous; as one set of texts, 'Eating Through Living',[20] suggests, living *is* eating – consuming and being consumed by speech. In the *Living* texts especially, Holzer meets the subtle subjections active in social discourse with wit and play. That is, she leads language astray. Thus, for example, she may turn our official tongue of efficacy and etiquette into its own parody:

> *Once you know how to do something you're prone to try it again. An unhappy example is compulsive murder. This is not to be confused with useful skills acquired through years of hard work.*

Or she may beguile officialdom with metal signs and bronze plaques that publicize the private (*The mouth is interesting because it is one of those places where the dry outside moves towards the slippery inside*) or pronounce the socially repressed (*It takes a while before you can step over inert bodies and go ahead with what you were wanting to do*). A sign is a social directive; a plaque is a marker of official truth which exalts a place or proper name as the very presence of history. The Holzer signs and plaques foil this marking, traduce this official language and proper speech which, like an old chauvinist in the hands of a supple feminist, undoes itself [...]

In her panels, posters and books Kruger appropriates photographs (mostly of women) from media sources, blows them up and crops them severely, then combines them with short texts. She has alternated image and text in a way reminiscent of photo-stories, montaged them in a parody of display ads, and combined them in the declarative address of signs in the street. In her first series of photo-texts Kruger represented various images (e.g., of a woman slumped among fashion magazines or with her hands clasped in prayer) stamped will) single words (e.g., 'deluded' or 'perfect') that rendered them invalid, took them out of circulation. This 'inception' of the stereotype is her principal device, yet in these early works it was only blasted and its maimed reality not redeemed. Such foreclosure implied not only that such cultural fictions and subject positions are more absolute than they are but also that the artist is in a transcendent relation to them.

Aware of these problems, Kruger has suggested that image appropriation, rather than question 'the "original" use and exchange value' of representations, contradict 'the surety of our initial readings' and strain 'the appearance of naturalism', may in fact confirm them.[21] Her later work evades this closure, for in its oscillation 'from implicit to explicit, from inference to declaration'[22] neither photograph nor text, neither connotation nor denotation is privileged as a stable site or mode of truth; in fact, the usual coordination of the two (as employed in the media to fix unstable meanings) is undone. More important, her photo-texts shift address and block identification in a way that allows for no certain or essential subject position. This is not to say that they are arbitrary. Her re-minting of the image is as motivated as her target is specific: the transparent naturalism of masculine readings which position women as objects of scopophilic pleasure (*We are being made spectacles of*); as figures of nature or otherness which support the patriarchal order of things (*We won't play nature to your culture*); as fetishistic images which serve to allay the anxiety (*I am your immaculate conception*) about the castration that woman otherwise suggests to man (*I am your almost nothing*). It is this phallocentric surety that Kruger literally contradicts. First, she sets up 'suave entrapments' with the very representations which position 'woman as image and man as bearer of the look',[23] then manipulates that pose, catches out that gaze. Though as seductive as any mass-media ad, her photo-texts work to reflect the masculine look that subjects women via a false feminine ideal and to block the feminine identification that submits to this construct [...]

1 See Benjamin H.D. Buchloh, 'Allegorical Procedures: Appropriation and Montage in Contemporary Art', *Artforum* (September 1982) 43-56.

2 See in particular Daniel Buren, 'Function of the Museum', Museum of Modern Art, Oxford, 1970; reprinted in *Artforum* (September 1973) [see above, 273-74].

3 See Peter Bürger, *Theory of the Avant-Garde*, trans. Michael Shaw (Minneapolis: University of Minnesota Press, 1984). First published in 1974, this important essay takes no account of the artists mentioned here who are involved in institutional critique.

4 Buren, 'Function of the Museum', *op. cit.* Duchamp may have 'accepted' this system, but he was certainly aware of its function. In *La boite-en-valise* (1936-41), a collection of miniature reproductions of his works, he in effect acculturated his own art in his own museum allegorically and before the fact.

5 See Douglas Crimp, 'The End of Painting', *October*, 16 (Spring 1981): 69-86; and Buchloh, 'Michael Asher and the Conclusion of Modernist Sculpture', in *Performance, Text(e)s & Documents*, ed. Chantal Pontbriand (Montreal: les editions Parachute, 1981) 55-65.

6 Yet this remains the measure of art devoted to institutional critique: 'the ambition, not of fitting in more or less adequately with the game, nor even of contradicting it, but of abolishing its rules by playing with them, and playing another game, on another or the same ground, as a dissident' (Buren, *Reboundings*, trans. Philippe Hunt [Brussels: Daled & Gevaert, 1977], 73).

7 Walter Benjamin, 'The Work of Art in the Age of Mechanical Reproduction', in *Illuminations*, ed. Hannah Arendt, trans. Harry Zohn (New York: Schocken Books, 1969), 225.

8 See Andrea Fraser, 'In and Out of Place', *Art in America* (June 1985), the notion 'sumptuary expenditure' is derived from Jean Baudrillard ('Art Auction: Sign Exchange and Sumptuary Value', in *For a Critique of the Political Economy of the Sign*, trans. Charles Levin [St. Louis: Telos Press, 1981], 112-22). In her work Lawler seems to catch out a new motivation or emphasis in art patronage - beyond noble social obligation or subtle

cultural legitimation to outright economic manipulation.

9 See Craig Owens, 'Allan McCollum: Repetition and Difference', *Art in America* (September 1983): 130-32.

10 Allan McCollum quoted in press release for 1985 Cash/Newhouse Gallery show.

11 Buchloh, 'Allegorical Procedures', 48. The analogy below between the art world and the race track is hinted at by Baudrillard in 'Art Auction'.

12 See Rosalind Krauss, 'Sculpture in the Expanded Field', in *The Anti-Aesthetic: Essays on Postmodern Culture*, ed. Hal Foster (Port Townsend: Bay Press, 1983).

13 Fraser, 'In and Out of Place'. I disagree with her representation of this work as a 'counterpractice'.

14 Apropos this remark, Norman Bryson writes of Roland Barthes: 'analysis omits the essential term of transformation through labour on which any theory of practice worthy of the name must rest; an omission accomplished by conceiving the signs within the social formation (discourse) as a finite mass, subject only to redistribution: this is a mercantilist theory of the signifying economy' (*Vision and Painting: The Logic of the Gaze* [New Haven; Yale University Press, 1983] 141).

15 Roland Barthes, 'Lecture in Inauguration of the Chair of Literary Semiology, Collège de France', *October*, 8 (Spring 1979) 5.

16 Ibid.

17 Dan Graham, 'Signs', *Artforum* (April 1981) 39.

18 Some of the *Essays* were published in the *Black Book* (a parody of the manuals of messianic leaders?), others with the *Truisms* in *Abuse of Power Comes As No Surprise* (Halifax: The Press of the Nova Scotia College of Art and Design, 1983).

19 Barthes, *Writing Degree Zero*, trans. Annette Lavers and Colin Smith (New York; Hill and Wang, 1978) 25.

20 See 'The Expressive Fallacy' elsewhere in this volume [*Recodings: Art, Spectacle, Cultural Politics*].

21 Barbara Kruger, *Screen*, 23:1 (1982).

22 Ibid.

23 Laura Mulvey, ('Visual Pleasure and Narrative Cinema', *Screen*, 16:3 (Autumn 1975); reprinted in *Art After Modernism*, 366. For important essays on Kruger and related matters, see Craig Owens, 'The Medusa Effect, or The Specular Ruse', and Jane Weinstock, 'What She Means, to You', in *We Won't Play Nature to Your Culture* (London: Institute of Contemporary Arts, 1983), 5-16; and Kate Linker, 'Representation and Sexuality', *Parachute*, 32 (Fall 1983), reprinted in *Art After Modernism*.

Hal Foster, *Recodings: Art, Spectacle, Cultural Politics* (Seattle: Bay Press, 1985) 98-222.

14. Richard Prince

Michael NEWMAN
Conceptual Art from the 1960s to the 1990s: An Unfinished Project? [1996]

[...] It is clear that since the late 1980s there has been an upsurge in activity by artists that could and have been called 'conceptual', and artists whose work emerged from Conceptual art – Jeff Wall and Rodney Graham from Canada, James Coleman from the Republic of Ireland would be obvious examples of the latter – have been receiving increasing attention. [...]

In much Conceptual art extreme positivism meets hyper-idealism, to the exclusion of questions of subjectivity and its construction – which, while already present in the Conceptual generation (Eleanor Antin) were taken up by a subsequent generation of feminist Conceptualists, including Mary Kelly. Revisionist accounts of Conceptual art have largely been through the issues raised by subsequent developments in feminist post-Conceptualism, and the artists whose critical stock has risen – Dan Graham, Vito Acconci, Bruce Nauman, Bas Jan Ader – have tended to be those whose interests were in subjectivity rather than the more positivistic and idealist-tautological artists. The other area of interest has been in those who took an architectural turn – Michael Asher, Dan Graham, Robert Smithson, Gordon Matta-Clark – completing the telos outlined by Buchloh from the end of painting ('Black Square') to the end of sculpture (Minimalist cube) to institutional intervention in an architectural site (Asher and Broodthaers), which has provided legitimation for the current interest in installation and curation (even if such 'interventions' have largely lost their critical point and turned into promotion with low overhead costs). The problem now is to provide a constructive critique of Conceptual art which does not turn into an assault on criticality, as it did in the iconophilic 'counter-reformation' of the 1980s which followed the iconoclastic 'reform' of Conceptual art.

INTERNAL AND EXTERNAL DEVELOPMENTS

The problems seem to arise in so far as the oppositional stance taken by Conceptual art remains abstract. Therefore we might suppose that the Conceptual art that succeeds would be that which takes a more dialectical relation to its object of critique, maintaining its identity at the same time as its difference. This is the case with Graham and Asher, the condition of whose interventions lies in maintaining the identity of their art with the conditions that it is supposed to critique (the museum, the system of publicity). But, conversely, the identity is not so complete that the only way out is the dead end of abstract negativity. And the difference lies in precisely what the artist cannot control, the dimension of social interaction where possibilities of subjectivity other than totally reified and dominated are intimated.

Only in this way is Conceptual art prevented from becoming merely academic. Becoming academic is a particular problem for Conceptual art since it is actually more dependant on institutions – including, particularly in Britain, teaching institutions – for its existence than painting and sculpture. For Conceptual art existence is identical with recognition (which is both its strength and its weakness) whereas for the 'object' arts material existence and recognition are more able to be distinguished. Thus, ironically, in the very act of drawing critical attention to the institutionalization of art Conceptual art renders itself all the more dependent on those institutions that reify art and recuperate cognitive critical discourse, including its own. This is one reason why artists formed by the student movements who began with 'linguistic' Conceptualism, turned increasingly to object making of one form or another, most frequently using photography, film and video (Victor Burgin, James Coleman, Jeff Wall, *et al.*) but also painting (Art & Language). Their problem then became how to produce objects which, while inevitably becoming commodities, could at the same time enable a critical reflection on the process as one involving social relations and institutions, rather than falling back on a reifying perceptualism.

In relation to this critique, as I have already suggested, certain subsequent developments *internal* to Conceptual art may be better understood. Perhaps most important is the emphasis on subjectivity and turn to psychoanalysis, from the mid 1970s, coming from film theory (Laura Mulvey being especially influential), Althusser and Lacan (1968 version of the Frankfurt School's attempt to fuse Marx and Freud), and feminism (the fusion of Lacan and Conceptualist art documentation can be seen in Mary Kelly's *Post-Partum Document*). The Conceptualist withdrawal of visuality comes to be allied with the attempt to extract a politics from psychoanalysis (mediated by Althusser) by advocating the epistemological gain of a move from the Imaginary to the Symbolic. Along with this, theory becomes a component of art training and practice (Burgin is an important figure both as exemplar and as teacher). Out of its use in documentation in Conceptual art, photography comes to be taken as a fundamental paradigm of the art object (Burgin again, but also Wall, Richard Prince, Cindy Sherman, Sherrie Levine and John Stezaker in his photo-collages).'

It is perhaps pre-eminently through photography that questions of reference, signification, authorship and ontology have been pursued since Conceptual art. One effect of this turn to photography, coupled with the interest in subjectivity, has been the breakdown of the distinction between representation and 'real' space/time in the rejection of the residual Anglo-American positivism carried over from Minimalism. The auto-critique of Conceptual art involved in these internal mutations and shifts of interest should not be confused with the effects of the economic and ideological forces at work in the Thatcherism and Reaganism of the 1980s as they made themselves felt in the art world (return to traditional modes, spurious claims to national identity). But two developments have affected subsequent Conceptualism to some degree: a reaction against theory and the re-emphasis on the object. While part of a regressive reaction against Conceptualism's institutional critique, both of these tendencies have affected the neo-Conceptualism, the emergence of which coincided with the post-inflationary recession of the late 1980s and the near collapse of the art market. If this has led to a 'rediscovery' of European and American Conceptual art, not only has this not been accompanied by any new theoretical developments of any interest, in addition the Conceptual artists who have received most attention have been either those European artists who tend towards the late Romantic, Symbolist and ironic modes of conceiving art, which were the *fin-de-siècle* sources of Modernism – Piero Manzoni, Yves Klein, Marcel Broodthaers, a tradition continued by Jan Vercruysse – or towards the synthesis of Conceptualism and Pop (Dan Graham). To take another example, there has recently been far more interest in Bas Jan Ader than at the time he made his films and photoworks, perhaps because of his combination of an ironic Conceptualism with a Romantic-melancholy stance, his films in particular prefiguring the work of a number of contemporary artists who use video and film, such as Jaki Irvine, Georgina Starr and Gillian Wearing. In addition, the significance of the current level of interest in Gerhard Richter lies in the realization that Conceptual art does not *a priori* involve a linguistic, architectural or photographic turn – just as the 'traditional' Conceptual modes are not immune to recuperation, equally it is possible to make paintings or three-dimensional objects without necessarily 'betraying' Conceptualist aims. Marcel Broodthaers prefigures the interest in curating, both by artists and by curators, as an 'aesthetic' activity in its own right, even if the orientation now is towards an art world career, whereas Broodthaers' interventions at the time functioned as a critical-ironic investigation of the conditions of exhibition value.

15. Gerhard Richter

In speaking of a resurgence of Conceptualism, it should also be emphasized that Conceptual art never really went away: not only have Conceptual artists who emerged in the 1960s and 1970s continued to produce work, exerting a manifest or subterranean influence, also artists with a later formation – Jenny Holzer for example, who would be unthinkable without the joint influence of Lawrence Weiner and Dan Graham, and Silvia Kolbowski – have developed Conceptual approaches in interesting new directions, including interventions in public urban space as well as the gallery, raising the question, among others, of the changing relations between public and private.

THE LEGACY OF CONCEPTUAL ART

To treat Conceptual art as a purely positive phenomenon or as a definitive overcoming of contradictions would be to deny its own project. However Conceptual art can neither exclude nor include its own critique. In retrospect it may be seen that Conceptual art was a part of what it opposed: that it both involved a defensive mimicry of bureaucratic culture and remained parasitic on the institutions it subjected to critique. We can summarize the developments out of Conceptual art, linked with political and economic shifts, as follows:

1 Conceptual art initially coincides with radical student movements and calls for real changes in social relations of art production and use;

2 Conceptual art takes a turn to both subjectivity and psychoanalytic theory during a period of recession and the failure of radical student movements to achieve their goals;

3 Conceptual art is marginalized during the hyper-inflation of the art market which only acknowledged commodifiable art and ended up treating Conceptual art 'documentation' as any other commodity;

4 neo-Conceptual art emerges in the 1980s on the one hand allied with popular culture, and on the other hand as a reinvigoration of Conceptual art as reflection on the status of the object, site and social relations. Such work continues to embody contradictory possibilities and its fate is by no means yet decided.

The legacy of Conceptual art is not a solution, nor is it a 'style' to be imitated, but is rather a problematic: the laying bare on the one hand of the conditions which *all* art has to face whether Conceptual or not (with the risk of ontologizing those conditions in the direction of a neo-Symbolist revival), and on the other hand, the *specific* conditions of its historical moment and socio-political milieu (with the risk of dissolving the work into a purely contingent, pragmatic interest). Perhaps in this dual exigency Conceptual art renders explicit the aporia of modern art. If modern art remains a project of consciousness, an unfinished work of enlightenment, it must at the same time deal with its own limits, which must include the *limits* to its self-consciousness. The most clear and emphatic change in Conceptual art since the 1960s has been the move from an epistemological model for the artwork to a psychoanalytic model on the one hand and an ontological model on the other.[2] Questions of knowledge, whether analytical or social, have given way to questions of subjectivity and questions of being; and self-consciousness as the self-transparency of a reflexive relation to conditions which may be known, forming part of a political, defetishizing project, has given way to the recognition of fundamental opacity or blind-spots as constitutive of both subjectivity, as an Other within the self not susceptible to self-knowledge, and the very manifestness of the work, as the work can only be present within a finite and limited historical-cultural order which can never be fully transparent to itself. It would be a mistake to suppose that knowledge and being are simply opposed, as reason to unreason, since they are mutually interdependent, and an inquiry into the limits of knowledge must turn to questions of being (the blind-spot of knowledge), just as being needs to be articulated in terms of knowledge (receptivity to the way being appears at a particular place and time). While Conceptual art opened up possibilities for critical artistic intervention the range of which has not yet been exhausted, its original epistemic bias towards reflexive self-transparency, which appears in retrospect not so far as may have seemed at the time from the modernist drive towards full presence through the self-critique and self-limitation of the work to its irreducible conditions (Greenberg and Fried), is no longer compatible with the exigencies of art-making in a multicultural world.

If under the conditions of a concern with 'art in general' no way of making a work can be *a priori* excluded from Conceptual art as non-conceptual then this must apply to painting and sculpture, therefore is it not impossible that one way of perpetuating Conceptual art may be by making paintings or objects. If Art & Language's claim that the important thing about Conceptual art is not fidelity to the 'purity' of, say, language-as-work, but rather its homelessness,[3] a shift may be observed from an emphasis on the displacement of or from the object (Robert Smithson, Marcel Broodthaers) to the displacement of or from the subject (mediated through Dan Graham in USA and film-studies influenced post-Conceptual art and photowork in the UK). It is possible that the current interest in blind-spots and opacities may indicate an attempt to indicate that site or scene in which subject-object relations are given, including the defensive, fetishizing structures that Conceptual art itself has sought to dissolve. If there is a danger of psychologizing or ontologizing political questions here, there is equally the possibility of an acknowledgment of finitude and alterity which may form the starting point for another politics. And if Conceptual art needs to be continually reinvented in order to stay one step ahead of its own reification – a 'revolutionary' temporality of invention first identified in art by Kant – it is by no means excluded that the best way of continuing Conceptual art in the only way that is possible, which is to say to maintain its *critical* potential, might therefore be to *not* be faithful to it, to betray it. How to do so without entering into alliance with the actually existing forces of reaction remains the problem all neo-Conceptual art has to face.

1 Cf. Jeff Wall, '"Marks of Indifference": Aspects of Photography in, or as, Conceptual Art' in Ann Goldstein and Anne Rorimer, *Reconsidering the Object of Art: 1965–1975* (Los Angeles: The Museum of Contemporary Art; Cambridge, Massachusetts: MIT Press, 1995) [reprinted above, 249–51].

2 For the relation of the epistemological to the ontological, see Stephen Melville, 'Aspects' in Goldstein and Rorimer, *Reconsidering the Object of Art*, *op. cit.*

3 In Art & Language members' papers by Michael Baldwin and Mel Ramsden read at the conference 'Who's afraid of Conceptual Art', Institute of Contemporary Arts, London, 19 March 1995.

Michael Newman, 'Conceptual Art from the 1960s to the 1990s: An Unfinished Project?', *Kunst & Museum Journaal*, 7:1,2,3 (1996) 95–104.

ARTISTS' BIOGRAPHIES

Vito **ACCONCI** [b. 1940, New York] lives in New York. Initially a poet, from 1969 he extended his work conceptually to explore individual and social interaction, through actions related to everyday situations. From 1974 his work progressed to the construction of environments. In 1988 he founded the architectural practice Acconci Studio. He was included in 'Information', The Museum of Modern Art, New York [1970] and Documenta 5, 7 and X [1972; 1982; 1997]. Solo shows include Stedelijk Museum, Amsterdam [1978] and the Museum of Contemporary Art, Chicago [1980].

Bas Jan **ADER** [b. 1942, Winschoten, The Netherlands, d. *c.* 1975, Atlantic Ocean] lived in California from 1963 onwards. His works from 1970-75 record actions which explore existential vulnerability. As part of his final work, *In Search of the Miraculous* [1975], he set sail alone from Cape Cod to England; the boat's wreckage was found in 1976, his body was never recovered. Solo shows include Art & Project, Amsterdam [1972] and 'In Search of the Miraculous', Claire Copley Gallery, Los Angeles [1975]. Retrospectives include Stedelijk Museum, Amsterdam [1988] and the University of California, Irvine [1999].

AKASEGAWA Genpei [b. 1937, Yokohama, Japan] lives in Machida, Tokyo Prefecture. An artist and writer, he was a participant member of the Japanese anti-art groups Neo Dada [1960] and Hi Red Center [1963-64]. From the mid 1960s he made a series of works using the 'model' of printed currency to question notions of cultural authority. He was included in 'Japanese Art after 1945: Scream against the Sky', Yokohama Museum of Art [1994] and US tour, and 'Global Conceptualism', Queens Museum of Art, New York [1999]. Solo shows include Nagoya City Art Museum [1995].

Eleanor **ANTIN** [b. 1935, New York] lives in California. Since the late 1960s, much of her work has examined social meanings via constructed personae placed in tableaux documented in photographic or video formats, combined with text. She was included in 'Video Art USA' and the São Paulo Bienal [1975]. Solo shows include The Museum of Modern Art, New York [1973] and Los Angeles County Museum of Art [1999].

ARAKAWA [b. 1936, Nagoya, Japan] moved to New York in 1961. In Tokyo in the late 1950s he made 'anti-art' works; he joined the Neo Dada group in 1960. His drawings and mixed media works progressively reduce subject matter to the demarcation of thought processes. Since 1963 he has collaborated with Madeline Gins [b. 1941, New York] on works such as their ongoing project *The Mechanism of Meaning*. He was included in 'Japanese Art after 1945: Scream against the Sky', Yokohama Museum of Art [1994] and US tour. Retrospectives include the Solomon R. Guggenheim Museum, New York, 1997.

ARMAN [Armand Fernandez, b. 1928, Nice] lives in New York. He met Yves Klein in 1947 and moved to Paris in 1949. There he encountered the work of Schwitters and Duchamp and began making assemblages, focusing by the early 1960s on accumulated similar objects. He was included in '1960: Les Nouveaux Réalistes', Musée d'art moderne de la Ville de Paris [1980]. Solo shows include Galerie Iris Clert, Paris [1958; 1960] and La Jolla Museum of Contemporary Art [1974] and tour.

ART & LANGUAGE [Michael Baldwin, b. 1945, Chipping Norton, Oxfordshire; Mel Ramsden, b. 1944, Ilkestone, Derbyshire]. Art & Language was the name given in 1968 to a collaborative practice developed initially in England by Terry Atkinson, David Bainbridge, Michael Baldwin and Harold Hurrell. Drawing on linguistic philosophy they investigated the conceptual and ideological presuppositions underlying art's institutionalization, through discussions, the exhibition of their working materials in various forms such as indexes, and in the journal *Art-Language*, launched in 1969 and edited from 1971 by the critic Charles Harrison. They acquired associates in New York among whom were the Australian artist Ian Burn, another British artist, Mel Ramsden, and US artists Joseph Kosuth, Christine Kozlov and Kathryn Bigelow. By 1979 only Baldwin and Ramsden continued to operate under the group's original name, producing works that investigate relationships between formalism and ideology. Art & Language were included in 'Conceptual Art and Conceptual Aspects', New York Cultural Center; 'Information', The Museum of Modern Art, New York; 'Idea Structures', Camden Arts Centre, London [1970] and Documenta 5 and X, Kassel [1972; 1997]. Solo shows include Stedelijk Van Abbemuseum, Eindhoven [1980].

ART WORKERS COALITION [New York, founded 1968] was a radical artists' organization which included Carl Andre, Mel Bochner, Peter Brandt, Robert Morris and Ronald Haeberle. They staged protest actions against social injustices embedded in institutions of power, initially in New York; their influence spread nationally and internationally via printed media.

Michael **ASHER** [b. 1943, Los Angeles] lives in Los Angeles. Since 1966 he has made site specific interventions which focus on the ideological nature of the physical environments of galleries and art institutions. He was included in Documenta 5, Kassel [1972] and the Venice Biennale [1976]. Solo shows include Pomona Gallery, Los Angeles [1970], Galleria Toselli, Milan [1973], Claire Copley Gallery, Los Angeles [1974] and the Art Institute of Chicago [1979].

Terry **ATKINSON** [b. 1939] lives in Leeds. A founder member of Art & Language, he left the group in 1974, since when he has worked as an individual. Solo shows include the Irish Museum of Modern Art, Dublin [1992] and Kunstwerke, Berlin [1995].

John **BALDESSARI** [b. 1931, National City, California] lives in California. Initially a painter, in the mid 1960s he incorporated texts and photography into his works on canvas, explicitly questioning the status of painting, which he rejected entirely in 1970. His works use photography and text or audio-visual media to investigate meaning and symbolism in everyday cultural signs. He was included in 'Information', The Museum of Modern Art, New York [1970]. Solo shows include Stedelijk Van Abbemuseum, Eindhoven [1981] and The Museum of Contemporary Art, Los Angeles [1990].

Robert **BARRY** [b. 1936, New York] lives in New Jersey. Initially a painter concerned with demarcations of space, in the late 1960s he continued this investigation using concepts and materials imperceptible to sight, such as radio waves. His later work is language-based. He was included in 'January 5-31, 1969', Seth Siegelaub, New York [1969], 'When Attitudes Become Form', Kunsthalle Bern and Institute of Contemporary Arts, London [1969] and 'Conceptual Art, Arte Povera, Land Art', Galleria Civica d'Arte Moderna, Turin [1970]. Solo shows include Art & Project, Amsterdam [1969] and Stedelijk Van Abbemuseum, Eindhoven [1977].

Bernd & Hilla **BECHER** [Bernhard Becher, b. 1931, Siegen; Hilla Wobeser, b. 1934, Potsdam] live in Dusseldorf. Since 1959 they have collaborated on a systematic photographic documentation of types of industrial and vernacular buildings. Their work follows rigorous criteria in its objective exploration of typologies. They were included in 'Information', The Museum of Modern Art, New York [1970] and Documenta 6, Kassel [1977]. Solo shows include Staatliche Kunstakademie, Dusseldorf [1966] and Centre Georges Pompidou, Paris [1985].

Joseph **BEUYS** [b. 1921, Krefeld, Germany, d. 1986, Dusseldorf, Germany]. Initially a sculptor, he collaborated with the Fluxus group [1962-63], subsequently combining various media and systems of thought in projects which fused lived experience with creativity. He taught sculpture at the Dusseldorf Academy until his dismissal in 1973 after which he founded the Free International School of Creativity and Interdisciplinary Research. He was included in Documenta 3, 4, 5 and 7, Kassel [1964; 1968; 1972; 1982] and the Venice Biennale [1976]. Retrospectives include Centre Georges Pompidou, Paris [1994].

Mel **BOCHNER** [b. 1940, Pittsburgh, Pennsylvania] lives in New York. An artist and theoretical writer on art, he explores relationships between thinking and seeing, measurement and counting. He curated 'Art in Series', Finch College, New York [1967] and was included in 'Information', The Museum of Modern Art, New York [1970]. Retrospectives include Baltimore Museum of Art [1976] and Yale University Art Gallery, New Haven, Connecticut [1996].

Alighiero BOETTI [b. 1940, Turin, d. 1994, Rome] was a key participant in the Arte Povera movement. In much of his work he explored conventional and arbitrary systems of classification and relationships between chance and necessity, order and disorder. He was included in 'When Attitudes Become Form', Kunsthalle Bern and Institute of Contemporary Arts, London [1969] and 'Conceptual Art, Arte Povera, Land Art', Galleria Civica d'Arte Moderna, Turin [1970], where a major retrospective of his work was presented in 1996.

Oscar BONY [b. 1941, Posadas, Misiones, Argentina] lives in Buenos Aires. Since 1964 his politicized work has intervened in and negated media such as sculpture and photography. He was included in the Venice Biennale [1982], the Havana Bienal and Istanbul Biennale [1997] and 'Global Conceptualism', Queens Museum of Art, New York [1999]. Solo shows include Museo de Arte Moderno, Buenos Aires [1967].

George BRECHT [b. 1926, New York] lives in Cologne. A central member of the Fluxus movement, from 1962-66 he worked closely with John Cage, LaMonte Young, Nam June Paik and others in the writing of scores for and enactment of 'events' involving everyday materials, situations and actions. He is also a theorist of Fluxus and of contemporary musical composition. He was included in Documenta 5, 6 and 8, Kassel [1972; 1977; 1987]. Solo shows include Kunsthalle Bern [1978].

Marcel BROODTHAERS [b. 1924, Brussels, d. 1976, Cologne]. Originally a poet, from the mid 1960s Broodthaers drew from a wide range of influences including Pop art and Fluxus, producing books, objects, films and installations which questioned the condition of art's media and institutions. He was included in Documenta 5 [1972]. Retrospectives include Tate Gallery, London [1980] and Galerie Nationale du Jeu de Paume, Paris [1991].

Stanley BROUWN [b. 1935, Paramaribo, Surinam] lives in Amsterdam. Originally associated with Fluxus, in the early 1960s he made works which related simple diagrams or maps of routes with a series of options open to participants in the process. His work has continued to centre on minimal means and resources. He was included in Documenta 5 [1972]. Solo shows include Stedelijk Museum, Schiedam [1970] and Kunsthalle Bern [1976].

Daniel BUREN [b. 1938, Boulogne-Billancourt, France] lives in Paris. Since 1965 he questioned the status of painting, working solely with stripes of a single colour of a specified width, alternated with white. Since 1967 he has worked *in situ*. He was included in 'Conceptual Art and Conceptual Aspects', New York Cultural Center [1970] and Documenta 5, Kassel [1972]. Solo shows include Wide White Space, Antwerp [1969] and Stedelijk Van Abbemuseum, Eindhoven [1981].

Victor BURGIN [b. 1941, Sheffield] lives in London. An artist and theoretical writer, during the 1970s he was a key influence in the introduction of semiological, Marxist, psychoanalytic and feminist perspectives within conceptual art. He was included in 'When Attitudes Become Form' [second version of exhibition], Institute of Contemporary Arts, London [1969], 'Idea Structures', Camden Arts Centre, London [1970], 'Information', The Museum of Modern Art, New York [1970] and Documenta 5, Kassel [1972]. Solo shows include Stedelijk Van Abbemuseum [1977].

Ian BURN [b. 1939, Geelong, Australia, d. 1993, Australia] was a founder of The Society for Theoretical Art and Analyses and joined Art & Language in 1969. He later worked on the New York based conceptual journal *The Fox*. In 1977 he returned to Australia and worked as a journalist and graphic artist in the trade union movement before returning to art practice in the late 1980s. He was included in 'Minimal-Conceptual Work, 1965-1970', Art Gallery of Western Australia, Perth [1992].

John CAGE [b. 1912, Los Angeles, d. 1992, New York] was a musical composer, writer and artist. In the early 1950s, influenced by Asian systems of thought, his work developed from chromatic composition to investigations of the role of chance and randomness in scores and performance. A major influence on subsequent Fluxus and conceptual artists through his teaching and writing, in this period he also collaborated on scored 'events' with the artist Robert Rauschenberg, among others.

Sophie CALLE [b.1953, Paris] lives in Paris. A photographer and installation artist, she documents life situations that evidence desire and loss. Retrospectives include Museum Boijmans Van Beuningen, Rotterdam [1994].

Judy CHICAGO [b. Judy Cohen Gerowitz 1939, Chicago] lives in New Mexico. A key figure in US feminist art, she is renowned for her collaborative sculpture *The Dinner Party* [1974-79]. She was included in 'Sexual Politics: Judy Chicago's Dinner Party in Feminist Art History', UCLA/Armand Hammer Museum of Art, Los Angeles [1996]. Solo shows include 'Trials and Tributes', Florida State University Museum of Fine Arts, Tallahassee [1999].

CHRISTO & JEANNE-CLAUDE [Christo Javacheff, b. 1935, Gabrovo, Bulgaria; Jeanne-Claude de Guillebon, b. 1935, Casablanca] live in New York. Since 1961 they have collaborated on large scale works in both urban and natural environments, in which experience of a location and its context is altered by its being wrapped and obscured by huge sheets. Their work was included in Documenta 4, Kassel [1968]. Solo shows include The Museum of Modern Art, New York [1968] and Stedelijk Museum, Amsterdam [1973].

Lygia CLARK [b. 1920, Belo Horizonte, Minas Gerais, Brazil, d. 1988, Rio de Janeiro] lived in Rio de Janeiro and Paris. Initially a Neo-Concretist sculptor, from the late 1960s onwards she focused, in participatory works, on phenomenological perceptions of physical environment, time and relationship, informed by her practice as a psychoanalyst. Retrospectives include Fundació Antoni Tàpies, Barcelona [1997].

James COLEMAN [b. 1941, Ballaghaderreen, Ireland] lives in Ireland. Working in a range of audio-visual media and performance, Coleman constructs enigmatic works which draw the viewer into an interpretive position in which the role of language is highlighted. He was included in the Venice Biennale [1978]. Solo shows include the Renaissance Society at the University of Chicago [1985].

Hanne DARBOVEN [b. 1941, Munich] lives in Hamburg and New York. From 1966-68 she engaged with minimalist conceptual art, making serial numerical drawings. From 1968 a calendar schema became integral to her work. In the early 1970s she introduced handwritten text and from 1978 also incorporated visual documentation. She was included in 'Language II', Dwan Gallery, New York [1968], 'When Attitudes Become Form', Kunsthalle Bern and Institute of Contemporary Arts, London [1969], 'Conceptual Art, Arte Povera, Land Art', Galleria Civica d'Arte Moderna, Turin [1970] and Documenta 5, Kassel [1972]. Solo shows include Musée d'art moderne de la Ville de Paris [1989].

Guy DEBORD [b. 1931, Paris, d. 1994, Paris] was a theorist, artist and filmmaker. With Asger Jorn and others he formed the Situationist International in 1957. He was the author of *Theses on the Paris Commune* [1962] and *Society of the Spectacle* [1967]. The Situationist International had a central role in the 1968 student revolution in Paris; it officially disbanded in 1972 but its intentionally uncopyrighted texts continue to be influential in critiques of capitalism and its sign systems.

Jan DIBBETS [b. 1941, Weert, The Netherlands] lives in Amsterdam. Since 1967 he has produced mostly photographically based work which investigates the constructed nature of perception, focusing on perspective, conditions of light and ephemeral events. He was included in 'When Attitudes Become Form', Kunsthalle Bern and Institute of Contemporary Arts, London [1969] and Documenta 8, Kassel [1987]. Solo shows include Stedelijk Van Abbemuseum, Eindhoven [1980] and Walker Art Center, Minneapolis [1987].

Braco DIMITRIJEVIC [b. 1948, Sarajevo, Yugoslavia] moved to London in 1971. In the early 1970s he made street interventions such as the series of publicly placed photo portraits *Casual Passer-by I Met …* In 1976 he published the theoretical text *Tryptichos Post Historicos*. He was included in Documenta 5, 6 and 9 [1972; 1977; 1992] and the Venice Biennale [1976]. Solo shows include Stedelijk Van Abbemuseum, Eindhoven [1979] and Museum Ludwig, Cologne [1984].

Willie DOHERTY [b. 1959, Derry, Northern Ireland] lives in Derry. Since the early 1990s he has used the visual language of documentary film and photography in a conceptual framework to highlight media constructions in representations of people, places and events. He was included in 'NowHere', Louisiana Museum of Modern Art, Humlebæk; and 'Face à l'Histoire 1933-1996', Centre Georges Pompidou, Paris [1996]. Solo shows include Matt's Gallery, London [1990] and Kunsthalle Bern [1996].

Marcel **DUCHAMP** [b. 1887, Blainville-Crevon, France; d. 1968, Neuilly-sur-Seine] since his first use of readymade objects in France in 1913, extended the anti-art impetus of Dada into a radical investigation of what constitutes art. After 1915 he spent much of his life in the USA, gradually becoming recognized as the most influential avant-garde artist of the century. His legacy was central to the development of Fluxus and conceptual art. Retrospectives include Tate Gallery, London [1966] and The Museum of Modern Art, New York [1973].

Hamish **FULTON** [b. 1946, London] lives in Kent. Since 1968 his work has centred on the act of walking. He uses predominantly photographs and text to document his experience. He was included in 'Konzeption/Conception', Städtisches Museum, Leverkusen, Germany [1969], 'Information', The Museum of Modern Art, New York [1970] and Documenta 5, Kassel [1972]. Retrospectives include Stedelijk Van Abbemuseum, Eindhoven [1985] and Tate Britain, London [2002].

Robert **GOBER** [b. 1954, Wallingford, Connecticut] lives in New York. Since the early 1990s his sculptural installations have presented fabricated objects which often allude to Duchamp's work but are layered with contemporary political and psychoanalytic resonance. He was included in Documenta IX, Kassel [1992]. Solo shows include Dia Center for the Arts, New York [1994] and The Museum of Contemporary Art, Los Angeles [1997].

Felix **GONZALEZ-TORRES** [b. 1957, Güaimaro, Cuba, d. 1996, New York] moved to New York in 1979. He became a member of Group Material, founded in that year, who aimed to build public dialogue on social change through institutional critique. Since the late 1980s he worked independently, directing conceptual strategies and minimalist and art photography aesthetics towards democratic engagement with contemporary crises such as AIDS. Retrospectives include Solomon R. Guggenheim Museum, New York [1995].

Zbigniew **GOSTOMSKI** [b. 1932, Bydgoszcz, Pomerania] lives in Poland. His early work explored abstract painting's boundaries. Since the 1980s he has devised 'empty' representational models – works of painting, photography or installation in which representational means such as perspective, illusionism and symbolism are negated. He was included in 'Présences polonaises', Centre Georges Pompidou, Paris [1983]. He has exhibited at Galeria Foksal, Warsaw, from 1968 onwards.

Dan **GRAHAM** [b. 1942, Urbana, Illinois] lives in New York. First associated with early Minimalism, from 1966 he operated outside recognized art systems, inserting works into general circulation magazines. In the 1970s his performance and video work explored individual and group consciousness and the limits of public and private space; from this emerged his architectural projects, from 1976 onwards. He was included in 'Konzeption/Conception', Städtisches Museum, Leverkusen, Germany [1969], 'Information', The Museum of Modern Art, New York [1970], Documenta 5, 6 and 7, Kassel [1972; 1977; 1982] and the Venice Biennale [1976]. Solo shows include Musée d'art moderne de la Ville de Paris [2001].

GRUPO DE ARTISTAS DE VANGUARDIA [Argentina] was a coalition of Argentinian artists who were joined by sociologists, theorists, film directors and photographers in a participatory political action, *Tucumán Arde* [*Tucumán Burns*] in 1968. This was a political protest against a hypocritical government oppression of workers in Tucumán, Rosario. It involved direct collaboration with workers and their participation in testimonials, actions and the dissemination of material through banners, posters and other means.

Hans **HAACKE** [b. 1936, Cologne] moved to New York in 1965. His work of the early 1960s was concerned with the objective analysis of natural phenomena and ecological systems. From these models he developed his systematic critique of the interconnected ideological, political and economic inequities underlying the institutions of art and society. He was included in Documenta 5, 7, 8 and X [1972; 1982; 1987; 1997] and the Venice Biennale [1993]. Solo shows include Tate Gallery, London [1984] and New Museum of Contemporary Art, New York [1997].

Tibor **HAJAS** [b. 1946, Budapest, d. 1980] was initially a poet. In the 1970s he became the foremost performance artist in Hungary, staging actions in Hungary, Poland, Belgium and the Netherlands in which a flashlight was used to delineate seconds of action. He also made photocopied works which investigated relationships between original and copy. Retrospectives include Atelier Hongrois, Paris [1985] and István Király Múzeum, Székesfehérvár, Hungary [1987].

Margaret **HARRISON** [b. 1940, Wakefield, Yorkshire] lives in Manchester and San Francisco. Working in painting, drawing and mixed media installation, she was a key artist and activist of the British feminist movement. She was included in 'Lives', Hayward Gallery, London [1977]. Solo shows include New Museum of Contemporary Art, New York [1989].

Eva **HESSE** [b. 1936, Hamburg; d. 1970, New York] lived in New York. Her sculpture and drawings of the 1960s and 1970s implicitly questioned aspects of the Minimalist idiom of serialism. She was included in 'When Attitudes Become Form', Kunsthalle Bern and Institute of Contemporary Arts, London [1969]. Retrospectives include Solomon R. Guggenheim Museum, New York [1972] and IVAM Centre Julio Gonzàlez, Valencia [1993].

HI RED CENTER was an artist's group, active in Tokyo [1962-64]. The three founding members were Akasegawa Genpei, Takamatsu Jiro and Nakanishi Natsuyuki. They staged actions which they called 'agitations', throughout Tokyo, involving everyday activities, such as cleaning the streets, to convey political messages. They were included in 'Japanese Art after 1945: Scream Against the Sky', Yokohama Museum of Art [1994] and US tour, and 'Out of Actions: Between Performance and the Object 1949-79', The Museum of Contemporary Art, Los Angeles [1998].

Susan **HILLER** [b. 1940, Tallahassee, Florida] moved to London in 1970. An artist, writer and curator, she has worked in media including painting, sculpture, video, photography, installation and artist's books. She investigates cultural processes of classification and their undercurrents in projects that are sometimes participatory. Solo shows include Tate Gallery, Liverpool [1996] and São Paulo Bienal [2000].

John **HILLIARD** [b. 1945, Lancaster] lives in London. In the early 1970s he investigated phenomena through the construction of experimental situations documented photographically, such as a camera recording its own condition in graded light conditions. In his later work he has addressed social issues through photography. He was included in 'The New Art', Hayward Gallery, London [1970]. Solo shows include Nova Scotia College of Art and Design, Halifax [1972] and Institute of Contemporary Arts, London [1984].

Jenny **HOLZER** [b. 1950, Gallipolis, Ohio] lives in New York state. Her work is language-based, subtly inverting the messages of mass culture. Since 1977 she has distributed messages via media ranging from printed ephemera to electronic sign boards. Retrospectives include the Solomon R. Guggenheim Museum, New York [1989].

Douglas **HUEBLER** [b. 1924, Ann Arbor, Michigan, d. 1997, Truro, Massachusetts]. From the late 1960s onwards he made work stating the existence of things in terms of time and/or place; as their interrelationships are beyond direct perceptual experience, the works rely on documentation. He was included in 'January 5-31, 1969', Seth Siegelaub, New York; 'When Attitudes Become Form', Kunsthalle Bern and Institute of Contemporary Arts, London; '557,087', Seattle Art Museum [1969] and 'Information', The Museum of Modern Art, New York [1970]. Retrospectives include F.R.A.C. Limousin, Limoges [1992] and Camden Arts Centre, London [2002].

Kay **HUNT** [b. 1933, London] now Kay Fido Hunt, lives in London. Since the late 1960s she has made documentary work which reflects personal experience and community history. Since 1975 she has researched women's labour history for anti-war projects. Solo shows include Courtauld Institute, London [1973].

Alfredo **JAAR** [b. 1956, Santiago, Chile] moved to New York in 1982. In photographic and sculptural installation works he has addressed preconceived notions of the relationship between art and politics, focusing on issues of global injustice. Solo shows include Museum of Contemporary Art, Chicago [1992] and Moderna Museet, Stockholm [1994].

Jasper **JOHNS** [b. 1930, Augusta, Georgia] lives in New York and the Caribbean. With Robert Rauschenberg, he is among the most influential artists who emerged from and criticized the values of abstract painting of the 1950s. He was included in 'New York Painting and Sculpture, 1940-1970',

Metropolitan Museum of Art, New York [1970]. Solo shows include Whitney Museum of American Art, New York [1977] and Centre Georges Pompidou, Paris [1978].

Ilya **KABAKOV** [b. 1933, Dnepropetrovsk, Russia] lives in New York. He worked unofficially as an artist in the Soviet Union until 1985. His early work took the form of fables in graphic form, related to his profession as a children's book illustrator. From 1970 he has made installations which comment on the values of collective life. He was included in Documenta IX, Kassel [1992] and the Venice Biennale [1993]. Solo shows include Kunsthalle Bern [1985] and Centre Georges Pompidou, Paris [1995].

Tadeusz **KANTOR** [b. 1915, Wielopole, Poland; d. 1990, Cracow, Poland] was a set designer in the 1930s, influenced by Surrealism. From 1945 he made abstract *informel* paintings. He ceased painting from 1949 to 1954 in protest at state-imposed social realism. In 1955 he began to direct experimental theatre, staging happenings and conceptual actions from 1965. He was included in Documenta 2, 6 and 8 [1958; 1977; 1987]. Retrospectives include Kunsthalle, Nurenberg [1968] and Cracow National Museum [1992].

Allan **KAPROW** [b. 1927, Atlantic City] lives in California. Taught painting by Hans Hofmann, 1950-51, and influenced by Jackson Pollock and the Gutai group, from 1957-59 he studied at the New School for Social Research, New York, under John Cage. He progressed from constructing environments to staging Happenings, an artform he pioneered, abandoning the term in 1967 after which he pursued other participatory models. He was included in 'Environments, Situations, Spaces', Martha Jackson Gallery, New York [1961]. Solo shows include Pasadena Art Museum [1967].

On **KAWARA** [b. 1933, Kariya, Aichi Prefecture, Japan] moved to New York in 1965. Since his first *Date Paintings* in 1966 he has attempted to unify the poles of individuality and universality in his work through systematic documentation of temporal and spatial situation. He was included in 'Language I; II; and III, Dwan Gallery, New York [1967; 1968; 1969], '557,087', Seattle Art Museum, 'Konzeption/Conception', Städtische Museum, Leverkusen [both 1969], 'Information', The Museum of Modern Art, New York, 'Conceptual Art and Conceptual Aspects', New York Cultural Center [both 1970] and Documenta 6 and 7 [1977; 1982]. Solo shows include Stedelijk Van Abbemuseum, Eindhoven [1980].

Mary **KELLY** [b. 1941, Fort Dodge, Iowa] lives in Los Angeles. Her installations and theoretical texts have been highly influential in introducing feminist interpretations of psychoanalytic theory into the arena of conceptual art. She was included in 'Difference: On Representation and Sexuality', New Museum of Contemporary Art, New York [1984]. Solo shows include 'Post-Partum Document', Institute of Contemporary Arts, London [1976].

Edward **KIENHOLZ** [b. 1927, Fairfield, Washington, d. 1994, Idaho] was a sculptor who worked in Los Angeles from 1953 until the late 1970s, since when he divided his time between Idaho and Berlin. He made large-scale assemblage works, often taking the form of tableaux, and devised 'concepts' which he offered for sale prior to the physical realization of a piece. Retrospectives include the Whitney Museum of American Art [1996].

Yves **KLEIN** [b. 1928, Nice, d. 1962, Paris] From 1947 onwards he theorized and produced monochrome works, by the late 1950s extending his notion of a 'zone of immaterial pictorial sensibility' to the presentation of a void space, *Le Vide*, at Iris Clert Gallery, Paris [1958]. In the early 1960s he sold certificates for such zones. Retrospectives include Centre Georges Pompidou, Paris [1983] and Ludwig Museum, Cologne [1994].

KOMAR & MELAMID [Vitaly Komar, b. 1943, Moscow; Alexandr Melamid, b. 1945, Moscow] moved to New York in 1978. Their collaboration began in 1965. In 1967 they initiated the SOTS Art movement, a Soviet version of Pop art. Since the late 1970s they have produced paintings and installations which pastiche and conceptually question the meaning of artforms such as social realism. They were included in Documenta 8 [1987] and the Venice Biennale [1997; 1999].

Joseph **KOSUTH** [b. 1945, Toledo, Ohio] lives in New York. A key artist and theorist in conceptual art practice, he has exhibited works since 1967 which examine the relationship between linguistic definitions and their referents. He was included in 'When Attitudes Become Form', Kunsthalle Bern and Institute of Contemporary Arts, London [1969], 'Idea Structures', Camden Arts Centre, London [1970], Documenta 6, 7 and IX [1977; 1982; 1992]. Solo shows include Museum of Normal Art, New York [1967] and Stedelijk Van Abbemuseum, Eindhoven [1978].

Christine **KOZLOV** [b. 1945, New York] has lived in London since the late 1970s. In New York in the mid 1960s she exhibited at Lannis Gallery and the Museum of Normal Art in a group which included Darboven and Kosuth. Her work uses photographs, audio-visual and printed media to explore self-referentiality, systematic ordering and diaristic chronicling. She was included in 'Information', The Museum of Modern Art, New York; 'Conceptual Art and Conceptual Aspects', New York Cultural Center [1970] and '*c*. 7,500', California Institute of the Arts, Valencia [1973].

Jaroslaw **KOZLOWSKI** [b. 1945, Poznań, Poland] lives in Poznań. His work is concerned with language as an independent structure. In works such as *Metaphysics-Physics-Ics* [1972-74] he examines the relationship between numerical classification and its referents in photographs. He was the founding director of the gallery Akumulatory 2 in Poznań [1972-90] and has exhibited in many alternative galleries in Poland and internationally.

Barbara **KRUGER** [b. 1945, New Jersey] lives in New York. An artist and critical writer on contemporary culture, since the early 1980s she has used photomontage to recontextualize fragments of images from media sources with texts that subvert the manipulations of corporate capitalist culture. Retrospectives include The Museum of Contemporary Art, Los Angeles and Whitney Museum of American Art [2000].

Shigeko **KUBOTA** [b. 1937, Niigata, Japan] lives in New York. Originally involved in Fluxus, she makes innovative video installations. Much of her work re-examines the legacies of Modernism's 'father' figures such as Marcel Duchamp from a feminist perspective. She was included in Documenta 7, Kassel [1982]. Solo shows include the National Museum of Art, Osaka [1992].

John **LATHAM** [b. 1921, Zambesi River, Rhodesia, now Zimbabwe] lives in London. Central to his experimental work, which has taken many forms since the mid 1950s, is the proposal that traditional ways of apprehension based on extension in space should be replaced by experience of extendedness in time, in which events form the basic unit. He was included in 'Information', The Museum of Modern Art, New York [1970] and Documenta 6, Kassel [1977]. Solo shows include Institute of Contemporary Arts, London [1960] and Stedelijk Van Abbemuseum, Eindhoven [1983].

Louise **LAWLER** [b. 1947, Bronxville, New York] lives in New York. In much of her work she has photographed or recreated arrangements of works of art in private or public collections, inviting consideration of the political dimensions of display and reception of artworks. Solo shows include The Museum of Modern Art, New York [1987].

Sherrie **LEVINE** [b. 1947, Hazleton, Pennsylvania] lives in New York. In her work of the 1980s she reproduced and re-appropriated artworks by canonical artists and photographers, drawing attention to contextual frames. She was included in 'Difference: On Sexuality and Representation', New Museum of Contemporary Art, New York [1984]. Solo shows include The Museum of Contemporary Art, Los Angeles [1995].

Sol **LEWITT** [b. 1928, Hartford, Connecticut] lives in Connecticut and Spoleto, Italy. He began producing minimal structures and reliefs in 1962. His *Serial Project No. 1 [ABCD]* [1966] bridged the gap between the formal abstraction of Minimalism and conceptual art. This was followed by his texts 'Paragraphs on Conceptual Art' [1967] and 'Sentences on Conceptual Art' [1969]. He was included in 'Primary Structures', Jewish Museum, New York [1966] and Documenta 4, 6 and 7, Kassel [1968; 1977; 1982]. Retrospectives include The Museum of Modern Art, New York [1978] and San Francisco Museum of Modern Art [2000].

Richard **LONG** [b. 1942, Bristol] lives in Bristol, England. His work centres on the activity of walking, documented through photographs, maps and text. In a number of early works he left ephemeral marks in the landscape; in later works natural materials are removed from their environment and installed in gallery spaces. He was included in 'When Attitudes Become Form', Kunsthalle Bern and Institute of Contemporary Arts, London

[1969] and Documenta 5 and 7, Kassel [1972; 1982]. Solo shows include Konrad Fischer, Dusseldorf [1968] and Solomon R. Guggenheim Museum, New York [1986].

George **MACIUNAS** [b. 1931, Kaunas, Lithuania, d. 1978, New York] was a founder and the key organizer of the Fluxus movement. He met La Monte Young, George Brecht and others who were to form the movement while studying under John Cage at the New School for Social Research, New York, in the late 1950s. He organized the first Fluxus festivals in New York and Europe in the early 1960s and wrote a Fluxus manifesto in 1963.

Piero **MANZONI** [b. 1933, Soncino, Italy, d. 1963, Milan] lived in Milan. His work of the 1950s and 1960s criticized the Romantic avant-garde strategies of his artistic contemporaries. Reflecting industrial conditions of production, his work ranged from white monochrome assemblages [*Achromes*] to packaged ephemeral matter such as breath or a drawn line, to 'certificates of authenticity'. Retrospectives include Centre Georges Pompidou, Paris [1991] and Serpentine Gallery, London [1998].

Gordon **MATTA-CLARK** [b. 1942, New York, d. 1978, New York] lived in New York. After studying architecture, from 1970 he developed an interventionist approach towards urban sites, which he named anarchitecture. This involved making sections through buildings, removals, or other strategies which highlighted site specific context in unprecedented ways. He was included in 'Pier 18', The Museum of Modern Art, New York [1971]. Solo shows include 112 Greene Street, New York [1972] and Holly Solomon Gallery, New York [1976]; retrospectives, Museum of Contemporary Art, Chicago [1985] and IVAM Centro Julio González, Valencia [1993].

MATSUZAWA Yutaka [b. 1922, Suwa, Nagano Prefecture, Japan] lives in Suwa. From the mid 1940s to the early 1960s he studied architecture, mathematics, religious philosophy and contemporary art. From the late 1950s he exhibited collages and assemblages. He made his first text-only work [*Ψ Corpse*] in 1964, since when he has continued to make anti-materialist, language-based work. Solo shows include Saito Memorial Kawaguchi Museum of Contemporary Art, Japan [1997].

Cildo **MEIRELES** [b. 1948, Rio de Janeiro] lives in Rio de Janeiro. In the late 1960s he developed mathematically derived conceptualizations of space in both small sculptures and large installations. From 1970 his work became more directly political as he made 'interventions into ideological circuits'. He was included in 'Information', The Museum of Modern Art, New York [1970] and Documenta IX [1992]. Solo shows include IVAM Centre del Carme, Valencia [1995] and New Museum of Contemporary Art, New York [1999].

Ana **MENDIETA** [b. 1948, Havana, Cuba; d. 1986, New York] lived in Iowa and New York. Her work of the 1960s and 1970s was characterized by ritual; she staged tableaux or inscribed her silhouette into natural environments. Her work addressed issues of violation and displacement. She was included in 'Inside the Visible', Whitechapel Art Gallery, London [1998]. Retrospectives include New Museum of Contemporary Art, New York [1987].

MIYAJIMA Tatsuo [b. 1957, Tokyo] lives in Tokyo. Since 1988 he has made works displaying changing arabic numerals on digital screens in darkness. Based on the concept 1. Keep Changing; 2. Connect with Everything; 3. Continue Forever, the work makes conceptual links with Zen, Sanskrit and pre-Socratic notions of the condition symbolized by zero, in relation to constant change. He was included in the Venice Biennale [1988; 1999]. Solo shows include Hayward Gallery, London [1997].

Robert **MORRIS** [b. 1931, Kansas City, Missouri] lives in New York. In the early 1960s he was a central figure in experimental dance theatre in New York and made a conceptual series of works influenced by Marcel Duchamp. In the mid to late 1960s he was a leading exponent of minimalist sculpture. He was included in Documenta 4, 6 and 8 [Kassel [1968; 1977; 1987], 'Information', The Museum of Modern Art, New York [1970] and the Venice Biennale [1980]. Solo shows include Green Gallery, New York [1963], Tate Gallery, London [1971] and Solomon R. Guggenheim Museum, New York [1994].

MURAKAMI Saburo [b. 1925, Kobe, Japan] lives in Nishinomiya. A leading member of the Gutai group, he made actions in which he intervened with a range of materials onto surfaces, leaving traces of his activity and gestures. He was included in the Second Gutai Art Exhibition, Ohara Kaikan Hall, Tokyo [1956] and 'Out of Actions: Between Performance and the Object 1949-79', Museum of Contemporary Art, Los Angeles [1998].

Bruce **NAUMAN** [b. 1941, Fort Wayne, Indiana] lives in New Mexico. Originally a sculptor, he began applying conceptual schema in diagrams, photographs, sculpture, performance and film in the mid 1960s. He was included in 'American Sculpture of the 1960s', Los Angeles County Museum of Art [1967]. Solo shows include Leo Castelli, New York, and Konrad Fischer, Dusseldorf [1968], Galleria Sperone, Turin [1970], Los Angeles County Museum of Art [1972] and tour, Centre Georges Pompidou, Paris [1998] and tour.

N.E. THING CO. [Iain Baxter, b. 1936, Middlesborough, England; Ingrid Baxter, b. 1938, Spokane, Washington] was founded in 1966 in Toronto and disbanded in 1978. It mimicked corporate concepts and protocols in works that explored the appropriation of everyday life into exchange value systems. N.E. Thing Co. was included in 'Konzeption/Conception', Städtische Museum, Leverkusen; '557,087', Seattle Art Museum [1969], 'Conceptual Art, Arte Povera, Land Art', Galleria Civica d'Arte Moderna, Turin; 'Conceptual Art and Conceptual Aspects', New York Cultural Center' and 'Information', The Museum of Modern Art, New York [1970].

Hélio **OITICICA** [b. 1937, Rio de Janeiro, d. 1980, Rio de Janeiro] lived in Rio de Janeiro and New York. From the Neo-Concrete sculptural environments he had developed since 1954, he redirected his work from the mid 1960s towards participatory, politicized engagement with 'sensorial objects', often centred on the material environment of the poor and disposessed. He was included in 'Information', The Museum of Modern Art, New York [1970]. Retrospectives include Galerie nationale du Jeu de Paume, Paris [1992].

Yoko **ONO** [b. 1933, Tokyo] lives in New York. She studied piano and composition as a child in Japan and moved to New York with her family in 1952. She became associated with John Cage and the Fluxus artists in the late 1950s. Her Chambers Street loft in Manhattan was the venue for a series of concerts and performances during 1960-61 that prefigured the formation of Fluxus. An early practitioner of 'scores' for events, from 1961-62 she exhibited textual 'instructions for paintings' in Tokyo and New York. In the mid 1960s she expanded her work into the field of film. She was included in 'Japanese Art after 1945: Scream Against the Sky', Yokohama Museum of Art, Japan [1994] and US tour. Solo shows include 'Yes. Yoko Ono', Japan Society Gallery, New York [2000].

Roman **OPALKA** [b. 1931, Hocquincourt, France] lives in France. Since 1963 he has explored the phenomenon of time as it is conceptualized in linear form by numbers. From 1965 he began his ongoing series of 'infinity' paintings, in which basic numerical units progress, by the addition of one unit in each sequence, towards infinity. He was included in the Venice Biennale [1970] and Documenta 6, Kassel [1977]. Solo shows include Musée d'art moderne de la Ville de Paris [1993].

Adrian **PIPER** [b. 1948, New York] lives in New York and Massachusetts. An artist and philosopher, in the late 1960s she made works on paper based on schematic approaches to the work of definition. From 1970 onwards she developed a 'catalytic' method to address issues of racial, gender and class identity, by interventionist actions and installations. She was included in 'Global Conceptualism', Queens Museum of Art, New York [1999]. Solo shows include the New Museum of Contemporary Art, New York [2000].

Viktor **PIVOVAROV** [b. 1937, Moscow] moved to Prague in 1982. A key member of the Moscow conceptual circle in the late 1970s, he makes cartoon illustration-like paintings with text panels which present everyday life incidents for interpretation in a wider cultural context. Solo shows include Washington Project for the Arts [1991], Galerie Studio Opatov, Prague [1992], Kunstverein, Graz [1995] and Musée d'art moderne, Saint-Étienne [1997].

Robert **RAUSCHENBERG** [b. 1925, Port Arthur, Texas] lives in New York. From 1948-49 he studied painting at Black Mountain College, North Carolina. A pioneer of Pop art, in the early 1950s he collaborated with the composer John Cage and the choreographer Merce Cunningham on events which prefigured Fluxus and Happenings. Solo shows include Centre Georges Pompidou, Paris [1981] and Solomon R. Guggenheim Museum, New York [1997].

Martha ROSLER [b. 1943, Brooklyn, New York] lives in New York. An artist and writer, she works in photography, video, performance and installation. Her work offers a feminist analysis of society, politics and the media. She was included in 'Difference: On Representation and Sexuality', New Museum of Contemporary Art, New York [1984]. Retrospectives include Ikon Gallery, Birmingham [2000].

Edward RUSCHA [b. 1937, Omaha, Nebraska] lives in California. A key figure in Pop art, he has explored relationships between word and image, in paintings and drawings, often of words themselves, and in photography in artist's books he produced mainly from 1963 to 1972. He was included in Documenta 5, 6, 7 and IX, Kassel [1972; 1977; 1982; 1992]. Solo shows include San Francisco Museum of Modern Art [1982] and the Hirshorn Museum and Sculpture Garden, Washington, D.C. [2000] and tour.

Richard SERRA [b. 1939, San Francisco] moved to New York in 1966, after encountering Arte Povera in Italy that year. Until 1969 his work engaged with process through language and actions such as casting or splashing, recorded on film. From 1969 he has conceived and fabricated sculptures made from large sheets of steel. He was included in Documenta 5, 6, 7 and 8, Kassel [1972; 1977; 1982; 1987]. Solo shows include Galleria La Salita, Rome [1966] and Stedelijk Van Abbemuseum, Eindhoven [1990].

SHIMAMOTO Shozo [b. 1928, Osaka] lives in Nishinomiya, Japan. A member of the Gutai group, in the mid 1950s he made ephemeral paintings by destructive means such as hurling bottles of paint. He was included in the Second Gutai Exhibition, Tokyo [1956] 'Gutai', Ashiya City Museum of Art, Osaka [1993], 'Japanese Art after 1945: Scream Against the Sky', Yokohama Museum of Art [1994] and US tour, and 'Out of Actions: Between Performance and the Object 1949-79', The Museum of Contemporary Art, Los Angeles [1998].

Mieko [Chieko] SHIOMI [b. 1938, Okayama, Japan] lives in Osaka. An improvised music performer in Tokyo in the early 1960s, she visited New York in 1964, encountering the Fluxus group. She formulated *Spatial Poem* [1965-75], an international work based on interchanges between artists by mail. Solo shows include 'Seven Performances', Okayama Cultural Centre [1963], 'Flux Concert: Mieko Shiomi', Washington Square Gallery, New York [1964] and 'Water Music, Air Event, Music for Two Players IV', Crystal Gallery, Tokyo [1965].

SHIRAGA Fujiko [b. 1928, Osaka, Japan] lives in Japan. A member of the Gutai group until 1961, in the 1950s she made ephemeral works using materials such as paper, which involved a minimal intervention with the object. She was included in 'Gutai Group', Gallery of Modern Art, Rome [1990], 'Gutai', Ashiya City Museum of Art, Osaka [1993] and 'Japanese Art after 1945: Scream Against the Sky', Yokohama Museum of Art [1994] and US tour.

SHIRAGA Kazuo [b. 1924, Amagasaki City, Japan] lives in Amagasaki. A member of the Gutai group, he experimented with many forms of action painting using diverse methods. From the mid 1950s he established the technique of painting with his feet. He was included in 'Gutai Group', Gallery of Modern Art, Rome [1990] and 'Japanese Art after 1945: Scream Against the Sky', Yokohama Museum of Art [1994] and US tour.

Robert SMITHSON [b. 1938, Rutherford, New Jersey, d. 1973, Amarillo, Texas] was from the mid 1960s a central figure in the intersections between conceptual art, Minimalism and Land art, both as an artist and as a writer. Much of his work offered a critique of current practice as well as extending its boundaries. He was included in 'When Attitudes Become Form', Kunsthalle Bern and Institute of Contemporary Arts, London [1969], Documenta 5 and 6, Kassel [1972; 1977]. Retrospectives include Musée d'art moderne de la Ville de Paris [1982] and Centro Julio González, Valencia [1993].

Michael SNOW [b. 1929, Toronto] lives in Toronto. Since the early 1960s his works, such as the influential film *Wavelength* [1967] which inspired a generation of structural filmmakers, have explored the basic conceptual structures of film. He has also worked with photography and sound. Solo shows include Venice Biennale Canadian Pavilion [1970], Art Gallery of Ontario, Toronto [1970; 1994].

Niele TORONI [b. 1937, Locarno] lives in Paris. Since 1966 his work has consisted of the imprints of a No. 50 paintbrush repeated at regular intervals of 30 cm. The work, like that of Buren and Kawara, draws attention to its context as well as the traces of its making. He was included in the Paris Biennale [1967] and Documenta 7 [1982]. Solo shows include Stedelijk Van Abbemuseum, Eindhoven [1977] and Museum van Hedendaagse Kunst, Ghent [1982].

Mierle Laderman UKELES [b. 1939, Denver, Colorado] reflects on the opposing Western cultural systems of free creativity, on the one hand, and regulation and maintenance, on the other, in interventionist works such as *Touch Sanitation* [1978-84] – a citywide action in collaboration with 8,500 sanitation workers in New York. Solo shows include 'Unburning Freedom Hall', The Museum of Contemporary Art, Los Angeles [1997].

Jeff WALL [b. 1946, Vancouver] lives in Vancouver. A key practitioner since the late 1960s of conceptual photography, he has engaged as both an artist and theorist with the social dimensions of Modernism and contemporary visual representation. Solo shows include Museum of Contemporary Art, Chicago [1995]; Galerie Nationale du Jeu de Paume, Paris [1995] and Musée d'Art Contemporain, Montreal [1999].

Andy WARHOL [b. 1928, Pittsburgh; d. 1987, New York] lived in New York. One of the most influential figures in late twentieth-century art, he established his New York studio as The Factory in 1962, where serial reproduction became a central feature of his work as an artist and filmmaker. Retrospectives include The Museum of Modern Art, New York, and Museum Ludwig, Cologne [1989] and Tate Modern, London [2002].

Lawrence WEINER [b. 1942, Bronx, New York] lives in New York. Since 1965 his work has taken the form of statements in relation to sculptural or other propositions which may or may not be realized in a form other than language. He was included in 'January 5-31, 1969', Seth Siegelaub, New York; 'When Attitudes Become Form', Kunsthalle Bern and Institute of Contemporary Arts, London; 'Op losse schroeven', Stedelijk Museum, Amsterdam [1969], Documenta 5 and 7, Kassel [1972; 1982]. Solo shows include Musée d'art moderne de la Ville de Paris [1984], Kunsthalle Bern [1983] and Stedelijk Museum, Amsterdam [1988].

Hannah WILKE [b. 1943, d. 1993] lived in New York. Originally a sculptor, she invented an iconography based on vaginal imagery, using clay, latex and gum. Her own body became increasingly the focus of her work, and featured in 'performalist portraits'. Solo shows include the posthumous 'Intra-Venus', Ronald Feldman Gallery, New York [1994]. Retrospectives include Santa Monica Museum of Art, California [1996].

Fred WILSON [b. 1954, New York] lives in New York. Making installations within institutional spaces, he draws attention to the ideological assumptions towards non-western and other marginal cultures which underly Modernism's emphasis on visuality in representation, display and critical framing. He was included in 'The Museum as Muse', The Museum of Modern Art, New York [1999]. Solo shows include Museum of Contemporary Art, Chicago [1994].

La Monte YOUNG [b. 1935, Berne, Idaho] is an experimental composer. After initial work in the twelve-note tradition of Schoenberg, he studied with Stockhausen in Darmstadt in 1958, encountering the work of John Cage. Returning to New York, he began composing 'scores' for ephemeral events, in collaboration with members of the Fluxus group. These were published in *An Anthology* [1963].

ZHANG Huan [b. 1965, An Yang, Henan Province, China] lives in New York. From 1994-97 he made both collaborative and solo actions on Beijing's outskirts which tested the boundaries between conceptual instruction and documentation and lived experience. He was included in the Venice Biennale [1999]. Solo performances include P.S. 1, New York [1998].

AUTHORS' BIOGRAPHIES

Theodor **ADORNO** [b. 1903, Frankfurt, d. 1969, Switzerland] was a philosopher, musicologist and cultural critic. A member of the Frankfurt School of critical theory, he spent 1930-50 in exile from Germany, mainly in the USA. There, in *Dialektik der Aufklarung* [1947; trans. *Dialectic of Enlightenment*, 1973], with Max Horkheimer, he developed the thesis of the dialectical character of enlightenment and an analysis of the culture industry as a form of 'mass deception'. Focusing on the deleterious consequences of the separation of the universality of reason from the particularity of the senses, he saw the autonomous character of modern art as the residual but threatened site of critical experience, and a 'promise of happiness', broken in society at large. His major works are *Negative Dialektik* [1966; *Negative Dialectics*, 1973] and the posthumously published *Äesthetische Theorie* [1970; *Aesthetic Theory*, 1984; 1997].

Alexander **ALBERRO** is Assistant Professor of Modern Art at the University of Florida, Gainesville. A scholar of conceptual art, he regularly contributes to *October* and *Artforum*. He is the author of *The Best Dishwashing Liquid Around: Conceptual Art and the Politics of Publicity* [2002] and the editor of *Two-Way Mirror Power: Selected Writings by Dan Graham on His Art* [1999]. He co-edited, with Blake Stimson, *Conceptual Art: A Critical Anthology* [1999].

Roland **BARTHES** [b. 1915, Cherbourg, d. 1980, Paris] was a French critic, literary theorist and exponent of semiology. In texts such as those collected in *Mythologies* [1957], Barthes analysed the process of 'naturalization' whereby we absorb ideological values through the sign systems of the cultural forms that surround us. His work influenced in particular Victor Burgin, who first encountered it in 1967. Key studies include *Elements de Sémiologie* [*Elements of Semiology*, 1964] and *La Chambre Claire* [*Camera Lucida*, 1980].

Jean **BAUDRILLARD** lives and works in Paris. As a critical theorist he has developed an influential portrayal of a society in which all sense of the real has been replaced by simulations. In this analysis, late capitalist culture increasingly 'mediatizes' the systems of cultural signs by which we understand the world. The signs become so estranged from their referents that they produce a 'hyperreal' condition. They have become transformed into simulacra, pure simulations. His works include *Le système des objets* [1968]; *Pour une critique de l'économie du signe* [1972; trans. *For a Critique of the Political Economy of the Sign*, 1981]; *Simulacres et simulations* [1981; trans. *Simulations*, 1983].

Samuel **BECKETT** [b. 1906, Dublin, d. 1989, Paris] was among the most innovative Irish literary writers of the twentieth century. Most of his major works were written initially in French from 1946 onwards, and include the novels *Murphy* [1938] and *Watt* [published in 1953] and the plays *Waiting for Godot* [1952] and *Endgame* [1957]. His works tragi-comically explore the absurdities of existence. Each work can be interpreted both as an existential metaphor and as a philosophical discussion. Part of the interest of his work for a number of early conceptual artists was its exploration of language games.

Benjamin H.D. **BUCHLOH** is an art historian and critic who teaches twentieth-century and contemporary art at Barnard College, Columbia University, New York. He has written extensively on the work of conceptual artists of the 1960s and 1970s, with many of whom he has had a close association over a long period. He is a regular contributor to *October*. His key early critical writings are collected in his *Neo-Avantgarde and Culture Industry: Essays on European and American Art from 1955 to 1975* [2001].

Jack **BURNHAM** [b. 1931] is an artist and critical theorist based in Connecticut. He has written extensively on contemporary art for art journals such as *Artforum* and was one of the most significant US writers on cybernetics and systems art in the 1960s. He is the author of *Beyond Modern Sculpture* [1968], *The Structure of Art* [1971] and *Great Western Salt Works: Essays on the Meaning of Post-Formalist Art* [1974].

Luis **CAMNITZER** [b. 1937, Lübeck, Germany] lives in New York state. He is an artist and critic and since 1969 has been Professor of Art at the State University of New York, Old Westbury. In 1939 he emigrated to Uruguay, where he was a citizen until he moved to the USA in 1964. In 1988 his work represented Uruguay at the Venice Biennale. He is the author of *New Art of Cuba* [University of Texas Press, 1994]. His essays have been published in periodicals including *Third Text*, *Art in America* and *New Art Examiner*.

Michel **CLAURA** is a French art critic and curator based in Paris who from the mid 1960s has written on the work of artists such as Daniel Buren, Niele Toroni and Lawrence Weiner.

Eduardo **COSTA** [b. 1940, Buenos Aires, Argentina] lives in New York. An artist and writer, in Buenos Aires with Raul Escari and Roberto Jacoby he created the first 'mass-media art work' [1966] and wrote *Un arte de los medios de comunicación [An Art of Communication Media]* [1965-66], both manifestations of *arte de los medios* [mass-mediatic art] a strategy of 'constituting the work inside mass-media itself'. In late 1966 he moved to New York where he met Vito Acconci and other artists with whom he collaborated. In 1978 he moved to Rio de Janeiro, where he was closely associated with Hélio Oiticica, Lygia Clark and others. In 1981 he returned to New York. Solo shows include the Museum of Modern Art, Buenos Aires [2002], and tour.

Johanna **DRUCKER** is Professor of Media Studies at the University of Virginia. She is also a book artist and the author of the authoritative survey *The Century of Artists' Books* [1996]. Her other publications include *The Visible Word: Experimental Typography and Modern Art* [1994] and *Theorizing Modernism* [1994].

Anton **EHRENZWEIG** [b. 1908, Vienna, d. 1966, London] was a Freudian art historian. His principal work was *The Hidden Order of Art: A Study in the Psychology of Artistic Imagination* [1967]. His specific contribution was his concept of 'dedifferentiation', a process by which the ego represses and disperses surface imagery, thus creating a structure which can only be grasped by a 'syncretistic vision'. One example he cited was the drip painting of Jackson Pollock. His theories were influential on a number of conceptual artists and were alluded to by Robert Smithson as pertinent to understanding the relationship between site and non-site.

Raúl **ESCARI** collaborated with Eduardo Costa and Roberto Jacoby in 1966 on the first 'mass-media art work' in Buenos Aires, and the manifesto *Un arte de los medios de comunicación [An Art of Communication Media]* [1965-66] [see Eduardo Costa]. The artwork was titled *Happening para un jabalí difunto* [*Happening for a Dead Boar*]. A detailed written and photographic report of a non-existent event was sent to the news media, who were encouraged to transmit it. It was then denounced as false.

Hal **FOSTER** is a scholar of twentieth-century art who focuses on relationships between avant-garde and neo-avant-garde movements and contemporary art. Professor of Modern Art at Princeton University, he is a co-editor of *October*. His publications include *Recodings – Art, Spectacle, Cultural Politics* [1985], *Compulsive Beauty* [1993] and *The Return of the Real: The Avant-Garde at the End of the Century* [1996]. Foster also edited the influential anthology *The Anti-Aesthetic* [1982].

Irving **GOFFMAN** [b. 1922, Manville, Alta, Canada, d. 1982, Philadelphia] was an American sociologist. His influential work based on field research in social interaction, *The Presentation of Self in Everyday Life* [1959], analysed social behaviour in terms of performance and role play, drawing analogies between theatre and the everyday.

Nelson **GOODMAN** [b. 1906, Somerville, Massachusetts] is an American philosopher. A proponent of nominalism – the thesis that only particulars are real – he has argued that philosophy should focus on precise structural descriptions of phenomena. His investigations of theories of representation involve analysis of the visual arts, musical notation and maps. His works include *The Structure of Appearance* [1951] and *Languages of Art* [1968].

Max **HORKHEIMER** [b. 1895, Stuttgart, d. 1973, Nuremberg] was a philosopher and social theorist of the Frankfurt School. Like Adorno he was exiled in the USA from the mid 1930s; he returned to Frankfurt in 1950. He expanded Marxism beyond its focus on the material forces of history, forming a critique of contemporary society which took into account broader issues of social psychology. In conjunction with Adorno,

Horkheimer wrote *Dialectik der Aufklarung* [1947; trans. *Dialectic of Enlightenment*, 1973], a historical account of the ways in which reason has self-destructively turned against itself during the development of modern, technocratic societies.

Roberto JACOBY [b. 1944, Buenos Aires] is an artist and theorist. He produced with Eduardo Costa and Rául Escari the manifesto *Un arte de los medios de comunicación [An Art of Communication Media]* [1965-66] [see Costa; Escari]. In the early 1970s he studied sociology at the University of Buenos Aires. From 1979 to 1985 he produced a manuscript on the epistemology of revolutionary thought. In 1979 he founded the musical group *Virus*. Since the 1980s he has organized experimental rock concerts.

George KUBLER [b. 1912, Los Angeles, d. 1996] was an art historian, best known for his books on the art and architecture of ancient South America. His book *The Shape of Time* [1962] brought into question the notion of stylistic development as a way of understanding art and also questioned the centrality of European art. His work anticipated subsequent postcolonial perspectives on cultural relativity.

Thomas S. KUHN [b. 1922, Cincinnati, Ohio, d. 1996] was an American philosopher and historian of science. In *The Structure of Scientific Revolutions* [1962], he differentiated two generic kinds of scientific enquiry. The 'normal' scientist works within the limits of a specific paradigm, such as Newtonian physics. The 'revolutionary' scientist, however, embarks on a process whereby one paradigm becomes replaced by another. The two paradigms are 'incommensurable'; the fundamental concepts of one cannot be rendered by the terms of the other.

Curt LEWIN [b. 1890, Mogilno, Posen, Germany [now Poland], d. 1947, Newtonville, Massachusetts] was a German-born psychologist who emigrated to the USA in 1933. From 1944 he was Founder-Director of the Research Center for Group Dynamics at Massachusetts Institute of Technology. A pioneer of environmental studies in psychology, he addressed problems of individual and group motivation as determined by given situations. His writings include *Principles of Topological Psychology* [1936] and *The Conceptual Representation and Measurement of Psychological Forces* [1938].

Lucy R. LIPPARD [b. 1937, New York] lives in New Mexico. She is a freelance writer, curator and activist. She is the author of seventeen books on contemporary art in addition to articles, reviews and catalogue essays. Lippard has curated exhibitions internationally; in 1969 she organized the conceptual art exhibition '557,087' in Seattle, and in 1973 the first all-women exhibition of conceptual art, 'C.7,500', in Valencia, California. She has written on a wide range of art practices and issues including conceptual, feminist, performance and environmental art. Her books include *Six Years: The Dematerialization of the Art Object from 1966 to 1972 ...* [1973] and *The Lure of the Local* [1997].

André MALRAUX [b. 1901, Paris, d. 1975, Paris] was a French novelist, art critic and politician. One of the most committed left-wing writers of the 1930s, he fought on the Republican side in the Spanish civil war and later in the French resistance, but from 1947 onwards moved to the right, serving in De Gaulle's governments. His writings on art include *Les voix du silence* [1951; trans. *The Voices of Silence*, 1960].

Herbert MARCUSE [b. 1898, Berlin, d. 1979, Sternberg, East Germany] was a social theorist of the Frankfurt School who became a US citizen in 1940. His works made pioneering links between Freudian and Marxist theory. In *Eros and Civilization* [1955] he argued for the erotic liberation of the unconscious from repression via liberation from capitalist oppression. In *One-Dimensional Man* [1964] he analysed the defusion of social discontent by capitalism's manipulation of communication media – individual desires being replaced with artificially induced materialistic ones.

Karl MARX [b. 1818, Trier, Germany, d. 1883, London], the German philosopher and critic of political economy, studied law and Hegelian philosophy at Berlin and Bonn universities. When the liberal journal he edited, *Rheinisch Zeitung*, was suppressed in 1842 he fled to Paris and was converted to the emerging idea of communism, which he developed, with Friedrich Engels, in *The Communist Manifesto* [1848] and *Das Kapital [Capital]*, the first volume of which was published in 1867. Several of his major works were published posthumously in the twentieth century, such as *The German Ideology* [1932; trans. 1964] and the drafts known as *Grundrisse [Outlines]* [1939; trans. 1973], contributing to the regeneration of Marxist social and cultural analysis in the 1960s.

Gustav METZGER [b. 1926, Nürnberg] lives in London. He came to Britain in 1939 as a Polish citizen and began making art in 1945, after coming into contact with Marxists, pacifists and early environmentalists, who influenced his subsequent work. In 1959 he published the manifesto *Auto-Destructive Art*, followed by a second manifesto in 1960, when his first auto-destructive works, such as 'action paintings' made with acid on nylon, were exhibited. In September 1966 he organized the Destruction in Art Symposium, held at the Africa Centre, London.

Michael NEWMAN is Associate Professor of Art History, Theory, and Criticism at the School of the Art Institute of Chicago. He has written on modern and contemporary art, and on the relationships between criticism and philosophy. He co-edited, with Jon Bird, *Rewriting Conceptual Art* [1999].

Brian O'DOHERTY [also known as Patrick Ireland] lives in Ireland. He is an artist and critical writer. His work has been shown in numerous galleries and museums in the USA and Europe. His books include *Object and Idea* [1967], *American Masters: The Voice and the Myth* [1973; revised 1988] and *Inside the White Cube: The Ideology of the Gallery Space* [1976; revised 1986].

Rozsika PARKER [b. 1945, London] works in London as a psychoanalytical therapist and writer. With Griselda Pollock, she is a key writer on British art of the women's movement and was a founder member of the *Spare Rib* magazine collective. Her publications include *The Subversive Stitch: Embroidery and the Making of the Feminine* [1989] and *Torn in Two: The Experience of Natural Ambivalence* [2000].

Ferdinand de SAUSSURE [b. 1857, Geneva, d. 1913, near Geneva] is regarded as the founder of modern linguistics and also the chief precursor of structuralism. In his key work, *Cours de linguistique générale* [Paris, 1915; trans. *Course in General Linguistics*, New York, 1959] he defined linguistic signs as arbitrary in two senses. 1. There is no intrinsic link between a signifier [such as a word] and the signified [meaning]. 2. Signifiers are not labels applied to autonomous entities, but are evidence of the arbitrary nature of the entire system of definition; every item within a given system both defines and is defined by all the other items. This was a central tenet of structuralism from the late 1940s to the 1970s.

Seth SIEGELAUB lives in Amsterdam. An exhibition organizer, publisher and dealer, he organized over 35 exhibitions, publications and catalogues in New York and Europe between 1964 and 1971. These included the installation of works by Andre, Barry and Weiner at Windham College, Putney, Vermont [1968], considered the first outdoor on-site installation exhibition; 'January 5-31, 1969' [1969] at the McLendon Building, New York, with Barry, Weiner, Kosuth and Huebler, in which the catalogue was the exhibition; and the so-called 'Xeroxbook' [1968] in which seven artists each made a 25-page work. In 1971 he produced *The Artist's Reserved Rights Transfer and Sale Agreement*.

Ludwig WITTGENSTEIN [b. 1889, Vienna, d. 1951, Cambridge, England] was a philosopher who made two quite distinct seminal contributions to the philosophy of language. The first, *Tractatus Logico-Philosophicus* [1922], located the condition of meaning in the formal logical components of language ['atomic propositions']. The second, the posthumously published *Philosophical Investigations* [1953], rejected this view in favour of a contextual approach to meaning, which situated individual propositions within 'language games', and language games within 'forms of life'. Both theories were hugely influential on philosophically oriented conceptual artists, such as Joseph Kosuth and Art & Language, at different stages of their development as artists.

BIBLIOGRAPHY

Alberro, Alexander 'The Turn of the Screw: Daniel Buren, Dan Flavin, and the Sixth Guggenheim International Exhibition', *October*, 80 [Spring 1997], 57-84

_____, *et al.*, *Lawrence Weiner*, Phaidon Press, London, 1998

_____ 'A Media Art: Conceptualism in Latin America in the 1960s', in Bird and Newman [eds], *Rewriting Conceptual Art*, 140-51

_____ and Norvell, Patricia [eds], *Recording Conceptual Art*, California University Press, Berkeley, 2001

_____ and Stimson, Blake [eds], *Conceptual Art: A Critical Anthology*, MIT Press, Cambridge, Massachusetts, 1999

Analytical Art Nos 1 & 2 [1971, 1972]

Art & Language [Michael Baldwin, Charles Harrison, Mel Ramsden], *Art & Language in Practice. Vol. 1: Illustrated Handbook; Vol. 2: Critical Symposium*, edited by Charles Harrison, Fundació Antoni Tàpies, Barcelona, 1999

Art in Process: The Visual Development of a Structure Finch College Museum of Art, New York, 1966

Art–Language, Vols 1-5 [1969-1985]

_____ New series, Nos 1-3 [1994-1999]

Aspen No.5-6, Fall-Winter 1967

Atkinson, Terry 'Concerning the Article "The Dematerialization of Art"' [1968], in Alberro and Stimson, *Conceptual Art*, 52-58; reprinted in this volume, 220-21

_____, 'From an Art & Language Point of View', *Art-Language*, 1, 2 [February 1970], 25-60; reprinted in this volume, 234-36

_____ *The Index, The World War One Moves and the Ruins of Conceptualism*, Cornerhouse, Manchester/Irish Museum of Modern Art, Dublin, 1992

_____ 'If We are Historical and Logical Monsters Then So Much the Better ... v2', *Art-Language*, New Series, 3 [September 1999], 62-75

_____ and Michael Baldwin, 'Unnatural Rules and Excuses', *Art-Language*, 2, 1 [February 1972], 1-27

Avalanche, Nos 1-13 [1970-1976].

Baldwin, Michael [see **Art & Language**]

Battcock, Gregory [ed.], *Idea Art: A Critical Anthology*, Dutton, New York, 1973

Benezra, Neal *et al.*, *Bruce Nauman*, Walker Art Center, Minneapolis, 1994

Berger, Maurice *Labyrinths: Robert Morris, Minimalism and the 1960s*, Harper and Row, New York, 1989

_____ [ed.], *Adrian Piper: A Retrospective*, Fine Arts Gallery, University of Maryland, Baltimore, 1999

Bird, Jon and **Newman, Michael** [eds], *Rewriting Conceptual Art*, Reaktion Books, London 1999. Contains essays by Alexander Alberro, Stephen Bann, Jon Bird, David Campany, Helen Molesworth, Michael Newman, Peter Osborne, Birgit Pelzer, Desa Philippi, Anne Rorimer, Peter Wollen, Willian Wood.

Branden, W. Joseph 'Robert Morris and John Cage: Reconstructing a Dialogue', *October*, 81 [Summer 1997], 59-69.

Brecht, George *Notebooks I-IV*, Verlag der Buchhandlung Walther König, Cologne, 1991, 1997

Broodthaers, Marcel *Writings, Interviews, Photographs*, edited by Benjamin H.D. Buchloh, MIT Press, Cambridge, Massachusetts, 1988

Buchloh, Benjamin H.D. 'Context-Function-Use Value: Michael Asher's Re-Materialization of the Artwork', in *Michael Asher: Exhibitions in Europe 1972-1977*, Stedelijk Van Abbemuseum, Eindhoven, 1980

_____ 'Marcel Broodthaers: Allegories of the Avant-Garde', *Artforum*, 18:9 [May 1980], 52-59

_____ 'Conceptual Art 1962-1969: From the Aesthetics of Administration to the Critique of Institutions', *October*, 55 [Winter 1990], 105-43. Extracts reprinted in this volume, 224; 278-80

_____ 'Benjamin Buchloh Replies to Joseph Kosuth and Seth Siegelaub', *October*, 57 [Summer 1991], 158-61

_____ *et al*, 'Conceptual Art and the Reception of Duchamp', *October*, 70 [Fall 1994], 127-46

Buren, Daniel 'The Function of the Studio',

_____ 'The Function of the Museum', *Artforum*, 12, 1 [September 1973]

_____ 'The Function of the Exhibition', *Studio International*, 186: 961 [December 1973]

_____ *Five Texts*, John Weber Gallery, New York, and Jack Wendler Gallery, London, 1973

_____ *Reboundings*, trans. Philippe Hunt, Daled and Gevaert, Brussels, 1977

Burgin, Victor 'Rules of Thumb', *Studio International*, 161: 933 [May 1971], 237-39

_____ 'In Reply', *Art-Language*, 2:2 [Summer 1972], 32-34

_____ 'Socialist Formalism', *Studio International*, 191: 980 [March-April, 1976], 148-54

_____ *Between*, Basil Blackwell, Oxford/Institute of Contemporary Arts, London, 1986

_____ *The End of Art Theory: Criticism and Postmodernity*, Macmillan, Basingstoke, 1986

Burn, Ian 'Dialogue', *Art-Language*, 2:1 [February 1970], 24

Cabanne, Pierre *Dialogues with Marcel Duchamp*, Da Capo, New York, n.d.

Cage, John *Silence*, Wesleyan University Press, Middletown, 1961

Calle, Sophie *à suivre*, ARC Musée d'art moderne de la Ville de Paris, 1991

Camnitzer, Luis 'Contemporary Colonial Art' [1969], in Alberro and Stimson [eds], *Conceptual Art*, 224-30

Chicago, Judy *The Dinner Party: A Symbol of our Heritage*, Anchor/Doubleday, Garden City, New York, 1979

Chiong, Kathyrn 'Kawara On Kawara', *October*, 90 [Fall 1999], 51-75

Conceptual Art, Conceptual Aspects, New York Cultural Center/Madison, New Jersey, 1970

Crane, Diana *The Transformation of the Avant-Garde: The New York Art World, 1940-1985*, Chicago University Press, Chicago, 1987

Crimp, Douglas 'Daniel Buren's New York Work', in Rudi Fuchs *et al.*, *Discordance/Cohérence*, Stedelijk Van Abbemuseum, Eindhoven, 1976, 75-78.

_____ 'This is Not a Museum of Art', *October*, 13 [Summer 1980]; reprinted in his *On the Museum's Ruins*, MIT Press, Cambridge, Massachusetts, 1993, 200-234

Crow, Thomas *The Rise of the Sixties: American and European Art in the Era of Dissent 1955-1969*, Harry N. Abrams, New York/Everyman Art Library, London, 1996

_____ 'Unwritten Histories of Conceptual Art', in his *Modern Art in the Common Culture*, Yale University Press, 1996, 212-42

De Duve, Thierry *Pictorial Nominalism: On Marcel Duchamp's Passage from Painting to the Readymade* [1984], trans. Dana Polan, University of Minnesota Press, Minneapolis, 1991

_____ *Kant After Duchamp*, MIT Press, Cambridge, Massachusetts, 1996

De Oliveira, Nicholas, Oxley, Nicola and Petry, Michael *Installation Art*, Thames and Hudson, London, 1994

Documenta 5 Documenta GmbH and Bertelsmann, Kassel, 1972

Duchamp, Marcel *The Writings of Marcel Duchamp*, edited by Michel Sanouillet and Elmer Peterson, Da Capo, New York, n.d. [reprint of Oxford University Press, 1973]

Field, Richard S. *et al.*, *Mel Bochner: Thought Made Visible 1966-1973*, Yale University Art Gallery, 1996

Flynt, Henry 'Concept Art', La Monte Young [ed.], *An Anthology of Chance Operations, Indeterminacy, Improvisation, Concept Art, Anti-Art, Meaningless Work, Natural Disasters, Stories, Diagrams, Music, Dance, Constructions, Compositions, Mathematics, Plans of Action*, New York, 1963

_____ *Fragments and Reconstructions from a Destroyed Oeuvre*, 1959-1963, Backworks, New York, 1982

Foster, Hal *Recodings: Art, Spectacle, Cultural Politics*, Bay Press, Seattle, 1985

_____ *The Return of the Real: The Avant-Garde at the End of the Century*, MIT Press, Cambridge, Massachusetts, 1996

The Fox, Nos 1-3 [1975-6]

Friedman, Ken [ed.], *The Fluxus Reader*, Academy Editions, Chichester, 1998

Gintz, Claude 'Michael Asher and the Transformation of "Situational Aesthetics"', *October*, 66 [Fall 1993], 113-31

_____ *et al.*, *L'art conceptual, une perspective*, ARC Musée d'art moderne de la Ville de Paris, 1989

Global Conceptualism: Points of Origin, 1950s–1980s, Queens Museum of Art, New York, 1999. Contains essays by Lázló Beke, Okwui Enwezor, Gao Minglu, Claude Gintz, Apinan Poshyananda, Mari Carmen Ramírez, Terry Smith, Reiko Tomii and Chiba Shigeo, Margarita Tupitsyn, Sung Wan-Kyung, Peter Wollen

Godfrey, Tony *Conceptual Art*, Art and Ideas Series, Phaidon Press, London, 1998

Goldberg, RoseLee *Performance Art: From Futurism to the Present*, Thames and Hudson, London, 1988

Goldstein, Ann and **Rorimer, Anne** [eds], *Reconsidering the Object of Art, 1965-1975*, Museum of Contemporary Art, Los Angeles/MIT Press, Cambridge, Massachusetts, 1995

Goodman, Nelson *Languages of Art: An Approach to a Theory of Symbols* [1968], Hackett, Indianapolis, 1976; excerpted in this volume, 202-6

Graham, Dan *Rock My Religion: Writings and Art Projects*, 1965-1990, edited by Brian Wallis, MIT Press, Cambridge, Massachusetts, 1993

_____ *Two-Way Mirror Power: Selected Writings by Dan Graham on his Art*, edited by Alexander Alberro, MIT Press,

Cambridge, Massachusetts, 1999

Gutai Galerie Nationale du Jeu de Paume, Paris, 1999

Haacke, Hans *Hans Haacke: Unfinished Business*, edited by Brian Wallis, New Museum of Contemporary Art, New York/MIT Press, Cambridge, Massachusetts, 1986

Harris, Mary Emma *The Arts at Black Mountain College*, MIT Press, Cambridge, Massachusetts, 1987

Harrison, Charles *Essays on Art & Language*, Blackwell, Oxford, 1991

_____ 'Artist's Writing', in *Art-Language*, New Series, 3 [September 1999], 15-35

_____ [see also **Art & Language**]

_____ and Wood, Paul [eds], *Art in Theory, 1900-1990: An Anthology of Changing Ideas*, Blackwell, Oxford, 1992

Hendricks, Jon [ed.], *Paintings and Drawings by Yoko Ono: July 17-30 1961, Preview July 16, Sunday*, Galeria 56, Budapest, 1993

_____ [ed.], *Instructions for Paintings by Yoko Ono, 24 May 1962*, Galeria 56, Budapest, 1993

Herkenhoff, Paulo *et al.*, *Cildo Meireles*, Phaidon Press, London, 1999

Higgins, Dick *A Dialectic of Centuries: Towards a Theory of the New Arts*, Printed Editions, New York, 1976

Hobbs, Robert *et al.*, *Robert Smithson: Sculpture*, Cornell University Press, Ithaca, New York, 1981

Huebler, Douglas *<Variable>, etc*, FRAC Limousin, Limoges, 1993

Idea Structures: Survey '70 Camden Arts Centre, London, 1970

Information The Museum of Modern Art, New York, 1970

Kelley, Mike 'Shall We Kill Daddy?', in Marianne Van Leeuw and Anne Pontégnie, *Origin and Destination: Alighiero E. Boetti, Douglas Huebler*, Societé des Expositions du Palais des Beaux Arts de Bruxelles, 1997, 155-72

Kelly, Mary *Post-Partum Document*, Routledge and Kegan Paul, London, 1983

Kolbowski, Silvia 'An Inadequate History of Conceptual Art', *October*, 92 [Spring 2000], 53-70

Kosuth, Joseph 'Art After Philosophy', *Studio International*, 178, 915-17 [November-December 1969], 134-37, 160-61, 212-13; reprinted in his *Art After Philosophy and After: Collected Writings, 1966-1990*, MIT Press, Cambridge, Massachusetts, 1991; excerpted in this volume, 232-34

_____ and Seth Siegelaub, 'Reply to Benjamin Buchloh on Conceptual Art', *October*, 57 [Summer 1991], 152-57

Kotz, Liz 'Post-Cagean Aesthetics and the "Event" Score', *October*, 95 [Winter 2001], 55-90

Krauss, Rosalind *'A Voyage on the North Sea': Art in the Age of the Post-Medium Condition*, Thames and Hudson, London, 1999

Lee, Pamela M. *Object to be Destroyed: The Work of Gordon Matta-Clark*, MIT Press, Cambridge, Massachusetts, 2000

Linker, Kate *Vito Acconci*, Rizzoli, New York, 1994

LeWitt, Sol 'Paragraphs on Conceptual Art', *Artforum*, 5:10 [Summer 1967], 79-83; reprinted in this volume, 213-15

_____ 'Sentences on Conceptual Art', *Art-Language*, 1:1 [1969], 11-13; reprinted in this volume, 222

Lippard, Lucy R. 'New York Letter: Carl Andre', *Art International*, 20, September 1965, 58-59

_____ [ed.], *Six Years: The dematerialization of the art object from 1966 to 1972: a cross-reference book of information on some aesthetic boundaries: consisting of a bibliography into which are inserted a fragmented text, art works, documents, interviews, and symposia, arranged chronologically and focused on so-called conceptual or information or idea art with mentions of such vaguely designated areas as minimal, anti-form, systems, earth, or process art, occurring now in the Americas, Europe, England, Australia, and Asia [with occasional political overtones]*, Praeger Publishers, New York, 1973; reprinted University of California Press, Berkeley and Los Angeles, 1997

_____, 'Escape Attempts', in Ann Goldstein and Anne Rorimer [eds], *Reconsidering the Object of Art: 1965-1975*, Museum of Contemporary Art, Los Angeles/MIT Press, Cambridge, Massachusetts, 1995, 17-39

_____, Chandler, John 'The Dematerialization of Art', *Art International*, 12:2 [February 1968], 31-36; reprinted in this volume, 218-20

Meyer, Ursula [ed.], *Conceptual Art*, Dutton, New York, 1972

Morgan, Robert C. *Art into Ideas: Essays on Conceptual Art*, Cambridge University Press, Cambridge, 1996

Morris, Robert *Continuous Project Altered Daily: The Writings of Robert Morris*, MIT Press, Cambridge, Massachusetts, 1993

_____ *The Mind-Body Problem*, Solomon R. Guggenheim Museum, New York, 1994

Munroe, Alexandra [ed.], *Japanese Art After 1945: Scream Against the Sky*, Harry N. Abrams, New York, 1994

_____ with Hendricks, Jon, *Yes Yoko Ono*, Japan Society/Harry N.Abrams, New York, 2000

The New Art Hayward Gallery/Arts Council of Great Britain, London, 1972

Newman, Michael 'Conceptual Art from the 1960s to the 1990s: An Unfinished Project?', *Kunst & Museum Journaal*, VII:1-3 [1996], 95-104; extract reprinted in this volume, 288-89

O'Doherty, Brian *Inside the White Cube: The Ideology of the Gallery Space* [1976; 1986], University of California Press, Berkeley and Los Angeles, 1999

Pelzer, Birgit 'Dissociated Objects: The Statements/Sculptures of Lawrence Weiner, *October*, 90 [Fall 1999], 77-108

_____ *et al.*, *Dan Graham*, Phaidon Press, London, 2001

Pepper, Ian 'From the "Aesthetics of Indifference" to "Negative Aesthetics": John Cage and Germany 1958-1972, *October*, 82 [Fall 1997], 31-48

Phillpot, Clive and **Tarsia, Andrea** *Live in Your Head: Concept and Experiment in Britain 1965-1975*, Whitechapel Art Gallery, London, 2000

Piper, Adrian *Out of Order, Out of Sight. Volume 1: Selected Writings in Meta-Art 1968-1992; Volume 2: Selected Writings in Art Criticism 1967-1992*, MIT Press, Cambridge, Massachusetts, 1996

Pollock, Griselda and **Parker, Rozsika** [eds], *Framing Feminism: Art and the Women's Movement 1970-1985*, Pandora, London, 1987

Primary Structures: Younger American and British Sculptors, Jewish Museum, New York, 1966

Ramírez, Mari Carmen 'Tactics for Thriving on Adversity: Conceptualism in Latin America, 1960-1980', in *Global Conceptualism*, 53-71

Ramsden, Mel 'Artist's Language 1', *Art-Language*, New Series, No. 3, September 1999, 35-46

_____ [see also **Art & Language**]

Reinhardt, Ad *Art as Art: The Selected Writings of Ad Reinhardt*, edited by Barbara Rose, University of California Press, Berkeley and Los Angeles, 1975

Reiss, Julie H. *From Margin to Center: The Spaces of Installation Art*, MIT Press, Cambridge, Massachusetts, 1999

Roberts, John [ed.], *The Impossible Document: Photography and Conceptual Art in Britain, 1966-1976*, Camerawork, London, 1997

Rorimer, Anne *New Art in the 60s and 70s: Redefining Reality*, Thames and Hudson, London, 2001

Rose, Bernice *et al.*, *Sol LeWitt*, The Museum of Modern Art, New York, 1978

Schimmel, Paul *Out of Actions: Between Performance and the Object, 1949-1979*, The Museum of Contemporary Art, Los Angeles/Thames and Hudson, London, 1998

Software: Information Technology: Its Meaning for Art Jewish Museum, New York, 1970

Smith, Roberta 'Conceptual Art', in Nikos Stangos [ed.], *Concepts of Modern Art*, Thames and Hudson, London, 1981, 256-70

Smithson, Robert *Robert Smithson: The Collected Writings*, edited by Jack Flam, University of California Press, Berkeley and Los Angeles, 1996

Stimson, Blake 'Dada-Situationism /*Tumamaros*-Conceptualism: An Interview with Luis Camnitzer', in Alberro and Stimson [eds], *Conceptual Art*, 492-500

Suderburg, Erika [ed.], *Space, Site, Intervention: Situating Installation Art*, University of Minnesota Press, Minneapolis, 2000

van Bruggen, Coosje *Bruce Nauman*, Rizzoli, New York, 1988

_____ *John Baldessari*, The Museum of Contemporary Art, Los Angeles, 1990

Wall, Jeff *Dan Graham's Kammerspeil*, Art Metropole, Toronto, 1991

_____ '"Marks of Indifference": Aspects of Photography in, or as, Conceptual Art,' in Goldstein and Rorimer [eds], *Reconsidering the Object of Art*, 1995, 247-67

_____ 'Monochrome and Photojournalism in On Kawara's Paintings', in Lynne Cooke and Karen Kelly [eds], *Robert Lehman Lectures on Contemporary Art*, Dia Center for the Arts, New York, 1996, 135-56

_____ 'Introduction: Partially Reflective Mirror Writings' in *Dan Graham, Two-Way Mirror Power*, 1999, xvii.

Ward, Frazer 'The Haunted Museum: Institutional Critique and Publicity', *October*, 73 [Summer 1995], 71-90

Weiner, Lawrence 'Statements', Art-Language 1:1 [May 1969], 17-18

When Attitudes Become Form: Works–Concepts –Processes–Situations–Information: Live in Your Head Kunsthalle, Bern, 1969

Young, La Monte [ed.], *An Anthology of Chance Operations, Indeterminacy, Improvisation, Concept Art, Anti-Art, Meaningless Work, Natural Disasters, Stories, Diagrams, Music, Dance, Constructions, Compositions, Mathematics, Plans of Action*, New York, 1963

de Zheger, M. Catherine [ed.], *Inside the Visible: An Elliptical Traverse of Twentieth-Century Art*, Institute of Contemporary Art, Boston/MIT Press, Cambridge, Massachusetts, 1996

INDEX

PUBLISHER'S ACKNOWLEDGEMENTS

We would like to thank all those who gave their generous permission to reproduce the listed material. Every effort has been made to secure all permissions and the editors and publisher apologize for any inadvertent errors or ommissions. If notified, the publisher will endeavour to correct these at the earliest opportunity.

We would like to express our gratitude to all the artists, authors and their representatives who have contributed to the making of this volume; in particular: Vito Acconci, New York; Estate of Bas Jan Ader/Patrick Painter Inc., Vancouver; Akasegawa Genpei and Nagoya City Art Museum, Japan; Laurie Anderson, New York; Carl Andre, New York; Arakawa and Madeline Gins, New York; Arman, New York; Michael Asher, Los Angeles; Ashiya City Museum of Art and History and the former members of Gutai Art Association, Ashiya, Japan; John Baldessari, Santa Monica, California; Art & Language [Michael Baldwin, Mel Ramsden], Banbury, England; Robert Barry, New Jersey; Bernd and Hilla Becher, Dusseldorf; Bibliothèque nationale de France, Paris; Mel Bochner, New York; Archivio Alighiero Boetti, Rome; Oscar Bony, Buenos Aires; Mary Boone Gallery, New York; Stanley Brouwn, Amsterdam; Daniel Buren, Paris; Victor Burgin, London; Avril Burn, Sydney; The John Cage Trust, New York; Leo Castelli Gallery, New York; Christo and Jeanne-Claude, New York; Estate of Lygia Clark/Museu de Arte Moderna, Rio de Janeiro; James Coleman, Dublin; Paula Cooper Gallery, New York; Eduardo Costa, New York; Anny De Decker, Antwerp; Dia Center for the Arts, New York; Jan Dibbets, Amsterdam; Braco Dimitrijevic, Paris; Willie Doherty, Derry, Northern Ireland; Electronic Arts Intermix, New York; Ronald Feldman Fine Arts, New York; Konrad Fischer Galerie, Dusseldorf; Estate of Dan Flavin, New York; Foksal Gallery Foundation, Warsaw; Hamish Fulton, Canterbury, England; Research Library, The Getty Research Institute, Los Angeles; Maria Gilissen, Brussels; Barbara Gladstone Gallery, New York; Robert Gober, New York; Estate of Felix Gonzalez Torres/Andrea Rosen Gallery, New York; Gorney, Bravin + Lee, New York; Dan Graham, New York; Wenda Gu, New York; Solomon R. Guggenheim Museum, New York; Hans Haacke, New York; Estate of Tibor Hajas, Budapest; Estate of Eva Hesse/Robert Miller Gallery, New York; Susan Hiller, London; Jenny Holzer, Hoosick, New York; Douglas Huebler Art Trust, Valencia, California; Kay Fido Hunt, London; Alfredo Jaar/Galerie LeLong, New York; The Japan Foundation, Tokyo; Catriona Jeffries Gallery, Vancouver; Philip Johnson, New York; Donald Judd Foundation, Marfa, Texas; Ilya and Emilia Kabakov, New York; Allan Kaprow, Encinitas, California; On Kawara, New York; Mary Kelly, Los Angeles; Estate of Edward Kienholz/L.A. Louver Gallery, Venice, California; Yves Klein Archives, Paris; Vitaly Komar, New York; Walther König, Cologne; Joseph Kosuth, New York; Christine Kozlov, London; Jaroslaw Kozlowski, Poznan, Poland; Irwin Kremen, Durham, North Carolina; Barbara Kruger, New York; L.A. Louver Gallery, Venice, California; John Latham and Barbara Steveni, London; Galerie LeLong, New York; Lisson Gallery, London; Richard Long, Bristol, England; Sol LeWitt, New York; Archivio Opere Piero Manzoni, Milan; Matsuzawa Yutaka, Nagano, Japan; Estate of Gordon Matta-Clark/David Zwirner Gallery, New York; Matt's Gallery, London; Cildo Meireles, Rio de Janeiro; Aleksandr Melamid, New York; Estate of Ana Mendieta/Galerie LeLong, New York; Metro Pictures, New York; Metropolitan Art Museum, Tokyo; Gustav Metzger, London; The Minneapolis Institute of Arts; Miyajima Tatsuo and Miyajima Yoriko, Japan; Moderna Museet, Stockholm; Robert Morris, New York; The Museum of Modern Art, New York; Nagoya City Art Museum, Japan; Projeto Hélio Oiticica, Rio de Janeiro; Yoko Ono, New York; Roman Opalka, Tournon d'Agenais, France; Lygia Pape, Rio de Janeiro; Galerie Emmanuel Perrotin, Paris; Peters Edition Ltd., London; Philadelphia Museum of Art; Adrian Piper, New York; Victor Pivovarov, Prague; Centre Georges Pompidou, Paris; Richard Prince, New York; Max Protetch Gallery, New York; Yvonne Rainer, New York; Robert Rauschenberg, New York; Gerhard Richter, Cologne; Andrea Rosen Gallery, New York; Martha Rosler, New York; Edward Ruscha, Venice, California; San Francisco Museum of Modern Art; Carolee Schneemann, New York; Richard Serra, New York; Shiraga Fujiko and Takamatsu City Museum of Art, Japan; Gilbert and Lila Silverman Fluxus Collection, New York; Susanna Singer, New York; Sonnabend Gallery, New York; Estate of Robert Smithson/James Cohan Gallery, New York; Michael Snow, Toronto; Tate Gallery, London; South London Gallery Archives; Through the Flower, Belen, New Mexico; Niele Toroni, Paris; Stedelijk Van Abbemuseum, Eindhoven; Ronny Van de Velde, Antwerp; Jeff Wall, Vancouver; The Andy Warhol Museum, Pittsburgh; John Weber Gallery, New York; Lawrence Weiner, New York; Städtisches Museum, Wiesbaden, Germany; Wesleyan University Press, Middletown, Connecticut; Estate of Hannah Wilke/Ronald Feldman Fine Arts, New York; Stephen Willats, London; La Monte Young, New York; David Zwirner Gallery, New York.

PHOTOGRAPHERS

Shigeo Anzai: p. 189; Orazio Bacci: pp. 42; 64 [bottom]; Ray Barrie: p. 156 [top right]; Leonardo Bezzola: p. 97; Guy Brett: p. 149 [right]; Rudolph Burckhardt: pp. 75; 191 [fig. 1]; D. James Dee: p. 129 [bottom]; Pierre Descargues: p. 63 [top, middle]; dpa: p. 65; Chris Gergley: pp. 144–45 [top]; Maria Gilissen: p. 169; John Groo: p. 96; Aurora Hendricks: p. 70 [bottom]; Konstantinos Ignatiadis: p. 122; Hiro Ihara: pp. 78; 93; 148; Bill Jacobson: p. 181; Robert McElroy: p. 113; George Maciunas: pp. 21; 67 [top]; 71; J. C. Mazur: p. 68 [bottom]; Peter Moore: pp. 20; 133 [top]; Billy Name: p. 24; Claudio Oiticica: p. 149 [top]; Adam Reich: p. 139 [top]; Walter Russell: pp. 137 [top], 171; Fred Scruton: p. 154; Harry Shunk: pp. 164–65; Richard Steinmetz: pp. 144–45; Akira Takahashi: p. 60 [top]; Zygmunt Targowski: p. 72 [bottom]; Nic Tenwiggenhorn: p. 32; Caroline Tisdall: p. 153 [bottom]; Franco Toselli: p. 175 [top]; Jacek Tureyk: p. 4; Donald Woodman: p. 161 [bottom].

AUTHOR'S ACKNOWLEDGEMENTS

This book is in numerous ways the product of a collaborative effort. I am grateful to Gilda Williams for initiating this project and to my editor, Ian Farr, who oversaw all aspects of its conception and production with exemplary patience and care. Thanks also to Elizabeth Manchester for her careful, intelligent research for the extended captions, and to the team at Phaidon: editor/researcher Clair Joy and researcher Clare Stent; the designer, Roger Fawcett-Tang; and Sarah McLaughlin, Production Controller.

I am grateful for critical conversations about conceptual art to David Batchelor, Andrew Benjamin, Jon Bird, Tony Godfrey, Michael Newman, Stewart Martin, Adrian Piper, Pawel Polit, John Roberts, Stella Sandford and Milada Slizinska.

Most importantly, I would like to thank the artists and authors who have provided the images and texts which make up the bulk of the book and whose work collectively contributed so much to the most profound transformation yet in the modern conception of art.

THEMES AND MOVEMENTS

The development of modern and contemporary art has been dominated by fundamental, revolutionary movements and recurring themes. The Themes and Movements series is the first fully to examine twentieth-century and recent art by combining expert narrative, key works and original documents. Each book is introduced by a comprehensive Survey from a distinguished scholar who provides a thorough analysis of the theme or movement. The second section is dedicated to numerous illustrations of the Works themselves. This selection of key images is accompanied by extended captions which describe the principal ideas, processes and contexts underlying each artwork. Finally, with the Documents section, the series also offers direct access to the voice of the artist and to primary texts by critics, historians, curators, philosophers and theorists. A unique archive of the innovations, discourses and controversies that have shaped art today, these books are as exhaustive as a full-scale museum overview, presenting many of the most significant works of art associated with a particular tendency.